Pronunciation Table

Consonants

Symbol	Keyword
p	pen
b	back
t	ten
d	day
k	key
g	get
f	fat
v	view
θ	thing
ð	then
s	soon
z	zero
ʃ	ship
ʒ	pleasure
h	hot
x	loch
tʃ	cheer
dʒ	jump
m	sum
n	sun
ŋ	sung
w	wet
l	let
r	red
j	yet

Vowels

short

Symbol	Keyword
ɪ	bit
e	bed
æ	cat
ɒ	dog *(BrE)*
ʌ	but
ʊ	put
ə	about
i	happy
u	actuality

long

Symbol	Keyword
iː	sheep
ɑː	father
ɒː	dog *(AmE)*
ɔː	four
uː	boot
ɜː	bird

diphthongs

Symbol	Keyword
eɪ	make
aɪ	lie
ɔɪ	boy
əʊ	note *(BrE)*
oʊ	note *(AmE)*
aʊ	now
ɪə	real
eə	hair *(BrE)*
ʊə	sure *(BrE)*
uə	actual
iə	peculiar

Special signs

ǁ	separates British and American pronunciations; British on the left, American on the right
/ˈ/	shows main stress
/ˌ/	shows secondary stress
/◂/	shows stress shift
/ɪ ə/	means that some speakers use /ɪ/ and some use /ə/
/ʊ ə/	means that some speakers use /ʊ/ and some use /ə/
/ə/	means that /ə/ may or may not be used.

LONGMAN BUSINESS ENGLISH DICTIONARY

ACKNOWLEDGEMENTS

Director	Della Summers
Editorial Director	Adam Gadsby
Senior Editors	Michael Murphy Bill Mascull
Editor	Sheila Dignen
Lexicographers	Rosalind Combley Laura Wedgeworth Martin Stark Andrew Delahunty Deborah Yuill Tammy Gales
US Editor	Julie Plier
Pronunciation Editor	Dinah Jackson
Project Manager	Alan Savill
Project Administrator	Denise Denney
Editorial Manager	Sheila Dallas
Production Editor	Michael Brooks
Editorial Assistance	Peter Braaksma
Corpus Development	Steve Crowdy
Computational Assistance	Trevor Satchell
Keyboarder	Pauline Savill
Designers	Mike Brain Alex Ingr

LONGMAN BUSINESS ENGLISH DICTIONARY

Pearson Education Limited
Edinburgh Gate, Harlow, Essex CM20 2JE, England
and Associated Companies throughout the World

Visit our website: http://www.longman.com/dictionaries

First published 2000
13 15 17 19 20 18 16 14 12

Words that the editors have reason to believe constitute trademarks have been described as such. However, neither the presence nor the absence of such a description should be regraded as affecting the legal status of any trademark.

ISBN
0-582-30607-8 (Cased edition)
ISBN-13: 978-0-582-30607-3
0 582 30606-X (Paperback edition)
ISBN-13: 978-0-582-30606-6

British Library Cataloguing-in-Publication Data
A catalogue record for this book is available from the British Library

Set in Nimrod by RefineCatch Ltd, Bungay, Suffolk, England
Printed in China
GCC

CONTENTS

Explanatory Notes

1 Finding the word you are looking for

In this dictionary, words are listed in two ways, depending on whether they are a single word or a compound word (groups of two or more words with a fixed form and a special meaning).

The ordering system we have used is a combination of alphabetical ordering and "nesting". Nesting is a way of holding a family of words that have closely related meanings together in one place, grouping them under the word that carries the general meaning that they all share. You will find most compound nouns are recorded in this way, under the final word in the group.

1.1 Compound words

Compound nouns make up a large part of the vocabulary of business English. They are made up of a word that refers to a general thing or subject (typically the final word of the group) and another word or words that identify a particular type of that thing or part of that subject. There are, for example, many different types of shares: advancing shares, capital shares, fully paid shares, split shares, etc. Share has an entry at its alphabetical place and all the different compound words referring to different types of share are ordered within that main entry. In every case, there is also a cross-reference to each of these different shares, at its place in the general alphabetical order, making certain that you always find the word you are looking for.

Structuring entries in this way brings together words from the same family and explains the similarities and differences between them in one place, helping to increase your understanding of the whole subject. In the real world, these words are used in the same context or appear together in the same discussion. In this dictionary, these words are defined in the same context and explained in relation to each other.

1.2 Phrasal verbs

Verbs made up of two or more words are listed in alphabetical order after the entry for the main verb. For example:

pay off *phr v* **1** [T] **pay sb/sth off** to pay all the money you owe a person or company: *BHC also has* ***paid off*** *all its long-term* ***debt***...
2 [I] if a plan, idea etc pays off, it is successful: *He predicted the company's modernization program would result in higher sales. So far, it has paid off*...

1.3 Phrases

Some words are used in relatively fixed phrases, and these phrases are given separate meanings in this dictionary. For example:

mar•ket[1] /ˈmɑːkɪ̈t‖ˈmɑːr-/ *n* [C]
5 corner the market if a seller corners the market, they own or produce most of the goods on sale, and can therefore set prices: *In order to prevent one firm from cornering the market on a new Treasury bill issue, the law limits any dealer from purchasing*...

Phrases are held at the first main word with an entry in the dictionary, not at words such as *the*, or *to*, or *in*.

1.4 Derived words

Words that are derived from a headword by adding a suffix do not need a definition because their meaning is simply that of the main word plus the meaning of the suffix.

In this dictionary, derived words are held at the meaning of the word that they are derived from. For example:

re·cy·cle /ˌriːˈsaɪkəl/ *v* [I,T] to put used objects or materials through a special process, so that they can be used again: *We recycle all our cans and bottles.* | *Environmentalists have attacked the material because it doesn't recycle as well as steel.* —**recyclable** *adj*: *recyclable materials* —**recycled** *adj*: *recycled paper* —**recycling** *n* [U] *a metals recycling plant.*

2 British and American English

British and American English are equally important in the world of business and this dictionary has been written by both British and American lexicographers. The definitions are written in British English and examples are taken from both British and American financial sources, such as *The Financial Times* and *The Wall St. Journal*. Words or meanings of words are marked *BrE* if they are only used in British English, or *AmE* if the word or meaning is restricted to American English. If they are much more frequent in one variety than the other, they are marked *especially BrE* or *especially AmE*.

2.1 Spelling differences

When words are spelt differently in British and American English, both spellings are shown. For example:

la·bour *BrE*, **labor** *AmE* /ˈleɪbə‖-ər/ *n* [U] **1** work involving a lot of physical or mental effort: *The garage charges £30 an hour for labour.*

If a word can have more than one spelling in a variety of English, the alternative spelling is shown. For example:

rea·li·za·tion also **realisation** *BrE* /ˌrɪəlaɪˈzeɪʃən‖-lə-/ *n* [singular, U] the act of changing something into money by selling it.

2.2 Meaning differences

Sometimes there is a completely different word in British and American English for the same thing. In cases like this, both British and American words are included in the entry, the second one shown after a semi-colon at the end of the definition. For example:

out-basket *n* [C] *AmE* a container used to hold letters, papers etc that have been dealt with; OUT-TRAY *BrE* —compare IN-BASKET
out-tray *n* [C] *BrE* a container used to hold letters, papers etc that have been dealt with; OUT-BASKET *AmE* —compare IN-TRAY

Irregular forms of a verb are shown like this.

The meaning of a word is explained simply, using a limited defining vocabulary of about 2000 words.

This tells you that a word is used to talk about a particular subject.

This tells you that a word is a verb, noun, adjective, etc.

Grammatical information is shown in square brackets, or in bold type before an example.

This tells you that the meaning of a word is formal (used mainly in writing or in formal speech).

This tells you that a meaning of a word is only used in British English, not American English.

Different types of a particular entry appear as a separate element under that entry.

If a word can be spelt differently in British and American English, both spellings are shown.

Words that are often used together are shown like this, followed if necessary by an explanation.

sub·poe·na[1] /sə'pi:nə, səb-/ *v* past tense and past participle **subpoenaed** [T] LAW to order someone to come to court and be a witness, or to order someone to give documents to the court: *Telephone companies' records can be subpoenaed.* **subpoena sb to do sth**: *We will subpoena him to give evidence.*

subpoena[2] *n* [C] LAW a document ordering someone to come to court and be a witness, or ordering someone to give documents to the court: *The regulators issued a subpoena for documents relating to 23 company audits.*

sub·rou·tine /ˌsʌbru:'ti:n/ *n* [C] COMPUTING a part of a computer program containing a set of instructions that will be followed every time the main program calls for it. This is used when the same small job may need to be done several different times as part of a larger job: *Subroutines can increase productivity by simplifying common programming tasks.*

sub·scribe /səb'skraɪb/ *v* **1** [I] to pay money regularly in order to have a newspaper or magazine sent to you, or to receive a broadcasting or telephone service + **to**: *Only 1% of Japanese households now subscribe to any cable TV network.*

2 [I] FINANCE to ask or agree to buy shares in a company that has offered shares to investors + **for**: *Each rights holder will be entitled to subscribe for one share of IBP common stock.*

3 subscribe to to pay money regularly to be a member of an organization or to help its work: *Chris subscribes to an environmental action group.*

4 [T] *formal* to sign your name: *Please subscribe your name to the document.*

sub·scrip·tion /səb'skrɪpʃən/ *n* [C] *BrE* an amount of money that you pay regularly to be a member of an organization or to help its work; DUES + **for/to**: *his subscription for the Student Union*

sub·sid·i·a·ry[1] /səb'sɪdiəri‖-dieri/ *n* plural **subsidiaries** [C] a company that is at least half-owned by another company: *Among Berkshire's holdings is an 80.1%-owned subsidiary, Wesco Financial Corp.* + **of**: *Chase Manhattan Bank is a subsidiary of Chase Manhattan Corp.*

partly-owned subsidiary a company that is partly owned by another company, and also has other owners: *BNP Intercontinentale, a partly-owned subsidiary of Banque Nationale de Paris*

wholly-owned subsidiary a company that is completely owned by another company: *A parent company in the UK will be legally responsible for the debts of its wholly-owned subsidiaries.*

sub·si·dize also **subsidise** *BrE* /'sʌbsɪdaɪz/ *v* [T] if a government or organization subsidizes a company, activity etc, it pays part of the cost: *The railroad company is partially subsidized by the federal government.* | *Some companies subsidize high-quality childcare facilities.* —**subsidized** *adj* [only before a noun] *heavily subsidized agricultural exports*

sub·sis·tence /səb'sɪstəns/ *n* [U] **1** a small amount of money or food that is just enough to survive: *refugees who are dependent for subsistence on support from aid agencies* | *Unfortunately, these people have become used to living at* ***subsistence levels*** (=with just enough food etc to survive). | *Foreign staff are paid* ***subsistence wages*** *by local standards.*

sub·sti·tute[1] /ˈsʌbstɪtjuːt‖-tuːt/ *n* [C] **1** something new or different that can be used instead of something else: *a sugar substitute used by the soft drinks industry* + **for**: *Money is no substitute for* (=cannot take the place of) *management.*

substitute[2] *v* **1** [T] to use or do something new or different instead of something else **substitute sth for/with sth**: *Corporations have been able to avoid some tax by substituting debt for equity.* | *Byproducts are reduced if a different bleaching agent is substituted for pure chlorine.*

sue /sjuː‖suː/ *v* [I,T] to make a legal claim against someone, especially for an amount of money, because you have been harmed in some way: *If the builders don't fulfil their side of the contract, we'll sue.* + **for**: *The company was sued for nonpayment by their supplier.* | *The council were sued for £2.2 million because of delays in building the bypass.*

suit /suːt, sjuːt‖suːt/ *n* **1** [C] LAW a case brought to a court of law by a private person or company, not by the police or government; LAWSUIT: *Ms. Sobel* ***filed a suit****, claiming sex discrimination.*
2 [C] a set of clothes made from the same material and including a JACKET (=short coat) and trousers or a skirt
3 [C usually plural] *informal* someone such as a manager working for a company that produces books, advertisements, or films, and who has to wear a suit when they are at work: *He looks more like a copywriter than an account managing 'suit'.* —compare CREATIVE[2]

sum[1] /sʌm/ *n* [C] **1** an amount of money: *trading schemes involving* ***large sums of money*** | *The company was sold for a sum estimated at $2.3 billion.*
2 the sum of the total produced when you add two or more numbers together: *The sum of the fraudulently obtained loans was nearly 360 billion yen.*

sum insured also **sum assured** *n* [C] the maximum amount of money that an insurer will have to pay, according to an insurance contract: *Their Policy schedule shows a sum insured of £1,000.*

sum·mons[1] /ˈsʌmənz/ *n* plural **summonses** [C] LAW an official order to appear in a court of law: *Administrators of his estate have* ***issued a summons*** *to get him to return to Australia.*

sum of the digits also **sum of the years' digits**, abbreviation **SOFTY** *n* [singular] ACCOUNTING one of the ways of calculating the DEPRECIATION (=loss of value over time) of an asset. For example, if an asset has a life of four years, 4+3+2+1=10, so in the company's accounts the asset is depreciated 40% in the first year, 30% in the second year and so on

sundries account —see under ACCOUNT[1]

su·per·vise /ˈsuːpəvaɪz, ˈsjuː-‖ˈsuːpər-/ *v* [I,T] to be in charge of a group of people or a particular area of work: *She* ***supervises*** *26* ***workers*** *in a business with annual sales of £4 million.* | *As managing director, he is supervising a portfolio of investments.* | *The fund manager pleaded guilty to failing to supervise properly.* —**supervised** *adj* [only before a noun] *The company will qualify for* ***court-supervised*** *debt restructuring.* | *the biggest* ***government-supervised*** *election in U.S. labor history*

Words that are spelt the same but belong to different parts of speech are shown like this.

Sentence patterns show how a word is typically used.

Useful natural examples taken from financial newspapers held on the Longman Corpus Network.

A word that can be used instead of the word being defined is shown after the definition in capital letters.

This tells you that a word is informal (used mainly in conversation).

Related words that are useful are shown like this.

Fixed phrases are shown in bold type and include a definition explaining the whole phrase.

If there are two similar words with the same meaning both are defined under the same entry.

Irregular forms of a noun are shown like this.

An abbreviation of a word is shown like this.

Cross-references tell you that a word is defined at another entry.

Words that can be understood if you know the meaning of the word they are derived from.

A1 also **A-1**, **A-one** *adj* INSURANCE in the LLOYDS REGISTER OF SHIPPING, an A1 ship is of the highest quality or in excellent condition; FIRST CLASS

A3 *n* [U] a standard paper size used in Europe, measuring 297×420 mm: *You can enlarge documents to A3 on the photocopier.*

A4 *n* [U] a standard paper size used in Europe, measuring 210×297 mm: *It should be typed on **A4 paper** with double spacing.*

AAA abbreviation for AMERICAN ACCOUNTING ASSOCIATION

AAA rating —see under RATING

AA rating —see under RATING

ABA abbreviation for AMERICAN BANKERS ASSOCIATION; AMERICAN BAR ASSOCIATION

a•ban•don /əˈbændən/ *v* [T] **1** to stop doing or using something because it is too difficult or unsuccessful: *Mr Knighton abandoned his takeover bid for the club.* | *The power plant was abandoned before it was even completed.*
2 INSURANCE if you abandon a ship or its cargo, you accept that it is too badly damaged to be saved, and so give it up to an insurance company in exchange for an insurance payment
3 abandon ship to leave an organization because you believe that it is going to fail soon: *Law firms facing difficult times are trying to prevent partners from abandoning ship and taking clients with them.*
4 abandon a case/claim/action etc to no longer continue with a legal case etc: *You cannot be asked to pay the defendant's legal costs, even if you decide to abandon your claim.* —**abandonment** *n* [U] *Disagreements about policy led to the abandonment of the plan.* (=insured cannot abandon partly damaged property to insurer and claim total loss)

a•bate /əˈbeɪt/ *v* [I,T] *formal* to become less strong or damaging, or to make something do this: *The level of wage settlements has shown no signs of abating in recent months.* | *Industry must use the best available techniques to abate pollution.* —**abatement** *n* [U] *the cost of investing in pollution abatement equipment*

ABC /ˌeɪ biː ˈsiː/ abbreviation for AUDIT BUREAU OF CIRCULATION

ABC method —see under METHOD

a•bode /əˈbəʊd‖əˈboʊd/ *n* [C usually singular] *formal* LAW the place where someone lives: *An 18-year-old man **of no fixed abode*** (=with no home) *appeared in court yesterday charged with burglary.*

a•bol•ish /əˈbɒlɪʃ‖əˈbɑː-/ *v* [T] to officially end a law, a system for doing something, an organization etc, especially one that has existed for a long time: *The new contracts will abolish the current 12-month redundancy notice.* | *All price controls are to be abolished by December.* —**abolition** *n* [U] *Many experts are now calling for the abolition of farm subsidies.*

above board also **aboveboard** *AmE adj* honest and legal: *The stock exchange aims to ensure that all deals are above board.* | *aboveboard negotiations*

above-men•tioned *adj* [only before a noun] *written formal* already mentioned on the same page or on a previous page; AFORESAID: *the above-mentioned sale of the company*

above the line *adj* **1** ACCOUNTING relating to a figure included in a statement of a company's profits and losses before tax has been paid, not after tax: *£31 million of the property profit has been **taken above the line*** (=counted as profit before tax).
2 MARKETING relating to a company's spending on advertising, as compared to other marketing activities such as research: *The company spent less than £500,000 above the line last year, compared to £3.5m this year on TV ads.*

ab•ro•gate /ˈæbrəgeɪt/ *v* [T] *formal* to officially end a law, agreement, or practice: *They accused the company of abrogating its contract.*

ABS abbreviation for AMERICAN BUREAU OF SHIPPING

ab•sence /ˈæbsəns/ *n* [C,U] HUMAN RESOURCES when a person is not at work, for example because they are ill: *Evelyn took charge **in his absence**.* | *The work of the department suffered because of her frequent absences.*
leave of absence plural **leaves of absence** permission given to someone not to be at work when normally they should be: *Employees may only **take leave of absence** in special circumstances such as the death of a close relative.*

ab•sen•tee /ˌæbsənˈtiː◂/ *n* [C] HUMAN RESOURCES someone not at work when they should be: *A time will come when a frequent absentee can be fairly dismissed.*

ab•sen•tee•is•m /ˌæbsənˈtiːɪzəm/ *n* [U] HUMAN RESOURCES the problem of employees not being at work when they should be: *About 25% of its workforce are alcoholics, causing **high absenteeism**.* | *An **absenteeism rate** of 16% was destroying the company.*

absentee land•lord —see under LANDLORD

absolute advantage —see under ADVANTAGE

absolute auction —see under AUCTION[1]

absolute majority —see under MAJORITY[1]

absolute ownership —see under OWNERSHIP

absolute title —see under TITLE

ab•sorb /əbˈsɔːb, əbˈzɔːb‖-ɔːrb/ *v* [T] **1** if a large organization absorbs a smaller one, it takes control of it and makes it part of one larger organization: *The best option would be for Costain to be absorbed by another construction company.* + **into**: *Thomson Electronics was absorbed into CEA Industrie.*
2 if a business absorbs costs, it manages to pay them without them having a very bad effect on the business: *The company has absorbed $10 million in losses.* | *The bank said that careful cost control had allowed it to absorb the costs of the merger.*
3 if a market absorbs a product, it takes it up and is able to sell it: *Trading was cautious and quiet as the market prepared to absorb £55 billion of government securities to be sold this week.* | *Canada absorbs about 20% of US exports.*
4 if an activity absorbs money or time, it uses a lot of it: *They must reduce the proportion of income absorbed by operating costs.*

ab•sorp•tion /əbˈsɔːpʃən, -ˈzɔːp-‖-ɔːr-/ *n* [U] when a larger organization takes control of a smaller one: *Rolo's absorption by Credito will lead to the loss of over 1,000 jobs.*

absorption costing —see under COSTING

absorption rate —see under RATE[1]

ab•stract /ˈæbstrækt/ *n* [C] a short written statement that contains the most important details of a longer piece of writing such as a newspaper article, a report, or a speech: *According to the abstract of Digital's presentation, the new chip processes information much more quickly.*

abstract of title —see under TITLE

A

a/c *BrE* written abbreviation for ACCOUNT

ACA *n* Associate of the Institute of Chartered Accountants; used after someone's name to show that they are a member of this organization: *David Bradley, ACA*

ACAS /ˈeɪkæs/ *n* Advisory, Conciliation and Arbitration Service; a government organization in Britain that attempts to solve disagreements between employers and employees: *Under terms agreed with ACAS, both sides have agreed not to comment during negotiations.*

ACCA *n* Association of Certified and Corporate Accountants; a British professional organization for accountants working in business

ac·cel·e·rate /əkˈseləreɪt/ *v* **1** [I,T] to happen more quickly, or make something happen more quickly: *Economic growth should accelerate as the year goes on.* | *There are fears that higher oil prices would accelerate inflation.*
2 [I] ECONOMICS when the economy accelerates, demand for goods increases: *The President will strive to keep the economy accelerating as the election nears.*
3 [T] FINANCE to agree that a debt should be repaid more quickly, either because the borrower and lender both want this, or because the borrower has failed to make necessary payments and the lender has the right to demand full repayment: *He sued the firm, charging that it had defaulted and seeking to* ***accelerate the debt.*** | *A demand has now been made for* ***accelerated payment*** *of the debt.* —**acceleration** *n* [U] *The new tobacco tax has been blamed for a sharp acceleration in inflation.* | *59 consecutive months of economic acceleration* | *Failure to resolve the default within 30 days could trigger acceleration of the repayment schedule.*

accelerated cost recovery system —see under SYSTEM

accelerated depreciation —see under DEPRECIATION

accelerated payment —see under PAYMENT

ac·cel·e·ra·tor /əkˈseləreɪtə‖-ər/ *n* [singular] ECONOMICS **1** the principle that when demand for goods rises and falls, investment rises and falls by even larger amounts
2 when a government uses the accelerator, it encourages demand as a way of controlling the economy: *Ministers need to time their use of the economic brake or accelerator carefully.*

ac·cept /əkˈsept/ *v* [I,T] **1** to take or agree to take something that has been offered: *German steel workers have accepted a 3% wage offer.* | *About 3,000 employees accepted early retirement.* **accept sth from sb**: *Doctors should not accept gifts of value from pharmaceuticals companies.*
2 to agree to a plan, idea, agreement etc: *The US is ready to accept the deal.* | *Canada voted to accept the GATT plan.*
3 to agree to take goods that have been ordered: *The company has shipped three supercomputers, but only two have been accepted.*
4 MARKETING when people accept a new product, they like it and are willing to buy it: *The machine is too highly priced to be accepted by the mass of US consumers.*
5 accept cash/dollars/cheques/credit cards etc to allow customers to pay using these forms of payment: *Do you accept Visa?*
6 accept a bill of exchange to agree to pay a BILL OF EXCHANGE
7 accept a risk INSURANCE to agree to insure something under a contract of insurance: *The insurance company reserves the right to make checks prior to accepting a risk on health insurance.*

ac·cept·ance /əkˈseptəns/ *n* **1** [U] taking or agreeing to take something offered: *Russia's acceptance of aid from western countries*
2 [U] when someone accepts a plan, idea, agreement etc: *A judge can force acceptance of a bankruptcy plan.*
3 [U] when a buyer agrees to take goods from a seller and must therefore pay for them
4 [U] MARKETING the willingness of people to buy a product, especially a new or changed product: *The company's earnings have fallen in the last four years owing to poor acceptance of new products.* | *Doubts about* ***consumer acceptance*** *have kept US food companies from using irradiation technology.*
5 [C] FINANCE in a takeover, agreement by individual shareholders to the offer: *The Rank takeover offer has received acceptances from Mecca shareholders representing 160 million Mecca shares.*
6 [C,U] BANKING agreement to pay a BILL OF EXCHANGE, the words on a bill showing this agreement, or the accepted bill itself: ***Bankers' acceptances*** *require actual certificates to be delivered the same day.*
partial acceptance [C usually singular] agreement by someone to pay part of the value of a BILL OF EXCHANGE, with other acceptors responsible for paying the rest

acceptance bank —see under BANK[1]

acceptance of proposal *n* plural **acceptances of proposal** [C] INSURANCE an agreement by an insurance company to provide the insurance asked for

acceptance sampling —see under SAMPLING

acceptance trial —see under TRIAL

accepting house also **acceptance house** —see under HOUSE

ac·cept·or also **accepter** *AmE* /əkˈseptə‖-ər/ *n* [C] BANKING a financial institution that accepts a BILL OF EXCHANGE: *In the case of bank bills the Bank has to be sure that the* ***acceptor bank*** *will be in a position to pay.*

ac·cess[1] /ˈækses/ *n* [U] **1** the right to sell goods to a particular market or country without breaking any laws or agreements + **to**: *Japan agreed to allow foreign manufacturers of satellite equipment equal access to the Japanese market.*
2 the way in which you are able to find information held on a computer + **to**: *In order to simplify access to the data, the computer program enables users to specify their own requirements.*
direct access a system of storing information on a computer which makes it possible to go directly to a particular piece of information without sorting through all the records: *The police national computer's direct access capacity is 190 million bytes.*
3 when you are allowed to see official documents + **to**: *The National Union of Teachers has proposed that parents should have access to their children's files.*
4 the ability to buy a product or make use of a service: *The move is intended to widen the access to credit.* | *Many poorer residents have no access to health care.*
5 the right to remove money from where it is invested in order to use it: *Policyholders often feel more confident if they have access to their funds.*

access[2] *v* [T] to be able to find, change, or run programs or information held on a computer: *The software enables each client to access data from other IBM databases.*

ac·ces·so·ry /əkˈsesəri/ *n* plural **accessories** **1** [C] something that you add to a machine, tool, car etc so that it can do other things or in order to make it look attractive: *They sell software and computer accessories.* | *a manufacturer of motor vehicle parts and accessories*
2 accessories [plural] small things that are used for a particular activity: *a retail chain that sells cooking items, kitchen accessories and home furnishings* | *a maker of plastic folders, binders and other office accessories*
3 [C] LAW someone who helps a criminal, but is not dir-

ectly involved in a crime + **to**: *He was an accessory to murder.*

accident and health benefit —see under BENEFIT[1]

accident insurance —see under INSURANCE

accommodation address —see under ADDRESS[1]

ac·count[1] /əˈkaʊnt/ *n* **1** [C] written abbreviation **a/c** or **acct** BANKING an arrangement between a bank and a customer that allows the customer to pay in and take out money; BANK ACCOUNT: *She used her first pay check to* ***open an account*** (=to start one). | *80% of people have* ***held an account*** (=had one) *with the same bank for five years or more.* | *They were unhappy with service at the bank and* ***closed*** *their* ***account*** *there.* —see also MONEY OF ACCOUNT, STATEMENT OF ACCOUNT, UNIT OF ACCOUNT, AGRICULTURAL UNIT OF ACCOUNT

2 no account BANKING words written on a cheque to show that the account to which it relates has been closed

3 [C] ACCOUNTING a record showing a particular part of the finances of a business

4 accounts [plural] ACCOUNTING the complete set of records showing money coming into and going out of a business, its profits, and its financial situation: *The new accounts contain more bad news for shareholders.* —see also BOOKS OF ACCOUNT

5 accounts [plural] the department of a company that deals with its accounts: *She works in accounts.*

6 [C] an arrangement between a buyer and a seller for payment to be made some time after the buyer receives the goods or services: *No interest is charged provided* ***the account is settled*** (=the money owed is paid) *in full every month.* | *All clients are sent a monthly* ***account statement*** (=list of goods or services bought and money owed).

7 on account paid as part of the total amount that needs to be paid: *We'll pay you half of your fee on account.*

8 on account to be paid for later: *Most of this equipment was bought on account.*

9 [C] an organization that is a regular client of a company, especially an ADVERTISING AGENCY: *He would like to win back the Xerox account, which went to Young and Rubicam.* | *He's always on the road calling on* ***key accounts*** (=important clients).

adjustment account also **control account** [C] ACCOUNTING a record of money spent and received, kept to check that no mistakes have been made in the official set of accounts kept in a LEDGER

annual accounts [plural] FINANCE the complete set of accounts produced by a business every year showing the results of trading during the year and the financial state of the company: *Everton's annual accounts showed a loss last year of £1.8 million.*

appropriation account *BrE* ◆ [C] FINANCE an account showing how a company's profits have been used, for example to re-invest in the company or to pay out to shareholders

◆ [C] in Britain, money that PARLIAMENT has voted to use for a particular purpose

approved accounts [plural] FINANCE accounts that have been formally accepted by a company's directors: *If the approved accounts do not comply with the law, every director who was a party to their approval is guilty of an offence.*

audited accounts [plural] FINANCE accounts that have been checked and approved by AUDITORS (=outside specialists): *Elders expects to report its unaudited annual results in September and audited accounts in October.*

balance of payments capital account [singular] ECONOMICS movements of money into and out of a country relating to investment and other exchanges of capital: *The US balance of payments capital account situation undermined confidence in the dollar.*

balance of payments current account [singular] ECONOMICS movements of money into and out of a country, relating to trade between private individuals, for example workers sending money to their family in another country

bank account [C] an account that a customer has with a bank: *Anyone can go into a bank and* ***open a bank account.***

blocked account [C] a bank account from which money cannot be taken out while a particular situation continues: *Payments due on the oil will be made into a blocked account rather than to Iraq.*

cash account ◆ [C] ACCOUNTING in a set of accounts, the account that records details of all amounts paid or received in cash

◆ [C] ACCOUNTING in arrangements for payment by customers, an account that is settled quickly in cash, rather than one which is paid later or in several payments

◆ [C] another name for a CHECKING ACCOUNT, CHEQUE ACCOUNT, or CURRENT ACCOUNT

cash management account abbreviation **CMA** [C] BANKING a personal bank account offered by a BROKER: *Merrill's cash management account combines a securities account with check-writing and credit-card facilities.*

charge account [C] *AmE* an account you have with a shop or a supplier that allows you to pay for goods at the end of a particular period of time in the future rather than when you buy them; CREDIT ACCOUNT *BrE*: *We have a charge account with a limousine service.*

cheque account *BrE* **checking account** *AmE*, also **current account** *BrE* [C] BANKING an account that allows the customer to use a CHEQUEBOOK and provides services such as bill payments: *It's better to transfer large amounts of money out of your cheque account.*

client account [C] BANKING a bank account operated by a professional person or organization for one of their clients: *Client money should be paid into a client account without delay.*

club account [C] a type of SAVINGS ACCOUNT

club accounts [plural] ACCOUNTING in Britain, accounting systems for organizations such as clubs and associations which do not operate to make a profit

company accounts [plural] financial information that a company is required to produce at the end of every year, including details of its profits or losses

consignment account [C] an account made for goods sent to someone acting on behalf of the owner, who must either sell them or return them to the owner

consolidated accounts [plural] FINANCE accounts showing the combined trading results and financial position of a group of companies: *Philips is removing Grundig from its consolidated accounts as from the start of the year.*

contra account [C] ACCOUNTING an account which is CREDITED or DEBITED against another account

contra-asset account [C] ACCOUNTING an account to record the DEPRECIATION (=loss in value) of assets

credit account *BrE* written abbreviation **C/A** [C] an arrangement with a shop that allows customers to buy goods up to a certain value every month and pay for them later within an agreed time; CHARGE ACCOUNT *AmE*: *My parents had a credit account at the city's major department store which they kept up to date every month.*

current account [C] *BrE* BANKING another name for CHEQUE ACCOUNT: *Your clearing bank will be able to transfer cash directly to and from your current account.*

custodial account [C] *AmE* BANKING a bank account that parents open for a child who is legally too young to control the account

demand account [C] *AmE* BANKING a bank account that you can take money out of without having to warn the bank in advance; INSTANT ACCESS ACCOUNT *BrE*: *There is no minimum balance on our demand account.*

A

deposit account [C] BANKING a bank account that pays interest, often used for saving money not needed immediately: *Before the stock market existed here, the only way for people to manage their money was to put it in a deposit account.*

depreciation account [C] ACCOUNTING a business account in which the amount of depreciation on a FIXED ASSET is entered in the DEBIT side and then also added to the account as a CREDIT, allowing the asset's value to be reduced by the correct amount each year

dormant account [C] a bank account that is still open but not being used: *Dormant bank accounts are often those that are forgotten when someone dies.*

entertainment account [C] the account in a company's set of accounts to which all entertainment costs are charged: *Profit comes from slim-line companies and bosses who keep a slim-line entertainment account.*

escrow account [C] BANKING a special account for money being held in ESCROW (=by a third party while a deal is completed): *Prospective borrowers generally avoid paying advance loan fees; if they do pay any, the money should be put into an escrow account with a third party until the loan is funded.*

Exchange equalization account also **Exchange equalisation account** *BrE* [singular] ECONOMICS an account at the Bank of England that is used by the British government to influence the price of the British pound by buying and selling gold and foreign currencies: *The Bank uses the Exchange Equalization Account to intervene in the foreign exchange market by buying up surplus sterling to keep up the external value of the pound.*

expense account [C] a company account that an employee can use for money that they have to spend as part of their job, for example on hotels, meals etc: *I have an expense account and spend about £20,000 a year on entertaining clients.*

external account [C] ECONOMICS another name for BALANCE OF PAYMENTS CURRENT ACCOUNT: *Hungary has export- and investment-led growth that will not lead to a worsening in the external account.*

final accounts [plural] FINANCE accounts showing the trading results and financial position of a company at the end of its financial year: *Only the final accounts are fully reviewed by external auditors.*

foreign currency account [C] BANKING a bank account held in one country, containing money in the currency of another: *The removal of controls will allow individuals to invest money overseas or in a foreign currency account.*

group accounts [plural] FINANCE accounts showing the trading results and financial position of each company in a group individually or in combined form: *BFE began to be consolidated in the group's accounts last year.*

inactive account ◆ [C] FINANCE a collection of shares or other investments in which the shareholder does not invest any more money, but does not wish to sell: *Every major Wall Street broker now imposes an* ***inactive account fee*** *on investors who don't generate enough commissions.*

◆ [C] a bank account which has not been used for a long time

income and expenditure account [C] FINANCE a record showing the amounts of money coming into and going out of an organization, during a particular period of time. In British companies, this is usually called the PROFIT AND LOSS ACCOUNT; in US companies, it is called the INCOME STATEMENT: *The Society's Income and Expenditure Account for the year ended 31 December shows a surplus of £3.7 million.*

individual retirement account abbreviation **IRA** [C] HUMAN RESOURCES in the US, a savings account for a worker whose employer does not offer a RETIREMENT PLAN. The worker usually puts a specific amount of money into the account at regular times in order to save money for when they stop work: *Some firms allow you to borrow from your Individual Retirement Account without penalty provided you return the money within 60 days.*

instant access account [C] *BrE* a bank account that you can take money out of without having to warn the bank in advance; DEMAND ACCOUNT *AmE*: *These savings accounts pay twice as much interest as many ordinary instant access accounts.*

interim accounts [plural] accounts prepared during the financial year to show a company's current progress and financial position: *Detailed interim accounts are prepared at monthly intervals.*

joint account [C] a bank account that two people can use, for example two people who are married: *Although we have a joint account, he is the one who has taken it into overdraft.*

loro account [C] BANKING an account held by a bank with another bank, usually one in a foreign country

margin account [C] FINANCE money lent by a BROKER (=a buyer and seller of shares etc for others) so that investors can buy shares and other investments with it: *Some alleged that brokers encouraged unsuitable investors to use margin accounts.*

nominal accounts [plural] ACCOUNTING a company's accounts showing all REVENUES (=money received over a period of time) and expenses —compare ***real accounts***

nostro account [C] BANKING a bank account that belongs to one bank and which is held by another bank in another country. The phrase nostro account is used by the bank which owns the account, rather than the bank which holds it —compare ***vostro account***

notice account [C] *BrE* BANKING a bank account that you can take money out of only if you warn the bank a certain number of days before. If you do not give this warning, you lose interest on the money in the account: *Nationwide is offering 4.5% interest on its 90-day notice account.*

NOW account [C] BANKING negotiable order of withdrawal account; a type of CURRENT ACCOUNT in the US that pays interest: *NOW account customers tend to maintain high balances.*

numbered account [C] BANKING a bank account with only a number, so the name of the customer is kept secret: *BCCI shipped $13.9 million to a numbered account in the Cayman Islands.*

postal account [C] a bank account that you can pay into and take money out of by post, rather than at a bank

profit and loss account abbreviation **P&L** [C] *BrE* FINANCE a FINANCIAL STATEMENT showing the financial results of a company's normal activities for a particular period of time, usually the financial year; INCOME STATEMENT *AmE*: *Ferguson will charge redundancy costs of about £3 million to the profit and loss account.*

public account [C] BANKING a bank account where public money is kept by tax authorities, government departments etc

purchases account [C] ACCOUNTING the account in the PURCHASE LEDGER where totals of entries in the purchases book are entered on the DEBIT side: *Total returns outwards are deducted from the purchases account.*

real accounts [plural] ACCOUNTING company accounts relating to the buying and selling of assets such as property and equipment —compare ***nominal accounts***

sales account [C] ACCOUNTING an account in which totals from the SALES DAY BOOK are added as credits every month, year etc

sales returns account [C] ACCOUNTING an account in which totals from the SALES DAY BOOK are added as debits every month, year etc

savings account [C] ACCOUNTING a bank account for

saving money over a long period of time, usually with higher interest than an ordinary DEPOSIT ACCOUNT: *Most savings accounts pay higher interest on larger balances.*

sundries account [C] ACCOUNTING an account in a SALES LEDGER or PURCHASE LEDGER for recording things bought or sold from companies who are not regular customers or suppliers and who therefore do not need their own separate accounts

suspense account [C] BANKING a bank account used to keep income for a short time until it has been decided how to deal with it: *More than $1 million remains in suspense accounts awaiting processing.*

vostro account [C] BANKING a bank account that belongs to one bank and which is held by another bank in another country. The phrase vostro account is used by the bank which holds the account, rather than the bank which owns it —compare ***nostro account***

account² *v*

account for sth *phr v* [T] **1** to be a particular amount or part of something: *Japanese cars accounted for 31% of the US market last year.*

2 ACCOUNTING to show something in a company's accounts in a particular way: *In financial statements, the bonds should be accounted for as debt.*

ac·coun·tan·cy /ə'kaʊntənsi/ *n* [U] *especially BrE* the profession or work done by accountants in keeping the financial records of organizations and in giving advice to clients on tax and other financial matters; ACCOUNTING: *She did a one-year accountancy course.* | *the accountancy profession*

ac·coun·tant /ə'kaʊntənt/ *n* [C] a professional person whose job is to keep and check the financial records of an organization, or to advise clients on tax and other financial matters: *People setting up in business on their own really need to employ an accountant.*

certified accountant in Britain, an accountant who is a member of the Association of Certified Accountants and is therefore allowed by law to officially check a company's accounts

certified management accountant abbreviation **CMA** in the US, an accountant who has passed examinations and is a member of the Institute of Management Accounting of the National Association of Accountants

certified public accountant abbreviation **CPA** in the US, an accountant who is a member of the American Institute of Certified Public Accountants and who holds a licence from the State to work as an accountant

chartered accountant in Britain, an accountant who has spent time working for a fully qualified accountant and has passed all the examinations set by the INSTITUTE OF CHARTERED ACCOUNTANTS

chief accountant the highest ranking accountant in a large organization

cost accountant also **management accountant** an accountant who examines the costs relating to different parts of a business and the cost of producing different products or services rather than doing accounting for formal, legal, or tax requirements: *The cost accountant needs to advise on whether the product can be supplied at the target price.*

forensic accountant an accountant who is trained to examine the facts in criminal cases that involve financial matters: *the role of the forensic accountant in criminal proceedings*

account balance —see under BALANCE¹

account executive —see under EXECUTIVE¹

ac·coun·ting /ə'kaʊntɪŋ/ *n* [U] **1** the usual word for the profession of ACCOUNTANCY in the US

2 the work of keeping a company's financial records, recording its income and expenses, and its business deals: *traditional methods of accounting* | *The 1985 Companies Act requires companies to keep accounting records.*

accrual accounting also **accruals accounting** accounting based on the principle that when a business buys or sells something, this should affect the profit for the period of time when it happens, not when the related payment is sent or received, even if the payment occurs in a different accounting period: *With accruals accounting, postponing or bringing forward cash payments or receipts has no effect.*

budgetary accounting a method of accounting in which the planned amounts and actual amounts spent and received are both included in the accounts, so that you can see at any time how much of the planned amount remains

cash accounting a system of accounting in which only amounts of money coming in and going out are shown in the accounts: *Cash accounting provides measures of cash inflows and cash outflows.*

cost accounting also **management accounting** accounting that studies the costs and profits relating to different parts of a business

creative accounting using unusual but not illegal methods in a set of accounts to make them look better than they really are: *Analysts have criticized his company for relying too much on number-juggling and creative tax accounting to boost profit.*

current cost accounting also **current value accounting** a form of accounting in which a business takes account of rising prices in the amounts it records for costs, sales etc: *In current cost accounting, land is measured in terms of its current value, which in many cases is its replacement cost.*

equity accounting when a company owns 20 to 50% of another company, and shows RETAINED EARNINGS from this company in its own accounts: *TNT earned a profit after tax of A$139.9 million; the figures reflect equity accounting of TNT's share of associated companies.*

false accounting the crime of dishonestly changing figures, records etc or writing false information in a company's financial accounts, deceiving people in order to obtain money by deceiving people: *Jones was found guilty of four charges of false accounting.*

financial accounting accounting concerned with the preparation of FINANCIAL STATEMENTS rather than with examining the costs and profits in each part of a business: *Financial accounting allows you to calculate profit, but is not concerned with how the profit arises.*

inflation accounting accounting that takes account of changing prices, for example the current cost of replacing an existing asset: *inflation accounting techniques in which all costs, revenues, profits and losses are fully adjusted for inflation*

social accounting ECONOMICS when a set of accounts is made from government figures, showing the income and spending of the various parts of the economy

accounting equation —see under EQUATION

accounting period —see under PERIOD

accounting principle —see under PRINCIPLE

accounting rate of return —see under RETURN¹

accounting rule also **accounting standard** —see under RULE¹

Accounting Standards Board abbreviation **ASB** *n* the organization that sets accounting rules in Britain —see also FINANCIAL ACCOUNTING STANDARDS BOARD

accounting system —see under SYSTEM

account manager —see under MANAGER

account payee —see A/C PAYEE (ONLY)

accounts payable —see under PAYABLE

accounts receivable —see under RECEIVABLE

account terms —see under TERM¹

A

ac•cred•it•ed /ə'kredətəd/ *adj* officially accepted as being of a satisfactory or high standard, or permitted to do a particular kind of work: *We are working towards a nationally accredited system of training.* | *The data is available to accredited researchers.* —**accreditation** *n* [U] *The new rules will make it easier for other European accountants to gain accreditation in the US.*

ac•cre•tion /ə'kriːʃən/ *n* [C,U] a slow, gradual increase in an amount, level, value etc: *We will solve our trade problem not by big contracts, but by an accretion of hundreds of smaller deals.*

ac•cru•al /ə'kruːəl/ *n* [C] an increase in an amount of money, usually over a period of time: *The airline is asking employees to allow a one-year freeze on pension accruals.* | *the accrual of $21 million in interest*

accrual accounting —see under ACCOUNTING

accrual basis also **accruals basis, accrual method,** or **accruals method** *n* [singular] ACCOUNTING a principle used in accounting that when a business buys or sells something, this should affect the results for the period of time when it happens, not when the related payment is sent or received, even if the payment occurs in a different accounting period: *Some businesses have to compute tax* ***on an accruals basis,*** *which means they account for it when work is carried out.* —compare CASH BASIS

ac•crue /ə'kruː/ *v* [I,T] *formal* **1** if an amount of money accrues, or is accrued, it gradually increases over a period of time: *The tax falls due at the end of the month, and interest will accrue from that date.*
2 if profits or benefits accrue to you, or are accrued, you have the right to receive them: *If profits are insufficient, no additional rights accrue to the holder of the bond.* | *pension benefits accrued during his 20 years as a businessman*

accrued cost —see under COST[1]

accrued expense —see under EXPENSE

accrued income —see under INCOME

accrued interest —see under INTEREST

acct. written abbreviation for ACCOUNT

ac•cu•mu•late /ə'kjuːmjəleɪt/ *v* **1** [T] to get, earn, or obtain something gradually over a period of time: *He had accumulated $20,000 in interest.* | *A lot of companies have accumulated significant debts.*
2 [I] to increase or develop gradually over a period of time: *the funds that had accumulated in their accounts* | *The arrears have been accumulating since last year.* —**accumulated** *adj* [only before a noun] *The firm now has $300,000 of accumulated debt.*

accumulated depreciation —see under DEPRECIATION

accumulated dividend —see under DIVIDEND

accumulated fund —see under FUND[1]

accumulated profit —see under PROFIT[1]

accumulation unit —see under UNIT

ac•cused /ə'kjuːzd/ *n* **the accused** the person or group of people who have been officially charged with a crime in a court of law

ACE abbreviation for ACTIVE CORPS OF EXECUTIVES

acid ratio —see under RATIO

ac•knowl•edge /ək'nɒlɪdʒ‖-'nɑː-/ *v* [T] **1** to tell someone that you have received something such as a letter they have sent to you: *We shall be grateful if you will kindly* ***acknowledge receipt of*** *this letter.*
2 to admit or accept that something is true or exists: *The government acknowledged that there had been irregularities at a number of voting centres.*

ac•knowl•edge•ment /ək'nɒlɪdʒmənt‖-'nɑː-/ also **acknowledgment** *n* [C,U] **1** a letter sent to someone, saying that you have received something from them: *When we receive an enquiry, a* ***letter of acknowledgement*** *is sent back immediately, enclosing a hotel brochure.* | *a standard* ***acknowledgement letter***
2 LAW a formal statement agreeing that something is correct or true: *The letter should include acknowledgement of the situation from both parties.*

acknowledgement of debt *n* plural **acknowledgements of debt** [C] an official written statement in which someone agrees that they have a debt and will pay it back

ACORN /'eɪkɔːn‖-ɔːrn, -ərn/ *n* A Classification of Residential Neighbourhoods; a system in Britain of putting areas of the country into different classes according to the incomes of the people who live there: *the five local authorities with the worst housing conditions under the ACORN scheme*

a/c payee (only) —see ***account payee (only)*** under PAYEE

ac•quire /ə'kwaɪə‖ə'kwaɪr/ *v* [I] **1** FINANCE if one company acquires another, it buys it: *Hays, the business services group, acquired a document management company, DEI, for £17 million.*
2 acquire a holding/an interest/a stake to buy part of the shares of a company: *P&O has acquired a 50% stake in Gruppo Investimenti Portuali.*

ac•qui•si•tion /ˌækwəˈzɪʃən/ *n* FINANCE **1** [C,U] when one company buys another one, or part of another one: *the group's acquisition of 85 stores in California* | *Sales from a recent acquisition increased revenue to $2.74 billion.*

bootstrap acquisition [C,U] a way of buying a company over a period of time. You buy some shares which you then use to borrow more money to buy more shares, each time promising to give them to the lender if you fail to make repayments on your loan: *WorldCom has been growing through a series of bootstrap acquisitions.*

bust-up acquisition [C,U] when one company is buying another and uses the assets of the company they want to buy as SECURITY to obtain a loan with which to buy that company

2 [C] a company or part of a company that is bought by another company: *Renault's US trucks subsidiary would make an ideal acquisition, but the French say the company is not for sale.*

ac•quis•i•tive /ə'kwɪzətɪv/ *adj* an acquisitive company often buys other companies or parts of other companies: *Conseco, the acquisitive life assurance company, has bought 22 life companies in the past decade.*

ac•ro•nym /'ækrənɪm/ *n* [C] a word made up of the first letters of the name of something such as an organization. For example, NATO is an acronym for the North Atlantic Treaty Organization

a•cross the board also **across-the-board** *adj* affecting everyone or everything in an organization or situation: *They have agreed to production cuts as long as they are across the board.* | *Unions are calling for a 5.9% across-the-board pay increase.* —**across the board** *adv*: *Jobs will be lost across the board in manufacturing.*

ACRS abbreviation for ACCELERATED COST RECOVERY SYSTEM

act[1] /ækt/ *n* [C] **1** a law that has been officially accepted by the governing body of a country: *an act to regulate the carrying on of investment business* | *the 1986 Tax Reform Act* —see also ACT OF CONGRESS

consolidating act a law that combines two or more previous acts

2 a written agreement that has legal force

act[2] *v* **1 act as sth** to do a particular job or have a particular role: *We will act as the company's agent for the* *sale.* | *mortgage brokers who act as middlemen between borrowers and lenders*

2 act for sb if a lawyer acts for someone, he or she represents them in a legal case: *the lawyer acting for the insurance company*

3 act on sb's behalf to represent someone: *The two parties may agree a price for the land or ask an agent to act on their behalf.*

4 act on sth to take action as a result of something that has been said, written, suggested etc: *Congress is eager to act on the report.* | *The administration hasn't yet acted on the request.*

act·ing /'æktɪŋ/ *adj* **acting head/chairman/director etc** someone who does an important job while the usual person is not there, or until a new person is chosen for the job: *Mr Rothers is currently acting general manager of the development company.*

ac·tion /'ækʃən/ *n* **1** [C,U] when someone does something in order to deal with a problem or difficult situation: *The government's action was prompted by shortages of foreign exchange.* | *We must* ***take action*** *to make our shares accessible to a broader segment of the investing public.* —see also RIGHT OF ACTION

affirmative action [U] HUMAN RESOURCES when employers give jobs or other opportunities to people who are normally treated unfairly because of their race, sex etc: *Raised in poverty, Mr Thomas nevertheless opposes the sort of* ***affirmative action programs*** *which got him to Yale law school.*

direct action [U] anything other than talking that is done by an organized group of people in order to try and change something or to get what they want, for example striking: *Scottish fishermen's leaders tried to distance themselves from the threat of direct action.*

industrial action [U] *BrE* when workers do something as a protest against their employer, for example stopping work for a period of time or by only doing certain types of work: *The union is threatening further industrial action.*

job action [C,U] *AmE* an occasion when workers STRIKE (=refuse to work) for a period of time as a protest against their employer: *The government's plan brought threats of job actions from postal employees.*

secondary action *n BrE* [U] a situation in which workers in one factory, company etc STRIKE in order to support the striking workers in a different factory etc: *The Court of Appeal ruled that the absence of a contract between the shipbuilders and the port authority made secondary action illegal.*

strike action [U] when workers STRIKE as a protest against their employer: *Postal workers have voted in support of strike action.* | *the number of man-hours lost through strike action*

2 [U] when important things happen, for example when there is a lot of buying or selling or prices rise or fall: *The tax cut was intended to restore some market action in the banking and real-estate sectors.*

3 [C,U] LAW the process of taking a case or a claim against someone to a court of law: *They began* ***an action to*** *repossess the house.* | *The European Commission is threatening* ***legal action*** *against Britain and France to protect the environment.* | *They will* ***bring an action against*** *him if he does not repay the loan.*

class action [C,U] when a group of people who have all suffered in the same way take a person or organization to court together: *class action lawsuits brought on behalf of smokers against tobacco companies*

frivolous action [C,U] a legal action that does not have serious legal reasons behind it: *The company said it would mount a vigorous defense 'against this frivolous action.'*

action point —see under POINT[1]

ac·tive /'æktɪv/ *adj* **1** if trading or a market is active, there is a lot of buying and selling: *Hong Kong shares advanced in* ***active trading.*** | *These markets are among the most active and volatile in the world.* | *Shares of Lotus, Novell and Microsoft were among the day's most active.* | *Gold was active again today, with nearly 70,000 contracts changing hands.*

2 [not before a noun] a company that is active is selling products or services: *Kraft has been active in Italy for more than 25 years.*

3 if someone is active in doing something, they do it: *Foreign companies have been active in making friendly acquisitions.* | *Australian gold mines are the most active in selling their future production at current prices.* | *Mr Mahlmann is not active in the day-to-day management of the company.*

4 taking definite action rather than just giving advice or waiting to see what will happen: *They are calling for active government intervention.* | *Sudbury will begin an active asset sale program.* | *She wanted to take a more active role in the running of the company.*

5 actually employed in doing a job: *They have looked at data on their active and retired employees' medical records.*

6 an active bank account is being used: *Active credit-card accounts dropped to 30,000 from 50,000 in the mid 1980s.*

active bond —see under BOND

Active Corps of Executives abbreviation **ACE** *n* an organization of US executives willing to work for little or no pay on activities with a social purpose

active population —see under POPULATION

active stock —see under STOCK[1]

active trading —see under TRADING

active trustee —see under TRUSTEE

act of bankruptcy —see under BANKRUPTCY

Act of Congress *n* plural **Acts of Congress** [C] a law made by the central national elected body of the US: *Increasing foreign voting control in US companies requires an Act of Congress.*

act of God *n* plural **acts of God** [C] LAW, INSURANCE a natural event such as a storm or an EARTHQUAKE. No one can be held to be legally liable for damage caused by an act of God, and insurance companies will not usually make payments for such damage: *The Court held that the rainfall was not an act of God and that the Corporation were liable.*

Act of Parliament *n* plural **Acts of Parliament** [C] a law made by the central national elected bodies of Britain and some other countries: *A recent Act of Parliament has for the first time enabled citizens to own and operate radio stations.*

actual damages —see under DAMAGE[1]

actual loss —see under LOSS

actual price —see under PRICE[1]

ac·tu·als /'æktʃuəlz/ *n* [plural] figures relating to something that has actually happened, rather than what was expected; OUTTURN: *Mobile phone operators had expected monthly usage of 250 minutes. Actuals are very different, at 100 minutes.*

actual total loss —see under LOSS

actuarial risk —see under RISK[1]

ac·tu·a·ry /'æktʃuəri‖-tʃueri/ *n* plural **actuaries** [C] INSURANCE someone whose job is to calculate risks, in order to advise INSURANCE companies or PENSION FUNDS: *Such information needs to be made available to actuaries, insurers, and those advising employers.* —**actuarial** *adj* [only before a noun] *He has calculated that, based on* ***actuarial tables*** (=lists of figures used to calculate risks), *he can count on living about 9,000 more days.*

A/D also **a/d** BANKING written abbreviation for AFTER DATE

A

ad /æd/ *n* [C] an informal word for ADVERTISEMENT; ADVERT *BrE*: *The TV ad is excellent and gives us a massive target audience.*

small ad also **classified ad** *BrE*, **want ad** *AmE* an advertisement put in a newspaper by someone wanting to buy or sell something: *He got his first clients through the small ads he put in the newspaper.*

teaser ad an advertisement that is used to get the public interested by giving very little information about the product. The purpose is to get attention for the full ADVERTISING CAMPAIGN that follows

ad agency —see under AGENCY

Ad Alley *n AmE informal* Madison Ave in New York City, where many companies in the advertising industry have offices

ADB abbreviation for ASIAN DEVELOPMENT BANK

added value —see under VALUE[1]

additional damages —see under DAMAGE[1]

ad·di·tion·al·i·ty /əˌdɪʃəˈnæləti/ *n* [U] *BrE* a rule or principle stating that the money spent by a government on public services such as health and education can be added to from other funds, especially European Union GRANTS, but cannot be replaced by those grants altogether: *Additionality has varied considerably amongst zones: while Portugal's additionality amounts to 60 per cent, others, such as Ireland, reveal totals of about 30 per cent.* | *Under the additionality regulations, estimates of local government spending must identify European structural funds separately.*

add-on *n* [C] a product that is sold to be used with another product: *Hewlett Packard now offers its own fax add-on, a bigger unit called the Laser Jet Fax.* —**add-on** *adj* [only before a noun] *There is always the option of buying extra add-on software.*

add-on interest —see under INTEREST

ad·dress[1] /əˈdres‖əˈdres, ˈædres/ *n* [C] the number of the building and the name of the street and town etc where someone lives or works, especially when written on a letter or package: *I wrote the wrong address on the envelope.* | *Please notify us of any* ***change of address****.*

accommodation address an address that is used by people to receive letters, packages etc, that is not the place where they live

e-mail address a name you use for sending and receiving e-mails. It usually consists of your name, followed by the sign @, followed by a company or university name: *You will be prompted to enter your e-mail address as the password.*

forwarding address an address showing the place where you live now, which you leave at the place you used to live so that people can send mail on to you

memory address COMPUTING a number that shows where a piece of information is stored in a computer's memory —see also FORM OF ADDRESS

ad·dress[2] /əˈdres/ *v* [T] **1** to write on an envelope, package etc the name of the person you are sending it to: *If you address the letter, I'll mail it to you.* **address sth to sb**: *The letter is addressed to you, not me.*

2 address a meeting/conference etc to make a speech to a large group of people: *The meeting was addressed by Senator Howard.*

3 *formal* to discuss, think about, or do something about a particular problem or question, especially with the aim of solving a problem: *This use of technology has enabled NatWest to* ***address a problem*** *facing many businesses across the UK.*

ad·here /ədˈhɪə‖-ˈhɪr/ *v*

adhere to sth *phr v* [T] to behave according to a rule, agreement etc: *Now companies must adhere to stricter guidelines on the disposal of toxic waste.* —**adherence** *n* [U] *Aid to these countries is linked to their strict adherence to disarmament agreements.*

ad·journ /əˈdʒɜːn‖-ɜːrn/ *v* [I,T] if a meeting or law court adjourns, or if the person in charge adjourns it, it finishes or stops, either for a short time, or until the next time it meets: *The chairman has the power to adjourn the meeting at any time.* + **for/until**: *The committee adjourned for lunch.* —**adjournment** *n* [C,U] *The adjournment will allow more time to receive votes from shareholders on the proposal.*

ad·ju·di·cate /əˈdʒuːdɪkeɪt/ *v* [I,T] **1** LAW to officially decide who is right in an argument between two groups or organizations: *The union has offered to adjudicate the claim.* + **on**: *The court refused to adjudicate on the issue until all construction activities on the disputed site had ceased.*

2 be adjudicated bankrupt to be judged by a court of law to be unable to pay debts: *In 1985 the two brothers were adjudicated bankrupt.* —**adjudication** *n* [U] *This is a matter for adjudication.* —**adjudicator** *n* [C] *The Banking Ombudsman is there to act as an impartial adjudicator.*

ad·just /əˈdʒʌst/ *v* [T] **1** to make small changes to something in order to correct or improve it: *Their monthly repayments are adjusted once a year.*

2 seasonally adjusted seasonally adjusted figures have been changed slightly according to influences that affect them regularly at particular times of the year, so that they can be compared with figures from other times of the year: *Orders totalled a seasonally adjusted $132.8 billion.*

3 INSURANCE to settle an insurance CLAIM: *The claim has been adjusted.*

adjustable-rate mortgage —see under MORTGAGE[1]

adjusted share price —see under PRICE[1]

ad·just·er /əˈdʒʌstə‖-ər/ *n* [C] **claims/insurance/loss adjuster** INSURANCE a person or company whose job is to assess the value of loss or damage for someone who has claimed on their insurance: *The loss adjuster feels there is likely to be a valid subsidence claim.*

average adjuster an adjuster whose job is to calculate payments by insurers following CLAIMS relating to ships and the goods they carry

ad·just·ment /əˈdʒʌstmənt/ *n* [C,U] **1** a change that is made to something in order to correct or improve it: *Upon devolution there would have to be an adjustment in government spending.* | *Grants are to be slashed by 33%, after adjustment for inflation.*

cost of living adjustment abbreviation **COLA** plural **cost of living adjustments** in the US, a small increase in someone's pay or pension, made to cover increases in the cost of living

debt adjustment when someone in financial difficulty makes new arrangements on when and how they will pay people that they owe money to: *Write to creditors with debt adjustment proposals, negotiate and finally agree a scheme.*

2 INSURANCE the agreement between an INSURER and someone who has claimed on their insurance over the amount that will be paid, or the amount itself: *We are still waiting for the adjustment to be paid.*

adjustment account —see under ACCOUNT[1]

adjustment factor —see under FACTOR[1]

ad·man /ˈædmæn/ *n* plural **admen** [C] *informal* someone who works in advertising: *It may very well be that the adman invented the teenager.*

ad·min /ˈædmɪn/ *n* [U] *especially BrE informal* the activities involved with managing or organizing the work of a company, organization etc; ADMINISTRATION: *She works in admin.*

ad·min·is·ter /ədˈmɪnəstə‖-ər/ *v* [T] **1** to manage, organize, and control something and make sure it is

dealt with correctly: *A new national fund will be administered by the insurance industry.* | *the bureaucrats who administer welfare programs*
2 administer justice to punish crimes: *They were responsible for maintaining order and administering justice within their community.*

ad·min·i·strate /ədˈmɪnəstreɪt/ *v* [T] another word for ADMINISTER[1]: *The system controls personnel records and administrates the payroll.*

ad·min·is·tra·tion /ədˌmɪnəˈstreɪʃən/ *n* **1** [U] the activities involved with managing and organizing the work of a company or organization: *I want to spend my time on research and development rather than administration.*
2 [U] the part of a company or organization involved with managing and organizing its work: *The job cuts will affect those in sales support and administration.*
3 [C usually singular] the government of a country at a particular time, especially in the United States: *He said that the Clinton administration had created one million new jobs.* | *The problem has been ignored by successive administrations.*
4 [U] in Britain and some other countries, when a company in financial difficulty is reorganized by an outside specialist with the aim of continuing some of its activities so that it can avoid LIQUIDATION (=being broken up and sold): *The company is currently* ***in administration****, but Mr Brown hopes that it will be possible to keep it going in some form.* | *Hamlet has* ***gone into administration*** *with debts of about £40 million.* | *The group should continue trading despite its financial problems, rather than be* ***put into administration****.* —see also BANKRUPTCY, CHAPTER 11, LIQUIDATION, RECEIVERSHIP

administration order —see under ORDER[1]

administrative assistant —see under ASSISTANT

administrative tribunal —see under TRIBUNAL

ad·min·is·tra·tor /ədˈmɪnəstreɪtə‖-ər/ *n* [C] **1** someone who manages and organizes the work of a company or organization: *He was a superb marketer, but as an administrator he was disorganized.*
2 someone who manages a company that has been put into administration: *The company might have to be put into the hands of an administrator.* —compare RECEIVER

Admiralty court —see under COURT[1]

ad·mis·sion /ədˈmɪʃən/ *n* [U] **1** the cost of entrance to a cinema, sports event etc: *Admission prices have been kept at £6 for adults and £3 for children.*
2 permission given to someone to enter a place, or become a member of a group, organization, school etc + **to**: *Many applicants are unable to* ***gain admission*** *to courses leading to these qualifications.* | *Greece was granted full admission to the EC in 1981.*
3 FINANCE permission given by a stockmarket to a company for its shares to be bought and sold there: *the admission of securities to official Stock Exchange listing*

admission of liability *n* plural **admissions of liability** [C] when a person or organization accepts legal liability for something: *The company maintains that the settlement accord is not an admission of liability.*

ad·mit /ədˈmɪt/ *v* past tense and past participle **admitted** present participle **admitting** [T] **1** to allow someone to enter a place or become a member of a group, organization, school etc **admit sb/sth to sth**: *Both republics are now hoping to be admitted to the IMF.*
2 admit liability to accept legal liability for something: *The multinational has now admitted liability for its negligence.*

a·dopt /əˈdɒpt‖əˈdɑːpt/ *n* [T] **1** if you adopt a new method, process etc, you start to use it: *All US companies are required to adopt the new standards.*
2 MARKETING to start using a product, especially a new product, usually with the intention of continuing to buy and use it: *More than 300 companies have adopted the Java toolkit.* —**adoption** *n* [C,U] *the adoption of sophisticated production techniques* | *adoption of new textbooks by the education department*

adoption curve —see under CURVE

ADR *n* **1** [C] FINANCE American Depositary Receipt; a type of investment that allows investors in the US to trade indirectly in the shares of non-US companies without trading in the shares themselves: *ADRs provide the opportunity to buy into Asian companies without incurring currency risks.*
2 [U] LAW alternative dispute resolution; a method in the US of settling legal disagreements without using an ordinary court: *Deere resolves its product liability cases through a company that provides ADR services.*

ad valorem duty —see under DUTY

ad valorem tariff —see under TARIFF

ad valorem tax —see under TAX[1]

ad·vance[1] /ədˈvɑːns‖ədˈvæns/ *adj* [only before a noun] done before an event happens: *A small fee is charged for this service and* ***advance notice*** *of at least two weeks is required.* | *A fair-minded employer will usually give employees plenty of* ***advance warning*** *of possible redundancies.*

advance[2] *n* [C] **1** an amount of money paid to someone before the usual time, or before a piece of work has been completed + **of**: *We could offer you an advance of £1,000 and the rest on satisfactory completion of the book.* + **on**: *He had received an advance on his wages.*
bank advance money lent by a bank to a customer: *The primary source of finance has been bank advances.*
2 an increase in the amount, level, or price of something: *UK stocks have risen sharply, with further advances expected.* + **in**: *Analysts forecast a 6% decline in Italian car sales and an 8% advance in French sales.*

advance[3] *v* **1** [T] if you advance someone money, you lend it to them or give it to them, perhaps before they have earned it: *Patrons advanced sums of money for building an art gallery.* **advance sb sth**: *Random House had advanced him the money to write a book.*
2 [I] FINANCE when the price of shares, currencies, goods etc advances, it increases: *Gold prices advanced slightly in early trading.* | *Crude oil advanced $2.88 a barrel.* + **against**: *The dollar advanced against the yen.*
3 [I] FINANCE when profits or sales advance, they increase: *The bank's pretax profit advanced 37% to $205.3 million.* | *First-quarter sales advanced 36%.*
4 [I] FINANCE when a company advances, its profit increases: *Corporation Bank advanced 19.5%, lifting net profits to 1.25 billion rupees.*

advance copy —see under COPY[1]

ad·vanced /ədˈvɑːnst‖ədˈvænst/ *adj* using the most modern ideas, equipment, and methods: *The country increased foreign-currency reserves by selling some of its* ***advanced technology*** *to foreign companies.*

advance fee —see under FEE

advance payment —see under PAYMENT

advance purchase fare —see under FARE

ad·van·cer /ədˈvɑːnsə‖-ˈvænsər/ *n* [C] FINANCE a share that increases in value on a particular day of trading on a stockmarket; ADVANCING SHARE: *Advancers beat decliners on the Big Board,* ***922 to 831*** (=shares in 922 companies rose and shares in 831 companies fell). —compare DECLINER

advancing shares —see under SHARE

advancing stocks —see under STOCK[2]

ad·van·tage /ədˈvɑːntɪdʒ‖ədˈvæn-/ *n* [C] something that helps you to be better or more successful than others: *America's lead in aerospace is one of its most important* ***competitive advantages.*** | *Government subsidies* ***give*** *these industries an* ***unfair advantage.*** + **over**: *It has an advantage over foreign manufacturers because of its flexible workforce.*

absolute advantage [C] ECONOMICS the advantage that one country has over another because it can make a product more cheaply: *UK growth rates were below those of Europe and as a result an absolute advantage was turned into an absolute disadvantage.*

comparative advantage ◆ [C] ECONOMICS the advantage that one country has over another because it is better at making a particular product: *America's comparative advantage in high technology*

◆ [U] ECONOMICS the idea that countries should specialize in making the products that they are particularly good at making, and should import products that other countries are better at making. People who support this idea believe that it is the best way for all countries to become wealthier: *Removing quotas allows comparative advantage to enrich the world.*

competitive advantage [C] an advantage that makes a company more able to succeed in competing with others: *Advanced Micro's chip carries the competitive advantage of using less power than Intel's.*

adverse balance —see under BALANCE[1]

adverse trade balance —see under BALANCE OF TRADE

ad•vert /ˈædvɜːt‖-ɜːrt/ *BrE n* [C] an informal word for advertisement

ad•ver•tise /ˈædvətaɪz‖-ər-/ *v* [I,T] **1** to tell people publicly about a product or service in order to persuade them to buy it: *Beer and wine are both advertised on TV.* | *They are among the most* ***heavily advertised*** *cigarettes in the US.* + **as**: *The cars are advertised as being more economical to run.*

2 to inform people publicly, for example in a newspaper or magazine, that a job is available and invite them to apply for it + **for**: *They have advertised for two engineers.*

ad•ver•tise•ment /ədˈvɜːtəsmənt‖ˌædvərˈtaɪz-/ also **advert** *BrE — n* [C] a picture, piece of film, or piece of writing that is used to tell people publicly about a product or service in order to persuade them to buy it: *She was used in an advertisement promoting slimming food.* | *the new* ***television advertisement*** *for the Volkswagen Golf* | *Next has* ***placed advertisements*** *today in the Wall Street Journal.* | *The importers of the faulty driers have* ***run advertisements*** *asking owners to contact them.*

classified advertisement a small advertisement you put in a newspaper if you want to buy or sell something

job advertisement an announcement in a newspaper or magazine, informing people that a job is available: *He condemned the practice of putting age limits in job advertisements.*

print advertisement advertisements that appear in newspapers, magazines etc: *In addition to print advertisements, Smirnoff will broadcast the commercial on cable TV channels.* | *Randolph is planning a print advertisement campaign.*

ad•ver•tis•er /ˈædvətaɪzə‖-vərtaɪzər/ *n* [C] a person or organization that puts out an advertisement: *The BCAP is the code with which all advertisers must comply.*

ad•ver•tis•ing /ˈædvətaɪzɪŋ‖-ər-/ *n* [U] telling people publicly about a product or service in order to persuade them to buy it: *Most organizations underestimate the benefits of advertising.* | ***Television advertising*** *revenues declined by 2.9%.*

business-to-business advertising MARKETING when a company advertises its products or services to other companies or to professional people, not to the general public

comparative advertising advertising that directly compares one company's products with another company's. Comparative advertising is illegal in some countries

direct advertising ◆ advertising that uses traditional methods such as television or magazine advertisements: *Because direct advertising of cigarettes is forbidden in Italy, other strategies for cigarette promotion are being developed.*

◆ advertising that involves contacting people directly, for example by writing to them, to tell them about a product or service: *We are planning to launch a direct advertising campaign.*

direct response advertising advertising which a customer has to respond to directly, by returning a form, making a phone call etc rather than simply going to a shop to buy the product

drip advertising when advertisements for a product or service are shown repeatedly over a long period of time

image advertising advertising that tries to give people a specific image about a product or company, for example an IMAGE of luxury, excitement, adventure etc: *Be wary of image advertising featuring posh offices, when all you really need is basic, reliable service.*

institutional advertising advertising that aims to improve the image of an organization or industry, or of a product in general such as fish or milk: *institutional advertising such as the 'See a Solicitor' series of leaflets*

issue advertising advertising that is not intended to sell a product or service, but rather to change people's opinions or behaviour: *anti-smoking campaigns and other issue advertising*

mass advertising advertising designed to reach large numbers of people, for example through newspapers and television: *The retail industry has focused too much on mass advertising and not enough on service.*

point-of-purchase advertising also **point-of-sale advertising** advertising for a product in places where it is sold: *point-of-sale advertising designed to prevent a last-minute change of mind*

product advertising advertising for particular products, rather than a brand or a company: *Heinz decided to withdraw all product advertising from television to concentrate its resources on direct marketing.*

subliminal advertising advertising that has hidden messages and pictures in it, that are supposed to give people information without them being conscious of it

advertising agency —see under AGENCY

Advertising Association *n* a professional association of British advertising companies and executives

advertising budget —see under BUDGET[1]

advertising campaign —see under CAMPAIGN

advertising executive —see under EXECUTIVE[1]

advertising space —see under SPACE

Advertising Standards Authority abbreviation **ASA** *n* a British organization that makes sure that advertising is honest and truthful: *Advertisements with flight prices must include all taxes and other charges, the Advertising Standards Authority has ruled.*

ad•ver•to•ri•al /ˌædvəˈtɔːriəl‖-vər-/ *n* [C] MARKETING an advertisement that uses the style of a newspaper or magazine article so that it appears to be giving facts rather than trying to sell a product: *The advertorial is intended to look as much like the other editorial pages as possible.*

ad•vice /ədˈvaɪs/ *n* **1** [U] information given to someone, especially by an expert, so that they know what to do and can make the right decision: *She will remain on the board and provide* ***financial advice*** *to the company.* | *US law firms began providing* ***legal advice*** *to government agencies.*

2 also **advice note** *BrE* [C] a document giving someone details about a sale or purchase that they are involved in, for example a note to a buyer giving details of goods that they are being sent

credit advice [U] a note from a bank informing a customer that an amount of money has been put into their account

advice note —see under NOTE[1]

advice of delivery *BrE n* [singular] a document sent by the POST OFFICE telling someone who has sent a letter by RECORDED DELIVERY that it has been delivered; DELIVERY CONFIRMATION *AmE*

advice of despatch *n* [singular] a document sent by someone sending goods abroad, telling the buyer that the goods they have ordered have been sent

ad·vis·er also **advisor** *AmE* /ədˈvaɪzə‖-ər/ *n* [C] **1** an expert who gives information to someone so that they are able to make a good decision: *An* ***independent financial adviser*** *can pick a pension plan to suit you.* | *an investment advisor*

2 in Britain, someone whose job is selling investment products like PENSIONS and LIFE INSURANCE from different companies, rather than someone selling the investment products of one company. However, some financial services companies have IFAs who sell their own company's products as well as those of other companies: *An independent financial adviser can pick a pension plan to suit you from a wide range.*

ad·vis·o·ry /ədˈvaɪzəri/ *adj* existing to give advice or having the purpose of giving advice: *He is a member of Franklin's investment* ***advisory board****.* | *She resigned as president, but will continue in an* ***advisory capacity****.*

Advisory, Conciliation and Arbitration Service —see ACAS

advisory fee —see under FEE

AEA abbreviation for AMERICAN ECONOMICS ASSOCIATION

aer·o·nau·tics /ˌeərəˈnɔːtɪks‖ˌerəˈnɒː-/ *n* [U] the science of designing, making, and flying planes: *South Korea is building an* ***aeronautics industry****.* —see also AVIATION —**aeronautic** *adj* —**aeronautical** *adj*: *Embraer, a Brazilian aeronautical firm*

aer·o·space /ˈeərəʊspeɪs‖ˈeroʊ-/ *n* [U] the making of aircraft and space vehicles: *US* ***aerospace companies*** *are developing a new plane in cooperation with the US Air Force.*

af·fil·i·ate[1] /əˈfɪliət/ *n* [C] a small company or organization that is connected with or controlled by a larger one: *Fuji Xerox Co., the Japanese affiliate of Xerox Corp*

af·fi·li·ate[2] /əˈfɪlieɪt/ *v* [I,T] if a group or organization affiliates to or is affiliated to a larger one, it is connected with it or controlled by it + **to**: *Ginsen is affiliated to the giant Sumitomo group.* | *Student associations almost all affiliate to the National Union of Students.* —**affiliated** *adj*: *a complicated network of affiliated companies* | *Most local TV stations are affiliated with one of the major networks.* —**affiliation** *n* [U] *The group is closely involved with developments in the rest of Europe via its affiliation to Euroserv.*

affiliated company —see under COMPANY

affinity card —see under CARD

affirmative ac·tion —see under ACTION

AFL-CIO *n* American Federation of Labor and Confederation of Industrial Organizations; the professional organization for LABOR UNIONs in the US, which represents them in discussions with the government, employers etc: *The AFL-CIO fears that the trade pact will harm the interests of its members.*

a·float /əˈfləʊt‖əˈfloʊt/ *adj* having enough money to operate or stay out of debt: *Matthew has been selling key assets just to* ***keep*** *the business* ***afloat****.* | *The Treasury will have to borrow at least £40 billion next year, just to* ***stay afloat****.*

a·fore·said /əˈfɔːsed‖ əˈfɔːr-/ also **a·fore·men·tioned** /əˈfɔːmenʃənd‖-ɔːr-/ *adj* [only before a noun] *written formal* already mentioned on the same page or on a previous page; ABOVE-MENTIONED: *an order which contains both the aforesaid provisions*

after date written abbreviations **A/D, a/d** *adv* BANKING words written on a BILL OF EXCHANGE to show that payment will be made after a particular period of time from the date on the bill: *two promissory notes promising to pay £110 six months after date*

after-hours *adj* [only before a noun] after-hours activities happen after the normal hours of opening for a business, financial market etc: *He asked Mr Gray to come to his office for an after-hours meeting.*

after-hours dealing —see under DEALING

after-hours trading —see under TRADING

af·ter·mar·ket /ˈɑːftəˌmɑːkət‖ˈæftərˌmɑːr-/ *n* [C] *BrE* **1** FINANCE the period of trading immediately after a new bond, share etc is ISSUED (=first sold), when its future price is still uncertain: *The stock issue traded at a premium in the aftermarket.*

2 MARKETING the market for products that people buy after they have bought another related product, for example spare parts or extra pieces of equipment: *the large US aftermarket for replacement car parts*

after-sales *adj* **after-sales service/support** help that is given to someone who has bought a product, for example free repairs or help in using the product: *O'Neill Cycles provides very good after-sales services, with a ten-year guarantee and a one-year parts guarantee.*

after-sales service —see under SERVICE[1]

after sight —see under SIGHT

after-tax *adj* [only before a noun] relating to the amount that remains after tax has been paid: *These measures would cost you about £825 of your* ***after-tax income****.* | *The bank has just announced* ***after-tax profits*** *of $22 billion.* —**after tax** *adv*: *TNT earned a profit after tax of £139 million.*

after-tax loss —see under LOSS

after-tax profit —see under PROFIT[1]

against all risks *adv* INSURANCE if something is insured against all risks, it is insured against any kind of loss or damage: *You will insure the aforesaid items against all risks.*

age discrimination —see under DISCRIMINATION

age·is·m also **agism** /ˈeɪdʒɪzəm/ *n* [U] treating people unfairly because of their age, especially because they are old: *Ageism in recruitment is an increasing problem.*

a·gen·cy /ˈeɪdʒənsi/ *n* plural **agencies** [C] **1** a government department with a particular responsibility: *the Atomic Energy Agency* | *the Environmental Protection Agency*

aid agency a government or private organization which helps people who are suffering from war, hunger etc by providing them with doctors, food, medicine, money etc: *international aid agencies, such as UNICEF*

2 a business that provides a particular service or provides information about other businesses and their products: *Association Marketing Inc, an insurance agency and brokerage company*

advertising agency also **ad agency** a business that gives advice to companies about how they should advertise their products, and produces advertisements for them: *Kerr is planning director at the advertising agency J. Walter Thompson.*

collection agency a business that buys debts from other businesses for a reduced amount and obtains payment of them

commercial agency *BrE* ◆ an organization offering information on the finances of a company or person, especially information on whether or not they can be expected to pay for something you provide them with; CREDIT AGENCY *AmE*

◆ any kind of profit-making agency

credit agency an organization that gives information about the financial strength of companies and governments to financial institutions and suppliers, so that they can decide whether to lend money or allow goods to be bought on credit: *The credit agency lowered the rating of California's public debt to double-A from the top rank of triple-A.*

employment agency also **employment bureau** a business that works for organizations to find people for jobs when the organizations need them; RECRUITMENT AGENCY: *There are many employment agencies who deal with advertising personnel.*

estate agency *BrE* a REAL ESTATE AGENCY

rating agency also **ratings agency** FINANCE an independent organization that calculates the risk of investing in or lending to a company and gives it a rating based on this. Examples of rating agencies are Moody's and Standard & Poors: *The ratings agency lowered the fund's rating to triple-B-plus from single-A-minus.*

real estate agency *AmE* a company that sells houses or land for other people; ESTATE AGENCY *BrE*: *She works as a real estate agent in Boston.*

recruitment agency also **recruitment firm** a business that works for organizations to find people for jobs when the organizations need them; EMPLOYMENT AGENCY

staff agency also **employment agency** HUMAN RESOURCES a company whose business is to find new employees for other companies; EMPLOYMENT AGENCY

3 a business that represents a company in a particular area and sells its products

agency broker —see under BROKER[1]

a·gen·da /əˈdʒendə/ *n* [C] **1** a list of the subjects to be discussed at a meeting: *What's the first item* ***on the agenda****?*

2 a list of things that someone considers important or that they are planning to do: *The recent strengthening of the dollar – and how to stop it – should be* ***at the top of the agenda****.* | *Free trade was still* ***high on the agenda****, but other aims began to seem even more important.*

3 hidden agenda someone's secret plan or aims, rather than the ones that they say that they have: *The union accused the company board of having a hidden agenda.*

a·gent /ˈeɪdʒənt/ *n* [C] **1** a person or company that is paid by another person or company to represent them in business, in their legal problems etc: *trading companies who act as agents for manufacturers* —see also SUB-AGENT

average agent INSURANCE a person or organization whose job is to arrange for insurance claims relating to ships to be examined

bargaining agent in the US, a union chosen by a group of workers in an organization

business agent ◆ in Britain, someone whose job is to represent another person in business matters and make important decisions for them, especially relating to contracts: *He is now acting as the business agent of the industrialist John de Verdun.*

◆ in the US, an employee who represents their LABOR UNION in a particular place or organization: *the business agent for Laborers Local 394*

buying agent a person or organization that represents people buying property and looks for suitable properties for them

commercial agent ◆ the business representative of a person or organization: *PepsiCo's negotiations in Argentina have been conducted through the local football authorities' commercial agent, the IMG Group.*

◆ PROPERTY *BrE* a person or organization that buys and sells commercial property for others; COMMERCIAL BROKER *AmE*: *The plan is to build 495 new houses and Healey and Baker are the commercial agents for the scheme.*

commission agent an independent seller of products or services who is paid a COMMISSION: *The Axa-UAP insurance group now has 4,500 commission agents.*

customs agent a person or company that is paid to make the formal arrangements for imported goods to go through customs

del credere agent someone who agrees to sell goods for another person and who will pay for the goods even if they do not manage to sell them. In exchange for this they usually receive a larger amount as payment

disbursing agent another name for a PAYING AGENT

economic agent a person, company etc that has an effect on the economy of a country, for example by buying, selling, or investing: *The two main economic agents in the diagram are individuals and firms.*

enrolled agent TAX in the US, a tax advisor who has worked for the IRS or passed an IRS examination

escrow agent a person or organization that accepts money, documents etc in ESCROW (=kept by a third party): *As an escrow agent, Ms Harrell collected money from the sales of property purchased with guaranteed loans that had been foreclosed.*

estate agent *BrE* someone whose job is to sell houses or land for other people; REAL ESTATE AGENT *AmE*; REALTOR *AmE*

forwarding agent a company that arranges for goods to be delivered to other countries

free agent a person or organization that is free to do what they want, without legal or other restrictions: *After the contract expires, the Zuckers will be free agents, producing movies at various studios.*

house agent someone whose business is to help people buy and sell their houses; ESTATE AGENT *BrE*; REAL ESTATE AGENT *AmE*; REAL ESTATE BROKER *AmE*

insurance agent a person or organization whose business is giving advice about and selling insurance, either the policies of one insurance company or the policies of different insurance companies: *Insurance agents rely heavily on a company's ratings and many will sell only policies of companies with a top rating.*

land agent a person or organization that works for a large landowner, managing the land and property, collecting rents etc: *a land agent representing several landowners and farmers*

literary agent someone who is paid by an author to find companies to PUBLISH their books, and to discuss the author's contract etc with the publishers

managing agent someone who works for or represents a property owner, managing properties, collecting rents etc: *Letting property today is very complex and it is essential you have a competent managing agent.*

overseas agent a person or company that sells another company's goods abroad: *Licensed overseas agents receive 15% commission on all videocassettes distributed by them.*

patent agent someone whose job involves helping people or companies protect their rights for their new products, methods of doing things etc by arranging PATENTS: *an application by the company's patent agents for litigation rights*

paying agent FINANCE a company, usually a bank, that receives money from companies that sell stocks, shares etc and pays the interest and DIVIDENDS on them to shareholders. Paying agents charge a fee for this service; DISBURSING AGENT: *An issuer will need to appoint a paying agent, to be responsible for the safekeeping of the notes.*

real estate agent someone whose job is to sell houses or land for other people; REAL ESTATE BROKER *AmE*; ESTATE AGENT *BrE*

shipping agent a person or company that organizes

the documents, insurance etc necessary for sending goods

transfer agent FINANCE someone whose job is to keep a list of all the people owning shares in a company, and who makes the necessary changes if the shares are sold to someone else

2 someone who is paid by actors, musicians etc to find work for them: *He instructed his agent to say no to the TV series.*

agent bank —see under BANK[1]

age profile —see under PROFILE[1]

ag·gre·gate[1] /'ægrɪgɪt/ *n* [C] **1** the total after a lot of different parts or figures have been added together: *If workers seek greater increases in wages, they will* ***in the aggregate*** (=in total) *bring about higher inflation.*

2 ECONOMICS one of the measurements used when calculating the amount of money in an economy at a particular time: *M2, the aggregate most closely tracked by the Federal Reserve Board* —see also MONEY SUPPLY

monetary aggregate one of the parts of the MONEY SUPPLY, for example cash, money held in banks etc: *The M2 and M3 monetary aggregates have not increased since April.*

aggregate[2] *adj* [only before a noun] total and combined: *The conglomerate reported an aggregate loss of 1.2 billion Australian dollars.* | *Analysts expect aggregate earnings of the top 500 companies to be down 1%.*

aggregate demand —see under DEMAND

ag·gre·ga·tion /ˌægrɪ'geɪʃən/ *n* [C,U] *formal* **1** when figures are combined to make a total, or the total amount produced: *Japanese banks represent perhaps 35% of South Korea's borrowings, but the precise aggregation is uncertain.*

2 when different things are combined to make a whole, or the whole that is produced: *The key in Internet TV will be in* ***content aggregation****: bringing TV together with facilities such as information services and shopping.*

ag·gres·sive /ə'gresɪv/ *adj* **1** an aggressive action uses direct and forceful methods in order to achieve the result that someone wants: *aggressive marketing tactics to promote smoking among teenagers* | *aggressive cost-cutting* | *Aggressive buying from foreign investors has led the Nikkei's recent recovery.*

2 an aggressive person or organization is very determined to be successful and achieve what they want: *AT&T is struggling to fight off aggressive competitors.*

aging schedule —see under SCHEDULE[1]

a·gi·o /'ædʒiəʊ‖-oʊ/ *n* [C usually singular] **1** BANKING the difference between the interest rate a bank pays on deposits and the interest rate it charges on loans

2 FINANCE the difference between the buying price and the selling price of a currency

AGM *BrE* abbreviation for ANNUAL GENERAL MEETING —see under MEETING

a·gree /ə'griː/ *v* [I,T] to make a decision with someone after a discussion with them: *AMV failed to agree a price with WPP.* | *Loughlin has agreed a new two-year contract.* **agree to do sth**: *The company agreed in principle to sell the paper mill to local managers.* + **on**: *Exxon and Alaska agreed on the broad terms of a settlement.* —**agreed** *adj*: *They are no longer prepared to pay the agreed price.* | *an agreed code of conduct*

agreed-value insurance —see under INSURANCE

a·gree·ment /ə'griːmənt/ *n* **1** [C] an arrangement or promise to do something, made by two or more people or organizations: ***Under the agreement****, Cail will distribute Lynwood's products in North America.* | *What happens if the warring parties fail to* ***reach an agreement****?* + **on**: *an agreement on arms reduction* —see also BREACH OF AGREEMENT, MEMORANDUM OF AGREEMENT

buy-and-sell agreement [C] LAW an agreement between owners of a non-public company, that if one of them sells their share in the company, they must offer it first to the other owners

collective agreement [C] a formal agreement between an employer and a TRADE UNION in which the agreed conditions of employment such as wages and hours are stated: *Contract workers fall outside collective agreements.*

concession agreement [C] an arrangement between a country and a company for the company to carry out activities such as MINING: *Union Texas has signed a new petroleum concession agreement with the Pakistan government.*

fair-trade agreement [C] *AmE* an agreement between a manufacturer and a retailer that the manufacturer's product will not be sold below a certain price. This is now illegal in many places

forward rate agreement abbreviation **FRA** [C] an agreement to buy a particular amount of currency for delivery at a fixed price on a fixed date in the future: *You can protect yourself against future rises in interest rates by negotiating a forward rate agreement.*

freeze agreement [C] an agreement made by a company looking for investment from other companies with a company that might be investing in it, stating that it will not look for investment from any other companies: *Nissan would have to sign a freeze agreement preventing it from approaching other carmakers until talks with Renault were completed or called off.*

gentleman's agreement [C] an informal agreement that is not written down, made between people who trust and respect each other: *It suited both parties for their arrangements to be* ***by gentleman's agreement****.*

heads of agreement [plural] *BrE* a document signed by the people involved in a deal, showing that they definitely want to be involved in it: *We have a heads of agreement signed by both parties, proving their commitment to the project.*

labour agreement *BrE* **labor agreement** *AmE* [C] an agreement between managers and workers about the conditions under which work is done: *The company* ***reached*** *a new* ***labor agreement*** *with its workers.* | *The United Auto Workers union and Chrysler Corp. begin talks soon on a new labor agreement.*

non-disclosure agreement [C] an agreement by two organizations not to give information to others about formal discussions they are having or plans they are making: *GTE has been looking at buying companies involved in privatizations, and in many cases is bound by non-disclosure agreements.*

repurchase agreement also **repo agreement** [C] FINANCE an occasion when the holder of particular bonds sells them and agrees to buy them back on a specific date in the future at a fixed price. CENTRAL BANKS use repos to control the MONEY SUPPLY (=the amount of money in the economy) by buying back government bonds for specific periods of time; SALE AND REPURCHASE AGREEMENT: *When it wants to inject cash into the banking system, the Bundesbank* ***enters repurchase agreements****. It takes securities from banks and gives them cash that they can invest or lend to clients.* —see also REPO[1]

sale and repurchase agreement [C] another name for REPURCHASE AGREEMENT

service agreement [C] ◆ an agreement between a company and its DIRECTOR, stating what the director will do, how much they will be paid etc; SERVICE CONTRACT: *If a director's service agreement is to last for more than five years, it must be approved by the shareholders.*
◆ [C] an agreement between a company and a customer, stating what product or service the company will provide, and any arrangements for delivery, payment etc; SERVICE CONTRACT: *Users must* ***sign a*** *12-month* ***service agreement*** *when they first receive the phone.*

A

standstill agreement [C] FINANCE in an unwanted takeover, an agreement between a company and the BIDDER (=someone trying to take control of it) in which the bidder agrees not to buy any more shares in the company for a particular period of time in return for more power on the board etc: *Dataproducts Inc. alleges that the hostile offer by DPC Acquisition Partners breaks a standstill agreement between the two concerns.*

voluntary restraint agreement [C] *AmE* an agreement between countries to limit imports or exports to a fixed number that is not set down in any laws or regulations: *Auto manufacturers claim the voluntary restraint agreement has hurt US exports.*

2 [C] an official document that people sign to show that they have agreed to something: *Please read the agreement and sign it.*

ag•ri•busi•ness /ˈægrɪˌbɪznəs/ *n* [U] farming using modern methods and equipment, considered as a business: *The influence of agribusiness is felt throughout the Third World.*

agricultural bank —see under BANK[1]

agricultural co-operative —see under CO-OPERATIVE

agricultural show —see under SHOW

agricultural unit of account abbreviation **AUA** *n* plural **agricultural units of account** [C] ECONOMICS a special form of the ECU used in the European Union to calculate minimum prices promised to farmers by governments

ag•ri•cul•ture /ˈægrɪˌkʌltʃə‖-ər/ *n* [U] the practice or science of farming: *Agriculture accounts for over 25% of net domestic production.* —**agricultural** *adj*: *sales of **agricultural machinery***

extensive agriculture farming of large areas, usually with low production for each unit of land farmed: *Replace unorganized extensive agriculture, which often involves the destruction of natural wealth, with one which will become progressively intensive.*

intensive agriculture farming of smaller areas, usually with higher production for each unit of land farmed

agro-industry *n* [U] agriculture and food production seen as an industry: *The region has excellent potential for investment in mining, tourism, and agro-industry.*

a•gron•o•my /əˈgrɒnəmi‖əˈgrɑː-/ *n* [U] the study, practice, and organization of animal and crop production in farming: *the single-crop agronomy of the Maya*

a•head /əˈhed/ *adv* if the value of something is ahead of a previous level, it has increased: *The shares were ahead more than 11% at one stage, and closed 85 up at 944p.*

AI abbreviation for ARTIFICIAL INTELLIGENCE

AICPA abbreviation for AMERICAN INSTITUTE OF CERTIFIED PUBLIC ACCOUNTANTS

aid /eɪd/ *n* [U] help, such as food, medicines, or money, given by a government or private organization to help people who are suffering from war, hunger etc: *UN workers have been trying to move **food aid** to an estimated 2 million starving people.* | *Aid is being flown out by several of the major **aid agencies**.* + **to**: *the crisis over aid to Somalia*

development aid financial help given by richer countries to poorer ones to help their industrial and economic development: *All the development aid that has gone to many third-world countries comes back through interest payments on the debt and underpayment for commodities.*

foreign aid also **overseas aid** *BrE* aid, usually in the form of money, given by one country to another: *The economy has very little industry, leading to a reliance on foreign aid.*

legal aid financial help given by a government organization to people involved in legal cases who cannot afford to pay for a lawyer themselves: *Clients who **qualify for legal aid** can choose between a salaried government lawyer or a lawyer in private practice.*

overseas aid *BrE* another name for FOREIGN AID

regional aid money given by a government, the EU etc to particular areas to help their economic development: *There was considerable regional aid to Scotland, which partly reversed the country's relative economic decline.*

aid agency —see under AGENCY

ai•ling /ˈeɪlɪŋ/ *adj* in financial difficulty: *This may be the best cure for China's ailing industries.* | *Many economists think the economy is still ailing.*

AIM *n* /eɪm/ Alternative Investment Market; a stock market in Britain for new, small companies, part of the **London Stock Exchange**

air•bill /ˈeəˌbɪl‖ˈer-/ *n* [C] a document that goes with a package sent by COURIER (=a fast delivery service), giving details of its contents, value, the name of the person it is addressed to etc

air broker —see under BROKER[1]

air cargo —see under CARGO

air•craft /ˈeəkrɑːft‖ˈerkræft/ *n* plural **aircraft** [C] a plane or other vehicle that can fly: *South Korea's **aircraft industry** is still in its infancy.*

commuter aircraft an aircraft used mainly by business people for travelling short distances: *USAir will switch from jets to smaller commuter aircraft.*

aircraft lease —see under LEASE[2]

air•line /ˈeəlaɪn‖ˈer-/ *n* [C] an organization offering transport by plane for passengers and goods: *Swissair, the shareholder-owned **state airline** of Switzerland* | *Intair is considering operating as a **charter airline**.* | *Delta had to restructure its business in the 1980s, as **no-frills airlines** began to cut into its profits.*

air•mail also **air mail** /ˈeəmeɪl‖ˈer-/ *n* [U] letters that are sent by plane, or the system of doing this: *an express airmail service* | *All letters are sent **by airmail**.*

air•port /ˈeəpɔːt‖ˈerpɔːrt/ *n* [C] a place where planes fly to and from, that has buildings for passengers to wait in and for cargo: *The site for the new airport has yet to be decided.*

free on board airport —see under INCOTERM

hub airport an airport with a lot of flights where people can easily change planes to travel on to another airport

international airport an airport designed for air travel to and from other countries, with space for the largest aircraft: *Heathrow, the world's busiest international airport*

regional airport an airport that serves a particular area but that has few international flights

air rage —see under RAGE

air time —see under TIME

air•wor•thy /ˈeəˌwɜːði‖ˈerˌwɜːrði/ *adj* a plane that is airworthy is safe enough to fly: *Substantial investment is required to maintain aircraft in an airworthy condition.*

aleatory contract —see under CONTRACT[1]

ALGOL /ˈælgɒl‖-gɑːl/ *n* [U] COMPUTING Algorithmic Oriented Language; a computer language used mainly for solving mathematical and scientific problems

a•li•en /ˈeɪliən/ *n* [C] someone who lives and works in a foreign country: *measures to prevent **illegal aliens** entering the country*

alienable right —see under RIGHT

A

al·i·mo·ny /ˈæləməni‖-mouni/ *n* [U] money that a court orders someone to pay regularly to their former wife or husband after their marriage has ended: *He is said to have paid £300,000 alimony to his first wife.* —compare MAINTENANCE

all·fi·nanz /ˌɔːlˈfaɪnæns, ˌælfɪˈnænts‖ˌɒːl-/ *n* [singular] the combining of banking and insurance activities in one organization; BANCASSURANCE: *Colonial is attempting to turn itself from a life insurance company into an allfinanz group.*

al·li·ance /əˈlaɪəns/ *n* **1** [C] an agreement between two or more organizations to work together: *Warner-Lambert said it* ***entered an alliance*** *with Boots to co-promote two new drugs.* | *The two insurance companies agreed to* ***form an alliance***. + **between**: *an alliance between AOL and Bertelsmann* + **with**: *Fokker said it may need to form an alliance with another company to survive.*

strategic alliance [C] an alliance formed as part of a plan with important aims: *Singapore Airlines and Lufthansa have announced a strategic alliance with broad implications for competition in the industry.*

2 in alliance with if two or more organizations are in alliance with each other, they work together: *Nissan said it would only enter Eastern Europe in alliance with a European manufacturer.*

all-in *adj BrE* an all-in rate or price is one that includes all services, parts etc, with no additional costs: *For an all-in price of £990, investors get an annual subscription as well as the hardware and software required.* —**all-in** *adv*: *The holiday will cost you about £1000 a week, all-in.*

all-inclusive *adj* an all-inclusive arrangement, for example a holiday, includes in its price all the services that people will need or expect, with no additional costs: *They operate all-inclusive holidays in Jamaica.*

all-in price —see under PRICE[1]

all-loss insurance —see under INSURANCE

al·lo·cate /ˈæləkeɪt/ *v* [T] **1** to decide officially that a particular amount of money, time etc should be used for a particular purpose **allocate sth for sth**: *Du Pont has allocated funds for the design of four plants.* **allocate sth to sth**: *Directors allocated $100 million to the search for oil.*

2 to decide officially that something such as a house or job should be given to a particular person **allocate sth to sb**: *Their job is to allocate homes to ordinary people.* **allocate sb sth**: *They allocated me a window seat at check-in.*

3 ACCOUNTING to decide where a particular amount, cost, or expense should be held in a company's accounts **allocate sth to sth**: *The regulators did not like the way in which the company allocated expenses to its bank units.*

al·lo·ca·tion /ˌæləˈkeɪʃən/ *n* **1** [C,U] the amount or share of something allocated to a person or organization, or the act of deciding how much of something each person or organization should get: *New airlines at the airport are being given priority in the allocation of take-off and landing slots.*

resource allocation [C,U] the way that the resources of a company, country etc are used for different purposes, and how this is decided: *Resource-allocation decisions should be based on all costs of production, not merely those costs reflected in market prices.*

2 [C] ACCOUNTING, FINANCE an amount, cost, or expense allocated to a particular part of a company's accounts: *BMW's per-share earnings rose to DM57 after excluding extraordinary items and allocations to reserves.*

cost allocation [U] when a business attaches particular costs to particular activities, products etc: *Confusing engineering and product costs would have resulted in the wrong product costs on any basis of cost allocation.*

3 [C] FINANCE the number of shares allocated to each possible buyer when new shares are first made available: *They will be sent details of their* ***share allocation*** *and will receive a minimum of 450 shares each.*

allocation letter —see under LETTER

al·lot /əˈlɒt‖əˈlɑːt/ *v* past tense and past participle **allotted** present participle **allotting** [T] to decide officially to give something to someone or to use something for a particular purpose: *Each worker was allotted only two uniforms a year.*

al·lot·ment /əˈlɒtmənt‖əˈlɑːt-/ *n* [C] **1** an amount or share of something such as money or time that is given to a person or organization: *They argued that they needed their full allotment of vacation days as the job is very stressful.*

2 FINANCE the number of shares allocated to each possible buyer when new shares are first made available; ALLOCATION: *Investors may wish to buy more than the 9 million* ***share allotment***. —see also LETTER OF ALLOTMENT

allotment letter —see under LETTER

al·lot·tee /əˌlɒˈtiː‖əˌlɑː-/ *n* [C] FINANCE a person or organization that is offered new shares when they are first made available: *Only 3.85 million of the 13.2 million shares offered had been taken up by provisional allottees.*

all-out strike —see under STRIKE[1]

al·low /əˈlaʊ/ *v* [T] **1** ACCOUNTING when the tax authorities allow an amount, cost, or expense, they permit it not to be counted as part of income or profits: *The ruling on takeover costs is important, because we feared the IRS might not allow any such costs.*

2 allow a claim to decide that an amount of money claimed for insurance, damages etc is correct and should be paid: *The judge allowed claims against the company involving unpaid dividends and disallowed others.*

allow for sth *phr v* [T] to take something into account when doing a calculation or making a decision: *Southern Electricity said its prices were 26% lower than six years ago after* ***allowing for inflation***.

al·low·a·ble /əˈlaʊəbəl/ *adj* **1** acceptable according to the rules: *The Canadian government has cut by 35% this year's allowable catch of fish.*

2 ACCOUNTING an allowable amount, cost, or expense does not need to be counted as part of income or profits: *Allowable deductions include travel and office supplies.*

al·low·ance /əˈlaʊəns/ *n* **1** [C] an amount of money that someone is given regularly or for a special reason: *She earns a package worth $1 million, including a $15,000* ***clothing allowance***.

cost of living allowance [C] money some people receive in addition to their normal pay to cover increases in the cost of living. The amount is related to changes in the cost-of-living index

entertainment allowance [C] an amount of money given regularly to an employee to pay for meals, hotels, drinks etc for company business clients: *He had an entertainment allowance of around £20,000 a year.*

family allowance [U] the old name for CHILD BENEFIT —see under BENEFIT[1]

job-seeker's allowance [C] *BrE* money that the British government pays to people who do not have a job but who are looking for one. The job-seeker's allowance replaced UNEMPLOYMENT BENEFIT

subsistence allowance [C] money that you are given to pay for food and other small costs, for example when you have to travel somewhere for your employer: *You can claim a £29 a day subsistence allowance to cover meals, taxis, and other incidental expenses.*

2 [C] ACCOUNTING an amount that a company thinks it may lose in the future, and includes in its accounts as a PROVISION + **for**: *The company has made an increase in its allowance for bad debt.*

A

loan-loss allowance [C] BANKING an amount that a bank thinks it may lose in the future because loans it has made will probably not be repaid: *Worsening economic conditions could force it to increase its loan-loss allowances.*

3 [C] TAX an amount of money that a person can earn without paying tax on it

income tax allowance [C] *BrE* a part of someone's income that is not taxed, for example because it comes from a particular source, or because they have children; INCOME TAX DEDUCTION *AmE*: *The married couple's income tax allowance is nearly £2,000 in the coming tax year.*

4 [C] TAX a maximum amount of goods that you can buy without paying tax on them when taking them into another country: *They may introduce higher sales taxes on purchases above the $100 Canadian **duty-free allowance**.*

5 [C] TAX an amount that can be taken off a business's profit figure when calculating tax. Allowances are often used to encourage particular business decisions, such as spending on new machinery

auto-expense allowance *AmE* **car allowance** *BrE* [C] an amount that can be taken off a business's profit figure when calculating tax, to allow for the cost of using cars for business purposes: *a big increase in taxes on company cars and a cut in the auto-expense allowance*

capital allowance [C] TAX a particular amount of a business's profit that is not taxed if it is invested in equipment etc: *Small and medium businesses will benefit from a doubling of capital allowances on machinery and plant.*

depreciation allowance [C] an amount that can be taken off a business's profit figure when calculating tax, to allow for the fact that an asset has lost part of its value during a particular period of time: *The finance minister should increase business depreciation allowances to encourage investment.*

writing-down allowance [C] in Britain, an amount allowed for DEPRECIATION (=fall in value) of an asset that is not taxed: *Only 25 per cent writing-down allowance is given in the first year.*

6 [C] MARKETING a reduction in price given to retailers by manufacturers or WHOLESALERS: *P&G had to give retailers special allowances so they could lower the price.* —see also OVERSUBSCRIPTION ALLOWANCE

all-risks also **all-risk**, written abbreviation **a/r** *adj* [only before a noun] INSURANCE providing insurance against any kind of loss or damage: *Expensive items of jewellery may be insured under an all-risks policy.*

all-risks insurance —see under INSURANCE

all-time *adj* **all-time low/high/peak/record** the lowest or highest that something has ever been: *The news caused the dollar to fall to an all-time low against the German mark.* | *Orders rose 35% to an all-time high for May.*

alternate director —see under DIRECTOR

alternative dispute resolution —see ADR

alternative investment —see under INVESTMENT

Alternative Investment Market —see AIM

alternative investments —see under INVESTMENT

alt key /ˈɔːlt kiː‖ˈɒːlt-/ —see under KEY[1]

Am written abbreviation for America; American

AMA abbreviation for AMERICAN MANAGEMENT ASSOCIATION; AMERICAN MARKETING ASSOCIATION

a·mal·ga·mate /əˈmælgəmeɪt/ *v* [I,T] if two organizations amalgamate, or if one amalgamates with another, they join together to form a bigger organization: *The two banks amalgamated earlier this year.* + **with**: *The agency is expected to amalgamate with the National Rivers Authority.* | *It is a big job to amalgamate four companies.* —**amalgamated** *adj*: *the Amalgamated Clothing and Textile Workers Union*

a·mal·ga·ma·tion /əˌmælgəˈmeɪʃən/ *n* [C,U] when two or more organizations amalgamate, often in order to increase profits by cutting costs: *the amalgamation of the regional sales operations into one national salesforce* | *There are plans for the reorganization of the industry, including amalgamations and some closures.*

horizontal amalgamation also **lateral amalgamation** when companies from the same industry amalgamate to form a larger company; HORIZONTAL INTEGRATION

vertical amalgamation when companies that make different parts of a product, or make parts at different stages in the manufacturing process, amalgamate, for example a leather manufacturer and a shoe factory; VERTICAL INTEGRATION

a·mass /əˈmæs/ *v* [T] to collect a large amount of something gradually over a period of time, especially money or information: *She has amassed a £94 million fortune through her family's hotel and banking chain.*

am·a·teur /ˈæmətə, -tʃʊə, -tʃə, ˌæməˈtɜː‖ˈæmətʃʊr, -tər/ *n* [C] someone who does an activity for pleasure, not as a job: *He thinks the drawings could be the work of an amateur.* | *amateur photographers*

a·mend /əˈmend/ *v* [T] to make small changes to a law or a document, for example to improve it, to make it more accurate, or to take account of new conditions: *a controversial plan to amend the Constitution* —**amendment** *n* [C,U] *The Securities Subcommittee is considering amendments to the proposal.*

American Accounting Association abbreviation **AAA** *n* a professional organization for ACCOUNTANTS in the US

American Bankers Association abbreviation **ABA** *n* a professional organization for commercial banks in the US that defends bank interests

American Bar Association abbreviation **ABA** *n* a professional organization for lawyers in the US

American Bureau of Shipping abbreviation **ABS** *n* the organization in the US that checks ships and puts them on an official list —compare ***Lloyds Register of Shipping*** under REGISTER[1]

American Depository Receipt —see ADR

American Economics Association abbreviation **AEA** *n* a professional organization of economists, working mainly in US universities

American Federation of Labor and Confederation of Industrial Organizations —see AFL-CIO

American Institute of Certified Public Accountants abbreviation **AICPA** *n* a professional organization of accountants in the US that represents the interests and views of accountants —compare FINANCIAL ACCOUNTING STANDARDS BOARD

American Management Association abbreviation **AMA** *n* an organization in the US that gives information and training to managers

American Marketing Association abbreviation **AMA** *n* a professional organization in the US for people working in marketing and MARKET RESEARCH

American National Standards Institute —see ANSI

American option —see under OPTION

American Society of Appraisers abbreviation **ASA** *n* a professional organization for APPRAISERS in the US

American Standard Code for Information Interchange —see ASCII

American Statistical Association abbreviation

A

ASA *n* a professional organization for STATISTICIANS in the US

American Stock Exchange abbreviation **AMEX** *n* the second largest STOCK EXCHANGE in the US after the NEW YORK STOCK EXCHANGE. It is based in New York and deals mainly in OPTIONS and in shares of new and foreign companies. It combined in 1998 with NASDAQ; KERB EXCHANGE: *The warrants will be listed on the American Stock Exchange.*

American ton —see under TON

a·mor·tiz·a·ble also **amortisable** *BrE* /əˈmɔːtaɪzəbəl‖ ˈæmər-/ *adj* ACCOUNTING if an asset is amortizable, its cost can be taken off the taxable profits of a business over several years: *The new law will increase the value of trade names, which haven't been amortizable in the past.*

a·mor·ti·za·tion also **amortisation** *BrE* /əˌmɔːtaɪˈzeɪʃən‖ˈæmərtə-/ *n* **1** [C,U] ACCOUNTING, FINANCE when an asset is amortized: *The law provides for five-year amortization of the first $5 million of acquisition expenses.* | *The drop in operating profit reflected a rise in amortizations, following an increase in industrial investments.* | *Operating profits rose due to smaller* ***amortization charges.*** —compare DEPRECIATION, WRITE-OFF

2 [U] FINANCE when repayments are made on a loan: *The lenders will extend the term of the loan and reduce the amortization of that debt.* | *He asked for a change in the* ***amortization schedule,*** *with interest payments spread over a longer period.* —see also EARNINGS BEFORE INTEREST, TAX, DEPRECIATION AND AMORTIZATION

a·mor·tize also **amortise** *BrE* /əˈmɔːtaɪz‖ˈæmər-/ *v* [T] **1** ACCOUNTING to show the reduction in the value of an asset in a company's accounts over a period of time: *All acquisition expenses are amortized over 10 years.* —see also DEPRECIATE

2 FINANCE to make repayments on a loan: *G&M reached agreement with its banks to amortize a loan balance of $73 million over two years.*

a·mount[1] /əˈmaʊnt/ *n* [C,U] a quantity of something: *debts that vary in amount* | *Figures show a big rise in the amount of money in the economy.* | *You must pay the* ***full amount*** *in advance.* | *a cheque in settlement of* ***the amount owing***

face amount ◆ [C] *AmE* INSURANCE a sum of money paid to someone who has an insurance POLICY when that policy MATURES (=it is time for it to be paid); SUM ASSURED *BrE*

◆ [C] the stated value of a share, bond etc when it is ISSUED (=sold for the first time). This is not necessarily the price that is really paid for it. Bonds, for example, may be sold slightly above or below their face amount. This value is used to calculate YIELD (=how much profit bonds make for the investor); FACE VALUE; NOMINAL VALUE; PAR VALUE

◆ [C] the value shown on a coin or BANKNOTE; FACE VALUE

amount[2] *v*

amount to sth *phr v* [T] if something amounts to a particular total, the different parts add up to that total: *Earnings per share amounted to 16.8p.* | *Total government income amounted to about £180,000 million.*

Am·trak /ˈæmtræk/ *n* the national railway company in the US, responsible for operating passenger train services between important American cities whether the service makes a profit or a loss: *The White House will seek to reduce – though not to eliminate – subsidies for Amtrak.*

a·nal·y·sis /əˈnælǝsǝs/ *n* plural **analyses** [C,U] a careful examination of something in order to understand it better: *In a regional* ***economic analysis,*** *they found the South and the West were recovering fastest.* | *By using* ***statistical analysis,*** *we determined which parts the engineers were most likely to use.* —see also CERTIFICATE OF ANALYSIS

break-even analysis ACCOUNTING a method of studying how much profit a business or product can make, by showing at what level of production costs are just covered by income and neither a profit nor a loss is being made

competitive analysis the study of competing companies in an industry to see how each works, what makes them successful etc: *Competitive analysis is a powerful tool in formulating a strategy, because it can spot gaps between you and your competitor in cost, quality and timeliness.*

cost-benefit analysis written abbreviation **CBA** a study of the advantages of buying equipment, building new buildings etc in relation to their cost: *The airport will have to do a cost-benefit analysis before building the new runway.*

cluster analysis STATISTICS the process of studying things in order to find groups that have characteristics in common: *Where cluster analysis can show the existence of large groupings, then these may be used as marketing targets.*

credit analysis *AmE* BANKING a check on someone's financial situation to see if it is safe to lend them money; CREDIT APPRAISAL *BrE* —see also CREDIT CHECK

critical path analysis also **critical path method (CPM)**, **critical path planning (CPP)** a method of planning a large piece of work by planning the different stages of it so that there will be few delays and the cost will be as low as possible

economic analysis study of economic systems or a study of a production process or an industry to see if it is operating effectively and how much profit it is making: *a detailed economic analysis of the plant's conversion to gas power*

factor analysis STATISTICS a way of understanding a large amount of DATA by putting similar results together in a group: *A factor analysis identified ten significant factors affecting women's rights in the workplace.*

financial analysis analysis of the financial state of a company or person: *Decisions about where we invest the stockholders' money will be based on financial analysis.*

gap analysis a method of examining an area of business and comparing what customers want with what is already available, and used especially when developing new products

industry analysis analysis of conditions in an industry at a particular time, including the behaviour of and relations between competitors, suppliers, and customers: *The director of industry analysis at Alcan says he can see signs of a pickup in aluminum demand.*

job analysis analysis of a job to see what it involves and what skills and experience are needed in order to do it, so that an employer can choose the right person for the job

lifecycle analysis the study of all the effects that a product has on the environment during its life: *Lifecycle analyses are difficult because no one knows just how to measure and compare all the environmental risks associated with products.*

ratio analysis a method of calculating how a company is performing by comparing the relationships between different figures, for example the ratio of profits to sales: *Ratio analysis can provide a useful snapshot of a company's finances.*

regression analysis STATISTICS a method of measuring the relationship between the changing value of one thing and the changing values of other related things: *Regression analysis is a statistical technique for predicting demand for a product from the value of one or more other factors.*

risk analysis ◆ when you calculate how much risk there is of not being paid if you supply a company in a foreign country with goods or services

A

◆ BANKING when a bank calculates how much risk there is of not being paid if it makes a loan to a foreign country: *Despite the use of* ***country risk analysis****, it must be admitted that competition for loan business has sometimes encouraged banks to indulge in unwise lending.*

◆ MANUFACTURING when a check is made on a factory to see that it is operating safely: *The plant, which treats hazardous wastes, had a risk analysis carried out last year in response to public concern.* —**risk analyst** *n* [C] *A bank's country risk analysts must consider a country's political structure.*

sensitivity analysis STATISTICS a careful analysis of a particular situation, that measures how possible changes in the future will affect it: *A sensitivity analysis will improve the quality of the final decision.*

strategic analysis a careful examination of the most important things which have an influence on the success of an organization: *a strategic analysis of competitive strengths* | *the links between strategic analysis and accounting*

structural analysis ◆ the careful examination of the structure of a whole industry, organization etc in order to find out how its parts relate to each other and to make plans for the future

◆ the careful examination of the physical structure of a material, building etc in order to find out what it is made of or whether there is anything wrong with it: *A structural analysis showed that the roof was sound.*

technical analysis FINANCE a method of working out how share prices will change in the future by carefully examining the quantities that have been bought and sold, changes in price etc, rather than by examining the financial details of particular companies

an•a•lyst /ˈænəl-ɪ̇st/ *n* [C] someone who is a specialist in a particular subject, market, industry etc and examines information relating to it in order to give their views about what will happen or should be done: *The company's senior oil analyst said that OPEC may need to cut production to balance the market.* | *an analyst with the Ministry of Defence* | *Mary Meeker, the bank's US* ***Internet analyst****, will help write the research for the IPO on the London Stock Exchange.*

computer (industry) analyst someone whose job is to examine the computer industry for a financial institution: *A computer analyst with Salomon Bros., says he is optimistic about the merger of the combined computer companies.*

credit analyst someone whose job is to estimate the financial strength of companies, for example in a credit agency: *Credit analysts see no signs that the health of companies that issue junk bonds will improve anytime soon.*

financial analyst someone who does FINANCIAL ANALYSIS (=analysis of the financial state of a company or person): *He is now a senior financial analyst for EDS.*

industry analyst someone who does INDUSTRY ANALYSIS (=analysis of conditions in an industry at a particular time): *a chemical-industry analyst at Morgan Stanley & Co*

investment analyst someone at a financial institution whose job is to look at the performance of different types of investment and make recommendations for future investments: *PolyGram is expected to report that its first-half net income fell 15% to 25%, London investment analysts said.*

systems analyst someone whose job involves studying business or industrial operations, and who uses computers to plan improvements, changes etc: *A systems analyst will assess the feasibility of the proposals.*

an•a•lyze also **analyse** *BrE* /ˈænəl-aɪz/ *v* [T] **1** to examine or think about something carefully in order to see what it is like or to understand it: *A computer analyzes the photographs sent by satellite.*

2 ACCOUNTING to separate and examine different types of costs, sales figures etc in order to understand them or take decisions based on them: *Cost control has been tightened, with costs being analysed even down to the 100-yen level.*

anchor tenant —see under TENANT

and Company also **& Co**, or **and Co** words forming part of the name of a company owned by more than one person: *Merrill Lynch & Co* | *Campbell, Parker and Co Ltd*

An•de•an Pact /ˌændiən ˈpækt/ *n* a trade association formed in 1969 by the South American countries of Bolivia, Columbia, Ecuador, Peru, Venezuela, and Chile that aimed to develop industry in the area. Chile left the association in 1976

and/or *conjunction* written in business letters and documents to mean that either or both of the things stated may apply: *It is important to establish that the increase in profit and/or sales* (=the increase in profit only, sales only, or in profit and sales combined) *is maintained.*

an•nu•al /ˈænjuəl/ *adj* **1** annual events happen once a year: *Shareholders can vote at the annual meeting.* | *an annual audit* —see also SEMI-ANNUAL

2 calculated over a period of a year: *What is an editor's annual income these days?* | *an annual growth rate of 6%*

Annual Abstract of Statistics *n* a book produced once every year by the British government, containing figures collected by the OFFICE OF NATIONAL STATISTICS, for example on unemployment, imports, exports etc

annual accounts —see under ACCOUNT[1]

annual dividend —see under DIVIDEND

annual earnings —see under EARNINGS

annual general meeting —see under MEETING

annual income —see under INCOME

annualized growth rate —see under GROWTH RATE

annual leave —see under LEAVE

annual loss —see under LOSS

annual percentage rate —see under RATE[1]

annual report —see under REPORT[1]

annual return —see under RETURN[2]

annual value —see under VALUE[1]

an•nu•i•tant /əˈnjuːɪ̇tənt‖əˈnuː-/ *n* [C] INSURANCE someone who has an annuity and receives a sum of money from it, usually monthly or yearly: *Money purchase schemes are likely to lose value through inflation if the annuitant lives a long time.*

an•nu•i•ty /əˈnjuːɪ̇ti‖əˈnuː-/ *n* plural **annuities** [C] INSURANCE **1** the right to regular future payments bought from an insurer. Many people buy an annuity to provide income for them when they stop working: *They have put most of their life savings into* ***annuity contracts****.*

2 the payments from an annuity contract: *Her annual annuity is $50,000.*

deferred annuity an annuity where the first payment is made by the insurer at a fixed time after it is bought: *Members of the pension scheme will be able to make regular contributions to a deferred annuity contract.*

immediate annuity an annuity where the first payment is made immediately or soon after the annuity contract is bought: *a 65-year-old man with $100,000 to invest in an immediate annuity that would give him a check a month for life*

joint annuity an annuity shared by two people

annuity insurance —see under INSURANCE

annuity policy —see under INSURANCE POLICY

ANSI /ˈænsi/ *n* American National Standards Institute; an organization that fixes rules on the design, quality, and safety of products: *The machines aren't meant for*

indoor use and ANSI calls for a warning to be put in the instructions.

answering machine —see under MACHINE[1]

an•swer•phone also **ansaphone** /ˈɑːnsəfəʊn‖ ˈænsərfoʊn/ *n* [C] a machine connected to a telephone which records your telephone messages when you are not able to answer the telephone; ANSWERING MACHINE: *She played back the messages on her answerphone and jotted down the numbers.*

an•te /ˈænti/ *n* **raise/up the ante** *informal* to make a situation more competitive, so that individuals or companies have more to gain or lose: *HP's lead may be short-lived as rivals raise the ante with faster machines.*

ante-date *v* [T] **1** to put a date on a document, letter, cheque etc that is earlier than the date it was actually signed, usually so that it takes effect from the earlier date

2 to be from an earlier period in history than something else: *The first Advertisements Regulation Act of 1907 ante-dated by two years the first Planning Act.*

ante-dated cheque —see under CHEQUE

anti- /ˈæntɪ‖ˈæntɪ, ˈæntaɪ/ *prefix* opposed to or against something: *the anti-business climate of the 1960s and 1970s* | *The bill is anti-consumer and anti-competitive.*

anticipatory breach —see under BREACH[1]

anti-dumping *adj* [only before a noun] ECONOMICS anti-dumping taxes and laws are introduced by a government to protect its economy from unfair competition, usually to stop imported goods being sold at prices which are lower than in the country where they were made: *China is working on* ***anti-dumping laws*** *to combat cheap imports.*

anti-inflation also **anti-inflationary** *adj* ECONOMICS anti-inflation policies or laws are aimed at preventing or reducing the effect of things that cause inflation, for example wages that rise too quickly: *Tough new* ***anti-inflation measures*** *include tight controls on credit.*

anti-spam *adj* COMPUTING **anti-spam features/measures** ways that a computer program finds and removes E-MAIL that someone has not asked for and does not want to read, for example messages sent by advertisers: *Outlook Express was to include an anti-spam feature that automatically separated all suspected junk mail into a special folder.*

an•ti•trust also **anti-trust** /ˌænti ˈtrʌst/ *adj* [only before a noun] LAW relating to laws in the US that make it illegal for a company or group of companies to restrict competition, set up a MONOPOLY, or limit another person's freedom to run a business: *The point of* ***antitrust laws*** *is to prevent restrictions on competition.* | *The US Department of Justice has dropped its* ***anti-trust case*** *against the company.*

AOB any other business; the time during a meeting when people can discuss things that were not on the AGENDA (=list of subjects to be discussed)

APACS /ˈeɪpæks/ abbreviation for ASSOCIATION FOR PAYMENT CLEARING SERVICES

a•part•ment /əˈpɑːtmənt‖əˈpɑːr-/ *n* [C] *AmE* a place where people live that consists of a set of rooms, usually on one floor and part of a larger building; FLAT

APEX fare —see under FARE

APL *n* COMPUTING Advanced Programming Language; a high-level computer programming language

apparent damage —see under DAMAGE[1]

ap•peal[1] /əˈpiːl/ *n* **1** [C,U] LAW an official request to a higher authority for a decision made by a court, committee etc to be changed: *The company's appeal against the assessment will be determined at the tribunal.* | *the accused's rights of appeal*

2 [C] an urgent request for something such as money or help: *a United Nations appeal for aid*

3 [U] a quality that makes people like something or want to buy it: *CD-ROMs now have wider* ***popular appeal.*** | *the* ***mass appeal*** *of the Internet*

appeal[2] *v* **1** [I,T] LAW to make a formal request to a higher authority for a decision made by a court, committee etc to be changed **appeal against sth**: *The accused applied for* ***leave to appeal*** *against the conviction.* **appeal to sb/sth**: *Applicants refused planning permission can appeal to the ministry.*

2 [I] to ask for money, help, or information from someone **appeal to sb**: *We appeal to our sisters all over the world to stand by us.* **appeal for sth**: *The President went on nationwide television and radio to appeal for a yes vote.*

3 appeal to sb if a product appeals to a particular type of person, that type of person likes it and is likely to buy it: *A lot of their products appeal to the older consumer.*

appeal bond —see under BOND

Appeal Court *n* [C] another name for COURT OF APPEALS

appeal court —see under COURT[1]

Appeals Court *n* [C] another name for COURT OF APPEAL

ap•pel•lant /əˈpelənt/ *n* [C] LAW a person who makes an APPEAL to a higher court against a judgement made in a lower court: *The appellant was found guilty of contempt of court.*

appellate court —see under COURT[1]

ap•pend /əˈpend/ *v* [T] to attach or add something to a piece of writing: *I have appended a letter which you sent to us last year.* **append sth to sth**: *The director has the right to append comments to the final report.*

ap•pen•dix /əˈpendɪks/ *n* plural **appendixes** or **appendices** [C] a part at the end of a book, document, or report, containing additional or useful information: *Further details of the 60 films used in this study are given in Appendix 2.*

ap•plet /ˈæplət/ *n* [C] COMPUTING a small computer program, for example one that is put onto your computer when you look at a particular WEBSITE on the INTERNET, and which allows you to use the website to do something: *You download an applet from the site to make the interactive animations work.*

ap•pli•cant /ˈæplɪkənt/ *n* [C] **1** a person who applies for a job or a place at a university, or for official permission to do something: *The starting salary of the* ***successful applicant*** *will be fixed according to experience.* + **for**: *applicants for EU membership*

2 FINANCE a person or organization who asks to buy new shares when they are first made available: *Individuals who apply for the shares through a PEP will be entitled to more shares than other applicants.*

ap•pli•ca•tion /ˌæplɪˈkeɪʃən/ *n* **1** [C] a formal, usually written, request for something or for permission to do something **an application to do sth**: *ABB* ***submitted an application*** *to establish a distribution company.* | *Immunogen* ***filed an application with*** *the Food and Drug Administration to begin trials on the drug.* + **for**: *Teleport's application for permission to offer more services to customers* | *Fill in your* ***application form*** *and return it to us before 30 April.*

job application [C] a formal request to be considered for a job: *His job application showed experience running warehouses.*

multiple (share) application [C] FINANCE in a SHARE ISSUE where each buyer can only buy a maximum number of shares, an occasion when someone tries to buy more shares by using more than one name. Multiple share applications are often illegal

originating application [C] *BrE* LAW a document which formally begins a legal case; ORIGINATING SUMMONS: *The Crown struck out the originating application on the grounds that the case was outside its jurisdiction.*

planning application [C] PROPERTY a request to the

authorities for permission to build or change a building, or to use land in a particular way: *The council is supporting General's planning application to build a £400 million shopping centre.*

share application [C] a request for shares in a SHARE ISSUE (=when shares in a company are sold for the first time); APPLICATION FOR SHARES

2 [C] a practical use for something: *Silicone has a wide range of applications in telecommunications equipment.*

3 [C] COMPUTING a piece of software for a particular use or job: *The top-selling application last year was Microsoft Office.*

multiple applications [plural] if a computer can deal with multiple applications, it can work with more than one application at a time: *Early PCs didn't have enough internal memory to handle multiple applications.*

application money —see under MONEY

application of funds —see SOURCE AND APPLICATION OF FUNDS

application program —see under PROGRAM[1]

application software —see under SOFTWARE

applied economics —see under ECONOMICS

applied research —see under RESEARCH

ap·ply /ə'plaɪ/ *v* past tense and past participle **applied**
1 [I] to make a formal, usually written, request for something, especially a job, a place at university, or permission to do something + **for**: *She had applied for a full-time job as an English teacher.* | *I recently applied for a home-improvement loan from my bank.* + **to**: *I applied to four universities and was accepted by all of them.* | *Mr Walton applied to Darlington Council for permission to change agricultural buildings into dwellings.* **apply to do sth**: *Another 156 hospitals have applied to become trusts from April 1998.*
2 [T] to use something such as a law or an idea in a particular situation: *When there are disputes about expert determination, the courts apply the law of contract.* **apply sth to sth**: *New technology is being applied to almost every industrial process.*
3 [I] to have an effect on someone or something, or to concern a person, group, or situation: *The restrictions on goods coming into Britain do not apply in this case.* **apply to sb/sth**: *Questions 3 and 4 only apply to married men.*

ap·point /ə'pɔɪnt/ *v* [T] **1** to choose someone for a job or position: *Advest last week appointed a new chairman.* **appoint sb to do sth**: *It can appoint a foreign company to manufacture its product under licence.* **appoint sb as sth**: *Scholtz Research and Development have appointed P&R Global Services as their sole distributors for the UK.* **appoint sb sth**: *Donald Chambers was appointed Chief Executive Officer.* **appoint sb to sth**: *Only accredited organisations are entitled to appoint delegates to the General Committee.*
2 *formal* to arrange or decide when something will happen or where it will happen: *The Lord Chancellor can* ***appoint a day*** *for the new rule to come into effect.* | *We met at* ***the appointed time.***

ap·poin·tee /ə,pɔɪn'tiː, ˌæpɔɪn-/ *n* [C] someone appointed to a position or job: *new appointees to the board*

ap·point·ment /ə'pɔɪntmənt/ *n* **1** [C] an arrangement to meet someone at a particular time and place: *Erlich was 25 minutes early for his appointment.* | *He* ***had an appointment*** *with a delegate of the Slaters union at the Grand Hotel.* | *Were you able to* ***make an appointment*** *to meet the area manager?* | *Visits to the doctor's surgery are strictly* ***by appointment*** (=you must make an appointment before coming).
2 [C,U] when someone is chosen to do a job, or the job itself: *I am pleased to accept the appointment and have taken note of the terms laid down in your letter.* | *a coherent policy for the dismissal and appointment of state employees*

appointment letter [C] a letter from an organization to someone to say that they have been given a job; LETTER OF APPOINTMENT: *Your entitlement to pay will be as set out in your letter of appointment.*

3 [C] a person who is chosen to do a particular job: *Our new appointment, Ms Baynes, seems to be working out very well.*

ap·por·tion /ə'pɔːʃən‖-ɔːr-/ *v* [T] to divide and share something between a number of people or organizations **apportion sth to/amongst/between**: *a scheme which will apportion shares in state enterprises to the general public* | *Funding will be apportioned between the country's local education authorities.*

ap·por·tion·ment /ə'pɔːʃənmənt‖-ɔːr-/ *n* [C,U] **1** when something is divided and shared out, or an amount of something that has been divided and shared out: *the apportionment of Japanese financial support to those states worst affected by the crisis* | *financial apportionments*
2 ACCOUNTING when each expense is placed in its proper account, or the amount placed in each account
3 INSURANCE, LAW when insurance companies or their clients agree to share the cost of something that goes wrong, or the amount that each person or company agrees to pay: *The excess shall be deducted prior to apportionment between the two insurers.*
4 LAW when the buyer and seller of a property agree to share the cost of a bill, for example property tax, that is paid to cover a period during which they will each be owners for a time: *You should stipulate the apportionment of any service charge liability in the sale agreement.*

ap·prais·al /ə'preɪzəl/ *n* [C,U] a statement or opinion judging the worth, value, or condition of something: *What's your appraisal of the situation?*

credit appraisal *BrE* BANKING a check on someone's financial situation to see if it is safe to lend them money; CREDIT ANALYSIS *AmE*: *There will have to be improvement in their credit appraisal systems if they want to avoid bad debts.* —see also CREDIT CHECK

performance appraisal also **performance evaluation, performance assessment** HUMAN RESOURCES a meeting between an employee and a manager to discuss the quality of the employee's work, and areas for future progress; PERFORMANCE REVIEW: *He has changed the organization's performance appraisal system, which used to rate 90% of personnel as 'outstanding'.*

ap·praise /ə'preɪz/ *v* [T] to officially judge how successful, effective, or valuable someone or something is: *It is the line manager's job to appraise staff.* **appraise sth at**: *The property was appraised at $28 million.*

ap·prais·ee /ə,preɪ'ziː/ *n* [C] an employee who is receiving a PERFORMANCE APPRAISAL from their manager

ap·prais·er /ə'preɪzə‖-ər/ *n* [C] **1** *AmE* someone whose job is to judge the condition and value of something, especially property; VALUER: *If the two sides cannot agree, the price will be determined by an independent appraiser.*
2 a manager who is responsible for carrying out a PERFORMANCE APPRAISAL

ap·pre·ci·ate /ə'priːʃieɪt/ *v* [I] **1** to increase in value: *Their art collection has appreciated substantially, almost doubling in value.*
2 when a currency appreciates, it increases in value compared to other currencies + **against**: *The Egyptian pound has appreciated against European currencies, and this is not good for Egyptian exporters.*

ap·pre·ci·a·tion /ə,priːʃi'eɪʃən/ *n* [U] **1** an increase in the value of something: *There has been a sharp appreciation in the share prices of US companies.*

capital appreciation also **asset appreciation** FINANCE an increase in the value of an asset, especially

property or financial investments: *Investors invest in companies because they expect a flow of income plus capital appreciation over time.*
2 an increase in the value of one currency compared to other currencies: *He estimated that **currency appreciation** had cost the company £700,000 last year.* + **against**: *UK import prices have fallen steadily because of the appreciation of sterling against EU currencies.*

ap·pren·tice /əˈprentɪs/ *n* [C] a young person being trained to do a skilled job, who has signed a contract agreeing to work a fixed number of years for the employer who is training them: *the announcement that BAe plans to take on apprentices again*

ap·pren·tice·ship /əˈprentɪsʃɪp/ *n* [C,U] the period of time when someone is an apprentice, or the job of an apprentice: *Bell **served an apprenticeship*** (=worked as an apprentice) *with the shipbuilders Shaw and Hart.* | *young people applying for apprenticeships in engineering*

ap·pro·pri·ate /əˈprəʊpri-eɪt‖əˈproʊ-/ *v* [T] **1** to take something for yourself when you have no right to do this: *The generals appropriated defence funds, leaving their men unpaid for months.*
2 to take something, especially money, officially for a particular purpose: *Congress has appropriated funds for the railroad for the next two years.*

ap·pro·pri·a·tion /əˌprəʊpriˈeɪʃən‖əˌproʊ-/ *n* [C,U] **1** the official use of money for a particular purpose, or an amount of money that is used: *They each receive a state appropriation of $50,000 to cover education costs.*
2 the act of taking control of something, especially by a government, perhaps against the wishes of the owners: *appropriation of oil companies' assets*

appropriation account —see under ACCOUNT[1]

ap·prov·al /əˈpruːvəl/ *n* [U] **1** when someone officially accepts something: *His proposals cannot become law until they have obtained Congressional approval.* | *Approval for the new buildings was given in July.*
2 on approval if you buy a product on approval, it is sent to you and you are allowed to look at it or use it before deciding whether you will buy it —see also SEAL OF APPROVAL

approved accounts —see under ACCOUNT[1]

approved contractor —see under CONTRACTOR

approx. written abbreviation for APPROXIMATE or APPROXIMATELY

ap·prox·i·mate /əˈprɒksɪmɪt‖əˈprɑːk-/ *adj* an approximate amount or number is not exact, but is more or less correct: *an approximate calculation of the overall cost of the project* —**approximately** *adv*: *Travelling time from London is approximately 4 hours.* | *an area of approximately 72 hectares*

APR *n* [C usually singular] FINANCE annual percentage rate; the rate of interest that you must pay when you borrow money. In many countries, APR must be shown in advertisements offering to lend money to people, to give the true cost of borrowing: *AT&T plans to lower the APR it charges to customers on its card to 17.9%.* | *The bank's charges are 21.9% to 25.3% APR for unsecured personal loans.*

Apr. written abbreviation for APRIL

ap·ti·tude /ˈæptɪtjuːd‖-tuːd/ *n* [C,U] the natural ability to do a particular activity or job + **for**: *He had a remarkable aptitude for accountancy.* | *staff who show aptitude for managerial responsibility*

aptitude test —see under TEST[1]

a/r written abbreviation for ALL-RISKS

Arab League *n* an association of Arab states based in Cairo whose aim is to protect and develop Arab interests

arable land —see under LAND[1]

arb /ɑːb‖ɑːrb/ *n* [C] FINANCE a person or organization whose job is arbitrage; ARBITRAGEUR

ar·bi·ter /ˈɑːbɪtə‖ˈɑːrbɪtər/ *n* [C] **1** a person or organization with the authority to decide how something should be done: *The Food and Drug Administration is the **final arbiter** of food labeling.*
2 a person or organization that tries to find solutions to disagreements: *Businessmen here often hire freelance arbiters to settle disputes.*

ar·bi·trage /ˈɑːbɪtrɑːʒ‖ˈɑːr-/ *n* [U] FINANCE **1** buying something such as a raw material or currency in one place and selling it immediately in another, in order to make a profit from price differences between the two places: *Analysts attributed the activity to arbitrage buying: traders bought cocoa in New York to sell at a profit in London.*
2 buying and selling shares of two companies involved, or that may be involved, in a takeover, in order to make a profit from differences in the share values of the two companies: *Wertheim incurred losses in **risk arbitrage** – or takeover-stock speculation – arising from last year's slump in U.S. merger activity.*
exchange arbitrage a situation in which dealers can make a profit because of the temporary difference in the value between two currencies in relation to a third currency

ar·bi·tra·geur /ˌɑːbɪtrɑːˈʒɜː‖ˌɑːrbɪtrɑːˈʒɜːr/ also **ar·bi·tra·ger** /ˈɑːbɪtrɑːʒə‖ˈɑːrbɪˌtrɑːʒər/ *especially AmE* — *n* [C] FINANCE a person or organization whose job is arbitrage; ARB: *ICI shares rose as investors and arbitrageurs bought in anticipation of a bid from Hanson.*

ar·bi·tra·tion /ˌɑːbɪˈtreɪʃən‖ˌɑːr-/ *n* [U] **1** LAW when a legal disagreement is dealt with by independent officials who have the authority to make a legal decision about it, rather than the case being dealt with in a court of law: *Disputes within the partnership can be **referred to arbitration**, avoiding the risks and costs of litigation.*
2 HUMAN RESOURCES when a disagreement between an employer and employees is dealt with by independent officials who try to reach an agreement between both sides in order to prevent a STRIKE or a legal battle: *Contract negotiations between them have reached deadlock and are likely to **go to arbitration**.* | *The **arbitration agreement** only applied to the missing oil, not to the other allegations of wrongdoing.*

ar·bi·trat·or /ˈɑːbɪtreɪtə‖ˈɑːrbɪtreɪtər/ *n* [C] LAW, HUMAN RESOURCES a professional person whose job is to act as a judge in legal or industrial disagreements: *If we accept your claim but disagree with the amount due to you, the matter will be passed to a legally appointed arbitrator.*

ar·chi·tect /ˈɑːkɪtekt‖ˈɑːr-/ *n* [C] **1** a person whose job is to plan and design buildings: *The mill was built in 1872 to the design of an architect.*
2 the architect of sth the person who originally thought of an important idea or who made an important event happen: *Mr Levin was a principal architect of the 1989 merger.*

ar·chi·tec·ture /ˈɑːkɪtektʃə‖ˈɑːrkɪtektʃər/ *n* [U] **1** the style or design of a building: *The architecture of their head offices is strikingly modern.*
2 the study and practice of planning and designing buildings: *Stirling went to Trinity College to study architecture.*
3 COMPUTING the design of the different parts inside a computer and the way they work together: *Microsoft is working with the European manufacturers to combine its operating system with the existing hardware architecture of each.*
client/server architecture COMPUTING a NETWORK in which a SERVER (=powerful central computer) is connected to a number of CLIENTS (=smaller computers)

A

ar•chive[1] /ˈɑːkaɪv‖ˈɑːr-/ *v* [T] COMPUTING to make a permanent copy of information held in a computer or to store the information so that it cannot be changed or lost: *Once a month the files will be archived.* —**archiving** *n* [U] *the scanning and archiving of paper documents onto optical disks* | *electronic archiving systems*

archive[2] *n* [C] COMPUTING the part of a computer or computer system where information is stored in such a way that it cannot be changed or lost: *You could rebuild your hard disk's contents from this archive.*

ar•e•a /ˈeəriə‖ˈeriə/ *n* [C] **1** a part of a city or country: *What area of Bristol do you live in?* | *the New York* ***metropolitan area*** (=New York city and the area around it)

assisted area in Britain, an area which receives financial help from the government because it has a high level of UNEMPLOYMENT and is in need of economic development: *Regional programme grants are used to encourage investment in assisted areas.*

development area a relatively poor area that the government tries to make richer by attracting industry, for example by offering money, lower taxes etc to businesses that move there: *Development Area status is vital to the Wirral in its efforts to bring more investment into the area.*

depressed area an area in a large city or a part of a country where houses and other buildings are in a bad condition, the level of unemployment is high, and a lot of people are poor: *Local councils are obliged to allocate 15% of council housing to people from depressed areas.*

dollar area the countries of the world where the US dollar is used as the main currency or where the value of the currency is directly connected to the US dollar: *Most of the expenditure was outside the dollar area, and did not give rise to immediate dollar payments.*

sales area a part of a city or country that a particular person or organization sells in and is responsible for; SALES TERRITORY *AmE*: *For each sales area there is one sales representative.*

wilderness area an area of public land in the US where no buildings or roads are allowed to be built: *Most of the forests have long been owned and maintained as wilderness areas by timber and paper companies.*

2 the part of a shop or SHOPPING CENTRE where goods are sold: *You enter its sales area straight off the street.*

3 a particular subject, field of activity, or type of business: *the areas of video games, electronic organizers and cellular phones*

growth area an area of business where sales are growing fast: *Sales rose 9% to 13 billion marks in certain key growth areas like electronics, automation and railroad systems.*

area code —see under CODE

Area Health Authority *n* plural **Area Health Authorities** [C] an organization in Britain which is responsible for managing and controlling all the NATIONAL HEALTH SERVICE hospital services and medical activities in a particular area: *the Camden and Islington Area Health Authority*

arithmetic mean —see under MEAN[2]

arithmetic unit —see under UNIT

ARM abbreviation for ADJUSTABLE RATE MORTGAGE —see under MORTGAGE[1]

arm's length *adj* involving normal business dealings, in which the people or companies taking part have no financial connections with each other and so do not receive any specially favourable terms: *Fujitsu insists that it is an arm's length owner of ICL, and emphasizes its lack of interference in ICL's affairs.*

ar•ray /əˈreɪ/ *n* [C] **1** a range of many different things: ***a vast array*** *of electronic and consumer products*

2 COMPUTING a set of computer memory units arranged in rows across or down: *Iceberg is a device that stores massive amounts of computer data on arrays of disk drives.*

ar•rears /əˈrɪəz‖əˈrɪrz/ *n* [plural] **1** money that is owed because it has not been paid on time: *Unemployment is the biggest cause of* ***mortgage arrears***. + **of**: *outstanding arrears of rent*

debt arrears debt or interest that was not paid when it should have been and is still owed: *Brazil recently agreed to pay banks 25% of its $8 billion debt arrears this year.*

2 be in arrears if someone is in arrears, or if their payments are in arrears, they are late in paying something that they should pay regularly: *One in eight mortgage payers is in arrears.* | *221,900 mortgages were more than* ***six months in arrears***. | *Thousands of couples are almost* ***£1000 in arrears***.

3 fall/get into arrears to start to be in arrears: *Borrowers couldn't afford to keep up their payments and so fell into arrears.*

4 be paid in arrears *BrE* to receive your wages or payment for a service at the end of a period of time you have worked: *You will be paid monthly in arrears.*

ar•ti•cle /ˈɑːtɪkəl‖ˈɑːr-/ *n* LAW **1** [C] one part of a law or legal agreement, especially a numbered part: *Articles 2 and 3 of the Constitution*

2 articles [plural] in Britain, a period of training with a firm of SOLICITORS which someone who wants to be a lawyer must complete before they can become fully qualified: *After graduation, she returned to her father's solicitor's practice to* ***take her articles***.

articles of association *BrE*, **articles of incorporation** *AmE* — *n* [plural] LAW an official document giving details of the structure and running of a company, for example the powers of directors, the rights of shareholders, the way in which the accounts will be approved, etc: *Rolls Royce announced the level of foreign ownership of shares has reached 29.5%, the maximum permitted by the company's articles of association.*

artificial intelligence abbreviation **AI** *n* [U] the study of how to make computers do things in the way that humans do them, for example take in information and make decisions: *Symbolics has been a pioneer in artificial intelligence technology.*

artificial person —see under PERSON

artistic property —see under PROPERTY

ASA abbreviation for ADVERTISING STANDARDS AUTHORITY; AMERICAN SOCIETY OF APPRAISERS; AMERICAN STATISTICAL ASSOCIATION

asap /ˌeɪ es eɪˈpiː, ˈeɪsæp/ abbreviation for as soon as possible: *Please fill in your questionnaire and return it to us asap.*

as at *BrE prep* ACCOUNTING on a particular date: *balance as at 20th March 1999*

ASCII /ˈæski/ *n* [U] COMPUTING American Standard Code for Information Interchange; a simple computer code in which letters are represented by numbers. Many different computers can read information stored in ASCII, so people often change documents into ASCII form before sending them to someone else: *converting word-processor files into standard ASCII format*

ASEAN /ˈæsiˌæn/ *n* Association of South East Asian Nations; an organization whose members are Brunei, Indonesia, Malaysia, the Philippines, Singapore, and Thailand, founded in 1967 to develop their political and economic relations

as from *prep* from a particular date or time onwards: *Museums will be introducing entrance charges as from early next year.*

A shares —see under SHARE

Asian Development Bank abbreviation **ADB** *n* a bank owned by the governments of several Asian governments, which tries to encourage economic development in the region

as is, where is *adj, adv* if something is being sold as is, where is, it is being sold in its present condition and place, even though this may not be very good: *The USAF agreed to make its last C-121 available on an as is, where is basis.*

ask /ɑːsk‖æsk/ *v* [T] if someone is asking a particular price for something, that is the price at which they are selling it **ask sth for sth**: *How much are they asking for their house?*

asking price —see under PRICE[1]

as of *AmE prep* **1** ACCOUNTING on a particular date; AS AT *BrE*: *As of August 1, the company had $44 million in long-term debt.*
2 from a particular date: *As of July, the company will be based in New York*

as per *prep* according to: *I'll make a note of your new address as per your request.*

as•say[1] /əˈseɪ, ˈæseɪ/ *n* [C,U] a test to show how pure a metal, drug etc is: *The experiments were done under standard assay conditions.*

as•say[2] /əˈseɪ/ *v* [T] to test something such as a metal or drug to find out how pure it is: *All samples were assayed in duplicate.*

as•say•er /əˈseɪə‖-ər/ *n* [C] someone who tests rocks containing metals, and mixtures of metals, to find out how much pure and valuable metal they contain

assay office —see under OFFICE

as seen *adv* if you sell something as seen, you sell it in the condition it is in now and accept no responsibility for it after it is sold: *Most second-hand cars are sold as seen.*

as•sem•ble /əˈsembəl/ *v* **1** [T] MANUFACTURING to make a product by putting parts together: *The factory will assemble GM pickup trucks for sale in the Chinese market.*
2 [T] FINANCE if a financial institution assembles a loan, it finds lenders who are willing to make part of the loan: *J.P. Morgan is attempting to assemble $1 billion of credit for MNC.*
3 [I] if an organization assembles, it meets officially: *The 12,000-member International Bar Association will assemble in New York City, Sept 19–23.*

as•sem•bly /əˈsembli/ *n* plural **assemblies** **1** [U] MANUFACTURING the process of putting the parts of products together: *Routine assembly of colour televisions eventually shifted to Taiwan.* | *a car* ***assembly plant***
2 [C] a group of people who are elected to make laws or decisions for a particular country or area: *plans for a regional assembly in the North-East*

assembly language —see under LANGUAGE

assembly line —see under LINE

assembly plant —see under PLANT

as•sent /əˈsent/ *n* **1** [U] LAW formal agreement by someone: *Any such decision would require the assent of two thirds of shareholders.*
2 [C] LAW a document that legally makes someone the new owner of a dead person's property

as•ser•tive /əˈsɜːtɪv‖-ɜːr-/ *adj* behaving in a confident way so that people listen to your opinions and ideas —**assertiveness** *n* [U] *The move shows Japan's new assertiveness on the question of global aid.* | ***assertiveness training*** *classes for female employees*

assertiveness training —see under TRAINING

as•sess /əˈses/ *v* [I,T] **1** to make a judgement about a person or situation after considering all the information: *This information is needed to assess efficiency and effectiveness.* + **that**: *The federal government assessed that the assets had been acquired illegally.*
2 to calculate how much something will cost to repair, how much something is worth, how much money someone should be given etc: *Ten loss adjusters are still assessing the extent of the damage.* **assess sth at**: *The net value of his estate was assessed at around £6,250,000.*
3 to calculate the amount of tax someone should pay **assess sb/sth on sth** to take sth into account when calculating tax: *The payroll tax isn't assessed on wages above a certain level.*

as•sess•ment /əˈsesmənt/ *n* **1** [C,U] a judgement that you make about a person or situation after considering all the information: *They will have to* ***make an assessment*** *of the services required to meet the health needs of the population.*
2 [C,U] a calculation of how much something will cost to repair, how much something is worth, how much money someone should be given etc: *Charges for students were based on an individual assessment of ability to pay.*
3 [C] a calculation of the amount of tax that someone has to pay: *Anyone facing a tax assessment which they consider unreasonable should seek professional advice.*
environmental impact assessment [C] an examination of the possible effects of a new project on the environment: *A full environmental impact assessment will be required before any development within 25 miles of the coast.*
risk assessment *n* [C,U] an examination of the possible risks involved in doing something, so that organizations can decide whether something is worth doing and how they can reduce the risks: *Any organisation employing more than four people must carry out a health and safety risk assessment.*
self-assessment ◆ [C,U] TAX a tax system in which people present information on how much they have earned and calculate for themselves how much tax they have to pay in a particular year: *For self-assessment to work, the tax has to be simple enough for taxpayers to be able to fill in their own tax returns.*
◆ [C,U] a process in which a company judges how good its own methods, staff etc are: *A campaign strategy needs to have an in-built system of self-assessment.*
standard spending assessment [C] in Britain, the amount of money that the government calculates a local council needs to spend on providing a particular service, and which they give to the council for this purpose

assessment centre —see under CENTRE

as•ses•sor /əˈsesə‖-ər/ *n* [C] **1** someone whose job is to examine places, systems, or people to decide how good or suitable they are: *I worked for a travel agency as an assessor of foreign locations.*
2 someone whose job is to assess the value of houses or other buildings to calculate how much tax the people who own them must pay: *It is the Regional Assessor who determines the tax band for the property.*
3 INSURANCE a person or company whose job is to assess the value of loss or damage for someone who has made an insurance claim; CLAIMS ADJUSTER; INSURANCE ADJUSTER; LOSS ADJUSTER: *Her car was still in the garage waiting for a visit from the insurance assessor.*
4 LAW someone who helps a judge in a court of law by advising them on technical or scientific matters, or on other matters on which special knowledge is needed: *Mr Watt, who is a specialist in insolvency, was an assessor to the Bingham Inquiry.*

as•set /ˈæset/ *n* [C] ACCOUNTING, FINANCE something belonging to an individual or a business that has value or the power to earn money: *The company has a tremendous asset – 50 hectares of real estate right next to an international airport.*

A

capital asset *AmE* **chargeable asset** *BrE* [C] TAX ◆ something such as land, buildings, or machinery used by a business to produce its goods or services; FIXED ASSET: *One estimate puts total investment in capital assets in Hong Kong by mainland China at $30 billion.*
◆ an asset on which CAPITAL GAINS TAX must be paid if it is sold
current asset [C usually plural] money that a business has or is owed, or something that could easily be turned into money, for example raw materials and goods that have been produced but not sold: *Investment properties are now shown as current assets.*
fixed asset [C usually plural] something that a business owns and that it uses in order to produce goods, for example a piece of land, a building, or a piece of machinery: *Lego doubled its investment in fixed assets as it prepared to produce a new range of toys.*
frozen asset [C usually plural] something that a business owns, for example money, property, or machinery, that cannot be sold because it has been put under outside control, for example by a court: *Thousands of legal claims are being made by individuals attempting to get their frozen assets returned.*
intangible asset [C usually plural] something that a business has and can make money from, but that is not something physical and so cannot easily be valued, for example a name of a product, technical knowledge, loyalty from customers etc: *Intangible assets such as information, image, and people are the main drivers of business today.*
liquid asset [C usually plural] anything that a business has that is either cash or something that can be easily turned into cash, such as money owed by customers and shares that can be easily sold: *Roche has been under pressure to invest some of its SFr15 billion of liquid assets.*
net assets [plural] the overall value of a business, the difference between its assets and its liabilities: *He recommended that the company be dissolved and its net assets distributed to shareholders.*
net current assets [plural] the difference between a company's CURRENT ASSETS and its CURRENT LIABILITIES
operating assets [plural] assets that are used in the production activities of a company: *Scala plans to sell the operating assets of its consumer tapes business for about £2 million.*
tangible asset [C usually plural] an asset that is physical and can be valued easily, rather than an intangible asset that is difficult to value: *Investors fled financial markets, putting their money into gold, collectibles and other tangible assets.*
underlying assets [plural] assets in relation to the SECURITIES that are based on them: *The stocks are trading at about 2.7 times the value of underlying assets, while the average for the last 50 years is 1.5 times.*
wasting asset [C] an asset, such as property or a business, that is losing money over time: *It's been quite clear for some time that the airline is a wasting asset.*

asset-backed security —see under SECURITY

asset backing —see under BACKING

asset cover *n* [U] another name for asset backing

asset deflation —see under DEFLATION

asset inflation —see under INFLATION

asset management —see under MANAGEMENT

asset mix —see under MIX

asset shuffling also **asset-chopping** *n* [U] FINANCE when a company reorganizes its assets, for example by splitting up businesses and creating new businesses, in the belief that this can improve their value: *Asset shuffling was an approach toward investing that was much in favor in the 1980s.*

asset-stripping *v* [U] FINANCE the practice of buying a company whose shares are worth less than its assets, then selling its assets in order to make a quick profit: *The new owners turned out to be more interested in asset-stripping than investment.* —**asset-stripper** *n* [C] *There was a fear we were going to come in as asset-strippers, sell everything quickly, and then run.*

asset turnover —see under TURNOVER

asset value —see under VALUE[1]

asset value per share —see under VALUE[1]

as•sign /ə'saɪn/ *v* [T] **1** to give someone a particular job or task, or send them to work in a particular place or for a particular person **assign sth to sb**: *His duties have now been assigned to the deputy chairman.* | *The case was assigned to US Bankruptcy Court Judge Burton Lifland.* **assign sb to sth**: *Workers are expected to do the jobs assigned to them.* | *She was assigned to the US Embassy in Moscow.* **assign sb to do sth**: *He was assigned to work in a Chicago bank.*
2 to give a particular amount of time, money, or resources to something: *How much time have you assigned for the meeting?*
3 to decide that something has a particular value or is of a particular quality: *the difficulty of* ***assigning a value*** *to an hour of housework* | *The group has been assigned a triple A rating by Standard and Poor's.*
4 LAW to give something such as property to another person formally, by contract: *They only assign ownership when the house is complete.* —see also DEED OF ASSIGNMENT —**assignor** *n* [C] *The assignor of the lease is released from future liability under this lease.*

assignable debt —see under DEBT

as•sign•ee /əˌsaɪ'niː/ *n* [C] LAW someone to whom something such as property has been formally given by contract

as•sign•ment /ə'saɪnmənt/ *n* **1** [C] a piece of work that someone is given: *My assignment was to save the company, whatever it took.*
2 [U] when someone is given a particular job or task, or sent to work in a particular place or for a particular person: *With the agreement, GM got more control over the assignment of skilled workers in the plant.*
3 [U] the act of deciding that something has a particular value or is of a particular quality: *Moody's said assignment of the highest rating reflects the company's improved performance.*
4 [U] LAW the act of giving something such as property to someone formally, by contract: *a change of tenant halfway through the rental period through assignment of the lease* —see also DEED OF ASSIGNMENT
wage assignment [U] when someone agrees to have part of the money they earn taken away, for example to pay a debt or pay into a PENSION

as•sis•tant /ə'sɪstənt/ *n* [C] **1** also **shop assistant** someone who sells things in a shop; SALES CLERK *AmE*: *a shop assistant in the men's department of a large store*
2 someone whose job is to help someone else of higher rank do their job: *manager Jean Cundy and her assistant Cherrie Elliott* + **to**: *an assistant to a stud-farm manager* | *I spoke to the* ***assistant director***. | *IBM's* ***assistant general manager***
administrative assistant someone whose job is to help make an organization or department run smoothly by helping other staff to organize their work: *staff carrying out routine clerical duties under the Administrative Assistant's direction*
clerical assistant someone who works in an office helping other people by doing jobs such as putting documents away in their correct place and typing information onto computer: *clerical assistants and office support staff*
executive assistant someone whose job is to help

an important manager do his or her job: *Lynn Schofield is Executive Assistant to the President of Scotiabank.*

personal assistant abbreviation **PA** ◆ a secretary who works for one person, organizing their work, meetings etc: *I phoned his personal assistant to arrange an interview.*

◆ someone whose job is to help an employee of a higher rank by doing some of their work for them: *Kate Pallis, personal assistant to Mr Aghajan, said negotiations had hit a snag.*

3 someone who works in a bank, office etc but who is not a manager: ***Bank assistants** cannot afford to live on their current basic salary.*

assistant manager —see under MANAGER

assisted area —see under AREA

assn written abbreviation for ASSOCIATION

as·so·ci·ate¹ /əˈsəʊʃiət, əˈsəʊsi-‖əˈsoʊ-/ *n* [C] **1** someone who you work with or do business with: *He manipulated government funds to benefit himself and his associates.* | *a merchant bank run by his **business associate**, Laurie Connell*

2 a member of an organization who has some but not all the rights of a full member: *Barry S. Rosenstein, a former associate of corporate buy-out specialist Asher Edelman* | *Michele Lord, senior research associate of the Family and Work Institute*

associate² *adj* **1 associate member** someone who is a member of an organization and has some but not all of the rights that full members have: *Hungary applied for associate membership of the EU.*

2 associate editor/producer/publisher etc someone whose job is closely connected to that of someone else and who shares responsibility or authority with them: *associate curator at the Metropolitan Museum of Art*

associated com·pa·ny also **associate company** —see under COMPANY

Associate of the Institute of Chartered Accountants —see ACA

As·so·ci·ates /əˈsəʊʃiəts, əˈsəʊsi-‖əˈsoʊ-/ *n* [plural] used in the name of PARTNERSHIPS and similar organizations of professional people: *Venture Growth Associates* | *Raymond James & Associates*

as·so·ci·a·tion /əˌsəʊsiˈeɪʃən, əˌsəʊʃi-‖əˌsoʊ-/ *n* written abbreviation **assn** **1** a group of people or organizations who have the same aims or do the same kind of work: *the National Association of Purchasing Managers*

housing association in Britain, one of the independent CHARITIES (=organizations run not for profit but in order to help people) that provide houses and flats for people to buy or rent at low cost: *The housing association CHA aims to provide affordable housing to people on low incomes.*

industry association also **trade association** an association that supports and protects the rights of a particular industry and the people who work in that industry: *the transport industry association* | *the machine tool builders' trade association*

staff association an organization that represents employees during discussions with management, and which also arranges social activities: *Legal advice may be available to you if you are a trade union member or a member of a staff association* —see also ARTICLES OF ASSOCIATION, BRAND ASSOCIATION, MEMORANDUM OF ASSOCIATION

Association for Payments Clearing Services abbreviation **APACS** *n* FINANCE an organization in Britain that manages and controls the movement of money between banks through CLEARING —see also BACS

Association of British Chambers of Commerce *n* a central organization of local CHAMBERS OF COMMERCE based in London

Association of Certified and Corporate Accountants —see ACCA

Association of South-East Asian Nations —see ASEAN

assumed liabilities —see under LIABILITY

as·sur·ance /əˈʃʊərəns‖əˈʃʊr-/ *n* [U] *BrE* insurance that a company agrees to pay on someone's death: *Abbey National has set up a new unit, Abbey National Life PLC, to sell its own **life assurance** products directly to its banking customers.*

decreasing term assurance an insurance agreement over a fixed period of time, in which the sum insured gets smaller each year: *This type of mortgage is usually arranged in conjunction with decreasing term assurance.*

endowment assurance a type of assurance in which someone pays a regular amount to an insurance company, and in return the company agrees to pay a sum of money either on a particular date, or when someone dies, if this is sooner: *Endowment assurance is a form of saving as your life will be covered for a fixed term.*

term assurance a type of life assurance in which someone pays a regular amount of money for a limited period of time. In return, the insurance company agrees to pay a sum of money if the person dies, but does not repay anything if the person does not die: *Term assurance is not a form of saving, as you lose the premium money if you survive the term.* —see also QUALITY ASSURANCE

as·sured¹ /əˈʃʊəd‖əˈʃʊrd/ *n* **the (life) assured** *BrE* the person or organization that will receive the money from an assurance agreement, or the person whose life is covered by the agreement; THE INSURED *AmE*: *A policy is of no effect until the certificate is delivered to the assured.*

assured² *adj* **an assured income/supply/market etc** something that you can rely on to be available: *Joe's assured income persuaded the bank to lend him the money.* | *Plentiful raw materials and assured markets had improved living standards.*

assured tenancy —see under TENANCY

assured value —see under VALUE¹

as·sur·er /əˈʃʊərə‖əˈʃʊrər/ *n* [C] *BrE* a person or company that provides assurance; INSURER *AmE*: *the largest British industrial assurer, The Prudential*

asynchronous transfer mode —see ATM

at best *adv* FINANCE if someone buys or sells a SECURITY at best, they buy or sell it at the most profitable price available —compare LIMIT ORDER

at call also **on call** *adv BrE* FINANCE if money is lent at call, it must be repaid immediately if the lender asks for it; ON DEMAND *AmE*

money at call also **money on call** *n* [U] money that a lender can make the borrower return immediately: *Money at call is the main reserve that banks draw on if they are short of cash.*

ATL abbreviation for ACTUAL TOTAL LOSS —see under LOSS

ATM /ˌeɪ tiː ˈem/ *n* **1** [C] BANKING automated teller machine or automatic teller machine; an electronic machine inside or outside a bank, which customers use, by means of a special card and a code number, to take out money and to get information about their accounts; CASH DISPENSER *BrE*; CASH MACHINE *BrE*; CASHPOINT *BrE*: *Obtaining cash by credit card incurs a commission whether it's across the counter or at an ATM.*

2 [U] COMPUTING asynchronous transfer mode; a way of sending MULTIMEDIA information (=writing, sound, pictures, or film) very quickly over a computer NETWORK (=a system of connected computers)

A

Atomic Energy Authority *n* the organization that is responsible for the production of NUCLEAR ENERGY in Britain, and for ensuring that it is safe

Atomic Energy Commission *n* the organization that is responsible for the production of NUCLEAR ENERGY in the US, and for ensuring that it is safe

at par —see under PAR

at sight —see under SIGHT

at·tach /əˈtætʃ/ *v* [T] **1** if conditions are attached to an agreement, they are added to it and made a part of it: *The US government has attached conditions to economic aid.*
2 if there are benefits, rights etc attached to something, they are associated with that thing: *Few companies have chosen to use tax advantages attached to the revaluation.*
3 if a letter or document is attached to something, it is sent with it: *information given in a memo attached to his tax return*

at·tach·ment /əˈtætʃmənt/ *n* **1** [C,U] LAW when part of someone's earnings or money that is owed to them is taken by a court and used to pay their debts: *Organizations can apply to have an* ***attachment of earnings*** *made on someone who owes them money.*
2 [C] a piece of paper fastened to a document such as an insurance agreement, which shows a special condition of the agreement
3 [C] COMPUTING a document which is sent as part of an E-MAIL message: *You can send me the spreadsheet as an attachment.*

at·tend /əˈtend/ *v* [I,T] to go to an event such as a meeting: *The two men both attended a 90-minute board meeting yesterday.* | *a conference attended by 200 people*

at·tend·ance /əˈtendəns/ *n* [C,U] **1** the number of people who attend something such as a meeting, or who go to see an event such as a football match etc: *Seven jobs were axed at the zoo after a 50% drop in attendances.*
2 the fact that you go to something that is held regularly, or the number of times that you go: *the attendance of Scottish companies at European events* | *The school has introduced rewards for good attendance.*

at·ten·tion /əˈtenʃən/ *n* **for the attention of** written abbreviations **attn**, **FAO** written on the front or at the top of a letter when you want a particular person to read it or deal with it: *for the attention of the manager*

at·test /əˈtest/ *v* [T] LAW to officially state that you believe something is true or real: *It must be signed in the presence of a witness who attests the signature.* —**attestation** *n* [C,U] *the attestation of financial statements by auditors*

attested copy —see under COPY[1]

at the money —see under MONEY

attn. written abbreviation for FOR THE ATTENTION OF —see under ATTENTION

at·tor·ney /əˈtɜːni‖-ɜːr-/ *n* plural **attorneys** [C] **1** LAW a person who has the legal right to do things and make decisions on someone else's behalf: *He appointed her his attorney.* —see also POWER OF ATTORNEY
2 LAW *AmE* a LAWYER, especially one who represents clients and speaks in court: *Acting on the advice of his attorney, he remained silent.*
district attorney a lawyer in the US who is responsible for bringing charges against people who are accused of crimes in a particular area: *Charges of unlawful business practices were filed against the company by the LA district attorney's office.*

attorney-at-law *n* plural **attorneys-at-law** [C] LAW a formal word for a lawyer in the US: *the business card of Robert McInnes, attorney-at-law*

attorney general *n* plural **attorneys general** [C] the chief lawyer in the legal system of the US and Britain: *The state attorney general alleged that Mitsubishi forced its dealers to agree to charge minimum prices for certain televisions.*

at·tract /əˈtrækt/ *v* [T] **1** to make someone want to buy something, do something, or take part in something: *Advertisements for a new headmaster attracted 120 candidates.* **attract sb to sth**: *What attracted me most to the job was the chance to travel.*
2 attract business/funding/interest/investment to create conditions where you start getting business or people start investing in your company etc: *France attracts 9% of all foreign investment in OECD countries.*
3 attract tax *BrE* if something attracts tax, tax must be paid on it: *They expect their post-retirement income to attract basic rate tax only.*

at·tri·bute /ˈætrɪbjuːt/ *n* [C] **1** MARKETING a characteristic, feature, or quality of a product: *In selling cars, product quality and product attributes are complex.*
2 STATISTICS a quality that people in a group either have or do not have, used as the basis for ATTRIBUTE SAMPLING

attribute sampling —see under SAMPLING

at·tri·tion /əˈtrɪʃən/ *n* [U] **1** the process of reducing the number of employees by not replacing those who leave for normal reasons, such as changing jobs, RETIREMENT (=leaving a job when you reach a certain age) etc: *The bank plans to reduce its staff by as much as 5% this year by* ***natural attrition****, it doesn't currently plan lay-offs.*
2 when customers are lost, for example because they start buying a competitor's product: *The success of this credit card has contributed to the attrition of card holders from other issuers.*

AUA abbreviation for AGRICULTURAL UNIT OF ACCOUNT

auc·tion[1] /ˈɔːkʃən‖ˈɒːk-/ *n* [C] **1** a public meeting where land, buildings, paintings etc are sold to the person who offers the most money for them: *Sotheby's estimated that its Impressionist paintings auction would take in about $80 million.* | *The buildings will be* ***sold at auction*** *next month.*
2 put sth up for auction to offer something for sale in an auction: *The house was put up for auction.*
absolute auction *AmE* an auction where there is no minimum price set by the seller, and something is sold to the person offering the most money
Dutch auction ◆ an auction at which the price of something is gradually reduced until someone buys it ◆ a system sometimes used in the US when a company buys back its shares or bonds. It sets a price range, and holders of the shares or bonds give a price at which they are willing to sell. The buyer then chooses a price and buys from holders who offered to sell at that price or lower
open-cry auction also **open-outcry** an auction at which buyers shout out the prices they are willing to pay
sealed-bid auction an auction in which buyers write down the price they are willing to pay and hand it in so that other buyers do not know how much they have offered: *The houses are to be sold by sealed-bid auction.*

auction[2] *v* [T] to offer something for sale at an auction: *Repossessed houses are often auctioned.* **auction sth off**: *Fleet arranged to auction off the company's inventory and equipment.*

auc·tio·neer /ˌɔːkʃəˈnɪə‖ˌɒːkʃəˈnɪr/ *n* [C] someone who is in charge of selling goods at an auction: *Each bid is a separate offer and a contract is not made until the auctioneer accepts one of them.*

au·di·ence /ˈɔːdiəns‖ˈɒː-, ˈɑː-/ *n* [C] the number or kind of people who watch or listen to something that is broadcast on radio or television, or listen to a particular type of music: *The ad was broadcast on all major channels, giving it an audience of millions.*
core audience the main kind of people who watch a

particular type of programme, listen to a particular type of music etc: *The Sporting News' core audience is score-mad baseball fans.*

target audience the kind of people that broadcasters are trying to reach with a particular programme, advertisement etc: *The target audience is kids under 12, but the station figures it will also reach parents.*

audience research —see under RESEARCH

au•di•o•tape /'ɔːdiəʊteɪp‖'ɒːdioʊ-/ *n* [C,U] a long thin band of MAGNETIC material used to record sound —compare VIDEOTAPE

au•di•o•vi•su•al also **audio-visual** /'ɔːdiəʊ'vɪʒuəl◂‖ˌɒːdioʊ-/ *adj* involving the use of recorded pictures and sound: *There is lots of scope for livening up your presentation with* ***audiovisual aids****.* | *high-definition television, the next major advance in* ***audio-visual equipment***

au•dit¹ /'ɔːdɪt‖'ɒː-/ *n* [C] **1** ACCOUNTING an official examination of a person's or organization's accounts by an expert, to check that they are true and honest: *An audit of the company showed accumulated losses of £1.5 billion.* | *The accounts will need to have an* ***independent audit*** *before they can be submitted.* | *We carry out a full* ***internal audit*** *once a year.*

continuous audit an audit where a company's financial records are checked for mistakes etc through the whole year, rather than just once a year

external audit an audit done by an expert from outside a company or organization that is being audited

2 an examination of an organization's activities or performance: *The prison population has risen by 2,500 in the last six months, according to a government audit.* | *She wants the oil company to agree to an* ***external audit*** *of its environmental policies.*

green audit an official examination of the effects of a company's activities on the environment

social audit also **ethical audit** an official examination of how well a company behaves, for example how it treats its employees, the environment etc: *The social audit of Ben and Jerry's in general commends the company, which gives 7.5% of pre-tax profits to charity.*

audit² *v* [T] **1** ACCOUNTING to officially check that an individual's or organization's accounts are true and honest: *To taxpayers who've been audited, the Internal Revenue Service is a frightening organization.*

2 to check a particular part of an organization's activities or performance: *When the cars it builds in Canada were audited, they were accepted as having the 50% North American content required under trade rules.*

Audit Bureau of Circulation *BrE*, **Audit Bureau of Circulations** *AmE*, abbreviation **ABC** *n* an organization which collects, checks, and publishes sales figures for newpapers and magazines: *The magazine 'Sailing' had a circulation of 163,000 in December, according to the Audit Bureau of Circulations.*

Audit Commission *n* an official organization in Britain that inspects the finances and work of local government authorities: *An Audit Commission study found that councillors spend too much time in meetings.*

audited accounts —see under ACCOUNT¹

audit failure —see under FAILURE

Audit Office *n* another name for the NATIONAL AUDIT OFFICE

au•di•tor /'ɔːdɪtə‖'ɒːdɪtər/ *n* [C] ACCOUNTING an outside specialist ACCOUNTANT that checks that an individual's or organization's accounts are true and honest: *Under pressure from the auditor, the company had to increase its reported loss for the year.* | *The shareholder group is pressing for* ***external auditors*** *to be appointed so that it can obtain reliable financial information.* | *The airline has said that* ***internal auditors*** *will look into the allegations that improper payments were made.*

district auditor in Britain, someone whose job is to make sure that local government finance is run as it should be according to law: *Traditionally, government-appointed district auditors have been responsible for examining most local authority accounts.*

auditor's report —see under REPORT¹

audit trail *n* [C] ACCOUNTING accounting records showing a series of steps leading up to a present financial situation: *The lack of a physical audit trail in electronic commerce increases the possibilities for tax avoidance.*

Aug. written abbreviation for AUGUST

aus•ter•i•ty /ɔː'sterɪti, ɒ-‖ɒː-/ *n* [U] ECONOMICS bad economic conditions in which people do not have much money to spend: *her childhood memories of war-time austerity*

austerity budget —see under BUDGET¹

austerity measure —see under MEASURE¹

au•thor•i•ty /ɔː'θɒrɪti, ə-‖ə'θɑː-, ə'θɔː-/ *n* plural **authorities** **1** [C] an official organization which controls a particular activity and checks that the rules and laws relating to it are being obeyed: *Illinois' metropolitan rail authority* | *the Financial Services Authority* —see also ADVERTISING STANDARDS AUTHORITY, ATOMIC ENERGY AUTHORITY, SECURITIES AND FUTURES AUTHORITY

health authority [C] a government organization in Britain that is responsible for providing health services in a particular area: *the Bolton Area Health Authority*

local authority [C] a government organization in Britain that is responsible for providing public services such as schools, the collection of rubbish etc in a particular area: *Local authorities have been told that they must cut their spending.*

port authority [C] an independent public organization that controls a PORT: *the Port Authority of New York and New Jersey*

2 the authorities [plural] the organizations that are in charge of a particular country or area or a particular activity: *The weak currency could force the authorities to raise interest rates.*

3 [U] the power that a person or organization has because of their official or legal position **the authority to do sth**: *I wouldn't have taken the job unless I had the authority to run the division.* | *The bankruptcy court lacked the authority to rule on this subject.*

4 authority to negotiate/purchase BANKING the power given by an importer to a bank in the exporter's country to allow the exporter to arrange a BILL OF EXCHANGE

5 authority to pay BANKING the power given by an importer to a bank in the exporter's country to pay a BILL OF EXCHANGE

au•thor•ize also **authorise** *BrE v* [T] /'ɔːθəraɪz‖'ɒː-/to give official or legal permission for something: *The board has authorized the buy-back of 85,000 shares.* | *The bill would authorize $850 million a year in grants to states to carry out school-improvement plans.* **authorize sb to do sth**: *The Food and Drug Administration authorized the company to restart production.* —**authorized** also **authorised** *BrE adj*: *For years, Sony has depended on a large network of authorized dealers.* —**authorization** also **authorisation** *BrE n* [C,U] *Japan Air Lines got authorization for four weekly cargo flights to Chicago.* | *He was accused of taking $38,000 from the company without authorization.* | *The government is threatening to reduce export authorizations.*

authorized capital —see under CAPITAL

authorized fund —see under FUND¹

authorized issue —see ***authorized capital*** under CAPITAL

authorized shares —see under SHARE

authorized stock —see ***authorized capital*** under CAPITAL

au•to /ˈɔːtəʊ‖ˈɒːtoʊ/ *n AmE* **1** [C] another name for AUTOMOBILE, especially when talking about the car industry: *The Big Three US **auto makers** | Japan's **auto dealerships** are controlled by the producers.*
2 autos [plural] FINANCE shares in companies that make cars: *He is avoiding airlines, autos and retailers.*

auto-expense allowance —see under ALLOWANCE

auto-financing *adj* FINANCE if a business is auto-financing, it gets enough money from its sales to pay for its operations and investment without having to increase capital or borrow money; SELF-FINANCING

au•to•mate /ˈɔːtəmeɪt‖ˈɒː-/ *v* [T] to change to a system where goods are produced or jobs are done by machines rather than by people: *a huge software project, designed to automate all the routine tasks in offices* —**automated** *adj*: *the industry's first **fully automated** warehouse* —**automation** *n* [U] *Costs have been reduced by automation and heavy job cuts. | software for **office automation***

automated teller machine —see ATM

au•to•mat•ic check•off /ˌɔːtəmætɪk ˈtʃekɒf‖ˌɒːtəmætɪkˈtʃekɒːf/ *n* [C,U] *AmE* HUMAN RESOURCES in the US, money that is taken off an employee's salary by the employer and sent directly to the union to pay for the employee's union membership —see also DUES CHECKOFF

automatic teller machine —see ATM

au•to•mo•bile /ˈɔːtəməbiːl‖ˈɒːtəmoʊ-/ *n* [C] *especially AmE* a car: *AGES makes rubber parts for the **automobile industry**.*

automobile insurance —see under INSURANCE

au•to•mo•tive /ˌɔːtəˈməʊtɪv◂‖ˌɒːtəˈmoʊ-/ *adj* [only before a noun] relating to cars or the car industry: *demand in the **automotive market** | They make truck parts, **automotive parts** and electronic controls.*

autonomous investment —see under INVESTMENT

av. written abbreviation for AVERAGE

a•vail•a•bil•i•ty /əˌveɪləˈbɪləti/ *n* [U] **1** the fact that something is able to be used or can easily be bought or found: *the availability of affordable housing*
2 subject to availability a phrase meaning that it is possible to buy or choose something if it is still available: *The weekend breaks can be taken any weekend, subject to availability.*

a•vai•la•ble /əˈveɪləbəl/ *adj* **1** able to be bought, used, seen etc: *They plan to make the product **widely available** in vending machines. | Full-year 1999 results aren't yet available.*
2 if someone is available, they are not busy and can see or talk to people: *I'm afraid the chairman isn't available at the moment. | Are you available for a meeting next Wednesday?*

a•val /əˈvæl/ *n* [C] BANKING a GUARANTEE given by a bank, for example an importer's bank, that a BILL OF EXCHANGE will be paid

av•e•rage[1] /ˈævərɪdʒ/ *adj* **1** [only before a noun] the average amount is the amount you get when you add together several amounts and divide this by the number of amounts you have added together; MEAN: *Oil companies are basing their budgets on an **average price** of $20.40 a barrel. | The electronics industry has increased output by an **average rate** of 14% a year. | **Average earnings** in the state are about $2500 a month.*
2 having qualities that are typical of most of the people or things in a group: *The average employee in Chicago must work 18 minutes to buy a hamburger. | Coffee production in an average year here totals 450,000 tonnes.*

average[2] *n* **1** [C] STATISTICS the amount calculated by adding together several amounts, and then dividing this amount by the total number of amounts added together: *Sales in the various markets improved by an average of 40% last year.*

moving average [C] an average of figures from a certain number of the most recent previous periods of time. For example, the average for the most recent 12-month period is re-calculated every month, with the latest month's figure replacing the first month from the previous series

weighted average [C] STATISTICS an average calculated by giving more value to some figures than others, depending on their relative importance: *Barclays de Zoete says its weighted average of Dutch company earnings fell 2%. | The weighted average term of the bonds is 1.71 years.*

2 on average based on a calculation of how many times something happens, how much money someone usually gets, how often people usually do something etc: *On average, people in their 50s require 45% more drug prescriptions than people in their 30s. | Visitors to Legoland on average spend $26 each.*
3 [C,U] the usual level or amount for most people or things in a group: *Employee pay and benefits are **above average** here. | Stockmarket volume was **below average** at 12.1 million shares traded. | Tea productivity in Assam is over 2,000 kg a hectare, compared with a **national average** in India of 1,790 kg a hectare.*
4 [C usually singular] FINANCE a list of shares on a stock market, showing the general level of shares at a particular moment; INDEX: *The **industrial average*** (=shares in industrial companies on a particular stockmarket) *surged 535.17 points, or 20.3%.*

Dow Jones averages [plural] a number of SHARE INDEXES showing the performance of company shares on the NEW YORK STOCK EXCHANGE: *We normally remove a stock from the Dow Jones Averages whenever the company enters bankruptcy proceedings.*

Dow Jones Industrial Average *trademark* abbreviation **DJIA** [singular] a share index of about 30 leading companies, whose movements show the direction of the New York stockmarket as a whole. The Dow Jones Industrial Average is the most important index, often referred to as the Dow Jones: *The Dow Jones Industrial Average closed down 147.49, a loss of 1.41%, to 10,463.00.*

Dow Jones Transportation Average *trademark* abbreviation **DJTA** [singular] an share index of 20 companies involved in the moving, storing, and selling of goods: *Rises among airline stocks sent the Dow Jones Transportation Average more than 1.2% ahead at 3,359.*

Dow Jones Utilities Average *trademark* abbreviation **DJUA** [singular] a share index of electricity, gas, and water companies. The movement of their shares is seen as a sign of the way interest rates may develop. These companies are big borrowers and, when interest rates go down, their results improve: *The Dow Jones Utilities Average rose 2.89 points yesterday to 212.90, which many traders interpret as signaling lower interest rates ahead.*

Nikkei average also **Nikkei index** [singular] the main share index of shares in companies on the Tokyo stockmarket: *The Nikkei index fell by 40% during the year.*

5 [U] INSURANCE a loss relating to damage to a ship or the CARGO (=goods it is carrying)

general average [U] INSURANCE when the owner of a ship and the owner of the CARGO share the cost of a loss caused by doing something to save either the ship or the goods: *The losses were shared by the shippers as 'general average' losses.*

particular average [U] INSURANCE the cost of damage to or loss of a ship or the CARGO it is carrying, paid to the owner of the goods actually damaged; PARTIAL LOSS —see also FREE OF PARTICULAR AVERAGE

average[3] *v* **1** [linking verb] if something averages a particular amount or rate, that is its average amount or

rate: *In Europe, budget deficits average 5% of GDP.* | *The store is averaging sales of $300,000 on an annual basis.*

2 [T] to calculate the average of a number of amounts: *The new system works by averaging the payments made to local authorities.*

average out *phr v* **1** [T] **average** sth ↔ **out** to calculate the average of a number of amounts: *They were found to earn only £60 a week when their seasonal and casual earnings were averaged out.*

2 average out at/to sth if something averages out a particular amount or rate, that is its average amount or rate: *Our training costs last year averaged out at £5,100 per trainee.* | *Basketball players' salaries average out at $3.3 million.*

average adjuster —see under ADJUSTER

average agent —see under AGENT

average audience rating —see under RATING

average clause —see under CLAUSE

average date —see under DATE[1]

average rate —see under RATE[1]

average revenue —see under REVENUE

average statement —see under STATEMENT

average stock —see under STOCK[1]

a•vi•a•tion /ˌeɪviˈeɪʃən‖ˌeɪ-, ˌæ-/ *n* [U] **1** the business of making aircraft: *job losses in the* ***aviation industry***

2 the business of transporting people and goods in aircraft: *More competition in aviation means more choice, better service and lower fares.* —see also AERONAUTICS

civil aviation the business of transporting passengers and goods by aircraft, rather than the use of aircraft for military purposes: *The Gulf War had an impact on civil aviation earnings.*

aviation insurance —see under INSURANCE

a•void /əˈvɔɪd/ *v* [T] if you avoid tax, you manage to not pay it legally, for example by the way that you enter profits or losses into your accounts: *Investing in this way allows savers to avoid tax upon withdrawal.* —compare EVADE —**avoidance** *n* [U] *There is a very thin line between* ***tax avoidance*** *and tax evasion.*

av•oir•du•pois /ˌævədəˈpɔɪz, ˌævwɑːdjuːˈpwɑː‖ˌævərdəˈpɔɪz/ *n* [U] a system of weighing things used in the UK and US, based on the standard measures of the OUNCE, POUND, and TON, which is being replaced in the UK by the METRIC SYSTEM: *There are 16 ounces to one avoirdupois pound.*

a•ward[1] /əˈwɔːd‖-ɔːrd/ *n* [C] **1** an amount of money that is given to someone as a result of an official decision or judgment: *The basic award for unfair dismissal is £6,150.* | *The nurses'* ***pay award*** (=increase in pay) *was not nearly as much as they had expected.*

2 something such as a prize or an amount of money given to a person or company to reward them for something they have done: *85% of the company's product is sold overseas, a feat which won it the Queen's Award for Export.*

award[2] *v* [T] **1** to officially decide that someone should have something such as an amount of money **be awarded sth**: *Devonport dockyard has been awarded the contract to refit Trident nuclear submarines.* **award sb sth**: *The tribunal can award you up to £14,000 compensation or order your reinstatement.*

2 to officially give a prize or an amount of money to a person or company, to reward them for what they have done **be awarded sth**: *He has been awarded the MBE for services to the electricity supply industry.* **award sb sth**: *The university awarded her a scholarship.*

a•ware•ness /əˈweənəs‖əˈwer-/ *n* [U] knowledge or understanding of a particular subject, situation, or thing: *US investors' awareness of international bond markets* | *They need to* ***raise awareness*** *of the product in markets such as France and the US, where it is less well known.*

brand awareness the degree to which people know about a particular brand: *Although Philips is well known in consumer electronics, it didn't enjoy much brand awareness in PCs.*

consumer awareness awareness by buyers of a particular product, company etc: *The car maker's problem is low consumer awareness in a crowded car market.*

axe[1] also **ax** *AmE* /æks/ *v* [T] *informal* **1** if a company axes jobs, it suddenly dismisses people in those jobs in order to reduce costs: *East Midlands Electricity last month axed 300 jobs.*

2 to suddenly get rid of a plan or service, or reduce the amount of money spent on it: *Stansted Airport's transatlantic service is to be axed next month.*

axe[2] also **ax** *AmE* — *n* **1 get/be given the axe** if someone gets the axe or is given the axe, they are suddenly dismissed from their job because the company wants to reduce costs. If a plan, project, or service gets the axe, it is stopped in order to reduce costs: *A lot of managers are now getting the axe.*

2 the axe falls if the axe falls, someone is dismissed from their job or a plan, project, or service is stopped because a company needs to reduce its costs: *The axe is now falling on people whose talents have been praised only months earlier.*

B

baby bond —see under BOND

Bachelor of Business Administration —see BBA

back /bæk/ *v* [T] **1** to support someone or something, especially by giving money or using your influence: *The board backed Mr Standley, who plans to cut costs.* | *Shareholders have backed a plan to build a second plant.* **2** FINANCE if SECURITIES are backed by particular assets, they are supported by income from them: *This new generation of securities is backed by aircraft leases, royalty streams from films, student loans and auto loans.* —see also ***asset-backed security*** under SECURITY

back sth ↔ **up** *phr v* [T] COMPUTING to put copies of information held on a computer onto a disk, so that the information is not lost if there is a problem with the computer: *This allows users to back up the database without shutting it down.* —see also BACKUP

back catalogue —see under CATALOGUE[1]

back·chan·nel also **back-channel** /ˈbækˌtʃænl/ *n* [C] someone or something that passes information secretly or unofficially from one person to another: *Woodward might well have served as a backchannel between ministers, carrying information so sensitive that it could only have been conveyed by a special officer.* | *You'll find out more in this organization through the backchannels than any number of staff briefings.* | *back-channel diplomacy*

back·date /ˌbækˈdeɪt‖ˈbækdeɪt/ *v* [T] **1** if a change in an amount paid is backdated, it has its effect from an earlier date **be backdated to**: *Postal workers are getting a 3.3% wage rise backdated to October.*
2 to put a date on a document that is earlier than the real date: *It was alleged that he had backdated the sale documents to evade a court order.*

backed bill —see under BILL OF EXCHANGE

back·er /ˈbækə‖-ər/ *n* [C] someone who supports a plan, person, or company, usually by giving money: *The directors closed down the operation after the company's **financial backers** pulled out.*

back·ground /ˈbækgraʊnd/ *n* [C] **1** HUMAN RESOURCES someone's past, for example their education, qualifications, and the jobs they have had: *We are looking for someone with a background in tourism.*
2 in the background COMPUTING a computer program working in the background continues to function and do calculations while the user is working with another program

background check —see under CHECK[1]

back·hand·er /ˈbækhændə‖-ər/ *n* [C] *BrE informal* an amount of money or something valuable that someone gives you to persuade you to help them or do something dishonest for them; BRIBE: *A former Ministry of Defence worker, has been found guilty of accepting £1.5 million in backhanders from arms companies.*

back·ing /ˈbækɪŋ/ *n* [U] support or help, especially financial help: *The proposals **have the backing of** the EU Commissioner for the Environment.* | *The consultancy was formed with **financial backing** from Saatchi and Saatchi.*

asset backing also **asset cover** the total value of all the assets that a company has, divided by the number of shares that the company has issued; ASSET VALUE PER SHARE

net asset backing the value of a company's assets less its liabilities, except its liabilities to shareholders: *News Corp. said it ended the year with net asset backing of A$27.91 a share.*

back·list /ˈbæklɪst/ *n* [C usually singular] a list of books that a PUBLISHER continues to produce and sell as well as the new books that it produces each year: *Most of the titles they publish are drawn from Everyman's backlist.*

back-load *n* [C] a load for a road transport vehicle to carry on its return journey: *Costs rise when hauliers are unable to fill their back-loads.*

back·log /ˈbæklɒg‖-lɔːg, -lɑːg/ *n* [C usually singular] an amount of work that should already have been completed: *The company has a backlog of 165 orders for the MD500 series helicopter.*

back office —see under OFFICE

back order —see under ORDER[1]

back pay —see under PAY[1]

back·room /ˈbækrʊm, -ruːm/ *adj* [only before a noun] **backroom staff/boys** people whose work is important but who do not get much attention and are not well-known

back·space /ˈbækspeɪs/ *n* [singular] the part of a computer KEYBOARD or TYPEWRITER that you press to move backwards towards the beginning of a line or to remove something that you have just written

back-to-back *adj* [only before a noun] back-to-back increases or decreases happen very quickly one after the other: *The Dow Jones finished up 5.96 to 10,571.29, the second advance this week and the first back-to-back gain since August.*

back-to-back loan —see under LOAN[1]

back·up /ˈbækʌp/ *n* [C] COMPUTING a copy of information held on a computer that is put onto a DISK so that the information is not lost if there is a problem with the computer: *Take a **backup copy** of the file to be converted.* —see also ***back up*** under BACK

back-up copy —see under COPY[1]

backup withholding *n* [U] FINANCE a system in the US in which banks and companies paying out investment earnings to people whose SOCIAL SECURITY numbers they do not have, send a percentage of the earnings directly to the tax authorities: *The start of this backup withholding has been delayed, giving taxpayers more time to supply their numbers.*

back·ward·a·tion /ˌbækwəˈdeɪʃən‖-wər-/ *n* [U] FINANCE when a COMMODITY due for delivery soon has a higher price than one due for future delivery: *In an economic slowdown it is surprising to see the copper market in backwardation.*

backward integration —see under INTEGRATION

ba·con /ˈbeɪkən/ *n informal* **bring home the bacon** to earn money: *He is counting on healthcare, food and technology companies to bring home the bacon for shareholders.*

BACS /bæks/ *n* [U] Bankers' Automated Clearing Services; an electronic system for making payments between accounts in different banks in the UK. BACS is part of the ASSOCIATION FOR PAYMENT CLEARING SERVICES: *Payments are made direct to employees' bank accounts via BACS.*

bad[1] /bæd/ *n* **to the bad** if you are a particular amount of money to the bad, you have lost or owe that amount: *Thanks to your mistake, I'm £500 to the bad!*

bad[2] *adj* **bad debt/loan/investment/stock/asset** a bad debt, loan, investment etc is one from which you will not be able to get your money back: *Barclays have sharply increased their provision for bad corporate debts.* | *The bank has more than a half billion dollars of bad assets.*

bad debt —see under DEBT

bad debt provision —see under PROVISION

bad debt recovery —see under RECOVERY

bad debt reserves —see under RESERVES

bad faith —see under FAITH

bad loan —see under LOAN[1]

badly off *adj* not having enough money to live comfortably: *My wife and I are not badly off as we have the state pension and my police pension.* —opposite WELL OFF

bad title —see under TITLE

bail[1] /beɪl/ *n* [U] LAW **1** when someone who has been accused of a crime is allowed to remain free until their court case starts, usually because an amount of money has been given to the court which the court will keep if the prisoner does not return: *The magistrates refused their* ***application for bail****.* | *Six former members of staff have been arrested and* ***released on bail*** *while the inquiry continues.*

2 the amount of money paid for bail: ***Bail was set at*** *£100,000 each on condition that the defendants did not leave the country.*

3 post bail to leave a sum of money with a court of law as bail: *If a defendant can post bail and presents no threat to the community, he can await trial at home.*

bail[2] *v*

bail out *phr v* **1** [T] **bail** sb/sth ↔ **out** to provide money to get a person or organization out of financial trouble: *These enterprises think they can force the banks to bail them out.* —see also BAIL-OUT

2 [T] **bail** sb ↔ **out** LAW to help someone to be set free on bail, usually by providing an amount of money that can be left with the court: *Somehow she raised the $500 to bail him out.*

3 [I] if you bail out of investments that are not doing well, you sell them: *Lockheed's stock has climbed to the low $40s from the low $30s, giving him a chance to bail out at a loss he could live with.*

bail•a•ble /ˈbeɪləbəl/ *adj* LAW a bailable offence is one for which an accused person is allowed by law to be set free on bail

bail bond —see under BOND

bail•ee /beɪˈliː/ *n* [C] LAW someone who has the right to use someone else's property, but without becoming its owner: *Under this arrangement, the bailee has an option to purchase the goods at a later date.*

bai•liff /ˈbeɪlɪf/ *n* [C] **1** *BrE* an official of the legal system who has the right to take the goods or property of a person or organization in debt, in order to pay off the debts: *Bailiffs entered the premises and took possession.*

2 *AmE* an official of the legal system who watches prisoners and keeps order in a court of law

bail•ment /ˈbeɪlmənt/ *n* [U] LAW the right to use someone else's property without, however, becoming its owner

bail•or /ˈbeɪlə, beɪˈlɔː‖-lər, -ˈlɔːr/ *n* [C] someone who gives or sells the right to use their property to someone else without selling it to them

bail-out also **bailout** *n* [C] FINANCE providing money to a person or organization to get them out of financial trouble: *Losses totaling hundreds of million dollars led to an expensive bailout by its parent company.* | *IMF directors approved a second tranche of funds for Thailand from its $17 billion* ***bail-out package****.* —see also ***bail out*** under BAIL[2]

bait-and-switch *adj* [only before a noun] *AmE* MARKETING if sellers use bait and switch methods, they attract customers by telling them about a cheap product which may or may not exist, and then persuade them to buy a more expensive one: *Airlines often promote bargain fares that are not available on all flights, classic bait and switch tactics.*

bal•ance[1] /ˈbæləns/ **1** *n* [C] ACCOUNTING, BANKING the difference between the total amounts of money coming into and going out of an account in a particular period of time

account balance ACCOUNTING the difference between the total of all the debit and all the credit entries in an account, which is the amount required to make the two sides of the account equal to each other

adverse balance *BrE* the amount by which a bank account is in debt; NEGATIVE BALANCE *AmE*: *His statement showed an adverse balance of £835.65.*

bank balance the balance of a bank account showing how much the account contains, or how much it is in debt: *He wears hand-made suits and has a healthy bank balance.*

cash balance the amount of money a company has in its bank accounts: *Anglia generated cash of £5.35 million in the period, lifting its cash balance to £26 million.*

closing balance the balance of an account at the end of an accounting period

compensating balance *AmE* in the US, an amount of money that must be left with a bank from which a loan has been received

credit balance a balance showing that more money has been received or is owed to a company than has been paid out or is owed by the company: *The bank statement shows a credit balance of £298.75.*

debit balance a balance showing that more money has been paid out or is owed by a company than has been received or is owed to the company: *The account was liquidated, and had a debit balance of almost $3.4 million.*

double declining balance ACCOUNTING a method of calculating DEPRECIATION (=the gradual loss in something's value) where twice the normal rate is subtracted in each period of time. For example, for an asset depreciated over five years, 40% of its remaining value is depreciated each year, not 20%.

idle balance *BrE* money kept in a bank account that does not pay interest, for example a CURRENT ACCOUNT: *As interest rates begin to rise, people choose to hold less idle balances.*

negative balance *AmE* the amount by which a bank is in debt; ADVERSE BALANCE *BrE*

opening balance ◆ the balance of an account at the beginning of an accounting period: *an opening balance of £1000, income of £500 pounds, expenditure of £700 and a closing balance of £800*

trial balance a way of checking that a set of accounts is accurate, by adding up the amounts received and the amounts paid out to see whether they are the same

unsold balance the value of the shares, bonds etc that have not been bought at the end of an ISSUE (=offer to the public to buy): *Bank of America reported an unsold balance of about $28 million on an issue of $121 million bonds.* —see also COMPETITIVE BALANCE

2 an amount still owed after some money has been paid: *The firm has paid $128,000, but whether it will ever pay the balance remains uncertain.* | *Most people have an* ***outstanding balance*** *on their credit cards for a couple of months, then pay it off.*

3 the rest or remaining part of an amount: *20,000 barrels a day are shipped to San Francisco, and the balance is delivered by pipeline directly to Los Angeles.*

balance[2] *v* **1** [T] ACCOUNTING to calculate the amount needed to make the debit side and the credit side of an account equal, perhaps by looking for mistakes

2 [I] ACCOUNTING if the debit and credit sides of an account balance, they show the same amounts

3 balance the accounts/books/budget to do what is necessary to spend no more than the amount of money received, usually by a government: *Costa Rica has*

worked on programs with the International Monetary Fund to balance its accounts. | *Real differences exist between the administration and Congress over how to balance the budget and where to cut taxes.*

balance brought down abbreviation **balance b/d**, also **balance brought forward** abbreviation **balance b/fwd** *n* [C] ACCOUNTING the balance of an account at the beginning of a new accounting period, which was also the balance at the end of the previous period

balance carried down abbreviation **balance c/d**, also **balance carried forward** abbreviation **balance c/fwd** *n* [C] ACCOUNTING the balance of an account at the end of an accounting period, which will be taken forward to become the balance at the beginning of a new period.

balance date —see under DATE[1]

balanced budget —see under BUDGET[1]

balanced fund —see under FUND[1]

balance of payments *n* [singular] ECONOMICS the difference between the amount of money coming into a country, for example in payment for its exports, and the amount of money going out, for example to pay for its imports: *Exports are expected to increase in the current quarter, which would improve Britain's balance of payments.*

balance of payments capital account —see under ACCOUNT[1]

balance of payments current account —see under ACCOUNT[1]

balance of payments deficit —see under DEFICIT

balance of payments surplus —see under SURPLUS[1]

balance of trade *n* [singular] ECONOMICS **1** the part of a country's balance of payments that relates to the value of goods and services imported and exported; TRADE BALANCE: *The overall balance of trade in the UK is improving as a result of the strong currency.*

2 the difference in the total value of imports and exports between two countries or areas: *The US and Europe sell nearly $100 billion worth of goods and services a year to each other. For the moment, the balance of trade is in the US's favor.*

adverse balance of trade ECONOMICS when the value of a country's imports is greater than the value of its exports

favourable balance of trade *BrE* **favorable balance of trade** *AmE* ECONOMICS when the value of the country's exports is greater than the value of its imports

balance sheet *n* [C] a document showing a company's financial position and wealth at a particular time, often the last day of its financial year: *IFF performed well last year, and has a* ***healthy balance sheet*** *with a good amount of cash.* | *a* ***strong balance sheet*** | *a* ***clean balance sheet*** (=without debt or without too much debt)

off-balance sheet *adj* [only before a noun] off-balance sheet items, activities, debts etc are ones that a company does not need to show on its balance sheet, but in notes added to it: *The leasing company said a Chinese airline has signed for an aircraft operating lease – a relatively short-term, off-balance sheet rental.*

bale[1] /beɪl/ *v*

bale sb/sth ↔ **out** *phr v* [T] FINANCE to provide money to get a person or organization out of financial trouble; BAIL OUT: *The restructuring was aimed at baling out Renong, freeing cash to allow the company to continue with key projects.*

bale[2] *n* [C] a large quantity of something such as paper, hay, or cotton that is tightly tied together: *The Agriculture Department is forecasting a 5% increase in world cotton production to 91 million bales.*

balloon loan —see under LOAN[1]

balloon mortgage —see under MORTGAGE[1]

balloon payment —see under PAYMENT

bal•lot[1] /ˈbælət/ *n* [C,U] **1** an occasion when people can vote, usually secretly, or a system of voting like this: *A ballot of the workforce resulted in a 2–1 vote in favour of industrial action.* | *a committee elected by* ***secret ballot*** | *Her union called an immediate* ***strike ballot*** *to decide whether a strike should go ahead.*

2 FINANCE a way of choosing who will get shares when there are too many requests for shares that are being made available for the first time

ballot[2] *v* past tense and past participle **balloted** or **ballotted** *BrE* present participle **balloting** or **ballotting** *BrE* [I,T] **1** to ask people to vote in order to decide something: *The chairman is elected by ballotting all the shareholders.* | *My union is at present ballotting to decide on industrial action.*

2 FINANCE to choose who will get shares when there are too many requests for shares that are being made available for the first time

ballpark /ˈbɔːlpɑːk‖ˈbɒːlpɑːrk/ also **ball park** *n* **1 ballpark estimate/figure** a number or amount that is approximately correct, though not exact: *A spokeswoman said that Baker and Arens had discussed a ballpark figure for financial aid.*

2 in the right/wrong/same ballpark used to say that an amount or price is approximately right, wrong, the same: *Pricing is being left to each of the six manufacturers, but all are expected to be in the same ballpark.*

Bal•tic Ex•change /ˌbɔːltɪk ɪksˈtʃeɪndʒ‖ˌbɒːl-/ also **Baltic Mercantile and Shipping Exchange** *n* FINANCE an international market for shipping and FREIGHT in the City of London

ban[1] /bæn/ *n* [C] an official order or law that forbids something from being used or done: *The* ***export ban*** *on live cattle was imposed almost three years ago.* | *Nurses at the hospital last night ended their* ***overtime ban***. (=ban on working more than the normal number of hours) + **on**: *The Environment Minister announced a ban on imports of potentially harmful industrial waste.*

ban[2] *v* past tense and past participle **banned** present participle **banning** [T] to say officially that something must not be done, used etc: *We propose to ban smoking in large areas of the Wimpey offices.* **ban sb from doing sth**: *Industries will be banned from using high-sulphur content fuels.*

banc•as•sur•ance /ˈbæŋkəˌʃʊərəns‖-ˌʃʊr-/ *n* [U] the combining of banking and insurance activities in one organization; ALLFINANZ

band•width /ˈbændwɪdθ/ *n* [C usually singular] **1** COMPUTING a measurement of the amount of information that can be sent from one computer to another on the Internet in a particular length of time: *The new* ***bandwidth capacity*** *will promote introduction of cheap, interactive services such as home shopping, banking and games.*

2 *informal* a measure of human intelligence, especially the ability of businesspeople to understand things quickly, to see how things are related etc: *Many of the individuals in this book possess super-high bandwidth, incredible mental ability.*

Bank /bæŋk/ *n* **The Bank** the BANK OF ENGLAND, Britain's central bank: *The Bank is worried that strong demand for labour could lead to higher wages and prices.*

bank[1] *n* [C] **1** a business that makes its profit by paying interest to people who keep money there and charging a higher rate of interest to borrowers who borrow money from the bank. Different types of bank provide a variety of other financial services: *The major banks have announced an increase in interest rates.* —see also GIROBANK

acceptance bank another name for ACCEPTING HOUSE
agent bank the bank which has been chosen to look after a SYNDICATED LOAN (=a loan to one borrower by many lenders), sending interest payments to lenders etc
agricultural bank a bank that lends money to farmers, often over a long period of time and at low rates of interest
banker's bank a bank offering services to other banks: *It has positioned itself as a banker's bank, handling other banks' processing and cash management business in the region.*
central bank the official bank of a country, which is responsible for setting interest rates, controlling the MONEY SUPPLY, producing bank notes and making them available, and keeping the country's supply of foreign currency and gold etc: *China's central bank said that a further decline in interest rates is unlikely.* | *Germany has no plans to sell gold from its* ***central bank reserves****.*
City Bank one of the RETAIL BANKS in Japan
clearing bank *BrE* one of the High Street banks that ISSUES and accepts cheques and passes them through the banking system
commercial bank ◆ a bank involved in international trading and providing services for businesses and organizations rather than for individuals
◆ a bank owned by shareholders rather than by a government
confirming bank also **confirming house** BANKING a bank which promises to make payment for goods bought by an importer if the importer has documents to show that the goods have been sent and that they will accept the goods
co-operative bank a bank that lends money, collected from its members, at low rates of interest
credit bank a bank that lends money to businesses and individuals
discount bank a bank that buys BILLS OF EXCHANGE (=documents ordering someone to pay a particular amount on a fixed date), often relating to trade
eligible bank in Britain, one of the banks officially approved to accept certain BILLS OF EXCHANGE that the BANK OF ENGLAND will then accept: *Bills accepted by banks designated as eligible banks by the Bank of England become first-class bills which the Bank of England is willing to deal in on the market.*
Export-Import Bank also **Eximbank** a US bank set up to encourage companies to export their goods by offering them loans at reduced rates of interest, GUARANTEEING loans made to them by other banks, giving credit to foreign borrowers so they can import goods etc: *Export-Import Bank financing of business with China*
foreign bank a bank based in another country
High Street bank *BrE* a bank that has branches in many towns and cities: *Several High Street banks have already announced a cut in interest rates.*
investment bank a bank that buys stocks and shares and then sells them to members of the public. Investment banks also offer advice on things such as MERGERS and TAKEOVERS: *Oxford Energy Co. announced it had hired an investment bank to explore options, including the possible merger with another entity.*
joint-stock bank a bank which is a public company with shares owned by investors rather than a government
lead bank a financial institution that organizes SYNDICATED LOANS (=loans to one borrower by many lenders)
merchant bank a bank that deals with business rather than the general public. Merchant banks advise on and arrange finance for investment and takeovers, and advise financial institutions on where to make investments etc: *Sudbury have hired Gordian Group, a New York merchant bank, to propose a financial restructuring of the company.*
mutual savings bank in the US, a savings bank that is owned by the people who put their savings into it and does not have shareholders
national bank in the US, a bank that operates in several parts of the country rather than at local level. National banks must be members of the FEDERAL RESERVE SYSTEM
paying bank a bank that is responsible for paying the amount of money on a cheque relating to one of its customers' accounts: *A County Court has decided that a paying bank is under no obligation to pay a forged cheque even if it is supported by the bank's guarantee card.*
private bank a bank which is a small LIMITED COMPANY
retail bank a bank that provides services to individual customers rather than to businesses or large organizations
savings bank a bank where people can save small amounts of money and receive interest on it. Savings banks do not offer other general banking services —see also NATIONAL SAVINGS BANK
state bank in the US, a bank that is controlled by the laws of a state rather than of the whole country. Unlike a NATIONAL BANK, a state bank does not have to be a member of the FEDERAL RESERVE SYSTEM: *He needed the funds to secure a personal loan at Iowa State Bank.*
stock savings bank in the US, a savings bank that invests small amounts of money for people and is owned by shareholders
2 the local branch of a particular bank: *I have to go to the bank at lunchtime.*
3 break the bank to cost or need so much money that a person or organization is unable to pay: *customers who want to get a reasonable PC without breaking the bank*
4 a store of something that can be used when needed
data bank a large amount of information held on a computer: *a computerized data bank to track customers' buying habits*
job bank a computer databank containing details of available jobs, created by an EMPLOYMENT AGENCY or by a large company: *Operators key data into an electronic job bank, trying to match unemployed workers with new opportunities.*
land bank the land that a company owns considered as an asset that can make money for the company: *WI has one of the largest land banks in Hong Kong, and its property units are almost fully rented.*

bank² *v* **1** [T] to put or keep money in a bank: *Did you bank that check?* | *He banked rather than spent $3,800 in tax refunds.*
2 [I] to keep your money in a particular bank + **with**: *Some families have banked with Hoare since the 17th century.* —see also OVERBANKED

bank (credit) line *n* [C] *AmE* another name for a CREDIT LINE

bank·a·ble /ˈbæŋkəbəl/ *adj* profitable and valuable: *If I didn't believe this was a bankable transaction, I wouldn't have made this decision.*

bank account —see under ACCOUNT¹
bank advance —see under ADVANCE²
bank balance —see under BALANCE¹
bank bill —see under BILL OF EXCHANGE
bank book —see under BOOK¹
bank borrowing —see under BORROWING
bank card —see under CARD
bank certificate —see under CERTIFICATE
bank cheque —see under CHEQUE
bank clerk —see under CLERK

bank credit —see under CREDIT[1]

bank credit line —see under CREDIT LINE

bank debt —see under DEBT

bank deposits —see under DEPOSIT[1]

bank discount —see under DISCOUNT[1]

B

bank draft also **banker's draft** *n* [C] a cheque written by a bank and therefore certain to be paid. A customer can use a bank draft to pay someone who will not accept a personal cheque: *Payment may be made by a bank draft drawn on a UK bank.*

bank•er /ˈbæŋkə‖-ər/ *n* [C] **1** someone who works in the management of a bank: *Mr Hartmann is a senior Swiss banker who sits on many company boards.*
2 an organization that performs banking activities: *GE Capital is a very skilled banker.*
investment banker a person who works in the management of an investment bank, or an organization that works as an investment bank

banker's bank —see under BANK[1]

banker's card —see under CARD

banker's discount —see under DISCOUNT[1]

banker's enquiry *n* plural **banker's enquiries** [C] another name for BANKER'S REFERENCE

banker's lien —see under LIEN

banker's order *n* [C,U] an instruction by a customer to their bank to make a regular payment to someone; STANDING ORDER: *Monthly repayments on the loans must be made by banker's order.* —compare DIRECT DEBIT

banker's reference —see under REFERENCE

Bank for International Settlements abbreviation **BIS** *n* an organization that organizes regular meetings between representatives from the main banks from different countries, to exchange information on international trade, payment systems etc

bank guarantee —see under GUARANTEE[2]

bank guarantee fund —see under FUND[1]

bank holiday *n* [C] **1** *BrE* an official holiday when banks and most businesses are closed; NATIONAL HOLIDAY *AmE*: *a quiet* ***bank holiday Monday***
2 *AmE* a day when banks are closed by law because of problems in the banking system: *The Argentinian currency lost 20% of its value against the dollar on Monday, forcing the resignation of the central bank governor. A two-day bank holiday was declared.*

bank•ing /ˈbæŋkɪŋ/ *n* [U] **1** the business activity of banks and similar institutions: *a large, New York-based banking company* | *The banking industry will strongly oppose these new regulations.*
investment banking the work done by INVESTMENT BANKS
offshore banking when banks are based abroad in a country where you pay less tax than in your own country: *Government officials dislike the rise of offshore banking.* | *Cyprus is becoming an international* ***offshore banking center.***
retail banking the work done by RETAIL BANKS
universal banking when a bank performs a range of banking activities: *Banco Central is a classic institution of the universal banking type, covering all areas of banking and with a strong industrial portfolio.*
2 using the services that a bank provides by a particular means: *With* ***Internet banking****, customers can carry out transactions, money transfers and other business 24 hours a day.*
electronic banking a service provided by banks that allows people to pay money from one account to another, pay bills etc over the INTERNET: *With electronic banking, consumers can pay credit card, utility and other bills and check their bank accounts via personal computer.*
home banking a service provided by banks that allows people to pay money from one account into another, pay bills etc by E-MAIL or telephone: *The First Direct Bank of England operates solely as a home-banking company with its customers tethered by phone lines to a regional computerized banking centre in Leeds.*
telephone banking when customers have an arrangement with a bank to be able to find out by telephone how much money they have in their account, ask for payments to be made etc

Banking Department *n* the part of the BANK OF ENGLAND that deals with general banking business, for example keeping DEPOSITS —compare ISSUE DEPARTMENT

banking power —see under POWER[1]

Banking Supervision —see BOARD OF BANKING SUPERVISION

banking system —see under SYSTEM

bank interest —see under INTEREST

bank loan —see under LOAN[1]

bank manager —see under MANAGER

bank money —see under MONEY

bank•note /ˈbæŋknəʊt‖-noʊt/ also **bank note** *n* [C] *BrE* a piece of printed paper money made available by a bank, usually a country's main bank; BANK BILL *AmE*: *Switzerland is* ***issuing a*** *SFr200* ***banknote*** *and withdrawing the SFr500 one.*

Bank of America *n* a COMMERCIAL BANK based in California

Bank of England written abbreviation **B of E** *n* Britain's CENTRAL BANK: *The Bank of England says growth in the UK economy will slow next year.*

Bank of England minimum lending rate —see ***base rate*** under RATE[1]

bank of issue *n* plural **banks of issue** [C] a bank that officially produces bank notes and makes them available for use

bank overdraft —see under OVERDRAFT

bank paper —see under PAPER

bank rate —see ***base rate*** under RATE[1]

bank reconciliation *n* [U] explaining the differences between the amount of money you really have in your bank account and the amount shown in your BANK STATEMENT, for example by taking into account cheques you have written that have not yet been paid: *The product offers all the things you would expect from a home finance software package, such as bank reconciliation.*

bank reserves —see under RESERVES

Bank Return *n* [singular] the report of the BANK OF ENGLAND*'s* financial situation that it makes available every week for the department in its organization dealing with general banking activities and the department responsible for producing and making available banknotes

bank•roll[1] /ˈbæŋkrəʊl‖-roʊl/ *v* [T] *informal* to provide the money a person or company needs to operate a business, find new markets, develop new products etc: *Friends Provident also pumped money into the business, bankrolling its expansion until it was floated in 1985.*

bankroll[2] *n* [C] *informal* **1** a supply of money for a particular purpose: *Credit Lyonnais could be one of his major backers for the project, providing a bankroll of $100 million or more.*
2 a large amount of paper money rolled together

bank run —see under RUN[2]

bank•rupt[1] /ˈbæŋkrʌpt/ *adj* LAW not having enough money to pay your debts: *Many people would lose their jobs if the firm were to* ***go bankrupt.*** | *He was* ***declared bankrupt*** *at Londons High Court yesterday.*

bankrupt² *n* [C] LAW someone judged to be unable to pay their debts by a court of law, and whose financial affairs are handled by a court official until the debts are settled

certificated bankrupt someone who has been officially declared bankrupt by a court of law

discharged bankrupt someone who has been declared bankrupt in the past but has obeyed the orders of the court and can now do business again

undischarged bankrupt someone who has been declared bankrupt and who is not yet allowed by the court to stop paying money back or to do business: *The Court heard that one of the directors had acted while an undischarged bankrupt.*

bankrupt³ *v* [T] to make a person, business, or country go bankrupt: *The new legislation would help restore pride in farming without bankrupting farmers in the process.*

bank•rupt•cy /ˈbæŋkrʌptsi/ *n* plural **bankruptcies** [C,U] LAW when someone is judged to be unable to pay their debts by a court of law, and their assets are shared among the people and businesses that they owe money to: *Many state-operated companies had experienced difficulties and some had faced bankruptcy.* | *The number of bankruptcies in the first half of the year soared by 60%.*

act of bankruptcy plural **acts of bankruptcy** [C] when someone does something which breaks a condition made by the court when they were declared bankrupt

discharge from bankruptcy plural **discharges from bankruptcy** [C,U] when the court decides that someone who has been declared bankrupt in the past has obeyed the orders of the court and can do business again

involuntary bankruptcy [C,U] when someone's CREDITORS (=people or companies who are owed money) ask the court to make the person bankrupt

trustee in bankruptcy plural **trustees in bankruptcy** [C] someone who is given the power to take control of a bankrupt business's property, to sell it, and to divide the money made from the sale between the people that the bankrupt company owes money to

voluntary bankruptcy [C,U] when someone asks the court to make them bankrupt

bankruptcy court —see under COURT¹

bankruptcy judge —see under JUDGE¹

bankruptcy order —see under ORDER¹

bankruptcy petition —see under PETITION

bankruptcy proceedings —see under PROCEEDINGS

bankruptcy protection —see under PROTECTION

bank statement —see under STATEMENT

bank transfer —see under TRANSFER²

bank trust department —see under DEPARTMENT

bar¹ /bɑː‖bɑːr/ *v* past tense and past participle **barred** present participle **barring** [T] to officially stop someone from doing something or from entering a place **bar sb from (doing) sth**: *Taiwan-made electronics products will be barred from countries that have signed the protocol.* | *Foreign investors would be barred from buying majority stakes.*

bar² also **Bar** *n* LAW **1 the bar** *BrE* the profession of a BARRISTER, or barristers in general: *In 1988, she **was called to the bar*** (=became a barrister) *and now practises in London, specialising in criminal and family law.* | *He has now passed his **Bar Examination*** (=the examination you must pass in order to become a barrister).

2 the bar *AmE* a word for the legal profession, used in the names of professional associations of lawyers: *the New Jersey State Bar Association* —see also AMERICAN BAR ASSOCIATION

bar chart —see under CHART¹

bar code —see under CODE

bare /beə‖ber/ *adj* **go bare** INSURANCE if a business goes bare, it decides not to buy insurance to protect it against claims for damage or harm done by its products: *Some firms choose to go bare, preferring possible bankruptcy to the certainty of huge insurance premiums.*

bareboat charter —see under CHARTER²

bare-bones *adj* [only before a noun] involving or providing the minimum and no more: *bare bones health insurance policies that provide minimum protection*

bare trustee —see under TRUSTEE

bar•gain¹ /ˈbɑːgᵻn‖ˈbɑːr-/ *n* [C] **1** something you buy cheaply or for less than the usual price: *Philips shares **are a bargain** at the current level.* | *He made a lot of money by buying houses at **bargain prices** and reselling them.*

2 an agreement between two people or groups to do something in return for something else: *Management and unions have managed to **strike a bargain** whereby unions have accepted more flexible working in return for better pay.* | *Football is important to Sky TV, and the clubs will now try to **drive a hard bargain*** (=make an bargaining agreement very much to their advantage) *on future TV rights.*

Dutch bargain a deal giving all of the advantage to one side

3 FINANCE *BrE* an occasion when particular shares, bonds etc are bought or sold on a financial market. The number of bargains in a particular period of time is one measurement of the level of economic activity: *In government securities, the number of bargains per day has averaged nearly 3,300.*

bargain² *v* [I] to discuss the conditions of a sale, agreement etc in order to get the greatest advantage for yourself

bargain-basement *adj* [only before a noun] bargain-basement goods and services cost much less than you would normally expect: *The Internet is a mass telecommunications network, offering global connections at **bargain-basement prices**.*

bargain-basement price —see under PRICE¹

bar•gain•ing /ˈbɑːgənɪŋ‖ˈbɑːr-/ *n* [U] discussion to reach agreement about something, for example trade, levels of pay etc: *There will be some **hard bargaining** between the US and Europe.*

collective bargaining the discussions held between an employer and a TRADE UNION in order to reach an agreement on wages and working conditions: *Contract workers fall outside collective bargaining agreements.* | *This ballot is about the right of our members to have their pay determined by **free collective bargaining** not controlled by the government or legal rules.*

pay bargaining another name for WAGE BARGAINING: *Pay bargaining does not begin until early next year in Germany.*

wage bargaining discussions between representatives of employees and employers in order to agree levels of pay: *A major round of wage bargaining is due to start later this week.*

bargaining agent —see under AGENT

bargaining chip *n* [C] something that can be used to your advantage during bargaining: *Management seemed intent on using potential purchases of new planes as a bargaining chip to win concessions from the pilots.*

bargaining position *n* [C] **1** the opinions and demands that one person or group puts forward during bargaining: *Both parties seem reluctant to modify their original bargaining position.*

2 the power that a person or group has during bargaining: *Those countries are in a **strong bargaining position** because the US will need their votes in the next round of GATT talks.*

bargaining power —see under POWER[1]

bargaining unit —see under UNIT

bargain price —see under PRICE[1]

bar graph —see under GRAPH[1]

ba•rom•e•ter /bəˈrɒmɨtə‖-ˈrɑːmɨtər/ *n* [C] ECONOMICS if something is a barometer of the economy, it gives important information about the condition of the economy as a whole: *The growth in demand for electricity is one of the most accurate barometers of the economy.* —see also INDICATOR

B

barometer stock —see under STOCK[1]

bar•on /ˈbærən/ *n* [C] *journalism* **1** FINANCE a business person who is in charge of a large industrial or financial organization: *an **oil baron***

press baron also **media baron** someone who owns several newspapers and is therefore important and has a lot of influence

2 a powerful criminal who is in charge of a large group of drug producers or smugglers: ***Drugs baron*** *Rene Black was jailed for 15 years yesterday.*

bar•rel /ˈbærəl/ *n* [C] **1** a large round container with a flat top and bottom, used for storing and carrying liquids such as oil and beer: *barrels of beer*

2 an amount of a liquid contained in a barrel, used as unit of measurement, especially in the oil industry: *There were fears that the price of crude would drop as far as $15 a barrel.* | *Oman produces more than 650,000 **barrels per day** of crude oil.* —see also PORK BARREL

barrier to entry *n* plural **barriers to entry** [C] something that prevents companies entering an industry, for example the need for a lot of capital or strict government regulations: *The aircraft engine business has **high barriers to entry** and requires a lot of technological capital.*

barrier to trade *n* plural **barriers to trade** [C] ECONOMICS something that makes trade between two countries more difficult or expensive, for example a tax on imports; TRADE BARRIER: *Companies have located production abroad to overcome barriers to trade.*

bar•ris•ter /ˈbærɨstə‖-ər/ *n* [C] LAW a lawyer in Britain who has joined the BAR and is qualified to represent a case in the higher courts —compare LAWYER, SOLICITOR

bar•ter[1] /ˈbɑːtə‖ˈbɑːrtər/ *v* [I,T] to exchange goods for other goods or to do work for someone in exchange for work they do for you, rather than using money **barter (sth) for sth**: *They import used cars, which they then barter for consumer goods.*

barter[2] *n* [U] a system of exchanging goods or work for other goods or work, rather than using money: *When people want to exchange any goods, they do so by barter.*

base[1] /beɪs/ *n* **1** [C,U] the main place from which a company or organization controls its activities: *Reps will be invited to Bristol, the company's base, for a briefing.* | *The Group's operating base is in Norway.*

2 [C usually singular] the part of something from which new things can be developed or achieved: *Small-scale industries provide a better base for employment growth.*

3 [C usually singular] in a series of figures or amounts, the figure against which later amounts are compared: *The wholesale price index stood at 190.5 last month, with its 1985 level at a base of 100.*

4 [C usually singular] all of the people or things that something depends on, considered as a whole

consumer base also **customer base** [C usually singular] all the people who buy or use a particular product: *computer manufacturers' general marketing problem of capturing and retaining a customer base*

cost base [C usually singular] the costs involved in operating a company or making a product: *ICL is to undertake further restructuring to reduce its cost base.*

manufacturing base also **industrial base** [C usually singular] all the factories or companies producing goods in a country or area, especially when considered in relation to the economy as a whole: *The country needs a strong manufacturing base.*

tax base [C usually singular] all the people who pay tax, and the total amount that they pay: *The country now faces the difficulty of a small tax base supporting a large welfare burden.*

base[2] *v*

base sth **on/upon** sth *phr v* [T] if one thing is based on another, it develops from it: *forming judgements based on evidence*

based /beɪst/ *adj* if a company is based somewhere, that is the place where it carries out its business: *The existing business is based in London but the owners may be willing to move.* | *a Chicago-based publisher*

base rate —see under RATE[1]

BASIC /ˈbeɪsɪk/ *n* [U] COMPUTING Beginner's All-Purpose Symbolic Instruction Code; a simple computer programming language used especially in personal computers or by students

basic industry —see under INDUSTRY

basic price —see under PRICE[1]

basic rate —see under RATE[1]

basic salary —see under SALARY

basic wage —see under WAGE

ba•sis /ˈbeɪsɨs/ *n* plural **bases** [C] **1** the facts or ideas from which something can be developed + **for**: *If talks restart, this package is likely to be a basis for negotiation.*

2 the original figures from which something can be calculated or valued + **for/of**: *1998 figures are the basis for future price calculations.* —see also ACCRUAL BASIS, CARE AND MAINTENANCE BASIS, CASH BASIS, EARNINGS BASIS

basis point —see under POINT[1]

basket case *n* [C usually singular] *AmE journalism* a company, country, or economy that is doing so badly and has so many problems that it is likely to fail completely: *By any standard, the area is an **economic basket case**.* | *The best known basket cases included Campeau Corp., which sought protection from creditors early in the year.*

basket of currencies *n* plural **baskets of currencies** [C usually singular] a group of currencies against which the value of another currency is measured: *The yen's exchange rate against a basket of currencies has fallen to its lowest level for three months.* —see also MARKET BASKET

Basle Con•cor•dat /ˌbɑːl kɒnˈkɔːdæt‖-kɑːnˈkɔːr-/ *n* **the Basle Concordat** an agreement between the GROUP OF TEN leading industrialized countries in 1975, relating to the control by banks of their foreign branches

Basle ratios *n* **the Basle ratios** [plural] an international agreement on the amount of capital financial institutions must have in relation to the amount they lend out

batch /bætʃ/ *n* **1** [C] a group of similar things or people arriving or being dealt with at the same time: *the process of indexing each new batch of documents*

2 [C] a quantity of food, goods, work etc prepared or produced at the same time: *The paper is always from a single batch, to ensure evenness of shade.*

batch costing —see under COSTING

batch processing —see under PROCESSING

batch production —see under PRODUCTION

bath /bɑːθ‖bæθ/ *n* **take a bath** *AmE informal* to lose a lot of money when buying or selling something: *CBS took a bath estimated at $275 million on the baseball television coverage deal.*

ba•zaar /bəˈzɑː‖-ˈzɑːr/ *n* [C] **1** a market, especially in India, North Africa, or the Middle East: *Chandni Chowk, a bustling local market and bazaar*

2 *journalism* a place where things are bought and sold in a disorganized or unofficial way: *The free market's arrival turned Poland's cities into cut-price bazaars.*

BBA *n* **1** British Banker's Association; a professional association of banks in Britain, that collects and distributes information about the banking industry and represents its views

2 [C] *AmE* Bachelor of Business Administration; a university business qualification

BCG matrix /ˌbiː siː dʒiː ˈmeɪtrɪks/ *n* another name for the GROWTH/SHARE MATRIX

b/e written abbreviation for BILL OF EXCHANGE

beach·head /ˈbiːtʃhed/ *n* [C] part of a market that a company obtains, hoping to obtain more of the same market or part of another larger market that is near the first one: *Telefonica **gained a** key **beachhead** in Brazil when it won control of CRT, the operator in Rio Grande do Sul.*

bean counter *n* [C] *informal disapproving* someone whose job is to study financial figures and work out the cost of doing something, and who is only concerned with making a profit: *Few love working at KGO now. The bean counters bought the place a while back and it's never been the same.* | *the bean counters and go-by-the-book types who can so easily undermine a creative enterprise*

bear /beə‖ber/ *n* [C] FINANCE someone who thinks that prices of shares, bonds, currencies, or basic goods are going to fall, and who may sell shares, bonds etc they do not actually own, expecting to be able to obtain them more cheaply later, before they have to deliver them to the buyer: *The bears argue that after the stock market's dramatic rise, shares are bound to fall again.* | *The bears took hold of Asda, sending the shares 5p lower to 159p.* | *A contingent of **dollar bears*** (=people who think that the price of the dollar is going to fall) *still persists in the market.* —compare BULL

bear·er /ˈbeərə‖ˈberər/ *n* FINANCE **1** [C] someone who owns or possesses a document such as a bond, cheque, or a BILL OF EXCHANGE: *The firm became suspicious about the bonds and asked the bearer for confirmation.*

2 payable to bearer words written on a document to say that the amount of money stated on the document should be paid to the person who has it in their possession, rather than to a named person: *I took a check marked 'payable to bearer' to a bank to cash.*

3 bearer bond/cheque/share etc a bond, cheque, share etc that is considered to be owned by or payable to the person who has it in their possession, even though their name may not appear on it or may not be on the official list of owners

bearer bond —see under BOND

bearer certificate —see under CERTIFICATE

bearer cheque —see under CHEQUE

bearer paper —see under PAPER

bearer security —see under SECURITY

bearer share —see under SHARE

bearer stock —see under STOCK[1]

bear hug *n* [C] an offer to take over a company in which more money is offered than the company is actually worth, and which people who own shares in the company will therefore find it hard to refuse: *The Schneider offer is considered a bear hug.*

bear·ish /ˈbeərɪʃ‖ˈber-/ *adj* FINANCE expecting prices on a financial market to fall or economic activity to slow down: *Trading was bearish after pessimistic weekend news.* | *Japan's ruling Liberal Democratic Party was considering measures to prop up the bearish market.* | *Today's report on declining auto sales will provide bearish news for the market.* | *Losses in New York added to the **bearish mood**.* + **on**: *He is still bearish on aluminum stocks.* —compare BULLISH

bear market —see under MARKET[1]

bear position —see under POSITION[1]

bear raid —see under RAID

bear run —see under RUN[2]

bear squeeze *n* [C] when share prices rise because it is known that people have sold these shares without actually owning them, hoping to be able to obtain them more cheaply later, before they have to deliver them to the buyer. Because it is known that these people will have to buy the shares, the price is forced up

beauty parade *n* [C] *informal* an occasion when several companies try to persuade another company to use their services: *The tender exercise should not be an opportunity for an unrestricted beauty parade; pre-selection should already have weeded out unsuitable candidates.*

bed-and-breakfasting *n* [U] FINANCE *informal* in Britain, when someone sells shares one day and buys them back the next day in order to reduce the amount of CAPITAL GAINS TAX that they have to pay in a particular period of time. This was made illegal in 1998: *Investors with large portfolios could consider bed-and-breakfasting to use up their capital gains tax allowance, but this is no longer possible.*

bed·room /ˈbedrʊm, -ruːm/ *n* [C] *AmE* an area just outside a large town where many of the people working in the town live; DORMITORY *BrE*: *workers who commute between Aspen, with its million-dollar homes, and cheaper **bedroom communities***

before-tax *adj* relating to the amount that has been earned before tax is paid on it: *This accounted for 6% of their **before-tax income**.* | *Their **before-tax profits** rose sharply last year.*

Beginner's All-Purpose Symbolic Instruction Code —see BASIC

beginning of year —see BOY

be·have /bɪˈheɪv/ *v* [I] to act or to do something in a particular way: *Citibank behaves in every market like a local bank.* | *Both gold and oil prices behaved exactly as analysts and investors had been predicting.*

be·hav·iour *BrE* **behavior** *AmE* /bɪˈheɪvjə‖-ər/ *n* **1** [U] the way that someone or something acts in different situations: *They have changed their **buying behavior** and are postponing major purchases.* | *The market's crash forced money managers to rethink basic assumptions about **market behaviour**.*

2 [C] particular ways of acting in different situations: *seminars that attempt to change attitudes and behaviors among white male managers*

consumer behaviour *BrE* **consumer behavior** *AmE* [U] MARKETING the study of where and how people buy things, why they choose one thing and not another etc: *The family is still a major factor in consumer behaviour.*

organizational behaviour *BrE* **organizational behavior** *AmE* also **organisational behaviour** *BrE* [U] HUMAN RESOURCES the study of how the people in an organization work together, and the effect this has on the organization as a whole, its effectiveness etc: *organisational behaviour, a combination of psychology and management theory*

be·he·moth /bəˈhiːmɒθ‖-mɑːθ/ *n* [C] *journalism* a very large and powerful international company, business, industry etc; GIANT: *a company that grew into a behemoth in New Zealand and today controls billions of dollars in assets worldwide* | *Time Warner Inc., the media and entertainment behemoth that J. Richard Munro helped to create*

be·hind[1] /bɪˈhaɪnd/ *adv* **be/get/fall behind (with sth)** to be late making a regular payment or doing work: *Over 4% of British borrowers are likely to be a month or more*

B

behind with their repayments. | *You may be putting your tenancy at risk if you fall behind with the rent.* | *I can't sleep at night because I'm worried about getting behind with my work.*

behind² *prep* **1 be behind sb/sth** to support a person, an idea, or the work they are doing: *Cabinet Ministers rallied behind the Prime Minister yesterday.*
2 not as advanced or successful as someone or something else: *Their social and economic development is so far behind the rest of the world that they can never compete on equal terms.*
3 behind schedule not arriving or happening at the right time: *Commuters were delayed for up to 35 minutes as trains ran behind schedule.* | *Contractors who* ***fall behind schedule*** *will incur financial penalties.*

B

Beige Book *n* **the Beige Book** ECONOMICS in the US, a regular report on economic activity by the FEDERAL RESERVE (=the US central bank): *The Beige Book said conditions are improving slowly in much of the country.*

bells and whistles *n* [plural] extra things that are offered with a product or system to make it more attractive to buyers: *Fax systems on the market today offer bells and whistles such as answering-machine capability.* | *The basic rule about computer memory is this: Buy as much as you can afford, even if it means sacrificing other bells and whistles.*

bell•weth•er /ˈbelˌweðə‖-ər/ *n* [C] FINANCE a type of stock, share etc whose price is thought to show the probable future direction of the market as a whole: *He periodically checks on a few properties chosen as bellwethers to see if prices are rising or falling.* | *With 40% of sales of pharmaceuticals, Glaxo is the* ***bellwether stock*** *of the sector.*

bellwether bond —see under BOND

belly up *adv informal* **go belly up** if a company goes belly up, it stops trading because it cannot pay its debts

below-cost price —see under PRICE¹

below-investment-grade —see under INVESTMENT-GRADE

below the line *adj* **1** ACCOUNTING, FINANCE relating to profits after EXCEPTIONAL ITEMS (=profits and losses that are made in a particular period of time but do not occur regularly) have been taken into account: *Provisions on doubtful property loans taken below the line reduced taxable profits to £3.95 million.*
2 MARKETING relating to a company's spending on marketing activities other than advertising, for example research: *Agencies offer strategic advice as well as below the line services like market research, pack design and direct marketing.* —compare ABOVE THE LINE

bench•mark¹ /ˈbentʃmɑːk‖-mɑːrk/ *n* [C] **1** something that can be used as a comparison by which to judge or measure other things: *The newest Treasury bond is the* ***benchmark bond,*** *the one that trades most heavily.* | *The fund's performance is rated by comparing it with a* ***benchmark index*** *for the sector.*
2 a good performance that one company has achieved, that can be used as a standard to judge other companies of the same type: *Companies need to know how much return they can expect from their IT investments: they need benchmarks to see how their systems are performing.*

benchmark² *v* [T] to use a company's good performance as a standard by which to judge the performance of other companies of the same type **benchmark sb/sth against sth**: *British Steel have benchmarked themselves against the best operations anywhere in the world.* —**benchmarking** *n* [U] *Mr O'Neill, a newcomer to the industry, heeds theories of cost control and benchmarking against other industries.*

benchmark index —see under INDEX¹

ben•e•fac•tor /ˈbenɪ̈fæktə‖-ər/ *n* [C] someone who gives money for a good purpose: *An* ***anonymous benefactor*** *has donated $100,000 towards building the hospital.*

beneficial interest —see under INTEREST

beneficial owner —see under OWNER

beneficial ownership —see under OWNERSHIP

ben•e•fi•cia•ry /ˌbenɪ̈ˈfɪʃəri‖-ˈfɪʃieri/ *n* plural **beneficiaries** [C] **1** LAW, INSURANCE a person who receives money or property from someone who has died: *Dorothy's son was her sole beneficiary.*
2 any person or organization that gets an advantage or help from something: *Oil companies were the main beneficiaries of the budget, on news that the Petroleum Revenue Tax is to be cut on North Sea oil fields.*

ben•e•fit¹ /ˈbenɪ̈fɪt/ *n* **1** [C] an advantage that a particular product or service has: *We will focus our marketing message on the environmental benefits of the product.*
2 [C,U] *BrE* money provided by the government to people who are old and no longer work, or to people who are unemployed, ill, or on a low income etc; WELFARE *AmE*: *the number of people out of work and receiving* ***unemployment benefit*** | *Two thirds of lone parents* ***on benefit*** *receive income support.*
accident and health benefit [C,U] money paid by a government or insurance company to people who are not able to work because of an accident or an illness
child benefit [C,U] money provided by the government to parents of children until they reach the age of eighteen, or nineteen if they remain in full-time education
disability benefit [C,U] money provided by the government to people who need extra help or cannot work because they cannot use part of their body properly
housing benefit [C,U] money given by the government to people who have no job, who have a low income, or who are sick to help them pay for somewhere to live: *You might be entitled to housing benefit.*
incapacity benefit also **invalidity benefit** [C,U] names used at different times in Britain for benefits received by those who are too ill to work: *In 1995, sickness benefit and invalidity benefit were merged to form incapacity benefit.*
maternity benefit [C,U] *BrE* money paid by the government or an employer to a woman when she has a baby: *In order to* ***claim maternity benefit,*** *you need to have worked for at least two years and 16 hours each week.* | *Maternity benefits are being offered by some companies.*
sickness benefit [C,U] *BrE* money paid, especially by the government, to someone who is too ill to work: *She is entitled* (=has an official right) *to receive State Sickness Benefit from the Department of Social Security.* | *Denmark has made cuts in sickness benefits.*
state benefit [C usually plural] *BrE* money provided by the government to people who are old and no longer work, or to people who are unemployed, ill, or on a low income etc: *One in five pensioners rely entirely on state benefits for their income.*
unemployment benefit [C,U] *BrE* money paid regularly by the government to people who do not have a job; UNEMPLOYMENT COMPENSATION *AmE*: *How long have you been receiving unemployment benefit?*
welfare benefit [C usually plural] *BrE* money provided by the government to people who are old and no longer work, or to people who are unemployed, ill, or on a low income etc: *Full details of welfare benefits for elderly people are published each April by Age Concern.*
3 [C] INSURANCE money paid out on certain insurance policies, especially health insurance: *In the event of a justified claim, permanent total disablement benefit will be payable from the date of the claimant's disablement.*
death benefit [C] a single sum of money paid by an

insurance company to the relatives of someone who has died: *Relatives of the deceased employees did not receive the expected death benefits even though the insurance company had paid out the cheques to the fund.*

4 [C] HUMAN RESOURCES something, especially money, that an employer gives to workers in addition to their normal pay, to encourage them to work harder or be satisfied where they work: *The company offers an excellent salary and **benefits package**, including relocation costs.*

employee benefits [plural] things that are offered to the employees of a company in addition to their normal pay, such as company cars, loans at low rates of interest, and the possibility of buying shares

fringe benefit [C] an additional advantage or service given with a job besides wages. PENSIONS, company cars, and loans at low rates of interest are examples of fringe benefits; PERK: *A competitive salary with fringe benefits will be offered.*

benefit[2] *v* **1** [I] to get help or an advantage from something: *The taxpayer benefits because we do not have to borrow public money from the Treasury.* + **from**: *Small firms benefited from a reform of the Uniform Business Rate, which effectively freezes increases for a year.*

2 [T] to give someone help or advantage: *The increase in house prices in the past 30 years has mainly benefited the comfortably-off.*

benefit club *n* [C] in Britain, an organization that raises money and provides members with financial help if they have an accident or are ill, or when they are too old to work

benefit in kind *n* plural **benefits in kind** [C] something other than money, for example free meals or a company car, that an employer gives to a worker in addition to their normal pay: *All benefits in kind are now taxed.*

benefit principle —see under PRINCIPLE

benefits package —see under PACKAGE[1]

Ben•e•lux /ˈbenəlʌks/ *n* Belgium, the Netherlands, and Luxembourg considered as a group: *TopLog says there will be no changes to how its subsidiaries operate in France, Benelux, Germany, the UK, and Spain.* | *The merger of Douwe Egberts and Van Nelle in 1988 gave them a 70% market share of the **Benelux countries**.*

bent /bent/ *adj BrE informal* financially dishonest: *a bent accountant*

be•queath /bɪˈkwiːð, bɪˈkwiːθ/ *v* [T] *formal* LAW to officially arrange for someone to have money or property that you own after your death, by writing it in your WILL **bequeath sth to sb**: *Sharp left the museum nothing, instead bequeathing his collection to a charitable foundation.* **bequeath sb sth**: *He bequeathed his wife 514 acres of arable land.*

be•quest /bɪˈkwest/ *n* [C] LAW money or property that you officially arrange for someone to have after your death, by writing it in your WILL: *Covenants and bequests form an essential part of the hospice's income.*

best-before date —see under DATE[1]

best buy —see under BUY[2]

best-efforts *adj* [only before a noun] FINANCE a best-efforts arrangement is one in which a financial institution agrees to try to sell a company's new shares without having to buy the shares itself if they are not sold to investors: *Bear Stearns agreed to try to privately place one million Angeion shares **on a best-efforts basis**.*

best price —see under PRICE[1]

Best rating —see under RATING

best seller *n* [C] a very popular book or other product, that many people buy: *The book has been on the New York Times fiction best-seller list for more than 30 weeks.* | *Biotech's best sellers are its biotechnology drugs* —**best-selling** *adj* [only before a noun] *America's best-selling pickup truck*

bet[1] /bet/ *v* past tense and past participle **bet** or **betted** present participle **betting** [I,T] **1** to risk money on a future event, for example by investing in a company or product or buying stocks or shares **bet (sth) on**: *Investors were willing to bet on Oncogene, and its shares jumped $1.94 to $9.06.* | *The New Jersey fund has bet $40 million on small stocks.* **bet (sb) that**: *The market bet heavily that the dollar would fall.*

2 bet the farm/ranch *AmE* to risk a lot of money on a future event, for example by investing in a company or product or buying stocks or shares: *Sony's support for CD-I is less than enthusiastic, and they won't bet the farm on it.*

bet[2] *n* [C] when you risk money on a future event, for example by investing in a company or product or buying stocks or shares: *They like selling short, or **making a bet** that share prices will decline.* | *Shearson **placed a** big **bet** on junk bonds and lost.* | *a huge $11 billion bet on US interest rates that went wrong*

beta coefficient also **beta factor**, **beta** *n* [singular] FINANCE a measurement of the amount of change in a share price over a period of time, compared with the average amount of change in all share prices: ***High beta** stocks fall by more in stock market crashes than **low beta** stocks.*

beta version —see under VERSION

Better Business Bureau *n* [C] in the US, a local organization, belonging to a national group of similar organizations, that gives advice and information about business to companies and consumers

bet•ter•ment /ˈbetəmənt‖-tər-/ *n* [U] *BrE* an increase in the value of property caused by improvements in the area surrounding the property: *It is logical to balance the compensation paid to aggrieved owners by collecting a **betterment charge** on owners who benefit from new developments.*

bi•an•nu•al /baɪˈænjuəl/ *adj* happening twice each year: *Wildlife Link's biannual liaison meeting with the Forestry Committee* —compare BIENNIAL

bi•as /ˈbaɪəs/ *n* plural **biases** [C,U] MARKETING in MARKET RESEARCH, errors in results, usually caused by working with a group of people who are not typical of the group you want to know about, or by asking confusing questions: *Sampling has its problems and bias must be guarded against at every step.* —see also GENDER BIAS

bid[1] /bɪd/ *n* [C] **1** a price offered to buy something such as goods, property, shares, or bonds: *bids from buyers in the Drouot auction rooms* | *Bids for the bonds totalled M$2.26 billion.* | *Avery shares were quoted yesterday at a **bid price** of 31 cents a share.*

cabinet bid *BrE* FINANCE the sale of an investor's OUT-OF-THE-MONEY OPTION for 1 penny in order to reduce the amount of tax they have to pay

open bid when possible buyers are invited to offer a price for something, with no restrictions on who can make an offer: *The enterprises will be sold through open bids.*

2 also **takeover bid** an offer by one company to buy another, or the value of this offer: *Hollinger **made a bid** for Southern at C$23.50 a share.* | *Leicester City Football Club **accepted a** £24 million **takeover bid** from Soccer Investments.* | *Coal and Allied directors rejected CRA's offer, saying the **bid price** significantly undervalues the company.*

cash bid a takeover bid in which the buyer offers to pay shareholders of the company they are buying in cash: *Publicis has made a $28-a-share cash bid to acquire just over 50% of True North.*

counter bid also **counter-bid** a bid that is higher than a previous bid, for example when more than one company is trying to take control of another company: *BT wants to go ahead with its merger with MCI, despite the counter-bid from WorldCom of the US.*

friendly bid a takeover bid that is wanted by the company that the bid is for
hostile bid a takeover bid that is not wanted by the company that the bid is for: *The company fought off a hostile bid from the American food giant.*
opposed bid a takeover bid that the DIRECTORS of the company that is bid for do not agree with and advise their shareholders to refuse
paper bid a takeover bid in which the buyer offers to pay shareholders of the company they are buying in the form of shares, bonds etc, rather than in cash: *Lowndes may make a paper bid, with investors in Fenchurch offered shares in the new company.*
3 an offer to do work or provide services for a fixed price, in competition with other offers: *Carlisle invited bids to run the whole hospital.* | *The company did not* ***put in a bid*** *for the contract.*
sealed bid an offer to buy something, do work, or provide a service at a price that is not known to anyone else. All the offers are then looked at together in order to find the best price: *Most loan auctions are conducted by sealed bid.* —see also ***sealed-bid tender*** under TENDER[1]

bid[2] *v* past tense and past participle **bid** present participle **bidding** [I,T] **1** to offer to pay a particular price for something such as goods, property, or bonds **bid (sth) for**: *He bid £69,000 at Sotheby's for an 18th century wine glass.*
2 to offer to buy a large number of shares in a company and so take over the company **bid (sth) for**: *Nestle and Exor are bidding F1,475 a share for Perrier.*
3 to offer to do work or provide services for a fixed price, in competition with others **bid (sth) for**: *Investors have bid a record amount of cash for Venezuela's oil operating licences.* | *The government has invited companies to bid for gas exploration rights in the west of the country.*
—**bidder** *n* [C] *Cinecitta has invited bidders from the film and TV industries to invest $30 million in a new company.*
—**bidding** *n* [U] *Klimt's 'Schloss Kammer am Attersee' made $14 million in frenzied bidding at Christie's.*
bid sth ↔ **up** *phr v* [T] if people bid up a price, they cause it to increase because of the competition between them in bidding: *Investors have bid up the company's shares about 25%, despite disappointing operating results.*

bid and asked *adj* FINANCE relating to the highest price a buyer is willing to pay and the lowest price a seller is willing to accept: *The OTC Bulletin Board will provide bid and asked quotes on the smaller stocks.*

bid bond —see under BOND

bid costs —see under COST[1]

bidders' ring —see under RING[1]

bid-offer spread —see under SPREAD[2]

bid price —see under PRICE[1]

bi•en•ni•al /baɪˈeniəl/ *adj* happening once every two years: *the biennial report published by the BDDA* —compare BIANNUAL

Big Bang *n* **1 The Big Bang** a popular name for the major changes that happened on the London STOCK EXCHANGE in 1986, that ended the differences between JOBBERS and BROKERS, and the system of fixed COMMISSIONS on buying and selling shares
2 The Big Bang a name for similar events in other financial centres: *The Big Bang opened the protected world of French broking to powerful and well-capitalized banks.*

Big Blue *n* a popular name for the computer company, IBM: *Big Blue grew into the world's biggest computer company.*

Big Board *n* **The Big Board** a popular name for the New York STOCK EXCHANGE: *WordPerfect Corp. filed to go public on the Big Board.*

Big Board stock —see under STOCK[1]

big business —see under BUSINESS

Big Eight *n* **The Big Eight** in Britain, the eight largest banks and BUILDING SOCIETIES that have branches in many towns and cities: *The Big Eight aren't all bad, and some have good value current accounts and mortgages.*

Big Four *n* **The Big Four** in Britain, the four largest banks that have branches in many towns and cities: Barclays, Lloyds TSB, HSBC, and NatWest: *Traditional credit cards, such as those available from the Big Four, are a very poor deal.*

big-league *adj* [only before a noun] another name for MAJOR-LEAGUE: *big-league sponsors in motor racing such as Marlboro and Budweiser.*

Big Steel *n* [U] large US steel producers seen as a group: *Bethlehem's departure from light steels marks yet another retreat by Big Steel from a business it once dominated.*

Big Three *n* **The Big Three** the largest US car makers: General Motors, Ford, and Chrysler, especially before Chrysler and Mercedes joined together in 1998: *The Big Three have lost much of the passenger car market to the Japanese and others.*

big-ticket *adj* [only before a noun] *informal* expensive: *Are they low value, high volume products, or single, big ticket items?*

bil. *AmE* written abbreviation for BILLION; BN *BrE*

bi•lat•er•al /baɪˈlætərəl/ *adj* involving two countries: *Mr Bush announced tentative agreement on a bilateral investment treaty with Singapore.* | *a bilateral trade agreement*

bilateral contract —see under CONTRACT[1]

bi•lat•e•ral•is•m /baɪˈlætərəlɪzəm/ *n* [U] ECONOMICS when trade agreements are negotiated between two countries at a time, rather than a larger number of countries: *He noted the US preference for bilateralism, especially when dealing with the Japanese.* —compare MULTILATERALISM

bill[1] /bɪl/ *n* [C] **1** a list showing how much you have to pay for services or goods received; INVOICE[1]: *big companies that fail to* ***settle*** *their* ***bills*** *with smaller businesses on time* | *The government will no longer* ***foot the bill*** (=pay the bill) *if banks run into difficulty.* + **for**: *The average bill for electricity is £270 a year.*
due bill *AmE* an amount of money that is owed: *MGM/UA shares have been trading on the basis of one share of stock plus a 'due bill' of $4 since July 3.*
past due bill *AmE* an amount of money that should already have been paid: *Child World said it will propose a plan to pay substantially all past due bills owed to smaller vendors.*
2 *BrE* a list showing how much you have to pay for food you have eaten in a restaurant; CHECK *AmE*: *We finished coffee and asked for the bill.*
3 LAW a written proposal for a new law: *The wording of the bill was vague.* | *Democrats met earlier this month to* ***draft*** (=write) *a new tax* ***bill.*** | *The Brazilian senate has* ***passed a bill*** (=voted for one and made it law) *to reform the social security system.* —see also FINANCE BILL
4 BANKING *AmE* a BANKNOTE: *A dollar bill costs 3.2 cents to produce.*
5 BANKING a BILL OF EXCHANGE
6 FINANCE a form of borrowing for short periods of time
Treasury bill also **T-bill**, **government bill** a form of borrowing for short periods of time by a government: *Three-month Treasury bills now yield less than 4%.* | *an auction of short-term US government bills*

bill[2] *v* [T] to send a bill to someone saying how much they owe; INVOICE[2] **bill sb for sth**: *They billed the Air Force for the work that they had carried out.*

bill•board /ˈbɪlbɔːd‖-bɔːrd/ *n* [C] a large sign used for advertising; HOARDING *BrE*: *tobacco ads in magazines, newspapers and on billboards*

bill•ing /ˈbɪlɪŋ/ *n* **1** [U] preparing and sending to customers lists of amounts of money owed for goods or services: *Ineffective credit control and* ***billing procedures*** *resulted in an unacceptable level of bad debts.*

itemized billing also **itemised billing** *BrE* [U] preparing and sending to customers detailed lists showing all goods and services they have received and are being charged for, rather than just a total amount

2 billings [plural] the total value of sales made by a company in a particular period of time: *Tyzack's UK turnover was £2.5 million, with world-wide billings around £7 million.*

3 [U] MARKETING the way that something is described in advertisements: *Only a small number of overseas visitors attend each year, and the festival hardly merits its 'International' billing.*

billing cycle —see under CYCLE

bil•lion /ˈbɪljən/ *number* written abbreviation **bn** *BrE*, **bil.** *AmE* plural **billion** or **billions** **1** one thousand million; 1,000,000,000: *The group has estimated debts of £1.2 billion.*

2 *BrE old-fashioned* a million million

bil•lion•aire /ˌbɪljəˈneə‖-ˈner/ *n* [C] someone who has assets worth at least a billion pounds, dollars etc: *Billionaire A. Alfred Taubman took over Sotheby's in 1983.*

bill of entry *n* plural **bills of entry** [C] an official document that gives details of goods that are being brought into or taken out of the country

bill of exchange abbreviation **b/e**, or **bill** *n* plural **bills of exchange** [C] BANKING a document ordering someone to pay a particular amount on a fixed date, used especially in international trade: *The exporter's bank sends the bill of exchange to its overseas branch in the importer's country.* | *When the buyer* ***accepts a bill of exchange*** (=agrees to pay it), *the exporter may arrange for it to be discounted.* | *Essing* ***dishonoured*** *four* ***bills of exchange*** (=failed to pay them) *drawn by Byrd to the amount of £2.39 million.*

backed bill [C] a bill of exchange accepted by a bank

bank bill [C] a bill of exchange given by a bank and instructing another bank to pay money to someone

bills in a set [plural] three copies of a bill of exchange, sent separately by an exporter to an importer in case one gets lost. The importer only needs to accept one copy

bills payable [plural] ACCOUNTING bills of exchange which a company has accepted and will have to pay as part of the company's LIABILITIES

bills receivable [plural] ACCOUNTING bills of exchange which will be paid to a company as part of the company's assets

commercial bill also **trade bill** [C] a bill of exchange used in the buying and selling of goods: *Most trade bills are discounted once and then held to maturity.*

discharged bill [C] a bill of exchange that has been paid

discounted bill [C] a bill of exchange that has been bought by a bank for less than it will be worth when it becomes due for payment

documents-against-acceptance bill [C] a bill of exchange addressed to a person such as an importer who is due to receive goods. The person must accept the bill of exchange before the bank will give them the documents needed to get possession of the goods

documents-against-payment bill [C] a bill of exchange addressed to a person such as an importer who is due to receive goods. The person must pay the bill of exchange before the bank will give them the documents needed to get possession of the goods

eligible bill [C] in Britain, a bank bill that has been accepted by one of about 100 banks officially approved by the Bank of England, and which the Bank of England has agreed to DISCOUNT (=give immediate payment for) again: *The eligible bill market is one of the largest elements of the London money market.*

fine trade bill [C] a bill of exchange which has little risk of not being paid, and is therefore sold at a lower DISCOUNT

non-prime bill [C] a bill of exchange which has quite a high risk of not being paid and is therefore sold at a higher DISCOUNT

sight bill [C] a bill of exchange that must be paid as soon as it is received: *Sight bills must be paid by the importer on presentation.*

term bill also **time bill**, or **usance bill** [C] a bill of exchange that must be paid at a specified time after it is written: *More useful are term bills where a period of credit is allowed.*

bill of lading written abbreviation **b/l** *n* plural **bills of lading** [C] a document that gives information about goods being transported. A bill of lading is also a contract to transport the goods, and shows that the transporter has received the goods: *If the buyer finds the bill of lading is not in order, he can refuse it.* | *With general cargo vessels, hundreds of bills of lading may have to be issued.*

claused bill of lading another name for an unclean bill of lading

clean bill of lading a bill of lading that shows that the goods and packaging are in good condition: *Bankers require clean bills of lading.*

container bill of lading also **combined transport bill of lading** a bill of lading relating to the transport of goods in CONTAINERS (=large metal boxes)

dirty bill of lading another name for an unclean bill of lading

electronic bill of lading a bill of lading held on a computer, not on paper: *Holders of the electronic bill of lading receive a password to access the carrier's computer network.*

foul bill of lading another name for an unclean bill of lading

ocean bill of lading a bill of lading for the transport of goods by sea

unclean bill of lading a bill of lading that shows that goods or packaging are damaged in some way: *Knowing what makes a bill of lading 'unclean' is essential to sellers and buyers.*

bill of materials *n* plural **bills of materials** [C] a list of the parts and materials needed in making, building, or producing something: *Product control will provide the bill of materials for given products and assemblies.*

bill of quantities *n* plural **bills of quantities** [C] a list of all the materials and costs in a planned building: *The contract documents include drawings and specifications, a schedule of work and bills of quantities.*

bill of sale *n* plural **bills of sale** [C] **1** a document giving details of something that someone has bought: *British ships can only be transferred by means of a bill of sale registered in the shipping register.*

2 in former times, a document used by money lenders to claim property if a loan was not repaid: *He held a bill of sale over her furniture and put a man into her house to remove it.*

bill rate —see under RATE[1]

bills in a set —see under BILL OF EXCHANGE

bills payable —see under BILL OF EXCHANGE

bills receivable —see under BILL OF EXCHANGE

bi•na•ry /ˈbaɪnəri/ *adj* COMPUTING relating to the system of numbers used in computers, that uses only the numbers 0 and 1: *All information inside the computer is stored in binary code.* | *the binary system*

bind /baɪnd/ *v* past tense and past participle **bound** present participle **binding** [T] if a legal agreement binds someone, it makes them promise to do something: *If a person signs a document which contains contract terms, he or she is bound by those terms.* **bind sb to do sth**: *the agreement with industry that binds companies to reduce the weight of packaging*

B

bind·er /ˈbaɪndə‖-ər/ *n* [C] LAW, INSURANCE a temporary contract that shows an agreement has been made, and is used until the formal contract has been prepared

bind·ing /ˈbaɪndɪŋ/ *adj* **a binding contract/promise/agreement etc** a promise, agreement etc that must be kept: *Participants in the world trade talks have agreed to negotiate specific binding commitments.* | *a* ***legally binding*** *agreement between the parties* **+ on/upon**: *No addition to these terms is binding on the buyer unless agreed in writing.*

bi·o·mass /ˈbaɪəʊmæs‖ˈbaɪoʊ-/ *n* [U] plant or animal matter used to provide fuel or energy: *If the 'green' biomass approach is taken there's the problem of finding enough ground to grow crops for ethanol* (=a type of fuel).

bi·o·phar·ma·ceu·ti·cal /ˈbaɪəʊfaːməˈsjuːtɪkəl‖-oʊfaːrməˈsuː-/ *adj* [only before a noun] concerned with BIOTECHNOLOGY (=the industrial use of living things to make drugs and chemicals) and with PHARMACEUTICALS (=the development and production of drugs and medicines): *Immune Response is a biopharmaceutical concern engaged in developing products for treatment of HIV infection.* —**biopharmaceuticals** *n* [plural] *life sciences, such as biopharmaceuticals and health care*

bi·o·tech /ˈbaɪəʊtek‖ˈbaɪoʊ-/ *adj* [only before a noun] relating to biotechnology: *biotech companies* | *the biotech industry* | *Biotech stocks have been the market's hottest performers.*

bi·o·tech·nol·o·gy /ˌbaɪəʊtekˈnɒlədʒi‖ˌbaɪoʊtekˈnɑː-/ *n* [U] the industrial use of living things to make drugs and chemicals, to destroy waste matter etc: *ATS is a biotechnology concern that develops products based on human tissue.*

BIS abbreviation for BANK FOR INTERNATIONAL SETTLEMENTS

bit /bɪt/ *n* [C] COMPUTING the smallest unit of information that can be used by a computer: *The total memory is approximately 64,000 bits.*

bite /baɪt/ *n* [C] another spelling of BYTE —see also TAX BITE

biz /bɪz/ *n informal* **show/music/glamour biz** a particular type of business, especially one connected with entertainment: *the latest* ***show biz*** *news*

biz·jet /ˈbɪzdʒet/ *n* [C] *informal* an aircraft used especially by business people: *There is no question of BAe's bizjets business being sold in total to another manufacturer.*

b/l written abbreviation for BILL OF LADING

black[1] /blæk/ *adj* not allowed by TRADE UNIONS to be handled or used by their members during a disagreement between management and employees: *The British Seamen's Union declared the ship black and picketed her on her return from Loch Fyne.*

black[2] *v* [T] *BrE* if a TRADE UNION blacks a company or blacks goods, it refuses to work with them or deal with them; BOYCOTT

black[3] *n* **in the black** if a business is in the black, it is making a profit: *The group is still in the black but trading in the first two months of the year has been difficult.* —compare ***in the red*** under RED

black box *n* [C] *informal* **1** an electronic unit that records information on an aircraft about its height, speed etc. If the plane crashes, the black box can be examined to find the causes: *Data from the black box recovered from the destroyed helicopter has been played back satisfactorily.*

2 a machine that works in a secret way that is not normally explained to people: *We found out what formulas were inside the black boxes that firms used to determine when to set off computer-driven program trades.*

black economy —see under ECONOMY[1]

Black Friday *n* [U] **1** FINANCE September 24, 1869, when a group of investors tried to take control of the US gold market and were considered to have caused a RECESSION

2 any Friday when something bad happens: *The latest cuts at Salomon were made on what staffers referred to as Black Friday.*

black hole *n* [C] a business activity or product on which large amounts of money are spent, but that does not produce any income or other useful result: *Anyone who launches a bid for Ferranti will want to be sure there are no more black holes lurking in the company's books.*

black knight *n* [C] a company that tries to take control of another company by offering to buy large numbers of its shares: *While not particularly welcome, the black knight is considered more favourably than the hostile bidder.* —compare WHITE KNIGHT

black·leg /ˈblækleg/ *n* [C] *BrE* a worker who continues to work during a strike or who does the work of someone who is on strike: *Chinese seamen were brought in from outside and used as blacklegs by the employers.* —see also STRIKEBREAKER

black·list /ˈblækˌlɪst/ *n* [C] a list of people, organizations, or countries that are disapproved of and that people avoid doing business with, for example because they are dishonest: *The companies had been placed on the blacklist after being accused of offering kickbacks to win a contract.* —**blacklist** *v* [T] *The company's near-monopoly of television has enabled it to blacklist artists who deal with its rivals.*

black·mail[1] /ˈblækmeɪl/ *n* [U] demanding money from a person or organization by threatening them, for example threatening to tell secrets about them if they do not pay: *Most of his wealth had been acquired through blackmail.*

blackmail[2] *v* [I,T] to demand money from a person or organization by threatening them, for example threatening to tell secrets about them if they do not pay: *a man who blackmailed gay businessmen by threatening to expose their homosexuality*

black market —see under MARKET[1]

black marketeer —see under MARKETEER

Black Monday *n* [U] **1** the world stockmarket CRASH of October 19, 1987: *What are we going to tell the victims if Black Monday happens again? That we thought Amgen was a good stock?*

2 any Monday when something bad happens: *The Mexican bolsa plunged 13.3% on Black Monday, its worst crash since 1987.*

Black-Scholes op·tion pric·ing mod·el /ˈblæk ˈskəʊlz ˈɒpʃən ˈpraɪsɪŋ ˈmɒdl‖-skoʊlz ˈɑːpʃən ˈpraɪsɪŋ ˈmɑːdl/ —see under MODEL

Black Thursday *n* [U] **1** October 24, 1929, when markets first began to fall heavily in the WALL STREET CRASH: *You're depressed and you've been behaving like a broker on Black Thursday.*

2 any Thursday when something bad happens: *Unemployment hit 20,000 workers yesterday. The biggest job losses during Black Thursday were announced by the Post Office.*

Black Tuesday *n* [U] **1** October 29, 1929, the worst day of the WALL STREET CRASH
2 any Tuesday when something bad happens: *Mr Dubinin was unfairly blamed for the currency crash known as Black Tuesday.*

Black Wednesday *n* [U] **1** September 9, 1992, when SPECULATORS forced the British pound out of the EXCHANGE RATE MECHANISM: *Black Wednesday is seen as a great defeat in British postwar history.*
2 any Wednesday when something bad happens

blank¹ /blæŋk/ *adj* without any writing or print: ***Leave** the last page **blank**.*

blank² *n* [C] **1** an empty space on a piece of paper or a computer screen where you are supposed to write information: ***Fill in the blanks,** taking care to use the right form.*
2 *AmE* a complete piece of paper or computer screen with spaces for writing information; FORM: *Blanks will be made available to all competition participants.*

blank check offering —see under OFFERING

blank cheque —see under CHEQUE

blan·ket /ˈblæŋkət/ *adj* [only before a noun] affecting or including everything or everyone: *The authorities have introduced a **blanket ban** on all deals of this kind.* | *The agency is offering a blanket settlement to all groups.*

blanket insurance —see under INSURANCE

blank transfer —see under TRANSFER²

bleed /bliːd/ *v* past tense and past participle **bled** **1** [I] to lose money: *Ford's Jaguar unit continued to bleed, with an operating loss of $100 million.*
2 [T] to make someone pay an unreasonable amount of money **bleed sb for sth**: *She bled him for every last cent that she could.*
3 bleed sb/sth dry/white to take a lot or all of someone's money: *developing countries bled dry by massive loan repayments*

blind call —see under CALL²

blind pool —see under POOL¹

blind test —see under TEST¹

blind trial —see under TRIAL

blind trust —see under TRUST

blister pack —see under PACK¹

blitz /blɪts/ *n* [C usually singular] a lot of activity designed to produce a particular result: *a blitz of television commercials* | *a year-long AT&T **marketing blitz** that attracted millions of customers back to its service*

bloat·ware /ˈbləʊtweə‖ˈbloʊtwer/ *n* [U] *informal* COMPUTING **1** computer software with many features that are not really needed
2 software which uses a large amount of computer memory and which is therefore not effective or useful: *Disgruntled users complained about the excessive time spent waiting for 'bloatware' to perform even the simplest operations.*

bloc /blɒk‖blɑːk/ *n* [C] **1** ECONOMICS a group of countries, usually with the same economic system, who have an official trading agreement with each other: *negotiations for the incorporation of Mexico into a trade bloc with the USA*
2 a group of countries or people who have been united together for a particular political purpose: *the former Eastern bloc*

block¹ /blɒk‖blɑːk/ *n* [C] **1** FINANCE a large number of shares in a particular company held by one owner or traded at one time. A block of shares usually involves 10,000 shares or more: *Enfield paid C$17.5 million to acquire a block of 1,224,489 Consumers Packaging shares.* | *A 10 million-share **block trade** in Avon at 39⅛ excited traders early in the day.* | *Wall Street's best-known and most aggressive **block trader***
2 a large building divided into separate parts: *a block of apartments* | *office blocks*
3 a solid mass of something or an amount of something solid: *a block of concrete*

block² *v* [T] if a government or other authority blocks something, they prevent it happening, developing, or succeeding: *The French government blocked the import of New Zealand agricultural products into the Common Market.*

block·ade¹ /blɒˈkeɪd‖blɑː-/ *n* [C] **1** the surrounding of a country or an area during a war in order to stop goods from entering or leaving: *On Oct. 3rd the Yugoslav navy began a blockade of seven Croatian ports.*
2 a refusal to trade with a country or state: *an economic blockade of Cuba by the USA*
3 the blocking of a place such as a port to stop people or goods from entering or leaving, done as a protest against something: *In 1989, drivers of Italian heavy goods vehicles began a blockade of customs posts at the border with Austria, causing traffic chaos.*

blockade² *v* [T] to surround a place and prevent goods from entering or leaving, either during a war or as a protest: *the use of warships to blockade Iraq and enforce UN Security Council sanctions*

block booking —see under BOOKING

block·bust·er /ˈblɒkˌbʌstə‖ˈblɑːkˌbʌstər/ *n* [C] *informal* a very successful film or book, usually one that is full of action or adventure but is not very serious: *the new Hollywood blockbuster 'The Phantom Menace'*

block·bust·ing¹ /ˈblɒkˌbʌstɪŋ‖ˈblɑːk-/ *adj* [only before a noun] a blockbusting film, book, or performance has high sales and is usually full of action or adventure but is not very serious: *a blockbusting sci-fi thriller*

blockbusting² *n* [U] when property prices in an area are intentionally forced down either by SPECULATORS saying falsely that the area is becoming poorer or less popular, or by factories that deliberately cause noise, POLLUTION etc, hoping that people living nearby will sell their houses for less than they are worth

blocked /blɒkt‖blɑːkt/ *adj* money that is blocked cannot be taken out of the country or changed into another currency: *The company managed to find a loophole to unblock its blocked money.* | *The funds are in blocked deposits at the Bank of New York and HSBC Bank in Britain*

blocked account —see under ACCOUNT¹

blocked currency —see under CURRENCY

block grant —see under GRANT¹

block insurance —see under INSURANCE

block move *n* [C] COMPUTING moving a complete part of a document to another part of the document or to a different document: *The program has a graphics engine for quick block moves.*

block vote —see under VOTE²

blood·let·ting /ˈblʌdˌletɪŋ/ *n* [U] *journalism* HUMAN RESOURCES dismissing employees in large numbers: *After two years of layoffs, bloodletting at the company may be over.*

blow /bləʊ‖bloʊ/ *v* past tense **blew** past participle **blown** [T] *informal* if you blow money on something, you spend a lot of money on it, often money that you cannot afford: *He blew his wages on a new stereo.*

blow·out /ˈbləʊaʊt‖ˈbloʊ-/ *n* [C] *informal* **1** when a business fails or a financial market falls very quickly: *Bull markets always end in a speculative blowout.*
2 a very successful period of time for sales or profits:

Microsoft's performance was slightly better than expectations, but it wasn't a blowout quarter.
3 in oil exploration, when pressure from under the ground causes oil to flow in an uncontrolled way: *a platform blowout that spilled thousands of barrels of oil into Santa Barbara Channel*

B

Blue Book *n* [singular] the British government's official annual accounts: *According to the government's estimates in its annual Blue Book, the central government owns £122 billion in buildings, machinery and vehicles.*

blue chip —see under CHIP

blue chip company —see under COMPANY

blue chip share —see under SHARE

blue chip stock —see under STOCK[1]

blue-collar *adj* [only before a noun] HUMAN RESOURCES blue-collar work is unskilled work that may be hard and dirty: *the loss of a lot of* ***blue-collar jobs*** *in the docks* | *a strike by* ***blue-collar workers*** —compare WHITE-COLLAR

blue-collar worker —see under WORKER

Blue Cross *n* INSURANCE a US medical insurance company: *If Blue Cross patients accounted for one-third of a hospital's patient days, the hospital would bill Blue Cross for one-third of its total costs.* —see also BLUE SHIELD

blue laws —see under LAW

blue•print /ˈbluːˌprɪnt/ *n* [C] **1** a plan for achieving or improving something: *an economic blueprint calling for new investment in training and infrastructure* + **for**: *Labour's blueprint for an integrated transport system*
2 a detailed photographic copy of a plan for a building or a machine, appearing as white lines on a blue background, used by builders or people who make or repair machines: *a blueprint drawn up by a firm of local architects*

Blue Shield *n* INSURANCE a US medical insurance company: *Blue Shield of California says increased fraud-detection efforts saved subscribers $9.2 million last year.* —see also BLUE CROSS

blue-sky laws —see under LAW

blurb /blɜːb‖blɜːrb/ *n* [C usually singular] *informal* MARKETING a short piece of writing describing and advertising a book, film, or a new product: *The blurb for her latest book describes her as 'one of Britain's best-loved art critics'.*

bn *BrE* written abbreviation for BILLION; BIL. *AmE*

board[1] /bɔːd‖bɔːrd/ *n* **1** [C] also **board of directors** the group of people who have been elected to manage a company by those holding shares in the company: *These accounts were approved by the Board of Directors on 15th July last year.* | *The executive committee effectively runs the company between monthly* ***board meetings***.
management board [C] a board directly responsible for managing a company: *Three of the company's five management board members have resigned in the past several months.*
supervisory board [C] in some countries, for example Germany, a board that does not directly manage a company, but that checks the actions and decisions of the management board: *The supervisory board can appoint and dismiss management board members and also rules on major policies of the company.*
2 [C] a group of people who make important decisions or rules about how an institution operates and make sure that these rules are obeyed: *The city's* ***licensing board*** *voted yesterday for restrictions on opening hours.* + **of**: *the board of examiners*
marketing board [C] an official organization responsible for organizing and encouraging the sale of a particular product, especially one where the government influences prices etc: *the Milk Marketing Board*
oversight board [C] in some public institutions in the US, a group of people who check that the institution is working correctly and who decide what it should do: *a special fiscal oversight board that will monitor city finances*
3 also **circuit board** [C] COMPUTING the part of a computer containing the CHIPS that govern a particular function: *A good sound board will really liven up your games and multimedia applications.*
4 [U] also **board and lodging** the meals and the room provided for you when you stay or live somewhere
full board [U] a room and breakfast, lunch, and an evening meal at a hotel: *13 nights in Cuba with an evening and full board in Prague on the return flight.*
half board [U] a room and two meals a day, usually breakfast and lunch at a hotel: *14 nights' half board for £239 in Alcudia*
5 on board on a ship, plane, or train: *All the crew must be on board by four o'clock this afternoon.*
6 take sth on board *informal* to listen to or accept a suggestion: *He was not able to comment, but he took on board the strength of feeling against the proposal.*
7 be on board/bring sb on board *informal* to join an organization or agree with someone's plans, ideas etc, or to make someone do this: *The response was to look for a way to accommodate the Danish Government, to bring the Danes back on board.* —see also ACROSS THE BOARD, BULLETIN BOARD

board[2] *v* [I,T] to get on a bus, plane, train, or ship: *Flight TA134 for Boston is now boarding at Gate 16.* | *I boarded a bus and headed off out of Lesotho.*

Board of Banking Supervision *n* BANKING the Bank of England department that establishes the rules of the banking system in Britain, and makes sure they are followed

Board of Customs and Excise *n* in Britain, the government department responsible for collecting certain taxes, especially taxes on goods coming into a country and VAT, and for preventing people from bringing goods into the country illegally

board of directors also **board** *n* plural **boards of directors** [C] the group of people who have been elected to manage a company by those holding shares in the company: *Bank of Boston's board of directors will vote on the merger proposal at a meeting today.*

board of equalization *n* plural **boards of equalization** [C] a department in each US state that makes decisions about how property, sales, and other taxes are calculated

Board of Inland Revenue *n* in Britain, the government department responsible for collecting direct taxes such as INCOME TAX and CORPORATION TAX, but not indirect taxes such as VAT. The comparable organization in the US is the INTERNAL REVENUE SERVICE

board of realtors *n* plural **boards of realtors** [C] in the US, a local professional association of people whose job is selling REAL ESTATE (=land and property)

Board of Trade *n* in Britain, the former government department dealing with trade, now known as the DEPARTMENT OF TRADE AND INDUSTRY

board representation —see under REPRESENTATION

board•room /ˈbɔːdruːm, -rʊm‖ˈbɔːrd-/ *n* [C] **1** the place in a company where its board of directors meets
2 boardroom battle/dispute/row/split etc a disagreement between two or more directors of a company: *a boardroom battle at Enersis, the Chilean electricity company, over the terms of its alliance with Spain's Endesa*
3 boardroom pay/salaries etc the amount that company directors are paid: *Boardroom pay has raced ahead,*

offering an inflationary example to workers being lectured about the need for restraint.

body copy —see under COPY[1]

body corporate —see under CORPORATE[2]

B of E written abbreviation for BANK OF ENGLAND

bo•gus /'bəʊgəs‖'boʊ-/ *adj informal* not real, but dishonestly pretending to be something or someone: *They issue certificates of deposits, often based on fictitious assets such as bogus gold mines.* | *bogus claims of injury by their workers*

boil•er•plate /'bɔɪləˌpleɪt‖-lər-/ *n* [C] LAW an agreement, contract etc with standard wording: *WillMaker adapts its boilerplate to the laws of the home state of the user.* | *boilerplate contract terms that can be transferred from scheme to scheme to cut costs*

boiler room also **boiler shop** *n* [C] FINANCE an organization selling investments by telephone using unfair and sometimes dishonest methods

bolt /bəʊlt‖boʊlt/ *n* [C] MANUFACTURING a large roll containing many metres of cloth

bomb[1] /bɒm‖bɑːm/ *n* **1 cost a bomb** *BrE informal* to cost a lot of money: *a new office development that must have cost a bomb*

2 make a bomb *BrE informal* to make a lot of money: *She made a bomb coaching movie stars in Palm Springs.*

bomb[2] *v* [I] *AmE informal* if a product or an activity bombs, it fails badly: *His original computer design bombed because it lacked power and software applications.* —see also CARPET BOMB

bo•na fi•de /'bəʊnə ˌfaɪdi‖'boʊnə faɪd/ *adj formal* real, true, and not intended to deceive: *a bona fide commercial transaction* | *a bona fide charity*

bona fides *n* [plural] LAW if you check someone's bona fides, you make sure they are the person they say they are or that what they say is true

bo•nan•za /bə'nænzə, bəʊ-‖bə-, boʊ-/ *n* [C] a lucky or successful situation in which a person or business makes a lot of money: *a £5 million export sales bonanza in the United States* | *a bonanza year for the computer industry*

bond /bɒnd‖bɑːnd/ *n* [C] **1** FINANCE an amount of money borrowed by a government or an organization. The government or organization produces a document promising that it will pay back the money that it has borrowed, usually with interest. The document, which can be bought and sold, is also called a bond: *Many investors switched out of shares into bonds yesterday.* —see also PREMIUM BOND

active bond a bond that is actively traded after it is first sold: *Prices of active bonds declined, ending with losses of about 1/8 to 1/4 point.*

baby bond ◆ in the US, a bond with a value of $1,000 or less

◆ a way of saving money for children by investing it in bonds so that they can receive it when they reach a particular age: *the With-Profit Baby Bond Plan from the Tunbridge Wells Equitable Friendly Society*

bearer bond a bond where the owner is considered to be the person who has it in their possession, whose name may not be recorded on an official list of owners —compare ***registered bond***

bellwether bond a government bond whose movements are considered to show the probable future direction of the bond market as a whole, and whose price is used to refer to prices of other bonds: *The bonds were priced at a spread of 1.2 percentage points above the Treasury's 30-year bellwether bond.*

bulldog bond a bond issued in pounds on the British markets by a non-British borrower

callable bond a bond that can be repaid when the borrower chooses, within the conditions made known when it is sold

called bond a bond that has been repaid before the usual time

convertible bond a bond that can be repaid by a company in the form of shares in the company: *Convertible bonds, which are bonds that can be converted into stock at a later date, jumped 32% last year.*

corporate bond a bond issued by a company: *Yields on corporate bonds are more attractive than on Treasuries at the moment.*

Eurodollar bond also **euro bond** a bond sold in a currency which is not that of the borrower's country, usually US dollars: *Sumitomo will issue 500 billion yen of yen bonds and $2 billion of Eurodollar bonds.*

guaranteed income bond a bond where you invest a sum for a fixed period of time, and the financial institution promises that the return will not be below a particular amount. Guaranteed income bonds are sometimes combined with life insurance: *A £3000 investment in the five-year guaranteed income bond from Pinnacle Insurance will earn 6.4% net of basic rate tax.*

guaranty bond also **guarenteed bond** a bond where the amount of money and the interest are guaranteed by someone other than the person who gave it to you, used especially in bonds related to large investments: *Mr. Davies claims he helped Mr. Parretti secure a guaranty bond for a major loan but was never paid the $1,750,000 premium he was owed.*

government bond a bond issued by a government: *Prices of French government bonds soared yesterday in heavy trading.*

income bond a bond pays a regular income in the form of interest

indexed bond also **stabilized bond** a bond ISSUED by a government where the interest rate follows changes in the CONSUMER PRICE INDEX (=the rate of increase of prices of goods that people buy)

junk bond a bond with a high rate of interest, but with a high risk of not being repaid: *He estimates that 38% of junk bonds will default at some point.*

municipal bond also **muni** a bond issued by a state or local government authority, usually in the US: *Rhode Island's municipal bonds held firm.*

registered bond a bond that has the name of the holder officially recorded by the company that has ISSUED it —compare ***bearer bond***

Samurai bond a bond issued in yen on the Japanese markets by a non-Japanese borrower: *The Ukraine hopes to issue Samurai bonds in Japan in September.*

savings bond a government bond sold to encourage people to save and invest small amounts of money: *US savings bonds cannot be redeemed before six months has elapsed.*

stabilized bond also **stabilised bond** *BrE* another name for INDEXED BOND

sterling bond a bond ISSUED by a country that is not the United Kingdom, but payable in British pounds

super sinker bond [C] a bond which MATURES (=becomes due for payment) after a short period of time of between 3 and 5 years, although it is expected to make the same amount of profit as investments which take longer to mature

sushi bond a bond with a fixed rate of interest, sold by Japanese companies usually to Japanese institutional investors in a foreign currency, usually US dollars

Treasury bond also **T-bond** a bond issued by the US federal government

Yankee bond a bond issued in dollars on the US markets by a non-US borrower

yearling bond another name for YEARLING

zero-coupon bond a bond bought at well below its actual value. It does not pay interest during its life, but the gain is made when it is resold; ZERO: *Zero-coupon bonds, though they put nothing in investors' pockets, can still generate tax liability.*

B

2 LAW a contract in which someone agrees to pay a sum of money if they do not do something they have promised to do: *Importers of Mexican cement must* ***post bonds*** (=leave money with a court) *to cover penalties that may apply later.*

appeal bond a sum of money that is sometimes left with a court when someone APPEALS (=asks the court to change a decision it has made). If the appeal is not successful, the person loses their money

bail bond a sum of money left with a court when an accused person is waiting for trial. If the person does not return for trial, they lose the money: *The judges decided to double the bail bonds for protesters who get arrested.*

bid bond a sum of money that the lowest bidder on a project pays to the developer to cover extra costs that the developer will have if the bidder later refuses to do the work: *Charter withdrew from bidding for the Saudi Arabian hospital project, and its $6 million bid bond was returned.*

indemnity bond the general name given to all bonds that promise to pay money to someone if someone else does not perform a specific duty

performance bond a sum of money provided by an organization that is working on a contract to another organization. The contractor loses this money if they fail to carry out the work in the contract correctly

surety bond a formal agreement in which one person or company promises to pay another company's debts if that company fails to do so: *The loan is backed by a surety bond issued by Financial Guaranty Insurance Corp.*

3 in bond if imported goods are in bond, they are kept in a BONDED WAREHOUSE until tax has been paid on them

customs bond an official document where an importer promises to pay import taxes to the authorities for particular goods: *With this computerised system, the holder of the customs bond can be informed immediately the consignment arrives.*

4 INSURANCE used to talk about certain types of insurance contract

commercial blanket bond an insurance policy providing insurance for damage caused by any of a company's employees

completion bond an insurance agreement that provides insurance against the risk that a project, for example a film or a property development, will not be completed or that it will cost more than planned: *Saab-Scania has SKr2.4 billion in completion bonds for continuing military projects.*

fidelity bond an insurance policy taken out by an organization against illegal acts by its employees, for example FRAUD: *Most small businesses lack fidelity bonds and other forms of loss insurance.*

bond broker —see under BROKER[1]

bond certificate —see under CERTIFICATE

bond creditor —see under CREDITOR

bond discount —see under DISCOUNT[1]

bond•ed /ˈbɒndɨd‖ˈbɑːn-/ *adj* [only before a noun] *BrE* related to goods that have been brought into a country, but for which no import taxes have yet been paid. The goods must be kept in buildings licensed by the government until the import tax is paid or until they are exported again

bonded factory —see under FACTORY

bonded goods —see under GOODS

bonded vault —see under VAULT[1]

bonded warehouse —see under WAREHOUSE

bond fund —see under FUND[1]

bond•hold•er /ˈbɒndˌhəʊldə‖ˈbɑːndˌhoʊldər/ *n* [C] a person or organization that owns bonds: *The company can seek bankruptcy court approval for a reorganization plan if it receives approval from at least half of the bondholders*

junior bondholder a bondholder who will only be repaid after other lenders if the borrower gets into financial difficulty: *The airline cannot purchase junior bondholders' debt until it has paid all the senior note defaults.*

senior bondholder a bondholder who will be repaid before other lenders are repaid if the borrower gets into financial difficulty

bond•ing /ˈbɒndɪŋ‖ˈbɑːn-/ *n* [U] the practice of keeping goods that have been imported in a special building and officially promising to pay the import tax when it is due: *a $100 auction-licensing fee and $80 a month to cover bonding*

bond interest —see under INTEREST

bond market —see under MARKET[1]

bond note —see under NOTE[1]

bond premium —see under PREMIUM[1]

bond rating —see under RATING

bond warrant —see under WARRANT[1]

bond yield —see under YIELD[1]

bo•nus /ˈbəʊnəs‖ˈboʊ-/ *n* [C] **1** an extra amount of money added to an employee's wages, usually as a reward for doing difficult or good work: *The bonus is discretionary but linked to performance.* | *Rover is offering its workforce a £3,000 cash bonus to take voluntary redundancy.*

loyalty bonus a sum of money that someone is paid as a reward for being a regular customer or for continuing to work for someone: *Payments might include a loyalty bonus for those who stay for the full period.*

performance bonus also **merit bonus** a bonus paid to a manager for increasing sales or profits, saving money, etc: *Our managers are offered a salary plus a small performance bonus for achieving monthly targets.*

productivity bonus an extra payment to workers for producing more of something than normal: *We now operate factory-wide productivity bonus and payment-by-results schemes.*

2 also **capital bonus** INSURANCE an extra payment from a life insurance company's profits to people who have certain types of life insurance: *On with-profits policies, bonuses are maintained at 6%.*

terminal bonus in Britain, an extra payment made at the end of some types of life insurance contract: *There is no chance of an endowment mortgage paying off the mortgage early. A large part of the policy's value is often added on the last day as a terminal bonus.*

3 INSURANCE a reduction in the cost of insurance when no claims are made during a particular period of time: *If you make a claim in any period of insurance, any* ***no-claim bonus*** *which you have earned may be reduced at your next renewal.*

bonus dividend —see under DIVIDEND

bonus issue —see under ISSUE[2]

bonus payment —see under PAYMENT

bonus share —see under SHARE

bonus stock —see under STOCK[1]

book[1] /bʊk/ *n* **1 books** [plural] ACCOUNTING the accounting records of a business; ACCOUNT BOOKS; BOOKS OF ACCOUNT: *The company's books are in such chaos that we won't know the truth for some time.*

cash received book [C] an account book in which the amounts of cash received are recorded

purchase (day) book also **purchases (day) book** [C] a record of all the INVOICES received by a business from its suppliers: *Most establishments keep their purchase book in the form of a weekly invoice summary sheet.*

sales day book [C] an account book in which you record all sales of goods on credit

sales returns book [C] an account book in which you record details of all goods returned by customers

2 books [plural] MANUFACTURING a list of a company's clients and orders for goods: *De Havilland has 100 firm orders for two different aircraft* ***on its books.***

3 books [plural] HUMAN RESOURCES a company's records of the people working for it: *The 206,000 employees* ***on*** *Italian railway's* ***books*** *last summer have now fallen to 185,000.*

4 a book containing an official record or list

bank book [C] a book that shows money paid into and taken out of a bank account

duplicate book [C] a book used to keep a record of sales, invoices etc. There are two pages for each entry, and when you write on the top page you also produce a copy on the second page

log book [C] ◆ an official detailed record of something: *differences between driving times entered on log books and on drivers' pay slips*

◆ *BrE* an official document containing details about a vehicle and the name of its owner

minute book [C] a book containing the official written record of what is said and decided at a meeting: *I have looked through the minute books from 1991 but can find no record of the proposal.*

plat book [C] PROPERTY *AmE* a public record of maps, showing how land in a particular area is divided

rule book [C] [C] a book of rules, especially one that is given to workers in a job

statutory book [C] in Britain, one of the five books that must be kept by every limited company by law. The statutory books are the THE REGISTER OF MEMBERS, the REGISTER OF DIRECTORS, the REGISTER OF DIRECTORS' SHAREHOLDINGS, the REGISTER OF CHARGES, and the MINUTE BOOK

5 FINANCE a list of the bonds, shares etc that a dealer has to offer at a particular time: *Marketmakers were running down their books ahead of the holiday.*

6 manage/run a book FINANCE to be responsible for organizing a SECURITIES ISSUE (=when new bonds, shares etc are sold): *Jardine Fleming will run the book for the Indian Gas Authority privatisation issue.*

book² *v* [T] ACCOUNTING to enter a figure in a company's account books: *The restructuring charge is to be booked in Electrolux's second-quarter accounts.*

book•build•ing /ˈbʊkˌbɪldɪŋ/ also **book building** *n* [U] FINANCE when financial advisers ask institutional investors how many shares they might buy and at what price before new shares are made available and sold: *Book-building will start today for the 270 to 320 billion drachma privatisation issue of OTE.*

book debt —see under DEBT

book depreciation —see under DEPRECIATION

book entry —see under ENTRY

book equity —see under EQUITY

book•ing /ˈbʊkɪŋ/ *n* [C] an arrangement in which a place on a plane, in a hotel, restaurant etc is kept for a customer who will arrive later; RESERVATION: *There's a problem over a* ***double booking*** (=one where two people have been given the same booking) *and you're being offered a different room.*

block booking a number of tickets sold as a unit to one group of people: *To make block bookings at Harlow Sportcentre, please ask for the Booking Secretary.*

book-keeper also **book keeper** *n* [C] ACCOUNTING a person whose job is to make an official record of all the money received into and paid out from a business: *the need to find an experienced and competent book-keeper*

book-keeping also **book keeping** *n* [U] ACCOUNTING the recording of all the money received into and paid out from a business: *Every business must have an accounts function where income and expenditure book-keeping is done.*

double entry book-keeping ACCOUNTING the accounting system in which each TRANSACTION is recorded twice, as a DEBIT in one account and as a CREDIT in another. For example, a sale is recorded as a credit in one account and the money owed by the buyer is recorded as a debit in another: *In double entry book-keeping the total debits must equal the total credits and by adding the two a check can be made on the double entry.*

single entry book-keeping the accounting system in which each TRANSACTION is recorded once in a single account, instead of being recorded as a DEBIT in one account and as a CREDIT in another

book•mark /ˈbʊkmaːk‖-maːrk/ *n* [C] COMPUTING a way of saving something such as the address of a WEBSITE or the place in a computer file, so that you can return to it more easily: *The bookmark function allows users to resume from the point where they left by electronically 'marking' it before switching the unit off.* —**bookmark** *v* [T] *You can bookmark your favourite web pages.*

book of final entry *n* plural **books of final entry** [C usually plural] one of the books or computer records showing the totals of items shown separately in the BOOKS OF FIRST ENTRY or DAY BOOKS; LEDGER

book profit —see under PROFIT¹

book•sel•ler /ˈbʊkˌselə‖-ər/ *n* [C] a company that owns or manages a bookshop or several bookshops: *a leading chain of booksellers*

books of account *n* [plural] the accounting records of a business; BOOKS

books of first entry also **books of prime entry** *n* [plural] books or computer records in which amounts that a company receives and spends are first recorded before total amounts are entered in LEDGERS (=official records): *Check each item in the ledger with the book of first entry.*

book-to-bill ratio —see under RATIO

book token —see under TOKEN¹

book value —see under VALUE¹

Boo•le•an /ˈbuːliən/ *adj* [only before a noun] COMPUTING relating to a type of LOGIC in which something can be either true or false, but not both: *online systems which make use of* ***Boolean logic*** | *a* ***Boolean search*** (=a search for information on a computer, using Boolean logic)

boom¹ /buːm/ *n* [C,U] **1** ECONOMICS a time when business activity increases rapidly, so that the demand for goods increases, prices and wages go up, and unemployment falls: *a boom in the building sector* | *After four years of* ***economic boom,*** *1990 saw a slowing down of the Spanish economy.* | *Government economic policy encouraged a* ***consumer boom*** *followed by a deep recession.* | *A system of low taxation on land sales helped fuel a* ***property boom.*** —compare SLUMP

2 FINANCE a time when activity on the stockmarket reaches a high level and share prices are very high: *Hopes of further interest rate cuts sparked off a shares boom yesterday.*

boom² *v* [I] if business, trade, or the economy is booming, it is very successful and growing: *Since the 1980s tourism has boomed here.* | *Cellnet has 600,000 mobile phone subscribers and business is booming.*

boom and bust *n* [U] ECONOMICS a situation in which an economy regularly becomes more active and successful and then suddenly fails: *We must try to break this economic cycle of boom and bust.*

B

boom•let /ˈbuːmlət/ *n* [C] a small boom that does not last very long: *The tax increases will do nothing to stop the current boomlet developing into a fully-fledged boom.*

boon•dog•gle /ˈbuːnˌdɒgl‖-ˌdɒːgl/ *n* [C] *AmE informal* an officially organized plan or action that wastes a lot of money: *Opponents say the Houston monorail plan is a boondoggle; projected routes would travel to places that would attract few riders.*

B

boost[1] /buːst/ *v* [T] **1** to increase something such as production, sales, or prices: *The advertising campaign is intended to boost sales.* | *Another cut in interest rates would boost stock prices.* | *800 jobs have been cut in an attempt to boost productivity.*
2 boost the economy to make the economy stronger, so that business activity increases, prices and wages go up, and unemployment falls: *The US Treasury ordered the Fed to lift the yen against the dollar in hopes of boosting the US economy before the November election.*
3 boost confidence to increase confidence: *The economy needs a positive jolt to boost consumer confidence.*
4 to advertise a product: *a special promotion to boost their new product*

boost[2] *n* [singular] **1** something that helps to increase something such as production, sales, or prices: *That optimistic outlook* ***gave*** *stocks and the dollar* ***a boost.*** | *Sales could* ***get a boost*** *in January and February.*
2 something that helps something to improve or become more successful: *The price of oil could soon be $15 a barrel or less, which would be a welcome boost to the American economy.* | *The sale of such a large nuclear power reactor is expected to give a boost to Canada's nuclear industry.* | *The market got a boost on Friday when the Federal Reserve Board cut the interest rate that it charges member banks.*
3 something that helps to improve confidence or encourage people: *The end of the war would almost certainly provide some sort of boost to business and consumer confidence.*

boot /buːt/ also **boot up** *v* [I,T] COMPUTING to make a computer ready to be used by getting all the programs it needs into its memory: *Try booting the system from a floppy.* | *The virus scanner will not run every time you boot up, only the first time you boot up each day.*

boot•leg /ˈbuːtleg/ *adj* [only before a noun] made or sold illegally: *900 bootleg videos of pop concerts have been seized by trading standards officers.* | *bootleg whisky*

boot•leg•ger /ˈbuːtˌlegə‖-ər/ *n* [C] someone who makes or sells something, especially alcohol, illegally: *a former bootlegger, now a gambling mogul*

bootstrap acquisition —see under ACQUISITION

bor•row /ˈbɒrəʊ‖ˈbɑːroʊ, ˈbɔː-/ *v* [I,T] to receive money from a person or organization which you must pay back later: *Nowhere else in Europe can home-buyers borrow 100% of the purchase price.* **borrow sth from sb**: *Your business can borrow money from your pension fund on normal commercial terms.* —compare LEND

bor•row•er /ˈbɒrəʊə‖ˈbɑːroʊər, ˈbɔː-/ *n* [C] someone who has borrowed money, especially from a bank or BUILDING SOCIETY: *Borrowers pay 14% interest, due to rise to 15.5% on 1 November.*

bor•row•ing /ˈbɒrəʊɪŋ‖ˈbɑːroʊ-, ˈbɔː-/ *n* **1** [U] when a person, company, or country borrows money, or the amount of money that is borrowed: *Interest rates are low and borrowing is cheap.* | *Israel relies heavily upon foreign aid and borrowing to maintain its economy.*
bank borrowing [U] when people or companies borrow from banks, rather than using other forms of finance, such as shares or bonds: *Parker said it will finance the acquisition partly through bank borrowing.*
consumer borrowing [U] borrowing by people for their own spending, rather than by businesses: *Consumer borrowing went down in February.*
corporate borrowing [U] borrowing by businesses rather than by individuals: *An increase in corporate borrowing can be a good sign because it means companies are preparing for more demand for their own products and services.*
distress borrowing [U] when a person or company is forced to borrow money because they are in need of money or just in order to keep going or keep trading: *A rise in interest rates, particularly if it deepens a recession, may force many firms into distress borrowing merely to survive.*
federal borrowing [U] borrowing by the US government: *Federal borrowing has increased in the last decade.*
government borrowing [U] borrowing by a government in a particular country: *The chancellor shocked analysts with the news that government borrowing would double to £28 billion next year.*
2 borrowings [plural] the amount of money that a company or organization has borrowed: *Riva Group has completed a refinancing programme to reduce borrowings by £5.8 million to £6.9 million.*
net borrowings [plural] the difference between the amount a business has borrowed and the amount it has in cash: *The new share issue will reduce Sainsbury's net borrowings to about 13% of shareholders' funds from 44%.*

borrowing powers —see under POWER[1]

boss /bɒs‖bɒːs/ *n* [C] *informal* **1** the person who employs you or who is in charge of you at work: *I'll have to ask my boss for a day off.*
2 a manager with an important position in an organization: *What they need to do is lobby strongly for more women bosses.* | *Prison bosses launched an investigation into major security lapses.*
3 be your own boss to work for yourself rather than being employed by someone else: *He's looking forward to the day when he will be his own boss.*

Bos•ton ma•trix /ˌbɒstən ˈmeɪtrɪks/ *n* another name for the GROWTH/SHARE MATRIX

bot•tle•neck /ˈbɒtlnek‖ˈbɑː-/ *n* [C] a delay in one stage of a process that makes the whole process slower and more difficult: *He said the company would not be vulnerable to production bottlenecks because it has 10 subcontractors in the Far East where it does all its manufacturing.*

bot•tom[1] /ˈbɒtəm‖ˈbɑː-/ *n* [C usually singular] **1** the lowest point, position, or level: *Hopefully, we are finally seeing the bottom of this recession.* | *Short-term interest rates are now probably near their bottom.*
2 hit/reach (rock) bottom to get to the lowest possible point, position, or level in price or performance: *He believes gold prices have hit bottom or are close to it.* | *Thailand's economic slowdown may have reached bottom and signs are some sectors are recovering.*
3 the bottom drops/falls out of the market used to say that prices reach extremely low levels, with many businesses and people in financial difficulty: *The recession came and the bottom dropped out of the market for luxury houses.* | *The bottom fell out of the wool market and many farmers went bust.*

bottom[2] *v*
bottom out *phr v* [I] to stop getting worse and begin to improve again: *We think the business jet market has bottomed out and we see steady growth in the years ahead.*

bottom fisher *n* [C] FINANCE someone who invests in something when its value is at a very low level, expecting the situation to improve and the investment to increase in value: *McColl made his name as a bottom fisher, buying distressed banks at giveaway prices.*

bottom line *n* [C] *informal* **1** the figure showing a company's total profit or loss: *Club Med's bottom line* *showed a net profit of FFr173 million.* | *Cost-cutting moves under way at the banks should help bottom lines.*

2 the end result of something or the most important point about something: *Accounting doesn't change how much money you bring in; the bottom line is that their movies didn't do well.*

bought deal —see under DEAL[2]

bought ledger —see under LEDGER

bought note —see under NOTE[1]

bounce[1] /baʊns/ *v* **1** [I,T] BANKING if a cheque bounces or a bank bounces it, the bank will not pay any money because there is not enough money in the account of the person who wrote the cheque: *Every time a cheque bounces it costs me £3 in bank charges.* | *The TSB bounced the cheque and cancelled his overdraft.*

2 [I] FINANCE, ECONOMICS to quickly increase in price or amount, especially after having fallen: *Wolseley's shares bounced to 617p before settling back to 604p.* | *In February last year production bounced 1.4%.*

3 [I] FINANCE if a stockmarket bounces, it suddenly becomes very active and share prices rise: *Tokyo's beleaguered stock market bounced dramatically to erase some of its recent losses.*

bounce back *phr v* [I] to quickly increase or become successful again after falling or having problems: *Morgan Grenfell shares dropped immediately to 430p, before bouncing back almost as quickly to close at 468p.*

bounce[2] *n* [C] a sudden rise in something such as prices, sales, or share prices: *Economists agree that there could be a bounce in prices next year.* | *a bounce on Wall Street*

dead cat bounce FINANCE when a share price or stockmarket rises a small amount after a large fall, perhaps before falling further: *Manila ended seven straight days on the downside by pushing the index up 1.4% as investors bought property and banking bargains. 'It looks like a classic dead cat bounce,' said one broker.*

bound /baʊnd/ *adj* LAW **be bound** if someone is bound by a law, promise, or agreement, they have to do what it says: *The Ashford Railway Company is still bound by its contract with Riche.* | *The developer is* ***legally bound*** *to abide by the conditions in the planning permission.* | *The company was* ***bound by law*** *to provide electricity to all homes in the area.*

bourse /bʊəs‖bʊrs/ *n* [C] FINANCE the French word for a stockmarket, used to refer to a stockmarket anywhere outside Britain and North America: *The company has recently joined the* ***Paris bourse.***

bou•tique /buːˈtiːk/ *n* [C] **1** a small, specialized shop selling fashionable goods: *boutiques such as Cartier and Christian Dior.*

2 FINANCE a small, specialized financial services organization: *Independent Strategy, a new investment research boutique.*

box•car /ˈbɒkskɑː‖ˈbɑːkskɑːr/ *n* [C] *AmE* a railway carriage with high sides and a roof, used for carrying goods; BOX WAGON *BrE*

box number —see under NUMBER[1]

box office also **box-office** —see under OFFICE

box wagon *n* [C] *BrE* a railway carriage with high sides and a roof, used for carrying goods; BOXCAR *AmE*

BOY FINANCE beginning of year; used in documents when talking about the beginning of a financial year

boy•cott[1] /ˈbɔɪkɒt‖-kɑːt/ *v* [T] to refuse to buy something, use something, or take part in something, as a way of protesting: *In the past, Mandela had called for people to boycott South African goods.* | *Palestinian leaders threatened to boycott the talks.*

boycott[2] *n* [C] when people boycott something, or the period of time when it is boycotted: *In 1937 the cocoa farmers* ***imposed a boycott*** *on European imports.* | *He called for an end to the Arab* ***economic boycott*** *of Israel.*

secondary boycott a situation in which workers refuse to deal with goods made or sold by a different company, because the workers at that company are on STRIKE (=refusing to work) or have a serious disagreement with their management: *The legislation applies to airlines and railroads, where secondary boycotts are still legal.*

bpd *n* barrels per day; a way of measuring how much oil a country or area produces: *Venezuela's oil production has risen to over 3.5 million bpd.*

BPR abbreviation for BUSINESS PROCESS RE-ENGINEERING

brack•et /ˈbrækɪ̇t/ *n* [C] **1** a particular range that an amount or number, such as someone's income or age, falls into: *people in the 55–64* ***age bracket***

2 also **(income) tax bracket** one of the ranges of amounts that people's income is divided into for the purpose of deciding how much tax they should pay: *taxpayers in the 15% bracket* | *a rate of 35% in the* ***top bracket*** (=for people with the highest incomes)

bracket creep *n* [U] *AmE* when people earn more money, move to a higher tax bracket, and pay a higher percentage of their income in tax: *Bracket creep and high inflation raise real tax rates.*

brain•storm•ing /ˈbreɪnˌstɔːmɪŋ‖-ɔːr-/ *n* [U] a way of developing new ideas and solving problems by having a meeting where everyone makes suggestions and these are discussed: *Executives held a* ***brainstorming session*** *involving the sales force, editors, and others.*

branch /brɑːntʃ‖bræntʃ/ *n* [C] **1** an individual bank, shop, office etc that is part of a large organization: *HSS Hire Shops has 170 branches throughout the UK.* | *To talk to one of our specialist financial advisers, just contact your* ***local branch.***

2 a part of a government or a large organization that deals with one particular type of work: *The executive and judicial branches of government would be totally separate.*

3 *BrE* a small local organization that is part of a TRADE UNION; LOCAL *AmE*: *He is a former chairman of the Belfast branch of the National Union of Journalists.* | *She joined the strike support committee and started going to* ***branch meetings.***

branch manager —see under MANAGER

branch office —see under OFFICE

brand[1] /brænd/ *n* [C] MARKETING a name given to a product by a company so that the product can easily be recognized by its name or its design: *Virgin's aim is to ensure that all its products and services match and exploit the brand.* | *the Lancôme brand of cosmetics* | *This is a company with* ***strong brands*** *and a good position in many markets.* | *We* ***built*** *the Veuve Clicquot* ***brand*** *slowly over seven years.* | *Argos bought five factories and* ***developed*** *its own* ***brand*** *called Fortuna.*

consumer brand a brand for goods bought by the public rather than by businesses: *CPC provides major consumer brands such as Knorr soups and Hellmann's mayonnaise.*

dealer's brand a product sold in a supermarket or other large shop with a label that shows the name of the shop selling it. Dealer's brands are usually cheaper than other products of the same type

house brand also **own brand**, **store brand** *AmE* a brand for goods sold with the name of a shop, rather than the producer of the goods. House brands are usually cheaper than others: *Many supermarket chains have their own house brand cereals.*

stand-alone brand a brand that is only used for one type of product, rather than for several different types: *stand-alone brands like Ariel and Häagen-Dazs ice-cream*

B

B

brand² *v* [T] MARKETING to give a name to a product or group of products so that they can be easily recognized by their name or design: *We have made great efforts to brand Phaidon books, putting the Phaidon name on the front and back of all our books.* —**branding** *n* [U] *Branding has grown enormously this century, and there is hardly a consumer product which does not have a brand name or designation of some kind.*

brand association *n* [U] the way in which people think of a particular brand of product when they think of a particular activity because they are closely connected with each other: *Nike has started to build the same brand association it has with basketball with other sports.*

brand awareness —see under AWARENESS

brand development —see under DEVELOPMENT

brand development index —see under INDEX[1]

brand·ed /ˈbrændɨd/ *adj* branded goods or products have brand names and so can easily be recognized by their name or design: *The world's big drinks companies will increasingly displace local drinks with branded products.* —compare GENERIC, OWN-LABEL

brand equity —see under EQUITY

brand extension *n* [C,U] MARKETING adding a new product to an existing branded group of products: *Keystone Dry beer is a brand extension of the company's Keystone and Keystone Light brands.* —see also LINE EXTENSION

brand image —see under IMAGE

brand·ing /ˈbrændɪŋ/ *n* [U] when a company gives the same brand name to a number of its products. This helps to make the brand name well known and makes it more likely that people will buy new products from the same range

brand leader —see under LEADER

brand loyalty —see under LOYALTY

brand management —see under MANAGEMENT

brand manager —see under MANAGER

brand name *n* [C] the name given to a product by a company so that the product can easily be recognized by its name or design: *The company's brand names include Izond, Lacoste, and Evan Picone.* | *Swatch is a* ***well-known brand name*** *worldwide.*

brand potential —see under POTENTIAL[1]

brand share —see under SHARE

brand stretching *n* [U] MARKETING when a company starts to use an existing brand name on another different type of product, hoping that people will buy it because they recognize the name: *Virgin, the most quoted example of brand stretching, is in a delicate position because it relies on the reputation of one man: Richard Branson.*

brass /brɑːs‖bræs/ *n* [U] *AmE informal* the top managers in an organization; TOP BRASS: *Mr Sprey and the Air Force brass clashed continually over major elements of the plane's design.*

breach¹ /briːtʃ/ *n* **1** [C,U] LAW an action that breaks an agreement, rule, law etc: *The company wrote a letter of apology to the Israeli government, saying that any breach of the rules was unintentional.* | *They were* ***in breach of*** *London stock exchange regulations.*

anticipatory breach [C,U] LAW when one person or organization that has signed a contract says in advance that they cannot or will not perform their responsibilities. When this happens, the other person or organization involved can ask a court to make a decision about it

2 [C] a serious disagreement between people: *a new and serious breach between the US and Germany*

breach² *v* [T] LAW if someone breaches an agreement, rule, law etc, they break it: *Sumitomo asserted that the agency* ***breached its contract*** *to buy 41 cars.* | *They claim that the supplier had* ***breached their agreement.***

breach of agreement *n* plural **breaches of agreement** [C,U] LAW when someone fails to do something that they had promised to do in an agreement: *The company sued him for breach of agreement.* | *She was held to be* ***in breach of agreement.***

breach of confidence *n* plural **breaches of confidence** [C,U] LAW when someone gives away information that had been given to them as a secret: *For me to reveal the identities of these individuals would be a breach of confidence.* | *The knowledge was disclosed* ***in breach of confidence.***

breach of contract *n* plural **breaches of contract** [C,U] LAW when someone fails to do something that they have agreed to do in a contract: *Watson had to pay more than £55 million in damages for breach of contract.* | *Their tactic was to say that all striking drivers were* ***in breach of contract****, and fire them.*

breach of duty *n* plural **breaches of duty** [C,U] LAW when someone fails to do something that it is their duty to do according to the law or an agreement: *Their failure to reveal the risks associated with this product amounted to a serious breach of duty.*

breach of fi·du·ci·a·ry du·ty /ˌbriːtʃ əv fɪˌdjuːʃiəri ˈdjuːti‖-fɪˌduːʃieri ˈduːti/ *n* [singular] LAW when a person or company who has responsibility for managing other people's money fails to protect the interests of the people whose money they are managing

breach of trust *n* plural **breaches of trust** [C,U] LAW when someone does something illegal or wrong with money that they are trusted to take care of, or when someone fails to do something that they have been trusted to do as part of their job: *The former Minister was found guilty of appropriation of public funds, forgery and breach of trust.*

breach of warranty *n* plural **breaches of warranty** [C,U] LAW when someone fails to do something that they have agreed to do as part of a contract

bread and butter *n* [singular] if you earn your bread and butter doing something, you earn money from it to live: *Composing music for TV ads only earns my bread and butter – it's nothing creative.*

bread·line /ˈbredlaɪn/ *n* **1 be on/near the breadline** to be extremely poor: *They are not well-off, but they are not on the breadline.*

2 be below the breadline to be below the level which is officially considered to be extremely poor: *an estimate that over half the population was* ***living below the breadline***

bread·win·ner /ˈbredˌwɪnə‖-ər/ *n* [C] the member of a family who earns the money, or most of the money, to support the others: *She is now the family's main breadwinner.*

break¹ /breɪk/ *v* past tense **broke** past participle **broken** [T] **1** if someone breaks a law, rule, agreement etc, they do not do what it says they should do: *The survey claimed most motor dealers were* ***breaking the law*** *by not displaying vehicle prices properly.* | *If any direct debit is paid which breaks the terms of this instruction, the bank will make a refund.*

2 if employers break a STRIKE, they force the strikers to end it, perhaps with the help of the army or the police: *He broke the ambulancemen's strike by getting the army to answer emergency calls.* —see also STRIKEBREAKER

3 break even to neither make a profit nor lose money: *The company needs to charge $13 a ton to break even.* | *Retix Inc. warns that it expects sales to be down by 15%, and it may only break even.*

break down *phr v* **1** [T] **break** sth ↔ **down** to separate information or a total amount into parts, especially so that it is easier to understand: *Once the statistics are broken down, some clear patterns of employment begin to emerge.*
2 [I] if talks break down, they fail and come to an end because the people involved cannot agree: *The meeting between management and unions broke down and no progress was made.* —see alsobreakdown
break sth ↔ **up** *phr v* [I,T] **1** if a company or group breaks up or is broken up, it is divided into smaller companies: *The new chairman plans to break up the group into more autonomous subsidiaries.* —see also BREAK-UP
2 if someone breaks up an arrangement or agreement, or if it is broken up, it ends: *Japan's Fair Trade Commission ordered 13 ink makers to break up a price-fixing cartel.*

break² *n* [C] **1** a period of time when you stop working or stop what you are doing in order to rest, eat etc: *He was entitled to a forty-five minute* ***lunch break****. | Employers must provide people who work at computers with* ***rest breaks****.*
2 also **commercial break** a pause for advertisements during a television or radio programme: *We'll be back with more music after the break.*
3 FINANCE a sudden, large fall in market prices, especially the price of shares on a stockmarket: *The big break in cattle prices has forced ranchers to stop selling young cattle.*
4 a sudden or unexpected chance to do something, especially to be successful in your job: *She got her first break in 1951 on Broadway. | He did small commercials for Yellow Pages before getting his* ***big break*** *with the Porsche advert.*
5 a period of several weeks or years during which something stops, before continuing again + **in**: *If you have a break in paid employment for two complete consecutive tax years, you must pay full-rate contributions when you return to work.*
career break a period of time when you do not work in your usual job or profession, for example because you want to take care of your children: *women taking a career break to bring up a family* —see also TAX BREAK

break·ag·es /ˈbreɪkɪdʒɪ̈z/ *n* [plural] things that have been broken while you were using them, or the charges made for doing this: *Claims can arise between builders and sub-contractors for items such as damage, breakages and delays.*

break·down /ˈbreɪkdaʊn/ *n* **1** [C] a statement showing information or a total amount separated into parts so that it is easier to understand: *A spending breakdown showed the average household spent £47.70 on food per week. | Also in the report is a breakdown of when delays are most likely to occur.*
2 [C,U] when something fails or stops working properly, especially because people cannot agree + **of/in**: *At its worst, this legislation represents a total breakdown of the US budget process. | The company issued an apology, and said there had been a****breakdown in communications****.* —see also ***break down*** under BREAK¹

breakdown clause —see under CLAUSE

break·e·ven /ˌbreɪkˈiːvən◂/ also **break-even** *n* [U] when a company is neither making a profit or a loss: *Lump sum transfers would be required to ensure breakeven.*

break-even analysis —see under ANALYSIS

break-even chart —see under CHART¹

break-even point —see under POINT¹

break·out /ˈbreɪkaʊt/ *n* [C] **1** a very successful product, especially one that comes after a company has produced some less successful ones: *Iceberg is a potential breakout product that could make StorageTek the IBM of the '90s.*
2 more detailed information referring to part of a set of figures: *The report gives detailed breakouts of wage changes.*
3 a sudden increase: *Oil prices were on the edge of a major breakout, but turned down in late trading.*

break-up *n* [C] an occasion when a company or group is broken up into smaller units: *Break-ups create added tax, interest and management costs.* —see also ***break up*** under BREAK¹

break-up value —see under VALUE¹

brew·er /ˈbruːə‖-ər/ *n* [C] another name for a BREWERY

brew·er·y /ˈbruːəri/ also **brewer** *n* plural **breweries** [C] a company that makes and sells beer, or a factory where beer is made: *What makes this campaign unusual is that it's backed by a major brewery, Courage. | production manager of a large modern brewery*
independent brewery a company that makes and sells beer, especially one that has only one factory, or only a small number of factories, and that sells beers to any bar, restaurant etc

bribe¹ /braɪb/ *n* [C] an amount of money or something valuable that someone gives you to persuade you to help them or do something dishonest for them: *US citizens are forbidden by law to* ***offer bribes*** *to officials of foreign governments. | He was to be included in the investigation for allegedly* ***accepting bribes****.*

bribe² *v* [T] to dishonestly give money to someone to persuade them to do something that will help you: *His office-equipment firm had bribed politicians to win public-works contracts.*

brib·er·y /ˈbraɪbəri/ *n* [U] dishonestly giving money to someone to persuade them to do something to help you: *The International Chamber of Commerce has had rules against bribery and extortion since 1977.*

bricks and mortar *n* [U] *informal* buildings such as houses, offices, and factories: *The hospital would cost about £37 million in bricks and mortar and another £10 million for equipment.*

bridge loan —see under LOAN¹

brief¹ /briːf/ *n* [C] **1** official instructions that explain what someone's job is or what their duties are: *The auditor's brief is to monitor and report upon agencies' effectiveness. | The topic of your talk is specified in advance, and you will be expected to* ***keep to your brief****.*
creative brief MARKETING a document which gives details about how a product is to be advertised: *Many agencies have now arrived at a very similar format for creative briefs.*
design brief a set of instructions about what a new product should look like or what features it should have: *Part of Carvin's design brief was to keep the controls as simple and as familiar-looking as possible.*
watching brief when someone is given the job of watching the progress of part of a business, a series of events, or a court case for someone else: *Phil Coughlan had* ***kept a watching brief*** *in MRPII for some time.*
2 LAW a document prepared for a lawyer to use when representing a client in a court of law. The brief includes all the details of the case and all the points of law relating to it: *In the various briefs prepared for the Supreme Court, the major argument surrounded the notion of 'service abroad'.*
3 *BrE informal* a SOLICITOR: *It's time you got yourself a brief.*

brief² *v* [T] **1** to give someone the information they need about something, for example so that they can do work related to it: *Allen was in London yesterday to brief investors about the company's efforts to return to profitability.*

2 LAW to give instructions to a lawyer who will represent a client in court: *The usual action must be taken to retain and brief counsel.*

brief•case /'bri:fkeɪs/ *n* [C] a case used for carrying papers or documents

brief•ing /'bri:fɪŋ/ *n* [C] a meeting at which information or instructions are given: *The revenue estimates will be announced* ***at a news briefing*** *today.* | *More details will be given* ***in a briefing*** *for reporters later this week.*

B

bright /braɪt/ *adj* FINANCE if share trading is bright, there is a lot of activity and prices are rising: *Trading will be 'relatively bright' in the first half, with the Nikkei rising above 30,000.*

bring /brɪŋ/ *v* past tense and past participle **brought**
bring a case/charge/suit/lawsuit to organize a legal case against someone: *a string of lawsuits brought by jobseekers who think they're the victims of discrimination* | *Company directors are meeting with law enforcement officials to determine whether to bring criminal charges.*
bring sth ↔ **down** *phr v* [T] **1** to reduce a price or rate: *The bank has hinted that it might bring interest rates down even further.* | *The government hopes to bring inflation down to 5% this year.*
2 to cause a government or other authority to fail: *a bank scandal that helped to bring down the socialist administration*
bring sth ↔ **forward** *phr v* [T] **1** if you bring forward a meeting or other event that is going to take place in the future, you arrange for it to take place at an earlier time: *The next departmental meeting has been brought forward to the 10th.*
2 to move the total from a set of numbers that you are calculating onto the next page, so that you can add or take away other numbers from it: *The balance brought forward from the previous bank statement is £356.78.*
bring in *phr v* [T] **1 bring** sth ↔ **in** if something brings money in, it earns it: *Brokerage firms have been moving steadily toward paying brokers for the client money they bring in to the firm.*
2 bring sb ↔ **in** to employ someone from outside an organization to solve a problem or do a difficult job: *Mr. Edell has brought in an experienced Supreme Court lawyer and academic, Prof. Laurence Tribe of Harvard, to handle the case.*
bring sth ↔ **out** *phr v* [T] if a company brings out a new product, it starts producing and selling it: *Ford is set to bring out three new models this month.*

brisk /brɪsk/ *adj* business or trading that is brisk is very busy, with a lot of products, shares etc bought and sold: *Restaurants do brisk business at Thanksgiving.* | *Following several days of brisk trading, the junk bond market was quiet.*

Brit /brɪt/ written abbreviation for Britain or British

British Bankers' Association —see BBA

British Institute of Management *n* a professional organization for managers in Britain, that provides information, education, and training

British Standard abbreviation **BS** *n* [C] a standard of quality set by the British Standards Institution

British Standards Institution abbreviation **BSI** *n* a British organization that sets standards of quality in building, ENGINEERING, and products used in the home. Products that are recognized by the Bitish Standards Institution have a special symbol on them to show that they are of good quality: *a lock bearing the British Standards Institution 'Kite mark'*

British ton —see under TON

broad money —see under MONEY

bro•chure /'brəʊʃə, -ʃʊə‖broʊ'ʃʊr/ *n* [C] a thin book giving information or advertising something: *Send for a free brochure today.* | *A company brochure says Lifetime expects sales of $250 million next year.*

broke /brəʊk/ *adj informal* **1** having no money at all or very little money: *By 1933 his career was over and he was broke.*
2 flat broke *AmE* **stony broke** *BrE* completely without money; PENNILESS: *The Contra Costa County district is flat broke and says it will not keep schools open past Tuesday.*

bro•ker[1] /'brəʊkə‖'broʊkər/ *n* [C] FINANCE a person or organization that buys and sells SECURITIES, currencies, property, insurance etc for others: *The success of Independent Insurance comes from a close relationship with its brokers, who take a commission for acting as go-betweens with clients.*
agency broker a broker that buys and sells shares for clients without keeping supplies of shares itself, unlike BROKER-DEALERS and MARKETMAKERS: *The trend in London is towards US-style agency brokers, despite James Capel's recent switch to marketmaking.*
air broker a person or organization whose job is selling space on aircraft for the transport of goods
bond broker a person or organization that trades in bonds
commercial broker a person or organization that buys and sells commercial property for others
commission broker a broker who is paid a percentage of what they buy or sell
commodity broker a broker that buys and sells things such as oil, metals, and agricultural products
deposit broker someone whose job is to arrange for money to be paid by one bank into accounts at other banks: *Wall Street deposit brokers, who transfer government-insured $100,000 blocks of certificates of deposit to S&Ls paying the highest interest rates*
discount broker a broker that buys and sells shares at low cost: *One thing discount brokers don't offer is investment advice.*
electronic broker a broker that buys and sells using a completely electronic system
floor broker a broker that trades on a market face-to-face, not on a computer or the telephone
foreign exchange broker a broker that trades in currencies
government broker the STOCKBROKER in Britain who is employed by the government to buy and sell GOVERNMENT SECURITIES on the London STOCK EXCHANGE under the instructions of the Bank of England. Usually the government broker buys government securities when their price is weak and needs support, and sells them later when their price is stronger
honest broker *n* [C] someone who tries to help people or organizations do a deal or solve a disagreement, by talking to each side, seeing what each one wants, and being fair to all of them: *He acted as an honest broker in the dispute.*
insurance broker a person or organization whose job is to give people advice about insurance and to sell the insurance policies of different insurance companies
issue broker a broker that sells shares that are being made available for the first time in a SHARE ISSUE
marine insurance broker INSURANCE a person or company that earns money by providing independent advice about the best type of insurance to buy for a ship or its cargo (=goods carried by a ship) in order to decide how much money the insurer must pay when a CLAIM for loss or damage is made. The insurer asks a SURVEYOR to do the examination and produce a report based on it
money broker a broker that arranges deals between banks lending money to each other

real estate broker *AmE* a broker that buys and sells land, property, and buildings; REAL ESTATE AGENT *AmE*; ESTATE AGENT *BrE* —see also SHIPBROKER, STOCKBROKER

broker² *v* [T] to arrange the details of a deal etc so that everyone can agree to it: *Ovitz brokered the multibillion-dollar Japanese acquisitions of Columbia and MCA.* | *IBM eventually* ***brokered a deal*** *in which Silicon Valley Group bought the business from Perkin-Elmer.*

bro•ker•age /ˈbrəʊkərɪdʒ‖ˈbroʊ-/ *n* **1** [C] also **brokerage house** an organization of brokers: *Brunswick, a Moscow-based brokerage* | *The credibility of a brokerage or bank can disappear overnight, and when it does, so does the firm.*

discount brokerage [C] a brokerage that buys and sells investments for its clients, without offering them investment advice

full service brokerage [C] a brokerage that offers investment advice: *full-service brokerage firms such as Merrill Lynch & Co. which, unlike the discounters, provide investment advice and research along with trading*

on-line brokerage [C] a brokerage that allows clients to buy and sell investments over the INTERNET

2 [U] the work done by brokers: *Its basic business of retail brokerage is slow.* | *The electricity company saved $520,000 in* ***brokerage fees*** *by selling the bonds directly to investors.*

broker-dealer *n* [C] FINANCE a broker that buys and sells SECURITIES for clients and also trades on its own account

broker-dealer fund —see under FUND¹

broker's lien —see under LIEN

brok•ing /ˈbrəʊkɪŋ‖ˈbroʊ-/ especially *BrE n* [U] the business or profession of brokers: *the world's largest tea* ***broking firm*** | *Japanese brokers face intense competition from foreign* ***broking houses.*** | *Total* ***broking fees*** *for the Telstra flotation are put at A$125 million.*

Brook•ings In•sti•tu•tion /ˈbrʊkɪŋ ɪnstəˌtjuːʃən‖-ˌtuː-/ *n* a non-profit organization in the US that produces studies about economic and social subjects: *a paper soon to be published by the Brookings Institution*

Bros written abbreviation for brothers, used especially in the names of companies: *Warner Bros Records*

brownfield site —see under SITE¹

brown goods —see under GOODS

brows•er /ˈbraʊzə‖-ər/ *n* [C] COMPUTING a computer program that allows users to look at information from the INTERNET

B/S also **B.S.**, **b/s**, **b.s.** written abbreviation for BILL OF SALE

BS abbreviation for BRITISH STANDARD

B-school *n* [C] *journalism* another name for BUSINESS SCHOOL: *To find more and better MBA students, B-schools have talked about the vast quantity of money their students are likely to earn upon graduation.*

B shares —see under SHARE

BSI abbreviation for BRITISH STANDARDS INSTITUTION

bub•ble /ˈbʌbəl/ *n* [C] **1** when a lot of people buy shares in a company that is financially weak, with the result that the price of the shares becomes much higher than their real value: *A* ***speculative bubble*** *may have been responsible for the rapid rise in equity prices in 1987.* | *The 1980s boom, when property and stock prices soared and created the* ***bubble economy,*** *is over.*

2 the bubble bursts if the bubble bursts in a particular area of business, a period of growth and success ends suddenly: *Software companies enjoyed rapid expansion before the bubble burst and market growth slowed.*

bubblejet printer —see under PRINTER

buc•ca•neer /ˌbʌkəˈnɪə‖-ˈnɪr/ *n* [C] someone who succeeds in business by using strong and unusual methods, and perhaps by cheating: *Airlines attracted the attention of corporate buccaneers.* —**buccaneering** *n* [U] *The most infamous example of the new buccaneering spirit in British boardrooms was the Guinness affair.*

buck¹ /bʌk/ *n* [C] *AmE informal* a dollar: *I owe 500 bucks but I haven't paid yet.* | *I hope that you guys can* ***make a buck*** (=earn some money) *out of it.* | *There are* ***big bucks*** (=a lot of money) *to be made from sport.* | *We won't sacrifice investments in research and development for the sake of* ***a fast buck*** (=money that you can make quickly and easily).

buck² *v* **1 buck the system** to do something that goes against the rules or against the normal way of doing something: *Many inventors attempted to buck the system by making alterations to existing machinery.*

2 buck a trend to do well in business when other companies are doing badly: *Britain will buck the global recessionary trend next year with growth of around 1.1pc.*

bucket shop —see under SHOP¹

Bud•get /ˈbʌdʒət/ *n* [C] an official statement that a government makes about how much it intends to spend and what the rates of taxes will be for the next year or six months: *There is a great deal in the Budget to help investment.* | *This year's Budget is expected to include measures to help small businesses.*

budget¹ *n* [C] FINANCE, ACCOUNTING **1** a detailed plan made by an organization or a government of how much it will receive as income over a particular period of time, and how much it will spend, what it will spend the money on etc: *Each year business managers* ***draw up a budget*** *and suggest a series of financial targets.* | *The President has promised to* ***balance the*** *government's* ***budget*** (=make sure that no more is spent than is received as income) *within three years.*

advertising budget an organization's spending plan for advertising during a particular period of time: *Procter and Gamble spends nearly 90% of its $3 billion advertising budget on TV commercials.*

austerity budget a national budget which aims to reduce the amount of money that people spend, for example by increasing taxes, or to reduce the amount that the government spends: *The Danish government presented an austerity budget which it said would reduce the national deficit.*

balanced budget a budget in which no more is spent than is received: *New York state has failed to achieve a balanced budget in six of the past eight years.*

capital budget a business's plans for spending on land, property, equipment etc in a particular period of time: *The airline plans to cut its capital budget and said it won't buy some of the 437 jets it had planned to acquire.*

cash budget a financial document that shows how much money a business is expected to have at the beginning and end of a particular period of time and how much money it will receive and pay out within that period: *A cash budget is prepared to ensure that the organization has sufficient cash to meet the ongoing needs of the business.*

unbalanced budget a budget in which more money is spent than is received

2 the amount of money that an organization has to spend on a particular activity in a given period of time, usually a year: *Hospital caterers have a budget of about £10 per person per week.* | *The service operates on a very* ***tight budget*** (=with very little money to spare). | *The film was made on a* ***shoestring budget*** (=a very small budget). —see also MINI-BUDGET

3 on a budget if you are on a budget, you have to do something with as little money as possible: *Our self catering apartments are popular with those on a budget.*

budget² *v* [I,T] to carefully plan and control how much you spend **budget (sth) for sth**: *$100 million has been budgeted for fees and expenses.* —**budgeted** *adj*: *The group has been trading slightly below budgeted levels.* | *the gap between budgeted sales and turnover*

bud·get·a·ry /ˈbʌdʒətəri‖-teri/ *adj* [only before a noun] relating to a budget and how much money is available to spend: *This is not the first year in which **budgetary cuts** have had to be made.* | *He hired an extra bodyguard, but **budgetary constraints*** (=spending limits) *have prevented him from getting a bulletproof car.* | *About 30 states suffered **budgetary problems** during the past fiscal year.*

budgetary accounting —see under ACCOUNTING

budgetary control —see under CONTROL¹

Budget Day *n* the day on which the British government's Budget is presented to the House of Commons by the Chancellor of the Exchequer: *Even Cabinet ministers may not hear of these decisions until Budget Day.*

budget deficit —see under DEFICIT

bud·get·ing /ˈbʌdʒətɪŋ/ *n* [U] ACCOUNTING, FINANCE preparing budgets in order to plan and control the financial management of a person, business, or country: *The job includes business planning, budgeting and all financial and administrative systems.*

zero-based budgeting planning spending by looking at what actually needs to be done in the next period, without taking into account this period's budget: *Carter had zero-based budgeting, an attempt to justify anew every dollar federal agencies spent.*

budget surplus —see under SURPLUS¹

buff·er /ˈbʌfə‖-ər/ *n* [C] **1** COMPUTING a place in a computer's memory for storing information temporarily: *Any data still in the file buffer is written to the file before the file is closed.*
2 something that protects something from unpleasant effects: *Many managers raised cash as a buffer against falling stocks last year, easing their overall losses.*

buffer stock —see under STOCK¹

bug /bʌg/ *n* [C] COMPUTING a fault in the system of instructions that operates a computer: *Custom-made software is often more reliable and has fewer 'bugs' or faults.*

Millennium bug [singular] a problem with the way many computers were programmed, meaning that they could not recognize the change in the date at the beginning of the year 2000: *The design team is competing with four other companies for the contract to design a suitable 'Millennium bug' logo.*

build /bɪld/ *v* past tense and past participle **built** [T]
1 to make or put together large things such as buildings, cars, ships, roads etc: *New offices are being built on the site.* | *No new ships are being built at the yard now.* | *Sales of cars built in the US are falling.*
2 also **build up** to create something over a long period of time by adding to it gradually: *a peasant's son who built an enormous business empire* | *Gerald Ratner, the marketing whiz who built Ratners Group PLC into the world's biggest jewelery concern* | *Pierrel has built up a formidable sales force.* | *The government has recently built up currency reserves by buying U.S. dollars.*
3 when lawyers build a case, they put together facts, information etc to try to convince a court that someone is innocent or guilty: *He said prosecutors had built a case based on circumstantial evidence* (=evidence that can make you believe that something happened, but does not prove that it did).

build·er /ˈbɪldə‖-ər/ *n* [C] **1** a person or company that builds or repairs buildings: *He called in a local firm of builders.*

cowboy builder *informal* a house builder with no proper training or official QUALIFICATIONS who does work of a low standard: *Do-it-yourself decorators and cowboy builders are ruining Britain's historic towns.*

custom builder someone who builds houses that are specially designed and built for a particular customer

speculative builder a person or company that buys land and builds property in areas where they think people will want to buy it, but without having any definite orders before they start work: *the building of a new housing estate by a local speculative builder*

2 ship/car/bridge/railway etc builder a company that makes ships, cars, bridges etc: *Orders for 10 tankers were placed with NE ship builders.*

build·ing /ˈbɪldɪŋ/ *n* [U] the business of building houses, offices, factories etc: *The **building industry** is still in recession.*

building code —see under CODE

building contractor —see under CONTRACTOR

building lease —see under LEASE²

building permit —see under PERMIT

building regulation —see under REGULATION

buildings and contents insurance —see under INSURANCE

building society *n* plural **building societies** [C] *BrE* FINANCE an organization providing financial services to customers, especially lending money in the form of MORTGAGES to buy a house or flat and paying interest to savers. Building societies were originally formed to help people buy or build houses with money from people who saved with the society: *I would have been better off investing in a building society investment account.*

building society interest —see under INTEREST

build-to-order *adj* [only before a noun] build-to-order products are specially made for a particular customer, according to what the customer wants: *the success of build-to-order computers such as Dell's* —compare BUILD-TO-STOCK

build-to-stock *adj* [only before a noun] build-to-stock products are made in a standard way for all customers: *build-to-stock business platforms* —compare BUILD-TO-ORDER

bulk /bʌlk/ *n* **1 the bulk of sth** the main or largest part of something: *The change in the tax system will affect the bulk of the population.* | *The bulk of the meetings would be held in Washington.*
2 if you buy, sell, or make something in bulk, you buy, sell, or make large amounts of it: *Small traders are unable to compete with larger companies which buy and sell in bulk.* | *a bulk shipment of medical supplies*
3 in bulk stored loose, not packed in containers: *the first Grain Warehouse for the storage of grain in bulk*

bulk buying *n* [U] buying goods in large quantities, which is usually cheaper than buying in small quantities: *Costs might be lowered through bulk buying or the better management of production.*

bulk cargo —see under CARGO

bulk carrier —see under CARRIER

bulk discount —see under DISCOUNT¹

bulk freight —see under FREIGHT¹

bulk shipment —see under SHIPMENT

bull /bʊl/ *n* [C] FINANCE someone who thinks that prices of shares, bonds, currencies, etc are going to rise, and who will therefore keep and buy investments: *Bulls predict the Dow Jones will go beyond 13,000.* | *A growing group of **dollar bulls*** (=people who think the price of the dollar is going to rise) *has kept the dollar on a firm footing.* —compare BEAR

bulldog bond —see under BOND

bulletin board *n* [C] **1** *especially AmE* a large board fixed to a wall where people can put notes and messages for other people to read; NOTICE BOARD *BrE*
2 electronic bulletin board a place on an computer information system where you read or leave messages

bullet loan —see under LOAN[1]

bullet point *n* [C] a black circle appearing before each item in a list on a document made using a computer

bul·lion /ˈbʊljən/ *n* [U] FINANCE bars of gold, silver, or PLATINUM of an officially approved quality, valued by weight rather than what they would be worth as coins: *The price of gold bullion remains a sensitive index of confidence in the international market.*

bul·lish /ˈbʊlɪʃ/ *adj* FINANCE expecting prices on a financial market to rise or economic activity to increase: *We're not bullish in terms of an art market recovery this year.* | *Good results from Schering encouraged a* ***bullish mood*** *in pharmaceuticals.* + **on**: *It's hard to find analysts who aren't bullish on banks.* —compare BEARISH

bull market —see under MARKET[1]

bull position —see under POSITION[1]

bull run —see under RUN[2]

Bun·des·bank /ˈbʊndəz ˌbæŋk/ *n* BANKING Germany's central bank; DEUTSCHE BUNDESBANK: *The Bundesbank has announced increases in its discount and Lombard rates.*

bun·dle[1] /ˈbʌndl/ *n informal* **1** [singular] a lot of money: *Comdisco* ***made a bundle*** *selling its old equipment to a smaller dealer.*
2 [C] a group of products or services that are provided together with other products or services: *The $849 bundle includes two copies of the software, cables, and an electronic mail application.*

bundle[2] *v* [T] to provide a product or service together with other products or services: *Image editing software is bundled with many digital cameras.* —**bundling** *n* [U] *interactive media services, a bundling of Internet, video-on-demand, and home shopping*

buoy /bɔɪ‖ˈbuːi, bɔɪ/ *v* [T] if the market or prices are buoyed, people feel confident and buy stocks and shares, and prices rise: *In Britain, bond prices were buoyed by a rise in the pound.* | *The market was buoyed by gains in some large telecommunications shares.*

buoy·ant /ˈbɔɪənt‖ˈbɔɪənt, ˈbuːjənt/ *adj* a buoyant market, economy etc is successful and has a lot of trading activity, and prices are rising rather than falling: *There is also a buoyant market for expensive Swiss watches.* | *Sterling lost ground against a buoyant German mark.* —**buoyancy** *n* [U] *The trends in consumer spending scarcely suggest a lack of economic buoyancy.* | *the continued buoyancy of domestic demand, which grew by 7.7% this year*

bur·den /ˈbɜːdn‖ˈbɜːrdn/ *n* [C] **1** something that causes people a lot of difficulty or worry: *In less prosperous areas the taxes were, for many, such a burden that they lived in poverty.*
2 particular costs such as taxes or interest payments seen as a problem, especially when they are high: *the burden of local rates that each company located in the area must pay* | *New regulations can put a heavy* ***cost burden*** *on small businesses.* | *The rise in the US* ***tax burden*** (=the amount of tax that people and companies have to pay) *has not been due to military spending, but to welfare.* | *They want a $10,000 limit on deductions for state and local income taxes as a way to increase the tax burden on the rich.*
debt burden the amount of debt that a business or country has; DEBT LOAD: *a major restructuring by the company to cut its $500 million debt burden*
3 LAW a duty that someone has legally or officially promised to do: *The holder of the bill of lading would* ***assume the burden*** (=take the responsibility) *of becoming subject to contractual liabilities.*

burden of proof *n* [singular] LAW the task of proving that a statement made in a court of law is true, especially one accusing somebody of doing something illegal or wrong: *It will not be up to the defendant to prove his innocence, the burden of proof is on the prosecution.*

bu·reau /ˈbjʊərəʊ‖ˈbjʊroʊ/ *n* [C] plural **bureaux** *BrE* or **bureaus** **1** an office, organization, or department that collects or gives out information: *the Citizens Advice Bureau* | *the tourist information bureau* —see also BETTER BUSINESS BUREAU
credit bureau an organization that collects and sells information on whether individuals have borrowed money in the past and whether they have repaid it. The credit bureau sells this information to institutions that lend money so that they can decide whether or not to lend to a particular person
2 *AmE* a government department or part of a government department: *the Federal Bureau of Alcohol, Tobacco and Firearms*
3 an office of a company or organization that is not its main office or base: *The international environmental organization Greenpeace has established its own Moscow bureau.*

bu·reauc·ra·cy /bjʊəˈrɒkrəsi ‖bjʊˈrɑː-/ *n* plural **bureaucracies** **1** [C] a system of government that uses a large number of departments and officials: *a powerful centralized bureaucracy*
2 [U] *disapproving* all the complicated rules and processes of an official system, especially when they are confusing or responsible for causing a delay: *the mountain of bureaucracy which blocks the path of aid workers trying to bring help to a country in desperate need*

bu·reau·crat /ˈbjʊərəkræt‖ˈbjʊr-/ *n* [C] an official working in a bureaucracy, especially one who obeys the rules very strictly: *the politicians and bureaucrats who run the EU*

bu·reau·crat·ic /ˌbjʊərəˈkrætɪk◂‖ˌbjʊr-/ *adj disapproving* involving or having a lot of complicated and unnecessary official rules: *The group has had a history of being very bureaucratic and very slow moving*

bureau de change /ˌbjʊərəʊ də ʃɒndʒ‖ˌbjʊroʊ də ˈʃɑːndʒ/ *n* plural **bureaux de change** [C] an office where people can change foreign money into local currency or buy other currencies

Bureau of Customs *n* in the US, the part of the DEPARTMENT OF THE TREASURY responsible for collecting taxes on imports. In Britain the department is called the BOARD OF CUSTOMS AND EXCISE

bur·glar·y /ˈbɜːgləri‖ˈbɜːr-/ *n* plural **burglaries** [C,U] the crime of entering a building illegally and stealing things: *The figures show that household burglary rose by 17%.*

burn /bɜːn‖bɜːrn/ *v* past tense and past participle **burned** or **burnt** [T] **1** COMPUTING to copy information held on a computer's HARD DRIVE onto a CD ROM
2 be/get burned *informal* to lose a lot of money in a business deal, usually because it involves a high risk: *A lot of investors got burned buying junk bonds which turned out to be worthless.*
3 burn your fingers/get your fingers burnt *informal* to suffer from the results of an unsuccessful business activity: *Since burning their fingers on 100% lending that turned into bad debt, lenders have been limiting borrowing to 75% of the property's value.*

burn·out /ˈbɜːnaʊt‖ˈbɜːrn-/ *n* [C] **1** a feeling of extreme tiredness and lack of energy caused by working too hard: *With longer vacations you would see less burnout and higher productivity.*
2 *AmE* when people stop doing something because they are tired of doing it or feel they have been asked to do it

too much: *Donor burnout grows as requests for money increase and fewer people can afford to give.*

bur•sar /ˈbɜːsə‖ˈbɜːrsər/ *n* [C] **1** someone whose job is to deal with the accounts and finances of a college or university

2 a college or university student in Scotland who receives a bursary

bur•sa•ry /ˈbɜːsəri‖ˈbɜːr-/ *n* plural **bursaries** [C] **1** in the US, the place at a college or university where the accounts and finance are dealt with

2 in Britain, an amount of money given to some students by a college or university to help them study there. Bursaries are also given by the government or other organizations —compare GRANT[1]

busi•ness /ˈbɪznəs/ *n* **1** [U] the production, buying, and selling of goods or services for profit: *Students on the course learn about all aspects of business.* | *We are* ***in business*** *to create profit.* | *Colgate says it will never* ***do business with*** *the bank again.* | *Mr Guerlain learned the perfume business in Grasse.* —see also REPEAT BUSINESS

2 go into business to start working in the production, buying, and selling of goods or services: *She wanted to quit working as a hostess and go into business on her own.*

3 go out of business to stop operating as a company, usually because of BANKRUPTCY: *1,800 furniture store companies went out of business last year.*

4 business is business used to say that profit is the most important thing: *With these guys, business is business, and charity and public works are not part of it.*

5 [U] the work that you do as part of your job: *Adam's in Argentina* ***on business****.* | *Companies are looking hard at the need for many* ***business trips****.*

6 [C] a person or organization that produces and sells goods or services: *Do you want to manage your own business?* | *She* ***runs a business*** *finding and restoring old cars.* | *Levi says it will invest $20 million in a jeans business in Poland.*

big business [U] ◆ very large companies considered as a powerful group with a lot of influence: *Reformers are trying to cut the links between government and big business.*

◆ a product or activity where a lot of money is involved: *Pet food is big business.* | *Trafficking in stolen cars has become big business across eastern Europe.*

core business [C] the business that makes the most money for a company and that is considered to be its most important and central one: *US car maker Chrysler is to sell off its $1billion technology arm to concentrate resources on its core business.*

e-business [U] electronic business; the practice of buying and selling goods and services and carrying on other business activities by computer, especially over the INTERNET; E-COMMERCE

family business [C] a business that is owned and managed by members of the same family: *Diamond Publishing is a* ***small family business****.*

one-man business [C] a business run by one person only: *He runs a small one-man business as a builder.*

organizing business also **organising business** *BrE* [U] companies involved in making or selling things that help people organize their lives, such as personal computers, videos etc: *The growing organizing business is also taking advantage of a change in retailing habits.*

show business [U] the entertainment industry, for example television, films, and popular music: *Few industries rely on show business as heavily as magazines do.*

small business [C] a business with not many employees, or these businesses considered as a whole: *They run a small business in Dorset.* | *computers for the home, education and small business markets* —see also SME

7 [U] the amount of work a company has or is doing: *Soon he had so much business he had to subcontract.* | *The company isn't doing much business in Japan.* | *The economy is growing, jobs are plentiful and* ***business is good****.* | *The promotional fares are designed to* ***drum up business*** (=increase it) *during the slower fall period.*

8 [U] work that must be done in a particular job or period of time: *We discussed this week's business.* | *the routine business of government* —see also AOB

9 get down to business to start dealing with an important subject: *He offers juice or tea before getting down to business.*

10 business as usual used to tell you that a shop or business is working normally when you might think it was working in a different way, or was closed: *The retailer says it intends to do business as usual during its reorganization.* | *The market is shut today for Bastille day, but tomorrow it is business as usual.*

business activity code —see under CODE

business advice centre —see under CENTRE

business agent —see under AGENT

business angel /ˌbɪznəs eɪndʒəl/ *n* [C] FINANCE a private investor who puts money into new business activities, especially ones based on advanced technical ideas: *In the UK, business angels are a more important source of investment for start-ups than venture capital funds.*

business card —see under CARD

business class fare —see under FARE

business combination —see under COMBINATION

business community —see under COMMUNITY

business confidence —see under CONFIDENCE

business continuity services *n* [plural] services provided to companies so that they can continue operating if they are affected by a serious event such as a fire, computer failure etc: *Guardian are the largest supplier of business continuity services – disaster recovery is their speciality.*

business cycle —see under CYCLE

business development center —see under CENTRE

business empire —see under EMPIRE

business entity —see under ENTITY

business ethics —see under ETHICS

business finance —see under FINANCE[1]

business game —see under GAME

business gift —see under GIFT

business hours *n* [plural] the normal hours when shops, offices, and banks are open, usually between 9 am and 5 or 6 pm in the English-speaking world: *Deliveries are only accepted during normal business hours.*

business interruption insurance —see under INSURANCE

business interruption policy —see under INSURANCE POLICY

business liability insurance —see under INSURANCE

business life and health insurance —see under INSURANCE

busi•ness•like /ˈbɪznəs-laɪk/ *adj* practical and effective in the way you work and organize things, or in your behaviour and appearance: *an attempt to run the department in a businesslike way* | *Wearing a suit makes me feel more businesslike.*

busi•ness•man /ˈbɪznəsmən/ *n* plural **businessmen** [C] a man who works at a high level in a company, or who owns a company: *a successful American businessman*

business manager —see under MANAGER

business mix —see under MIX

business owner's insurance policy —see under INSURANCE POLICY

busi•ness•per•son /ˈbɪznɪsˌpɜːsən‖-ˌpɜːr-/ *n* plural **businesspeople** [C usually plural] a businessman or businesswoman: *The hotel is owned by a group of Japanese businesspeople.*

business plan —see under PLAN[2]

business process re-engineering abbreviation **BPR** *n* [U] when a business tries to improve its performance in every area, not just manufacturing, by completely redesigning systems, processes etc, rather than changing the existing ones: *Business process re-engineering totally reshapes the company to take advantage of new technologies.*

business property and liability insurance —see under INSURANCE

business reply mail —see under MAIL[1]

business reply service *n* [C] *BrE* in Britain, an arrangement between a company and the POST OFFICE that lets members of the public return mail to the company without paying. The cost of returning the mail is paid for by the company.

business strategy —see under STRATEGY

business-to-business advertising —see under ADVERTISING

business trust —see under TRUST

busi•ness•wom•an /ˈbɪznɪsˌwʊmən/ *n* plural **businesswomen** [C] a woman who works at a high level in a company, or who owns a company: *a highly successful businesswoman*

bust[1] /bʌst/ *adj informal* **go bust** if a business goes bust, it cannot continue to operate because it does not have enough money to pay its debts: *International Investments Ltd eventually went bust, leaving debts of £7 million.*

bust[2] *v* past tense and past participle **bust**

bust sth ↔ **up** *phr v* [T] *informal* to break a unit such as a company or department into parts, or to end it completely: *The auto maker may have to bust up the finance unit or sharply limit the credit it extends to buyers and dealers.*

bust-up *n* [C] **1** when a unit such as a company or department is broken into parts

2 *journalism* when people disagree strongly: *a boardroom bust-up, when the chief executive walked out after six weeks in the job*

bust-up acquisition —see under ACQUISITION

bus•y /ˈbɪzi/ *adj* comparative **busier** superlative **busiest**

1 *AmE* a telephone that is busy is being used; ENGAGED *BrE*

2 someone who is busy is working and is not available: *Mr Bullon is busy right now – can you phone back after lunch?* + **with**: *I've been busy with customers all morning*

3 a busy period is full of work: *Christmas is one of Oxford Street's busiest times of the year.*

button-down also **buttoned-down** *adj* [only before a noun] a button-down company or style is formal and traditional: *Wearing cowboy boots and open-necked shirts, he did not fit in with the button-down culture of IBM.*

buy[1] /baɪ/ *v* past tense and past participle **bought** [T]

1 to get something by paying money for it: *We just cannot afford to buy a new car.* **buy sb sth**: *Come on, I'll buy you lunch.*

2 if a sum of money buys something, you can get it for that amount of money: *£100,000 should buy a decent house, especially outside London.* **buy sb sth**: *A dollar won't even buy you a cup of coffee these days.*

3 buy a pig in a poke *informal* to buy something without seeing it or looking at it carefully, that turns out to be bad value: *House purchasers must satisfy themselves through legal advisers or surveyors that they are not buying a pig in a poke.*

4 buy a pup FINANCE *informal* to be cheated into buying something that is not good value: *If he has bought a pup, it is highly unlikely that any other shrewd financier would buy it from him.*

5 buy (sth) long FINANCE to buy and hold stocks, shares etc expecting their price to rise

buy sth ↔ **down** *phr v* [T] a lender who buys down interest rates makes them lower for the borrower: *RP Builders will buy down interest rates and provide lower down payments for black buyers.*

buy sth ↔ **forward** *phr v* [T] to agree a price for something now for delivery in the future

buy sth ↔ **in** *phr v* [T] if an organization buys in parts or services, it gets them from another company, rather than produce them itself: *Under the new system, schools have to buy in the services of advisers and librarians.*

buy into sth *phr v* [T] **1** to buy part of a company or business: *A lot of US companies are buying into Japanese firms.*

2 to invest in something: *In momentum investing, the name of the game is being the first investor to buy into a stock, and the first investor to sell out before bad news breaks.*

3 to believe in something completely: *My last employer expected us to buy into the ideas of every new American business guru, without question.*

buy sb ↔ **off** *phr v* [T] to pay someone money or give them something they want to stop them causing trouble or doing something that harms you: *Companies bought off the threat of trouble with high wage settlements in the prosperous 1950s.*

buy sb/sth ↔ **out** *phr v* [T] **1** to buy all of someone's shares in a business that you previously owned together, giving you complete control: *The publishing family plan to buy out the shares they do not own in Pergamon AGB.*

2 to buy a business: *Samsung has bought out American PC maker AST Research.* —see also BUYOUT

buy sth ↔ **up** *phr v* [T] to quickly buy as much as possible of something such as land or tickets: *Much of the land has been bought up by property developers.*

buy[2] *n* **be a good/bad etc buy** to be worth or not worth the money being paid: *Do you think a second-hand car is a good buy? | These prices are only a guide and it's worth shopping around for the best buy.*

best buy [C] a product that has been carefully tested and that a consumer organization says offers the best value for money in relation to other similar products: *Today's vacuum cleaners have a confusing array of features, so GHI tested a range of models to find the best buys.*

impulse buy [C] something which is bought without planning or choosing carefully: *Motorcycles are often an impulse buy.*

buy-and-sell agreement —see under AGREEMENT

buy•back /ˈbaɪbæk/ also **buy-back** *n* [C] **1** when someone buys something that they previously had sold: *Good economic data strengthened sterling and prompted buybacks of the currency. | Porsche's* ***buyback scheme*** *will guarantee a value of 55% of the car's purchase price at the end of three years.*

2 FINANCE when a company buys its own shares from existing shareholders; BUY-IN

3 FINANCE when the owners of a company previously sold to another become independent again by buying their shares from the new owners: *William A Robinson, a Chicago marketing agency acquired three years ago by Ketchum Communications, completed its buyback from Ketchum and renamed itself Robinson & Maites.*

B

buy·er /ˈbaɪə‖-ər/ *n* **1** [C] someone who is buying something: *After three weeks, the family had a buyer for their three-bedroomed home.*

impulse buyer [C] someone who buys goods without planning or choosing carefully: *Books with attractive jacket designs can be sold to impulse buyers.*

move-up buyers [plural] *AmE* PROPERTY people who own a house, but want to move into a bigger and better property: *The condos have been specifically designed to appeal to move-up buyers.*

2 (let the) buyer beware a phrase meaning that it is the responsibility of the person buying something to notice any faults that it may have: *'Let the buyer beware' has long served as an ominous warning to home buyers and a cherished protection for sellers.*

3 [C] someone whose job is to buy the goods, materials etc for a shop to sell or a company to use: *A wholesale buyer of women's clothing only inspects a sample of the goods.*

materials buyer [C] someone whose job is to buy the materials needed by a factory to produce goods; PROCUREMENT OFFICER; PURCHASING OFFICER

media buyer [C] a person or organization whose job is to buy advertising space in newspapers etc, or advertising time on television etc: *Carat is one of Europe's top media buyers, buying large blocks of ad space at a discount and then selling individual advertising slots to other agencies.*

special buyer [C] FINANCE someone whose job is to buy and sell bills and shares for the Bank of England as a way of controlling the amount of money in an economy

buyer concentration —see under CONCENTRATION

buyer power —see under POWER[1]

buyer risk —see under RISK[1]

buyer's market —see under MARKET[1]

buyer's risk —see under RISK[1]

buyers' surplus —see CONSUMER SURPLUS under SURPLUS[1]

buy-in *n* [C] FINANCE when a company buys its own shares from existing shareholders; BUYBACK: *A buy-in has the advantage of removing small shareholders and frees the parent company to run the unit.*

management buy-in when a management team previously not connected with a company buys a enough shares to gain control of it: *The management buy-in of the Donside Mill was led by Bill Gore, previously chief executive of Charles Letts.* —compare BUYOUT

buying agent —see under AGENT

buying power —see under POWER[1]

buying price —see under PRICE[1]

buying round *n* [U] obtaining goods directly from a producer instead of from a distributor

buy limit order —see under ORDER[1]

buy order —see under ORDER[1]

buy·out /ˈbaɪaʊt/ also **buy-out** *n* [C] FINANCE **1** when a person or organization buys a business: *The company has accepted a* ***buyout offer*** *of $44.50 a share.* —see also ***buy out*** under BUY[1]

employee buyout also **staff buyout** when employees buy the company they work for: *One of the airline's unions is refusing to participate in an employee buyout.*

leveraged buyout when a person or organization buys a company using a loan borrowed against the company's assets, some of which may then be sold to pay off the loan: *With debt taken on in a $4.9 billion leveraged buyout, Southland could not afford to pay all its bills.*

management buyout abbreviation **MBO** when a company's top managers buy the company they work for: *Commodore is to be relaunched following a management buyout of its Dutch manufacturing plant.*

2 FINANCE when a person or organization buys all the shares in a company owned by a particular shareholder: *Petrofina said it was continuing to negotiate a buyout of minority stakeholders in Fina Inc., the US subsidiary.*

3 HUMAN RESOURCES money given to someone to persuade them to leave a company: *JAL plans to cut its payroll by 5,000, mainly through buyouts.*

buy rating —see under RATING

by·law also **byelaw** /ˈbaɪlɔː‖-lɒː/ *n* [C] **1** LAW a local government law that must be obeyed by the people living in an area, or people visiting it: *a bylaw banning public drinking in the town centre*

2 a rule made a company or organization that must be obeyed by the people working for it

by-product also **byproduct** *n* [C] **1** something produced during the process of making something else, especially during an industrial process: *Bran is a byproduct of the milling process.*

2 something unexpected or unplanned that happens as a result of something else happening: *The fiscal crisis is a byproduct of the recession.*

byte also **bite** /baɪt/ *n* [C] COMPUTING a unit of computer information that can hold one number or letter. A byte is made up of eight BITS (=the smallest units of storage on a computer). The amount of processing space on a computer is measured in MEGABYTES (=a million bytes), so for example a PC with 32 megabytes of space has space for 32 million bytes of information

C

c written abbreviation for CENTIME

C&F also **c.a.f.** written abbreviation for COST AND FREIGHT

C&M written abbreviation for CARE AND MAINTENANCE BASIS

C/A written abbreviation for CAPITAL ACCOUNT; CREDIT ACCOUNT; CURRENT ACCOUNT

CAA abbreviation for CIVIL AVIATION AUTHORITY

CAB abbreviation for CITIZEN'S ADVICE BUREAU

cab•i•net /'kæbənət/ *n* [C] the group of politicians, including the leader of the government, who hold important positions in the government and meet regularly to discuss important issues: *a law approved by the prime minister and his cabinet* | ***Cabinet ministers** were ordered to reduce the size of their offices.* —see also FILING CABINET

cabinet bid —see under BID[1]

ca•ble /'keɪbəl/ *n* **1** [C,U] a tube containing wires that carry electronic signals or information: *Telecommunications is the transmission of information by cable or radio waves.*
2 [U] also **cable television** a system of broadcasting television programmes by means of cables under the ground instead of signals through the air: *At present it is providing cable television services to only 35,000 customers.* | *Only 2.5 percent of homes had cable installed by mid-1992.*

cable company —see under COMPANY

cab•o•tage /'kæbə,tɑːʒ/ *n* [U] **1** laws that allow ships, aircraft, or road vehicles to collect and move goods or passengers within a foreign country or to another country: *an agreement which extended the rights of cabotage by road haulage firms in other EU member countries*
2 the movement of ships from one port to another along the coast, usually within the same country

CAC 40 /,kæk 'fɔːti, ,siː eɪ siː-‖-'fɔːr-/ *n* a SHARE INDEX of shares in 40 leading companies on the Paris stockmarket: *The CAC 40 index of actively traded French stocks was up 1.62%.*

cache[1] /kæʃ/ *n* [C usually singular] COMPUTING part of a computer's memory

cache[2] *v* [T] COMPUTING to put something in a cache

CACM abbreviation for CENTRAL AMERICAN COMMON MARKET

CAD —see CAD/CAM

ca•das•tre /kə'dæstə‖-ər/ *n* [C] LAW a detailed record of who owns particular areas of land, used for collecting taxes

CAD/CAM /'kæd,kæm/ also **CAD-CAM** *n* [U] computer-aided design and manufacture; the use of computers to help design and make industrial products and buildings: *the need for new CAD/CAM systems*

caf•e•te•ri•a /,kæfə'tɪəriə‖-'tɪr-/*n* [C] *AmE* a place in a factory, office etc where meals are provided, usually quite cheaply; CANTEEN *BrE*

CAL /kæl/ *n* [U] Computer Assisted Learning or Computer Aided Learning; computer programs or teaching methods that involve using computers to help people learn something. CAL programs and materials are often used for teaching people who are not able to travel to a college, school etc: *Several colleges have developed flexible learning based around the Institute's CAL courses.*

cal•en•dar /'kæləndə‖-ər/ *n* [C] **1** pages showing the days, weeks, and months of a particular year
2 *AmE* a book with separate spaces or pages for each day of the year, where you write down the things you have to do on each day; DIARY *BrE*
3 all the events or dates in a year that are important for a particular organization, person, or activity: *The National Conference is the premier event in the Institute's calendar.* | *On today's **economic calendar** is the release of the December merchandise trade balance.*
4 calendar month one of the twelve months of the year: *Earnings have not exceeded £36,000 in any of the last 12 calendar months.*
5 calendar month a period of time from a certain date to the same date in the next month: *Payment terms are one calendar month from date of invoice.*
6 calendar year a period of time from January 1st to December 31st: *Italy's financial year closes at the end of the calendar year.*
7 calendar (year) 98/99 etc the year 1998, 1999 etc from January 1st to December 31st: *IBM's revenues from mainframe processors in calendar 1998*

call[1] /kɔːl‖kɒːl/ *v* **1** [I,T] to telephone someone: *She called the airport to ask about flights.* | *I was told that the office was closed and to call tomorrow.*
2 call (sb) collect *AmE* to make a telephone call which is paid for by the person you are telephoning; REVERSE THE CHARGES *BrE*
3 call a meeting/election to arrange for a meeting or an election to happen at a definite time: *The company called a shareholders meeting to discuss the takeover bid.*
4 [I] to make a short visit to a person or place in order to do something: *If you decide not to go ahead, just return the policy within 15 days. No salesman will call.*
5 [T] to ask or order someone to come to a place **call sb in/into/to**: *Mike was called into the manager's office and told there was no longer a job for him.* **call sb to do sth**: *They were called to give evidence before the committee.*
6 [T] FINANCE to repay a loan or bond to a lender, usually before it is normally due to be repaid: *Interest rates are so low now it's unlikely the bonds will ever be called.*

call back *phr v* **1** [T] **call** sth ↔ **back** to ask for something that you have lent or given to be paid or given back to you: *In conditions of liquidity shortage they will call back these loans.*
2 [I,T] **call** sb ↔ **back** to telephone someone again, usually because one of you was not in or was busy at the time of the first call: *No problem, I'll call back later.* | *Can you ask him to call me back when he gets in?*
3 [I] to visit a person or place again in order to do something: *I've got to do some shopping now. I'll call back later for my order.*

call for sth *phr v* [T] to ask publicly for something to happen: *United's second largest shareholder is calling for the public flotation of the shares.* **call for sb to do sth** He called for Europe to work towards economic integration.

call in *phr v* **1** [T] **call** sb ↔ **in** to ask for someone in authority to come and help with a difficult situation: *He threatened to call in the receiver to Mr Bond's corporation.*
2 [T] **call** sth ↔ **in** to ask for money that you have lent to be repaid: *UMF continued to trade at a loss and in November 1987 the Canadian Cooperative Credit Society called in its loan.*
3 [I] to telephone somewhere, especially the place where you work, to tell them what you are doing or where you are: *During the break I called in to the office.* | *I wasn't feeling very well, so I **called in sick*** (=telephoned to say I was too ill to come to work).

call sth ↔ **off** *phr v* [T] to decide and announce that something should be stopped or should not take place: *The union called off strike action planned for today.*

call on/upon sb *phr v* [T] **1** to formally ask someone to do something: *She called on local employers to commit themselves to equal opportunities.*
2 to visit someone for a short time: *Small booksellers often don't have time to see all the reps who call on them.*
call up *phr v* **1** [I,T] **call** sb ↔ **up** to telephone someone: *Several customers called up to complain.*
2 [T] **call** sth ↔ **up** if you call up information on a computer, you make the computer show it to you: *Here's how to call up the latest Stock Exchange prices.*

call[2] *n* [C] **1** an attempt to speak to someone by telephone: *Calls cost 36p a minute cheap rate, 48p at all other times.* | *If you wish to be added to the mailing list, please* ***give*** *me* ***a call*** *on the number above.* | *Andrew Walker telephoned this morning, and would like you to* ***return his call*** *as soon as possible.*
blind call also **cold call** if someone who is selling something makes a blind call or a cold call, they telephone someone they have never spoken to before to offer them a product or service: *Placing blind calls isn't entirely futile, insists Mr. Sobeck, who guesses that one out of 40 or 50 calls turns up a lead.* | *They used cold calls and pressure tactics to push stocks.* —**cold-calling** *n* [U] *His marketing efforts have been direct, including cold-calling.* —**cold-caller** *n* [C] *A cold-caller mistakenly called the company's boss.*
conference call a telephone call in which several people in different places are able to talk together at the same time
2 a request or demand for someone to do something + **for**: *He made a call for private companies to offer up to 25% of their shares to workers' co-operatives.* | *a strike call*
3 a short visit, especially for a particular reason: *I'll* ***pay a call on*** *our supplier later this week.*
4 BANKING a demand for money that can be made at any time and without warning, especially a demand for a loan to be repaid: *There are $200 million in bearer bonds still outstanding, held by people who did not hear about a call.*
cash call FINANCE when a company asks existing shareholders for more money for investment: *Ladbroke's said that under the terms of the cash call, it plans to issue 216 million new ordinary shares at 220p each.*
5 BANKING **at/on call** if a bank lends money at call or on call, the bank can demand to have it paid back at any time and without warning; ON DEMAND: *Overdrafts to customers are often granted for a few days or weeks. Some loans to other financial institutions may be loans at call.*
6 FINANCE a demand from a company to a shareholder to pay for shares that they have been given: *Kingfisher is raising £155 million from the first call of 225p a share.*
margin call an occasion when investors who have borrowed money to buy shares or other investments must repay it, for example because the value of their investments has gone down: *The firm clearing his account issued a $22 million margin call, which he didn't meet.*
7 another name for CALL OPTION (=the right to buy shares etc at a particular price within a specific period of time): *Total options volume was 33,000, with puts at 19,000 outnumbering calls.*
8 a decision that you have to make yourself: *Buy or don't buy – it's your call.* —see also YIELD TO CALL
judgement call *BrE* **judgment call** *AmE* a decision that you have to make yourself in a new or unfamiliar situation: *The company made a judgment call in proceeding with the project.*

call·a·ble /ˈkɔːləbəl‖ˈkɒːl-/ *adj* FINANCE if a loan, bonds, or shares are callable, they must be repaid whenever the lender or shareholder asks for them to be repaid, or when the borrower decides to repay them, within certain conditions when the loan is made or when the bonds or shares are first sold: *The notes, which are callable after 10 years, leave the company some flexibility to refinance if rates are lower then.*

callable bond —see under BOND

callable debenture —see under DEBENTURE

callable fixture *n* [C] FINANCE in Britain, money lent to DISCOUNT HOUSES by banks for a short period of time

call centre —see under CENTRE

call deposit —see under DEPOSIT[1]

called bond —see under BOND

call feature *n* [U] FINANCE in bonds, one of the conditions made by the borrower relating to early repayment: *Some investors avoided the New Jersey Turnpike Authority bonds maturing in 2014 because of an unfavorable call feature.*

call loan —see under LOAN[1]

call option —see under OPTION

CAM —see CAD/CAM

cam·paign /kæmˈpeɪn/ *n* [C] a series of actions intended to achieve a particular result + **for/against**: *the miners' continuing campaign against pit closures* **a campaign to do sth**: *a campaign to convince investors Swindon is the most desirable business site in the world.*
advertising campaign an organization's programme of advertising activities over a particular period of time with specific aims, for example to increase sales of a product: *Intel's success in establishing its brand name through multi-million dollar advertising campaigns*
drip campaign a way of advertising a product or service in which advertisements are shown repeatedly over a long period of time
sales campaign a series of events or activities aimed at advertising a product and increasing sales; SALES DRIVE: *Chrysler said its aggressive sales campaign has helped boost sales.*

can·cel /ˈkænsəl/ *v* **cancelled cancelling** *BrE* **canceled canceling** *AmE* [T] **1** to arrange that a planned activity or event will not now happen: *Airport security has been increased but there is no intention of cancelling flights.* | *Because of the takeover moves the meeting was cancelled.* | *Some airlines have been forced to cancel orders.*
2 to end an agreement or arrangement that exists in law: *You can suspend or even cancel your contract for the period you are away.*
3 LAW to draw lines across a document so that it no longer has any legal effect
cancel sth ↔ **out** *phr v* [T] if one thing cancels out another, it has an equal but opposite effect, so that the effects of the first thing are not felt: *The losses in our overseas division have cancelled out this year's profits.*

can·cel·la·tion /ˌkænsəˈleɪʃən/ *n* [C,U] a decision or statement that a planned activity will not happen, or that an agreement will be ended: *Rail passengers are fed up with cancellations and delays.* | *Britain's aircraft industry could face more job losses after the cancellation of a £2.3 billion order.*

can·di·date /ˈkændədət‖-deɪt, -dət/ *n* [C] **1** someone who is being considered for a job or is competing to be elected: *Candidates must have strong interpersonal skills.* + **for**: *They are interviewing three candidates for the post of sales manager.*
2 someone who is taking an examination

can·ni·bal·i·za·tion also **cannibalisation** *BrE* /ˌkænəbəlaɪˈzeɪʃən‖-bələ-/ *n* [U] MARKETING when one of a company's new products or activities takes sales away from an older one: *With Marks and Spencer starting a mail-order operation there was a danger of cannibalisation, with existing customers choosing to shop at home rather than creating any new business.*

can·ni·bal·ize also **cannibalise** *BrE* /ˈkænəbəlaɪz/ *v* [T] **1** MARKETING if one of a company's new products cannibalizes an older one, it takes sales away from it: *Healthy Choice was a best seller without cannibalizing sales of its other frozen food brands.*
2 MANUFACTURING to take parts from one machine to use in another, for example to repair it: *By the time the replacement part arrived, the helicopter had been cannibalized for spare parts.*

can·teen /kænˈtiːn/ *n* [C] *BrE* a place in a factory, office etc where meals are provided, usually quite cheaply; CAFETERIA *AmE*: *We usually have lunch in the works' canteen.*

can·vass /ˈkænvəs/ *v* [T] to try to get information or support from people, or try to sell something to them, by talking to them: *NASA will spend $4.5 million to canvass the public, aerospace companies and students for innovative technologies to send astronauts to the moon again.* —**canvasser** *n* [C] *You may get a brief visit from a canvasser.*

can·vas·sing /ˈkænvəsɪŋ/ *n* [U] the activity of trying to get information or support from people, or trying to sell something to them, by talking to them: *The election candidates have to learn the art of **doorstep canvassing**.* (=visiting people's houses to get their support) | *Members of the Finance Houses Association should discourage intrusive methods of canvassing.*
cold canvassing canvassing in which people are visited without being telephoned or warned in advance: *a very cost effective method of selling that eliminates a lot of cold canvassing by salespeople*

CAP abbreviation for COMMON AGRICULTURAL POLICY

cap /kæp/ *v* past tense and past participle **capped** present participle **capping** [T] *BrE* **1** to put a limit on the amount of money that can be charged or spent: *The total annual fee is capped at 1.5%.* | *Up to 150 local government jobs could go if the Council has its spending capped by the new Home Secretary.*
2 BANKING to put a limit on the amount of interest that can be charged on a loan, however much interest rates rise: *annual rate increases capped at two percentage points* —**capping** *n* [U] *They were the first local authorities hit by capping under the new Council Tax system.* —**cap** *n* [C] *The administration has put a cap on domestic spending.* | *The banks were instructed to **put a cap on** credit card interest rates.*

ca·pac·i·ty /kəˈpæsəti/ *n* **1** [U] the amount of space a container, room etc has to hold things or people: *The fuel tank has a capacity of 12 gallons.* | *a conference room with a seating capacity of 500.*
deadweight (carrying) capacity [U] the weight of goods and fuel that a ship is able to carry when it is floating in water that goes up to a line marked on its side; DEADWEIGHT TONNAGE
2 [U] the amount of something that a factory, company, machine etc can produce or deal with: *Our **production capacity** has gone up again, with a throughput* (=the amount dealt with) *of 800 tabloid pages per week.* | *When **working to full capacity*** (=producing as much as possible)*, the shipyard employed more than thirty craftsmen and apprentices.*
excess capacity [U] when a company or industry has the factories, equipment etc to produce more than it is actually producing, and needs to reduce this: *The US banking industry suffers from excess capacity – there are simply too many banks.*
spare capacity [U] when a company or industry has the factories, equipment etc to produce more than it is actually producing and could produce more if necessary: *Although Venezuela doesn't have much spare capacity, it could increase oil output.* —compare OVERCAPACITY
3 [singular] someone's job, position, or duty: *Rollins will be working **in an advisory capacity** on this project.* | *I attended **in my capacity as** chairman of the safety committee.*
legal capacity [singular] a person's or organization's right or duty to act in a particular way or to have a particular responsibility: *Some have questioned the legal capacity of the state guaranty funds to own and operate an insurance company.* —see also DEBT CAPACITY, DUAL CAPACITY

capacity to contract *n* [singular] someone's right or ability to be part of a legal contract, because there is nothing such as BANKRUPTCY which legally prevents them

cap and collar *n* [singular] **1** BANKING an agreement by a lender not to go above or below certain interest rates on a particular loan: *The mortgage lenders have introduced a cap and collar deal with an upper rate of 7.75% and a floor of 5.99%.*
2 FINANCE in a takeover, a maximum and minimum offer for shares: *WorldCom's bid for MCI includes a cap and collar designed to give MCI investors a fixed price and a greater sense of security.*

cap·i·tal /ˈkæpətl/ *n* [U] **1** ECONOMICS money or property used to produce wealth: *Countries around the world are hungry for capital and economic development.* —see also RETURN ON CAPITAL
human capital people and their skills considered as a FACTOR OF PRODUCTION (=one of the things an economy or organization must have to create wealth): *Governments must invest in health and education to develop human capital.*
social capital the people working for a company, and their combined skills, knowledge etc, or the skills etc of people in a country as a whole: *The Japanese are good at managing the social capital of large organisations.*
2 FINANCE money from shareholders and lenders that can be invested by a business in assets in order to produce profits: *There is a shortage of capital for the purchase of new aircraft.* | *Since the stockmarket fall, companies have been prevented from **raising capital** by selling new stock.* | *Because Mr Blech is **injecting** new **capital**, Ecogen said it is no longer seeking a buyer for the firm.* | *Jinno has bought lots of land over the last few years, which **ties up capital*** (=makes it unavailable for use) *as it waits to develop it.*
authorized capital also **authorised capital** *BrE* the largest amount of capital a company is allowed to have in the form of shares; AUTHORIZED ISSUE; AUTHORIZED STOCK: *To finance the expansion programme, PAL doubled its authorised capital from 5 billion to 10 billion pesos.*
core capital another name for SHARE CAPITAL when talking about the capital of financial institutions: *the proportion of the bank's total assets held as core capital*
equity capital capital in the form of shares, not debt: *The company will issue 30 million new shares and raise its equity capital by DM 1.56 billion.*
fixed capital capital invested in assets that produce goods or services, or the assets themselves; FIXED ASSETS: *The replacement of fixed capital is usually accompanied by an increased production capacity because of advances in technology.*
flight capital capital sent abroad because of economic or political uncertainty: *When Africa's flight capital comes home we will know that real recovery is in progress.*
issued capital capital in the form of shares already offered to and held by shareholders: *Carlsberg is to acquire 10% of the issued capital of Cruzcampo from Guinness.*
loan capital capital in the form of money lent to a company as loans, BONDS, or DEBENTURES, not shares;

DEBT: *The Welsh Development Agency provides loan capital for industrial projects.*

ordinary capital a company's main class of ordinary shares on which DIVIDENDs are paid only after those on more important classes of shares: *AT&T holds 91 million ordinary shares in CIR, representing 18.6% of its ordinary capital.*

paid-in capital also **paid-up capital** SHARE CAPITAL for which money has actually been received from shareholders, rather than for shares not yet paid for or not yet ISSUED (=made available): *The issue of new shares raises its paid-up capital to $620 million.*

preference capital *BrE* **preferred capital** *AmE* a special class of a company's shares, on which DIVIDENDs are paid before the dividends on ordinary shares, and whose holders are repaid before others if the company goes bankrupt

risk capital capital invested in a business activity that involves a lot of risk, but which may be very profitable; VENTURE CAPITAL

share capital capital that a company has from investors who have bought shares: *San Paolo said it plans to sell the shares, which represent 20% of the bank's share capital.*

split capital a way of dividing a TRUST COMPANY's capital into two kinds of shares, CAPITAL SHARES and INCOME SHARES

Tier 1 capital also **first-tier capital** BANKING one of the two categories which a bank's capital is divided into, consisting of the most central and important types of capital. According to banking rules, banks must keep a certain amount of Tier 1 capital to protect them against failing: *Tier 1 or 'core' capital consists of common stock, retained earnings, and preferred stock.* | *The agreement called for the bank to maintain Tier 1 capital of at least 6% of its assets.*

Tier 2 capital also **second-tier capital** BANKING one of the two categories which a bank's capital is divided into, consisting of the less important and central types of capital: *Tier 2 capital includes securities and subordinated loans.*

uncalled capital capital in the form of shares that have been ISSUED (=made available to investors) but not yet paid for: *the Company's property or assets, including its uncalled capital*

unissued capital shares that a company is allowed to issue but has not issued yet: *options on the* ***unissued share capital***

venture capital money lent to someone so that they can start a new business; RISK CAPITAL: *The fund provides venture capital and loans for US business projects.* | *Pullman has borrowed heavily from banks and* ***venture capital companies.***

working capital also **operating capital** money used by a business to carry on production and keep trading, for example to pay employees and suppliers before money is received for goods sold: *We will have to make our entire technical staff redundant because we have run out of operating capital.* | *the need for working capital to expand operations*

capital account —see under BALANCE OF PAYMENTS

capital accumulation *n* [U] ECONOMICS the process of saving money rather than spending it: *There should be a move from taxes on capital accumulation to taxes on consumption.*

capital adequacy *n* [U] *BrE* BANKING a measure of whether a bank has enough capital in relation to possible losses on loans to borrowers: *S&P said Security-Connecticut has excellent capital adequacy and a low-risk investment strategy.*

capital adequacy ratio —see under RATIO

capital allowance —see under ALLOWANCE

capital appreciation —see under APPRECIATION

capital asset —see under ASSET

capital asset pricing model —see under MODEL

capital bonus —see under BONUS

capital budget —see under BUDGET[1]

capital charge —see under CHARGE[1]

capital consumption —see under CONSUMPTION

capital dilution *n* [U] FINANCE when a company's profits are divided between more shares when new shares are sold

capital employed *n* [U] FINANCE the total amount of SHARE CAPITAL and debt that a company has and uses: *Amoco is faced with doubling the capital employed in its refining and marketing business to £6 billion in the next 10 years.*

return on capital employed [C] a company's profits for a particular year as a percentage of its capital; RETURN ON CAPITAL: *Balrampur has a return on capital employed of 19.25%, the highest in the Indian sugar industry.* —compare RETURN ON ASSETS, RETURN ON SALES

capital equipment —see under EQUIPMENT

capital expenditure —see under EXPENDITURE

capital expense —see under EXPENSE

capital flight —see under FLIGHT

capital flow *n* [C,U] FINANCE when money for investment goes from one country to another; CAPITAL MOVEMENT: *Freer capital flow makes it easier for funds to flow to economies with large trade deficits, like the US.* | *There has been a five-fold increase in capital flows to China – after the US, it receives more foreign investment than any other country.* | *the IMF's proposals to* ***liberalise capital flows*** (=to reduce limits on them)

capital formation *n* [U] ECONOMICS the process of collecting capital for use in investment: *After the fall of communism, the main problem was to facilitate capital formation and channel it into sectors capable of using it most efficiently.*

capital gain —see under GAIN[2]

capital gains tax —see under TAX[1]

capital gearing —see under GEARING

capital goods —see under GOODS

capital grant —see under GRANT[1]

capital-intensive *adj* FINANCE capital-intensive businesses or industries need large amounts of money to pay for the assets they need: *Glass making is capital-intensive, requiring huge investments and big production volumes to operate economically.*

capital-intensive industry —see under INDUSTRY

capital invested *n* [U] FINANCE the amount of money put into a particular business or activity: *This is the biggest cellular equipment venture of the last 10 years; capital invested will be several hundred million dollars.*

capital investment —see under INVESTMENT

cap·i·tal·is·m /ˈkæpətl-ɪzəm/ *n* [U] ECONOMICS a system of production and trade based on property and wealth being owned by private business and ordinary people, rather than the state: *Sweden's 'middle way' between communism and capitalism: a free-market economy committed to social justice*

popular capitalism *BrE* when ordinary members of the public buy shares in companies: *the wave of popular capitalism that spread through Britain in the 1980s*

state capitalism ECONOMICS a system of production and trade used in some SOCIALIST countries based on property and wealth being owned mostly by the government, but managed by private individuals.

cap·i·tal·ist[1] /ˈkæpətl-əst/ *n* [C] **1** someone who supports capitalism: *The country has really changed; it's OK to be a capitalist now.*

2 someone who owns or controls a lot of money and lends it to businesses to create more wealth: *Mexico has finally captured foreign capitalists' attention, if not yet their investment.*

venture capitalist someone who invests money in new businesses: *In the fourth quarter, venture capitalists invested $317 million in computer-related business start-ups.*

capitalist² also **capitalistic** *adj* using or supporting capitalism: *leaders of the Group of Seven largest* ***capitalist democracies*** | *Beijing agreed to maintain Hong Kong's* ***capitalist system*** *for at least 50 years.*

cap·i·tal·i·za·tion also **capitalisation** *BrE* /ˈkəpətlaɪˈzeɪʃən‖-əˈzeɪ-/ *n* [U] FINANCE **1** the total value of a company's shares: *IBM's capitalisation has increased to $81.5 billion.* | *There were strong gains in* ***large capitalization shares*** *such as shipbuilding and steel companies.* | *The early drop wiped around £800 million off the company's* ***market capitalisation.***

2 the total value of all the shares on a stockmarket at a particular time: *Share prices are so low that the total* ***market capitalization*** *of the Seoul bourse last week amounted to only 66,000 billion Won.*

capitalization issue —see under ISSUE²

capitalization of reserves also **capitalisation of reserves** *BrE* — *n* [U] FINANCE when RESERVES are paid out to shareholders in the form of extra shares

capitalization rate —see under RATE¹

cap·i·tal·ize also **capitalise** *BrE* /ˈkæpətl-aɪz/ *v* [T] FINANCE to make money available to a business in the form of loans and money invested in shares so that it can operate and grow: *Semiconductor Singapore will be capitalized with $80 million in cash from the four partners and about $250 million in debt.*

capitalize on sth *phr v* [T] to get as much advantage out of an event, situation etc as you can: *We are well-placed to capitalize on the growth of cable TV.*

cap·i·tal·ized also **capitalised** *BrE* /ˈkæpətl-aɪzd/ *adj* **1** FINANCE a business capitalized with a particular amount of money has that amount available in loans and money that has been invested in its shares: *JMB is very* ***well-capitalized*** *and in a strong financial position.* | *They will create a new fund to keep* ***poorly capitalized*** *banks from failing.*

2 ACCOUNTING if a cost is capitalized, it is shown in a company's BALANCE SHEET as a charge that is reduced over several years, rather than being shown in the PROFIT AND LOSS ACCOUNT as a charge for a particular year: *Software development costs will not be capitalised on the balance sheet.*

capital levy —see under LEVY²

capital loss —see under LOSS

capital market —see under MARKET¹

capital movement *n* [C,U] FINANCE when money for investment goes from one country to another; CAPITAL FLOWS, FREE MOVEMENT: *The increase in global trade and capital movements has made national governments less important.*

capital outlay —see under OUTLAY

capital project —see under PROJECT¹

capital ratio —see under RATIO

capital rationing *n* [U] FINANCE when there is not a lot of money available for investment

capital redemption reserves —see under RESERVES

capital requirement —see under REQUIREMENT

capital reserves —see under RESERVES

capital share —see under SHARE

capital stock —see under STOCK¹

capital structure —see under STRUCTURE

capital sum —see under SUM¹

capital surplus —see under SURPLUS¹

capital tax —see under TAX¹

capital taxation —see under TAXATION

capital transfer —see under TRANSFER²

capital turnover —see under TURNOVER

capital value —see under VALUE¹

capitation fee —see under FEE

capitation grant —see under GRANT¹

capped rate —see under RATE¹

capped-rate mortgage —see under MORTGAGE¹

captain of industry *n* plural **captains of industry** [C] someone who runs or owns an important company and has a lot of influence: *An aptitude for leadership is essential for a successful captain of industry.*

cap·tive /ˈkæptɪv/ *adj* [only before a noun] captive viewers or customers watch a company's advertisements or buy a company's products because they have no other choice: *Kids in the classroom are a* ***captive audience*** *to whom ads may seem a welcome break from studies.* | *Companies exporting to Third World countries often get a* ***captive market*** *for their goods.*

captive market —see under MARKET¹

captive outlet —see under OUTLET

cap·ture /ˈkæptʃə‖-ər/ *v* [T] **1** to get something that previously belonged to one of your competitors: *Japanese firms have captured over 60% of the electronics market.*

2 COMPUTING to put something such as information or a picture into a form that a computer can use: *The data is captured using an optical scanner.* —**capture** *n* [U] *a leading maker of bar code data-capture systems*

car·at /ˈkærət/ *n* [C] **1** also **karat** *AmE* a measurement used to show how pure gold is: *a 22-carat gold chain*

2 a measurement equal to 200 MILLIGRAMS on the scale of measurement for the weight of jewels: *a 23.11 carat yellow diamond*

car·boy /ˈkɑːbɔɪ‖ˈkɑːr-/ *n* [C] a large bottle protected by a strong frame, used for carrying liquid chemicals such as acids

card /kɑːd‖kɑːrd/ *n* [C] **1** a small piece of plastic or paper that shows that someone belongs to an organization, club etc: *Employees must show their* ***ID cards*** *at the gate.* | *All members are issued with a* ***membership card.***

green card also **Green Card** ◆ a document that a foreigner must have in order to live and work legally in the US: *She has applied for her green card.*

◆ INSURANCE a British motor insurance document that you need when you drive in a foreign country: *Most hauliers carry a Green Card to ensure an uninterrupted journey, although the regulations do not insist on this.*

loyalty card a card given by a shop, SUPERMARKET etc that gives regular customers lower prices, money back on goods etc: *The loyalty card offers a 5% discount on the store's own-brand goods.*

2 a small piece of stiff paper or plastic that shows information about someone or something, especially one that is part of a set used for storing information: *A helpful device is to print your presentation ideas on separate* ***index cards.***

smart card a small plastic card with an electronic CHIP that records and remembers information: *Travelers will carry a smart card that allows them to use their cellular phones in more than 15 countries, with all the bills going to a single account.* | *Nippondenso has* *estimated that its smart-card business will have revenue of 15 billion yen in five years' time.*

swipe card [C] a special plastic card containing information which can be read by a machine: *Customers will enter their orders, then pay with their swipe cards.*

3 a small piece of plastic that you use to pay for goods or to get money from a machine at a bank: *Lost or stolen cards must be reported immediately.*

affinity card a CREDIT CARD where a certain amount of money is given by the credit card company to a CHARITY every time the card is used

bank card also **banker's card** a CHEQUE CARD, CASH CARD, DEBIT CARD given to you by a bank: *RBS is putting photos of its clients on bank cards in order to fight card fraud.*

cash card a plastic card that you use for getting money from a machine at a bank

charge card a plastic card that you can use to buy goods in a particular shop and pay for them later

cheque (guarantee) card *BrE* **check (guarantee) card** *AmE* a plastic card that you show when paying for something by cheque to prove who you are and to show that your bank has promised to pay your cheques up to a certain amount: *Personal cheques will only be accepted if accompanied by a valid cheque card.*

credit card a plastic card that you can use to buy goods. At the end of each month you pay all or part of the total amount you have spent, and interest is charged on any amount not paid: *AT&T's entry into the credit-card business has also stirred up the already intense competition in the industry.*

debit card a plastic card which is used instead of money or a CHEQUE to pay for goods and services. The cost is taken directly from the user's BANK ACCOUNT. Debit cards can also be used to obtain money from CASH MACHINES

gold card a credit card that gives you extra advantages or services, such as a high spending limit: *Offers for free interior design consultations were sent to American Express gold card holders.*

plastic card *informal* a CREDIT CARD, CASH CARD, CHEQUE CARD, or STORE CARD: *People in Britain spend about £25 billion a year using plastic cards.*

store card a CREDIT CARD which can only be used to buy goods in one particular shop or chain of shops (=a number of shops owned by the same company)

4 also **business card** a small piece of thick stiff paper that shows your name, job, and the company you work for: *I'll leave my card and you can contact me when it suits you.*

5 COMPUTING a part inside a computer to which chips are fixed, that allows the computer to do specific things: *a **sound card***

chip card a card containing a computer chip, which allows it to store a lot more information than other types of card

expansion card a CIRCUIT BOARD that fits into a computer and makes it possible to add extra features to the computer. Examples of expansion cards are SOUNDCARDS, VIDEO CARDS, and MODEMS —see also RATE CARD, WILD CARD

card catalogue —see under CATALOGUE[1]

card·hold·er /ˈkɑːdˌhəʊldə‖ˈkɑːrdˌhoʊldər/ *n* [C] BANKING someone who has a credit card: *Each cardholder has a set limit that can be borrowed at any one time.*

card index system —see under SYSTEM

care and maintenance basis written abbreviation **C&M** *n* [singular] when a ship, building, or piece of machinery is kept on a care and maintenance basis, it is no longer used but is kept in good condition so that it can be used in the future if it is needed

care assistant —see under ASSISTANT

ca·reer /kəˈrɪə‖-ˈrɪr/ *n* [C] **1** a job or profession that you have been trained for and intend to do for your working life, and which offers the chance to be PROMOTED (=move up through different levels): *He has devoted his **legal career** to defending those facing execution.* | *You should think long and hard before **changing careers**.* + **in**: *I decided to take up a career in advertising.*

2 career soldier/teacher/diplomat etc someone who intends to be a soldier, teacher etc for most of their life, not just for a particular period of time: *a course designed for career linguists or anyone in language-related posts*

career break —see under BREAK[2]

career counselor *n* [C] *AmE* someone whose job is to give people advice about what jobs and professional training might be suitable for them; CAREERS OFFICER *BrE*

career ladder *n* [singular] a career, considered as a series of levels that lead to better and better jobs: *Women's chances to **climb the career ladder** have always been less than men's.*

career move *n* [C] something you do to make progress in your career, sometimes something not directly related to your job: *I joined the Labour Party because I believed in its values, not simply as a career move.*

careers officer also **careers advisor** *n* [C] *BrE* someone whose job is to give people advice about what jobs and professional training might be suitable for them; CAREER COUNSELOR *AmE*

care of written abbreviation **c/o** *prep* used when sending letters to someone at someone else's address: *Send it to me, care of Racal Electronics.*

car·go /ˈkɑːgəʊ‖ˈkɑːrgoʊ/ *n* plural **cargoes** or **cargos** [C,U] goods carried on a ship, plane, TRUCK etc: *What was the plane's cargo?* | *A Swedish **cargo boat** with some passenger accommodation* + **of**: *a freighter due to ship a cargo of highly radioactive plutonium from France*

air cargo cargo that is carried by plane: *the intensely competitive air cargo market*

bulk cargo cargo that is carried loose, not packed in containers: *B&H Maritime transports dry bulk cargo and refined petroleum products.*

containerized cargo also **containerised cargo** *BrE* cargo that is carried in very large metal containers, usually by ship or TRUCK: *The underfloor holds are capable of accommodating over five tonnes of containerised cargo.*

deadweight cargo heavy goods such as coal and stone. The cost of carrying deadweight cargo is calculated according to its weight, not according to the amount of space it fills

dry cargo cargo consisting of dry goods such as coal, iron, food grains, seeds etc: *revenue from export and cross-trading for both wet and dry cargo shipping*

general cargo cargo consisting of various kinds of goods, not one single type of goods: *General cargo continued to flow through the port.*

cargo handling —see under HANDLING

cargo ship —see under SHIP[1]

Caribbean Community and Common Market abbreviation **CARICOM** *n* an organization of the 13 former British states in the Caribbean, formed in 1973 to work together in political and economic matters such as FOREIGN POLICY, development of trade, health, and industrial relations

car insurance —see under INSURANCE

car lease —see under LEASE[2]

car·net /ˈkɑːneɪ‖kɑːrˈneɪ/ *n* [C] a CUSTOMS document allowing someone to import goods into a country without paying DUTY, if they export them again within a particular time

car•pen•ter /ˈkɑːpɪntə‖ˈkɑːrpɪntər/ *n* [C] someone whose job is making and repairing wooden things

car•pet•bag•ger /ˈkɑːpɪtˌbægə‖ˈkɑːrpɪtˌbægər/ *n* [C] *informal* **1** FINANCE *BrE* an investor who puts their money into a LIFE INSURANCE COMPANY or a BUILDING SOCIETY, hoping that it will DEMUTUALIZE (=become a company with shares) and that they will get a WINDFALL (=money paid to members if they agree to the change): *It has opened eight times the normal number of accounts, partly because of activity from carpetbaggers.* —**carpetbagging** *n* [U] *carpetbagging which brought record cash inflows*
2 *AmE* a politician who is active in an area that is not their home because they think they have more chance of being successful there than at home: *NSF supporters branded them carpetbaggers for the long period they had spent in exile abroad.*

carpet bomb *v* [T] MARKETING to send advertising material to as many people as possible, or to all the people in an area: *Members carpet-bomb voters in the area with propaganda publicizing their accomplishments.*

car pool[1] *n* [C] **1** *BrE* a group of cars owned by a company or other organization that its members can use; MOTOR POOL *AmE*
2 a group of car owners who agree to go to work together in one car: *highways with 'car pool lanes' for vehicles carrying more than two passengers*

carpool[2] *v* [I] *AmE* if a group of people CARPOOL, they go to work together in one car, often using cars owned by different people in the group on different days

carr fwd written abbreviation for CARRIAGE FORWARD

car•riage /ˈkærɪdʒ/ *n* [U] **1** when goods are moved by vehicle from one place to another; FREIGHT: *The receipts for carriage of timber have formed an important proportion of revenue.*
2 the cost of moving goods from one place to another: *Prices exclude carriage and VAT.* | *There is a* ***carriage fee*** *of £68.*
3 carriage forward *BrE* written abbreviation **carr fwd** used to show that the carriage of a delivery of goods will be paid for by their buyer: *All goods are sold carriage forward.*
4 carriage free *BrE* used to show that the seller will pay for the carriage of a delivery of goods
5 carriage inwards *BrE* ACCOUNTING used on the debit side of a TRADING ACCOUNT to show payments for the carriage on goods bought by a business. This amount is included as part of the cost of buying the goods
6 carriage outwards *BrE* ACCOUNTING used on the debit side of the profit and loss account to show payments for carriage on goods sold by a business. This amount is included in the sale price of the goods
7 carriage paid home *BrE* used to show that the seller will pay the carriage on a delivery of goods as far as the address of the buyer

carriage and insurance paid —see under INCOTERM

carriage paid —see under INCOTERM

carried down written abbreviation **c/d** *adj, adv* ACCOUNTING written at the end of an account to show that an amount has to be taken down to the beginning of the next account lower down the same page of the account book

carried forward abbreviation **cf** *adj, adv* ACCOUNTING used at the bottom of an account to show that an amount which is the BALANCE of the account has to be taken forward to the next account or to a later page in the account book

carried over *adj, adv* ACCOUNTING used at the bottom of an account to show that an amount which is the BALANCE of the account has been carried to the top of the next page

car•ri•er /ˈkæriə‖-ər/ *n* [C] a person or company whose job is to TRANSPORT goods from one place to another: *national carriers like Pickfords, with their own warehouses and regular clientele* | *the American overseas* ***air carrier****, United Airlines*
bulk carrier a large ship specially designed for carrying goods such as grain and oil that are transported loose, not packed in containers
common carrier a carrier that TRANSPORTS goods from one place to another for any member of the public, and is responsible for any loss of the goods while they are being transported: *Under U.S. law, an ocean freight forwarder cannot act as a common carrier.*
contract carrier *BrE* also **public carrier** a carrier that arranges contracts with a number of producers, dealers etc to TRANSPORT their goods from one place to another, and who can refuse to transport goods for anyone else
limited carrier a carrier that TRANSPORTS only certain kinds of goods
private carrier a carrier that used vehicles to TRANSPORT only their own goods
public carrier another name for a CONTRACT CARRIER

carrier's lien —see under LIEN

carrier's risk —see under RISK[1]

car•ry /ˈkæri/ *v* past tense and past participle **carried** [T]
1 to move goods or passengers from one place to another: *Airlines carried 262 million passengers on international flights last year.*
2 if a person or a company carries a debt, they have that amount of debt: *The company still carries a lot of debt.*
3 to have a particular thing: *Short-term loans carry higher interest rates.* | *The shares carry an annual dividend of $3.64 a share.* | *The issue carries triple-A ratings from both Moody's and S&P.*
4 if a shop carries goods, it has them available for sale: *All of their stores carry the same merchandise.*
carry sth ↔ **down** *phr v* [T] ACCOUNTING to take an amount down to the beginning of the next account lower down the same page of the account book
carry sth ↔ **forward** *phr v* [T] **1** ACCOUNTING to take an amount forward to the next account or to a later page in the account book: *The average assets carried forward from season to season varied from minus $630,000 to plus $770,000.*
2 TAX if you carry forward a loss or other amount not used in a particular accounting period, you use it in the next accounting period in order to reduce the amount of tax you have to pay: *Taxpayers were allowed to deduct losses carried forward from previous years from their net income.*
carry sth ↔ **over** *phr v* [T] another name for carry forward

car•ry•back /ˈkæribæk/ *n* [C,U] ACCOUNTING, TAX when an amount of money earned or spent in a particular year is included in the accounts for an earlier year: *A carry-back was introduced for BES investors, enabling them to carry back tax relief on £15,000 invested to the previous tax year.*

car•ry•for•ward /ˈkæriˌfɔːwəd‖-ˌfɔːrwərd/ *n* [C] *AmE* ACCOUNTING, TAX an amount of money earned or spent in a particular year which is carried forward from one accounting period to a later period, usually in order to reduce the amount of tax you have to pay: *Advest's results include an extraordinary credit of $1 million, or 10 cents a share, because of a* ***tax-loss carryforward****.*

carrying charge —see under CHARGE[1]

carrying cost —see under COST[1]

carry-over *n* [singular] **1** an amount of money earned in a particular year that is still available to be

C

spent the following year + **from/to**: *The £20 million included a £7 million carry-over from last year's budget.*
2 when a dealer on the stock exchange delays payment of an account until the following day; CONTINUATION

car•tel /kɑːˈtel‖kɑːr-/ *n* [C] a group of companies who agree to set the price of something they produce at a fixed level in order to limit competition and increase their own profits: *The **oil cartel**, OPEC, had just had its first major success in forcing up oil prices.* | *a cartel of coffee producers*

car•ton /ˈkɑːtn‖ˈkɑːrtn/ *n* [C] a light strong container made of CARDBOARD or plastic, usually in the form of a box

C

case /keɪs/ *n* [C] **1** a large box or container in which things can be stored or moved: ***packing cases** full of electrical drugs* + **of**: *a case of 10,000 cigarettes and several cases of spirits* —see also BASKET CASE
2 LAW a question or problem that will be dealt with by a court of law: *those claiming damages in personal injury cases* | *The Council appealed to them to **drop the case*** (=stop investigating it).
leading case a legal case that establishes a PRECEDENT and decides the outcome of other similar cases: *The leading case on exclusion of liability for negligence is Smith v.* Bush.
stated case a legal case that is used for reference when making a judgement in a court of law, and that influences the outcome of similar cases: *the principal stated case on diminished responsibility*
test case [C] a legal case that establishes a particular principle and can be used as a standard against which other, similar cases can be judged: *Everybody is looking at this as a test case. If Mrs Cooke is successful, you're going to see a lot more lawsuits against the tobacco companies.* —compare PRECEDENT
3 LAW all the reasons that one side in a legal argument can give against the other side: *The **prosecution case** was that the victim was stabbed by Reid during a general disturbance.* | *The plaintiff needed legal representation in order to **present** her **case** properly.*

case law —see under LAW

case load —see under LOAD[1]

case rate discount —see under DISCOUNT[1]

case study —see under STUDY[1]

cash[1] /kæʃ/ *n* [U] **1** money in the form of notes and coins, rather than cheques, credit cards etc: *I'm bringing $400 in traveller's cheques and $100 **in cash**.* | *All deals are done in **hard cash** or by bank transfer.*
2 pay cash to pay for something immediately with money or a cheque, rather than at a later time: *Are you paying cash or do you have an account?*
3 money rather than shares, bonds etc: *Instead of paying cash for their bonds, they can offer bondholders common shares.* | *The real debt crisis won't come until next year, when it must start paying cash instead of paper to some debt holders.* —see also DOCUMENTS AGAINST CASH
4 money that is immediately available, for example in bank accounts or in the form of shares etc that can be easily sold: *Power Corp has $1 billion in **ready cash** and the ability to borrow much more.*
vault cash *AmE* another name for RESERVES: *$2 billion came from the sale of assets, and $3 billion from surplus vault cash.*

cash[2] *v* **cash a cheque/postal order/draft etc** to exchange a cheque etc for cash: *Can you cash my traveller's cheques here?*
cash in *phr v* **1** [I] to profit from a situation, sometimes in a way that other people may consider wrong or unfair + **on**: *Counterfeiters are trying to cash in on the huge demand for Levi jeans.*
2 [T] **cash** sth ↔ **in** to exchange an investment for cash: *A cut in Spanish interest rates caused him to cash in his Spanish government bonds.* | *Computer-related shares, which have been strong performers lately, fell as investors **cashed in gains** to receive their profits.*
3 cash in your chips *informal* to sell all your investment in something
cash out *phr v* [I] *AmE* to sell an investment + **of**: *The fund doubled its money when it cashed out of Louisiana Gas.*
cash up also **cash out** *AmE phr v* [I] to add up and check the amount of money earned in a shop in a day

cash•a•ble /ˈkæʃəbəl/ *adj* easily exchanged for money: *readily cashable assets, such as Commonwealth securities*

cash account —see under ACCOUNT[1]

cash accounting —see under ACCOUNTING

cash against documents *n* [U] BANKING an arrangement in which an importer can only collect goods sent by an exporter after paying the related BILL OF EXCHANGE —compare DOCUMENTS AGAINST ACCEPTANCE

cash and carry *n* plural **cash and carrys** [C] a very large shop where customers representing a business or organization can buy large amounts of goods at cheap prices: *Cash and carrys tend to offer a 'no-frills' service.* | *a cash and carry warehouse*

cash-and-carry store —see under STORE[1]

cash at bank *n* [U] ACCOUNTING written on the assets side of a BALANCE SHEET to show the amount of a business's money held in a bank —compare CASH IN HAND[1]

cash•back /ˈkæʃbæk/ *n* [U] a way of getting cash from a SUPERMARKET (=a large shop selling food and other goods) when you are paying for your goods with a DEBIT CARD (=a plastic card made available by a bank that allows you to pay for goods and services, with the amounts taken immediately from your bank account)

cash balance —see under BALANCE[1]

cash basis *n* [singular] **1** ACCOUNTING a system of accounts in which the profit or loss for a particular period of time is based on the amounts of money received and paid out during that period, rather than on goods or services provided during that period: *Some firms are allowed to pay VAT on a cash basis: VAT need only be paid when the invoice bearing VAT has actually been paid.*
2 if you receive goods or services on a cash basis, you must pay for them as soon as you receive them rather than paying later: *If hotel guests have no credit cards they are usually asked to prepay for their stay on a cash basis.*

cash before delivery abbreviation **CBD** *n* [U] when a buyer must pay for goods before they are sent to them

cash bid —see under BID[1]

cash•book /ˈkæʃbʊk/ *n* [C] ACCOUNTING a book in which a record is kept of money received and paid: *The basic records which every practice should have include cashbook and wages and salaries record.*

cash-box *n* [C] a small, strong box for keeping cash in

cash budget —see under BUDGET[1]

cash call —see under CALL[2]

cash card —see under CARD

cash column —see under COLUMN

cash cow *n* [C] **1** FINANCE a very profitable business or part of a business: *Mail order should be seen as a cash cow that will generate cash for further moves into information services.* | *GM and Ford have used luxury cars as cash cows; giving those up could have a terrible impact on profitability.*
2 in the GROWTH/SHARE MATRIX, a product with high market share in a low-growth market

cash crop —see under CROP

cash discount —see under DISCOUNT[1]

cash dispenser *n* [C] another name for a CASH MACHINE —see under MACHINE[1]

cash dividend —see under DIVIDEND

cash equivalent —see under EQUIVALENT

cash flow also **cashflow** *n* **1** [U] FINANCE the amounts of money coming into and going out of a company, and the timing of these: *the lack of cash flow that results from customers not paying bills on time* | *The business is suffering severe* ***cash flow problems****.* | *Mr Trump will have to keep to a business plan with strict month-by-month* ***cash flow projections****.*

negative cash flow [U] a situation where more money is going out of a business from its commercial activities than there is coming in: *Vacancy rates of 25% or more indicate a negative cash flow on the property, meaning the owner must rely on other sources of cash to meet interest payments and other expenses.*

2 [C,U] profit made by a business in a particular period of time, measured in different ways by different businesses: *Time Warner defines cash flow as earnings before interest payments, taxes and depreciation.* | *Volvo needs to raise production to 500,000 units to* ***generate the cash flow*** (=to produce it) *required for expensive new model development programmes.* | *The company announced an increase in its* ***after-tax cash flow****.*

free cash flow [U] profit from a company's operating activities, less CAPITAL SPENDING (=money spent on machinery, buildings etc) and taxation: *Rentokil generated £200 million of free cashflow this year, so it could make another acquisition soon.*

cash generation —see under GENERATION

cash•ier /kæˈʃɪə‖-ˈʃɪr/ *n* [C] **1** someone whose job is to take and pay out money in a shop, bank, hotel etc: *a supermarket cashier*

2 someone who is responsible for keeping an account of the money received by and paid out by a bank or company: *The petty cash book, receipts and vouchers are presented to the head cashier, who audits them.*

petty cashier the person in charge of money kept ready in an office for making small payments: *The petty cashier is entrusted with a fixed sum of money.*

cashier's cheque —see under CHEQUE

cash in hand[1] *n* [U] **1** the amount of money in the form of cash that a company has after it has paid all its costs: *We have a sound balance sheet, no borrowings and net cash in hand of £23 million.*

2 ACCOUNTING written at the top of the assets side of a BALANCE SHEET to show the amount of money held by a company in the form of notes and coins —compare CASH AT BANK

cash in hand[2] *adj, adv* if someone is paid cash in hand, they are paid in notes and coins so there is no written record of the payment: *One dealer had been taking his commission payments cash in hand.*

cash-in-transit policy —see under INSURANCE POLICY

cash ISA —see under ISA

cash issue —see under ISSUE[2]

cash•less /ˈkæʃləs/ *adj* [only before a noun] a cashless system works without any money in the form of notes or coins being given from one person or company to another, for example by the use of BANK TRANSFERS or CREDIT CARDS: *Employees will no longer be able to opt out of cashless pay systems.* | *American Express has a strong core business because the* ***cashless society*** *is an unstoppable trend.*

cash machine —see under MACHINE[1]

cash management —see under MANAGEMENT

cash management account —see under ACCOUNT[1]

cash market —see under MARKET[1]

cash mountain *n* [C usually singular] money that a company has available to spend, for example to buy other companies, or to give to shareholders; CASH PILE: *Hongkong Telecom has accumulated a cash mountain of $HK15 billion and has said this would enable it to take advantage of investment opportunities.*

cash on delivery abbreviation **COD** *n* [U] when a buyer must pay for goods when they are delivered: *If you have reservations only accept orders on the basis of cash on delivery.*

cash pile *n* [C usually singular] another name for CASH MOUNTAIN: *Lonrho is* ***sitting on*** (=has) *a large* ***cash pile*** *that could be used for acquisitions.*

cash position —see under POSITION[1]

cash price —see under PRICE[1]

cash ratio —see under RATIO

cash ratio deposits —see under DEPOSIT[1]

cash received book —see under BOOK[1]

cash register *n* [C] a machine used in shops, restaurants etc to keep money in and record the amount of money received from each sale

cash sale —see under SALE

cash settlement —see under SETTLEMENT

cash-strapped *adj* [only before a noun] *journalism* not having enough money: *The cash-strapped airline isn't making lease payments on its aircraft.*

cash with order abbreviation **cwo** *adj, adv* if something is sold on a cash with order basis, payment must be sent with the order, before the goods are sent out: *Be wary of paying cash with order unless you know the supplier is reliable and solvent.* —compare ***payment in advance***

cask /kɑːsk‖kæsk/ *n* [C] a container for liquids, especially in the beer and wine trades: *The wine is transported in casks and bottled in London.*

cast /kɑːst‖kæst/ *v* past tense and past participle **cast** [T] **cast a vote** also **cast a ballot** *AmE* to vote for someone or vote in an election: *Justice Kennedy cast the deciding vote in the 5–4 ruling.*

casting vote —see under VOTE[2]

cas•u•al[1] /ˈkæʒuəl/ *adj BrE* casual workers are only employed when they are needed, and are not in permanent or continuous employment; TEMPORARY: *Traditionally, labour in the construction industry has been employed on a casual basis.* | *The job was completed using casual labour.*

casual[2] *n* [C] a casual worker; TEMP: *This latest recruitment drive is also aimed at casuals.*

casual labour —see under LABOUR

cas•u•al•ty /ˈkæʒuəlti/ *n* plural **casualties** [C] **1** a person, project, or company that suffers very badly or goes out of business as a result of something: *The airline is the latest casualty of the recession.* | *A rail project for the MX missile became the first casualty of the defense budget cutters.*

2 INSURANCE an accident that causes injury, damage, or loss

casualty insurance —see under INSURANCE

casual work —see under WORK[2]

cat•a•logue[1] also **catalog** *AmE* /ˈkætəlɒg‖-lɒːg, -lɑːg/ – *n* [C] **1** a book containing a list of products that are for sale together with their prices: *You will find the product listed on page 19 of our current catalogue.*

2 a mail order catalogue: *our new menswear catalogue*

3 a book containing a list of all the items stored in a place such as a library, and details of where they can be found: *the production and maintenance of library catalogues*

C

back catalogue a list of all the products a company has ever produced, and that it can still produce and sell: *The record label's entire back catalogue was up for sale.*
card catalogue a set of cards that are arranged in a particular order and contain details about a large group of items, for example books: *a series of card catalogues which allow retrieval by subject and author*
classified catalogue a catalogue in which things of the same type are together in groups: *a classified catalogue of British books published since 1950*
mail order catalogue a catalogue containing photographs and details of clothes and other goods for sale that people can order and have delivered to their home
online catalogue ♦ a catalogue of goods for sale that is displayed on a computer screen and from which you can order goods using your computer: *Place your order from our online catalogue.*
♦ a computer program that allows you to search for information on a particular subject: *monitoring user activity on an online catalog*

C

catalogue[2] also **catalog** *AmE* — *v* [T] to put a list of things into a particular order and write it in a catalogue: *Edward catalogued the stock and took charge of the paperwork.*

catalogue price —see under PRICE[1]

catastrophe risk —see under RISK[1]

catch /kætʃ/ *v* past tense and past participle **caught** [T]
1 be caught in sth to be in a situation that is difficult to escape from: *BNL is caught in the middle of the dispute.* | *The yen was caught in a downward spiral.*
2 catch sb by surprise/off guard/flatfooted etc *BrE* to happen when you are not expecting it or not ready to deal with it: *The sharp turn in share prices caught many investors by surprise.* | *Many oil companies were caught flatfooted when oil prices fell sharply with the start of the Gulf War.*
3 catch a cold *BrE informal* if a business catches a cold, it begins to have financial problems: *With the economic downturn, the recruitment industry will catch a cold.*
catch on *phr v* [I] **1** if a product or an idea catches on, it becomes popular: *Industry executives believe that RSA Data's products will catch on as customers become more security conscious.* | *The survey indicates computers are catching on at law firms.* | *The idea caught on fast.*
2 if someone catches on, they begin to understand or realize something: *Some investors clearly caught on that bad news was in the offing.* | *Foreign companies are catching on to the advantages of franchising.*

catch-22 *n* [U] a situation in which it seems impossible to make progress because you cannot do one thing until you have done another thing, but the second thing cannot happen until the first thing has happened: *'We've got a wonderful Catch-22 here,' Mr. Ratajczak says: 'The producers don't want to build up production and investment until they see stronger sales ahead, and consumers don't want to spend more until they see more jobs.* | *It's a **catch 22 situation**; without experience you can't get a job and without a job you can't get experience.*

category killer *n* [C] MARKETING a very big specialized international CHAIN STORE that causes local competitors to go out of business.

ca•ter•er /ˈkeɪtərə‖-rər/ *n* [C] a person or company that provides food and drink for organizations: *The caterers need to know how many people will be attending.* | *Hospital caterers are struggling with some severe economic constraints.*
contract caterer a company of caterers that is paid by a company or organization to prepare food in its kitchens for its staff: *Contract caterers are now providing nearly 55 per cent of meals served in business and industry.*

CAT standard —see under STANDARD[1]

cause /kɔːz‖kɒːz/ *n* [C]
proximate cause LAW the thing that is directly responsible for an event happening: *Pilots' breaches of duty and negligence were a proximate cause of the plane crash.*

cause of action *n* plural **causes of action** [C usually singular] LAW a legally recognized reason for starting a legal action against someone: *You've got to have a good cause of action and you've got to plead it well.*

cau•tion /ˈkɔːʃən‖ˈkɒː-/ *n* **1** [U] if there is caution in the financial markets, people are unwilling to buy or sell because they are worried that prices will fall: *British shares closed lower as caution over international events continued to suppress trading.*
2 [C] *BrE* a spoken official warning given by the police or someone in authority to a person who has done something wrong: *He got off with a caution.*

caution money —see under MONEY

cau•tious /ˈkɔːʃəs‖ˈkɒː-/ *adj* if buyers or investors are cautious, they are unwilling to buy because they feel uncertain about the future: *Seoul investors turned cautious about the market's rapid rises last week, and share prices ended lower.*

ca•ve•at emp•tor /ˌkeɪviæt ˈemptɔː, ˌkæv-‖-tɔːr/ *n* [U] a phrase meaning 'let the buyer beware', used to say that it is the buyer's responsibility to find out any problems with goods before buying them, and it is not the seller's responsibility to tell the buyer about them: *In the sale of property, the rule 'caveat emptor' generally applies.*

CBA written abbreviation for COST-BENEFIT ANALYSIS

CBD abbreviation for CASH BEFORE DELIVERY; CENTRAL BUSINESS DISTRICT

CBI abbreviation for CONFEDERATION OF BRITISH INDUSTRY

CBO abbreviation for COLLATERALIZED BOND OBLIGATION, CONGRESSIONAL BUDGET OFFICE

CBOE written abbreviation for CHICAGO BOARD OPTIONS EXCHANGE

CBOT also **CBT** abbreviation for CHICAGO BOARD OF TRADE

cbu abbreviation for COMPLETELY BUILT-UP

cc[1] used on letters, documents, and E-MAILs to show that a copy has also been sent to someone in addition to the person to whom it is addressed: *To Neil Fry, cc Anthea Baker, Matt Fox*

cc[2] *v* [T] *informal* to send a copy of a letter, document, or E-MAIL addressed to one person to another person: *Can you send a memo to Bill and cc it to the sales team.*

CCTV abbreviation for CLOSED CIRCUIT TELEVISION

CD abbreviation for CERTIFICATE OF DEPOSIT; COMPACT DISC

c/d also **C/D** written abbreviation for CARRIED DOWN

CD-ROM also **CD-Rom** /ˌsiː diː ˈrɒm‖-ˈrɑːm/ *n* [C,U] compact disc read only memory; a small disk on which large quantities of information can be stored to be used by a computer. On a standard CD-Rom, the information can only be read, not changed: *A CD-Rom holds the equivalent of 1,000 floppy discs.* | *the first newspaper available **on CD-ROM***

CD-ROM drive —see under DRIVE[2]

CDRW *n* [singular] compact disc read-write; a type of CD-Rom on which you can save information from your computer

cede /siːd/ *v* [T] to officially give property, land, or rights to someone else: *The deal calls for Mr Trump to cede 50% equity in the property to bondholders.* | *He has been forced to **cede control** of the company.* | *The airline plans to cede majority ownership to creditors.* —see also CESSION

Ce•del /se'del/ *n* a CLEARING HOUSE based in Luxembourg —see also EUROCLEAR

cei•ling /'siːlɪŋ/ *n* [C] the largest level, amount, or number of something that is officially allowed: *Oil **price ceilings** remained in place for a decade.* | *the strict **spending ceilings** imposed by last year's budget* | ***Wage ceilings** needed to be introduced and the state pension scheme overhauled.* + **on**: *The new government set a ceiling on prices for basic foodstuffs.* —see also GLASS CEILING

ceiling price —see under PRICE[1]

cel•lar•age /'selərɪdʒ/ *n* [U] **1** the cost of storing goods, especially in a room below ground
2 a space in a room below ground where things, for example wine, can be stored

cell phone —see ***cellular phone*** under PHONE

cel•lu•lar /'seljələ‖-ər/ *adj* [only before a noun] a cellular telephone system uses short-range radio signals so that users can carry telephones around with them: *a fleet of commuters equipped with **cellular phones*** | *Fast growth is forecast in the cellular market.* | *a large group of independent cellular companies*

cen•sus /'sensəs/ *n* plural **censuses** [C] **1** an occasion when the population of a country is officially counted and details about the people are recorded: *the 1991 Census of Great Britain and Northern Ireland*
2 an occasion when something is officially counted for government planning: *a traffic census*

cent /sent/ *n* [C] a unit of currency used in the United States, Canada, Australia, and some other countries, that is equal to 0.01 of the main currency unit: *The price of oil rose 35 cents to nearly $22 a barrel.* —see also PERCENT[2]

center the American spelling of centre

centi- /sentə/ *prefix* in the METRIC SYSTEM, one hundredth part of a unit: *a centimetre* (=0.01 metres)

cen•time /'sɒntiːm‖'sɑːn-/ written abbreviation **c** *n* [C] a unit of currency used in France, Belgium, Algeria, and some other countries, that is equal to 0.01 of the main currency unit

cen•ti•mo /'sentəməʊ‖-moʊ/ *n* [C] a unit of currency used in Spain, Venezuela, Peru, and some other countries, that is equal to 0.01 of the main currency unit

Central American Common Market abbreviation **CACM** *n* an organization of Central American countries, including Costa Rica, El Salvador, Guatemala, Honduras, and Nicaragua, set up to improve living standards and help the development of industry and trade in the region

central bank —see under BANK[1]

central business district abbreviation **CBD** *n* [C] the area in a city where a lot of businesses have their offices: *The survey of 35 central business districts showed that the office vacancy rate rose to 18.8%.*

central counterparty —see under COUNTERPARTY

Central Gilts Office *n* FINANCE the organization that manages the trading of British government bonds

central government borrowing requirement —see under REQUIREMENT

cen•tral•ize also **centralise** *BrE* /'sentrəlaɪz/ *v* [I,T] to organize the control of a company, organization, or country so that one central group has power and tells people in other places what to do: *Shippers are centralizing their European distribution activities.* | *The firm focused on centralizing its buying to cut costs.* —**centralization** also **centralisation** *BrE n* [U] *the increasing centralization of public sector employment* —**centralized** also **centralised** *BrE adj*: *The country is continuing its efforts to move away from a centralized economy.* | *a centralized computer system*

Central Moneymarkets Office *n* FINANCE an organization that manages trading on the London MONEY MARKETS

central processing unit —see under UNIT

central processor *n* [C] COMPUTING another name for a CENTRAL PROCESSING UNIT: *The PC's central processor is used to perform the calculations that end up as images on your monitor.*

Central Standard Time *n* [U] a TIMEZONE, six hours behind GREENWICH MEAN TIME, used in North America: *We advanced our watches two hours to Central Standard Time.*

cen•tre *BrE* **center** *AmE* /'sentə‖-ər/ *n* [C] **1** the place where most of the important things connected with a business or activity happen: *Already Bahrain has become a major international banking centre.* + **of**: *plans to turn the town into a centre of high-tech inward investment*

cost centre *BrE* **cost center** *AmE* part of a business that is used as a unit to calculate the costs related to operating it: *Mobil is splitting itself into four cost centres and four profit centres.*

financial centre *BrE* **financial center** *AmE* ◆ [C] a city where there are a lot of financial activities, such as banking and insurance. A financial centre may also have a stockmarket, currency market etc: *If the UK does not enter the euro, it could harm London's standing as an **international financial centre**.* | ***global financial centers** such as London, Paris, Tokyo and Frankfurt*
◆ [C] a city or country where there are fewer rules, less strict laws, lower taxes etc: *Dublin is promoting itself as an offshore financial centre.*

money center *AmE* a large, important bank, or a city where there are many such banks: *such major money centers as Tokyo, Hong Kong, London and Frankfurt* | *the big New York money-center banks*

profit centre *BrE* **profit center** *AmE* a part of a business that is expected to produce profits, or that is used as a unit in calculating profits in relation to other parts: *Porsche's research and development facility works for other auto makers, including Ford, and is run as a profit center.*

2 a building that is used for a particular activity: *the World Trade Center*

assessment centre *BrE* **assessment center** *AmE* HUMAN RESOURCES a way of selecting new employees by giving them a set of tests, interviews, and activities over a period of a day or more, or the place where this is carried out

business advice centre *BrE* **business development center** *AmE* a place where specially trained staff are available to give advice on running a small business: *Local authorities are playing a part in the promotion of co-operatives, in training schemes and business advice centres.*

call centre *BrE* **customer service center** *AmE* an office where people answer customers' questions, make sales etc over the telephone: *IBM has announced a big call centre investment in Ireland to provide worldwide PC support.*

conference centre *BrE* **conference center** *AmE* a building, especially one with several large rooms, designed to be used for large business meetings or gatherings: *Edinburgh's new international conference centre*

enterprise centre *BrE* **enterprise center** *AmE* a place where people can get advice on starting and running a small business and that may provide work space for such new businesses: *Deeside Enterprise Centre is getting a grant worth £99,840 for four additional workshop units.*

exhibition centre *BrE* **civic center** *AmE* a very

large building or set of buildings used for exhibitions, and often other events such as concerts: *Earl's Court Olympia is one of Europe's most popular and busiest exhibition centres.*

job centre *BrE* a place where jobs are advertised and training courses are provided for people looking for work. In Britain, job centres are provided by the government —see also EMPLOYMENT AGENCY

shopping centre *BrE* **shopping center** *AmE* a group of shops built together in one area, often under one roof: *The complex will include a shopping center and luxury apartments.*

3 the part of a town or city where most of the shops, offices, restaurants, cinemas etc are: *Our head office is located in the centre of London* | *shops in Birmingham city centre*

C

CEO abbreviation for CHIEF EXECUTIVE OFFICER

cer·tain /ˈsɜːtn‖ˈsɜːrtn/ *adj* **a sum certain** LAW an amount of money that cannot be changed or have anything added to it: *a written order requiring the importer to pay a sum certain in the exporter's domestic currency*

cer·tif·i·cate /səˈtɪfɪkət‖sər-/ *n* [C] **1** an official document that states that certain facts are true: *The mother's occupation is not routinely recorded on the* ***birth certificate.*** | *The merger was completed a year after the certificate of merger was filed.*

bank certificate a document showing how much money a business has in its bank account on a particular date, asked for by people checking the business's accounts

bearer certificate the document relating to a bond, share etc where the owner's name is not officially recorded, but the owner is considered to be the person who has it in their possession: *Bearer certificates are negotiable, but the holder has to demonstrate he has the title to them.*

bond certificate the document showing who owns a bond, now replaced in many places by computer records: *Some people like collecting old stock and bond certificates.*

charge certificate also **certificate of charge** in Britain, a document showing details about property if there is a loan related to it. It is normally kept by the borrower

delinquent tax certificate *AmE* TAX a document representing tax that has not been paid on a property, which can be bought at a reduced price as an investment. The buyer can then pay the tax and get the money from the owner of the property or, if the owner does not pay, take over the property

deposit certificate BANKING, FINANCE another name for CERTIFICATE OF DEPOSIT: *an illegal loans scheme using forged deposit certificates*

exemption certificate a document that gives a person or company official permission not to do something or not to pay something

insurance certificate a document you get from an insurance company, showing that you are insured against a particular risk: *The courts recognise the insurance certificate as evidence of being insured.*

Land Certificate PROPERTY LAW a formal document in Britain that shows who owns a particular piece of land or property

medical certificate a document signed by a doctor, stating that a person is not able to work for medical reasons: *For absences of more than three days, a medical certificate is required.*

practising certificate *BrE* a document held by an accountant or lawyer that states they have passed certain professional exams and are allowed to work as an accountant or lawyer; PRACTISING LICENSE *AmE*

share certificate also **stock certificate** a document that gives the details of the shares in a company owned by a particular shareholder: *Anyone who wants to become a shareholder must be entered on the register and issued with a share certificate.*

2 an official paper stating that you have completed a course of study: *All the students were congratulated on their work and presented with certificates.* —see also GIFT CERTIFICATE

certificated bankrupt —see under BANKRUPT[2]

certificate of analysis *n* plural **certificates of analysis** [C] MANUFACTURING a formal document showing what is in a chemical product after it has been officially tested: *The test results of each product are stored in computer files, from which a certificate of analysis is generated.*

certificate of charge —see ***charge certificate*** under CERTIFICATE

certificate of deposit abbreviation **CD**, also **deposit certificate** *n* plural **certificates of deposit** [C usually plural] FINANCE a sum of money left with a bank for a particular period of time, and the document showing details of this: *Holders of Bank of New England certificates of deposit* | *Philippine National Bank said it would issue $125 million worth of floating rate certificates of deposit with a maturity of three years.*

eurodollar certificate of deposit a certificate of deposit offered in dollars outside the US: *Investors have been earning about 8% on their money, which is invested in Eurodollar certificates of deposit.*

yankee dollar certificate of deposit a certificate of deposit offered by non-American banks in the US

certificate of existence *n* plural **certificates of existence** [C] INSURANCE a document signed by a responsible person saying that someone who is going to receive a PENSION is still alive

certificate of incorporation *n* plural **certificates of incorporation** [C] LAW a document needed before a new company can start doing business giving details of its directors, the money and assets that it has etc: *Edisto intends to change its certificate of incorporation to increase the number of authorized common shares.*

certificate of insurance *n* plural **certificates of insurance** [C] INSURANCE a document to be shown as proof that an insurance contract exists, with information about the risks that are covered and conditions relating to the insurance: *Insurance cover comes into force only when a certificate of insurance is actually received.*

certificate of manufacture *n* plural **certificates of manufacture** [C] an official document showing where something was made, the company that made it etc

certificate of origin *n* plural **certificates of origin** [C] an official document showing where goods or food products come from, which company produced them etc

certificate of posting *n* plural **certificates of posting** [C] *BrE* a document given to a customer by the post office as proof that a letter or package has been posted; REGISTERED MAIL RECEIPT *AmE*: *If you do not obtain a certificate of posting, we are not legally liable to pay compensation.*

certificate of protest *n* plural **certificates of protest** [C] BANKING, LAW a document showing that a BILL OF EXCHANGE was not paid when it should have been

certificate of registration *n* plural **certificates of registration** [C] a document giving information about a person or organization that appears on an official list: *After the incident, Gloucestershire County Council is proposing to cancel the nursing home's certificate of registration.*

certificate of search *n* plural **certificates of search** [C] LAW a legal document showing the results of looking for the name of an owner of land or property in a LAND REGISTER: *The certificate of search did not give notice of any transaction.* —compare ABSTRACT OF TITLE

certificate of tax deducted *n* plural **certificates of tax deducted** [C] TAX a document prepared by a bank showing the amount of tax on interest earned on a customer's account that has been paid directly by the bank to the tax authorities

cer·ti·fi·ca·tion /sə,tɪfɪ'keɪʃən‖sər-/ *n* [U] the official act of approving a person, organization, or product and saying that they reach particular standards of ability, quality etc: *Three prototype jets are currently undergoing tests, but certification by the US Federal Aviation Administration is not expected until next year.*

certified accountant —see under ACCOUNTANT

certified bankrupt —see under BANKRUPT[2]

certified cheque —see under CHEQUE

certified copy —see under COPY[1]

certified mail —see under MAIL[1]

certified management accountant —see under ACCOUNTANT

certified public accountant —see under ACCOUNTANT

cer·ti·fy /'sɜːtəfaɪ‖'sɜːr-/ *v* past tense and past participle **certified** [T] **1** to state that something is correct or suitable, especially after an official check or test: *Every delivery must be certified for consistent quality.* | *The farm has not yet been certified organic.*
2 to give an official paper to someone that states they have completed a course of training for a profession: *She was certified as an accountant in 1996.*

ces·sion /'seʃən/ *n* [C,U] when a person, company, or country officially gives property, land, or rights to someone else: *Russia was vehemently opposed to cession of the Liaodong Peninsula.* —see also CEDE

cf[1] also **c/f** abbreviation for CARRIED FORWARD

cf[2] compare; used in documents and reference books

CFA *n* Communauté Financière Africaine; a group of French-speaking countries in Africa with economic links: *In an effort to restore their competitiveness, the CFA countries have tried everything.*

CFI also **cfi** abbreviation for COST, FREIGHT, INSURANCE

CFTC *n* Commodity Futures Trading Commission; a US organization that checks and controls trading in FUTURES

CGBR abbreviation for CENTRAL GOVERNMENT BORROWING REQUIREMENT

CGT abbreviation for CAPITAL GAINS TAX —see under TAX[1]

chae·bol /'tʃeɪbol‖-bɑːl/ *n* plural **chaebol** or **chaebols** [C] an industrial group in South Korea: *The Samsung Group, like other chaebol, is investing heavily in petrochemicals.*

chain /tʃeɪn/ *n* [C] **1** a number of shops, hotels, cinemas etc owned or managed by the same company or person: *Britain's leading **supermarket chain*** + **of**: *Airtours is expanding its chain of travel agents.*
2 a series of people or organizations involved in different stages of the same activity

distribution chain also **chain of distribution**, **supply chain** the series of organizations that are involved in passing products from manufacturers to the public: *There are price advantages to be gained when middlemen, or retailers, are by-passed in the chain of distribution.* | *the various stages in the supply chain, from the fishing boat to the supermarket*

value chain ♦ how each part of an organization adds to the value of the goods or services produced: *We need to be aware of the complete value chain for the company's products and how investment will improve each part.*
♦ how each organization adds to the value of the goods or services produced —see also DAISY CHAIN

chain of title *n* plural **chains of title** [C usually singular] LAW, PROPERTY the complete list of owners of a property over a period of time: *You need to form a chain of title from the date of that document right up to the present time.*

chain store —see under STORE[1]

chair[1] /tʃeə‖tʃer/ *n* [singular] **1** the person who is in charge of a meeting, or the job of being in charge of it: *the Chair of the plenary session* | *If you have strong feelings about a situation, declare an interest and suggest that someone else **takes the chair*** (=takes charge of the meeting).
2 the chairman or chairwoman of a company or organization, or the job of chairman or chairwoman: *chair of the International Commercial Bank of China*

chair[2] *v* [T] to be in charge of a meeting: *He chaired his first board meeting yesterday afternoon.*

chair·man /'tʃeəmən‖'tʃer-/ *n* plural **chairmen** [C] **1** someone, especially a man, who is in charge of a meeting or who directs the work of a committee or organization; CHAIR: *The chairman then declared the meeting closed.* | *Morrison had **been elected chairman** of the party's Campaign Committee.*
2 also **chairman of the board** the person who is in charge of a large company or organization, especially the most senior member of its BOARD; CHAIR: *Microsoft chairman, Bill Gates* | *Lord Ashburton became Chairman of BP on 25 June 1992.*

deputy chairman someone who is directly below a chairman in rank: *Deputy Chairman of the advertising agency Saatchi and Saatchi*

executive chairman a chairman who is involved in the everyday running of a company or organization: *Would the executive chairman be ready to sell his shares for the sake of the company?*

vice chairman or **vice-chairman** the title given in some organizations to the person directly below the chairman in rank: *The post of Vice Chairman was left to be decided at the next Committee meeting.*

chairman's statement —see under STATEMENT

chair·per·son /'tʃeə,pɜːsən‖'tʃer,pɜːrsən/ *n* plural **chairpersons** or **chairpeople** [C] someone who is in charge of a meeting or who directs the work of a committee or organization; CHAIR: *CNIAG had no elected secretary, treasurer or chairperson.*

chair·wom·an /'tʃeə,wʊmən‖'tʃer-/ *n* plural **chairwomen** [C] a woman who is in charge of a meeting or who directs the work of a committee or organization; CHAIR: *the acting chairwoman of the Broadcasting Standards Council*

chalk /tʃɔːk‖tʃɒːk/ *v*

chalk up sth *phr v* [T] to succeed in getting something or reaching a total: *KLM chalked up profit of 192.5 million guilders.*

chal·lenge /'tʃæləndʒ/ *n* [C] **1** a careful check of the cash and shares etc held by the employees of a company, as part of an official check to discover if there has been any dishonesty
2 something difficult that you feel determined to solve or achieve: *Now the company's challenge is to work out a plan to settle its $1.5 billion in debts.* | *Making these vehicles was a formidable challenge.*
3 a refusal to accept that something is right and legal: *The suit is a major challenge to Georgia's election laws.*

chamber of commerce *n* plural **chambers of commerce** [C] an official group of business people in a town or area, working together to improve trade, collect and pass on business information etc: *A survey for the Birmingham Chamber of Commerce indicates a slow but steady gain for business in the region.*

chamber of trade *n* plural **chambers of trade** [C] a group of businesspeople in a town or area, working together to improve trade: *a meeting of the Teesside Chamber of Trade*

chance /tʃɑːns‖tʃæns/ *n* [U] the risk always present in certain business activities and accepted by business people: *Every commercial business is subject to chance or risk.*

Chancellor of the Exchequer also **Chancellor** *n* plural **Chancellors of the Exchequer** [C usually singular] the British government minister in charge of deciding levels of taxes and government spending: *In his autumn statement, the Chancellor of the Exchequer was forecasting an economic upturn.*

change¹ /tʃeɪndʒ/ *v* [T] **1** to exchange a unit of money for smaller units that add up to the same value: *Can you change a £20 note?*
2 to exchange money in one currency into money of another currency: *We had to change some Swiss francs into French ones to buy a cup of coffee.*
3 to exchange something that you have bought, especially because there is something wrong with it: *We will only change goods accompanied by a receipt.*
4 change hands if property changes hands, it passes from one owner to another: *The FT-SE 100-Share Index closed just 1.0 down, with just under 593 million shares changing hands.*

C

change² *n* [U] **1** the money you get back when you have paid for something with more money than it costs: *She received a forged banknote in her change.* | *You won't get much change from a ten pound note here.*
2 money in the form of coins and notes of low value: *I have about a dollar in change.* | *I didn't have any* ***small change*** *for the telephone.*

chan•nel¹ /'tʃænl/ *n* [C] **1** a system that is used for supplying information or goods: *A direct marketing channel moves goods directly from manufacturer to consumer.*
distribution channel also **channel of distribution** a system for moving goods from producers to buyers, and the people and organizations involved: *Until very recently, the company's 2,000 dealers were its only distribution channel.*
2 a television station and all the programmes broadcast on it: *a 24-hour channel devoted exclusively to football*
3 COMPUTING a route along which computer signals can be sent, for example a CABLE

channel² *v* **channelled channelling** *BrE* **channeled channeling** *AmE* [T] to control and direct something such as money or effort towards a particular purpose **channel sth into**: *BCE wanted to channel all its financial resources into completing several major office buildings.* **channel sth through**: *The International Finance Corp. will channel funds through Zivnobanka for other investment projects in the Czech republic.*

channel port —see under PORT¹

Channel Tunnel *n* **the Channel Tunnel** the railway tunnel built under the Channel linking England and France: *the Channel Tunnel high-speed rail link*

CHAPS /tʃæps/ abbreviation for CLEARING HOUSE AUTOMATED PAYMENT SYSTEM

chap•ter /'tʃæptə‖-ər/ *n* [C] *AmE* the local members of a professional organization or LABOR UNION: *the Illinois chapter of the AFL-CIO*

Chapter 11 *n* [U] LAW, FINANCE part of the US law that deals with the process by which companies officially become bankrupt. Chapter 11 gives companies in financial difficulty time to reorganize without having to pay people or organizations they owe money to: *The store chain* ***filed for Chapter 11 protection*** (=asked for protection under Chapter 11) *after failing to get an agreement with creditors to restructure debt.* | *Southmark* ***emerged from Chapter 11*** *and began distributions to creditors and shareholders.*

Chapter 11 bankruptcy protection —see under PROTECTION

Chapter 7 *n* [U] LAW, FINANCE the part of the US law that deals with the process of a company that is bankrupt going into LIQUIDATION: *The airline will liquidate its remaining assets through Chapter 7 proceedings in bankruptcy court.*

char•ac•ter /'kærɪktə‖-ər/ *n* [C] COMPUTING a number, letter, or other sign used on a computer

charge¹ /tʃɑːdʒ‖tʃɑːrdʒ/ *n* **1** [C,U] an amount of money paid for services or goods: *Vodafone is cutting its call charges by 15%.* | *You can search the D&B database* ***free of charge.*** + **for**: *Politicians are opposing higher charges for electricity.*
capital charge [C] ACCOUNTING the cost to a business of borrowing money and allowing for DEPRECIATION (=fall in value over time) of its assets: *A system of capital charges will show health authorities' use of existing capital assets and any new capital investment.*
carrying charge [C] ◆ ACCOUNTING the cost of storing assets that have not yet been sold or from which you have not received any profit
◆ *especially AmE* a charge added to the price of goods sold on CREDIT
cover charge [C] an amount of money you have to pay at some restaurants and clubs in addition to the cost of food and drinks
handling charge [C] a charge for dealing with goods or moving them from one place to another: *I received a handling charge of £2 for each set of travellers cheques.*
management charge ◆ [C] FINANCE an amount charged by a BROKER or INVESTMENT FUND for managing investors' money: *One of the advantages of investment trusts is the relatively low management charges and dealing costs.*
◆ [C] PROPERTY an amount charged by a company that manages property to the owner of a building or TENANTS (=those renting it)
service charge ◆ [C] an amount of money paid to the owner of a rented block of offices for services such as cleaning and repairing the building: *The firm negotiated a 25-year lease at a cost of £400,000 a year, including rates and service charge.*
◆ [C] an amount of money paid to a company, especially a bank, for arranging something such as a loan or special service for a customer: *A service charge is made on each withdrawal from the account.*
◆ *BrE* an amount of money added to a bill in a restaurant and given to the people who serve the food. A service charge is usually 10 or 15% of the total bill
surrender charge also **surrender penalty** [C] INSURANCE an amount of money someone owning an insurance policy has to pay if they stop the policy before it MATURES (=becomes due for payment): *Most annuities have steep surrender charges in the first seven years.* | *Investors should always compare surrender penalties.*
2 [C usually plural] money charged by a bank for services such as paying cheques, sending out bank statements etc: *concern at the level of* ***bank charges*** *charged by some of the High Street banks*
3 also **legal charge** [C] LAW a legal right to an asset belonging to another person if a particular event happens, for example if they do not repay a loan with which they bought the asset: *Fund the purchase of the house by a loan, with the lender holding a charge on the property as security.*
fixed charge [C] FINANCE the right of people who are owed money by a company to receive money from particular assets belonging to the company, for example a building or equipment, when these have been already agreed on
floating charge [C] FINANCE the right of people who are owed money by a company to receive money from

all the company's assets if the debt is not paid on time: *Typically, when lending money to a company, a bank will take as security a charge over all or most of the assets of the company, the charge being a fixed charge on land and certain other assets, and a floating charge over the remaining assets.*

4 [C] ACCOUNTING, FINANCE a cost, especially one that is not paid regularly: *Pyramid's net loss for the period will also include a restructuring charge of $12 million.* | *Denver said it will* ***take a charge*** (=pay a cost) *of about $590 million for the write-off of certain assets.*

5 be in charge (of) to be the person who manages a group of people, an organization, or an activity: *Under the new plan, each board member will be in charge of one product area.* | *He was* ***put in charge of*** *GM's worldwide truck operations.*

6 take charge (of) to take control of a group of people, an organization, or an activity: *After a brief power struggle, she took charge of the family firm.*

7 [C] LAW an official statement saying that someone has done something against the law: *He was arrested* ***on charges of*** *bribery.* + **against**: *The charges against him are expected to cover fraud, forgery and fraudulent bankruptcy.*

charge² *v* **1** [I,T] to ask someone to pay a particular amount of money for something: *She was charged $995 for a belt that really only cost $195.* | *The prices that producers charged for food fell by 0.8% in July.*

2 charge sth to sb's account to record the cost of something on someone's account so they can pay for it later: *Charge the room to the company's account.*

3 [T] *AmE* to pay for something with a CREDIT CARD: *I charged the shoes on Visa.*

4 [T] LAW to state officially that someone has done something against the law: *He* ***was charged with*** *theft.*

charge sth ↔ **off** *phr v* [T] ACCOUNTING, FINANCE to lose profit because money that is owed to you will not be repaid: *Banc One charged off $82.9 million in bad loans on the third quarter.* —see also CHARGE-OFF

charge·a·ble /ˈtʃɑːdʒəbəl‖ˈtʃɑːr-/ *adj* **1** an amount of money that is chargeable can be charged and must be paid: *The annual fees chargeable for the coming university year are £3,104.*

2 work or time that is chargeable must be paid for: *1,500 chargeable hours on a case is a common target for personal injury lawyers.*

3 if income or profits are chargeable, tax must be paid on them: *The company's chargeable profits for the period were agreed at £66,030,816.*

chargeable asset —see under ASSET

charge account —see under ACCOUNT¹

charge card —see under CARD

charge certificate —see under CERTIFICATE

charge-off *n* [C] when you lose profit because money that is owed to you will not be repaid: *Charge-offs for loan losses were only 0.7% of total loans, about half the average for regional banks.*

charge on assets *n* plural **charges on assets** [C] FINANCE the right of people who are owed money by a company to receive money from the company's assets if the debt is not paid on time

charges register —see under REGISTER¹

charitable trust —see under TRUST

char·i·ty /ˈtʃærəti/ *n* plural **charities** **1** [C] an organization that collects money to help people, for example those who are sick or poor, or to help certain types of activity such as artistic activity; NOT-FOR-PROFIT ORGANIZATION, NON-PROFIT ORGANIZATION *AmE*: *a charity set up to help Bosnian children* | *We are asking employees to make a regular donation to the charity.*

2 [U] money or gifts given to help people, for example those who are sick or poor: *All of the money raised will go to charity.* | *a sponsored cycle ride for charity*

Charity Commission *n* in Britain, an official organization that makes sure that charities act legally and honestly: *New trustees took over the running of the fund two years ago, after an inquiry by the Charity Commission.* —**Charity Commissioner** *n* [C] *Charity Commissioners are investigating the disappearance of thousands of pounds of funds.*

chart¹ /tʃɑːt‖tʃɑːrt/ *n* [C] a mathematical drawing or list, showing information arranged in a way that is clear and easy to understand: *European companies account for the remaining 89% of sales – see chart on next page.* —compare GRAPH¹, —see also FLIPCHART

bar chart *BrE* a mathematical drawing in the form of a series of long thin boxes next to each other, each box representing an amount being compared with all the others; BAR GRAPH *AmE*: *The bar chart shows what the average Westerner consumes in a year compared with someone from the Third World.*

break-even chart ACCOUNTING a drawing with lines and numbers that shows how costs and profits change according to the level of production of a product: *Break-even charts are useful for their indication of the effects of marginal changes in sales volume or costs on profit figures.*

flow chart also **flow diagram**, **flow sheet** a mathematical drawing in the form of shapes and lines, showing the series of stages in a process and how they are connected with each other: *We have used flow charts for the definition of some of the more complex legislation.* | *a simplified flow diagram of the economy*

Gantt chart a chart that shows the different stages of a piece of work, showing stages that can be done at the same time, and stages that have to be completed before other stages can begin

organization chart also **organisation chart** *BrE* a drawing of lines connected together, showing the structure of an organization, what each part does, and how it is related to others within the same organization and outside organizations: *an organization chart, showing lines of command, departmental responsibility, and broad fields of jurisdiction*

pie chart a drawing of a circle divided into several sections, each section representing an amount as a percentage of the whole: *If you look at a pie chart of how public money is spent in this country, it's difficult to find the slice that is the arts.*

chart² *v* [T] **1** to carefully record information about a situation over a period of time to see how it changes or develops: *We are collecting large amounts of information on households and companies in order to chart the effects of taxes and benefits.*

2 to plan something new in detail: *a national conference set up to chart a democratic future for the country*

char·ter¹ /ˈtʃɑːtə‖ˈtʃɑːrtər/ *v* [T] **1** to pay for the use of a plane, boat, train etc for a particular period of time or a particular journey: *The US government has chartered 41 commercial vessels to carry equipment to the Mideast.*

2 to officially allow a financial institution to operate in a particular place: *Banks chartered in Delaware are allowed to act as insurers.*

charter² *n* **1** [C,U] an arrangement in which a person or organization pays a company to use its ships, aircraft etc: *Two of its ships were being repaired and unavailable for charter.* | ***Charter rates*** (=rates charged for charter) *for oil tankers have risen to more than $50,000 a day.* | *No ship without a* ***charter party*** (=official contract between the owner and the user) *could be loaded.*

bareboat charter also **demise charter** *BrE* [C] a charter in which the owner rents out a ship or aircraft only, and the client provides fuel, people to work on it etc

time charter [C] a charter in which the owner rents out a ship for a particular period of time

voyage charter [C] a charter in which the owner rents out a ship for a particular journey

2 [C] LAW in the US, an official document that allows a business to operate and controls its activities: *Smith Barney, Harris Upham & Co was granted a New York state charter for its newly formed Smith Barney Trust Co, which will offer money management services.*

3 [C] a statement of the principles, duties, and aims of an organization: *The United Nations charter may be changed to allow Japan a seat on the security council.* | *Last year the BBC's charter was renewed for 10 years.*

citizen's charter [singular] in Britain and some other countries, a statement about standards of service that people should expect from local and national government departments: *Spain is considering a citizen's charter to cut bureaucracy.*

C

char·tered /ˈtʃɑːtəd‖ˈtʃɑːrtərd/ *adj* [only before a noun] **1** a chartered ship, aircraft etc is one that someone has paid to borrow: *Thirty people were killed when a chartered airliner carrying French tourists crashed in Senegal.*

2 in the US, a chartered organization is one that has an official document that allows it to operate: *the decision to close 45 state chartered banks* | *a federally chartered company*

chartered accountant —see under ACCOUNTANT

Chartered Association of Certified Accountants *n* one of the professional organizations for ACCOUNTANTS in Britain

Chartered Financial Consultant *n* [C] a member of the American society of Chartered Life Underwriters and Chartered Financial Consultants, qualified to give financial advice

Chartered Institute of Bankers abbreviation **CIB** *n* a professional organization offering training and information for people working in banking in Britain

Chartered Institute of Insurers abbreviation **CII** *n* a British professional organization for managers in the insurance industry

Chartered Institute of Marketing abbreviation **CIM** *n* a British professional organization for managers in marketing

Chartered Institute of Public Finance and Accountancy *n* a British professional organization for financial managers working for government departments or organizations

Chartered Life Underwriter abbreviation **CLU** *n* [C] someone who is a member of the American society of Chartered Life Underwriters and Chartered Financial Consultants and is qualified to sell and give advice about life insurance

char·ter·er /ˈtʃɑːtərə‖ˈtʃɑːrtərər/ *n* [C] a person or organization that rents a ship or plane from its owner: *Some shipping companies are passing the higher insurance costs on to charterers and shippers.*

chart·ist /ˈtʃɑːtɪst‖ˈtʃɑːr-/ *n* [C] FINANCE someone who studies past patterns in share prices and other market movements to say how they might change or move in the future: *Chartists get clues to future price changes by studying price and volume trends.*

chat room *n* [C] a place on the INTERNET where users can send and receive messages to other uses about something that interests them: *A conversation about the case took place in the WBS-Talk political chat room last week.*

chat·tels /ˈtʃætlz/ *n* [plural] LAW the things that someone owns, not including land or buildings: *the **goods and chattels** that made up the Duke's personal estate* | *a person whose chattels have been seized by the police*

chattels personal *n* [plural] LAW the things that a person owns that can be moved

chattels real *n* [plural] LAW **1** *BrE* property that someone owns LEASEHOLD

2 *AmE* things other than property that someone owns

cheap /tʃiːp/ *adj* **1** not costing very much to buy: *At least the accommodation and food are cheap.* | *Buyers got their orders in while shares were relatively cheap.* | *the introduction of special cheap fares to France*

2 not costing very much to produce, use, or employ: *the prospect of obtaining cheap electricity from sunlight* | *These taxes are cheap to administer.* —**cheaply** *adv*: *Pork is priced cheaply in relation to beef.* | *China is keen to buy metals cheaply.*

3 on the cheap *BrE* if work is done on the cheap, it is done for less money than you would expect and may not be done very well: *Much of the building work was done on the cheap, using materials salvaged from old buildings.*

cheat /tʃiːt/ *v* [I,T] to deceive someone, break rules, or behave dishonestly, especially in order to make money for yourself: *Not all publishers want to cheat authors.* | *There are stiff penalties for stockbrokers who cheat customers.* **cheat on sth**: *These new rules could lead more people to cheat on their taxes.* **cheat sb out of sth**: *He accused his employer of deliberately trying to cheat him out of his redundancy money.* —**cheating** *n* [U] *Auditors will check the information for any patterns that might indicate cheating by floor traders.*

check¹ /tʃek/ *n* **1** [C] *AmE* the American spelling of CHEQUE: *After a minute, she wrote out the check and placed it on the table.*

rubber check *informal* a cheque that a bank refuses to accept because the person who wrote it does not have enough money in their account

2 [C] an examination or investigation of something to see that it is correct, true, or safe and in the condition it should be: *The fund is monitored regularly by carrying out a check of all outgoing payments against the register.* | *You can get a free safety check on your gas fire from British Gas.* | *I passed my **medical check** and was then sent to HQ.*

background check also **background investigation** an examination by an employer of the background of someone who wants to work for them: *30% of all fraud losses would have been avoided if proper background checks had been done.*

credit check [C] a check carried out by a lender or employer, looking at someone's record in repaying loans before giving them a new loan or a job: *Then come a questionnaire, two interviews, credit checks, psychological and drug tests, police screening and 32 hours of training.*

spot check [C] a check on particular things or people from a group, done without warning: *A spot check of 140 vehicles entering the car park revealed 18 people not wearing a seatbelt.*

3 keep a check on to watch or examine something regularly to make sure that it is correct, true, or safe and in the condition it should be: *It's important to keep a constant check on cashflow.*

4 [C,U] something that controls another thing and stops it from happening more or getting worse: *Higher interest rates act as a check on government spending.*

5 keep/hold something in check to keep something under control: *The bank may have to raise interest rates further to keep inflation in check.*

6 [C] *AmE* the bill you are given in a restaurant at the end of your meal, showing what you have eaten and the cost; BILL *BrE*

7 [C] *AmE* a mark that you put next to an answer to show it is correct or against an item on a list to show that you have dealt with it; TICK *BrE*

check² *v* **1** [I,T] to find out whether something is

correct, true, or safe: *Insurance arrangements will be included in the pension scheme, but you should check that cover is adequate.* | *Employers have the right to check the criminal record of a potential employee.*

2 [T] to stop something bad from happening more or getting worse: *They welcomed the Bundesbank's tighter monetary policy to check inflation and provide for a healthier economic recovery next year.*

3 [T] to leave your bags at a place such as an airport: *We checked our baggage at left-luggage and went for a meal.*

4 [T] *AmE* to make a mark next to an answer or something on a list to show that it is correct or has been dealt with; TICK *BrE*: *Make sure that you check each item on the invoice against the original order.*

check sth ↔ **in** *phr v* [I,T] to go to the desk at a hotel or airport and say that you have arrived: *The keycard is authorised automatically when the guest checks in.* | *His suitcase was already checked in.*

check sth ↔ **off** *phr v* [T] to write a mark next to an item on a list, showing that you have dealt with it or it is correct: *Check people's names off as they arrive.*

check out *phr v* **1** [T] **check** sth ↔ **out** to make sure that something is true, correct, or safe: *I checked out the financial aspects of buying into the company.*

2 [I] if information or a document checks out, it proves to be correct or true: *If your credit limit checks out, you can make a purchase today.*

3 [I] to leave a hotel after paying the bill: *You've got to check out by 12:00.* —see also CHECKOUT

check•book /ˈtʃekbʊk/ *n* [C] *AmE* a book of checks given by a bank to its customers; CHEQUEBOOK *BrE*

check digit —see under DIGIT

check•er /ˈtʃekə‖-ər/ *n* [C] **1** COMPUTING **spell/spelling/grammar checker** a computer program that checks spelling or grammar: *an automatic grammar checker that searches for missing words, bad punctuation etc*

2 someone whose job is to check that things are correct or done correctly: *our quality control checker*

3 *AmE* someone who works in a SUPERMARKET, adding up the cost of the goods people buy

check kiting *n* [U] *AmE* when someone illegally obtains credit from one of their bank accounts by paying in a cheque from another account, taking money out against this cheque and using it for a few days before having to repay the original amount

check•list /ˈtʃekˌlɪst/ *n* [C] a list of things you need or have to do for a particular job or activity, written to help you remember to get or to do these things: *Use your tax return as a financial planning checklist for next year.*

check•out /ˈtʃek-aʊt/ *n* **1** [C] the place in a SUPERMARKET where you pay for the things you are buying: *a magazine for sale at* ***checkout*** *counters*

2 [U] the time by which you must leave a hotel room: *Checkout is at noon.*

chemical engineering —see under ENGINEERING

cheque *BrE* **check** *AmE* /tʃek/ *n* [C] **1** BANKING a printed form that you use to pay for something instead of using money. You write on it the amount in words and numbers, the date, the person being paid, and sign your name: *a cheque for £200* | *You can pay* ***by cheque*** *or credit card.* | *He* ***cashed the cheque*** (=exchanged it for cash) *at a High Street bank.* | *He had second thoughts, and phoned his bank to* ***stop the cheque*** (=tell the bank not to pay it). | *As long as you don't exceed the agreed limit, the bank won't* ***bounce your cheques*** (=refuse to pay them because there is not enough money in your account).

2 float a check *AmE* to write a cheque that you do not have money in the bank to pay

ante-dated cheque *BrE* **ante-dated check** *AmE* a cheque on which you write a date which is earlier than the actual date

bank cheque *BrE* also **banker's cheque** *BrE* **bank check** *AmE* a cheque written by a bank from one of its own accounts. A customer can use a bank cheque to pay someone who will not accept a personal cheque.

bearer cheque *BrE* **bearer check** *AmE* a cheque where the money can be paid to any person who presents it to the bank, not just to a person named on the cheque

blank cheque *BrE* **blank check** *AmE* a cheque that has been signed, but where no amount has been written in

cashier's cheque *BrE* **cashier's check** *AmE* a cheque written by a bank from one of its own accounts

certified cheque *BrE* **certified check** *AmE* a cheque that a bank promises in writing to pay: *Only a certified cheque, cashier's cheque or bank draft is acceptable.*

crossed cheque *BrE* a cheque with two lines across it, and the words 'account payee', showing that it can only be paid into a bank account of the person named on the cheque, and not exchanged for cash or paid into a different account; THIRD PARTY CHECK *AmE*: *A crossed cheque gives some protection against fraud.*

dud cheque *BrE* **dud check** *AmE* a cheque that cannot be paid because the person who wrote it has no money or not enough money in their bank account

endorsed cheque *BrE* **endorsed check** *AmE* a cheque on which the person the cheque is made out to has written someone else's name on it so that the other person can receive the money: *Banks could not confirm the signature on endorsed cheques, so stolen cheques could be easily cashed.*

open cheque *BrE* a cheque that is not a CROSSED CHEQUE. The person whose name appears on the cheque can write the name of another person on it, and the money will be paid to them

personal cheque *BrE* **personal check** *AmE* a cheque written by a private person, not an organization: *Personal cheques are accepted if accompanied by a valid cheque card.*

post-dated cheque *BrE* **post-dated check** *AmE* a cheque on which you write a date that is later than the actual date

stale cheque *BrE* a cheque which a bank will not accept and exchange for money or payment because it was written more than six months ago

third party check *AmE* a cheque with the name of the person it is being paid to written on it; CROSSED CHEQUE *BrE*

traveller's cheque *BrE* **traveler's check** *AmE* a cheque for a fixed amount that can be bought from a bank and cashed for local currency in another country: *Lists of stolen or lost traveller's cheques are circulated to hotels.* —see also EUROCHEQUE, PAYCHEQUE

cheque account —see under ACCOUNT[1]

cheque•book /ˈtʃekbʊk/ *n* [C] *BrE* a book of cheques given by a bank to its customers; CHECKBOOK *AmE*

cheque card —see under CARD

cheque rate —see under RATE[1]

cherry-pick *v* [T] *informal* to take or buy only the best things from a group: *Some banks have cherry-picked their investments to provide instant profits.* —**cherry-picking** *n* [U] *He called their actions "financial cherry-picking".*

Chicago Board of Trade written abbreviation **CBOT**, or **CBT** *n* FINANCE the main US market for trading in grain and some types of FUTURES

Chicago Board Options Exchange abbreviation **CBOE** *n* FINANCE the main US market for trading in OPTIONS

Chicago Mercantile Exchange abbreviation **CME** *n* FINANCE an important US market for trading in FUTURES, currencies, and LIVESTOCK (=animals)

Chicago School *n* ECONOMICS a group of economists at the University of Chicago who believe that economic success comes from letting the forces of supply and demand operate freely in a market and by controlling the amount of money in an economy at one time

chief accountant —see under ACCOUNTANT

chief executive —see under EXECUTIVE[1]

Chief Executive Officer —see under OFFICER

chief financial officer —see under OFFICER

chief information officer —see under OFFICER

chief knowledge officer —see under KNOWLEDGE OFFICER

chief operating officer —see under OFFICER

child allowance *n* [U] the old name for CHILD BENEFIT

child benefit —see under BENEFIT[1]

Chinese wall *n* [C usually plural] FINANCE in certain financial institutions, an action to stop secret information passing between departments where one department could gain from the information. For example, a department buying and selling shares might gain from information from the department that gives advice on MERGERS (=when one company joins with another to form one larger company): *The securities commission fined the financial group for failing to maintain Chinese Walls between its corporate finance and broking arms.*

chip /tʃɪp/ *n* **1** also **silicon chip** [C] COMPUTING a small electronic device, used in a computer to store information, organize the computer's operating system, run programs etc; MICROCHIP: *This new type of semiconductor allows designers to put more circuits on a chip.*

2 FINANCE *informal* a share in a company: *Brokers will start bidding for chips in MicroTech as soon as the London market opens.*

blue chip [C usually plural] a share in a well-managed, successful company with a long record of paying profits to shareholders during good and bad economic times: *FTSE 100 stocks posted gains as buyers returned to the quality blue chips.*

red chip [C usually plural] a share in a Chinese company that is listed on the Hong Kong stockmarket: *Hong Kong made strong gains in response to a surge in red chips.* —see also BARGAINING CHIP

chip card —see under CARD

CHIPS /tʃɪps/ abbreviation for CLEARING HOUSE INTERBANK PAYMENTS SYSTEM

chit /tʃɪt/ *n* [C] an official note giving you permission to do something, receive something etc: *You had to sign a chit to use any of the equipment in the lab.* | *expenses chits*

Chun•nel /ˈtʃʌnl/ *n* **the Chunnel** another name for the CHANNEL TUNNEL: *The opening of the Chunnel has prompted ferry companies to offer better deals.*

churn[1] /tʃɜːn‖tʃɜːrn/ *n* [U] MARKETING the number of customers who stop buying a service from a supplier in a particular period of time, either because they stop using the service or because they change to another supplier; TURNOVER: *The cable TV company's churn is 22% and is expected to rise when new prices come into effect.*

churn[2] *v*

churn sth ↔ **out** *phr v* [T] to produce large quantities of something, perhaps without caring about quality: *The plant turns out more than half a million cheap watches a month.*

churn•ing /ˈtʃɜːnɪŋ‖-ɜːr-/ *n* [U] *informal* FINANCE when a STOCKBROKER buys and sells different investments for their clients more often than they should, in order to increase the amount of COMMISSION they earn: *He will consider increasing taxes on short-term trades as a way to discourage churning of stocks.*

CIB abbreviation for CHARTERED INSTITUTE OF BANKERS

CIF abbreviation for COST, INSURANCE, FREIGHT

CIM abbreviation for COMPUTER-INTEGRATED MANUFACTURE

CIO abbreviation for CHIEF INFORMATION OFFICER —see AFL-CIO

CIP abbreviation for CARRIAGE AND INSURANCE PAID

circuit board —see under BOARD[1]

circuit judge —see under JUDGE[1]

cir•cu•lar /ˈsɜːkjələ‖ˈsɜːrkjələr/ *n* [C] an official letter or advertisement sent to a lot of people: *The government's instructions were issued to local authorities via circulars.* | *a **circular letter** sent out by one insurance company, urging people to 'Act Now And Beat The Tax Man'*

cir•cu•late /ˈsɜːkjəleɪt‖ˈsɜːr-/ *v* [T] to send a letter or information to people: *A summary of the report was circulated to all board members.*

circulating asset —see ***current asset*** under ASSET

cir•cu•la•tion /ˌsɜːkjəˈleɪʃən‖ˌsɜːr-/ *n* **1** [U] the exchange of money within an economy: *It was a bold anti-inflation plan, including a squeeze on the circulation of money.*

2 [U] if money is in circulation, it is being used by people in an economy. If money is out of circulation, it is not being used: *An obvious sign of hyperinflation is the massive increase in the quantity of money in circulation.* | *The Spanish government is withdrawing more than 500,000 million pesetas from circulation.*

3 [C usually singular] the average number of copies of a newspaper or magazine that are sold each day, week, or month: *The paper's circulation increased by 150,000.* | *a **mass circulation** (=selling a very large number of copies) newspaper*

CISCO also **Cisco** /ˈsɪskəʊ‖-koʊ/ *n* FINANCE the City Group for Smaller Companies; an organization that represents smaller companies whose shares are sold on the stockmarket: *The conference was run by the Guild of Shareholders and Cisco.*

Citizen's Advice Bureau abbreviation **CAB** *n* plural **Citizen's Advice Bureaux** **1** [singular] an organization in Britain with offices in many towns, which give free advice to members of the public who need help with legal, financial, or other problems

2 [C] an office of the Citizen's Advice Bureau

citizen's charter —see under CHARTER[2]

Cit•y /ˈsɪti/ *n* **1 The City** London's financial institutions, for example the INTERNATIONAL STOCK EXCHANGE and other markets, banks, and insurance companies considered together as a financial centre: *The City will keep its position as a leading financial centre whether the UK joins the single currency or not.*

2 The City the area of London where most financial institutions are based: *BZW left the City for brand new premises in Canary Wharf.*

City Bank —see under BANK[1]

City Code on Takeovers and Mergers —see under CODE

City desk *n* **the City desk** the department of a British newspaper that deals with financial news

City Group for Smaller Companies —see CISCO

civic center —see under CENTRE

civ•il /ˈsɪvəl/ *adj* [only before a noun] relating to legal cases concerning private problems or disagreements rather than crimes: *He brought a **civil suit** against Northrop.* | *a senior lawyer who supervises all criminal and civil litigation in the division*

civil aviation —see under AVIATION

Civil Aviation Authority abbreviation **CAA** *n* the organization responsible for air traffic control and airline safety in Britain —compare FEDERAL AVIATION ADMINISTRATION

civil commotion *n* [U] INSURANCE large-scale violence by members of the public, causing damage to people or property. This is not covered by normal insurance policies: *No cover is provided for loss or damage caused by riots or civil commotion.*

civil court —see under COURT[1]

civil damages —see under DAMAGE[1]

civil engineering —see under ENGINEERING

civil law —see under LAW

civil liability —see under LIABILITY

claim[1] /kleɪm/ *n* [C] **1** a request or demand for money, or the amount of money asked for: *The developer **made a claim** against the owner for extra building costs.* | *There were very large claims for loss of earnings.* | *The company finally agreed to **settle** her **claim*** (=pay it) *for damages.*

pay claim a demand by employees for more money: *Teaching unions are to take strike action in support of their pay claim.*

2 also **insurance claim** INSURANCE a request for a payment for damage, theft, injury etc for which you are insured: *Europ Assistance will deal with any claim received from the insured.* | *This form will be needed should you have to **make an insurance claim**.* | *Unocal's results included a net gain of $87.3 million from the **settlement of insurance claims** resulting from the interruption of its operations.* —see also STATEMENT OF CLAIM

damage claim an insurance claim for something that has been damaged but not completely lost: *There is the possibility of a damage claim, should an accident occur due to the event being held on the highway.*

exaggerated claim an exaggerated claim is one in which the insured person dishonestly says that the value of goods stolen or damaged is greater than their true value

3 LAW a right to have or get something such as land or other assets that belong to you: *Northern Telecom says it has a prior claim to the initials 'NT' and has told Microsoft it can't use them.*

counter-claim LAW when someone who is being taken to court by another person tries to take that other person to court and ask for money from them: *The four men are suing QM for wrongful dismissal; the company has filed defences against them, and made a counter-claim for damages.*

priority claim a request to a law court by a person or organization that is owed money by a bankrupt company, asking to be paid before others that are also owed money: *Some attempts to establish priority claims against companies in bankruptcy have met adverse court rulings.*

4 MARKETING a favourable statement made about a product by its producer that may or may not be true: *P&G has been forced by the Food and Drug Administration to remove 'no cholesterol' claims from its labels.*

claim[2] *v* [I,T] **1** to officially request, demand, or receive money from an organization: *The new rules mean young people between 16 and 18 can no longer claim unemployment benefit.* | *Alcan claimed damages for the losses that resulted from the government cancelling the project.*

2 INSURANCE to request and perhaps receive money for damage, theft, injury etc for which you are insured **claim (sth) on**: *Can you claim on your household insurance if the tiles on your roof are stolen?*

3 LAW to state that you have a right to something or to take something that belongs to you: *They wanted to expand the golf course on land that Indians had claimed.*

clai•mant /ˈkleɪmənt/ *n* [C] **1** someone who requests or receives money from the state because they are ill, unemployed etc: *claimants for long-term sickness benefits*

2 INSURANCE someone who requests and receives money from an insurer for damage, theft, injury etc for which they are insured: *No payment will be made if the claimant, at the time of effecting the insurance, was receiving medical treatment.*

3 LAW someone who demands money from a person or organization that has caused harm to them: *Claimants using a product while drunk will not receive damages.*

4 LAW someone who states that they have a right to take or receive something that belongs to them: *a claimant to an interest in land*

claims adjuster —see under ADJUSTER

class /klɑːs‖klæs/ *n* [C] **1** one of the groups that society can be divided into according to their jobs, income etc: *the professional classes* | ***Social class** 4 consists of semi-skilled manual occupations.*

the working class *especially BrE* the group of people in society who traditionally do physical work and do not have much money or power: *the power resources of the working class* —**working-class** *adj*: *working-class skilled manual labourers* | *a working class area of Newcastle*

2 a particular quality of product or service: *Many more women are now buying their own luxury class jewellery.* | *Boeing 767s have 174 seats – 14 for **first class**, 30 for **business class**, and 130 for **economy class**.*

3 a particular type of product or service: *The company is developing a new class of pharmaceuticals based on nucleotides.*

4 FINANCE a particular type of a company's liabilities, or the people to whom they are owed: *One class of secured creditors will receive 95% of the face value of their bonds.*

5 class A/B etc shares different types of shares in a company whose owners have different rights in the company, for example different voting rights and different rights to be repaid if the company goes bankrupt: *Class A shares in Meralco are available to Filipinos only and are 118 pesos each; class B shares cost 121 pesos.*

class action —see under ACTION

classical economics —see under ECONOMICS

classification society *BrE*, **classification authority** *AmE n* [C] INSURANCE an official organization that is responsible for making sure that ships are as safe as possible and for putting ships into classes according to their safety: *Shipbuilding contracts invariably say that the ship must comply with the rules of the relevant Classification Society.*

clas•si•fied /ˈklæsɪfaɪd/ *adj* classified information or documents are ones that the government has ordered to be kept secret: *classified documents relating to defence contracts*

classified ad —see under AD

classified advertisement —see under ADVERTISEMENT

classified catalogue —see under CATALOGUE[1]

classified common stock —see under STOCK[1]

clas•si•fy /ˈklæsɪfaɪ/ *v* past tense and past participle **classified** [T] to state officially that something belongs to a particular group or type **classify sth as sth**: *a substance that is officially classified as hazardous*

clause /klɔːz‖klɒːz/ *n* [C] a part of a written law, contract, or legal document that deals with a particular item or subject: *Clause 12 enables the Secretary of State to make orders to protect pension rights.* | *A confidentiality clause was added to the contract.*

average clause INSURANCE a condition set by an insurer that a payment for damage or loss will be in proportion to the value insured. For example, if a building worth £100,000 but insured for £50,000 is totally destroyed, the insurers will only pay £25,000

breakdown clause a condition in a contract, saying

that someone who pays to use a ship, aircraft, vehicle, or piece of machinery will not have to pay any money during any period of time when the ship, aircraft etc is not working properly

commerce clause a clause in the US CONSTITUTION, giving Congress the authority to control business, labour, and farming that takes place between the different states of the US: *Discrimination against waste from other states violates the interstate commerce clause of the American Constitution.*

confidentiality clause HUMAN RESOURCES a clause, especially in a contract of employment, that says you must not give other people or companies private information about your employer's activities: *He had breached the terms of a confidentiality clause in his agreement.*

continuation clause INSURANCE a clause in an insurance policy by which insurance cover will continue after the end of the policy until a new one is paid for

enabling clause part of a new law or bill that gives officials the power to start using the new law and to make sure it is obeyed: *Local authorities have the strategy and the enabling powers to make provision for housing, including for the homeless.*

escalator clause part of a contract that states that a price or other quantity may be increased if certain conditions occur: *Canada proposed an escalator clause for an airline to increase services if its aircraft were more than 65% full.*

escape clause part of a contract that states that someone is no longer bound by a particular part of a contract if certain conditions occur: *The wage deal has an escape clause: companies may pay their workers less if they exercise a 'hardship clause'.*

grandfather clause *AmE* a clause in a new rule stating that a person or business already doing the activity covered by the rule does not have to follow it: *The new rule has a good chance of winning approval because it has a generous grandfather clause.*

objects clause the clause in a company's MEMORANDUM OF ASSOCIATION (=a document giving all the details of a new company when it is formed), listing the things that the company will do, including the types of goods and services that it will deal with: *The objects clause did not provide for the construction and running of railway systems, only for the manufacture of railway equipment.*

penalty clause a condition in a contract that says what will happen if one of the people or organizations involved does not do what the contract states they should: *The defendants were liable to a penalty clause in the main contract if the work was not completed on time.* —see also INSTITUTE CLAUSES

claused bill of lading —see under BILL OF LADING

claw /klɔː‖klɒː/ *v*

claw back *phr v BrE* **1** [T] **claw** sth ↔ **back** FINANCE if a company claws back shares, it takes back new shares that it had offered to its present shareholders, but they do not want to buy, and offers them to other investors: *Shares worth £800 million have been set aside for new investors, rising to £1.2 billion if extra shares are clawed back from the members' offer.*

2 [T] **claw** sth ↔ **back** if an authority claws back money from someone, it gets back money previously received by that person: *If partners' earnings for the two years before the collapse of the partnership were judged excessive, then they could be clawed back to help pay debts.*

3 [I,T] **claw** sth ↔ **back** if a financial market or something traded on one claws back to a previous level, its value slowly goes back up to that level after a fall: *Telecom shares have now clawed back 40 cents from their low of NZ$7.70 hit last Tuesday.* | *Wall Street* ***clawed back*** *early losses to end the morning comfortably higher.*

claw-back *n* **1** [C] FINANCE when a company takes back new shares that it had offered to its present shareholders, but they do not want to buy, and offers them to other investors: *Just over 5.2 million new shares are being placed, with 3.1 million subject to clawback.*

2 [C,U] when an authority gets back money from a person who previously received it from them: *In the privatisation of Belfast airport, the Audit Office criticized the Treasury for not including a clawback clause on any future resale.*

clean[1] /kliːn/ *adj* **1** done in a fair or legal way, or showing that you have followed the rules or the law: *In ethical investment, investors try to buy shares in companies with a clean record.* | *His clean credit history will give him access to bank financing.*

2 clean products or industrial methods do not damage the environment; GREEN: *clean vehicles such as electric cars and natural-gas buses* | *clean coal technology*

clean[2] *v*

clean out *phr v* [T] **1 clean sb/sth out** to take all the money of a person or organization: *The 16 bankrupt financial institutions threatened to clean out the central bank's reserves.*

2 clean sth ↔ **out** to improve an organization by removing parts or people that are not making money or are not effective or honest: *The banks must restructure to cut costs and clean out portfolios that are full of bad loans.* —see also CLEAN-OUT

clean up *phr v* **1** [T] **clean** sth ↔ **up** to improve an organization by removing parts or people that are not making money or are not effective or honest: *Weyer is cleaning up its income statement and developing a more profitable business.* —see also CLEAN-UP

2 [I] to make a lot of money in a deal: *The traders buying the bonds cleaned up, because they carried high fixed interest rates when inflation was falling quickly.*

clean bill of health —see under HEALTH

clean bill of lading —see under BILL OF LADING

clean·ers /ˈkliːnəz‖-ərz/ *n* **take sb to the cleaners** *informal* to cheat someone out of a lot of money: *She took on an agent to make sure she was not taken to the cleaners in the contract.*

clean hands *n* [plural] someone with clean hands has not been involved in dishonest activities: *In a political scandal, it is rare to find anyone with clean hands.*

clean opinion *n* [singular] ACCOUNTING a good report that is given about a company's finances by someone who has officially checked them: *Peat issued a clean opinion of Penn Square's financial condition.*

clean-out *n* [C] when an organization is improved by removing parts or people that are not making money or are not effective or honest: *The country needs a clean-out of the balance sheets of its industrial companies.* —see also ***clean out*** under CLEAN[2]

clean-up *n* [C] when an organization is improved by removing parts or people that are not making money or are not effective or honest: *A clean-up may require financial help from the World Bank.* —see also ***clean up*** under CLEAN[2]

clear /klɪə‖klɪr/ *v* [T] **1** to give permission for a product to be sold or for a deal to be made: *Glaxo migraine medicine has been cleared by the Food and Drug Administration.* | *Venezuela's congress cleared the sale of the state telephone company CANTV.*

2 BANKING **clear trades/transactions** to make payments relating to trading on financial markets or trading of goods: *About 1,000 small brokerage firms are using the company to clear and settle their trades.* | *It takes ages for the banks here to clear transactions and it's very expensive.*

3 clear a cheque if a bank clears a cheque, or if a cheque clears, the money is sent from one bank to another and the cheque is paid: *The fraud relied on managers returning money before the original cheque had cleared.*

4 clear sth through customs/clear customs to be allowed to take things through CUSTOMS: *Bribery is needed to get goods cleared through customs.* | *They cleared customs, but never boarded their flight.*

5 clear a debt to pay a debt in full: *Russia is to pay France $400 million to clear its outstanding pre-revolution debts.*

6 *informal* to earn a particular amount of money, or to make a particular amount of profit: *Diane clears £20,000 a year.*

7 to sell goods cheaply in order to get rid of them: *Ford is offering discounts in order to clear out last year's models.*

clear sth ↔ **out** *phr v* [T] to sell goods cheaply in order to get rid of them: *We need to clear the old stock before we can bring in this season's range of products.*

clear·ance /ˈklɪərəns‖ˈklɪr-/ *n* [C,U] permission to sell a product or do a deal: *The government gave clearance to plans by Thorn to acquire Thames Television.* —see also CUSTOMS CLEARANCE

clearance sale —see under SALE

clear·er /ˈklɪərə‖ˈklɪrər/ *n* [C usually plural] **1** BANKING a bank that clears cheques; CLEARING BANK: *Compare Lloyds TSB, the smallest of the big four clearers, with HSBC.*

2 FINANCE an organization that makes payments between banks and other financial institutions; CLEARING HOUSE: *Technology is forcing change among the clearers – the houses that clear and settle the trades carried out on the world's markets.*

clear·ing /ˈklɪərɪŋ‖ˈklɪr-/ *n* [U] BANKING, FINANCE when banks and other financial institutions make payments to each other at the end of a period of trading so that they no longer owe each other any money: *a pan-European clearing system*

clearing agent *n* [C] FINANCE another name for a CLEARING HOUSE

clearing bank —see under BANK[1]

clearing house —see under HOUSE

Clearing House Automated Payment System abbreviation **CHAPS** *n* BANKING a computerized system for making high-value payments between banks in Britain and Europe, jointly owned by British banks and others

Clearing House Interbank Payments System **CHIPS** *n* BANKING a computerized system for making high-value international payments in dollars

cler·i·cal /ˈklerɪkəl/ *adj* connected with office work, especially with keeping records or accounts and dealing with letters: *He held a series of undemanding clerical jobs.* | *A spokesman blamed a* ***clerical error*** *for material going to the wrong address.* | *a* ***clerical assistant***

clerical assistant —see under ASSISTANT

clerical staff —see under STAFF[1]

clerk /klɑːk‖klɜːrk/ *n* [C] **1** someone who keeps records or accounts in an office: *a filing clerk*

bank clerk someone who works in a bank, serving customers and doing other jobs

correspondence clerk someone whose job is to receive, answer, and file letters and other documents in an office

filing clerk *old-fashioned* a person who works in an office whose job is to store all the papers and documents in the right order: *She tried a government training course in shorthand and typing but, lacking confidence, ended up as a filing clerk.*

ledger clerk ACCOUNTING someone whose job is to enter information in a LEDGER (=an accounting record showing what a business has bought or sold)

2 an official in charge of the records of a court, town council etc: *Plans of the land were deposited with the clerk of the county council.*

3 *AmE* someone who deals with people arriving in a hotel: *Leave the keys with the* ***desk clerk***. —see also SALESCLERK

cli·ent /ˈklaɪənt/ *n* [C] **1** someone who pays for services or advice from a professional person or organization: *British Aerospace is one of the stockbroking firm's* ***corporate clients*** (=clients that are companies). | *Defence lawyer Ronald Cole said his client was suffering from deep depression.*

2 someone who buys something from a seller; CUSTOMER: *Most of the shop's regular clients are men.*

3 COMPUTING a computer connected to another computer that controls it, for example in a NETWORK —compare SERVER

client account —see under ACCOUNT[1]

cli·en·tele /ˌkliːənˈtel‖ˌklaɪənˈtel, ˌkliː-/ *n* [singular] all the people who regularly use the services of a person or organization: *Sharelink has built up a clientele of about 57,000 in two years.* | *The bar's clientele was almost entirely male.*

client machine —see under MACHINE[1]

client/server architecture —see under ARCHITECTURE

clinch /klɪntʃ/ *v* [T] to finally succeed in getting or winning something: *Advertising creates the interest, but personal selling* ***clinches the deal***.

clinical governance —see under GOVERNANCE

clip·board /ˈklɪpbɔːd‖-bɔːrd/ *n* [C] **1** a small flat board with a piece of metal or plastic on top for holding pieces of paper so that you can write on them

2 COMPUTING a part of a computer memory that stores sections of text while you move them from one part of a document to another, or to another document

CLO abbreviation for COLLATERALIZED LOAN OBLIGATION

clock /klɒk‖klɑːk/ *v*

clock in also **clock on** *BrE phr v* [I] to record on a special card the time you arrive at work or begin work: *I clock on at 8:30.*

clock off *BrE* also **clock out** *phr v* [I] to record on a special card the time you stop work or leave work: *I'm clocking off early today.*

clock up sth *phr v* [T] to reach a particular number or amount: *Thomas has clocked up 40 years service with Llanidloes.* | *The UK clocked up record exports of £4.3 billion.*

clock·speed /ˈklɒkspiːd‖ˈklɑːk-/ *n* [C usually singular] COMPUTING the speed at which a computer operates and deals with information

clone /kləʊn‖kloʊn/ *n* [C] **1** COMPUTING a computer that is almost an exact copy of a different type of computer and can use programs that were written for it: *an IBM clone*

2 an animal or plant that is produced from the cells of another animal or plant and is exactly the same as it —**clone** *v* [T]

close[1] /kləʊz‖kloʊz/ *v* **1** [I,T] also **close down** if a company, shop etc closes or someone closes it, it stops operating permanently: *We have reluctantly decided to close the factory.* | *Banks are closing down branches by the hundred.*

2 [I,T] if a shop or building closes or someone closes it, it stops being open to the public for a period of time: *The shops close at 6.*

3 [I] FINANCE if a share or currency closes at a particular value, it is worth that amount at the end of the day's trading on a particular market: *Portland's shares closed down 4p at 112p.* | *The pound closed up slightly at $1.6080.*

4 [I] to finish on a particular date: *Special offer closes June 3.*

5 close a deal/sale to reach the point in a deal or sale where everyone involved agrees to it: *The objective of the negotiation phase is to close the deal.* | *He had to lower his price in order to close the sale.*

6 close an account to stop having a particular account with a bank: *Mr Samuels agreed to close the account and transfer the money to a company account.*

7 close the books to calculate the financial results at the end of a particular accounting period: *On Friday Project Software closed the books on its fiscal first quarter.*

8 close (out) a position if an investor or dealer on a financial market closes a position, they buy or sell the stocks, shares, currencies etc that they have agreed to buy or sell, even if this means that they lose money: *If a dealer buys a futures contract and its price declines, he buys another at a lower price rather than closing out his position.*

close sth ↔ **out** *phr v* [T] *AmE* if a store closes out a type of goods, it sells all of them cheaply: *We're closing out this line of swimwear.* —see also CLOSEOUT

close² *n* [singular] the end of the day's activity, for example on the stockmarket or in a bank: ***At the close,*** *the Dow Jones Industrial Average had climbed 17.49.* | *The dividend was payable to shareholders on the Register of Members* ***at close of business*** *on 7th May 1998.*

close company —see under COMPANY

closed /kləʊzd‖kloʊzd/ *adj* not open for business: *The markets were closed on Monday and Tuesday for the Christmas holiday.*

closed circuit television abbreviation **CCTV** *n* [C,U] a system in which cameras send pictures to television sets that is used in many buildings to prevent crime: *The offices are monitored via closed circuit television.*

closed-end *adj* [only before a noun] *AmE* FINANCE a closed-end fund or trust invests in a fixed number of shares, bonds etc: *a* ***closed-end mutual fund***

closed-end fund —see under FUND¹

closed-end investment company also **closed-ended investment company** *BrE* —see under COMPANY

closed market —see under MARKET¹

closed shop *n* [C usually singular] **1** HUMAN RESOURCES a place of work where only members of a particular TRADE UNION are employed: *Mr Blair was criticised by union leaders when he dropped his support of the closed shop.*

2 a market or organization where people from outside it are not allowed: *a closed shop membership structure invented in the Victorian era*

closely held *adj* [only before a noun] FINANCE in the US, a closely held company is one that does not have many shareholders, with five or less shareholders owning more than half of the stock: *WordPerfect, a closely held software supplier*

close•out /ˈkləʊzaʊt‖ˈkloʊz-/ *n* [C usually singular] *AmE* **1** when goods are sold cheaply in a sale: *a retail chain that buys manufacturers' closeout merchandise and sells it at big discounts to customers* | *a* ***closeout store*** —see also ***close out*** under CLOSE¹

2 FINANCE the end of a trading period on a financial market dealing in FUTURES or OPTIONS: *the closeout of August stock-index futures and options*

clos•ing¹ /ˈkləʊzɪŋ‖ˈkloʊ-/ *n* **1** [C,U] when a shop or company stops operating permanently: *The risk of injury did not justify the closing of the factory.* | *The firm has announced a series of short-term layoffs and plant closings.*

2 [U] the time at which shops, offices etc stop operating for the day: *Some pub landlords are content with 11 pm closing but others want to serve drinks beyond then.*

3 [U] the final point in a deal or sale, when all the conditions are agreed: *US West will pay $150 million on closing and the balance over four years.* | *The firm had insufficient funds to cover the downpayment and* ***closing costs.***

4 [U] ACCOUNTING the end of an accounting period

closing² *adj* [only before a noun] **1** coming at the end of a day's trading: *The shares ended at 65, down 7 points from Thursday's* ***closing price.*** | *The bond slipped to its lowest* ***closing level*** *for three years.* | *The official bank* ***closing rate*** (=the value of a currency at the end of a day's trading) *showed the pound at 2.7784 marks.*

2 final: *The* ***closing date*** *for the sale of the shares is expected to be May 9.*

3 closing statement/speech/arguments the final remarks made by a lawyer at the end of a court case: *He told the jury in his closing arguments that there wasn't a shred of evidence linking his client to any wrongdoing.*

closing balance —see under BALANCE¹

closing down sale —see under SALE

closing entry —see under ENTRY

closing price —see under PRICE¹

closing stock —see under STOCK¹

cloud on title *n* plural **clouds on title** [C,U] LAW something such as a CLAIM which, if found to be legally correct, would affect someone's right to own a particular piece of property

clout /klaʊt/ *n* [U] the power or authority to influence other people's decisions: *AT&T and BT have sufficient* ***market clout*** *to win the support of wireless equipment manufacturers to help develop the technology.*

club account —see under ACCOUNT¹

cluster analysis —see under ANALYSIS

clut•ter /ˈklʌtə‖-ər/ *n* [U] MARKETING when there is so much information available that people cannot easily understand or remember it: *CCC has moved most of its advertising to radio and print from television – the company is trying to break out of the clutter, it says.*

CME abbreviation for CHICAGO MERCANTILE EXCHANGE

CMO abbreviation for COLLATERALIZED MORTGAGE OBLIGATION

Co written abbreviation for Company

co /kəʊ‖koʊ/ *prefix* added to the front of a noun to show that someone does a job with someone else: *the co-chairman of Saatchi & Saatchi* | *Tom Barton, co-director of research for Feshbach Brothers* | *The claims will be paid by American International and six other co-insurers.*

c/o written abbreviation for CARE OF, used when you are sending something to someone who is living in someone else's house or receiving mail at their place of work: *John Hammond, c/o Dowling Music College, Bethesda, Maryland*

coach fare —see under FARE

coal•face /ˈkəʊlfeɪs‖ˈkoʊl-/ *n* [C usually singular] **1** the part of a coal mine where coal is cut from the earth

2 at the coalface *BrE* doing work and gaining experience yourself, rather than studying or reading: *his experiences in dealing with boards and managers at the coalface in retail banking*

co•a•li•tion /ˌkəʊəˈlɪʃən◂‖ˌkoʊə-/ *n* **1** [C] a group of people who join together to achieve a particular purpose: *A coalition of junior doctors, managers, and consultants must assess the working practices of all staff.*

2 [C] two or more political parties that join together to fight an election: *the centre-right coalition led by Chancellor Kohl* | *a* ***coalition government.***

3 [U] a process in which two or more political parties or groups join together

coast•er /ˈkəʊstə‖ˈkoʊstər/ also **coasting ship** *BrE*, **coasting vessel** *BrE* — *n* [C] a small ship that carries goods between ports within a country, but does not go to foreign ports: *A small coaster was discharging timber.*

COBOL also **Cobol** /ˈkəʊbɒl‖ˈkoʊbɑːl/ *n* [U] COMPUTING Common Business Oriented Language; a language used to write computer programs: *applications written in Cobol*

COD /ˌsiː əʊ ˈdiː‖-oʊ-/ *n* [U] abbreviation for CASH ON DELIVERY

code /kəʊd‖koʊd/ *n* **1** [C] LAW a complete set of written rules or laws: *Each state in the US has a different criminal and civil code.*

building code a set of rules that states what features a new building, bridge etc should have and what features it is not allowed to have, for reasons of safety or appearance: *The design of the suspension connections did not comply with the relevant building code.*

City Code also **City Code on Takeovers and Mergers** [singular] a set of rules that should be followed in Britain when one company is taking over another

Internal Revenue Code [singular] TAX the complete set of tax laws in the US

Takeover Code [singular] in Britain, a set of rules that companies buying other companies agree to follow, even though they do not have to by law

2 [C] a set of numbers, letters, or signs that are used to show what something is or give information about it: *It is all too easy to miss an employee off a list because a code has been entered incorrectly.*

bar code [C] a series of lines printed on products sold in a shop that can be read by a machine connected to a computer to give the price, keep a record of the sale etc: *The scanner at the checkout recognises the bar code and charges the correct amount.* —**bar coding** *n* [U] *The use of bar coding has meant that restocking is done automatically.*

sort code [C] *BrE* a set of six numbers found on a cheque book, bank card, or bank letter showing which BRANCH (=office) of a bank it relates to: *Do you know the sort code and account number?*

Universal Product Code abbreviation **UPC** [C] another name for BAR CODE: *the Universal Product Code that is used on packaged goods for checkout scanners*

3 [C,U] COMPUTING a set of instructions that tell a computer what to do: *a translator that will take the binary code from Windows applications and produce Alpha code* | *An ANDF version of the spreadsheet runs to 200,000 lines of code.*

4 [C] also **dialling code** *BrE*, **STD code** *BrE*, **area code** *AmE* the group of numbers that come before a telephone number when you are calling from a different area: *What's the code for Aberdeen?* | *Dial 0101 first, then your area code, followed by your home number.*

5 [C] *BrE* also **tax code**, **code number** a number that is given to an employee showing the amount of money that they are allowed to earn without paying any tax: *When you get married your code will change.*

business activity code [C] a number given to companies by the US tax authorities to show the type of business they are involved in —see also DRESS CODE, POSTCODE, ZIP CODE

Code of Banking Practice *n* [singular] a set of rules that banks in Britain agree to follow

code of conduct —see under CONDUCT²

code-sharing *n* [U] when two AIRLINES sell tickets together and use the same numbers for their flights: *Lufthansa and Singapore Airlines are expected to announce a strategic partnership which might include a code-sharing agreement.*

co•de•ter•min•a•tion /ˌkəʊdɪtɜːmɪ̵ˈneɪʃən‖ˌkoʊdɪ̵-tɜːr-/ *n* [U] when the employees of an organization are involved in making important decisions about what the organization will do

co•di•cil /ˈkɒdɪ̵sɪl‖ˈkɑː-/ *n* [C] LAW something that is added to a WILL (=document saying what will happen to someone's money when they die) which makes changes to part of it: *She specified in a codicil to her will that she wanted the house turned into an educational centre.*

cof•fers /ˈkɒfəz‖ˈkɒːfərz, ˈkɑː-/ *n* [plural] the money that an organization, government etc has available to spend: *The UK market has only been contributing £15,000 a month to the company's coffers.* | *Increased spending has drained government coffers.*

cognitive dissonance *n* [U] MARKETING, HUMAN RESOURCES when someone's behaviour goes completely against their beliefs: *The cognitive dissonance between the act of firing someone and the manager's beliefs about what is decent behaviour can be extremely painful.*

Cohesion Fund *n* part of the budget of the EUROPEAN UNION, given to relatively poorer countries such as Spain and Greece to help them develop economically: *Ireland will receive IR£1.1 billion under the Cohesion Fund set up to help finance infrastructure projects.*

coin¹ /kɔɪn/ *n* **1** [C] a piece of metal, usually flat and round, that is used as money: *Since the introduction of the £1 coin, the smallest English note is £5.*

2 [U] money in the form of metal coins: *They found £1,000 in coin.*

coin² *v* [T] **1** to make pieces of money from metal

2 *BrE informal* **coin money/coin it in** to earn a lot of money very quickly: *A rush of stock exchange takeover bids coined money for shareholders.*

coin•age /ˈkɔɪnɪdʒ/ *n* [U] **1** the system of coins used in a country: *Britain did not use decimal coinage until 1971.*

standard coinage a system where a coin's value is the same as the value of the metal it contains

token coinage a system like the one used now in Britain, where coins have a value that is much higher than the value of the metal they contain

2 money in the form of coins: *substantial amounts of silver and gold coinage*

3 the making of coins —see also DEBASEMENT OF COINAGE

coincident indicator —see under INDICATOR

co-insurance *n* [U] when two or more insurers share a particular risk: *Under co-insurance, private brokers assume 20% of the risk in insuring mortgages for multi-family apartment blocks, and the federal government is responsible for the remainder.*

COLA abbreviation for COST OF LIVING ADJUSTMENT

cold call —see under CALL²

cold canvassing —see under CANVASSING

Cold War *n* the unfriendly relationship between the US and the USSR after the Second World War, when there was very little trade between the two countries: *How has the end of the Cold War affected the Middle East?*

col•lab•o•rate /kəˈlæbəreɪt/ *v* [I] to work together with another person, company, or organization to achieve something + **with**: *Firms are collaborating with other firms to spread rising research and development costs.* + **on**: *They will collaborate on a series of research projects.*

col•lapse¹ /kəˈlæps/ *v* [I] if a company, organization, or system collapses, it suddenly fails or becomes too weak to continue: *We did not want existing company pension schemes to collapse.*

collapse² *n* [C,U] when a company, organization, or system suddenly fails or becomes too weak to continue: *The province has become sadly familiar with news of redundancies and company collapses.*

col•lat•e•ral /kəˈlætərəl/ *n* [U] FINANCE assets promised by a borrower to a lender if the borrower cannot repay a loan; SECURITY: *The firm went bankrupt, and because he had used his two homes as collateral when he borrowed money for the company, he lost almost everything he owned.*

col·lat·e·ral·ized also **collateralised** *BrE* /kəˈlætərəlaɪzd/ *adj* FINANCE **1** if loans, bonds etc are collateralized on particular assets of the borrower, the lender has the right to take these assets if the borrower fails to repay the loans etc: *Tobishima believes its credits are sufficiently collateralized to protect it from substantial losses.* | *In an effort to get rid of $1.1 billion in troubled loans, First Boston is preparing to pool the loans into a package and sell them as* ***collateralized bond obligations.*** | ***Collateralised loan obligations*** *are securities backed by claims on existing assets, in this case income from commercial leases.*

C

2 in ASSET-BACKED SECURITIES, income from lending is used to make interest payments on bonds that are collateralized on this lending. The money received from the bonds is often used to make more loans. The bonds are then traded on bond markets: *$400 million of credit card certificates are collateralized with Visa and MasterCard receivables, sold by Norwest Bank Iowa.*

col·league /ˈkɒliːg‖ˈkɑː-/ *n* [C] someone you work with, used especially by professional people or managers: *a colleague of mine at the bank*

col·lect[1] /kəˈlekt/ *v* [T] **1** BANKING **collect cheques** to arrange for cheques to be paid: *The district banks provide a variety of services for commercial banks, including collecting and clearing cheques.*

2 collect debts/taxes to obtain payment of debts or taxes: *Minuteman wasn't aggressive about collecting debts.* | *Russia's public finances must be brought into order by collecting more taxes and cutting spending.*

collect[2] *adv* **call/phone sb collect** *AmE* when you telephone someone collect, the person receiving the call pays for it: *Calling the US is very expensive from here – better to call collect.*

col·lect·i·ble /kəˈlektəbəl/ *n* [C] a valuable object bought as an investment: *diamonds, stamps, and other collectibles*

col·lec·tion /kəˈlekʃən/ *n* **1** [C,U] the activity of collecting payments from customers, and the payments themselves: *GE Capital will handle the collections for Ikea's new credit card.* | *Italy has made good progress in cleaning up public finances and improving* ***tax collection.***

debt collection [U] the activity of making individuals and businesses pay debts, usually ones that they have not paid on time or that they are refusing to pay: *Like hundreds of small-business people with debt collection problems, Mr Buschman has retained a lawyer to help him collect on an overdue bill.*

2 [C,U] BANKING the activity of organizing the payment of cheques, SECURITIES etc: *Security Pacific is the system's clearing bank, or channel for collection and disbursement of all funds and securities moving into and out of Delta.*

collection agency —see under AGENCY

collection and delivery *n* [U] when something is collected from one place and delivered back later or delivered to another place: *There is a free collection and delivery service for repairs within 10 miles.*

collection ratio —see under RATIO

col·lec·tive /kəˈlektɪv/ *adj* [only before a noun] **1 collective farm/factory** a farm or factory that is owned by a government and controlled by the people who work in it: *Russians who were in favour of the abolition of the collective farm system*

2 shared by several people: *This has to be a collective decision.* | *Management must take collective responsibility for the bank's collapse.*

collective agreement —see under AGREEMENT

collective bargaining —see under BARGAINING

collective policy *BrE* —see under INSURANCE POLICY

col·lec·tiv·is·m /kəˈlektɪvɪzəm/ *n* [U] when the state plans and controls the economy of a country and owns the means of production and distribution: *The Labour Party seems to be moving away from its traditional objectives of public ownership, trade union bargaining rights, and collectivism.* —**collectivist** *adj* [only before a noun] *the post-war collectivist welfare state*

col·lec·tor /kəˈlektə‖-ər/ *n* [C] **1** someone whose job is to collect something, for example taxes or debts: *a wave of strikes by* ***tax collectors*** | *When Tina fell behind on her credit-card bill,* ***debt collectors*** *bombarded her employer with phone calls.*

2 someone who collects things that are interesting or attractive: *An American* ***art collector*** *paid $1.2 million for a drawing by Matisse.* | *The table was sold to a dealer on behalf of a* ***private collector.***

col·li·er /ˈkɒliə‖ˈkɑːliər/ *n* [C] *BrE* someone whose job is to work under ground in a coal mine

col·lie·ry /ˈkɒljəri‖ˈkɑːl-/ *n* plural **collieries** [C] *BrE* a coal mine and the buildings and equipment connected with it: *Strikes halted production at collieries throughout the country.*

col·li·sion /kəˈlɪʒən/ *n* [C,U] **1** INSURANCE when a vehicle hits another vehicle or object, causing damage: *A Nissan car he was travelling in was in collision with another vehicle.* | *All aircraft are now fitted with collision-avoidance equipment.*

2 on a collision course (with) if two groups are on a collision course, they are very likely to have a serious disagreement at some time in the future: *This latest announcement may put the nation's largest cable operators on a collision course with telephone companies.*

collision damage waiver —see under WAIVER

col·lu·sion /kəˈluːʒən/ *n* [U] when people or businesses share information or secretly make arrangements among themselves to get an unfair advantage: *an investigation into alleged collusion among art dealers* | *The Wall Street Journal reported last month that collusion and price-fixing in the Treasury market have been routine for more than a decade.*

col·lu·sive /kəˈluːsɪv/ *adj* [only before a noun] collusive activities are ones in which people or businesses share information or secretly make arrangements among themselves to get an unfair advantage: *US companies feel they have been locked out of the market by* ***collusive practices.***

collusive tendering —see under TENDERING

co·lo·ni·al·is·m /kəˈləʊniəlɪzəm‖-ˈloʊ-/ *n* [U] when a powerful country rules a weaker one and establishes its own trade and culture there: *the new Third World states liberated from colonialism*

co·lo·ni·al·ist[1] /kəˈləʊniələst‖-ˈloʊ-/ *n* [C] someone who supports colonialism or who is part of a colonialist system: *The region was neglected by the colonialists.*

colonialist[2] *adj* [only before a noun] relating to colonialism: *old-fashioned colonialist ideas*

col·o·phon /ˈkɒləfɒn‖ˈkɑːləfɑːn/ *n* [C] **1** a statement at the end of the text of a book that gives information about its production

2 a design printed on a book to show that it is produced by a particular publisher or printer

col·umn /ˈkɒləm‖ˈkɑː-/ *n* [C] **1** ACCOUNTING a line of numbers written or printed under each other so that they can be easily added up, or a space on a page or on a computer screen for numbers to be arranged in this way

cash column ACCOUNTING in a CASH BOOK, the column in which cash amounts are entered: *Payments made in cash are shown in the cash column and payments made by cheque are shown in the bank column.*

2 one of two or more lines of print that go down the page of a newspaper or book and that are separated from each other by a narrow space: *Turn to page 5, column 2.*

column-inch *n* [C] MARKETING a unit of measurement used by people selling advertising space in newspapers and magazines. A column inch of text is a column wide and an inch deep: *Most small ads fill one or two column inches.*

co-manager *n* [C usually singular] **1** someone who shares the job of manager with someone else: *Mr Marshall was co-manager of Goldman Sachs's financial strategies group.*
2 BANKING a bank that is next in rank after a LEAD MANAGER in the marketing of certain financial products: *Alex Brown & Sons Inc. and Hambrecht & Quist Inc. are co-managers of the underwriting syndicate.*

com•bi•na•tion /ˌkɒmbəˈneɪʃən‖ˌkɑːm-/ *n* [U] *BrE* when two or more companies join together in a MERGER, takeover, or other financial arrangement affecting their ownership
business combination when two or more companies work together: *Triton may consider a sale, merger or other* ***business combination.***
horizontal combination when two or more companies involved in the same stage of the production or distribution process of a particular product join together in this way
vertical combination when two or more companies involved in different stages of the production or distribution process of a particular product join together in this way: *Vertical and horizontal combination produced those industrial empires which controlled the lives of thousands.* —compare INTEGRATION

com•bine[1] /kəmˈbaɪn/ *v* [I,T] if two or more groups or organizations combine, or if you combine them, they join together: *Qual-Med believes it can achieve operating efficiencies by combining its operations in Northern Carolina with those of Bridgeway.* **combine to do sth**: *Two old established practices combined to form The Anthony Clark Partnership.* —**combined** *adj* [only before a noun] *The new combined bank will have a market share of more than 50% in the central region.*

combine[2] /ˈkɒmbaɪn/ *n* [C] an association of two or more businesses or companies that work together on a temporary or permanent basis: *a large regional banking combine* | *There may be concern if one airline combine controls more than 25% of a relevant market.*

combined transport bill of lading —see under BILL OF LADING

Com•dex /ˈkɒmdeks‖ˈkɑːm-/ *n* COMPUTING the largest computer industry TRADE FAIR in the US, and the name of the company that organizes it and similar events in other countries

COMECON /ˈkɒmɪkɒn‖ˈkɑːmɪkɑːn/ *n* the Council for Mutual Economic Assistance; an organization set up in 1949 by countries in Eastern Europe to help the economic development of its member countries

Com•ex /ˈkɒmeks‖ˈkɑː-/ *n* FINANCE the New York Commodities Exchange; a large market for trading metals: *December silver was up 19.7 cents to $5.420 an ounce on Comex.*

comfort letter —see under LETTER

com•mand /kəˈmɑːnd‖kəˈmænd/ *n* [C] COMPUTING an instruction given to a computer using the KEYBOARD or the MOUSE: *When you have typed the document, use the save command to save it.*

command economy —see under ECONOMY[1]

com•merce /ˈkɒmɜːs‖ˈkɑːmɜːrs/ *n* **1** [U] the buying and selling of goods and services; TRADE: *Modern computing facilities are very much in demand by* ***industry and commerce.*** | *a guide to English for Commerce*
e-commerce electronic commerce; the practice of buying and selling goods and services and carrying on other business activities by computer, especially over the INTERNET; E-BUSINESS: *e-commerce applications such as online ticketing and reservations*
international commerce commerce between companies or industries in different countries: *The GATT trade agreement established a sound basis for international commerce.*
Internet commerce also **Net commerce** business done over the INTERNET; E-COMMERCE
interstate commerce commerce between companies in different states in the US: *It's a violation of interstate commerce to prevent us from shipping this medication across state lines.*
passive commerce commerce in which goods being exported or imported by one country are transported by another country
2 *old-fashioned* a school or university subject concerned with the principles and methods of business and how offices are run; BUSINESS STUDIES: *He was trying to finish a commerce degree at university.*

commerce clause —see under CLAUSE

com•mer•cial[1] /kəˈmɜːʃəl‖-ɜːr-/ *adj* **1** relating to business and the buying and selling of goods and services: *Oran is a large commercial city on the coast.* | *protests against commercial development on green field sites*
2 [only before a noun] relating to the ability of a product or business to make a profit: *We do not want to see ivory having a* ***commercial value.*** | *The invention enjoyed great* ***commercial success.***
3 [only before a noun] a commercial product is one that is produced in large quantities and sold to the public: *All commercial milk is pasteurized.* | *a large commercial fish farm*
4 commercial port/airline/flight etc a port etc that provides a service for the general public to use and is run to make a profit: *This aircraft was the first Boeing 727 to carry fare-paying passengers on a commercial flight.*
5 commercial radio/TV/channel etc radio and television broadcasts that are produced by companies that earn money through advertising, rather than ones owned by the state: *Atlantic 252 has become the most popular commercial radio station in Britain.*
6 more concerned with money than with quality: *The record company tried to make me write songs that were very commercial.*

commercial[2] *n* **1** [C] an advertisement on television, radio, or at the cinema: *The campaigns were designed to run as television or cinema commercials.* | *the Levi's 501 commercials of the mid-eighties*
2 commercials [plural] *BrE* FINANCE shares in companies that produce and sell consumer goods, rather than companies involved in industrial processes

commercial agency —see under AGENCY

commercial agent —see under AGENT

commercial art *n* [U] design work used in advertising, on product PACKAGING etc —**commercial artist** *n* [C] *Commercial artists and manufacturers began using these photographs on box tops and so on.*

commercial bank —see under BANK[1]

commercial bill —see under BILL OF EXCHANGE

commercial blanket bond —see under BOND

commercial break —see under BREAK[2]

commercial broker —see under BROKER[1]

commercial company —see under COMPANY

commercial correspondence —see under CORRESPONDENCE

commercial counsellor —see under COUNSELLOR

commercial court —see under COURT[1]

com·mer·cial·is·m /kəˈmɜːʃəlɪzəm‖-ɜːr-/ *n* [U] *disapproving* when people are more concerned about making money from something than about its real qualities, value etc: *the commercialism that turned the Raffles Hotel in Singapore into a shopping mall with rooms*

com·mer·cial·ize also **commercialise** *BrE* /kəˈmɜː-ʃəlaɪz‖-ɜːr-/ *v* [T] **1** to make something available to buyers for the first time: *He doesn't see any rush to commercialize the Sunpower technology for household use.*
2 to use something in a way that makes as much money as possible, without considering its quality: *the growing tendency to commercialize museums* —**commercialized** also **commercialised** *BrE adj*: *this ever more commercialised world* —**commercialization** also **commercialisation** *BrE n* [U] *Money and commercialisation are damaging the image of sport.*

C

commercial loan —see under LOAN[1]

commercial manager —see under MANAGER

commercial paper —see under PAPER

commercial product —see under PRODUCT

commercial property —see under PROPERTY

commercial set *n* [C] the four SHIPPING DOCUMENTS needed when exporting goods: BILL OF EXCHANGE, BILL OF LADING, CERTIFICATE OF INSURANCE, and INVOICE

commercial traveller —see under TRAVELLER

commercial treaty —see under TREATY

commercial vehicle —see under VEHICLE

com·min·gling /kɒˈmɪŋglɪŋ‖kə-/ *n* [U] when two organizations or business activities are mixed together and cannot easily be judged or valued separately: *The two concerns jointly own a distribution company, and the commingling of the two operations means that it's hard to determine Phar-Mor's profitability.*

com·mis·sion[1] /kəˈmɪʃən/ *n* **1** [C,U] an amount of money paid to someone according to the value of goods, shares, bonds etc they have sold: *He didn't charge a commission on trades, as other brokers do.* | *All of the sales staff are **on commission**.* —see also ERROR OF COMMISSION
2 [C] a request for a writer, musician, or artist to produce a piece of work for which they are paid: *a commission from the company for a new sculpture*
3 [C] an official organization that ensures that the law is obeyed in a particular activity: *the New Jersey Casino Control Commission* | *the Equal Employment Opportunity Commission*
Federal Communications Commission abbreviation **FCC** [singular] a US government organization responsible for making rules for the TELECOMMUNICATIONS industry and for making sure that they are obeyed: *The Federal Communications Commission will select the most effective way to protect consumers from unwanted phone calls.*
4 [C] a temporary official organization looking at problems in a particular area and suggesting changes: *A state senate commission was created last year to study tax reform.* —see also REGULATOR

commission[2] *v* [T] to formally ask someone to produce a report, work of art etc: *One of the new team's first acts was to commission a report on Fox's operations.*

commission agent —see under AGENT

commission broker —see under BROKER[1]

com·mis·sion·er /kəˈmɪʃənə‖-ər/ *n* [C] the head of a COMMISSION[1] or similar organization, or a member of one

Commissioners of Customs and Excise *n* [plural] *formal* the authority in Britain responsible for collecting tax on goods bought and sold or goods brought into the country; CUSTOMS AND EXCISE: *The judges ruled that the Commissioners of Customs and Excise had no authority to impose the charges.*

Commissioners of Inland Revenue *n* [plural] *formal* TAX Britain's tax collecting authority; INLAND REVENUE

com·mit /kəˈmɪt/ *v* past tense and past participle **committed** present participle **committing** **1** [I,T] to say that someone will definitely do something or must do something **commit sb to do sth**: *He committed his government to support Thailand's traditional free-market system.* **commit yourself to doing sth**: *Sorry, I've already committed myself to working for Clive.* **commit to sth**: *She would not want to commit to anything that would last more than a year.*
2 [T] to decide to use money, time, people etc for a particular purpose **commit sth to sth**: *A client needs to approve an idea before committing resources to it.*
3 [T] to do something wrong or illegal: *We are confident that we have not committed any fraud.*

com·mit·ment /kəˈmɪtmənt/ *n* **1** [C,U] a promise to do something or to behave in a particular way: *He's **made a commitment** to improve the quality of life for people in Gloucestershire.* + **to**: *a commitment to equal pay and opportunities*
contractual commitment [C,U] a commitment to do something that is made legal by being included in the terms of a contract: *Do not be afraid to seek professional advice before making a contractual commitment.*
2 [U] the hard work and loyalty that someone gives to an organization or activity: *Sue will be greatly missed for her enthusiasm and commitment.* + **to**: *The Group's success is a direct result of commitment by staff to high standards of service.*
3 [C] something that you have to do that prevents you from doing something else: *Mr Reid has a previous commitment and is unable to attend the meeting.* | *part time work for people with family commitments*
4 [C] an amount of money that you have to pay regularly and that prevents you from spending your money on other things: *A mortgage may be the largest financial commitment you will make in your life.*
5 [U] the use of money, time, people etc for a particular purpose: *The plan involves commitment of large amounts of money and staff time.*

commitment fee —see under FEE

com·mit·tee /kəˈmɪti/ *n* [C] a group of people within an organization such as a government, company, or political party who have been chosen or elected in order to do a particular job, take decisions etc: *They will discuss the issue at a **committee meeting** next month,* | *He resigned as chairman of the committee but remains a **committee member**.*
compliance committee a committee in a financial institution that makes sure the institution is obeying financial laws
creditors' committee *AmE* a group of creditors who act together to get back the money they are owed by a bankrupt company: *LTV's creditor committee, which represents holders of about $1.5 billion in claims, said it will try to block any sale of the company.*
executive committee ◆ a committee made up of the senior managers of a company, usually one chosen by the BOARD: *These executives will form an executive committee aimed at improving relations with the agency's largest global clients.*
◆ a committee at the head of a professional association or political party: *the executive committee of the Italian Bankers Association*
management committee a committee that takes decisions about how a company operates or is run: *GM's management committee met yesterday afternoon to discuss corporate reorganization.*
political action committee abbreviation **PAC** *AmE* an organization formed by a business or TRADE UNION which raises money to help elect its supporters

to Congress: *Arctic Alaska employees' political action committee gave Mr. Miller's campaign a total of $3,400.*

select committee an independent committee which examines and reports on different government departments and activities: *Under British parliamentary procedure, a select committee can force witnesses to answer questions.*

steering committee a committee with responsibility for making sure that particular tasks are carried out: *The corporate marketing steering committee coordinates marketing issues.*

Committee of Public Accounts *n* a group of members of the House of Commons in Britain who have been chosen to check that the spending of government departments has been according to levels agreed in parliament; PUBLIC ACCOUNTS COMMITTEE

Committee of Ways and Means —see under WAYS AND MEANS COMMITTEE

commodities fund —see under FUND[1]

com•mod•i•ty /kəˈmɒdəti‖kəˈmɑː-/ *n* plural **commodities** [C] **1** FINANCE a product that can be sold to make a profit, especially one in its basic form before it has been used or changed in an industrial process. Examples of commodities are farm products and metals: *IBC trades worldwide, buying and selling basic commodities such as timber, coal and cement.* | *Rice is the country's principle* ***export commodity****.* | *a* ***commodity broker*** | *The news has hit many* ***commodity markets*** *and prices have fallen.*

cyclical commodity a commodity whose price rises and falls by large amounts during periods of fast and slow economic growth

physical commodity an actual commodity that is to be delivered, rather than one in financial trading where the trader does not take delivery: *Most futures contracts are canceled out by opposing trades, so futures traders rarely take delivery of a physical commodity.*

2 also **commodity product** a product or service that is difficult to show as being different from similar products or services offered by competitors: *PCs have become commodity products.*

commodity broker —see under BROKER[1]

commodity fund —see under FUND[1]

Commodity Futures Trading Commission abbreviation **CFTC** *n* FINANCE in the US, a government organization that controls all trading in commodities

commodity market —see under MARKET[1]

commodity product —see under PRODUCT

Common Agricultural Policy abbreviation **CAP** *n* in the European Union, a system of controlling the production and sale of farm produce, especially by paying government money to farmers to produce certain crops: *The minister's plan to reduce beef production is in line with reforms of the Common Agricultural Policy announced by the European Commission.*

com•mon•al•i•ty /ˌkɒməˈnæləti‖ˌkɑː-/ *n* [U] MANUFACTURING when different products use the same parts in their production: *They will try to keep the proportion of common components as high as 90%, and this commonality could save the US government $60 billion over 10 years.*

common carrier —see under CARRIER

common law —see under LAW

Common Market *n* a former name for what became known as the EUROPEAN COMMUNITY and then the EUROPEAN UNION

common market *n* [C] a group of countries that encourages trade by reducing the CUSTOMS DUTIES that have to be paid when goods are traded between them: *The Buenos Aires Declaration aimed to establish a Latin American common market by 1992.*

common ownership —see under OWNERSHIP

common pricing —see under PRICING

common seal —see under SEAL[1]

common share —see under SHARE

common stock —see under STOCK[1]

Commonwealth also **Commonwealth of Nations** *n* an organization of about 50 countries that were once part of the British EMPIRE, and that are now connected politically and economically: *Britain's gradual conversion of the colonial Empire into the British Commonwealth of Nations*

Commonwealth Development Corporation *n* an organization set up to help the countries of the Commonwealth develop their own skills or products through financial and technical support

comm port —see under PORT[1]

comms /kɒmz‖kɑːmz/ *n* [plural] *BrE* COMPUTING communications; used when talking about computer programs that allow communication between different computers; COMMUNICATIONS SOFTWARE *AmE*: *Dataflex sells Transend comms software with its modems.*

com•mune /ˈkɒmjuːn‖ˈkɑː-, kəˈmjuːn/ *n* [C] **1** a group of people who live and work together and share what they produce

2 a group of people who work together on a farm owned by the state, and give what they produce to the state: *the communes of China*

3 the smallest division of local government in countries such as France and Belgium: *The Auvergne is divided into four Departments which are organised into Cantons and ultimately consist of 1,308 Communes.*

com•mu•ni•ca•tion /kəˌmjuːnəˈkeɪʃən/ *n* **1** [U] the process of exchanging information or ideas: *Because some editors work in San Fransisco and others in London, there is a greater need for communication in the decision-making process.* | *rules of confidentiality which limit communication* | *The industry will continue to evolve as communication technology changes and* ***mass communication*** (=ways of passing information to a large number of people) *becomes even more sophisticated.*

2 [C] *formal* a letter, message, or telephone call: *The CAA recently received a communication from the French Director of Civil Aviation, complaining about the matter.*

3 be in communication with sb *formal* to talk or write to someone on a regular basis, or be in the process of talking or writing to someone: *We are currently in communication with the Inland Revenue regarding the amount of training expenses that a sole trader can deduct from their tax bill.*

4 communications [plural] ways of sending information, especially using a telephone, radio, or computer: *The vodopaging network offers the most cost-effective form of mobile communications available.*

wireless communications communications that do not involve passing signals through electrical or telephone wires, for example mobile telephones: *a new product that blends wireless communications with portable computing*

5 communications [plural] used to talk about ways of travelling or sending goods on the roads, railways etc: *With its many airports and train stations, London has excellent communications with the rest of Europe.*

Com•mu•nis•m /ˈkɒmjənɪzəm‖ˈkɑː-/ *n* [U] a political system in which, in principle, the government or the workers control the production of food and goods, and there are no different social classes —**Communist** *adj*: *Communist countries* | *a Communist regime*

Com•mu•nist /ˈkɒmjənəst‖ˈkɑː-/ *n* [C] someone who believes in Communism or is a member of a political party that supports Communism

com•mu•ni•ty /kəˈmjuːnəti/ *n* plural **communities** [C] **1** all the people who live in the same area, city etc: *The new arts centre will serve the whole community.*

2 a group of people who all share the same nationality, religion, or interests: *Miami's* ***black community***
3 business community the companies, businesses, and businesspeople operating in an area: *Edinburgh's business community*
4 the business community businesspeople acting as a group in order to influence government or public opinion: *The business community isn't happy with some of the Democratic Party's proposals.*
5 the international community all the countries of the world: *The international community agreed that industrialised countries should allocate 4% of overall foreign aid to population programmes.*

C

community antenna television abbreviation **CATV** *n* [U] a television system in which television signals are received by one large piece of receiving equipment and then sold to people living in the local town, city, or area

community investment —see under INVESTMENT

Community preference —see under PREFERENCE

Community Reinvestment Act *n* LAW in the US, a law saying that banks must encourage investment in local areas, for example by lending money to people living in poor areas or who are on low incomes

com•mu•ta•tion /ˌkɒmjʊˈteɪʃən‖ˌkɑː-/ *n* [C] INSURANCE a single large payment instead of a series of future payments: *The assets of the insurer will be used to make a single, final payment, called a commutation, to policyholders.*

com•mute /kəˈmjuːt/ *v* [I] to regularly travel a long distance for your work + **between**: *a businessman who commutes between Northern Ireland and Hong Kong* —**commute** *n* [C usually singular] *He got fed up with the daily commute into London.* —**commuter** *n* [C] *British Rail networks carrying commuters into London*

commuter aircraft —see under AIRCRAFT

comp /kɒmp‖kɑːmp/ *n* [U] *AmE* HUMAN RESOURCES abbreviation for COMPENSATION: *Most workers' comp claims are for short absences with a minor injury.*

compact disc read only memory —see CD-ROM

compact disk —see under DISK

Companies House *n* LAW the place where the official list of companies in Britain is kept

companies register —see under REGISTER[1]

companies registry —see under REGISTRY

com•pa•ny /ˈkʌmpəni/ *n* plural **companies** [C] **1** an organization that makes or sells goods or services in order to make a profit: *It will be years before the company is strong enough to pay dividends.*
affiliated company a company owned by another company; SUBSIDIARY; RELATED COMPANY: *Hino Motors, a truck maker in the Toyota group of affiliated companies*
associated company also **associate company** a company of which more than 20% but less than 51% of the EQUITY is held by another company or group of companies: *Employees of the National Magazine Company and their associated companies may not enter this competition.*
blue chip company also **blue-chip company** a well-known, successful company whose shares are a very safe investment: *blue chip companies like Shell, BP and Unilever, which have well-defined, long-term business strategies*
cable company a company that uses cables under the ground to provide services such as cable television: *International Family Entertainment is one of the biggest cable companies in the US with over 56 million subscribers.*
close company also **closely held company** in the US, a close company is one that has five or fewer shareholders owning more than half of the stock: *WordPerfect, a closely held software supplier*
closed-end investment company also **closed-ended investment company** *BrE* an investment company with a fixed number of shares that an investor can only sell to another investor, not back to the company
commercial company ♦ a company that has to follow normal accepted business practices and operates in order to make a profit: *KLM is a commercial company and it uses all commercial possibilities in an active and creative manner.*
♦ a company that is not a financial institution: *As banks trade in cash, this is not such a simple financial calculation as it is for a commercial company.*
constituent company a company that is one of a group of organizations that have been joined together
controlling company a company that owns more than 50% of the shares of another company
credit company a company that lends money to people or businesses; FINANCE COMPANY
daughter company a company that is completely or partly owned by another company; SUBSIDIARY
dock company a company that owns and operates a port: *The firm told the dock company to deal with the timber.*
finance company also **finance house** *BrE* a financial institution that lends to people or businesses, so that they can buy things such as cars or machinery. Finance companies are often part of COMMERCIAL BANKS, but operate independently: *The major suppliers of construction equipment have their own finance houses, who can offer attractive loan finance or leasing packages to customers.*
holding company a company that completely or partly owns other companies and may also carry out normal business activities itself: *IRI, the Italian state holding company which controls Alitalia*
insurance company a company that sells insurance: *If the insurance company that issued your pension is in trouble, is your money safe?*
investment company also **investment trust** a company that invests its capital in SECURITIES (bonds, shares etc). The value of the company's shares and DIVIDENDS depends on the profit made on these investments: *Société Centrale d'Investissements, a French investment company with interests in several leading corporations*
investment trust company a company that manages MUTUAL FUNDS: *You will only receive the advantage of low charges if you buy directly from the investment trust company.*
open-end investment company also **open-ended investment company** *BrE* an investment company where new shares are created for new investors and which buys back shares from investors who want to sell: *a proposal to convert the fund from a closed-end to an open-end investment company.*
private company ♦ a company owned by people or other companies, rather than by the government
♦ also **privately held company** a company whose shares are not openly traded and can only pass to another person with the agreement of other shareholders
public company ♦ a company owned by people or other companies, rather than by the government
♦ also **publicly held company** a company whose shares are openly traded
red chip company also **red-chip company** a Chinese company that is listed on the Hong Kong stockmarket
limited (liability) company a company where the shareholders will lose only what they have invested if the company goes bankrupt, and will not lose other property that they own

listed company a large, successful company whose shares are traded on the main financial markets

management company a company that manages financial assets or property for people or businesses: *Sprind Gestione is the management company for the mutual funds of Finanza & Futuro SpA.*

mutual company a company that has members but no shareholders. Profits from a mutual company are not paid out in DIVIDENDS but in another form: *Equitable Insurance's plan to covert from a mutual company owned by its policyholders, to a stock-owned company*

mutual insurance company an insurance company whose owners are its POLICYHOLDERS (=people insured by the company) rather than shareholders

offshore company a company based outside the country in which it does business, usually for legal or tax reasons

off-the-shelf company another name for a SHELF COMPANY

parent company a company that owns other companies: *Costs are two thirds lower at Japan Air Charter, a subsidiary that employs foreigners, than at the parent company.*

private limited company a company whose shares are not openly traded and can only pass to another person with the agreement of other shareholders

property company a company that buys land and buildings in order to sell or rent them; REAL ESTATE COMPANY *AmE*

proprietary company a form of limited company in Australia and South Africa, with the letters Pty after its name

public limited company a limited company whose shares are freely sold and traded, in Britain with a minimum SHARE CAPITAL of £50,000 and the letters PLC after its name

registered company in Britain, a company which has been officially registered with the REGISTRAR OF COMPANIES

related company a company that is connected with or owned by another, larger company; AFFILIATED COMPANY: *He merged Royex with four related companies to form Corona Ltd.*

shelf company also **off the shelf company** a company that has already been legally formed, but is not active and can be bought by people who want to start a business quickly: *You will have to decide if a new company should be formed or if a shelf company will be enough.*

shell company ♦ a company that has been formed for legal or tax reasons but does not trade or do business

♦ a company that is used to hide criminal activities such as passing profits from criminal activities into the normal banking system: *Shell companies are often used to hide the owner's identity and money flows are disguised using false invoices and loans.*

sister company one of two or more companies that are owned by the same PARENT COMPANY: *Random House Inc. said that the chairman of its London-based sister company, Random Century Ltd, has resigned.*

small business investment company in the US, a small company in which investors can buy shares. If the shares make a loss, it is treated as an ordinary business loss

start-up company a company that has just been formed: *He told them that within five years the start-up company would become Japan's leading software distributor.*

subsidiary company a company of which more than half is owned by another company: *The Johnson Electric Group now controls 11 subsidiary companies locally and overseas.*

trading company a company that sells goods or services rather than one that makes its profit from investing in other companies

trust company ♦ *BrE* a company that invests peoples' money for them: *The investment manager of an* ***investment trust company*** *will not normally be regarded as an appropriate person to give independent advice about that company.*

♦ *AmE* a company that acts as a TRUSTEE (=person in charge of a trust) for the property of people who have died, or for property in trust for living people. A trust company may also advise people on investments and invest their money for them

unit trust company in Britain, an investment company that manages UNIT TRUSTS

unlimited company a company whose shareholders will lose all their money if the company goes bankrupt, and also risk losing their own property in order to pay the company's debts: *Unlimited companies are not subject to the strict accounting requirements which govern limited companies.*

unlisted company a small company whose shares are not on the official list of shares traded on a particular stockmarket: *Trading conditions were tough for smaller unlisted companies.*

company accounts —see under ACCOUNT[1]

company car *n* [C] a car provided by a company to an employee, especially a manager

company director —see under DIRECTOR

company doctor —see under DOCTOR[1]

company law —see under LAW

company limited by guarantee *n* plural **companies limited by guarantee** [C] LAW, FINANCE a company in which each shareholder is responsible for paying debts up to a certain amount if the company goes bankrupt

company limited by shares *n* plural **companies limited by shares** [C] LAW, FINANCE in Britain, a company whose shareholders are responsible for paying debts up to the amount of their UNPAID SHARES, if the company goes bankrupt

company meeting —see under MEETING

company officer —see under OFFICER

company promoter *n* [C] someone who organizes the starting of new companies, bringing together accountants, lawyers, and other specialists: *Solicitors guide company promoters through the legal technicalities of forming companies.*

company seal —see under SEAL[1]

company secretary —see under SECRETARY

company union —see under UNION

com·pa·ra·bles /ˈkɒmpərəbəlz‖ˈkɑːm-/ *n* [plural] PROPERTY properties similar to one being sold: *Check comparables, which should be on similar-sized lots in similar neighborhoods.*

comparable worth *n* [U] *AmE* HUMAN RESOURCES the principle that women doing the same type of job as men should be paid the same amount as men

comparative advantage —see under ADVANTAGE

comparative advertising —see under ADVERTISING

compassionate leave —see under LEAVE

com·pat·i·bil·ity /kəmˌpætəˈbɪləti/ *n* [U] COMPUTING the ability of one piece of computer equipment or software to be used with another: *Phoenix BIOS provides full MS-DOS, OS/2, SCO UNIX/XENIX and Novell compatibility.*

com·pat·i·ble[1] /kəmˈpætəbəl/ *adj* COMPUTING computer equipment or software that is compatible with other equipment or software can be used with it, even if the two are made by different companies or use different operating systems: *IBM compatible computers* + **with**:

C

Make sure that the software is compatible with the other applications you want to run.

compatible² *n* [C usually plural] a piece of computer equipment that can be used with other computers, even those made by a different company: *the IBM PC and its compatibles*

com·pen·sate /ˈkɒmpənseɪt‖ˈkɑːm-/ *v* [I,T] **1** to pay someone money because they have suffered injury, loss, or damage **compensate sb for sth**: *He has promised to compensate farmers for the price cuts.*

2 *AmE* HUMAN RESOURCES to pay someone in money and other ways for work that they do: *Nobody knows if compensating executives better makes their companies perform any better.*

C

compensating balance —see under BALANCE¹

compensating error —see under ERROR

com·pen·sa·tion /ˌkɒmpənˈseɪʃən‖ˌkɑːm-/ *n* [U] HUMAN RESOURCES **1** an amount paid to someone because they have been hurt or harmed: *Mr Lewis was **awarded** $75,000 **compensation** for injuries suffered in the accident.* | *The group will **pay compensation** to 800 people who have been made redundant.*

2 abbreviation **comp** *AmE* the total amount of money and other advantages that someone receives as an employee: *Japanese workers get 30% of their compensation in vacation pay and bonuses.* | *The firm has agreed to a new **compensation package** for Mr Eisner, including stock options worth $252 million.*

employee compensation *especially AmE* ◆ the total pay and benefits that a particular employee or group of employees receives: *An increasing proportion of the company's employee compensation is paid in stock.*

◆ money paid to an employee by an employer's insurers because they have been harmed in some way, for example in an accident at work: *Because of the limitations of employee compensation policies, more people are turning to the courts to seek additional disability awards.*

social security compensation in the US, the money people have to pay into a government run retirement plan and the money people received from the government when they retire

compensation package —see under PACKAGE¹

compensation payment —see under PAYMENT

compensatory damages —see under DAMAGE¹

com·pete /kəmˈpiːt/ *v* [I] when one company or country competes with another, it tries to get people to buy its goods or services rather than those available from another company or country: *measures to enable Irish industries to compete effectively in Europe* + **with**: *NatPower has to keep its own prices down so that it can compete with other major electricity suppliers.* + **for**: *If the pound continues at this level our exporters can't compete for sales across the Atlantic.*

com·pe·tence /ˈkɒmpɪtəns‖ˈkɑːm-/ *n* **1** [U] the ability or skill to do something well or to a satisfactory standard: *To remain in the guild, members must maintain their standards of professional competence.* | *Part of the job requirement is that the candidate has competence in English.*

2 [C] *formal* a skill that you need to do a particular job: *short residential courses designed to develop specific management competences*

3 [singular] *BrE* LAW the official authority of a court to hear a legal case; JURISDICTION: *The Court of Appeal possesses the competence to set aside convictions.*

4 [U] LAW when someone is old enough, well enough, or intelligent enough to make decisions, appear in a court of law, sign a legal document etc: *Many children's solicitors found it difficult to determine the child's competence to give instructions.*

com·pe·tent /ˈkɒmpɪtənt‖ˈkɑːm-/ *adj* **1** having enough skill, knowledge, or ability to do something to a satisfactory standard: *The farm would have to be run by a competent manager.* | *You need someone who is both competent at finance and honest.*

2 a piece of work or equipment that is competent is satisfactory but not particularly good: *The graphics test showed the portable photocopier to be competent, but no more.*

3 LAW having the official power to make legal decisions or deal with particular legal cases: *We are determined to ensure that those individuals appear before a **competent court** as speedily as possible.*

4 LAW old enough, well enough, or intelligent enough to make decisions, appear in a court of law, sign a legal document etc: *He was declared competent to stand trial.*

com·pe·ti·tion /ˌkɒmpɪˈtɪʃən‖ˌkɑːm-/ *n* **1** [U] a situation in which businesses are trying to be more successful than others by selling more goods and services and making more profit: *Competition between the two cable companies has driven down the price for program services.* | *They sell everything from food to furniture to fashion, often **in direct competition with** nearby stores.* | *Jaguar faces **stiff competition** from Japanese luxury brands.* —see also HYPERCOMPETITION

imperfect competition ECONOMICS in real markets, when the conditions for perfect competition do not exist

perfect competition also **pure competition** ECONOMICS in a model market, when there are many small businesses producing the same products, all workers do the same types of jobs, buyers and sellers have complete knowledge about market conditions, and businesses and factories are free to move anywhere

price competition when producers cannot charge as much as they would like to for their goods because others are charging less: *Japanese semiconductor manufacturers are under tough price competition from Korean and other makers.*

2 the competition all the businesses that compete with a particular business, seen as a group: *In the past, Honda has **kept ahead of the competition** because it was small and fast.*

com·pet·i·tive /kəmˈpetɪtɪv/ *adj* **1** used to describe situations and behaviour in which businesses are trying very hard to be more successful than others, for example by selling their goods or services more cheaply than others: *The food retail market in the UK is becoming increasingly competitive.* | *The airline industry remains intensely competitive. Average fares are at all-time lows.* —**competitiveness** also **competitivity** *n* [U] *The currency's higher value will hurt competitiveness by making Taiwan's exports more expensive for foreign buyers.*

2 competitive prices are similar to or less than other companies' prices for the same product: *Japanese consumers are being denied access to foreign goods at competitive prices.* + **with**: *Cutting the cost per unit would make nuclear fuel far more competitive with gas and coal.*

3 if a process is competitive, people have to compete with each other and those who do best will be successful: *Administrative service members are recruited through an annual competitive examination.*

competitive advantage —see under ADVANTAGE

competitive analysis —see under ANALYSIS

competitive balance *n* [C] a market situation where no business is too big or has an unfair advantage: *Sprint could be taken over by another telecoms company without upsetting the competitive balance.*

com·pet·i·tive·ness /kəmˈpetɪtɪvnɪs/ *n* [U] the ability of a product, company, or country to compete with others

com·pet·i·tiv·i·ty /kəmˌpetɪˈtɪvɪti/ *n* [U] another name for COMPETITIVENESS: *Another indicator of declin-*

ing Czech competitivity is the rapidly growing trade deficit.

com·pet·i·tor /kəm'petətə‖-ər/ *n* [C] a person, product, company, country etc that is competing with another: *NBC Cable operates a* ***direct competitor*** *to the Financial News Network, the Consumer News and Business Channel.* | *Britain has had higher long-term interest rates than most of its* ***major competitors****.*

com·pi·la·tion /ˌkɒmpə'leɪʃən‖ˌkɑːm-/ *n* [U] **1** the process of collecting information together and writing it into a list, report, book etc: *The auditor must see that proper accounting practices have been observed in the compilation of the accounts.* | *Everyone recognised the expertise and effort involved in the document's compilation.*
2 FINANCE in the US, when an accountant presents a financial statement without a promise that it meets GENERALLY ACCEPTED ACCOUNTING PRINCIPLES, but which has been prepared according to the rules set out by the AMERICAN INSTITUTE OF CERTIFIED PUBLIC ACCOUNTANTS

com·pile /kəm'paɪl/ *v* [T] **1** to collect information together and write it into a list, report, book etc: *Our staff are compiling the material for an on-line database.*
2 COMPUTING to put instructions into a computer in a form that the computer can understand and use: *You do not have to exit the editor, compile the program, run the program, then reload the editor to fix any bugs.*

com·pil·er /kəm'paɪlə‖-ər/ *n* [C] **1** a person who collects information together and writes it into a list, report, book etc
2 COMPUTING a computer program or piece of software that changes another program from its existing FORMAT into one that the computer can understand: *DEC will have its Alpha AXP compiler for Microsoft Corp Windows NT ready by early March.*

com·plain·ant /kəm'pleɪnənt/ *n* [C] *BrE* LAW a person who makes a complaint in a CIVIL LAW court; PLAINTIFF: *If the committee rejects a complaint, the complainant now has the right to apply for a rehearing.*

com·plaint /kəm'pleɪnt/ *n* **1** [C,U] a written or spoken statement by someone complaining about something: *Our sales assistants are trained to deal with customer complaints in a friendly manner.* | *a letter of complaint* + **about**: *Mr Jones was unable to* ***lodge a complaint*** *about the doctor because he missed the deadline.*
2 [C] LAW a statement made by a person bringing a case or making a claim in a court of law, stating the facts upon which the case or claim is based
3 [C] LAW a statement made by one person against another in a legal case, either in a court or to an officer of the court: *Defence counsel, Graham Bell, QC, pointed out that the complaint had not been served until 14 February this year.*

com·ple·men·ta·ry /ˌkɒmplə'mentəri◂‖ˌkɑːm-/ *adj* sold or used with other products: *complementary goods, for example videocassettes and videorecorders*

completely built-up abbreviation **cbu** *adj* MANUFACTURING a completely built-up product, machine etc is in one piece and does not need to be put together: *The new car might have to be imported in completely built-up form while a new plant is built.*

completely knocked-down abbreviation **ckd** *adj* MANUFACTURING a completely knocked-down product, machine etc is in several pieces and needs to be put together before it can be used: *The first Malaysian-built Elises will be made from completely knocked-down kits from Lotus.*

com·ple·tion /kəm'pliːʃən/ *n* [U] *BrE* LAW, PROPERTY the final point in the sale of a property, when the documents have all been signed and all the money has been paid; CLOSING *AmE*: *When you buy a house in an auction, completion normally takes place four weeks later.*

completion bond —see under BOND

completion statement —see under STATEMENT

com·pli·ance /kəm'plaɪəns/ *n* [U] when someone obeys a law or rule or keeps an agreement: *The Coast Guard can board any ship and check its compliance with safety rules.* | *The refinery is operating safely and* ***in compliance with*** *clean air standards.* —see also DECLARATION OF COMPLIANCE

compliance committee —see under COMMITTEE

compliance officer —see under OFFICER

com·pli·ant /kəm'plaɪənt/ *adj* if something is compliant with a law or rule, it does what the law says it must: *The Rolls-Royce engines are half as noisy as the other engines, making the planes compliant with the rules on noise levels set by some airports.*

C

com·pli·men·ta·ry /ˌkɒmplə'mentəri◂‖ˌkɑːm-/ *adj* complimentary food, goods, services etc are given free to customers or clients: *You will receive a complimentary bottle of wine on arrival at your hotel.*

complimentary close *n* [C usually singular] the usual way of ending a formal business letter. If you address the letter 'Dear Sir/Madam', you end it 'Yours faithfully'; if you address the letter to a particular person, you end it 'Yours sincerely'

com·pli·ments /'kɒmpləmənts‖'kɑːm-/ *n* [plural] **with the compliments of.../with our compliments** written on a compliments slip or used when a company or organization gives or send goods to someone without charging them: *These starter packs for new businesses are free, with the compliments of Barclays Bank.*

compliments slip —see under SLIP[2]

com·ply /kəm'plaɪ/ *v* past tense and past participle **complied** [I] to obey a law or rule, or to keep an agreement + **with**: *the high costs of upgrading aging mills to comply with environmental regulations*

com·po·nent /kəm'pəʊnənt‖-'poʊ-/ *n* [C] **1** one part of something + **of**: *The M2 component of the money supply grew $7.2 billion in April.* | *British Sugar is the* ***main component*** *of the Bristar food division.* | *Imported energy is a* ***major component*** *of the trade deficit.*
2 MANUFACTURING one part used in making a machine, vehicle etc: *Varity, a tractors, engine and* ***auto components*** (=ones used in cars) *company* | *a small company that makes* ***electronic components***

com·po·site /'kɒmpəzət‖kɑːm'pɑː-/ *adj* [only before a noun] made up of several different parts or things: *the Nasdaq composite index* | *Wachovia shares finished at $58.375 a share, down 37.5 cents, in composite trading on the New York Stock Exchange.*

composite supply —see under SUPPLY[2]

com·po·si·tion /ˌkɒmpə'zɪʃən‖ˌkɑːm-/ *n* [C usually singular] LAW an arrangement between a person or organization that owes money and the people or organizations the money is owed to concerning the way in which the debts should be repaid: *The debtor may then make a composition with his creditors, but if this is not done he will be made bankrupt.*

com·pos·i·tor /kəm'pɒzətə‖-'pɑːzətər/ *n* [C] someone whose job is to arrange the letters, photographs, drawings etc on the page of a book, magazine, or newspaper before it is printed: *The newspaper's compositors had refused to set an offending leading article.*

com·pound /kəm'paʊnd‖kɑːm'paʊnd, 'kɑːmpaʊnd/ *v* [T] *AmE* FINANCE to pay interest on both a sum of money and the interest already earned on it: *My bank compounds interest quarterly.*

compound annual rate of return *n* [C] FINANCE the amount of COMPOUND INTEREST paid or earned on a sum of money in twelve months

compound entry —see under ENTRY

compound growth rate —see under GROWTH RATE

compound interest —see under INTEREST

compound rate —see under RATE[1]

compound tariff —see under TARIFF

comprehensive insurance —see under INSURANCE

com•pro•mise[1] /ˈkɒmprəmaɪz‖ˈkɑːm-/ *n* [C,U] an agreement between two people or groups in which both sides agree to accept less than they first asked for and to give up something that they value: *Representatives of each side might well* ***come to*** *some sort of* ***compromise****.*

compromise[2] *v* [I] if two groups compromise, they each accept less than they first asked for, and each give up something that they value + **on**: *The company has refused to compromise on a reduction in the working week.* + **with**: *We agreed to compromise with the union on certain things.*

C

comp•trol•ler /kənˈtrəʊlə, kəmp-‖-ˈtroʊlər/ *n* [C] FINANCE, ACCOUNTING the chief accountant of the finance or accounts department of a company, or a government official in charge of a department that keeps a record of the money spent or received by the government; CONTROLLER: *the comptroller of the Audit Commission*

Comptroller and Auditor General *n* FINANCE in Britain, the government official in charge of the NATIONAL AUDIT OFFICE

Comptroller General *n* FINANCE in the US, the government official in charge of the GENERAL ACCOUNTING OFFICE

Comptroller of the Currency *n* FINANCE, BANKING in the US, the government official responsible for controlling the financial dealings of banks and other financial institutions

com•pul•so•ry /kəmˈpʌlsəri/ *adj* something that is compulsory must be done according to a law or rule: *The company has introduced compulsory overtime for all its workers.*

compulsory acquisition —see COMPULSORY PURCHASE

compulsory liquidation —see under LIQUIDATION

compulsory purchase also **compulsory acquisition** *n* [U] LAW in Britain, when a government organization has the legal power to make you sell them your land or property and pays you an amount of money as COMPENSATION. This usually happens when a new road etc is being built: *The Local Authority had certain powers of compulsory purchase in relation to land near the motorway.*

compulsory purchase order —see under ORDER[1]

compulsory retirement —see under RETIREMENT

compulsory winding up —see under WINDING UP

com•pute /kəmˈpjuːt/ *v* [I,T] *formal* to calculate a number or amount: *The amount assessed was computed by the Inland Revenue to include a proportion of the school's overheads as average costs.*

com•put•er /kəmˈpjuːtə‖-ər/ *n* [C,U] an electronic machine that can do calculations very quickly, store information or documents, or do tasks according to a set of instructions called a program: *We store all our clients' details* ***on computer****.* | *The winner is chosen* ***by computer****.* | *The popularity of the Internet is bringing a massive rise in* ***computer literacy*** (=when people understand computers and know how to work with them).

fifth generation computer a computer that uses ARTIFICIAL INTELLIGENCE to process information and perform tasks

home computer a small computer used by one person in their business or home; PC: *home computer games*

host computer the central computer that controls and communicates with all the other computers in a system: *Most computer printers receive their information from the host computer sequentially.*

mainframe computer a large powerful computer that can do a lot of complicated jobs quickly and which can be used by a lot of people at the same time: *terminals linked to the University's mainframe computer*

personal computer abbreviation **PC** a small computer used by one person in their business or home: *a wordprocessing program for a personal computer* —see also LAPTOP, MICROCOMPUTER, MINICOMPUTER, PALMTOP, SUPERCOMPUTER

computer (industry) analyst —see under ANALYST

computer-aided design —see CAD/CAM

computer-aided manufacture —see under MANUFACTURE[2]

computer-assisted *adj* done with the help of a computer: *computer-assisted telephone interviewing* | *computer-assisted trading*

Computer Assisted Learning —see CAL

computer-based training —see under TRAINING

computer-integrated manufacture —see under MANUFACTURE[2]

com•put•er•ize also **computerise** *BrE* /kəmˈpjuːtəraɪz/ *v* [T] to use computers to control an operation, system, process etc: *They computerized the accounts department back in 1985.* | *a computerized database* —**computerization** also **computerisation** *BrE n* [U] *The company has completed the computerization of specific things such as the alarm system.*

computer language —see under LANGUAGE

computer-literate *adj* able to use a computer

computer program —see under PROGRAM[1]

computer system —see under SYSTEM

con•ceal•ment /kənˈsiːlmənt/ *n* [U] **1** LAW the crime of not telling a court about something affecting a legal case, for example when a bankrupt person does not tell a court officer about any money or property they own: *It is a criminal offence to allow the concealment of documents which you know are relevant to the investigation.*
2 INSURANCE when an insured person or company does not tell the insurance company about something affecting the conditions of their policy

con•cen•tra•tion /ˌkɒnsənˈtreɪʃən‖ˌkɑːn-/ *n* [U] ECONOMICS when companies combine to form larger companies, resulting in fewer businesses in an industry; CONSOLIDATION: *Continental, in a move that underlines the growing concentration of the tire industry, announced the acquisition of a Fiat tire subsidiary.*

buyer concentration the situation in industries where there are relatively few possible buyers

concentration of industry *n* [U] ECONOMICS when a lot of industrial activity is found in one place: *In Scotch whisky, the greatest concentration of industry is along the River Spey.*

con•cept /ˈkɒnsept‖ˈkɑːn-/ *n* [C] MANUFACTURING, MARKETING an idea for a product: *the management of an R&D process, from an original concept through to marketing, manufacture and end-use*

marketing concept ◆ [C usually singular] an idea for a product, or related to a product, especially a new one: *The neighborhood factor was also an important marketing concept in trying to attract residents to move to Pittsburgh*
◆ [singular] when a business concentrates on designing and selling products that satisfy customer needs in order to be profitable; MARKET ORIENTATION: *Without adopting the marketing concept a company cannot possibly hope to develop future plans.* —see also CONSISTENCY CONCEPT, REALIZATION CONCEPT

concept testing *n* [U] MARKETING when groups of possible users are asked about an idea for a product

con•cern /kən'sɜːn‖-ɜːrn/ *n* [C] *formal* a business organization, usually a company: *the French defense and electronics concern, Matra SA*

going concern a business that is making a profit

concert party *n* plural **concert parties** [C] FINANCE a group of investors who join together, sometimes secretly, to buy shares in a company individually and then combine them in order to get control of the company: *Pemberstone's offer for Roman is unconditional, with the company and its concert parties now in control of 86.1% of the shares.*

con•ces•sion /kən'seʃən/ *n* [C] **1** the right to carry out a particular business activity, given or sold to a company by a government or other public organization: *Bell South has paid B$2.65 billion for the concession to operate cellular phones in São Paulo.* | *AW was* ***granted a concession*** *to build a 364 km stretch of the Warsaw-to-Berlin motorway.*

2 *AmE* a small shop in a hotel, theatre, office building etc owned and managed by another business: *Snack concession sales per person at cinemas have increased.*

3 an agreement or rule allowing someone to pay less money, tax etc than they would normally pay: *American Express offered a rate concession to Laura Ashley's UK operations.* | *The* ***tax concessions*** *apply only after the savings account has been held for five years.*

4 *AmE* FINANCE the amount paid to an UNDERWRITER when new shares or bonds are made available for the first time: *a public offering of 8 million common shares in Perrigo, priced at $16 a share through underwriters Morgan Stanley – selling concession is 61 cents*

concession agreement —see under AGREEMENT

con•ces•sion•aire /kənˌseʃə'neə‖-'ner/ *n* [C] a person or organization with a CONCESSION: *Concessionaires operating in national parks will pay 22% of gross revenues to the government.*

con•cil•i•a•tion /kənˌsɪli'eɪʃən/ *n* [U] HUMAN RESOURCES the process of getting an employer and employees who are involved in an argument to meet and discuss their differences, in the hope of ending the argument: *Procedures for conciliation and mediation between the two sides of industry should be encouraged.* | *the conciliation service ACAS* —see also ACAS —**conciliator** *n* [C] *The government has appointed an official conciliator in a last attempt to bring the unions and management to the negotiating table.*

con•clude /kən'kluːd/ *v* **1** [I] to decide that something is true after considering all the facts: *The Stock Exchange concluded that the accounts could be regarded as suspect because they made no reference to such businesses.* | *We can conclude from the statistics that there is still an imbalance between the opportunities for men and women.*

2 conclude an agreement/treaty/deal etc to finish arranging an agreement, deal etc: *We would like to conclude the deal by the end of the financial year.*

3 [I,T] when something concludes, or you conclude it, it ends: *By five the interview had at last concluded and we left.* | *Anxious to conclude the meeting, he added: "All the figures you need are in the business plan."*

con•di•tion /kən'dɪʃən/ *n* [C] LAW, INSURANCE something stated in a contract, agreement, or insurance policy that must be done or must be true otherwise the contract, agreement, or policy will be ended or will not remain in force: *You should read the conditions of your contact of employment carefully.* | ***Under the conditions of*** *the contract, all work must be completed by June 1st.* | *The bank agreed to extend the loan if we* ***met*** *certain* ***conditions****.*

express condition a condition that is written down in a contract, rather than one that is accepted or intended but not specifically mentioned: *The buyers were entitled to reject the goods primarily on the basis of breach of the express condition, since they were slightly damaged.*

implied condition a condition that is accepted or intended without actually being written down in a contract: *There is an implied condition that the goods will correspond with the description.*

con•di•tion•al /kən'dɪʃənəl/ *adj* if an offer, agreement etc is conditional, it will only be done if something else happens + **on/upon**: *The sale of the company is conditional upon approval by Farnell's shareholders.* | *Seeboard has accepted the new electricity price arrangements, but Scottish Hydro has only given* ***conditional acceptance****.*

conditional sale —see under SALE

condition precedent *n* [C] LAW a condition in a contract that will only come into force once something stated in the contract happens or becomes true: *The continuing existence of the lease was not a condition precedent to the right to review the rent.*

conditions of sale *n* [plural] the arrangements made by a seller for selling goods, which the buyer must accept, including how payment should be made, when the goods will be delivered etc: *To protect yourself it is important that your conditions of sale and your terms of credit are known and agreed to by your customer at or before the point of sale.*

condition subsequent *n* [C] LAW a condition that exists until a particular event happens, for example payment of a pension until someone dies

con•do•min•i•um also **condo** /ˌkɒndə'mɪniəm‖ˌkɑːn-/ *n* [C] *AmE* an apartment in a building with several apartments, each of which is owned by the people living in it, or the apartment building itself

con•duct[1] /kən'dʌkt/ *v* [T] **1** to manage or organize something: *In future, Mr O'Reilly will conduct his business within the rules and regulations.* | *The Special Fund may, in his name, conduct legal transactions and finalise contractual issues.*

2 to carry out an activity or process in order to obtain information or prove facts: *The European Parliament had asked its legal affairs committee to conduct an investigation into the case.*

3 conduct yourself *formal* to behave in a particular way, especially in a situation where other people judge your behaviour: *I am full of admiration for the way in which he has conducted himself while the horrible events have gone on and been reported in the press.*

con•duct[2] /'kɒndʌkt‖'kɑːn-/ *n* [U] **1** the way in which a person behaves: *They claimed that Nike had engaged in anti-competitive conduct.*

code of conduct also **code of practice** a set of rules that employees, companies, or professional people agree to follow in the way they behave and do business: *Companies wishing to join the PC Direct Marketers' Association will have to abide by a code of conduct.* | *a code of practice for sales staff*

2 the way in which something is managed or organized: *There has been a huge change in the conduct of monetary policy.* | *rules governing the conduct of shareholder meetings*

conduct money —see under MONEY

Confederation of British Industry abbreviation **CBI** *n* in Britain, an organization with members from many private businesses and large companies, which represents them in talks with the government, TRADE UNIONS, legal organizations etc

con•fer /kən'fɜː‖-'fɜːr/ *v* past tense and past participle **conferred** present participle **conferring** [I] to discuss something with other people in order to make a decision based on more than one person's opinion: *The chairwoman is conferring with the board later today.*

con•fe•rence /ˈkɒnfərəns‖ˈkɑːn-/ *n* [C] **1** a large formal meeting, usually lasting a day or several days, where people discuss things in order to exchange information or to come to an agreement: *a sales conference*
2 a private and formal meeting involving a small number of people + **with**: *After a brief conference with ministers, Mr Blair left for Germany.* | *I'm afraid the CEO is* ***in conference*** *and will not be able to see you today.*
press conference also **press briefing** a meeting at which someone makes an official statement to the people who write for the newspapers, radio, or television: *a high-security press conference*
teleconference a meeting in which people in different places can talk to each other using videos or computers, so that each person can see and speak to all the others: *I have arranged a teleconference with the export sales team.* —***teleconferencing*** *n* [U] *We are increasingly making use of teleconferencing.* | *a teleconferencing system*

C

conference call —see under CALL[2]

conference centre —see under CENTRE

con•fi•dence /ˈkɒnfədəns‖ˈkɑːn-/ *n* [U] **1** the feeling that you can trust someone or something to do what they say, work properly etc: *We have every confidence in the team.* | *Our top priority is to maintain* ***customer confidence*** *in our product.* —see also BREACH OF CONFIDENCE
2 the feeling felt by businesses and investors that the economic situation will not become very bad: *Economic confidence was raised further by trade deregulation and lower interest rates.* | *Confidence in the housing market stands at a 15-month high.* | *A report by the Confederation of British Industry says Britain is enjoying the biggest increase in* ***business confidence*** *for ten years.*

con•fi•den•tial /ˌkɒnfəˈdenʃəl◂‖ˌkɑːn-/ *adj* confidential information is spoken or written in private and intended to be kept secret: *These figures are* ***highly confidential.*** | *A confidential letter was leaked to the press.*

con•fi•den•ti•al•i•ty /ˌkɒnfədenʃiˈæləti‖ˌkɑːn-/ *n* [U] the practice of keeping private information secret: *He raised concerns that departmental confidentiality had been breached.* | *a confidentiality agreement*

confidentiality clause —see under CLAUSE

con•firm /kənˈfɜːm‖-ɜːrm/ *v* [T] **1** to say or show that something is definitely true: *Ferranti said the report confirmed what its own directors and accountants had already established.* + **that**: *Walsh confirmed that the money had been paid.*
2 to tell someone that a possible arrangement, date, or time is now definite: *Could you confirm the dates we discussed.* | *I am writing to confirm our order for a 500mm print.* | *If a confirmed booking is cancelled a 50% fee will be charged.* —**confirmation** *n* [U] *The bank has to receive confirmation that the check has cleared.*

confirmation hearing —see under HEARING

confirmed irrevocable credit —see under CREDIT[1]

confirmed letter of credit —see under LETTER OF CREDIT

confirming bank —see under BANK[1]

con•fis•cate /ˈkɒnfəskeɪt‖ˈkɑːn-/ *v* [T] to officially take private property away from someone, for example because a crime has been committed: *The state can confiscate criminals' profits from books or movies describing their crimes.* —**confiscation** *n* [U] *A judge ordered the confiscation of the smuggler's £1.5 million assets.*

con•flict /ˈkɒnflɪkt‖ˈkɑːn-/ *n* [C,U] **1** a state of disagreement between people, groups, countries etc: *The General Strike was the most important* ***industrial conflict*** *of British inter-war history.* + **between**: *They are both strong-willed managers, and associates have noted signs of conflict between them.*
2 a situation in which you need to choose between two or more different needs + **between**: *the conflict between housing the poor and minimizing taxpayer costs*

con•flict•ing /kənˈflɪktɪŋ/ *adj* conflicting ideas, beliefs, or opinions are different from each other and cannot both be true: *Customers are being given conflicting advice by manufacturers.*

conflict of interest *n* plural **conflicts of interest** [C,U] a situation in which you cannot do your job fairly because you have the power to decide something in a way that would be to your advantage, although this may not be the best decision: *There is a growing conflict of interest between her position as a politician and her business activities.*

conflict of laws *n* plural **conflicts of laws** [C,U] LAW a legal situation in which a case is covered by the laws of more than one country, state etc and these laws are different

confrère /ˈkɒnfreə‖ˈkɑːnfrer/ *n* [C] someone who works in the same profession as you do: *his confrères in the medical profession*

con•glom•e•rate /kənˈglɒmərət‖-ˈglɑː-/ *n* [C] a large business organization consisting of several different companies that have joined together: *TWE is a cable-TV and film subsidiary of the world's largest media conglomerate.*

conglomerate merger —see under MERGER

con•gress /ˈkɒŋgres‖ˈkɑːŋgrəs/ *n* **1** [C,U] a formal meeting of representatives of different groups, countries etc, to discuss ideas, give information, and make decisions: *the annual congress of the miners' union*
2 [C] also **Congress** the group of people chosen or elected to make the laws in some countries: *The law was drafted by the Paraguayan military in 1991 and approved by the Congress.*
3 Congress the group of people elected to make laws in the US, consisting of the Senate and the House of Representatives: *The President had lost the support of Congress.* —see also ***Act of Congress*** under ACT[1]

Congressional Budget Office abbreviation **CBO** *n* the department of the US Congress that analyzes economic information, makes economic FORECASTS (=calculates what it thinks will happen in the future) etc: *The CBO now forecasts that the economy will grow 2.8% next year.*

Congress of Industrial Organizations —see AFL-CIO

con•nec•tion also **connexion** *BrE* /kəˈnekʃən/ *n* **1** [C] a train, bus, or plane which leaves at a time that allows passengers from an earlier train, bus, or plane to use it to continue their journey: *The train was late, and we nearly* ***missed our connection.***
2 [C] a road, railway etc that joins two places and allows people to travel between them: *Cheshunt has good rail connections to London, with trains every half hour.*
3 connections [plural] people you know who can be useful to you in business or in your career: *He used his connections in the City to find Pablo another job.*

con•nois•seur /ˌkɒnəˈsɜː‖ˌkɑːnəˈsɜːr/ *n* [C] someone who knows a lot about something such as art, wine etc: *an art historian and connoisseur of drawings*

con•sen•su•al /kənˈsensjuəl‖-ʃuəl/ *adj* [only before a noun] consensual agreements, plans, or actions are ones in which all the people involved agree with what is being done: *We think we will be able to reach a* ***consensual plan*** *that's fair to all parties.* | *This move towards consensual politics replaces the traditional confrontational approach we used to see between the parties.*

con•sen•sus ad i•dem /kənˈsensəs æd ˈaɪdem, -ˈɪdem‖-ˈaɪdem/ *n* [U] LAW agreement between all the people or groups who make a contract on what they understand the contract to be about. Consensus ad idem must exist before a court can force any of the people or groups to obey the contract

con•sent /kən'sent/ *n* [U] **1** permission to do something, especially by someone who has authority or responsibility: *He took the car* ***without*** *the owner's* ***consent.*** | *The city authorities have* ***given their consent*** *to leases on two buildings.*
2 agreement about something: *The chairman was elected* ***by common consent*** (=with most people agreeing). | *His contract is to be terminated* ***by mutual consent*** (=by agreement between both sides).
3 LAW willing agreement to a contract and its conditions, without any force or dishonesty having been used. If someone has given consent, a court can force them to obey the contract: *Except under special circumstances the parents or guardians of the child must give their consent to the adoption.*

consent decree —see under DECREE

consequential damages —see under DAMAGE[1]

con•ser•va•tis•m /kən'sɜːvətɪzəm‖-ɜːr-/ *n* [U] **1** unwillingness to take unnecessary risks: *Honda's conservatism extends as well to capital spending.*
2 ACCOUNTING the principle of being careful not to state an asset value, profit etc to be bigger, or a loss to be smaller, than it actually might be

con•ser•va•tive /kən'sɜːvətɪv‖-ɜːr-/ *adj* **1** careful to avoid taking risks: *He would be better taking a conservative approach to his new mortgage and opting for a fixed rate.*
2 careful not to state a value or amount to be bigger or smaller than it actually might be: *For the purposes of our valuation we have used a conservative forecast of £8 million.* | *Realization of the asset would bring in, at a* ***conservative estimate****, around £15,000 extra income.*

con•ser•va•tor /kən'sɜːvətə, 'kɒnsəveɪtə‖-'sɜːrvətər, 'kɑːnsərveɪtər/ *n* [C] *AmE* LAW someone who is legally responsible for the property of a person who cannot take care of it themselves

consgt written abbreviation for CONSIGNMENT

con•sid•e•ra•tion /kənˌsɪdə'reɪʃən/ *n* [C,U] LAW something of value given by one person or group signing a contract in exchange for something given by the other: *The rent-free period is consideration for the tenant's building work.* | *The seller transfers the property in goods to the buyer for a* ***money consideration****, called the price.* | *The guarantee was void as having been made for an* ***illegal consideration*** (=payment that was against the law).

con•sign /kən'saɪn/ *v* [T] *formal* **1** to send or deliver goods to someone, usually someone who has bought them: *Another copy of the document is sent to the party to whom the goods are consigned.*
2 if you consign a work of art to an AUCTIONEER, you ask them to sell it: *The Earl of Rosebery has consigned to Sotheby's Rembrandt's 'Portrait of Johannes Uyttenbogaert'.*

con•sign•ee /ˌkɒnsaɪ'niː, -sə̇-‖ˌkɑːn-/ *n* [C] *formal* a person or organization that goods are sent to: *The consignees in New York reported to London that the diamonds were overdue.* —compare CONSIGNOR

con•sign•ment /kən'saɪnmənt/ written abbreviation **consgt** *n* **1** [C] a quantity of goods delivered at the same time: *Sixty eggs are removed from each consignment and tested for salmonella.* + **of**: *A large consignment of weapons was unloaded from the ship.*
2 [C,U] goods given to someone acting for the owner, who must either sell them or return them to the owner: *Instead of selling him your goods, you can let him have them* ***on consignment****. This means he gets physical possession of the goods but you keep legal title.*

consignment account —see under ACCOUNT[1]

consignment invoice —see under INVOICE[1]

consignment note —see under NOTE[1]

con•sign•or /kən'saɪnə‖-ər/ *n* [C] **1** a person or organization that sends goods to someone; SENDER
2 a person or organization that sends goods to someone acting for the owner, who has agreed to sell them for the owner: *The consignor has been paid by the auction house, but they have not yet been paid by the purchaser.* —compare CONSIGNEE

con•sis•ten•cy /kən'sɪstənsi/ *n* [U] ACCOUNTING when a company uses the same accounting methods each year when it reports its results, so that the results can be easily compared: *In his chairman's statement, Grossart spoke of the need for consistency in financial matters.*

consistency concept *n* [singular] ACCOUNTING one of the basic principles of accounting, which says that there should be consistency in accounting methods

con•sol•i•date /kən'sɒlə̇deɪt‖-'sɑː-/ *v* [I,T] **1** to make your position of power or success stronger and more likely to continue: *His successful negotiations with the Americans helped him to consolidate his position.* | *Canon has consolidated its hold on the European market.*
2 to join together a group of companies, organizations, departments etc or to become joined together: *Amdahl Corp. says it has been able to consolidate a number of operations and 1,100 jobs worldwide must go.* | *He remains convinced that the smaller oil and gas companies should consolidate to add value for shareholders.*

consolidated accounts —see under ACCOUNT[1]

Consolidated Annuities *n* [plural] another name for CONSOLS

consolidated profit —see under PROFIT[1]

Consolidated Stock *n* [U] another name for CONSOLS —see under STOCK[1]

consolidating act —see under ACT[1]

con•sol•i•da•tion /kənˌsɒlə̇'deɪʃən‖-ˌsɑːl-/ *n* [C,U] **1** ECONOMICS, FINANCE when companies combine in takeovers and MERGERS, resulting in fewer businesses in an industry: *In a move toward further consolidation in the trucking industry, P-I-E Nationwide is to take control of Transcon Lines Inc.*
2 when organizations or departments become joined together: *Other changes include the consolidation of all financial functions into one department.*
3 when a company's position of power or success is made stronger and more likely to continue: *This is a time for consolidation, not for expansion.*

con•sol•i•da•tor /kən'sɒlə̇deɪtə‖-'sɑːlə̇deɪtər/ *n* [C] **1** FINANCE a larger company that takes control of smaller ones: *In view of its size, Generali has been seen as a possible consolidator in the European insurance industry.*
2 a business that brings together and sells at a reduced price things that other producers or suppliers have not been able to sell: *Consolidators buy up surplus airline tickets and offer bargain prices.*
3 a transport company that combines small loads sent by different companies into bigger ones: *Container transport documents are issued frequently by freight forwarders or consolidators.*

Con•sols /'kɒnsɒlz, kən'sɒlz‖'kɑːnsɑːlz, kən'sɑːlz/ *n* [plural] FINANCE British government bonds that have no fixed date for repayment and so will continue to pay interest; CONSOLIDATED STOCK

con•sor•ti•um /kən'sɔːtiəm‖-ɔːr-/ *n* plural **consortiums** or **consortia** [C] a combination of several companies, banks etc working together for a particular purpose, for example in order to buy something or build something; SYNDICATE: *Transmanche Link, a consortium of 10 British and French construction firms who built the Channel tunnel*

C

conspicuous consumption —see under CONSUMPTION

con•spi•ra•cy /kən'spɪrəsi/ *n* plural **conspiracies** [C,U] a secret plan that is made by two or more people to do something harmful or illegal **conspiracy to do sth**: *All three men were charged with conspiracy to defraud.* **a conspiracy against sth/sb**: *The company appears to be looking for proof of an industry-wide conspiracy against it.*

constituent company —see under COMPANY

con•sti•tut•ed /'kɒnstətju:tədǁ'kɑ:nstəˌtu:-/ *adj* LAW a properly constituted group, meeting etc has been formed and organized in a correct and legal way: *The opposition group was banned from taking part, as it was not officially constituted as a political party.* | *the importance of properly constituted audit committees in raising standards*

C

con•sti•tu•tion /ˌkɒnstə'tju:ʃənǁˌkɑ:nstə'tu:-/ *n* [C] **1** the system of basic laws and principles that a DEMOCRATIC country is governed by, which cannot easily be changed by the political party in power: *The First Amendment of the American Constitution guarantees freedom of speech.*
2 the system of rules and principles that an organization must follow: *the article giving general managerial powers to company directors which is found in the constitution of most companies*
3 the way that something is formed, especially the people or parts that make it up: *This change would fundamentally alter the constitution of the company.*

con•struct /kən'strʌkt/ *v* [T] **1** to build houses, apartments, offices, factories, roads etc: *It was the world's costliest hotel to construct at an estimated $1 million a room.* | *The partners will construct and own a long-distance phone system.*
2 to manufacture things containing many parts, such as aircraft, vehicles etc: *The partners will construct and own a long-distance phone system.*

con•struc•tion /kən'strʌkʃən/ *n* **1** [U] the activity of building houses, apartments, offices, factories, roads etc: *Share prices of construction, building materials and property investment companies were particularly hard hit during the recession.* | *Five of the emirates have built their own international airports and a sixth is* ***under construction***. | *the construction industry*
2 [C] something that has been built: *a strange construction made of wood and glass*
3 [U] the activity of manufacturing aircraft, vehicles etc, using many parts: *Titanium is used in the construction of aircraft fuselages.*

constructive dismissal —see under DISMISSAL

constructive total loss —see under LOSS

constructive trust —see under TRUST

constructive trustee —see under TRUSTEE

con•sul also **Consul** /'kɒnsəlǁ'kɑ:n-/ *n* [C] a representative of a government who lives in a foreign country in order to help and protect the citizens of their own country who go there, and to do work connected with trade between the two countries: *The British consul advised all British visitors to return home.* —**consular** *adj*: *a consular official* | *consular fees*

con•su•lage /'kɒnsjələdʒǁ'kɑ:nsə-/ *n* [U] charges made by consulates for the work that they do

con•su•late also **Consulate** /'kɒnsjələtǁ'kɑ:nsələt/ *n* [C] the official building in which a consul lives and works: *The Embassy or Consulate of the country you are visiting will advise you what documents are required.*

Consul General *n* [C] a consul with the highest rank

con•sul•tan•cy /kən'sʌltənsi/ *n* plural **consultancies** [C] a company that gives advice and training in a particular area to people in other companies; CONSULTING FIRM

con•sul•tant /kən'sʌltənt/ *n* [C] someone whose job is to give people or businesses advice or training in a particular area: *The firm has appointed a consultant to advise on the restructuring of the company.* | *a firm of* ***tax consultants***

consulting firm —see under FIRM

con•sume /kən'sju:mǁ-'su:m/ *v* **1** [I,T] to buy and use goods, services, energy, or natural materials: *Never underestimate the power of the American citizen to consume.* | *The UK and France consume more gas than Italy, mainly because of their colder climates.*
2 [T] to use money or time that could be used for something else: *Expenses consume less than 16 cents of every revenue dollar at Wal-Mart.* | *Lawsuits consume time and hurt a company's image.*

con•sum•er /kən'sju:məǁ-'su:mər/ *n* [C] **1** a person who buys goods, products, and services for their own use, not for business use or to resell: *Demand for autos is increasing as consumers feel more confident about the economy.* | *Oil price rises will be passed on to* ***the consumer*** (=consumers in general) *in higher costs.* | *research on* ***consumer behaviour***
ultimate consumer the person who buys and uses a particular product in its final form; END-USER; ULTIMATE CUSTOMER: *Under the Act, an ultimate consumer can claim against the producer of a defective product.*
2 a person, organization, industry, or country that uses products, services, energy, or natural materials: *South Africa is one the world's major coal producers and a significant coal consumer.*

consumer awareness —see under AWARENESS

consumer base —see under BASE[1]

consumer behaviour —see under BEHAVIOUR

consumer borrowing —see under BORROWING

consumer brand —see under BRAND[1]

consumer confidence index —see under INDEX[1]

consumer credit —see under CREDIT[1]

consumer debt —see under DEBT

consumer demand —see under DEMAND

consumer durables —see under DURABLES

consumer electronics —see under ELECTRONICS

consumer finance —see under FINANCE[1]

consumer goods —see under GOODS

consumer group —see under GROUP

con•sum•er•ism /kən'sju:mərɪzəmǁ-'su:-/ *n* [U] **1** the idea or belief that buying things is very important for people: *Consumerism is the new religion, and department stores are important temples.*
2 the movement to protect consumers from bad products, dishonest producers etc

consumer loan —see under LOAN[1]

consumer non-durables —see under NON-DURABLES

consumer panel —see under PANEL

consumer price —see under PRICE[1]

consumer price index —see under INDEX[1]

consumer price inflation —see under INFLATION

consumer product —see under PRODUCT

consumer profile —see under PROFILE[1]

consumer protection —see under PROTECTION

consumer research —see under RESEARCH

consumer resistance —see under RESISTANCE

Consumers' Association *BrE* **Consumers' Union**

AmE — *n* an organization that does research into the safety and effectiveness of products, defends the interests of the people who buy them etc: *The Consumers' Association has called for minimum requirements for minerals in mineral water.*

consumers co-operative —see under CO-OPERATIVE

consumer surplus —see under SURPLUS[1]

con·sump·tion /kən'sʌmpʃən/ *n* [U] **1** the amount of goods, services, energy, or natural materials used in a particular period of time: *Texas is second only to California in beer consumption.* | *Cuban households have been asked to reduce their electricity consumption by 10%.*
2 the act of buying and using products, services etc: *The spread of mass production, mass consumption and urbanisation have all contributed to the pollution of Lake Biwa.*

capital consumption ECONOMICS the amount of money spent on buying goods such as machinery that are used to produce other goods and products

conspicuous consumption when consumers buy expensive goods to impress people and show how rich they are: *Customers might view the purchase of a $300 bottle of wine as conspicuous consumption.*

3 ECONOMICS the amount spent on goods by consumers in a particular period of time: *Developing countries keep their currencies' value low and this allows them to limit consumption and imports and to stimulate exports, investment and growth.* | *He recommends a tax system that would tax consumption rather than income.*

domestic consumption also **home consumption**, or **internal consumption** ECONOMICS goods and services consumed in the country where they are produced: *The recovery should be export-led rather than led by domestic consumption.*

consumption expenditures —see under EXPENDITURE

consumption function *n* [singular] ECONOMICS a measure of the changes in the way that consumers spend money on goods and services when there are changes to their income

consumption goods —see under GOODS

consumption tax —see under TAX[1]

cont. written abbreviation for continued, used to show that a letter, report etc is continued on the next page

con·tact /'kɒntækt‖'kɑːn-/ *n* [C] a person you know who may be able to help or advise you, especially because of the work they do: *He has a lot of contacts in the media.* | *There are some excellent opportunities around, if you ask friends and* ***business contacts****.*

con·ta·gion /kən'teɪdʒən/ *n* [C,U] when problems in one country, area etc spread to other countries etc: *Europe and Japan are feeling the effects as the slow US economy* ***spreads its contagion****.* | *The Japanese banking crisis has created the possibility of worldwide* ***financial contagion****.*

con·tain·er /kən'teɪnə‖-ər/ *n* [C] **1** something such as a box or bottle that can be used for keeping things in: *the EU directive on beverage containers*
2 a very large metal box, of a standard size, in which goods are packed to make it easy to lift or move them onto a ship or road vehicle: *The deck was full of cargo containers.* | *a* ***container ship*** (=one designed to carry containers)

container bill of lading —see under BILL OF LADING

con·tain·er·ize also **containerise** *BrE* /kən'teɪnəraɪz/ *v* [T] to put goods into standard sized containers in order to move them by road, rail, or ship: *the steadily increasing volumes of iron ore, oil and containerized trade crossing the Pacific* —**containerization** also **containerisation** *BrE n* [U] *The revolution in distribution costs introduced by containerization opened up the world into a single market.*

containerized cargo —see under CARGO

container port —see under PORT[1]

container ship —see under SHIP[1]

container traffic —see under TRAFFIC[1]

con·tam·i·nate /kən'tæmɪneɪt/ *v* [T] **1** to make something dirty and dangerous, for example with chemicals or poison: *A large number of eggs were contaminated with salmonella.*
2 INSURANCE to spoil goods carried by a ship, especially by sea water getting into them —**contamination** *n* [U] *The pollution could cause serious contamination of agricultural land.*

con·tan·go /kən'tæŋgəʊ‖-goʊ/ *n* [U] FINANCE a situation in which the price for COMMODITIES (=oil, metals, etc) being traded is lower for immediate delivery than it is for future delivery: *The market was* ***in contango*** *– the price for metal for three-month delivery was $24 a tonne above that for immediate delivery.*

con·tent /'kɒntent‖'kɑːn-/ *n* **1 contents** [plural] the things that are inside a bag, box, room etc: *The contents of the suitcase were seized by the police.*
2 contents [plural] the things that are written in a letter, document, book etc: *The contents of some news broadcasts have offended some parents.*
3 [U] the amount of a substance that is contained in something: *Rainier's light beer has an alcohol content of 2.6%.* | *Coal has a high sulfur content.*
4 [U] the materials, parts etc that a product contains: *Eight states require a minimum percentage of* ***recycled content*** (=materials that have already been used) *in packaging.*

local content also **domestic content** [U] when a foreign company makes products in a country, the materials, parts etc that have been made in that country rather than imported. A minimum level of local content is sometimes a requirement under trade laws when giving foreign companies the right to manufacture in a particular place: *Mitsubishi plans to exports 200 Eclipse models a month to Switzerland, Austria and Sweden, but the car will have 60% local content.*

con·ti·nent /'kɒntɪnənt‖'kɑːn-/ *n* **1** [C] one of the seven large masses of land in the world: *the continents of Asia and Africa*
2 the Continent *BrE* used to refer to Western Europe not including Britain: *There is now greater co-operation with Customs Officers on the Continent.*

continental cover —see under COVER[1]

con·tin·gen·cy /kən'tɪndʒənsi/ *n* plural **contingencies** [C] **1** an event or situation that might happen in the future, especially one that might cause problems: *Damage to television aerials is covered under the Contents section. Note: some contents policies do not cover this contingency.*
2 a plan for dealing with an event or situation that might happen or cause problems in the future: *Imagine a major crisis in your area of responsibility. Do you have a contingency for it?*

contingency account *n* [C] another name for a CONTINGENCY FUND

contingency fee —see under FEE

contingency fund —see under FUND[1]

contingency insurance —see under INSURANCE

contingency plan —see under PLAN[2]

contingency reserve *n* [C] another name for a CONTINGENCY FUND

con·tin·gent /kən'tɪndʒənt/ *adj* **be contingent on/upon sth** if one thing is contingent upon another, the second thing must happen in order for the first thing to happen or exist: *Further investment is contingent upon the company's profits continuing to grow at the present rate.*

contingent fee —see under FEE

contingent liabilities —see under LIABILITY

continuation clause —see under CLAUSE

continuing security —see under SECURITY

continuous audit —see under AUDIT[1]

continuous disability policy —see ***permanent health policy*** under INSURANCE POLICY

continuous employment —see under EMPLOYMENT

continuous inventory —see under INVENTORY

continuous production —see under PRODUCTION

contra account —see under ACCOUNT[1]

contra-asset account —see under ACCOUNT[1]

con·tra·band /ˈkɒntrəbænd‖ˈkɑːn-/ *n* [U] goods that are brought into a country illegally, especially without tax being paid on them: *He had been accused of smuggling contraband from Brazil.* | *traders dealing in contraband silver*

con·tract[1] /ˈkɒntrækt‖ˈkɑːn-/ *n* [C] **1** LAW a formal written agreement between two or more people or groups which says what each must do for the other, or must not do: *Informix signed a contract to provide software for Wal-Mart Stores' distribution and systems.* | *Lawyers are still **drawing up** the recording **contract**.* | *Gazprom has **entered into a contract** with NIOC to develop the South Pars gasfield.* | *He wasn't fired and he is still **under contract to** OGE.* | *All cargo-handling services are now **put out to contract*** (=companies compete to win the work). —see also BREACH OF CONTRACT, ESSENCE OF A CONTRACT, ***work to contract*** under WORK[1]

2 FINANCE an agreement to deliver a type of basic goods or material at a particular price and time in the future: *The wheat contract for March delivery rose 8.5 cents a bushel.*

aleatory contract an insurance agreement that provides cover against loss or damage caused by a chance event

bilateral contract a contract between two people or groups: *They made peace by a series of bilateral contracts with other cities.*

binding contract a contract that courts of law will recognize as legal: *The successful bidder is under a binding contract to purchase the relevant property.*

evergreen contract HUMAN RESOURCES a job contract for a top company manager that in principle must be agreed regularly, for example every three years, but is always continued automatically

executed contract LAW a contract where the people or groups involved have done the things that they agreed to do

express contract a contract which states clearly what has been agreed: *Apart from express contract, a tenant owes no duty to the landlord to keep the premises in repair.*

fixed-period contract also **fixed-term contract** HUMAN RESOURCES a contract offering someone work for a fixed period of time: *A lot of the staff are now on fixed-term contracts.*

fixed term contract LAW a job contract stating that you will be employed for a limited period of time only: *With fixed term contracts, people are wondering whether their contract will be renewed at the end of the season.*

formal contract a contract that is properly written down, rather than just a spoken agreement: *A Boeing official said the company hopes to sign a formal contract soon for the sale of the jets.*

forward contract FINANCE a private arrangement between two organizations for buying a particular amount of something for a fixed price on a fixed date in the future. This type of contract is not traded on any financial market: *A forward contract between the exporter and his bank will fix the rate at which payment in foreign currency will be converted when it is received in the UK.*

frustration of contract [U] LAW when a contract is ended because of an unexpected event such as war or sickness which makes it impossible to do what was stated in the contract

futures contract FINANCE a contract for a fixed amount of a COMMODITY or SECURITY to be delivered at a fixed price on a fixed date in the future. Unlike forward contracts, futures are traded on financial markets: *The fund sells Treasury-bond futures contracts that obligate it to sell its Treasury bonds for today's prices in three or six months.*

hire purchase contract an agreement to buy something by making payments over a period of time. With a hire purchase contract, you do not own the thing you are buying until you have made the final payment

implied contract a contract that is not specifically stated or written down: *The broker was said to have acted honestly and in good faith, and there was no implied contract that he would have any degree of skill.*

labor contract HUMAN RESOURCES *AmE* an agreement between a company and a LABOR UNION on pay, conditions etc: *Italian journalists, in talks to renew their national labor contract, began a three-day strike.*

naked contract also **nude contract**, or **nudum pactum** [U] FINANCE a FUTURES CONTRACT or OPTIONS CONTRACT where the seller does not own the related shares etc

onerous contract a contract that is unfair for one of the people or groups involved: *an onerous contract that called for Tucson Electric to buy much of the plant's power through 2014*

options contract FINANCE a contract that gives the right to buy or sell particular shares, currencies etc at a particular price on a particular date in the future or within a particular period of time: *Each crude-oil options contract entitles its holder to buy (a call option) or sell (a put option) the equivalent of 1,000 barrels of oil at a predetermined price.*

oral contract a contract that is not written down: *Oral contracts are possibilities in situations where well-established trade customs can be proved.*

performance contract LAW a contract which becomes legally acceptable because of something someone has done for someone else, such as a particular task: *Mexico has opened up its oil sector to performance contracts in which the drilling company would receive a premium if oil was found.*

rolling contract a contract that continues until an agreed PERIOD OF NOTICE (=amount of time before you are informed that you no longer have a job), rather than until a particular date: *When discussing terms with your employer, you may be asked to consider whether you prefer a fixed-term agreement or a rolling contract.*

service contract ◆ an agreement between a company and a customer in which the company agrees to repair equipment the customer has bought or rented from it: *The Revenue Service confirmed its award of a $1.4 billion service contract to AT&T.*

◆ an agreement between a company and one of its DIRECTORS, stating what the director will do, how much they will be paid etc; SERVICE AGREEMENT: *A director is likely to be restricted by his service contract from competing with his employer.*

◆ an agreement between a company and a customer, stating what product or service the company will provide, and any arrangements for delivery, payment etc; SERVICE AGREEMENT: *Shop Television had a service contract to provide programming for the satellite television channel.*

turnkey contract a contract for a building project in which the company doing the work must finish the work and leave the building, factory etc ready to operate: *GEC-Alsthom won a turnkey contract valued at FFr3.6 billion for a power station in Morocco.*

unenforceable contract a contract that cannot be recognized because of a legal detail that is not correct

unilateral contract a contract in which only one of the parties has to do something, which is therefore not legally a proper contract: *The seller has undertaken no obligation and there is only a unilateral contract under which the buyer is committed to pay if the seller delivers.*

void contract a contract that is not recognized by a law court because it is illegal

voidable contract a contract that can be ended because one of the people or groups involved has done something unfair

contract[2] *adj* [only before a noun] *BrE* contract builders, electricians etc do work for companies rather than for the general public

con·tract[3] /kənˈtrækt/ *v* **1** [I] if an economy, industry, or business activity contracts, it gets smaller or less successful: *European scheduled air traffic grew 1.1%, but domestic traffic contracted by 1.6%.* —**contraction** *n* [U] *The US remained the largest buyer of Japanese vehicles in May, despite a 17% contraction in shipments.*

2 contract to do sth to formally agree to do something, for example by signing a contract: *Last month, the shipbuilding industry contracted to export 16 vessels.*

contract in *phr v* [I] *BrE to agree officially to take part in an arrangement: The company pension scheme was started last June, and since then 1500 employees have contracted in.*

contract out *phr v BrE* **1** [I] to agree officially not to take part in an arrangement: *If your company uses the state pension scheme and you want to contract out, then you can also have a personal pension.*

2 [T] **contract** sth **out** to arrange to have a job done by a person outside your organization

contract carrier —see under CARRIER

contract caterer —see under CATERER

contract labour —see under LABOUR

contract note —see under NOTE[1]

contract of employment *n* plural **contracts of employment** [C] HUMAN RESOURCES a formal document giving the conditions of someone's job, how much they are paid etc; TERMS OF EMPLOYMENT: *Under his contract of employment, he is entitled to six months' notice.*

contract of insurance *n* plural **contracts of insurance** [C] HUMAN RESOURCES, LAW a formal document giving conditions relating to an insurance agreement: *This summary of benefits is not intended to form part of an offer relative to the contract of insurance.*

contract of service *n* plural **contracts of service** [C] HUMAN RESOURCES, LAW another name for CONTRACT OF EMPLOYMENT

con·trac·tor /kənˈtræktə‖ˈkɑːntræktər/ *n* [C] a person or company that makes an agreement to do work or provide goods in large amounts for another company: *The company has no plans to expand the use of contractors in place of its own staff.* | *a roofing contractor*

approved contractor a contractor put on a list by an official group to say that they can be trusted to do work in a satisfactory way: *Paint manufacturers will have to get themselves onto a list of approved contractors before they can even bid for orders to major customers.*

building contractor a person or company that builds houses, offices, public buildings etc under the terms of a contract: *a contract to supply building materials to a building contractor*

defence contractor *BrE* **defense contractor** *AmE* a company that provides goods, such as aircraft, to a country's armed forces: *major defence contractors, such as Boeing in Washington*

haulage contractor *BrE* a person or company whose business is carrying goods for other companies by road or rail; CONTRACT CARRIER: *A haulage contractor agreed to deliver mixed concrete to RMC's customers.*

contract to sell *n* plural **contracts to sell** [C usually singular] a contract in which one person or company agrees to sell something and another agrees to buy it at a future time, for example when it is made or built

con·trac·tu·al /kənˈtræktʃuəl/ *adj* relating to a contract or agreed in a contract: *Uncertainty can be reduced by strict* ***contractual agreements***. | *a* ***contractual dispute***

contractual commitment —see under COMMITMENT

contract worker —see under WORKER

contra entry —see under ENTRY

con·tra·ri·an /kənˈtreəriən‖-ˈtrer-/ *n* [C] FINANCE an investor who believes in doing the opposite to most other investors at any one time: *A long-sighted contrarian might now get rid of equities in favour of real estate.*

con·trib·ute /kənˈtrɪbjuːt/ *v* [I,T] to give money, help, ideas etc to something that a lot of other people are involved in + **to/towards**: *His department contributed £2.3 million towards the fund.* | *They contributed to a number of worthy causes.*

con·tri·bu·tion /ˌkɒntrəˈbjuːʃən‖ˌkɑːn-/ *n* **1** [C usually plural] a regular payment made to the government by an employee and their employer so that the employee has the right to receive money from the government when they are ill or unemployed: *To qualify for the full basic pension, someone would need to have paid national insurance* ***contributions*** *for most of their working life.* | *In many pension schemes, you're allowed to pay additional voluntary contributions to buy a bigger pension.*

2 [C] an amount given to CHARITY: *His contributions this year include gifts to the San Francisco library and Museum of Modern Art.*

3 [C usually singular] ACCOUNTING the amount a particular product or activity pays to a company's OVERHEADS: *the contribution the business makes to corporate overheads and the way it is linked to the company's other operations*

4 [C] INSURANCE where there is more than one insurer, the amount that each of these pays to the insurer who pays out when a client makes a CLAIM: *If the claim exceeds $100 then a contribution should be obtained from the Home Insurer on an independent liability basis.*

general average contribution [C] INSURANCE an amount payable by one person or organization involved in a contract to the others involved in the same contract when there is loss or damage to a ship or its cargo: *While your car is being transported by sea, general average contributions, salvage charges and labour charges will be covered.*

contribution holiday —see under HOLIDAY

con·trib·u·tor /kənˈtrɪbjətə‖-ər/ *n* [C] someone who makes CONTRIBUTIONS: *Nearly half of contributors changed from one pension fund to another last year.*

contributory neg·li·gence —see under NEGLIGENCE

contributory pension plan —see under PENSION PLAN

contributory pension scheme —see under SCHEME

con·trol[1] /kənˈtrəʊl‖-ˈtroʊl/ *n* **1** [C] an action taken to make sure that something does not increase too much: *Devaluations were combined with* ***wage*** *and* ***price controls*** *and reductions in state spending.* | *Private rented*

C

accommodation has been freed of ***rent controls****, taking it beyond the reach of the young homeless.*

budgetary control [U] a system of management control in which actual income and spending are compared with planned income and spending, so that you can see if plans are being followed and if those plans need to be changed in order to make a profit: *Improved budgetary control has yielded a healthy surplus of £419,000.*

cost control [U] the process of making sure that a company or organization does not spend too much: *Analysts said tight cost control had kept Sail in profit.*

credit control ◆ [U] actions by a business to make sure that its customers can pay and can pay on time: *A £1.5 million charge was made for bad debts; credit control procedures have now been strengthened.*

◆ [U] actions by a bank to make sure that it only lends to those who can repay their loans and that payments are made on time: *Strong credit control and loan discipline are the best tools for reducing a bank's credit risk.*

exchange control [C usually plural] a limit set by a country on how much of its currency can be exchanged for other currencies: *Exchange controls were completely removed in 1978, and since then offshore financial activities in Singapore have exploded.*

import control [C usually plural] an action taken by a government to limit the number of goods that can be brought into a country from abroad to sell: *The Fiji government announced the removal of import controls and the reduction of tariffs on most imports.*

inventory control [U] *AmE* the process of making sure that supplies of materials, goods being produced, and finished goods are managed correctly; STOCK CONTROL *BrE*: *Inventory control aims to answer two basic questions: how much should be ordered and when?*

management control ◆ [U] the ability of managers to make an organization work as they want it to, and the methods that they use: *The firm's failures included poor record-keeping and weak management control systems.*

◆ [U] the power that someone has to manage a company as they wish, for example because they own more shares in it than anyone else: *Gillette will have management control and a 65% equity stake in the venture.*

materials control ◆ [U] a system for checking that a company has enough materials in stock for its production needs, but is not storing more than it needs because this would use capital unnecessarily; STOCK CONTROL, INVENTORY CONTROL

◆ [U] a system for checking the quality of materials bought by a company

production control ◆ [C,U] an action taken by a government or authority to limit the production of something in order to influence its price: *This price for oil is a goal OPEC hopes to achieve through production controls.*

◆ [C,U] an action taken by a company to manage its production efficiently: *The reorganization means that Acustar's production control operations will be handled by the parent company.*

quality control [U] the process of making sure that an organization's goods and services are produced and sold as planned and designed and are of the right quality: *Airlines have been asked to check new 737s after a check by Boeing of its quality control records showed that a bolt may have been left off the forward door.*

stock control [U] *BrE* the process of making sure that supplies of materials, goods being produced, and finished goods are managed correctly; INVENTORY CONTROL *AmE*: *He will take responsibility for Laura Ashley's purchasing, distribution and stock control.*

2 [U] FINANCE if someone has control of shares in a company, they own them: *Krupp said it had control of other blocks of Hoesch shares.*

3 [U] if someone has control of a company, they own more than half its shares, or enough shares to be able to decide how the company is managed: *CFS and Mr Vernes were* ***battling for control*** *of the Victoire insurance group.* | *Publicis purchased a little over 50% of Inovasi to* ***gain control****.* | *India is to sell stakes in state-owned companies to overseas investors while retaining* ***majority control****.*

creeping control ◆ [U] when someone gets control of a company little by little, perhaps without others noticing: *Mr Arnaud has a history of establishing creeping control of companies.*

4 [U] [singular] COMPUTING also **control key** a button on a computer that allows you to do operations when used with another button: *Press control D to delete text.*

control² *v* past tense and past participle **controlled** present participle **controlling** [T] **1** to have the power to make someone or something do what you want: *U.S. offices of foreign banks now control roughly a quarter of U.S. banking assets.* | *The government controls the production and distribution of all national newspapers.*

2 to limit something or prevent it from increasing too much: *To help control costs, the company cut salaries by between 2% and 25% last month.* | *Romania will control skyrocketing food prices by setting ceilings for items such as meat.* | *new measures to control inflation*

3 to check that something is as it should be: *Checkers control the quality of products as they come off the production line.*

4 FINANCE to own shares: *Mr Kahn now controls 854,236 common shares, or about 40% of Mercury's stock.*

5 FINANCE to own more than half the shares of a company, or enough shares to decide how the company should be managed: *The Agnelli family controls the car group through a variety of holding companies.*

6 MARKETING if a company or product controls a particular part of a market, its products account for a large amount of the sales in that market: *De Beers controls 80% of the rough, uncut diamond market.*

control group *n* [C] STATISTICS in a test, a group of people or things that you do not test and that you then compare with the group being tested. By using a control group, you can see if the results of your test are caused by the thing you are testing or are caused by chance: *It found that households buying the magazine spent 7% more a week on groceries than a control group.*

control key —see under KEY¹

controlled economy —see under ECONOMY¹

con•trol•ler /kənˈtrəʊlə‖-ˈtroʊlər/ *n* [C] another name for COMPTROLLER

controlling company —see under COMPANY

controlling interest —see under INTEREST

controlling shareholder —see under SHAREHOLDER

controlling stockholder —see under STOCKHOLDER

control period —see under PERIOD

con•ur•ba•tion /ˌkɒnɜːˈbeɪʃən‖ˌkɑːnɜːr-/ *n* [C] *BrE* a group of towns that have spread and joined together to form an area with a high population, often with a large city as its centre: *the densely populated conurbations of Britain*

con•vene /kənˈviːn/ *v* [I,T] if a group of people convenes, or if someone convenes them, they come together for a formal meeting: *The conference established five committees which would convene in April or May.* | *It will be necessary to* ***convene a meeting*** *of shareholders.*

con•ve•ni•ence /kənˈviːniəns/ *adj* **convenience foods/meals/goods** food products that are made and packed in a way that makes them very quick and easy to use: *the growth in sales of frozen convenience meals* —see also FLAG OF CONVENIENCE

convenience store —see under STORE¹

con•ven•tion /kənˈvenʃən/ *n* **1** [C,U] behaviour and

attitudes that most people in a society believe to be normal and right
2 [C] a formal agreement, especially between countries, about rules for an activity such as war or trade: *The Berne convention, which requires its signatories to respect copyrights for the life of the author plus 50 years.*
3 [C] a large meeting of people who belong to the same profession or organization, or work in the same industry: *Business was so bad that many dealers decided not to go to that year's National Automobile Dealers Association convention.*

con•ven•tion•al /kən'venʃənəl/ *adj* a conventional way of doing something is the way that has been used or available for some time and is considered to be normal: *standard conventional fixed-rate mortgages* | *Conventional measures of stock prices really aren't good guides to value.*

con•verge /kən'vɜːdʒ‖-'vɜːrdʒ/ *v* [I] **1** if two or more rates of interest, unemployment etc converge, they move to the same level + **with**: *Irish productivity per worker has converged with the EU norms.*
2 ECONOMICS if two or more economies converge, they start to have the same characteristics such as the same levels of inflation, interest rates etc. The economies of countries wanting to join the EURO have to converge with those of existing members before they can join + **with**: *Britain's economy has not yet converged sufficiently with those of the present participants in the euromarket.* —compare DIVERGE —**convergent** *adj*: *The Asian crisis showed the convergent, rather than divergent, nature of emerging economies.* —**convergence** *n* [U] *employment policies that work against regional convergence*

con•ver•sion /kən'vɜːʃən‖-'vɜːrʒən/ *n* [U] **1** LAW when someone gives away or sells property that does not belong to them
2 when something changes from being one thing to another, for example when a BUILDING SOCIETY becomes a bank: *The majority of Halifax customers voted for conversion.*

conversion premium —see under PREMIUM[1]

conversion rate —see under RATE[1]

con•vert /kən'vɜːt‖-'vɜːrt/ *v* [T] to change or make something change from one thing to another **convert sth to/into sth**: *energy consumption that could readily be converted from oil to natural gas* | *bonds that can be converted into stock at a later date* | *A falling dollar means that foreign-currency profits are worth more when converted into dollars.*

con•ver•ti•ble /kən'vɜːtəbəl‖-3ːr-/ *adj* able to be changed from one thing to another: *The new preferred shares will be convertible immediately to common shares.* —**convertibility** *n* [U] *The step toward **currency convertibility** is part of an attempt to move to a free market.*

convertible bond —see under BOND

convertible currency —see under CURRENCY

convertible debenture —see under DEBENTURE

convertible loan stock —see under STOCK[1]

convertible notes —see under NOTE[1]

convertible security —see under SECURITY

convertible share —see under SHARE

convertible stock —see under STOCK[1]

con•vey•ance /kən'veɪəns/ *n* LAW **1** [C] a document that officially states that land or property has passed from one person to another: *the drafting of a legal document such as a will or a conveyance*
2 [C,U] when land or property that was owned by one person becomes the property of another person, and the legal process of doing this: *the conveyance of a legal estate to new trustees*

con•vey•anc•er /kən'veɪənsə‖-ər/ *n* [C] LAW someone whose job is to deal with the legal process of making land or property owned by one person become the land or property of another: *It is the duty of a buyer's conveyancer to consider whether a plan correctly describes the property.*

con•vic•tion /kən'vɪkʃən/ *n* **1** [C] a decision in a court of law that someone is guilty of a crime: *Smith, who had no previous motoring convictions, had been rushing home to see his family when he hit another car.* + **for**: *He had a conviction for burglary in South Africa.*
2 [U] the process of proving someone guilty in a court of law: *Even when crimes are known to the police, only a small proportion lead to arrest, conviction and sentence.* | *legal safeguards against **wrongful conviction***

C

cook /kʊk/ *v* **cook the books** to dishonestly change official records and figures: *The health authorities have been accused of cooking the books to give more acceptable waiting list figures.*

cooling-off period —see under PERIOD

co-op /'kəʊɒp‖'koʊɑːp/ *n* [C] another name for a CO-OPERATIVE or a CO-OPERATIVE STORE: *the development of co-ops to produce and distribute organic produce*

co-op•e•ra•tive also **cooperative** /'kəʊ'ɒpərətɪv‖koʊ'ɑːp-/ *n* [C] *BrE* also **co-operative society** a company, factory, or organization in which all the people working there own an equal share of it: *Ten years ago a small group of woodworkers formed a co-operative.* | *She founded the Maison Espérance, a co-operative dressmaking business.*

agricultural co-operative a co-operative that brings together and sells the products produced by small farmers: *Privately owned farms have replaced many agricultural co-operatives.*

consumers' co-operative a co-operative that buys goods from a WHOLESALE CO-OPERATIVE and sells them in a shop. Any profit that it makes is divided between the members

credit co-operative a co-operative that lends money, collected from its members, at low rates of interest; CREDIT SOCIETY: *the Tokyo Shinkin bank, an Osaka-based credit co-operative*

housing co-operative in Britain, a co-operative that provides low-cost housing for people to rent: *a complex of flats to be let by a housing co-operative*

industrial co-operative an industrial company that is owned by its employees rather than by outside shareholders: *The industrial co-operative is particularly unsuited to capital intensive business.*

marketing co-operative a co-operative where producers of a particular type of goods work together in order to sell them: *a marketing cooperative in which more than 140 small local producers take part*

retail co-operative another name for CONSUMERS' CO-OPERATIVE

wholesale co-operative a co-operative owned by a number of consumer co-operatives that buys or produces large quantities of goods and supplies them to its members and to other co-operatives. The profit it makes is shared between the members according to the value of the stock they have bought

co-operative bank —see under BANK[1]

co-operative farm —see under FARM[1]

co-operative marketing —see under MARKETING

co-operative shop —see under SHOP[1]

co-operative society *n* plural **co-operative societies** [C] another name for a CO-OPERATIVE

co-operative store —see under STORE[1]

co-operative wholesale society *n* plural **co-operative wholesale societies** [C] another name for a WHOLESALE CO-OPERATIVE

co-owner *n* [C] one of the owners of a business or an

asset when there is more than one owner: *Mr Soberay and his brother are co-owners of the small Soberay rubber processing equipment company.* —**co-ownership** *n* [U]

cop·per /ˈkɒpə‖ˈkɑːpər/ *n* **1** [U] a reddish-brown metal used, among other things, for making wire and CABLES: *On Friday, copper for March delivery ended at 98.9 cents a pound, up 1.9 cents.* | *Kabelmetal AG, a major producer of copper products*
2 coppers *BrE* [plural] coins of low value made of copper or other dark-coloured metals: *He counted out three pounds, all in coppers.*

copper-bottomed *adj* completely safe to buy, invest in, or have confidence in: *Under the Tories, state pensions have a* ***copper-bottomed guarantee****.*

cop·y[1] /ˈkɒpi‖ˈkɑːpi/ *n* plural **copies** **1** [C] one of many documents, books, magazines, computer software packages etc that are all exactly the same: *We are offering a free copy of Windows98 with all new PCs.* | *The book sold 24,000 copies in the first three months.*

advance copy [C] a book, magazine etc that is sent to someone before supplies become generally available to the public: *Advance copies of reports are provided to the press and other interested parties at a cost of about £6,000 a year.*

certified copy [C] LAW a copy of a document that contains a formal statement signed by an official to prove that it is a true copy: *A certified copy of the court order will be required by HM Land Registry.*

office copy [C] a copy of a letter or other document kept in a file by a company: *We keep an office copy of all invoices we send out.*

proof copy [C] a copy of the pages of a book or magazine provided by a printer to a PUBLISHING company for them to check before printing of the final copies: *Once the first draft is complete, a proof copy is sent up for checking.*

2 [C] a letter, document etc that has been made to look exactly like another one, for example by being PHOTOCOPIED (=copied using a special machine called a photocopier): *Please send copies of all the relevant documents to me as soon as possible.*

top copy [C] a piece of written material that is produced first and from which copies have been made: *Keep the top copy on file.* | *The top copy of the bill acts as a receipt if the customer pays cash.*

3 [U] written material that is to be printed in a newspaper, magazine etc: *Our closing date for copy for the next issue is February 14.* | *six pages of double-spaced copy*
4 [U] MARKETING the written part of an advertisement: *"The business of fitness and good health is healthier than ever," or so says the advertising copy for the National Exhibition of Health & Leisure.*

body copy [U] the main written part of an advertisement, not the picture or the HEADLINE: *The logo is in capital letters while the body copy is set in roman.*

5 [C] a computer program, CD etc that has been made by putting information or music from another one onto a disk. It is illegal to sell copies made in this way: *selling pirated copies of computer games*
6 [C] COMPUTING a file, DIRECTORY etc in which you have put all the same information as is in another one: *Before you run this software, you should make a copy of your autoexec.bat file.*

back-up copy [C] a file, DIRECTORY etc in which you have put all the same information as is in another one so that you can use it if something should happen to the original one: *Back-up copies of working disks should be made frequently so that if a disk is accidentally damaged, not too much work is lost.*

hard copy [C,U] COMPUTING information from a computer that is printed out onto paper: *The terminal can store up 37 pages in memory for review or printing to hard copy.*

copy[2] *v* past tense and past participle **copied** [T] **1** to make a copy of a letter, document etc: *Could you copy these letters before you send them out?* **copy sth to sb**: *The letter was copied to the managing director.*
2 to deliberately use an idea, design etc that legally belongs to someone else: *They have issued a patent infringement lawsuit accusing their rivals of copying their design for a range of ready meals.*
3 to illegally make a copy of a computer program, CD, etc: *a new way to protect software from being copied* | *illegal software copying*
4 COMPUTING to make a file, DIRECTORY, program etc that is exactly the same as another one so that you can use it if something happens to the original one: *The best way to save an email is to copy it to a file.* | *You can copy, delete, or tag files in a matter of seconds.*

copycat product —see under PRODUCT

copy order —see under ORDER[1]

cop·y·right[1] /ˈkɒpiraɪt‖ˈkɑː-/ *n* [C,U] LAW a legal right to be the only producer or seller of a book, play, film, or record for a particular length of time: *A lecturer normally* ***owns the copyright*** *in any book or article he writes.* | *Drawings are prepared for most designs and drawings* ***are protected by copyright*** *as artistic works.* | *She started High Court proceedings against her publishing house for* ***breach of copyright****.* | *The distributer must not tamper with the content of the videos, including the copyright notice.*

copyright[2] *v* [T] LAW to obtain a legal right to be the only producer or seller of a book, play, film, or record for a particular period of time: *It's impossible to copyright a number, as Intel has found to its cost in its failed attempts to sue rival '386' chip manufacturers.*

cop·y·writ·er /ˈkɒpiˌraɪtə‖ˈkɑːpiˌraɪtər/ *n* [C] MARKETING someone whose job is to write COPY (=written material) for advertisements: *Most brand managers or copywriters in advertising agencies are under the age of 40.*

core[1] /kɔː‖kɔːr/ *n* [C] a part of something that is important in relation to its growth, future etc **+ of**: *The business park has created a core of new technology businesses in a city long affected by economic decline.* | *A core of major states support the national organization's plan.* —see also HARD CORE

core[2] *adj* **core business/activity/product** the business, activity etc that makes most money for a company and that is considered to be its most important and central one: *US car maker Chrysler is to sell off its $1 billion technology arm to concentrate resources on its core business.*

core audience —see under AUDIENCE

core business —see under BUSINESS

core capital —see under CAPITAL

core deposits —see under DEPOSIT[1]

core inflation —see under INFLATION

core product —see under PRODUCT

core workers —see under WORKER

corn and dry measure —see under MEASURE[1]

cor·ner /ˈkɔːnə‖ˈkɔːrnər/ *v* **corner the market** to gain control of the whole supply of a particular type of goods or services: *Singapore has made significant efforts to corner the market in this type of specialised service company.*

corner shop —see under SHOP[1]

corp. also **Corp.** *BrE* written abbreviation for CORPORATION

cor·po·rate[1] /ˈkɔːpərɨt‖ˈkɔːr-/ *adj* [only before a noun] relating to a company, usually a large one, or business in general: *$5 million is to be used to open new stores, relocate to a new warehouse and for other corporate purposes.* |

More than half of companies restricted corporate air travel during the Gulf War.

corporate² *n* [C] **1** a company, rather than another type of organization: *Our customers are large corporates.*

body corporate LAW a group of people who have formed a CORPORATION: *An artificial entity such as an organisation cannot function except in the name of a body corporate.*

2 bonds in companies, rather than in other types of organization: *municipal bonds and investment-grade corporates*

corporate bond —see under BOND

corporate borrowing —see under BORROWING

corporate culture —see under CULTURE

corporate debt —see under DEBT

corporate finance —see under FINANCE¹

corporate funder —see under FUNDER

corporate governance —see under GOVERNANCE

corporate hospitality *n* [U] when companies entertain clients, take them on trips etc in order to get business: *The Seurat exhibition will be popular for corporate hospitality, mainly through breakfast meetings.*

corporate identity *n* plural **corporate identities** [C,U] the way in which a company uses similar designs and colours on all its products, advertisements, letters etc so that people will become familiar with the company

corporate income tax —see under INCOME TAX

corporate investment —see under INVESTMENT

corporate issuer —see under ISSUER

corporate loan —see under LOAN¹

corporate marketing —see under MARKETING

corporate planning —see under PLANNING

corporate raider *n* [C] a person or company that tries to gain control of another company by buying most of its shares: *The company became the subject of a hostile takeover bid from corporate raider Ronald O. Perelman.*

corporate sector —see under SECTOR

corporate state —see under STATE

corporate strategy —see under STRATEGY

corporate venturing *n* [U] when larger companies give financial and technical help to smaller ones to help them develop their ideas in return for a share in profits if the smaller company is successful: *GE regards human energy technology as an investment – a corporate venturing exercise rather than a strategic acquisition.*

cor·po·ra·tion /ˌkɔːpəˈreɪʃən‖ˌkɔːr-/ written abbreviation **corp.** *n* [C] **1** a particular type of company, for example in the US one with indefinite duration and LIMITED LIABILITY: *the Sony Corporation* | *Mesa has completed its conversion from a partnership to a corporation.*

2 in Britain, a large company or a public organization: *the British Steel Corporation* | *the Corporation of the City of London* | *the British Broadcasting Corporation*

de facto corporation in the US, a CORPORATION that has not been properly formed according to law, but is allowed to exist as if it has been

development corporation a government organization responsible for a development area: *The Teesside Development Corporation has planning powers over the site.*

global corporation a corporation that considers the whole world to be its market: *the market power of giant global corporations*

multinational corporation a corporation that operates in many different countries: *He contrasts strongly the modern global corporation with the ageing multinational corporation.*

private corporation ◆ a corporation owned by people or other companies, rather than by the government: *She opposes government aid to private corporations.*

◆ a corporation whose shares are not available for sale, for example because they are owned by the person who started the company: *his private corporation, in which he and his wife are sole shareholders*

public corporation ◆ a corporation that is owned and managed by the government: *Latin American governments are privatizing loss-making public corporations.*

◆ a corporation with shares that are traded on a stockmarket: *Granada Corp. rolled 11 limited partnerships into two public corporations, one of which is Granada BioSciences.*

◆ an organization established by the national government or a state for a particular purpose, but not to make money: *the Job Development Authority, a public corporation*

corporation tax —see under TAX¹

cor·po·ra·tize also **corporatise** *BrE* /ˈkɔːpərətaɪz‖ˈkɔːr-/ *v* [I,T] to change a government organization into a company: *New South Wales has corporatised the former Pacific Power monopoly.* —**corporatization** also **corporatisation** *BrE n* [U] *Deng's successors appear ready to allow gradual corporatisation of larger state enterprises.*

corporeal hereditament —see under HEREDITAMENT

cor·rec·tion /kəˈrekʃən/ *n* [C,U] FINANCE a change in the prices on a financial market, usually when they fall quickly because they have been too high and are no longer related to the real condition of companies and the economy: *Market watchers are expecting a* ***stock-market correction*** *in February.* | *The fall in equity prices in October 1987 may have been no more than a correction to the market.*

technical correction [C] FINANCE a rise or fall in the price of a share, bond, currency etc that follows a very large fall or rise and brings it back to its real value: *a technical correction in the market*

cor·re·spon·dence /ˌkɒrəˈspɒndəns‖ˌkɔːrəˈspɑːn-, ˌkɑː-/ *n* [U] **1** letters exchanged between people, especially business or official letters: *Any correspondence concerning the inquiry should be sent to Mr Alan Wood.*

commercial correspondence business letters, especially as a subject of study: *The book contains standard models for commercial correspondence and business communication.*

2 the process of sending and receiving letters: *Details eventually were given after correspondence with the Western Board.*

correspondence clerk —see under CLERK

correspondence course —see under COURSE

cor·re·spon·dent /ˌkɒrəˈspɒndənt‖ˌkɔːrəˈspɑːn-, ˌkɑː-/ *n* [C] **1** *BrE* a person or organization, especially one in a foreign country, that you regularly do business with: *Among a wide circle of friends and correspondents, Cayley seems to have been recognized as a generous and modest man.*

2 BANKING a bank in one country that acts for a bank in another country: *Banks, by overseas representation and correspondents, are able to provide advice on economic, financial and commercial conditions in other countries.* | *Instructions are sent by airmail to a* ***correspondent bank*** *requesting it to credit the exporter or his bank with an appropriate amount in the exporter's domestic currency.*

cor·rupt¹ /kəˈrʌpt/ *adj* **1** using power in a dishonest or illegal way in order to get money or an advantage of some kind: *Swiss justice, in our experience, is as tough on corrupt bankers as it is on all other criminals.* | *people wilfully involved in bribery or other corrupt practices*

2 COMPUTING information on a computer that is corrupt has been damaged and can no longer be read or used by the computer: *It's generally impossible to compress files when overlays have been used because the program sees each overlay as corrupt data.*

corrupt² *v* [T] **1** to encourage someone to behave in an immoral or dishonest way: *US politics has been corrupted by money and the influence of special interests.*

2 COMPUTING to damage information on a computer, so that it can no longer be read or used by a computer: *viruses which can corrupt and destroy computer data* —**corrupted** *adj* [only before a noun] *A corrupted file is a big problem; you might never recover the data.* —**corruptible** *adj*: *providing arms and money to a corruptible military regime*

C

cor·rup·tion /kəˈrʌpʃən/ *n* [U] **1** LAW the crime of giving or receiving money, gifts, a better job etc in exchange for doing something dishonest or illegal: *He denies twelve counts of corruption.* | *The Chamber of Deputies voted to allow Venice magistrates to investigate corruption charges against him.*

2 when someone who has power or authority uses it in a dishonest or illegal way to get money or an advantage: *As well as causing a breakdown in the economic system, hyper-inflation led to a spread of corruption.*

cos·me·ceu·ti·cals /ˌkɒzmə̇ˈsjuːtɪkəlz‖ˌkɑːzmə̇ˈsuː-/ *n* [plural] products that are combinations of COSMETICS and PHARMACEUTICALS, and the industry that makes them

cost¹ /kɒst‖kɒːst/ *n* **1** [C,U] the amount of money that you have to pay in order to buy, do, or produce something: *The distributor bears the* ***full cost*** *of promoting a film.* | *Siemens is moving production to* ***low cost*** *sites in Portugal and Mexico.* | *The policy covers all major illnesses and includes children's cover* ***at no extra cost.*** | *The loss of such people caused shortages in key areas of the economy and necessitated the importation of expatriate skills, often at high cost.* | *The company had to bring in skilled workers from abroad, often* ***at high cost.***

2 costs [plural] the money that a business or an individual must regularly spend: *The rising costs of land and labour have weakened the ship repair business in Singapore.* | *Delays in construction could increase costs significantly.* | *Kraft is seeking to* ***cut costs*** *by closing plants.* | *Rents will be sufficient to* ***cover costs*** (=pay for costs) *and allow the developer a profit.*

accrued cost [C] ACCOUNTING the value of goods or services bought by a business during a particular period of time, even if it pays for them in a later period; ACCRUED EXPENSE

bid costs [plural] the cost of accountants, advisers, bankers, lawyers etc involved when one company tries to take over another

carrying cost [C] a cost relating to owning assets such as buildings and machinery, for example the cost of repairs, storing machinery, replacing old machinery etc

current cost [C] the cost of buying an asset now, rather than the price that was paid for it in the past; REPLACEMENT COST: *The difference between the historical cost and the current cost of resources used up is shown as an expense in the profit and loss account.*

depreciated cost [C] the original cost of a FIXED ASSET less the total amount that has been claimed against tax for depreciation: *The balance sheet value of £12 million represents a surplus over depreciated cost of £8.9 million.*

direct cost [C] a cost related to a particular product or service rather than to general costs related to buildings, equipment etc

discretionary costs [plural] company costs that managers can easily increase or reduce, such as those for advertising or developing new products: *Telstra said its costs rose fairly modestly thanks to reduced growth in material costs and tighter management of discretionary costs.*

economic cost ◆ [C] the cost of something in money, rather than other costs: *the major social and economic costs of a high level of unemployment*

◆ [U] a price that people can afford to pay: *We must ensure a free flow of mineral products at economic cost.*

factor cost [C] ECONOMICS a cost related to a FACTOR OF PRODUCTION, such as land, capital, or LABOUR (=work): *Unusually high factor costs in the area make the London operation less profitable.*

factory cost —see ***factory-gate price*** under PRICE¹

fixed cost [C] a cost to a business that does not change when the amount of goods or services produced changes and is paid whether anything is produced or not: *Their retail branches are a fixed cost, so the more business they put through them the better.* —compare ***variable cost***

historic cost also **historical cost** [C] the price paid for an asset when it was bought, rather than what it is worth now

holding cost [C] the cost of owning or storing an asset, for example when it is not being used: *The holding costs for raw land aren't as high as for commercial and residential real estate, where buildings must be maintained.*

incremental cost [C usually singular] the extra cost of producing one more of something; MARGINAL COST: *Child-resistant packaging is available at a low incremental cost.*

indirect cost [C] a cost not directly related to a particular product or service, but related to general costs for buildings, equipment etc: *supervision, inspection, maintenance and other indirect costs*

landed cost [C] the price of goods including the cost of the goods, insurance, and transport to a particular place: *Ayr had to demonstrate that they could manufacture at a landed cost competitive with other Digital plants.*

lifecycle cost [C] ACCOUNTING a method of calculating the total cost of making or using a machine, system etc, including the cost of development, repairs, and changes for the period of time during which it will be used: *70% of a product's total lifecycle cost is in the design, before it even gets built.*

marginal cost [C usually singular] ECONOMICS the extra cost of producing one more of something; INCREMENTAL COST: *It would be hard to make a fixed charge for the right to travel by rail and a fare per journey reflecting marginal cost.*

one-off cost [C] a cost that is paid once and not repeated: *Daimler said there would be a one-off cost of DM50 billion for fitting the anti-roll system to cars already produced.*

opportunity cost ECONOMICS [U] the real cost of doing something, including the cost of things that you cannot do because of the choice you have made: *The opportunity cost of sending a child to a fee-paying school is all the things that you can't afford to buy as a result: the new car and the holidays that you can't afford.*

overhead cost [C] a cost not directly related to a particular product or service, but related to general costs for buildings, equipment etc; INDIRECT COST: *A number of overhead costs are seasonal, eg heating and lighting.*

replacement cost [C] the cost of buying an asset now, rather than the price that was paid for it in the past; CURRENT COST: *Your sum insured should be for the full replacement cost of all your possessions.*

running cost [C usually plural] a cost involved with operating a machine, factory, vehicle etc: *Dellorto quality and finish ensures longer life, reliability and low running costs.*

setup cost also **startup cost** [C usually plural] the amount of money needed to start a new business, project etc: *Setup costs for a program to recycle paper can be repaid in a few months by sales.*

standard cost [C] the planned and calculated cost of

producing goods, which is compared with the real cost after production: *Where standard costs are used, they need to be reviewed frequently to ensure that they bear a reasonable relationship to actual costs.*

standby cost [C] another name for FIXED COST

sunk cost [C] money that has been used to pay for something and that you cannot get back: *The original cost is a historical cost and is therefore an irrelevant sunk cost.*

transaction cost [C] the cost of buying or selling something relating to payments to agents who work for you, lawyers etc: *Shareholders can sell their Exxon shares for a small transaction cost of 10 cents a share.*

unit cost [C] the cost of producing one item, dealing with one customer etc: *The number of people seen is high – up to 100 patients a day – thus ensuring that unit costs are kept low.*

variable cost [C] a cost that changes when the amount of something produced changes: *The variable costs start from zero, since labour and material are not consumed until production starts.* —compare ***fixed cost***

cost² *v* **1** past tense and past participle **cost** [T] to have a particular price: *This dress cost $75.* **cost (sb) sth**: *How much did the work cost you?*

2 cost a (small) fortune/the earth to cost a lot of money: *The meal cost a small fortune, but it was well worth it.*

3 cost a bomb *BrE informal*: *What a fantastic dress. It must have cost a bomb!*

4 past tense and past participle **costed** [T usually passive] to calculate the cost of something or decide how much something should cost: *We'll get the plan costed before sending it to the board.*

cost accountant —see under ACCOUNTANT

cost accounting —see under ACCOUNTING

cost allocation —see under ALLOCATION

cost and freight —see under INCOTERM

cost apportionment *n* [U] another name for COST ALLOCATION

cost base —see under BASE¹

cost-benefit analysis —see under ANALYSIS

cost centre —see under CENTRE

cost containment *n* [U] when an organization keeps costs low, or within a limit that has been planned: *Despite intense cost containment efforts, corporate medical bills rose an average 21.6% last year.*

cost control —see under CONTROL¹

cost-effective *adj* bringing the best possible advantages in relation to costs: *Private banking isn't cost-effective for the consumer with less than about $200,000, as those customers can get most basic services at lower fees from regular banks.*

cost efficiency *n* plural **cost efficiencies** [C,U] the act of saving money by making a product or performing an activity in a better way: *The systems offer cost efficiencies in terms of easier administration and cheaper maintenance.*

cost, freight, insurance *n* [U] another name for COST, INSURANCE, FREIGHT

cost inflation —see under INFLATION

cost·ing /ˈkɒstɪŋ‖ˈkɒːst-/ *BrE n* [C,U] the process of calculating the cost of a future activity or product, or the calculation itself; COST ESTIMATE: *Railtrack originally said the scheme would cost £100 million, but last year produced revised costings of £350 million.*

absorption costing [U] a way of calculating the cost of a product, including the cost of producing it and also the general costs of running the business or factory

batch costing [U] a system where the cost of making a product is calculated by the BATCH rather than by the individual item, including comparing the costs of different sized batches made under different conditions

job costing [U] the costing of each piece of work in a production process as a separate cost

marginal costing also **standard costing** [U] a system of costing where OVERHEADS (=general costs not directly related to particular goods or services) are not included and are calculated separately

cost, insurance, freight —see under INCOTERM

cost leader —see under LEADER

cost of goods sold *n* [U] ACCOUNTING the total VARIABLE COSTS (=costs of materials, workers etc) of goods sold in a particular period of time, before other costs are taken into account: *Cost of goods sold dropped sharply when Microsoft switched most of the software it sells from magnetic disks to CD-Rom.*

cost of living *n* **the cost of living** the average amount of money people in a particular place spend on food, clothes, or a place to live: *The cost of living rose by over 2.5% in the first half of this year.*

cost of living adjustment —see under ADJUSTMENT

cost of living allowance —see under ALLOWANCE

cost of living index —see under INDEX¹

cost of possession *n* plural **costs of possession** [C] another name for CARRYING COST

Cost of Production Theory of Value *n* [singular] ECONOMICS a 19th century economic idea, saying that the value or price of something depends only upon the cost of making or growing it. This idea is now seen as too simple, especially because it does not take into consideration supply and demand

cost of sales *n* [U] another name for COST OF GOODS SOLD: *Fuel represented less than 3% of Carnival's cost of sales.*

cost overrun —see under OVERRUN¹

cost per thousand *n* plural **costs per thousand** [C,U] MARKETING used to talk about how much a particular form of advertising costs to reach one thousand viewers, readers etc: *Costs per thousand vary sharply by station, and it is especially expensive to advertise in the London area.*

cost-plus *adj* **cost-plus product/price/basis etc** if something is made or done on a cost-plus basis, it is made or done at an agreed price plus an extra amount. This is done when the cost of making a product etc is not known at the time the agreement to buy it is made: *In the past it has been the practice for research and development contracts to be on a cost-plus basis.*

cost price —see under PRICE¹

cost-push inflation —see under INFLATION

cost structure —see under STRUCTURE

cottage industry —see under INDUSTRY

cough /kɒf‖kɒːf/ *v*

cough sth ↔ **up** *phr v* [I,T] *informal* to pay money unwillingly: *Grumman finally coughed up $40 million in settlement of the legal claims against it.* | *We'll get a new TV as soon as the insurance company coughs up.*

Cou·lisse /kuːˈliːs/ *n* FINANCE **the Coulisse** a group of unofficial dealers on the Paris BOURSE

coun·cil /ˈkaʊnsəl/ *n* [C] **1** a group of people that are chosen to make rules, laws, or decisions, or to give advice: *the council for civil liberties*

works council HUMAN RESOURCES an organization in a company where employers and representatives of workers meet to discuss pay, working conditions etc: *A court ordered Renault to consult its European works council before making any move to close its Vilvoorde plant.*

C

2 in Britain, the organization that is responsible for local government in a particular region: *Bob Jones has been on the Borough Council for years.*
3 a group of people elected to the government of a city in the US: *the Los Angeles city council*

Council for Mutual Economic Assistance —see COMECON

Council of Economic Advisors *n* in the US, a group of economic advisers appointed by the President and the SENATE to give the President advice on economic matters: *The Council of Economic Advisers produced startling figures: 9.3 million (20%) Americans were living below the poverty line.*

Council of Ministers *n* the EUROPEAN UNION*'s* official organization for making economic decisions, consisting of a person from each member state or country: *a working directive which is to be considered by the Council of Ministers next week*

council tax —see under TAX[1]

coun·sel /ˈkaʊnsəl/ *n* [C usually singular] LAW a lawyer who represents a client in a court of law; BARRISTER *BrE*: *My **defence counsel** destroyed his evidence on that fact alone.* | *The **prosecuting counsel** told the jury that there was no further evidence to consider.* | *the **counsel for the defendant***

coun·sel·ling *BrE* **counseling** *AmE* /ˈkaʊnsəlɪŋ/ *n* [U] the process of listening to someone who has a problem and giving them professional advice: *All staff who are made redundant receive free employment counselling.*

counsellor *BrE*, **counselor** *AmE n* [C] someone whose job is to help or advise people

commercial counsellor *BrE* someone who represents their country abroad and advises companies on trade between the two countries; TRADE REPRESENTATIVE: *Mr Lee, commercial counsellor at the Korean embassy in Bonn, says his country's investment in Germany is still growing.*

debt counsellor *BrE* **debt counselor** *AmE* someone who helps and advises people who are having trouble paying their debts: *It is important that training courses in debt counselling include giving emotional as well as financial support.*

coun·ter /ˈkaʊntə‖-ər/ *n* **1** [C] the place where you are served in a shop, bank, etc: *Please pay at the checkout counter.*
2 across/over the counter if something can be done or obtained across or over the counter, it can be done easily in a shop, bank etc without making special arrangements: *You can also withdraw and deposit money across the counter in any of our branches just by presenting your card.*
3 under the counter something that is kept or sold under the counter can only be obtained illegally or unofficially —see also BEAN COUNTER

counter bid —see under BID[1]

counter-claim —see under CLAIM[1]

coun·ter·cyc·li·cal /ˈkaʊntəˈsɪklɪkəl, -ˈsaɪ-‖-tər-/ *adj* ECONOMICS **1** not following the normal pattern of business activity, for example increasing when other activities are decreasing: *The aircraft engineering division will not be sold, as its countercyclical performance helps balance the EIS Group.*
2 countercyclical actions are intended to change the way in which the economy is behaving at different times, for example actions to stop it growing too fast, or to help it grow when it is not growing: *Bank supervision is not a suitable tool of **countercyclical policy**.*

coun·ter·feit[1] /ˈkaʊntəfɪt‖-tər-/ *adj* made to look exactly like something, usually illegally: *Last year about $80 million in **counterfeit notes** were seized, compared with $77 billion in genuine notes produced.* | *the growing trade in **counterfeit goods***

counterfeit[2] *v* [T] to copy something so that it looks like something else, usually illegally: *We must mark coins in a way that makes them harder to counterfeit.* —**counterfeiter** *n* [C] *Calvin Klein is a popular target for counterfeiters.*

coun·ter·foil /ˈkaʊntəfɔɪl‖-tər-/ *n* [C] *BrE* the part of something such as a cheque that you complete and keep as a record of how much you have spent; CHEQUE STUB: *I enclose the ticket counterfoil as proof of purchase.*

counter-inflationary *adj* intended or able to help reduce INFLATION (=increase in prices): *A strong currency is a counter-inflationary anchor.*

coun·ter·mand /ˌkaʊntəˈmɑːnd, ˈkaʊntəmɑːnd‖ˌkaʊntərˈmænd/ *v* [T] to officially tell people to ignore an instruction, order etc: *The appeal countermanded a decision by the Federal Transportation Authority that the new system was illegal.*

counter-offer *n* [C] an offer that is higher than a previous one, for example when more than one company is trying to take control of another company: *Celebrity voted to accept the RCI bid, despite a counter-offer of $525 million from Carnival Corp.*

coun·ter·part /ˈkaʊntəpɑːt‖-tərpɑːrt/ *n* [C] someone or something that has the same job or purpose as someone or something in a different place: *A German steelmaker earned DM43.12 an hour and his Japanese counterpart the equivalent of DM35.11.*

coun·ter·par·ty /ˈkaʊntəpɑːti‖-tərpɑːrti/ *n* plural **counterparties** [C] FINANCE the person or company who you are buying from or selling to, when you buy or sell something such as a bond: *In traditional trading, each side of the trade must assume that the counterparty will make good on its obligation.*

central counterparty a system used in some stockmarkets in which investors do not buy and sell to each other directly, so that there is no risk that one side will not pay what is owed: *The central counterparty effectively stands between buyers and sellers, momentarily taking the shares onto its own books during the transaction.*

counter-purchase *n* [C] in international trade, the act of buying goods as part of a COUNTERTRADE agreement: *Iran proposed a counter-purchase system for buying Japanese goods in exchange for Iranian oil.*

coun·ter·sign /ˈkaʊntəsaɪn‖-ər-/ *v* [T] to sign a document that someone else has signed, for example to show your agreement: *The cheques had not been countersigned, and the bank had no authority to honour them.*

counter staff —see under STAFF[1]

coun·ter·trade /ˈkaʊntəˌtreɪd‖-tər-/ *n* [U] when two countries trade goods or services in exchange for other goods or services: *The jets were offered at $34 million each, but the price will be settled as part of a complicated countertrade deal in which the Russians will purchase Indonesian rubber and coffee.*

countervailing duty —see under DUTY

counting-house *n* [C] *BrE informal* ACCOUNTING the part of a large organization that is responsible for looking after money; FINANCE DEPARTMENT *AmE*

country risk —see under RISK[1]

county court —see under COURT[1]

cou·pon /ˈkuːpɒn‖-pɑːn/ *n* **1** [C] FINANCE a small piece of paper attached to certain types of bond, that you tear off and hand in so as to receive interest: *The frequency of coupon payments can differ between bonds; for example, some bonds pay coupons quarterly, others pay coupons annually.*
2 [singular] FINANCE the rate of interest paid on bonds: *a new two-year bond with a 10% coupon* | *The **high coupon** is there to compensate high risk.*

3 [C] a printed piece of paper given to customers by the seller of a product, allowing the customer to pay less than usual for the product when they next buy it, or to get a free gift: *a 20p-off coupon*
4 [C] a printed piece of paper given to people by the government, allowing them to buy a particular product or get something for free, usually during a war: *ration coupons* | *petrol coupons* —see also INTERNATIONAL REPLY COUPON

coupon rate —see under RATE[1]

coupon sheet *n* [C] FINANCE a number of coupons attached to a bond

cou•ri•er /ˈkʊriə‖-ər/ *n* [C] **1** a person or company whose job is to collect packages, documents etc and deliver them somewhere: *a motorcycle courier* | *Harrods had sent the garment by courier.*
2 *BrE* someone who is employed by a travel company to help people when they are on holiday, for example to give them information or organize trips to interesting places; ESCORT *AmE*: *a courier for a touring holiday company*

course /kɔːs‖kɔːrs/ *n* [C] *especially BrE* a series of classes, or studies in a particular subject: *a one-year journalism course*
correspondence course a course in which the student works at home and sends completed work to their teacher by mail: *a correspondence course in accountancy*
refresher course a training course that teaches you about new developments in a particular subject or skill, especially one that you need for your job: *Nurses must attend a five-day refresher course every three years.*
sandwich course *BrE* a college or university course that includes periods of time spent working in industry or business: *a sandwich course in Industrial Design*

course•ware /ˈkɔːsweə‖ˈkɔːrswer/ *n* [U] COMPUTING computer software designed for educational purposes

court[1] /kɔːt‖kɔːrt/ *n* **1 the court** the people in a court, especially the judge, other officials, and the JURY (=ordinary people who decide certain cases). The phrase is often used when talking about what a judge or jury think or decide about a case: *The court said the defendants had been denied a fair trial.*
2 [C] LAW a place where all the information concerning a crime or disagreement is given so that it can be judged: *The new laws haven't yet been tested* ***in court.*** | *Sexual harassment is a criminal offense in Germany, but few women complain or* ***go to court*** (=start the legal process to have a case dealt with in court). | *Federal authorities are free to* ***take*** *taxpayers* ***to court*** *to collect unpaid taxes.* | *The two sides agreed to* ***settle*** *the case* ***out of court*** (=without asking the court to make a decision).
Admiralty court in Britain, a court that makes decisions about ships and the sea
appeal court *BrE* also **appeals court**, **appellate court** *AmE* a court where someone can ask for a decision or judgement made in lower court to be changed: *An appeals court overturned the $5.2 million award.* | *A jury in a state court ruled in favor of the Morning News and an appellate court upheld the decision.*
bankruptcy court a court that decides cases where companies are unable to continue trading because they cannot pay their debts and have gone bankrupt: *The company has filed for protection from creditors in bankruptcy court.*
civil court a court that makes decisions on legal cases brought by private citizens that concern private problems or disagreements rather than crimes
commercial court a court that makes decisions in disagreements involving businesses
county court in Britain, a court that makes decisions on legal cases brought by private citizens within a particular area, that are not important enough to be heard in a HIGH COURT
criminal court a court where judgements about crimes are made: *Most lawyers without a criminal speciality aren't skilled enough to operate in criminal courts.*
Crown Court in Britain, a court that deals with serious criminal cases and is higher than a Magistrates' Court: *He admitted eight theft charges at Liverpool Crown Court.*
district court in the US, a federal court at which a trial is first heard: *the United States District Court for the Eastern District of New York*
family court in the US, a court that makes decisions about divorce cases
Federal Court in the US and some other countries, a court that makes decisions about cases at a national level rather than state level: *the high quality of justice the nation has long expected of the federal courts*
High Court *n* ◆ an important court in London, that deals mainly with CIVIL (=not criminal) cases for England and Wales: *A top sportswoman was awarded £230,981 damages in the High Court yesterday after being knocked down by a motorcycle.*
◆ an important court in Scotland for criminal and CIVIL cases: *A man who was caught in possession of a stolen famous painting has been jailed for 18 months at the High Court in Edinburgh.*
mercantile court *BrE* the name for a COMMERCIAL COURT in some places: *the Manchester mercantile court*
small claims court a court where disagreements between private citizens involving small amounts of money are decided without the use of lawyers: *Claims of up to £1,000 can be made in the small claims court, but in larger, more unusual cases you'll probably need a solicitor.*
state court in the US and some other countries, a court that makes decisions about cases at a state level rather than a national level: *Although some state courts allow cameras in courtrooms, they currently aren't permitted in federal court.*
Supreme Court *n* [singular] the most important court of law in some countries, and in some states of the US

court[2] *v* [T] **1** to behave nicely towards someone because you want them to do something for you or you want to get something from them: *IBM has courted teachers by offering them discounts.* | *Coke courted Mark Goldston, then the president of Fabergé's USA division. But Mr Goldston ended up taking a marketing job at Reebok.*
2 if one company courts another, it has discussions with the other company about the possibility of a friendly takeover or MERGER (=combining the companies): *While only Daimler-Benz has courted the luxury car company in public, Volkswagen is also said to be interested in buying it.*

cour•te•sy[1] /ˈkɜːtəsi‖ˈkɜːr-/ *adj* [only before a noun] *provided free to a customer or to the public*: *A* ***courtesy bus*** *runs to the Hotel Del Levante from the airport every day.*

courtesy[2] *n* **(by) courtesy of** if something is provided by courtesy of someone, it is provided for free by them: *We stayed in Leeds, courtesy of The Hilton Hotel.* | *My colleague and I flew courtesy of British Midland first class to Heathrow.*

Court of Appeal also **Appeal Court** *n* [singular] in Britain, the highest court of law that makes decisions about criminal and CIVIL cases that have been decided by lower courts but where people are not happy about the decision made. Appeals against a judgement in the Court of Appeal are heard in the HOUSE OF LORDS

Court of Appeals also **Appeals Court** *n* [singular] in the US, one of the federal or state law courts that makes decisions about criminal and CIVIL cases that have been decided by lower courts but where people are not happy about the decision made: *The 11th US Court of Appeals in Atlanta overturned a federal judge's dismissal of a water pollution suit against the company.*

Court of Queen's Bench *n* [singular] LAW in Britain, a part of the HIGH COURT OF JUSTICE that hears CIVIL cases

court order —see under ORDER[1]

cov•e•nant /ˈkʌvənənt/ *n* [C,U] LAW a formal written agreement to do something or not to do something, or to pay an amount of money: *We are tied by a covenant which prohibits the stadium from being put to any other use.* | *The covenant to pay the rent on the due date is absolutely fundamental.* | *Under this ruling, the landlord would not have a claim against the tenant for* ***breach of covenant*** (=breaking the agreement). —see also DEED OF COVENANT

restrictive covenant [C] a covenant where someone agrees not to do certain things: *Restrictive convenants are the most common legal restriction imposed on the purchaser.* —**covenant** *v* [I,T] *All the agency's profits are covenanted to third world charities.*

cov•er[1] /ˈkʌvə‖-ər/ *n* [U] **1** insurance against losing something or suffering damage, injury etc: *The policies provide cover for death of the Policyholder.* | *You have to pay an extra premium to have* ***insurance cover*** *on your personal possessions.*

continental cover insurance from a British insurer that covers vehicles and goods while they are in other European countries —see GREEN CARD

interest cover FINANCE a company's income in relation to the interest payments it has to make on the money it has borrowed: *He feels happy with interest cover (the ratio of operating profit to interest payable) of two and a half to three times.*

2 also **insurance cover** the value that someone or something is insured for: *insurance cover of up to £5000 per item for loss or damage*

3 *BrE* BANKING, FINANCE something valuable, for example property or an insurance policy, that you promise to give to a bank or someone who has lent you money if you fail to pay the money back; SECURITY; COLLATERAL

4 BANKING the amount of notes and coins kept by a bank to meet the needs of its customers —see also DIVIDEND COVER

cover[2] *v* [T] **1** when an insurance policy covers someone or something, the insurance company will pay out money if the person dies or is injured, or if something is damaged, stolen etc: *You are not covered by your medical insurance if an accident happens abroad.* **cover sb against sth**: *Our optional Payment Protector plan covers you against loss of income in the event of sickness, accident or compulsory redundancy.*

2 if an amount of money covers something, it is enough to pay for it: *It took a massive $1.68 billion pretax charge to* ***cover losses*** *from bad loans.*

3 if an institution covers a loan, it makes sure that it has something valuable, for example property or an insurance policy, that it can keep if the loan is not repaid: *Many of these banks' loans no longer have collateral that covers the amount of the loan.*

4 FINANCE to obtain and pay for a currency, bonds, shares etc that are needed to make a sale that has been agreed, for example in a FUTURES CONTRACT: *The price of zinc for immediate delivery rose sharply because Chinese zinc producers that had sold short had to cover their positions.*

cov•er•age /ˈkʌvərɪdʒ/ *n* [U] **1** the area served by a broadcaster or MOBILE PHONE company: *one-2-one now has nationwide coverage with its network.*

2 INSURANCE the amount of protection given to you by an insurance agreement: *Make sure the policy gives adequate coverage against burglary.*

extended coverage ◆ when an insurance agreement remains effective for longer or covers more risks than usual: *Employees were not properly informed of the right to purchase extended coverage on their health insurance.*

◆ when a GUARANTEE (=maker's agreement to replace or repair a product) is for longer than normal, or covers more things than normal: *Owners of the defective trucks will be provided with extended coverage of three years or 300,000 miles on the radiators.*

cover charge —see under CHARGE[1]

covered option —see under OPTION

covered warrant —see under WARRANT[1]

covering letter —see under LETTER

cover note —see under NOTE[1]

cow•boy /ˈkaʊbɔɪ/ *n* [C] *BrE informal* someone who is dishonest in business or does bad quality work, usually because they want to make money quickly

cowboy builder —see under BUILDER

co-worker *n* [C] someone who works with you and has a similar job or position: *The report criticized them for being bad team players, unable to communicate verbally with their co-workers.*

CPA abbreviation for CERTIFIED PUBLIC ACCOUNTANT; CRITICAL PATH ANALYSIS

CPI written abbreviation for CONSUMER PRICE INDEX

CPM abbreviation for CRITICAL PATH METHOD

CP/M *n* [U] COMPUTING an OPERATING SYSTEM previously used on some personal computers —see also MS-DOS, UNIX

CPU abbreviation for CENTRAL PROCESSING UNIT

cr written abbreviation for credit

craft /krɑːft‖kræft/ *n* [C] a job or activity that takes a lot of skill, usually one in which you make things using your hands and special tools: *the blacksmith's craft* | *He learnt the film-making craft at Pinewood studios.*

crafts•man /ˈkrɑːftsmən‖ˈkræfts-/ *n* plural **craftsmen** [C] a skilled male worker in a job that involves making things with your hands: *Each drawer is individually finished by craftsmen to bring out the full beauty of the wood.*

crafts•man•ship /ˈkrɑːftsmənʃɪp‖ˈkræfts-/ *n* [U] **1** the special skill someone uses to make something beautiful with their hands: *Hyundai's intention is to make world-class cars with craftsmanship.*

2 the quality that something has when it is made with a lot of skill or made by a craftsman or craftswoman: *The attention to detail seen in this furniture is evidence of the superb craftsmanship.*

crafts•wom•an /ˈkrɑːftsˌwʊmən‖ˈkræfts-/ *n* plural **craftswomen** [C] a skilled female worker in a job that involves making things with your hands

craft union —see under UNION

cram•down /ˈkræmdaʊn/ *n* [C] *AmE* FINANCE when a BANKRUPT company (=one that has to close because it owes too much money to continue operating) asks a court of law to decide how CREDITORS (=those to whom it owes money) should be paid, rather than trying to reach an agreement with them: *Fairfield will attempt to use cramdown procedures in court to impose the original repayment plan on shareholders.*

crane /kreɪn/ *n* [C] a large tall machine that lifts things and moves them from one place to another, used especially on building sites and for unloading ships

crash[1] /kræʃ/ *n* [C] **1** a time when many stocks and shares lose a lot of their value very quickly, usually when investors lose confidence in the market and want to sell quickly: *the stock market crash of October 1987*

2 an occasion when a computer or piece of computer software suddenly and unexpectedly stops working properly: *The major problem with our on-screen editor is that it is plagued by crashes.*

crash² *v* **1** [I] if stock markets or shares crash, they suddenly lose a lot of value: *The cost of the project has soared, causing the shares to crash 11p to 329p.*

2 [I,T] if a computer or a piece of software crashes, or if you crash it, it suddenly and unexpectedly stops working properly: *The memory was completely overloaded, causing the system to crash.* | *an error which crashed the whole system*

crate /kreɪt/ *n* [C] a strong wooden, metal, or plastic box with an open top used for keeping things in, especially when moving them from one place to another

crawling peg *n* [C] ECONOMICS a way of trying to stop a currency losing value too quickly by connecting value to another currency, but allowing it to change between upper and lower limits: *Russia's central bank is to introduce a* ***crawling-peg system****.*

cre•ate /kriˈeɪt/ *v* [T] **1** to make something exist that did not exist before: *The building boom has* ***created*** *50,000 construction* ***jobs*** *in the state.* | *Banesto and AGF will* ***create a company*** *to sell life insurance in Spain, with each providing 50% of the capital.* | *The Fed is now targeting a lower federal funds rate, which should help to* ***create money*** *and lead the economy out of recession.* | *These families have* ***created wealth*** *in businesses they've controlled.*

2 to design or invent something: *The agency has created a number of American Express ads.* | *They are rushing to* ***create a product*** *that combines wireless communications with portable computing.*

cre•a•tive¹ /kriˈeɪtɪv/ *adj* **1** producing or using new and interesting ideas: *The movie company has come under criticism for focusing too heavily on marketing and not enough on creative issues.* | *He regularly gives lectures and classes on creative thinking.*

2 MARKETING relating to the work of producing advertisements etc at an ADVERTISING AGENCY, rather than management of the agency: *She is leaving the agency to take a senior creative position elsewhere.* —**creativity** *n* [U] —**creativeness** *n* [U]

creative² *n* [C usually plural] *informal* someone working for a company that produces books, advertisements, or films whose job involves writing, drawing, or having new ideas, and who does not have to dress smartly when they are at work: *Calling All Creatives – WPP Group's J. Walter Thompson is seeking budding art directors and copywriters for their US offices.* —compare SUIT

creative accounting —see under ACCOUNTING

creative brief —see under BRIEF¹

creative director —see under DIRECTOR

creative financing —see under FINANCING

cre•den•tials /krɪˈdenʃəlz/ *n* [plural] **1** the training, education, or experience that give you the ability to do a particular job or task well, especially in the opinion of other people: *You'll be given a three-month probationary period to fully establish your credentials as an accountant.*

2 a letter or other document that proves that someone is who they say they are or has the ability to do a particular job or task: *Swiss police checked the drivers' credentials before allowing them to pick up the delegates.*

cred•it¹ /ˈkredɪt/ *n* **1** [U] an arrangement with a shop, supplier etc to buy something now and pay for it later: *They are saving for new furniture – instead of buying* ***on credit****.* | *Sales were helped by the introduction of* ***interest-free credit****.*

trade credit [U] when a supplier allows a business customer to pay for goods or services after they are delivered, usually 30, 60, or 90 days later: *Half of those giving trade credit said that payment was not received on time.*

2 [C,U] an amount by which a payment is reduced, relating for example to goods you have returned: *Buyers can return a new Oldsmobile within 30 days and get full credit toward the purchase of another Oldsmobile.* —see also LETTER OF CREDIT

3 the credit side [U] ACCOUNTING the right-hand side of each account in DOUBLE-ENTRY BOOKKEEPING, the side used for increases in LIABILITIES (=the amount of debt that must be paid) or REVENUES: *Every time an entry is made on the debit side, another entry of equal value must be made on the credit side somewhere in the books.*

4 in credit *BrE* if you are in credit, you have money in your bank account; be in the black: *There are no bank charges if you stay in credit.*

5 [U] another name for CREDIT HISTORY: *If your credit is good and you drive less than 15,000 miles a year, you should consider leasing your car rather than buying one.*

6 also **bank credit** [C,U] an arrangement with a bank for a loan, or bank lending in general: *Transco is to get an additional $225 million in credit with no strings attached.* | *In the economic recovery, bank credit is absolutely critical, particularly for small businesses.* | *Lloyds said it would continue to* ***extend credit*** (=make loans) *to Mirror Group to keep it in business.*

confirmed irrevocable credit [U] BANKING in foreign trade, a document in which a bank promises to pay an exporter when it receives proof that the goods have been sent

consumer credit also **personal credit** [U] lending to members of the public, rather than to businesses: *Declines in consumer credit usually occur during recessions and indicate that consumers don't want to commit themselves to long-term payments.*

documentary credit [U] BANKING a method of financing international trade where a bank agrees to pay the exporter when it receives the related trade documents; LETTER OF CREDIT: *The importer can be sure that no payment will be made until the exporter has provided evidence that the goods have been shipped in accordance with the terms of the documentary credit.*

export credit [C,U] money lent to an exporter to cover the period of time between producing and sending the goods to the country buying them and being paid: *Governments subsidize export credit through official guarantees and below-market interest rates.* | ***Export credit agencies*** (=organizations that specialize in lending in this way) *provide insurance against certain defaults to the exporter.*

extended credit [U] when money is lent for longer than usual, or longer than was originally agreed: *Extended credit often supports banks that should fail, thus increasing costs to the government when they do go under.*

long-term credit [C,U] loans for five to ten years or more: *long-term credits to finance the construction of warehouses*

medium-term credit [C,U] loans for periods of between one and five years: *Interbanca has shown steady growth by concentrating its business on the low-risk area of medium-term credits.*

personal credit [U] another name for CONSUMER CREDIT: *Mortgage loans are considered the safest form of personal credit.*

revolving credit [C,U] BANKING an arrangement with a bank for borrowing up to an agreed limit; if the limit is reached and the loan is then partly repaid, the borrower can later borrow up to the limit again: *The new eight-year debt package comprises a $20 million term loan and a $45 million revolving credit agreement.*

secured credit [U] loans where the lender has the right to claim some of the borrower's assets if they do not repay it: *Leaseway offered to give its bondholders* *ownership of the company and convert its bank debt to a secured credit facility.*

short-term credit [C,U] loans for a year or less: *They provided short-term credit to finance ongoing working capital and capital expenditure requirements.*

unsecured credit [U] a loan where the lender does not have the right to claim the borrower's assets if they do not repay it: *In the majority of bankruptcies secured credit is repaid before unsecured credit.*

7 [C,U] an amount of money given to you by the authorities, or an amount that you do not have to pay, which normally you would have to pay: *The couple may claim a credit of $800 for child care against their tax bill. The credit may be carried over to future years until used up.*

C

investment tax credit in the US, a reduction in the tax that companies pay on their profits if they invest in certain types of equipment. This credit has been introduced and ABOLISHED (=ended) several times: *An investment tax credit would encourage more investment, thereby creating more jobs.*

pollution credit [C,U] a form of tax credit that a company that does not cause much POLLUTION (=damage to the environment) can sell to one that does. The system is intended to decrease the general level of pollution: *How much pollution credit a company gets for scrapping old cars would depend on the city.* | *Plants whose emissions are well below the permitted level can sell pollution credits to units which find cleaning up more difficult.*

tax credit [C] an amount of money on which you do not have to pay tax. The amount is taken away from your total tax bill or, if you do not earn enough to pay tax, it may be given to you by the government: *Under the financing program, tax credits are available to individuals who invest between $10,000 and $50,000 in a Maine company.* | *They proposed a $300 tax credit for each child.*

credit[2] *v* [T] **1** to add money to a bank account: *The tax authorities have confirmed that interest credited to the income account will be taxable.*

2 ACCOUNTING to make an entry on the credit side of an account in DOUBLE-ENTRY BOOKKEEPING: *On selling an asset, any excess over cost of replacement is credited to capital reserve or a specific asset replacement account.*

credit account —see under ACCOUNT[1]

credit advice —see under ADVICE

credit agency —see under AGENCY

credit analyst —see under ANALYST

credit appraisal —see under APPRAISAL

credit balance —see under BALANCE[1]

credit bank —see under BANK[1]

credit bureau —see under BUREAU

credit card —see under CARD

credit-card loan —see under LOAN[1]

credit card payment —see under PAYMENT

credit check —see under CHECK[1]

credit company —see under COMPANY

credit control —see under CONTROL[1]

credit co-operative —see under CO-OPERATIVE

credit crunch *n* [singular] when borrowers find it difficult to borrow because banks are forced to reduce the amount they lend: *One reason for the credit crunch is that bankers fear that regulators are more likely to classify loans as bad.*

credit freeze —see under FREEZE[2]

credit history *n* plural **credit histories** [C usually singular] a person's record in repaying loans, which is checked when they ask for a new loan or credit card: *It bases the interest rate charged for a car loan on a consumer's credit history.*

credit information —see under INFORMATION

credit insurance —see under INSURANCE

credit limit —see under LIMIT[1]

credit line also **bank credit line, line of credit** *n* [C] an arrangement with a bank for a loan or a number of loans: *The auto maker is currently negotiating a new $1.8 billion credit line that would replace a much bigger, existing $2.6 billion credit.*

credit loss —see under LOSS

credit market —see under MARKET[1]

credit note —see under NOTE[1]

cred•i•tor /ˈkredɪtə‖-ər/ *n* **1** [C] a person or business to whom another person or business owes money: *The company said its largest creditor, Crédit Agricole of France, is owed $22 million.*

bond creditor [C] someone holding bonds where the borrower is unable to repay either the bonds or the interest on them: *Not all bond creditors receive equal treatment.*

general creditor [C] when a business goes bankrupt, a creditor who has no special rights to be repaid before others, and may not be repaid at all: *The claimants will all have to stand in line as general creditors.*

judgment creditor also **judgement creditor** [C] a creditor who has obtained the right from a court of law to demand that an amount owed to them should be paid back

junior creditor [C] another name for GENERAL CREDITOR: *Senior creditors could receive as much as 98% of their allowed claims under its plan to emerge from bankruptcy, while junior creditors could receive 5% to 10%.*

preferential creditor also **preferred creditor** [C] when a business goes bankrupt, a creditor who has the right to be paid before others: *Preferential creditors include Customs and Excise, which is investigating Olympic to see how much VAT the company has neglected to pay.*

secured creditor [C] when a business goes bankrupt, a creditor who has the right to specific assets of the business: *Bondholders were concerned that the secured creditors would take possession of assets worth the approximately $85 million owed to them and there'd be nothing left over for bondholders.*

senior creditor [C] when a business goes bankrupt, a creditor who will be paid before junior creditors, or who will get a larger percentage of what they are owed

trade creditor [C] a supplier who has not yet been paid by a business to which it has sold goods or services: *The company said it has enough money to keep paying trade creditors and operating expenses.*

unsecured creditor [C] when a business goes bankrupt, a creditor who does not have any rights to specific assets of the business: *Pan Am also said that it was likely that unsecured creditors would receive only a small fraction of their claims, if anything.*

2 creditors [plural] ACCOUNTING the money owed by a business to its suppliers and lenders, and the entry in the accounts showing this: *creditors falling due within one year*

creditor nation —see under NATION

creditors' committee —see under COMMITTEE

creditors' meeting —see under MEETING

creditor turnover rate *n* [C usually singular] ACCOUNTING the amount a company owes its suppliers at any one time as a percentage of the total amount it buys from suppliers during a year. The credit turnover rate shows how quickly a company usually pays its suppliers

credit policy —see under POLICY

credit rating —see under RATING

credit receipt —see under RECEIPT[1]

credit repair —see under REPAIR[2]

credit risk —see under RISK[1]

credit sale —see under SALE

credit scoring *n* [U] the activity of calculating the risk that an individual asking for a loan will not make repayments on the loan when they should, by checking the answers to specific questions about their job, how much they earn etc: *Most lenders have cut costs by moving to a credit scoring system to assess how likely you are to default on a loan.*

credit society —see under SOCIETY

credit squeeze —see under SQUEEZE[2]

credit standing —see under STANDING

credit status —see under STATUS

credit terms —see under TERM[1]

credit transfer —see under TRANSFER[2]

credit union *n* [C] *AmE* a group of people, for example in the place where they work, who save money together so that members can borrow at lower interest rates than at banks; CREDIT SOCIETY *BrE*: *an unofficial credit union where people group together to help each other with major purchases*

cred•it•wor•thy /ˈkredət͵wɜːθi‖-͵wɜːr-/ *adj* if a country, business, or individual is creditworthy, they are in a good position financially and have a good record of paying back loans on time, so institutions can lend money to them with confidence that the money will be paid back: *There is no general lack of credit for creditworthy borrowers.* —**creditworthiness** *n* [U] *There were doubts about Olympia's creditworthiness following reports that it was having difficulty repaying some of its loans.*

creep•ing /ˈkriːpɪŋ/ *adj* [only before a noun] gradually becoming stronger and gaining more influence, but so slowly that people do not notice: ***Creeping inflation***, *high interest rates, shrinking profits and a stagnant stock market – all the evidence points to an economic downturn.* | *legislation that paved the way for the creeping privatisation of British Rail*

creeping control —see under CONTROL[1]

creeping inflation —see under INFLATION

creeping takeover —see under TAKEOVER

Crest /krest/ *n* [U] FINANCE the name given to the London STOCK EXCHANGE's system of buying and selling stock, shares etc electronically, using computers. Members of the system keep an electronic record of their stocks and shares, and when one member wants to buy or sell from another, the system checks that the seller has the stocks or shares, then the buyer can order them and pay for them: *Investors can still use certificates with Crest, but brokers need to input each deal electronically.*

crew /kruː/ *n* [C] **1** all the people working on a ship or plane: *These planes carry over 300 passengers and crew.*

2 all the people working on a ship or plane except the most important officers: *No one would take responsibility for off-loading the cargo, and Captain Pintar and his crew would not fly with it.*

crime /kraɪm/ *n* **1** [C] a dishonest or immoral action that can be punished by law: *Insider trading is not a crime in Germany, although it is a breach of stockmarket rules.*

2 [U] illegal activities in general: *We moved here ten years ago because there was very little crime.*

white-collar crime *n* [U] crimes by professional people that involve ways of illegally getting money: *The government is determined to cut down on white-collar crime.*

crim•i•nal[1] /ˈkrɪmənəl/ *adj* [only before a noun] **1** not allowed by law and able to be punished by law: *The investigation uncovered serious criminal activity.* | *allegations of possible criminal conduct involving company directors*

2 dealing with legal cases that involve crime: *forensic tests involved in criminal and civil court cases* | *a criminal lawyer*

criminal[2] *n* [C] someone who is involved in illegal activity or has been found guilty of a crime

criminal court —see under COURT[1]

criminal injury —see under INJURY

criminal law —see under LAW

criminal liability —see under LIABILITY

cri•sis /ˈkraɪsəs/ *n* plural **crises** [C,U] **1** a period of great difficulty, danger, or uncertainty, especially in politics or economics: *the energy crisis of 1972* | *the Cuban missile crisis*

2 crisis of confidence a time when people no longer have confidence in something and no longer support it: *There seems to be a crisis of confidence in the economy.*

crisis management —see under MANAGEMENT

critical mass *n* [singular] the minimum number of users, buyers etc that is necessary for a product to succeed or for something to happen **+ of**: *A communications system is of no value to the users unless there is a critical mass of users.*

critical path analysis —see under ANALYSIS

critical success factor —see under FACTOR[1]

crook•ed /ˈkrʊkəd/ *adj informal* slightly dishonest: *a crooked deal*

crop /krɒp‖krɑːp/ *n* [C] **1** a plant such as wheat, rice, or fruit that is grown by farmers in order to be eaten or used in industry: *The main crop in China is rice.* | *the cotton crop*

2 the amount of wheat, rice, fruit etc that is produced in a season: *Wheat farmers have had a record crop this year.*

cash crop a crop that a farmer grows to sell for money rather than to live on or use: *Although illegal, cannabis is already the largest cash crop in several states.*

subsistence crop a crop that is grown to be used by the farmer rather than to be sold: *Coca plantations are interspersed with subsistence crops.*

cross /krɒs‖krɒːs/ *v* [T] **cross a cheque** *BrE* BANKING to draw two parallel lines across a cheque and write the words 'account payee', showing that it can only be paid into a bank account of a person named on the cheque, and not exchanged for cash or paid into a different account; ENDORSE: *If you ask another person to pay a cheque into your account for you, it is advisable to cross the cheque with the words 'account payee only'.*

cross-border *adj* [only before a noun] cross-border buying, selling etc involves organizations in two or more countries: ***cross-border mergers*** *in the European arms business* | *They want simpler regulations in order to make* ***cross-border trade*** *easier.*

cross-border merchant —see under MERCHANT

crossed cheque —see under CHEQUE

cross-examination —see under EXAMINATION

cross-examine *v* [T] to question a WITNESS very carefully during a court case, especially in order to show that they are not telling the truth: *You will get a chance to cross-examine the witness when she has finished giving her evidence.* —**cross-examination** *n* [U] *He conceded* ***under cross-examination*** *that he did know about the letter.*

cross guarantee —see under GUARANTEE[2]

cross-holding —see under HOLDING

cross merchandising —see under MERCHANDISING

cross ownership —see under OWNERSHIP

cross promotion —see under PROMOTION

cross rate —see under EXCHANGE RATE

cross-selling *n* [U] MARKETING when one company helps another to sell products by offering the second company's products at the same time as its own, for example in an advertisement or in a MAIL-SHOT: *We have good opportunities for cross-selling with KPMG.*

cross-trading also **crosstrading** *n* [U] when currency dealers in one country buy or sell the currency of a second country in exchange for the currency of a third country: *The dollar also benefited against the mark from selling of marks for yen in cross-trading.*

C

crown /kraʊn/ *n* **1 the Crown** the government of a country such as Britain that is officially led by a king or queen: *The islands are possessions of the Crown.*
2 [C] the English name for a unit of currency used in several European countries, for example Denmark, Norway, and Sweden: *Swedish drug company Pharmacia had pre-tax profits of 545 million crowns (£54 million).*

Crown Agents for Overseas Governments and Administrations *n* a British government organization that acts for foreign governments in buying goods and services and gives them financial advice

Crown Court —see under COURT[1]

crown jewels *n* [plural] a company's most important and valuable assets: *Unocal's two crown jewels are its huge natural gas reserves and an experimental oil business, which could yield major long-term benefits.*

crown jewels defence —see under DEFENCE

crude[1] /kruːd/ *adj* **1 crude oil/sugar etc** crude oil, sugar etc is in a natural condition, before it has been treated in an industrial process: *300 million tons of crude oil*
2 not calculated very exactly: *The level of income at which Supplementary Benefit is received is widely accepted as a crude measure of the 'poverty line'.*
3 STATISTICS crude figures have been found by simply counting the numbers of something, without considering things which may affect the numbers: *a crude analysis of the use of doctors by the various socio-economic groups*

crude[2] *n* [U] crude oil: *a fall in the price of crude*

crunch /krʌntʃ/ *v* **crunch (the) numbers** to do very complicated calculations on large amounts of DATA (=information stored on a computer) in order to find out about something: *Media buyers have to know what's going on, not just how to crunch numbers.* —see also CREDIT CRUNCH, SUPPLY CRUNCH

crys•tal•lize also **crystallise** *BrE* /ˈkrɪstəlaɪz/ *v* [T] FINANCE **crystallize a gain/loss** to actually obtain or lose an amount of money; REALIZE: *the practice of buying back shares the day after disposal to crystallize a capital gain* | *The failure of the Gulf Group would have crystallized large losses and put the bank's survival in doubt.*

C-suite *n* **the C-suite** the most important people in world business; the CHIEF EXECUTIVES and heads of finance and information at the 10,000 most successful companies in the world

CT abbreviation for CORPORATION TAX

CTT abbreviation for CAPITAL TRANSFER TAX

cu. also **cub** written abbreviation for CUBIC

cu•bic /ˈkjuːbɪk/ *adj* **cubic centimetre/metre/unit etc** a measurement of space which is calculated by multiplying the length of something by its width and height: *The well produced 19.4 million cubic metres of gas.*

cul•ti•vate /ˈkʌltɪveɪt/ *v* [T] **1** to prepare and use land for growing crops and plants: *Some of the land would be impossible to cultivate.* | *cultivated fields*
2 to develop a particular skill or quality in yourself: *The company has been successful in cultivating a very professional image.*
3 to make an effort to develop a friendly relationship with someone who could be useful to you: *Professor Gladwyn would be an acquaintance worth cultivating.*

cul•ture /ˈkʌltʃə‖-ər/ *n* **1** [C,U] the ideas, beliefs, and customs that are shared and accepted by people in a society: *Western culture places a high value on material acquisition.*
2 [C,U] the attitudes or beliefs that are shared by a particular group of people or in a particular organization: *Working late hours seems part of the **company culture**.* | *Can he transform Sabena's **corporate culture** from overstaffed public administration to profit-minded entrepreneurship?* | *Slim has succeeded in giving Telmex a much more business-like **management culture**.*
3 [U] activities that are related to art, music, literature etc: *If it's culture you're looking for, the city has plenty of museums and art galleries.*
4 [U] the practice of growing crops: *strawberry culture*

cum /kʊm, kʌm/ *prep* **cum dividend/cum div** when the price of shares is listed cum dividend or cum div, the person who buys them will receive the next DIVIDEND payment on them: *Marketmakers are able to claim against their tax liabilities any trading losses made by buying stock cum dividend and then selling it ex-dividend.*

cum interest —see under INTEREST

cu•mu•la•tive /ˈkjuːmjələtɪv‖-leɪtɪv/ *adj* increasing gradually and having a greater effect as more is added over a period of time: *The state is already saddled with a cumulative deficit of about $73 million.* | *The FHA faces cumulative losses approaching $7 billion.*

cumulative dividend —see under DIVIDEND

cumulative preference share —see under SHARE

cumulative preferred stock —see under STOCK[1]

cu•pro-nick•el /ˌkjuːprəʊˈnɪkəl‖ˌkuːproʊ-/ *n* [U] a mixture of COPPER with 25% NICKEL, used to make silver-coloured coins in Britain and many other countries

cur written abbreviation for currency

curb[1] /kɜːb‖kɜːrb/ *v* [T] to control or limit something that has a harmful effect: *He told the conference that his priority was to curb inflation.*

curb[2] *n* [C] a control or limit on something + **on**: *The plan called for curbs on government spending.*

curb market —see under MARKET[1]

cur•ren•cy /ˈkʌrənsi‖ˈkɜːr-/ written abbreviation **cur** *n* plural **currencies** **1** [C,U] the system or type of money used in a particular country: *The Bulgarian currency, the Lev, is fixed at 1,000 to the D-Mark.* | *The dollar was lower against European currencies.* —see also BASKET OF CURRENCIES

blocked currency [C,U] a currency which a government does not allow to be taken out of the country or changed into other currencies

convertible currency [C,U] a currency that can be freely exchanged for another: *Croatia has created a strong, convertible currency backed by growing foreign currency reserves.*

decimal currency [C,U] a currency whose main unit is divided into a hundred smaller units, for example dollars and cents

domestic currency also **local currency** [C,U] the currency of the home country of a particular user: *An importer might be able to make payment in his own domestic currency if this is acceptable to the exporter.*

floating currency [C,U] a currency whose value is allowed to change in relation to other currencies: *The South Korean Won had its first day as a fully floating* *currency yesterday, increasing in value against the US dollar.*

foreign currency [C,U] a currency or currencies not belonging to your own country: *Growing exports will give them more foreign currency.* | *He wasted billions of **foreign currency reserves** in trying to support the value of the pound.*

hard currency [C,U] a currency that keeps its value or whose value increases in relation to other currencies, and is used for international payments: *Vietnam was obliged to pay in hard currency, rather than in roubles, for goods imported from Russia.*

non-convertible currency also **inconvertible currency** [C,U] a currency that cannot be exchanged for other currencies: *There is no guarantee that earnings in the local, non-convertible currency, the Dong, can be exchanged for hard currency.*

paper currency [C,U] a currency based on paper notes rather than on gold and silver coins: *The creation of a paper currency was central to the financial revolution and the growth of commerce.*

pegged currency [C,U] a currency that is controlled by the CENTRAL BANK in a country so that it keeps the same value against other currencies

reserve currency [C,U] a currency held by governments because of its strength and its usefulness in making international payments: *The strong mark ranks as the world's second-largest reserve currency, next only to the US dollar.*

single currency [C,U] the common currency introduced in many European Union countries in 1999, the EURO: *The single currency is run by a national bank, but the supporting economic policies stay largely in national hands.*

soft currency also **weak currency** [C,U] a currency that regularly loses value in relation to others: *The euro may be seen as a soft currency due to its use by countries with histories of high budget deficits and inflation.*

2 [U] in the US, banknotes and coins, especially when considered as part of the MONEY SUPPLY (=the amount of money in an economy at a particular time): *The money supply, essentially the sum of all currency and bank deposits, barely grew in the fourth quarter.*

currency dealer —see under DEALER

currency deflation —see under DEFLATION

currency devaluation *n* [C,U] **1** another name for CURRENCY DEPRECIATION: *Mexico announced that it would slow down the rate of currency devaluation by 20%.*
2 when a country decides to reduce the value of its currency, usually to help its economy: *Recent currency devaluations by neighbouring countries have made Vietnam's exports less competitive.*

currency futures —see under FUTURES

currency market —see under MARKET[1]

currency movements *n* [plural] changes in value of a currency or currencies: *The latest results were helped by **favorable currency movements**.* (=ones to your advantage) | *The deficit increased from $2.9 million to $6.1 million due largely to **adverse currency movements*** (=ones to your disadvantage) *in Brazil.*

currency notes —see under NOTE[1]

currency option —see under OPTION

currency rate *n* [C usually plural] the value of one currency in relation to another: *The currency rate's move above 150 yen to the dollar was bad news for the Japanese bond market.*

currency reserves —see under RESERVES

currency risk —see under RISK[1]

currency swap —see under SWAP[2]

cur·rent /ˈkʌrənt‖ˈkɜːr-/ *adj* [only before a noun] happening, existing, or true now: *the current world price for crude oil* | *the budget for the current year*

current account —see under ACCOUNT[1]

current account deficit —see under DEFICIT

current asset —see under ASSET

current cost —see under COST[1]

current cost accounting —see under ACCOUNTING

current liabilities —see under LIABILITY

current prices —see under PRICE[1]

current ratio —see under RATIO

current value accounting —see under ACCOUNTING

current yield —see under YIELD[1]

cur·ric·u·lum vi·tae /kəˌrɪkjələm ˈviːtaɪ/ *n* [C] **1** *BrE* abbreviation **CV** a document giving details of your education and past employment, used when you are applying for a job; RESUME *AmE*: *Applicants who meet all the above requirements should send a covering letter and curriculum vitae by 31 January.*
2 *AmE* a document on which a university teacher writes a list of their teaching experience and articles, books etc they have written when they are applying for a job

cur·sor /ˈkɜːsə‖ˈkɜːrsər/ *n* [C] COMPUTING a small mark or light that can be moved around a computer screen to show where you are working: *Move the cursor onto the character you want to remove.*

cur·tail /kɜːˈteɪl‖kɜːr-/ *v* [T] to reduce or limit something: *The Federal Bank's critics in Congress are eager to curtail its power.* | *Investment plans may be curtailed by high interest rates.*

curve /kɜːv‖kɜːrv/ *n* [C] a diagram showing how a price or an amount changes in relation to another price, amount etc: *The capital constraints will hold down supply as the demand curve begins to rise.* | *The price curve is rising as the bond gets closer to maturity.*

adoption curve the rate at which people accept a new product: *There was a tremendous adoption curve for this software – a lot of people started to buy and use it very quickly.*

demand curve ECONOMICS a mathematical drawing showing how much of a product or service will be bought at different prices: *The demand curve for labour shows the relationship between the real wage and the demand for labour by employers.*

experience curve the pattern of falling costs as production of a particular product or service increases, because the company learns more about it, workers become more skilful etc

indifference curve ECONOMICS the degree to which people will continue to buy the same quantity of a product even if the price rises

yield curve FINANCE a curve that shows interest rates for bonds of the same type but with different MATURITIES (=lengths of time until they are repaid): *The yield curve for Treasury securities was practically a level line.* | *a **flat yield curve*** (=one where interest rates do not change over time) | *an **inverted yield curve*** (=one where interest rates are higher in the near future than later) —see also LAFFER CURVE, LEARNING CURVE

cus·to·di·al /kʌˈstəʊdiəl‖-ˈstoʊ-/ *adj* [only before a noun] **1** connected with keeping someone in prison: *He now faces a **custodial sentence**.*
2 connected with looking after and investing money for someone else: *Bank of New England Corp. agreed to sell its mutual fund custodial business to Investors Bank & Trust Co.* | *investment advisory and **custodial fees*** | *The firm makes two-thirds of its money from fees for providing custodial services for mutual and pension funds.*

custodial account —see under ACCOUNT[1]

cus•to•di•an /kʌˈstəʊdiən‖-ˈstoʊ-/ *n* [C] someone who is responsible for looking after something valuable for another person or for the public + **of**: *If the bank is the custodian of this company's money | plans by Edinburgh University to sell works from the Torrie art collection, of which it is custodian*

cus•to•dy /ˈkʌstədi/ *n* [U] **1 in/into custody** kept in prison by police until you go to court, because the police think you are guilty: *A man is being* ***held in police custody*** *in connection with the murder. | He was arrested and* ***taken into custody***.

2 when you look after someone's money or assets, or invest money for them: *The new subsidiary will offer custody services. | The shares are in a custody account.*

safe custody when a bank takes care of important documents or other valuable possessions for someone, in return for a regular charge: *Banks also provide safe custody facilities for their customers.*

cus•tom /ˈkʌstəm/ *n* [U] *BrE* when people use a particular shop or business: *the older consumer, whose custom is becoming too valuable to be ignored | Saturday is usually our busiest day and we have missed out on a great deal of custom through the closure.* —see also CUSTOMS

custom and practice —see under PRACTICE

custom builder —see under BUILDER

cus•tom•er /ˈkʌstəmə‖-ər/ *n* [C] a person or organization that buys goods or services from a shop or company: *We try to keep* ***regular customers*** *happy. | the* ***customer complaints*** *department*

ultimate customer the person who buys and uses a particular product in its final form; END-USER; ULTIMATE CONSUMER: *from the factory to the ultimate customer*

customer profile —see under PROFILE[1]

customer research —see under RESEARCH

customer service *n* [U] —see under SERVICE[1]

customer service center —see under CENTRE

Custom House also **Customs House** *n* [C] the offices, usually in a port, of the CUSTOMS service

Custom-House report —see under REPORT[1]

cus•tom•ize also **customise** *BrE* /ˈkʌstəmaɪz/ *v* [T usually passive] if something is customized for a customer, it is designed, built etc specially for that customer, making it different from other things of its kind: *We provide both standard and customized training schemes. | A menu system makes Screen Scenes easy to control and customize.*

custom-made *adj* designed or built specially for a particular customer, making it different to other things of its kind: *custom-made furniture manufactured to meet the client's specific requirements*

Cus•toms also **customs** /ˈkʌstəmz/ *n* [U] **1** the government department responsible for collecting the tax on goods that have been brought into the country and making sure that illegal goods are not imported or exported: *The shipment had come from Spain and had been tracked by Customs. | A collection of pornographic photos, films and books have been seized by* ***Customs officers***.

2 the place at an airport or port through which people and goods arriving in the country must pass and where any tax owed must be paid: *If you go over the limit you have to pay duty on the excess when you* ***go through customs***. *| The remainder of the money is allocated only after goods have* ***cleared customs*** (=been checked by customs officials).

customs agent —see under AGENT

Customs and Excise *n* the British government department responsible for collecting the tax on goods that are being bought or sold or have been brought into the country: *HM Customs & Excise have announced the introduction of a new warehouse facility from 1 January.* —see also BOARD OF CUSTOMS AND EXCISE

customs bond —see under BOND

customs broker *n* [C] another name for a CUSTOMS AGENT

customs clearance *n* [U] when customs officials agree to allow goods entering or leaving the country to continue on their journey after all the necessary checks have been made: *When you arrive at the continental airport you will be required to pass through passport control, claim your baggage and obtain customs clearance.*

customs declaration —see under DECLARATION

customs drawback —see under DRAWBACK

customs duty —see under DUTY

customs entry —see under ENTRY

customs specification —see under SPECIFICATION

customs tariff —see under TARIFF

customs union *n* [C usually singular] an agreement between two or more countries to reduce or stop customs duty on goods traded between them: *There will be a customs union, free trade in goods and services, and free movement of labour, money and capital.*

customs warehouse *n* [C] another name for BONDED WAREHOUSE —see under WAREHOUSE

cut[1] /kʌt/ *n* [C] **1** a planned reduction in the amount or level of something + **in**: *Amex's chairman took an $800,000 cut in pay last year because of poor profits. | the president's programme of* ***budget cuts*** *| The* ***price cuts*** *are aimed at making Compaq more competitive with lower cost PCs.*

2 *informal* the share of an amount of money that someone is allowed to take for themselves, especially as a reward or payment for helping someone to earn the total amount: *The video has been hugely popular, yet Jones received only £1,600 after his agents took their cut.*

cut[2] *v* past tense and past participle **cut** present participle **cutting** [T] to reduce prices, amounts, money etc: *She criticizes supermarkets for failing to pass on profits to customers by cutting prices. | There's always pressure on the organisation to increase productivity and cut costs. | Marston's is to cut its workforce by a third.*

cut•off /ˈkʌtɒf‖-ɒːf/ also **cut-off** *n* [singular] **1** the level at which you decide to stop doing something: *They will review cost estimates of the services and determine a* ***cut-off point*** *at which Medicaid will no longer provide coverage. | There was a rush by builders in January to obtain permits to beat the Jan. 13* ***cut-off date***.

2 when you stop making, paying, or providing something: *The Air Force's F-16 could face a production cutoff. | the cutoff of technical assistance*

cut•o•ver /ˈkʌtəʊvə‖-vər/ *n* [U] a very quick change from one stage of a business plan, deal etc to the next stage

cut-price also **cut-rate** *adj* [only before a noun] **1** selling products or services at extremely low prices: *Kwik Save, Britain's biggest cut-price supermarket chain, has been bought by Somerfield.*

2 costing much less than other products of the same type: *Jet, which already sells cut-price petrol, will knock 12p off a gallon of unleaded, | Families are snapping up cut-price holidays as travel agents slash the cost of trips to the sun.*

cut-throat *adj* [only before a noun] involving business competing very strongly with each other, for example by offering lower prices which may force some businesses to fail: *Cut-throat competition is keeping ticket prices low. | a cut-throat battle for market share*

cutting edge *n* [C] if a company or its work is at the

cutting edge of an activity, they are working in the most advanced area of it, using the newest methods, systems, equipment etc + **of**: *The scientific and engineering skills which we have developed are at the cutting edge of nuclear technology.* —**cutting-edge** *adj* [only before a noun] *exciting, cutting-edge media projects*

CV *n* [C] abbreviation for CURRICULUM VITAE: *Applicants should enclose a CV and covering letter.*

cwo abbreviation for CASH WITH ORDER

cwt written abbreviation for HUNDREDWEIGHT: *Copper metal sold for about £3 per cwt.*

cyber- /saɪbə‖-ər/ *prefix* used to form words that refer to activities involving the use of computers rather than the real world, especially activities on the INTERNET: *Users can browse in a synthesized world that's been dubbed 'cyberspace' by fans.* | *attempts to halt the spread of cybercrime*

cy·ber·net·ics /ˌsaɪbəˈnetɪks‖-bər-/ *n* [U] the scientific study of the way in which information is moved about and controlled in machines and in the human brain. In business, cybernetics is mainly concerned with making industrial processes fully automatic and presenting information so that decisions can be made —**cybernetic** *adj*

Cy·ber·port /ˈsaɪbəˌpɔːt‖-bərˌpɔːrt/ *n* an area in Hong Kong providing offices, telephone and computer links, and other things that are needed by IT companies

cy·ber·squat·ting /ˈsaɪbəˌskwɒtɪŋ‖-bərˌskwaː-/ *n* [U] COMPUTING the practice of REGISTERING (=including in an official list) company names as DOMAIN NAMES in order to try to sell the names to companies and make a profit: *The World Intellectual Property Organization has a procedure to combat cybersquatting.* —**cybersquatter** *n* [C]

cy·cle /ˈsaɪkəl/ *n* [C] a series of events that happen in an order that regularly repeats itself: *Approved Training Practices are monitored by the Association on a five-year cycle.*

billing cycle the usual time that is taken between sending a customer a list of the amount of money owed for goods or services and the money being received, taking into account the amount of time allowed to customers to pay: *Any change of year end could affect a firm's billing cycle, which may have been agreed with clients.*

business cycle a cycle in which business activity increases, decreases, then increases again

job cycle a cycle in which all the main tasks of a particular job are done: *The aim is to maximise the number of cars produced during each shift by reducing the job cycle time.*

trade cycle a cycle in which trade increases, decreases, then increases again: *the boom and slump periods of a trade cycle* —see also KONDRATIEV CYCLE

cyc·li·cal /ˈsɪklɪkəl, ˈsaɪ-/ also **cy·clic** /ˈsaɪklɪk/ *adj* happening in regular cycles: *Most of the UK's problems are cyclical and will disappear as the economic recovery begins.* | *It is interesting to note that our annual seasonal fluctuations are sharper than the typical cyclical fluctuations.*

cyclical commodity —see under COMMODITY

cyclical demand —see under DEMAND

cyclical share —see under SHARE

cyclical stock —see under STOCK[1]

C

D

d written abbreviation for date; died; DIVIDEND

D.A. *n* [C] a DISTRICT ATTORNEY

DAF abbreviation for DELIVERED AT FRONTIER —see INCOTERM

dai·ly[1] /ˈdeɪli/ *adj, adv* **1** happening or done every day: *daily flights to Miami* | *The office is open daily, from 9am to 5pm.*
2 connected with a single day: *daily rates of pay*

daily[2] *n* plural **dailies** [C] **1** also **daily paper** a newspaper that is printed and sold every day except Sunday: *Of eleven main dailies, six were tabloids with 80% of the circulation.*
2 *AmE* a newspaper that is printed and sold every day including Sunday

Daily Official List *n* [C] FINANCE an official list of share prices produced every day by the London Stock Exchange

daisy chain *n* [C] FINANCE a situation in the stockmarket when dealers buy and sell to each other so that investors will think that there is a lot of trading in the market. This will encourage investors to invest and prices to rise

dam·age[1] /ˈdæmɪdʒ/ *n* **1** [U] a bad effect on something that makes it weaker or less successful + **to**: *The result of this policy will be severe damage to the British economy.*
2 [U] physical harm caused to something: *a fire which caused hundreds of pounds worth of damage to property*
3 flood/storm/wind etc damage damage caused by a flood, storm etc: *The shop suffered severe smoke damage.*
apparent damage [U] damage that is noticed when goods are being unloaded from a ship and is reported to the ship's owners
4 damages [plural] LAW money that a court orders someone to pay to someone else for harming them or their property, or causing them financial loss: *The group is facing **claims for damages** due to faulty components.* | *They are being **sued for damages** by clients who they advised to invest in an insurance company that went bankrupt.* | *A federal jury **awarded damages** for breach of contract, negligence and fraud.*
actual damages [plural] money that a court orders someone to pay to someone else for harming them or their property, to cover the cost of the harm, rather than to punish them: *The jury's verdict included $17 million in actual damages.*
additional damages [plural] an additional amount of money that a court orders someone to pay as damages: *France Telecom was fined FFr30 million by the competition authorities; this opens the way for BT to seek additional damages and interest.*
civil damages [plural] damages that the court orders someone to pay following a court case between companies or people, using CIVIL LAW, rather than a case started by a government: *Exxon would have paid $100 million in fines related to criminal charges, and it would have paid up to an added $1 billion for civil damages.*
compensatory damages [plural] another name for ACTUAL DAMAGES
consequential damages [plural] damages paid by a person or organization, relating to the direct result of their mistake or NEGLIGENCE: *The company shall not be liable for any incidental or consequential damages resulting from the use of the Program.* —compare INCIDENTAL DAMAGES
exemplary damages [plural] damages that a court orders someone to pay as a punishment, rather than to pay for actual harm: *Prudential must pay about $1.4 million, including $600,000 in 'exemplary' damages, which typically are awarded to punish and deter a defendant.*
incidental damages [plural] damages paid by a person or organization, relating to the indirect result of their mistake or NEGLIGENCE —compare CONSEQUENTIAL DAMAGES
liquidated damages [plural] damages specified in a contract that are payable if a particular event is not performed: *If a contract states '£300 per day for each day delivery is delayed', this is a liquidated damages clause.*
money damages also **monetary damages** [plural] damages in the form of money, rather than another type of court judgement
nominal damages [plural] a small amount of damages that a court orders someone to pay to show that wrong has been done, but that it did not cause great harm or financial loss: *The Hortons asked the judge to award at least nominal damages.*
non-economic damages [plural] damages that are paid for physical harm that has been done rather than for financial loss: *Non-economic damages should be paid only to the victims of permanently disabling injuries.*
punitive damages [plural] another name for EXEMPLARY DAMAGES
treble damages also **triple damages** [plural] damages that are calculated on the basis of the financial loss multiplied by three: *The jury awarded the tour company $235,000, and under treble damages, the amount climbed to $705,000.*
unspecified damages [plural] when the person asking for damages does not state the amount they are asking for, but lets the court decide: *Intel is asking for an injunction to prevent Advanced Micro from using the software, plus unspecified damages.*

damage[2] *v* [T] **1** to cause physical harm to something: *Be careful not to damage the timer mechanism.* | *goods damaged in transit*
2 to have a bad effect on something in a way that makes it weaker or less successful: *Taylor felt her reputation had been damaged by the newspaper article.*

damage certificate *n* [C] another name for a CERTIFICATE OF DAMAGE

damage claim —see under CLAIM[1]

danger money —see under MONEY

da·ta /ˈdeɪtə, ˈdɑːtə/ *n* [U, plural] **1** information or facts about a particular subject that someone has collected: *We cannot tell you the results until we have looked at all the data.*
primary data information that an organization collects and examines itself, instead of using information that already exists: *For primary data, a marketing research organisation is likely to be used.*
secondary data information used in RESEARCH that has already been collected together in the past, rather than being collected specially: *Secondary data can pinpoint areas for further investigation.*
2 information in a form that can be stored and used, especially on a computer: *a new data retrieval system*

data bank also **databank** *n* [C] a collection of information on a particular subject that is stored somewhere, especially on a computer: *The Department of Employment plans to introduce a data bank of job vacancies throughout Europe.*

da·ta·base /ˈdeɪtəˌbeɪs/ *n* [C] a collection of information on a particular subject that is stored on a computer in an organized way so that you can find and use it easily: *A database of more than 14,000 training courses is being marketed by an information services company.* | *New customers are put on the database.*

database management —see under MANAGEMENT

database management system —see under SYSTEM

database software —see under SOFTWARE

data dictionary *n* plural **data dictionaries** [C] COMPUTING the part of a database that controls the way the information is stored and the way different pieces of information relate to each other

data file —see under FILE[1]

data interchange format file abbreviation **DIF file** —see under FILE[1]

data mining also **data-mining** *n* [U] analyzing large amounts of data about customers held on computer in order to get information about them that is not immediately available or obvious: *Data-mining tools allow marketing departments to identify groups of customers and develop highly targeted mail campaigns.*

data process•ing —see under PROCESSING

data protection —see under PROTECTION

data warehouse —see under WAREHOUSE

date[1] /deɪt/ written abbreviation **d** *n* [C] **1** the words you use to talk about a particular day, month, and year: *The date on the letter was 30th June 1998.*

average date also **average due date** a date when several payments which are owed to the same person are made, which is usually about halfway between the date that the first payment should be made and the date that the last payment should be made

balance date *BrE* ACCOUNTING, FINANCE the last day of a company's FINANCIAL YEAR: *The value of Pearl Group has risen from just over £1 billion in 1989 to twice that at last balance date.*

best-before date *BrE* a date printed on containers of food or drink and some other products that shows when they will be too old to eat, drink, or use; EXPIRATION DATE *especially AmE*; EXPIRY DATE: *Suppliers should put a best-before date on the boxes of test kits with a specific shelf life.*

delivery date ◆ the date that has been arranged for goods to be delivered: *The delivery date for the second cargo has already passed.*

◆ the date that a new product will be available: *IBM didn't quote a price or delivery date for these systems.*

◆ FINANCE the date when a SECURITY must be handed over, for example in FUTURES TRADING: *As the July delivery date for the futures contracts approached, the CBOT used emergency powers to force Ferruzzi to liquidate its position.*

drop dead date *AmE informal* a date by which it is very important that you have done or completed something, because after this date it is no longer worth doing or completing it: *The originally agreed-upon drop-dead date is June 23. However, if all parties agree, there could be another extension.*

due date the date by which an amount of money must be paid, a document received etc: *The loan wasn't paid on its Sept. 7 due date; it has been extended until May.* | *Taxpayers have until the due date of the tax return to make these arrangements.*

effective date the date on which a new law, agreement, contract, or system becomes effective: *The integration of NCR with AT&T's computer operations should be completed well in advance of the effective date of the merger.*

expiration date *especially AmE* also **expiry date** ◆ the date when an agreement or offer legally or officially ends: *The April 8 expiration date for the purchase offers remains unchanged.* | *the expiration date of Blum's contract*

◆ the last date when it is possible to exercise an OPTION or WARRANT: *DNA Plant Technology Corp. said it extended for one year the expiration date of its 2,111,006 public warrants outstanding.*

◆ *AmE* the last date that a product, especially food, should be sold; SELL-BY-DATE *BrE*

maturity date the date on which a bond is to be repaid or an investment agreement ends and a payment is made: *The debentures carried a 14% interest rate with a 2008 maturity date.*

off-sale date the date when a business selling newspapers and magazines calculates the amount sold and reports this to the WHOLESALER

prompt date FINANCE the date for delivery of a COMMODITY (=oil, metal, farm product etc) in a FUTURES CONTRACT (=agreement to deliver a commodity at a date in the future)

record date the date when a shareholder must possess shares in order to receive a related DIVIDEND or vote at a meeting of shareholders: *First Western set a record date of Jan 11 for an annual shareholders meeting on Feb 14.*

redemption date another name for MATURITY DATE

sell-by date *BrE* the last date that a product, especially food, should be sold; EXPIRATION DATE *AmE*: *This champagne should be drunk soon after it is released, but some wine merchants have been keeping it past its sell-by date.*

settlement date ◆ FINANCE the day when investors must pay for shares etc they have agreed to buy, often three working days after the original agreement; ACCOUNT DAY: *The first dividend consists of the interest accrued* (=gained) *from the settlement day to the first payment date.*

◆ LAW the day when property or goods are sold and they legally belong to the buyer; COMPLETION DATE: *The contract allows the vendor* (=person selling something) *to withdraw any time up to and including the settlement day.*

2 after date words written on a BILL OF EXCHANGE to show that the bill can be paid a particular period of time after the date on the bill —see also YEAR TO DATE

date[2] *v* [T] to write the date on a letter or cheque: *In a letter dated 1st August 1999, the inspector said he would need to examine the company's accounts.* —see also ANTEDATE, POSTDATE

dated security —see under SECURITY

date line *n* **the (International) date line** an imaginary line that goes from the NORTH POLE to the SOUTH POLE. The date to the east of this line is one day earlier than the date to the west: *Crossing the International Date Line means that we either gain a day (eastwards crossing) or lose one (westwards crossing).*

date stamp[1] *v* [T] **1** to print the date on a document or an envelope: *The Government is developing an electronic postmark to time and date stamp e-mail.* | *The form must be date stamped by the Post Office.*

2 to print the date on a product in order to show when it was made or the date by which it should be eaten, sold, or used

date stamp[2] —see under STAMP[1]

da•ting /ˈdeɪtɪŋ/ *n* [U] *AmE* when a supplier allows a customer a longer period of credit than they usually give

daughter company —see under COMPANY

dawn raid *n* [C] FINANCE when a company suddenly buys a large number of shares in another company, in an attempt to get control of it: *A dawn raid allows the build-up of a significant stake in a target company within a matter of hours, giving the board of the target company little time to react or advise its shareholders.*

DAX /dæks/ *n* Deutsche Aktienindex; a SHARE INDEX of shares in 30 leading companies on the Frankfurt stockmarket: *Twenty of DAX shares retreated, eight advanced, and two were unchanged.*

day book *n* [C] ACCOUNTING an account book in which goods and services bought on credit and sales are recorded: *Any purchase invoices should be checked and entered into the purchases day book and the ledger.*

day planner *n* [C] a chart used to help someone plan their activities on a particular day

day rate —see under RATE[1]

day release —see under RELEASE[2]

day·trad·er /ˈdeɪˌtreɪdə‖-ər/ *n* [C] someone who uses a computer to trade shares on the INTERNET, often buying and selling very quickly to take advantage of small price changes

DBMS abbreviation for DATABASE MANAGEMENT SYSTEM

DCP abbreviation for CARRIAGE PAID

DDP abbreviation for DELIVERED DUTY PAID

D

dead /ded/ *adj* **1** if the economy or an industry is dead, it is not growing or successful: *The plan is to lower interest rates in order to breathe life back into the dead economy.* | *The domestic gold industry is dead.*

2 no longer important, in use, or popular: *Toy companies sneered at Nintendo, saying the video-game craze was dead and buried.* | *Takeover investing isn't dead, despite all the new state anti-takeover laws.*

dead·beat /ˈdedbiːt/ *n* [C] *AmE informal* someone who does not pay their debts: *We ought to think about how to get the money from the deadbeats before we raise taxes on those who do pay.*

dead cat bounce —see under BOUNCE[2]

dead·head[1] /ˈdedhed/ *n* [C] *AmE informal* someone who avoids paying their fare on a train, bus etc

deadhead[2] *adj* [only before a noun] a deadhead journey by a truck, bus etc is one on which no goods or passengers are being carried: *With careful planning, and by avoiding out-of-the-way pickups and deliveries, the trucks usually operate with full loads, avoiding deadhead miles.*

deadhead[3] *v* [T] to drive a truck or bus without carrying any goods or passengers

dead·line /ˈdedlaɪn/ *n* [C] a date or time by which you have to do or to complete something: *Tomorrow is the deadline for creditors to vote on three rival reorganization plans for Revco.* | *I think we need to* ***set a deadline****.* | *The financially troubled company didn't* ***meet*** *yesterday's* ***deadline*** *for filing its annual report.* | *Algoma said the Ontario Court* ***extended the deadline*** *for filing its restructuring plan to Jan 31.* | *The successful applicant must have the ability to* ***work to a deadline*** *under pressure.* | *He was known as a demanding boss who imposed* ***tight deadlines****.*

dead season —see under SEASON

dead stock —see under STOCK[1]

dead time —see under TIME

dead·weight /ˈdedweɪt/ *adj* deadweight tons or tonnes are a measure of a ship's weight when it is empty: *The maximum size vessel that can use the Panama canal is a ship of about 65,000 deadweight tons.*

deadweight capacity —see under CAPACITY

deadweight cargo —see under CARGO

deadweight tonnage abbreviation **dwt** *n* [U] another name for DEADWEIGHT (CARRYING) CAPACITY

deal[1] /diːl/ *v* past tense and past participle **dealt**

deal in sth *phr v* [T] if a person or company deals in a particular type of product, they buy and sell it as their business: *The Salvage Shop deals in goods that have been the subject of insurance claims.* | *traders dealing in futures*

deal with sb/sth *phr v* [T] **1** to do business with a person or company or to have a business connection with them: *I've dealt with their company for a long time.* | *John now has an art studio that deals with advertising agencies.*

2 to have a particular job or function in an organization: *The banking department deals with all the other banking business.* | *insurance assessors who deal with accident claims*

deal[2] *n* [C] **1** an agreement or arrangement, especially one that involves the sale of something: *Baskin-Robbins has* ***signed a deal*** *with a group of dairy farmers, to supply the milk necessary for the factory.*

bought deal FINANCE a deal in which a company sells some of its own shares, or shares it owns in other companies, to a financial institution for a fixed amount. The financial institution then resells them to investors

fair deal an arrangement or agreement between two or more people that is reasonable and treats all the people involved equally: *To get a fair deal you need to be fully aware of your legal entitlements.*

package deal an offer or agreement that includes several things that must all be accepted together: *CNN's goal is to sign up four to five global advertisers for the package deal.*

2 an offer of a product at a lower price than usual, available only for a limited time: *There are some good deals on mortgages around at the moment.*

deal·er /ˈdiːlə‖-ər/ *n* [C] **1** someone who buys and sells a particular type of goods: *Collectors were looking for guidance from experienced art dealers.*

2 a shop that sells a particular type of goods: *Computers should always be bought from a reputable dealer.* | *a used car dealer*

3 FINANCE someone whose job is buying and selling bonds, shares, currencies, etc on a financial market; TRADER *AmE*: *On the London Futures & Options Exchange dealers rushed to obtain cocoa.*

currency dealer also **foreign exchange dealer** someone whose job is buying and selling currencies, usually at a financial institution; CURRENCY TRADER, FOREIGN EXCHANGE TRADER *AmE*: *Currency dealers had been pushing the dollar slowly but steadily lower last week.*

floor dealer also **floor trader**, **floor broker** *AmE* someone whose job is to deal on a financial market where there is a TRADING FLOOR: *The LIFFE conference hosts a number of floor traders who conduct business on their own account rather than on behalf of clients.*

primary dealer a financial institution that is allowed to deal directly in government bonds with a CENTRAL BANK (=bank that controls a country's currency): *The Belgian treasury will raise money by selling its paper directly to 14 primary dealers.*

dealer aids *n* [plural] MARKETING things given to a shop by a manufacturer or importer to help show or advertise their product, for example product magazines, models, shelves and price lists

dealer's brand —see under BRAND[1]

deal·er·ship /ˈdiːləʃɪp‖-ər-/ *n* [C] a business that sells products, especially cars, made by a particular company: *He works for a Peugeot dealership in Birmingham.*

deal·ing /ˈdiːlɪŋ/ *n* **1** [U] *BrE* FINANCE the job or activity of buying and selling stocks, shares, foreign currencies, etc on a financial market; TRADING *especially AmE*: *After the first hour of dealing, the FTSE had slipped 10.1 to 3025.3.* | ***Share dealings*** *in the new issue will begin on Dec. 8.* | *a full range of* ***currency dealing*** *services*

after-hours dealing [U] *BrE* FINANCE buying and selling stocks, shares, etc after the financial markets have officially closed for the day; AFTER HOURS TRADING *especially AmE*: *After hours dealing in the June Footsie contract suggested that market is all set to go better again today.*

fair dealing [U] a way of doing business that is honest and treats people equally: *Any reputable company or adviser will be keen to preserve a* ***reputation for fair dealing****.*

insider dealing [U] *BrE* when someone uses knowledge of a particular company, situation etc that is not available to other people in order to buy or sell shares. Insider dealing is illegal; INSIDER TRADING

over-the-counter dealing [U] *especially BrE* the buying and selling of shares etc directly between dealers over the telephone and computer systems; OVER-THE-COUNTER TRADING *especially AmE*: *In national over-the-counter trading, Collagen closed at $16.25 a share, up 75 cents.*

wheeling and dealing [U] business activities that involve a lot of complicated and sometimes dishonest deals: *With so much wheeling and dealing going on in the industry, we can expect to see more legal suits.* —**wheeler-dealer** *n* [C] *the famous wheeler-dealers of the 1980s takeover scene*

2 dealings [plural] the business relationships or activities that you have become involved in: *The secret dealings of his department were made public.* | *Anyone who has* ***had dealings with*** *an insurance company knows how long it takes for payment to be made.*

shady dealings [plural] illegal or dishonest dealings: *accusations of shady dealings, false documents and bribery schemes* —see also WHEELING AND DEALING

dealing floor —see under FLOOR

dealing-only service —see under SERVICE[1]

dear /dɪə‖dɪr/ *adj* **1** *especially BrE* costing a lot of money; EXPENSIVE: *I could never afford a house around here – they're far too dear.*

2 FINANCE, BANKING if money is dear, INTEREST RATES are high and it may be difficult and expensive to get loans from banks: *He was a critic of dear money and a supporter of public works.*

dear money —see under MONEY

dear-money policy —see under POLICY

dearth /dɜːθ‖dɜːrθ/ *n* [singular] a lack of something: *This is a critical time for small business, which faces a dearth of start-up financing.* —opposite GLUT[1]

death benefit *n* [C,U] INSURANCE an amount of money paid as a single sum to the relatives of someone who has died: *Relatives of the deceased employees did not receive the expected death benefits even though the insurance company had paid out the cheques to the fund.*

death duties *n* [plural] in Britain, taxes that must be paid by someone who is left property or money by someone who has died: *The government introduced death duties which were to lead to the gradual breaking up of the wealthy estates.*

death futures —see under FUTURES

death grant —see under GRANT[1]

death rate —see ***mortality rate*** under RATE[1]

death tax —see under TAX[1]

deb. abbreviation for DEBENTURE

debasement of coinage *n* [U] in the past, when gold and silver coins were dishonestly reduced in weight so they became worth less and caused increases in prices: *the debasement of the gold coinage of the Byzantine empire in the eleventh century*

de·ben·ture /dɪˈbentʃə‖-ər/ abbreviation **deb.** *n* [C usually plural] FINANCE an interest-paying loan which may be traded on bond markets. In Britain, debentures are normally SECURED on particular assets of the borrower, so that the person with the debenture will gain these assets if the loan is not repaid, but in the US they are not normally secured in this way: *Coca-Cola Enterprises* ***issued*** *$750 million of 30-year* ***debentures*** *yielding 8.61%.* | *First City* ***defaulted on*** (=fail to make interest payments on) *$97 million of* ***debentures****, but the company is optimistic that a restructuring agreement can be reached with debtholders.*

callable debenture a debenture that the borrower can choose to repay before the normal or agreed time: *$500 million of five-year callable debentures with a coupon of 7.95% the issue is callable at par in one year*

convertible debenture also **exchangeable debenture** a debenture that can be exchanged for another form of debt or for shares: *It also agreed to convert $3.2 million in Mountain Medical convertible debentures into 870,000 common shares.*

junior debenture a debenture which will not be repaid until senior debentures have been repaid if the borrower gets into financial difficulty

non-callable debenture a debenture that the borrower agrees not to repay before the normal or agreed time: *Dayton Hudson sold $100 million of 20-year non-callable debentures priced to yield 9.31%.*

pay-in-kind debenture a debenture that pays interest in the form of additional SECURITIES rather than cash

senior debenture a debenture that will be repaid before junior debentures if the borrower gets into financial difficulty

subordinated debenture a debenture that will not be repaid until other lenders have been repaid if the borrower gets into financial difficulty

debenture holder *n* [C] a person or organization that has lent money to a company in the form of debentures: *The next payment to debenture holders is due in February.*

debenture interest —see under INTEREST

debenture stock —see under STOCK[1]

debenture trust —see under TRUST

deb·it[1] /ˈdebɨt/ *n* [C] **1** a decrease in the amount of money in a bank account, for example when a payment is made from it —see also DIRECT DEBIT

2 ACCOUNTING the left-hand side of each account in DOUBLE-ENTRY BOOKKEEPING, the side used for decreases in liabilities or REVENUES: *Every time an entry is made on the debit side, another entry of equal value must be made on the credit side somewhere in the books.*

3 ACCOUNTING an amount recorded on the debit side of an account: *In the plant accounts there is a debit which supports the balance sheet item.*

debit[2] *v* [T] **1** to take money out of a bank account **debit sth from sth**: *The fee will be automatically debited from your account.* | *The money was debited from the account without even informing me.*

2 ACCOUNTING to record an amount on the debit side of an account in DOUBLE-ENTRY BOOKKEEPING: *Note that as the principal repayment reduces the loan outstanding so it is debited to that account.*

debit balance —see under BALANCE[1]

debit card —see under CARD

debit note —see under NOTE[1]

debit receipt —see under RECEIPT[1]

debt /det/ *n* **1** [C] money that one person, organization, country etc owes to another: *Honduras will not receive further funds after it failed to repay debts of $16 million.* | *The importer will have to* ***settle*** *his* ***debt*** *in the exporter's currency.* | *Once we have* ***cleared the debt*** (=paid it), *we could buy a car with another loan.*

2 [U] the state of owing money: *Families* ***in debt*** *on their fuel bills are already choosing between heating and eating.* | *People with children are much more likely to* ***get into debt*** *than people without children.* | *Daishowa was so* ***heavily in debt*** *that it had to sell off its corporate art collection.*

3 [U] FINANCE capital borrowed by a business or government organization on which it pays interest: *Mesa needs to sell assets to reduce its debt.* | *This company has enormous cash flow and it should have no problem* ***servicing its debt*** (=making interest payments on its debt). | *McFarland said it will use the cash to* ***pay down debt*** (=reduce the amount of debt owed). | *Lomas should be able to get cheaper loans,* ***retire*** *its costliest* ***debt*** (=repay loans) *and improve the capital structure of the company.* | *The IMF has failed to find money to help* ***write off debts*** (=to no longer expect or demand repayment) *of the poorest countries.* —see also ACKNOWLEDGEMENT OF DEBT

bad debt [C,U] a debt that will probably never be paid, and is therefore worthless to the person or company that is owed the money: *Bad debts caused by the recession will wipe out the bank's operating profit this year.* | *The company has been reluctant to* ***write off bad debts*** (=accept that they will never be paid).

bank debt [U] money owed to banks, rather than other types of lenders: *Fries has about $25 million in bank debt and $25 million of 7.5% bonds.*

book debt ◆ [C,U] ACCOUNTING money owed to a company by its customers, as shown in its financial records: *the administrative burden of collecting book debt*

◆ [C,U] FINANCE the amount of debt owed by a company to banks etc, as shown in its BALANCE SHEET

consumer debt [U] money owed by people, rather than businesses or countries: *The high level of consumer debt is holding house-building back.*

corporate debt [U] money owed by businesses, rather than governments or individuals

doubtful debt [C] a debt that is not likely to be repaid: *The recession reduced demand for financing and created more bad and doubtful debts.*

external debt [U] money that a country owes to other countries: *the external debt problems of developing countries*

fixed-rate debt [U] debt with an interest rate that does not change

floating debt [U] debt with an interest rate that changes: *Maintaining a safe relationship between amounts of floating and fixed-rate debt is a balancing act that tests every treasurer.*

foreign debt [C,U] money that a country owes to lenders abroad; EXTERNAL DEBT: *Most of Turkey's $43 billion in foreign debt is owed to private banks rather than to governments.*

investment-grade debt [U] debt that has a low risk of not being repaid: *securities ranging from risk-free Treasury bonds, investment-grade corporate debt, right down to junk bonds*

judgement debt also **judgment debt** [C] LAW a debt that a court has ordered to be paid: *The plan must be approved by banks and shareholders, and also depends on payment of a £50 million judgment debt owed to Grand Metropolitan.*

junior debt [U] debt that a borrower in financial difficulty will not repay until after other debts are repaid, or of which it will only repay a smaller percentage: *Price warned that the junior debt holders would get less favorable treatment.*

long-term debt [U] debt that is to be repaid a long time after the money is borrowed

medium-term debt [U] debt that is to be repaid between one and 10 years after the money is borrowed

mezzanine debt [U] debt that a borrower in financial difficulty will repay after senior debt, but before it repays other lenders and shareholders

national debt MONEY borrowed and still owed by a country

public debt ◆ [U] money owed by a local or national government

◆ debt in the form of loans obtained on financial markets, rather than other forms of lending

secured debt [U] debt that is supported by particular assets of the borrower. If the borrower is in financial difficulty, they must sell these assets to repay the lender

senior debt [U] debt that a borrower in financial difficulty will repay first, or of which they will pay a bigger percentage than other types of debt

short-term debt [U] debt that is to be repaid a short time after the money is borrowed, usually within one year

sovereign debt [U] money owed by a government, rather than a company or person

subordinated debt [U] debt that a borrower in financial difficulty will not repay until after other debts are repaid, or of which it will repay a smaller percentage

Third World debt [U] money owed by developing countries: *his much-publicized plan to solve the Third World debt crisis*

trade debt [U] money that a business owes to its SUPPLIERS: *The company owes about $300 million in trade debt and about $300 million in bank debt.*

unsecured debt [U] debt that is not supported by any assets of a borrower

debt adjustment —see under ADJUSTMENT

debt arrears —see under ARREARS

debt burden —see under BURDEN

debt capacity *n* [U] the possibility that a person or company has for borrowing more, depending on how much has already been borrowed and how able they are to repay the debts: *Cash flow is the typical measure for determining additional debt capacity*

debt collection —see under COLLECTION

debt consolidation loan —see under LOAN[1]

debt counselling —see under COUNSELLING

debt-equity ratio —see under RATIO

debt-equity swap —see under SWAP[2]

debt exposure —see under EXPOSURE

debt factoring —see under FACTORING

debt finance —see under FINANCE[1]

debt instrument —see under INSTRUMENT

debt leverage —see under LEVERAGE[1]

debt load —see under LOAD[1]

debt·or /ˈdetə‖-ər/ *n* **1** [C] a person, organization, or country that owes money: *Putting a debtor into jail means that he can't earn money to pay his debts.* | *The IMF turned to financing efforts to restructure the debts and economies of* ***debtor nations*** (=countries that owe money to others).

judgement debtor also **judgment debtor** [C] someone who has been ordered by a court of law to pay a particular debt: *Other partners will have the right to dissolve their partnership with the judgment debtor.*

sundry debtor a person or organization that owes money to a company for something other than goods or services that have been sold to them, for example money that the company has lent them

2 debtors [plural] ACCOUNTING *BrE* money owed to a business by its customers; ACCOUNTS RECEIVABLE *AmE*: *Current assets are typically finished goods, work in progress, raw materials, cash and debtors.*

debtor-in-possession financing —see under FINANCING

debt overhang *n* [U] when a business or government has so much debt that it is unable to make new investments: *the kind of debt overhang that has weighed down the Japanese economy throughout the 1990s*

debt payment —see under PAYMENT

debt rating —see under RATING

debt ratio —see under RATIO

debt relief —see under RELIEF

debt rescheduling also **debt restructuring** *n* [U] when a company or government arranges to pay its debts later or in another form than originally planned: *Nigeria has reached a debt rescheduling agreement with its foreign creditor banks that allows conversion of debt into bonds.*

debt retirement —see under RETIREMENT

debt-ridden *adj journalism* owing a lot of money and having difficulty in paying it: *Debt-ridden companies should be allowed to fail quickly.*

debt service also **debt servicing** *n* [U] paying interest on debt and repaying the debt itself: *The higher cost on that amount would result in an additional $80 million in debt service over the 20-year life of the bonds.*

debt service ratio —see under RATIO

debt swap —see under SWAP[2]

de·bug /ˌdiːˈbʌg/ *v* past tense and past participle **debugged** present participle **debugging** [T] to get rid of faults from a computer program: *He has to write, debug, and run his programs in the most basic form.*

de·but /ˈdeɪbjuː, ˈdebjuː‖deɪˈbjuː, dɪ-/ *n* [C] **1** the first public appearance of something: *The new machines will mark the debut of the next generation of memory chips.*
2 FINANCE an occasion when a company ISSUES (=makes available and sells) shares, bonds etc for the first time: *Bangkok Land **made a** notable **debut**, accounting for about 32% of the exchange's total trading volume.* —**debut** *v* [I,T] *AmE*: *When it debuted, Mazda's MPV was one of the few alternatives to Chrysler Corp.'s minivan.* | *In the fall, IBM debuted its first completely uniform, pan-European ad campaign for a product.*

Dec. written abbreviation for DECEMBER

de·ceased /dɪˈsiːst/ *n formal* **the deceased** the person who has died or the people who have died: *circumstances not foreseen by the deceased when the will was made* —**deceased** *adj*: *Relatives of the deceased employees did not receive the expected death benefits.*

de·ceit /dɪˈsiːt/ *n* [C,U] behaviour that is intended to make someone believe something that is not true

de·ceive /dɪˈsiːv/ *v* [T] to make someone believe something that is not true in order to get what you want: *Postal officials have long deceived the public on how slow mail delivery really is.* **deceive sb into sth**: *Applicants were deceived into thinking that their money would be invested and protected.*

de·cen·tral·ize also **decentralise** *BrE* /ˌdiːˈsentrəlaɪz/ *v* [I,T] if a large company, organization, or industry decentralizes or is decentralized, responsibility, services, or jobs are moved away from its centre in one place and spread between different parts of areas of it: *There may be a need to decentralize and set up semi-autonomous subsidiaries.* | *The 1970s saw a trend on the part of the 'nationals' to decentralize their operations.* —**decentralization** also **decentralisation** *BrE* — *n* [U] *the decentralization of local government services*

de·cep·tion /dɪˈsepʃən/ *n* [C,U] LAW another name for DECEIT: *He pleaded guilty to charges of forgery and deception.*

deci- /desɪ/ *prefix* used in the metric system to mean 'one tenth'. For example, a decimetre is equal to one tenth of a metre

de·cile /ˈdesəl, -saɪl‖ˈdɪsaɪl -səl/ *n* [C] in a set of VARIABLES arranged in order of value, any variable that is equal to one tenth of the amount of the highest one —see also MEDIAN, PERCENTILE, QUARTILE

decimal currency —see under CURRENCY

decision-making unit —see under UNIT

decision tree *n* [C] a mathematical drawing that shows all the courses of action that are available from a particular situation. Decision trees are used in planning: *a decision tree for a hypothetical development project to develop and market a new product*

deck /dek/ *n* [C] one of the levels on a ship: *Cargo is stored on the ship's lower deck.*

de·clar·ant /dɪˈkleərənt‖-ˈkler-/ *n* [C] *formal* someone who makes a declaration

dec·la·ra·tion /ˌdekləˈreɪʃən/ *n* [C] **1** a statement in which you officially give information, for example about your income or about goods you are importing, which is used to calculate how much tax you will pay
customs declaration a declaration by a traveller or an importer relating to goods brought into a country, used as a basis for calculating import tax: *It is important that customs declaration forms are correct and fully completed.*
tax declaration a declaration to the tax authorities of how much you have earned during a particular year, used to calculate how much tax you will have to pay: *The lawyers for the Pierre Matisse estate say that they are currently preparing an amended tax declaration.*
2 a statement in which you officially give information about yourself: *You have to **make a declaration** that your income is sufficient to meet your monthly payments.*
3 INSURANCE a statement signed by someone asking for insurance, promising that the details they have given on the insurance agreement are correct
4 INSURANCE a statement made by someone who has taken out insurance, giving details of the goods insured to the insurance company

declaration day *n* [singular] on a financial market, the last day on which someone who holds an OPTION may decide whether or not they accept it

declaration insurance —see under INSURANCE

Declaration of Association *n* plural **Declarations of Association** [C usually singular] LAW in Britain, a document in which seven or more people ask to be formed into a company and list the number of shares each one of them will take. The Declaration of Association is the last part of the MEMORANDUM OF ASSOCIATION

declaration of compliance *n* plural **declarations of compliance** [C usually singular] in Britain, a document stating that all the necessary official actions have been taken to set up a new LIMITED COMPANY. The declaration of compliance is signed by a lawyer, director, or secretary and sent to the REGISTRAR OF COMPANIES

declaration of intent *n* plural **declarations of intent** [C usually singular] an official document stating what a person or group intends to do, but which does not have the legal force of a formal contract: *To do this would be to reduce the contract to a mere declaration of intent.*

declaration of means *n* plural **declarations of means** [C usually singular] *BrE* a statement giving details of the amount of money you earn or have, used especially to calculate how much money you can receive from the state: *application for legal aid with declaration of means*

declaration of trust *n* plural **declarations of trust** [C usually singular] a statement in which a TRUSTEE officially states that property is held for someone: *As both the husband and the wife have an interest in the property, each should be provided with a copy of any declaration of trust.*

de·clare /dɪˈkleə‖-ˈkler/ *v* [T] **1** to make something known officially to the public: *Speyhawk, which declared a £216 million loss, fell 712p to 334p.* | *Two dominant*

D

companies have declared major redundancy programmes in the course of restructuring.

2 declare an interest to officially make it known that you are connected with something and that this might affect the decisions you make about it: *A director of a company who is in any way interested in a contract or proposed contract with his company is required to declare his interest at the meeting of the board.*

3 declare sb bankrupt to state officially that a person or company is unable to pay all their debts: *The consequences of being declared bankrupt would be harsh and severe.*

4 declare bankruptcy to state officially that you are unable to pay your debts: *The new law established a mechanism to declare bankruptcy.*

5 declare an option to state whether or not you are accepting an OPTION that you hold

6 declare a dividend when a company declares a DIVIDEND, it says that it will pay it to its shareholders: *Before declaring a dividend, the trustee must give notice of his intention to do so to all creditors of whom he is aware.*

7 to make an official statement saying how much money you have earned, what property you own etc: *A lot of childcare is in the black economy, with carers not declaring their cash payments.* | *Works whose value had not been declared for taxation purposes were subject to taxation on the full sale price.*

8 to formally say that something is done, open, closed etc: *I now declare this factory open.* | *Anything else? No? Then I declare the meeting closed.*

D

declared value —see under VALUE[1]

de•cline[1] /dɪˈklaɪn/ *v* [I] **1** if an industry or country declines, it becomes less profitable, productive, wealthy etc: *This type of business is a declining sector of the UK.*

2 if sales, profits, production etc decline, they become less: *The market share for nuclear electricity in the UK may slightly increase to about 25% next year, but it will decline to a mere 1% by the year 2020.* | *As profitability declines, people would go out of farming.*

decline[2] *n* [C,U] **1** when sales, profits, production etc become less: *The number of jobless is forecast to have risen about 15,000 in April after two unexpected months of decline.* | *The profit rise came despite a decline in sales.*

2 when an industry or country becomes less profitable, productive, wealthy etc: *Of concern to the economists is the decline in the province's manufacturing sector.* | *a false and damaging picture of a nation* ***in decline***

de•clin•er /dɪˈklaɪnə‖-ər/ *n* [C] FINANCE a share that falls in value on a particular day of trading on a stockmarket; DECLINING SHARE: *Hachette was the exchange's biggest decliner of the session.*

declining balance method *n* [singular] another name for REDUCING BALANCE METHOD

declining industry —see under INDUSTRY

declining shares —see under SHARE

declining stocks —see under STOCK[1]

de•cod•er /diːˈkəʊdə‖-ˈkoʊdər/ *n* [C] a piece of equipment that you need in order to receive certain types of television service: *antennas and decoders that consumers will need to receive Hughes' DirecTv*

de•com•mis•sion /ˌdiːkəˈmɪʃən/ *v* [T] to destroy a factory, POWER STATION or other industrial building that has closed down and to remove anything from it that might be harmful or dangerous: *25 of the mine's 260 full-time employees will be kept on to decommission the property.* | *an increase in electric rates to pay for two nuclear powerplants due to be decommissioned in 2045* —**decommission** *n* [C,U] *Campeche, based in Mexico City, specializes in the decommission of oil refineries.*

de•crease[1] /dɪˈkriːs/ *v* [I,T] to go down to a lower level, or to make something do this: *Network television viewing continues to decrease.* | *The bank decreased its dividend to 15 cents from 31.25 cents a share.* —**decreasing** *adj* [only before a noun] *The airline has been hurt by high fuel costs and decreasing passenger traffic.*

decrease[2] *n* [C,U] the process of reducing something, or the amount by which it reduces + **in**: *The government announced a 25% decrease in the price of fuel.* + **of**: *Industrial production last month rose 0.5%, after a decrease of 0.2% in December.*

decreasing term assurance —see under ASSURANCE

de•cree /dɪˈkriː/ *n* [C] **1** a judgement made in a court of law after a CIVIL action: *The council had already been successful in obtaining a court decree against the former MP.*

consent decree LAW an order by the court to end a CIVIL case when the accused person or company admits that the complaint against them is correct and agrees to a particular course of action

2 in certain forms of government, an order from a president, minister etc that has the force of a law: *He signed a decree permitting individuals to buy and sell goods without special permission.*

de•cruit /dɪˈkruːt/ *v* [I,T] HUMAN RESOURCES to reduce the number of people working for an organization, for example by no longer employing them or offering them early RETIREMENT

de•cruit•ment /dɪˈkruːtmənt/ *n* [U] when a company or an organization dismisses employees that it no longer needs

ded•i•cat•ed /ˈdedəkeɪtəd/ *adj* [only before a noun] COMPUTING a dedicated computer, computer system etc is only used for one particular job, such as controlling a particular machine: *The data can be accessed by a dedicated machine or an ordinary personal computer.*

deducing title —see under TITLE

de•duct /dɪˈdʌkt/ *v* [T] **1** to take away an amount from a total: *Brazil has about 48 million bags of coffee available for sale; from this, deduct about eight million bags for domestic use.*

2 to take away an amount from an employee's pay for a particular purpose before they receive it: *The firm makes it easy to donate to charity: it offers to deduct the contributions from employees' paychecks.*

3 TAX to take away particular costs from the amount you have earned before you calculate how much tax you will have to pay on what you have earned: *Self-employed people can deduct 100% of health-insurance costs against income.*

de•duct•i•ble[1] /dɪˈdʌktəbəl/ *n AmE* **1** [C usually plural] a payment that is taken away from an employee's pay for a particular purpose before they receive it: *Under the plan, an employer raises workers' deductibles, normally by about $250.*

2 [C] INSURANCE an amount that an insured person has to pay each time they make a CLAIM; EXCESS *BrE*: *A comprehensive pet plan, for $97.50 a year, has a $50 deductible, and pays a maximum of $1,000 per injury or illness.*

3 [C] an amount the owner of a product must pay if it is repaired while it is still under GUARANTEE: *Ford has eliminated the $50 deductible that owners of its cars had to pay on warranty repairs.*

deductible[2] *adj* TAX if an amount of money is deductible, you can take it away from the amount you have earned before you calculate how much tax you will have to pay on what you have earned: *Only 80% of dining and entertainment costs are deductible as a business expense.*

de•duc•tion /dɪˈdʌkʃən/ *n* [C,U] the process of taking away an amount from a total, or the amount that is taken away

income tax deduction [C] *AmE* a part of someone's

income that is not taxed, for example because it comes from a particular source, or because they have children; INCOME TAX ALLOWANCE *BrE*: *Gifts to charity can generate an income-tax deduction.*

standard deduction [C usually singular] TAX in the US, a fixed amount of the money you earn that you do not have to pay tax on: *The exemption and the standard deduction are the basic elements that determine how much of a person's income is subject to tax.*

deed /diːd/ *n* [C] LAW a formal written document recording an agreement, especially one relating to property: *The parties to a deed should sign it in the presence of a witness.*

title deed a legal document proving that someone owns a particular property

trust deed a formal document that creates a TRUST (=arrangement where someone controls another person's money for them). It states who will manage the trust, how it is to be managed, and who will gain from it: *Trustees for the stockholders and eurobond holders are appointed under trust deeds.*

deed of arrangement *n* plural **deeds of arrangement** [C] in Britain, a formal agreement arranged by a court for the assets of a person or company that owes money to be sold and the money divided between the people who are owed money

deed of assignment *n* plural **deeds of assignment** [C] a deed showing an agreement to give an asset to someone else: *The individual assigns his right to the property by a deed of assignment.*

deed of conveyance *n* plural **deeds of conveyance** [C] PROPERTY a formal document showing change of ownership of land, buildings etc: *The deed of conveyance of the land was executed on 21st January.*

deed of covenant *n* plural **deeds of covenant** [C] in Britain, a formal agreement to make regular payments to a CHARITY so that the charity avoids paying income tax: *If you use your Deed of Covenant form every £1 you give becomes £1.33 – so your gift can work even harder.*

deed of gift *n* plural **deeds of gift** [C] a formal arrangement to give property to someone without payment: *Make the house over to Benedict by deed of gift.*

deed of partnership *n* plural **deeds of partnership** [C] a formal agreement to begin a PARTNERSHIP

deed of transfer *n* plural **deeds of transfer** [C] a formal agreement relating to change of ownership or property or shares: *A deed of transfer was executed on 18 October, whereby the developers transferred the land in question to the Prudential.*

deed of trust *n* plural **deeds of trust** [C] in the US, a change of ownership of a property to a TRUSTEE as SECURITY in case the owner of the property fails to do something such as repay a loan: *A notary forged deeds of trust against people's houses and got away with $1.8 million.*

deep discounter —see under DISCOUNTER

def. written abbreviation for DEFICIT

de fac•to /ˌdeɪ ˈfæktəʊ‖ dɪ ˈfæktoʊ, ˌdeɪ-/ *adj, adv* really existing, even if there is no formal legal document etc to prove it: *Prior to the Companies Act 1976, resignation would have constituted a de facto breach of contract.*

de facto corporation —see under CORPORATION

de•fal•ca•tion /ˌdiːfælˈkeɪʃən‖ˌdiːfælˈkeɪʃən, ˌdefəl-/ *n* [U] LAW when someone who has been trusted to take care of money steals it or uses it dishonestly

de•fault[1] /dɪˈfɒlt‖-ˈfɒːlt/ *n* **1 by default** if something happens or is decided by default, it happens or is decided in that way because something else did not happen or someone did not do what they should have done: *They won the last election by default.*

2 [C,U] when someone fails to pay money that they owe at the right time: *An asset can be repossessed by a lessor in the event of* ***a default on*** *the lease payments.* | *The banks have decided that the company is* ***in default*** *on its loan agreements.*

3 [U] LAW when someone fails to do something that it is their duty to do: *The contract includes provisions for loss and expense suffered by the contractors due to default by the employer.*

4 [U] LAW when someone fails to come to court or make a written statement when they are supposed to: *The defendant will have to explain his default and satisfy the court that he has a defence which ought to be heard.* | *The landlords did not acknowledge the writ, so Debbie's solicitor requested a judgement in default for the full amount plus interest and court fees.*

5 [C,U] COMPUTING the way in which things will be arranged on a computer, or done by a computer, if you do not change them or give a different instruction: *If the defaults are acceptable the user can just press Return.* | *This icon appears* ***by default***. | *The default margin settings are 1.25 each for a page 8.5 wide.*

D

default[2] *v* [I] **1** to fail to pay money that you owe at the right time: *The Act covered what mortgage lenders could do to recover their money if borrowers defaulted.* + **on**: *He defaulted on his child support payments.*

2 LAW to not do something that it is your duty to do: *If a party defaults in its obligations so as to jeopardize the project, then the party's right to continue participating in the project shall be terminated.*

de•fault•er /dɪˈfɔːltə‖-ˈfɒːltər/ *n* [C] someone who fails to do something that it is their duty to do, especially someone who fails to pay money that they owe: *The number of mortgage defaulters is rising in Britain.*

default judgment —see under JUDGMENT

de•fect[1] /dɪˈfekt,ˈdiːfekt/ *n* [C] a fault in something that means it is not perfect: *They recalled the vehicles because of brake defects.* | *an effort to improve customer satisfaction and reduce* ***product defects*** | *a possible* ***safety defect*** *with the autopilot of the plane* —**defective** *adj*: *defective engine controls* —**defectively** *adv*: *The computer system was defectively designed.*

latent defect LAW [C] a fault something has, but which cannot be seen. When something is sold, for example a house or a car, the seller must tell the buyer about any latent defects which they know about: *There was a latent defect present in the goods at the time of delivery.*

zero defects [plural] when a product or system has no faults at all, especially when this is the aim of the company making the product or using the system: *We thought it would take three years to eliminate the problems. Instead, the plant ran with zero defects the day it opened.* | *They are moving from Total Quality Management toward* ***Zero-Defects Management*** (=a way of managing production so that there are no defects).

de•fect[2] /dɪˈfekt/ *v* [I] *journalism* **1** if the buyer of one product defects to another product, they stop buying the first one and start buying the second one: *They tried to retain customers who might defect to a credit card with a lower interest rate.*

2 if an employee working for a particular company defects, they leave it and start working for another: *Although several senior employees have defected, it's not true that there's any kind of mass walkout.* —**defector** *n* [C] *When a group of his partners announced they were leaving, the firm prevented the defectors from entering their offices.* —**defection** *n* [C,U] *The big investment bank has been hit by* ***client defections***.

defective title —see under TITLE

defence *BrE*, **defense** *AmE* /dɪˈfens/ *n* [C] **1** the things that are said in a court of law to try to prove that someone is not guilty of a crime: *I am unhappy about the way my barrister is conducting my defence.*

2 the defence the lawyers in a court of law who try to prove that someone is not guilty of a crime: *the chief witness for the defence* | *The defense argued that the case should be dropped.* —compare PROSECUTION

3 FINANCE actions taken by a company to prevent a takeover that it does not want

crown jewels defence *BrE* when a company avoids being taken over by selling important assets cheaply to a supporter, so that the company is less attractive to buy, and then buying them back later when the takeover is no longer likely to happen

Pacman defense *AmE* when one company tries to buy another in a TAKEOVER, but the second company buys the shares of the first, stopping it from happening: *American Brands executed a successful PacMan defense by acquiring E-II Holdings following a hostile bid.*

defence contractor —see under CONTRACTOR

defence document —see under DOCUMENT[1]

defence electronics —see under ELECTRONICS

D

de•fend /dɪˈfend/ *v* [T] **1** if a lawyer defends someone charged with a crime, he or she represents that person and argues that they are not guilty of the charge

2 to do something in order to stop something being taken away or to make sure that something continues: *The union said that they would take strike action to defend their members' jobs.*

de•fen•dant /dɪˈfendənt/ *n* [C] the person or organization in a court of law that has been ACCUSED of doing something illegal: *The defendant was convicted and sentenced to 7 years in state prison.*

defense the American spelling of DEFENCE

defensive merger —see under MERGER

defensive share —see under SHARE

defensive stock —see under STOCK[1]

de•fer /dɪˈfɜː‖-ˈfɜːr/ *v* past tense and past participle **deferred** present participle **deferring** [T] to delay something until a later time or date: *The president may defer decisions on future defense spending cuts.*

de•fer•ment /dɪˈfɜːmənt‖-ɜːr-/ also **de•fer•ral** /dɪˈfɜːrəl/ *n* [C,U] the act of delaying something, or the period of the delay itself: *The bank accepted a deferment of interest payments.*

deferment period —see under PERIOD

deferred annuity —see under ANNUITY

deferred credits *n* [plural] ACCOUNTING money received for goods to be supplied and for services to be performed in the future, shown as liabilities in the accounts: *Capital grants are treated as deferred credits and are credited to the profit and loss account on the same basis as the related tangible assets are depreciated.*

deferred equity —see under EQUITY

deferred income —see under INCOME

deferred income tax —see under INCOME TAX

deferred interest security —see under SECURITY

deferred liabilities —see under LIABILITY

deferred share —see under SHARE

deferred tax —see under TAX[1]

deferred taxation —see under TAXATION

deficiency judgment *n* [C] LAW a decision by a court that a borrower still owes money after the SECURITY for a loan is sold for less than the amount owed

deficiency notice —see under NOTICE

def•i•cit /ˈdefəsət/ abbreviation **def** *n* [C] **1** an amount of money that a business has lost in a particular period of time: *The heaviest loss was at Armco Steel Co, which had a deficit of $61.6 million.*

2 ECONOMICS the amount by which what a government spends is more than it receives in a particular period of time: *The budget did less than many bankers and businessmen would have liked to reduce public spending and the deficit.*

balance of payments deficit the amount by which money going out of a country is more than the amount coming in: *Italy's balance of payments deficit narrowed 3.757 trillion lire in November from 4.975 trillion lire a year earlier.*

budget deficit the amount by which what a government spends is more than it receives in taxes or other income, during a particular period of time: *Any savings on military spending should be used to reduce the budget deficit.*

current account deficit the amount by which money relating to trade, investment etc going out of a country is more than the amount coming in: *Germany's current account deficit deepened as more Germans went abroad on summer holidays, including first-time Western vacations for many eastern Germans.*

federal deficit the amount by which US government spending is greater than the money it receives from taxes in a particular year: *A five-year package of measures designed to reduce the federal deficit by almost $100 billion.*

trade deficit the amount by which the money going out of a country to pay for imports is more than the amount coming in from exports: *This year, the U.S. is expected to* ***run a trade deficit*** (=have one) *with China of as much as $15 billion.*

deficit financing —see under FINANCING

deficit spending —see under SPENDING

de•flate /ˌdiːˈfleɪt, dɪ-/ *v* [I,T] ECONOMICS **1** when a government deflates, or deflates the economy, it reduces the demand for goods and services by raising interest rates and taxes, limiting wage increases, reducing government spending, or a combination of these: *Raising interest rates too high could deflate the economy into a serious financial crisis.*

2 if the price of something deflates, or something deflates it, it goes down: *Without a takeover, they say, the company's stock is likely to deflate further.* —compare REFLATE

de•fla•tion /ˌdiːˈfleɪʃən, dɪ-/ *n* [U] ECONOMICS when a government reduces demand for goods and services by raising interest rates and taxes, limiting wage increases, or reducing government spending, or a combination of these: *Governments responded to the loss of competitiveness by deflation and incomes policies.*

asset deflation when the value of assets such as property is falling: *All around the world you have asset deflation going on. The whole world is slowing into a recession.*

currency deflation also **monetary deflation** a situation in which prices are falling: *Governments can't employ monetary deflation because it destroys private debtors.* —compare DISINFLATION, INFLATION —**deflationary** *adj*: *The government was unwilling to introduce adequate deflationary policies.*

de•flat•or /ˌdiːˈfleɪtə, dɪ-‖-ər/ *n* [C] in calculating economic statistics, something that is used to remove the effect of INFLATION from the figures so that figures from different periods of time can be compared: *Spending for each department is shown deflated by an average price index – the GDP deflator. The Treasury calls this 'real terms' spending.*

de•fraud /dɪˈfrɔːd‖-ˈfrɒːd/ *v* [I,T] to gain money or goods from someone by saying or doing something dishonest: *He admitted attempting to defraud the Provincial Insurance Company.* **defraud sb of sth**: *She defrauded her employers of thousands of pounds.*

de•fray /dɪˈfreɪ/ *v* [T] *formal* **defray costs/expenses/charges** to pay someone's costs etc: *The company will defray any expenses you have on the journey.*

de•gear•ing /ˌdiːˈɡɪərɪŋ‖-ˈɡɪr-/ *n* [U] *BrE* FINANCE when a company starts to get more of the money it needs by selling shares in the company, and less by borrowing in the form of loans or bonds; DELEVERAGE

degressive tax —see under TAX[1]

de•hir•ing /ˌdiːˈhaɪərɪŋ‖-ˈhaɪr-/ *n* [U] *AmE* when a company or an organization dismisses employees it no longer needs

de•in•dus•tri•a•li•za•tion also **deindustrialisation** *BrE* /ˌdiːɪnˌdʌstriəlaɪˈzeɪʃən‖ -lə-/ *n* [U] when there is less and less manufacturing industry in an area or country: *People entering the workforce in recent decades have increasingly taken jobs in service enterprises instead of working in factories. This change has come to be known as Britain's deindustrialization.*

de ju•re /ˌdiː ˈdʒʊəri,ˌdeɪ ˈdʒʊəreɪ‖-ˈdʒʊr-/ *adj, adv* LAW recognized and supported by law: *It declared that the independent Republic of Latvia, recognized internationally in 1920, was still in existence de jure.* | *He now has de jure control of the company.* —compare DE FACTO

de•lay•er /ˌdiːˈleɪə‖-ər/ *v* [I] when an organization delayers, it reduces the number of management levels it has —**delayering** *n* [U] *Whether it's called downsizing or delayering, the goal is the same: to reduce the number of middle managers.*

del cre•de•re a•gent /del ˈkreɪdəri ˌeɪdʒənt/ —see under AGENT

del•e•gate[1] /ˈdeləɡət/ *n* [C] someone who has been elected or chosen to speak, vote, or take decisions for a group: *Also at the conference were delegates from industry associations including the Building Employers' Federation.* | ***Delegates to*** *the union's annual meeting are expected to endorse the plans.*

del•e•gate[2] /ˈdeləɡeɪt/ *v* **1** [I,T] to give part of your power or work to someone else, usually someone in a lower position than you: *You can create organizational cultures which make it easier to delegate.* **delegate sth to sb**: *Decision making on a day-to-day basis will be delegated to team managers.*

2 [T] to choose someone to do a particular job, or to be a representative of a group **delegate sb to do sth**: *I've been delegated to organize the weekly meetings.*

delegated legislation —see under LEGISLATION

del•e•ga•tion /ˌdeləˈɡeɪʃən/ *n* **1** [C] a group of people who officially represent a company, organization, government etc: *A delegation of British business executives has arrived in Cuba for trade talks.* | *The company's chief executive led a powerful delegation to today's meeting.*

2 [U] the process of giving part of your power or work to someone else, usually someone in a lower position than you: *Mr Horton set out to establish a structure with minimum controls and maximum delegation of responsibility.*

de•lete /dɪˈliːt/ *v* [T] **1** to remove something written on a list, in a document etc: *Libelous remarks about living people have been deleted from the document.* | *The company will be deleted from the S & P 500 Index.*

2 COMPUTING to remove a document, program etc from a computer: *You can simply look at faxes on the screen and delete the ones you don't want.*

3 MARKETING if a company deletes a product, it stops making it or selling it —**deletion** *n* [C,U] *investigating the deletion of data from company files*

de•le•ver•age /ˌdiːˈliːvərɪdʒ‖-ˈlev-, -ˈliːv-/ *n* [U] FINANCE when a company starts to get more of the money it needs by selling shares in the company, and less by borrowing in the form of loans or bonds; DEGEARING *BrE*: *RJR Nabisco, which had a debt/equity ratio that was as high as 25 to one at the time of its leveraged buy-out, is now cited as a classic case of deleverage.* —**deleverage** *v* [T] *He encouraged corporations to deleverage their balance sheets in order to lower capital costs*

de•lin•quen•cy /dɪˈlɪŋkwənsi/ *n* plural **delinquencies** [C,U] *AmE* ACCOUNTING when money that is owed is not paid at the right time, or is not paid at all: *Mortgage* ***delinquency rates*** *fell to 4.52% in the second quarter.*

de•lin•quent /dɪˈlɪŋkwənt/ *adj* *AmE* ACCOUNTING **delinquent account/debt/payment etc** an account, debt etc that has not been paid at the right time, or has not been paid at all: *Creditor management allows lenders to reduce the risk of delinquent accounts.*

delinquent loan —see under LOAN[1]

delinquent tax certificate —see under CERTIFICATE

de•list /ˌdiːˈlɪst/ *v* [T] FINANCE to remove the name of a company from a Stock Exchange list, so that its stocks, shares etc can no longer be traded there: *The exchange said it would apply to the Securities and Exchange Commission to delist Schafer.* | *The New York Stock Exchange said it suspended trading in Citytrust Bancorp Inc. and will now seek to delist the shares.* —**delisting** *n* [U] *The Committee has not recommended any more drastic sanction, such as delisting.*

de•liv•er /dɪˈlɪvə‖-ər/ *v* **1** [T] to take goods or mail to a place: *An average of 52 tankers a day deliver 462 million gallons of crude oil, gasoline and other petroleum products to the U.S.* | *The new computers will be delivered next week.*

2 [I,T] to manage to provide or achieve something that other people benefit from: *The stocks delivered a compound annual return of 9.5%.* | *Good government can deliver a high level of services while maintaining fiscal discipline.* + **on**: *The question is whether the company can deliver on these commitments.*

delivered at frontier —see under INCOTERM

delivered duty paid —see under INCOTERM

delivered price —see under PRICE[1]

de•liv•er•y /dɪˈlɪvəri/ *n* plural **deliveries** **1** [C,U] the act or process of bringing goods, letters etc to the place or person they have been sent to: *Deliveries to the restaurant should be made at the back entrance.* | *a delivery charge* | *They have just* ***taken delivery of*** (=received) *ten new American fighter jets.*

part delivery [C] a delivery of only some of the goods that were ordered

recorded delivery [C,U] a service provided by the POST OFFICE in Britain where the person who receives a letter or package signs a document to prove to the sender that they have received it: *Warning notices were sent* ***by recorded delivery*** *on the first default of payment.* | *a recorded delivery letter* —compare DELIVERY CONFIRMATION

special delivery [C,U] a service that delivers a letter or package very quickly: *I'd like to* ***send*** *these letters* ***special delivery***.

spot delivery also **nearby delivery** [U] the delivery of COMMODITIES (=oil, metals, farm products etc) immediately, rather than in the future: *Copper for spot delivery now trades at a discount to copper for 3-month delivery.*

2 [U] LAW when a seller officially hands over something, for example a document relating to property or shares, to a buyer —see also ADVICE OF DELIVERY, CASH BEFORE DELIVERY, CASH ON DELIVERY, GENERAL DELIVERY

delivery confirmation *n* [C] *AmE* a service provided by the POST OFFICE where the person who receives a letter or package signs a document to prove to the sender that they have received it; ADVICE OF DELIVERY *BrE*

D

delivery date —see under DATE[1]

delivery note —see under NOTE[1]

delivery order —see under ORDER[1]

delivery receipt —see under RECEIPT[1]

delivery terms —see under TERM[1]

delivery time —see under TIME

Del•phi tech•nique /ˈdelfi tekˌniːk/ *n* [singular] a method of asking SPECIALISTS (=people who know a lot about a particular subject) to say if and when something might happen in the future. The average of their opinions is used to estimate how likely it is to happen

del•ta /ˈdeltə/ *n* [singular] STATISTICS a change in an amount

delta shares —see under SHARE

de•mand /dɪˈmɑːnd‖dɪˈmænd/ *n* [U] ECONOMICS **1** the amount of spending on goods and services by companies and people in a particular economy: *Demand in the US economy generated 23 million new jobs in the period 1974 to 1986.*
2 the total amount of a type of goods or services that people or companies buy in a particular period of time + **for**: *Lower interest rates did nothing to increase demand for loans to buy houses.* | *There was a very* ***strong demand*** *for jeans and T-shirts over the last month.* | *Chrysler said its Jeep plant won't operate next week because of* ***weak demand.***
3 the total amount of a type of goods or services that people or companies would buy if they were available: *Power companies have been forced to reduce voltage when demand exceeded available supplies during extreme cold or hot spells.* | *Demand for phone service in Thailand far outstrips the supply with back orders totaling about one million.*
4 law of demand the idea that the more something costs, the less demand for it there is
aggregate demand the total demand for goods and services in an economy: *The tax rises are aimed at reducing aggregate demand in the economy, particularly for cars and consumer durables.*
consumer demand demand for goods and services from people rather than businesses: *Consumer demand led to higher imports of manufactured goods.*
cyclical demand demand that changes in a regular way over time, depending on the part of the trade cycle that a country is in or the time of year: *The company is looking well placed in a world market that is prone to cyclical demand.*
derived demand demand for a type of goods or services that depends on demand for another type of goods or services: *An individual firm's demand for labour can be thought of as a derived demand – it is derived from the consumers' demand for the firm's product.*
domestic demand demand from within a particular country, not from abroad: *Japan agreed to reorient its economy, depending on domestic demand, rather than exports, for growth.*
elastic demand when a change in the price of something leads to a larger change in the amount of it that is sold or that could be sold if it was available: *Margins on goods in relatively elastic demand should be lower than those on relatively inelastic demand.*
excess demand when there is more demand for something than available supplies of it: *The greater the excess demand for labour, the greater will be the rate of wage inflation.*
global demand total demand from all over the world: *He also expressed concern about global demand for capital that is keeping interest rates firm in many major countries.*
inelastic demand when a large change in the price of something results in only a small change in the demand for it: *Alcohol is a product with a very inelastic demand.*
institutional demand demand for SECURITIES from financial institutions rather than other investors
market demand demand for a particular type of goods or services from a particular group of buyers: *Ford developed a 'modular' design for the engine, which allows it to vary the number of cylinders to meet market demand.* —see also ELASTICITY OF DEMAND, ON DEMAND

demand account —see under ACCOUNT[1]

demand and supply *n* [U] ECONOMICS the demand for goods and services in relation to the amount available and the price: *Perfectly competitive markets achieve an efficient allocation of resources by balancing demand and supply through the price mechanism.* —compare SUPPLY AND DEMAND

demand curve —see under CURVE

demand deposit —see under DEPOSIT[1]

demand inflation —see under INFLATION

demand note —see under NOTE[1]

demand price —see under PRICE[1]

demand-pull inflation —see under INFLATION

demand-side *adj* [only before a noun] demand-side ideas emphasize managing the economy through changes in interest rates and taxes in order to influence demand and so keep unemployment low —compare SUPPLY-SIDE

de•mar•ca•tion /ˌdiːmɑːˈkeɪʃən‖-ɑːr-/ *n* [U] HUMAN RESOURCES when different jobs are given to workers belonging to different trade unions: *the company's attempt to break down demarcation between skilled trades*

demarcation dispute —see under DISPUTE

de•mar•ket•ing /ˌdiːˈmɑːkᵻtɪŋ‖-ɑːr-/ *n* [U] MARKETING when actions are taken to reduce the amount of demand for a product, for example because it is dangerous: *the demarketing of cigarettes*

de•ma•te•ri•a•lize /ˌdiːməˈtɪəriəlaɪz‖-ˈtɪr-/ also **dematerialise** *BrE v* [T] FINANCE in trading shares, bonds etc, to change from a system based on CERTIFICATES (=official documents showing ownership) to PAPERLESS TRADING (=where records of ownership are kept on computer): *India has tens of billions of shares in issue, and only 500 million have been dematerialised – converted into electronic form – to date.* —**dematerialization** also **dematerialisation** *BrE* — *n* [U]

de•merge /ˌdiːˈmɜːdʒ‖-ˈmɜːrdʒ/ *v* [I,T] to make one part of a large company into a separate company: *A plan was announced yesterday to demerge its North American operations.* —**demerger** *n* [C] *Merchant bankers proposed a demerger of Ferranti International into two separate businesses.*

de•mise[1] /dɪˈmaɪz/ *n* [C usually singular] LAW, PROPERTY when a property owner rents property to someone, or the rented property itself: *Where the demise includes the whole of a building the airspace above the building may be excluded from the demise.*

demise[2] *v* [T] LAW, PROPERTY if the owner of a property demises it, they rent it to someone: *The plaintiff landlord had demised premises to the defendant for 21 years.* —**demised** *adj*: *a demised property*

demise charter —see ***bareboat charter*** under CHARTER[2]

dem•o /ˈdeməʊ‖-moʊ/ also **demo version** *n* [C] COMPUTING an example of a type of software that is produced to show customers what it can do, to encourage them to buy the complete form of the software

de•moc•ra•cy /dɪˈmɒkrəsi‖dɪˈmɑː-/ *n* plural **democracies** **1** [U] a system of government in which members of the government are elected by the people of a country: *They carried banners demanding democracy and a free press.*

social democracy ◆ [U] a political and economic system based on socialism combined with democratic principles, such as freedom and government by elected representatives: *the divide between modern social democracy*

◆ [C] a country with a government based on social democracy: *income policies in the European social democracies*

2 [C] a country that has a government which has been elected by the people of the country: *He said we should be increasing our support for Russia's democracy.*

3 [C,U] a situation or system in which everyone has the right to be involved in making decisions: *People will continue to view our party with suspicion until we display democracy within our organization.*

workplace democracy also **democracy in the workplace** [U] a way of running a company in which all employees are involved in making important decisions about the company

dem•o•crat /ˈdeməkræt/ *n* [C] **1** someone who believes in, or works to achieve, democracy: *She is a democrat who supports self-determination.*

2 Democrat a member or supporter of the Democratic party in the US: *My parents were lifelong Democrats.*

dem•o•crat•ic /ˌdeməˈkrætɪk◂/ *adj* **1** controlled by representatives who are elected by the people of a country: *a democratic government*

2 organized according to the principle that everyone has a right to be involved in making decisions: *a very democratic management style* —**democratically** *adv*: *a democratically elected council*

demographic profile —see under PROFILE[1]

dem•o•graph•ics /ˌdeməˈgræfɪks/ *n* MARKETING **1** [plural] details of the type of people that make up a particular group, in particular their age, sex, and income. This term is used especially in marketing to talk about the groups of people who buy a particular product: *When we look at the demographics of book buyers and project forward the changes in these groups, there is good news.*

2 [U] the study of human populations and the way in which they change, used especially in marketing when thinking about which people might buy a particular product: *Consumer targeting has been made increasingly effective by developments in demographics and statistics.* —**demographically** *adv*: *medical practitioners working in demographically less attractive parts of the city*

de•mog•ra•phy /dɪˈmɒgrəfi‖-ˈmɑː-/ *n* **1** [U] the study of human populations and the way in which they change: *economics, sociology, demography and other statistical social studies*

2 [singular] the type of people that make up a particular population: *changes in the demography of British cities over the past two decades*

de•mon•e•tize also **demonetise** *BrE* /ˌdiːˈmʌnɪtaɪz‖-ˈmɑːn-/ *v* [T] FINANCE to no longer allow the use of a particular coin or BANKNOTE as money: *The Philippines central bank said it would demonetize paper money printed during the late Ferdinand Marcos's administration.* —**demonetization** also **demonetisation** *BrE n* [U] *the demonetisation of silver a century ago*

dem•on•stra•tion /ˌdemənˈstreɪʃən/ *n* [C,U] an act of explaining and showing how a product works or how something is done: *He gave a demonstration of how the program works.* | *a* ***sales demonstration*** (=one done in order to sell something) *of vacuum cleaners*

demonstration effect —see under EFFECT

demonstrative legacy —see under LEGACY

de•mote /dɪˈməʊt‖-ˈmoʊt/ *v* [T] to give someone a job with a lower rank or position than they had before: *Constructive dismissal can include demoting you or reducing your salary.* **demote sb to sth**: *a Cabinet reshuffle in which he was demoted to Deputy Education Secretary* —**demotion** *n* [C,U] *She could remain on the staff if she accepted demotion to ordinary lecturer.*

de•mur•rage /dɪˈmʌrɪdʒ‖-ˈmɜː-, -ˈmʌ-/ *n* [U] **1** when a ship is kept by someone who has CHARTERED it for longer than the time agreed or allowed

2 money which someone who has CHARTERED a ship pays to its owner if the ship does not sail at the agreed time

de•mu•tu•a•lize also **demutualise** *BrE* /ˌdiːˈmjuːtʃuəlaɪz/ *v* [I,T] FINANCE if a MUTUAL COMPANY such as a life insurance company or a BUILDING SOCIETY demutualizes or is demutualized, it obtains the agreement of the people who invest in it, or are insured by it, to become a LIMITED COMPANY with shareholders, listed on the stockmarket: *Northern Rock is the latest of this year's building societies and life insurers to demutualise and float on the stock market.* —**demutualization** also **demutualisation** *BrE n* [C,U] *There has been a massive expansion in share ownership caused by privatisations and demutualisations.*

de•na•tion•al•ize also **denationalise** *BrE* /diːˈnæʃənəlaɪz/ *v* [T] to sell a business or industry that is owned by the state, so that it is owned privately; PRIVATIZE: *There was no attempt to denationalize the giant state monopolies.* | *British Telecom and other such denationalized companies* —**denationalization** also **denationalisation** *BrE n* [U] *the denationalization of British Rail*

de•nom•i•na•tion /dɪˌnɒmɪˈneɪʃən‖dɪˌnɑː-/ *n* [C] the value shown on a coin, BANKNOTE, stamp etc: *a handful of notes of different denominations* | *TV licence stamps in 50p denominations* | *A lot of our customers at the bank request* ***small denomination*** *notes.*

de•part•ment /dɪˈpɑːtmənt‖-ɑːr-/ written abbreviation **Dept** *n* [C] **1** one of the parts of a large organization such as a company or university where people do a particular kind of work: *She heads the customer services department.* | *the Department of Genetic Research* —see also BANKING DEPARTMENT

bank trust department [C] in the US, the part of a bank that deals with the money and property of people who have died, and manages other family financial matters

2 one of the parts that a government is divided into, which has a particular area of responsibility: *the Department of Employment* | *the Justice Department*

3 a part of a large shop that sells a particular type of product: *Joan works in the toy department.*

4 one of the areas that some countries, for example France, are divided into

5 be sb's department *spoken* to be something that a particular person is responsible for: *The website isn't really my department – ask Bill.*

Department of Social Security abbreviation **DSS** *n* the government department in Britain that deals with making payments to people who are unable to work, for example because they are ill or unemployed

Department of Trade and Industry abbreviation **DTI** *n* the government department in Britain that deals with matters relating to trade with other countries and the production and selling of goods and services within Britain

department store —see under STORE[1]

de•par•ture /dɪˈpɑːtʃə‖-ˈpɑːrtʃər/ *n* **1** [C,U] an act of leaving a place, especially at the start of a journey: *I saw Simon shortly before his departure for Russia.*

2 [C,U] an act of leaving an organization or position: *His sudden departure from the political scene took everyone by surprise.*
3 [C] a flight, train etc that leaves at a particular time: *There are several departures a day for New York.*

de·pen·dant /dɪˈpendənt/ *n* [C] someone, for example a child, who depends on you for money, food, clothes etc: *the effect of the budget on a middle-aged mother who has dependants, a job, a mortgage, and a car* | *those who retire early to look after an elderly dependant*

de·pen·dent /dɪˈpendənt/ *adj* needing another person to provide money, food, clothes etc: *Do you have any dependent children?* + **on/upon**: *Adequate provision must be made for any child who is dependent on either spouse.*

de·plete /dɪˈpliːt/ *v* [T] to greatly reduce the amount of something, using up nearly all of it: *Drastic measures will need to be taken if fish stocks in Europe's seas are not to be disastrously depleted.* —**depleted** *adj* [only before a noun] *Measures to build up the depleted foreign exchange reserves were supported by the International Monetary Fund.*

D

de·ple·tion /dɪˈpliːʃən/ *n* [U] when an amount of something is greatly reduced or nearly all used up: *Many businessmen judged the bank's measures insufficient to prevent the continuing depletion of foreign exchange reserves.* | *the depletion of the world's natural resources*
provision for depletion ACCOUNTING when the value of a FIXED ASSET is reduced by a particular amount every year in a company's accounts, so that the value of the asset is recorded as nothing by the time it is totally depleted

de·po·nent /dɪˈpəʊnənt‖-ˈpoʊ-/ *n* [C] LAW someone who makes a statement in a court of law which they promise is true. A deponent can appear in court as a WITNESS or make a written statement which is presented in court as evidence: *If the evidence has been given by affidavit, the court may order the deponent to attend for cross-examination.*

de·pos·it[1] /dɪˈpɒzɨt‖dɪˈpɑː-/ *n* **1** [C] an amount of money paid into a bank account or held in a bank account, especially when it is earning interest: *Residents have some $4 billion in deposits in local financial institutions.* | *BCC Hong Kong had more than US$1 billion* ***on deposit*** *when it was closed.* —see also CERTIFICATE OF DEPOSIT, MEMORANDUM OF DEPOSIT
fixed deposit [C] an amount of money held in a bank account and earning a particular rate of interest for a fixed period of time: *Investors are now able to obtain a better yield, 7%, from one-year fixed deposits at the Post Office Savings Bank.*
2 deposits [plural] the total amount of money held in bank accounts etc within an economy
bank deposits [plural] the total amount of money that customers have paid into a particular bank or into all banks in a particular area or economy: *The money supply, essentially the sum of all currency and bank deposits, barely grew in the fourth quarter.*
cash ratio deposits [plural] the amount of money that a country's banks must leave with its CENTRAL BANK. Interest on this money helps pay the central bank's costs: *Banks hope the rate for cash ratio deposits will drop from 0.35% of their sterling deposits to 0.2%.*
core deposits [plural] the money available to a bank in its customers' accounts, rather than through the MONEY MARKET: *CalFed added 68,000 new savings and checking accounts, to bring total core deposits to $13.2 billion.*
money market deposits [plural] money held on the MONEY MARKET rather than in bank accounts: *Investors have shifted their funds into short-term money market deposits, where they can earn interest rates as high as 8%.*
public deposits [plural] money belonging to the British government held by the BANK OF ENGLAND: *The public deposits are usually relatively small, as surplus cash is used for repayment of government debts.*
retail deposits [plural] another name for CORE DEPOSITS
3 [C] also **deposit account** a bank account in which money can be held and will earn interest
call deposit [C] a type of bank account from which you can take out money immediately without paying a charge and without informing the bank in advance: *For customers specifically wanting US dollars, it has a US Dollar Call Deposit Account, offering interest and immediate access to funds.*
demand deposit [C] another name for a CALL DEPOSIT: *Bank of America requires no minimum balance on its demand deposit account.*
sight deposit [C] another name for a CALL DEPOSIT: *The most familiar form of sight deposit are current accounts at banks.*
term deposit also **time deposit** [C] a bank account in which you must leave your money for a minimum period of time and from which you can only take out money after informing the bank in advance: *More than $150 billion was withdrawn from time deposits in thrifts and banks last year.*
4 [C] a small first payment that you make for a house, car, holiday etc: *You have to* ***put down a deposit*** *of 25% of the total cost.*
5 [C] an amount of money that you pay when you rent something which will be given back to you if you do not damage the thing you are renting: *You will have to pay one month's rent in advance, plus a deposit of $500.*

deposit[2] *v* [T] to leave money or other valuable things at a bank: *The Cubans gave Mr Arias $20,000, which he deposited in his personal account.* | *Someone deposited the silver in the vaults of a Zurich bank.*

deposit account —see under ACCOUNT[1]

de·pos·i·tary /dɪˈpɒzɨtəri‖-ˈpɑːzɨteri/ *n* [C] another spelling of DEPOSITORY

deposit broker —see under BROKER[1]

deposit certificate —see under CERTIFICATE

deposit insurance —see under INSURANCE

dep·o·si·tion /ˌdepəˈzɪʃən, ˌdiː-/ *n* [C] LAW a formal statement that someone makes to a court about facts relating to a court case: *The plant safety director said in a deposition that the broken cable should have been repaired the night before.*

deposit liabilities —see under LIABILITY

deposit money —see under MONEY

de·pos·i·tor /dɪˈpɒzɨtə‖dɪˈpɑːzɨtər/ *n* [C] a person or organization that puts money into a bank account so that it can be held there and earn interest

de·pos·i·to·ry /dɪˈpɒzɨtəri‖dɪˈpɑːzɨtɔːri/ *n* plural **depositories** [C] **1** an organization where the formal documents showing who owns shares, bonds, etc can be kept safely: *Bankers Trust, which served as depository for the Marathon shares during the takeover battle*
2 a place where goods can be kept safely: *the Dallas book depository*
night depository *AmE* a special hole in the outside wall of a bank into which a customer can put money or documents when the bank is closed; NIGHT SAFE *BrE*
3 LAW statements and EVIDENCE prepared for use in a court case: *The case depository – nearly 20,000 pages of evidence – was to be stored at Mr Petrone's law offices.*

depository institution —see under INSTITUTION

deposit protection fund —see under FUND[1]

deposit receipt —see under RECEIPT[1]

deposit slip *n* [C] another name for a deposit receipt

deposit-taking *adj* [only before a noun] a deposit-taking financial institution is one into which people can pay money so that it can be held there and earn interest: *The Bank of England earlier had refused to upgrade BCCI's status from a deposit-taking company to a bank.*

dep•ot /ˈdepəʊ‖ˈdiːpoʊ/ *n* [C] **1** a place where large quantities of goods, equipment, or materials are stored until they are needed: *a **fuel depot** | The business is opening a new **distribution depot** in the midlands.*
2 a place where buses or trains are kept until they are needed, and often repaired and maintained: *the main British Rail maintenance depot*
3 *AmE* a small bus or railway station

depreciable life —see under LIFE

de•pre•ci•ate /dɪˈpriːʃieɪt/ *v* **1** [I] to decrease in value over a period of time: *If you don't get your car serviced regularly, it will depreciate quickly.*
2 [I,T] FINANCE if a currency depreciates, it goes down in value compared to the currencies of other countries: *People will switch to dollars, depending on how much they think the exchange rate will depreciate. | Mexico's central bank is committed to depreciating the peso by no more than 6.6% against the dollar.*
3 [T] ACCOUNTING to reduce the value of a FIXED ASSET over the particular period of time allowed under tax law: *Other fixed assets are depreciated on a straight line basis at annual rates which vary according to the class of asset.*

depreciated cost —see under COST[1]

de•pre•ci•a•tion /dɪˌpriːʃiˈeɪʃən/ *n* [U] **1** when the value of something goes down, usually gradually: *The proposed site of the factory may lead to depreciation of property value in the immediate vicinity.*
2 FINANCE when the value of a currency falls compared to the currencies of other countries, causing imports to cost more and exports to be worth less: *A **currency depreciation** can have a serious effect on the domestic rate of inflation.*
3 ACCOUNTING the gradual loss in value of a FIXED ASSET that wears out over a number of years or needs to be replaced regularly. Under tax law, the amount lost each year can be taken away from a business's profits, reducing the amount of tax to be paid: *The calculation of depreciation for tax purposes is governed by the tax authority's rules. | Fixed assets are normally valued at cost, less provision for depreciation.*

accelerated depreciation a system where tax authorities allow larger amounts for depreciation at the beginning of the life of an asset, and for the whole value of the asset to be claimed before the end of its useful life: *Japan allows companies to use an accelerated depreciation method for investment costs.*

accumulated depreciation the total amounts allowed for depreciation of an asset up to a particular time: *The decline in pretax profit was due to higher costs for materials and accumulated depreciation.*

book depreciation the amount of depreciation for one or more assets, as shown in a business's books rather than the real value of the depreciation: *Capital allowances deducted from taxable income may be higher in the early years than book depreciation.*

depreciation account —see under ACCOUNT[1]

depreciation allowance —see under ALLOWANCE

depreciation fund —see under FUND[1]

depreciation method —see under METHOD

de•press /dɪˈpres/ *v* [T] **1** to prevent an economy, industry, market etc from working properly or being as active as it usually is: *Several factors combined to depress the American economy | Overproduction was blamed for depressing oil markets*
2 to reduce the value of something such as prices or wages: *Competition between workers will depress wage levels. | Profits have already been depressed by the recession*

de•pressed /dɪˈprest/ *adj* **1** an industry or economy that is depressed does not have enough manufacturing or business activity: *Glaxo was a major winner in an otherwise **depressed sector** as its yearly results provided welcome comfort for investors. | help for companies suffering from the **depressed** economic **climate***
2 if the price of something is depressed, it is lower than normal: *The timber was sold, albeit at prices depressed by the glut of timber on the market.*

depressed area —see under AREA

de•pres•sion /dɪˈpreʃən/ *n* **1** [C,U] a long period of time during which there is very little business activity and a lot of people do not have jobs: *The current **economic depression** can be turned around if companies can be persuaded to invest in the industry. | The nation as a whole was suffering from a period of **deep depression** following a boom which had peaked six or seven years before.* —compare RECESSION
2 The (Great) Depression the period from 1929 to 1934 during which economic activity was very low and unemployment reached very high levels in the US and Europe: *The American silk market collapsed in 1929–30 following the onset of the Great Depression. | Commodity prices were at their lowest since the Great Depression.*

deprival value —see under VALUE[1]

Dept. or **dept.** written abbreviation for department: *the U.S. Dept. of Commerce*

depth interview —see under INTERVIEW[1]

dep•u•ty /ˈdepjᵘ̮ti/ *n* plural **deputies** [C] someone in an organization who is immediately below the rank of another important person, and who is officially in charge when that other person is not there: *the **deputy chairman** and managing director, Geoffrey Whalen | the **deputy leader** of the Democrat Party*

deputy chairman —see under CHAIRMAN

d/e ratio written abbreviation for DEBT-EQUITY RATIO —see under RATIO

de•reg•u•late /ˌdiːˈregjᵘ̮leɪt/ *v* [I,T] to remove or reduce the number of government controls on a particular business activity, done to make companies work more effectively and to increase competition: *After internal US flights were deregulated in 1978, the industry quickly became more competitive. | The pressure to deregulate came from inside the Stock Exchange.* —compare REGULATE —**deregulated** *adj* [only before a noun] *Competition is intense in the **deregulated financial markets**.* —**deregulation** *n* [U] *The bank industry maintains deregulation has benefited consumers.*

de-requisition *v* [T] to give property that has been requisitioned (REQUISITION) back to its owner

de•riv•a•tive /dɪˈrɪvətɪv/ *n* [C usually plural] something such as an OPTION (=the right to buy or sell something at a particular price within a particular period) or a FUTURE (=paying a fixed price now for delivery of something in the future) based on UNDERLYING assets such as shares, bonds, and currencies: *Derivatives often offer investors an easy way to make bets in markets that might be otherwise inaccessible.*

derivative lease —see under LEASE[2]

derivative product —see under PRODUCT

derived demand —see under DEMAND

der•rick /ˈderɪk/ *n* [C] **1** a type of CRANE, used especially for loading and unloading ships
2 a tall tower built over an oil well, used to raise and lower the drill: *a massive **oil derrick***

de·sal·i·na·tion /diːˌsæləˈneɪʃən/ *n* [U] when salt is removed from sea water so that the water can be used in homes and factories, and on farm crops: ***Water desalination** is still an expensive prospect.* | *the world's largest seawater **desalination plant***

de·sert·i·fi·ca·tion /dɪˌzɜːtəfəˈkeɪʃən‖-ɜːr-/ *n* [U] when useful land, especially farm land, becomes dry and gradually turns into a desert. This can happen when trees and bushes are cut down, allowing the top layer of soil to blow away, or when too many farm animals are allowed to feed on an area of land

de·sign[1] /dɪˈzaɪn/ *n* **1** [C,U] the way in which something has been planned and made, including its appearance, how it works etc: *One or two changes have been made to the computer's basic design.* | *a company that believes in the importance of good design*

job design [U] the process of deciding what work and responsibilities a particular job should include: *Poor job design results in unhappy employees in boring jobs.*

2 [U] the process of making a drawing of something to show how it will be made or what it will look like

computer-aided design abbreviation **CAD** [U] the use of computers in designing something, especially buildings, cars etc: *Company officials say that the use of a computer-aided design process helps to keep project costs down.*

graphic design [U] the art of combining pictures and words in order to design books, magazines, newspapers, and advertisements: *Computerized graphic design is changing the publishing industry.*

industrial design [U] the designing of products which are made by machines, for example cars, computers, radios etc, or the job of doing this: *The new proposals will allow car makers to gain more legal protection on all their industrial designs.*

registered design [C] *BrE* a design which has been recorded with the PATENT OFFICE, but does not get a PATENT: *When an item is to be commercially reproduced, you need to be aware of its registered design rights.*

design[2] *v* [I,T] **1** to make a drawing or plan of something that will be made or built: *The theatre was designed by a local architect.* | *a **well-designed** office* | *There were too many badly built, **badly designed** vehicles.*

2 to plan or develop something for a specific purpose **be designed to do sth**: *Harvard Graphics software that is designed to work in Microsoft Windows.* **be designed for**: *The car's parts are designed for easy recycling.* **be designed as**: *The program is designed as an incentive for Iowa companies to create new jobs*

des·ig·nate[1] /ˈdezɪgneɪt/ *v* [T] to choose someone or something for a particular job or purpose: *Mr Timmer has been designated to succeed Mr van der Klugt.* | *The government designated the aircraft industry as a strategic sector.*

des·ig·nate[2] /ˈdezɪgnət, -neɪt/ *adj* [not before a noun] a word used after the name of an official job showing that someone has been chosen for that job but has not yet officially started work: *Mr Warren is currently group finance director designate.*

designated hitter *n* [C] *informal AmE* someone who represents someone or does a job in their place

des·ig·na·tion /ˌdezɪgˈneɪʃən/ *n* **1** [U] the act of choosing someone or something for a particular purpose, or of giving them a particular description: *Designation of the town as a historic site would increase tourism.*

2 [C] a name or title: *The 'tax adviser' designation requires a six-course program.*

design brief —see under BRIEF[1]

de·sign·er[1] /dɪˈzaɪnə‖-ər/ *n* [C] someone whose job is to design products, equipment, furniture, clothes etc: *Kelly Johnson, a former Lockheed aircraft designer who helped develop more than 40 airplanes and spacecraft*

fashion designer someone whose job is to design clothes

graphic designer someone whose job is combining pictures and words, for example in books and magazines or in advertising

industrial designer someone whose job is designing industrial equipment or products

designer[2] *adj* [only before a noun] designer clothes are fashionable and expensive and have been designed by a well-known fashion designer: *Fashion trends now move quickly from **designer clothes** to cheaper imitations.*

designer label —see under LABEL[1]

desk /desk/ *n* [C] **1** a piece of furniture like a table, usually with drawers in it, that you sit at to write and work: *My father has worked behind a desk for over forty-two years.*

2 a place where you can get information in a hotel, airport etc: *You may inquire at the **information desk** about tour times for the King's Palace.* | *the hotel's **front desk*** —see also CITY DESK, TRADING DESK

de·skill /ˌdiːˈskɪl/ *v* [T] to remove or reduce the level of skill needed to do a job, usually by getting a machine to do some or all of the work: *Recent analysis shows how employers have been driven to deskill the workforce in order to control the workprocess.*

de·skil·ling also **de-skilling** /ˌdiːˈskɪlɪŋ/ *n* [U] **1** when employees do not learn the skills required to be able to work with modern technology: *The application of information technology is often thought to lead to deskilling, unemployment and resistance to change.*

2 when employees in a particular job require a lower level of skills than before: *the de-skilling of jobs on the railways, where the traditional culture of safety is changing* —**deskill** *v* [T] *Advances in machine technology had deskilled numerous working-class jobs.* —**deskilled** *adj*: *a semi-skilled or deskilled labour force in personal services such as restaurants or hotels*

desk job —see under JOB[1]

desk jockey *n* [C] *informal AmE* someone who does all their work at a desk in an office: *Samuel began his career as a desk jockey at a government agency in Detroit.*

desktop publishing —see under PUBLISHING

desk-top publishing software —see under SOFTWARE

de·spatch /dɪˈspætʃ/ *v* [T] another spelling of DISPATCH —see also ADVICE OF DESPATCH

des·ti·na·tion /ˌdestəˈneɪʃən/ written abbreviation **destn** *n* [C] the place that someone or something is going to: *the most popular **holiday destinations*** | *The train reached its **final destination** after two hours of delay.*

des·ti·tute /ˈdestətjuːt‖-tuːt/ *adj* having no money, no food, and nowhere to live: *San Francisco has targeted the problems of street litter and homelessness by hiring destitute citizens to perform jobs cleaning up the city.* —**destitution** *n* [U] *The worker is kept on the margin of destitution in many manual-labor jobs.*

destn written abbreviation for DESTINATION

de·tached /dɪˈtætʃt/ *adj* PROPERTY a house or garage that is detached is not joined to another building on any side

detail person *n* plural **detail people** [C] *AmE* a person whose job is to visit a company's customers and give information about products

de·te·ri·o·rate /dɪˈtɪəriəreɪt‖-ˈtɪr-/ *v* [I] to become worse: *The economy deteriorated further in August, with orders for manufactured goods falling.* —**deterioration** *n* [C,U] *a deterioration in sales*

de•ter•mine /dɪˈtɜːmən‖-ɜːr-/ *v* [T] LAW **1** to make an official decision about something: *a hearing to determine the amount of back taxes owed by Drexel Burnham Lambert* | *The agency is investigating diet products to determine if they pose a health hazard.*

2 to decide the exact meaning of the conditions of a contract, for example when there are disagreements about it: *If there is a contract of employment, the employee's obligations were to be determined from the contract.* —**determination** *n* [U] *The final determination of how many employees will be laid off will be made in the next couple of weeks.*

Deutsche Aktienindex —see DAX

Deut•sche Bank /ˌdɔɪtʃə ˈbæŋk/ *n* a large German bank: *There were rumours that Deutsche Bank, Germany's biggest bank, was preparing to take over Commerzbank.*

Deut•sche Bun•des•bank /ˌdɔɪtʃə ˈbʊndəsbæŋk/ *n* Germany's CENTRAL BANK: *Speculation that the Deutsche Bundesbank might raise German interest rates undermined traders' confidence in buying the dollar against the mark.*

Deutsch•mark /ˈdɔɪtʃmɑːk‖-mɑːrk/ written abbreviation **DM** *n* [C] the standard unit of money used in Germany until the introduction of the EURO; MARK

de•val•ue /diːˈvæljuː/ *v* **1** [T] to cause something to lose its value: *Heavy price discounting will devalue our famous brands.*

2 [T] ECONOMICS when a country devalues its currency against other currencies, it decreases its value for economic reasons, for example to make its exports cheaper: *Hungary said it will devalue its currency an average of 15% against major Western currencies.*

3 [I] ECONOMICS when a country's currency devalues against others, it loses its value: *With more money coming into circulation, the ruble will likely devalue further.* —**devaluation** *n* [C,U] *the pound's devaluation after sterling withdrew from the European Exchange Rate Mechanism*

de•vel•op /dɪˈveləp/ *v* **1** [I,T] to grow or gradually change into a larger, stronger, or more advanced state: *Once a stock market develops in the Czech Republic, the bank's customers will be offered investment accounts.* **develop into**: *The city developed into a major trading center.* **develop from**: *The Pacific Basin Rim has developed from being a satellite to Japan into an economic base of its own.* **develop sth**: *The company wants to develop its European operations.* | *At Toshiba, he developed the company's laptop market, which was a great success.*

2 [T] to plan and make a new product or provide a new service: *Digital has developed a new-generation microprocessor that is expected to be the heart of most of its expensive computers.* | *It takes time to develop and market new software.*

3 [T] PROPERTY to build on land, or improve existing buildings: *Mountleigh is developing a site in Piccadilly Circus.*

4 [T] to use a natural substance or product in order to make a profit: *The Union Texas-led joint venture will explore for and develop oil and natural gas in the Sindh province of Pakistan.*

5 [T] to create a plan, policy, or idea: *The country must develop a viable national energy policy.* | *We have developed a very positive plan for Macy's future.*

developed country *n* plural **developed countries** [C] a rich industrial country with a lot of business activity

developed land —see under LAND[1]

de•vel•op•er /dɪˈveləpə‖-ər/ *n* [C] **1** a person or company that works on the planning and design of new products: *electric car developers* | *software developers*

2 PROPERTY a person or company whose business is buying land and building on it: *Developers say it could take at least two years for significant office construction to begin again.* | *one of the country's major* ***property developers*** | *a Los Angeles* ***real-estate developer***

merchant developer a company that builds commercial buildings and sells them

developing country *n* plural **developing countries** [C] a country that is changing its economy from one based mainly on farming to one based on industry: *Developing countries, including such giants as India and China, have insisted they need financial and technological help.*

de•vel•op•ment /dɪˈveləpmənt/ *n* **1** [U] the growth or improvement of something, so that it becomes bigger or more advanced: *promises of economic development and thousands of new jobs* | *This had stunted development of the Japanese PC market.* | *She saw the qualification as a part of her professional development.* | *helping staff with their* ***career development***

economic development [U] when a country or area increases its wealth, for example by changing from an economy based on agriculture to one based on industry, or by changing to more modern industries and services: *Free trade can be a powerful engine for economic development, creating new jobs and opening new markets.*

human resources development also **human resource development**, abbreviation **HRD** [U] the work of improving human resources in an organization through training etc: *Human resource development must be driven by all managers, not just the personnel director.*

management development [U] activities to improve the skills of managers in a company, such as training and MENTORING (=when more experienced managers give help and advice to less experienced ones) etc: *IBM's director of education and management development*

2 [U] the process of planning and making new products or providing a new services: *The new phone is the result of two years of development by AT&T units.* | *The Japanese approach to* ***product development*** *is spreading around Detroit.* —see also RESEARCH AND DEVELOPMENT

brand development [U] an attempt to make a brand more successful by changing it over time so that it remains popular and fashionable: *Grey Brand Futures is specifically looking at brand development – where consumers will be in the next five to 10 years.*

3 [U] the process of planning and building new houses, offices etc, or improving existing ones: *the development of office buildings, shopping centers and apartment complexes*

property development ◆ [C,U] *BrE* land on which houses are built or being built: *the sale of a commercial property development in Witney, Oxfordshire*

◆ [C] *AmE* the process of building new houses, offices etc

4 [U] the creating of a plan, policy, or idea: *the development of a coherent transport policy*

5 [U] the using of a natural substance or product in order to make a profit: *This includes $370 million for the development of the East Brae Field in the United Kingdom North Sea.*

6 [C] a new event or piece of news that will have an effect on the present situation: *The G-7 will discuss international financial developments, including the continued weakness of the yen.*

7 also **real-estate development** *AmE* [C] a group of new buildings that have all been planned and built together on the same piece of land: *low-income families living in high-rise housing developments*

development aid —see under AID

D

development area —see under AREA

development corporation *n* [C] a government organization responsible for a development area: *The Teesside Development Corporation has planning powers over the site.*

development economics —see under ECONOMICS

development grant —see under GRANT[1]

development land —see under LAND[1]

de•vi•a•tion /ˌdiːviˈeɪʃən/ *n* **1** [C,U] a noticeable difference from what is expected or acceptable: *Any deviation in the current inflation rate could send stocks sharply up or down.* + **from**: *The sudden rise in market prices was an unexpected deviation from the norm.*
2 [C] STATISTICS a difference between a number or measurement in a set and the average of all the numbers or measurements in that set

standard deviation [C] a number that shows how widely members of a mathematically related group vary from the average: *Volatility as measured by the standard deviation of daily stock price movements has frequently been much higher than it is today.*

D

de•vi•ous /ˈdiːviəs/ *adj* using dishonest tricks and deceiving people to get what you want: *He's an honest businessman, not the devious executive the government says he is.* —**deviously** *adv* —**deviousness** *n* [U] *the deviousness of tobacco advertising, promotion and sponsorship activities*

de•vise /dɪˈvaɪz/ *v* [T] LAW to give land or buildings to someone after you die by writing it in a WILL —**devise** *n* [U] —see also BEQUEST

de•vo•lu•tion /ˌdiːvəˈluːʃən/ *n* [U] when a national government or a large organization gives some or all of its power to a smaller group or an organization at a more local level: *the devolution of political power*

de•volve /dɪˈvɒlv‖dɪˈvɑːlv/ *v* **1** [T] to give work, responsibility or power to someone at a lower or more local level: *The goal of the welfare bill is to devolve power and responsibility to the states.*
2 [I] LAW if land, goods etc devolve to someone they become the property of that person when their owner dies: *In the event of the guardian dying before the child attains twenty-one years, all of the estate shall devolve upon the said child and be held for him in trust.*

di•a•gram /ˈdaɪəgræm/ *n* [C] a drawing or plan that shows where something is, what it looks like, or how it works: *See the attached diagram for details on current market projections.* | *the wiring diagram that goes with the system*

scatter diagram a diagram that shows the relationship between two sets of quantities using DOTS (=small points) drawn between two lines, one going up and one going across, each representing one of the quantities

di•a•gram•mat•ic /ˌdaɪəgrəˈmætɪk◂/ *adj* showing in a drawing or plan exactly where something is, what something looks like, or how something works: *The progress can be summarised in diagrammatic form, as shown in figure 15b.* —**diagrammatically** *adv*

di•a•ry /ˈdaɪəri‖ˈdaɪri/ *n* plural **diaries** [C] **1** a record of events that have happened, or a book containing these: *The bills in this case showed the attorney's diary entries and descriptions of the work done.*
2 *BrE* a book with marked spaces for separate days of the year where you write down the meetings, events etc which are planned for each day; ORGANIZER *AmE*: *A full diary of engagements has been booked for the months ahead.*

Dic•ta•phone /ˈdɪktəfəʊn‖-foʊn/*n* [C] *trademark* an office machine on which you can record speech so that someone can listen to it and TYPE it later: *Many new executive cars come equipped with a telephone and a dictaphone.*

dic•tate[1] /dɪkˈteɪt‖ˈdɪkteɪt/ *v* [T] to say words for someone else to write down: *When Laurie got back to the office, she dictated a letter to Stewart.* —**dictation** *n* [U] *Many computers can **take** voice-activated **dictation**.*

dic•tate[2] /ˈdɪkteɪt/ *n* [C] *formal* an order, rule, or principle that you have to obey: *Individual countries are free to follow their own dictates on matters concerning the economy.*

dictation machine —see under MACHINE[1]

did•dle /ˈdɪdl/ *v* [T] *informal* to get money from someone by deceiving them: *I'm sure he diddled me out of quite a lot of money!*

dif•fe•ren•tial[1] /ˌdɪfəˈrenʃəl◂/ *n* [C] the amount of difference that there is between two things + **in**: *There is a severe differential in the quality of jobs between north and south.*

duty differential a difference in the tax that has to be paid on different products to show their relative usefulness or value: *In the budget, the Chancellor introduced a 10p duty differential between leaded and unleaded petrol.*

earnings differential also **pay differential** a difference in the pay of two jobs that is supposed to show their relative importance: *I don't think the pay differentials in Grades 4 and above properly reflect the job's responsibilities.*

price differential a difference in the prices of two products or of the same product in different places: *The Commission is looking at the price differentials of the same car models in different member states.*

differential[2] *adj* [only before a noun] based on or depending on a difference between two things: *The change in the exchange rate over a period will equal the differential inflation rates between the two countries.*

differential pay —see under PAY[1]

dif•fe•ren•ti•ate /ˌdɪfəˈrenʃieɪt/ *v* [T] MARKETING when a company differentiates its products, it shows how they are different from each other and from competing products, for example in its advertising. This is done to show buyers the advantages of one product over another: *How does a computer maker differentiate between the relative goodness of their Windows machine versus someone else's Windows machine?* | *The only viable strategy was to differentiate Citibank credit cards from all the low-cost alternatives.*

dif•fe•ren•ti•a•tion /ˌdɪfərenʃiˈeɪʃən/ *n* [U] the process of showing or seeing that one thing is different to something else

product differentiation MARKETING when a company shows how its products are different from each other and from competing products, for example in its advertising. Differentiation is important in telling buyers the advantages of one product over another: *To maintain product differentiation, the new models have all been styled distinctively.*

di•ge•ra•ti /ˌdɪdʒəˈrɑːti/ *n* [plural] *informal, journalism* people who understand computers well and who are confident about their skill in using them —compare COMPUTER-LITERATE

di•git /ˈdɪdʒɪt/ *n* [C] one of the written signs that represent the numbers 0 to 9: *Binary code uses the digits 1 and 0.* —see also DOUBLE-DIGIT

check digit COMPUTING a number or series of numbers added to the end of a code (=set of numbers or letters) to prevent a computer from making a mistake: *a unique 5 digit staff number followed by a check digit*

di•gi•tal /ˈdɪdʒɪtl/ *adj* digital electronic equipment receives sound and pictures from BINARY electrical signals (=signals using the numbers 0 and 1): *SDI is an inexpensive, dialup digital service used to carry data, video, fax and voice traffic.* | *Two new home **digital** recording **systems** are expected in stores later this year.*

digital nervous system —see under SYSTEM

di·lap·i·da·tions /dɪˌlæpəˈdeɪʃənz/ *n* [plural] *BrE* LAW money you have to pay if you damage a house that you are renting: *Damages for dilapidations will be assessed at the end of your annual contract.*

dil·i·gence /ˈdɪlədʒəns/ *n* [U] **1** care that someone in a position of responsibility takes with their work: *All directors must act honestly and use reasonable diligence and skill in the discharge of their duties.*

due diligence ◆ when a company thinking of buying another looks carefully at its accounts, as it must do by law before the deal can be agreed: *The acquisition is subject to a* ***due diligence review*** *by Commonwealth Bank, as well as government and central bank approvals.*

◆ when an organization selling investments checks their quality before selling them in order to protect investors: *Discipline in the due-diligence area often breaks down when times are busy.*

2 INSURANCE the duty that the owners of a ship have to do everything they can to make sure that the ship and the people and goods on it are safe

di·lute /daɪˈluːt/ *v* [T] FINANCE if a company dilutes its shares or the earnings on its shares, it increases the number of its shares that are available and so reduces the amount that each share will earn: *They issued new shares which diluted the equity of the current Novell shareholders.* | *Westinghouse said the $900 million equity infusion could dilute earnings by 10% next year.* —**dilution** *n* [U] *The conversion of loan stock will give the new investors 58% of the ordinary share capital, representing a substantial dilution of equity.*

diluted shares —see under SHARE

diluted stock —see under STOCK[1]

dime /daɪm/ *n* [C] a coin in the US and Canada, worth one tenth of a dollar: *a man who made a lot of money but never had a dime on him* —compare CENT

di·men·sions /daɪˈmenʃənz, də-/ *n* [plural] the size of something, especially when this is given as its length, height, and width: *A box of larger dimensions can be ordered.* | *a small aluminium case, dimensions 152mm by 102mm by 51mm.*

dime store —see under STORE[1]

diminishing returns *n* [plural] ECONOMICS **1** the idea that a point can be reached where the advantage or profit you are getting stops increasing in relation to the effort you are making: *For a time, companies concentrated on cost-cutting and restructuring; by the mid-1990s, that was producing diminishing returns and the emphasis swung back to growth in revenues.*

2 the law of diminishing returns the idea that when workers use a particular amount of something such as land or machinery, each additional worker will produce less and create less profit than the previous worker

din·er /ˈdaɪnə‖-ər/ *n* [C] *AmE* a small restaurant that serves cheap meals: *She's a waitress in an all-night diner.*

DINKS /dɪŋks/ *n* [plural] *journalism* double income no kids; professional couples with no children who have a lot of money available to spend

dip[1] /dɪp/ *v* past tense and past participle **dipped** present participle **dipping** [I,T] FINANCE to become lower, often before increasing again: *An oil glut would weaken prices as demand dipped in the spring.* | *Shares in Costain, the building and construction group, dipped 6p after the company revealed massive losses last year.* | *Data General's annual revenues dipped from $1.36 billion to $1.31 billion.*

dip[2] *n* [C] FINANCE a decrease in the amount of something: *an unexpected dip in profits*

direct access —see under ACCESS[1]

direct action —see under ACTION

direct advertising —see under ADVERTISING

direct cost —see under COST[1]

direct deb·it *n* [C,U] *especially BrE* an instruction that you give your bank to regularly pay money directly out of your account to a particular person or organization: *Payment can be made by direct debit.* | *We set up a direct debit to pay the monthly instalments.* —compare STANDING ORDER

direct expense —see under EXPENSE

direct exporting —see under EXPORTING

direct investment —see under INVESTMENT

di·rec·tive /dəˈrektɪv, daɪ-/ *n* [C] an official order or instruction: *The software will enable companies to conform fully with the EC directives on cross-border VAT payment.*

direct labour —see under LABOUR

direct mail —see under MAIL[1]

direct-mail marketer —see under MARKETER

direct marketer —see under MARKETER

direct marketing —see under MARKETING

di·rec·tor /dəˈrektə, daɪ-‖-ər/ also **company director** *n* [C] **1** one of the committee of top managers who control a company: *Westinghouse directors are expected to cut the 35-cent quarterly dividend when they meet later this month.* —see also BOARD OF DIRECTORS

alternate director *AmE* someone who is chosen by a company director to carry out his or her duties during their absence: *The appointment of any alternate Director shall terminate if the Director who appointed him vacates his office.*

creative director MARKETING someone in a company or ADVERTISING AGENCY whose job is to manage the advertising and selling of a product or range of products: *Tom Ford took over at Gucci as creative director with the aim of taking the brand to the cutting edge of fashion.*

executive director a director who is also in charge of the daily management of part of an organization: *Dennis Coleman, executive director of the county economic council in St Louis*

guineapig director *informal* a company director who is not involved in managing the company and does not have any real power to make decisions: *Because they couldn't fire Jackson, Robertson Enterprises gave him the position of guineapig director.*

managing director abbreviation **MD** the person in charge of the daily management of a company. The job is often combined with that of CHAIRMAN: *Ron Garrick, managing director of Weir Group* | *Jan Murray, chairman and managing director of PC World*

non-executive director also **outside director** a director who is not involved in the daily management of an organization

2 financial/sales/personnel etc director someone who is in charge of a particular department of an organization: *James Kiser, a regional director of operations at Marriott Corp*

di·rec·tor·ate /dəˈrektərət, daɪ-/ *n* [C] the committee in charge of an organization, especially a government organization: *the Food Safety Directorate* | *The Bundesbank confirmed that it plans to reorganize its seven-member directorate.*

Director-General of Fair Trading *n* in Britain, an official whose job is to protect consumers by checking that there is fair competition between companies in areas such as pricing, takeovers etc: *The Director-General of Fair Trading said that ties between the company and its exclusive wholesalers restricted competition between wholesalers and ice cream manufacturers.*

D

Director of Public Prosecutions abbreviation **DPP** *n* LAW in England, an important official who advises the government on legal subjects and decides which cases should go before a court of law: *A file was sent to the Director of Public Prosecutions, but the DPP decided not to press charges against the individuals concerned.*

di·rec·tor·ship /dəˈrektəʃɪp, daɪ-‖-ər-/ *n* [C] the position of being director of a company or organization: *Mr Runciman holds a number of directorships, including Scottish Eastern Investment Trust and British Steel.*

directors' interest *n* [C usually plural] the pay, benefits etc that a company's directors receive, and the records of these that a company must keep by law: *The notification must include the nature of the transaction, the nature and extent of the director's interest in it and the date on which the transaction was effected.*

directors register —see under REGISTER[1]

directors' report —see under REPORT[1]

di·rec·to·ry /daɪˈrektəri, də-/ *n* plural **directories** [C] **1** a book or list of names, facts etc, usually arranged in alphabetical order: *I couldn't find your number in the telephone directory.* | *a new business directory* | *the* ***Classified Directory*** *of Wisconsin Manufacturers* —see also EX-DIRECTORY
2 COMPUTING part of a computer's memory where information is stored, containing one or more FILES: *I suggest you create a separate directory to keep these files in.*

directory enquiries *BrE*, **directory assistance** *AmE n* [U] the telephone service that provides telephone numbers to people who ask for them; INFORMATION *AmE*

direct overhead —see under OVERHEAD

direct production —see under PRODUCTION

direct-reduction mortgage —see under MORTGAGE[1]

direct response advertising —see under ADVERTISING

direct sale —see under SALE

direct sales —see under SALE

direct selling —see under SELLING

direct tax —see under TAX[1]

direct taxation —see under TAXATION

di·ri·gisme /ˌdiːriːˈʒiːzəm‖ˌdɪrɪˈʒɪ-/ *n* [U] ECONOMICS the idea that a government should be very active in planning and running a country's economy: *He insists the project won't entail any protectionism or dirigisme, with the government dictating to industry.* —**dirigiste** *adj*: *French socialists remain instinctively dirigiste and nationalist at the first sign of economic trouble.*

dirt·y /ˈdɜːti‖ˈdɜːr-/ *adj* comparative **dirtier** superlative **dirtiest** unfair or dishonest: *a dirty political campaign* | *revelations about dirty dealing in the Treasury bond market* | *He accused the government of* ***dirty tricks*** *against the Republicans.*

dirty bill of lading —see under BILL OF LADING

dirty float —see under FLOAT[2]

dirty ship —see under SHIP[1]

dis·a·bil·i·ty /ˌdɪsəˈbɪləti/ plural **disabilities** also **dis·a·ble·ment** /dɪsˈeɪbəlmənt/ *n* **1** [C] a physical problem that makes someone unable to use a part of their body: *She leads a normal life in spite of her disabilities.*
2 [U] when someone is unable to use parts of their body properly: *learning to cope with disability* | *You may be able to claim* ***disability benefit*** *if you are unable to work.* | *He also receives a* ***disability pension*** *from the army.*

disability benefit —see under BENEFIT[1]

disability insurance —see under INSURANCE

disability payment —see under PAYMENT

disability pension —see under PENSION[1]

disabled quota —see under QUOTA

dis·al·low /ˌdɪsəˈlaʊ/ *v* [T] to officially refuse to allow or accept something: *The court will examine the costs and expenses sought and disallow those that it considers have not been 'properly incurred'.*

di·sas·ter /dɪˈzɑːstə‖dɪˈzæstər/ *n* [C,U] **1** a sudden event such as a flood, storm, or accident which causes great damage or suffering: *100 people died in the mining disaster.* | *The 1987 hurricane was the worst* ***natural disaster*** *to hit England for decades.*
2 a complete failure: *Disaster could strike if the company is outbid by many of its expected rivals for the franchise.* | *What is good news for shoppers can be a disaster for shareholders.*

dis·burse /dɪsˈbɜːs‖-ɜːrs/ *v* [T] *formal* to officially give or pay money to someone: *The state health department will disburse funds to local health departments for anti-smoking education.*

dis·burse·ment /dɪsˈbɜːsmənt‖-ɜːr-/ *n formal* [C,U] a payment of money made by a professional person such as a lawyer when doing work for their client. The professional person can then claim the money back from their client later

disbursing agent —see under AGENT

disc /dɪsk/ *n* [C] **1** a COMPACT DISC
2 *BrE* a computer DISK

dis·charge[1] /dɪsˈtʃɑːdʒ‖-ɑːr-/ *v* **1** [T] to officially allow or tell someone to leave hospital, the army, a job etc: *The men were treated for minor injuries and discharged.* | *He was discharged from the RAF last August.*
2 [T] to remove someone from their job: *In December, Carolco discharged 49 employees and said it might need to make further cuts.*
3 discharge a duty/responsibility/function etc *formal* to do properly everything that is part of a particular duty etc: *The committee said that the Bank had failed to discharge its supervisory duties.*
4 discharge a debt/claim/liability etc LAW to completely pay an amount that is owed: *The payment of £4,000 together with the monthly sum of £1,000 was not enough to discharge in full the invoice for January's work.*
5 [I,T] to send out gas, liquid, smoke etc or allow it to escape: *Gas leaked from the tanker as it discharged crude oil at the Fawley refinery.* | *pollutants being discharged into the atmosphere*
6 [I,T] to take goods off a ship, plane etc; UNLOAD: *The ship discharged the 2,911 tonne cargo of 330 concrete coated steel pipes in less than a day.*
7 [T] to state officially that someone who was bankrupt has obeyed the court and can do business again

dis·charge[2] /ˈdɪstʃɑːdʒ‖-ɑːrdʒ/ *n* **1** [C,U] when someone is officially allowed or told to leave hospital, the army, a job etc: *The organization helps ex-servicemen and their dependants following discharge from the forces.*
2 [C,U] when someone is removed from their job: *He threatened to sue the firm for wrongful discharge.*
3 [U] *formal* when someone does properly everything that is part of a particular duty, responsibility etc: *Although we do not consider Mr Gray's conduct to have been dishonest, the discharge of his responsibilities as company secretary was most unsatisfactory.*
4 [U] LAW, INSURANCE when an amount such as a debt or money claimed on an insurance policy is completely paid: *the residue of the estate after the discharge of all debts and liabilities*
5 [C,U] when gas, liquid, smoke etc is sent out or allowed to escape: *the discharge of toxic waste into the sea* | *£1 billion has been spent to control sewage discharges.*

6 [C,U] when goods are taken off a ship, plane etc; UNLOADING: *I would sometimes help repaint the ships or check the discharge of cargo.*

discharged bankrupt —see under BANKRUPT[1]

discharged bill —see under BILL[1]

discharge from bankruptcy —see under BANKRUPTCY

discharge of contract *n* [U] LAW when the duties that someone has under a contract are ended, for example because they have carried out those duties, because there has been an agreement to end the contract, or because someone has broken the contract

dis·ci·pli·na·ry /ˈdɪsəplɪnəri, ˌdɪsəˈplɪ-‖ˈdɪsəpləneri/ *adj* HUMAN RESOURCES concerned with how people in an organization or group should behave, and how they should be punished if they do not obey the rules: *If a member of staff is continually late for work, a* ***disciplinary code*** (=set of rules about behaviour and punishments) *should be available to give guidance to the supervisor about what steps to take.* | *The investigation led to* ***disciplinary action*** *being taken against several officers.*

disciplinary hearing —see under HEARING

dis·claim·er /dɪsˈkleɪmə‖-ər/ *n* [C] LAW a statement that you are not responsible for something or not connected with it: *a case concerned with a disclaimer of liability in a surveyor's report*

dis·clo·sure /dɪsˈkləʊʒə‖-ˈkloʊʒər/ *n* **1** [C,U] the duty of someone in a professional position to inform customers, shareholders etc about facts that will influence their decisions: *The code of conduct is based on the need for disclosure, which ensures that all those with a legitimate interest in a company have the information which they need.*

2 [U] LAW when a person or organization gives information that would normally be kept secret, for example when a bank gives information about a customer's accounts to the police: *In America 'shield' laws allow journalists to protect their sources, with certain exceptions, for example if public interest is better served by disclosure.*

3 [U] INSURANCE the duty of someone who is insured to tell the insurance company every important fact that relates to the insurance

4 [C] a fact which is made known after being kept secret: *There was criticism of his salary and tax arrangements following disclosures in the newspapers.*

dis·con·tin·ue /ˌdɪskənˈtɪnjuː/ *v* [T] to stop doing, making or providing something that you have regularly done, made or provided until now: *Ibanez guitar manufacturers discontinued almost their entire range to concentrate on the RG450 and JEM series.* | *Bus Route 51 is being discontinued as of March 1st.* | *This is a* ***discontinued line*** (=product that is no longer being made) *that we are selling off cheaply.*

dis·count[1] /ˈdɪskaʊnt/ *n* [C] **1** a reduction in the cost of goods or services in relation to the normal cost: *You can nearly always get books there* ***at a discount.*** | *Reebok is trying to increase market share by selling its shoes at* ***discount prices.***

bulk discount a lower price that is offered for buying a large number or amount of something: *As twenty are required it might pay to ask your supplier for a bulk discount.*

case rate discount the discount when you pay less for something because you buy a complete CASE (=box of goods) rather than just one thing

cash discount a lower price that is offered for quick payment or payment in cash

no claims discount INSURANCE a lower price for insurance offered to an insured person or organization if they do not make a claim during a particular period of time: *A motoring breakdown scheme is offering members a 20% no claims discount if they do not call out the service during the year.*

trade discount a lower price offered by a producer to a shop or business: *Our normal trade discount (33.3%) will be applied.*

volume discount another name for BULK DISCOUNT

2 FINANCE the amount by which the price of a SECURITY is less than the value shown on it: *Zero-coupon bonds are sold at a discount to their face value and pay no interest until maturity.*

3 fine rate of discount if a BILL OF EXCHANGE is traded at a fine rate of discount, it is bought and sold at a price near to the amount shown on it, because the buyer knows there is little risk of it not being paid: *Accepting Houses accept bills of exchange for a fee. This enables the bill to be traded at a fine rate of discount.*

4 FINANCE if something in a financial market is traded at a discount, it is bought and sold at lower prices than something else to which it is compared: *The premium of platinum over gold narrowed to $11, but there is a good chance platinum will trade at a discount to gold soon.*

banker's discount also **bank discount** the difference between the value shown on a bond, share etc that is bought by a bank from a customer, and the amount that the customer actually receives from the bank. The banker's discount is kept by the bank as payment

bond discount the difference between a bond's present price in the market and its actual value

dis·count[2] /ˈdɪskaʊnt/ *v* [T] **1** to offer something for sale at a lower price than usual: *The retailers discounted the goods below prices set by Sony.* | *The one-way fares are now discounted 15% off regular fares.*

2 FINANCE to change the price of something in a financial market by taking into account good or bad news that affects it: *I think the market has discounted almost all of what can go right with the economy this year.*

3 FINANCE to sell SECURITIES at less than the value shown on them. The person who buys the securities makes a profit when the borrower buys them back at their full value at the repayment date

4 to sell a BILL OF EXCHANGE or other COMMERCIAL BILL before its normal payment date for less than it will be worth on that date. The buyer makes a profit when the bill is paid in full by the borrower at the repayment date

discount bank —see under BANK[1]

discount broker —see under BROKER[1]

discount brokerage —see under BROKERAGE

discounted bill —see under BILL OF EXCHANGE

discounted cash flow *n* [C usually singular] a way of finding out if a planned investment will be profitable by using a particular interest rate to calculate the present value of future income from the investment over time. The interest rate used is the present market rate to which is added an extra amount for the risk involved. If, using this rate, the investment will bring in more money than its current cost, it is considered worth making

dis·count·er /ˈdɪsˌkaʊntə‖-ər/ *n* [C] **1** a seller of goods or services that sells at lower prices than normal: *The cameras list for under $1,000, and will be available soon from discounters for as little as $600.*

deep discounter a commercial organization or financial institution offering the lowest prices, often offering only a very basic service

2 a large shop that has very low prices and a limited number of different products

3 also **invoice discounter** a financial institution that lends a business an amount of money equal to that owed by the business's suppliers: *The specialist invoice discounters have increasingly sought to distinguish their activities from those of the factoring companies.*

discount house —see under HOUSE

dis•count•ing /ˈdɪsˌkaʊntɪŋ/ also **invoice discounting** *n* [U] when a financial institution lends a business an amount of money equal to that owed to the business by its suppliers, in return for a percentage. This is good for the business because it gets the money immediately, improving its CASH FLOW. Discounting is a form of finance that can be cheaper than bank loans or OVERDRAFTS: *For invoice discounting, fees are typically between 0.2% and 0.5% of the value of invoices.* | *You may have a lot of money tied up in your sales ledger in unpaid bills. Invoice discounting is a way to release this money for you.* —**invoice discounter** *n* [C] *The specialist invoice discounters have increasingly sought to distinguish their activities from those of the factoring companies.* —compare FACTORING

discount market —see under MARKET[1]

discount price —see under PRICE[1]

discount pricing —see under PRICING

discount rate —see under RATE[1]

discount store —see under STORE[1]

discount window *n* [C] in the US, a way in which banks can borrow from the US central bank at special low rates of interest: *Some big New York banks are expected to borrow needed funds at the Fed's discount window instead of through the market.*

di•screp•an•cy /dɪˈskrepənsi/ *n* plural **discrepancies** [C,U] a difference between two numbers, amounts, details etc that ought to be the same: *Money managers warn that individual investors may find wide discrepancies in the prices they are quoted.*

di•scre•tion /dɪˈskreʃən/ *n* [U] the ability, right, or freedom that someone has to take decisions in a particular situation: *The licensee is supposed to have complete discretion over how the station is operated.*

discretionary costs —see under COST[1]

discretionary fund —see under FUND[1]

discretionary income —see under INCOME

discretionary service —see under SERVICE[1]

discretionary spending —see under SPENDING

discretionary trust —see under TRUST

di•scrim•i•nate /dɪˈskrɪmɨneɪt/ *v* [I] to behave unfairly towards one group of people or one type of company or product: *employment practices that discriminate against women* | *The court ruled that the state's highway-use tax discriminated in favor of trucking companies based in Arkansas and against companies based in other states.*

discriminating duty —see under DUTY

discriminating tariff —see under TARIFF

di•scrim•i•na•tion /dɪˌskrɪmɨˈneɪʃən/ *n* [U] **1** ECONOMICS the process of treating one market, country, type of product etc differently from another: *the discrimination in favour of imported wine when it comes to excise duty*

price discrimination the practice of charging different prices for the same product in different markets: *Peak load pricing is a system of price discrimination whereby peak time users pay higher prices.*

2 HUMAN RESOURCES when a worker in a company is treated unfairly because of their race, sex, age etc, especially by not being considered for a job. This is illegal in many countries: *The survey showed that there was unofficial discrimination against women in the engineering industry.* | *The Bill sought to prohibit* ***employment discrimination*** *against qualified disabled persons on the ground of their disability.*

age discrimination unfair treatment of someone because of their age, especially when they are not given a job because they are too old; AGEISM

genetic discrimination unfair treatment of someone who has an illness that they were born with and that their parents also had: *In one case of genetic discrimination, a patient with Gaucher's disease was denied a government job.*

positive discrimination also **reverse discrimination** when one group of people are treated more favourably than another, often because they have been treated unfairly in the past: *positive discrimination in favour of female candidates for public sector appointments*

race discrimination also **racial discrimination** when people from one race are treated less favourably than those from another: *Race discrimination is still quite widespread.*

sex discrimination also **sexual discrimination** when people, especially women, are treated unfairly because of their sex, especially when this stops them getting a job or making progress in their job: *Sex discrimination in private pension plans is illegal.*

discriminatory tax —see under TAX[1]

discriminatory taxation —see under TAXATION

dis•e•con•o•mies /ˌdɪsɪˈkɒnəmiːz‖-ˈkɑː-/ *n* [plural] extra costs that make something less profitable: *There will be some diseconomies when the two companies merge.*

diseconomies of scale —see under SCALE

dis•em•bark /ˌdɪsɨmˈbɑːk‖-ɑːrk/ *v* **1** [I] to get off a ship or plane: *We took our luggage down to the lower deck, eager to disembark.*

2 [T] to put people or goods onto land from a ship or plane: *Smith landed at Westcott to disembark its passengers.* —**disembarkation** *n* [U] *Have your dinner on board the ferry before disembarkation in France.*

dis•e•qui•lib•ri•um /ˌdɪsekwɨˈlɪbriəm, ˌdɪsiː-/ *n* [U] ECONOMICS when an economy or a particular market is not in a balanced state: *The competitive process arises out of disequilibrium in markets giving opportunities for entrepreneurs to exploit their superior information and earn profits.*

disguised unemployment —see under EMPLOYMENT

dis•hoard•ing /ˈdɪshɔːdɪŋ‖-ɔːr-/ *n* [U] ECONOMICS when money or goods that have been kept are brought back into the economy, for example by spending or investing money rather than saving it as cash —compare HOARDING

dis•hon•our *BrE*, **dishonor** *AmE* /dɪsˈɒnə‖-ˈɑːnər/ *v* [T] **1** if a bank dishonours a cheque, it refuses to pay out money for it, usually because the person who has written it does not have enough money in their account: *The law is that people who obtain goods by presenting a cheque which they know will be dishonoured are not guilty of theft.*

2 if someone dishonours a BILL OF EXCHANGE, they do not accept it when it is presented, or do not pay it after they have accepted it

dis•in•fla•tion /ˌdɪsɪnˈfleɪʃən/ *n* [U] ECONOMICS when a government reduces the rate of inflation without also reducing the general level of economic activity or increasing unemployment. This may be done by raising interest rates, controlling the amount of credit available to people, and limiting the availability of goods which are in short supply. Disinflation is a gentle form of DEFLATION: *In 1930, the inflation-disinflation sequence ended in outright deflation.* —**disinflationary** *adj*: *Some argue that disinflationary forces are so strong that movements in the exchange rate pose no threat.*

D

dis•in•te•gra•tion /dɪsˌɪntəˈgreɪʃən/ *n* [U] ECONOMICS when a group of producers stops producing particular products themselves and start buying them from other producers —opposite INTEGRATION

dis•in•ter•me•di•a•tion /dɪsˌɪntəmiːdiˈeɪʃən‖-tər-/ *n* [U] FINANCE, BANKING when financial products are sold directly to customers rather than through financial institutions: *Many banks were keen to move into Stock Exchange activities in order to capture some of the business they were losing through disintermediation.* —opposite INTERMEDIATION

dis•in•vest /ˌdɪsɪnˈvest/ *v* [I] to invest less or to stop investing in an activity or area of business + **from**: *Many funds are disinvesting from stocks that fail to deliver shareholder value.* | *His two brothers decided to disinvest from the family business.* —opposite INVEST —**disinvestment** *n* [C,U] *Germany recorded disinvestment last year, after attracting inflows of $12 billion the year before.* | *17 of these disinvestments were the result of restructuring.*

disk /dɪsk/ *n* [C,U] a flat circular piece of plastic or metal used for storing computer information: *There are a number of products which allow* ***PC disks*** *to be read or written from a Macintosh.* | *Can you send me your report* ***on disk?***

compact disk also **compact disc** [C,U] a small circular piece of hard plastic on which music or information is stored

floppy disk also **floppy** [C,U] a disk on which computer information is stored

hard disk also **hard drive** [C] the part of a computer that permanently stores programs and information: *Hard drive capacity has been growing by 60% per year and will continue that way for several more years.*

disk drive —see under DRIVE[2]

dis•kette /dɪsˈket‖ˈdɪsket/ *n* [C] another name for a FLOPPY DISK

disk operating system —see under SYSTEM

dis•miss /dɪsˈmɪs/ *v* [T] **1** to remove someone from their job, usually because they have done something wrong: *He was dismissed from his job at a bank for repeatedly turning up to work late.*

2 LAW to state officially that a court case cannot continue because there is not enough evidence against the accused person: *The prosecution offered no evidence and the case was dismissed.*

dis•miss•al /dɪsˈmɪsəl/ *n* [C,U] when someone is removed from their job by their employer: *The 11 employees would face disciplinary action, ranging from reprimand to suspension or dismissal.* | *There will not be any dismissals of teachers.*

constructive dismissal when someone chooses to leave their job but feels they have been forced to leave because their employer has treated them badly or asked them to do something that is not in their contract: *Mr Rump was ordered to work outside the south of England and he refused; he was not dismissed; he resigned, claiming constructive dismissal.*

unfair dismissal also **wrongful dismissal** when someone is unfairly removed from their job by their employer: *Two employees complained of unfair dismissal.* | *a claim of unfair dismissal*

di•spatch also **despatch** *BrE* /dɪˈspætʃ/ *v* [T] to send something or someone to a place: *Manufacturers dispatch vials of vaccine in large, insulated cartons.* | *A rescue team was dispatched to the mountain.* —**dispatch** *n* [U] *Six weeks should be allowed for the dispatch of tickets.*

dispatch-case *n* [C] a flat case with a handle used to carry papers, books etc; BRIEFCASE

dis•patch•er /dɪˈspætʃə‖-ər/ *n* [C] **1** someone whose job is to make sure that goods or workers are sent out at the right time: *At the centre, dispatchers keep track of taxis on monitor screens.*

2 the person, company etc that sent something: *The person receiving the parcel in prison could be prosecuted but the dispatcher could not be dealt with.*

dispatch note —see under NOTE[1]

di•spense /dɪˈspens/ *v* [I,T] **1** if a machine dispenses something, it gives it to someone who puts in money, a special number etc: *Four machines dispense a wide range of drinks and snacks.* | *a cash dispensing machine*

2 to sell or give medicines to people: *A pharmacist will never dispense a prescription unless he or she is sure it is correct.*

di•splay[1] /dɪˈspleɪ/ *n* **1** [C,U] an attractive arrangement of objects for people to look at or buy, for example in a shop: *enormous shops with beautiful window displays* | *the wide range of goods* ***on display***

2 [U] MARKETING printing or page design to attract people's attention, used especially in advertisements: *big* ***display adverts*** *with prominent slogans*

3 [C] COMPUTING the text or pictures you see on a computer screen, or the style, colour, brightness etc of this: *the use of different kinds of devices to control a display on the computer monitor* | *Select 'Display' and a dialogue box will appear with a choice of screen display options.*

display[2] *v* [T] to arrange objects in an attractive way for people to look at or buy, for example in a shop: *The clothes were beautifully displayed.*

display pack —see under PACK[1]

dis•pos•a•ble /dɪˈspəʊzəbəl‖-ˈspoʊ-/ *adj* **1** intended to be used once or for a short time and then thrown away: *disposable coffee cups*

2 available to be used: *disposable resources*

disposable in•come —see under INCOME

dis•pos•al /dɪˈspəʊzəl‖-ˈspoʊ-/ *n* **1** [U] when someone gets rid of something that is no longer needed or wanted + **of**: *European Community environment ministers agreed to tighten controls on the production, transport and disposal of waste.*

2 [C] an asset that is sold, and the act of selling it: *The disposal of the 34 stores will allow the company to concentrate on its most profitable operations.* | *Volvo, continuing an* ***asset disposal*** *program, agreed to sell its 12.5% stake in Saga Petroleum.*

dis•pose /dɪˈspəʊz‖-ˈspoʊz/ *v*

dispose of sth *phr v* [T] **1** to get rid of something that is no longer needed or wanted: *IBM accepts return of all its products for recycling, charging customers as little as DM50 to dispose of a computer terminal.*

2 to sell an asset: *Most of those properties will be disposed of over the next five years.*

dis•pos•sess /ˌdɪspəˈzes/ *v* [T] to take property or land away from someone, often illegally: *black South Africans who had been dispossessed of their homes* —**dispossession** *n* [U]

di•spute /dɪˈspjuːt,ˈdɪspjuːt/ *n* [C] **1** a serious disagreement between two groups of people, especially a disagreement between workers and their employers in which the workers take action to protest: *The amount of working time lost through disputes and stoppages has fallen dramatically.* | *A dustmen's dispute left. tons of rat-infested refuse in city centres.* | *a pay dispute involving 450 staff in the finance department* | *their long-running dispute over copyright*

demarcation dispute HUMAN RESOURCES a disagreement between different trade unions about which workers should do which jobs: *The company has a flexible workforce in that workers can each carry out a number of different jobs without demarcation disputes.*

industrial dispute *BrE* another name for LABOUR DISPUTE: *a prolonged industrial dispute*

D

labour dispute *BrE*, **labor dispute** *AmE* a disagreement between the managers and workers of a company, sometimes resulting in a STRIKE: *A labor dispute at the Southern Peru Copper Corp. was recently settled.*
2 be in dispute (with sb) if two groups of people are in dispute, they are involved in a disagreement: *Cork is in dispute with a number of American firms of lawyers over unpaid fees.*

dis·qual·i·fy /dɪs'kwɒlǝ̇faɪ‖-'kwɑː-/ *v* past tense and past participle **disqualified** [T] to officially or legally stop someone being allowed to do something, because they have done something wrong: *The General Medical Council had disqualified a doctor for misconduct.* | *He was disqualified from driving for a drink-driving offence.*

dis·rupt /dɪs'rʌpt/ *v* [T] to prevent a situation, event, system etc from working in the normal way: *Traders are worried that war would disrupt ocean shipping.* | *Train drivers have threatened to disrupt services if they are not happy with the pay award.* —**disruption** *n* [C,U] *Oil markets appear to be expecting severe disruptions of supplies.*

dis-saving *n* [U] ECONOMICS when people spend the money they have saved: *About 40% of net personal income in these three regions was financed out of net dissaving.*

dis·so·lu·tion /ˌdɪsə'luːʃən/ *n* [U] when a company or PARTNERSHIP comes to an end officially: *Any member or creditor aggrieved by the dissolution can apply within the following 20 years for restoration of the company name.*

dis·solve /dɪ'zɒlv‖dɪ'zɑːlv/ *v* [T] to bring a company or PARTNERSHIP to an end officially: *Samsung Electronics Co Ltd has abandoned its facsimile software for Unix unit, Samsung Software America, and dissolved the operation after about a year.*

dis·train /dɪ'streɪn/ *v* [T] LAW to take goods from someone to be sold in order to pay rent that is owed: *Legislation has largely restricted the right to distrain goods found upon the premises but not belonging to the tenant.* —**distraint** *n* [U] *We believe the payment of debt by manageable amounts to be more civilised than distraint.*

dis·tress /dɪ'stres/ *n* [U] LAW when someone's goods are taken with the permission of a court of law so that they can be sold to pay unpaid rent, bills etc: *The corporation had a power of absolute and immediate distress in the event of non-payment of dues.*

distress borrowing —see under BORROWING

distressed property —see under PROPERTY

distress selling —see under SELLING

distributable profit —see under PROFIT[1]

distributable profits —see under PROFIT[1]

dis·trib·ute /dɪ'strɪbjuːt/ *v* [T] **1** to make goods available to customers after they have been produced: *The new products will be sold under the Lipton brand and distributed by Pepsi.*
2 to divide up a company's profits for a particular period of time and give them to shareholders in the form of DIVIDENDS or new shares: *One share of Celtrix will be distributed for every four Collagen shares held.*

distributed processing —see under PROCESSING

distributed profit —see under PROFIT[1]

dis·tri·bu·tion /ˌdɪstrǝ̇'bjuːʃən/ *n* **1** [U] the actions involved in making goods available to customers after they have been produced, for example moving, storing, and selling the goods: *The company plans to establish a network of central warehouses to make product distribution more efficient.* | *General Motors Corp's Canadian sales arm will take over distribution of Saab cars in Canada.*
2 [U] FINANCE when a company's profits are divided up and given to shareholders in the form of DIVIDENDS or new shares: *The company anticipates that about $1.20 to $1.25 a share will be available for distribution.*
final distribution [singular] FINANCE the last DIVIDEND paid during a financial year, if a company pays dividends more than once during the year
3 [U] ECONOMICS the way in which wealth is divided among people in a particular economy: *During periods of economic expansion, those who are in the top one-third of the **income distribution** will always benefit.*

distribution chain —see under CHAIN

distribution channel —see under CHANNEL[1]

distribution fee —see under FEE

distribution warehouse —see under WAREHOUSE

dis·trib·u·tive /dɪ'strɪbjǝ̇tɪv/ *adj* [only before a noun] *formal* connected with or relating to distribution: *marketing, designers and other distributive agencies*

distributive trades *n* [plural] industries involved in distribution, for example those involved in moving, storing, or selling goods: *The latest monthly survey of distributive trades found low growth in retailing activity.*

dis·trib·u·tor /dɪ'strɪbjǝ̇tə‖-ər/ *n* [C] a person or business responsible for making goods available to customers after they have been produced, either one that sells directly to the public or one that sells to shops etc: *We make sure that the distributors are always stocked adequately with the fast-moving standard items.*

district attorney —see under ATTORNEY

district auditor —see under AUDITOR

district court —see under COURT[1]

district judge —see under JUDGE[1]

dis·u·ti·l·ity /ˌdɪsjuː'tɪlǝ̇ti/ *n* [U] ECONOMICS the trouble or lack of satisfaction caused by having too much of something —opposite UTILITY

dit·to /'dɪtəʊ‖-toʊ/ *n* [C] a mark (") used instead of repeating what you have already written, usually immediately above in a list

di·verge /daɪ'vɜːdʒ, dǝ̇-‖-ɜːrdʒ/ *v* [I] if two or more rates of interest, unemployment etc diverge, the difference between them becomes larger: *Business cycles in different EU countries currently diverge significantly.* —compare CONVERGE —**divergent** *adj*: *US stocks had widely divergent performances, with blue chips weakening as many technology issues made gains.* —**divergence** *n* [U] *the divergence between British and continental interest rates*

di·ver·si·fieds /daɪ'vɜːsǝ̇faɪdz‖dǝ̇'vɜːr-, daɪ-/ *n* [plural] FINANCE shares in diversified companies

di·ver·si·fy /daɪ'vɜːsǝ̇faɪ‖dǝ̇'vɜːr-, daɪ-/ *v* past tense and past participle **diversified** [I] **1** if a company or economy diversifies, it increases the range of goods or services it produces + **into**: *Singapore has diversified into a wider range of industries.* + **from**: *The UK Department of Energy is urging farmers to diversify from traditional crops and consider using land to grow wood for fuel.*
2 to start to put your money into different types of investments in addition to the investments you already have: *Depositors in the eurocurrency markets sought to diversify into dollar bonds.* —**diversification** *n* [C,U] *The company intends school software to be a major new area of diversification for their business.* | *a policy of gradual economic diversification away from fishing* | *The process of financial deregulation in Japan has been accompanied by increasing international diversification of investment portfolios.* | *Bic's diversifications into sports clothing and perfumes*

di·ver·sion /daɪ'vɜːʃən, dǝ̇-‖-ɜːrʒən/ *n* [singular] FINANCE when money stops being spent in one area of business or on one type of product, and starts being spent on another: *a diversion of resources away from the competitive export market*

di•vert /daɪˈvɜːt, d½-‖-ɜːrt/ *v* [T] to spend money or make an effort in a new area of business or a new product **divert sth into**: *The company should divert more resources into research.*

di•vest /daɪˈvest, d½-/ *v* FINANCE **1** [T] if a group divests one of the companies that it owns, it gets rid of it by selling it: *We fulfilled our commitment to shareholders to divest Ultramar's downstream business by creating a new company.*

2 [T] if a company divests assets, it sells them, for example because it needs cash for another activity or to repay debts: *Where our competitive position is weak, we have continued to divest assets to help fund more profitable ventures elsewhere.*

3 [I] to reduce the number of your investments by selling some of them: *performance reports which may signal that it is time to divest rather than invest* —**divestment** *n* [C,U] *The string of divestments is part of the holding company's effort to lighten its debt load.* —**divestiture** *n* [C,U] *The divestiture of AT&T, effective in January 1984, opened the US telecommunications equipment market.*

di•vi also **divvy** /ˈdɪvi/ *n* [C] an informal word for a DIVIDEND: *The divi is being held at 8.8p.*

div•i•dend /ˈdɪv½dənd, -dend/ written abbreviation **d** *n* [C] **1** a part of the profits of a company for a particular period of time that is paid to shareholders for each share that they own: *Oneok raised its regular dividend on common shares 19% to 25 cents.* | *Consolidated Press forecasts a dividend of 29.8 cents a share.*

accumulated dividend a dividend on PREFERRED SHARES which is not paid out in each financial year, but allowed to build up: *The redemption price is $100,000 a share, plus accumulated dividends of $926.92 a share.*

annual dividend a dividend paid on each share held in a company for one financial year, or the total amount that the company pays out in dividends in that year: *Fuji intends to cut the annual dividend to six yen a share, including a 0.5 yen special payout already paid.*

bonus dividend an extra dividend paid in addition to a normal dividend: *The airline is proposing a bonus dividend of 7.5 cents a share to celebrate its 50th anniversary.*

cash dividend a dividend paid in cash, rather than in the form of new shares: *BBL said it would offer shareholders the option of receiving new shares in place of cash dividends.*

cumulative dividend interest paid on PREFERENCE SHARES which, if not paid out, will be added to the value of these shares: *Comcast agreed to issue preferred stock with an 8% cumulative dividend.*

extraordinary dividend a dividend paid for a particular reason, and not paid in every period of time: *BCI will receive 24.8 rand a share. In addition, an extraordinary dividend totaling 11.0 rand a share will be paid out of Blue Circle Ltd.'s reserves.*

final dividend the last dividend payment relating to a company's financial year: *Asda will pay a final dividend of 0.85 pence, making for a full-year dividend of 2.10 pence a share.*

gross dividend a dividend before tax is taken off: *If the total of gross dividends and other distributions exceeded $400, report it on Schedule B of your tax return.*

interim dividend a dividend paid during a company's financial year, usually every three or six months

ordinary dividend a dividend that does not depend on particular conditions: *Lend Lease raised its ordinary dividend to 63 cents a share for the year from 60 cents.*

preference dividend a dividend paid on PREFERENCE SHARES (=a kind of shares on which dividends must be paid before dividends on ordinary shares are paid)

quarterly dividend a dividend relating to a three-month period of a company's financial year

share dividend *especially BrE*, also **stock dividend** *especially AmE* a dividend paid to shareholders in the form of new shares in the company: *New Line Corp. declared a 25% stock dividend, in the form of one new share for each four common shares owned.*

special dividend a dividend paid in addition to the normal dividend, perhaps in a period of especially high profits: *ICN said it declared the special dividend to recognize the continued growth and strong performance of the company.*

stock dividend *AmE* a dividend that is paid to shareholders in the form of new shares rather than cash; BONUS ISSUE *BrE*: *CSM said shareholders will have the option of either a cash dividend or a stock dividend.*

unpaid dividend a dividend that has been announced by a company but has not yet been paid: *Unpaid dividends are recognized as liabilities until paid.*

2 a fixed rate of interest that is paid on certain types of company STOCK: *If Ford common stock remains depressed, they will still collect an 8.4% dividend on the preferred stock.*

3 INSURANCE a part of the profits of a LIFE INSURANCE company paid out to those who have insurance agreements with the company: *Holders of some types of policies, such as whole life, may see increases in their dividends.*

4 omit/pass/suspend a dividend to decide not to pay a dividend, usually because of bad financial results: *Poor profitability forced JAL to pass its dividend for the sixth year running.* | *The board voted to omit the dividend.* —see also ***ex dividend*** under EX[1]

dividend check *n* [C] the American for a DIVIDEND WARRANT

dividend cover *n* [singular] *BrE* a company's profits for a particular period measured in relation to the amount that it pays out in dividends for the period of time: *Body Shop wants to bring down its dividend cover down from 2.8 times to the sector average of 2.3 times.*

dividend payment —see under PAYMENT

dividend payout ratio —see under RATIO

dividend per share written abbreviation **Div/Share, DPS** *n* [C] the dividend paid out by a company for each of its shares: *KDD pays a 25-yen dividend per share, a 0.2% yield on Thursday's closing price of 12,200 yen.*

dividend-price ratio —see under RATIO

dividend reinvestment plan *n* [C] in the US, an arrangement offered by companies to shareholders for their dividends to be paid in the form of new shares rather than cash: *The company also announced a dividend-reinvestment plan yesterday to encourage shareholders to buy new stock at a 3% discount.*

dividend roll *n* [C usually singular] *AmE* when shares are bought in order to get a dividend payment and then sold again

dividends payable —see under PAYABLE

dividend-stripping *n* [U] when someone sells shares just before a dividend payment and buys them again after the payment in order to avoid paying tax on the dividend: *Dividend stripping is to some extent considered legitimate tax planning by the Inland Revenue.*

dividend warrant —see under WARRANT[1]

dividend yield —see under YIELD[1]

di•vi•sion /d½ˈvɪʒən/ *n* [C] one of the large parts into which a large organization or company is divided: *Each division has its own editorial, production, and marketing sales staff.* | *Thomson acquired the TV manufacturing division of America's General Electric.*

di•vi•sion•al /d½ˈvɪʒənəl/ *adj* [only before a noun] connected with a division of an organization, company etc: *marketing areas to be run on a local level by divisional managers*

D

di•vi•sion•a•li•za•tion /də̇ˌvɪʒənəlaɪˈzeɪʃən‖-lə-/ also **divisionalisation** *BrE n* [U] when an organization, company etc is divided into several divisions or separate companies

division of labour *BrE*, **division of labor** *AmE* — *n* plural **divisions of labour** *BrE*, **divisions of labor** *AmE* [C,U] ECONOMICS a way of organizing work in which each member of a group has one particular job to do instead of each member doing a share of all the jobs: *Greater efficiency can be achieved through the division of labour.*

Div/Share written abbreviation for DIVIDEND PER SHARE

divvy another spelling of DIVI

DIY /ˌdiː aɪ ˈwaɪ/ *n* [U] do-it-yourself; the activity of making or repairing things yourself instead of buying them or paying someone else to do it: *The British DIY business has been fiercely competitive with stores Do-It-All, B&Q and Texas all battling for supremacy.* | *expensive DIY equipment*

D

DJIA *trademark* FINANCE abbreviation for DOW JONES INDUSTRIAL AVERAGE —see under AVERAGE

DJTA *trademark* FINANCE abbreviation for DOW JONES TRANSPORTATION AVERAGE —see under AVERAGE

DJUA *trademark* FINANCE abbreviation for DOW JONES UTILITIES AVERAGE —see under AVERAGE

DM written abbreviation for DEUTSCHMARK, the currency of Germany until the introduction of the EURO: *The costs of the project are estimated at DM 93 million.*

DMU abbreviation for DECISION MAKING UNIT

DO or **d/o** written abbreviation for DELIVERY ORDER

dock[1] /dɒk‖dɑːk/ *n* **1** [C] a place in a port where ships are loaded and unloaded: *Oil can go by pipeline to a nearby dock where tankers can load it.*

2 docks [plural] a port area: *James turned up at the docks expecting a luxury liner, only to find a cargo ship.* —see also DRY DOCK

3 LAW **the dock** the part of a law court where the person who is accused of a crime stands: *With him in the dock and receiving the same sentence was his business partner.*

dock[2] *v* **1** [I] if a ship docks, it sails into a dock: *The ferry left Ramsgate for Dunkirk at 9.00am and docked two hours later.*

2 dock sb's wages/pay to reduce the amount of money you pay someone, usually as a punishment

dock company —see under COMPANY

dock dues —see under DUES

dock•er /ˈdɒkə‖ˈdɑːkər/ *n* [C] *BrE* someone whose job is loading and unloading ships; LONGSHOREMAN *AmE*; STEVEDORE *AmE*: *Dockers were on strike in the port of Durres.*

dock•et /ˈdɒkə̇t‖ˈdɑː-/ *n* [C] **1** a document giving details of goods that have been sold or delivered, the contents of a package etc: *the old system of having to write out an individual docket for every transaction*

2 *AmE* LAW a list of legal cases that will take place in a particular court: *Once your case is on the court's docket, you and your attorney will have the opportunity to meet with IRS lawyers.*

dock•lands /ˈdɒkləndz‖ˈdɑːk-/ *n* [plural] **1** *BrE* an area of a city that contains or used to contain docks: *This is an opportunity for the docklands to be redeveloped as a high quality, high density part of the city of Cardiff itself.*

2 Docklands an area of London formerly containing DOCKS and now a centre for business with many office buildings: *All three firms have decided to move to London's Docklands.*

dock receipt —see under RECEIPT[1]

dock•side /ˈdɒksaɪd‖ˈdɑːk-/ *n* [singular] the area around the place in a port where ships are loaded and unloaded: *The union is demanding a contract for dockside workers similar to that covering cargo handlers working on ships.*

dock•yard /ˈdɒkjɑːd‖ˈdɑːkjɑːrd/ *n* [C] a place where ships are built or repaired: *Falmouth has dockyards which now are used mainly for the repair of oil tankers and naval ships.*

doc•tor[1] /ˈdɒktə‖ˈdɑːktər/ *n* [C] **1** someone who is trained to treat sick or injured people

2 someone who has a DOCTORATE from a university

company doctor ♦ someone with special knowledge and experience who is employed to help a business that is losing money and which may have to close: *The ailing engineering firm has called in a company doctor after shedding 90 staff.*

♦ a medical doctor who is employed by a company to treat people who are sick or injured at work, and to give general advice on health: *Both my own doctor and the company doctor failed to diagnose my illness.*

doctor[2] *v* [T] to change something, especially in order to deceive people: *Police uncovered 43 cars for sale with doctored mileage readings.*

doc•tor•ate /ˈdɒktərə̇t‖ˈdɑːk-/ *n* [C] the highest university degree: *Goodwin* ***earned*** *her* ***doctorate in*** *political science from Harvard in 1978.* | *an* ***honorary doctorate*** *from Oxford University*

doc•u•ment[1] /ˈdɒkjʊ̈mənt‖ˈdɑːk-/ *n* [C] a record of important information on paper or computer disk: *His main expense is photocopying thousands of legal documents.* | *Cimtech advises on all aspects of traditional and electronic document management systems.*

defence document *BrE*, **defense document** *AmE* [C] a statement by a company which is the subject of a takeover offer giving reasons why its shareholders should not accept the offer: *In its defence document, Capital, which owns Crockfords and the Colony Club casinos, attacked London Clubs' record of managing casinos.*

export documents [plural] documents sent by an exporter's bank to a bank or other organization in the importer's country, who delivers them to the importer when the importer pays for the goods or accepts a BILL OF EXCHANGE. These documents are needed by the importer to get permission for the goods to come through CUSTOMS and to make insurance claims if the goods are lost or damaged; SHIPPING DOCUMENTS: *The exporter presents the required export documents to his bank and receives immediate payment from the bank of up to 100% of invoice value.*

offer document [C] a statement by a company that wants to buy another company in a takeover. In the offer document, the buyer says what its aims are, why shareholders of the company to be bought should accept the offer etc: *Before the offer document is published, it must be submitted to the supervisory authority and the management of the target company.*

shipping documents [plural] documents, including the BILL OF LADING, CUSTOMS DOCUMENTS, and insurance documents that relate to particular goods that are being shipped: *We recommend that companies match orders, shipping documents and invoices and follow up inconsistencies.*

doc•u•ment[2] /ˈdɒkjʊ̈ment‖ˈdɑːk-/ *v* [T] to record important information on paper, film, or computer disk: *The New York agency documented 60 attacks on journalists.*

documentary credit —see under CREDIT[1]

doc•u•men•ta•tion /ˌdɒkjʊ̈mənˈteɪʃən, -men-‖ˌdɑːk-/ *n* [U] **1** documents that are used to prove that something is true or correct, or as a record of something: *He was asked to provide documentation of his personal finances.*

2 documents that explain how a piece of equipment

works: *The lack of documentation has caused customers a significant amount of frustration.*

document of title —see under TITLE

documents against acceptance *n* [plural] an arrangement in which an importer will be given the documents giving them ownership of goods only after accepting and promising to pay the related BILL OF EXCHANGE —compare DOCUMENTS AGAINST CASH

documents-against-acceptance bill —see under BILL OF EXCHANGE

documents against cash also **documents against payment**, **documents against presentation** *n* [plural] an arrangement in which an importer will be given the documents giving them ownership of goods only after paying the related BILL OF EXCHANGE —compare DOCUMENTS AGAINST ACCEPTANCE

documents-against-payment bill —see under BILL OF EXCHANGE

dodge[1] /dɒdʒ‖dɑːdʒ/ *v* [T] *informal* to avoid doing something, especially paying for something, even though it is illegal not to do it or pay it: *We suspected they were dodging VAT and alerted Customs and Excise.* | *ways in which the tobacco industry had dodged bans on advertising*

dodge[2] *n* [C] *informal* something dishonest that is done to avoid a rule or law

tax dodge an illegal way of paying less tax: *Tax relief on forest ownership was abolished after it was revealed that business corporations were investing in conifer plantations as a tax dodge.* —**tax dodger** *n* [C] *the Inland Revenue's work in seeking out tax dodgers*

Dodge index —see under INDEX[1]

dodg•er /ˈdɒdʒə‖ˈdɑːdʒər/ *n* [C] *informal* **tax/licence dodger** someone who does something dishonest to avoid paying taxes: *When cases reach the courts, convicted tax dodgers can expect to receive a severe sentence.*

dodg•y /ˈdɒdʒi‖ˈdɑː-/ *adj* comparative **dodgier** superlative **dodgiest** *informal* **1** slightly dangerous or likely to cause problems: *Norton Disk Doctor can perform miracles on a dodgy hard disk.* | *It's always a bit dodgy, sacking a manager.*

2 dishonest or illegal: *Some dealers have an inkling which shares are dodgy.* | *dodgy land deals*

DoE /ˌdiː əʊ ˈiː‖-oʊ-/ *n* **1** Department of the Environment; a government department in Britain which is responsible for laws affecting, for example the land, sea, and rivers

2 Department of Energy; a government agency in the United States which is responsible for laws affecting the supply of, for example electricity, gas and NUCLEAR POWER

dog /dɒg‖dɒːg/ *n* [C] in the GROWTH/SHARE MATRIX, a product with low market share in a low-growth market

dogs•bod•y /ˈdɒgzˌbɒdi‖ˈdɒːgzˌbɑːdi/ *n* plural **dogsbodies** [C] *BrE informal* someone who is given the uninteresting or unpleasant jobs to do: *I got myself a job as typist and general dogsbody on a small magazine.*

do it yourself —see under DIY

dol. written abbreviation for DOLLAR

dol•drums /ˈdɒldrəmz‖ˈdoʊl-, ˈdɑːl-, ˈdɒːl-/ *n* [plural] *informal* if an industry or market is in the doldrums, there is very little increase in prices or very little trade taking place: *The mortgage market has been in the doldrums for three years and lending is falling.*

dole /dəʊl‖doʊl/ *n* [U] *BrE informal old-fashioned* in Britain, money that the government gives to people who are looking for work; WELFARE *AmE*: *There are few vacancies for horticulturists, and he is again **on the dole**.* | *unemployed demonstrators protesting at dole cuts*

dole queue —see under QUEUE[1]

dol•lar /ˈdɒlə‖ˈdɑːlər/ written abbreviation **dol.** *n* [C] **1** the name of the currency unit used in the United States, Australia, New Zealand, Hong Kong, Singapore and some other countries. The symbol for the dollar is $: *Chewing gum importers face a fine of as much as 10,000 Singapore dollars (US$6,171).*

2 the almighty dollar the idea that money is more important than any other thing, often used to criticize activities done only for profit: *responsible executives who put public interest and taste before the almighty dollar* —see also HALF-DOLLAR

dollar area —see under AREA

dollar-cost averaging *n* [U] FINANCE when a small amount of money is invested in the same stock over a period of time: *If the stock market continues to rise over the long-term, dollar-cost averaging almost guarantees investment gains.*

dol•lar•i•za•tion also **dollarisation** *BrE* /ˌdɒləraɪˈzeɪʃən‖ˌdɑːlərə-/ *n* [U] **1** when people in countries outside the US prefer to use the dollar, rather than their country's own currency: *High inflation has led many Russians to hold US dollars rather than roubles. This dollarisation is only now starting to reverse.*

2 when a country makes its currency the same value as the dollar, or keeps its currency at the same rate in relation to the dollar —**dollarized** also **dollarised** *BrE adj*: *As a dollarised economy, the Argentinian peso has the same value as the US dollar.*

dols. written abbreviation for dollars

do•main /dəˈmeɪn, dəʊ-‖də-, doʊ-/ *n* [C] **1** an area of activity, interest, or knowledge: *the scientific domain.*

2 sb/sth's domain an activity controlled by one person, organization, industry etc: *Marketing treasury bills had been the **exclusive domain** of banks* (=only banks could do it).

3 an area of land or property owned and controlled by one person or organization: *Mr Li now controls a vast domain of container terminals, supermarkets and power plants.*

4 the public domain if information or property is in the public domain, it is available for everyone to use and not kept secret, or not kept as the property of a particular person or organization: *Company lawyers believe the word 'deluxe' is **in the public domain**.* | *A change in the law extended copyright protection to many books that otherwise would have **entered the public domain*** (=become available for anyone to publish).

domain name *n* [C] COMPUTING the address of a computer NETWORK connected to the INTERNET. A domain name is followed by an abbreviation which could show its type, for example .com for a company, or its country of origin, for example .uk for the United Kingdom

do•mes•tic /dəˈmestɪk/ *adj* [only before a noun] **1** relating to the home or the family: *dramatic rises planned on domestic fuel bills*

2 relating to the country you live in, rather than abroad: *The government hoped to halt the overall decline in **domestic investment** by restructuring industrial production.* | *Only farmers with a federal license can sell peanuts on the **domestic market**.* | *Foreign concern over human rights issues does not constitute interference in **domestic affairs**.*

domestic consumption —see under CONSUMPTION

domestic credit expansion —see under EXPANSION

domestic currency —see under CURRENCY

domestic demand —see under DEMAND

domestic investment —see under INVESTMENT

D

domestic market —see under MARKET[1]

domestic policy —see under POLICY

domestic port —see under PORT[1]

dom•i•cile /ˈdɒmɪsaɪl‖ˈdɑː-, ˈdoʊ-/ *n* [C,U] LAW the country in which a person normally lives, and that is thought of as their permanent home: *Formerly the domicile of a wife was necessarily the same as that of her husband.* —compare RESIDENCE

domicile of choice [singular] a country in which a person decides to live, although it is not the country in which they were born: *If he marries a German woman, he has a domicile of choice in Germany.*

domicile of origin [singular] the country in which a person was born: *Every person receives at birth a domicile of origin.*

dom•i•ciled /ˈdɒmɪsaɪld‖ˈdɑː-,ˈdoʊ-/ *adj* LAW **be domiciled in** if a person is domiciled in a particular country, they live there, and it is thought of as their permanent home: *the requirement for all owners to reside and be domiciled in the United Kingdom*

do•nate /dəʊˈneɪt‖ˈdoʊneɪt/ *v* [T] to give money or something valuable to a person or organization in order to help them **donate sth to sb**: *Laurance S. Rockefeller donated $21 million to Princeton University for a center to study and teach human values.* —**donation** [C,U] *The maximum individual donation to political candidates, now $1,000, will be cut in half.*

do•nee /ˌdəʊˈniː◂‖ˌdoʊ-/ *n* [C] LAW **1** someone who receives money or other valuable things from another person: *All the property given to the donee by the donor will be subject to tax.* —compare BENEFICIARY
2 someone who has been given a POWER OF ATTORNEY: *She was of sufficient capability to be a suitable donee.*

do•nor /ˈdəʊnə‖ˈdoʊnər/ *n* [C] someone who gives money or other valuable things to people who are ill, hungry, poor etc: *His fines were paid by an* ***anonymous donor***. | *Japan is Asia's biggest* ***foreign aid donor***, *giving over $1.1 billion in official development assistance and loans.*

door to door *adv* **1** someone who works or goes door to door goes to each house in a street: *In the past, most insurance plans were sold strictly door to door by companies such as Prudential and Pearl.*
2 goods that are delivered door to door are brought from the factory to a person's home: *a unique system to deliver carpets door to door from Scotland to anywhere in Europe*

door-to-door *adj* [only before a noun] **1** door-to-door sales, collections etc involve going to each house in a street in order sell something, to collect information etc: *They will be raising funds through door-to-door collections.* | ***door-to-door salesmen***
2 a door-to-door service delivers goods directly from a factory to a person's house: *Although its home market is Europe, the company can offer* ***door-to-door transport*** *to other destinations.* | *the closure of British Rail's* ***door-to-door parcels service***

dor•mant /ˈdɔːmənt‖ˈdɔːr-/ *adj* something that is dormant has not been active for a long time, although it may become active in the future: *The project* ***lay dormant*** *for two years until we found a co-sponsor.* | *Someone tampered with IBM systems by planting a dormant bug due to wipe out whole data banks on Friday 13th.*

dormant account —see under ACCOUNT[1]

dor•mi•to•ry /ˈdɔːmɪtəri‖ˈdɔːrmɪtɔːri/ *n* plural **dormitories** [C] *BrE* an area just outside a large town where many of the people working in the town live: *The development could reduce it to just another dormitory for Hull.* | *a* ***dormitory suburb*** *of Lyons*

DOS /dɒs‖dɑːs/ *n* [U] COMPUTING Disk Operating System; computer software that controls and manages the different operations done by a computer, especially storing and finding information: *The package will run on Unix, DOS and Novell networks.*

dosh /dɒʃ‖dɑːʃ/ *n* [U] *BrE informal* money: *Cycling is good fun and saves you heaps of dosh!*

dos•si•er /ˈdɒsieɪ‖ˈdɒːsjeɪ, ˈdɑː-/ *n* [C] a collection of written papers which contain detailed information about a particular subject or person: *a thick dossier containing new information about the alleged confessions* | *She had* ***a dossier of*** *complaints about her neighbours.* | *The FBI have* ***kept a dossier on*** *him since his radical student days.*

DOT *n* Department of Transportation, a government department in the US which is responsible for laws affecting, for example, roads and vehicles

DoT /ˌdiː əʊ ˈtiː‖-oʊ-/ *n* Department of Transport; a government department in Britain which is responsible for laws affecting, for example, roads and vehicles

dot /dɒt‖dɑːt/ *n* **1** a small round mark, for example the one used over the letter i. If you are telling someone your E-MAIL address, you refer to the round mark between the words as dot: *If you need to email me, you can contact me at mick dot murphy at AWL dot com.*
2 on the dot if something happens at a certain time on the dot, it happens at exactly that time: *The meeting begins at 9.30 on the dot.*

dot ma•trix print•er —see under PRINTER

dotted line *n* **sign on the dotted line** to agree officially to something by writing your name on an official or legal document: *Demand that the repairs are done before you sign on the dotted line.*

doub•le[1] /ˈdʌbəl/ *adj* twice as big, twice as much, or twice as many as usual, or twice as big, much, or many as something else: *The number of men receiving professional degrees today is still nearly double that of women.*

double[2] *n* [C,U] something that is nearly twice the size, quantity, value or strength of something else: *'What did they offer you?' 'Ten thousand.' 'I'll give you double.'*

double[3] *v* [I,T] to become twice as much or as many, or to make something twice as big: *The costs of providing medical insurance for employees has doubled in recent years.* | *GE plans to more than double the size of its railcar leasing operation.*

double-cross *v* [T] to cheat someone who you are involved in an illegal or dishonest activity with: *He was living in fear of drug traffickers he had double-crossed.*

double dealing *n* [U] *informal* cheating and deceiving people: *Politicians are always being accused of duplicity and double dealing for party or personal advantage.*

double declining balance —see under BALANCE[1]

double density *adj* [only before a noun] COMPUTING a double density computer disk has twice as much space for storing information as some earlier kinds of disk had

double-digit *adj* [only before a noun] relating to numbers between 10 and 99: *Few economists expect a return to the double-digit inflation and interest rates seen at the end of the 1980s.* | *double-digit growth in the Chinese market*

double-digit inflation —see under INFLATION

double dipping *n* [U] *disapproving* when someone receives money from two different sources for doing the same job: *Double dipping, using subsidized water to grow crops like cotton and rice that are also subsidized because of oversupply, costs taxpayers hundreds of millions of dollars a year.*

double-dip recession —see under RECESSION

double entry book-keeping —see under BOOK-KEEPING

double figures *n* [plural] the numbers between 10 and 99: *Inflation reached 9.4% in April, and is expected to top double figures before falling.*

double income no kids —see DINKS

double-income tax relief —see under TAX RELIEF

double indemnity —see under INDEMNITY

double insurance —see under INSURANCE

double option —see under OPTION

double taxation —see under TAXATION

double time —see under TIME

double-witching also **double-witching hour** *n* [singular] *informal* FINANCE a time on a financial market when two types of FUTURES (=contracts to buy or sell shares etc at a fixed price on a fixed date) or OPTIONS (=rights to buy or sell shares etc at a fixed price within a fixed period of time) both EXPIRE (=reach the end of their life) at the same time: *London had to cope with the first double-witching – simultaneous endings of the FTSE 100 future and FTSE 100 index options.* —compare TRIPLE-WITCHING

doubtful debt —see under DEBT

dough /dəʊ‖doʊ/ *n* [U] *informal* money: *His family stake is worth just over £1.2bn – a lot of dough.*

dove /dʌv/ *n* [C] a politician or official who does not believe in using force or firm action when dealing with problems —compare HAWK[1]

Dow Jones averages —see under AVERAGE[2]

Dow Jones Industrial Average —see under AVERAGE[2]

Dow Jones industrials —see under INDUSTRIALS

Dow Jones Transportation Average —see under AVERAGE[2]

Dow Jones Utilities Average —see under AVERAGE[2]

down[1] /daʊn/ *adv* **1** if an amount or the level of something goes down, it falls to a lower amount or level: *The cuts have taken Wimpey's UK workforce* ***down by*** *30% | By lunchtime, the 100-index was down 4.2 at 3053.1. | 59% of companies report sales volume down on a year ago.*

2 cash/money down FINANCE a money paid as a first payment towards a larger sum. Cash down can also mean paying for something immediately in notes and coins rather than with a cheque: *The sum of money to be paid is $50 cash down and ten monthly installments of $5.* —see also DOWN PAYMENT

down[2] *adj* COMPUTING if a machine, system or piece of electrical equipment is down, it is not working: *My system went down over the weekend and I didn't get any emails. | The printer can be used even when the telecommunication lines are down.*

down[3] *v* **down tools** if the people who work in a factory down tools, they refuse to work: *The lads from the nail factory were in an angry mood and had just downed tools in protest against their foreman.* —compare STRIKE[2]

down·grade /ˈdaʊngreɪd/ *v* [T] **1** to give something less importance, for example by spending less money on it or reducing its value: *Glaxo is planning to downgrade some of its products from prescription status.*

2 to make someone's job less important or well-paid than it was before: *Eighty-eight middle managers had been made redundant, downgraded or fired. | Services have been reduced and temporary contracts are being used to downgrade or replace qualified staff.* —compare UPGRADE[1]

3 ECONOMICS to reduce an amount or value that you had calculated or guessed: *Analysts downgraded four-year profit projections and exposed Lincat to the harsher side of stockmarket life. | The company's long-term debt-rating has been downgraded from triple-A to double-A-2.* —compare UPGRADE[1]

down·hill /ˌdaʊnˈhɪl◂/ *adv* if something that was successful is going downhill, it is starting to fail, and is getting gradually worse: *Sales had peaked in 1997 at $3.8 million but had* ***gone*** *steadily* ***downhill****.*

down·load /ˌdaʊnˈləʊd‖-ˈloʊd/ *v* [T] COMPUTING to move computer software or information from one computer to another, usually from a large computer to a smaller one: *If you have a modem you can log on to a bulletin board and download it. | The advantage of COMMUNITEL is that pages of information can* ***be downloaded from*** *Prestel.*

down·mar·ket[1] /ˌdaʊnˈmɑːkɪ̍t◂‖-ɑːr-/ also **downscale** *AmE* *adj* involving goods and services that are cheap and perhaps not of very good quality compared to other goods etc of the same type, or the people that buy them: *The mail order business has never been able to break away from its traditional downmarket image. | downscale, blue-collar consumers*

downmarket[2] also **downscale** *AmE* — *adv* **1 go/move downmarket/downscale** to start buying or selling cheaper goods or services: *Mercedes will move further downmarket with the Smart, a tiny two seater for urban use.*

2 take sth downmarket/downscale to change a product or a service, or people's ideas about it, so that it is cheaper or seems cheaper and more popular: *He was accused of taking BBC Radio 3 downmarket to compete with a new commercial station. | He opened some 60 more stores and took the chain downscale.*

down payment —see under PAYMENT

down·scale /ˈdaʊnskeɪl/ *v* [I,T] MARKETING *AmE* to sell or buy cheaper goods of lower quality: *She predicts that American consumers will downscale in reaction to the recession. | Other organisations will downscale their programs, sell more t-shirts and work for other sources of revenue.*

down·shift /ˈdaʊnʃɪft/ *v* [I] if someone downshifts, they willingly choose to do a less important, difficult, or STRESSFUL job, so that they are under less pressure and have more time to enjoy their life —**downshifting** *n* [U]

downside risk —see under RISK[1]

down·size /ˈdaʊnsaɪz/ *v journalism* **1** [T] to make a product, part etc smaller: *Sales of copper suffered as many items in which it is used were downsized, and less of the metal was needed.*

2 [I,T] if a company downsizes, or someone downsizes it, the company reduces the number of employees and levels of management that it has: *If your company downsizes and you are over 50, your working life may be over. | We have cut expenses and downsized our operations so that we will be in a position to capitalize on a gradually improving market.* —see also RESTRUCTURE —**downsized** *adj*: *In downsized organisations, there may not be anyone who has been on the staff long enough to teach the other managers anything.*

down·siz·ing /ˈdaʊnˌsaɪzɪŋ/ *n* [U] HUMAN RESOURCES when the managers of a company decide to reduce the number of people working for the company in order to save money or increase profits: *Digital has not yet put a figure on the number of job losses involved in the downsizing. | Middle managers are the usual victims of downsizing.*

down·stream /ˌdaʊnˈstriːm◂/ *adj* relating to an activity, product etc that depends on or happens after another activity etc: *With co-operatives, farmers have more control over downstream activities such as the marketing of their crops.* —**downstream** *adv* —compare UPSTREAM

down·swing /ˈdaʊnswɪŋ/ *n* [C] another name for a DOWNTURN

down•tick /ˈdaʊntɪk/ *n* [C] FINANCE the sale of a SECURITY at a price lower than the original or earlier price: *The short sale was barred at the 4 pm closing price during the regular session because it was on a downtick.* | *The New York Stock Exchange's* ***downtick rule*** *seeks to stabilize the market by curbing stock index arbitrage trades.*

down time —see under TIME

down•time /ˈdaʊntaɪm/ *n* [U] **1** MANUFACTURING time lost in producing goods because something has gone wrong, for example because a machine has broken or materials have not arrived: *loss of revenue due to downtime* | *With less downtime at the plant, customers can start to expect significant savings.*
2 COMPUTING time lost on a computer NETWORK (=a system of connected computers) because the system is not working properly: *Last year alone, computer downtime cost the company $4,000 in lost productivity.*

down•town /ˌdaʊnˈtaʊn◂/ *adj* [only before a noun] *AmE* the downtown area of a city is the main business district where many shops and offices are located: *Price Waterhouse has about 100 personnel in its downtown San Diego office.* —**downtown** *adv*: *I* ***went downtown*** *to open up the store.*

D

down•turn /ˈdaʊntɜːn‖-tɜːrn/ *n* [C,U] ECONOMICS the part of the economic cycle when prices or the value of stocks, shares etc fall: *Aspreys has proved largely immune to* ***economic downturn.*** | *The decade of the 1980s had its upturns as well as* ***downturns in*** *food production.* —compare RECESSION, UPTURN, —see also ***turn down*** under TURN[1]

down•ward /ˈdaʊnwəd‖-wərd/ also **downwards** *adv* towards a lower position or level: *Inflation for June was lower at 3.9%, and the underlying trend appears downward.* | *Competition among the owners of a particular resource may tend to force its price downwards.* —**downward** *adj*: *Brazil's debt had an important role to play in creating* ***downward pressure*** *on the currency.*

down•zon•ing /ˈdaʊnˌzəʊnɪŋ‖-ˌzoʊ-/ *n* [U] *AmE* when official rules restrict the type of buildings allowed on a particular area of land, or on the type of work that can be done in those buildings

dow•ry /ˈdaʊəri‖ˈdaʊri/ *n* plural **dowries** [C] **1** FINANCE *journalism* money which is given by one company to a company it is trying to buy. The dowry is meant to encourage the second company to agree to the arrangement: *The government has already written off £5 billion worth of debts and thrown in an extra £1.6 billion dowry.* | *7% of group revenue comes from its subsidiaries in Zimbabwe, the dowry from South African investor Allied Electronics Pty.*
2 money or valuable gifts that in some cultures the family of a BRIDE gives to her husband when she gets married

doz. written abbreviation for DOZEN

doz•en /ˈdʌzən/ written abbreviation **doz.** *n* plural **dozens** or **dozen** [C] a group of twelve things: *More than a dozen managers have come and gone.* | *The extension to a wider base has won them at least* ***half a dozen*** (=six) *valuable new clients.*

DPP abbreviation for DIRECTOR OF PUBLIC PROSECUTIONS

DPS FINANCE written abbreviation for DIVIDEND PER SHARE

Dr. written abbreviation for Doctor

draft[1] /drɑːft‖dræft/ *n* [C] a document or piece of writing that has to be checked and possibly changed, and so is not yet in its finished form: *This is only a rough draft of the letter.* | *When can I have the* ***first draft*** *of your proposal?* | *a* ***draft report****, which the Committee has read and considered in detail.*

exposure draft *BrE* ACCOUNTING a document distributed by the FINANCIAL STANDARDS ACCOUNTING BOARD which suggests a change in the ACCOUNTING rules. People who are affected by the rules are asked to comment on the exposure draft before it becomes law —see also BANK DRAFT

draft[2] *v* [T] to write a letter, report etc that will need to be changed before it is in its finished form: *I'll ask our contracts department to draft an agreement.*

draft terms —see under TERM[1]

drain[1] /dreɪn/ *n* [C usually singular] **a drain on sth** something that continuously uses up a lot of money, time, or effort: *This project has been a serious drain on our financial resources.*

drain[2] *v* [T] to use too much of something so that there is not enough left: *The high cost of road maintenance is draining funds from the local government budget.* **drain sb/sth of sth**: *Savings and loans losses are continuing to drain the Treasury of $20 million weekly.*

draining reserves —see under RESERVES

draught /drɑːft‖dræft/ *n* [C] a ship's draught is the distance from the bottom of the ship to the level of the water. This distance is the depth of water that a ship needs to float in

laden draught the draught when a ship is loaded

light draught the draught before a ship is loaded

load draught the distance from the bottom of a ship to the level of the water when the ship is loaded. This is the line to which the ship is allowed to load

draw /drɔː‖drɒː/ *v* past tense **drew** past participle **drawn** [T] **1** also **draw out** to take money from your bank account: *Many credit cards can now be used to draw cash from ATMs around the world.* | *All the money in his account has been drawn out.*
2 to receive an amount of money regularly from your employer or from the government: *In the first year of the partnership, Jenny drew a salary of £30,000.* | *You are entitled to draw unemployment benefit.*
3 to write out and sign a cheque or BANK ORDER: *I'll draw a cheque on the company account.*
4 BANKING to write a BILL OF EXCHANGE: *Bills are drawn by the exporter on the issuing or confirming bank.*

draw sth ↔ **down** *phr v* [T] **1** to obtain money as part of a loan that has already been agreed, or to use money that has been saved: *He drew down the final $25 million of the Bankers Trust loan.* | *A huge wave of Japanese will soon reach retirement and begin to draw down their life savings.*
2 to use something that has been reserved or stored: *Consuming nations should draw down their high oil inventories before asking OPEC to produce more.*

draw sth ↔ **up** *phr v* [T] to write out or prepare an agreement, list, plan etc: *The chairman had drawn up an agenda.* | *The first thing you need to do is draw up a business plan.* | *Our selection committee drew up the list of candidates.*

draw•back /ˈdrɔːbæk‖ˈdrɒː-/ *n* **1** [C] a disadvantage of a situation, product etc that makes it less attractive: *There are drawbacks to being a sole trader, but they are outweighed by the benefits.* | *one of the main drawbacks of this scheme*

customs drawback ◆ [C] a Customs document given to an exporter so that they can claim back customs duty paid on goods they earlier imported
◆ [U] a repayment of customs duty when goods or materials on which import duty has been paid are later exported

draw•down /ˈdrɔːdaʊn‖ˈdrɒː-/ also **draw-down** *n* **1** [C,U] when a stock or supply of something is used: *Strong import demand for coarse grains will result in a large drawdown in world coarse grain stocks.* | *a drawdown of 6.4 million barrels in gasoline stocks*
2 [U] when someone obtains money as part of a loan that has already been agreed or uses money that they

have saved: *an income drawdown plan that allows you to keep your fund invested while drawing a regular income*
3 [C] a reduction in the value of an investment: *Even if an investor says he is prepared for a 30% drawdown, he always finds it a worse experience then he imagined when it happens.*

draw•ee /ˌdrɔːˈiː‖ˌdrɒː-/ *n* [C] BANKING **1** the bank that is given an instruction to pay a sum of money to someone when a person who has an account with that bank writes a cheque or BANK DRAFT
2 the person named on a BILL OF EXCHANGE who is expected to accept it and to pay it

draw•er /ˈdrɔːər‖ˈdrɒːər/ *n* [C] BANKING **1** a person who writes a cheque and so gives an instruction to his or her bank to pay a sum of money to someone
2 refer to drawer written abbreviation **R/D** words written by a bank on a cheque that has not been paid, usually because there is not enough money in the account of the person who wrote it
3 a person who signs a BILL OF EXCHANGE that gives an instruction to another person to pay a sum of money at a particular time

dress code *n* [C] the way that you are expected to dress in a particular situation, especially as an employee of a particular company: *The company liberalized its dress code to allow women to wear slacks* (=trousers) *to the office.*

drift[1] /drɪft/ *v* [I] to go slowly up or down in value, without any particular direction: *London shares drifted in the absence of fresh news.* | *The dollar* ***drifted lower*** *against other major currencies in thin trading.* | *The pound* ***drifted down*** *again yesterday.* | *The Nasdaq Composite Index* ***drifted higher*** *throughout the session to close with a gain of 1.27%,*

drift[2] *n* [C] a slow change or development from one situation, opinion etc to another **+to/towards**: *What marked out the drift towards recession was that the service sector would be as badly hit as manufacturing.*

drip advertising —see under ADVERTISING

drip campaign —see under CAMPAIGN

drip method *n* [singular] MARKETING a way of selling goods or services to people by making regular telephone calls to them over a long period of time to persuade them to buy

drive[1] /draɪv/ *v* past tense **drove** past participle **driven**
drive a hard bargain to succeed by arguing in a very determined way in making an agreement that is very much to your advantage: *Sorrell drives a hard bargain and may not sell at all if he can't get a suitable price.*
drive sth ↔ **down** *phr v* [T] to force prices, costs etc to fall: *pressures that could drive down interest rates*
drive sth ↔ **up** *phr v* [T] to force prices, costs etc to rise quickly: *A shortage is all it would take to tighten supplies and drive up prices.*

drive[2] *n* [C] **1** a planned effort by an organization to achieve something: *They have decided to sell some parts of the business in a drive to raise capital.* | *The airlines will step up their* ***recruitment drive*** *for pilots in North America.*
sales drive a series of events or activities aimed at advertising a product and increasing sales; SALES CAMPAIGN: *The company expects its* ***sales drive*** *in SE Asia to lift exports to the region by 20%.*
2 COMPUTING part of a computer that reads information from a disk: *Insert the floppy disk into Drive A.*
CD-ROM drive a part of a computer into which you can put CD-ROMs and read information from them: *an ordinary personal computer with a built-in CD-ROM drive*
disk drive COMPUTING a piece of equipment in a computer system used to pass information to or from a disk: *The software scans all the disk drives to check for viruses.* | *a 6GB hard disk drive*
tape drive a small machine attached to a computer that passes information from a computer to a tape or from a tape to a computer

drive-in *adj* [only before a noun] a drive-in restaurant, cinema, bank etc allows you to buy food, watch a film etc without leaving your car —**drive-in** *n* [C] *The only theater in town is a drive-in.*

drive-in store —see under STORE[1]

-driv•en /ˈdrɪvən/ *suffix* **1** if something is petrol-driven, computer-driven etc, it is operated or controlled by petrol, a computer etc: *Lower interest rates set off computer-driven 'buy' programs that sent stocks soaring late in the day.* | *Changes in transmission regulations will allow the company to sell satellite-driven phone services worldwide.*
2 if something is market-driven, client-driven etc, the market or the client is the main force or influence on it: *We listen to our customers. We are a* ***client-driven firm.*** | *In a* ***market-driven economy,*** *people are forced to invest by the need to make profits.* | *As the PC market has become* ***price-driven,*** *Compaq's market share has dropped.* | *Japan is less export-driven than in the past.* —compare -LED, -ORIENTED

driv•er /ˈdraɪvə‖-ər/ *n* [C] **1** a person who drives a car, bus, train etc
2 something that has an important influence on other things: *Population growth is the biggest single driver of atmospheric pollution.*
3 COMPUTING a program that controls the operation of a piece of equipment: *The program automatically chooses the correct driver for whatever option you're configuring.* | *a 32 bit ScSC driver, featuring a Solaris operating system*

drive-through *adj* [only before a noun] *AmE* a drive-through bank, restaurant etc that you can use without getting out of your car: *drive-through pizza restaurants* —**drive-through** *n* [C]

drive-up window *n* [C] *AmE* a place at a restaurant, shop, or pharmacy where people can collect their food or shopping without getting out of their cars

droop /druːp/ *v* [I] if prices, sales etc droop, they start to fall: *In Tokyo share prices drooped during Emperor Hirohito's illness.*

drop[1] /drɒp‖drɑːp/ *v* past tense and past participle **dropped** present participle **dropping** **1** [I] to fall to a lower level or amount **+ to/from**: *Second quarter earnings this year dropped to $157 million from $182 million.* | *Stock prices* ***dropped sharply*** *today.* | *The dollar dropped against the Japanese yen today.* | *Demand has dropped by 7%.*
2 [T] to stop doing or planning something: *Plans to expand the business have been quietly dropped.* | *She was persuaded to drop the harassment lawsuit.*
3 [T] *informal* to lose money in business, a game etc: *He dropped £1000 on the stockmarket.*
drop off also **drop away** *phr v* [I] to become lower in level or amount: *Sales have dropped off in recent months.* | *With the strong pound, tourism has dropped off.* —see also DROP-OFF

drop[2] *n* [C usually singular] if there is a drop in the amount, level, or number of something, it goes down or becomes less: *Yesterday saw a* ***sharp drop*** *in stock prices.* | *Business is expecting* ***a drop in*** *interest rates later this year.* | *The first quarter total shows a drop from the same quarter last year.* —see also LEAFLET DROP, MAIL DROP

drop dead date —see under DATE[1]

drop-lock *n* [C] a bond or loan with an interest rate that changes but does not go below a level decided in advance

drop-off *n* [C] **1** if there is a drop-off in the amount,

level, or number of something, it goes down or becomes less: *There has been a drop-off in tourism this year.* | *temporary drop-offs in sales*
2 a delivery, or the place where something is delivered to: *A truckload carrier takes a full cargo from one point to another, without any intervening pickups or drop-offs.*

drop-shipping *n* [U] **1** an arrangement between a company that sells goods and the supplier or producer of the goods. The goods are advertised and marketed by the company selling them, but delivered directly from the supplier or producer to the customer
2 *AmE* when letters, packages etc are taken to a place nearer to the postal address before being posted, in order to save US postal service charges

drug /drʌg/ *n* [C] **1** a medicine or substance for making medicines; PHARMACEUTICAL: *a drug used in the treatment of cancer* | *a drugs company*
over-the-counter drug abbreviation **OTC drug** a drug that you can buy in a shop without a written order from a doctor
prescription drug a drug that you can only obtain with a written order from a doctor
2 an illegal substance that people take to make them feel happy or excited: *The business was secretly laundering drug money.*

D

drug·store /ˈdrʌgstɔː‖-stɔːr/ *n* [C] *AmE* a shop where you can buy medicines, beauty products etc; PHARMACY, CHEMIST'S *BrE*

drum¹ /drʌm/ *n* [C] a large round container for storing liquids such as oil, chemicals etc: *a stack of oil drums*

drum² *v* past tense and past participle **drummed** present participle **drumming**
drum sth ↔ **up** *phr v* [T] if you drum up business or support, you make an effort to get more of it: *We have been looking for new ways to* ***drum up business.***

dry /draɪ/ *v* past tense and past participle **dried**
dry up *phr v* [I] to no longer be available or active: *There are fears that investment could dry up.* | *Sales could dry up if this trend continues.*

dry cargo —see under CARGO

dry dock *n* [C,U] an enclosed place used for repairing or building ships, from which the water can be pumped in and out: *We were towed to a dry dock in New York.* | *The ship is in dry dock for an overhaul.*

dry farming —see under FARMING

dry goods —see under GOODS

dry lease —see under LEASE²

dry measure —see under MEASURE¹

dry ship —see under SHIP¹

DSS abbreviation for DEPARTMENT OF SOCIAL SECURITY

DST *n* [singular] *AmE* daylight saving time; the time during the summer when clocks are one hour ahead of standard time

DTI abbreviation for DEPARTMENT OF TRADE AND INDUSTRY

DTP abbreviation for DESKTOP PUBLISHING

dual capacity *n* [U] FINANCE when MARKETMAKERS are allowed to buy and sell shares on their own account, as well as acting as buying and selling agent on behalf of others, the situation that has existed on the London stockmarket since BIG BANG: *Under dual capacity a member firm can act as both agent and principal whereas previously jobbers and brokers were separated.*

dual purpose fund —see under FUND¹

dual sourcing —see under SOURCING

dud /dʌd/ *n* [C] *informal* something that is useless or of bad quality, especially because it does not work correctly: *The new system turned out to be a market dud.* —**dud** *adj*: *dud results from biotech companies*

dud cheque —see under CHEQUE

due /djuː‖duː/ *adj* **1** [not before a noun] an amount of money that is due is an amount that should be paid at a particular time: *Breakwater said it was unable to meet an interest payment due yesterday.* —see also PAST DUE
2 [only before a noun] proper and expected by law: *He was charged with driving without due care and attention.*

due bill —see under BILL¹

due date —see under DATE¹

due diligence —see under DILIGENCE

due process —see under PROCESS¹

dues /djuːz‖duːz/ *n* [plural] regular payments made to an organization such as a professional association or TRADE UNION by its members; SUBSCRIPTION *BrE*: *Institute dues, which average $112 per member, were last raised three years ago.*
dock dues charges paid to a port by a shipping company that uses it to load or unload goods: *the dock dues levied by Rochester Corporation on coal and coke*
harbour dues *BrE*, **harbor dues** *AmE* money that a ship owner must pay for keeping a ship in a harbour. The amount of money charged is usually based on the number of tons of CARGO the ship is carrying: *The money collected at the port included customs duties, excise on spirits and harbour dues.*

dues checkoff *n* [C] when dues for membership of a TRADE UNION are taken out of people's wages by their employer and paid directly to the union: *Unions can't finance benefit plans with union dues checkoffs.* —see also AUTOMATIC CHECKOFF

dull /dʌl/ *adj* if business on a financial market is dull, not many people are buying or selling: *Investors were busy moving in and out of two-year Treasury notes yesterday, providing a bit of excitement to an otherwise dull session.* | *The unusually light calendar of economic releases this week is largely responsible for the* ***dull trading.***

du·ly /ˈdjuːli‖ˈduːli/ *adv* in the proper, expected, or legal way: *State officials were duly authorized by the state legislature to enter into the agreement.*

dumb /dʌm/ *v*
dumb sth ↔ **down** *phr v* [I,T] *disapproving* if something dumbs down, or someone dumbs it down, it is made so simple to understand that it is no longer interesting or useful: *British television is dumbing down to even greater levels of stupidity.* | *Expert users of Windows may feel that their computer has been dumbed down to suit less sophisticated users.*

dumb·size /ˈdʌmsaɪz/ *v* [T] *journalism* to reduce the number of people working for a company to a level where it is no longer possible to do the work effectively or well —compare DOWNSIZE

dumb terminal —see under TERMINAL

dum·my¹ /ˈdʌmi/ *n* plural **dummies** [C] **1** a product that is made to look like a real product and is used for testing, obtaining people's opinions etc
2 a test advertisement or design
3 a model of a human used for showing clothes in a shop window or for testing car safety

dummy² *adj* [only before a noun] **1** a dummy product is made to look like a real one and is used for tests, getting people's opinions etc: *72% of the men in the group taking a dummy pill continued to lose hair.*
2 a dummy organization is used to hide the real owner of assets, or to hide criminal activities: *They had set up a series of dummy corporations to buy and sell 8,000 acres of useless New Mexico desert.*
3 a dummy activity is used to make people think that something is happening when it is not: *They used dummy trades to create a false impression of a more active market than really existed.*

dump /dʌmp/ *v* [T] **1** to put waste in a particular place, especially illegally: *11 million gallons of crude oil were illegally dumped into Prince William Sound.*
2 to sell something that you do not want: *But before you call your broker and dump all your stockholdings, consider some other data.*
3 to sell products cheaply in an export market, perhaps in order to increase your share of the market there: *Japanese-made display screens are being dumped in the US at below-market prices.* —**dumping** *n* [U] *Anti-dumping duties are intended to eliminate the difference between an allegedly unfair import price and a higher home-market price.*
4 COMPUTING to copy information from a computer onto another computer, or onto a TAPE or a DISK: *Orders can be placed by credit card; they are then automatically dumped into the Flowers computer system.*

dun /dʌn/ *v* past tense and past participle **dunned** present participle **dunning** [T] *AmE informal* to demand payment of an unpaid debt: *The IRS dunned the Chagras for $6.3 million in back tax and penalties.*

Dun and Brad•street /ˌdʌn ənd ˈbrædstriːt/ *n* an international organization that gathers and sells information about companies, especially about their ability to pay for goods and materials that they order: *The rate of business failures rose nearly 50% in the first seven months of the year, according to Dun & Bradstreet.*

Dun's number *n* [C] a number used by Dun and Bradstreet to describe a company according to the industry it is in, the number of employees it has etc

du•op•o•ly /djuˈɒpəli‖duˈɑː-/ *n* plural **duopolies** [C usually singular] a market in which there are only two producers or sellers: *With the merger of Greyhound and Trailways, the bus duopoly has become a monopoly.*

du•plex /ˈdjuːpleks‖ˈduː-/ *n* [C] *AmE* **1** an apartment on two levels, or a house divided into two homes
2 COMPUTING when information is sent along a wire in both directions at once: *Users of videoconferencing need a good sound card with full duplex sound capabilities.*

du•pli•cate[1] /ˈdjuːplɪkɪt‖ˈduː-/ *n* [C] **1** an exact copy of a document: *Did you keep a duplicate of the contract?*
2 in duplicate if a document is written in duplicate, there are two copies of it: *Provide a separate invoice in duplicate for each purchase order.*

du•pli•cate[2] /ˈdjuːplɪkeɪt‖ˈdu-/ *v* [T] to repeat, perhaps unnecessarily, something that has already been done: *Duplicating research is costly and time-consuming.* | *The report merely duplicates earlier findings.* —**duplication** *n* [U] *We need to eliminate such wasteful duplication of effort.*

duplicate book —see under BOOK[1]

duplicate of exchange *n* plural **duplicates of exchange** [C] BANKING the second copy of a BILL OF EXCHANGE

du•plic•i•ty /djuːˈplɪsɪti‖duː-/ *n* [U] *formal* dishonest behaviour that is intended to deceive someone: *She accused him of duplicity in the negotiations.* —**duplicitous** *adj*

dur•a•ble /ˈdjʊərəbəl‖ˈdʊr-/ *adj* **1** if something is durable, it lasts a long time, even if it is used a lot: *These materials are used in televisions to make them more durable and more fire-resistant.*
2 continuing, or continuing to be successful, for a long time: *The U.S. economy is a durable beast.* —**durability** *n* [U] *The car maker has spent decades building its image of safety and durability.* | *They failed to predict the durability of the German boom.*

durable goods —see under GOODS

dur•a•bles /ˈdjʊərəbəlz‖ˈdʊr-/ *n* [plural] ECONOMICS products that are intended to have a life of more than three years from when they are made or bought; DURABLE GOODS: *Spending on durables was down in the period before Christmas*
consumer durables products that people do not buy regularly or often: *Spending is slowing; especially hard hit are consumer durables – nobody seems to want to buy a new automobile.* —compare CONSUMER NON-DURABLES

du•ra•tion /djʊˈreɪʃən‖dʊ-/ *n* [singular, U] the length of time that something continues: *We have hired her* ***for the duration of*** *the project.* | *Economists predict that the recession will be limited* ***in duration.***

du•ress /djʊˈres‖dʊ-/ *n* [U] LAW the illegal or unfair use of force or threats to make someone do something: *He claimed that he had signed the contract* ***under duress.***

dust bowl *n* [C] an area of land where farming is not possible because it is too dry, used especially to talk about parts of the mid-western United States during the 1930s: *Many Americans abandoned the dust bowl in search of jobs.*

D

Dutch auction —see under AUCTION[1]

Dutch bargain —see under BARGAIN[1]

du•ti•a•ble /ˈdjuːtiəbəl‖ˈduː-/ *adj* TAX dutiable goods are goods on which you must pay CUSTOMS DUTY: *the usual US tariffs on dutiable Canadian goods*

du•ty /ˈdjuːti‖ˈduː-/ *n* plural **duties** **1** [C usually plural] something that you have to do as part of your job: *Thomas J Hutchison was named chief executive officer, adding to his duties as president and chief operating officer.* —see also BREACH OF DUTY, BREACH OF FIDUCIARY DUTY
fiduciary duty [U] LAW the legal duty of someone who is responsible for the assets of others to protect their interests
2 [C,U] a tax you pay on something you buy, import etc: *Democrats want these imported vans classified as trucks and hit with a 25% duty.* | ***Duty is levied*** (=charged) *on every bottle of wine brought into the country.*
ad valorem duty [C,U] duty calculated as a percentage of the value of goods, rather than on their weight or the number of units
countervailing duty [C,U] a tax on goods brought into a country that is intended to protect an industry in that country from competition from abroad
customs duty [C,U] a tax on goods brought into a country that is used to raise money for the government and to protect industries in the country from competition from abroad; CUSTOMS TARIFF: *Privately imported cars are subject to a 19% customs duty.*
death duties [plural] in Britain, taxes that must be paid by someone who is left property or money by someone who has died
discriminating duty [C,U] a tax on goods brought into a country which varies according to the country that the goods are coming from
estate duty [C,U] another name for DEATH DUTIES
excise duty [C,U] a government tax on certain goods such as tobacco, alcoholic drinks, and petrol that are sold in the country
export duty [C,U] tax that is paid on goods leaving a country: *the export duties collected on timber shipped south to the US*
import duty [C,U] a tax on goods coming into a country from abroad, often used by governments as a way of reducing imports and protecting local industries; IMPORT LEVY, IMPORT TARIFF, IMPORT SURCHARGE + **on**: *a US decision to impose import duties on Honda's Canadian-assembled cars*
specific duty [C,U] duty based on a fixed amount of money for each unit of quantity or weight of a product,

rather than its value: *specific duties on tobacco and alcohol to replace the old ad valorem system*
stamp duty [U] tax that has to be paid in some countries when buying and selling things such as shares, property etc: *Dealings in the certificates will incur the 1% stamp duty levied on all share dealings.*

duty differential —see under DIFFERENTIAL[1]

duty-free *adj* duty-free goods can be bought without paying tax on them, for example at ports and airports when you are travelling abroad: *The drop in air traffic is expected to cut into duty-free perfume sales.* —**duty-free** *adv*: *Although the US had many high tariff rates in 1900, some 60% of imports came in duty-free.*

duty-free goods —see under GOODS

duty-frees *n* [plural] goods such as alcoholic drinks, tobacco etc that you can buy at ports and airports when travelling abroad without paying tax on them: *Many charter airlines make more out of duty-frees than from carrying passengers.*

duty of faith —see under FAITH

duty paid *adj* if goods are duty paid, duty has already been paid on them: *boats imported into the UK on a duty paid basis*

DVD *n* [C] digital versatile disk, digital video disk; a type of advanced COMPACT DISK that can carry data, sound, and pictures and that has enough space for a full-length cinema film

dwell·ing /ˈdwelɪŋ/ *n* [C] LAW a place where someone lives: *Housing starts are expected to rise 15% this year to 180,000 dwellings.*

dwell time —see under TIME

dwt written abbreviation for DEADWEIGHT TONNAGE: *two 5,600 dwt, 22 knot ships*

D

E

E written abbreviation for east

e- also **E-** *prefix* electronic; used before another word to mean something that is sent between computers or is done using information sent between computers, especially over the INTERNET: *Schwab was the dominant* ***e-broker*** *last year, conducting 65% of its trades on-line* (=by computer). | *Hard copy* (=documents on paper) *has some functions which e-documents can never replace.*

E & OE errors and omissions excepted; used in formal documents to say that mistakes and things that have been forgotten should also be taken into account

Ea·gle /'iːgəl/ *n* [C] a US gold coin worth ten dollars: *Coin dealers have been loading up on American Eagle gold coins, a popular choice for small investors whenever they rush to buy gold.*

EAP abbreviation for EMPLOYEE ASSISTANCE PROGRAM; EMPLOYMENT ASSISTANCE PROGRAM

early adopter *n* [C] MARKETING a person or organization that is among the first to buy and use a new product: *Early adopters are willing to pay heavily for new gadgets – up to $1,700 for the first video players.*

early retirement —see under RETIREMENT

ear·mark /'ɪəmɑːk‖'ɪrmɑːrk/ *v* [T] to plan to use something for a particular purpose or to give someone a particular role **earmark sb/sth for**: *Of the money provided, 80% was earmarked for use in metropolitan areas.* **earmark sb/sth as**: *He had been earmarked as a possible successor to Bolcarro.*

earn /ɜːn‖ɜːrn/ *v* **1** [I,T] to be paid money for the work you do: *The managing director's personal assistant earned £35,000 last year.* | *She earns a very respectable wage.* | *Some young people want to start earning as soon as possible.*

2 [T] if an investment earns money, it makes a profit: *If a bond is not redeemed at maturity, it continues to earn interest.*

3 earn a/your living to earn the money that you need to live: *It's impossible to earn a decent living in this country.* —see also SAVE AS YOU EARN

earned income —see under INCOME

earn·er /'ɜːnə‖'ɜːrnər/ *n* [C] **1** someone who earns money by working: *He's the highest earner in the company at the moment.* | *It is hard when there is only one* ***wage earner*** *in the family.*

2 an investment or asset that earns money: *The Suez Canal is one of Egypt's main foreign exchange earners.*

3 a nice (little) earner *BrE informal* something that earns quite a lot of money for you: *The shop could be quite a nice little earner.*

earnest money —see under MONEY

earning power —see under POWER[1]

earn·ings /'ɜːnɪŋz‖'ɜːr-/ *n* [plural] **1** the money that a person receives for the work they do in a particular period of time: *He always thought he'd be satisfied even if his earnings didn't reach $20,000 a year.* | *the gap between the* ***gross earnings*** (=income before tax) *of manual and non-manual workers*

2 the total amount that people receive for the work they do in a particular industry or economy in a particular period of time: *Figures on inflation, industrial production,* ***average earnings*** (=the average amount that people earn) *and unemployment are expected to show continuing economic weakness.*

3 FINANCE the profit that a company makes in a particular period of time, or the total profits that companies make in a particular industry or economy in a particular period of time: *British Airways counts on North Atlantic flights for about half its earnings.* | *This year, the steel industry's earnings should be higher with the completion of costly modernization programs.* | *Few can match Quality's* ***earnings growth*** *of 40% per year over the past five years.*

annual earnings ♦ the amount someone earns in a year, or the average amount earned by people in an area or industry in a year: *Growth in annual earnings in services slowed last year.*

♦ a company's profits for a particular year: *General Electric reported annual earnings that make it the most profitable company in the US.*

retained earnings a company's profit for a particular period of time not paid out in DIVIDENDS to people owning shares, but put into its RESERVES: *Retained earnings are piling up fast; Geico's per-share earnings last year of $13.74 far exceeded its current $2-a-year dividend rate.*

undistributed earnings net profit for a particular period of time, or for several periods of time, that are not paid to shareholders in DIVIDENDS; RETAINED PROFIT

4 buy earnings growth FINANCE an investor buys earnings growth by buying shares that are quite cheap in relation to the amount of profit the company made in the previous year, hoping that the value of the shares will increase: *Associated British Ports could buy earnings growth for its shareholders by buying ports overseas with its excess capital.* —see also PE RATIO

earnings basis *n* [singular] used to discuss a company's performance based on its profits, rather than other measures of performance: *While not cheap on an earnings basis, the stock's $2-a-share in operating cash flow makes Mr Kass see it as a bargain.*

earnings before interest and tax abbreviation **EBIT** *n* [plural] a company's profits for a particular period of time, without counting interest payments on its debt and payment of tax: *In the supermarkets division, sales rose from A$6.4 billion to A$6.9 billion, with earnings before interest and tax (EBIT) increasing from A$217 million to A$234 million.*

earnings before interest, tax, depreciation and amortization abbreviation **EBITDA** *n* [plural] a company's profits for a particular period of time, not including interest payments on its debt, tax payments and amounts to cover the decreasing value of machinery, equipment etc

earnings differential —see under DIFFERENTIAL[1]

earnings per share abbreviation **EPS** *n* [plural] a company's profits for a period of time divided by the number of its shares: *Sales advanced 42% to £1.59 billion from £1.12 billion a year earlier; earnings per share, however, slipped 2% to 9.9 pence from 10.1 pence because of the larger number of shares in issue in the latest period.*

earnings rule —see under RULE[1]

earnings yield —see under YIELD[1]

earn-out period —see under PERIOD

Easdaq /'iːzdæk/ *n* FINANCE a stockmarket based in Brussels for new, growing European companies, in which a computer network is used to buy and sell shares. The equivalent of Easdaq in the US is NASDAQ

ease /iːz/ *v* **1** [I,T] if limits, rules, restrictions etc are eased, or someone eases them, they become less strict: *India is easing rules for joint ventures with foreign concerns.*

2 [I,T] if interest rates ease, or someone eases them, they fall slightly: *The central bank is prepared to ease interest rates further.*

3 [I] if prices on a financial market ease, they fall slightly: *Stock prices eased in a slow trading session.* | *Tokyo Gas eased 2 to 565, and Marubeni lost 5 to 660.* —**easing** *n* [C,U] *the easing of restrictions on non-refundable fares* | *Profit-taking in the oil sector led to an easing of prices.* | *Rates are now around 7%, following a series of easings by the Reserve Bank of Australia.*

ease off also **ease up** *phr v* [I] to become less strong or less active: *The demand for personal pensions has eased off slightly.*

ease·ment /ˈiːzmənt/ *n* [C] LAW a limited right for people to use someone's land for a particular purpose: *California will have to pay owners of beach-front property for an easement to allow other people to walk across their land to get to the water.*

Eastern Time also **Eastern Standard Time**, abbreviation **EST** *n* [U] the time in the eastern part of the US and Canada, five hours behind GREENWICH MEAN TIME and one hour ahead of CENTRAL STANDARD TIME: *L'Oreal says its offer for Maybilline will expire at 12.00 midnight Eastern Standard Time.*

eas·y /ˈiːzi/ *adj* comparative **easier** superlative **easiest**
1 (on) easy terms if you buy something on easy terms, you pay for it with several small payments, rather than paying the whole amount at once: *Farmers can obtain credit on very easy terms from a variety of government sources.*
2 be easier when prices are easier, they are slightly lower: *Gold was slightly easier yesterday, ending in London at $362.50 an ounce.*
3 on easy street *AmE informal* having all the money you need: *The $2 million he has to invest will produce enough money to keep him on easy street for the rest of his life.*

easy money —see under MONEY

EBA *n* the European Banking Association; an organization that makes and manages payments between banks

EBIT abbreviation for EARNINGS BEFORE INTEREST AND TAX

EBITDA abbreviation for EARNINGS BEFORE INTEREST, TAX, DEPRECIATION AND AMORTIZATION

EBRD written abbreviation for EUROPEAN BANK FOR RECONSTRUCTION AND DEVELOPMENT

EC /ˌiː ˈsiː◂/ *n* **1** abbreviation for EUROPEAN COMMUNITY —see also EEC, EUROPEAN UNION
2 written abbreviation for EUROPEAN COMMISSION

ECA *n* [singular] Economic Commission for Africa; an organization that is part of the UNITED NATIONS and aims to encourage economic development in Africa. It is based in Addis Ababa

ECB abbreviation for EUROPEAN CENTRAL BANK

ECE *n* [singular] Economic Commission for Europe; an organization that is part of the UNITED NATIONS and aims to encourage economic development in Europe. It is based in Geneva

ECGD written abbreviation for EXPORT CREDITS GUARANTEE DEPARTMENT

ech·e·lon /ˈeʃəlɒn‖-lɑːn/ *n* [C] a rank or level of responsibility within an organization, group of businesses etc, or a person at that level: *those in the **highest echelons** of management* | *The banking system normally helps allocate money to the **lower echelon** but at the moment there is a credit squeeze.*

ECLAC *n* the Economic Commission for Latin America and the Caribbean; a UNITED NATIONS department based in Santiago, Chile that studies economies of the area, gives information about them etc

e-com·merce /ˈiː ˌkɒmɜːs‖-ˌkɑːmɜːrs/ also **e-business** *n* [U] electronic commerce; the practice of buying and selling goods and services and carrying on other business activities by computer, especially over the INTERNET: *e-commerce applications such as online ticketing and reservations*

e·con·o·me·tri·cian /ɪˌkɒnəməˈtrɪʃən‖ɪˌkɑː-/ *n* [C] a person who has studied econometrics or works using econometrics

e·con·o·met·rics /ɪˌkɒnəˈmetrɪks‖ɪˌkɑː-/ *n* [U] the branch of economics that uses mathematical and STATISTICAL methods to understand how economic systems work. Econometrics looks at important factors, for example interest rates, levels of employment, and government policies, and tests how changes to them could affect the economy in the future —**econometric** *adj* [only before a noun] *They use econometric models to search for the effects of the tax-reform law on the economy in general.*

ec·o·nom·ic /ˌekəˈnɒmɪk◂, ˌiː-‖-ˈnɑː-/ *adj* **1** [only before a noun] relating to or involving economics, money, finance, industry, trade etc: *The **economic climate** (=general state of the economy) is not likely to improve significantly in the current year.* | *The country is facing a severe **economic crisis**.* | *The government is trying to promote political stability and **economic growth**.* | *What are the prospects for **economic recovery**?*
2 a business or an investment that is economic produces enough profit to make it worth continuing with: *Oil that is today marginal or not economic suddenly becomes considerably more attractive when oil prices increase.*

Economic Advisors —see COUNCIL OF ECONOMIC ADVISORS

economic agent —see under AGENT

ec·o·nom·i·cal /ˌekəˈnɒmɪkəl, ˌiː-‖-ˈnɑː-/ *adj* using time, money, goods etc carefully and without wasting any: *Adults generally watch a movie on video once or twice, making it more economical to rent than buy.* | *Environmentalists insist that polystyrene recycling can be economical.*

ec·o·nom·i·cally /ˌekəˈnɒmɪkli, ˌiː-‖-ˈnɑː-/ *adv* **1** in a way that is related to systems of trade, money, business, industry etc: *The country is in danger of collapsing economically and politically.* | *an economically depressed area*
2 in a way that makes a profit: *Electric cars are not yet **economically viable** (=possible to produce and sell with a profit).* | *They are seeking new ways to produce the oil economically.*
3 in a way that uses time, money, goods etc carefully and without wasting any: *We must use these resources economically.*

economic analysis —see under ANALYSIS

Economic and Monetary Union —see EMU

Economic Commission for Africa —see ECA

Economic Commission for Europe —see ECE

Economic Commission for Latin America —see ECLA

Economic Commission for Latin America and the Caribbean —see ECLAC

economic co-operation *n* [U] when two or more countries work together to develop their economies through trade, financial help etc: *Mr Hashimoto and Chinese officials will discuss development loans from Japan to China and economic cooperation between the two countries.*

economic cost —see under COST[1]

economic development —see under DEVELOPMENT

economic efficiency —see under EFFICIENCY

economic geography *n* [U] the way in which industries and wealth are distributed in an area, and the effect that the landscape, climate etc has in this distribution: *The rise of the cloth industry considerably changed the economic geography of England.*

economic goods —see under GOODS

economic growth —see under GROWTH

economic history *n* [U] the history of economic development in different parts of the world: *a new study of the economic history of Japan*

economic indicator —see under INDICATOR

economic life —see under LIFE

economic nationalism *n* [U] the idea that a country's economy will perform best if its industries are protected from competition, for example by taxes on imported goods

economic order quantity —see under QUANTITY

economic paradigm —see under PARADIGM

economic planning —see under PLANNING

ec•o•nom•ics /ˌekəˈnɒmɪks, ˌiː-‖-ˈnɑː-/ *n* **1** [U] the study of the way in which wealth is produced and used: *While economics is important, man must never be reduced to the merely economic.*

applied economics [U] economics used to understand and solve problems in the world of business and government, rather than just as ideas: *a one-year course in applied economics for government policymakers*

classical economics [U] the ideas that people had about economics between the 18th and early 20th centuries, for example that wealth increases as a result of people following their own interest, and that there is a natural state of balance in the economy that will happen if nothing is done to disturb it

development economics [U] the study of how to increase wealth in countries that are changing from an agricultural economy to an industrial one: *A knowledge of development economics and the challenges faced by a small, developing country would be an advantage for this job.*

industrial economics [U] the study of how businesses compete against each other in different industries, and what makes businesses succeed or fail

mathematical economics [U] another name for ECONOMETRICS

supply-side economics *n* [U] ECONOMICS a theory stating that governments should cut taxes in order to encourage investment, rather than making more money available in the economy

welfare economics [U] the part of economics that deals with how a country's economy should be managed to increase the wealth and standard of living of people in the country: *In welfare economics the existence of market failure is sufficient reason for government intervention.*

2 [plural] calculations of whether an activity or business will be profitable or not: *The economics of producing oil from coal do not look attractive.* —see also MACROECONOMICS, MICROECONOMICS

economic sanctions —see under SANCTION

economic system —see under SYSTEM

economic theory —see under THEORY

economic value —see under VALUE[1]

economic value added abbreviation **EVA** *n* [U] the difference between the amount of profit a company makes from capital it invests and the amount it pays out to get that capital: *Economic value added indicates whether managers are creating value for shareholders or destroying it.*

economies of scale —see under SCALE

Economist *n* **The Economist** a British weekly magazine that deals with business, economics, and politics

e•con•o•mist /ɪˈkɒnəmɪ̇st‖ɪˈkɑː-/ *n* [C] someone who studies the way in which wealth is produced and used in an area: *Many economists believe the recession is ending.*

e•con•o•mize also **economise** *BrE* /ɪˈkɒnəmaɪz‖ɪˈkɑː-/ *v* [I] to reduce the amount of time, money, goods etc that you use: *The company will continue to economize by shedding a further 2,000 jobs this year.* + **on**: *New machines were brought in to economize on labor.*

e•con•o•my[1] /ɪˈkɒnəmi‖ɪˈkɑː-/ *n* plural **economies**
1 [C] the system by which a country's goods and services are produced and used, or a country considered in this way: *the transformation from a centrally planned socialist economy to a market-led one* | *He expects Europe's economies over the long run to grow faster than the US.*

black economy [C] business activities that take place unofficially, especially in order to avoid paying tax: *It is impossible to quantify exactly the extent of the black economy.*

command economy also **controlled economy** [C] an economy in which the government of a country owns most of the industry and makes all economic decisions: *Russia began a program to switch from a centrally planned, command economy to a free market within 500 days.* —compare MARKET ECONOMY

exchange economy [C] an economy in which goods are traded using money or exchanged for other goods: *the establishment of an exchange economy, with markets and a single accepted currency*

free economy [C] another name for MARKET ECONOMY

global economy [singular] the economy of the world seen as a whole: *an interconnected global economy where billions of dollars and other currencies can be shifted at the touch of a button*

Goldilocks economy [C] an economy that is not growing too slowly, with the risk of RECESSION, or too fast, with the danger of OVERHEATING: *Americans thought the Goldilocks economy of the 1990s would last forever.*

market economy also **free economy** [C] an economy in which companies are not controlled by the government but decide for themselves what to produce and sell, based on what they believe they can make a profit from: *The Colombian government has demonstrated its belief in a market economy by privatizing inefficient state companies.*

political economy ◆ [U] the study of the way countries organize the production and the use of wealth
◆ [C,U] the way an economy is organized in a particular country: *Haiti is the American country with the worst political economy – whether measured by per capita income, life expectancy, or inflation.*

service economy [U] an economic system in a country which depends on selling services such as banking, transport, TOURISM etc, rather than on manufacturing, industry, farming etc: *Following the industrial decline of the 1980s, all the evidence suggests that Britain has become a service economy.*

shadow economy [C] business activities that are difficult for the authorities to find out about, for example because they are against the law; SHADOW MARKET: *The lack of reliable statistics comes from the growing shadow economies that have escaped accurate analysis.*

2 [U] the careful use of money, goods, time etc so that nothing is wasted: *In the achievement of economy the National Health Service is well served by the present system of budgeting.* | *The post office was closed as part of an* ***economy drive*** (=a planned effort to cut costs).

3 [C] a way of spending less money: *Following AXA-UAP's merger, the group should* ***make economies*** *of about FFr200 million next year.* | *As an* ***economy measure,*** *those all-expenses-paid tickets have been withdrawn.*

false economy [C] something that seems to be a way

E

of spending less money, but actually costs you more money in the end: *Buying cheaper, poorer quality materials is often a false economy.*

economy[2] *adj* [only before a noun] **1** an economy fare, hotel etc is cheaper than other things of the same type: *Kuoni Travel offers a range of economy and medium-priced hotels.*

2 an economy size product or packet contains more than a normal one and is cheap compared to the normal size product: *The small-size-only offerings that used to fill shelves have been replaced with economy-size packages.*

economy class —see under CLASS

ECU /ˈekjuː‖eɪˈkuː/ *n* [C] European Currency Unit; a currency used in the EUROPEAN MONETARY SYSTEM before the introduction of the EURO. The value of the ECU was based on the value of the currencies of different countries, but was not used as the currency of any particular country: *A market in bonds denominated in ECUs grew rapidly.*

e·cur·ren·cy /ˈiː ˌkʌrənsi‖-ˌkɜː-/ *n* plural **e-currencies** [C] one of the types of E-MONEY (=money that can be used on the INTERNET): *One type of e-currency is beenz.*

edge[1] /edʒ/ *n* [singular] **have/give sb an edge (over sb/sth)** if a person, company, or country has an edge over others, they are more successful, profitable etc because they have an advantage that the others do not have: *They have a slight edge over their competitors.* | *Commercial Textiles service orders faster than many similar companies, giving the company an important **competitive edge**.* —see also LEADING EDGE

edge[2] *v* [I] **1 edge up/upwards/higher/ahead** to increase by a small amount: *Consumer prices edged up 0.2% last month.* | *Hong Kong edged ahead after a day of sharp swings.* | *Turnover edged forward 2% to £43.6 million.*

2 edge down/downwards/lower/back to decrease by a small amount: *Sales of cars, trucks and buses in Japan edged down 0.9% in January.* | *The index, which had climbed to 106.6 in late July, edged back to 100.4.*

EDI abbreviation for ELECTRONIC DATA INTERCHANGE

ed·it /ˈedᵻt/ *v* [T] **1** to make changes to a piece of writing, a film, or a recording in order to improve it and remove any mistakes: *After you have created and edited a document, you will want to format it.*

2 to be the editor of a newspaper or magazine: *He edited the New Statesman from 1994 to 1998.*

edit sth ↔ **out** *phr v* [T] to remove sth from a piece of writing, a film, or a recording: *The interviewer's questions may be edited out so that all we see is the individual talking.*

e·di·tion /ɪˈdɪʃən/ *n* [C] **1** a copy of a book that is printed at one particular time. Second, third etc editions of a book may contain changes to the previous book: *These chapters did not appear in the **first edition**.* | *A **new edition** is due out next month.* | *A **paperback edition** of the book is now available.*

limited edition a fixed number of a product, especially a car or book, produced at one time. Limited editions are often valuable because no more will be made: *A signed, limited edition of 1,250 copies sold out at $325 each.* | *Honda Motor Co., working with Kobe Steel of Japan, has introduced a limited-edition aluminum car.*

2 a copy of a newspaper or magazine that is produced on a particular day or at a particular time: *The story made it into **later editions** of the Times and Telegraph.*

ed·i·tor /ˈedᵻtə‖-ər/ *n* [C] **1** the person who has responsibility for deciding what should be included in a newspaper or magazine: *Lawson had seen many financial scandals when working as a **City Editor**.* | *the **foreign editor** of the New York Herald Tribune* | *the **Deputy Editor** of the Arab Observer*

2 a person who prepares a book for printing or a film for broadcasting by checking it and making changes to improve it: *For the past four years she's been an editor at Waverly Place Books.*

3 a computer program that allows you to make changes to a piece of writing. An editor only allows you to change the writing in a document, not the way in which the writing will appear on the page when it is printed out

EDP abbreviation for ELECTRONIC DATA PROCESSING

ed·u·ca·tion /ˌedjʊˈkeɪʃən‖ˌedʒə-/ *n* [U] the process of learning, for example at schools and universities, and the process by which your mind develops through doing this: *The most important element of **business education** (=learning about business) is teaching kids that business is more than just 'chasing after big bucks.'* | *a consulting firm specializing in **management education** and organization development* | *Russian immigrants have very high levels of **technical education**.*

tertiary education *BrE* education at university level

ed·u·tain /ˌedjʊˈteɪn‖ˌedʒə-/ *v* [I,T] *journalism* to educate and entertain people at the same time: *Microsoft, the world's biggest software company, has a mission to edutain.* —**edutainment** *n* [U] *The edutainment program, designed for kids up to five, will teach them about the inner workings of a computer.*

EEA abbreviation for EUROPEAN ECONOMIC AREA

EEC abbreviation for EUROPEAN ECONOMIC COMMUNITY

EEOC abbreviation for EQUAL EMPLOYMENT OPPORTUNITY COMMISSION

ef·fect /ɪˈfekt/ *n* **1** [C,U] the way in which an action, event, or person changes someone or something: *Inflation is **having a** disastrous **effect on** the economy.*

demonstration effect [singular] ECONOMICS the idea that people expect or want to buy or have things because they see that other people are able to have them: *The demonstration effect of rising real wages in Europe was another powerful stimulus to trade unionist expectations.*

halo effect [singular] when people think that a company is good because it is owned by or connected with another company that is famous and important: *The big companies are luring investors back and creating a halo effect for the rest of the group.* | *The Parcelforce ads have had a halo effect on international delivery services in general.*

Hawthorne effect [singular] HUMAN RESOURCES the way that the performance of workers improves when special attention is given to them during tests, even if these tests might be expected to have negative effects: *Some job enrichment programmes were initially successful and then failed, suggesting that they owed their success more to the Hawthorne effect than to a deeper understanding of people.*

impact effect [singular] ECONOMICS when demand for a product suddenly increases, but the supply cannot be increased for a long period of time: *Analysts are monitoring the impact effect that has been caused by the product's sudden rise in popularity.*

price effect [C,U] the effect of an event on the price of something: *The further away from maturity that the instrument is, the greater is the price effect following an interest rate change.*

substitution effect [singular] ECONOMICS the effect on customers' behaviour when the price or value of something changes. For example, if the price of a product rises in relation to other, similar products, some customers may replace it with the cheaper product

wealth effect [singular] ECONOMICS the effect of share prices on spending. For example, when share prices are high, investors feel that they can afford to spend a lot of money: *After the 1987 stockmarket crash,* *pessimists cited the wealth effect to support forecasts of deep recession.*

2 put/bring sth into effect to make a plan or idea happen: *It won't be easy to put the changes into effect.*

3 come into effect/take effect if a new arrangement, law, system etc comes into effect or takes effect, it officially starts: *The new tax rates come into effect in April.*

4 with immediate effect/with effect from starting to happen immediately, or from a particular date: *Hoskins is appointed manager, with immediate effect.*

5 effects [plural] *formal* the things that someone owns: *Insurance also covers* ***personal effects*** *required during travel on company business.*

uncleared effects [plural] *BrE* BANKING cheques etc that have been handed to a bank to be paid into an account but have not yet gone through the banking system and been paid into the account; UNCLEARED CHECK *AmE*

ef•fec•tive /ɪˈfektɪv/ *adj* **1** working well and producing the result or effect that was wanted or intended: *The company mounted a very effective publicity campaign.* | *The 7% increase in sales shows that AT&T have become more effective in marketing their services.* —see also COST-EFFECTIVE

2 [not before a noun] if a law, agreement, or system becomes effective, it officially starts + **from**: *The new rates are effective from 22 February.*

3 [only before a noun] real, although not obvious or officially recognized: *Digital Equipment Corp. now has* ***effective control*** *of the German company's computer operations.*

effective date —see under DATE[1]

effective rate —see under RATE[1]

effective tax rate —see under RATE[1]

effective yield —see under YIELD[1]

effects not cleared also **uncleared effects** *n* [plural] *BrE* BANKING cheques that a customer has paid into a bank account but for which the bank has not yet received any money. Usually the customer cannot take out or use this money until it has been received by the bank

ef•fi•cien•cy /ɪˈfɪʃənsi/ *n* [U] **1** how well an industrial process, factory, or business works so that it produces as much as possible from the time, money, and resources that are put into it: *A charity like ours must constantly strive for* ***greater efficiency***. | *The increase in profitability is the result of* ***improved efficiency***.

2 how well and quickly a person or machine works: *He was impressed by the speed and efficiency of the Japanese trains.* | *I had to admire his efficiency.*

3 cost efficiency/fuel efficiency etc when something costs as little as possible, uses as little fuel as possible etc: *Auto makers will increase the fuel efficiency of their cars by 20% over the next five years.*

economic efficiency the ability of a factory or process to produce goods cheaply so that they can be sold at a low price and still make a profit: *Minor adjustments have been made to the system to improve its economic efficiency.*

industrial efficiency the ability of an industry to produce goods cheaply so that they can be sold at a low price and still make a profit: *The result could be a more efficient use of resources in Japan, which would improve the country's industrial efficiency.*

technical efficiency how well and quickly a machine produces high quality goods. When measuring the technical efficiency of a machine, the production costs are not considered important: *Improvements in technical efficiency have led to a more streamlined manufacturing process.*

ef•fi•cient /ɪˈfɪʃənt/ *adj* **1** producing goods using as little time, money etc as possible: *Food production and distribution is vitally important, and the United States has developed the most efficient methods.* | *Is this really an efficient use of resources?*

2 cost-efficient, fuel-efficient etc costing as little as possible, using as little fuel as possible etc: *energy-efficient light bulbs*

3 doing a job quickly and well: *a very efficient young secretary* | *a fast and efficient transport system* —**efficiently** *adv*: *an efficiently run restaurant* | *equipment that distributes electrical power more efficiently*

efficient market —see under MARKET[1]

EFTA /ˈeftə/ abbreviation for EUROPEAN FREE TRADE ASSOCIATION

EFTPOS /ˈeftpɒs‖-pɑːs/ *n* [U] BANKING Electronic Funds Transfer at Point of Sale; a system in Britain for paying for goods without using cash or cheques. The buyer's DEBIT CARD or CREDIT CARD is put into a special machine connected to a central computer that automatically takes money out of their account and puts it into the seller's account

eg /ˌiː ˈdʒiː/ abbreviation for example, used when you are listing some examples of things you are talking about

EGM *n* [C] *BrE* extraordinary general meeting; a meeting of those who own shares in a company, to discuss and vote on important subjects that cannot wait until the next AGM: *An EGM to decide the company's fate will be held on Thursday.*

EIB abbreviation for EUROPEAN INVESTMENT BANK

EIS abbreviation for ENTERPRISE INVESTMENT SCHEME, ENVIRONMENTAL IMPACT STATEMENT

elastic demand —see under DEMAND

elasticity of demand also **price elasticity (of demand)** *n* [U] ECONOMICS the degree to which a change in the price of something leads to a change in the amount of it that is sold or that could be sold if available: *Economists may have over-estimated the elasticity of demand for electricity.*

income elasticity of demand the degree to which a change in people's incomes leads to a change in the amount of something that is sold or could be sold if available: *a high UK income elasticity of demand for imports, compared with a much lower world income elasticity of demand for UK exports*

elasticity of substitution *n* [U] ECONOMICS the degree to which one INPUT can replaced by another. For example, in producing goods, if the cost of wages increases and the cost of machinery and capital used to pay for it stays the same, it may be possible to increase the amount of machinery used and so decrease the amount of wages paid: *The effect of the corporation tax on employment has a direct effect on the use of labour in the corporate sector, which depends on the elasticity of substitution.*

e•lect[1] /ɪˈlekt/ *v* [T] to choose someone for an official position by voting: *the country's first democratically elected president* **elect sb to**: *John Rodewig was elected to the board, filling a vacancy.* **elect sb (as) president/chairman etc**: *Steven J. Shapiro was elected vice president, corporate planning.* —**elected** *adj*: *an elected member of the board*

elect[2] *adj* [only after a noun] **chairman/president elect** a person who has been elected to a particular job but has not yet started doing that job: *Dan Connell, the Jacksonville Chamber of Commerce's chairman-elect*

e•lec•tion /ɪˈlekʃən/ *n* **1** [C] when people vote to choose someone for a job: *Ronald W. Allen was nominated to* ***stand for election*** *as a Coca-Cola director.* | *Mr Buntrock is also up for election to the board of directors at rival First Chicago Corp.*

2 [singular] the fact of being elected to an official

position: *Her election to the board expands American Brands' board to 16 members.*

electrical engineering —see under ENGINEERING

electrically programmable read-only memory —see EPROM

e·lec·tron·ic /ɪˌlekˈtrɒnɪk, ˌelɪk-‖-ˈtrɑː-/ *adj* **1** electronic equipment uses electricity and computer CHIPS: *a new electronic organizer that could replace the traditional diary*
2 made or produced using electronic equipment: *electronic music* —**electronically** *adv*: *video libraries stored electronically*

electronic banking —see under BANKING

electronic bill of lading —see under BILL OF LADING

electronic broker —see under BROKER[1]

electronic commerce —see E-COMMERCE

electronic cottage *n* [C] *journalism* a building, usually in the country, equipped with computers etc so that people can work there without travelling to an ordinary company office in a town; TELECOTTAGE —see also TELEWORKING

electronic data interchange abbreviation **EDI** *n* [U] COMPUTING a way for companies and banks to send information to each other by computer. Documents are sent in an agreed FORMAT so that the company receiving them can easily read them on their computer and print them out on paper: *software designed to facilitate Electronic Data Interchange*

E

electronic data processing —see under PROCESSING

electronic funds transfer (at point of sale) —see EFTPOS

electronic invoice —see under INVOICE[1]

electronic mail —see under MAIL[1]

electronic media *n* [plural] devices such as televisions, computers and CD ROMS that make information available to people

e·lec·tron·ics /ɪˌlekˈtrɒnɪks, ˌelɪk-‖-ˈtrɑː-/ *n* [U] **1** the study of making equipment that works using electricity and computer CHIPS: *She studied electronics at Manchester University.*
2 equipment that works using electricity and computer CHIPS, and the industry of making it: *SCI Systems makes electronics and computer parts.* | *Electronics is a strategic area in which government aid is justified.*

consumer electronics the industry of making electronic products for sale to people for their own use, rather than for industrial purposes: *high-definition TV and other consumer electronics products*

defence electronics *BrE*, **defense electronics** *AmE* the industry of making electronic parts and equipment for military purposes: *Raytheon makes missiles, defense electronics, appliances and aircraft.*

home electronics another name for CONSUMER ELECTRONICS

industrial electronics the industry of making electronic products for industrial purposes

el·i·gi·ble /ˈelɪ̈dʒɪ̈bəl/ *adj* allowed to do something or receive something + **for**: *Are you eligible for social security benefits?* —**eligibility** *n* [U] *Turkish eligibility to join the European Union*

eligible bank —see under BANK[1]

eligible bill —see under BILL OF EXCHANGE

e·lim·i·nate /ɪˈlɪmɪ̈neɪt/ *v* [T] to get rid of something unnecessary or unwanted: *Deere & Co. said it plans to eliminate 2,100 jobs.* | *The administration's goal was to eliminate all spending restrictions on federal grants.*

El·li·ott wave theo·ry /ˌeliət ˈweɪv ˌθɪəri‖-ˌθiːəri/ —see under THEORY

e-mail[1] also **email** /ˈiː meɪl/ *n* **1** [U] electronic mail; a system that allows people to send messages and documents to each other by computer: *Do you have e-mail* (=is your computer set up to send and receive e-mail) *at home?* | *The file had been sent* ***by email*** *and then transferred to a floppy disk.* | *We automatically delete all* ***e-mail messages*** *more than three months old.*
2 [C,U] a message or document sent by e-mail: *Send me an e-mail telling me how many books you want to buy.* | *I had just finished reading my e-mail.*

e-mail[2] also **email** *v* [T] to send someone a message or a computer file by e-mail: *You can phone, fax, or e-mail me.* **email sb with sth**: *I e-mailed you with my order six weeks ago.* **e-mail sb sth**: *Please will you e-mail me the latest set of accounts?*

e-mail address —see under ADDRESS[1]

em·bar·go[1] /ɪmˈbɑːgəʊ‖-ˈbɑːrgoʊ/ *n* plural **embargoes** [C] **1** an official order stopping trade with a country. Governments and organizations put embargoes on countries with whom they have a political disagreement: *Union officials then* ***put an embargo on*** *the importation of yarn by ordering dockers not to handle such yarn.* | *The UN was urged to* ***lift the embargo*** (=end it). | *An oil embargo would also hurt Italy and Germany, the main importers of Libya's high quality crude.*
2 an official order stopping information from being made public until a particular date or time: *We need to know whether there is an embargo on the use of the press release, and when the embargo will be lifted.*
3 when there is a possibility of war, a government order stopping ships from an enemy country from entering or leaving its ports

embargo[2] *v* [T] to put an embargo on a country: *Israel had made it clear that new military contracts would remain formally embargoed.*

em·bark /ɪmˈbɑːk‖-ɑːrk/ *v* [I] if passengers embark on a ship, they get on it: *Passengers should assemble in the lounge before embarking.*

em·bar·ka·tion /ˌembɑːˈkeɪʃən‖-bɑːr-/ *n* [U] when passengers get on a ship: *Embarkation will take place at 17.00 hours.*

em·bez·zle /ɪmˈbezəl/ *v* [I,T] if someone embezzles money from the company or organization they work for, they steal it, perhaps over a period of time, and use it for themselves: *An American banker, accused of embezzling $13 million, yesterday gave himself up to the authorities.* —**embezzlement** *n* [U] *An employee of his was once convicted for embezzlement.* | *charges relating to the embezzlement of public funds.*

e·mend /ɪˈmend/ *v* [T] to remove the mistakes from a piece of writing before it is made available for people to read: *Software and support should take account of the possible need to emend the data after it has been released.* —**emendation** *n* [C,U] *He has his own methods of textual editing and emendation.*

e·mer·gen·cy /ɪˈmɜːdʒənsi‖-ɜːr-/ *n* plural **emergencies** [C] **1** an unexpected and dangerous situation that must be dealt with immediately: *Ring this number in case of an emergency.*
2 emergency repairs/meeting/reserves etc work, a meeting, money etc needed to deal with an urgent and unexpected problem: *In addition to providing a regular preventative maintenance service they are also well set up for dealing with emergency work.* | *emergency reserves held at the Bank of England*

e·mer·ging /ɪˈmɜːdʒɪŋ‖-ɜːr-/ *adj* [only before a noun] **1** in an early state of development: *Around 1911, a similar crisis was facing the newly emerging car industry.*
2 the emerging nations/countries/economies countries, especially those in Asia, Africa, and South America that are just starting to have influence or power in trade,

finance etc: *The EC is politically, morally and economically bound to respond to those emerging economies by allowing freer access to their products.*

em·i·grant /ˈemɪɡrənt/ *n* [C] someone who leaves their own country to live permanently in another country: *the 1830s, when a tide of emigrants left Europe for Australia* —compare IMMIGRANT

em·i·grate /ˈemɪɡreɪt/ *v* [I] to leave your own country to live permanently in another country: *About 8000 people emigrate from the region each year.* —compare IMMIGRATE

em·i·gra·tion /ˌemɪˈɡreɪʃən/ *n* [U] the process of leaving your own country and going to live in another one —compare IMMIGRATION

net emigration the amount by which the number of EMIGRANTS is greater than the number of IMMIGRANTS: *The rate of net emigration from the UK is estimated to have increased by 47,000 a year.*

e·mol·u·ment /ɪˈmɒljəmənt‖ɪˈmɑːl-/ *n* [C usually plural] *formal* money and any other form of payment that someone, especially a lawyer, doctor, accountant etc, gets for the work that they do. The money earned by company directors who are not employees of the companies concerned can also be referred to as emoluments: *His pay was described as 'director emoluments' and he paid tax as a self-employed person.*

e-money /ˈiː ˌmʌni/ also **e-cash** *n* [U] currency that can be used to buy things on the INTERNET. It does not exist in physical form or belong to any particular country: *The wholly disembodied currency that can be used on the Net is known interchangeably as e-money or e-cash.*

e·mo·ti·con /ɪˈməʊtɪkɒn‖ɪˈmoʊtɪkɑːn/ *n* [C] COMPUTING one of a set of characters used to express feeling in writing, for example in an E-MAIL message. For example, the emoticon :-> is used after a comment to show that the comment is not intended to be serious

em·pire /ˈempaɪə‖-paɪr/ *n* [C] *informal* a group of companies or organizations controlled by one powerful company or person: *Their cautious and unflamboyant management style has created a retailing empire of solid reliability.* | *The Bond* ***business empire*** *was once worth about £3.5 billion.*

em·ploy /ɪmˈplɔɪ/ *v* [T] to pay someone to work for you: *The company employs 2000 people worldwide.* **employ sb as sth**: *He is employed as a baggage handler at the airport.* **employ sb to do sth**: *Freelance consultants have been employed to look at ways of reducting waste.*

em·ploy·a·ble /ɪmˈplɔɪəbəl/ *adj* suitable to be employed: *Universities should be providing skills to make their students more employable.* —**employability** *n* [U] *Employers have a responsibility to maintain employability through continuous training, even if they cannot always maintain employment levels.*

em·ploy·ee /ɪmˈplɔɪ-iː, ˌemplɔɪˈiː/ *n* [C] someone who is paid to work for an organization, especially someone who has a job of low rank: *A large proportion of the company's employees work outside the UK.* | *Managers and employees met several times to discuss our organisation structure.*

public employee someone who works for a local or national government: *Philadelphia ranked seventh of 11 major cities in terms of the number of public employees per 10,000 citizens.*

employee assistance program abbreviation **EAP** *n* [C] HUMAN RESOURCES in the US, a set of organized actions by employers to help employees with personal or family problems: *More than two thirds of major firms now support employee assistance programs for drug abusers.*

employee benefits —see under BENEFIT[1]

employee buyout —see under BUYOUT

employee compensation —see under COMPENSATION

employee involvement *n* [U] ways of making employees feel more interested in their work so that they produce more, produce work of better quality etc: *With more employee involvement in workplace functions such as ordering supplies, setting schedules, and keeping quality records, morale is higher and productivity climbs.*

employee leasing —see under LEASING

employee ownership —see under OWNERSHIP

employee participation *n* [U] **1** another name for EMPLOYEE INVOLVEMENT: *The company also encourages employee participation in this process through small groups in which workers discuss ideas.*
2 another name for EMPLOYEE OWNERSHIP: *There is a high level of employee participation through an employee share ownership plan.*

employee profit sharing *n* [U] **1** another name for EMPLOYEE OWNERSHIP: *The employee profit-sharing plan holds about a 45% stake in Carter Hawley.*
2 *AmE* a way of rewarding workers who have helped a company achieve high profits

employee representation —see under REPRESENTATION

Employee Retirement Income Security Act —see ERISA

employee stock option —see under OPTION

employee stock ownership plan —see ESOP

em·ploy·er /ɪmˈplɔɪə‖-ər/ *n* [C] a person or company that pays people to work for them: *Every employer should spend money on training.* | *Who is your current employer?* | *Potential employers feel they can tell a lot about a person by looking at their handwriting.*

employer liability —see under LIABILITY

employers' liability policy —see under INSURANCE POLICY

employers' organization —see under ORGANIZATION

em·ploy·ment /ɪmˈplɔɪmənt/ *n* [U] **1** work that you do to earn money: *students seeking employment after college* | *Part-time employment was often the only paid employment women could find.*

continuous employment a period of time when you work for a single employer, and do not have a break to work for another employer, go to college etc: *Maternity leave does not break your period of continuous employment and indeed it counts as part of that period.*

2 the number of people in an area or a country who have jobs, the types of jobs they have etc: *key factors for the for U.S. standard of living – employment, productivity, research and development, wage levels and technological development*

full employment when almost everyone in an area or country who wants a job has one: *Since we are very close to full employment, the economy needs to grow a little less slowly to fight inflation.* —see also CONTRACT OF EMPLOYMENT, TERMS OF EMPLOYMENT

employment agency —see under AGENCY

employment assistance program —see under PROGRAM[1]

employment bureau *n* plural **employment bureaux** *BrE* or **employment bureaus** [C] another name for EMPLOYMENT AGENCY

employment discrimination —see under DISCRIMINATION

employment protection *n* [U] protection of the rights of workers in a company, for example the right for women to go on MATERNITY LEAVE or the right to be given a reasonable REDUNDANCY payment if you lose your job.

E

Employment protection also refers to the system of laws, agreements, and processes that make this possible: *British workers had the worst employment protection laws in Europe.*

employment report —see under REPORT[1]

employment theory —see under THEORY

em•po•ri•um /ɪm'pɔːriəm/ *n* plural **emporia** [C] *old-fashioned* a large shop: *Kennedy's Furniture Emporium*

em•pow•er /ɪm'paʊə‖-ər/ *v* [T] *formal* to give a person or an organization the power or the legal right to do something **empower sb to do sth**: *The region's policy and resources committee yesterday empowered the administration leader to take whatever action is necessary to try to retain the service.* —**empowered** *adj*: *I want every employee to have access to the same knowledge as I have. Then they are empowered to do their job better.*

em•pow•er•ment /ɪm'paʊəmənt‖-'paʊr-/ *n* [U] when workers in a company are given more responsibility by allowing them to organize their own work, make decisions without asking their managers etc. For the company, this has the advantage of making their employees more involved and able to help clients more quickly: *The trend is towards empowerment and allowing junior employees to take personal initiatives that normally would have been beyond the scope of their jobs.* —see also ***participative management*** *under* MANAGEMENT

E

emp•ties /'emptiz/ *n* [plural] **1** empty containers that will be used again: *The landlord may wish to ensure that a yard adjoining a building does not become obstructed by trade empties.*
2 houses in which no-one is living: *All his empties could be let at low rents for perhaps three years.*

empty nesters *n* [plural] MARKETING a couple whose children have left home. Marketers see them as a group ready to buy certain types of things such as smaller houses, particular types of holidays etc: *Married couples without children, including 'empty nesters' as well as newly-married partners, form the largest single group of households at 36% of the total.*

EMS abbreviation for EUROPEAN MONETARY SYSTEM

EMTN abbreviation for EURO MEDIUM-TERM NOTE

EMU /'iːmjuː/ *n* [U] European Monetary Union or Economic and Monetary Union; the use by many EUROPEAN UNION countries of the same currency, the EURO, starting in 1999 for payments between banks and companies and in 2002 for the general public, when coins and BANKNOTES are made available

enabling clause —see under CLAUSE

enc also **encl** written abbreviation for ENCLOSED or ENCLOSURE, used at the end of an official letter to show that something is in the envelope with the letter

en•cash /ɪn'kæʃ/ *v* [T] *BrE* FINANCE, BANKING to exchange a CHEQUE, BOND, or other investment for cash: *After the payment of one full year's contribution you may encash your bond at any time.* —**encashment** *n* [U] *The ultimate encashment value of a PEP should be far greater than an endowment plan.*

en•clo•sure /ɪn'kləʊʒə‖-'kloʊʒər/ *n* [C] written abbreviation **enc, encl** something, for example an information pack or a contract, put inside an envelope with a letter: *I refer to your letter and enclosure of 26 January 1999.*

en•croach /ɪn'krəʊtʃ‖-'kroʊtʃ/ *v*
encroach on/upon sth *phr v* [T] to gradually take more control of someone's rights, property, responsibility etc than you should: *With Hewlett-Packard Co threatening to encroach on its market area, Pyramid Technology is expected to fight back next month with new hardware.* —**encroachment** *n* [C,U] *The Government should legislate to give better protection from encroachment on the green belts.*

en•crypt /ɪn'krɪpt/ *v* [T] COMPUTING to write information in the form of CODE, especially to prevent certain people from being able to use it: *LIFESPAN RDBI will encrypt this password the first time the data transfer program is run.* —**encryption** *n* [U] *a data encryption facility so data can be saved to disk in encoded form*

en•cum•bered /ɪn'kʌmbəd‖-ərd/ *adj* encumbered property has a MORTGAGE, LEASE, charge etc on it: *an executor of the ex-lord general's encumbered estate*

en•cum•brance /ɪn'kʌmbrəns/ *n* [C,U] something such as a MORTGAGE, LEASE, or charge on property, that may cause difficulties when the property is passed on to someone else: *Most directors would like to keep the company's business premises free from further encumbrances if at all possible.*

end /end/ *n* **1 top/bottom end** a figure that is at the top or bottom end of a range is high or low in the range of possible figures that were expected: *The results were at the top end of previous market forecasts.*
2 top/expensive/bottom/cheap end a product that is at the top or bottom end of a range is the most expensive or cheapest in the range: *It won't be easy competing at the top end of the market.* | *Bombay dealers, the main suppliers of the cheap end of the US diamond jewelry market* —see also FRONT END, HIGH END, YEAR END

end-consumer also **end consumer** *n* [C] the person who buys and uses a product after it has passed through all the stages of production: *the margin between the cost of producing the oil and the price it fetches from the end-consumer*

end of month —see EOM

end-of-season sale —see under SALE

en•dorse also **indorse** /ɪn'dɔːs‖-ɔːrs/ *v* [T] **1** LAW to sign a formal document for something that you own so that ownership changes to someone else
2 to sign your name on the back of a cheque, a BILL OF EXCHANGE etc so that it can be paid to someone other than the person whose name is written on it: *The bank could not confirm the endorsed signature so stolen cheques could be cashed long before anyone realised it.*
3 MARKETING if a well-known person endorses a product, they say how good it is in advertisements. People will buy the product because they like or trust the person

endorsed cheque —see under CHEQUE

en•dor•see /ɪnˌdɔː'siː, ˌendɔː'siː‖ˌendɔːr'si/ *n* [C] the person who will benefit from a cheque, BILL OF EXCHANGE etc when it is endorsed: *when an endorser becomes insolvent before the endorsee has taken possession of the bill of lading* —compare ENDORSER

en•dorse•ment also **indorsement** /ɪn'dɔːsmənt‖-ɔːr-/ *n* **1** [C,U] LAW when someone signs a formal document for something they own so that ownership changes to someone else: *A bill of lading was transferable by endorsement, and capable of transferring title to the goods.*
2 [C,U] BANKING when someone signs a cheque, BILL OF EXCHANGE etc that was payable to them so that it becomes payable to someone else
3 [C,U] BANKING when a bank official signs a BILL OF EXCHANGE or PROMISSORY NOTE as a promise that the bank will pay it. The bank will then get the money from the person who originally should have paid it after DISCOUNTING it
4 [C] INSURANCE a written condition added to an insurance agreement: *Under the policy terms and endorsements, we will insure you against certain legal liability, loss or damage.*
product endorsement [C,U] MARKETING when a well-known person says how good a product is in

advertisements. People will buy the product because they like or trust the person: *He committed the Spice Girls to product endorsement deals for everything from Asda supermarkets to Polaroid cameras.*

en·dors·er /ɪn'dɔːsə‖-ər/ *n* [C] someone who endorses a document, for example a document showing ownership, a BILL OF EXCHANGE or a PROMISSORY NOTE: *If the original payee cannot pay at maturity, the final holder can approach the last endorser for payment, who in turn can claim from the previous endorser, etc.*

en·dow /ɪn'daʊ/ *v* [T] to give a sum of money to a college, hospital etc in order to give it an income: *He planned the museum and helped raise the $55 million to build and endow it.* —**endowment** *n* [C,U] *King's School received generous new endowments.*

endowment assurance —see under ASSURANCE

endowment mortgage —see under MORTGAGE[1]

endowment policy —see under INSURANCE POLICY

end-product also **end product** *n* **1** [C] the final thing produced in a manufacturing process: *chemicals that are processed to make fibers, detergents and other end-products*

2 [C usually singular] the final result of a series of actions or events: *The end-product of our training was for us to become independent in every way.* —compare BY-PRODUCT

end-to-end *adj* [only before a noun] **1** MARKETING involving products that cover all the stages of a particular process, service etc: *The demand for end-to-end product development and manufacturing solutions is turning suppliers such as Parametric into one-stop shops* (=companies which supply everything related to a particular activity).

2 COMPUTING end-to-end services provide everything that is needed to connect someone to a COMPUTER NETWORK and let them send and receive information using it: *The company will offer end-to-end videoconferencing products* (=including camera and screen at both ends, network connections etc).

end user —see under USER

en·gage /ɪn'geɪdʒ/ *v* [T] *formal* to arrange to employ someone or to pay someone to do something for you **engage sb to do sth**: *You will need to engage a commercial lawyer to protect your interests in the drafting of a contract.*

en·gaged /ɪn'geɪdʒd/ *adj BrE* a telephone that is engaged is being used; BUSY *AmE*: *I can't get through – her line's engaged.* | *Every time I call I get the* ***engaged tone*** (=the sound you hear when the telephone is engaged).

en·gage·ment /ɪn'geɪdʒmənt/ *n formal* **1** [C,U] when you arrange to employ someone or to pay someone to do something for you: *the engagement of supply teachers by schools*

engagement letter [C] a letter in which the conditions under which someone is employed are stated; employment contract. In the US, letters of engagement are usually given to a CONTRACTOR who has been employed to carry out a particular service or job; LETTER OF ENGAGEMENT: *If you deviate from the conditions laid down in this letter of engagement, we will be free to terminate the engagement at any time.*

terms of engagement [plural] the official conditions that someone must agree to before they can start to be employed by someone: *Set out the detailed terms of engagement as agreed with the instructing clients.*

2 [C] an arrangement to meet someone or attend an event: *the Prime Minister's official engagements* | *He was unable to attend because of a* ***prior engagement*** (=one already arranged).

3 **without engagement** used to show that a price given by a seller can be changed

en·gi·neer[1] /ˌendʒ₅ˈnɪə‖-ˈnɪr/ *n* [C] **1** someone who designs the way roads, bridges, machines, electrical equipment etc are built: *He is an engineer with an oil company.*

2 **chemical/civil/electrical etc engineer** one who works in chemical etc engineering: *software engineers and computer scientists*

engineer[2] *v* [T] **1** to arrange something by clever, careful, and often secret, planning: *Nobody knew who had engineered the minister's downfall.*

2 to design and plan the construction of roads, machines, software etc: *Portec makes engineered products for various industries, including railroads.* | *Unlike car and aerospace parts, new drugs can't be engineered based on existing knowledge.*

en·gi·neer·ing /ˌendʒ₅ˈnɪərɪŋ‖-ˈnɪr-/ *n* [U] **1** the profession and activity of designing the way roads, bridges, machines, electrical equipment etc are built: *the benefits of using computers in engineering* | *the French* ***engineering company*** *AFE*

chemical engineering engineering that involves the use of chemistry in large-scale industrial processes, for example in the production of oil and the manufacture of plastics: *He wanted to join ICI to work in chemical engineering.*

civil engineering the design, building, and repair of roads, bridges, large buildings, etc: *the world's biggest civil engineering project*

electrical engineering the design and building of electrical equipment

financial engineering arranging finances and investments in a clever, profitable, and sometimes slightly dishonest way: *A strong relationship with a client enables a bank to find innovative solutions, using the latest financial engineering techniques, to the client's problems.* | *How long can earnings grow if sales are flat, no matter how clever the financial engineering?*

genetic engineering a scientific method used to affect the way a human, animal, or plant develops: *The mice, developed through genetic engineering, are expected to provide important clues about Alzheimer's disease.*

heavy engineering the design and building of large machines and equipment: *companies involved with heavy engineering, eg the production of electricity generating plant*

light engineering the design and building of small machines, equipment etc: *Industrially, the area is dominated by light engineering and manufacturing.*

mechanical engineering the design and building of machines and tools

precision engineering the design and building of complicated tools and instruments whose parts must be exactly right in size and position: *In the 1970s and 1980s, higher value-added industries such as precision engineering were attracted to Singapore.*

reverse engineering when a product is studied to see how it is made, so that it can be copied

software engineering the design and producing of computer software: *a computer-aided software engineering tool*

structural engineering the planning and building of large structures such as bridges: *Tudor Engineering Co. will provide structural engineering services for the new mass-transit system.*

2 doing or constructing something in a carefully planned and effective way

social engineering the practice of making changes in the law in order to change society according to a political idea: *He called the ad ban an example of 'social engineering' and 'state moralism'.*

engineering insurance —see under INSURANCE

E

en•hance /ɪn'hɑːns‖ɪn'hæns/ *v* [T] to improve the quality or value of something: *The performance of some Windows programs should be enhanced by the Unix hardware.* —**enhanced** *adj*: *The plan was to offer senior officers enhanced pensions.*

en•joy /ɪn'dʒɔɪ/ *v* [T] **1** to use a legal right and benefit from it: *Local producers enjoy tariff protection at home.* —**enjoyment** *n* [U] *Golf development will not be permitted if it causes disruption to the public enjoyment of rights of way.*
2 to experience something good such as high profits or increased sales: *Stratus Computer Inc. has also enjoyed revenue growth this year.* | *Oil companies enjoyed windfall profits as a result of the Gulf War.*

en•quire /ɪn'kwaɪə‖-'kwaɪr/ *v* [I,T] *especially BrE* another spelling of INQUIRE

en•quir•er /ɪn'kwaɪərə‖-'kwaɪrər/ *n* [C] *especially BrE* another spelling of INQUIRER

en•qui•ry /ɪn'kwaɪəri‖'ɪŋkwəri, ɪn'kwaɪri, 'ɪŋkwɨri/ *especially BrE* another spelling of INQUIRY

en•rich•ment /ɪn'rɪtʃmənt/ *n* [U]
job enrichment when employees are given more rewarding work or more responsibility in their job, in an effort to make them feel happier and perform better: *There has been increased interest in job enrichment programmes.*

E

enrolled agent —see under AGENT

en•tail /ɪn'teɪl/ *n* [U] LAW when ownership of land and property can only pass to a certain person, especially the oldest son, when the owner dies: *Until the eighteenth century aristocratic landed property was generally governed by entail, which worked to secure large estates.*

en•ter /'entə‖-ər/ *v* [T] **1** if people or goods enter a country, they arrive there: *A lot of goods are fraudulently and illegally entering the US.*
2 if a company enters a market, it starts selling goods or services in that market: *Banc One entered the Texas market last year by buying MCorp's 20 failed banks.* | *Konica entered the underwater camera market with a basic model costing $8.95.*
3 if a possible buyer enters a market, they start looking for something to buy there: *Property prices soared as more young people entered the housing market.*
4 if someone enters a financial market, they buy or sell something there: *Institutional investors repeatedly entered the market to sell into the rally.*
5 to write something in an account book, on a list etc.: *Any deposits received in advance are entered in the cash book.*
6 to put information into a computer by pressing the KEYS: *If a command is entered incorrectly, the machine will not recognize it.*
7 to legally make an agreement: *a customer who enters a contract as a result of doorstep canvassing*
8 to start a particular career: *Britain's agriculture industry could be plunged into crisis as fewer young people enter farming.*
9 enter a plea of guilty/not guilty LAW to say that you are guilty or not guilty of a crime in a court of law: *He entered a plea of not guilty to the charge of causing death by reckless driving.*
enter into sth *phr v* [T] to officially make an agreement, contract etc: *When we entered into a sponsorship agreement with the Rugby World Cup Limited, no one believed that the event would be such an outstanding success.*

en•ter•prise /'entəpraɪz‖-ər-/ *n* **1** [C] a company or business: *Good financial accounts are vital to any enterprise.* | *The company started as a* ***family enterprise***.
2 [C] a business activity: *Bell Canada and Systemhouse will establish an enterprise to provide computer services to the telecommunications industry.*
3 [U] business activity considered as a whole, especially in relation to other parts of the economy, society etc: *French-style 'economic programmes' between government and enterprise*
free enterprise [U] *approving* when people can own capital and organize their businesses in any way they like, without begin prevented or controlled by the government: *Encouragement has been given to individualism, free enterprise and the pursuit of profit.*
private enterprise ◆ [U] the economic system in which private businesses compete freely with each other: *laws permitting private enterprise and the establishment of joint stock companies*
◆ [C] a company owned by people or other companies, rather than by the government: *They are transforming state-owned industries into private enterprises.*
public enterprise ◆ [C] a business that is owned and run by the government: *the difference between a vast public enterprise, and a local farmer making a living as economically as he could*
◆ [U] businesses and companies that are owned and run by the government, considered as a whole: *He believed in privatization and the dismantling of public enterprise.*
4 [U] the ability to think of new activities and ideas and to take risks in business, especially by starting and running new businesses: *Managers seemed to lack enterprise and initiative.* | *Mrs Thatcher's calls for an* ***enterprise culture*** (=an environment in which enterprise is encouraged)

enterprise centre —see under CENTRE

Enterprise Investment Scheme abbreviation **EIS** *n* a British government arrangement to encourage investors to put money into new businesses: *The company is trying to raise £750,000 through the Enterprise Investment Scheme.*

enterprise zone —see under ZONE[1]

en•ter•pris•ing /'entəpraɪzɪŋ‖-tər-/ *adj* showing the ability to think of new activities and ideas and to take financial risks in business, especially by starting and running new businesses: *There are enterprising men like Richard Branson wanting to put trains on the line complete with champagne and bathrooms.*

en•ter•tain•ment /ˌentə'teɪnmənt‖-tər-/ *n* [U]
1 when a company or business person spends money on taking customers to restaurants, bars, theatres etc, as a way of making business deals easier to complete: *the necessary expenses of entertainment in securing a new contract*
2 the business of films, television, theatre productions etc: *people employed in retailing and entertainment* | *Virgin sold 25% of its music business to Japanese media and entertainment group, Fujisankei.* | *the worldwide impact of the American* ***entertainment industry***
home entertainment entertainment that you enjoy in your home, for example films on VIDEO or music played on CD PLAYERS: *In today's fast-moving home entertainment industry advances in product technology are occurring at a very fast rate.*

entertainment account —see under ACCOUNT[1]

entertainment allowance —see under ALLOWANCE

entertainment expense —see under EXPENSE

en•ti•ty /'entɨti/ *n* plural **entities** [C usually singular] ACCOUNTING, LAW **1** used to talk about any business that is a single unit from a legal or financial point of view: *The thrift was declared insolvent and merged with seven other Texas thrifts into a new entity, Sunbelt Savings FSB.*
business entity ACCOUNTING, LAW a company involved in the production, buying, and selling of goods

or services for profit: *AT&T's recent reorganization into a much more efficient and competitive business entity*

legal entity an organization considered as a separate, independent unit for legal purposes: *Having to keep separate legal entities in every state is an irritation to Iveco's integrated European operation.*

2 the entity convention the principle that a business is separate from the people who own it, so that they do not have to use their own money to pay the company's debts

en·trant /'entrənt/ *n* [C] MARKETING a company that starts to sell goods or services in a market where they have not sold them before, or one of these types of goods or services: *Some **foreign entrants** such as BT and others have recently come into the market.* | *Any **new entrant** is a threat in such a competitive industry.*

en·tre·pot /'ɒntrəpəʊ‖'ɑːntrəpoʊ/ *n* [C] a port through which goods pass before going somewhere else: *London grew faster than all other ports as a point of transit for English exports and so became a major entrepot of international trade.*

en·tre·pre·neur /ˌɒntrəprə'nɜː‖ˌɑːntrəprə'nɜːr/ *n* [C] someone who starts a company, arranges business deals, and takes risks in order to make a profit: *State governments had sought to promote economic development through close links with local entrepreneurs.* —compare INTRAPRENEUR —**entrepreneurial** *adj*: *design graduates with an entrepreneurial approach to the subject* —**entrepreneurship** *n* [U] *Once again private entrepreneurship has not waited for government to take the initiative.*

en·trust or **intrust** /ɪn'trʌst/ *v* [T] to make someone responsible for doing something or dealing with something **entrust sb with sth**: *a presidentially appointed panel entrusted with keeping the stock markets fair and honest* | *an 85-year-old widow who had entrusted her life savings to Home State and now stood to lose it all*

en·try /'entri/ *n* plural **entries** **1** [U] *formal* the arrival of people or goods in a country: *border patrol officers who control illegal entry into the US*

customs entry [U] when official documents are presented and signed giving details of goods that are being brought into or taken out of a country: *the introduction of a new much improved customs entry processing system* —see also BILL OF ENTRY

2 [U] also **market entry** when a company starts selling goods or services in a market where they have not sold them before: *In South Korea, smoking rates among teenage boys nearly doubled after the entry of US brands.* | *Technological changes have helped reduce the costs of market entry, especially in telecommunications.* —see also BARRIER TO ENTRY

3 [C] ACCOUNTING a figure or other piece of information entered in a set of accounts: *In a double-entry system of bookkeeping, each debit has a corresponding credit entry.*

book entry ◆ [C] ACCOUNTING a record of an amount spent or received, as shown in a company's accounting records: *The company had falsified book entries.*

◆ [U] FINANCE where names of owners of bonds, shares etc are held on computer rather than on documents: *Mutual funds are generally book entry, but certificates are available for investors who want them.* | *The issue will be available in book-entry form only.*

closing entry [C] an entry made at the end of an accounting period, moving an amount from a NOMINAL ACCOUNT (=which records income and spending) to a PROFIT AND LOSS ACCOUNT (=which calculates profit)

compound entry [C] an entry in a bookkeeping LEDGER that includes items relating to several different accounts or several different items relating to one account

contra entry [C] an entry made in one side of an account equal in amount to an entry in the other side of the account: *If a cheque is cashed for office use, a contra entry is made, which means an entry is made on the debit and credit side of the cash book.* —see also BOOK OF FINAL ENTRY

4 [U] when you put information into a computer: *Press Esc to return to menu at any time during **data entry**.*

entry fee —see under FEE

entry level *adj* **an entry level product/model/computer/car etc** a type or design of product that is most suitable for people with little money to spend or who have no experience of using that kind of product, and that usually has fewer extra features and is cheaper than other types: *Digital Equipment Corp launched three new Alpha workstations, adding a new high end model and two entry level machines.* —see also ***entry level*** under LEVEL[1]

entry-level product —see under PRODUCT

entry visa —see under VISA

en·ve·lope /'envələʊp‖-loʊp/ *n* [C] a thin paper cover in which you put a letter

self addressed envelope written abbreviation **sae** an envelope that you put your own name and address on

stamped addressed envelope *BrE* an envelope that you put your name, address, and a stamp on, so that someone can send you something

en·vi·ron·ment /ɪn'vaɪərənmənt‖-'vaɪr-/ *n* [C] **1 the environment** the air, water, and land in which people, animals, and plants live: *Since these chemicals were banned, pesticide levels in the environment have been declining.*

2 the general conditions that influence something: *Moving forward in a changing environment is never easy.* | *In the new global **business environment** the exchange of information is the key to success.* | *It is going to be a very **competitive environment** in which Primestar operates.* | *The results were in line with what we expected internally, in spite of the difficult **economic environment**.* | *Despite the poor **retail environment**, the company is doing well.*

3 COMPUTING the kind of OPERATING SYSTEM used by a computer: *the Windows environment*

environmental health —see under HEALTH

environmental impact assessment —see under ASSESSMENT

environmental impact statement —see under STATEMENT

EOM end of month; used on INVOICES to show that they should be paid within 30 days of the end of the month following. For example, invoices sent before the end of March should be paid by the end of May

EOQ abbreviation for ECONOMIC ORDER QUANTITY

EPROM /'iːprɒm‖-prɑːm/ *n* [C] COMPUTING electrically programmable read-only memory; a type of computer CHIP where the contents can only be replaced or changed by a specialized machine, not by a normal user. Eproms are used in SMART CARDS

EPS abbreviation for EARNINGS PER SHARE

EQ test —see under TEST[1]

Equal Credit Opportunity Act *n* a law passed in the US in the 1970s stating that when financial institutions are giving out credit, they should not treat people unfairly because of their age, sex, RACE, religion etc

Equal Employment Opportunity Commission abbreviation **EEOC** *n* a US organization whose job is to make sure that employers do not treat people unfairly because of their age, sex, RACE, religion etc

e·qual·i·ty /ɪ'kwɒləti‖ɪ'kwɑː-/ *n* [U] when all people are treated in the same way and have the same opportunities: *Young women are insisting on career equality* + **of**: *We believe in equality of opportunity*

racial equality when people of different races are

E

treated in the same way and have the same opportunities: *the Commission for Racial Equality*

equalization board —see BOARD OF EQUALIZATION

equal opportunities *n* [plural] when the same chances and opportunities for employment are given to everyone whatever their age, sex, RACE, religion etc: *We must establish a balanced work force that will help guarantee equal opportunities for all – whites and blacks, men and women.* | *The Civil Service is an* ***equal opportunities employer***.

equal pay *n* [U] the principle that men and women should be paid the same amount if they do the same work: *The campaign for equal pay has been continued by the trade-union movement.*

equal rights amendment abbreviation **ERA** *n* [singular] a suggested law in the US, not accepted by every state, that would make it illegal to use the sex of the people involved as the basis for legal decisions: *Under the state's anti-discrimination law and equal rights amendment, anything in the insurance code that allows sex discrimination in setting payment rates would be illegal.*

e•qua•tion /ɪˈkweɪʒən/ *n* [C] a statement in mathematics, showing that two quantities are equal

accounting equation one of the relationships between assets and liabilities used in accounting: *The accounting equation here is: assets minus liabilities equals shareholders' equity.*

E

e•qui•lib•ri•um /ˌiːkwəˈlɪbriəm/ *n* [U] ECONOMICS the idea that there is a situation in an economy where supply and demand are naturally in balance. For example, the supply and demand of goods would be in balance through price changes, or the supply and demand of employment would be in balance through changes in wages

general equilibrium a situation of balance in all markets and areas of the economy: *The factors of uncertainty, information, and market power have quite far reaching implications for the way in which we view the general equilibrium of the economy.*

market equilibrium a situation of balance in a particular market: *The nearly parallel descending paths of supply and demand for office space make it clear that market equilibrium is several years away.*

partial equilibrium equilibirium in one part of the economy, for example the supply and demand of a particular product

equilibrium exchange rate —see under EXCHANGE RATE

e•quip•ment /ɪˈkwɪpmənt/ *n* [U] all the special machines, tools etc that you need for a particular activity: *The company has invested heavily in new equipment.*

capital equipment FINANCE buildings, machinery etc used by a business to produce its goods or services, or by a country in its buildings, roads, water supplies etc; FIXED ASSETS: *Farrel makes capital equipment used to process rubber and plastics.* | *Proceeds from the share issue will be used to repay debt and purchase capital equipment.*

heavy equipment large machines, for example those used to make cars: *Manufacturers of heavy equipment and the electric utilities consume most of Britain's coal.*

equipment lease —see under LEASE[2]

equipment leasing —see under LEASING

equitable mortgage —see under MORTGAGE[1]

eq•ui•ty /ˈekwəti/ *n* plural **equities** **1** [U] FINANCE the capital that a company has from shares rather than from loans: *Turner has been moving toward the use of equity rather than debt.* | *The strong stock market will encourage more companies to use equity to finance acquisitions.* | *SAS will need to* ***raise*** *additional* ***equity*** *to complete the SKr20 billion of aircraft purchases it plans.* —see also RETURN ON EQUITY

book equity [U] the value of a company's shares, as shown in its statement of its financial position at the end of a particular period of time: *The write-down of oil and gas assets will reduce its shareholders' book equity by 50%.*

deferred equity [U] money that a company borrows, for example in the form of CONVERTIBLE LOAN STOCK that can later be exchanged for shares

negative equity ◆ [U] when an asset, usually property, bought by a borrower with a loan is worth less than the loan remaining to be paid: *the growing number of home owners with negative equity*

◆ [U] when a company's liabilities are more than its assets: *The level of bad debts at some Thai banks may mean that some have negative equity.*

owners' equity [U] the difference between the value of a company's assets and its liabilities other than those to shareholders. In principle, this is what the company would be worth to shareholders if it stopped trading, its assets were sold and its debts paid

shareholder equity also **shareholders' equity** [U] another name for OWNERS' EQUITY: *If News Corp revalues its assets by A$1 billion, that will increase shareholders' equity to A$8.2 billion.*

stockholder equity also **stockholders' equity** [U] another name for OWNERS' EQUITY

stub equity [U] the share capital that is left in a company after it has been financially reorganized using a large amount of debt borrowed against the company's assets

tier-1 equity [U] shareholders' equity in a bank. By law, banks must have a minimum amount of tier-one equity in relation to other forms of capital: *The bank currently has $8.894 billion in core equity capital, giving it a 4.08% tier-one equity capital ratio.*

2 equities [plural] trading in companies' shares on a stockmarket, rather than trading on other types of market: *investors seeking to place funds in equities* | *Milan equities finished mostly higher.*

3 [U] in MORTGAGE or HIRE PURCHASE lending, the amount that would be left for the borrower if the property or asset was sold and the remaining loan repaid: *homeowners who have lost the ability to pay but still retain equity in their homes*

4 [U] LAW the principle that a fair judgement must be made where the existing laws do not provide a clear answer in a particular case: *The courts have been willing to look at the settlement of arguments on the basis of equity rather than strict legal principle.*

brand equity [U] MARKETING the value of a brand to the company that owns it and to possible buyers of the company. Brand equity is included as an asset on the BALANCE SHEETS of some companies, but some people think this is not acceptable because it is difficult to give an exact value to a brand: *The company has strong brand equity in the UK, where Walkers crisps is the market leader.*

equity accounting —see under ACCOUNTING

equity capital —see under CAPITAL

equity finance —see under FINANCE[1]

equity financing —see under FINANCING

equity fund —see under FUND[1]

equity funder —see under FUNDER

equity instrument —see under INSTRUMENT

equity investment —see under INVESTMENT

equity ISA —see under ISA

equity kicker *n* [C] when a company raises money by issuing (ISSUE) debt, with the right for investors of the debt to exchange it at a later date for shares in the company, perhaps with a right to buy shares at a lower price than usual: *16 Japanese debt issues with equity kickers were brought to market in April alone.*

equity market —see under MARKET[1]

equity method *n* [singular] another name for EQUITY ACCOUNTING: *Telerate's share of Trading Service losses wasn't included in operating results but was reported as an investment by the equity method of accounting.*

equity of redemption *n* [U] LAW the right of someone who has borrowed money to buy property to keep their property even if they do not make repayments on the loan for a period of time, but then continue with repayments or repay the loan and pay any costs to the lender: *The debtor has an equity of redemption, which he is only to lose after the court has given him ample opportunity to repay, and it becomes plain to the court that he can not or will not pay.*

equity of taxation *n* [U] the principle that taxes should be fair and should be based on different people's ability to pay, which is usually related to their income

equity stake —see under STAKE[1]

equity sweetener —see under SWEETENER

equity yield —see under YIELD[1]

e·quiv·a·lent /ɪˈkwɪvələnt/ *n* [C] something that is equal in value, amount, quality etc to something else: *Nippon Credit had the equivalent of $131 billion in assets on March 31.* —**equivalent** *adj*: *Silicon Graphics said it must issue 5 million new shares or equivalent convertible securities to complete the deal.*

cash equivalent ◆ the value of something expressed in cash: *It is quite easy to work out the cash equivalent of company pension to an employee.*
◆ FINANCE a very safe investment that can easily be sold for cash: *Investors would have been better off putting their money into cash and cash equivalents such as short-term Treasury bills.*

ERA abbreviation for EQUAL RIGHTS AMENDMENT

e·rase /ɪˈreɪz‖ɪˈreɪs/ *v* [T] COMPUTING if you erase information on a computer, you remove it; DELETE 2 —**erasure** *n* [C,U]

er·go·nom·ics /ˌɜːgəˈnɒmɪks‖ˌɜːrgəˈnɑː-/ *n* [U] the study of how the design of equipment affects how well people can do their work: *the ergonomics of computer keyboards* —**ergonomic** *adj*: *a comfortable, ergonomic design* —**ergonomical** *adj* —**ergonomically** *adv*: *The factory is well-lit, ergonomically designed and air-conditioned.*

ERISA /ɪˈriːsə/ *n* Employee Retirement Income Security Act; a US law that says how private PENSION plans should be operated

ERM *n* abbreviation for EXCHANGE RATE MECHANISM: *Luxembourg says it remains fully committed to keeping its currency within the ERM.*

e·rode /ɪˈrəʊd‖ɪˈroʊd/ *v* [T] if an amount or value is eroded, it is slowly reduced: *Stock prices were eroded by profit-taking and ended down.* | *The real value of the capital was slowly being eroded by inflation.* —**erosion** *n* [U] *They were striking over the erosion of salaries.*

er·rat·ic /ɪˈrætɪk/ *adj* having no pattern or plan, making it difficult to know what is going to happen: *Erratic currency markets led to intervention by the major central banks.* | *the erratic performance of exports*

er·ror /ˈerə‖ˈerər/ *n* [C] **1** a mistake: *The confusion was the result of a computer error.* | *The company has made some strategic errors.*

compensating error ACCOUNTING a mistake in keeping accounts that is hard to find because it cancels out another mistake

unrecoverable error COMPUTING a problem that occurs when you are working on a computer, in which information is lost and it is impossible to get it back: *Any sudden loss of power can cause unrecoverable file and disk errors.*

2 errors and omissions excepted used in formal documents to say that mistakes and things that have been forgotten should also be taken into account

error of commission *n* plural **errors of commission** [C] ACCOUNTING when an entry is put in the wrong account in a set of account books, or is of the wrong amount

error of omission *n* plural **errors of omission** [C] ACCOUNTING when an entry is completely missed out from a set of account books

error of posting also **posting error** *n* plural **errors of posting** [C] ACCOUNTING a mistake made in BOOK-KEEPING: *A posting error can be corrected by using a correction or void key.*

error of principle *n* plural **errors of principle** [C] ACCOUNTING when an entry is put into the wrong kind of an account in a set of accounts, for example a RECEIPT entered as a payment, or a PURCHASE entered as a sale

es·ca·late /ˈeskəleɪt/ *v* [I] if amounts, prices etc escalate, they increase: *They saw costs escalating and sales slumping as the effect of rising oil prices hit the company.* —**escalation** *n* [U] *The rapid escalation of loan defaults in the area has caused concern.*

escalator clause —see under CLAUSE

escape clause —see under CLAUSE

es·cheat /ɪsˈtʃiːt/ *n* [U] LAW when the government has the right to someone's property if they die if there is no one who has a right to claim their property and if they have not left formal instructions about what should happen to the property: *By the old doctrine of escheat, states and municipalities may capture unclaimed and dormant bank deposits.* —**escheatment** *n* [U]

es·crow /ˈeskrəʊ‖-kroʊ/ *n* [U] LAW **1** when money or SECURITIES related to a business deal or disagreement between two people or organizations is kept by a THIRD PARTY while the deal is completed or the disagreement is settled: *Amdura said most of the proceeds from the sale will be held **in escrow** for future payments to creditors.*
2 when documents, software etc are kept by a third party to make sure that someone performs their part of an agreement

escrow account —see under ACCOUNT[1]

escrow agent —see under AGENT

ESOP /ˈiːsɒp‖ˈiːsɑːp/ *n* [C] Employee Stock Ownership Plan; a scheme by which employees can buy shares in the company they work for: *a new tax incentive to encourage companies to establish or extend an ESOP*

es·pi·o·nage /ˈespiənɑːʒ/ *n* [U] when people secretly find out a country's or company's secrets: *He was cleared of mounting a campaign of **industrial espionage** against his main rival.*

Esq. *n* abbreviation for ESQUIRE, written after a man's name, especially on the address of an official letter or after the name of a lawyer in the US

essence of a contract *n* [U] the most important condition of a contract, and its main purpose

essential industry —see under INDUSTRY

EST *n* [U] Eastern Standard Time; the time used in the eastern US

Est. also **est.** written abbreviation for ESTABLISHED, used to say when a company was first formed: *Mulligan's Fabrics, Est. 1936*

es·tab·lish /ɪˈstæblɪʃ/ *v* [T] to start a company, organization, system etc that is intended to exist for a long time: *My grandfather established the family business in 1938.*

E

es•tab•lish•ment /ɪˈstæblɪʃmənt/ *n* **1** [C] *formal* a business organization such as a shop or hotel: *Microwave ovens are now an essential piece of equipment in catering establishments.* | *a financial establishment*
2 [U] when a company, organization, system etc is established: *the establishment of the Personal Investment Authority*
3 the Establishment the group of people in a society who have a lot of power and influence and who are often opposed to any kind of change or new ideas

es•tate /ɪˈsteɪt/ *n* [C] **1** PROPERTY a large piece of land in the country, usually with one large house on it and one owner: *The estate consists of the main villa, several outbuildings and barns, a swimming pool, a farm house and an old mill.*
2 land used for growing a particular crop, especially tea, coffee, or rubber: *efficiently run coffee estates*
3 an area of land with factories and offices; INDUSTRIAL PARK *AmE*: *The firm's plant employs 92 people on the town's **industrial estate**.*
trading estate *BrE* an area just outside a city or town where there are small factories and businesses; BUSINESS PARK *AmE*
4 LAW, PROPERTY when someone owns all or part of a piece of land, and any buildings on it, or has a right to use it
freehold estate when land and buildings are owned by someone completely and with no limit in time: *Until 1540 freehold estates could not be left by will.*
leasehold estate when land and buildings are held and used by someone for a period of time and then return to their original owner: *A leasehold estate is measured by a fixed period of time.*
legal estate the legal ownership of land, for a particular time or permanently: *To have a legal estate, whether freehold or leasehold, is to enjoy quite a considerable degree of individual freedom.*
life estate when someone owns all or part of a piece of land and its buildings, or has a right to use them, but only for the length of time they are alive: *Limitation in time is most clearly seen in the case of a life estate, where the estate is held for the life of the tenant.*
5 LAW all of someone's money and property, especially everything that is left after they die: *In her original will, Georgette Magritte left her whole estate to Belgium's Musée Royale des Beaux-Arts.*

estate agent —see under AGENT

estate duty —see under DUTY

estate planning —see under PLANNING

estate tax —see under TAX[1]

es•ti•mate[1] /ˈestɪmɪt/ *n* [C] **1** a calculation of what the value, size, amount etc of something will probably be: *They were able to give us a **rough estimate** (=a not very exact one) of the cost.* | *Even the most **conservative estimates** (=deliberately low) suggest we need to build one million new homes.*
2 a statement of how much it will probably cost to build or repair something; QUOTATION, QUOTE: *Get several estimates before starting any building work.* | *Nuclear power stations are notoriously unreliable and construction costs go way over original estimates.*

es•ti•mate[2] /ˈestɪmeɪt/ *v* [I,T] to calculate what you think the value, size, amount etc of something is or will probably be: *Officials estimate that supply has exceeded demand by £7.5 billion since the beginning of 1988.* | *The value of the deal **is estimated at** £12 million.*

es•ti•ma•tion /ˌestɪˈmeɪʃən/ *n* [C] **1** your opinion of the value, nature etc of someone or something: *His skills and abilities make him, **in my estimation**, an ideal candidate for the board of governors.*
2 a calculation of what the value, size, amount etc of something will probably be; ESTIMATE: *the agriculture department's report, with its estimations of higher pork production to come*

es•ti•ma•tor /ˈestɪmeɪtə‖-ər/ *n* [C] someone whose job is to calculate the probable cost, value, or price of something: *An estimator can call at the customer's home, take measurements and quote a price.*

es•top•pel /ɪˈstɒpəl‖eəˈstɑː-/ *n* [C] LAW a legal rule that prevents someone from saying that something they said earlier in a COURT is untrue, or from saying that it should not now be taken into account

e-tail•ing /ˈiː ˌteɪlɪŋ/ *n* [U] the practice of selling goods and services directly over the INTERNET: *We have all the best bargains in retailing and e-tailing.*

et al /ˌet ˈæl/ *adv written* used after a name or list of names to mean that other people are also involved in something, for example the writing of a report, article etc: *the 'Time for Action' study by Godlove et al*

et alii also **et alia** *adv* a more formal way of writing ET AL

etc /et ˈsetərə/ *adv written* et cetera; used after a list to show that there are other similar things or people that could have been added: *loans taken out to cover the cost of repairs, new equipment etc*

et cet•e•ra /et ˈsetərə/ *adv* the full form of ETC

eth•i•cal /ˈeθɪkəl/ *adj* **1** connected with principles of what is right and wrong: *The practice of analysts owning shares raises tough ethical questions.*
2 morally good or correct: *We know our actions are completely legal and ethical.* —**ethically** *adv*: *Hospitals are trying to behave ethically, and balance the medical needs of a patient against their own financial concerns.*

ethical investment —see under INVESTMENT

eth•ics /ˈeθɪks/ *n* [plural] moral rules or principles of behaviour that should guide members of a profession or organization and make them deal honestly and fairly with each other and with their customers: *Besides sales techniques, salespeople will get training in contract law, psychology, and **business ethics**.* | *The firm observes high standards of **professional ethics**.* | *a journalistic **code of ethics*** (=list of moral rules for a particular activity or profession)

e•thos /ˈiːθɒs‖ˈiːθɑːs/ *n* [singular] the set of ideas, aims and moral attitudes belonging to the members of an organization: *Getting a bit of the American ethos into the business has been a good thing.* | *the company ethos of valuing part-time workers as much as full-time ones* —see also CORPORATE CULTURE

et•i•quette /ˈetɪket‖-kət/ *n* [U] the formal rules for behaviour: *the professional rules of etiquette imposed by the Law Society* | ***Business etiquette*** (=rules for behaviour by businesspeople) *is still very important in corporate Japan.* —see also NETIQUETTE

et seq *adv written* used after a figure, date etc to refer to everything that follows that figure, date etc: *This change of practice applies to settlement income for 1981–82 et seq.*

EU *n* [singular] abbreviation for EUROPEAN UNION: *the member countries of the EU*

EURATOM /jʊəˈrætəm‖jʊrˈæ-/ *n* the European Atomic Energy Community; an organization set up in 1958 to develop and control the use of NUCLEAR POWER in Europe

Eur•i•bor /ˈjʊərɪbɔː‖ˈjʊrɪbɔːr/ *n* [singular] BANKING European interbank offered rate; the interest rate for lending between banks in EUROS: *We need to know which central banks will continue to use national rates and which will be using Euribor.*

Eu•ro /ˈjʊərəʊ‖ˈjʊroʊ/ *n* [C] the currency of many countries of the EUROPEAN UNION, introduced in 1999 for companies, with BANKNOTES and coins available in 2002: *The Euro got off to a strong start on its first day of trading.*

Euro- /jʊərəʊ‖jʊroʊ/ *prefix journalism* European, especially in relation to the EUROPEAN UNION: *We are seeing the*

E

emergence of a new breed of Euro-retailer, using ideas picked up in different markets to add interest to their stores.

Eu•ro•bond /ˈjʊərəʊbɒnd‖ˈjʊroʊbɑːnd/ *n* [C] a bond made available and sold in a currency outside the country of origin of that currency: *Sibneft became the first Russian company to tap the international debt markets by issuing a $150 million Eurobond.*

Eu•ro•card /ˈjʊərəʊkɑːd‖ˈjʊroʊkɑːrd/ *n* [singular] *trademark* a CREDIT CARD made available by European banks, part of the MASTERCARD organization

Eu•ro•cheque /ˈjʊərəʊtʃek‖ˈjʊroʊ-/ *n* [C] *trademark* a payment system that allows users to pay by CHEQUE or to cash cheques in banks in many European countries, with the amounts taken from the user's bank account in their own country: *With your Eurocheques and Eurocheque card, you will find that paying at restaurants, hotels and shops in Europe is as easy as using your cheque book in the UK.*

Eu•ro•clear /ˈjʊərəʊklɪə‖ˈjʊroʊklɪr/ *n* [singular] an international CLEARING HOUSE (=payment system) for bonds and other SECURITIES operated by Morgan Guaranty Brussels for the banks that own it

Eu•ro•crat /ˈjʊərəʊkræt‖ˈjʊroʊ-/ *n* [C] *journalism disapproving* someone who works for and has power in the organization of the European Union: *The price of a pint of cider could double if Eurocrats in Brussels have their way.*

eu•ro•cur•ren•cy /ˈjʊərəʊˌkʌrənsi‖ˈjʊroʊˌkɜː-/ *n* plural **eurocurrencies** [C] any currency bought and sold outside its country of origin, not just in Europe: *In the Eurocurrency market, three-month Eurodollar deposits currently yield 8.19%.*

Eurodollar bond —see under BOND

eurodollar certificate of deposit —see under CERTIFICATE OF DEPOSIT

eurodollar deposits *n* [plural] US dollars held by banks outside the US on which interest is paid: *Three-month eurodollar deposits yield 6.69%, compared with 9.125% for equivalent deutschemark deposits.*

eurodollar market —see under MARKET[1]

eu•ro•dol•lars /ˈjʊərəʊˌdɒləz‖ˈjʊroʊˌdɑːlərz/ *n* [plural] US dollars held and lent by banks outside the US: *If a large sum of eurodollars is borrowed and then used in a transaction, the recipient of the dollars does not see that they are eurodollars rather than 'domestic' US dollars.*

euro-equity issue —see under ISSUE[1]

eu•ro•francs /ˈjʊərəʊfræŋks‖ˈjʊroʊ-/ *n* [plural] French francs and bonds etc in French francs that are held and lent by banks outside France

Eu•ro•land /ˈjʊərəʊlænd‖ˌjʊroʊ-/ also **Euro-zone** *n* [U] the countries of the EUROPEAN UNION that use the euro

eu•ro•mar•ket /ˈjʊərəʊˌmɑːkɪt‖ˈjʊroʊˌmɑːr-/ *n* [C] the buying and selling of currencies and bonds etc in currencies outside their countries of origin: *The currency euromarkets were kept active yesterday with South African rand and Philippine peso offerings for retail investors.*

eu•ro•marks /ˈjʊərəʊmɑːks‖ˈjʊroʊmɑːrks/ *n* [plural] German marks or bonds etc in them that are held and lent by banks outside Germany: *Euromark futures contracts rose yesterday, as traders decided that the Bundesbank might cut interest rates soon.*

Euro medium-term note —see under NOTE[1]

eu•ro•mon•ey /ˈjʊərəʊˌmʌni‖ˈjʊroʊ-/ *n* [U] money in any currency that is bought and sold outside its country of origin

EURO.NM /ˌjʊərəʊ en ˈem‖ˌjʊroʊ-/ *n* FINANCE a group of European stockmarkets that trade in the shares of companies which have new, original ideas or products and are likely to grow and become successful: *Euro.NM member markets currently include Le Nouveau Marche and Neuer Markt.*

eu•ro•notes /ˈjʊərəʊnəʊts‖ˈjʊroʊnoʊts/ *n* [plural] a type of MEDIUM-TERM bonds that are made available and sold as a series but under one single selling arrangement: *Moldova's recent $30 million euronote issue*

European Atomic Energy Community —see EURATOM

European Bank for Reconstruction and Development abbreviation **EBRD** *n* a bank established in 1991 to provide loans and financial advice to countries in Europe that used to be economies controlled by the state but are changing to FREE MARKET economies

European Banking Association —see EBA

European Central Bank abbreviation **ECB** *n* the CENTRAL BANK of the EUROPEAN UNION based in Frankfurt, responsible for setting interest rates, controlling MONEY SUPPLY etc of countries using the EURO: *an independent European Central Bank modelled on the Bundesbank with a low inflation target*

European Coal and Steel Community *n* an organization established in order to gradually remove import taxes and to encourage fair competition in coal and steel between the six countries that later formed the EEC

European Commission written abbreviation **EC** *n* a central organization of the EUROPEAN UNION with political and administrative responsibilities. It is directed by officials from member countries, each with a particular responsibility: *Around 40 multi-million pound takeovers are subject to the approval of the European Commission in Brussels each year.*

European Commission for Europe —see ECE

European Common Market *n* an unofficial name for the EUROPEAN ECONOMIC COMMUNITY, used in the past

European Community abbreviation **EC** *n* an organization of Western European countries established by Belgium, France, Germany, Italy, Luxembourg, and the Netherlands by the TREATY OF ROME in 1957 with the aim of encouraging member countries to work together more closely in economic and political matters. After other countries had joined, it became the EUROPEAN UNION: *The narrow European Economic Community of the 1960s is developing into a wider European Community which could eventually stretch from the Atlantic to the Urals, from the Arctic Circle to the Bosphorus.*

European Council —see COUNCIL OF MINISTERS

European Court of Justice *n* one of the institutions of the EUROPEAN UNION, that explains and decides the meaning of European law, decides if member states have broken the law, and deals with complaints from people and organizations that feel they have not received justice in their national courts: *The European Court of Justice held that once a product had been lawfully produced and marketed in a member state, other member states must recognise that fact and allow it to be imported and sold in its own territory.*

European Currency Unit —see ECU

European Economic Area *n* an area in which goods and services can be traded freely, formed in 1993 by the countries of the EUROPEAN UNION with Norway and Iceland: *Norway's membership of the European Economic Area will continue to provide the main resource for export trade and access to the single market.*

European Economic Community abbreviation **EEC** *n* an old name for the EUROPEAN COMMUNITY, used especially when it was referred to in relation to its economic institutions, for example the agreement to allow goods and services to be traded freely between member countries

European Free Trade Association abbreviation **EFTA** *n* an area in which goods and services can be traded freely, with no taxes on imports, established by Austria, Denmark, Norway, Portugal, Sweden, Switzerland, and Britain in 1958 to compete with the EUROPEAN ECONOMIC COMMUNITY. Both groups are now part of the EUROPEAN ECONOMIC AREA

European interbank offered rate —see under RATE[1]

European Investment Bank abbreviation **EIB** *n* an institution of the EUROPEAN UNION that lends money for investment for roads, communications etc and business development inside and outside the EU: *The European Investment Bank will finance up to 30% of Poland's first big toll motorway linking Berlin and Warsaw at a cost of Ecu2.2 billion ($2.5 billion).*

European Monetary System abbreviation **EMS** *n* an arrangement established in 1979 between some members of the EUROPEAN UNION to make their currencies steady against each other by taking action in the currency markets when one member's currency moves too far from its normal rate against other currencies: *The Portuguese escudo has stayed within a narrow range against the other currencies of the European monetary system since 1993.* —see also EXCHANGE RATE MECHANISM

E

European Monetary Union —see EMU

European option —see under OPTION

European Parliament *n* the directly elected PARLIAMENT of the European Union: *The European Parliament has still to establish itself as an effective channel between citizens and decision makers.*

European Regional Development Fund *n* money given by the EUROPEAN UNION for investment in areas that are less economically developed: *The Broadnet project will receive more than £2.4 million in funding from the European Regional Development Fund.*

European Union abbreviation **EU** *n* an association of European countries, formerly known as the EUROPEAN COMMUNITY. Following the MAASTRICHT TREATY most member countries of the EU are moving towards common economic, foreign, and social POLICIES: *European Union integration will not be complete without a Europe-wide industrial relations system.*

Eu·ro·port /ˈjʊərəʊpɔːt‖ˈjʊroʊpɔːrt/ *n* [C] used in the names of several large European ports: *Thames Europort at Dartford*

Eu·ro·ster·ling /ˈjʊərəʊˌstɜːlɪŋ‖ˈjʊroʊˌstɜːr-/ *n* [U] British pounds and bonds etc in British pounds that are held and lent by banks outside Britain: *last month's £150 million issue by Reliance, the first eurosterling issue by an Indian company*

Eu·ro·tun·nel /ˈjʊərəʊˌtʌnl‖ˈjʊroʊ-/ *n* the company that operates the CHANNEL TUNNEL, or the tunnel itself: *The ferry companies claimed competition from Eurotunnel would ensure prices were kept down.*

eu·ro·yen /ˈjʊərəʊjen‖ˈjʊroʊ-/ *n* [plural] Japanese yen and bonds etc in Japanese yen that are held and lent by banks outside Japan: *The Korea Development Bank yesterday issued its first euroyen bond.*

euro-zone —see under ZONE[1]

EVA abbreviation for ECONOMIC VALUE ADDED

e·vade /ɪˈveɪd/ *v* [T] to not do something that you should do according to the law, for example to not pay tax: *He was charged with evading $12.6 million of taxes.* —**evasion** *n* [U] *charged with fraud, bribery, and* ***tax evasion*** —compare AVOID

e·val·u·ate /ɪˈvæljueɪt/ *v* [T] to carefully consider something to see how useful or valuable it is: *An important element of this process will be to evaluate the effectiveness of the services on offer.* —**evaluation** *n* [C,U] *the development and evaluation of new products* | *There are fears that job evaluation could lead to pay cuts for many employees.*

e·ven /ˈiːvən/ *adj* **1** staying at the same level, rather than frequently changing from one level to the other: *Strong trade will encourage more even selling.*
2 giving two sides, things, ideas etc equal or fair treatment: *ideas on how we can create a more even balance between work and recreation*
3 even tens/hundreds/thousands in whole numbers, to the nearest ten, hundred etc
4 ACCOUNTING an even account is the same on each side, so that there is neither a credit nor a debit balance

event management —see under MANAGEMENT

event marketing —see under MARKETING

evergreen contract —see under CONTRACT[1]

e·vict /ɪˈvɪkt/ *v* [T] to legally force someone to leave the house they are living in or land they are living on: *the US government's plan to evict suspected drug users from public housing projects* —**eviction** *n* [C,U] *Foreclosure and eviction are nothing new in mortgage lending.*

ev·i·dence /ˈevɪ̇dəns/ *n* [U] LAW information or facts given in a court of law to prove that someone is guilty: *The former chairman of the Bank of Crete gave evidence at the trial in which four leading politicians faced charges of corruption.*

evidence of title *n* [U] documents such as DEEDs that prove that someone owns property: *It is common practice for evidence of title to be supplied before contracts are exchanged.*

ex[1] /eks/ *prep* **1** used with a price for goods to show from which place the buyer will be responsible for paying for transport of the goods
2 ex dock/quay/wharf an ex dock, ex quay, or ex wharf price is one where the seller is responsible for taking the goods off the ship in a particular port, and making them available there, but not for transporting them anywhere
3 ex quay duty paid if a price is ex quay duty paid, it is ex quay with the seller responsible for paying any import taxes
4 ex quay duties on buyer's account if a price is ex quay duties on buyer's account, it is ex quay with the buyer responsible for paying any import taxes
5 ex factory/works an ex factory or ex works price is one where the seller makes goods available to the buyer at the seller's factory, and the buyer is responsible for paying for them to be transported to where they are needed
6 ex ship an ex ship price is one where the seller will make the goods available on a ship in a particular port, and the buyer is responsible for paying for the goods to be put on land and transported to where they are needed
7 ex warehouse an ex warehouse price is one where the seller makes the goods available at a particular warehouse, and the buyer is responsible for arranging and paying for the goods to be transported to where they are needed
8 used with a share price or bond price to show that the price does not include particular advantages that have been or will soon be available and that might be included, but which instead go the seller —compare CUM
9 ex all an ex all price for shares is one without any of the advantages that have been or will soon be available, for example DIVIDENDS or RIGHTS ISSUES
10 ex capitalization also **ex capitalisation** *BrE* if shares are sold ex capitalization, the buyer does not have the right to a BONUS ISSUE that has been made
11 ex coupon/interest if bonds are sold ex coupon or ex interest, the buyer does not have the right to a particular interest payment: *RJR Nabisco's 15% debentures were*

quoted 6 5/8 points lower at 113 3/8, reflecting the fact the bonds went ex-coupon yesterday.
12 ex dividend if shares or bonds are sold ex dividend, the buyer does not have the right to a particular DIVIDEND payment, or with bonds, to a particular interest payment: *Shares in BT, which issued a profits warning last month, are expected to fall further today when the stock goes ex-dividend.*
13 ex interest when the price of bonds is ex interest, the person who buys them will not receive the next interest payment on them
14 ex rights if shares are sold ex rights, the buyer does not have the right to new shares in a particular RIGHTS ISSUE: *Novartis, traded ex-rights, finished SFr17 higher at 1,718; Tuesday's closing price was adjusted down SFr79 for the rights.*

ex² abbreviation for excluding, used to show that an amount is not included: *Pastel retails for £349* ***ex VAT.***

ex•act /ɪg'zækt/ *v* [T] *formal* to demand and get something from someone, especially using forceful methods: *The corporation exacted the payments under a mistake of fact.* | *the return of taxes exacted under an unlawful demand* —**exaction** *n* [U] *The company supervises the exaction of tolls at the port.*

exaggerated claim —see under CLAIM¹

ex•am•i•na•tion /ɪgˌzæmə̇'neɪʃən/ *n* **1** [C,U] when you look closely at something in order to see what it is like or whether it is in good condition: *a cover-up designed to obstruct the SEC's examination of his company's books* | *The department was considering the accounting questions as part of a routine examination of the company.*
regulatory examination [C,U] when a government official formally looks at the activities of a company or financial institution to see that it is not doing anything illegal or wrong: *Some banks haven't had a full regulatory examination for as long as two years.*
2 [C,U] LAW when someone is formally asked questions in a court of law, after having promised to tell the truth: *A re-investigation would involve a fresh examination of witnesses.*
cross-examination [C,U] when someone in a court of law is asked questions by a lawyer for the other side after being asked questions by their own lawyer. The purpose of the cross-examination is to check facts and try to find out whether the person is telling the truth: *Mr Coghill finished his cross-examination on Thursday night.*
public examination [C] in Britain, a meeting that is open to members of the public where someone who has become bankrupt is questioned by people who are owed money and by officials
re-examination [C,U] when someone in a court of law is asked further questions by their own lawyer after the cross-examination: *witnesses who were subject to both cross-examination and re-examination*
3 [C] a spoken or written test of knowledge: *an accountancy examination*

examination-in-chief *n* [C,U] LAW when someone who is a WITNESS in a court of law is asked questions by the person who calls the witnesses: *A witness cannot be asked in examination-in-chief about any previous statement made out of court which is inconsistent with his testimony.*

examination of title *n* [U] LAW when research is done into who owns property

ex•ceed /ɪk'siːd/ *v* [T] **1** to be more than a particular number or amount: *Working hours must not exceed 42 hours a week.* | *individuals with assets exceeding £500,000*
2 to go beyond an official or legal limit: *Pesticide levels will be allowed to exceed the EC limits until at least 31 December 2000.*

ex•cel•lence /'eksələns/ *n* [U] when someone is very good at something, or when something is of very high quality. Excellence was a popular word and idea in management in the 1980s: *By reading these books, executives can learn how to achieve excellence.*

excepted perils *n* [plural] INSURANCE risks involved in moving goods from one place to another, that are not covered by a normal insurance policy and for which the company moving the goods is not responsible

ex•cep•tion /ɪk'sepʃən/ *n* [C] INSURANCE a particular event or risk that is mentioned in an insurance policy as something that the policy does not cover; EXCLUSION: *Unless the claim presented is ruled out by one of the policy exceptions, then every consideration should be given for settlement of the claim.*

ex•cep•tion•al /ɪk'sepʃənəl/ *adj* ACCOUNTING **1** an exceptional cost etc is one that does not occur regularly: *a $34 million exceptional restructuring charge*
2 very good, or much better than usual: *The decade of the 1980s produced exceptional returns on many kinds of investments.*

exceptional loss —see under LOSS

ex•cep•tion•als /ɪk'sepʃənəlz/ *n* also **exceptional items, extraordinary items** [plural] FINANCE amounts in a company's accounts that relate to events that are not normally repeated in every period, such as asset sales or charges for RESTRUCTURING (=reorganizing): *Profit, including exceptionals, will be helped by unit sales but hurt by merger costs.*

ex•cess¹ /ɪk'ses, 'ekses/ *n* [C,U] **1** a larger amount of something than is allowed or needed: *He told the Federal Assembly that the devaluation would compensate for an excess in public spending during the past nine months.*
2 in excess of more than a particular amount: *ships carrying in excess of 20,000 tonnes of cargo*
3 INSURANCE a condition in an insurance policy that states that the insured person will pay a particular amount towards any damage and the insurance company will pay the rest. This condition makes people less likely to claim for small amounts: *The insurance company will pay the insured value less the policy excess.*

ex•cess² /'ekses/ *adj* [only before a noun] **1** additional and not wanted or needed because there is already enough of something: *An excess supply of goods and services on the market will exert downward pressure on prices.*
2 excess baggage/luggage bags or cases that weigh more than the legal limit that you can take on a plane: *As I checked in at Baghdad airport, I found that I had 100kg of excess baggage.* | *an excess baggage charge*

excess capacity —see under CAPACITY

excess demand —see under DEMAND

excess fare —see under FARE

excess-of-loss reinsurance —see ***reinsurance*** under INSURANCE

excess profit —see under PROFIT¹

Exch *n* [singular] written abbreviation for EXCHEQUER

ex•change¹ /ɪks'tʃeɪndʒ/ *n* **1** FINANCE [C] a market where goods, services, or shares are bought and sold, in return for money: *the London International Financial Futures Exchange* | *the London Metal Exchange*
futures exchange [C] a place where FUTURES CONTRACTS (=contracts to pay a particular price for the delivery of a particular amount of something in the future) are bought and sold: *At the Chicago Board of Trade, the world's largest futures exchange, total futures and options volume fell 9.7% last year.*
mercantile exchange [C] a place where people meet to buy and sell things, often COMMODITIES (=oil, metals, farm products etc): *the Chicago Mercantile Exchange*

stock exchange [C] a market where company shares are traded; STOCKMARKET: *Companies listed on the Madrid stock exchange dropped about 3% this year.* | *the New York Stock Exchange*

2 corn/wool/cotton exchange a large building in a town, that was used in the past for buying and selling corn, wool etc: *a derelict corn exchange in Cardiff docks*

3 [U] also **foreign exchange** FINANCE the activity of buying and selling currencies; FOREX: *We have recently seen the removal of* ***exchange controls*** (=limits on the amount of currency you are allowed to exchange). | *huge foreign exchange deals* | *Goldman this year has also made healthy profits in its* ***foreign exchange operations.*** —see also EXCHANGE RATE

direct exchange [U] when one currency is exchanged directly for another, without using that of a third country

indirect exchange [U] exchange between two countries using the currency of a third country

4 [U] ECONOMICS money in the currency of a foreign country, for example money obtained through exports: *Since oil prices collapsed, Mexico has made a great effort to promote manufactured exports as an alternative source of* ***foreign exchange.*** | *The Suez Canal is one of Egypt's main foreign exchange earners.*

5 [C,U] when you accept one thing in return for another: *the exchange of goods and services* | *Tickets cannot be accepted back for exchange or re-sale.*

information exchange [U] when information is passed between people and organizations, by means of computer equipment: *The traditional role of telecommunications in voice communication is being rapidly superseded by 'information exchange' made possible by the merger of computer and communications systems.*

6 [C] an arrangement in which two people from different countries, areas etc do each others jobs for a period of time: *He was on a six-month exchange at the factory where her father was works manager.* —see also BILL OF EXCHANGE, DUPLICATE OF EXCHANGE, MEDIUM OF EXCHANGE, TELEPHONE EXCHANGE

exchange² *v* [T] **1** to give someone something and receive something in return: *The new system allows marketing data as well as orders and invoices to be exchanged.* **exchange sth for sth**: *Around £2 billion is exchanged for chips in casinos every year.*

2 if a shop or company exchanges something you have bought, they take it back and give you a new one, for example because the thing you first bought has a fault: *The store will not exchange goods without a receipt.*

3 if you exchange money, you get money in one currency for money in another: *Where can I exchange my dollars for pounds?*

4 exchange contracts *BrE* PROPERTY to complete the final stage of buying a house or other property by signing a contract with the person you are buying it from: *The firm had just exchanged contracts on a nine-acre site.* —see also EXCHANGE OF CONTRACTS

ex·change·a·ble /ɪks'tʃeɪndʒəbəl/ *adj* if something is exchangeable, it can be given to someone who will give something back in return + **for**: *Each bond is priced at FFr680 and is exchangeable for one share from July 1 next year.* + **into**: *When people lend dollars, they lend because they trust that they will be repaid in money that will be exchangeable into goods.*

exchange arbitrage —see under ARBITRAGE

exchange control —see under CONTROL[1]

exchange cross rate —see CROSS RATE

exchange dealer —see under DEALER

exchange economy —see under ECONOMY[1]

Exchange Equalization Account —see under ACCOUNT[1]

exchange of contracts *n* plural **exchanges of contract** [C usually singular] PROPERTY when property is being bought and sold, the moment when the buyer signs the contract of sale and sends it to the seller, who also signs it, making the sale effective: *Exchange of contracts is the vital moment of agreement, after which it is very difficult to withdraw without stiff financial penalties.*

exchange office —see under OFFICE

exchange of shares *n* plural **exchanges of shares** [C] when one company takes over another or joins with it, a part of the agreement that gives shareholders in each company shares in the other: *AT&T and Telecom Italia have moved closer to an alliance by announcing they will pursue an exchange of shares.*

exchange rate *n* [C] the price at which one currency can be bought with another: *If the yen-dollar exchange rate remains at its current level, U.S. exporters could lose $5 billion to $10 billion in business annually.*

cross rate the rate of exchange between two currencies, calculated by comparing them to another currency: *In the foreign exchange market all currencies are quoted against the dollar, so market operators can quickly work out cross rates between various currencies.*

equilibrium exchange rate an exchange rate that would take account of differences in INFLATION, INTEREST RATES, and other aspects of the economic situation: *The head of currency research at JP Morgan calculates an equilibrium exchange rate of DM2.95 to the pound, based on current yield gaps and an assumption the UK joins the Euro in 2002.*

fixed exchange rate an exchange rate that is not allowed to change in relation to others, for example under the BRETTON WOODS AGREEMENT: *Given a fixed exchange rate and a UK inflation rate higher than that in the rest of the world, UK exports will become less competitive in world markets while imports will become more attractive to UK buyers.*

floating exchange rate also **free exchange rate** an exchange rate when the value of a currency is allowed to change in relation to others

forward exchange rate a fixed price given for buying a currency today to be delivered in the future, for example in three months' time, used in international trade to avoid the extra costs that could occur if the exchange rate changes

intervention rate the rate of exchange, either high or low, at which a country's national bank must buy or sell its own currency in order to return it to the same value that it had before: *The Bank of France pushed up its intervention rate by 0.75% to 9.5%.*

official exchange rate an exchange rate set by the government: *America also lets exiles send money to Cuba in lots of $100 a household, delivered in Cuban pesos at the official exchange rate of two pesos to the dollar; in Havana, the black market rate for pesos is 60 to the dollar.*

spot (exchange) rate the price of a currency to be delivered now, rather than in the future: *the percentage difference between the forward exchange rate and the spot exchange rate*

trade-weighted exchange rate an exchange rate calculated in relation to different country's currencies to take account of the amount of trade that is done with each country

unofficial exchange rate an exchange rate that is not set by a government but is one that people really use, for example on the BLACK MARKET: *His official monthly salary of 500 rubles is now worth only about $9.60 at the widely used unofficial exchange rate.*

exchange rate dirty float —see DIRTY FLOAT

Exchange Rate Mechanism abbreviation **ERM** *n* in the EUROPEAN UNION, an arrangement for keeping the currencies of most member countries nearly the same in relation to each other through actions by members' CENTRAL BANKS, and which is continuing for currencies of some of the countries not taking part in the EURO: *There are fears that other EU currencies will be more subject to big price movements than the currencies of the Exchange Rate Mechanism because of the arrival in 1999 of the Euro.*

exchange risk —see under RISK[1]

Ex·cheq·uer /ɪks'tʃekə‖'ekstʃekər/ written abbreviation **Exch** *n* **the Exchequer** the British government department responsible for collecting taxes and paying out public money: *In 1988–89, the Exchequer received some £17 billion from motoring taxation.* —see also CHANCELLOR OF THE EXCHEQUER

Exchequer stock —see under STOCK[1]

ex·cise /'eksaɪz/ *n* **1** [C,U] a government tax that is charged on certain goods that are sold in the country, for example alcoholic drinks and petrol: *In theory, an excise on home production of tobacco could have produced the same revenue as a tax on imports.* | *The Chancellor decided not to increase excise on whisky.*

2 the Excise in Britain, a group of government officials whose job is to collect excise and some other taxes: *By 1780 the Excise had watch over 35,500 tea and coffee dealers.* | *an excise officer* —see also CUSTOMS AND EXCISE

excise duty also **excise tax** —see under DUTY

excise tax —see under TAX[1]

ex·cite /ɪk'saɪt/ *v* [T] FINANCE to produce a lot of activity in a market, with a lot of people buying and selling stocks and shares: *Shute excited the market again yesterday by reporting sharply higher profits for BM Group.* —**excited** *adj*: *The markets have been excited all week.* —**excitement** *n* [U]

excl written abbreviation for EXCLUDING

ex·clud·ing /ɪk'skluːdɪŋ/ written abbreviation **excl** *prep* used to say that something is not included in a total or a set of things: *Deficit, excluding invisible items such as banking and insurance, was £4.5 billion.* | *an allowance for plant and machinery, excluding cars*

ex·clu·sion /ɪk'skluːʒən/ *n* [C] **1** INSURANCE a particular event or risk that is mentioned in an insurance policy as something that the policy does not cover; EXCEPTION: *Common exclusions in medical insurance policies are pregnancy, cosmetic surgery and treatment of AIDS.*

2 FINANCE an amount that would normally form part of a person or company's total income, but that is kept separate because a particular part of tax law states that tax does not have to be paid on it: *Customs are reviewing the current range of exclusions.*

ex·clu·sive /ɪk'skluːsɪv/ *adj* **1** an exclusive agreement, contract or right is one that a single person or organization has and no one else has: *They have signed an* ***exclusive agreement*** *to market and sell the diamonds to retail jewelers in Switzerland.* | *Nippon Systemhouse will have an* ***exclusive license*** (=a right that no one else has) *to make and market the systems in Japan.* | *FMC has* ***exclusive rights*** *to any commercial product that exploits the research.* + **to**: *This offer is exclusive to readers of The Economist.*

2 exclusive places, products etc are so expensive that not many people can afford to buy them: *Bel Air, an exclusive suburb of Los Angeles*

3 if a figure is exclusive of a particular amount, it does not include that amount: *GM's operating costs, exclusive of depreciation and amortization, fell 8%.* | *It costs £200, exclusive of VAT.*

exclusive economic zone —see under ZONE[1]

ex·clu·siv·i·ty /ˌeksklυː'sɪvəti/ *n* [U] **1** the fact that a place or product is so expensive that not many people can afford to buy it: *Porsche highlighted its exclusivity by aiming at the high end of the luxury-car segment.*

2 the fact of having an exclusive agreement, contract or right: *SmithKline will have seven-year marketing exclusivity for the drug.*

3 when a business that is in the process of being bought agrees not to speak to any other person or company that may be interested in buying it

ex coupon —see under EX[1]

ex-directory *adj BrE* an ex-directory telephone number is deliberately not given in a public telephone book; UNLISTED *AmE*: *You can change your number and* ***go ex-directory*** (=no longer have your number in the phone book).

ex dividend —see under EX[1]

ex dock —see under EX[1]

ex·ec /ɪg'zek/ *n* [C] *informal* an executive: *Employers want execs skilled in marketing, the environment, accounting and controlling costs.*

ex·e·cute /'eksəkjuːt/ *v* [T] **1** to do what is written in a contract, plan etc: *The directors make the decisions but the managers have to execute them.* | *UK companies with a proven management ability to execute a business plan*

2 COMPUTING **execute a command/query/instruction** to do something to make a computer carry out an instruction

executed contract —see under CONTRACT[1]

executed trust —see under TRUST

ex·ec·u·tive[1] /ɪg'zekjətɪv/ *n* [C] **1** someone who has an important job as a manager in a company or business: *She is Scottish Power's most senior woman executive.* | *a* ***senior executive*** *with a major pharmaceuticals company* | *One of the BBC's* ***top executives*** *was working under a freelance contract.* —see also ACTIVE CORPS OF EXECUTIVES

account executive written abbreviation **AE** an executive who works for an ADVERTISING AGENCY and deals directly with clients, communicating their ideas to the company and making sure that their accounts are managed in a satisfactory way: *An account executive will be expected to know when a client can see the proofs of the latest press advertisement.*

advertising executive a senior person in an ADVERTISING AGENCY: *a dynamic young advertising executive*

chief executive ◆ the person who has the highest position in a company or other organization and who makes all the important decisions about how it is run: *John Smale, former chairman and chief executive of Procter & Gamble*

◆ **the Chief Executive** *AmE* the President of the United States

legal executive *BrE* someone who works in a law firm, preparing cases and advising clients, but who has not studied and trained to be a lawyer: *She took a post as a trainee legal executive with a firm of solicitors.*

2 the executive the part of a government responsible for taking decisions on policy, running the government etc, rather than for making laws: *an audit on behalf of both the legislative and the executive*

3 a government organization responsible for deciding policy and taking decisions to do with one particular thing

Health and Safety Executive [singular] a government organization in Britain that controls the risks to people's health and safety from work activities: *The Health and Safety Executive has published three free guidance leaflets for chemical manufacturers.* —compare OCCUPATIONAL SAFETY AND HEALTH ADMINISTRATION

4 the group of people in a political organization, society etc that make the rules and make sure that they work in the way that was planned: *The executive deferred a decision on his future until mid-January.* | *the Labour party executive*

E

national executive an executive representing all the parts of a political organization etc within a country: *the National Executive of the Labour Party*

executive[2] *adj* [only before a noun] **1** connected with making decisions and managing and organizing things, especially within a company or government: *Some of the members of the* ***executive board*** *decided to rethink the organizational culture.* | *When he reached the company's retirement age of 60, he decided to give up his* ***executive duties***. | *the legislative and executive functions of government*
2 for the use of people who have important jobs in the management of a company or business: *The Falcon 20 is one of the most versatile* ***executive jets*** (=small jet planes for the use of a company's top managers) *flying in the world today.* | *the executive lounge at Heathrow airport*
3 used to suggest that something is of high quality, even if executives do not actually use it: *an executive coach service*

executive assistant —see under ASSISTANT

executive chairman —see under CHAIRMAN

executive committee —see under COMMITTEE

executive director —see under DIRECTOR

executive perk —see under PERK

executive search —see under SEARCH[1]

executive secretary —see under SECRETARY

ex•ec•u•tor /ɪɡˈzekjətə‖-ər/ *n* [C] LAW a person, lawyer, or bank that deals with the instructions in someone's WILL (=a document that says who should receive their property after they die): *His executors hope that the money raised by the painting will pay off the last of his debts.* | *The major banks now provide insurance, security-dealing, trustee and executor services.*

executory trust —see under TRUST

ex•ec•u•trix /ɪɡˈzekjətrɪks/ *n* [C] LAW a woman who acts as an executor: *Mary Wilding, executrix of William Wilding*

exemplary damages —see under DAMAGE[1]

ex•empt[1] /ɪɡˈzempt/ *v* [T] **1** to allow something that would normally be affected by a tax, law etc not to be affected: *Democrats would also tax the entire cost of private planes, while Republicans would exempt them.* **exempt sth from**: *a simple change in the tax law to exempt dividends from the recipient's income taxes*
2 to give permission to someone or to an organization not to do something that they would normally have to do **exempt sb from**: *The new rules also exempt established companies from having to comply with all the new safety regulations.*

exempt[2] *adj* **1** something that is exempt from a law, tax etc is not affected by that law etc when normally it might be + **from**: *Restaurant and delicatessen food will be exempt from the labeling requirements.*
2 someone who is exempt from something has special permission not to do it + **from**: *Students are not exempt from compulsory military service.*

exemption certificate —see under CERTIFICATE

ex•er•cise /ˈeksəsaɪz‖-ər-/ *v* [T] **1** *formal* **exercise power/influence/a right etc** to use your power, influence or a right that you have: *the symbolic power that creditor exercises over debtor*
2 exercise an option to buy the property mentioned in an OPTION: *The seller is likely to exercise the option if the market value of the property is above the repurchase price.* —**exercise** *n* [U] *A time should be given for exercise of any option.*

exercise price —see under PRICE[1]

ex factory —see under EX[1]

ex gra•tia /ˌeks ˈɡreɪʃə/ *adj, adv* an ex gratia payment is one made to help someone or as a gift, not because you have a legal duty to make it: *The government had announced that it would make ex gratia payments to all investors who had suffered loss, while stressing that it had no legal liability to pay compensation.*

ex gratia payment —see under PAYMENT

ex•haust /ɪɡˈzɔːst‖-ˈzɒːst/ *v* [T] **1** if you exhaust a supply of something, you use it all, so that there is none left: *The museum was unable to buy the painting as its funds were exhausted by the purchase of two huge albums of eighteenth-century architectural drawings.*
2 to take all the natural supplies of something from a place such as a mine so that there is none left: *Cut-and-run logging is expected to exhaust the primary rainforest by the end of the decade.* | *an exhausted coal mine*

ex•hib•it[1] /ɪɡˈzɪbət/ *v* [I,T] to put something in a public place such as a TRADE SHOW so that people can go and see it: *Last month, Toyota exhibited at a London company-car show for the first time.*

exhibit[2] *n* [C] **1** something exhibited in a public place such as a TRADE SHOW: *The centrepiece of the exhibit was the central section of an ART 700 filter system for use on diesel powered buses.*
2 a picture, drawing or chart used in a talk to help someone present information: *An example of a typical integrated capital budgeting system is shown in Exhibit 1.*
3 LAW an object, piece of clothing etc that is used in a court of law to try to prove that someone is guilty or not guilty: *In total, the jury heard 94 prosecution witnesses and saw over 950 pages of exhibits.*

ex•hi•bi•tion /ˌeksəˈbɪʃən/ *n* [C] a public event where businesses and other organizations show their products and services so that people can go and see them: *Exhibitions and trade shows are expensive but good ways to promote a message or an image.* | *the Expo 99 exhibition*
trade exhibition a public event where businesses and other organizations show their products and services so that people from other companies can look at them and decide whether to buy them; TRADE FAIR, TRADE SHOW

exhibition centre —see under CENTRE

exhibition hall *n* [C] a very large room used for exhibitions

exhibition stand —see under STAND[2]

ex•hib•i•tor /ɪɡˈzɪbətə‖-ər/ *n* [C] a business or other organization showing its products at an exhibition: *The exhibitors are all market leaders in their respective fields and are of special interest and value to all in the credit profession.*

Ex•im•bank /ˈeksɪmˌbæŋk/ also **Ex-Im Bank** *n* another name for the US EXPORT-IMPORT BANK

ex interest —see under EX[1]

ex•it /ˈeɡzət, ˈeksət/ *v* [I,T] to leave a market, a type of business, or an agreement: *the bank's four-year effort to exit the long-term lending business* + **from**: *The company plans to exit from the real estate business and concentrate on insurance.* —**exit** *n* [singular] *The deal marks their exit from the auto insurance market.*

exit interview —see under INTERVIEW[1]

exit poll —see under POLL[1]

ex of•fi•ci•o /ˌeks əˈfɪʃiəʊ‖-oʊ/ *adj* an ex officio member of a group or organization is a member because of their senior rank or position, not because they have been chosen by others: *The National Assembly is composed of 228 members – 168 directly elected, 25 ex officio, and 35 indirectly elected.*

ex•or•bi•tant /ɪɡˈzɔːbətənt‖-ɔːr-/ *adj* an exorbitant price, rate, demand etc is much higher than is reasonable or usual: *a businessman who claims his bank is* *forcing him to pay exorbitant charges* | *On the black market prices were particularly exorbitant.*

ex•pand /ɪk'spænd/ *v* [I,T] **1** to become larger in size, amount, or number, or to make something larger in size, amount, or number: *If a bank increases its lending, other things being equal, the money supply will expand.* | *The money will be invested on upgrading sorting offices and expanding the Post Office vehicle fleet.*
2 if an economy, industry, or business activity expands, it gets bigger or more successful: *The business was growing very rapidly and expanding abroad.* | *Many firms borrowed heavily to expand their businesses.* | *The Chancellor is predicting that the economy will expand at 3% a year.* **expand into**: *western car makers hoping to expand into the new consumer markets of eastern Europe*

ex•pan•sion /ɪk'spænʃən/ *n* [U] **1** when something increases or is increased in size, amount, or number: *An expansion of demand can give rise to inflationary pressures* | *There was enormous expansion of credit to finance cumulative budget deficits of $1,400 billion.*
2 when an economy becomes more successful, and there is increased economic activity, more jobs etc: *the continued expansion of the Japanese economy* | *The study was carried out at a time of* ***economic expansion*** *and three out of four of the firms had experienced growth in the year prior to the study.*
3 when an industry or company becomes bigger or more successful: *a strategy of modest but steady expansion* | *Many small businesses are already benefiting from lower interest rates as they accelerate their expansion plans and product introductions.* | *More expansion into Europe is likely, but the company will not be hurried.*
domestic credit expansion ECONOMICS a way of measuring growth in the total amount of money in a country's economy at a particular time. It includes bank loans to private customers in the UK and abroad, and the PUBLIC SECTOR BORROWING REQUIREMENT (=the amount of money the government will need to borrow in the future for all its different departments). It does not include the amount of money owed by the government to private companies: *Increased government borrowing tends to lead to increased domestic credit expansion.*
vertical expansion when a company starts to take on the business activities that are carried out by its suppliers or customers: *Vertical expansion so that suppliers can be controlled may also be a short-run goal.*

expansion card —see under CARD

expansion slot *n* [C] COMPUTING a CONNECTOR on a computer system board that can hold an expansion card: *Internal modems fit into an expansion slot and don't require a physical serial port socket.*

ex par•te /eks 'pɑːti‖'pɑːr-/ *adj, adv* LAW **1** made by one side only in a legal disagreement, without first telling the other side: *Ex parte applications are frequently made to the courts and granted without hearing the party affected.*
2 made by someone who is not one of the sides in a legal disagreement, but who will be affected in some way by the court's final decision

ex•pat•ri•ate /eks'pætriət, -trieɪt‖eks'peɪ-/ also **expat** *n* [C] someone who has moved to a foreign country to live and work: *The State of Bahrain is the banking and commercial centre of the Arabian Gulf, with a large community of expatriates.*

ex•pec•tan•cy /ɪk'spektənsi/ *n* [U] HUMAN RESOURCES the amount of effort an employee believes will be necessary to do his or her job. Expectancy is important to managers because, by knowing about it, they know what they have to do to make their employees want to work harder: *Expectancy theories of motivation are based on the premise that people are motivated by the expected outcomes of their actions.* —see also LIFE EXPECTANCY

expectation of life *n* [U] *BrE* INSURANCE the length of time that a person is expected to live, depending on where they live, their job, sex etc. Insurance companies use this information to calculate the cost of insuring someone's life, and therefore the amount that people have to pay for that insurance; LIFE EXPECTANCY

ex•pec•ta•tions /ˌekspek'teɪʃənz/ *n* [plural] **1** ECONOMICS what people in the business world believe will happen in the economy in the future. Expectations are important because they affect the level of investment in an economy: *The current level of economic activity will certainly influence business expectations and confidence.*
2 LAW someone's chances of being given money or property owned by someone else when that person dies

expected value —see under VALUE[1]

ex•pel /ɪk'spel/ *v* past tense and past participle **expelled** present participle **expelling** [T] to officially make someone leave a country or an organization: *They found it legally difficult to identify and expel illegal immigrants.* **expel sb from sth**: *an attempt to expel a member from a trade union*

ex•pend•a•ble /ɪk'spendəbəl/ *adj* expendable supplies or items are ones of little value. Companies do not have to keep records of who has expendable items, and what they are being used for

ex•pen•di•ture /ɪk'spendɪtʃə‖-ər/ *n* [C,U] the total amount of money that a government, organization or person spends during a particular period of time: *It's a rare advertiser who knows what their return on investment in advertising expenditures is.* + **on**: *a 58% increase in expenditure on books and teaching materials*
capital expenditure [C,U] spending by a company on buildings, machinery, equipment etc; CAPITAL OUTLAY: *Tight credit markets could make heavy capital expenditures on new technology difficult now.* | *Asahi increased capital expenditure to increase production capacity.*
consumption expenditures [plural] amounts of money spent by people buying goods and services in an economy: *Economists generally expect personal income to have risen in December and consumption expenditures to have been flat.*
government expenditure also **public expenditure** [C,U] spending by a government, usually a national government: *Falling oil prices coupled with increased public expenditure are widening Venezuela's budget deficit.*
marketing expenditure [C,U] the amount of money spent by a company on marketing activities in a particular period of time: *The company said discount pricing that began last summer requires heavy marketing expenditures.*
public expenditure [C,U] another name for GOVERNMENT EXPENDITURE
state expenditure [C,U] spending by a government, or, in the US, one of its states: *Tennesseans can count the absence of an income tax as one reason their state expenditure problem isn't as bad as Kentucky's next door.*

expenditure tax —see under TAX[1]

ex•pense /ɪk'spens/ *n* **1** [C,U] an amount of money that a business or organization has to spend on something: *Most advertisers look upon advertising as an expense and not an investment, which is a mistake.* | *The company's cost-cutting program is expected to reduce expenses by $28 million next year.*
accrued expense [C usually plural] the value of goods or services that were bought by a business or organization during a particular period of time, even if it pays for them in a later period

E

capital expense [C usually plural] money that a business or organization spends on investing in new equipment, buildings etc, rather than on running the business or producing goods: *Japan Airlines and All Nippon, with plans for new airport facilities and aircraft, are both facing a lot of capital expenses.*

direct expense [C usually plural] money that is spent directly on making one particular product or performing one particular service, rather than money spent on general costs, such as management costs

entertainment expense [C usually plural] money that a business or organization spends on taking customers to restaurants, bars, theatres etc, as a way of making business deals easier to complete: *a breakdown of average entertainment expenses for large Japanese companies – bars, nightclubs: 47%, gifts: 20, restaurants: 17, golf: 10, other: 6.*

fixed expense [C usually plural] money that a business or organization has to pay that does not change with the amount of goods or services it produces or sells

general expense [C usually plural] money that is spent on the general running of a business or organization, rather than money spent on producing goods or selling services: *Operating profit was knocked down 15% by higher sales, administrative and general expenses.*

handling expense [C usually plural] the extra costs of buying and selling goods, for example packaging, shipping, storing and insurance: *Last year sales of paintings totalled £1.3 million, out of which the administration and handling expenses had to be paid.*

indirect expense [C usually plural] money that is spent on general costs, such as management costs, rather than money spent directly on making one particular product or performing one particular service —compare ***direct expense***

interest expense [C usually plural] money that a business or organization has to spend on paying interest on money that it has borrowed: *Planned debt reductions will reduce annual interest expenses by about $15 million.*

marketing expense [C usually plural] money that a business or organization spends on advertising and marketing: *Research and development went from $28 million to $45 million, while sales and marketing expenses increased even more.*

overhead expense also **operating expense** [C usually plural] other names for GENERAL EXPENSE: *A reduction in overhead expenses would free funds for workers' pay.*

sales expense also **selling expense** [C usually plural] the money that a business or organization spends on selling its products, for example running sales offices, paying salespeople etc: *Sprint's first-quarter earnings are likely to be hurt by higher selling expenses related to new marketing programs.*

travel expense also **travelling expense** *BrE* [C usually plural] money that a business or organization spends to pay for its employees to travel to attend meetings etc

2 expenses [plural] money that an employee spends while doing their job on things such as travel and food, and which their employer then pays back to them: *Come on, have another drink – it's* ***on expenses.*** | *Mr Pistner gets an annual salary of $1.5 million; in addition he gets reimbursed for travel and other expenses.*

expense account —see under ACCOUNT[1]

expense ratio —see under RATIO

ex·pen·sive /ɪk'spensɪv/ *adj* **1** costing a lot of money: *expensive computer equipment* | *Many manufacturers would find it* ***prohibitively expensive*** (=so expensive that they could not afford it) *to set up their own High Street stores.*

2 charging a lot of money: *We don't have luxury yachts or go to expensive hotels.*

ex·pe·ri·ence /ɪk'spɪəriəns‖-'spɪr-/ *n* **1** [U] knowledge or skill gained from doing a particular job: *a high-up executive who had years of experience in advising investors* | *Applicants will normally have at least two year's experience teaching English for Business.* | *You will receive a salary in the range of £15,586 to £20,176 pa depending on qualifications and experience.* | *His bank manager pointed out that Jack had no* ***business experience*** *and was therefore a high risk from the bank's point of view.* | *They are prepared to take young people with* ***no previous experience*** *and train them.*

hands-on experience [U] experience gained from doing a job rather than studying it: *On this course there is an emphasis on hands-on experience and practical work.*

work experience [U] a short period of time during which a young person works for a company in order to learn about a job and about working life in general: *Shell is working on projects to help find training and work experience for some of Brazil's 13 million street children.*

2 [U] INSURANCE a record of the difference in amount between claims made by insured people and money they pay for their insurance policies. This information is used by insurance companies to calculate the amount people should pay for their insurance policies: *A fleet insurance means an insurance under a motor policy covering a number of vehicles in respect of which the risk is rated on its own experience.*

experience curve —see under CURVE

ex·pe·ri·enced /ɪk'spɪəriənst‖-'spɪr-/ *adj* someone who is experienced has done a particular type of job before and therefore has knowledge and skills connected with the job: *The company has a small team of experienced sales people.* + **in**: *Some of the smaller firms are less experienced in foreign trade.*

ex·pert /'ekspɜːt‖-ɜːrt/ *n* [C] **1** someone who has a special skill or special knowledge of an area of work or study, usually as the result of many years experience: *One of the functions of the marketing expert in commerce is to develop a clear idea of the target market.* + **in/on**: *You don't have to be an expert in accountancy to use this software package.*

2 expert advice/evidence/guidance etc advice etc given by an expert: *It will normally be necessary to seek expert advice on this kind of investment.*

ex·per·tise /ˌekspɜː'tiːz‖-ɜːr-/ *n* [U] special skills or knowledge in an area of work or study: *KPMG's international tax and accounting expertise* | *An independant financial advisor's* ***area of expertise*** *includes products such as pension plans and insurance policies.* + **in**: *Renault's expertise in corrosion protection is confirmed by the new eight year anti-corrosion warranty covering all models of the Clio.*

expert system —see under SYSTEM

expert witness —see under WITNESS[1]

expiration date —see under DATE[1]

ex·pire /ɪk'spaɪə‖-'spaɪr/ *v* [I] **1** if an official document such as a contract, agreement, or licence expires, the period of time during which it can be used ends: *If your Program disk should prove defective after the warranty expires, LD will replace it for a fee of £200.* | *The existing lease expires at the end of this year.*

2 if a period of time expires, it comes to an end: *The Panel will not take any action until the appeal period of two business days has expired.* | *If you can't do what you said you'd do, then you should contact the client before the deadline expires.*

3 FINANCE if an OPTION (=the right to buy a particular amount of shares, currency etc in the future) expires, it can no longer be EXERCISED (=it is no longer possible to buy the shares, currency etc that it relates to): *When the October options expire, the clearing house for the market will create a new series of options for July expiry.*

ex·pir·y /ɪk'spaɪəri‖-'spaɪri/ *n* [U] *BrE* when an official document, period of time, or right to buy shares, currency etc expires; EXPIRATION *AmE*: *The sellers' right to repossess the goods did not arise until the expiry of the credit period.* | *The first cycle of options have* ***expiry dates*** *in January, April, July, and October.*

ex·ploit /ɪk'splɔɪt/ *v* [T] **1** to use something fully and effectively in order to gain a profit or advantage: *Institutions like Lloyd's have been slow to exploit computers.* | *the ways in which natural resources are exploited*
2 to treat someone unfairly in order to make money or to get an advantage for yourself: *The system is unjust in that it enables the owners to exploit the workers.* —**exploitation** *n* [U] *International oil companies have been seen as symbols of imperialist exploitation.*

ex·po·nen·tial /ˌekspə'nenʃəl◂/ *adj* **exponential growth/increase/rise etc** a rate of growth that becomes faster and faster over time: *This simple model shows an* ***exponential increase*** *in sales during the period of the advertising campaign.* | *The social security budget was rising at an* ***exponential rate***. —**exponentially** *adv*: *Demand for eye tests from the over-60s is increasing exponentially.*

ex·port[1] /'ekspɔːt‖-ɔːrt/ *n* **1** [C usually plural] a product or service that is sold to another country: *A third of America's exports go to American-owned firms abroad.* | *Shiseido, a Japanese cosmetics giant, plans to* ***boost exports*** (=increase them).
invisible exports [plural] exports such as financial services that are not physical goods or products: *The overseas earning capacity of banking and insurance are referred to as 'invisible exports'.*
visible exports [plural] exports that are physical goods, for example industrial products and food: *In the year to 1999, the value of United Kingdom visible exports to the United States of America was almost double the level of a decade earlier.*
2 [U] the sale of goods to other countries: *The import and export of goods is more complicated than conducting domestic business within a single country.* | *the availability of cash crops, for example coffee, for export*

export[2] /ek'spɔːt‖-ɔːrt/ *v* [I,T] **1** to sell goods to other countries: *In the first 11 months of last year, Brazil exported 15 million bags of coffee.* | *The mine will produce 9 million tonnes of coal annually of which 5.3 million tonnes will be exported to Japan.*
2 to introduce an activity, idea etc to another country: *We are retailers, and our skills may not be easily exported.*

ex·por·ta·tion /ˌekspɔː'teɪʃən‖-ɔːr-/ *n* [U] when goods or services are exported: *the campaign against the exportation of live animals*

export credit —see under CREDIT[1]

export credit guarantee —see under GUARANTEE[2]

Export Credits Guarantee Department written abbreviation **ECGD** *n* the Export Credits Guarantee Department; a British government organization that provides British companies with export credit insurance and so encourages them to export their goods abroad: *The ECGD last year insured £200 million of UK investments against war, expropriation, restrictions on remittances and other political risks.*

export documents —see under DOCUMENT[1]

export duty —see under DUTY

ex·port·er /ɪk'spɔːtə‖-'spɔːrtər/ *n* [C] a person, company, or country that exports goods: *If the yen rose above 115 to the dollar, virtually every exporter in Japan would be losing money.* | *Britain's leading exporter of manufactured goods*
net exporter a country that exports more of a particular thing than it imports: *France will never be a net exporter of fossil fuel.*

export factoring —see under FACTORING

Export-Import Bank —see under BANK[1]

ex·port·ing /ɪk'spɔːtɪŋ‖-ɔːr-/ *n* [U] selling goods to other countries
direct exporting selling goods directly to consumers in other countries
indirect exporting selling goods in other countries by using another company to carry, market or sell the goods for you

export insurance —see under INSURANCE

export invoice —see under INVOICE[1]

export licence —see under LICENCE

export market —see under MARKET[1]

export permit —see ***export licence*** under LICENCE

ex·pose /ɪk'spəʊz‖-'spoʊz/ *v* [T] **1** to reveal the truth about someone or something that was hidden, especially when it involves something illegal, dishonest or wrong: *a popular politician who achieved prominence by exposing high-level corruption*
2 MARKETING to put goods in a place where people can see them or buy them: *The products do not have to be exposed at the supplier's premises.* | *Instead of offering high-quality digital TV, they could expose the cheaper sets.*

ex·po·sé /ɪk'spəʊzeɪ‖ˌekspə'zeɪ/ *n* [C] a newspaper article or a television programme which tells people the truth for the first time about something bad, or someone who has done something illegal, dishonest or wrong: *a sensational* ***exposé of*** *insider dealing and corruption in the City*

ex·po·si·tion /ˌekspə'zɪʃən/ *n* [C] *formal* **1** MARKETING a large international show that is open to the public, where new products, especially industrial products, can be seen; EXHIBITION: *Comdex is launching the Enterprise Computing Exposition and Conference in July.*
2 a detailed explanation of a particular idea or THEORY: *Great care must be taken to make the exposition clear to a non-technical audience.*

ex·po·sure /ɪk'spəʊʒə‖-'spoʊʒər/ *n* **1** [U] MARKETING advertising and PUBLICITY which is used to sell a product or service: *Our unrivalled advertising exposure gets fast results.* | *I'd probably get some personal* ***media exposure*** *– an interview on Going Live, perhaps.*
2 [C,U] when a newspaper article or a television programme tells people the truth for the first time about something bad, or someone who has done something illegal, dishonest or wrong: *Other exposures such as the irregular payments to Graham Roberts have come largely from the Press or club officials.*
3 [C,U] FINANCE the amount of money that a bank lends to a customer, and which the bank therefore risks losing: *Rising government debt will be a worry, though most of us will be concentrating on dealing with our own* ***borrowing exposures***. | *Concern over* ***exposure to*** *the troubled Heron International group hit the banking sector, with Barclays the main casualty.*
4 [C,U] FINANCE the amount of money an investor risks losing if their investments do badly, for example on the stockmarket: *Some companies overlook the fact that* ***foreign exchange exposures*** *rise when the contract is signed.* | *The fund is aiming to raise $200 million from banks looking to reduce their exposure to Eastern Europe.*
debt exposure [C,U] when a company's or country's financial situation is at risk because it is owed a lot of money that may not be repaid: *Germany, with its large debt exposure to some of the republics, could be hurt.*

E

exposure draft —see under DRAFT[1]

ex·press[1] /ɪk'spres/ *v* [T] **1** to say what you think or feel about something: *The sales manager expressed caution about the deal.* | *Worries have been expressed within the industry about the trend.*
2 LAW to state clearly and openly something that has been agreed: *Such warranties are implied, unless a contract expresses a contrary intention.*
3 to write a quantity or amount in numbers, letters or other figures **express sth as**: *The level of expenditure is usually expressed as a percentage of the measure of economic activity of a particular country.*

express[2] *adj* [only before a noun] **1** stated or written clearly and openly, and showing a clear purpose or intention: *the distinction between* ***express authority*** *and mere consent* | *Copyright prevents use of this material without the* ***express permission*** *of the author.* | *There is an* ***express agreement*** *by the plaintiff to pay £10 towards the ground-rent.*
2 an express service is one that is quicker than the normal service: *overnight express trains* | *It takes anything from 2 to 5 days, depending on whether or not you use an express transfer.*

ex·pres·sage /ɪk'spresɪdʒ/ *n* [U] *AmE* the system of using an express service, or the charges made for that service

express condition —see under CONDITION

express contract —see under CONTRACT[1]

expression of interest *n* plural **expressions of interest** [C] a formal statement by an organization, company, or investor, stating that they want to become involved in a particular project or do a particular job: *BP have* ***invited expressions of interest*** *in a new program to reopen the oil fields.* | *Several investor groups are considering submitting bids to acquire First Capital Life Insurance Co. At least three groups have made expressions of interest.* —compare LETTER OF INTENT

express term —see under TERM[1]

express trust —see under TRUST

express warranty —see under WARRANTY

ex·pro·pri·ate /ɪk'sprəʊprieɪt‖-'sproʊ-/ *v* [T] LAW if a government expropriates someone's property, it legally takes that person's property from them for public use: *There is a risk that an investment abroad may be expropriated by the overseas government.* | *The Court ruled that Yeltsin had been correct to expropriate property which belonged to the state.* —**expropriation** *n* [U] *There was little resistance to the purchase or expropriation of their land for cash crops.*

ex·pul·sion /ɪk'spʌlʃən/ *n* [C,U] when someone is forced to leave a place or an organization: *Bankruptcy results in instant expulsion from the group.* | *Companies which seriously breach the code* ***face expulsion from*** *the Direct Marketing Association.*

EXQ abbreviation for EX QUAY

ex quay —see under INCOTERM

EXS abbreviation for EX SHIP

ex ship —see under INCOTERM

Ex·tel /'ekstel/ *n* a company belonging to the Financial Times that provides information on business and financial services: *In the Extel ranking of investment analysts, NatWest Securities came first in overall quality.*

ex·tend /ɪk'stend/ *v* **1** [T] to increase the period of time for which an agreement, contract etc is effective: *The company decided not to extend his employment contract.* | *The lease has been extended to five years.*
2 [T] to make something bigger or increase its range: *The group successfully blocked a plan to extend a golf course over Tunstall Hills.* | *If the program is successful it will be extended to cover the whole country.*
3 extend credit to sb to make credit available to someone: *the first time banks have extended credit to a Mexican government agency*

extended coverage —see under COVERAGE

extended credit —see under CREDIT[1]

ex·ten·sion /ɪk'stenʃən/ *n* **1** [C] one of many telephone lines in a large building that all have different numbers, but that can be contacted through one central number: *All staff who have a telephone extension will now in effect have their own direct telephone line.*
2 [C usually singular] an additional period of time given to someone to finish a job, repay money that they owe etc: *You can request an automatic four-month extension of the due date for paying your tax.*
3 [C usually singular] when lenders agree to lend money for longer than was originally agreed: *Horne's lenders have given the retailer a five-year extension of a $87.4 million credit line.*
4 [C usually singular] when a law, tax etc is changed to affect more things than before: *an extension of the sales tax to various personal services and power utilities*
5 [C] another room or rooms that are added to a building: *A 250-bedroom extension to the Excelsior will increase total capacity to 1,576 rooms.* —see also BRAND EXTENSION, LINE EXTENSION

extensive agriculture —see under AGRICULTURE

ex·ter·nal /ɪk'stɜːnl‖-ɜːr-/ *adj* coming from outside a company, organization or country: *the repayment of external debts* | *Domestic demand fell in the latest quarter, while external demand rose.*

external account —see under ACCOUNT[1]

external audit —see under AUDIT[1]

external debt —see under DEBT

external growth —see under GROWTH

ex·ter·nal·i·ty /ˌekstɜː'næləti‖-ɜːr-/ *n* plural **externalities** [C usually plural] ECONOMICS something that is not directly connected to an industrial process or economic activity but has an effect on it: *Clean-air rules are all about what economists call externalities, with one person's pollution causing problems for others.*

ex·ter·nal·ize also **externalise** *BrE* /ɪk'stɜːnəl-aɪz‖-ɜːr-/ *v* [T] if a company externalizes supplies or services, it buys them from other companies rather than making them or performing them itself; OUTSOURCE: *Jobs are transferred from manufacturing to service industries as the former externalize services previously provided in-house.*

external liabilities —see under LIABILITY

external trade —see under TRADE[1]

ex·tin·guish /ɪk'stɪŋgwɪʃ/ *v* [T] **1** LAW to remove someone's permission or right to do something: *Any settlement extinguishes the plaintiff's title to that interest in the goods.* | *The contract would be valid only where such rights had not been extinguished by the government.*
2 FINANCE, LAW to agree that a debt does not have to be paid: *Death does not automatically extinguish debts on bank accounts.*

ex·tort /ɪk'stɔːt‖-ɔːrt/ *v* [T] to illegally force someone to give you money by threatening them **extort money from/out of sb**: *Vogel was arrested on suspicion of having extorted property and money from at least 18 clients.* —**extortion** *n* [U] *He pled guilty to charges of extortion, fraud, tax evasion and obstruction of justice.* —**extortioner** *n* [C] —**extortionist** *n* [C]

extortion racket —see under RACKET

ex·tra[1] /'ekstrə/ *adj* [only before a noun] more than normal, or in addition to something else: *Mitubishi will be advertising for 200 extra staff.* | *an extra 1% on National Insurance contributions* —**extra** *adv*: *Full*

English breakfast is £17 extra. | *Mr Chase* ***paid extra*** *for a room to himself.*

extra² *n* [C] something which is added on, especially charges on a bill: *Curtain linings are available as an* ***optional extra.*** | *Be clear about what you are paying for, as there may be hidden extras.*

extra cost —see ***marginal cost*** under COST¹

ex·tract¹ /ɪk'strækt/ *v* [T] **1** to remove RAW MATERIALS, such as gold or oil, from a place, for example the sea or the ground, so that they can be sold or used in an industrial or manufacturing process: *The landowner has appealed for planning permission to extract the peat.* | *The three most heavily taxed commodities are alcohol, tobacco, and the oil being extracted from the North Sea.*

2 to separate a substance or chemical from RAW MATERIALS: *collecting and burning seaweed to extract alkali* | *Cocoa butter and cocoa powder are extracted from the beans.*

3 to get information or facts from a piece of writing or set of figures: *The software extracts data directly from the accounting system.* | *He would not leave until he'd extracted every detail.*

4 to get information or an agreement from someone, although it is difficult to do so: *The full employment of the 1950s gave trade unions the power to extract better terms and conditions from employers.*

extract² *n* [C] **1** a small part of a piece of writing, music or a film + **from**: *an extract from a memorandum to a US delegate*

2 a substance or chemical which has been removed from RAW MATERIALS: *vanilla extract*

extractive industry —see under INDUSTRY

ex·trac·tor /ɪk'stræktə‖-ər/ *n* [C] **1** a machine which removes dirt, dust etc from the air: *An efficient steam extractor, the Aquafresh, fits neatly into the ceiling.* | *We're probably breaking Health and Safety regulations: there should be* ***extractor fans.***

2 a company which removes RAW MATERIALS such as gold or oil, from a place, for example the sea or the ground, and sells them to companies which use them in an industrial or manufacturing process: *Many Third World countries are the extractors of raw materials rather than being the refiners or processors of them.*

ex·tra·net /'ekstrənet/ *n* [C] COMPUTING a computer NETWORK (=series of connected computers) used for exchanging or seeing information within a group of companies that have business connections, that works in the same way as the INTERNET: *Extranets extend a private corporate network to business associates.* —compare INTRANET

ex·tra·or·di·na·ry /ɪk'strɔːdənəri‖ɪk'strɔːrdn-eri, ˌekstrə'ɔːr-/ *adj* [only before a noun] ACCOUNTING an extraordinary cost etc is one that does not occur regularly; EXCEPTIONAL: *The results represent an operating loss of DM170 million, combined with extraordinary write-offs and costs connected with the layoff of 840 workers at three of its plants.*

extraordinary dividend —see under DIVIDEND

extraordinary general meeting —see under MEETING

extraordinary item —see under ITEM

extraordinary meeting —see under MEETING

ex·trap·o·late /ɪk'stræpəleɪt/ *v* [T] *formal* to separate and examine the facts about something, and to form an opinion or come to a conclusion based on your knowledge of those facts: *The figures are wildly optimistic, and could only have been extrapolated from a very small medical trial.* | *We obtained a picture of the economy by extrapolating past trends.* —**extrapolation** *n* [U] *By a process of extrapolation, it can be estimated that there are about 3,500 professionals employed in the industry.*

ex·trav·a·gant /ɪk'strævəgənt/ *adj* **1** *disapproving* spending a lot of money when it is not necessary: *Vauxhall's new Corsa cars featured in an extravagant £3m TV commercial.* | *Even when in debt, he continued to enjoy an* ***extravagant lifestyle.***

2 very extreme and not based on real facts: *The advertisements make* ***extravagant claims,*** *guaranteeing that you will stop smoking within 10 days.*

ex·trin·sic /ɪk'strɪnsɪk, -zɪk/ *adj* [only before a noun] *formal* relating to matters which affect the outer appearance or behaviour of something

extrinsic value —see under VALUE¹

ex VAT *adj* in Britain, used with a price to show that it does not include VAT: *The price is about £940,403 ex VAT, which represents very good value for a yacht of this class.*

EXW abbreviation for EX WORKS

ex warehouse —see under EX¹

ex wharf —see under EX¹

ex works —see under INCOTERM

E

F also **f** written abbreviation for FOLLOWING (PAGE); FRANC

FA abbreviation for FACULTY OF ACTUARIES

FAA abbreviation for FEDERAL AVIATION ADMINISTRATION

fab·ri·cate /ˈfæbrɪkeɪt/ *v* [T] MANUFACTURING to make something, using tools, special machines, or an industrial process; MANUFACTURE: *Samsung will fabricate its own microprocessor.* | *The steel frame was fabricated by McKenzie & Brown of Caernarfon.* —**fabricated** *adj* [only before a noun] *fabricated metal products*

fab·ri·ca·tion /ˌfæbrɪˈkeɪʃən/ *n* [U] MANUFACTURING the process of manufacturing something: *No figures on gold going into jewelry fabrication are available yet.* | *a fabrication press, used to shape metal*

fabrication plant —see under PLANT

fab·ri·cat·or /ˈfəbrɪkeɪtə‖-ər/ *n* [C] MANUFACTURING a company that makes industrial products, such as computers, cars, or machine parts: *trade talks between US and Japanese fabricators* | *Mitsubishi, a fabricator of microprocessors, is negotiating a merger with DEC.*

face amount —see under AMOUNT[1]

face·lift /ˈfeɪslɪft/ *n* [C usually singular] **1** if a building or area is given a facelift, it is cleaned and improved to make it look more attractive; RENOVATION: *Singapore's Raffles Hotel reopened after a facelift costing £55 million.* | *San Jose's downtown has* ***undergone*** *an extensive* ***facelift*** *recently.*

2 if a company gives one of its products or services a facelift, it improves it and makes it more attractive: *Nissan's six-year old supermini is due for a facelift next year.*

face validity —see under VALIDITY

face value —see under VALUE[1]

facilities management —see under MANAGEMENT

fa·cil·i·ty /fəˈsɪlǝti/ *n* plural **facilities** **1 facilities** [plural] special buildings or equipment that have been provided for a particular use, such as sports activities, shopping or travelling: *The Schloss Lebenberg's* ***leisure facilities*** *include a large indoor pool, sauna and sun terrace.* | *modern* ***health-care facilities***

2 [C] a place or large building which is used to make or provide a particular product or service; PLANT: *Torness Harbour has the best permanent docking facility on Scotland's south-east coast.*

3 [C] an arrangement made by a bank for its customers which lets them use the services the bank offers. These services would include, for example, borrowing or investing money: *MIT has put in place a £20 million* ***loan facility*** *for investment in European bonds.* | *INTERCO secured new* ***credit facilities*** *to finance the purchase of Thomasville plc.*

note issuance facility abbreviation **NIF** an arrangement that allows a company to borrow money a number of times over a period of time without going through the usual formal arrangements each time: *A note issuance facility is a medium-term commitment between a borrowing corporate and a bank.*

4 [C] a special feature of a piece of equipment that allows it to do certain useful things, in addition to the things the equipment normally does: *IBM have urged businesses to increase their* ***back-up facilities*** (=a system that can be used if the main one does not work).

fac·sim·i·le /fækˈsɪmǝli/ *n* [C] **1** *formal* another name for a FAX

2 an exact copy of something, especially something old and valuable such as a book or picture etc: *The collection includes facsimiles of early English postage stamps.*

facsimile signature —see under SIGNATURE

fac·tion /ˈfækʃən/ *n* [C] a small group of people who belong to a larger group but who have different ideas and opinions from the larger group, and may argue or fight with them: ***Rival factions*** *at the department store are preparing to face each other at tomorrow's extraordinary meeting.*

fac·tor[1] /ˈfæktə‖-ər/ *n* **1** [C] one of many things that influence or affect a situation: *The council will take a number of factors into account when making its decision.* | *The law should not be concerned solely with* ***economic factors.***

adjustment factor [C] when calculating something, a figure introduced to balance the effect of something that is not typical or representative: *Because the data did not include numbers of employees in all companies, an adjustment factor of 5% was applied.*

critical success factor abbreviation **CSF** [C usually plural] the most important things that a company does to make it successful and likely to make a profit: *A critical success factor was the establishment of a close relationship with Geco-Prakla.* | *What is important is how IT serves* ***the critical success factors of*** *business across all sectors.*

hygiene factors [C plural] HUMAN RESOURCES things such as salary and working conditions that are not enough in themselves to make employees satisfied with their work, but can cause dissatisfaction if they are not good enough. Some of the things that give satisfaction are responsibility and the work itself. The idea of hygiene factors was developed by Frederick Herzberg: *Managers should not expect to motivate employees with hygiene factors alone.*

load factor [singular] the number of seats on a bus, train, or plane that are occupied by passengers who have paid the full fare, used when calculating profits: *Passenger load factor on international flights was 66% last year, down from 69% a year earlier.* | *The* ***break-even load factor*** (=the number of passengers needed to start making a profit) *was 61%.*

weighting factor [C] STATISTICS if you are calculating an average for a group of different things, a weighting factor can be used to give more importance to certain things in the group. For example, to share money between people who need different amounts, a weighting factor could be used so that the people who needed more money would get more: *NERC has recently announced its intention to* ***introduce a weighting factor*** *which takes departmental size into account.*

2 the deciding/decisive/determining factor the most important thing that affects a decision: *The chancellor's achievements on exchange and interest rates could be the deciding factor.* | *The size of the firm is likely to be the determining factor as to whether decisions should be unanimous or taken by majority vote.*

3 the feelgood factor *journalism* when people have positive feelings about the economy and their own financial situation, and the way that this influences the popularity of the government: *An opinion poll of voters showed a big drop in the feelgood factor.*

4 [C] also **invoice factor** FINANCE a financial institution that pays a business the money that suppliers owe it immediately, in return for a small percentage. The business benefits by getting the money immediately, improving its CASH FLOW. Factoring is a form of finance that can be cheaper than bank loans or OVERDRAFTS: *New technology used by modern factors shows what cheques have been*

paid in and whether there are disputed invoices. | *a member of the Association of Invoice Factors*
5 [C] STATISTICS one of two or more numbers which divide into another number exactly. For example, 5 and 7 are factors of 35
6 by a factor of five/ten etc if an amount increases or decreases by a factor of five, ten etc, it increases or decreases by five times, ten times etc: *A computer system can speed up administration by a factor of about 4.*

factor² *v* [T] FINANCE to buy debts that are owed to another company for less than the debts are worth, and then obtain payment directly from those who owe these debts: *Some companies prefer not to disclose cashflow details, making it impossible to know how much merchandise in stores is factored.*
factor sth ↔ **in/into/out** *phr v* [T] if you factor an amount in or into a figure or sum, you include it. If you factor an amount out of a figure or sum, you do not include it: *The purchaser paying cash often pays more because the retailer has factored into the pricing structure the credit card company's fee.* | *Even after factoring out gains, earnings still fell by 67%.*

factor analysis —see under ANALYSIS

factor cost —see under COST¹

fac•tor•ing /ˈfæktərɪŋ/ *n* [U] also **debt factoring, invoice factoring** FINANCE when a financial institution called a FACTOR takes over the administration of a company's RECEIVABLES (=money owed by suppliers). The factor pays the business the money that suppliers owe to it immediately, in return for a percentage. The business benefits by getting the money immediately, improving its CASH FLOW. Invoice factoring is a form of finance that can be cheaper than bank loans or OVERDRAFTS: *With invoice factoring, we provide an immediate advance of up to 80% of the value of invoices.* | *The* ***factoring companies*** *have been heartened by signs of increased demand after a difficult year.*
export factoring a service provided by some large international banks for an exporter, in which the bank arranges to obtain payment directly from the importer. This allows the exporter to borrow part of the importer's debt before being paid in full and therefore improves the exporter's CASH FLOW: *If international trade continues to grow, export factoring should increase in importance.*

fac•tor•ize also **factorise** *BrE* /ˈfæktəraɪz/ *v* [T] STATISTICS to divide a sum into the numbers that, when multiplied, equal that sum. For example, if you factorise the number 10, you get 2 and 5: *These numbers can be factorised uniquely into primes (3, 7 and 13).*

factor of production *n* plural **factors of production** [C] ECONOMICS something that is needed to produce a particular product. The main factors of production are land, labour, and capital: *Inner-urban areas provide ideal factors of production for new companies, such as cheap premises and labour.*

factor price —see under PRICE¹

fac•to•ry /ˈfæktəri/ *n* plural **factories** [C] a large building or group of buildings where goods are made, using large industrial machinery and usually employing many people: *The owner wouldn't comment on the factory's future.* | *the textile factories of Catalonia* | *No one was injured but factory inspectors say there could easily have been casualties.*
bonded factory a factory officially licensed by the government to store imported goods and use them in manufacturing without paying tax for importing the goods until they leave the factory

factory cost —see ***factory-gate price*** under PRICE¹

factory farming —see under FARMING

factory floor —see under FLOOR

factory-gate price —see under PRICE¹

factory pre•set /ˌfæktəri ˈpriːset/ *n* [C] the way that a computer, machine etc is set when you buy it, which you can change if you want to: *The A4 contains 60 programs, half of which are factory presets.* | *It is possible to customise a factory preset so that you can use icons and sounds of your own choosing.*

factory price —see ***factory-gate price*** under PRICE¹

factory ship —see under SHIP¹

factory shop —see under SHOP¹

factory worker —see under WORKER

fail /feɪl/ *v* **1** [I] if a business fails, it is not successful and loses so much money that it has to close: *The company failed amid charges that the chairman had stolen $17 million.* | *More than 10,000 companies failed with debts of more than 10 million yen.* —**failed** *adj* only before a noun *the failed Bank of Credit & Commerce International*
2 [I] if something you try to do fails, it is not successful: *A move to vote the chairman off the Bell Resources board failed.* **fail to do sth**: *A salesman may communicate perfectly well with a customer but fail to make a sale.* —**failed** *adj* [only before a noun] *The firm collapsed after a failed bid for Skandia, a Swedish insurer.*
3 [I] if something fails to happen, it does not happen, although you expected or wanted it to **fail to do sth**: *The new projects have failed to gain general acceptance from the board.* | *If the recovery fails to cut the deficit sharply, a rise in taxes will be needed.*
4 [I] if equipment or a machine fails, it stops working because there is a fault
5 [I] if crops fail, they do not grow or produce any food: *The corn harvest failed after a terrible drought.*
6 [I,T] to not pass an examination, test or INSPECTION: *The railway line failed its Board of Trade inspection earlier this year.*

fail•ure /ˈfeɪljə‖-ər/ *n* **1** [C,U] a situation in which a business that is not successful has to close because it is losing money: *The Official Receiver recommended a detailed investigation into* ***the reasons for*** *the company's* ***failure.*** | *Business failures rose by 31% to 62,767, according to Dun & Bradstreet.*
2 [U] not doing something which you should do or which people expect you to do **failure to do sth**: *the failure of some large firms to adhere to a strict policy on wages*
3 [C,U] a situation in which equipment or a machine stops working: *potential financial loss as a result of computer failure*
audit failure [C,U] when an AUDIT (=an official examination of a company's financial records) does not find things which it should, such as FRAUD: *Some audit failures have resulted in professional disciplining.*
market failure [U] ECONOMICS when a market does not work efficiently, for example because buyers and sellers do not have all the information they require to make sensible decisions, or because it does not take into account costs such as damage to the environment: *Firms refuse to take on more labour because the effective demand for their goods is too low. The government can correct for this type of market failure by increasing demand.*

fair¹ /feə‖fer/ *adj* a situation or arrangement which is fair is reasonable, honest, and acceptable: *The committee takes seriously the need to be* ***fair and just*** *in everything it does.* | *fair voting procedures*

fair² *n* [C] a large show where business people producing a particular product or service can meet to advertise or sell their products: *the Frankfurt* ***book fair*** | *Many businesses deal less formally, for example at* ***trade fairs.***

fair deal —see under DEAL[2]

fair dealing —see under DEALING

Fair Labor Standards Act *n* a US law passed in 1938 that deals with the level of wages, amount of hours of work etc

fair price —see under PRICE[1]

fair rent —see under RENT[2]

fair trade —see under TRADE[1]

fair-trade agreement —see under AGREEMENT

fair trading —see under TRADING

fair value —see under VALUE[1]

fair wear and tear —see under WEAR

faith /feɪθ/ *n* **1** [U] confidence that someone or something can be trusted or will work properly + **in**: *We **have faith** in our staff.* | *Don't **put** too much **faith** in competition.* | *Foreign investors were **losing faith** in the country.*

duty of faith [singular] LAW a duty that an employee has to their employer not to do anything that would harm the employer: *The duty of good faith will be broken if an employee copies a list of the customers of the employer for use after his employment ends.*

2 good faith if you do something in good faith, you do not intend to deceive anyone and believe that what you are doing is honest: *As a gesture of good faith, he deposited £1,000 with the business agents.* | *A bank is not liable if it has accepted the cheque **in good faith**.* | *Throughout the negotiations we **acted in good faith**.*

3 bad faith if you do something in bad faith, you intend to deceive people: *The jury found that all three accountants had **acted in bad faith**.*

F

faith•ful•ly /ˈfeɪθfəl-i/ *adv* **Yours faithfully** *especially BrE* the usual polite way of ending a formal letter which you have begun with 'Dear Sir' or 'Dear Madam' —compare ***Yours sincerely*** *under* SINCERELY

fake[1] /feɪk/ *adj* made to look like something valuable or GENUINE (=real) in order to deceive people: *fake Rolex watches* | *Three bank employees had issued fake certificates for collateral on loans.*

fake[2] *n* [C] a copy of an original document, valuable object etc that is intended to deceive people into believing it is the real document, object etc: *The signature on the contract proved to be a fake.*

fake[3] *v* [T] to make an exact copy of something, or invent figures or results, in order to deceive people: *She had faked her boss's signature on the cheque.*

fall[1] /fɔːl‖fɒːl/ past tense **fell** past participle **fallen** *v* **1** [I] to go down to a lower price, level, amount etc: *Sales of new passenger cars in Europe fell 9.6%.* + **to**: *The British pound fell to $1.7520 from $1.7850.* | *The company went public at $17 a share, but its stock price has **fallen sharply** since then.* | *The consumer confidence index **fell steeply** by a large amount from 79.3 in May to 50.9 in October.*

2 fall due if a payment falls due on or by a particular date, it must be made on or by that date: *Subscriptions are payable annually and fall due on 1 December.* | *Of these sums, $44.2 million fell due for repayment within one year and a further $22 million fell due after more than one year.*

fall away *phr v* [I] **1** another word for fall: *Dealers said activity in equities had fallen away sharply last week.* **2** to lose in a competitive situation: *After the weak carriers fall away, American, Delta, and UAL will be the dominant airlines.*

fall back *phr v* [I] if prices on a financial market fall back, they go down after a period of time when they have been going up + **from**: *In Tokyo, stocks fell back from early gains.*

fall behind *phr v* **1** [I,T] **fall behind** sb/sth to make less progress than others in a competitive situation: *Small firms that fall behind technologically can be rapidly wiped out.*

2 [I] to fail to make payments on time, for example for rent or on a loan + **with/on**: *He had fallen behind with his mortgage after losing his job.*

3 [I,T] **fall behind** sth to fail to finish work on time: *Contractors who **fall behind schedule** incur financial penalties.*

fall off *phr v* [I] another word for fall: *The charity reported that gifts have fallen off by more than 60% in value.*

fall through *phr v* [I] if a deal, arrangement etc falls through, it does not start or is not completed successfully: *When an offer to buy the airline fell through, Midway were forced to stop operating.*

fall[2] *n* **1** [C] a reduction in the amount, level, price etc of something + **in**: *Japanese companies have tried to make up for a fall in domestic demand by increasing sales overseas.*

2 [singular] when a person or organization loses their position of power or becomes unsuccessful: *the **rise and fall** of the British motorcycle industry*

fall•back /ˈfɔːlbæk‖ˈfɒːl-/ *n* [C] **1** another word for FALL[2] + **in**: *The March consumer price index is also expected to benefit from a fallback in clothing prices.*

2 something that can be done if the original plan does not succeed, or that can be used if the thing that you want is not available: *Nobody admits to having a **fallback position** in case European monetary union does not work out.* | *Fallbacks are essential to ensure you are not putting your home at risk if your saving plans go wrong.*

fallen angel *n* [C] *informal* an investment that is not performing well but that performed well in the past: *Those bonds in recent months have turned into fallen angels, as rating agencies downgrade them.*

fall guy *n* [C] *informal AmE* someone who is punished for someone else's mistakes: *Like many fall guys, he was a loyal manager who was hardly the only person to blame for his employer's troubles.*

falling-off *n* [singular] a slow reduction in the amount, level, price etc of something + **in**: *Worldwide, TV audiences for Formula One racing are as high as ever, despite a falling-off in the UK.*

fall money —see under MONEY

fall•off /ˈfɔːlɒf‖ˈfɒːlɒːf/ also **fall-off** *n* [C] another word for FALL[2] + **in**: *The stronger mark has led to a sharp falloff in German import prices.*

fal•low /ˈfæləʊ‖-loʊ/ *adj* **1** fallow land has been dug but is not being used for growing crops, giving the quality of the soil a chance to improve: *Fallow land rose by nearly 30% to 37,000 hectares.*

2 lie fallow if land lies fallow, it is not being used to grow crops: *EU incentives for farmers to let land lie fallow in order to reduce grain surpluses*

3 a fallow period of time for a person or organization is one when they are not very active, productive, profitable etc: *ICI's pharmaceutical division emerged from a relatively fallow period, with increased profits this year.*

false /fɔːls‖fɒːls/ *adj* **1** not true or real, but intended to look real in order to deceive people: ***false and misleading** advertisements* | *Firms issuing false certificates might be subject to lawsuits.*

2 a false economy something that you think will save money but which will really cost you more: *It's a false economy to hire unqualified staff.*

false accounting —see under ACCOUNTING

false economy —see under ECONOMY[1]

false invoice —see under INVOICE[1]

false pretences —see under PRETENCES

false representation *n* [C,U] LAW the crime of obtaining money from someone by deceiving them, especially by pretending that something is true when it is not; FRAUD: *When a mailing violates the law, the mailer faces civil penalties for false representation.* | *The company was accused of a lack of duty of care and false representations.*

fal·si·fy /ˈfɔːlsəfaɪ‖ˈfɒːl-/ *v* past tense and past participle **falsified** [T] to change figures, records etc so that they contain false information: *The financial director was charged with **falsifying** the company's **accounts**.* —**falsification** *n* [C,U] *the falsification of expense accounts* | *a lawsuit alleging weight falsification* (=when scales in a shop have been changed, cheating customers)

family allowance —see under ALLOWANCE

family business —see under BUSINESS

family lifecycle —see under LIFECYCLE

fan club *n* [C] *BrE* FINANCE investors who buy shares in a company involved in a TAKEOVER in order to increase its share price —compare CONCERT PARTY, FRIENDS

fan·cy /ˈfænsi/ *adj informal* a very high and often unreasonable price: *Designer labels tend to come with **fancy prices** to match.*

fancy goods —see under GOODS

fand /fænd/ *n* [C] *AmE* FINANCE another name for a PFANDBRIEF (=type of bond issued in Germany)

Fan·nie Mae /ˌfæni ˈmeɪ/ *n* an informal name for the FEDERAL NATIONAL MORTGAGE ASSOCIATION

FAO *n* the Food and Agricultural Organization; a department of the UNITED NATIONS that has the aim of improving food production and distribution throughout the world and improving NUTRITION (= the qualities in food that help people grow and be healthy)

fao written abbreviation for FOR THE ATTENTION OF

faq /fæk/ *n* [plural] frequently asked questions; on INTERNET SITES a list of questions that users often ask about the site, and their answers

fare /feə‖fer/ *n* [C] the price paid to travel by plane, train etc: *With cheaper **air fares**, travelers have more vacation choices.* | *South Yorkshire's low **bus fares** are persuading drivers to leave their cars at home.*

advance purchase fare apex fare a cheap plane or train fare that must be bought a particular number of days before you travel: *bargain advance purchase fares, which require Saturday-night stayovers* | *new all-year-round low apex fares*

business class fare a fare designed for business people that can be exchanged, CANCELLED etc without charge: *British Midland is undercutting rival business class fares by up to 40%.*

coach fare *AmE* a standard air fare that costs less than the first class fare but is more expensive than the cheapest fares: *Most business fliers travel on full coach fares that are readily acceptable for travel on any available flight.*

excess fare ◆ an amount of money a passenger has to pay if they want to change from a lower class of seat to a higher one on a train, plane etc

◆ an amount of money a passenger has to pay when they do not have the right ticket for their trip

first-class fare a plane or train fare with the best seats, meals etc: *Profit margins on first-class fares are often 10 times greater than they are in economy class.*

off-peak fare a fare at a time of the day, week, or year when not many people travel: *The limits on fare increases apply to most rush-hour commuter fares, but not to off-peak fares.*

one-way fare *AmE* a fare for travel to a place, but not back again; SINGLE FARE *BrE*: *Continental has announced new one-way fares from the US to Europe.*

open-jaw fare a fare for travel to a place and travel back from a different place, the passenger making other travel arrangements between the two places

peak fare a fare at a time of the day, week, or year when a lot of people travel: *Peak fares are available noon Thursday through noon Monday.*

peak season fare a fare at a time of the year when a lot of people travel: *KLM announced sharply lower peak season fares to the US from Amsterdam.*

return fare *BrE*, **round-trip fare** *AmE* a fare for travel to a place and back again: *Willy agreed to take the job in London as long as he was given the return fare.* | *USAir cut round-trip fares for Thanksgiving holiday travel.*

single fare *BrE* a fare for travel to a place but not back again; ONE-WAY FARE: *Virgin is offering return tickets to New York from Heathrow for £186; the single fare is £93.*

farm[1] /fɑːm‖fɑːrm/ *n* [C] **1** an area of land, used for growing crops or keeping animals as a business: *a 3000-hectare maize farm* | *Farm exports account for 70% of New Zealand's exports.* | *a **dairy farm*** (=one for producing milk and milk products)

co-operative farm a farm owned and run by a group of farmers as a CO-OPERATIVE

truck farm *AmE* an area for growing fruit and vegetables for sale; MARKET GARDEN *BrE*

2 a place where particular fish or animals are bred as a business: *a trout farm* | *a mink farm*

farm[2] *v* [I,T] to use land for growing crops, keeping animals etc: *His family has been farming the same land for generations.* | *organically farmed produce*

farm sth ↔ **out** *phr v* [T] to send work to other people, especially people outside your company, instead of doing it yourself: *Some of the work can be farmed out to freelancers.*

farm·er /ˈfɑːmə‖ˈfɑːrmər/ *n* [C] a person who owns or manages a farm: *Government subsidies to farmers have been reduced.* | *a sheep farmer*

tenant farmer someone who farms land that is rented from someone else

farm·ing /ˈfɑːmɪŋ‖ˈfɑːrmɪŋ/ *n* [U] the practice or business of growing crops or keeping animals on a farm: *modern methods of farming* | *the UK's **farming industry***

dry farming farming methods used in dry areas where there is very little water and no IRRIGATION (=way of supplying water to land)

factory farming also **battery farming** when large numbers of animals such as cows, pigs, and chickens are kept in buildings so that food from them can be produced quickly and cheaply: *the use of antibiotics in factory farming* | *branches of the industry which have been turned over to **factory farming methods***

intensive farming also **intensive agriculture** farming which produces a lot of food from a small area of land: *consumer reaction to intensive farming*

farm land —see under LAND[1]

farm worker —see under WORKER

FAS abbreviation for FREE ALONGSIDE SHIP —see under INCOTERM

fash·ion[1] /ˈfæʃən/ *n* **1** [C,U] a way of doing something or behaving that is popular at a particular time + **for**: *How do you explain the current fashion for takeovers?* | *Good design will never **go out of fashion*** (=become unfashionable). | *Big companies seem to be **in fashion*** (=acceptable and popular) *again.*

2 [U] the business of making and selling clothes, shoes etc in new and changing styles: *Emma wants to work in **the fashion industry**.* | *leading **fashion designers***

3 [C,U] a style of clothes or hair that is popular at a particular time: *We sell only the latest fashions.* | *Long skirts are **back in fashion**.* (=are in fashion again after a period of time when they were not)

fashion[2] *v* [T] *journalism* to produce something: *Houston has fashioned a substantial economic recovery.* | *The two sides have been unable to fashion a compromise.*

F

fash•ion•a•ble /ˈfæʃənəbəl/ *adj* popular at a particular time: *fashionable management theories* | *Commuting became fashionable again in the 1980s.*

fashion designer —see under DESIGNER[1]

fashion goods —see under GOODS

fast[1] /fɑːst‖fæst/ *adv* quickly or without delay: *Exports are still* ***growing fast***. | *The Bundesbank has been criticized for not cutting interest rates fast enough.* | *How fast can you get that report done?*

fast[2] *adj* happening quickly or without delay: *The IT industry is expanding at an incredibly fast rate.* | *Trading has been* ***fast and furious*** (=full of excitement and activity) *this afternoon.* | *We guarantee a fast response to all inquiries.*

fast-moving consumer goods —see under GOODS

fast track *n* [singular] a quick and direct path to getting jobs that are more important and better paid: *He is a middle manager in his 30s,* ***on the fast track*** *for promotion.* | *one of the bank's fast track graduates* —**fast tracking** *n* [U] *Fast tracking of managers with high potential can slow down managerial development of the company as a whole.*

fat cat *n* [C usually plural] *journalism disapproving*
1 a rich person, especially someone who does not deserve to be rich: *Pilots have a bad image among their co-workers, who view them as fat cats who earn higher salaries.* | *corporate fat cats and their big bonuses*
2 in Britain, a businessperson who became rich when they became the director of one of the government companies that were PRIVATIZED (=sold to the public) in the 1990s: *Criticisms of railway privatisation include underinvestment in track improvements, and fat cat managers.*

F

fault /fɔːlt‖fɒːlt/ *n* [C] **1** MANUFACTURING something that is wrong with a machine, system etc that prevents it from working correctly + **in**: *They have spent FF100 million repairing engineering* ***design faults*** *in the model.*
2 fault-tolerant computer/machine a computer that can go on working even if it has a fault, or there is a fault in the PROGRAM: *Its fault-tolerant computers will be used in applications such as branch banking.*
3 MANUFACTURING a mistake in the way something is made, that spoils its appearance; FLAW: *The sweater had a fault in it and I had to take it back.*
4 LAW the responsibility of a person or organization for damage or injury to someone, or for a criminal act: *The borrowers were* ***at fault*** *for signing fraudulent applications.*
5 no-fault LAW used to talk about arrangements where it is not necessary to prove that someone was at fault for the person who was injured or hurt to receive money: *no-fault systems for medical malpractice cases that would provide limited but guaranteed benefits* | *no-fault auto insurance*

fault•y /ˈfɔːlti‖ˈfɒːlti/ *adj* if a machine, system etc is faulty, there is something wrong with it that prevents it from working correctly: *Owners of affected cars can go to their dealerships to have the* ***faulty part*** *replaced.*

favourable balance of trade —see under BALANCE OF TRADE

fax[1] /fæks/ *n* [C] **1** a written document that is sent in electronic form down a telephone line and then printed using a special machine: *Could you send this fax for me?*
2 also **fax machine** a machine used for sending and receiving faxes: *His home office is equipped with a PC, fax and photocopier.* | *I sent the details* ***by fax***. | *What's your* ***fax number****?*

fax[2] *v* [T] to send someone a message by fax **fax sth to sb**: *He faxed the printout to his agent.* **fax sb sth**: *Can you fax me your details?*

fax machine —see under MACHINE[1]

FCA *n* used after the name of a Fellow of the Association of Chartered Accountants; a CHARTERED ACCOUNTANT who is a member of the ASSOCIATION OF CHARTERED ACCOUNTANTS and who has reached a certain level of skill in his or her profession: *Ian Fleming FCA was appointed Group financial controller.*

fcs also **Fcs** written abbreviation for FRANCS

FDIC abbreviation for FEDERAL DEPOSIT INSURANCE CORPORATION

feasibility study —see under STUDY[1]

fea•si•ble /ˈfiːzəbəl/ *adj* a plan, idea, or method that is feasible is possible and likely to work: *the only feasible way of solving the problem* **feasible to do sth**: *Powerful computers have made it feasible to search through millions of records at great speed.*

feath•er•bed•ding /ˈfeðəˌbedɪŋ‖-ðər-/ *n* [U] when there are more workers to do a job than are really needed. TRADE UNIONS are often accused of forcing employers to do this when workers risk losing their jobs because new machines are being introduced: *Management says it needs to get rid of featherbedding and other labor abuses and save $50 million annually.*

Feb. written abbreviation for FEBRUARY

Fed /fed/ *n informal* **the Fed** another name for the FEDERAL RESERVE BANK, the FEDERAL RESERVE BOARD, or the FEDERAL RESERVE SYSTEM: *The bond market rallied as the Fed eased monetary conditions.*

Federal Aviation Administration abbreviation **FAA** *n* a US government organization responsible for making rules for airports and aircraft and for making sure that they are obeyed: *The Federal Aviation Administration has ordered extensive repairs to about 1400 aging airliners.* —compare CIVIL AVIATION AUTHORITY

federal borrowing —see under BORROWING

Federal Communications Commission abbreviation **FCC** *n* a US government organization responsible for making rules for the TELECOMMUNICATIONS industry and for making sure that they are obeyed: *The Federal Communications Commission will select the most effective way to protect consumers from unwanted phone calls.*

federal court —see under COURT[1]

federal deficit —see under DEFICIT

Federal Deposit Insurance Corporation abbreviation **FDIC** *n* BANKING a US government organization that insures DEPOSITS of up to $100,000 if a member bank fails, and that can act to prevent bank failures and finance TAKEOVERS of failed banks: *The Federal Deposit Insurance Corporation wants to encourage bank mergers as a way to improve credit conditions.*

Federal Express *n trademark* a US company that delivers mail and packages —see also FEDEX

federal funding —see under FUNDING

Federal funds —see under FUND[1]

federal grant —see under GRANT[1]

Federal Home Loan Mortgage Corporation abbreviation **FHLMC** *n* a US government organization that buys home loans from commercial banks and arranges for them to be resold as SECURITIES on the financial markets. The money obtained is then used to make more loans to home buyers; FREDDIE MAC: *One of the biggest issuers was Federal Home Loan Mortgage Corp., which sold $300 million of seven-year debentures priced to yield 6.86%.*

Federal Housing Administration abbreviation **FHA** *n* a US government organization that insures lenders of money to people buying homes against the risk of the loans not being repaid: *Mortgage insurance policies* *issued by the Federal Housing Administration made full repayments to lenders on the loans at the greatest risk of default.*

federal income tax —see under INCOME TAX

federal judge —see under JUDGE[1]

federal land —see under LAND[1]

Federal National Mortgage Association abbreviation **FNMA** *n* a US government organization that buys home loans that have been GUARANTEED by the Federal Housing Administration and some other insurers, and arranges for these to be resold as SECURITIES on financial markets. The money obtained is then used to make more loans to home buyers; FANNIE MAE: *The Federal National Mortgage Association reported that earnings rose 16% in the first quarter.*

Federal Open Market Committee abbreviation **FOMC** *n* a committee of the Federal Reserve Board that sets MONETARY POLICY: *Bond investors will be watching closely as the Federal Open Market Committee meets on Tuesday.*

Federal Reserve Bank abbreviation **FRB** *n* one of the 12 banks based in different US cities that make up the Federal Reserve System. Each one carries out the System's decisions and makes sure that national and state banks with branches in its area follow banking rules: *The New York Federal Reserve Bank could sell more securities, providing as much new debt as the market needs.*

Federal Reserve Board abbreviation **FRB** *n* the management board of the Federal Reserve System, whose seven members are chosen by the US president. It decides the POLICIES of the Federal Reserve System: *With the Federal Reserve Board's latest discount rate cut, mortgage rates have been driven to their lowest level in nearly 20 years.*

Federal Reserve System *n* the US CENTRAL BANK. It consists of the 12 Federal Reserve Banks and sets banking rules, controls the MONEY SUPPLY, (=the amount of money in the economy) and manages the CLEARING SYSTEM (=the system for making payments between banks): *The Federal Reserve System has committed itself to fighting the recession with lower interest rates.*

federal tax —see under TAX[1]

federal tax lien —see under LIEN

Federal Trade Commission abbreviation **FTC** *n* a US government organization that fights unfair or illegal activities such as false advertising, PRICE FIXING, and FRAUD: *The Federal Trade Commission is investigating the promotional claims of some 25 marketers of diet products.*

fed·e·ra·tion /ˌfedəˈreɪʃən/ *n* [C] **1** a group of organizations, clubs, or people that have joined together to form a single group to represent their interests, and often used in the names of professional associations and TRADE UNIONS: *the American Federation of State, County and Municipal Employees* | *the National Federation of Independent Business*

labor federation *AmE* a large TRADE UNION organization to which many smaller local trade unions are connected: *The 70,000-member National Federation of Workers' Unions is Honduras' most powerful labor federation.*

2 a group of states that have joined together to form a single group: *Was the Soviet Union to be a federation or a looser arrangement of independent states?* —**federated** *adj*: *Some Europeans want a federated nation state.*

Fed·ex /ˈfedeks/ or **Fed Ex** *n* [singular] *trademark* another name for FEDERAL EXPRESS: *FedEx reported that its average daily volume during November was up only 3.8% from the year before.* —**Fedex** *v* [T] *While Americans often speak of 'Fedexing' an important document, in London, Paris or Berlin people 'DHL' it, referring to the major competitor.*

Fed·wire /ˈfedwaɪə‖-waɪr/ *n* [singular] the main technical system for payments between banks in the US: *Fedwire, the Federal Reserve's electronic-payments system couldn't operate after generators failed.*

fee /fiː/ *n* **1** [C] an amount of money paid to a professional person or organization for their services: *The company can't afford the fees that some supermarkets charge food manufacturers for shelf space.* | *If you want help selecting a policy, you might want to use an insurance adviser who* ***charges a fee****, but earns no commission.* —see also NO WIN NO FEE

advance fee [C] an amount of money paid for services before they are delivered: *Thousands of people have been conned in advance fee loan schemes.*

advisory fee [C] a sum of money paid for investment advice given by a MUTUAL FUND: *other annual expenses such as the investment advisory fee and the cost of administering the fund*

capitation fee [C] a payment or charge that is made for each person: *Schools received a capitation fee for every pupil in the school.*

commitment fee [C] a sum of money paid to a bank for agreeing to make a loan: *Philip Morris will pay a commitment fee of 0.15% for the new bank credit line.*

contingency fee also **contingent fee** [C] LAW when a lawyer is paid a percentage of any DAMAGES (=money for loss or injury) that they win for their client: *In settling a personal injury case, a contingency fee contract with his client gave Mr Goodman one-third of the $3 million award.*

distribution fee [C] a sum of money charged by a film-making company to make a film available to cinemas: *'Batman' has returned revenue to Warner of $253.4 million; from that sum, Warner deducted $80.4 million for the studio's distribution fee.*

entry fee [C] a sum of money charged to join an organization, to go into a particular place, or to take part in a competition: *We sell products in bulk and at reduced prices to selected customers who pay an entry fee.*

fixed fee also **flat fee** [C] a set amount paid for work or a service, that does not change with the time the work takes or the amount the service is used: *Quebec doctors get a fixed fee for each medical service performed.* | *Airlines usually charge a flat fee for unlimited use of their reservation systems.*

incentive fee ◆ [C] an amount paid to a person or organization for carrying out their work to a high standard: *Harrah's will receive an incentive fee if it hits certain goals.*

◆ [C] an amount of money an investor pays to a dealer who is working for them if the dealer succeeds in making an agreed profit: *The rate includes an incentive fee of 12.5%.*

landing fees [plural] the money that the owner of a port or airport charges owners of ships or aircraft to pay for using it: *Landing fees at airports are based on aircraft weight – jetliners pay thousands of dollars for each flight.*

licence fee *BrE*, **license fee** *AmE* [C] money paid to a person or organization for permission to use their ideas or designs: *Imatron received a $4 million license fee from Siemens for use of its technology in developing medical diagnostic products.*

licencing fee *BrE*, **licensing fee** *AmE* [C] another name for LICENCE FEE

management fee [C] money paid to a person or organization that operates a business activity for another person or organization: *Geodyne receives a management fee from the investors for managing and operating the properties.*

sales fee [C] money paid to a MUTUAL FUND by an investor when putting money into the fund: *If an* *investor puts $10,000 into a mutual fund that charges a 5% sales commission, $500 would go toward the sales fee, and, as a result, only $9,500 would be invested in the fund.*

scale fee [C] a way of charging for legal work based on a standard scale, rather than based on the amount of work done: *The maximum conveyancing charge of £350 was a considerable saving on the scale fee traditionally charged by solicitors.*

transfer fee [C] an amount of money charged for transferring money, shares, property etc from one person to another: *The Save & Prosper Society ensures customer loyalty by* ***imposing*** *a £50* ***transfer fee****.*

tuition fees [plural] money paid by or for a student to a university or similar institution for its courses: *State universities, strapped for cash because of budget cuts, are being forced to raise tuition fees.*

upfront fee ◆ [C] another name for ADVANCE FEE: *In return for a $500 up-front fee, the broker promised to help Mr Haze find money.*

◆ [C] an amount of money paid by an investor to a MUTUAL FUND to manage their investment; LOAD: *An investor who places $10,000 for 15 years in a fund that charges a fee of 0.75% of assets pays the equivalent of a $900 load.*

2 [C] an amount of money paid to an author, musician etc for a book, piece of music etc that they have written; ROYALTY: *Simon & Schuster canceled publication and refused to pay the author a promised $900,000 fee.*

fee absolute also **fee simple**, **fee simple absolute** *n* [singular] PROPERTY, LAW complete possession of property, with the right to give or sell it freely, or leave it to someone in a WILL (=a document that says who should get your property when you die): *Ownership of the freehold is defined as ownership in 'fee simple absolute in possession'.*

F

feed¹ /fiːd/ *v* past tense and past participle **fed** [I,T] to pass to a later stage in a process or system **feed into sth**: *The data are fed into computers for analysis.* | *tax increases and spending curbs by state and local governments that feed into the private sector* **feed through sth**: *the route through which a rise in interest rates feeds through the system* **feed through into sth**: *Growth across the portfolio was 7%, which feeds through into higher dividend income.*

feed² *n* **1** [C] a way of supplying something that is needed for a particular process or activity: *Traders on each of the four markets will be able to view listings on the others via a common* ***data feed****.* | *French television has agreed to provide a feed if BBC coverage of the World Cup is disrupted by strike action.*

2 [U] food for farm animals: *cattle feed*

feed·back /ˈfiːdbæk/ *n* [U] **1** advice or criticism about how well you are doing your job and what you could do to improve. Managers usually give feedback to their employees: *The line manager judges the trainee's work and provides feedback.*

2 advice or criticism about products or ideas for new products. Employees or the public usually give this kind of feedback to a company's managers: *We launched a customer survey to obtain feedback on customer perception of our products, service and performance.*

feed·stock /ˈfeːdstɒk‖-stɑːk/ *n* [C] **1** a main RAW MATERIAL (=a material such as coal or oil in its natural state before being treated in order to make things) used for making products such as plastics and NYLON: *Coal tar was the feedstock for all kinds of chemicals until it was replaced by oil.*

2 food such as grain given to animals on farms: *Its activities included supplying feedstock and seeds, managing the sale of produce and supplying agricultural machinery.*

feelgood factor —see under FACTOR¹

feet /fiːt/ —see FOOT¹

fel·on /ˈfelən/ *n* [C] LAW someone who is guilty of a felony: *The aim of the bill was to stop the sale of firearms to convicted felons.*

fel·o·ny /ˈfeləni/ *n* plural **felonies** [C,U] LAW a serious crime such as murder: *Citizens had a legal duty to reveal felonies known to them.* | *a previous conviction for felony* —compare MISDEMEANOUR —**felonious** *adj*: *Prosecuters have charged him with* ***felonious assault*** *for attacking a woman near the square.*

fence /fens/ *v* [I] *informal* to buy and sell stolen goods: *The police suspect he has been fencing electronic equipment.*

fer·ry /ˈferi/ *n* plural **ferries** [C] a ship that carries people, vehicles, or goods across a narrow part of a sea: *Faster ferries will improve service timings.* | *Work has already started on a new 14-acre* ***ferry terminal*** (=place where ferries arrive and leave) | *The* ***ferry operators*** *undertook not to reduce services.*

FF also **FFr** written abbreviations for FRENCH FRANCS: *Exclusive properties are offered with prices ranging from FF 3,000,000.*

ff written abbreviation for FOLLOWING PAGES

FHA abbreviation for FEDERAL HOUSING ADMINISTRATION; FINANCE HOUSES ASSOCIATION

FHLMC abbreviation for FEDERAL HOME LOAN MORTGAGE CORPORATION

FIA *n* [C] used after the name of a Fellow of the Institute of Actuaries; an ACTUARY who is a member of the INSTITUTE OF ACTUARIES and who has reached a particular level of skill in the profession

FIBOR /ˈfiːbɔː‖-ɔːr/ *n* BANKING the Frankfurt Inter-Bank Offered Rate; the rate of interest that German banks offer for loans between each other —compare EURIBOR, LIBOR, SIBOR

fibre op·tics *BrE*, **fiber optics** *AmE* — *n* [U] the process of using very thin threads of glass or plastic to carry information in the form of light, especially on telephone lines: *the use of fibre optics in cable television*

fictitious person —see under PERSON

fictitious precision *n* [U] when a set of figures look correct because of their detail and presentation but are in fact not correct: *Fictitious precision is just one of many ways in which managers can be misled by numbers.*

fid·dle /ˈfɪdl/ *v* [T] *informal* to give false information about something in order to avoid paying money, or to get extra money: *It would be naive to think that staff never* ***fiddle their expenses****.* | *Auditors ensure that employers or directors have not been* ***fiddling the books****.* —**fiddle** *n* [C] *an alleged* ***insurance fiddle***

fidelity bond —see under BOND

fidelity insurance —see under INSURANCE

fi·du·ci·a·ry¹ /fɪˈduːʃiəri‖-eri/ *n* plural **fiduciaries** **1** [C] someone who is responsible for the assets of people, organizations etc and, by law, must protect their interests: *Where corporate information is revealed legitimately to a consultant working for the corporation, they may become fiduciaries of the shareholders.*

2 [U] coins and BANK NOTES put into CIRCULATION (=made available for public use) by a bank, usually a CENTRAL BANK: *The issue of banknotes is the sole function of the issue department, the notes being fiduciary backed by government securities rather than backed by gold.*

fiduciary² *adj* involving the relationship of trust that a fiduciary must have with the person or organization whose assets or interests they are responsible for: *A person in a* ***fiduciary position*** *is not entitled to make a profit or to put himself in a position where his interest and duty conflict.*

breach of fiduciary duty *n* plural **breaches of fiduciary duty** [C,U] LAW when a fiduciary does not protect the interests of the people whose assets they are responsible for: *The company was in breach of fiduciary duty to the song-writers by keeping 75% of their royalties.*

fiduciary duty —see under DUTY

field[1] /fiːld/ *n* [C] **1** a subject that people study or are involved in as part of their work: *We are looking for graduates with degrees in artificial intelligence, languages and related fields.* | *Until recently, NEC was alone **in the field of** wireless communication.*
2 studies, testing etc that are done in the field are done in the real world rather than in a LABORATORY, factory etc: *We need someone who can test the drilling machinery **in the field**.*
3 coal/oil/gas field a large area where coal, oil etc is found: *Even the largest oil corporations have to rely on external finance to develop new oil fields.*
4 COMPUTING a space made available for a particular kind of information: *The database contains 10 free-text fields.*

field[2] *v* [T] to deal with a question, enquiry, telephone call etc, usually successfully: *He fielded several angry calls from franchisees asking for their money back.*

field research —see under RESEARCH

field staff —see under STAFF[1]

field test —see under TEST[1]

field trial —see under TRIAL

fieri facias —see WRIT OF FIERI FACIAS

FIFO /ˈfaɪfəʊ‖-foʊ/ abbreviation for FIRST IN, FIRST OUT: *the FIFO basis of stock valuation*

fifth generation computer —see under COMPUTER

fifty-fifty *adj* **1** divided or shared equally between two people, companies etc: *It was suggested that they continue the Skybolt development on a fifty-fifty cost-sharing basis.* —**fifty-fifty** *adv*: *We decided to split the costs fifty-fifty.*
2 having an equal chance of happening in one of two ways: *When people lose their jobs, they now stand a worse than fifty-fifty chance of being out of work for more than three months.*

fig·ure[1] /ˈfɪɡə‖ˈfɪɡjər/ *n* **1 figures** [plural] a number representing an amount, especially an officially published number: *I need this week's **sales figures**.* | *These are the worst **unemployment figures** in three years.* | *February figures showed growth in lending had slowed to 5.5%.*
2 [C] a number written as a sign rather than a word: *In management reports, it is often worth adding up the columns of figures that are presented.*
3 double figures numbers between 10 and 99: *Sir Terence is still furious that inflation went back into double figures, after all the pain of getting it below 5%.*
4 six-figure/seven-figure etc a number in the hundred thousands, millions etc, often used to talk about someone's income: *What's the point of a six-figure salary with no time to enjoy it?*
5 [C] a particular amount of money: *The event raised $200,000 for charity, and this is not the **final figure**.* (=the amount that will be obtained in the end)
6 put a figure on sth to say exactly how much something costs, is worth etc: *Police are waiting to hear from the accountants before they can put an exact figure on the amount missing.*
7 [C] written abbreviation **fig** a numbered drawing or DIAGRAM in a book: *Figure 3.1 shows the important position of planning in the decision-making process.*

figure[2] *v* **1** [T] *AmE informal* to calculate an amount: *Did you figure your expenses for last month yet?*
2 [I] to be involved in an important part of an activity, process, or situation + **in**: *IBM and a number of British companies all figure in his career background.*

file[1] /faɪl/ *n* [C] **1** information about a person or subject that is kept by a company or other organization: *I see from my files that we still have not received payment from you.* | *A credit reference agency is a company which **keeps files on** individuals' debt records.*
2 on file if information is kept on file, it is kept so it can be used when it is needed: *We will keep your application on file.*
3 a box or a cover made of heavy paper or plastic, used to store papers, letters, or documents: *Copies of every letter are kept in a file to record what was agreed.*
4 a collection of information on a computer that is stored under a particular name: *Be careful not to **delete** (=remove) any important **files**.* | *You might want to **rename the file** at a later date.*
5 save sth to disk/file to put information onto disk or in a particular file: *Save a copy of the file to disk and send it to me.*
data file COMPUTING a file containing information that a computer program changes into a form that can be used by the user. An example of a data file is a help file that provides the user with information on using their computer: *The files on the floppy were data files which can not reveal their contents without the assistance of program files.*
data interchange format file abbreviation **DIF file** COMPUTING a computer file in which information has been taken from a file in one program and is held in such a way that it can be moved to a file in a different program
log file COMPUTING a file that records the progress of computer operations, including error messages, that you can use to find out why a particular operation did not work: *Ensure that the log file is deleted periodically so it remains a sensible size.*
PostScript file COMPUTING a file in a form that can be printed. Post Script is a trademark: *The final stage is to have the documents typeset which usually means taking PostScript files to a bureau.*
program file COMPUTING a computer program containing a series of instructions that it sends to a computer's CENTRAL PROCESSING UNIT so that the user can create documents. The names of program files usually end with .exe or .com: *If a program file gets deleted by a virus, simply reinstall it from the master disk.* —compare DATA FILE
text file COMPUTING a simple file containing a written document: *Format and print is an excellent facility for adding page numbers to a standard text file.*
zip file COMPUTING a file that has been COMPRESSED (=made smaller) by changing the information in it into a special code, so that it uses less space when you store it. To read or use the file, you change it back into its original form: *I was sent the work in the form of a compressed zip file.* —see also PAY AND FILE, RANK AND FILE

file[2] *v* **1** [T] to keep or put papers with information on them in a particular place, so that you can find them easily: *The reservation form and confirmation slip are then filed alphabetically.*
2 [T] ACCOUNTING to officially send your accounts to the authorities: *You could be prosecuted for failing to file your accounts before February 28.* —see also PAY AND FILE
3 [I,T] LAW to officially record a complaint, law case, official document etc: *Chevron filed a lawsuit to remove Pennzoil as a shareholder.* | *America's federal bankruptcy code was rewritten in order to make it easier to **file for bankruptcy**.* (=inform the authorities that a business is bankrupt)

file cabinet *n* [C] *AmE* another name for a FILING CABINET: *Paper copies and the traditional file cabinet still play a major role in many offices.*

file manager —see under MANAGER

F

file·name /ˈfaɪlneɪm/ *n* [C] the name that you give to a computer FILE and which you use when you want to open it, remove it, put it on disk etc: *Enter the filename, or press F1 for a list of available filenames.*

file server —see under SERVER

file transfer —see under TRANSFER²

filing cabinet *n* [C] a piece of office furniture with two or more deep drawers. Filing cabinets are used to store documents and other paper records; FILE CABINET *AmE*: *He drew a sheaf of papers from the top drawer of the filing cabinet.*

filing clerk —see under CLERK

filing system —see under SYSTEM

filing tray *n* [C] a flat container, used in an office to hold letters, papers etc that are being dealt with; IN-TRAY; OUT-TRAY: *The papers were piled into two filing trays on Jefferson's desk.*

fill /fɪl/ *v* **1 fill a job/post/vacancy etc** to find and employ a suitable person to do a job that has been advertised: *Headhunters are charging up to 60% of annual salary to fill a top job.* | *The post cannot be filled by a British executive because it requires a more south-east Asian background.*
2 fill a gap/hole/niche MARKETING to provide a product or service that is needed but is not available or has not been provided before: *Stagecoach jumped in to fill a gap with its overnight buses when InterCity ended seated accommodation on most sleeping car trains.* | *IBM introduced a mainframe that fills a hole in its product line.* + **with**: *The plan is to produce a credible set of proposals for filling this niche with new sales of hi-tech machines.*
3 fill a need/demand to provide a service that will deal with a problem: *The futures and options business has filled a need for managing the fluctuating exchange rates.*
4 fill an order to supply the goods a customer has ordered: *After filling an order for the car from other Eastern European countries, the plant will be shut down.*
fill sth ↔ **in** *phr v* [T] to write all the information that is requested on an official form; FILL OUT: *He filled in the usual trader's form offering to sell the car to the finance company.* | *The time sheet is filled in by your supervisor.*
fill in for sb *phr v* [I] to do another person's job for a short period of time because they are not there or are unable to do it + **for**: *The supervisor is forbidden by the union contract to fill in for an employee who is on a break.* —see also FILL-IN
fill sth ↔ **out** *phr v* [T] another name for FILL-IN
fill up *phr v* [I] to gradually become full of people, things, or a substance: *Disks eventually fill up, since new data can only be written after what has gone before.* | *Britain was given a boost as shares on the Stock Market rose, and industry reported order books filling up.* + **with**: *The Antrim Technology Park is filling up with high technology software companies.*

fill·er /ˈfɪlə‖-ər/ *n* [C] a short newspaper article or programme on television or radio, used to take up extra space or time, and to keep people interested: *'A Healthy Step' is the first of a series of short fillers for television.*

fill-in *n* [C] a person who does another person's job for a short period of time, because the other person is not there: *I was just a fill-in when she wasn't available.* —see also ***fill in for*** under FILL

fill or kill *adj informal* fill or kill orders are instructions given to a BROKER or a DEALER to buy or sell stocks or shares. If the instructions are not performed immediately, the deal is stopped, and nothing is bought or sold

Fi·lo·fax /ˈfaɪləfæks/ *n* [C] *trademark* a small book filled with separate sheets of paper on which you write names, addresses, telephone numbers etc: *a Filofax containing lists of clients and orders.* —compare ***personal organizer*** under ORGANIZER

filthy lucre —see under LUCRE

Fin also **fin** written abbreviation for FINANCE

fi·nal /ˈfaɪnəl/ *adj* **1** [only before a noun] the last in a series of things, actions, or events: *An official announcement was expected following* ***a final meeting*** *at Pirelli's Milan headquarters.* | *The US-based company is still arguing with several contractors over the* ***final bill.*** | *foreign currency receipts from the* ***final instalment*** *of the sale of British Steel shares* —**finally** *adv*: *He has finally decided to settle down after six months as a freelance trouble-shooter.*
2 a decision, offer, agreement etc that is final cannot be changed: *Members must vote in favor again next year for the* ***decision*** *to become* ***final.*** | *Now that the ECJ has issued its opinion, it is up to the Conseil d'Etat to make a* ***final ruling.***
3 [only before a noun] a final piece of writing or set of figures has been prepared in several stages, and is now considered to be correct: *The report, prepared by the National Audit Office, has just been circulated as a* ***final draft.*** | *The provisional estimate of retail sales volume for October was 119.0; the* ***final estimate*** *is closer to 116.9.*
4 final and binding LAW a legal judgement or decision which is final and binding has to be obeyed because it has been decided in a court of law: *Some contracts refer technical disputes to an expert whose* ***decision is final and binding.***

final accounts —see under ACCOUNT¹

final distribution —see under DISTRIBUTION

final dividend —see under DIVIDEND

final invoice —see under INVOICE¹

fi·nal·ize also **finalise** *BrE* /ˈfaɪnəl-aɪz/ *v* [T] to finish and agree to an arrangement, plan, business deal etc: *In the last two weeks, Whitbread has finalised the purchase of two breweries from Manchester-based Boddington's.* | *British Aerospace is about to finalise a £240 million joint venture with Taiwan Aerospace to manufacture regional jets.*

final payment —see under PAYMENT

final reminder —see under REMINDER

fi·nance¹ /ˈfaɪnæns, fɪ̈ˈnæns‖fɪ̈ˈnæns, ˈfaɪnæns/ *n* **1** [U] *BrE* money provided or lent, for example by a bank for INVESTMENT (=when money is put into buildings, equipment, etc to produce goods and services) or CONSUMPTION (=when people buy goods and services) + **for**: *Scottish Homes is the nation's biggest source of finance for house building.* | *The European Investment Bank would* ***provide finance*** *for a range of activities including regional development activity.* | *The next step was to* ***obtain finance*** *in order to start manufacturing and selling full-sized engines.* | *If you are selling a larger property, which is paid for, and buying a smaller one, then you will not have to* ***raise finance*** *to obtain it*
2 [U] the management of money by countries, organizations, and people: *McDonald's named Jack Greenberg, the fast-food concern's top finance executive, to be vice chairman, suggesting finance will play a prominent role in the company's future.* | *Russia's* ***finance minister*** *said he expects the ruble to stabilize soon.*
3 [U] the study of the management and use of money: *He is professor of finance at Wharton Business School.*
4 finances [plural] the money that an organization or person has, and their way of managing it: *Italian state finances are about the worst of any major world economy.* | *CBS hired McKinsey to conduct an overall strategic review of its structure, operations and finances.*
business finance money lent by a bank or other financial organization to a business for a particular purpose, and the lending of money in this way: *leasing and other forms of business finance*
consumer finance finance that is provided to people, usually so that they can buy particular goods:

The PSM consumer finance company hands out loans for motorcycles.

corporate finance finance that is provided to companies, and the banking activity of providing it: *The corporate finance group will act as advisers to corporate clients on such matters as strategic restructuring and mergers.*

debt finance borrowing by companies or governments in the form of loans on which interest is paid, for example bonds: *Most European companies use only one form of debt finance – the traditional bank credit.* | *If taxation is not available to cover public expenditure, governments must resort to debt finance or increases in the money supply to finance their activities.*

equity finance finance obtained by companies in the form of shares, rather than in the form of debt: *They fell into the trap of relying too little on equity finance and too much on bank credit.*

high finance financial activities involving very large amounts of money, for example with governments or large companies: *Their influence has spread as they have moved into the corridors of high finance and big business.*

mortgage finance finance for people and companies to buy property: *Banks, federal credit agencies and mortgage brokers now provide the vast majority of mortgage finance to the nation's homeowners.*

personal finance people's management of their own money: *Mr Givens turned his life around with strategies he devised in personal finance, tax reduction and investing.*

public finance the management of money by a local or national government: *New York's office of public finance*

finance[2] *v* [T] to give or lend money, especially a large amount of money, to pay for something: *The new company will be financed by a total of $200 million in equity and $300 million in bank debt.* —see also FINANCING, REFINANCE

Finance Act *n* in Britain, the law that puts into effect the decisions announced by the CHANCELLOR (=the British finance minister) in the BUDGET (=the plans for government taxation, borrowing, and spending for the coming year): *The Finance Act brings into force the Windfall Tax.*

Finance Bill *n* the proposals for the Finance Act that are discussed in the British Parliament before they become law: *The opposition will oppose any Finance Bill that puts tax cuts before investment in education.*

finance company also **finance house** *BrE* —see under COMPANY

Finance Houses Association abbreviation **FHA** *n* a professional association of British finance houses, that represents their views, checks that standards are kept etc: *The Finance Houses Association were also anxious to ensure that collection practices conformed to the highest ethical standards.*

finance lease —see under LEASE[2]

finance market —see under MARKET[1]

fi•nan•cial /fɪ̆ˈnænʃəl, faɪ-/ *adj* related to or involving finance or money: *a law barring* ***financial transactions*** *between American corporations and countries accused of supporting terrorism* | *Hong Kong's* ***financial system*** —see also FINANCIALS

financial accounting —see under ACCOUNTING

Financial Accounting Standards Board abbreviation **FASB** *n* ACCOUNTING the organization that sets the standard rules for ACCOUNTING in the US. These rules are referred to as the GENERALLY ACCEPTED ACCOUNTING PRINCIPLES: *The Financial Accounting Standards Board has adopted a less complex rule on deferred taxes.* —see also ACCOUNTING STANDARDS BOARD

financial analysis —see under ANALYSIS

financial analyst —see under ANALYST

financial books *n* [plural] another name for BOOKS OF ACCOUNT: *The company is being fined £50,000 for not keeping proper financial books.*

financial centre —see under CENTRE

financial engineering —see under ENGINEERING

financial futures —see under FUTURES

financial indicator —see under INDICATOR

financial institution —see under INSTITUTION

financial instrument —see under INSTRUMENT

financial intermediary —see under INTERMEDIARY

financial investment —see under INVESTMENT

financial leverage —see under LEVERAGE[1]

financial obligations —see under OBLIGATION

financial product —see under PRODUCT

financial ratio —see under RATIO

financial reporting —see under REPORTING

Financial Reporting Standard abbreviation **FRS** *n* [C usually plural] ACCOUNTING in Britain, one of the rules about how company's financial information must be shown, set by the ACCOUNTING STANDARDS BOARD. Similar rules in the US are the GENERALLY ACCEPTED ACCOUNTING PRINCIPLES: *Financial Reporting Standard no. 3 requires asset disposals to be separated from other components of the profit and loss account.*

fi•nan•cials /fɪ̆ˈnænʃəlz, faɪ-/ *n* [plural] FINANCE stocks and shares in financial companies: *Financials began firmly but ran out of steam.*

financial services —see under SERVICE[1]

Financial Services Act *n* in Britain, a law that in 1986 REGULATED (=established rules and laws for) investment advice and services in order to protect investors, and that prepared for BIG BANG: *The aim of the Financial Services Act 1986 was to introduce self-regulation within a legal framework.*

Financial Services Authority abbreviation **FSA** *n* an organization that in 1997 took control of REGULATION (=making sure that laws are obeyed) of the British financial services industry from the nine separate organizations which previously had been responsible for banking, insurance etc: *The Financial Services Authority regulates the sale and marketing of most investment products.*

financial standing —see under STANDING

financial statement —see under STATEMENT

financial structure —see under STRUCTURE

financial supermarket —see under SUPERMARKET

Financial Times abbreviation **FT** *n* an important financial newspaper based in London, with EDITIONS in Europe, Asia, and North America

Financial Times indices —see ***FTSE indices*** under INDICES

financial year —see under YEAR

fi•nan•cier /fɪ̆ˈnænsɪə, faɪˈnæn-‖ˌfɪnənˈsɪr/ *n* [C] **1** a person or organization that provides money for investment: *The firm has a value only if it is earning more than its cost of capital; otherwise, the financiers should have put their money elsewhere.*

2 someone who works in a financial institution and is responsible for particular investments: *A successful* ***corporate financier*** (=one who arranges investments in companies) *needs to be more commercial, more extrovert and more ambitious than the average number cruncher.*

3 a person who controls large sums of money and investments: *Benlox, a £45 million group, 23% owned by Egyptian financier Ashraf Marwan*

F

fi·nan·cing /ˈfaɪnænsɪŋ, fəˈnænsɪŋ‖fəˈnænsɪŋ, ˈfaɪnænsɪŋ/ *n* [U] the money provided for an investment, and the arrangements for providing it: *the financing of new roads* | *He said he hadn't carefully considered the project's financing.* | *They put together a* ***financing package*** (=a set of different forms of financing) *to back their takeover bid for Dixons.* | *An equity offering is the most important part of the company's* ***financing plan.***

creative financing unusual but not necessarily illegal ways of getting or providing finance: *Mr Goodman, with little cash but a talent for creative financing, helped build Corona into a major company.*

debtor-in-possession financing when a debtor company is allowed to keep possession of its assets while it is given financial help to organize a way to pay its debt: *Anthonys said normal operations will continue, thanks largely to $50 million in debtor-in-possession financing secured from GE Capital.*

deficit financing when government spending not paid for by taxes is paid for by borrowing: *The government might have to issue deficit financing bonds to cover falling tax revenues during the coming fiscal year.*

equity financing when a company obtains money for investment by making shares available, rather than by using bonds or bank loans: *The new Class C common shares will improve Nichols' ability to use equity financing to support and expand its operations.*

find /faɪnd/ past tense and past participle **found** *v* [T]
1 if you find work or employment, you get a job or some work. If you find someone to do a job, you employ them to do that job: *Karen* ***found a job with*** *a major travel company after she completed her course.* | *an assignment to* ***find*** *a chief executive* ***for*** *the American Council of Life Insurance*
2 to discover or learn something by study or RESEARCH: *We found 36% of customers interviewed said they had to wait between five and 10 minutes to be served.* | *The survey found that these drivers were more likely to drive badly and break the law.* —**findings** *n* plural *As a result of these findings, Glaxo stopped clinical trials for ethical reasons.* | *Following the on-site inspection, the findings are analysed and the surveyor prepares a written report.*
3 LAW if someone ACCUSED of a crime is found guilty or innocent, a court of law decides that they are guilty or innocent of that crime **be found guilty/innocent of sth**: *All the senior executives were found guilty of conspiring to mislead the markets during the £837 million Blue Arrow rights issue.*
4 find for/against sb LAW to decide in a court of law whether someone is innocent or guilty of a crime: *The Board of Review allowed the taxpayer's appeal, but the High Court found for the Commissioner.* | *If the court finds against the bank, its bosses might be replaced with central-bank appointees.* —**finding** *n* [C usually plural] *Accountants inevitably greeted the court's finding with some concern.* | *If the appellant is dissatisfied with* ***the findings of*** *the Appeal Committee, he may seek judicial review of the decision in the courts.*
5 if you find a computer file, you bring it up on your screen so that you can read it or write in it: *Windows lets you find a file without having to remember which package you were using when you created it.*
6 *informal* if you find an amount of money, you have enough money to allow you to do something: *The first-time buyer has to find a deposit of 5% or more of the property price.*

fine[1] /faɪn/ *n* [C] money that someone has to pay as a punishment: *Mr Boesky served 22 months in jail and paid a $100 million fine to settle insider trading charges.* | *If convicted, they face* ***heavy fines.***

fine[2] *v* [T] to make someone pay money as a punishment **fine sb for doing sth**: *The company has been fined for illegal nuclear exports to North Korea.*

fine[3] *adj* of a very high quality or standard: *fine wines*

fine paper —see under PAPER

fine trade bill —see under BILL OF EXCHANGE

fin·ish /ˈfɪnɪʃ/ *v* [I,T] if shares etc finish at a certain level or price on a financial market, they are at that level or price when trading ends for the day: *Shares finished marginally weaker, with the All Ordinaries index down 3.1 points at 1,772.5.* | *The* ***FTSE 100 index*** *finished 16.4 points lower at 2,342.1.*

finished goods —see under GOODS

fire /faɪə‖faɪr/ *v* [T] to dismiss someone from their job; SACK: *Lee Iacocca worked his way up to the presidency of Ford Motor Company, from which he was abruptly fired by Henry Ford II.* | *The government aimed to sell off state assets and fire about 80,000 workers.*

fire·fight·ing /ˈfaɪəˌfaɪtɪŋ‖ˈfaɪr-/ *n* [U] **1** the work of preventing fires and stopping them burning
2 the work of dealing with sudden problems in an organization, rather than its normal work: *Many computer departments are fire-fighting operations, going from crisis to crisis.* | *The Ministry needs a strategy that goes beyond just firefighting.*

fire insurance —see under INSURANCE

fire insurance policy —see under INSURANCE POLICY

fire loss —see under LOSS

fire policy —see under INSURANCE POLICY

fire risk only —see FRO

fire·sale /ˈfaɪəˌseɪl‖ˈfaɪr-/also **fire sale** *n* [C] FINANCE an occasion when someone sells something very cheaply because they need to raise money quickly: *Bankruptcy could lead to a firesale, with creditors receiving a smaller dividend.* | *Stores have resorted to fire sale tactics this month because they have more inventory than they want to talk about.*

firesale price —see under PRICE[1]

fire·wall /ˈfaɪəwɔːl‖ˈfaɪrwɒːl/ *n* [C] **1** COMPUTING a system which stops people looking at certain information on a computer, especially information on the INTERNET: *British Aerospace uses a firewall so that individuals cannot be looked up in the directory of users.*
2 FINANCE a system which is used by large financial and law companies to stop sensitive or confidential information being passed from one department to another; CHINESE WALL: *It is in the interests of the universal bank to put in effect internal precautions such as firewalls.*

fir·ing /ˈfaɪərɪŋ‖ˈfaɪr-/ *n* **hiring and firing** the process of employing people and dismissing them from employment, often with very little time in between: *The alternative to temporary working would probably be more hiring and firing.*

firm[1] /fɜːm‖fɜːrm/ *n* [C] a company or business, especially one which is quite small: *The eight-volume guide contains entries for 700,000 lawyers and 44,000* ***law firms.*** | *a* ***firm of chartered accountants*** | *The auditing services market is dominated by a small number of large* ***accounting firms.***

consulting firm a company that gives advice and training in a particular area to people in other companies; CONSULTANCY

search firm a company that finds people with the right skills and experience to do a particular job for employers that need them; HEAD-HUNTER: *A search firm contacted him and said Hughes wanted to talk to him about a chief executive position.* | *The company has hired an* ***executive search firm*** *to help identify candidates.*

firm[2] *v* [I,T] FINANCE if prices on a financial market firm to a particular level, they rise to that level **+ to**: *Sales volume hit £53 million as the shares firmed 19p to 126p.* | *The austral had stabilized, firming from around US$1=6,000 australs in March to US$1=5,000 australs as at May 31.*

firm[3] *adj* **1** [only before a noun] firm decisions, judgements, or offers are final and not likely to be changed: *Mr Perelmann said it was too early to make* ***firm forecasts*** *about demand.* | *The airline has* ***firm orders*** *for 20 Airbus A321 medium-range jets.*
2 FINANCE stocks, shares, prices etc which are firm have been rising and do not seem likely to fall: *The Federal Reserve chairman implied that the US would keep* ***interest rates firm.*** | *OPEC members need* ***firm prices*** *to maintain their revenues.* | *The dollar ended the week* ***on a firm note.*** (=with a steady price)

firm name *n* [C] LAW the name of a firm, rather than the names of the people who own it, used in legal documents or for trading purposes: *Any one of the partners may incur liabilities in the firm name.*

firm offer —see under OFFER[2]

firm price —see under PRICE[1]

firm sale —see under SALE

firm•ware /ˈfɜːmweə‖ˈfɜːrmwer/ *n* [U] COMPUTING instructions to computers that are stored on CHIPS so that they can be done much faster, and cannot be changed or lost: *Manufacturers are considering incorporating the window manager into their firmware products.* | *A pen-plotter normally has built-in firmware that will automatically join two points with a straight line.* —see also HARDWARE, SOFTWARE

first /fɜːst‖fɜːrst/ *adj* **first half/quarter/period** the first half, quarter etc of the financial year

first-class also **first class** *adj* **1** if something is first-class, it is of very good quality and much better than other things of the same type: *We provide a first-class, professional service for our customers.*
2 using first-class mail: *a first-class stamp*
3 first class seats, accommodation etc are the most comfortable and expensive available: ***first-class*** *airline* ***tickets*** | *The airline claims its 9,000 daily* ***first-class seats*** *are 65% full.* —**first class** *adv*: *If you* ***send the letter first class,*** *it should arrive tomorrow.* | *Company policy says we cannot* ***fly first class,*** *but we can fly business class on trips over a thousand miles.*

first-class fare —see under FARE

first-class mail —see under MAIL[1]

first entry —see BOOKS OF FIRST ENTRY

first-half *adj* [only before a noun] ACCOUNTING, FINANCE first-half profits, losses, sales etc are ones made in the first six months of the financial year: *Shares of Dixons Group Plc increased in price after the UK electronics retailer reported a 41% increase in* ***first-half*** *pretax* ***profit.*** | ***First-half sales*** *grew 11% to $1,025 billion.*

first-half loss —see under LOSS

first in, first out abbreviation **FIFO** *n* [U] ACCOUNTING, FINANCE a method of calculating the value of goods or materials a company has in stock, based on the idea that those put in stock first were the first ones sold or used. Any stock that is left at the end of the year is valued at the cost of the most recently bought stock: *Since inventory is costed on a* ***first in, first out basis*** *it is assumed the oldest inventory is used up first, leaving the newest inventory to be priced at the current higher prices.* —compare LAST IN, FIRST OUT

first lien —see under LIEN

first mortgage —see under MORTGAGE[1]

first-rate *adj* excellent or of the very best quality: *This is a first-rate company with a 58-year history.* | *The service is first-rate and the prices are very reasonable.*

first refusal —see under REFUSAL

first section —see under SECTION

first-tier *adj* FINANCE **first-tier shares/bonds etc** shares, bonds etc in companies that are considered to be the biggest or most important: *Many* ***first-tier*** *investment* ***bonds*** *gained on speculation of a rise in US interest rates.* —compare BLUE CHIP, SECOND-TIER —see also ***Tier 1 capital*** under CAPITAL, ***Tier 1 equity*** under CAPITAL

fis•cal /ˈfɪskəl/ *adj* [only before a noun] FINANCE connected with government taxes, debts, and spending: *The* ***fiscal deficit*** *was estimated at $53,800,000 or 3.5% of gross national product.* | *Pérez stated that the current fiscal crisis was the result of the collapse of the oil industry.* —**fiscally** *adv*: *countries with* ***fiscally sound*** (=well-managed) *governments* | *The President is pro-business and* ***fiscally conservative.***

fiscal drag *n* [U] ECONOMICS when rising incomes mean that the government receives increasing amounts of tax, as people move up into higher TAX BRACKETS (=levels of income with a particular tax rate). Taxes have to be adjusted to take account of this, if it is not to have an effect on the economy as a whole: *If we do not cut taxes, the normal process of fiscal drag means that the tax burden rises over time.*

fiscal policy —see under POLICY

fiscal stimulus —see under STIMULUS

fiscal year —see under YEAR

fish•e•ry /ˈfɪʃəri/ *n* plural **fisheries** **1** [U] the fishing industry: *the agriculture, forest and fishery sectors*
2 [C] a part of the sea where fish are caught as a business: *the Peruvian anchovy fishery, one of the largest in the world*
3 fisheries [plural] the fishing industry. Fisheries is often used in the names of organizations involved in industrial fishing: *The National Fisheries Institute, a trade group representing seafood producers, processors, distributors and brokers.*

fit[1] /fɪt/ *v* past tense **fitted** also **fit** *AmE* past participle **fitted** present participle **fitting** [T] to put a piece of equipment into place, or a new part on a machine **fit sth on/to sth**: *An interactive entertainment system will be fitted on Virgin's 747s.* **fit sth with sth**: *Insurance is cheaper for homes fitted with alarms.*
fit sth ↔ **out** *phr v* [T] to provide a room, building etc with decorations or equipment + **with**: *Used boats are usually fitted out with electronic gear that would cost thousands when added to the base price of a new boat.*

fit[2] *n* [C,U] if there is a fit between a company's different activities, they go well together and can be managed together profitably + **between**: *The fit between the two merged supermarket chains is excellent.*
strategic fit when a particular plan, product etc is suitable in relation to an organization's STRATEGY: *Head office reviewed these proposals on the basis of financial criteria, but also looked for strategic fit.* | *Corporate planners ensure that projects, however viable, possess 'strategic fit'.*

fit•ter /ˈfɪtə‖-ər/ *n* [C] *BrE* someone who repairs or puts together machines or electrical equipment: *a gas fitter*

five nines also **five nines reliability** *n* [U] COMPUTING a computer or computer system with five nines reliability, or which has five nines, is almost certain never to break or go wrong: *Our server has just five minutes of downtime a year – that's 99.999 per cent availability, the five nines to which other hardware companies can only aspire.*

five Ps /ˌfaɪv ˈpiːz/ *n* **the five Ps** MARKETING the FOUR PS, and, in addition, PACKAGING

fix[1] /fɪks/ *v* [T] **1** *informal* to repair something: *We had to* ***fix*** *some computer* ***problems.*** | *It will cost millions of dollars to* ***fix the system.***
2 to decide on a level, value etc for something: *It is very difficult to* ***fix*** *an offer* ***price*** *several weeks in advance.* + **at**: *The interest* ***rate*** *has been* ***fixed*** *at 6.5%.*

F

3 also **fix up** to make arrangements for something: *They agreed to **fix a time** for the interview.* | *Mike wants to **fix up a meeting** with you.*
4 to arrange something dishonestly in order to get the result you want: *We suspected that the **deal had been fixed** in advance.*

fix² *n* **1** [C] something that has been dishonestly arranged: *Allegations of a fix were not proven.* | *Obviously his appointment to the position was a fix.*
2 [C] a solution to a problem, especially if the solution is temporary: *They do not want a **quick fix**, but a resolution of the issues.* | *a fix for the suffering American economy*
3 [C] COMPUTING a solution to a computer software problem: *Sometimes new software can be uploaded into the machine to create a fix.* | *The software checks for the latest bug fixes.*
4 get a fix on sb/sth to understand what someone or something is really like: *Investors are trying to get a fix on Chrysler's future.*

fixed /fɪkst/ *adj* not movable or changeable: *Consumers spend a fixed amount on books regardless of price changes.* | *The lira and peseta will keep their fixed levels against each other.* —compare FLEXIBLE

fixed asset —see under ASSET

fixed capital —see under CAPITAL

fixed charge —see under CHARGE[1]

fixed cost —see under COST[1]

fixed deposit —see under DEPOSIT[1]

fixed disk *n* [C] COMPUTING another name for HARD DISK

fixed exchange rate —see under EXCHANGE RATE

fixed expense —see under EXPENSE

fixed fee —see under FEE

fixed income —see under INCOME

fixed-income investment —see under INVESTMENT

fixed instalment system —see under SYSTEM

fixed-interest securities —see under SECURITY

fixed-interest security —see under SECURITY

fixed investment —see under INVESTMENT

fixed liabilities —see under LIABILITY

fixed parity —see under PARITY

fixed-period contract —see under CONTRACT[1]

fixed price —see under PRICE[1]

fixed rate —see under RATE[1]

fixed-rate debt —see under DEBT

fixed-rate mortgage —see under MORTGAGE[1]

fixed term contract —see under CONTRACT[1]

fixed trust —see under TRUST

fixtures and fittings *BrE* abbreviation **f & f**, **fixtures** *AmE n* [plural] LAW, PROPERTY things such as lights etc that are fixed or fastened to a house or building and are included as part of the property when it is sold: *Ask the seller of the house to list the smaller fixtures and fittings that are to be left.*

flack also **flak** /flæk/ *n* [C] *AmE informal* a person whose job is to represent an organization and talk to newspaper and television reporters, answering their questions about a negative story involving the organization: *He put a shield between himself and the press by hiring a flack to handle media calls.*

flag of convenience *n* plural **flags of convenience** [C] the national flag of certain countries, especially Panama, Liberia, Honduras, and Costa Rica which are willing to REGISTER a ship owned by someone who is a citizen of another country. Owners sometimes register their ships in one of these countries in order to avoid paying heavy taxes and because of their lower safety standards and rates of pay: *The ferry, registered under a flag of convenience, was unprepared to handle a disaster, investigators say.*

flag·ship /ˈflægʃɪp/ *adj* [only before a noun] **1** a flagship product is the best and most important one that a company produces: *Anheuser-Busch has just launched a new advertising campaign for its **flagship brand**, Budweiser.*
2 a flagship company is one of the best in its industry: *Pan Am was once regarded as the **flaghip airline** of the United States.*
3 a flagship building is the best and most important one that a company owns: *27% of Tiffany's sales still come from the company's **flagship store** on Fifth Avenue in Manhattan.* —**flagship** *n* [C] *This new microprocessor will be Intel's future flagship.* | *Croch's and Brentano's Inc. is a chain of 19 bookstores, including a five-story flagship in downtown Chicago.*

flame /fleɪm/ *v* [T] *informal* COMPUTING to send someone a message that criticizes them on the INTERNET, especially in a rude or angry way. If someone breaks the rules of NETIQUETTE, they may be flamed —**flame** *n* [C] —**flaming** *n* [U]

flat¹ /flæt/ *adj* comparative **flatter** superlative **flattest**
1 [only before a noun] a flat fee, price etc is fixed and does not change or have anything added to it: *We charge a **flat fee** for car hire.* | *Subscribers to the service have to pay a **flat charge** each month.*
2 if a market, economy etc is flat or sales are flat, levels of trade or sales are not increasing: *In the USA, car **sales were flat** although truck sales increased.* | *As demand for Pilkington's products stays flat and costs remain high, half-year profits have fallen by 70% to £15.1 million.*
3 FINANCE if the stockmarket is flat, prices are not rising or falling: *The share market closed flat after spending the day trapped in a 10 point range.*

flat² *n* [C] *BrE* a place where people live that consists of a set of rooms, usually on one floor and part of a larger building; APARTMENT *AmE*: *Prices start from £80,995 for a studio and £89,995 for one-bedroom flats.*

flat³ *adv* **1 fall flat** if something you are doing or planning falls flat, it is unsuccessful: *The Ryans' **plans** to build a retirement dream home **fell flat**.*
2 flat out *informal* if you work flat out, you work as fast as possible: ***Working flat out**, the men completed the work by about ten-thirty on Saturday morning.*

flat fee —see ***fixed fee*** under FEE

flat rate —see under RATE[1]

flat-rate *adj* **1 flat-rate charge/fee/pricing etc** a flat-rate charge etc is always the same and does not change depending on the time spent doing something, the results that are produced etc: *Some property shops charge a **flat-rate fee**, whether they sell your home or not.* | *Many Internet service providers have moved toward a **flat-rate pricing system**, in which users pay little attention to the clock because they are not charged based on how long they spend online.*
2 [only before a noun] TAX a flat-rate tax is one, usually on income, where the rate does not change in relation to the amount earned, and where there are no ALLOWANCES (=income on which tax is not paid) FLAT TAX: *The chancellor will replace individual and corporate income taxes with a flat-rate 13% income tax*

flat tax —see under TAX[1]

flaw /flɔː‖flɒː/ *n* [C] **1** a mistake or weakness in a machine, system etc that prevents it from working correctly + **in**: *The manufacturers agreed to spend about $10 million to fix a flaw in the missile.* | *The cause of the leak is a **design flaw** in the assembly.* | *The space telescope had a **fundamental flaw*** (=very serious one) *in one of its* *two mirrors.* | *There is no cause to disrupt the program. There is no* ***fatal flaw*** (=extremely serious one) *in the B-2.*

2 a mistake in an argument, plan, or set of ideas: *Small banks are missing from the plan and this is the main flaw in the Treasury's approach.*

flawed /flɔːd‖flɒːd/ *adj* having a mistake or weakness: *The plane crashed as a result of a flawed engine fan disk.* | *Outside experts warned the study could be flawed.*

fledg·ling /ˈfledʒlɪŋ/ *adj* [only before a noun] a fledgling company is fairly new: *a fledgling phone company with barely $1 billion in annual sales*

fleece /fliːs/ *v* [T] *informal* to charge someone too much money for something, usually by tricking them: *The former singer is suspected of fleecing investors of more than $500,000 by selling rights to recordings he didn't own.*

fleet /fliːt/ *n* [C] **1** a group of cars, buses, trucks, planes, or ships owned or controlled by one company: *WAM Beverage Distributors owns half the fleet of 25 trucks that distribute Tropical Fantasy.* | *All Nippon Airways' new fleet of Boeing 777 supertwin aircraft* | ***fleet*** *car* ***insurance***

2 a group of ships or boats sailing together: *a fleet of fishing vessels*

fleet rating —see under RATING

fleet rental —see under RENTAL

Fleet Street *n* a street in London where many important newspaper offices used to be, and still often used as a name for the British newspaper industry: *He was interested in working in the communications industry, or Fleet Street.* | *Fleet Street journalists*

fleet terms —see under TERM[1]

flex·i·ble /ˈfleksəbəl/ *adj* **1** a person, plan etc that is flexible can change or be changed easily to suit any new situation: *flexible investment opportunities* | *a flexible factory capable of building several different models* | *90% of people would pick a job with* ***flexible benefits*** (=ones between which they can choose) *over one without them.*

2 HUMAN RESOURCES if arrangements for work are flexible, employers can ask workers to do different jobs, work part-time rather than full-time, give them contracts for short periods of time etc. Flexible working also includes flexitime, JOB-SHARING, and TELEWORKING (=working at home): *More employees are seeking* ***flexible hours*** (=being able to choose the times they work) *family leave or work-at-home deals.* | *attempts by organizations to increase efficiency by adopting* ***flexible manning arrangements*** | *German companies have been moving production abroad to take advantage of more* ***flexible working practices.*** —**flexibility** *n* [U] *Flexibility for working mothers including teleworking and automatic leave if a parent is very ill.*

flexible trust —see under TRUST

flex·i·time /ˈfleksitaɪm/ also **flex·time** /ˈflekstaɪm/ *AmE* — *n* [U] a system in which people who work in a company work for a fixed number of hours each week, but can choose what time they start or finish work: *Staff wishing to avail themselves of this* ***flexitime arrangement*** *should discuss it with the manager.* | *family-friendly businesses that offer flextime*

flier *n* [C] another spelling of FLYER

flight /flaɪt/ *n* **1** [C] a journey by plane: *American Airlines began the* ***regular flights*** *to Santiago less than a year ago.* | *a* ***return flight*** *to Hong Kong*

2 top-flight *BrE*, **topflight** *AmE* a top-flight manager is one who is in a very high position in an organization and who is very good at the job: *It is worth investing in a selection procedure to find a top-flight sales person.*

3 [singular] ECONOMICS the rapid movement of money, goods etc out of a country or particular type of investment: *Employers warned of or into* ***a flight of*** *investment and manufacturing overseas.* | ***the flight into*** *deposit-based savings after the 1987 crash*

capital flight [U] when large amounts of money are sent out of a country because of fears about its economic future: *Chinese missile tests near Taiwan made share prices fall and prompted capital flight.*

flight capital —see under CAPITAL

flip /flɪp/ *v* past tense and past participle **flipped** present participle **flipping** [T] FINANCE to buy shares and sell them soon after to make a quick profit: *selling by some speculative accounts that were flipping the stock for a profit* —**flipper** *n* [C] *Stock jumped as high as $33 in frenetic trading as flippers — investors who buy a hot deal and then immediately sell it for a quick profit — turned over their shares.*

flip·chart /ˈflɪptʃɑːrt‖-tʃɑːrt/ *n* [C] a large board with pieces of paper attached at the top. Flipcharts are used to present information written on the paper to a group of people: *A good technique is to have a flipchart, draw a line down the middle and ask someone to write up the arguments for and against.* —compare WHITEBOARD

float[1] /fləʊt‖floʊt/ *v* **1** [I,T] to sell new shares, bonds etc on a financial market: *To finance the expansion, airports have floated $30 billion in bonds, which typically cover 75% of construction costs.*

2 float a company on the stockmarket to sell shares in a company on a stockmarket for the first time: *The price of Northern Rock's shares on the day it floated on the stock market beat all expectations.*

3 [I,T] if a country floats its currency or if the currency floats, its value is allowed to change in relation to other currencies after a period of time when it has been fixed: *The Labor government floated the New Zealand dollar and deregulated various areas of the economy.*

4 [I] if a price, amount etc floats, it moves up or down slowly: *The oil market let crude prices float lower.* | *In the 1970s, rural areas suffered, but the stock and bond markets floated up.* —see also ***float a cheque*** under CHEQUE

float[2] *n* [C usually singular] **1** when shares, bonds etc are sold on a financial market, or when a company sells shares for the first time; FLOTATION: *GPA is still talking with its investment bankers about the timing and terms of the float, which is expected to value the company at between $3 billion and $4 billion.*

2 when a currency is allowed to change in value in relation to others: *the European Monetary System, a joint float of currencies centering on the mark*

dirty float when a currency that is supposed to be floating is actually being kept close to a particular value by the actions of a country's central bank

3 the money made available to banks while customers' cheques go through the banking system: *Many consumers have long believed that bankers have lengthened the check-clearing process to use the float for their own benefit.*

4 the amount of notes and coins in the TILL of a shop, restaurant etc when they open for business: *Cash floats should be rechecked to ensure that cashiers have enough change for the evening business.*

5 *BrE* a fixed sum of money that is kept in an office and can be used to buy small items needed in the office; PETTY CASH: *The use of business credit cards removes the need for unproductive and costly cash floats.*

floa·ta·tion /fləʊˈteɪʃən‖floʊ-/ *n* [C] another spelling of FLOTATION

float·er /ˈfləʊtə‖ˈfloʊtər/ *n* [C] **1** a bond with a VARIABLE interest rate: *The issue was split into three fixed-rate tranches and one floater.*

2 INSURANCE insurance which covers risks in a number of different places in addition to the particular insurance for each place, for example so that goods stored in different WAREHOUSES are covered without the insured having to say in advance which warehouse they will be stored in

F

floating charge —see under CHARGE[1]

floating currency —see under CURRENCY

floating debt —see under DEBT

floating exchange rate —see under EXCHANGE RATE

floating insurance —see under INSURANCE

floating rate —see under RATE[1]

floating rate note —see under NOTE[1]

flog /flɒg‖flɑːg/ *v* past tense and past participle **flogged** present participle **flogging** [T] *informal* to sell something: *The Russians, in their new entrepreneurial mode, were flogging their most advanced military hardware.*
flog sth ↔ **off** *phr v* [T] to sell something in order to get rid of it: *The government wants to flog off the National Air Traffic Control Service.*

flood[1] /flʌd/ *v* **1** [T] to send a large number of things such as letters or requests to an organization **flood sth with**: *Dealers flooded Congress with angry letters.* | *Swiss banks have been flooded with deposits and loan requests from blue-chip American firms.*
2 [I] to arrive in large numbers **flood in/into/across etc**: *The eastern states need judges and lawyers to deal with thousands of property claims flooding in from the west.* | *As his corruption became evident, the usually tolerant Brazilians flooded onto the streets and drove Mr Collor out.*
3 flood the market to make a product available in large quantities, perhaps with the result that its price falls: *Auto-makers are flooding the market with late-model used cars.* | *the potential for GE and Tungsram, with 8% of world sales in light bulbs, to flood the western European market*

F

flood[2] *n* [U] a large number of things or people that arrive at the same time + **of**: *The last-minute* ***flood of applications*** *means most small investors will probably be allocated fewer than 400 shares.* | *The flood of credit into the housing market fuelled house-price inflation.*

flood•gates /ˈflʌdgeɪts/ *n* **open the floodgates** to suddenly make it possible for a lot of people to do or have something for the first time: *The exception, once granted, could* ***open the floodgates to*** *similar demands by other companies.*

flood insurance —see under INSURANCE

floor /flɔː‖flɔːr/ *n* [C] **1** ECONOMICS the lowest EXCHANGE RATE a currency is permitted to fall to: *The pound ended the day less than 1% away from* ***its floor of*** *241.5 against the Portuguese escudo.* | *Before the lira was devalued, traders were buying lira at prices well below* ***the currency's floor against*** *the Deutschmark.* —compare CEILING
2 ECONOMICS a level below which prices, wages etc are not allowed to fall: *The agreement might also act as* ***a floor to wages*** *during the recession.* | *Quarterly* ***price floors*** *were established for Japanese commodities.* —compare CAP
3 dealing/trading/exchange floor FINANCE the part of a financial market where shares, COMMODITIES (=oil, metals, farm products) etc are bought and sold. In American English, only trading floor and exchange floor are used, not dealing floor: *He eventually took responsibility for running the dealing floor.* | *People say he has less influence now because of opposition on the exchange floors.*
4 the floor *AmE* FINANCE a dealing, trading, or exchange floor
5 the floor the place where a public meeting or discussion happens, or the people who attend it: *The AGM was turbulent, with the administration being recommended by the floor to reconsider the deal they had earlier rejected.*
6 get in on the ground floor *BrE*, **get in on the first floor** *AmE* if you get in on the ground floor, you get involved in a business activity when it begins: *The scope for an entrepreneur to get in on the ground floor and turn petrol stations into shops was obvious to those with an eye for business.*
7 shop/factory floor used to refer to the workers who make the goods in a factory or sell the product: *the union's influence on the factory floor* | *Workers celebrated news of the deal with free beer at a shop floor meeting.*
8 the shop floor the area in a factory where the ordinary workers do their work: *The chairwoman started her working life on the shop floor.*

floor broker —see under BROKER[1]

floor dealer —see under DEALER

floor limit —see under LIMIT[1]

floor price —see under PRICE[1]

floor•space /ˈflɔːspeɪs‖ˈflɔːr-/ *n* [U] the area of the floor in an office or other building: *Industry now requires fewer workers per unit of factory floorspace.*

floor trader —see under DEALER

flop /flɒp‖flɑːp/ *v* past tense and past participle **flopped** present participle **flopping** [I] if a product or an attempt to do something flops, it fails completely: *A £16 million rights issue from Addison Consultancy flopped yesterday with only 2.4 % of the 151 million shares on offer taken up.* | *Some members of the board pointed out that many of sales director's schemes have flopped.* —compare BOMB 2
—**flop** *n* [C] *Another famous invention, the Sinclair C5 electric car, was a spectacular flop, but he's still inventing.*—see also ISSUE FLOP

flop•py /ˈflɒpi‖ˈflɑːpi/ *n* plural **floppies** [C] another name for a FLOPPY DISK

floppy disk —see under DISK

flo•ta•tion /fləʊˈteɪʃən‖floʊ-/ *n* [C,U] ECONOMICS making shares in a company available for people to buy for the first time: *3i group has decided to postpone its* ***stock-market flotation*** *until next year.* | *If the dividend had been cut, it might have made investors nervous about the BT3* ***share flotation.*** | *Between flotation in 1980 and sales peak in 1988, Amstrad saw profits rise to £160.4 million.*

flour•ish /ˈflʌrɪʃ‖ˈflɜːr-/ *v* [I] if a business or industry flourishes, it is very successful and makes a profit: *While most supermarket chains in Europe have been suffering in the recession, discount stores like Aldi and Netto have flourished.*

flour•ish•ing /ˈflʌrɪʃɪŋ‖ˈflɜːr-/ *adj* a business or industry that is flourishing is very successful and is making a profit: *Thailand's flourishing tourist industry*

flow /fləʊ‖floʊ/ *v* [I] **1** if money flows somewhere, such as into a bank account or into a particular country, it is moved there **flow from/into/between etc**: *A record $10 billion in foreign capital flowed into Mexican stocks last year.* | *Throughout the summer, new savings flowed away from building society accounts.* | *Investment trust money has been flowing back into blue chip companies such as Sony, Honda and Pioneer.*
2 *formal* if an event or action flows from something, it is caused by it **flow from**: *The regulations which flow from the Charities Act will mean that charities will have to improve their accounts.*
3 if information or ideas flow, people start to exchange information or their ideas so that they can discuss them: *To discover what had gone wrong, the team examined the way in which information* ***flowed between*** *Bow Valley's 300 employees.* | *As brainstorming* (=when a group of people discuss all the ideas they have about something) *gets underway, the suggestions start to flow.*

flow•back /ˈfləʊbæk‖ˈfloʊ-/ *n* [C] FINANCE when investors who own shares in a company abroad sell their shares to people living in that country: *1999 saw a steady flowback of shares across the Atlantic as US investors withdrew from the UK tobacco sector.*

flow chart also **flow diagram**, **flow sheet** —see under CHART[1]

Flow of Funds *n* in the US, official information published on borrowing and lending by banks: *the Federal Reserve's Flow of Funds data on net new commercial bank loans to non-financial corporations*

flow of funds *n* plural **flows of funds** [C,U] **1** when money is moved from one place to another, for example for investment: *Capital constraints continue to hurt the flow of funds to small businesses.* | *"There is a nice flow of funds into the stock," he says.*

2 movements of money into, within, and out of a business, as shown in the SOURCES AND USES OF FUNDS STATEMENT

fluc·tu·ate /ˈflʌktʃueɪt/ *v* [I] if prices, income, rates etc fluctuate, they change, increasing or falling often or regularly: *Dealers know that prices fluctuate and that capital losses can be expected.* + **around**: *The income of many charities tends to fluctuate around £100,000* —**fluctuating** *adj*: *Exports to non-EC countries will still be subject to* ***fluctuating exchange rates****.*

fluc·tu·a·tion /ˌflʌktʃuˈeɪʃən/ *n* [C,U] the movement of prices, income, rates etc as they increase and fall: *Fluctuations* ***in profits*** *resulted from differences between the volume of sales and the volume of production.* | *Buying patterns are usually subject to upward or downward fluctuation caused by changes in the market.* | *Although* ***market fluctuations*** *are inevitable, the stock and futures markets are basically solid.*

flush /flʌʃ/ *adj* **1 be flush (with cash/funds)** *informal* to have a lot of money at a particular time: *Singapore's savings rate is so high that the banks are flush with funds.* | *Asprey, 5p higher at 290p, is flush and has been making more acquisitions.*

2 be flushed with/by success to be very successful, and keen to achieve more success: *Flushed by success in selling homes in the slump, Pidgeley now plans to do the same in the commercial property sector.*

3 a busted flush a complete failure: *You can get a dealer who is a busted flush at 30.*

flut·ter /ˈflʌtə‖-ər/ *n informal* **have a flutter (on sth)** to risk a small amount of money on the result of a horse race, football game etc; BET,; GAMBLE: *The majority of Spaniards like to have a flutter on the Christmas lottery.*

fly /flaɪ/ *v* past tense **flew** past participle **flown** **1** [I] to travel by plane: *From Belfast, British Airways Cargo flies to London Heathrow, Manchester and Glasgow.* | *Mr McGovern always flies economy class.*

2 [T] to take goods or people to a place by plane: *It was more cost-effective to fly the chemicals direct to each country.* | *Waiting helicopters flew the executives to a second meeting.*

3 [I] *AmE* if a product or idea flies, it succeeds: *We were never confident the system was going to fly.* | *a product which the market has clearly rejected and which cannot be made to fly*

4 fly in the face of sth to be or do the opposite of what most people think is reasonable, sensible or normal: *A sales tax would fly in the face of EC moves towards greater standardisation of indirect taxes.* | *Anita Roddick has made a virtue of flying in the face of business convention.*

fly a kite —see under KITE[1]

fly-by-night *adj* [only before a noun] *informal* a fly-by-night company or businessperson is not reliable and is only interested in making a quick profit and then disappearing: *The authority requires surety bonds of $50,000 from health agencies to deter fly-by-night operations from joining the program.*

fly-by-wire *adj* [only before a noun] *informal* fly-by-wire planes are controlled mainly by computers: *In January, an Air Inter fly-by-wire A320 went down near Strasbourg with the loss of 87 lives.*

fly-drive *adj* **fly-drive package/holiday** an arrangement for which you pay a fixed price that includes your flight, a car to drive and places to stay: *Several airlines, notably American and Delta, offer a wide variety of fly-drive packages.*

fly·er also **flier** /ˈflaɪə‖-ər/ *n* [C] a small sheet of paper that is used to advertise something. Flyers are usually handed out in the street or delivered to people's houses: *a succession of flyers announcing special events*

FMCG also **fmcg** *BrE* abbreviation for FAST-MOVING CONSUMER GOODS

FNMA *n* abbreviation for FEDERAL NATIONAL MORTGAGE ASSOCIATION

FOB abbreviation for FREE ON BOARD —see under INCOTERM

fob /fɒb‖fɑːb/ *v* past tense and past participle **fobbed** present participle **fobbing**

fob sb ↔ **off** *phr v* [T] **1** to make someone accept something that is not as good as the thing they wanted + **with**: *East Europeans are highly sensitive about being fobbed off with out-of-date stock.*

2 to try to stop someone complaining or asking questions by giving them explanations, excuses etc that are obviously untrue + **with**: *I'm tired of being fobbed off with excuses and promises.*

fob sth ↔ **off on** sb *phr v* [T] to persuade or deceive someone into buying or accepting something: *You can't just fob off last year's model on customers.*

FOB airport abbreviation for FREE ON BOARD AIRPORT see under INCOTERM

fo·cus /ˈfəʊkəs‖ˈfoʊ-/ *n* [U] when a company tries to serve particular groups of customers in a market with particular needs, rather that trying to serve the whole market —**focuser** *n* [C] *The focuser seeks to achieve a competitive advantage in its target segments even though it does not possess a competitive advantage overall.*

focus group —see under GROUP

focus list —see under LIST[1]

FOD INSURANCE abbreviation for FREE OF DAMAGE

foist /fɔɪst/ *v*

foist sth **on/upon** sb *phr v* [T] to force someone to accept something that they do not want: *The company attempted to foist a defective brake-disc system on to a customer.* | *Decisions have been foisted on the staff by the board of directors.*

fold /fəʊld‖foʊld/ also **fold up** *v* [I] if a business folds or folds up, it stops operating or trading because it does not have enough money to continue: *A Merseyside engineering firm has folded today with the loss of 30 jobs.* | *His jewellery importing business folded in less than a year.* | *As the recession deepened, the company folded up.*

fold sth **into** sth *phr v* [T] to make a company become part of a larger company so that it is no longer separate: *Factories devoted exclusively to producing products for Radio Shack will be folded back into Tandy.* | *American Mitac has folded itself into a distributor company.*

fold·er /ˈfəʊldə‖ˈfoʊldər/ *n* [C] **1** a cover for keeping loose papers in, made of card or plastic: *All the correspondence is in this folder.*

2 COMPUTING a place in a computer where FILES are stored, often appearing on the screen as a picture of a folder

follow /ˈfɒləʊ‖ˈfɑːloʊ/ *v* **1** [I,T] to come or happen afterwards: *The company's decision to diversify follows a sharp decline in demand for its products.* | *As the recession worsened, further closures followed.*

2 [I] also **follow on** to be sent or paid later: *Pay a deposit of £400 now, with the balance to follow within 30 days.*

3 [T] to do something in the way that someone has told or advised you to do it, or according to the instructions that say how it should be done: *If you'd followed my advice, we'd still be in profit.* | *failure to follow proper safety procedures* | *Just follow the guidelines contained in this report.*

F

4 [T] to act according to a particular plan or set of ideas: *The Chancellor is expected to **follow** a cautious economic **policy**.* | *The company had **followed** the wrong **strategy**.*
5 [T] to happen or develop in the same way as something else: *These recent mergers appear to be **following a trend**.* | *If one company drops its prices, the others have to **follow suit*** (=do the same thing).
6 follow an occupation/trade/career etc *formal* to do a particular job or trade: *He intends to follow a legal career.*
follow sth ↔ **up** *phr v* [T] to do something as a result of something someone has suggested or something you have found out: *Many of the report's recommendations are worth following up.*
follow sth **up with** sth *phr v* [T] to do something to make sure that earlier actions have been successful or effective: *It is important to follow the initial phone call up with a letter.* —see also FOLLOW-UP

fol•low•er /ˈfɒləʊə‖ˈfɑːloʊər/ *n* [C] **1** also **market follower** a company or product which is not one of the main ones in a particular market and does not have a large share of the market: *They returned to the business last fall with three laptop computers. But those machines were market followers.*
2 a company or product which is technically less advanced than others: *It will take this competitor, a traditional follower behind Gillette, some time to come up with anything as good.*

follow-up *adj* [only before a noun] a follow-up letter, visit etc is done to make sure that earlier actions have been effective or successful, or to continue a plan of action that was started earlier: *to send out a **follow-up letter*** | *Follow-up interviews have indicated that the advertising campaign was widely misunderstood.* —**follow-up** *n* [C] *Have you sent a follow-up yet?*

font /fɒnt‖fɑːnt/ *n* [C] a set of printed letters of a particular design, used to refer to letters in a magazine, book etc: *Choose the font style from the list in the dialog box.*

Food and Agriculture Organization —see FAO

food stamp —see under STAMP[1]

food•stuff /ˈfuːdstʌf/ *n* [C,U] a substance regularly used as food, especially one that is produced and sold as a product: *a sharp rise in the price of foodstuffs* | *the subsidising of **essential foodstuffs*** (=extremely important food, such as grain, bread or rice) | *shortages of **basic foodstuffs** and consumer goods* | *one of Japan's staple foodstuffs, the soya bean*

fools•cap /ˈfuːlskæp/ *n BrE* [U] a large size of paper for writing or printing, usually 432×343 mm: *a sheet of foolscap* | *a foolscap envelope*

foot[1] /fʊt/ *n* plural **feet 1** [C] **ft** a unit for measuring length, equal to 12 inches or 30.48 centimetres
2 [singular] the lowest part of something: *the foot of a page*

foot[2] *v* **foot the bill** to pay for something, especially something expensive that you do not want to pay for: *Colombia is footing the bill for what is really an international problem.* | *Who is going to foot the repair bill?*

foot•age /ˈfʊtɪdʒ/ *n* [U] a length or quantity measured in feet: *The new site will double the **square footage** that the company presently occupies.*

foot•er /ˈfʊtə‖-ər/ *n* [C] the line of information at the bottom of a computer screen or a printed page —compare HEADER

foot•hold /ˈfʊthəʊld‖-hoʊld/ *n* [C usually singular] part of a market that a company obtains, hoping to obtain more of the same market or part of another larger market that is related to it; BEACHHEAD: *Several U.S. companies have teamed up with Mexican retailers to **get a foothold** in the huge Mexican market.*

foot•ing /ˈfʊtɪŋ/ *n* **1 a sound/firm/solid footing** good financial arrangements under which a business operates: *He has put the company **on a sound financial footing**.*
2 on an equal footing/on the same footing if two people, companies etc deal with one another on an equal footing or on the same footing, they do so on the basis that neither side is more important or in a stronger position than the other: *The new guidelines are intended to put women **on an equal footing with** men.* | *It is vital that all parties to takeovers proceed on an equal footing.*

foot•print /ˈfʊtˌprɪnt/ *n* [C] COMPUTING the space on the surface of a desk that is filled by a computer: *These PCs have a 50% smaller footprint than previous models.* | *a desktop footprint of about 9' by 6'*

Foot•sie /ˈfʊtsi/ *n* FINANCE *journalism* an informal name for the FINANCIAL TIMES-STOCK EXCHANGE INDEX OF 100 SHARES (FT-SE 100): *The Footsie closed 2.3 points higher at 2,840.0.* | *an eventual 9.5 point gain on the Footsie to 2600.5* | *the Footsie index*

foot•wear /ˈfʊtweə‖-wer/ *n* [U] things that people wear on their feet, such as shoes and boots: *price increases for **clothing and footwear*** | *the footwear industry* | *a wide range of sports footwear at favourable prices*

FOR abbreviation for FREE ON RAIL —see under INCOTERM

force[1] /fɔːs‖fɔːrs/ *n* **1** [C] a group of people who have been trained and organized for a particular purpose: *Our division has expanded its **sales force*** (=the people in a company who sell the company's products) *to 160.*
labour force *BrE*, **labor force** *AmE* [C] all the people who work for a company or in a country: *Out of Minnesota's labor force of 2.1 million, only 110,000 are reckoned to be earning the minimum wage.*
task force [C] a group formed for a short time to deal with a particular problem: *Management gave a task force only five months to do two years of research-and-development work.*
2 in force if a law or rule is in force, it exists and must be obeyed: *These regulations **have been in force** since 1997.* | *New EC directives **come into force*** (=start to operate) *in April.*
3 [C usually singular] something or someone that has a strong influence on an activity or the way events develop: *Margaret Curran is the **driving force*** (=person or thing that has the strongest influence on the way things happen) *behind the group's creation.* | *Rebuck is certainly **a force to be reckoned with*** (=has a lot of power and influence) *in the publishing industry.*
4 market forces [plural] the way that the behaviour of buyers and sellers affects the levels of SUPPLY AND DEMAND in a particular market, especially when the government does nothing to change this: *By ending the electricity monopoly, market forces rather than state utilities will set prices.* | *The question of whether there is enough demand to sustain all of the engine makers, we will have to **leave to market forces**.* (=allow market forces to take effect so that the market works in the most efficient way)
5 [U] influence or authority: *The City's code of practice does not have the **force of law**.* (=the same authority as the law)

force[2] *v* [T] **1** if a situation forces you to do something, it makes you do it, even though you do not want to **force sb to do sth**: *Massive debts have forced them to close the store.* | *We were forced to raise prices because of increased costs.*
2 to make something happen against the wishes of the people who are affected: *The imposition of VAT would force the closure of 20% of regional newspapers.* | *fears of a forced takeover*
force sth ↔ **down** *phr v* [T] to make something go down in price: *The price could fall to £100, forced down by competition from Asian producers.*
force sth ↔ **up** *phr v* [T] to make something go higher in price: *Oil shortages forced up the price.*

forced labour —see under LABOUR

forced saving —see under SAVING

force ma·jeure /ˌfɔːs mæˈʒɜː‖ˌfɔːrs mɑːˈʒɜːr/ *n* [U] LAW unexpected events that prevent people from doing what they officially promised or agreed to do. Such events, usually including war, strikes, and natural disasters, may allow the agreement or contract to be ended or changed: *I want a force majeure clause added to the contract.*

fore·cast¹ /ˈfɔːkɑːst‖ˈfɔːrkæst/ *n* [C] a description of what is likely to happen in the future, based on information that is available now: *The figures for 2001 are forecasts, the others are actuals.* | *a gloomy* ***sales forecast*** | *a* ***cash-flow forecast*** | ***Economic forecasts*** *are widely used by policy makers.* | *It is too early to* ***make forecasts*** *about demand.* | *He has cut his full-year* ***profit forecast*** *from £235 million to £220 million.* + **of**: *an inflation forecast of 3.5%* | *The IMF had reduced its forecasts of economic growth among the world's largest industrialized nations.*

forecast² *v* past tense and past participle **forecast** or **forecasted** [T] to make a statement saying what is likely to happen in the future, based on information that is available now: *Turnover is forecast to grow 6.7% this year.* | *This year we* ***forecast growth*** *of 30%.* + **that**: *The bank's chief economist has forecast that interest rates will fall within two months.* **forecast sth at sth**: *GDP growth was forecast at 1%.* —**forecasting** *n* [U] *Economic forecasting is not an exact science.*

fore·close /fɔːˈkləʊz‖fɔːrˈkloʊz/ *v* **1** [I] if a bank or BUILDING SOCIETY forecloses, it take possession of someone's property because they have failed to pay back an agreed part of a loan: *They ran out of money and the bank foreclosed.* + **on**: *Building societies may* ***foreclose on a mortgage*** *if the repayments are not kept up.*
2 [T] to decide that something is not a possibility: *The government did not want to* ***foreclose*** *other* ***options***.

fore·clo·sure /fɔːˈkləʊʒə‖fɔːrˈkloʊʒər/ *n* [C,U] the act of foreclosing on a loan, or the right to do this: *As an alternative to foreclosure, the court may direct a sale of the property.* | *the growing number of redundancies and* ***mortgage foreclosures***

foreign aid —see under AID

foreign bank —see under BANK¹

Foreign Credit Insurance Association abbreviation **FCIA** *n* a US organization that insures exporters against the risk of not being paid: *Movies can receive loan guarantees from the federal Export-Import Bank and backing by the Foreign Credit Insurance Association.*

foreign currency —see under CURRENCY

foreign currency account —see under ACCOUNT¹

foreign debt —see under DEBT

foreign exchange —see under EXCHANGE¹

foreign exchange broker —see under BROKER¹

foreign exchange dealer —see under DEALER

foreign exchange market —see under MARKET¹

foreign investment —see under INVESTMENT

foreign loan —see under LOAN¹

foreign ownership —see under OWNERSHIP

foreign policy —see under POLICY

foreign trade —see under TRADE¹

foreign trade zone —see ***free zone*** under ZONE¹

fore·man /ˈfɔːmən‖ˈfɔːr-/ *n* plural **foremen** [C] **1** a man who is in charge of a group of workers, for example in a factory: *a factory foreman* | *the foreman of a building site*
2 a person who is the leader of a JURY (=the group of ordinary people who decide whether someone is guilty in some courts of law): *Would the foreman please stand?*

forensic accountant —see under ACCOUNTANT

for·est·ry /ˈfɒrəstri‖ˈfɔː-, ˈfɑː-/ *n* [U] the activity and industry of producing wood and other products from trees: *the minister of agriculture, fisheries and forestry* | *Finland's big* ***forestry-products industry***

fore·wom·an /ˈfɔːˌwʊmən‖ˈfɔːr-/ *n* plural **forewomen** [C] **1** a woman who is in charge of a group of workers, for example in a factory: *the forewoman at a watch factory*
2 a woman who is the leader of a JURY (=the group of ordinary people who decide whether someone is guilty in some courts of law): *The forewoman refused to comment on deliberations and so did the other jurors.*

for·ex /ˈfɒreks‖ˈfɔː-/ *n* [U] another name for FOREIGN EXCHANGE: *The remittances may be exchanged by beneficiaries at any forex bureau.*

for·fait·ing /ˈfɔːˌfeɪtɪŋ‖ˈfɔːr-/ *n* [U] FINANCE when a specialized financial institution buys the debt to an exporter on or shortly after the delivery of goods to an importer: *With forfaiting, we can provide liquidity and remove the political and credit risks for local exporters.* —**forfaited** *adj* [only before a noun] *investors that buy* ***forfaited paper*** (=debts related to exported goods) —**forfaiter** *n* [C] *Specialist forfaiters have begun to finance significant trade deals in Kazakhstan.*

for·feit /ˈfɔːfət‖ˈfɔːr-/ *v* [T] **1** to lose property or the legal right to something because you have broken the law: *The company will forfeit all its assets to the federal government.*
2 to lose rights, benefits etc: *Maryland's judges are to forfeit vacation days or salary due to the fiscal crisis.* | *He will have to persuade investors to forfeit $215 million in principal and interest payments over the next year.*

for·fei·ture /ˈfɔːfətʃə‖ˈfɔːrfətʃər/ *n* [U] **1** when someone loses property or the legal right to have something because they have broken the law: *Under racketeering law, prosecutors are seeking forfeiture of certain properties.*
2 when someone loses rights, benefits etc: *Employees should be able to move from one institution to another without worrying about forfeiture of pension benefits.*

forge /fɔːdʒ‖fɔːrdʒ/ *v* [T] **1** to produce a document or money that is not GENUINE (=real), or to sign something with a false name: *They had* ***forged documents*** *and set up phoney* (=false) *bank accounts.* —**forged** *adj*: *He is currently in prison accused of trying to use forged banknotes.*
2 forge an alliance/partnership/relationship etc to establish a relationship of working together with another person, organization or country + **with**: *Foote, Cone and Belding Communications forged an alliance with France's Publicis.* + **between**: *A number of links have been forged between Danish and American companies.* | *Both General Motors and Ford would like to forge a liaison with Jaguar.* | *The US hopes to forge a closer economic relationship with East European countries.*
3 forge an agreement to make an agreement with another person, organization, or country + **with**: *They forged an agreement with Philips Electronics to produce two games using Philips's Compact Disc-Interactive format.*

forge ahead *phr v* [I] **1** to increase quickly and by a large amount: *The dollar forged ahead to a 16-month high against the German mark.*
2 to move forward with a plan or course of action + **with**: *Petro-Canada, Canada's state-owned oil and gas company, is forging ahead with plans to sell as much as 15% of its shares to the public.*
3 to become bigger and more successful: *Company officials said the company is ready to forge ahead in Europe.*

for·ge·ry /ˈfɔːdʒəri‖ˈfɔːr-/ *n* plural **forgeries** **1** [C] a document, piece of money, or SIGNATURE that is not GENUINE (=real): *It turned out that the will was a forgery.*
2 [U] the crime of producing a document or money that is not GENUINE (=real), or of signing something with a false name: *The 55 year old businessman was called home from his vacation and charged with embezzlement, forgery and misappropriation of client funds.* | *The State Attorney General is seeking to stop a rising tide of forgeries in the $1.5 billion-a-year industry of autographed sports memorabilia.*

for·give /fəˈgɪv‖fər-/ *v* past tense **forgave** past participle **forgiven** [T] FINANCE to state that a debt does not have to be paid: *Under the plan, the US forgave $2.6 billion, or about 70%, of Poland's debt to the US government.* —**forgiveness** *n* [U] *a comprehensive restructuring agreement that would include* ***debt forgiveness***

fork /fɔːk‖fɔːrk/ *v*
fork out sth *phr v* [I,T] *informal* to spend a lot of money on something when you do not really want to and are not very happy about it; SHELL OUT: *Even more embarrassingly for the struggling bank, it had to fork out a further $2.4 million to end the agreement.* + **for**: *Companies will have to fork out for the extra equipment needed to reduce greenhouse gas emissions.* + **on**: *The company forks out a small fortune on telephone line rentals.*
fork over sth *phr v* [T] *informal AmE* another name for fork out: *Congress will simply continue to fork over subsidies to special interests.*

fork-lift also **fork-lift truck** *n* [C] a small vehicle with special equipment on the front for lifting and moving heavy things, for example large boxes of goods, on PALLETS (=large wooden objects specially designed for this)

F

form[1] /fɔːm‖fɔːrm/ *n* [C] an official document with spaces to answer questions and add information: *a Medicare Benefits form* | *We need to receive your* ***application form*** *by July 31.* | *There was no delivery address on the* ***order form***. | *If you would just like to* ***fill in a form*** *we will process your request as quickly as possible.*

form[2] *v* **1** [T] to establish a company, an organization, or a committee: *Coca-Cola Amatil formed a joint venture with Tirtalina Group of Indonesia.* | *A committee was formed to look at the whole issue of bonuses for staff.* | *North American Vehicle Imports is a* ***newly formed*** *company with two principal partners.*
2 [I] when a company, organization, or committee forms, it is established: *This was something that was not considered when the United Nations first formed.*
3 form an alliance/partnership/coalition to establish a relationship of working together: *Electronic Data Systems Corp. and Australian-based Mincom formed an alliance to jointly market computer services and software to the mining industry.* —**forming** *n* [U] *The forming of US Steel marked a turning point in his career.*

form·al /ˈfɔːməl‖ˈfɔːr-/ *adj* done or given officially and publicly: *The companies said they expect to sign a* ***formal agreement*** *before year's end.* | *No* ***formal announcement*** *has yet been made.* | *The British authorities have decided to launch a* ***formal investigation*** *into the company's trading practices.* —**formally** *adv*: *The merger was formally announced late yesterday afternoon.*

formal contract —see under CONTRACT[1]

for·mal·i·ty /fɔːˈmælɪti‖fɔːr-/ *n* plural **formalities**
1 [C usually plural] something formal or official that you have to do so that a process can be completed properly: *immigration and customs formalities* | *Certain formalities have to be completed before the legal transfer can take effect.*
2 a formality something that has to be done for official reasons but will not have any real effect on something that has already been planned or agreed: *It would only be a formality to renew the agreement on a long-term basis.* | *Although the sale still requires the approval of the Chinese government, such approval is a mere formality.*

for·mat[1] /ˈfɔːmæt‖ˈfɔːr-/ *n* [C] **1** COMPUTING the way in which information is arranged and stored in a computer file or on a DISK. If the format is not right, a computer will not be able to read the information: *The firm markets software that automates the conversion of data from one computer format to another.*
2 the size, shape, and design in which a book or magazine is produced: *A larger format often means an increase in price.*
3 a way of organizing, arranging or presenting something: *The stores face competition from other retailers using the megastore format.* | *News stations are searching for a new format that holds viewers and attracts the younger audience that advertisers seek.*

format[2] *v* past tense and past participle **formatted** present participle **formatting** [T] **1** COMPUTING to put an instruction into a computer in order to prepare a DISK so that information can be stored on it in a way that the computer can read it: *You'll need to* ***format the disk*** *before you can copy the files across.*
2 to arrange information in a computer file, for example using particular software or a particular type of writing, page size etc + **in**: *The documents are all formatted in WordPerfect.* | *Documents are generally formatted for A4.*
3 to arrange a book, magazine, or page according to a particular design: *The text has not been very well formatted.* —**formatting** *n* [U] *If we transfer the file, we may lose the formatting.*

for·ma·tion /fɔːˈmeɪʃən‖fɔːr-/ *n* [U] the forming of a company, organization, or committee: *Aberdeen-based Wood Group Production technology has branched out into the United States, with the formation of Wood Group Production technology Inc.* —see also CAPITAL FORMATION

for·mer /ˈfɔːmə‖ˈfɔːrmər/ *adj* [only before a noun] happening or existing in the past, but not now: *the former chairman of United Telecommunications Inc*

for·mer·ly /ˈfɔːməli‖ˈfɔːrmərli/ *adv* in the past: *She was formerly the company's chief financial officer.*

form letter —see under LETTER

form of address *n* plural **forms of address** [C] a word or expression used as the correct polite way of speaking or writing to someone. For example, 'Sir', 'Dear Madam', and 'Messrs' are forms of address: *He was careful always to use the correct form of address.*

for·mu·la /ˈfɔːmjᵊlə‖ˈfɔːrm-/ *n* plural **formulae** or **formulas** **1** [C] a fixed way of doing something that can be used successfully many times: *Mr Sussman has boasted that he can make a success of any firm, but his rivals are not convinced that he has a* ***magic formula***. | *a formula for long-term growth* | *The company has owned three chains in Canada for nearly two decades, but management has failed to discover a* ***winning formula***.
2 [C] a list of the substances used to make a drug, food, or drink: *the secret formula for Coke*

for·mu·late /ˈfɔːmjᵊleɪt‖ˈfɔːrm-/ *v* **formulate a plan/policy/strategy etc** to decide on a plan or a way of doing something and work out in detail how it should be done: *The company has hired a financial adviser to assist in formulating a growth strategy.* | *The company has another 120 days to formulate a plan for repaying its creditors.*

FORTRAN /ˈfɔːtræn‖ˈfɔːr-/ *n* [U] COMPUTING abbreviation for formula translation; a language used for computer programming, especially for complicated scientific and mathematical uses: *the task of writing programs in FORTRAN* | *These figures were all produced using a FORTRAN program.* —compare COBOL

for·tune /ˈfɔːtʃən‖ˈfɔːr-/ *n* **1** [C] a very large amount of money: *Working on the Stock Exchange, he* ***made a***

fortune in just a few years. | *It would **cost a fortune** to treat all the waste.* | *Producers pay stars as much as $3,000 per film, a **small fortune** in Pakistan.*
2 fortunes [plural] how successful or unsuccessful a person, business, or industry is at a particular time: *The company suffered a sudden **decline in its fortunes**.* | *Over the last couple of years we have seen a **change in the fortunes** of the Japanese car industry.*

Fortune 500 /ˌfɔːtʃən faɪv ˈhʌndrɨd‖ˌfɔːr-/ *n* [U] *trademark* the 500 largest companies in the US, listed each year in the magazine Fortune: *a survey of how many Fortune 500 companies are run by women*

for·ward¹ /ˈfɔːwəd‖ˈfɔːrwərd/ *v* [T] to send goods, documents, money etc somewhere, often after receiving them from somewhere else: *These investors get company financial reports and dividends forwarded to them by their brokers.* **forward sth to sb**: *The US embassy in San Jose had already forwarded the papers to the Costa Rican government.*

forward² *adj* [only before a noun] a forward TRANSACTION (=when something is bought and sold) is when a fixed amount of a currency or a COMMODITY (=oil, metal, farm product etc) is bought at a fixed price for delivery on a fixed future date: *Zinc producers should view any strong rises in forward prices as **forward selling** opportunities.* | *The government plans to open a futures market for **forward trading** of agricultural goods vulnerable to price changes.* —**forward** *adv*: *Royal Oak Mines had sold forward 100,000 ounces of gold for future delivery at $465 an ounce.* —see also ***bring forward*** under BRING, ***carry forward*** under CARRY

freight forward also **freight collect** *n* [U] used on a BILL OF LADING to show that the costs of sending goods is to be paid by the person receiving them when they are delivered

forward contract —see under CONTRACT¹

for·ward·er /ˈfɔːwədə‖ˈfɔːrwərdər/ *n* [C] a company that takes goods somewhere or arranges for them to be taken there, buying the services of other companies; FREIGHT FORWARDER: *Bilspedition act as forwarders – or organizers of traffic – often using small subcontractors to do the actual hauling.*

freight forwarder a company that takes goods somewhere or arranges for them to be taken there, buying the services of other companies; FORWARDER: *For years, Harper Group Inc., a San Francisco freight forwarder, mainly transported goods from one location to another.* | *Banks will reject a transport document issued by a freight forwarder unless it is the FIATA Combined Transport Bill of Lading.*

forward exchange rate —see under EXCHANGE RATE

forwarding address —see under ADDRESS¹

forwarding agent —see under AGENT

forward integration —see under INTEGRATION

forward market —see under MARKET¹

forward multiple —see under MULTIPLE²

forward price —see under PRICE¹

forward rate agreement —see under AGREEMENT

FOT abbreviation for FREE ON TRUCK —see ***free on rail*** under INCOTERM

foul bill of lading —see under BILL OF LADING

found /faʊnd/ *v* [T] to start a new company or organization: *The company was founded back in 1947.*

found·er¹ /ˈfaʊndə‖-ər/ *n* [C] a person who starts a new company or organization: *The company's founder and chairman, Charles Munch, has resigned.* | *He was a **founder member** of the Institute of Mechanical Engineers.*

founder² *v* [I] if a company, plan, job etc founders, it fails or is unsuccessful: *Two major companies foundered this week.* | *A potential rescue deal foundered after Gannett rebuffed an offer of $2.5 million.* + **on**: *The institution foundered on huge loan losses.*

Four A *n* the AMERICAN ASSOCIATION OF ADVERTISING AGENCIES

401(k) plan *n* [singular] in the US, a type of PENSION PLAN where a company pays an amount of money into the plan that matches the amount that an employee pays into it, with tax advantages for both

four Os /ˌfɔːr ˈəʊz‖-ˈoʊz/ *n* MARKETING **the four Os** used to analyse the marketing of a product in relation to object of PURCHASE (=the product being bought) OBJECTIVES (=aims) of the purchase, organization of purchasing (the person buying it), and operation (where it is bought)

four Ps /ˌfɔː ˈpiːz‖ˌfɔːr-/ *n* MARKETING **the four Ps** used to talk about the marketing activities of product (what to sell), price, place (where it is sold), and PROMOTION (=special activities to help sell a product) —see also ***marketing mix*** under MIX

fourth /fɔːθ‖fɔːrθ/ *adj* **fourth half/quarter/period** the fourth half, quarter etc of the financial year

FPA abbreviation for FREE OF PARTICULAR AVERAGE

Fr. written abbreviation for Friday

fr. written abbreviation for from

frac·tion·al /ˈfrækʃənəl/ *adj* **1** a fractional amount, change, gain etc is very small: *July's Consumer Price Index was 231.2, a fractional change from the 231 index reported in June.* | *While blue-chip stocks ended lower, the broader market held onto fractional gains.* —**fractionally** *adv*: *Revenue for the period fell fractionally to $22,056,000 from $22,722,000.*
2 related to part of a larger whole: *BTR owns a fractional stake in Norton*

fractional share —see under SHARE

frag·ment·ed /frægˈmentɨd‖ˈfrægmentɨd/ *adj* if an industry or business activity is fragmented, there are many companies involved in it; SEGMENTED: *In healthcare, Hillhaven and Manor Care Inc. are larger chains in a fragmented industry dominated by smaller companies.*

franc /fræŋk/ written abbreviation **F** *n* [C] the standard unit of money used in France, Belgium, and Luxembourg until the introduction of the EURO, and in some other countries: *Repairs are expected to cost over five million francs.* | *150 million **Swiss francs** of 6 3/4% public bonds*

fran·chise¹ /ˈfræntʃaɪz/ *n* [C] **1** an arrangement in which a company gives a business the right to sell its goods or services in return for a fee or a share of the profits: *Roddick operates most of her Body Shop stores **under a franchise**.* | *Disputes in the **franchise industry** typically involve such issues as contract termination, unpaid fees and territorial rights.*
2 a particular shop, restaurant etc that is run under a franchise, or a company that owns a number of these: *The franchise, with 10 dealerships in suburban Chicago, sold just 50 vehicles in December.*

franchise² *v* [I,T] to sell franchises to people: *An increasing number of companies are expected to franchise their operations rather expand in traditional ways.* —**franchising** *n* [U] *We have a specialist team to give expert advice and assistance to people interested in franchising.* | *an information sheet about **franchising opportunities***

fran·chi·see /ˌfræntʃaɪˈziː/ *n* [C] someone who is sold a franchise: *The franchisors consistently over-estimated the level of sales that franchisees might expect.*

F

fran·chis·or also **franchiser** *AmE* /ˈfræntʃaɪzə‖-ər/ *n* [C] a company that sells a franchise

frank /fræŋk/ *v* [T] to print a sign on an envelope or package to show that the cost of sending it has been paid: *All mail for despatch should be franked.* | *If the volume of mail is high, a* ***franking machine*** *can save time.*

Frankfurt Inter-Bank Offered Rate —see FIBOR

franking machine —see under MACHINE[1]

fran·tic /ˈfræntɪk/ *adj* if there is frantic trading on the stock market, people buy and sell a lot of currency, shares, COMMODITIES, etc in an urgent and unorganized way: *The Bundesbank's assistance was crucial in a day of* ***frantic trading*** *on the currency markets.* | *New York Stock Exchange trading was active but less frantic than on Monday.*

fraud /frɔːd‖frɒːd/ *n* [C,U] a method of illegally getting money from a person or organization, often using clever and complicated methods: *Should audits be expected to detect every fraud?* | *He had a criminal conviction for* ***credit card fraud***. | *Hood was convicted of* ***tax fraud*** *and sent to prison.*

Fraud Squad *n* the department in the British police force that examines fraud in business: *According to the Fraud Squad, he is alleged to have stolen more than £130,000 from the Inland Revenue.* —see also SERIOUS FRAUD OFFICE

fraud·u·lent /ˈfrɔːdjələnt‖ˈfrɒːdʒə-/ *adj* fraudulent activities, documents etc are intended to deceive: *Winchester Crown Court found him guilty of theft, perjury and* ***fraudulent trading***. | *It is difficult to estimate the exact number of* ***fraudulent insurance claims***.

fraudulent misrepresentation —see under MISREPRESENTATION

F

FRB —see FEDERAL RESERVE BOARD

FRC abbreviation for FREE CARRIER —see under INCOTERM

Fred·die Mac /ˌfredi ˈmæk/ *n informal AmE* FINANCE an informal name for the FEDERAL HOME LOAN MORTGAGE CORPORATION: *Enterprises like Freddie Mac have a unique advantage over private-sector competitors: they can keep all their profits, but their losses are picked up by the taxpayer.*

-free /friː/ *suffix* without something, often something that you do not want: *Earnings will be* ***tax-free*** *if the money remains on deposit for seven years.* | *Heathrow Airport gets more money from* ***duty-free sales*** *than from landing fees.* | *pollution-free electric cars*

free[1] /friː/ *adj* **1** costing nothing: *First-class passengers will have four films to choose from, all of them free.* | *Like pizza, Chinese food is more expensive than hamburgers and can bear the cost of free delivery.*

2 no free lunch/no such thing as a free lunch used to say that something may seem to be free, but that in fact somebody must pay for it: *The economic principle of 'no free lunch' applies – people get the services they pay for.* | *There's no such thing as a free lunch. If you receive 'free' shares, you're bound to pay for them in other ways.*

3 free of/from sth without something, usually something that you do not want: *The data reflect an economy that remains slow but relatively free of inflation.* | *The interest on savings bonds is free from state and local tax.* | *Personal Equity Plans, which have a £6,000 investment limit each financial year, are* ***free of income tax*** *and capital gains tax.*

4 not restricted, limited, or controlled: *We can talk about privatization, but the main condition for a market economy is free prices.* + **to**: *The company is free to impose whatever work rules and pay it chooses.*

free[2] *v* [T] **1** to remove laws, rules etc + **from**: *More prices, including that of milk, will be freed from state control.*

2 also **free up** to make something available so that it can be used: *Ford said the sale of its heavy truck unit will* ***free resources*** *to concentrate on its light and medium truck business.* | *The government have freed up several million dollars of federal money that was reserved for development but never spent.*

free[3] *adv* without payment: *Senior citizens can travel free at off-peak times.* | *NASA has a wealth of technology that it will gladly transfer* ***free of charge***. | *In the '80s, Apple sold overpriced hardware and gave away neat software* ***for free***.

free agent —see under AGENT

free alongside ship —see under INCOTERM

free·bie /ˈfriːbiː/ *n* [C] *informal* something that you are given free, for example to encourage you to buy more of the same thing or to buy something else: *You get three freebies for every 20 cases of soda purchased.*

free carrier —see under INCOTERM

free cash flow —see under CASH FLOW

free collective bargaining —see under COLLECTIVE BARGAINING

free economy —see under ECONOMY[1]

free enterprise —see under ENTERPRISE

free-fall also **free fall** *n* [singular, U] *journalism* when prices on a financial market go down or the economy gets worse very quickly: *After closing at $19.125 per share on Tuesday, First City's price* ***went into a free fall***, *ending at $14.50 at Friday's close.* | *Mexico's peso went into free fall last December.* | *AT&Ts have gone into a two-point free fall overnight.*

Free·fone /ˈfriːfəʊn‖-foʊn/ *adj* [only before a noun] *trademark BrE* a Freefone number is one you can call without paying;: *Readers wishing to contribute to the Wildlife Hospital Appeal can ring Freefone 0800 400478.* —**Freefone** *n* —compare WATS

free gift —see under GIFT

free·hold /ˈfriːhəʊld‖-hoʊld/ *n* [C,U] PROPERTY complete ownership of a building or land for an unlimited time: *Residential leaseholders living in blocks of flats have the right to* ***acquire the freehold*** *of their block at the market rate.* | *He was forced to* ***sell the freehold*** *of Balderton.* | *The cost of* ***freehold land*** *is so high that only a wealthy man who farms intensively can hope to make a living on his own farm.* | *The increase in fixed assets reflects two major* ***freehold property*** *purchases.*

free·hold·er /ˈfriːhəʊldə‖-hoʊldər/ *n* [C] PROPERTY someone who owns freehold land or property: *Kentish families were either freeholders or held their land on a yearly basis.*

freehold estate —see under ESTATE

freehold possession —see under POSSESSION

freehold property —see under PROPERTY

free·lance[1] /ˈfriːlɑːns‖-læns/ also **free-lance** *adj* working for different companies or organizations rather than being directly employed by one: *The company does not directly employ such specialists as designers, but operates on a* ***freelance basis***. | *a* ***freelance journalist*** —**freelance** *adv*: *Sheila set up her own business called Editorial Services and now* ***works freelance*** *from home.*

freelance[2] also **free-lance** *n* [C] someone who does freelance work: *I'm basically a freelance, and most of my work comes through various agencies.*

freelance[3] also **free-lance** *v* [I] to work for different companies or organizations rather than being directly employed by one: *They began freelancing for UK magazines and, occasionally, BBC radio.*

free·lan·cer /ˈfriːˌlɑːnsə‖-ˌlænsər/ also **free-lancer** *n* [C] another name for FREELANCE[2]

free market —see under MARKET[1]

free marketeer —see under MARKETEER

free movement *n* [U] FINANCE when money for investment goes freely from one country to another; CAPITAL FLOWS, CAPITAL MOVEMENT

free offer —see under OFFER[2]

free of particular average abbreviation **FPA** *adj* [not before a noun] INSURANCE a condition stating that insurance is only against TOTAL LOSS (=when the thing insured is totally lost or destroyed), not PARTIAL LOSS (=when the thing insured is not totally lost or destroyed). Free of particular average is one of the INSTITUTE CARGO CLAUSES

free on board —see under INCOTERM

free on board airport —see under INCOTERM

free on rail —see under INCOTERM

free on truck *n* [U] another name for FREE ON RAIL

free pay —see under PAY[1]

free port —see under PORT[1]

Free·post /ˈfriːpəʊst‖-poʊst/ *n* in Britain, an arrangement where a company or organization pays the cost of letters that are sent to it by post: *Send donations to Iona Cathedral Trust, Freepost, Edinburgh EH8 0LL.* | *Simply complete the coupon below and send it to us, using the Freepost address given.*

free ride *n* [C usually singular] something that you do not have to pay for, because someone else is paying for it: *Government employees are getting a free ride on taxpayers' money.*

free trade —see under TRADE[1]

free-trader *n* [C] someone who believes that free trade is good for the economy: *Free-traders say a trade treaty would create more jobs on both sides of the border.*

free·ware /ˈfriːweə‖-wer/ *n* [U] computer software that is given away free: *Since being published as freeware in 1991, PGP has rapidly become the standard for encryption of e-mail.* —compare SHAREWARE

freeze[1] /friːz/ *v* past tense **froze** past participle **frozen** [T] **1** if a government or company freezes prices, wages etc, they keep them at a particular level: *IDT cut salaries 10% for company executives, and 4% for other employees; remaining salaries were frozen.* | *Perez froze fuel prices and set a ceiling on prices for basic foodstuffs.*
2 to legally prevent money in a bank from being taken out, property from being sold etc, for example because there is a disagreement concerning it: *A federal judge froze more than $20 million in FundAmerica bank accounts last Friday after several California investors sued Mr Edwards.*
3 to stop an activity or a proposed activity for a period of time: *American Electric froze hiring and instructed employees to reduce spending.* | *Mr Smith has frozen plans to develop the record company.* —see also FROZEN

freeze[2] *n* **1** [C] when prices, wages etc are fixed at a particular level: *They said the cable television industry was abusing its market position, and called for a mandatory* ***price freeze*** *in cable rates.* | *demands for a national two-year* ***rent freeze*** | *The prime minister called for a* ***pay freeze*** *to help keep inflation down.*
credit freeze [singular] ECONOMICS when banks are forced by the government to stop lending completely
2 [C] when an activity is stopped for a period of time + **on**: *If a Labour Government imposes a freeze on the roads programme, up to 20,000 jobs could be lost.* | *a cost-cutting program that includes a* ***hiring freeze*** (=when a company does not take new employees) *and layoffs*

free zone —see under ZONE[1]

freight[1] /freɪt/ *n* [U] **1** goods carried in large quantities by ship, plane, train etc: *A 747 can* ***carry freight*** *as well as passengers.* | *The volume of* ***rail freight*** *is only 8% of the rail-and-road total.* | *The Panama Canal has lost some of its importance because of* ***air freight***. | *The railroad is now only used by* ***freight trains***. | *a* ***freight car*** (=a wagon pulled by a train in which freight is carried)
bulk freight ♦ goods such as coal, steel, and grain carried as freight: *Among foodstuffs, grain was the principal bulk freight.*
2 the cost of carrying goods in large quantities by ship, plane, train etc: *The goods had been loaded on board the vessel and freight had been paid.* | *The railways adopted a negative attitude to the milk trade, refusing to grant concessionary* ***freight rates***.

freight[2] *v* [T] to TRANSPORT goods in large quantities by ship, plane, train etc: *There was no time to send it by ship, so it was freighted in a B747F aircraft.* —**freighting** *n* [U] *The Aero Club is involved in freighting and also passenger flights.*

freight and insurance paid *n* [U] another name for CARRIAGE AND INSURANCE PAID

freight collect *n* [U] another name for FREIGHT FORWARD —see under FORWARD[2]

freight·er /ˈfreɪtə‖-ər/ *n* [C] a ship or aircraft that carries FREIGHT: *a Japanese freighter due to ship a cargo of highly radioactive plutonium*

freight forward —see under FORWARD[2]

freight forwarder —see under FORWARDER

freight inwards —see under INWARD

freight outwards —see under OUTWARD

freight paid *n* [U] another name for CARRIAGE PAID

freight prepaid *n* [U] used on a BILL OF LADING to show that the cost of TRANSPORTING the goods has already been paid: *They issue their own bills on a 'freight prepaid' basis.*

frequent flyer —see under FLYER

frequently asked questions —see FAQ

fresh money —see under MONEY

frictional unemployment —see under UNEMPLOYMENT

friendly bid —see under BID[1]

friendly merger —see under MERGER

friendly society —see under SOCIETY

friendly takeover —see under TAKEOVER

friends /frendz/ *n* [plural] FINANCE investors who buy the shares of a company that wants to take over another, and sell shares of the company that is the TARGET of the takeover. This results in a fall in the value of the shares of the company that is the target of the takeover, making it cheaper to buy —see also CONCERT PARTY, FAN CLUB

fringe /frɪndʒ/ *adj* [only before a noun] relating to something that is in addition to the main or most important part of something: *The company is a fringe player in the US with less than 2% of the car market.* | *We were spending a lot of money on the fringe areas that weren't producing results.*

fringe benefit —see under BENEFIT[1]

frivolous action —see under ACTION

FRN abbreviation for FLOATING RATE NOTE

FRO *n* [U] INSURANCE fire risk only; used on an insurance policy to show that it only covers the risk of fire

front[1] /frʌnt/ *n* **1** [C] a person, organization, system etc used to hide something secret or illegal: *His family kept a shop as a front for dealing in stolen goods.*
2 a plan for achieving something: *The soft-loan proposal would open a new front in the bank's financing of reform in the east.*

3 on the financial/inflation/employment etc front used to talk about something in relation to money, inflation, employment etc: *There is a slight improvement on the **jobs front** with 30% of directors saying they expect to recruit more this year.*
4 in front (of) more successful than other people or organizations in a business or activity: *The Data System is just part of a massive development programme to keep us in front and to offer our clients the best licensed taxi service there is.*
5 be brought/called/hauled in front of sb to have to see someone in authority because you have done something wrong: *My whole section was called in front of the manager.*
6 up front if you pay for something up front, you pay for it before you receive it: *You have to pay a lot up front before you start getting the benefits of the system.* —see also SHOP FRONT, STOREFRONT

front[2] *v* [T] to lead an organization because you are the person with the highest rank: *AVS's European operation is fronted by Peter Collins.*

front end *n* [singular] **1** if a company is at the front end of a business or activity, they have a lot of success, especially because they are producing a lot of new products: *Japanese corporations in the front end of the innovation process*
2 front end charge/cost charges or costs you have to pay before you can receive something or before an investment can start making you money: *Initial charges are 4% for the managed funds and there is no front end charge for the single funds.*

front·line /ˈfrʌntlaɪn/ *adj* [only before a noun] **1 frontline manager/supervisor** a manager or SUPERVISOR whose job involves meeting or communicating directly with workers: *Efforts are being made to improve the relationship between frontline managers and shop stewards.*
2 frontline worker/employee an ordinary worker who is directly involved in making a product or providing a service: *Frontline workers are closest to most problems and opportunities: they know what actually happens.* | *a loss in productivity by so-called frontline workers*

front loading also **front end loading** —see under LOADING

front man *n* plural **front men** [C] someone who represents an organization to the public, but who does not lead it: *He was a good front man, but the real work was done by his team of four assistants.*

front money —see under MONEY

front office —see under OFFICE

front-running *n* [U] FINANCE when a share dealer takes an order from a client to buy a company's shares, but buys shares in the same company for their own account before carrying out the order. As an order often makes share prices rise, the dealer can then sell the shares they bought at a profit: *The five men were found to have systematically practised front-running and were banned for life from trading on London's financial markets.*

fro·zen /ˈfrəʊzən‖ˈfroʊ-/ *adj* **1** frozen food is stored at very low temperatures in order to preserve it: *Europe's $30 billion **frozen-food industry*** | *frozen fish*
2 frozen assets, accounts etc cannot be used by their owners, for example because there is a legal disagreement concerning them: *Tens of thousands of legal claims are being made by companies attempting to have their frozen assets returned.* | *The frozen accounts at banks in Miami had received illegal proceeds from the operations of cocaine traffickers* —see also FREEZE[1]

frozen asset —see under ASSET

fru·gal /ˈfruːgəl/ *adj* careful to buy only what is necessary: *The pay settlement must be frugal in order to avoid layoffs.* | *People who rely on the basic retirement pension must live a **frugal existence**.* | *We're having to be very frugal with our training budget this year.* —**frugality** *n* [U] *Most departments were being told to cut spending and practise frugality again this year.* —**frugally** *adv*: *If you want to retire young, you'll have to live frugally and invest wisely.*

frustration of contract —see under CONTRACT[1]

FT —see FINANCIAL TIMES

ft. written abbreviation for FOOT or FEET

FT Actuaries share indices —see under INDICES

FTC abbreviation for FEDERAL TRADE COMMISSION

FTSE 30 Share Index —see under INDEX[1]

FTSE 100 Share Index —see under INDEX[1]

FTSE All-Share Index —see under INDEX[1]

FTSE Eurotop 100 Index —see under INDEX[1]

FTSE Eurotop 300 Index —see under INDEX[1]

FTSE Fledgling Index —see under INDEX[1]

FTSE indices —see under INDICES

FTSE Mid 250 Index —see under INDEX[1]

FTSE SmallCap Index —see under INDEX[1]

fu·el /ˈfjuːəl/[1] *n* [C,U] a substance such as coal, gas, or oil that can be burned to produce heat or energy: ***fuel prices*** | *The Postal Service lost $450 million last year, primarily because of higher labor and **fuel costs**.*

fuel[2] *v* **fuelled fuelling** *BrE*, **fueled fueling** *AmE* [T] to cause a situation to change quickly: *Consumers will continue to fuel economic growth.*

ful·fil *BrE*, **fulfill** *AmE* /fʊlˈfɪl/ *v* past tense and past participle **fulfilled** present participle **fulfilling** [T] **1** if a hope, promise etc is fulfilled, the thing that you had hoped for, promised etc happens or is done: *Our aim is to **fulfill** our clients' **wishes** as efficiently as possible.* | *To **fulfil** this **ambition** he was prepared to go to any lengths.*
2 fulfil an order to supply the things that have been ordered: *a UK company that acquires goods from a Belgian supplier to fulfil an order from a German customer*
3 fulfil a contract to do the things that a contract says you must do: *The seller can fulfil his contract only by delivery of 500 tons from the specified cargo.* | *The company is struggling to fulfill its contracts.*
4 fulfil a condition/specification/requirement etc to reach a standard that is necessary, especially one that has been officially decided: *Much of the electrical equipment failed to fulfill safety requirements.* | *the conditions which the tenant is required to fulfil*
5 fulfil a need/requirement to provide something that someone needs: *other rewards such as responsibility or advancement that companies can provide to fulfill employees' needs* | *Electricity driven vehicles fulfil most of the basic requirements of the consumer.*
6 fulfil a role/function/duty etc to do the things a person, organization, or machine must do or is expected to do: *He fulfilled his role as manager very effectively.* | *Robots fulfil many dull and tedious jobs on the production line.*
7 fulfil an aim/objective/goal etc to achieve what you were hoping to do: *The managers must decide on the policies and priorities that help the company to fulfil its aims.* | *There are major goals which businesses fulfill such as maximising the return on capital.*
8 if your work fulfils you, it makes you feel satisfied because you are using all your skills or qualities: *I have rarely seen a person so **fulfilled by** his **work**.* —**fulfilled** *adj*: *I'm sure I'd feel more fulfilled if I had a job that involved working with people.*—**fulfilling** *adj*: *Managers and executives often hope to become consultants or do something more fulfilling, perhaps turn a hobby into a business.*

F

9 fulfil your potential to be as successful as you could possibly be: *We are confident that the new sales manager will fulfil his potential.*

fulfillment house —see under HOUSE

ful·fil·ment *BrE*, **fulfillment** *AmE* /fʊlˈfɪlmənt/ *n* [U] **1** fulfilment of a hope, promise etc is when the thing that you had hoped for, promised etc happens or is done: *the **fulfillment** of a life-long **ambition***
2 fulfilment of an order the action of supplying the things that have been ordered: *produce already allocated for fulfilment of state orders*
3 fulfilment of a contract when you do in a satisfactory way the things that a contact says you must do: *The clearing house guarantees fulfilment of all contracts by becoming a party to every transaction.*
4 fulfilment of a condition/specification/requirement etc the action of reaching a standard that is necessary, especially one that has been officially decided: *The offer of this contract is subject to the fulfilment of certain conditions.* | *The Bundesbank said that the fulfillment of conditions of economic convergence between EC countries should not be linked to a specific time frame.*
5 fulfilment of a need/requirement an occasion when something that is wanted, needed etc happens or is given: *The effective leader must perform two functions successfully, namely the achievement of the task which has been set and the fulfilment of colleagues' needs.*
6 fulfilment of a role/function/duty etc when people, organizations, or machines do the things they must do or are expected to do: *The fulfilment of the Bank's public duty overrides its duty of confidence to their customers.*
7 fulfilment of an aim/objective/goal etc when you achieve what you were hoping to do: *tasks aimed at the fulfillment of our strategic goals* | *This aid money is crucial to the fulfilment of the government's economic policies.*
8 the feeling of being satisfied, especially in your job, because you are using all your skills and qualities: *He gained great fulfillment from teaching and training others for the profession.* | *Working on a conveyor belt does little for a **sense of personal fulfilment**.*

full board —see under BOARD[1]

full employment —see under EMPLOYMENT

full-fledged *adj AmE* something full fledged is complete and total in its progress or development; FULLY-FLEDGED *BrE*: *It has been more than eight years since the economy and stock market went through a full-fledged recession and recovery.*

full line —see under LINE

full merger —see under MERGER

full ownership —see under OWNERSHIP

full-page *adj* [only before a noun] a full-page advertisement or article covers all of one page, especially in a newspaper or magazine: *intensive direct mail campaigns and **full-page advertisements***

full-service *adj* [only before a noun] *AmE* full-service companies, hotels etc offer a complete range of activities or services: *Companies need to hire managers who have the skills to direct a full-service drug company, not just a research boutique.* | *Nations Bank Corp. operates full-service banking centres in nine states.*

full service brokerage —see under BROKERAGE

full-size *adj* also **full-sized** a full-sized product is of the proper or standard size, rather than a smaller version: *'Preview', a monthly distributed free in movie theaters, is a shortened version of K-III's full-sized 'Premiere' magazine.*

full-time *adj* **1** working or studying for the complete number of hours that this is usually done: *He was unable physically to handle the demands of a **full-time** sales **position**.* | *Mr Kasal slashed his **full-time staff** to six from 13 as revenue dropped.* | *5.5 million Americans are working part-time because they can't find **full-time work**.* | *Ohio has been gaining in part-time jobs, while losing many thousands of **full-time jobs**.* —**full-time** *adv*: *I can't work full time because of my illness.*
2 full-time job/occupation hard work that you are not paid for that takes a lot of time: *A job search is a full-time job.*

full-year *adj* [only before a noun] FINANCE full-year earnings, profits, results etc are for a complete period of 12 months, rather than a shorter period of time: *Despite the fourth-quarter deficit, UAL had a full-year profit of $94.5 million.*

full-year loss —see under LOSS

fully-fledged *adj BrE* something fully-fledged is complete and total in its progress or development; FULL-FLEDGED *AmE*: *Belgium was the first European country to possess a fully-fledged rail network.*

fully-paid share —see under SHARE

fully-subscribed *adj* FINANCE if a bond or share ISSUE (=when new bonds or shares are sold for the first time) is fully-subscribed, all the available bonds or shares are bought: *If the offering is fully-subscribed, we're looking to increase our capital base by 20%.*

func·tion[1] /ˈfʌŋkʃən/ *n* **1** [C] the purpose for which something is made or used, or the job that someone does; ROLE: *The original function of a cash-machine was to provide people with cash when the bank was shut.* | *He was once asked what he considered the function of a chairman to be.* | *In your new job you will be expected to **perform** many different **functions**.* | *For accounting purposes the Bank's function as the issuer of currency notes is shown separately from its banking activities.*
2 [U] the way in which something works or operates, or the way in which it is used: *People buy design rather than function; otherwise why bother to design a beer can? The beer stays the same.*
3 sales/personnel/accounting etc function [C usually singular] the part of a company that is responsible for sales, accounting etc: *Why do companies use headhunters instead of their own in-house recruiting facilities and personnel function?* | *The more efficient a company's accounting function might be, the less time it should take to do the audit.*
4 [C] COMPUTING an operation or series of operations performed by a computer or a computer program: *You press the Ins key once to **turn on a function** and press it again to **turn off** the same **function**.*
5 a function of if one thing is a function of another, it is produced by or varies according to the other thing: *The unit price at any time is a function of the prevailing interest rates and the risk involved.* | *For marketing purposes, purchases by customers are assumed to be a function of advertising and promotional expenditure.* —see also CONSUMPTION FUNCTION

function[2] *v* [I] **1** to work or operate: *Can you explain exactly how this new system will function?* | *Different types of organizations will require differing types of budgets to enable them to **function effectively**.* | *factors stopping a member of staff from **functioning properly***
2 if a machine or system functions, it works or operates in the way that it is supposed to: *a test run to check that the air conditioning system is functioning* | *Hospitals function in spite of the system, but only because of the enormous professional devotion of their staffs.*
function as sth *phr v* [T] to become something else or to do the work of another person or thing: *The BCC cannot function as a holding company, but can carry*

out service activities for the group. | *It took a year to train a group of people to function as general managers.*

func•tion•al /ˈfʌŋkʃənəl/ *adj* **1** [only before a noun] connected with the purpose for which something is made or used, or with the job that someone does: *Three key functional areas of management are marketing, production and personnel management.* | *The project manager is responsible for ensuring that time and money are properly budgeted between* ***functional departments.***

2 designed to be useful rather than beautiful or decorative: *We now have premises which are both smart and functional.* | *a functional environment that is organized, uncluttered and convenient*

3 working in a way that something is supposed to: *Intel is sending* ***fully functional*** *samples of the chips for shipment to manufacturers.* —**functionally** *adv*: *AEI wanted a product which functionally met its needs.* | *Management set up functionally differentiated work groups.* | *functionally specialised and precisely defined jobs*

func•tion•a•ry /ˈfʌŋkʃənəri‖-neri/ *n* plural **functionaries** [C] someone who has a job doing unimportant or boring official duties, especially for a government or political party: *At that time a ranking* ***government functionary*** *earned 200 Iraqi dinars a month.*

fund[1] /fʌnd/ *n* **1** [C] an amount of money that is obtained and used for a particular purpose: *They agreed to* ***set up*** (=start) *a $240 million international* ***fund*** *through which industrialized nations can help developing countries.*

accumulated fund [C] a fund built up over a period of time, usually for a particular purpose: *Interest earned on the accumulated fund will supplement future Social Security tax receipts to finance the increased benefits.*

bank guarantee fund [C] a sum of money held by a government to help banks in financial difficulty: *Norway's national bank guarantee fund has pumped more than NKr7 billion into ailing banks.*

contingency fund also **contingency account, contingency reserve** [C] an amount of money that is kept in case of an event that causes losses in the future: *Under the five-year plan a contingency fund was to be created to cope with any international or domestic variables.* | *Remington is confident the contingency reserve will cover these additional expenses.*

deposit protection fund *n* [C] BANKING in Britain, an amount of money that is paid into a central organization by banks and will be paid to people who lose money if a bank goes BANKRUPT: *The Isle of Man has a deposit protection fund but has yet to pay 5,000 savers who lost £42 million when its Savings and Investment Bank collapsed.*

depreciation fund [C] a fund set up by a company to provide money to buy new FIXED ASSETS. Every year, the fund invests an amount of money equal to an existing asset's depreciation allowance in GILT-EDGED SECURITIES, giving the company money that can be used to buy new assets

discretionary fund [C] an amount of money which can be used for purposes to be decided later

guarantee fund [C] a sum of money designed to pay people or organizations who would lose money if an organization goes BANKRUPT: *Tuffier was the first brokerage to qualify for protection under the guarantee fund for clients who cannot recover their cash from a bankrupt broker.*

pension fund [C] a fund that is used to pay PENSIONS (=money for people who no longer work) to those who have regularly paid money into the fund: *the Dallas Police and Fire Pension Fund*

revolving fund [C] a fund from which money can be taken when it is needed but must be replaced, so that the full amount is again available: *a self-financed revolving fund for energy efficiency projects*

sinking fund [C] a fund into which regular payments are made so that future expenses can be paid: *The building's management company set up a sinking fund to which all flat owners contributed to pay for repairs.*

slush fund *informal disapproving* [C] a fund of money obtained secretly and illegally and used for illegal purposes: *He operated an $18 million slush fund intended to corrupt Pentagon officials.*

strike fund [C] a fund used to pay money to workers who are members of a TRADE UNION who are on strike

trust fund [C] a fund for money or property held for the benefit of others or for a particular purpose. The person in charge of the fund is responsible for the money etc and can only act in certain ways: *the 0.1-cent-a-gallon gasoline tax that flows into a trust fund to clean up leaking underground storage tanks at filling stations* | *the Yorkshire Miners' Welfare Trust Fund* —see also SUPERFUND

2 [C] an organization that is responsible for obtaining and spending money for a particular purpose: *Thanks to the European Development Fund, a fourth station will reopen in Wales this October.* | *The fund invests in money market deposits with a range of banks and financial institutions.* | *the World Wildlife Fund*

3 funds [plural] money that a person or organization has available: *With the additional bank financing, we'll have sufficient funds to pay our suppliers.*

Federal funds also **Fed funds** ◆ [plural] money that US banks lend to each other for short periods of time. The FEDERAL RESERVE (=the US central bank) influences this lending as one of its controls on MONEY SUPPLY (=the amount of money in the economy): *The Federal Reserve Bank of New York arranged repurchase agreements, and traders took this as a signal that the Fed's new target for the* ***Federal Funds rate*** (=the interest rate banks charge each other) *was 6.25%, down from 6.75%.*
◆ [plural] money from the national government that a US state has available for spending: *The state's budget plan is 6% larger than last year's budget, though after subtracting $17.85 billion in federal funds, state spending would only go up 2.8%.*

public funds [plural] money that belongs to a local or national government, available for PUBLIC SPENDING: *Despite infusions of over $800 million in public funds to help develop the technology, MAC was a failure on the marketplace.*

shareholders' funds [plural] *BrE* money in a company that legally belongs to shareholders including capital and RESERVES (=earlier profits not paid out) in the form of DIVIDENDS: *Losses from operations may have wiped out more than half its remaining shareholders' funds.*

state funds [plural] money available for spending by a national or state government: *There is a further argument for investing more state funds in the troubled company.*

4 in funds having money, or enough money for a particular purpose: *He promised to send repayment when he was next in funds.* | *A new spending bill was needed to* ***keep*** *the government* ***in funds*** (=make sure the government has enough money).

5 be short of funds/run out of funds to have little or no money: *The government is short of funds and needs additional revenue quickly.* | *ITC ran out of funds, leaving gross debts of £900 million.*

6 funds [plural] used to talk about borrowing for different periods of time

long-term funds [plural] borrowing over 10 to 15 years or longer: *The assistance corporation is an authority created last year to raise long-term funds and eliminate the state's need to sell a large amount of short-term notes each year in its spring borrowing.*

short-term funds [plural] borrowing that is repaid after a short time, up to five years: *Gulf Power invested $500,000 of short-term funds in a 90-day Ginnie Mae certificate.*

7 also **investment fund** [C] FINANCE a company whose activity is putting money from investors into a particular type of investment or a range of investments, or an amount of money invested in this way: *The investment fund, which is newly organized, will invest primarily in Brazilian companies.* | *The small investor will increasingly be found mostly under the umbrella of large investment funds.*

authorized fund also **authorised fund** *BrE* [C] another name for a MUTUAL FUND or a UNIT TRUST: *There will need to be a lot of co-ordination with the new authorised funds to avoid affecting the existing stock market.*

balanced fund [C] a fund that invests in shares and bonds: *the old-fashioned balanced fund, many of which keep a fairly stable 60%–40% mix of stocks and bonds*

bond fund [C] a fund that invests in bonds: *Investors switched from certificates of deposit, which now yield less than 5%, and into bond funds, many of which are still paying 7% and above.*

broker-dealer fund [C] a fund that is open only to BROKER-DEALERS (=financial institutions that invest their own money and the money of other investors)

closed-end fund also **closed-ended fund** *BrE* [C] a fund that has a fixed number of shares. Investors can sell their shares only to other investors, not back to the fund: *The closed-end funds don't have to worry about daily sales and withdrawals and thus can remain fully invested.*

commodity fund [C] a mutual fund that invests in COMMODITIES (=metals, farm products etc): *A lot of commodity funds have been coming into precious metals markets over the past month.*

dual-purpose fund [C] a fund that has two classes of shares, income shares that produce income in the form of DIVIDENDS, and capital shares that increase or decrease in value with the value of the shares in which the fund has invested: *The portfolio strategy of dual-purpose funds often ends up helping the income shareholders at the expense of the capital shareholders.*

equity fund [C] a fund that invests in company shares: *Since the stockmarket crash, the average equity fund has gone up 61.24%.*

fund of funds also **fund fund** [C] an investment fund that invests in other funds: *The SFr400 million Private Equity Holding operates as a fund of funds, investing in between 15 and 20 venture capital partnerships.*

general-purpose fund [C] a fund open to all types of investors, rather than one just open to financial institutions: *Assets of 280 general-purpose funds declined $2.89 billion, to $173.81 billion.*

go-go fund [C] a fund that makes SPECULATIVE investments (=ones with a high risk but the chance of high profitability): *Go-go funds constantly adjust what they are doing and investing in.*

growth fund [C] a fund that specializes in producing growth in the value of its shares rather than producing income: *Investors should own both growth funds and value funds, because these two investment styles tend to do well at different times.*

hedge fund [C] a fund that makes investments that are unlikely to fall in value as well as in those that go up or down in value, to reduce the risk of losing a lot of money: *He manages a $40 million hedge fund.*

high-yield fund [C] a fund designed to produce high income, for example by investing in high-risk bonds: *Many newly issued junk bonds yield about 11%, which many high yield fund managers consider too low when they were used to buying bonds that were yielding 15% or more.*

income fund [C] a fund that makes investments designed to produce income, rather than growth in the value of its shares: *Global income funds were star performers last year, because of higher overseas interest rates.*

index fund also **tracker fund** *BrE* [C] a fund with a combination of shares that are in a particular SHARE INDEX. The fund is not managed, and follows the movements of the index: *the Vanguard Index Trust-500 Portfolio, an index fund that buys and holds the stocks that make up the Standard & Poor's 500* | *Picking an investment manager is itself an investment decision. You can avoid this by using a tracker fund.*

institutional fund [C] a fund open only to financial institutions

managed fund [C] a fund where INVESTMENT MANAGERS actively buy and sell investements and try to increase the fund's value by more than the general increase in the value of the markets they invest in: *When managed funds get very large, it might be impossible for a manager to deploy them effectively.* | *Managed funds allow investors to give the investment manager all responsibility for choosing a diversified range of investments.*

money fund also **money-market fund** [C] a fund that invests in CERTIFICATES OF DEPOSIT (=money put into banks for a particular period of time), COMMERCIAL PAPER (=money lent to companies for short periods of time), and TREASURY BILLS (=government borrowing over short periods of time) rather than shares, company bonds etc: *Assets of the nation's money market funds increased significantly despite a rising stock market.*

mutual fund [C] a particular legal form of fund in the US, often one that is open to the general public for saving and investing in particular financial markets; UNIT TRUST *BrE*: *Each year, a mutual fund is obliged by law to distribute to shareholders nearly all the capital gains and all the income that the fund earned.*

no-load fund [C] a fund that does not charge a fee to investors when they put their money into it: *The fund's success came from the fact that it's a no-load fund, which means investors can buy shares without paying a sales commission.*

open-end fund also **open-ended fund** *BrE* [C] a fund where investors can freely buy and sell shares from the fund, rather than only being able to buy them from and sell them to other investors: *Prudential Intermediate Income Fund Inc. began continuous offering as an open-end fund.*

performance fund [C] a fund that specializes in producing growth in the value of its shares rather than producing income. A performance fund may invest in companies that are growing fast but are not yet profitable

stock fund *AmE* [C] a fund that invests in company shares: *The average stock fund posted a total return of 17.19% in the first quarter.* | *You may want to divide money equally between large-company funds and* ***small-stock funds*** (=ones that invest in the shares of small companies).

tracker fund *BrE* [C] another name for INDEX FUND

umbrella fund [C] a fund that is made up of a number of different investments: *Their umbrella fund consists of up to 22 sub-funds, each designed to track different markets, including Australia, Hong Kong, Italy, Malaysia, USA and Sweden.*

value fund [C] another name for INCOME FUND: *If you take the recent poor performance of value funds as a signal to dump value and buy growth, you could be making a bad mistake.*

vulture fund [C] a fund that invests in companies in difficulty, hoping to gain control of them and improve their performance: *Zell's vulture fund offered to buy* *about $550 million in bonds and supplier claims of Carter Hawley Hale Stores for 40 cents on the dollar.*

fund² *v* [T] **1** to provide money for an activity, organization, or event: *This year's profits will be used to help fund a record £1.5 billion programme of investment over the next five years.* | *Mr Murdoch remains relatively unworried about the group's ability to fund its expansion.* —see also OVERFUNDED, UNDERFUNDED

2 to change the arrangements for paying a debt, so that you have more time to pay: *Proposals to fund part of the state debt faced stubborn resistance.*

fun·da·men·tal·ist /ˌfʌndəˈmentəlɪst/ *n* [C] FINANCE someone who looks at basic information about the economy, an industry, or a company, rather than other information: *If the pound reaches $1.65, some think it could shoot up into the $1.70s or 1.80s, but few fundamentalist analysts are as positive.*

fun·da·men·tals /ˌfʌndəˈmentlz/ *n* [plural] FINANCE basic information about a company, the economy etc that must not be forgotten when looking at share prices, currencies etc: *Silver's fundamentals don't justify its current high price, he said.* | *The* ***underlying fundamentals*** *of the economy are strong and interest rates are low, factors consistent with a strong market.* —compare TECHNICALS

fund·er /ˈfʌndə‖-ər/ *n* [C] a government, organization, or person that makes money available to others, for example in the form of loans: *The initiatives were funded by VSO, the Department of Trade and Industry, and a number of private sector funders, including BP.*

corporate funder a company that gives money to a CHARITY, or other NON-PROFIT MAKING organization: *New York's art museums hope that several corporate funders may be willing to subsidise the new project.*

equity funder an organization that provides capital for an investment: *Innisfree, the equity funder, announced a £60 million investment in South Buckinghamshire.*

fund·ing /ˈfʌndɪŋ/ *n* [U] money provided to an organization, for example in the form of loans, or GRANTS (=money given for a particular purpose): *Ted Turner got his early funding for CNN from Drexel Burnham Lambert's much-criticized junk bonds.*

federal funding *AmE* money provided by the US government: *Arts groups should stand on their own without federal funding.*

state funding *AmE* money provided by a particular state: *Texas lawmakers approved a five-year education plan that adds $528 million to state funding for public schools.*

fund manager —see under MANAGER

fund of funds —see under FUND¹

fund·rais·er /ˈfʌndˌreɪzə‖-ər/ *n* [C] a person or event that collects money for a political party, CHARITY etc: *"We hope for support from telecomms and computer companies," says the Science Museum's main fundraiser.* | *Mr Clinton picked up $600,000 at a $1,500-a-plate New York fundraiser this week.*

fund·rais·ing /ˈfʌndˌreɪzɪŋ/ *n* [U] **1** the activity of obtaining money for political parties, CHARITIES etc: *The rules of campaign fundraising are brutally simple: money follows a winner.* | *'Literaturnaya Rossiya' has launched a fundraising drive for the cathedral.*

2 the activity of obtaining money for investment: *Moody's downgrading probably will have only minimal effects on the fundraising abilities of the bank.*

funds flow statement —see under STATEMENT

fund share —see under SHARE

fun·gi·ble /ˈfʌndʒɪbəl/ *adj* **1** fungible things can be exchanged for another amount of the same thing, or used instead of another thing: *External PC and Mac modems are generally fungible. Swapping them just requires new cable settings.*

2 if one amount of money, bonds, shares etc is fungible with another, they are of the same type and can exchanged for each other, and treated in exactly the same way + **with**: *The inability to offer securities within the US that are genuinely fungible with the same securities offered outside it limits the opportunities available to issuers.* | *The $10 billion it seeks to borrow isn't earmarked for particular projects. But, as any banker or borrower knows, money is fungible.*

funny money —see under MONEY

fur·nish /ˈfɜːnɪʃ‖ˈfɜːr-/ *v* [T] **1** to provide or supply something: *Each company is required to* ***furnish details*** *of its market position to the Bank at the close of business each day.* | *The company entered into a hire-purchase agreement to* ***furnish the goods.*** | *The Andean oil pipeline furnishes about half of Ecuador's exports.* **furnish sb/sth with sth**: *The rules require brokers to furnish potential buyers with documents outlining the potential risks of their investment.*

2 to put furniture and other things into a house or room: *the heavy expense of furnishing a home* **furnish sth with sth**: *an office furnished with a desk and swivel chair* —**furnished** *adj*: *a furnished flat*

fur·ni·ture /ˈfɜːnɪtʃə‖ˈfɜːrnɪtʃər/ *n* [U] large movable objects such as chairs, tables, and beds that you use in a room to make it comfortable to live or work in: *He built up a substantial* ***furniture business.*** | *Business Superstore has everything from* ***office furniture*** *to paper-clips.*

fuse /fjuːz/ *v* [I,T] to join two or more companies together, forming a single organization: *We intend to fuse the separate companies into a single business organization.*

fu·tures /ˈfjuːtʃəz‖-ərz/ *n* [plural] FINANCE buying and selling futures contracts: ***Corn futures*** *prices rose as forecasts raised fears that the weather may damage the corn crop at a critical stage of its development.* | ***Precious metals futures*** *prices declined, with silver temporarily dropping below the critical $5-an-ounce level.*

currency futures agreements to buy or sell a fixed amount of currency on a fixed date in the future at a fixed price

death futures *informal, disapproving* life insurance policies owned by people who are very ill and expected to die soon, and which are bought cheaply by investors as short-term investments

financial futures agreements to buy or sell on a fixed date at a fixed price a particular amount of currency or a particular SECURITY: *By trading financial futures contracts, companies such as Archer-Daniels try to hedge against swings in the value of its securities holdings.*

index futures futures in the value of a SHARE INDEX (=the average value of a group of shares on a particular stockmarket): *He has bought stock index futures – contracts that give him the right to purchase a basket of stocks at specified prices.*

interest-rate futures futures contracts based on the value of changes on interest rates at a point in the future: *At the London Futures & Options Exchange, there is an interest rate futures contract on UK mortgages.*

stock index futures futures contracts based on the value of a STOCK INDEX at a point in the future, for example 3 or 6 months later: *Stock index futures let investors bet on a basket of stocks without owning the actual shares.*

futures contract —see under CONTRACT¹

futures exchange —see under EXCHANGE¹

futures market —see under MARKET¹

futures price —see under PRICE¹

F

future value —see under VALUE[1]

fv abbreviation for FUTURE VALUE

fwd written abbreviation for FORWARD

fy also **FY** written abbreviation for FISCAL YEAR; FINANCIAL YEAR

FYI written abbreviation for FOR YOUR INFORMATION

F

G

G abbreviation for GRAND

g written abbreviation for GRAM(S)

G & A written abbreviation for GENERAL AND ADMINISTRATIVE EXPENSES

G5 —see under GROUP OF FIVE

G7 —see under GROUP OF SEVEN

G10 —see under GROUP OF TEN

GAAP written abbreviation for GENERALLY ACCEPTED ACCOUNTING PRINCIPLES

GAB written abbreviation for GENERAL ARRANGEMENTS TO BORROW

gage /geɪdʒ/ *n* [C] LAW something you give to someone when you borrow money from them. The person lending the money will keep the asset if you cannot pay back the loan; PLEDGE

gagging order —see under ORDER[1]

gain[1] /geɪn/ *v* **1** [T] to get or achieve something important or valuable, usually by working very hard: *We hope to* ***gain a*** *larger* ***share of*** *the local market.* | *BP America says* ***knowledge gained*** *from the disaster has been shared with other oil companies.*
2 [I,T] to gradually get more of a useful or valuable quality, skill etc: *Donald* ***gained*** *a lot of useful* ***experience*** *when he was working for a merchant bank.* | *Employees will* ***gain in knowledge*** *and confidence by making full use of the training opportunities.*
3 [I,T] to increase in value or amount: *Standard & Poor's 500-stock index gained slightly, closing up 3.75 points.* | *Production in both China and India gained while domestic consumption slowed.* | *For the week, the Dow industrials gained 39.85 points.*
4 gain ground if a currency, share, or financial market gains ground, it increases in value: *The stock market gained ground after two days of losses.* + **against** (=compared to): *The dollar gained ground against foreign currencies.*
5 gain ground to gradually become more popular, successful etc: *Grolsch has also gained ground, with sales up 12.2%.* + **against/on** (=compared to): *Aluminium has been gaining ground against more traditional metals.* | *GM's trucks are gaining ground on Ford's F series.*
6 [I,T] to get an advantage from a situation, opportunity, or event: *Some countries depreciated their currencies so as to* ***gain a competitive advantage*** *over their trading rivals.* **gain (sth) from sth**: *Malaysia has not always gained greatly from the sales of assets such as shares in its airline.* | *People with higher incomes clearly gained more from the tax cuts.* | *The management group owns about 18% of the stock and would stand to gain millions of dollars if the company were sold.*
7 gain a foothold to reach a position from which you can start to make progress and achieve your aims: *European television groups will be ready to pay substantial amounts to gain a foothold in the UK market.*
8 gain currency to become more popular: *The new idea was gaining currency.*
9 gain access to sth if a country or company gains access to a place, it is able to sell its products there for the first time: *The government's aim is to help US companies gain access to foreign markets.* | *US computer makers have accused the Japanese of selling machines at steep discounts to gain access to markets where they are not competitive.*
10 gain access to sth to manage to use something, especially something that is difficult to obtain: *The program allows a hacker to secretly gain access to computer systems.*
11 gain approval if a plan, proposal etc gains approval, it is officially accepted: *The company did not gain approval from the planning commission for the new building.*
12 gain in popularity become more popular: *Insurance-funded plans are gaining in popularity because they are not subject to tax.*

gain[2] *n* **1** [C] an increase in the amount or level of something: *The Sainsbury share price ended the year with a near 60% gain.* | *The Nikkei average ended with a gain of 140.19 points at 35,522.99.* + **in**: *gains in consumer spending* | *a 50 point gain in the Dow Jones industrial average on the New York Stock Exchange*
2 [U] financial profit: *Developers cut down the forests* ***for economic gain.*** | *The politician denied the charge that he was using his office* ***for personal gain.***
capital gain [C] FINANCE, TAX profit that is made when an asset is sold for more than it cost, or more than its BOOK VALUE: *Parisbas said much of its profit increase came from the sale of an office building for a capital gain of FF1.3 billion.* | *Electrolux* ***realized a capital gain*** *of SKr100 million on the sale of its laundry and textile units.* | *You may* ***incur a capital gain*** (=make a capital gain) *that will be taxed every time you transfer money from one mutual fund to another.*
short-term gain [C] FINANCE, TAX profit made from the sale of an asset within a short time of buying it, usually one year
3 [C] an advantage or improvement: *The new machinery has produced big* ***efficiency gains.***
4 ill-gotten gains [plural] money or an advantage obtained dishonestly: *The ruling requires the banks to return 'ill-gotten gains' to hundreds of thousands of past customers.*

gain•er /ˈgeɪnə‖-ər/ *n* [C] FINANCE a share that increases in value on a particular day of trading on a stockmarket; ADVANCER: *One of the day's biggest gainers was Thorn EMI, which added 21 to 733.*

gain•ful /ˈgeɪnfəl/ *adj* [only before a noun] *formal* **gainful employment/work/activity** work or activity for which you are paid: *The United States now has a far higher proportion of its population in gainful employment than any other Western industrial economy.*

gains tax *n* [U] —see ***capital gains tax*** under TAX[1]

gal. also gall *BrE* written abbreviation for GALLON

gal•lon /ˈgælən/ *n* [C] **1** *BrE* a unit for measuring liquids, equal to 4.5435 litres: *The price of petrol will increase by around 11p* ***a gallon.*** | *a 12.6 million-gallon cargo of industrial oil*
2 *AmE* a unit for measuring liquids, equal to 3.785 litres: *Unleaded gasoline fell 0.53 cent to 59.89 cents* ***a gallon.*** | *An improvement in car mileage of just one mile* ***per gallon*** *would save 350,000 barrels of crude oil per day*

galloping inflation —see under INFLATION

Gallup poll —see under POLL[1]

gam•ble[1] /ˈgæmbəl/ *v* [I,T] **1** to risk money on the stockmarket or a new business activity in the hope of making a profit + **on**: *The company is gambling on new merchandise lines aimed at expanding its business.* **gamble sth on sth**: *Spielberg is to gamble £20 million on making the most expensive black-and-white film ever.* + **with**: *The two men gambled with £6,000 of their savings to establish a research company.*
2 to risk money on the result of something uncertain

such as a card game or race: *While on Madeira, he gambled at the island's casino.*

gamble[2] *n* [C usually singular] an action or plan that involves a risk but that you hope will succeed: *All stock exchange investment is a gamble.* | *The board decided to embark on aggressive overseas expansion, the biggest **gamble** it had ever **taken**.*

gam•bling /ˈgæmblɪŋ/ *n* [U] the practice of risking money or possessions on the result of something uncertain, for example a card game or a race: *The defendants are accused of illegal gambling and conspiracy.*

game /geɪm/ *n* [C] **1** an activity in which people compete with each other according to agreed rules: *The market is a game which creates wealth through the process of production exchange.*

business game also **management game** a method of teaching business skills, where teams of managers act as companies competing with each other

2 the advertising/public relations etc game *informal* the profession of advertising, public relations etc: *The company is certainly not new to the publishing game.*

3 beat/play sb at their own game to beat someone or fight back against them by using the same methods that they use: *Compaq built its reputation by beating IBM at their own game.* —see also ZERO-SUM GAME

game plan *n* [C] a plan for achieving success: *Investors should first look at their long-term objectives and their investment game plan.*

game theory —see under THEORY

gam•ing /ˈgeɪmɪŋ/ *n* [U] LAW playing cards or other games of chance for money; GAMBLING: *Reno's hotel-casino owners hope to breathe new life into the city's **gaming business**.* | *Isutani made an application for a **gaming license** for a small casino.* | *fees payable under the provisions of the Gaming Act 1968*

Gantt chart —see under CHART[1]

GAO *n* General Accountancy Office; an independent organization established by the US Congress to examine the accounts of US government departments, checking whether public money is being received and spent correctly

gap /gæp/ *n* [C] **1 gap in the market** an opportunity to develop and sell a particular product or service because no other company is doing this yet: *DASA thinks there is a gap in the market for small jets.* | *Just Mums, a mail-order company, is aiming to **fill the gap in the market** with a range of swimwear in different styles and colours.*

2 a difference between two situations, amounts, groups of people etc: *Brazil had a **trade gap*** (=difference in value of what a country buys from abroad and what it sells) *of $3.16 billion last year.* + **between**: *the gap between the earnings of manual and non-manual workers*

3 something that is missing that stops something else from being complete + **in**: *Lotus, trying to **fill a gap** in its product line, announced it would buy an Atlanta software firm for $65 million.*

gap analysis —see under ANALYSIS

gar•bage /ˈgɑːbɪdʒ‖ˈgɑːr-/ *n* [U] COMPUTING information in a computer memory that is no longer needed or wanted: *These areas of dead memory are called garbage.*

garbage in, garbage out written abbreviation **GIGO** COMPUTING used to say that if you put bad information into a computer, you will get bad results

Garment District also **garment district** *n AmE* **the Garment district** an area of New York where many offices and factories connected with the women's clothing industry are

gar•ni•shee /ˌgɑːnɪˈʃiː‖ˌgɑːr-/ also **gar•nish** /ˈgɑːnɪʃ‖ˈgɑːr-/ *v* [T] LAW when a court of law garnishees someone's money or property, it orders an organization holding it, for example a bank or an employer, to send it to the court in order to pay that person's debts: *Military law holds armed forces personnel responsible for their debts, and wages can be garnisheed to pay them.* | *One method of getting your money back is to obtain a **garnishee order** requiring money to be paid out of your debtor's bank account.* —**garnishment** *n* [C,U] *Five states, including Texas, don't permit garnishment of wages.*

gas /gæs/ *n* plural **gases** or **gasses** [C,U] a substance which is not solid or liquid at normal temperatures, and which usually cannot be seen: *Greenhouse gases are the direct result of pollution.* | *Over 40% of Pakistan's energy needs are supplied by gas.*

natural gas [U] gas used for heating and lighting, taken from under the earth or under the sea: *Tehran planned to sell the Ukraine 75 billion cubic meters of natural gas a year.* | *vehicles powered by natural gas*

gate /geɪt/ *n* **1** [C] the door leading to the planes at an airport: *a new 10-gate passenger terminal at La Guardia Airport*

2 [singular] the number of people attending a public place or event such as a football match, amusement park, film etc. The gate also refers to the total sum of money received in entrance fees: *revenue for local television rights and **gate receipts*** | *Universal Studios Hollywood concedes its **total gate** is slightly lower this year.*

3 open/close its gates if a company or organization opens its gates, it opens for business for the first time. If it closes its gates, it is no longer in business: *By the time Disneyland opened its gates, the city of Anaheim had increased to four times its size.* | *Within the next few years, the factory will close its gates, supplanted by the modern technology.*

4 be left at/first out of the starting gate if you are left at the starting gate, you are not able to take part in an activity or succeed in it because you have been too slow to get involved when it began. If you are first out of the starting gate, you are likely to succeed in an activity because you were quick to get involved in it: *His campaign never even left the starting gate.* | *This is the first time that the traditionally slow Hitachi has been first out of the starting gate.*

gate•fold /ˈgeɪtfəʊld‖-foʊld/ *adj* [only before a noun] a gatefold page in a book or magazine is bigger than the other pages, with the edges folded to the middle so that it can be opened out. Gatefold pages are used for large pictures, photographs etc: *a campaign featuring **gatefold ads** in trade magazines*

gate•keep•er /ˈgeɪtˌkiːpə‖-ər/ *n* [C] **1** MARKETING someone in an organization who has a lot of influence over which products it buys, which company it buys them from etc: *For technology gatekeepers, the challenge is to keep ahead of new computer developments.*

2 *informal* someone in an organization who decides who should deal with particular enquiries and customers. Gatekeepers may also restrict who is allowed to talk to certain people in the organization: *The receptionist has an important role to play as the firm's gatekeeper.*

gate•way /ˈgeɪt-weɪ/ *n* [C] **1** something that gives a person, company or country the opportunity to do something successfully or make progress in some way + **to/into/between**: *The British are heading for Texas in an attempt to open a gateway to Mexico's potentially huge markets.* | *Hong Kong is a critical **economic gateway** between the mainland and the outside world.*

2 COMPUTING a device on a computer that makes it possible to connect it to another computer of a different type or on a different NETWORK; ROUTER: *Email gateways already connect various US networks to a growing global infrastructure.* | *the introduction of **gateway facilities** on Prestel*

3 *BrE* LAW in Britain, arrangements that allow companies to do things that would not normally be allowed. Gateways mainly relate to the RESTRICTIVE TRADES

G

PRACTICES ACT: *The regional unemployment gateway was successfully pleaded, where it was argued that sales restrictions would increase unemployment in the area.*

GATT /gæt/ *n* the General Agreement on Tariffs and Trade; an international organization set up to reduce restrictions on trading between its members. It was replaced in 1995 by the WORLD TRADE ORGANISATION

gauge[1] /geɪdʒ/ *v* [T] **1** to measure how people feel about something or the effect that something is likely to have on them: *'Management Today' commissioned research to* ***gauge opinions*** *on how British industry is meeting its environmental responsibilities.* | *extensive testing to* ***gauge*** *consumer* ***reactions***

2 to calculate what is likely to happen in the future, using a particular method or set of figures: *US retail sales will help gauge how the economy is faring.* | *Bristol and West hopes to gauge the likely demand for each property before the auction starts.*

gauge[2] *n* [C] **1** a measurement of how people feel about something or the effect that something is likely to have on them: *The survey is an important* ***gauge of*** *attitudes and aspirations among college freshmen.*

2 a method or set of figures that helps to calculate what is likely to happen in the future: *The government's* ***economic forecasting gauge*** *rose for the fifth month in a row.*

ga·zette /gəˈzet/ *n* [C] a newspaper, often one listing official announcements such as legal notices or the names of people who have taken up a position in government. The word 'Gazette' is often used in newspaper titles: *Before any new statute can be enacted, it must be announced in the official gazette.* | *the Arkansas Gazette*

gaz·et·teer /ˌgæzəˈtɪə‖-ˈtɪr/ *n* [C] a book listing the names of places and information about each place. The word 'Gazetteer' is sometimes used in the title of such books: *Bartholomew's Gazetteer shows trading facts about each country, region, or regional organisation.*

G

ga·zump /gəˈzʌmp/ *v* [T] *BrE* PROPERTY *disapproving* **be gazumped** if you are gazumped, someone who has agreed to sell you a house at an agreed price sells it to someone else for more money: *If the potential buyer is gazumped, Skipton's customers will receive a voucher towards any fees.* —**gazumping** *n* [U] *In some areas of London, gazumping has returned, as buyers have found a shortage of good properties.*

ga·zunder /gəˈzʌndə‖-ər/ *v* [T] *BrE* PROPERTY *disapproving* **be gazundered** if you are gazundered, someone who has agreed to buy your house says that they will only buy it for less than the amount originally agreed —**gazundering** *n* [U]

gb COMPUTING written abbreviation for GIGABYTE

GCC *n* the Gulf Co-operation Council; an international organization which encourages its members to work together on matters such as the economy and defence. Its members are Bahrain, Kuwait, Oman, Qatar, Saudi Arabia and the United Arab Emirates

GCSE *n* [C] General Certificate of Secondary Education; a school examination in a range of subjects that is taken by students aged 15 or over in Britain

GDP abbreviation for GROSS DOMESTIC PRODUCT

gear[1] /gɪə‖gɪr/ *n* [U] **1** special equipment or clothing used for a particular purpose: *Pneumo Abex makes airplane landing gear and other aerospace parts.* | *police in* ***riot gear*** (=special clothing that protects them if they are attacked)

2 in/into high/top gear if an activity moves into high gear, it becomes much more important, and people put more effort into making it succeed: *The alliance with Mattel is part of Disney's strategy to keep its merchandising efforts in top gear.*

3 in/into low gear if a financial or industrial activity is in low gear, it is not growing, or it is not at a high level: *The Japanese economy has been stuck in low gear since 1992.* | *Wall Street* ***shifted into low gear*** (=started working more slowly than usual) *ahead of the Memorial Day weekend.*

gear[2] *v* [T] **1 be geared at/to/towards** to be designed or organized in a way that is suitable for a particular purpose: *Honda's advertisements are geared at consumers who normally prefer buying American cars.* | *Fiji's policies are geared towards reducing reliance on sugar exports and tourism.*

2 be geared to to be connected to something, so that if one thing changes, so does the other: *They were borrowing large sums that were* ***geared to interest rates*** *that might rise.* | *The minimum notice period is geared to the length of time you have been employed.*

gear up *phr v* [I] to prepare for something that is about to happen, usually something exciting or difficult: *The Postal Service is gearing up to absorb some of the United Parcels Service business if there's a strike.* + **for**: *Deutsche Morgan Grenfell has been gearing up for a major push into investment banking.*

gear·ing /ˈgɪərɪŋ‖ˈgɪr-/ *n* [U] FINANCE *BrE* also **capital gearing** the amount of borrowing that a company has in relation to its SHARE CAPITAL. If the company makes more profit by investing this borrowed money in its business activities than it pays to lenders in interest, the company's shareholders will obtain higher DIVIDENDS (=payments from their shares) than they would without the use of borrowed money. But if the company makes less profit by investing this borrowed money in its business activities than it pays to lenders in interest, dividends will be lower, so high gearing involves a higher degree of risk; LEVERAGE: *Microvitec Plc has cut gearing to between 40% and 50% from approximately 80% over the past two years.* | *the company's target of lowering its gearing to the 1:1 level* | *With higher levels of capital gearing, debt service payments stood at record levels.*

geek /giːk/ *n* [C] *informal* someone who knows a lot about a technical subject, usually computers, but who is not good at communicating with people; NERD: *This book is about a geek, written by a geek for a geek readership.* | *Who's the* ***alpha geek*** (=the person who knows most about computers) *round here?* —**geeky** *adj*: *I surf the Internet but I'm not at all geeky.*

gen·der /ˈdʒendə‖-ər/ *n* [C,U] the fact of being male or female: *Discrimination on the grounds of sex, race or gender is illegal.*

gender-awareness *n* [U] HUMAN RESOURCES when you are sensitive to the differences between men and women, and treat them both fairly and equally: *Arthur Andersen & Co. has started a gender-awareness program called 'Men and Women as Colleagues'.*

gender bias *n* plural **gender biases** [C,U] HUMAN RESOURCES when men and women are treated differently in a way that is unfair: *the rights of women to sue in cases of gender bias and harassment* | *Women have advanced into the higher ranks of the legal profession, but unfair gender-biases persist.* —**gender-biased** *adj*: *The tests are gender-biased because the questions do not draw on female areas of knowledge.*

General Agreement on Tariffs and Trade —see under GATT

General Arrangements to Borrow *n* [plural] an agreement between the GROUP OF TEN countries and Switzerland, made in 1962 to provide loans to each other and to the IMF: *The GAB facility was designed to meet serious balance-of-payment problems that could threaten the stability of the international monetary system.*

general average —see under AVERAGE[2]

general average contribution —see under CONTRIBUTION

general average loss —see under LOSS

general cargo —see under CARGO

General Certificate of Secondary Education —see under GCSE

general creditor —see under CREDITOR

general delivery *n* [U] *AmE* a post office department to which you can send letters for someone, and which will keep them until they are collected; POSTE RESTANTE *BrE*

general equilibrium —see under EQUILIBRIUM

general expense —see under EXPENSE

general haulage —see under HAULAGE

gen•e•ral•ist /ˈdʒenərəlɪst/ *n* [C] someone with knowledge of many subjects, rather than detailed knowledge of one subject: *The state can no longer be governed by generalists; each policy area demands considerable expertise.* —compare SPECIALIST

general ledger —see under LEDGER

general legacy —see under LEGACY

general lien —see under LIEN

Generally Accepted Accounting Principles abbreviation **GAAP** *n* [plural] ACCOUNTING in the US, official rules about how things should be dealt with and shown in company accounts. A similar arrangement in Britain is the FINANCIAL REPORTING STANDARDS: *New York state now requires the city to balance its budget on the basis of Generally Accepted Accounting Principles.*

general management trust —see under TRUST

general manager —see under MANAGER

general meeting —see ***annual general meeting***, under MEETING

general partner —see under PARTNER

general partnership —see under PARTNERSHIP

general-pur•pose *adj* [only before a noun] **1** a general-purpose product is suitable for most uses or situations that such products are normally used for: *general-purpose computers*
2 FINANCE general-purpose lending is used to finance a number of different things: *New York Power Authority said it plans to issue about $180 million of **general-purpose bonds** to finance two projects.*

general-purpose fund —see under FUND[1]

general reserve —see under RESERVE

general ship —see under SHIP[1]

general store —see under STORE[1]

general strike —see under STRIKE[1]

gen•e•rate /ˈdʒenəreɪt/ *v* [T] **1** to produce energy or power: *lower prices for the fuels used to **generate power***
2 to do something that will create or increase sales, income, profit etc: *The Clariant sale **generated proceeds** of FFr2.3 billion.* | *the percentage of sales generated abroad*

gen•e•ra•tion /ˌdʒenəˈreɪʃən/ *n* **1** [U] the process of producing energy or power: *the **generation of electricity***
2 [U] the process of creating or increasing income, profits, sales etc: *Losses of about $27 million weakened Zenith's **internal cash generation**.* (=its ability to produce cash from its activities) | *Capital assets play a major role in **the generation of income** within the economy.*

cash generation [U] when a company or organization makes money that can be invested, after all the other business costs have been paid: *The group's accelerating cash generation will attract increased market attention.*

3 [C] a product which is at a certain stage in its technical development: *McDonnell Douglas has firm orders for its **new generation of** Delta-3 rocket scheduled for launch in 2003.* | *The **previous generation of** phototypesetters cost anything up to $300,000 each.*

Generation X *n* [U] MARKETING the group of people who are between about 20 and 35 years old: *The company sees Generation X as a market eager for new products.* | *The president's campaign overlooked the Generation X voters.* —**generation X-er** *n* [C] *94% of Generation X-ers put home ownership at the top of their list.*

gen•e•ra•tor /ˈdʒenəreɪtə‖-ər/ *n* [C] **1** a product which makes a profit or has other advantages: *The company's biggest **profit generator** is its snack-food operation.* | *The auto industry is a huge generator of employment and foreign exchange for Mexico.*
2 COMPUTING a computer program that is used to produce a particular set of figures, results etc: *A **report generator** solves the problem of information management.*
3 a machine that produces power: *factors governing the use of **wind generators*** (=ones which run using wind power)

ge•ner•ic /dʒəˈnerɪk/ *adj* [only before a noun] **1** *AmE* a generic product such as a type of food or a drug is one which is sold under its own name, rather than under the name of a particular manufacturer: *Cardizem, also known by its **generic name** of diltiazem* | *Cut-price **generic brands** have stolen millions of customers from the big-name cigarettes.* | *Companies will increasingly share the **generic market*** (=people buying generic products) *with bigger brand-name firms.*
2 MARKETING generic advertising involves all the makers of a particular product working together to sell the product, rather than competing against each other: *The Video Software Dealers Association announced a funding mechanism for its planned **generic campaign**.*
3 LAW a generic word, name etc is used to talk about a whole group of things, and therefore cannot be used as a TRADEMARK: *The court ruled that 'champagne' is not a generic word and that wine sold under that name had to be produced in the Champagne region of France.*

generic pharmaceuticals —see under PHARMACEUTICALS

generic product —see under PRODUCT

genetically-modified abbreviation **GM** *adj* genetically-modified foods and plants have had their GENETIC (=the materials that control the development of particular qualities) structure changed so that they are not affected by certain diseases or harmful insects: *Consumers are turning their backs on **genetically-modified ingredients**, and demanding more organic products.* | *Iceland is the first store refusing to stock genetically-modified produce.*

genetically modified organism —see GMO

genetic discrimination —see under DISCRIMINATION

genetic engineering —see under ENGINEERING

genetic modification *n* [U] abbreviation **GM** a method of producing crops by changing the GENETIC (=the materials that control the development of particular qualities) structure of plants so that they are not affected by certain diseases or harmful insects: *an international forum on the environmental effects of genetic modification*

gentleman's agreement —see under AGREEMENT

gen•tri•fy /ˈdʒentrəfaɪ/ *v* past tense and past participle **gentrified** [T] **be gentrified** if an area of a city where poor people live is gentrified, people with more money go to live there, and the buildings are improved and become more expensive as a result: *Now that the neighbourhood has been gentrified, the houses are not available to tenants.* | *the gentrified Lincoln Park area* —**gentrification** *n* [U] *This gentrification is taking place alongside large public-housing projects.*

get /get/ *v* past tense **got** past participle **got** *BrE* **gotten** *AmE* present participle **getting** [T] **1** to receive a

G

particular amount of money: *Uganda continues to get about $100 million a year in foreign aid.* | *The company still gets a good return on its investments.*

2 to be given or obtain a job or work: *Just out of Oxford University, Jonathan was trying to get a job in journalism.* | *They should be getting a lot of work through the Channel Tunnel project.*

get sth ↔ **across** *phr v* [T] to succeed in making people understand what you are telling them: *To* ***get its message across****, Reebok will boost its advertising budget this year to $220 million.*

get ahead *phr v* [I] to be more successful than other people or companies who are doing similar work: *Working overseas is important to getting ahead in many companies.* + **of**: *BP and Unipart are combining forces to get ahead of the competition.*

get around sth also **get round** *phr v* [T] to find a way of dealing with a problem, especially by avoiding it altogether: *Gasoline was smuggled across the border to get around an international trade embargo.* | *The US banks searched for ways to get round these restrictions.*

get back to sb *phr v* [T] to talk or write to someone about something you had discussed together earlier: *I left my name and number so they could get back to me.*

get by *phr v* [I] to manage to deal with a difficult situation, using whatever money, equipment etc you have; manage + **on/with**: *The Fed made several changes designed to make it easier for banks to get by on fewer reserves.* | *In Microsoft Windows, you can get by with just 2 megabytes of memory.*

get down to sth *phr v* [T] to finally start doing something that needs a lot of time or energy: *Conflicts in meetings disappear rapidly once you get down to the details.*

get into sth *phr v* [T] to start working or trading in a particular product or service: *Many young people want to get into advertising or public relations.* —compare ***get out (of)***

get on with sth *phr v* [T] to make progress with a particular activity, plan etc: *BTR's headquarters leaves its management teams to get on with the day-to-day running of each business.*

G

get out *phr v* **1** [I] to stop investing in or making a particular product or performing a particular activity, usually because it is no longer making a profit: *Investors can get out early if trouble arises.* + **of**: *Most banks are now getting out of development finance.*

2 [I] to avoid meeting the terms of a contract, agreement etc + **of**: *The company hopes the move will let it get out of costly gas supply contracts.*

3 [T] **get** sth **out** to succeed in producing something and making it available: *We must get those letters out on time.* | *IBM wanted to get out a system that the novice could use.*

get out ahead *phr v* [I] *AmE* to have an advantage over the people you are competing against: *The way to deal with the pressure is to get out ahead.*

get round sth *phr v* [T] another name for get around

get through *phr v* **1** [I] to succeed in making someone understand something, especially when this is difficult: *Including a joke gives your message impact and more chance of getting through.* + **to**: *We've been trying to change the way we get through to the voters.*

2 [I] to succeed in having a plan, law etc approved by an official group: *His deficit reduction plan eventually got through Congress.*

3 [I] to succeed in reaching someone by telephone: *The brokers received so many phone calls that many investors couldn't get through.* + **to**: *It could take a client up to half an hour to get through to his dealer.*

4 [T] **get through** sth to deal with a large number of things in a particular order: *We never seem to get through all the items on the agenda.*

5 [T] **get through** sth to manage to come to the end of a difficult situation or experience: *Cadbury's got through a major restructuring without making any redundancies.*

6 [T] **get through** sth to use a lot of something or spend a lot of money: *He got through at least $500 every weekend.*

7 [T] **get through** sth FINANCE if the price of something gets through a particular level on a financial market, it rises above that level: *The failure of the dollar to get through 79.15 yen prompted the sudden sell-off.*

ghost[1] /gəʊst‖goʊst/ *n* [C] people who are listed as workers on a company's books and PAYROLL, but who in reality do little or no work for the company: *Some contractors, in the interest of labor harmony, hire ghosts.* | *Exhibitors complained that their bills are inflated by* ***ghost workers*** *supposedly employed by the exhibition centre.*

ghost[2] *v* [T] to write something as a GHOSTWRITER: *She received a generous advance fee for the book she's ghosting.*

ghost•writ•er /ˈgəʊstˌraɪtə‖ˈgoʊstˌraɪtər/ *n* [C] someone who writes books, articles or speeches for other people, who then presents it as their own work: *Her company in Washington has three ghostwriters on its staff.* —**ghostwrite** *v* [T] *Mr Petrie got the contract to ghostwrite Mr Watson's autobiography.*

gi•ant /ˈdʒaɪənt/ *n* [C] a very large, successful company: *The world's soft drinks market is dominated by the US giants, Pepsi and Coke.* | *ICI, the* ***chemicals giant****, paid $193 million to buy an American explosives manufacturer.* | *Shell and other giant organisations like IBM and Unilever*

giant-size also **giant-sized** *adj* a giant-size version of a product is a very large one, or the largest one available in a range: *Food containers regarded as giant-sized in other countries are considered individual size in the US.*

gift /gɪft/ *n* [C] **1** something given to someone on a special occasion or to thank them; PRESENT: *Sales of* ***Christmas gifts*** *are expected to grow about 20%.* —**gift** *adj* [only before a noun] *She has several years of experience in the gift business.*

2 something given free of charge to a customer by an organization in return for buying their products or using their services: *Your* ***free gift*** *will be sent to you once your first month's premium has been paid.*

3 LAW money or property given to someone with nothing expected in return. For a gift to be recognized by law, it must be clear that the giver intended to give it and that he or she did give it.: *Pension contributions or* ***charitable gifts*** *are deducted from pay for tax purposes.* | *You might want to* ***make a gift of*** *your whole estate to your partner.*

business gift ◆ money given by a business to an organization that does not make a profit, such as a CHARITY, on which the company receives TAX RELIEF: *a guide to tax relief on business gifts to schools*

◆ a gift given by a company or one of its employees to a customer: *the use of business gifts where the 'giving' was tied to the placing of orders* —see also DEED OF GIFT

gift certificate *n* [C] *AmE* a piece of paper worth a particular amount of money which can be exchanged for goods in a shop; GIFT TOKEN, GIFT VOUCHER *BrE*: *The promotion gives customers gift certificates valued at $25 on purchases over $100.*

gift pack —see under PACK[1]

gift tax —see under TAX[1]

gift token also **gift voucher** —see under TOKEN[1]

gift-wrap *v* past tense and past participle **gift-wrapped** present participle **gift-wrapping** [T] if someone working in a shop gift-wraps something you are buying, they wrap it in attractive coloured paper, so that you can give it to someone as a gift: *a gift-wrapped bottle of Moet Chandon champagne*

gift-wrapping *n* [U] **1** attractive coloured paper, used to wrap gifts

2 when a shop wraps goods you have bought in attractive coloured paper: *a* ***gift-wrapping service***

gig•a- /ˈɡɪɡə/ *prefix* used in units of measurement to mean one thousand million. For example, one GIGAWATT of electricity is equal to one thousand million WATTS: *177 gigatons of coal*

gig•a•bit /ˈɡɪɡəbɪt/ *n* [C] COMPUTING a unit of computer information equal to one thousand million BITS: *Five gigabits is equal to 5,000 200-page books.*

gig•a•byte /ˈɡɪɡəbaɪt/ written abbreviation **Gb** *n* [C] COMPUTING a unit of computer information equal to one thousand million BYTES: *cassettes that can hold up to 96 gigabytes of data*

GIGO COMPUTING written abbreviation for GARBAGE IN GARBAGE OUT

gilt-edged *adj* gilt-edged investments are the safest available, usually in government bonds: *The safest place to put your money is with the government. Over hundreds of years, it has never defaulted on gilt-edged bonds.* | *its gilt-edged triple-A bond rating*

gilt-edged market also **gilts market** —see under MARKET[1]

gilt-edged security —see under SECURITY

gilts /ɡɪlts/ *n* [plural] FINANCE British government bonds sold by the BANK OF ENGLAND, done to finance the British NATIONAL DEBT: *Gilts fell sharply despite continued firmness in the pound.*

index-linked gilts gilts whose value is linked to the RETAIL PRICE INDEX (=the general level of prices): *Despite being linked to the RPI, index-linked gilts are subject to a six-month delay in indexation, which means that the bond is not inflation-protected for the last six months of its life.*

irredeemable gilts another name for UNDATED GILTS

long gilts also **long-term gilts** gilts with a MATURITY (=repayment date) more than 15 years in the future; LONGS: *The Bank is worried about refinancing short-term debt and will not, therefore, stop issuing long-term gilts.*

medium-term gilts gilts with a MATURITY (=repayment date) between five and 15 years in the future;: *Confidence in the future of the economy has pushed down yields on medium-term gilts.*

short-term gilts gilts with a MATURITY (=repayment date) less than seven years in the future; SHORTS: *A cut in interest rates makes short-term gilts an attractive buy because of their fixed interest payments.*

undated gilts gilts with no MATURITY DATE (=repayment date) that will go on paying interest for ever

variable rate gilts gilts with an interest rate that changes during their life, linked to general market interest rates: *The UK government has issued floating rate notes under the name of variable-rate gilts.* —see also REPO[1]

gilt stocks —see under STOCK[1]

gilt yields —see under YIELD[1]

gim•mick /ˈɡɪmɪk/ *n* [C] *disapproving* a trick or object that makes you notice a product and want to buy it: *It would be foolish to dismiss the videophone as nothing more than a gimmick.* —**gimmicky** *adj*: *a gimmicky new product for gadget-hungry consumers*

Gin•nie Mae /ˌdʒɪni ˈmeɪ/ *n* **1** [singular] the familiar name for the GOVERNMENT NATIONAL MORTGAGE ASSOCIATION, a US government organization that buys home loans from lenders, GUARANTEES them (=promises to repay them if the borrowers do not repay), and arranges for them to be sold and traded on financial markets as SECURITIES. The money obtained is then used for more loans to home buyers: *mortgage-backed securities, such as those issued by the Ginnie Mae.*

2 Ginnie Maes [plural] bonds sold by the GOVERNMENT NATIONAL MORTGAGE ASSOCIATION: *Ginnie Maes are backed by the full faith and credit of the US government.* —see also FANNIE MAE, FREDDIE MAC

gi•ro /ˈdʒaɪrəʊ‖-roʊ/ *n BrE* **1** [U] also **National Giro** BANKING in Britain and some other countries, a system for sending money electronically from one bank account to another: *You can pay your gas bill* ***by giro***. | ***bank giro*** *credits*

2 [C] a cheque paid by the government to someone who is unemployed or who cannot work because of bad health: *Have you cashed your giro?* | *an income support* ***giro cheque***

Gi•ro•bank /ˈdʒaɪrəʊbæŋk‖-roʊ-/ *n* a bank in Britain where customers can use post offices to put money into and take money out of their account, to pay bills etc

give•a•way /ˈɡɪvəweɪ/ *n* [C] **1** *informal* used, especially by advertisers, to say that something is extremely cheap to buy: *At £400, these computers are a giveaway.* | *No airline could afford to carry passengers for long at such* ***giveaway prices***.

2 something that is given to customers free of charge: *Comic books were first published in the US in 1933, for use as advertising giveaways.*

give•back /ˈɡɪvbæk/ *n* [C] *AmE* something a company or employee does for the benefit of the economy as a whole or their employer, even though it is bad for the company or person themselves. It might take the form of an employee taking a reduction in wages when their employer's business is in difficulty: *The union was not forced into any givebacks.*

giv•er /ˈɡɪvə‖-ər/ *n* [C] FINANCE a person or organization that gives money to a political party, CHARITY (=an organization that exists to help people, in health, education) etc; DONOR: *32% of the country's givers say they are reducing contributions.*

glamour stocks —see under STOCK[1]

glass ceiling *n* [C] also **glass wall** the attitudes in an organization that prevent women from rising beyond a certain level, despite having the necessary skills and ability: *the glass ceiling keeping women executives out of top corporate jobs* | *Women aren't the only victims of glass walls; it's an issue that concerns men as well.*

glass wall *n* [C] another name for GLASS CEILING

glitch /ɡlɪtʃ/ *n* [C] a small fault in the working of something: *a computer glitch*

glit•te•ra•ti /ˌɡlɪtəˈrɑːti/ *n* [plural] *journalism* rich, famous, and fashionable people whose activities are often reported in newspapers and magazines: *At Christie's auction house, the crowd of glitterati was so big it overwhelmed the place.*

glo•bal /ˈɡləʊbəl‖ˈɡloʊ-/ *adj* **1** including and considering all the parts of a situation together, rather than the individual parts separately: *The auditor's report takes a global view of the figures.*

2 affecting or involving the whole world: *Information and money are becoming increasingly global.* | *Global banks must be able to serve the financing needs of corporations, big and small, anywhere in the world.* | *the need to reduce operating costs in the face of increased* ***global competition*** | *The US competes in a* ***global market*** *and can't ignore interest rates in other countries.*

3 go global if a company or industry goes global, it starts doing business all over the world: *Arco Chemical went global in the 90s and today deals with Nissan, Toyota, Honda, Renault, Peugeot, Volkswagen, and the US car makers.* —**globally** *adv*: *The Wall Street Journal has learned to think globally while operating regionally.*

global corporation —see under CORPORATION

global demand —see under DEMAND

global economy —see under ECONOMY[1]

glo•bal•i•za•tion also **globalisation** *BrE* /ˌɡləʊbəlaɪˈzeɪʃən‖ˌɡloʊbələ-/ *n* [U] the tendency for the world economy to work as one unit, led by large international

G

companies doing business all over the world. Some of the things that have led to globalization are the ending of TRADE BARRIERS, the free movement of capital, cheap transport, and the increased use of electronic systems of communication such as the INTERNET: *"By being everywhere and working in different products, you also spread risk," Mr Maucher of Nestle says. "That is part of the beauty of real globalization."* | *Bertelsmann is stepping up its globalisation and moving into new media such as the Internet and digital broadcasting.* | *The* ***rapid globalization*** *of the world economy and the creation of a single European currency has doubled cross-border capital flows.*

glo•bal•ize also **globalise** *BrE* /ˈgləʊbəlaɪz‖ˈgloʊ-/ *v* [I,T] if a company, industry, or economy globalizes or is globalized, it no longer depends on conditions in one country, but on conditions all over the world: *the corporate alliances that have globalized the aerospace industry* | *Most African companies are seeking to globalise, liberalising trade and opening the door to foreign investment.*

global marketing —see under MARKETING

global music network —see under GMN

Global System for Mobiles —see under GSM

global village *n* [singular] the idea that the world can be considered as one unit for business and communication purposes: *the avalanche of information freely available in the global village of the 21st century*

global warming *n* [U] a general increase of world temperatures caused by increased amounts of CARBON DIOXIDE around the Earth: *An efficient policy to deal with global warming would be a tax on the carbon content of fuels.*

GLOBEX /ˈgləʊbeks‖ˈgloʊ-/ *n trademark* FINANCE a computer network for trading FUTURES (=contracts to buy or sell shares etc at a fixed price on a fixed date), run by the CHICAGO MERCANTILE EXCHANGE that can be used by traders all over the world

G

glo•cal•i•za•tion /ˌgləʊkəlaɪˈzeɪʃən‖ˌgloʊkələ-/ also **glocalisation** *BrE n* [U] *journalism* the idea that companies should think globally, but use methods in each particular place that are suited to it: *Mitsubishi Bank believes in 'glocalization' – adopting local ways in each of its global locations.*

glut¹ /glʌt/ *n* [C usually singular] a supply of something that is more than is needed, caused by producing too much of it: *A* ***world-wide glut*** *of memory chips should prevent prices from rising.* | *production cuts in an effort to prevent an* ***oil glut***

glut² past tense and past participle **glutted** present participle **glutting** *v* **glut the market** to produce a supply of something that is more than is needed, causing its price to fall: *The market is already glutted with unsold properties.* —**glutted** *adj* [only before a noun] *Hawaii's glutted luxury-hotel industry*

GM abbreviation for GENETICALLY MODIFIED; GENETIC MODIFICATION

gm written abbreviation for GRAM; GROSS MARGIN

GmbH used in the names of German companies or businesses when the company is a LIMITED LIABILITY COMPANY: *BMW Rolls-Royce GmbH*

GMN *n* global music network; a system to DISTRIBUTE (=make available and sell) music all over the world through the INTERNET

GMO *n* [C] genetically modified organism; a substance used to change the GENETIC (= the materials that control the development of particular qualities) structure of plants so that they are not affected by certain diseases or harmful insects: *GMOs could revolutionise crop production in less than five years.*

GMT /ˌdʒiː em ˈtiː/ *n* [U] Greenwich Mean Time; the time as measured at Greenwich in London, used as an international standard for measuring time: *The accident happened at 9.33 a.m. GMT on 14 May.*

GNMA *n* abbreviation for GOVERNMENT NATIONAL MORTGAGE ASSOCIATION —see under GINNIE MAE

Gnomes of Zu•rich /ˌnəʊmz əv ˈzjʊərɪk‖ˌnoumz əv ˈzʊrɪk/ *n* [plural] *informal* used to refer to important bankers and FINANCIERS from central Europe, especially Switzerland, who are considered to have a powerful but secret political influence: *People who imagine that some small group of powerful investors move the market often talk about the Gnomes of Zurich.*

GNP *n* abbreviation for GROSS NATIONAL PRODUCT: *If the project is successful it could account within five years for at least 10% of the Philippines' GNP.*

go /gəʊ‖goʊ/ *v* past tense **went** past participle **gone**
1 [I] to be sold for a particular amount or to a particular person **go for sth**: *He believes GM shares will fetch $45 by the year-end, while Ford will go for 40.* **go to sb**: *Government spending in the area doubled, but most of it went to the oil industry.*
2 go it alone to do something on your own, for example to start a new business: *Unless an entrepreneur wants to go it alone and has the necessary money and talents, he or she may have to take on a partner.*
3 used before an adjective or adjectival phrase to mean that something has happened or been done in a particular way. For example, if someone goes BANKRUPT, they become bankrupt; if a company goes GLOBAL, it starts doing business all over the world
go after *phr v* [T] **1 go after** sth to try to obtain something, such as a new job, a business contract etc: *Sega plans to go after the core of the video game playing market – children eight to 12 years old.*
2 go after sb to take actions to punish someone who has done something wrong or illegal: *Rules are needed to go after brokers who sell unsuitable investments.*
go back on sth *phr v* **go back on your promise/word** to break a promise: *You can rely on her. She won't go back on her word.*
go down *phr v* [I] if a computer or machine goes down, it stops working because of a fault: *When the machines went down, employees kept the bank open until 8:30 pm.*
go under *phr v* [I] if a business goes under, it fails because of financial difficulties: *As their smaller competitors go under, the large home-building companies grab more and more of the market.*
go with sth *phr v* [T] to accept someone's idea, plan etc: *We're asking importers to go with the domestic rules and customs.*

goal /gəʊl‖goʊl/ *n* [C] something that you hope to achieve in the future; AIM: *The Sensor razor is helping Gillette* ***achieve its goal*** *of getting new customers.* | *Our* ***long-term goal*** *is universal private education.* | *His goal was to see Security Pacific with banks in 35 states by the end of the decade.*

goal definition *n* [U] when an employee agrees with their employer what they want to achieve in their job over a future period of time, especially during an APPRAISAL (=a meeting in which they discuss the employee's performance)

go-between *n* [C] a person or company that acts for another person or company as their representative or AGENT: *We* ***act as a go-between for*** *supplier and buyers and help them develop trading links.*

go•fer /ˈgəʊfə‖ˈgoʊfər/ *n* [C] *informal* someone who carries messages or gets things for their employer: *If you are appearing on television or radio or making a significant speech, always have a company gofer with you.* —see also GOPHER

go-go fund —see under FUND[1]

going concern —see under CONCERN

gold[1] /gəʊld‖goʊld/ *n* **1** [U] a valuable soft metal used to make jewellery, coins etc, and formerly used in a system in which the value of the standard unit of a currency is equal to a fixed weight of gold of a particular quality: *Last year was also a difficult time for gold investors who began to doubt the metal's traditional role as a safe investment.* | *On the Commodity Exchange in New York, gold for current delivery settled at $394 an ounce, up $8.60.* | *South African* ***gold stocks*** (=shares in gold mining companies) *closed weaker.* **—gold** *adj*: *gold bars* | *a gold watch*

2 hit/strike gold *BrE informal* to make a useful or valuable discovery that will make a lot of money; STRIKE PAYDIRT *AmE*

gold•brick /ˈgəʊldbrɪk‖ˈgoʊld-/ *v* [I] *AmE informal* to do no work when you are at your place of work or to stay away from your place of work when you should be there: *Working from home, once considered an opportunity to goldbrick, has become the norm in many industries.* **—goldbricking** *n* [U] *She noticed workers taking a coffee break and accused them of goldbricking.*

gold card —see under CARD

golden handcuffs *n* [plural] things that make important employees stay with a company rather than going to work for a COMPETITOR: *Company pensions were the golden handcuffs which chained staff to a company.*

golden handshake also **handshake** *n* [C] *BrE* a large amount of money given to a senior employee when he or she leaves a company, especially when they are being forced to leave: *200 university lecturers were made redundant with golden handshakes averaging £80,000.* | *The retiring chief executive received a handshake of $27 million.*

golden hello *n* [C] a large amount of money given to an employee by their new employer to try to persuade them not to go to work for another company: *They hired anybody, giving six-figure golden hellos to anyone willing to break a contract.*

golden parachute *n* [C] an arrangement in which a senior employee of a company will be paid a large amount of money if they lose their job, for example if the company is sold: *The golden parachutes were in place to give the top people a big pay-off should the company be acquired.*

golden share —see under SHARE

gold•field /ˈgəʊldfiːld‖ˈgoʊld-/ *n* [C] an area of land where gold can be found

Goldilocks economy —see under ECONOMY[1]

gold•mine /ˈgəʊldmaɪn‖ˈgoʊld-/ also **gold mine** *n* [C] **1** *informal* a business or activity that produces large profits: *Pay-per-view television, under the right circumstances, is a proven gold mine.*

2 be sitting on a goldmine to own something very valuable, especially without realizing it: *The three companies realized they were sitting on a gold mine: a computerized directory containing the names and addresses of most people in America*

3 a deep hole or system of holes under ground from which rock containing gold is taken: *The Hayden Hill gold mine is expected to produce about 145,000 ounces of gold a year.*

gold reserves —see under RESERVES

gold-rush also **gold rush** *n* [C] when a lot of companies or people hurry to invest in a place or activity that they expect to make them a lot of money: *The internet sparked a gold-rush for powerful desktop computers.* | *Eager to take part in the gold rush, all the big Japanese trading companies have set up offices in Vietnam.*

golds /gəʊldz‖goʊldz/ *n* [plural] FINANCE stocks and shares in gold companies: *Golds fell 3.6%.*

gold standard —see under STANDARD[1]

gon•do•la /ˈgɒndələ‖ˈgɑːn-, gɑːnˈdoʊlə/ *n* [C] a large set of shelves in a supermarket which displays goods on both sides

good /gʊd/ *n* **1** [singular] ECONOMICS used by economists to talk about something that has been produced in order to be used or sold. It is not usual for non-specialists to use this singular form: *In the real free market, the users bear the costs of a good or service.*

2 be £10/$50 etc to the good to have £10, $50 etc more than before or to have made a profit of £10, $50 etc: *Guinness shares closed 6.5p to the good at 608.5p.*

good faith —see under FAITH

good faith money —see under MONEY

goods /gʊdz/ *n* [plural] **1** things that are produced in order to be used or sold: *North Korea has no hard currency reserves to* ***buy goods***. | *The strike is expected to delay payments to companies that* ***sell goods*** *to the government.* | *Suppliers have refused to* ***ship goods*** *since the company filed for bankruptcy last month.* | *If Mexico develops its economy, it will* ***export goods*** *and not its workers.* | *Manaus became a free-trade zone where companies could freely* ***import goods*** *and components.*

2 *BrE* heavy things that are carried by road, train etc; FREIGHT: *The report criticises the transport industry for the distances over which goods are moved by road.*

bonded goods goods that have been brought into a country and are kept in a special building until import tax has been paid on them

brown goods small electrical equipment such as televisions, tape recorders etc: *The market for small domestic appliances and brown goods fell by 6% last year.*

capital goods goods such as machinery, equipment etc, used by businesses to produce other goods; INDUSTRIAL GOODS: *Last year, Japan invested 23.4% of its GDP in new factories, machinery and other capital goods.*

consumer goods goods bought by people for their own use, rather than by businesses and organizations: *Rising incomes have brought higher demand for cars and other western consumer goods.*

consumption goods ECONOMICS another name for consumer goods: *There were more and more labour-saving devices among consumption goods in the modern home.*

dry goods ◆ goods such as tobacco, tea, coffee, and sugar that are not in liquid form

◆ *AmE* things such as clothes, sheets, and curtains that are made from cotton or other cloth: *a dry goods store*

durable goods large expensive products that consumers do not buy regularly or often, for example refrigerators, televisions etc; CONSUMER DURABLES; DURABLES: *Orders to factories for durable goods, which include machinery, household appliances, cars and other items designed to last at least three years, fell to $123.27 billion last month.*

duty-free goods goods on which you do not have to pay taxes, especially IMPORT DUTY: *The Kasbah is excellent for duty free goods such as cameras and audio equipment which can often be half the price they are in the UK.*

economic goods ECONOMICS goods seen from the point of view of their value and place in the economy: *The accounts provide measures of the economic goods and services consumed, transformed and earned.*

fancy goods small attractive objects that are sold as gifts or SOUVENIRS (=things you buy in a place to remind you of it after you have left it): *a kiosk selling snacks, postcards and fancy goods*

G

fashion goods clothes or other goods that manufacturers and retailers need to regularly replace with new styles because of changing fashions

fast-moving consumer goods abbreviation **FMCG** *BrE* goods, especially food, that sell very quickly and in large amounts. They are usually sold in SUPERMARKETS: *By concentrating on only fast-moving consumer goods, they keep their stock at a minimum.*

finished goods goods have been made completely and are ready to be sold: *converting raw materials and components into the* ***finished goods***

hard goods *AmE* goods bought by people for their own use that they expect to last for a long time; CONSUMER DURABLES: *Consumer doubts about the economy continue to depress sales of hard goods such as appliances and furniture.*

industrial goods another name for CAPITAL GOODS

intermediate goods ECONOMICS goods that have had some work done on them, but which are not finished: *Japan runs a massive trade surplus with Malaysia, due primarily to the export of intermediate goods, which are then finished and re-exported.*

investment goods ECONOMICS another name for CAPITAL GOODS: *Production of investment goods trebled, while consumption rose by less that 50%.*

luxury goods expensive goods bought for comfort and pleasure, not as a basic need: *Luxury goods makers such as Chanel, Yves Saint Laurent and Cartier say the problem of fakes is getting worse.*

manufactured goods goods that are made using machines: *A country does not get rich by importing manufactured goods.*

non-durable goods ECONOMICS goods that have a short life, for example food products; NON-DURABLES: *Outputs of non-durable goods fell by 1.1% with clothing, footwear and food all showing significant declines.*

packaged goods consumer goods that are sold in packages under a BRAND NAME: *packaged goods from tobacco to shampoo* | *The advertising firm has signed up a number of packaged-goods marketers, including Procter & Gamble, Unilever and Colgate-Palmolive.*

perishable goods goods such as food products that must be used within a short period of time; PERISHABLES: *Customs delays – particularly for perishable goods – have been costly to foreign companies.*

piece goods goods, especially TEXTILES (=woven material made in large quantities) that are made and sold in standard sizes

red goods goods, such as food, that consumers use quickly after buying them and that produce a low profit

soft goods goods made of cotton and similar materials such as curtains etc: *The home-furnishing retailer's sales of soft goods remain strong.*

sporting goods also **sports goods** goods used to play sports: *Adidas, the sports goods manufacturer*

wet goods goods that are in liquid form

white goods equipment used in homes that is usually painted white, for example washing machines, REFRIGERATORS etc: *Consumers are buying more clothes, furniture, white goods and electronic equipment.*

goods and chattels *n* [plural] LAW personal possessions: *The goods and chattels do not include the value of buildings and land, which come under real estate.*

goods and services *n* [plural] ECONOMICS used to talk about everything produced or sold in an economy: *Consumer spending on goods and services rose 0.6% in September, after adjusting for inflation.*

goods and services tax —see under TAX[1]

goods train —see under TRAIN[1]

goods vehicle —see under VEHICLE

good·will /ɡʊdˈwɪl/ *n* [U] ACCOUNTING the value that a business has in addition to the value of its ASSETS. Goodwill includes things such as the good REPUTATION that a business has, the names of its products, and the good relations it has with its customers: *The company believes the economic recession has damaged the financial value of the goodwill related to most of its recent acquisitions.* | *LSI said it was* ***writing off goodwill*** *associated with a 1988 acquisition of a graphics board company.*

goodwill payment —see under PAYMENT

go·pher /ˈɡəʊfə‖ˈɡoʊfər/ also **GOPHER** *n* [U] COMPUTING a computer PROGRAM that quickly collects information from many different places across the INTERNET: *Significant developments are taking place in the use of software, such as WAIS and GOPHER, to enable users to search multiple catalogues of holdings.* —see also GOFER

go-slow *n* [C] *BrE* a form of industrial protest in which people deliberately work as slowly as possible; SLOWDOWN *AmE*: *The union carried out a series of strikes and go-slows as part of its campaign for higher wages.*

gov·ern /ˈɡʌvən‖-ərn/ *v* **1** [I,T] to officially and legally run a country and make decisions about taxes, laws, public services etc: *A small military elite has been governing for just seven months.*

2 [T] if rules, principles etc govern the way a system or organization works, they control how things are done: *Law Society members are highly qualified and governed by a strict code of ethics.* | *The current regime governing credit card transactions in the UK runs counter to basic trading practices.*

gov·er·nance /ˈɡʌvənəns‖-vər-/ *n* [U] also **corporate governance** the way a company is managed at the highest level: *There is growing interest by institutional investors in the governance of companies in which they own stock.* | *At the shareholders' meeting, directors should expect questions about corporate governance, executive pay and internal financial controls.*

clinical governance the way HEALTHCARE is managed at the highest level

gov·ern·ment also **Government** /ˈɡʌvəmənt, ˈɡʌvənmənt‖ˈɡʌvərn-/ *n* [C] the group of people responsible for running a country or state and making decisions about taxes, laws, public services etc: *The Government is planning further cuts in public spending.*

government bond —see under BOND

government borrowing —see under BORROWING

government broker —see under BROKER[1]

government expenditure —see under EXPENDITURE

government investment —see under INVESTMENT

Government National Mortgage Association abbreviation **GNMA** —see under GINNIE MAE

government owned —see under -OWNED

government ownership —see under OWNERSHIP

government security —see under SECURITY

government stock —see under STOCK[1]

gov·er·nor /ˈɡʌvənə‖-ərnər/ *n* [C] **1** the person in charge of an important organization such as a country's CENTRAL BANK: *the governor of the Bank of England*

2 *BrE* a member of the committee in control of an institution such as a school, or of some official organizations: *The BBC's* ***board of governors*** *meets today to discuss the whole issue of funding.*

govt. written abbreviation for GOVERNMENT

Gp written abbreviation for GROUP, used in the names of companies: *Pacific Telesis Gp.*

gr. written abbreviation for GROSS; GRAM(S); GRAMM(ES); GRAIN(S)

grab[1] /ɡræb/ *v* past tense and past participle **grabbed** present participle **grabbing** [I,T] to take or obtain something that other people also want: *Both companies are looking to grab a share of the overseas market.* | *Sega grabbed a substantial market lead in the home video game market.*

G

grab² *n* [singular] **1** an attempt to take or obtain something that other people also want: *The company's recent growth could slow if competitors* ***make a grab for*** *some of its markets.* | *British and Spanish officials complain that the idea looks suspiciously like a* ***power-grab*** *by Brussels.*
2 be up for grabs *informal* if something is up for grabs, it is available for anyone who wants to try to obtain it: *Argentina has already sold off its telephone company, and dozens of other assets are up for grabs.* | *The assets of several carriers are* ***coming up for grabs****.* | *A large part of the business might be* ***put up for grabs****.*

grace /greɪs/ *n* [U] **1** additional time that is allowed before a payment must be made: *Paraguay was granted a new period of 20 years, with eight years' grace, for the payment of its $436 million debt to Brazil.* | *They have a* ***grace period*** *of ten years on the payment.*
2 a fall from grace when someone or something suddenly becomes much less successful or much less popular: *Philadelphia's economy has escaped the fall from grace seen in other Northeastern cities.*
3 to fall from grace to become suddenly much less successful or much less popular: *As drug stocks fell from grace, prices of oil stocks rose.*

grad·ing /ˈgreɪdɪŋ/ *n* [U] the process of judging goods or materials and giving them a number or name to show their size or quality: *Canada's* ***grading system*** *for grain* | *Currently, only a fraction of the 4 billion pounds of seafood consumed each year undergoes some form of product-grading or inspection.*

grad·u·ate¹ /ˈgrædʒueɪt/ *n* [C] **1** a person who has completed a university degree course, especially for a first degree: *a science graduate from Oxford University* | *The company is looking for a graduate engineer with the ability to lead and motivate a team of four people.*
2 *AmE* a person who has completed a course at a college or school: *a Harvard business-school graduate*

graduate² *adj* [only before a noun] *AmE* a graduate student is someone studying for their second degree

grad·u·ate³ /ˈgrædʒueɪt/ *v* **1** [I] to obtain a degree, especially a first degree, from a college or university + **from**: *He graduated from the University of California with a degree in mathematics.*
2 [I] *AmE* to complete your education at HIGH SCHOOL
3 [T] *AmE* to give a degree or DIPLOMA to someone who has completed a course
4 graduate (from sth) to to start doing something that is bigger, better, or more important: *Some ghetto children graduate from painting graffiti on subway trains to careers in the visual arts.*
5 graduate (from sth) to MARKETING to start buying a product etc that is better than the one you bought before: *They bought low-priced homes after graduating from rooming houses and apartments.*

grad·u·at·ed /ˈgrædʒueɪtɪ̆d/ *adj* TAX if a tax on income is graduated, the more you earn, the more tax you pay: *They pay a flat 34% tax, not the regular graduated rates on income up to $75,000.*

graduated tax —see under TAX¹

graduate recruitment —see under RECRUITMENT

graft¹ /grɑːft‖græft/ *n* [U] **1** *informal, BrE* hard work: *He put his success down to stamina, resilience, and sheer* ***hard graft****.*
2 *especially AmE* when money or advantage is obtained by using power or influence in a dishonest way: *The whole system is full of corruption and graft.*

graft² *v*
graft sth **onto** sth *phr v* [T] to try to combine a new idea or system with one that already exists: *Now Mr Vincent is preparing to graft onto Perrier an entirely new senior-management structure.*

grain /greɪn/ written abbreviation **gr** *n* [U] crops such as corn, wheat, and rice: *Grain futures declined sharply this week.*

gram also **gramme** /græm/ written abbreviation **g**, **gm**, **gr**, or **grm** *n* [C] the basic unit for measuring weight in the METRIC SYSTEM

Gramm-Rud·man Act /ˌgræm ˈrʌdmən ˌækt/ *n* [singular] a US law passed in 1985 that forced the government to BALANCE the BUDGET (=spend no more than it gets in taxes) by 1991: *Under the Gramm-Rudman Act, lawmakers were bound by fixed deficit targets.*

grand /grænd/ *n* plural **grand** abbreviation **G** [C] *informal* a thousand pounds or dollars: *ten grand's worth of goods*

grandfather clause —see under CLAUSE

grandfather provision —see under PROVISION

grandfather rights *n* [plural] at an airport, the rights of AIRLINES to use TAKE-OFF and LANDING SLOTS (=times at which aircraft can leave and arrive) that they have always had, and not to be forced to give or sell them to other airlines: *At present, airlines hold the slots in perpetuity* (=for ever) *giving them so-called grandfather rights.*

grand jury —see under JURY

grant¹ /grɑːnt‖grænt/ *n* [C] a sum of money given to a person or organization for a particular purpose, often by a government: *West Berlin's Free University was founded with major grants from the Ford Foundation.* | *The Arts Council* ***awarded*** (=gave) *her* ***a grant*** *of £2200 for a photographic mission to the Andes.*
block grant money given by central government to local government to help pay for services such as the police, roads etc: *It is difficult to know whether a regional authority is using the money allocated for transport in the block grant for transport matters.*
capital grant in Britain, a sum given by a government department to an organization for a particular investment: *The UK has never given farmers cheap loans for investment schemes, as in France, instead of capital grants.*
death grant in Britain, an amount of money paid to the relatives of someone who has just died to help pay the cost of their funeral: *Among the benefits to be abolished was the death grant.*
development grant money given by a government authority for economic development in a particular region: *As poorer members of the EC, most regions in Spain and Portugal qualify for sizeable EC development grants.*
federal grant a sum of money given by the central US government for a particular purpose: *The communities will receive federal grants to carry out health care programs.*
investment grant money given by the government to a business so that it can invest in buildings, machinery etc usually in order to help economic development in a particular area: *There are generous investment grants to car manufacturers from local authorities in Latin America.*
research grant a sum given by an organization to a person or institution in order to perform research: *Glasgow University has just received a £1.5 million research grant from the Science and Engineering Research Council to carry out a project to increase the capacity of fibre-optic cables.*

grant² *v* [T] to officially give a person or an organization something they have asked for **grant sb sth**: *The government granted Alberta-Pacific timber rights to a 28,000-square-mile area.* | *The Dutch industry department is to decide today whether to* ***grant a license*** *for a proposed sale of Dutch-built submarines to Taiwan's navy.*

G

gran·tee /ˌɡrɑːn'tiː‖ˌɡræn-/ *n* [C] LAW a person who is given the legal ownership of land, property, or money: *The legal ownership of the land was vested in the grantee.*

grant-in-aid *n* [U] money that is paid by the central government to government organizations or local government: *Some local authorities are expected to inflate next year's figures to increase their grant-in-aid.*

gran·tor /ˌɡrɑːn'tɔː, 'ɡrɑːntə‖'ɡræntər, -tɔːr/ *n* [C]
1 LAW a person who gives their legal ownership of land, property, or money to someone else
2 a person or company that allows someone to have something: *AT&T is the first big* ***credit grantor*** *to respond to complaints that consumers have difficulty obtaining their credit reports.*

grantor trust —see under TRUST

graph[1] /ɡrɑːf‖ɡræf/ *n* [C] a drawing that uses a line or lines to show the relationship between two or more sets of figures, measurements etc: *To enhance a presentation, you can utilize visuals such as charts and graphs to reinforce the information.* —compare CHART[1]

bar graph *AmE* a mathematical drawing in the form of a series of long thin boxes next to each other, each box representing an amount being compared with all the others; BAR CHART *BrE*

graph[2] *v* [T] *AmE* to draw a line or lines on a graph, showing the relationship between two or more sets of figures, measurements etc: *Using the above data, graph the demand for wheat and the supply of wheat.*

graph·ic /'ɡræfɪk/ *adj* [only before a noun] relating to drawing, printing, designing etc: *the best* ***graphic designer*** | *displays of* ***graphic arts****, including architectural drawings*

graphical user interface also **graphical interface**, abbreviation **GUI** *n* [C] COMPUTING a computer interface (=way of showing and organizing information on screen) that is easy to use and understand

graphic design —see under DESIGN[1]

graphic designer —see under DESIGNER[1]

graph·ics /'ɡræfɪks/ *n* [plural] drawings, designs, or pictures that are used to represent objects or facts, especially in computer programs: *exciting Disney animation using the latest* ***computer graphics***

graphic software —see under SOFTWARE

grass /ɡrɑːs‖ɡræs/ *n informal* **put sb out to grass** *BrE* another phrase for PUT SOMEONE OUT TO PASTURE *AmE*: *I'll be 60 in September, and when you turn 60, the military puts you out to grass.*

grat·is /'ɡrætəs, 'ɡreɪtəs/ *adv* provided without payment, free: *His work for the charity is performed gratis.* —**gratis** *adj*: *There's a small charge for some programs; others are gratis.*

gra·tu·i·tous /ɡrə'tjuːətəs‖-'tuː-/ *adj* LAW provided without payment, free: *Inheritance tax is concerned with gratuitous transactions.*

gra·tu·i·ty /ɡrə'tjuːəti‖-'tuː-/ *n* plural **gratuities** [C] *formal* **1** a small amount of money given to someone for a service they provided; TIP: *In many restaurants, a small gratuity given in advance may greatly improve service.*
2 *BrE* a large amount of money given to someone when they leave their job, especially when they leave the army, navy etc: *He received a gratuity of £5000 when he left the services.*

graveyard market —see under MARKET[1]

graveyard shift —see under SHIFT[1]

gravy train *n informal* **1 the gravy train** a business or activity where people can make money or profit without much effort: *The question is how, in otherwise very competitive capital markets, this gravy train has survived so long.*
2 the gravy train a government organization where people can get jobs and earn money without working much or at all, for example because they know the right people: *Mr Cardenas has campaigned strongly against corruption, warning that his government will not be a gravy train for his party's supporters.*

grease /ɡriːs/ *v informal* **1 grease sb's palm** to give someone money in a secret or dishonest way in order to persuade them to do something: *The chairman finally admitted that he too, was forced to grease a few palms along the way.*
2 grease the wheels to help a person, organization, system etc to work better, especially in order to get an advantage: *By exempting pension funds and unit trusts from income tax, the chancellor has done a lot to grease the wheels of the City's securities business.*

Great Britain abbreviation **GB**, also **Britain** *n* [singular] the island consisting of England, Scotland, and Wales, which together with Northern Ireland forms the United Kingdom: *a report on retailing in Great Britain*

Great Depression —see under DEPRESSION

green /ɡriːn/ *adj* connected with protecting the environment or harming it as little as possible: *These revelations will damage the company's green image.* | *a revolutionary new 'green' car*

green audit —see under AUDIT[1]

green·back /'ɡriːnbæk/ *n* [C] *informal AmE* an American BANKNOTE, especially a dollar note: *The Singapore dollar has been rising against the greenback.*

green belt *n* [C,U] an area of land around a city where building is not allowed

green card —see under CARD

green currency —see under CURRENCY

greenfield project *n* [C] a new company that is formed without assets or capital in order to take part in a new area of activity involving a lot of financial risk

greenfield site —see under SITE[1]

green·mail /'ɡriːnmeɪl/ *n* [U] when a company buys back its stock from a SUITOR (=a company that is trying to take it over), often for a very high price, to try to prevent a TAKEOVER: *One of Japan's wealthiest men, he has a history of speculation in stocks and real estate and is renowned for his attempts at greenmail.* | *The director told shareholders he had no intention of accepting* ***greenmail payments****.*

Green Revolution *n* [singular] **1** the increase in the amount produced by crops, such as wheat and rice, in several poorer countries in the 1960s and 1970s. This is due to improved scientific methods of farming: *The extra food production is the result of the Green Revolution, which has transformed agriculture in Asia and Latin America.*
2 the interest in protecting the environment that has recently developed in many parts of the world

green·shoe /'ɡriːnʃuː/ *n* [U] FINANCE when a financial institution sells all the available shares in a company's SHARE ISSUE or SECONDARY OFFERING and then sells more, or the number of shares sold in this way; OVERALLOTMENT: *The issue will raise DM1.7 billion, and the* ***greenshoe option****, to satisfy extra demand, is likely to increase this to nearly DM2 billion.*

green shoots *n* [plural] *journalism* used to talk about the first signs of economic improvement during a RECESSION: *To claim that a packed Oxford street is an indication of* ***the green shoots of recovery*** *is surely premature.* | *The latest manufacturing figures confirm the recent growth of green shoots in the economy.*

Green·wich Mean Time /ˌgrenɪtʃ ˈmiːn taɪm, ˌgrɪ-, -nɪdʒ-/ —see under GMT

greet·ing /ˈgriːtɪŋ/ *n* [C,U] words you use or something you do when you meet someone or write to them: *They briskly* ***exchanged greetings*** *before sitting down to start negotiations.* | *There followed an official greeting from the local Mayor.*

grey market —see under MARKET[1]

grey pound —see under POUND

grey power —see under POWER[1]

griev·ance /ˈgriːvəns/ *n* **1** [C] HUMAN RESOURCES a complaint made by a worker to an employer, usually because they feel they have been treated unfairly: *All shopfloor grievances will be passed on to management.* | *You must pursue your complaint through* ***the grievance procedure*** (=the system that a company has to examine and discuss workers' complaints) | *Make sure you* ***air your grievances*** *to your superiors* (=tell them you feel you have been treated unfairly).
2 [C,U] the feeling that you have been treated unfairly by someone: *Although she had been effectively demoted, she felt no grounds for grievance.* + **against**: *The fire may have been started by someone with a grievance against the oil industry.*

grind[1] /graɪnd/ *n* [singular] **1** something that is hard work and physically or mentally tiring: *I find the journey to work a real grind.* + **of**: *the relentless grind of international conferences*
2 the daily grind the boring things that you have to do at work every day: *workers emerging from their daily grind in the factory*

grind[2] *v* past tense and past participle **ground grind to a halt** to gradually stop working: *If the strikes continue, steel production will grind to a halt.* | *These latest figures are further evidence of Britain's economy grinding to a halt.*
grind sb ↔ **down** *phr v* [T] to spend a long time arguing with someone so that they are finally no longer able to oppose you: *He's a brilliant negotiator and eventually grinds down his opponents.*

gross[1] /grəʊs‖groʊs/ *adj* [only before a noun] **1** a gross amount of money is the total amount before any costs or taxes have been taken away: *The Tyson-Holyfield fight will generate a huge amount of money. The gross total is likely to exceed $100 million.*
2 gross behaviour is seriously wrong and unacceptable: *The inquiry uncovered widespread abuses, monumental waste and* ***gross mismanagement*** *at the Department.*

gross[2] *n* plural **gross** **1** [singular] the amount paid by people to go and see a film in a particular period of time; GROSS RECEIPTS: *During its first weekend, 'Dick Tracy' had a* ***box office gross*** *of $95 million.*
2 [U] the amount earned by a person or a business before costs and taxes are taken away: *While album sales once accounted for only a tiny share of his revenue, they now account for the majority of his* ***annual gross*** *of about $100,000.*
3 [C] a quantity of 144 things: *a cardboard box containing two gross of packets of Maltesers*

gross[3] *v* [T] **1** *especially AmE* if a film grosses a particular amount, people pay that total amount of money to see it: *'Titanic' broke a three-day box office record last weekend when it grossed $36 million.*
2 *especially AmE* if a person or business grosses a particular amount, they earn that total amount of money before costs and tax have been taken away: *Oprah Winfrey, the US's number one talkshow host, grossed more than $100 million last year.*
gross sth ↔ **up** *phr v* [T] to calculate an amount, including in it all the things, for example tax relief, that are normally taken away: *A basic rate taxpayer currently receives a net dividend of £75 on his personal saving plan. This dividend will be grossed up to £100.*

gross[4] *adv* if a person, business, or investment earns a particular amount gross, they earn that amount before tax has been taken away: *Leading shares now earn just 6% gross and pay dividends of 4% after tax.*

gross dividend —see under DIVIDEND

gross domestic product abbreviation **GDP** *n* [singular] the total value of goods and services produced in a country's economy, not including income from abroad: *Canada's annual* ***growth in gross domestic product*** *will decline to about 1% next year.*
inflation-adjusted gross domestic product gross domestic product after increases in prices are taken into account: *Economists expect inflation-adjusted gross domestic product to edge upward by 0.5%.*
per capita gross domestic product gross domestic product of a country divided by the number of people living there: *Luxembourgers, with a per capita gross domestic product above $30,000, rank as some the wealthiest people in the EC.*

gross income —see under INCOME

gross interest —see under INTEREST

gross investment —see under INVESTMENT

gross margin —see under MARGIN

gross misconduct —see under MISCONDUCT

gross national product abbreviation **GNP** *n* [singular] ECONOMICS the total value of goods and services produced in a country's economy, including income from abroad: *The Bundesbank expects the German gross national product to grow at a rate of 1.5% to 2.0% this year.*
inflation-adjusted gross national product gross national product after increases in prices are taken into account: *Forecasters now look for the inflation-adjusted gross national product to decline by 1.3%.*
per capita gross national product gross national product divided by the number of people living in the country: *The Doba oil project could transform the fortunes of Chad, which has a per capita gross national product of just $180.*

gross negligence —see under NEGLIGENCE

gross player —see under PLAYER

gross product *n* [U] ECONOMICS the total value of goods and services produced in a particular place: *In California, farmers produce about 10% of the state's gross product.*

gross profit —see under PROFIT[1]

gross receipts —see under RECEIPT[1]

gross registered tonnage —see under TONNAGE

gross return —see under RETURN[2]

gross salary —see under SALARY

gross sales —see under SALE

gross weight —see under WEIGHT[1]

gross yield —see under YIELD[1]

Gro t written abbreviation for GROSS TONNAGE; GROSS TONS

ground[1] /graʊnd/ *n* **1** [C usually plural] a reason, often a legal or official one, for doing or believing something + **for**: *There are grounds for optimism that the slump in the housing market may end.* | *Are there grounds for dismissing him?* | *The factory was closed* ***on health and safety grounds.***
2 gain ground to get an advantage or to rise in price: *The dollar gained ground against sterling.*
3 lose ground to lose an advantage or to fall in price: *Prices were lower across the board, with nearly all blue-chip stocks losing ground.*

G

4 get off the ground if a plan, business idea etc gets off the ground, it gets started or it starts to be successful: *This fund is intended to help new projects get off the ground.*

5 break new ground to do something completely new that no one has ever done before or discover something new about a subject: *Our scientists are breaking new ground in AIDS research.*

ground[2] *v* **be grounded in sth** to be based on a particular idea, principle etc: *His fiscal strategy is firmly grounded in Keynesian economics.*

ground floor —see under FLOOR

ground·ing /ˈgraʊndɪŋ/ *n* [singular] training in the basic knowledge of a subject or skill + **in**: *Applicants should have a* ***basic grounding*** *in personal injury work.* | *This course provides* ***a good grounding*** *in the management side of distribution.*

ground rent —see under RENT[2]

group /gruːp/ *n* [C] **1** also **group of companies** a large business organization that consists of several companies that all have the same owner: *Burmah Castrol, the lubricants group* | *the sale of the Rover Group to BMW* | *a dramatic surge in* ***group profits*** | *the group chairman*

2 several people or things considered together

consumer group an organization for protecting the interests and rights of consumers: *Consumer groups say that alliances between airlines could push up fares.*

focus group MARKETING a group of consumers brought together by a company to help it do MARKET RESEARCH. The group is asked to discuss their feelings and opinions about products, advertisements, companies etc: *The company has set up focus groups to talk to a range of PC users.*

income group people who earn similar amounts of money, especially when considered as a social group for purposes of marketing, public opinion etc: *Even among people in the same income group, those with less education were much less healthy.*

peer group ◆ a group of companies or products that can be compared because they are similar in a number of ways: *He promised to make Campbell a premier performer in the peer group of food companies.* | *The stock isn't significantly more expensive than others in its peer group.*

◆ a group of people who influence each other because they are the same age, have the same job, social position, etc: *Trainees can discuss the job with their peer group at an induction day.* | ***Peer group pressure*** (=the influence that people like you have on you) *is effective when selling ideas.*

special interest group a group of people who all share the same aims, especially one that tries to influence government policy on a particular issue: *special-interest groups, such as the American Insurance Association and the National Venture Capital Association* —see also CONTROL GROUP, NEWSGROUP

group accounts —see under ACCOUNT[1]

group·age /ˈgruːpɪdʒ/ *n* [U] when several small CONSIGNMENTS (= quantities of goods) from different exporters that are being sent to the same place are packed and sent together by the FORWARDING AGENT to save costs and reduce charges. These consignments are listed together on one BILL OF LADING: *The Port of Rotterdam Distriparks offer groupage services and warehousing.* | *to take advantage of* ***groupage rates***

group insurance —see under INSURANCE

group of companies *n* plural **groups of companies** [C] FINANCE another name for a GROUP[1]

Group of Five abbreviation **G5** *n* Japan, Germany, France, UK, and the US, that agreed in 1986 to try to control the value of their currencies against each other more closely: *The central banks of the Group of Five agreed that they should regulate the decline in the dollar's foreign exchange value.*

Group of Seven abbreviation **G7** *n* a group of countries with the seven largest economies, Britain, Canada, France, Germany, Italy, Japan, and the US, whose finance ministers meet regularly to discuss economic and financial subjects that affect them and other countries. Russia is also usually invited to these meetings: *The Group of Seven industrialised countries should act against financial market speculation and stabilise exchange rates.*

Group of Ten abbreviation **G10** *n* a group of industrialized countries: the Group of Seven plus Belgium, the Netherlands, Sweden, and Switzerland, and others whose CENTRAL BANK officials meet regularly. A meeting of the Group of Ten may involve representatives from up to 20 countries: *The chairman of the bank governors' committee of the Group of Ten countries said that the G10 countries did not intend to sell more gold 'for the time being'.*

group·ware /ˈgruːpweə‖-wer/ *n* [U] COMPUTING software designed to be used on a number of different computers at the same time: *the availability of groupware such as Lotus Notes* | *a range of groupware applications*

grow /grəʊ‖groʊ/ *v* past tense **grew** past participle **grown** **1** [I] to increase in amount, size, or degree: *Seaman grew rapidly, becoming one of the largest advertisers in the New York area.* | *As the US starts to grow again, it will be a more attractive place in which to invest.* + **by**: *In the past 12 months, the labor force has grown by only 660,000.*

2 [T] *journalism* if you grow a business activity, you make it bigger: *As general manager of IBM Global Network, Whiteside has helped* ***grow the business*** *by more than 20% a year for the past three years.*

growth /grəʊθ‖groʊθ/ *n* [U] an increase in size, amount, or degree + **in**: ***Annual growth*** *in the $400 million ready-to-drink tea market is running at 15 to 20%.* | *To help its clients keep up with the* ***exponential*** (=extremely fast) ***growth*** *of market data, the bank has created the world's first integrated financial information system.* | *Paper cup manufacturing, an area with high profit margins, showed* ***strong growth.*** | *Officials have argued for lower interest rates because of recent* ***slow growth in*** *the economy.* | *There is likely to be very* ***low growth in*** *the industrial countries – perhaps in the 1% to 1.5% range.* | *China' slumping economy recorded* ***zero growth in*** (=no growth) *industrial output during the first quarter, although some signs of recovery were seen in March.* | *The last time the telecommunications industry had* ***negative growth*** (=when sth gets smaller) *was in the Great Depression.*

economic growth an increase in the value of goods and services produced in a country or area: *At 7% economic growth a year, the economy would double in size in less than a decade.* | *Spain will have* ***strong economic growth*** *and reduced unemployment through next year.*

external growth when a company increases its sales and profits by buying other companies, rather than from its own operations: *In view of the need to digest acquisitions made in the past two years, he said, Usinor Sacilor's external growth will pause this year.*

monetary growth an increase in the amount of money in the economy: *They want to cut high interest rates and inflation; to control monetary growth and reduce budget deficits.*

sustainable growth ◆ growth that it is possible SUSTAIN (=make continue) without causing economic problems: *The finance minister's goal was to put the economy on track for stable and sustainable growth.*

◆ economic growth that it is possible to sustain without causing environmental problems: *We want to unlock the resources of the living world, at the same time promoting competitive and sustainable growth.*

unsustainable growth ◆ growth that it is not possible to SUSTAIN (=make continue) without causing economic problems: *Even the health-care industry, which created 425,000 jobs in the past year, will eventually slow its unsustainable growth as efforts to cut costs take effect.*

◆ economic growth that it is not possible to sustain without causing environmental problems: *Ever since Malthus forecast a population explosion among the poor, there have been prophecies of unsustainable growth.*

growth area —see under AREA

growth fund —see under FUND[1]

growth industry —see under INDUSTRY

growth rate *n* [C] the speed at which something grows: *The main attraction of investing in the world's emerging stock markets is their much faster growth rates than those of developed countries.* | *The company said its* ***low growth rate*** *stems from the recession's impact on commercial and industrial customers.*

annualized growth rate also **annualised growth rate** *BrE* a rate for a whole year, calculated using the rate for a shorter period of time: *The economy raced ahead at a remarkable annualized growth rate of 10.4% in the first three months of the year.*

compound growth rate also **compounded growth rate** growth calculated over a period of years, showing the percentage increase for each year in relation to the year before, rather than the percentage increase over the whole period of time. The compound growth rate is the usual way of calculating growth rates: *Dividend per share has increased from 3.0p nine years ago to 15.8p today – a compound growth rate of 20% per annum.*

projected growth rate the rate something is expected to grow in the future: *growth stocks, as measured by the 50 stocks with the highest five-year projected growth rates*

growth share —see under SHARE

growth/share matrix *n* [singular] the idea that the profit obtained from a product depends on the growth rate of the particular market it is in and its share of that market. A product with high market share in a high-growth market is a STAR, and one with high market share in a low-growth market is a CASH COW. A product with low market share in a high-growth market is a PROBLEM CHILD, and one with low market share in a low-growth market is a DOG; BCG MATRIX; BOSTON MATRIX: *In 1970, the Boston Consulting Group's growth/share matrix still has a major influence on strategic thinking in many companies.* —see also EXPERIENCE CURVE, PORTFOLIO

growth stock —see under STOCK[1]

growth vector matrix *n* [singular] in CORPORATE PLANNING, the idea developed by Igor Ansoff in the 1960s that a company can grow by increasing its market share with its existing products, by introducing new products into the same market, by introducing its existing products into a new market, or by DIVERSIFYING (=developing new products in new markets): *The growth vector matrix indicates the directions a company can move in relation to its current product-market position.*

Grs. written abbreviation for GROSS; GRAMMES

GRT abbreviation for GROSS REGISTER TONNAGE

Gr. T. abbreviation for GROSS TON

grub·stake /ˈgrʌbˌsteɪk/ *n* [U] *informal AmE* money provided to develop a new business in return for a share of the profits

gr. wt. abbreviation for GROSS WEIGHT

GSM **1** Global System for Mobiles; a system that makes it possible for people to use MOBILE PHONES (=telephones you can carry with you and use in any place): *France Telecom wanted the Swiss PTT to pay a fee for the use of the French GSM network.*

2 abbreviation for GENERAL SALES MANAGER

guar. written abbreviation for GUARANTEE

guar·an·tee[1] /ˌgærənˈtiː/ *v* [T] **1** to make a formal written promise to repair or replace a product if it has a fault within a specific period of time after you buy it **guarantee sth against**: *The S2's galvanized bodyshell is guaranteed a full ten years against corrosion.*

2 to make a legal promise to repay a loan if the original borrower DEFAULTS (=fails to repay it or make interest payments on it): *The loan will finance Asia Cement's purchase of equipment from Fuller, and the loan will be guaranteed by Bangkok Bank.*

guarantee[2] *n* [C] **1** a formal written promise to repair or replace a product if it has a fault within a specific period of time after you buy it + **against**: *For new home-owners, some builders have now given a 20-year guarantee against structural defects.* **be under guarantee** (=be protected by a guarantee): *As the video camera was still under guarantee, he took it back to the shop to be repaired.*

performance guarantee ◆ another name for GUARANTEE: *We must restore reliability and the engines are covered by performance guarantees.*

◆ in selling a property or other investment, a guarantee by the seller that the property etc will reach a minimum level of profitability: *The sale of the ski resort is subject to performance guarantees that it will live up to expectations.*

◆ a contract between a supplier and a manufacturer that specifies conditions for the design and delivery of parts by the supplier: *Micro Compact Car has risk-sharing and performance guarantees with the component companies that are system partners on the project.*

2 FINANCE an agreement to be responsible for someone else's promise, especially a promise to repay a loan if the original borrower DEFAULTS (=fails to repay it or make interest payments on it)

3 FINANCE money or assets held by an organization until someone has paid their debts, or debts that they might have in the future: *Creditor banks holding part of the airline's assets as guarantees of earlier debts.*

bank guarantee a promise by a bank to repay a loan if the original borrower DEFAULTS: *Majestic would offer film producers financing, in the form of bank guarantees, in exchange for distribution rights.*

cross guarantee a guarantee given to a bank by several companies that are part of the same group of companies, when the bank lends money to one of the companies in the group

export credit guarantee a promise by a government organization to an exporter that they will repay loans taken out to finance the goods being exported if the importer fails to pay for them: *The 1990 farm law forbids the Agriculture Department from extending agricultural export credit guarantees to any country that can't adequately service the debt.*

loan guarantee a promise to repay a loan if the original borrower DEFAULTS: *The Canadian government agreed to contribute $2.3 billion in cash and loan guarantees toward Hibernia's development costs.*

guaranteed income bond —see under BOND

guaranteed price —see under PRICE[1]

guarantee fund —see under FUND[1]

guar·an·tor /ˌgærənˈtɔː‖-ˈtɔːr/ *n* [C] LAW a person or organization that promises to repay a loan if the borrower DEFAULTS (=fails to repay it): *EAC said that its Goodren unit is a borrower under the credit facilities and that EAC is a guarantor.* | *The federal government is the* ***ultimate guarantor*** (=the one that will repay if no one else does) *of these loans.*

G

guar·an·ty /ˈɡærənti/ *n* plural **guaranties** [C] *AmE* LAW a formal promise, especially of payment: *Our corporation is now owned by the federal government, but our debt doesn't carry an explicit government guaranty.* | ***Guaranty funds*** *provide the best system for protecting policyholders.*

guaranty bond also **guaranteed bond** —see under BOND

guard·i·an /ˈɡɑːdiən‖ˈɡɑːr-/ *n* [C] LAW someone who is legally responsible for looking after someone else, especially a child or someone who is mentally ill: *Mr. Gonzales became his young cousin's* ***legal guardian*** *after the child's parents died.*

guess·ti·mate /ˈgestɪmɪt/ *n* [C] *informal* an attempt to judge an amount or quantity by guessing it: *In these uncertain economic times, Wall Street earnings estimates more closely resemble guesstimates.* —**guesstimate** *v* [I,T] *In the absence of usable pricing information, the best most lawyers can do is to guesstimate a fee before they start work.*

guest worker —see under WORKER

GUI abbreviation for GRAPHICAL USER INTERFACE

guide[1] /ɡaɪd/ *n* [C] **1** something that provides you with information, figures etc on which you can base your judgement or method of doing something: *The key US and foreign annual interest rates below are a guide to general levels but don't always represent actual transactions.*

2 a book that provides information on a particular subject or explains how to do something: *the latest version of the company guide*

3 someone whose job is to show a place to people visiting it: *Saundra, who liked traveling, started a new career in her forties as a professional* ***tour guide****.*

guide[2] *v* [T] **1** to show someone the right way to do something, especially something difficult or complicated: *The Justice Department issued regulations to guide businesses on how to deal with their customers under the new laws.*

2 to take someone through or to a place that you know very well, showing them the way: *On the tour, we were personally guided through five of the rooms in the White House.*

guide price —see under PRICE[1]

guineapig director —see under DIRECTOR

gulf /ɡʌlf/ *n* [C] **1** a great difference or lack of understanding between two groups of people, especially in their beliefs, opinions, and way of life + **between**: *The South African Government must intervene to reduce the gulf between white wealth and black poverty.*

2 a big difference between two amounts, levels etc + **between**: *The result is a 30% gulf between actual company hirings this year and projected hiring next year.*

Gulf Co-operation Council —see under GCC

gu·ru /ˈɡʊruː/ *n* [C] *informal* **fashion/management etc guru** someone who knows a lot about fashion, managing businesses etc, that people consider to be a leader in their area and that they go to for advice: *Management gurus have looked at world-class firms in the hope of finding the magic formula for success.* | *a computer-science guru*

gyp /dʒɪp/ *v* past tense and past participle **gypped** present participle **gypping** [T] *informal AmE* to cheat someone: *You paid 50 bucks for those shoes? You were gypped!* —**gyp** *n* [C] *That new car I just bought was really a gyp – it already needs repairs!*

ha written abbreviation for HECTARE

ha•be•as cor•pus /ˌheɪbiəs ˈkɔːpəs‖-ˈkɔːr-/ *n* [U] LAW the right of someone in prison to come to a court of law so that the court can decide whether they should stay in prison: *40% of habeas corpus appeals are successful.*

hack[1] /hæk/ also **hack into** *v* [T] to secretly find a way to reach the information on someone else's computer system so that you can use, change, or damage it: *The police are investigating a series of computer crimes involving people thought to have hacked confidential databases.* | *He didn't have to hack into my personal computer to get the information.* —**hacking** *n* [U] *Hacking is easy if you know how to do it.*

hack away at sth *phr v* [T] to work slowly and with difficulty in order to reduce something: *Budget cutters are being forced to hack away at their favorite domestic programs.*

hack[2] *n* [C] **1** a writer who does a lot of low quality work, especially writing newspaper articles: *The paper printed a series of letters from an English hack living in Australia.*

2 *AmE informal* a taxi, or someone whose job is to drive a taxi

hack•er /ˈhækə‖-ər/ *n* [C] someone who secretly gets into another person's or company's computer system in order to use or change the information it holds, or to damage the system: *Intercepting messages on the Internet is easy for a smart hacker.*

had /hæd/ *adj* **be had** *informal* to be tricked or made to look stupid: *Skilled counterfeiting led stores to sell goods they thought were the real thing, only to find they'd been had.*

hae•mor•rhage *BrE*, **hemorrhage** *AmE* /ˈhemərɪdʒ/ *v* **haemorrhage red ink** *journalism* if a business, organization etc haemorrhages red ink, it loses a lot of money: *The state's long-term fiscal management has been solid, although the current budget threatens to hemorrhage red ink.*

hag•gle /ˈhægəl/ *v* [I] to argue about the price of something before reaching an agreement + **over**: *The Maine Legislature has been haggling over the state's budget for months.* —**haggling** *n* [U] *If the haggling continues and there is no budget by July 30, it'll mean no paychecks for 199,000 state workers.*

Hague Rules /ˈheɪg ruːlz/ *n* [plural] LAW a set of internationally accepted rules that must be followed when sending goods by sea: *Any damages caused by reckless acts are not covered under the Hague Rules.*

hair•cut /ˈheəkʌt‖ˈher-/ *n* [C] *AmE* FINANCE **1** a small amount off the normal selling price of a bond, share etc: *Congress forced depositors to take a mandatory 10 to 15% haircut in order to regulate the industry.*

2 a reduction in the BUDGET (=the amount of money to be spent) for a plan, investment etc: *By year end, the project had been given three haircuts, and the managers began to worry about its final outcome.*

half board —see under BOARD[1]

half-commission man *n* plural **half-commission men** [C] a person who introduces customers to a STOCKBROKER, or who works for one, and gets half of the COMMISSION for selling shares to a client as payment

half-dollar *n* [C] an American or Canadian coin worth 50 cents —see also DOLLAR

hall•mark[1] /ˈhɔːlmɑːk‖ˈhɒːlmɑːrk/ *n* [C] **1** an idea, quality, or skill that is typical of a particular person or thing: *Their ability to work under tight deadlines is a hallmark of their professionalism.*

2 a mark put on an object made of silver, gold, or PLATINUM that shows the quality of the metal, and where and when it was made: *a 1998 Philadelphia hallmark*

hallmark[2] *v* [T] to put a hallmark on silver, gold, or PLATINUM

hall test —see under TEST[1]

halo effect —see under EFFECT

halve /hɑːv‖hæv/ *v* [I,T] to go down to half of a previous amount, level etc, or to make something do this: *Since the boom, the currency halved and the bottom fell out of the luxury-car market.* | *He announced plans to sell more than $1 billion in assets and halve the company's dividend.*

halves /hɑːvz‖hævz/ *adv* **go halves** *informal* to share something equally: *We decided to go halves on the investment.*

ham•mer[1] /ˈhæmə‖-ər/ *n* **come/go under the hammer** to be sold at an AUCTION: *The paintings come under the hammer at Sotheby's in November.*

hammer[2] *v* **hammer the market** to sell a large amount of stocks, shares etc at one time, causing prices to fall: *Selling continued to hammer the market's larger corporations.*

hammer sth ↔ **out** *phr v* [T] to decide on an agreement, contract etc after a lot of discussion and disagreement: *The two companies will take several months to hammer out an agreement for splitting the profits.*

hand /hænd/ *n* **1** [C] someone who does physical work on a farm, in a factory etc: *Cooper held several odd jobs before coming to California to work as a* ***factory hand***. | *Jones hired himself out as a* ***deck hand*** *and cook on a Mexican fishing boat.*

2 by hand using your hands, not a machine: *Workers at the factory sand and* ***finish*** *the furniture* ***by hand***.

3 by hand delivered directly by one person to another, not sent through the post: *His letter of confirmation will leave today by hand.*

4 change hands if goods, property etc change hands, they pass from the old owner to the new owner: *More than 1.2 million IBM shares changed hands on Friday.*

5 on hand *AmE*, **to hand** *BrE* close by and ready when needed: *The company had to turn out orders on a reliable schedule and to keep enough cash on hand to pay the bills.*

6 time/money in hand extra time or money that is available to be used: *He has enough money in hand to stay on the airwaves through election day.*

7 at hand a situation or problem that is at hand is happening now: *Not all indicators of European economic performance suggest that a crisis is at hand.*

8 in hand being dealt with: *Don't worry – all the contract arrangements are in hand.*

9 show of hands a situation where people vote by raising their hands: *A show of hands revealed that nearly half of the people agreed with the chairman's resolution.*

10 shake hands to hold someone's hand when you meet in order to greet them or to show that you have reached an agreement: *Smiling broadly, the two leaders shook hands.* —see also HANDSHAKE

hand•book /ˈhændbʊk/ *n* [C] a book that provides information on a particular subject or explains how to do something; GUIDE: *Safety regulations are discussed in section 3 of the handbook.*

hand•i•craft /ˈhændikrɑːft‖-kræft/ *n* [C usually plural] objects produced by people using their hands skilfully: *Today, many small-scale handicrafts are being produced by larger factories.*

han•dle /ˈhændl/ *v* [T] **1** to deal with a difficult situation or problem: *First-time travelers get some peace of mind when an agency handles everything.*
2 to deal with a particular client or product: *Lintas currently handles Sara Lee baked goods and meat products.*
3 if you handle a particular job, you are responsible for doing it: *Christophson will handle merchandising and advertising as well as retaining his duties as president.*
4 to buy, sell, or deal with goods or services in business or trade: *Domestic car manufacturers have said their dealers are free to handle foreign cars if they wish.*
5 to move goods etc from one place to another: *We handle large volumes of imported goods.*

hand•ling /ˈhændlɪŋ/ *n* [U] **1** the way in which a problem, situation, or person is dealt with: *He is charged with securities fraud in the handling of his clients' accounts.* | *Inept handling of sackings is bad not just for those dismissed but for the employer as well.*
2 when goods etc are moved from one place to another: *The environmental unit deals with waste handling and clean-up.*
cargo handling the activity of moving cargo onto and off the ships, planes, or TRUCKS that are going to take it somewhere: *The Port of Belfast can offer its customers the most up-to-date, cost effective cargo handling facilities.*
materials handling the movement of materials within the same factory, or from one factory to another: *Materials handling is already commonly performed by robots in the manufacturing industry.*

handling charge also **handling fee** —see under CHARGE[1]

handling expense —see under EXPENSE

hand•out /ˈhændaʊt/ *n* [C] **1** money or goods that are given to someone, for example because they are poor: *Veterans said they're asking for jobs, not handouts.*
2 a piece of paper with information on it, given to the people at a meeting, event etc: *The Air Force gave reporters a handout listing staff locations and times of buses to the areas.*

hand-picked *adj* someone who is hand-picked is carefully chosen: *The environment we set up at Mac assumes that this special, hand-picked team is the best in the world.*

hand•shake /ˈhændʃeɪk/ *n* [C] **1** another name for GOLDEN HANDSHAKE
2 COMPUTING when one computer gives information to another computer, telling it that a connection has been made: *You will get a handshake telling you what system is on the other end.*
3 on a handshake if you do a deal on a handshake, you do it without making a formal contract or agreement: *I always did business on a handshake, but now you need 10-page contracts for everything.*

hand•shak•ing /ˈhændˌʃeɪkɪŋ/ *n* [U] COMPUTING the exchange of messages between computers that makes it possible for two machines in different places to work together: *The hardware handshaking is always active.*

hands-on experience —see under EXPERIENCE

hand•y /ˈhændi/ *adj* comparative **handier** superlative **handiest** used to describe things that are easy to use or carry, especially because they are small and light: *Look out for **handy size** packs of plasters.* | *a detergent in a handy 100 ml tube*

hang•ar /ˈhæŋə‖-ər/ *n* [C] a very large building where aircraft are kept

Hang Seng Index /ˌhæŋ ˈseŋ ˌɪndeks/ also **Hang Seng** —see under INDEX[1]

happy talk *n* [U] *journalism* news or other information that is intended to entertain or please people, rather than present a meaningful or realistic discussion of a situation or event: *They don't want happy talk, they want stories that give them solutions to problems.* | *Clinton listened to what his advisors had to say even when he didn't want to hear it. As a result, he got good information, not just happy talk.*

har•ass•ment /ˈhærəsmənt, həˈræsmənt/ *n* [U] when someone is treated in an unpleasant or threatening way: *The alleged harassment took place at the company's head office.*
racial harassment harassment of someone because of their race: *He alleged persistent racial harassment by his colleagues.*
sexual harassment harassment of someone because of their sex: *There have been a number of sexual harassment complaints.*

har•bour *BrE*, **harbor** *AmE* /ˈhɑːbə‖ˈhɑːrbər/ *n* [C] an area of calm water next to the land, where boats arrive and leave; PORT: *The island has a fine modern harbour.* | *The **harbour master** (=someone in charge of a harbour) may request the ship owner to remove the vessel.*

harbour dues —see under DUES

hard /hɑːd‖hɑːrd/ *adj* **hard facts/numbers** information based on things that can be measured, rather than feelings or opinions: *Investors are again showing respect for hard numbers like quarterly earnings.* | *We have to separate the myths from the hard facts.*

hard•ball /ˈhɑːdbɔːl‖ˈhɑːrdbɒːl/ *n informal* **play hardball** to be very determined to get what you want, especially in business or politics, without considering the feelings of others: *The car company is ready to play hardball in negotiations with the union.*

hard copy —see under COPY[1]

hard core *n* [C usually singular] those most involved or active in something, or who support something very strongly: *There is a hard core of users for videoconferencing, but it is certainly not a mass medium.*

hard-core unemployment —see under UNEMPLOYMENT

hard currency —see under CURRENCY

hard disk also **hard drive** —see under DISK

hard•en /ˈhɑːdn‖ˈhɑːrdn/ *v* [I] *BrE* if prices on a financial market harden, they go up: *Sainsbury advanced a penny to 296 pence, and Tesco hardened 4 pence to 225.5 pence.*

hard goods —see under GOODS

hard hat *n* [C] **1** a protective hat worn by builders: *Hard hats are now required by the Occupational Safety and Health Administration for all construction workers.*
2 *AmE informal* a worker in the building industry: *People working in television tend not to feel at home with hard hats and blue collars and view them as a form of exotic creature.*

hard loan —see under LOAN[1]

hard money —see under MONEY

hard sell *n* [singular] **1** when it is difficult to sell something: *It's a hard sell to convince young people who are the big spenders that cider is a fashionable drink.*
2 when someone uses a lot of pressure to get you to buy something or persuade you to do something: *Securities firms are encouraging brokers to soften their hard sell and win back the clients' faith.* | *Dealers are turning to **hard sell tactics** to convince customers to buy now*

hard selling —see under SELLING

hard up *adj informal* **1** not having enough money, especially for a short period of time: *We expected quite a bit of income from the Las Vegas project, but this has been postponed, so we're financially hard up.*
2 be hard up for something to not have enough of something for a particular period of time, especially work: *The media are obviously hard up for stories because they seem interested in this very mundane (=not interesting, ordinary) case.*

hard•ware /ˈhɑːdweə‖ˈhɑːrdwer/ *n* [U] **1** COMPUTING computer equipment, rather than the programs that make it work: *Unix runs on most types of* ***computer hardware****.* | *An* ***upgrade*** (=improvement) *in our* ***hardware*** *helped us cope with an expected rise in demand.* —compare SOFTWARE, FIRMWARE

2 equipment and tools for homes and gardens: *If the housing market is strong, hardware and electrical products benefit.*

3 the machinery and equipment needed to do something: *the shipment of US tanks and other* ***military hardware*** *to Saudi Arabia*

har•mo•nize also **harmonise** *BrE* /ˈhɑːmənaɪz‖ˈhɑːr-/ *v* [T] to make two or more systems, sets of rules etc more similar so that they work better together: *a European Commission directive to harmonise rules on copyright in different EU countries* —**harmonization** also **harmonisation** *BrE n* [U] *monetary union, followed by rapid harmonisation of tax and social laws*

harvesting strategy —see under STRATEGY

hatchet man *n* plural **hatchet men** [C] *informal* someone employed to make unpopular changes in an organization, especially ones which involve people losing their jobs: *He came in as a hatchet man and scared a lot of people.*

haul[1] /hɔːl‖hɒːl/ *v* [T] **1** if a train or TRUCK hauls goods, it takes them from one place to another: *The freight train hauled the load of 240 tons with ease.* | *Union Pacific hauls garbage from Seattle to a landfill in eastern Oregon.*

2 also **haul up** to officially make someone go to a senior manager, committee, or court to be judged on something they have done, especially something bad **+ before/in front of**: *Officials can be hauled before Congressional committees and asked to justify their policies.* | *Bar staff who serve drunk drivers may get hauled up in front of the local judge if those people are later involved in accidents.*

3 haul sb over the coals to speak to someone angrily and severely because they have done something wrong: *He might be hauled over the coals and forced to resign if his manager did not agree with his actions.*

haul[2] *n* [C] **1** the amount of fish caught in one net or in one period of time: *Demand for fishing boats depends on estimated sizes of fish hauls.*

2 a large amount of stolen or illegal goods that has been found by the police or CUSTOMS **+ of**: *A* ***haul of*** *stolen cars has been seized by police.* | *a £1million* ***drugs haul***

3 long/short haul connected with long or short journeys by plane: *KLM earns most of its revenue on* ***long-haul flights****.* | *a popular short-haul destination*

haul•age /ˈhɔːlɪdʒ‖ˈhɒːl-/ *BrE*, **haul•ing** *AmE* /ˈhɔːlɪŋ‖ˈhɒː-/ *n* [U] the business of carrying goods by road or rail: *Rail freight charges are high compared with those of* ***road haulage****.* | *a successful* ***haulage company***

general haulage the business of carrying goods of any kind by road or rail: *General haulage is expensive and it is more profitable for companies to specialize.*

heavy haulage the business of carrying heavy goods such as coal and steel by road or rail: *a heavy haulage company based in Sheffield*

haulage contractor —see under CONTRACTOR

haul•i•er /ˈhɔːliə‖ˈhɒːliər/ *BrE*, **haul•er** *AmE* /ˈhɔːlə‖ˈhɒːlər/ *n* [C] someone who owns or manages a haulage business

hawk[1] /hɔːk‖hɒːk/ *n* [C] a politician or official who believes in using force or firm action when dealing with problems, rather than a more peaceful approach: *Mr George has a reputation as* ***a hawk on*** *inflation.* | *He has always been* ***a deficit hawk*** (=a politician who wants to reduce the amount of money the government owes). —compare DOVE —**hawkish** *adj*: *Mr. Iacocca's hawkish stance didn't do much for Cherokee's image in Japan.*

hawk[2] *v* [T] **1** *journalism* to sell: *Jenner is an ex-athlete who now hawks exercise equipment.*

2 *disapproving* to try to make people interested in something or to try to make them buy something: *He's been on every chat show hawking his new movie.*

Haw•thorne ef•fect /ˈhɔːθɔːn ɪˌfekt‖ˈhɔːrɔːrn-/ —see under EFFECT

Hay system —see under SYSTEM

haz•ard /ˈhæzəd‖-ərd/ *n* [C] something that may be dangerous, cause problems, accidents etc: *There may be other workplaces with similar* ***fire hazards****.* | *One of the company's biggest* ***financial hazards****, the C-17 military cargo plane, appears to being doing better now.* | *We want to take waste away from places where it poses a* ***health hazard****.* | ***environmental hazards***

moral hazard INSURANCE the idea that some people or companies are a bigger insurance risk than others, because of their past behaviour or their present situation. For example, someone who has spent time in prison is more likely to make a dishonest claim: *Certain groups must pay higher premiums, to account for the moral hazard problem.*

occupational hazard a risk that always exists in a particular job: *Coal dust exposure is an occupational hazard for coal miners.*

head[1] /hed/ *n* [C] **1** the leader or person in charge of a group, organization, or part of an organization **+ of**: *The head of each division is responsible for its operating performance.* | *Stone was head of corporate finance at Coopers & Lybrand.* | *Work is divided into different areas and is supervised by* ***section heads****.*

2 head receptionist/trader/cashier etc the most senior RECEPTIONIST etc: *Any cash received must be double-checked by the head receptionist.*

3 have a (good) business head to be able to make sensible and PROFITABLE business decisions

4 a head/per head for each person: *A conference for 70 people will work out at around £30 a head per day.* | *Expenditure per head on training had been growing rapidly.*

5 head on if you deal with a problem head on, you deal with it in a very brave and direct way: *The issue has to be tackled head on.*

6 head on if two companies compete head on, they each try to be successful selling the same product or service: *Instead of trying to* ***compete head on*** *with stores like Our Price and HMV, he moved down-market, stocking cheaper CDs and tapes.*

7 have/be given a head start to have an advantage that helps you to be successful **+ over**: *Banks will have a head start over their non-banking rivals in selling products across the EC.*

8 keep your head above water to only just manage to keep your company in business or live on the income you earn: *These are savings that defence companies have to make to keep their heads above water.*

9 go over sb's head *disapproving* if you go over the head of your BOSS (=the person who you normally take orders from at work), you ask his or her boss something instead of asking him or her directly: *My boss was angry because I went over his head to the department manager.*

10 heads will roll *spoken* used to say that someone will lose their job or be punished for a mistake they have made

head[2] *v* [T] **1** also **head up** to be in charge of a group, an organization, or part of an organization: *Perelman heads the Revlon cosmetics empire.*

2 be headed if a page is headed with a particular word or sentence, it has it on the top: *The three columns are headed budget, actual and variance.*

3 head north/south *informal* FINANCE if a share price, currency etc heads north, it rises in value. If it heads south, it falls in value: *He expects investors to push the*

Dow Jones industrials to yet another high in coming weeks. "My best guess is that there will be another try to head north from here." | *Right now, the rouble is heading south.*

head down *phr v* [I] if a share price, currency etc heads down, or is headed down, it falls in value: *Futures markets suggest oil prices may be headed down.*

head sth ↔ **off** *phr v* [T] to take action to prevent something bad from happening: *China needs to find oil in time to head off a serious energy crisis.*

head up *phr v* **1** [T] **head** sth ↔ **up** to be in charge of an organization, part of an organization, or group: *Perkins left his post to head up marketing at Pizza Hut.*
2 [I] if a share price, currency etc heads up, or is headed up, it increases in value: *Commodity prices began heading up just after the recession ended.*

head·count /ˈhedkaʊnt/ also **head count** *n* [C] **1** *informal* the number of people employed by an organization: *The new company will operate out of its parent's offices with an initial headcount of 20 staff.*
2 do a headcount to count how many people are present at a place or event: *I **did a** quick **headcount** to see how many people had come to the meeting.*

head·ed /ˈhedɨd/ *adj* **headed notepaper/paper** paper for writing letters that has your name and address, or that of your company, at the top: *All letters to clients must be printed on headed paper.*

head·er /ˈhedə‖-ər/ *n* [C] the line of information at the top of a computer screen or a printed page —compare FOOTER

head honcho —see under HONCHO

head·hunt /ˈhedhʌnt/ *v* [T] to find a manager with the right skills and experience to do a particular job, often by persuading a suitable person to leave their present job: *Mr Birt **was headhunted** to be director of the BBC.* —**headhunter** *n* [C] *They hired a headhunter to search out a replacement.* —**headhunting** *n* [U] *Most **headhunting firms** offer a professional and high-quality service.*

head·line /ˈhedlaɪn/ *adj* **1 headline figure/rate** *BrE* in Britain, a figure that shows the general level of inflation, including MORTGAGE payments (=repayments on a loan for buying a house): *The headline rate of inflation is being pushed towards 4% by higher mortgage costs.* —compare UNDERLYING
2 headline trading/investment when a person or company trades or invests on the basis of information they get from the news

headline inflation —see under INFLATION

head office —see under OFFICE

head·quar·tered /ˈhedˌkwɔːtəd, hedˈkwɔːtəd‖-ɔːrtərd/ *adj* [not before a noun] having your headquarters in a particular place: *Pearson is a media company with worldwide operations headquartered in the UK.*

head·quar·ters /ˈhedˌkwɔːtəz, ˌhedˈkwɔːtəz‖-ɔːrtərz/ *n* [plural] the head office or main building of an organization: *The company moved its **corporate headquarters** to Houston.*

heads of agreement —see under AGREEMENT

head tax —see under TAX[1]

health /helθ/ *n* [U] **1** the business of providing medical services to keep people healthy; HEALTHCARE: *Increased resources had been made available for health, housing, and education.* | *Rentokil specialises in industrial products in the field of **public health**.* | *Health inspectors came to check the factory's canteen.*
environmental health the activity of protecting people from things that could damage their health or affect their life in some other bad way: *Your **environmental health officer** will check the temperature of your refrigeration equipment.*
2 used to talk about how successful an organization, system, or economy is: *This is a serious threat to the health of Japan's banking system.* | *The balance sheet provides a lot of information on the **financial health** of the company.*
3 a clean bill of health if a system or an organization gets a clean bill of health, it is said to be in a good financial position after a detailed examination of it has been made: *A meeting of EC finance ministers **gave** the European exchange-rate mechanism **a clean bill of health**.*
4 give sth a clean bill of health to make an official statement that a product is not harmful or dangerous: *Lawyers said the company had something to hide about the drug's development, but the FDA gave Prozac a clean bill of health.*

health and safety *n* [U] the activity of protecting employees from illness or injury at work: *In the construction industry, health and safety is of considerable importance.* | *It is a well-run center that **meets health and safety standards**.*

Health and Safety Executive abbreviation **HSE** *n* HUMAN RESOURCES the official British government organization that makes sure that companies are using safe methods of production etc

health authority —see under AUTHORITY

health·care /ˈhelθkeə‖-ker/ also **health care** *n* [U] the activity of looking after people's health, considered as an industry: *An ageing population creates greater expenditure on health care.* | *a New York investment banking firm specializing in **healthcare companies***

health insurance —see under INSURANCE

health maintenance organization —see HMO

health plan *n* [C] INSURANCE an insurance policy that pays for medical treatment if you are sick or injured

Health Service *n* another name for the NATIONAL HEALTH SERVICE, the national government system for health care in Britain; NHS: *a management position in the Health Service*

health warning *n* [C] **1** a warning that certain products must display by law, telling customers that the product is bad for their health: *Cigarettes carry a **government health warning**.*
2 FINANCE in Britain, a warning that advertisements for financial products must contain, telling people that the value of their investments can go down as well as up: *If ever an investment needed a health warning, it was the Channel Tunnel, which might never have produced a penny of income.*

health·y /ˈhelθi/ *adj* comparative **healthier** superlative **healthiest** **1** a healthy organization, system, economy etc is working effectively and successfully: *Banks should invest only in financially healthy companies.*
2 a healthy amount of something is large: *They are predicting **healthy profits** on the shares.* | *I hope to see a **healthy return** on my investment.* | *Industry needs a **healthy supply** of graduates.*

hear·ing /ˈhɪərɪŋ‖ˈhɪr-/ *n* [C] a meeting of a court or special committee to find out the facts about a case: *A **court hearing** is unlikely before the end of next year.* | *The attorneys' actions prevented the defendant from **getting a fair hearing**.*
confirmation hearing ◆ in the US, a hearing to approve the choice of someone for an official job: *At her confirmation hearing, she said she opposed Treasury-backed legislation concerning futures trading.*
◆ in the US, a hearing to approve an earlier decision of another court of law: *A confirmation hearing on the reorganization plan is scheduled for July 11.*
disciplinary hearing a meeting between senior people at a company and a worker who has done something wrong in order to judge the case and decide what his or her punishment will be: *You may wish to have a solicitor present at your disciplinary hearing.*

H

public hearing a hearing where anyone affected by a particular problem can give their views: *The Food and Drug Administration plans to schedule a public hearing on whether anti-depressant drugs can encourage suicide.*

heav·y /ˈhevi/ *adj* comparative **heavier** superlative **heaviest** if the price of shares in a particular company is heavy, it is high in relation to the prices of other shares on the same stockmarket. A company with a heavy share price may divide its shares into a larger number of units to make them easier to buy and sell

heavy duty also **heavy-duty** *adj* [only before a noun] heavy duty materials, equipment etc are strong and suitable for hard work: *heavy-duty gearboxes used in tanks* | *heavy duty workwear* —compare LIGHT-DUTY, MEDIUM-DUTY

heavy engineering —see under ENGINEERING

heavy equipment —see under EQUIPMENT

heavy goods vehicle —see under VEHICLE

heavy haulage —see under HAULAGE

heavy hitter *n* [C] *journalism* a person or organization with a lot of influence and power: *We wanted a heavy hitter as chairman and felt that share options were a good way to attract one.*

heavy industry —see under INDUSTRY

heavy machinery —see under MACHINERY

heavy share —see under SHARE

heavy trading —see under TRADING

heav·y·weight /ˈheviweɪt/ *n* [C] *informal* a person or organization with a lot of influence and power: *Among the oil companies involved in production are **industry heavyweights** Chevron Corp, Texaco Inc and Exxon Corp.* | *The agency's heavyweight clients include RJR Nabisco.*

hec·tare /ˈhektɑː, -teə‖-ter/ *n* [C] a unit for measuring area, equal to 10,000 square metres

hec·tic /ˈhektɪk/ *adj* hectic trading is when a lot of people buy and sell shares, currencies etc; FRANTIC: *hectic trading in which 3.1 million shares changed hands*

hecto- /hektəʊ‖-toʊ/ *prefix* used in units of measurement to mean 100. For example, one hectogram is equal to 100 grams

hedge[1] /hedʒ/ *n* [C] FINANCE something that gives you protection against a financial risk, for example FUTURES (=agreements to buy or sell currencies etc on a fixed date in the future at a fixed price) or OPTIONS (=rights to buy or sell currencies etc at a particular price within a particular period of time or on a particular date in the future): *They decided that diesel fuel for the company's trucks would rise by at least 10 cents a gallon, and have done some forward buying as a hedge.* | *The firm provides many option **hedge strategies** to accommodate customers' risk management requirements.* + **against**: *Investors often buy precious metals as a hedge against inflation.*

hedge[2] *v* **1** [I,T] FINANCE if you hedge a financial risk, you protect yourself against it, for example with FUTURES (=agreements to buy or sell currencies etc on a fixed date in the future at a fixed price) or OPTIONS (=rights to buy or sell currencies etc at a particular price within a particular period of time or on a particular date in the future): *I've never hedged currencies before. But I could see the dollar was getting lower, and I hedged for the first time, betting that the dollar would rise.* | *Northwest Airlines saved more than $7 million in fuel costs because it hedged 4.2 million gallons of its fuel purchases for each month by buying futures contracts.* —**hedging** *n* [U] *Manufacturers have been doing more hedging because they expect prices for copper to rise.* | *sophisticated currency hedging techniques*

hedge against sth *phr v* [T] if you hedge against, or hedge yourself against, a financial risk, you protect yourself against it by hedging: *Consumers of a raw material can hedge against price movements through the futures markets.* | *Many companies have not hedged themselves against a rising yen.* | *Although invested in Europe, they weren't sufficiently hedged against currency changes.*
2 hedge your bets to reduce your chances of failure or loss by having several choices available to you: *Promoters, uncertain whether losing weight was going to stay popular, hedged their bets by advertising that their products would either help you add weight or reduce it.*

hedge fund —see under FUND[1]

hedging instrument —see under INSTRUMENT

heir /eə‖er/ *n* [C] the person who has the legal right to receive another person's money, property, or business after that person has died + **to**: *Taki is heir to a Greek shipping fortune.*

heir apparent *n* [singular] *journalism* someone who is expected to become head of an organization after the present head leaves: *Mr O'Reilly is to be succeeded as chief executive at Heinz by William Johnson, for a long time his heir apparent.*

heir·loom /ˈeəluːm‖ˈer-/ *n* [C] a valuable object that has been owned by a family for many years and that is passed, for example, from grandfather to father to son: *The clock is a **family heirloom**.*

hel·i·port /ˈhelipɔːt‖-pɔːrt/ *n* [C] a small airport for HELICOPTERS

help /help/ *n* [U] people that organizations employ, especially for a short time; TEMPS *BrE*: *To meet increased demand, companies have hired temporary help.*

help menu —see under MENU

her·e·dit·a·ment /ˌherɪˈdɪtəmənt/ *n* [U] LAW land and buildings, and the advantages in owning them: *Rates are not payable on any unoccupied hereditament for any period during which the owner was prohibited by law from occupying the property.*

corporeal hereditament an advantage relating to the ownership of property that exists physically: *buildings or parts of buildings (however they are divided) and other corporeal hereditaments*

incorporeal hereditament an advantage relating to the ownership of land or buildings that does not exist physically: *Additional rights include incorporeal hereditaments such as rights of way.*

her·i·ta·ble /ˈherɪtəbəl/ *adj* LAW heritable property can be passed from the older members of a family to the younger members when the older ones die: *tenants with no heritable interest in the buildings they occupy*

heritage industry —see under INDUSTRY

heu·ris·tics /hjʊˈrɪstɪks/ *n* [U] *formal* a method of solving problems by trying different things and seeing what happens, rather than using specific tests that you know will produce particular results: *Expert Systems use knowledge and heuristics to solve complex problems.*

HGV abbreviation for HEAVY GOODS VEHICLE: *an HGV licence*

hid·den /ˈhɪdn/ *adj* hidden costs, charges etc are difficult to notice, for example because they are not included in the basic price of something: *Make sure you're clear about what you are paying for, as there may be **hidden extras**.* | *The current system imposes dozens of **hidden subsidies** and **taxes** on each enterprise.*

hidden agenda —see under AGENDA

hidden reserves —see under RESERVES

hidden unemployment —see under UNEMPLOYMENT

hi•er•ar•chy /ˈhaɪrɑːki‖-ɑːr-/ *n* plural **hierarchies** **1** [C,U] an organization or structure in which the staff are organized in levels and the people at one level have authority over those below them: *Many companies have restructured their* ***organizational hierarchies.*** | *the key men in the* ***company hierarchy*** —see also MASLOW'S HIERARCHY OF NEEDS
2 [C] COMPUTING a structure in which files, information etc are organized in levels, each one being reached from the previous one: *Each disk is divided into a hierarchy of directories.* —**hierarchical** *adj*: *Research shows that hierarchical organisations are slow to respond to change.* | *a hierarchical structure of files* —**hierarchically** *adv*: *The police bureaucracy is organized hierarchically.*

high[1] /haɪ/ *n* [C] a maximum amount, figure, value etc in a particular period of time: *Advancing stocks again led as 162 issues* ***reached new highs*** *and only 14 dropped to new lows.*
historic high also **historical high** the highest level ever reached: *Oil stocks are at historic highs.*
intraday high the highest level reached in a financial market on a particular day: *The dollar reached an intraday high of DM1.5350 and later approached that level several times.*
life-of-contract high in FUTURES TRADING, the highest level reached during a particular CONTRACT: *Cotton futures prices set life-of-contract highs on continued concerns about tight supply.*
record high the highest level ever reached: *London share prices closed at record highs Thursday.*
session high the highest level reached on a financial market in a particular TRADING SESSION: *Centocor ended up at 33 1/2, although below its session high.*

high[2] *adj* **1** a high amount, number, or level is more than normal, more than average, or more than it was before: ***high interest rates*** | *Gas prices were high and expected to go higher.* | *A* ***high proportion*** *of female directors are in the 35-to-55 age range.* | *Sales to rental car companies made up a* ***high percentage*** *of the vehicles sold by General Motors.* | *There is still a* ***high risk*** *that the US currency will fall back during the year.*
2 containing a lot of a particular substance or quality: *coal with high energy content, low sulfur and low ash*
high in sth: *Diets high in sodium can increase the risk of heart disease.*
3 having an important position in an organization: *Western-educated technocrats* ***high up*** *in powerful bureaucracies* —compare LOW[1]

high[3] *adv* at or to a high amount, number, level etc: *Prices could go even higher early this year.* | *The corn harvest could range* ***as high as*** *8.5 billion bushels, up roughly one billion bushels from last year.*

high and low *n* plural **highs and lows** [C] the maximum and minimum levels reached in a particular period of time: *The 12-month high and low for the index are 278.40 and 202.99.* | *He likes to see how strong the market is by comparing the number of new highs with the total of new highs and lows.*

High Commission *n* [C] a building in a COMMONWEALTH country where the official representatives of another Commonwealth country work. A High Commission is similar to an EMBASSY: *the UK High Commission in Harare*

High Commissioner *n* [C] the chief representative of one COMMONWEALTH country in another Commonwealth country. A High Commissioner is similar to an AMBASSADOR

high coupon —see under COUPON

High Court —see under COURT[1]

high end *n* [singular] **1** if a figure, amount etc is at the high end of what people expected it to be, it is near the top of that range + **of**: *Dreyer's Grand Ice Cream Inc.'s fourth-quarter profit was near the high end of analysts' estimates of 11 to 14 cents a share.*
2 the high end of a market or product range consists of the most expensive products in that market or range + **of**: *Maytag continued to aim at the high end of the dishwasher market, where sales weren't large but profits were.* | *Blaupunkt, maker of high-end car stereo equipment*

high-end product —see under PRODUCT

higher-up *AmE*, **high-up** *BrE* —*n* [C] *informal* someone who has a high rank in an organization: *Restaurant managers have been known to fill in customer comment cards themselves just to impress their higher-ups.*

high finance —see under FINANCE[1]

high flyer also **high flier** *n* [C] **1** an extremely successful person, organization, etc: *Retailing is not generally the first career choice of young high fliers.* | *The Albert Fisher group was a high flier in the 1980s when it expanded rapidly through acquisitions, but profits later collapsed.*
2 FINANCE shares or other investments that are doing well on the stock exchange: *Other high fliers included water and electricity shares.* —**high-flying** *adj*: *The day's most active and high-flying tech stock was Octel Communications, which jumped 4 to close at 23 5/8.*

high-grade *adj* [only before a noun] **1** of high quality: *750 million barrels high-grade crude oil* | *high-grade beef*
2 FINANCE high-grade bonds etc have a low risk of DEFAULT (=not being repaid): *While high-grade corporate bonds ended between 1/4 and 3/8 point higher, junk bonds finished only marginally higher.*

high-level language —see under LANGUAGE

high-level management —see under MANAGEMENT

highly geared *BrE*, **highly leveraged** *AmE* —*adj* FINANCE **1** having a lot of debt in relation to SHARE CAPITAL. This is important when considering the cost of repaying debt in relation to paying DIVIDENDS to SHAREHOLDERS, and in questions of ownership of the company: *Many firms are highly geared, having borrowed to expand their businesses. Now, with incomes falling, interest payments are almost impossible to meet.* | *There still are many highly leveraged companies that are close to defaulting.*
2 a highly leveraged or highly geared loan etc is one where a lot of money is borrowed in relation to the amount of capital already held by the borrower: *Highly geared first-time buyers were especially at risk when interest rates began rising.* | *a bank that lent money to finance a* ***highly leveraged transaction*** *that failed*

highly leveraged capital structure —see under STRUCTURE

high net worth individual abbreviation **HNWI** *n* [C] *journalism* a very rich person: *High net worth individuals increasingly turn to their private banks for corporate finance advice.*

high-pow•ered *adj* **1** having a powerful and important job: *a high-powered, Yale University-educated lawyer*
2 a high-powered machine, vehicle, or piece of equipment is very powerful: *high-powered computers with massive storage capabilities*

high-pres•sure *adj* [only before a noun] **1** a high-pressure job or situation is one where you need to work extremely hard; STRESSFUL: *He helped launch the television network and then left the high-pressure job after disagreements with a colleague.*
2 high-pressure sales/selling methods etc very direct methods of selling that try to force people to buy:

H

They used high pressure sales tactics to force unwary customers to buy securities that were worthless.

high-price also **high-priced** *adj* expensive in relation to other things of the same kind: *high-powered, high-priced cars such as Porsches and BMWs*

high-ranking *adj* [only before a noun] having a high position in a government or other organization: *The firm's new management has slashed costs – dismissing many highly paid, high-ranking employees.*

high-rise *adj* [only before a noun] high-rise buildings are tall with many floors: *3,000,000 square feet of office space in three high-rise towers in downtown Dallas* —**high-rise** *n* [C] *It differed from the other projects in that it included both high-rises and houses.* —compare LOW-RISE

high-roller *n* [C] *informal AmE* someone who spends a lot of money carelessly or who risks a lot of money, especially in GAMBLING (=risking money on the results of card games, races etc): *For really high rollers there is Marquis Louis Roederer Crystal champagne at $205 a bottle.*

high seas *n* [plural] the areas of ocean that do not belong to any particular country: *the need to establish regional organizations which would regulate fishing on the high seas and settle disputes* —compare TERRITORIAL WATERS

high season —see under SEASON

high street *n* [C] *BrE* the main street of a town where many shops and businesses are: *The fashion industry has established better links through design and manufacturing to the high street.* | *Retailers hope the interest rate cut may boost shoppers' confidence and **high street spending** in the run-up to Christmas.*

High Street bank —see under BANK[1]

high-tech also **hi-tech** /ˌhaɪ ˈtek◂/ *adj* high-tech equipment, activities etc involve or use advanced technology: ***High-tech companies** must keep their specialized personnel in order to explore emerging technologies.* | *Like most **high-tech products** when they first hit the market, Sony's latest offering won't be cheap.* | ***high-tech industries*** —opposite LOW-TECH

high-tech industry —see under INDUSTRY

high technology —see under TECHNOLOGY

high-tech product —see under PRODUCT

high-up *n* [C] *BrE informal* someone who has a high rank in an organization; HIGHER-UP *AmE*

highway robbery *n* [U] *informal* a situation where something costs much more than it should: *National Football League pricing is highway robbery, and way out of reach for the average family.*

high-yield also **high-yielding** *adj* **1** FINANCE a high-yield investment gives a high level of interest or a high DIVIDEND: *Kroger Co. will buy back as much as $100 million of its high-yield debt in a move to lighten its debt load.* | *Owens-Illinois has retired about $1 billion of high-yielding junk bonds by replacing them with new, lower yielding senior notes.* —**high-yielder** *n* [C] *High-yielders such as the Canadian and Australian dollars are backed by high domestic interest rates.*

2 a high-yield crop is one that produces large quantities of grain etc: *Africa is now getting high-yield crop varieties and farming systems.*

high-yield fund —see under FUND[1]

high-yield market —see under MARKET[1]

hike[1] /haɪk/ *n* [C] *informal* a large increase in prices, taxes, or INTEREST RATES + **in**: *The government is proposing massive hikes in taxation.* | *There is growing public concern over **price hikes** and joblessness.*

hike[2] *v* [T] *informal* to increase prices, taxes, or INTEREST RATES by a large amount: *The Chancellor introduced VAT on domestic fuel and power bills as well as hiking National Insurance contributions.*

hin·ter·land /ˈhɪntəlænd‖-ər-/ *n* [singular] ECONOMICS the area around a particular place, especially a large city, that is economically important for that place: *Shanghai, and the vast hinterland of the Yangtze River delta*

Hip *n* [C] *BrE* PROPERTY home income plan; an arrangement that allows you to have an income from the EQUITY in your home (=the part of your home's value that would belong to you if the house was sold): *The alternative to the mortgage-based Hip is a plan where you sell, rather than mortgage, part or all of your house.* —see also SHIP

hire[1] /haɪə‖haɪr/ *v* [T] **1** to employ a person or an organization for a short time to do a particular job for you: *The company has hired an investment banking firm to assist with managing its pension fund.*

2 to agree to give someone a permanent job: *The company has just hired 250 new staff.* | *The board has **hired and fired** a number of top chief executives in the past few years.* + **as**: *He was hired as the company's chairman last year.*

3 *BrE* to pay money to use something for a period of time; RENT *AmE*: *You can hire a car at the airport.*

hire sth/sb ↔ **out** *phr v* [T] *BrE* to allow someone to use something or someone for a period of time in exchange for money: *They hire out photocopiers and other office equipment.* | *a company that hires out computer engineers*

hire[2] *n* **1** [U] *BrE* an arrangement by which someone borrows something for a period of time in exchange for money; RENTAL: *All our equipment is available **for hire**.* | *The engine is **on hire** from a local firm.* | *We want to keep **hire charges** on plant and machinery to a minimum.*

2 [C] *AmE* someone who starts to work for an organization; RECRUIT: *The firm's hires included economist Richard Hoey and investment strategist Joseph Cohen.* | *Nearly half Andersen's **new hires** are women.*

hire purchase *n* [U] *BrE* a way of buying expensive goods by making regular payments over a period of time. Under hire purchase, the person buying the goods has a right to use the goods during the time they are paying for them, but does not become the legal owner until the final payment has been made; INSTALLMENT PLAN *AmE*: *A lot of new cars are bought **on hire purchase**.* | *a **hire purchase agreement*** | ***Hire purchase sales** have fallen in recent months.* | *The **hire purchase price** is always higher than the cash price.*

hire purchase contract —see under CONTRACT[1]

hir·er /ˈhaɪərə‖ˈhaɪrər/ *n* [C] *BrE* **1** a person or organization that hires someone or something: *The hirer of equipment must provide proof that they carry the necessary insurance.* | *tax breaks for hirers of disadvantaged workers*

2 *BrE* LAW a person who is buying something on hire purchase: *Under a hire purchase agreement, the goods become the hirer's property only when the final installment has been paid.*

his·to·gram /ˈhɪstəgræm/ *n* [C] another name for BAR CHART —see under CHART[1]

historical cost —see under COST[1]

historic cost —see under COST[1]

historic high —see under HIGH[1]

hit[1] /hɪt/ *v* past tense and past participle **hit** present participle **hitting** **1** [T] to reach a particular level or number: *Profits should hit $23 million this year.* | *The company's shares hit a 52-week high of $34 last Friday.*

2 [T] to have a bad effect on something: *Strikes hit several ports in Australia last month.* | *The industry has been **badly hit** by the rise in oil prices.* | *A number of computer*

H

retail chains have been ***hit hard*** *by the recession.*
3 [I] when a RECESSION hits, it begins: *A final blow to the company came when the recession hit in 1990.*
4 hit the market/shops/shelves to become available for people to buy: *This new generation of computers is expected to hit the market some time next year.*
5 hit the jackpot to be very successful and make a lot of money: *The company hit the jackpot with its New Kids range of clothing.*

hit² *n* [C] **1** something that is extremely popular and successful: *Their latest computer game has been a* ***big hit*** *with customers.* | *The group is currently on tour promoting its latest* ***hit single.***
2 take a hit *AmE* if a person or organization takes a hit, they suffer from a problem: *The construction industry took a serious hit as jobs declined by 37,000 during the first 10 months of the year.*
3 take a hit *AmE* FINANCE if a company takes a hit in its financial results, it pays a CHARGE (=a cost related to a particular event, usually one that is not repeated in later periods of time): *After charges for the sale of some European operations, Campbell will take a hit of $302 million, or $2.33 a share.* | *The bank took a huge hit in charges to clean up the mess in its African subsidiaries.*
4 COMPUTING an occasion when someone looks at a particular WEBSITE on the INTERNET: *The Winter Olympics website had over 600 million hits in 16 days.*

hit list —see under LIST¹

hive /haɪv/ *v*
hive sth ↔ **off** *phr v* [T] *BrE* to separate one part of a business or organization from the rest, for example by selling it or using it to form a new company + **into**: *The computer software part of the business has been hived off into a new company.*

HMG *n* Her Majesty's Government or His Majesty's Government; the British government at a particular time: *HMG will not be able to ignore the arguments set out in this report.*

HMO *n* [C] health maintenance organization; a form of health insurance in the US where the person who is insured can use particular doctors, hospitals etc that are taking part in the arrangement: *The health center serves 63,000 HMO members and 8,000 Medicare beneficiaries.* | *HMO premiums have increased significantly in recent years.*

H

HMSO *n* Her/His Majesty's Stationery Office; a British government organization which prints and sells government papers, documents, and books. It became The Stationery Office or TSO in 1997, and is now run as a COMMERCIAL COMPANY (=one that is run for profit): *The document is available price £5 from TSO and booksellers.*

HNWI abbreviation for HIGH NET WORTH INDIVIDUAL

HO written abbreviation for HEAD OFFICE

Ho written abbreviation for house, used in addresses

hoard¹ /hɔːd‖hɔːrd/ *v* [T] to collect and save large amounts of something in order to sell it later at a high price or because you think there might not be enough available in the future: *Banks must be discouraged from hoarding dollars.* | *He accused big companies of hoarding available stocks of grain.* —**hoarder** *n* [C] *America is the biggest official gold hoarder.*

hoard² *n* [C] a store of money or goods kept to be used or sold in the future: *a huge institution with a cash hoard of more than 10 billion marks*

hoard·ing /ˈhɔːdɪŋ‖ˈhɔːr-/ *n* **1** [U] when you collect and save large amounts of something in order to sell it later at a high price or because you think there might not be enough available in the future: *There has been an increase in cash hoarding ahead of the government's proposed tax on interest income.*
2 [C] *BrE* a large sign used for advertising; BILLBOARD *AmE*

hock /hɒk‖hɑːk/ *n informal* **1 be in hock** to be in debt: *The newspaper is now in hock to a group of business tycoons.* | *The Egyptian economy was effectively in hock.*
2 go into hock to go into debt: *The company went $1.5 billion into hock.*
3 put sth in hock *BrE* if you put something in hock, you sell it temporarily because you need the money; PAWN: *Most of their possessions are already in hock.*

hoist /hɔɪst/ *v* [T] to increase something quickly or suddenly: *California is getting ready to hoist its sales tax next week.* | *The new line helped Reebok regain brand momentum, boost profits, and hoist its stock price.* —**hoist** *n* [C] *High Street banks raised their lending rates by 2% following the Government's initial* ***interest rate hoist.***

hold¹ /həʊld‖hoʊld/ *v* past tense and past participle **held** [T] **1** FINANCE if you hold an investment, you own it: *Brierley Investments said it holds 1,883,600 La Quinta shares.* | *First Executive holds billions of dollars of junk bonds.*
2 FINANCE to keep an investment, rather than sell it: *I don't sell anything. I buy stocks to hold. That's what I'm living on.*
3 hold an interest/position/stake in sth FINANCE to own part of company, asset etc: *Phillips Petroleum, which operates the well,* ***holds an*** *89.4%* ***interest*** *in it, and Opicoil of Taiwan holds the rest.*
4 to hold a patent to own a PATENT (=the right to profits from a product based on a new idea): *Inventor Charles Fritz holds the patent to the Tripledge windshield wiper.*
5 to keep supplies in a particular place: *British Steel holds stocks at the terminals in order to make just-in-time deliveries to local customers.*
6 hold (its) value if something holds value or holds its value, it does not lose its value, or it loses value more slowly than you might expect: *Magritte and Miro, two artists that continue to hold their value at auctions despite the art-market slump* | *In an increasingly disposable society, luxury cars are one of the few items that hold value.*
7 hold office if a political party holds office, it governs a country
8 hold office to have an important job in the government or in a company: *The original directors of the company would hold office only for the first year of privatization.*
9 hold a job/position/post etc *formal* to have a particular job: *Mr Andrews is the first black to hold the top position in a national law firm.*
hold sth ↔ **down** *phr v* [T] to prevent something such as prices from rising: *RTZ has intensified efforts to hold down costs and improve efficiency.* | *To fight inflation, the government held down gasoline prices.*
10 hold down a job *informal* to succeed in keeping a job: *Mr Mills had to hold down a full-time job while attending night school.*
hold out *phr v* [I] if, when discussing a possible agreement, you hold out for more, you refuse to accept an offer, hoping to get a better one **hold out for sth** *Anybody holding out for a better deal is being unreasonable, considering the economic environment we're in now.*
hold up *phr v* [I] if a price, value etc holds up, it stays at or near the same level, especially when it was expected to fall: *Copper prices held up surprisingly well during the recession.*

hold² *n* [C] **1** the part of a ship or plane where goods are stored for transport: *The Mega Borg had 38 million gallons of crude in its hold.*
2 if a company has a hold on a market or large part of a market, it makes it difficult for others to compete + **on**: *MCI is fighting to weaken Sprint's hold on 40% of the federal long-distance phone contract.*

3 FINANCE if someone says that an investment is a hold, they mean that people who have it should keep it and not sell it, but that they should not buy any more of it: *He rates the stock a hold, but figures it 'might go down before it goes up.'*

hold•er /ˈhəʊldə‖ˈhoʊldər/ *n* [C] **1** someone who possesses land, investments etc + **of**: *JPS said holders of 62.3% of its bonds have already approved its restructuring plan.* —see also BONDHOLDER, CARDHOLDER, DEBENTURE HOLDER, POLICYHOLDER, SHAREHOLDER, STOCKHOLDER
2 the person who has a particular job +**of**: *The holder of this post is supposed to speak independently of Congress and the White House on policy matters.*

Hold•ing /ˈhəʊldɪŋ‖ˈhoʊl-/ also **Holdings** *n* used in the name of holding companies: *Glaxo Holdings PLC*

hold•ing /ˈhəʊldɪŋ‖ˈhoʊl-/ *n* [C] **1** an amount of a particular type of investment owned by a person or organization + **of**: *Mr Gross has doubled his usual holdings of government securities to more than $10 billion.* | *O&Y's* ***real estate holdings*** *are concentrated in Toronto, New York and London.*
2 a quantity of shares held in a company by a particular SHAREHOLDER; STAKE: *Kerr Addison Mines is seeking a buyer for its 30.5% holding in Anderson Exploration.*
cross-holding when one company owns part of another company, which itself owns part of a third etc: *In a complicated series of cross-holdings, Jardine Matheson owns 54% of Jardine Strategic, which in turn owns 33% of Hongkong Land.*

holding company —see under COMPANY

holding cost —see under COST[1]

hold•out /ˈhəʊldaʊt‖ˈhoʊld-/ *n* [C] **1** a person or organization that does not follow the generally accepted way of doing something: *West New York, with its 'three miracle miles' of shops and restaurants, one of the last great holdouts in the Northeast against suburban shopping malls*
2 a CREDITOR (=a person or organization to whom money is owed) that refuses the official plan to reorganize a bankrupt company: *With its reorganization plan approved by creditors representing two-thirds or more of its debt, holdouts are obliged by court order to go along with the plan.*

hold rating —see under RATING

hold-up *n* [C] **1** a delay, for example in transport or production: *motorway holdups*
2 an attempt to rob someone by threatening them with a gun: *He pleaded guilty to a street robbery and two restaurant hold-ups.*

hole-in-the-wall *n* [C usually singular] *BrE informal* another name for ATM: *The Bank of Scotland is to update its hole-in-the-wall cash dispensers to make them faster and safer.*

hol•i•day /ˈhɒlɪdi‖ˈhɑːlɪdeɪ/ *n* **1** [C] a day fixed by law on which people do not go to work or school and shops and businesses are closed: *The Zurich stock market was closed yesterday for a* ***national holiday***. | *This Monday is a* ***public holiday*** *in France.*
bank holiday [C] *BrE* an official holiday when banks and most businesses are closed; NATIONAL HOLIDAY *AmE*: *The London stockmarket will reopen tomorrow after the* ***bank holiday***.
2 [C,U] a time of rest from work or school. Most employees are allowed a fixed number of days each year as paid holiday: *My secretary's* ***on holiday*** *this week.* | *You have to* ***take your holiday*** *by the end of the year.* | *Most employees would like to have more* ***holiday entitlement*** (=the right to take longer holidays).
3 [C] also **holidays** *BrE* a period of time spent in a place for pleasure: *They're* ***on holiday*** *in the Caribbean.* | *Make sure you have adequate* ***holiday insurance*** *before you leave.* | *a popular* ***holiday resort***
4 [C] a period of time when it is not necessary to make payments that must normally be made
contribution holiday also **contributions holiday** [C] a period of time when an employer does not make payments into the PENSION FUND of its employees, for example because it believes there is enough money in it to make necessary payments: *Larger pension schemes took a complete employer contribution holiday or paid reduced contributions.*
tax holiday [C] a period of time during which a company does not have to pay tax on all or part of their profits, for example when they first open a new factory. Governments often offer tax holidays to encourage new business in an area or country: *The Hungarian government gave GM Hungary a 10-year tax holiday and a customs allowance on imported parts.*

holiday pay —see under PAY[1]

home /həʊm‖hoʊm/ *adj* [only before a noun] connected with or happening in the country where goods are produced, rather than foreign countries; DOMESTIC: *The company faces very little competition in the* ***home market***. | ***Home consumption*** *of whisky has continued to decline.* —see also STARTER HOME

home banking —see under BANKING

home computer —see under COMPUTER

home electronics —see under ELECTRONICS

home entertainment —see under ENTERTAINMENT

home equity loan —see under LOAN[1]

home income plan —see HIP

home loan —see under LOAN[1]

home•own•er /ˈhəʊmˌəʊnə‖ˈhoʊmˌoʊnər/ *n* [C] a person who owns their own home: *The average cost of* ***homeowner's insurance*** *was $800 last year.*

homeowner's insurance —see under INSURANCE

home•page /ˈhəʊmpeɪdʒ‖ˈhoʊm-/ also **home page** *n* [C] the part of an INTERNET WEBSITE that contains all the basic information about a person or an organization. The homepage is the first place you go to on a website, and it is the place from which you can go to all other areas

home port —see under PORT[1]

home product —see under PRODUCT

home repair —see under REPAIR[2]

home•stead /ˈhəʊmsted, -stɪd‖ˈhoʊm-/ *n* [C] *AmE* **1** LAW property that is someone's home and that they cannot be forced to sell to pay their debts: *Texas homestead law protects your home from being seized if you go bankrupt.*
2 a farm and the area of land around it: *the homestead his grandfather left him*

home•stead•ing /ˈhəʊmˌstedɪŋ‖ˈhoʊm-/ *n* [U] *AmE* when people are given financial help to improve the condition of their homes, especially in poor areas: *a new project to promote homesteading*

home worker —see under WORKER

hon. also **Hon.** written abbreviation for HONORARY: *Mrs M Grattan, Hon Treasurer, Management Committee*

hon•cho /ˈhɒntʃəʊ‖ˈhɑːntʃoʊ/ *n* [C] *informal* **head honcho** someone who is in charge of an organization: *Gyllenhammar is the Volvo group's head honcho.*

honest broker *n* [C] —see under BROKER[1]

hon•o•rar•i•um /ˌɒnəˈreəriəm‖ˌɑːnəˈrer-/ *n* plural **honorariums** or **honoraria** [C] *formal* a sum of money offered to someone for their services; FEE: *He was paid $100,000 for writing the book, and the honorarium is now the subject of an inquiry.*

hon•or•ar•y /ˈɒnərəri‖ˈɑːnəreri/ *adj* [only before a noun] **1** an honorary title, rank, or university degree is given to someone as an honour: *They made him an*

H

honorary member of the club. | *She received an honorary doctorate from Harvard.*
2 written abbreviation **Hon** an honorary position in an organization is held without receiving any payment: *The* ***Honorary Secretary*** *read the minutes of the previous meeting.*

hon•our¹ *BrE*, **honor** *AmE* /ˈɒnə‖ˈɑːnər/ *v* [T] **1 honour a cheque/ticket/voucher etc** if a bank, store etc honours a cheque, ticket etc, it allows it to be used: *Any cheque you write up to £50 will be honoured.* | *Carriers must honor tickets issued by airlines that go bankrupt.*
2 honour a contract/agreement/promise etc to do what you have agreed or promised to do: *This company always honours its contracts.* | *They have not honoured their promise to reduce prices.*
3 honour your debts/commitments/obligations etc to pay money that you owe: *Burundi was unable to honor its foreign debt commitments.* | *Is the company able to honour its pensions obligations?*

honour² *BrE*, **honor** *AmE* —*n* **1** [U] the respect that people have for a person, organization etc: *The incident damaged the company's honour and credibility.*
2 honours written abbreviation **Hons**, or **hons** [plural] *BrE* a level of university degree that is higher than the most basic level: *You will need a good 2.1* ***honours degree.*** | *He passed his degree* ***with honours.***
3 Your Honour *BrE* used when speaking to a judge: *"Has the jury reached a verdict?" — "Yes, Your Honour. Not guilty."*

hons also **Hons** *BrE* written abbreviation for HONOURS

hook¹ /hʊk/ *v* [T] **1** *AmE informal* to succeed in attracting someone: *These tactics have helped hook such big clients as CocaCola.*
2 to connect one piece of electronic equipment to another piece of equipment or to an electricity supply **hook sth to/into sth**: *Hook one of the telephone lines to the fax machine.*
hook into sth *phr v* [T] to connect to a computer, telephone, television etc system: *The sales force can hook into a central computer and find out the latest product information.*
hook sth ↔ **up** *phr v* [T] to connect one piece of electronic equipment to another piece of equipment or to an electricity supply: *Don't forget to hook up the printer.* —see also HOOKUP
hook up to sth *phr v* [T] to become connected to the Internet, a telephone system etc: *Many companies are hooking up electronically to the Stock Exchange.*
hook up with sb/sth *phr v* [T] *informal* to agree to work with another organization for a particular purpose: *Japanese companies are rushing to hook up with foreign designers.*

hook² *n* **1** [C] something that attracts customers: *Free hotel rooms are one of the hooks designed to bring in new clients.*
2 off the hook if a person or business is off the hook, they are allowed to get out of a difficult situation, especially one they might have been punished for: *The broker isn't off the hook yet for the security violations.*
3 be on the hook (for sth) *AmE* to have to pay for something, especially something that is not really your responsibility: *Two dozen banks are on the hook for at least $100 million each.*

hook•up /ˈhʊkʌp/ *n* [C] **1** a connection to a computer or telephone system, to the INTERNET etc: *I work from home via a* ***computer hookup.*** | *an office complete with fax, cellular phones and* ***satellite hookup***
2 an agreement between two organizations to work together for a particular purpose + **with**: *a McDonnell Douglas hookup with Taiwan Aerospace Corp. to build the MD-12 jet*

hop•per /ˈhɒpə‖ˈhɑːpər/ *n* [C] a large container for waste, animal food, coal etc with a narrow opening at the bottom from where it can be emptied

H

horizontal amalgamation —see under AMALGAMATION

horizontal combination —see under COMBINATION

horizontal integration —see under INTEGRATION

horizontal merger —see under MERGER

horse•pow•er /ˈhɔːsˌpaʊə‖ˈhɔːrsˌpaʊr/ written abbreviation **hp** *n* [U] a unit for measuring the power of an engine: *The test vehicle's horsepower was increased by 11%.*

horse-trading *n* [U] FINANCE *journalism* when two sides discuss a business deal in a very forceful way, each one trying to get as much as they can without making the other want to stop the deal: *There has been some intense horse-trading today.*

hor•ti•cul•ture /ˈhɔːtəˌkʌltʃə‖ˈhɔːrtəˌkʌltʃər/ *n* [U] the activity or science of growing flowers, fruit, and vegetables

host /həʊst‖hoʊst/ *n* [C] COMPUTING the computer that controls and communicates with all the other computers in a REMOTE PROCESSING system such as a NETWORK (=a group of connected computers): *You can share the work between the host and your workstation.*

host computer —see under COMPUTER

hos•tile /ˈhɒstaɪl‖ˈhɑːstl, ˈhɑːstaɪl/ *adj* a hostile BID or TAKEOVER is one in which a company tries to buy another company whose SHAREHOLDERS do not want to sell: *Kerry Packer launched a hostile bid for Bond's media interests.*

hostile bid —see under BID¹

hostile takeover —see under TAKEOVER

hot-desking *n* [U] *BrE* HUMAN RESOURCES when people working in an office do not each have their own desk, but work where there is one available: *Hot-desking ensures that desks are never left unoccupied while people are away from the office.*

hot key —see under KEY¹

hot•line /ˈhɒtlaɪn‖ˈhɑːt-/ also **hot line** *n* [C] a special telephone line for people to ask for information, give their opinions about something etc: *American Express operates a 24-hour hotline with Japanese-speaking operators and travel counselors in several cities.*

hot money —see under MONEY

house /haʊs/ *n* [C] **1** a company, especially one that produces books, lends money, or designs clothes: *America's oldest publishing house* | *the French fashion house, Yves Saint Laurent*
accepting house also **acceptance house** *BrE* BANKING an old name for one of the London banks that accepted BILLS OF EXCHANGE
brokerage house another name for BROKERAGE
clearing house BANKING an organization that makes payments between banks and other financial institutions that trade regularly with each other: *Banks' and brokers' back offices are linked to a central clearing house in a single computer network.*
discount house BANKING in Britain until the 1990s, a specialist bank that borrowed from COMMERCIAL BANKS and used the money to buy TREASURY BILLS etc. These were bought by the Bank of England if the discount houses needed to repay commercial banks. Discount houses were therefore important in controlling the MONEY SUPPLY
finance house —see ***finance company*** under COMPANY
fulfillment house *AmE* a company that provides a service for a manufacturer before goods are delivered to customers, for example labelling or packaging: *The fulfillment house hired by Kraft to handle the promotion accidentally mailed some out-of-date coupons.*
issuing house a financial institution that arranges

for a company's shares to be sold on a stockmarket: *The issuing house was active in turning small- and medium-sized firms into public companies.*

securities house FINANCE an organization that ISSUES (=makes available and sells) companies' shares, bonds etc, trades in shares, bonds etc for itself and for its clients, and provides other financial services to companies. Most securities houses form part of large international financial institutions: *Bear Stearns, the Wall Street securities house, upgraded its recommendation on shares in Heinz to 'buy'.*

2 in house/out of house if work is done in house, it is done in a company's offices by the company's own staff. If work is done out of house, it is done outside the offices by people who are not directly employed by the company: *We used to handle our advertising in house.* | *a team of out-of-house lawyers*

3 clean/clear house *AmE* to try to make your business more PROFITABLE by getting rid of parts of the business or staff that are making you lose money: *They have been clearing house before the relaunch of the company.*

4 on the house provided free to a customer by a restaurant, bar etc

house agent —see under AGENT

house brand —see under BRAND[1]

house•hold[1] /ˈhaʊshəʊld‖-hoʊld/ *adj* connected with looking after a house and the people in it: *retailers of furniture, carpets, and **household goods*** | *Video phones won't become a **household appliance** for a long time.*

household[2] *n* [C] all the people who live together in one house: *The Labour Force Survey collects information from around 80,000 households.* | *people whose **household income** doesn't exceed $60,000*

house•hold•er /ˈhaʊsˌhəʊldə‖-ˌhoʊldər/ *n* [C] someone who owns or is in charge of a house: *More and more householders are living on reduced income.*

household insurance —see under INSURANCE

household name *n* [C] a name of a product, company etc that is very well known: *Nintendo is now a household name.*

household policy —see under INSURANCE POLICY

household product —see under PRODUCT

house•keep•ing /ˈhaʊsˌkiːpɪŋ/ *n* [U] **1** the work and organization of the things that need to be done in a house or hotel, such as cleaning and cooking: *Guests must vacate their rooms by 11 a.m. so that the housekeeping staff can clean the rooms.*

2 jobs that need to be done regularly to keep a system, organization etc working properly: *The scandal at the bank was first dismissed as a housekeeping problem.*

house magazine —see ***inhouse magazine*** under MAGAZINE

House of Commons *n* the part of the British or Canadian parliament whose members are elected by the people: *It was the new Chancellor's first speech in the House of Commons.*

House of Lords *n* the part of the British parliament, some of whose members are not elected but have positions because they have been given a rank or title: *The bill will be discussed in the House of Lords this week.*

House of Representatives *n* the larger of the two parts of the US Congress or of the parliament of Australia or New Zealand: *The measure requires approval by the Senate before it can go to the House of Representatives.* —compare SENATE

Houses of Parliament *n* [plural] the buildings where the British parliament meets, or the parliament itself: *2000 people demonstrated outside the Houses of Parliament.*

house style —see under STYLE

hous•ing /ˈhaʊzɪŋ/ *n* **1** [U] the houses or conditions that people live in: *The smartest new **housing developments** in Malaysia often come with golf courses attached.* | *the link between poor housing and health* | *Falling prices in **the housing market** have made lenders more cautious.* | *a **housing boom*** (=when a lot of people are buying and selling houses and prices are rising)

public housing [U] housing built by the government, usually for people with low incomes: *Chicago Housing Authority is cleaning up **public housing projects*** (=groups of buildings) *by throwing out people who are caught with drugs.*

2 [U] the work of providing people with houses to live in: *More money had been made available for health, housing, and education.*

3 [C] a cover that protects a machine or part of a machine: *a catalytic converter housing*

housing association —see under ASSOCIATION

housing benefit —see under BENEFIT[1]

housing co-operative —see under CO-OPERATIVE

housing market —see under MARKET[1]

housing starts —see under START[2]

HP abbreviation for HIRE PURCHASE

hp written abbreviation for HORSEPOWER: *a 112 hp electric motor*

HQ abbreviation for HEADQUARTERS: *Films are sent to the company's HQ for processing.*

HRD abbreviation for HUMAN RESOURCE DEVELOPMENT

HRM abbreviation for HUMAN RESOURCE MANAGEMENT

hrs. written abbreviation for HOURS: *The meeting will start at 1830 hrs.*

HTML *n* [U] COMPUTING Hypertext Markup Language; a computer language for creating documents on the WORLDWIDE WEB, using a system of codes to design the document and create LINKS to other documents: *You can convert Quark documents into HTML.* | *an HTML document*

hub /hʌb/ *n* [C] **1** a city or country where there is a lot of business activity because it is central in relation to other places, there are good communications etc: *Taiwan will become a hub for Asian markets and a financial center.*

2 also **hub airport** an airport with a lot of flights where people can easily change planes to go on to somewhere else: *As its Nashville hub expands, it plans to begin a daily nonstop service between Nashville and Las Vegas.*

hub airport —see under AIRPORT

huck•ster /ˈhʌkstə‖-ər/ *n* [C] *AmE disapproving* someone who uses forceful selling methods, especially dishonest ones: *time-share hucksters waiting hotel lobbies for unwary tourists*

human capital —see under CAPITAL

human resource development —see under DEVELOPMENT

human resource management —see under MANAGEMENT

human resources *n* [plural] **1** the abilities and skills of people, especially the employees of an organization: *We believe we have the human resources, the management resources and the capital for this project.* | *Continuing investment in capital and human resources resulted in steady productivity gains.*

2 written abbreviation **HR** the department in an organization that deals with employing, training, and helping employees; PERSONNEL

human resources manager —see under MANAGER

hun•dred•weight /ˈhʌndrɨ̈dweɪt/ written abbreviation **cwt** *n* [C] a unit for measuring weight equal to 112 pounds or 50.9 kilograms: *a hundredweight of flour*

hush money —see under MONEY

hy•draul•ic /haɪˈdrɒlɪk, -ˈdrɔː-‖-ˈdrɒː-/ *adj* moved or operated by the pressure of water on other liquids: *The factory makes hydraulic cylinders for use in the steel industry.* —**hydraulically** *adv*: *hydraulically operated doors*

hy•dro•e•lec•tric /ˌhaɪdrəʊ-ɪˈlektrɪk◂‖-droʊ-/ *adj* using water power to produce electricity: *The dams produce cheap* ***hydroelectric power***. —**hydroelectricity** *n* [U] *Oil was abandoned in favour of hydroelectricity and nuclear power.*

hy•giene /ˈhaɪdʒiːn/ *n* [U] the practice of preventing illness or stopping it from spreading by keeping things clean: *The layout of the kitchen does not conform to* ***food hygiene*** *regulations.*

industrial hygiene the practice of protecting the health of industrial workers: *They have only just begun to train engineers in industrial hygiene.*

hygiene factor —see under FACTOR[1]

hype[1] /haɪp/ *n* [U] *disapproving* when advertisers try to make the public interested in a person, product, or company through advertisements that make people talk about it a lot on television and radio: *Their status has been gained through their pursuit of quality, not through public relations hype.* | *the hype surrounding any new film*

hype[2] *v* [T] **1** also **hype up** to try to make the public interested in a product or company through advertisements or by getting it talked about a lot on television and radio: *The unit trust industry is usually quick to hype its products.* | *Competitors criticized the group for hyping up products it can't deliver.*

2 to deceive people by changing figures or results, usually to make a situation look better than it really is: *The company admitted that it had hyped customer orders and faked records to match those orders.*

hy•per•com•pet•i•tion /ˈhaɪpəkɒmpɨ̈ˌtɪʃən‖-pərkɑːm-/ *n* [U] a situation in which there is a lot of very strong competition between companies, markets are changing very quickly, and it is easy to enter a new market, so that it is not possible for one company to keep a COMPETITIVE ADVANTAGE for a long time: *According to Mr. D'Aveni, business has entered a new era of hypercompetition.*

hy•per•in•fla•tion /ˌhaɪpərɪnˈfleɪʃən/ —see under INFLATION

hy•per•link /ˈhaɪpəlɪŋk‖-pər-/ *n* [C] COMPUTING a way of organizing and storing a HYPERTEXT document on a computer, so that you can easily move to other parts of the document or to other documents using a MOUSE. Words with a hyperlink have a line under them: *We should encourage hyperlinks to each others' documents.*

hy•per•mar•ket /ˈhaɪpəˌmɑːkɨ̈t‖-pərˌmɑːr-/ *n* [C] *BrE* a very large SUPERMARKET, usually one built outside a town

hy•per•text /ˈhaɪpəˌtekst‖-pər-/ *n* [U] COMPUTING written information containing references to other documents or parts of documents that can be displayed by choosing them with the mouse: *a simple system of networked hypertext* | *He put everything on one page instead of using* ***hypertext links***.

Hypertext Markup Language —see HTML

hy•poth•e•cat•ed tax /haɪˈpɒθɨ̈keɪtɨ̈d ˌtæks‖-ˈpɑː-/ —see under TAX[1]

hy•poth•e•sis /haɪˈpɒθɨ̈sɨ̈s‖-ˈpɑː-/ *n* plural **hypotheses** [C] STATISTICS an idea that can be tested to see if it is true or not: *The survey was aimed at testing a hypothesis that happily-married couples tend to vote more conservatively.*

null hypothesis the fact that there is no relation between two things. In science, tests are done to see if the null hypothesis can be shown to be untrue: *The null hypothesis is that there is difference in medical outcome between community care and hospital clinic care.*

H

I

IATA /aɪˈɑːtə, iː-/ abbreviation for INTERNATIONAL AIR TRANSPORT ASSOCIATION

ib•id /ˈɪbɪd/ also **ib** *written* used to explain that something is from the same book, writer, or article as the one that has just been mentioned: *These data are reflected in the estimates (ibid. p. 7).* —see also ID

IBRD abbreviation for INTERNATIONAL BANK FOR RECONSTRUCTION AND DEVELOPMENT

i/c written abbreviation for IN CHARGE

ICAO abbreviation for INTERNATIONAL CIVIL AVIATION ORGANIZATION

ICC abbreviation for INTERNATIONAL CHAMBER OF COMMERCE; INTERSTATE COMMERCE COMMISSION

i•con /ˈaɪkɒn‖-kɑːn/ *n* [C] COMPUTING a small sign or picture on a computer SCREEN that is used to start a particular operation: *First open your File Manager by clicking on the icon.*

id /ɪd/ *written* used to explain that something is from the same book, writer, or article as the one that has just been mentioned —see also IBID

IDA abbreviation for INTERNATIONAL DEVELOPMENT ASSOCIATION

i•den•ti•fi•er /aɪˈdentəfaɪə‖-ər/ *n* [C] COMPUTING a group of letters, numbers, or symbols that a computer has been programmed to recognize and uses to process information: *For companies, Social Security numbers serve as a universal identifier that can help them link information about an individual from several separate data bases.*

i•dle /ˈaɪdl/ *adj* not active or being used: *Today, San Diego's airplane manufacturing plants are largely idle.* | *Carefully planned loading can reduce* ***idle time*** (=time when people or machines are not working).

idle balance —see under BALANCE[1]

idle money —see under MONEY

ie used to explain the exact meaning of something that you have just said: *The key to success is engaging the workforce – i.e. getting workers to show the same enthusiasm for their work as they do for their hobbies.*

IFC abbreviation for INTERNATIONAL FINANCE CORPORATION

il•le•gal /ɪˈliːgəl/ *adj* **1** not allowed by the law **illegal to do sth**: *It's illegal to copy copyrighted movie cassettes.* | *Despite knowing about the* ***illegal activity****, the executives failed to tell the government for months.* | *He made* ***illegal payments*** *in connection with contracts awarded to his company.* | *Anyone knowingly hiding the origins of* ***illegal profits*** *faces a fine or imprisonment.* —**illegally** *adv*: *An investigation is being conducted to see if anyone illegally profited from the takeover.*

2 COMPUTING involving an instruction, CHARACTER etc that is not allowed in a particular computer program

il•le•gal•i•ty /ˌɪlɪˈgæləti/ *n* plural **illegalities** **1** [U] the state of being illegal: *a political regime characterized by lies and illegality*

2 [C] an illegal act: *There is so much chaos on trading floors that proving illegalities is difficult.*

il•le•gi•ble /ɪˈledʒəbəl/ *adj* not written or printed clearly, and difficult or impossible to read: *Midwest refused to honor the check, saying that the endorsement was illegible.* —opposite LEGIBLE

il•li•cit /ɪˈlɪsət/ *adj* not allowed by laws or rules, or strongly disapproved of by society: *Officials are hoping prosecution of certain gun dealers will curb* ***illicit sales.*** | *They were convicted of racketeering and were ordered to repay $100 million in* ***illicit profits.***

il•liq•uid /ɪˈlɪkwəd/ *adj* FINANCE involving things that cannot easily be changed into cash, or things that are difficult to buy and sell: *real estate and other* ***illiquid assets*** | *Because bank loans are typically illiquid, they are difficult for outsiders to value.* —opposite LIQUID —**illiquidity** *n* [U] *The drawback is that small shares may be difficult to sell because of illiquidity.*

ILO abbreviation for INTERNATIONAL LABOUR ORGANIZATION

ILU abbreviation for INSTITUTE OF LONDON UNDERWRITERS

im•age /ˈɪmɪdʒ/ *n* [C] **1** MARKETING the general opinion that most people have of a person, organization, product etc: *Law suits hurt a company's image and may hinder future fund raising.* | *A good advertising campaign will promote a company's* ***corporate image*** *while reminding consumers of the products it makes.*

brand image the collection of ideas and beliefs that people have about a brand: *Both BMW and Honda have built their brand images on engineering excellence and high performance with a heavy accent on motorsport.*

2 a picture on the SCREEN of a computer or television: *When someone sends a fax, the fax modem answers the call and turns the transmission into a computer image that can be displayed on your screen.*

image advertising —see under ADVERTISING

image marketing —see under MARKETING

IMF abbreviation for INTERNATIONAL MONETARY FUND

IMF quota —see under QUOTA

immediate annuity —see under ANNUITY

immediate possession —see under POSSESSION

im•mi•grant /ˈɪməgrənt/ *n* [C] someone who comes from abroad to live permanently in another country: *The college has a large* ***immigrant population.*** —compare EMIGRANT

im•mi•grate /ˈɪməgreɪt/ *v* [I] to come into a country in order to live there permanently: *Born in the Philippines, Celeste immigrated to the United States when she was 15.* —compare EMIGRATE

im•mi•gra•tion /ˌɪməˈgreɪʃən/ *n* [U] **1** the process of entering another country, state etc in order to live there: *In the past, California has had the highest rate of immigration.* —compare EMIGRATION

2 also **immigration control** the place at an airport, port etc where officials check the documents of people entering the country

net immigration the amount by which the number of IMMIGRANTS is greater than the number of EMIGRANTS: *Over the past decade, the south that has experienced a net immigration of more than a million persons.* —compare ***net emigration*** under EMIGRATION

imminent peril *n* [U] INSURANCE a situation of great danger, which will cause something very bad to happen soon: *Our policies will only cover abortion counselling for a woman whose pregnancy places her life in imminent peril.*

im•mo•bil•i•ty /ˌɪməˈbɪləti/ *n* [U] ECONOMICS when land, labour, or capital cannot be easily moved from one kind of use or employment to another, for example, when skilled workers cannot be easily employed in another job that uses different skills: *urban problems such as housing shortages and* ***labour immobility***

im•mo•bi•lize *AmE* also **immobilise** *BrE* /ɪˈməʊbəlaɪz‖ɪˈmoʊ-/ *v* [T] FINANCE **1** if a company immobilizes its capital, it uses it to buy CAPITAL GOODS

I

(=machinery and equipment that is used to make other goods)
2 if something immobilizes an organization, machine etc, it prevents it from working: *A miners' strike has immobilised all power plants.*

im•mov•a•ble also **immoveable** /ɪˈmuːvəbəl/ *adj* something immovable cannot be moved or changed: *Tax will be levied on the worth of* ***immovable property****.* (=buildings etc)

immovable property —see under PROPERTY

im•pact¹ /ˈɪmpækt/ *n* [C] the effect or influence that an event, situation etc has on someone or something + **on**: *High interest rates have a negative* ***impact on*** *spending.* | *The new advertising campaign has had little impact on sales.*

im•pact² /ɪmˈpækt/ *v* [I,T] *especially AmE* to have an important or noticeable effect on someone or something: *The recession has impacted the domestic business market.* + **on**: *How will this program impact on the local community?*

impact effect —see under EFFECT

im•pe•cu•ni•ous /ˌɪmpɪˈkjuːniəs◂/ *adj formal* having very little money: *She was not the first person to leave the impecunious world of politics for the big bucks world of TV news.*

im•per•fect /ɪmˈpɜːfɪkt‖-ɜːr-/ *adj* **1** imperfect goods, products etc have not been made completely correctly: *Years ago, manufacturers used shopping malls to unload imperfect goods.*
2 ECONOMICS used to describe markets or competition where competing products cannot be compared exactly because they are not exactly the same, not everyone has complete information about them etc. Most real markets are imperfect: *The inability of a firm to gain infinite demand for its services if it sells at below market prices suggests imperfect rather than perfect competition: firms do not compete on price alone.*

imperfect competition —see under COMPETITION

im•per•fec•tion /ˌɪmpəˈfekʃən‖-pər-/ *n* [C] something that is not completely correct or perfect in a system, product etc; FLAW: *The CD had several small imperfections.*

imperfect market —see under MARKET¹

im•plied /ɪmˈplaɪd/ *adj* not stated openly, but understood to exist or to be true: *Disney argues that it had an oral contract and an implied license to use the Muppet characters.*

implied condition —see under CONDITION

implied contract —see under CONTRACT¹

implied term —see under TERM¹

implied trust —see under TRUST

implied warranty —see under WARRANTY

im•port¹ /ˈɪmpɔːt‖-ɔːrt/ *n* **1** [C usually plural] something that is made in one country and brought into another, usually in order to be sold there + **of**: *French fishermen protesting over imports of fish from Scandinavia* | *Singapore has* ***banned imports*** *of fighting dogs.* | *A slowdown in Japan's domestic economy has led to a sharp* ***decline in imports*** *of luxury cars.*
2 [U] the activity or process of bringing goods into a country; IMPORTATION + **of**: *US regulations on the import of four-wheel drive vehicles*
parallel imports *n* [plural] goods that are imported avoiding the DISTRIBUTION CHANNELS (=ways of buying goods to sell to the public) approved by the makers: *a recent increase in parallel imports, where British retailers purchase CDs from European countries where prices are lower than in the UK*

im•port² /ɪmˈpɔːt‖-ɔːrt/ *v* [T] **1** to bring something into a country from abroad, usually in order to sell it + **from**: *Bees were imported from Africa in an effort to improve honey production.* + **into**: *These raw materials are all imported into Korea, as there are no local producers.* | *We must reduce the country's dependence on* ***imported oil****.*
2 COMPUTING to move information from one computer or software program into another: *You can either type your data into this form or you can* ***import data*** *from a spreadsheet.*

im•por•ta•tion /ˌɪmpɔːˈteɪʃən‖-ɔːr-/ *n* [U] the activity or process of bringing things into a country from abroad in order to sell them: *US law prohibits importation of prison-made goods.*

import control —see under CONTROL¹

import duty —see under DUTY

im•port•er /ɪmˈpɔːtə‖-ˈpɔːrtər/ *n* [C] a person, organization, or country that imports goods: *The US remains by far the world's biggest importer.* + **of**: *Geest is a major importer of bananas into the UK.*
net importer a country that imports more of something than it exports: *Because of a construction boom in Seoul, South Korea was a net importer of steel products.*

import levy —see under LEVY²

import licence —see under LICENCE

import quota —see under QUOTA

import surcharge —see under SURCHARGE¹

import tariff —see under TARIFF

import trade —see under TRADE¹

im•pose /ɪmˈpəʊz‖-ˈpoʊz/ *v* **impose a ban/tax/fine etc** to officially order that something should be forbidden, taxed etc: *The city council can not impose a utility tax without voter approval.* | *The US Commerce Department threatened to impose a 15% fee on subsidized lumber flooding U.S. markets.*

im•pound /ɪmˈpaʊnd/ *v* [T] LAW if the police or law courts impound your possessions, they take them and keep them because a law has been broken: *Courts are authorized to impound any vehicle driven by a person without a valid license.* | *The courts granted the request to impound all documents relevant to the case.*

im•pre•sa•ri•o /ˌɪmprᵻˈsɑːriəʊ‖-rioʊ/ *n* [C] someone who owns a business that organizes performances in theatres, concert halls etc: *a rock impresario*

im•prest /ɪmˈprest/ *n* [U] ACCOUNTING a sum of money given to someone in an organization to make small payments: *This petty cash is kept on the* ***imprest system****, whereby the petty cashier is entrusted with a fixed sum of money.*

im•pri•ma•tur /ˌɪmprᵻˈmeɪtə, -ˈmɑː-‖-ər/ *n* [singular] *formal* **1** approval of something, given by an official authority or an important person + **of**: *The administration hopes that having the imprimatur of the White House will improve the chances that the changes will occur.*
2 permission to print a book: *The work was published* ***under the imprimatur of*** *Goldman Sachs Investment Research.*

im•print /ˈɪmprɪnt/ *n* [C] **1** the names of the PUBLISHER and the PRINTER as they appear on a book: *books published* ***under the*** *Books For Young Readers* ***imprint***
2 a publishing company: *Over the next three years, the imprint will publish between 300 and 400 books from Everyman's backlist.*

im•pro•pri•e•ty /ˌɪmprəˈpraɪᵻti/ *n* plural **improprieties** [C,U] *formal* behaviour that is unacceptable according to moral or professional standards: *He faced* ***allegations of impropriety*** *over the insider trading scandal.* | *They argued that these were minor improprieties, not crimes.*

im•prove /ɪmˈpruːv/ *v* **1** [I,T] if shares, prices etc improve by a particular amount, they rise by that amount: *Jaguar improved 21p, closing at 665p.* + **by**: *Hungary's dollar current account improved by a remarkable 5% of GDP.*

2 [T] to make something better: *work to improve access for people with disabilities* | *The marketing team will need to* ***improve communication*** *with the suppliers.*

3 [I] to become better: *The AAPA is confident that audit standards will improve.* | *Business started to improve again in January.*

improve on/upon sth *phr v* [T] to do something better than it was done before, or to make something better than it was before: *The government hopes to improve on the 3% economic growth of the past two years.*

im·proved /ɪm'pruːvd/ *adj* [only before a noun] better than before: *improved banking arrangements* | *the introduction of* ***new and improved*** *products*

im·prove·ment /ɪm'pruːvmənt/ *n* [C,U] the act or state of getting better + **in**: *Canandaigua Wine Co reported a 70% improvement in net income for the third quarter.* | *An economist said he was optimistic that September sales will* ***show an improvement****.*

im·pru·dent /ɪm'pruːdənt/ *adj* a decision, plan etc that is imprudent is not sensible or wise: *The finance house took action against some employers for imprudent decisions in buying annuities.* —**imprudently** *adv*: *The committee is focusing on whether Drexel acted imprudently in granting the bonuses.* —**imprudence** *n* [C,U] *The commission has never identified any specific area of fault, or imprudence, on the part of the company.*

impulse buy —see under BUY[2]

impulse buyer —see under BUYER

im·pu·ta·tion /ˌɪmpjʊ'teɪʃən/ *n* **1** [C,U] LAW a suggestion that someone or something is the cause of a particular situation, or is responsible for a particular action, especially something bad + **on**: *A corporation may sue for an imputation on its trading reputation.* + **of**: *Exxon wished to avoid the imputation of blame for the accident.*

2 [U] STATISTICS a method of calculating the value of something when you do not know what the actual value is: *The Population Census used a procedure of imputation to infer values for those households which failed to return their forms.*

imputation system —see under SYSTEM

im·pute /ɪm'pjuːt/ *v* [T] **1** LAW to suggest that someone or something is the cause of a particular situation, or is responsible for a particular action, especially something bad: *The court ruled that the newspaper report did impute a criminal offense.*

2 TAX, STATISTICS to calculate the value of something which cannot easily be measured in the usual way by giving it a value based on similar things: *The Inland Revenue imputes a set amount of taxable income according to the size of a car's engine.* + **to**: *CableWest imputes to its costs an amount for connection to its exchange.*

3 be imputed to TAX if the interest on a loan is imputed to the loan agreement, the interest is calculated at market rates, even though the actual rate of interest paid may be lower than the market rates

imputed interest —see under INTEREST

imputed value —see under VALUE[1]

in written abbreviation for INCH or INCHES

in·ac·tive /ɪn'æktɪv/ *adj* **1** FINANCE if investors or dealers in a financial market are inactive, they are buying and selling very little: *Institutions continued to buy stocks selectively, while small investors remained inactive.*

2 FINANCE if a company's shares are inactive, very few people are buying or selling them: *The Pacific Stock Exchange announced a plan to list a category of inactive stocks.*

3 if a company is inactive, it still exists but does not do any business: *Sterling Electric Inc., a now inactive subsidiary of A.O. Smith Corp.*

4 if a loan is inactive, interest payments are not being made on it as agreed: *The bank itself ran up losses of $15 billion, with extensive outstanding but inactive loans.*

inactive account —see under ACCOUNT[1]

in·ad·mis·si·ble /ˌɪnəd'mɪsəbəl◂/ *adv* LAW if something produced as EVIDENCE in a court of law is inadmissible, it is not allowed to be used: *The tape recording was* ***ruled inadmissible*** *because it had been illegally obtained.* —**inadmissible** *adj*: *His statement contained damaging but* ***inadmissible evidence****.*

in·au·gu·ral /ɪ'nɔːgjʊrəl‖ɪ'nɒː-/ *adj* **1 inaugural meeting/flight/voyage etc** the first in a series of meetings, flights etc: *The problem was detected on the plane's inaugural flight.*

2 inaugural speech/lecture etc a speech, lecture etc given by a person who has taken up an important position, to introduce themselves and their ideas: *In his* ***inaugural address****, the new president called attention to the needs of the homeless.*

in·au·gu·rate /ɪ'nɔːgjʊreɪt‖-'nɒː-/ *v* [T] **1** to begin a new system, service, project etc: *Iberia airlines inaugurated their first nonstop flight from Madrid to Moscow.* | *a billion dollar aid package inaugurated at the economic summit in Paris*

2 to officially celebrate when a person takes up an important position such as that of president, by holding a special ceremony: *He is keeping quiet about his budget plans until after he is inaugurated on Jan 7.* —**inauguration** *n* [C,U] *the inauguration of a Hungarian stock exchange* | *the third anniversary of President Roh Tae Woo's inauguration*

in-basket *n* [C] *AmE* a container used to hold letters, papers etc that need to be dealt with; IN-TRAY *BrE*: *The in-basket was full of a load of fresh paperwork.* —compare OUT-BASKET

in bond —see under BOND

in·bound /'ɪnbaʊnd/ *adj* [only before a noun] *AmE* **1** FINANCE inbound investment is investment in a country from abroad: *Inbound foreign investment, he claims, is never the solution to a nation's competitive problems.*

2 an inbound plane, train etc is arriving at a place; INCOMING *BrE*: *It would be impossible to divert all inbound rail shipments to truck.* —compare OUTBOUND

inbound telemarketing —see under TELEMARKETING

Inc. written abbreviation for INCORPORATED

inc written abbreviation for INCLUDING; INCLUSIVE (OF); INCREASE

in·cal·cu·la·ble /ɪn'kælkjʊləbəl/ *adj formal* not possible to calculate: *The social cost of unemployment is incalculable.* | *Countries are insuring against the* ***incalculable risk*** *of the consequences of climate change.*

incapacity benefit —see under BENEFIT[1]

in·cen·tive /ɪn'sentɪv/ *n* [C] something which is used to encourage people, especially to make them work harder, produce more or spend more money: ***tax incentives*** *for first-time home buyers* | *Greyhound proposed a package of incentive-based pay raises.*

incentive fee —see under FEE

in·cen·tiv·ize also **incentivise** *BrE* /ɪn'sentɪvaɪz/ *v* [T] to give someone an incentive to do something, especially to buy something: *We will reward and incentivise customers with these new programs.*

in·cep·tion /ɪn'sepʃən/ *n* [singular] **1** the start of a business, organization etc: ***Since its inception*** *in 1965, Medicare has based the payments it makes for each claim on what individual doctors charge.*

2 the date on which an agreement or system becomes effective: *The customer agrees to guaranteed monthly payments* ***at the inception of*** *the agreement.*

I

inch /ɪntʃ/ *n* [C] a unit for measuring length, equal to 2.54 centimetres

in•ci•dence /ˈɪnsɪ̇dəns/ *n* [singular] **1** TAX the effect of a particular tax on people or organizations, and how much they have to pay: *The structure of production may influence **the incidence of taxation**.*

2 the number of times something happens: *The incidence of new product failure is very high.*

in•ci•den•tal /ˌɪnsɪ̇ˈdentl◂/ *adj* **incidental costs/expenses etc** small amounts of money which are spent at various times as part of a larger bill: *The Law Centre has to meet the incidental expenses of the committee, such as phone bills, petrol and stationery.*

incidental damages —see under DAMAGE[1]

in•ci•den•tals /ˌɪnsɪ̇ˈdentlz/ *n* [plural] *informal* another name for INCIDENTAL COSTS/EXPENSES: *If hotel guests have no credit cards they are usually asked to pay all incidentals in bars and restaurants in cash.*

incl. written abbreviation for INCLUSIVE; INCLUDING

inclosure —see ENCLOSURE

in•clude /ɪnˈkluːd/ *v* [T] if an offer, payment, bill etc includes something, it is counted as part of the offer, payment, bill etc: *The public issue will include 1,025,000 shares offered by Body Drama.* **include sth in sth**: *The auditors included the restructuring charge of $9 million in the final assessment of the accounts.* —**including** *prep*: *The current staff numbers 40 attorneys, including 10 partners.*

in•clu•sion /ɪnˈkluːʒən/ *n* [U] the act of including something as part of a larger amount or group of things: *the inclusion of cash flow information* + **in**: *The agency is still reviewing two other widely used ingredients for possible inclusion in the ban.* —compare EXCLUSION

in•clu•sive /ɪnˈkluːsɪv/ *adj* **1** an inclusive price, cost etc includes everything that has to be paid **be inclusive of**: *The stated price is inclusive of meals.*

2 1-10 inclusive/July to January inclusive etc including 1 and 10 and all the numbers in between, July and January and all the months in between etc: *paragraphs 2 to 4 inclusive*

3 inclusive holiday/vacation/package including everything, for example flight, hotel and meals, in the price; ALL-INCLUSIVE: *inclusive package tours to the Costa Brava*

in•come /ˈɪŋkʌm, ˈɪn-/ *n* [C,U] money that you earn from your job or that you receive from investments: *The family pays more than 50% of its income for rent.* | *Transferring interest from a deposit account can provide you with a **regular income** from your savings.* | *People **on low incomes** will be getting some help to pay their fuel bills.*

accrued income [U] the total amount of money earned by a company during a particular ACCOUNTING PERIOD, whether paid or still owed to them

annual income [U] the total amount of money earned or obtained by a business, organization, country etc during a year: *This is the first fall in BT's annual income for five years.* | *Business travellers provided a fifth of the country's annual income before the war.*

deferred income [U] income relating to things that will happen or be done in the future for which payment has already been received: *Included in deferred income is £14 million which relates to a pre-payment received under a contract for sale of gas.*

discretionary income [U] income that you can spend on things that are not completely necessary for living: *White-collar employees are usually furniture stores' best customers because they have the most discretionary income.*

disposable income [U] income that is available for someone to spend or save after they have paid tax and paid for the things that they need such as accommodation and food: *Mexicans have more disposable income now that the economy is healthier.*

earned income [U] **1** money that you earn from work that you do, for example wages from your job or profit from your business. Earned income is usually taxed at a different rate to UNEARNED INCOME: *Your pension is taxable as earned income.*

2 money that a company makes from its activities, after taking away some costs. Companies calculate their income in different ways according to the ACCOUNTING SYSTEM they use and the type of business they are in: *The casino **reported income** of $21.8 million on revenue of $269 million.*

fixed income [C,U] income that does not increase over time, for example from a PENSION or an ANNUITY: *widows, retirees and others living on fixed incomes*

gross income [C,U] the total amount of income received before taking off tax, expenses etc: *The average gross income before overhead of a US doctor is $400,000.*

investment income [U] income from investments in the form of interest, DIVIDENDs etc, rather than income from your job or a company's income from its normal operating activities: *In addition to his investment income, Mr. Alexander earned $303,072 last year.*

money income [U] people's income in the form of money, rather than BENEFITS IN KIND etc: *The difference in real income between the university graduates and other groups is greater than those shown by money income alone, because of better fringe benefits.*

national income [C,U] ECONOMICS the value of all the goods and services sold in a country in a particular period of time, usually a year: *Roughly 25% of Norway's national income comes from petroleum.*

net income ◆ [C,U] TAX the amount of income left after paying INCOME TAX and SOCIAL SECURITY CONTRIBUTIONS: *Last year, the average net income of pensioner couples was £270 a week.*

◆ [C,U] TAX the amount of income that a company has after paying costs and tax; NET PROFIT: *EC had third-quarter net income of $483,000 on revenue of $15.1 million.*

operating income [C,U] income from a company's normal operating activities, not including EXCEPTIONAL ITEMS: *Theme parks are responsible for 60% to 65% of Disney's operating income.*

per-capita income [C,U] the income of a country, its GDP, divided by the number of people living there. This shows how rich or poor the people are on average: *Africa's per-capita income fell by a quarter in the 1980s.*

personal income [C,U] the income of a person, rather than of a government, organization, or company: *Personal incomes are falling as unemployment rises.*

premium income [U] INSURANCE income that an insurance company gets from people and organizations paying for insurance: *Premium income from life insurance rose 8.5% to 1.109 trillion lire.*

private income [C,U] money that someone gets from investments rather than from working: *The government has promised to lower taxation on private income.*

psychic income also **psych pay** [U] something apart from money that you get from your job, and which gives you emotional satisfaction such as a feeling of being powerful or important.

real income [C,U] someone's income measured over a period of time in relation to what they can buy with it, after taking rising prices into account: *Most middle-income people here have had their taxes go up and their real incomes down.*

taxable income [C,U] TAX the amount of income used as a basis to calculate tax after taking away ALLOWANCEs, DEDUCTIONs etc from gross income: *Someone with a taxable income of $90,000 has, on average, a gross income of $125,000.*

tax-exempt income also **tax-free income** [C,U] a part of personal income on which you do not have to pay income tax: *His tax return shows that he earned $217,000 in taxable and tax-exempt income last year.* | *A unit investment trust generates tax-free income from interest over the life of the trust.*

unearned income [U] another name for INVESTMENT INCOME: *a high tax on unearned income*

unreported income [U] income that someone does not show in their TAX RETURN, in order to avoid paying tax on it: *Argentina's GNP is underestimated by as much as 40% because of unreported income in the black market.*

income and expenditure account —see under ACCOUNT[1]

income bond —see under BOND

income bracket —see under BRACKET

income elasticity of demand —see under ELASTICITY OF DEMAND

income fund —see under FUND[1]

income group —see under GROUP

income insurance —see under INSURANCE

income share —see under SHARE

incomes policy —see under POLICY

income statement —see under STATEMENT

income stock —see under STOCK[1]

income stream —see under STREAM

income tax *n* [C,U] in Britain, a tax on money people earn, paid to the national government. In the US, a tax on the money people earn or on the profits companies make, paid to the national, state, or local government: *Florida and Texas have no income tax, which is one reason that many people with substantial assets live there.* | *He failed to report and **pay income tax** on his portion of this income.* —see also separate entry for TAX[1]

corporate income tax a tax on company profits in the US; CORPORATION TAX *BrE*: *a reduction in corporate income taxes that will benefit small businesses*

deferred income tax income tax to be paid by a company in a later tax year on profits made in an earlier year: *Breakwater had $83.8 million of liabilities as of Sept. 30, excluding deferred income taxes.*

federal income tax a tax paid by people on what they earn or by companies on their profits to the US government: *They were charged with evading federal income taxes on millions of dollars of income.*

individual income tax income tax on what people earn rather than a tax on company profits: *Individual income taxes, which account for close to half of all federal receipts, were down 4.5%.*

local income tax an income tax paid to a city in the US: *These figures include local income tax of $138 in Denver and $1,903 in New York.*

negative income tax a proposal by some economists and politicians to make payments to people on low wages to bring their incomes up to a minimum level: *I want to bring in a negative income tax to bring income up to the level needed for family subsistence.*

personal income tax another name for INDIVIDUAL INCOME TAX: *The state's budget includes a 4.5% personal income tax.*

state income tax income tax paid to a US state government: *Municipal bonds are typically free of state income taxes in the state where issued.*

income tax allowance —see under ALLOWANCE

income tax deduction —see under DEDUCTION

income tax rate —see ***tax rate*** under RATE[1]

in·com·ing /ˈɪnkʌmɪŋ/ *adj* [only before a noun] **1** an incoming plane, train etc is arriving at a place; INBOUND *AmE*: *Fog is causing delays to incoming flights.*

2 incoming telephone calls, enquiries etc are received by someone rather than being made by them: *automatic filing of **incoming** and outgoing **mail*** | ***Incoming messages** can be stored in the teleprinter's memory.*

3 an incoming government, president, leader etc has just been elected or has just started a new job: *Many analysts expect the incoming chief executive to streamline the company.* —compare OUTGOING

in·com·pat·i·ble /ˌɪnkəmˈpætəbəl◂/ *adj* COMPUTING computers, computer systems, or programs that are incompatible cannot be used together + **with**: *Most PCs in Japan run on software based on NEC Corp's architecture, which is incompatible with IBM machines.*

in·com·pe·tent /ɪnˈkɒmpətənt‖-ˈkɑːm-/ *adj* not having the skill or ability to do a job properly: *Police demonstrated to demand the resignation of incompetent commanders.* —**incompetence** *n* [U] *He was accused of medical incompetence.* —**incompetently** *adv*: *If lawyers perform incompetently, clients are entitled to a refund.*

in·cor·po·rate /ɪnˈkɔːpəreɪt‖-ɔːr-/ *v* [T] **1** if a company is incorporated, it is listed officially as a company by meeting certain legal REQUIREMENTS which apply in a particular country or a particular state. Companies which are incorporated become CORPORATIONS: *Zapata Trading was founded in 1986 and incorporated in 1989.* | *The law gave corporations that are incorporated in Pennsylvania 90 days to opt out of certain provisions.*

2 to include or add something to a group, system, plan etc: *Volvo hopes to incorporate Japanese concepts of worker participation.* **incorporate sth in/into sth**: *Apple Computer agreed to incorporate Adobe's printer software in the basic program for all Macintosh PCs.* —**incorporation** *n* [C,U] *During the first quarter, new business incorporations increased 8.5%.* | *the incorporation of previous price increases into current wage bargaining*

In·cor·po·ra·ted /ɪnˈkɔːpəreɪtəd‖-ɔːr-/ abbreviation **Inc** *adj AmE* used after the name of a company in the US to show that it is a CORPORATION

incorporeal hereditament —see under HEREDITAMENT

In·co·term /ˈɪŋkəʊˌtɜːm‖-koʊˌtɜːrm/ *n* [C] a word on a list from the International Chamber of Commerce that is used in international trade contracts. The list provides the exact meaning of terms, for example FOB, in order to avoid confusion between people in different countries: *The ICC's Incoterms are widely used by exporters and forwarders involved in the shipment of goods.*

carriage and insurance paid abbreviation **CIP**, also **freight and insurance paid** *n* [U] an INCOTERM stating that the seller pays for the goods to be taken as far as a named place and is responsible for insuring them until then

carriage paid abbreviation **DCP**, also **freight paid** *n* [U] an INCOTERM stating that the seller pays for the goods to be taken to a named place. The buyer is responsible for insuring the goods after they have been given to the first CARRIER (=company moving the goods)

cost and freight abbreviation **C&F** *n* [U] an INCOTERM stating that the seller pays for the goods to be taken as far as a named place but is not responsible for insuring them

cost, insurance, freight abbreviation **CIF**, also **cost, freight, insurance**, abbreviation **CFI** *n* [U] an INCOTERM stating that the seller pays the cost of the goods, the cost of transporting them to an agreed place, and the cost of insuring them

delivered at frontier abbreviation **DAF** *n* [U] an INCOTERM stating that the seller pays for the goods to be taken, usually by road or train, as far as the border of the buyer's country and is responsible for insuring them up to that point

delivered duty paid abbreviation **DDP** *n* [U] an INCOTERM stating that the seller pays for the goods to be delivered to the buyer, is responsible for insuring them for the whole journey and pays all related taxes

ex quay abbreviation **EXQ** *n* [U] an INCOTERM stating that the seller is responsible for taking the goods off the ship in a particular port, and making them available there, but not for transporting them anywhere

ex ship abbreviation **EXS** *n* [U] an INCOTERM stating that the seller will make the goods available on a ship in a particular port, and the buyer is responsible for paying for the goods to be put on land and transported to where they are needed

ex works abbreviation **EXW** *n* [U] an INCOTERM stating that the seller will make goods available to the buyer at the seller's factory, and the buyer is responsible for paying for them to be transported to where they are needed

free alongside ship abbreviation **FAS** *n* [U] an INCOTERM stating that the seller is responsible for paying for the goods to be taken to a port for export, and any loss or damage to them, up to the time when the goods are ready to be loaded on a ship at the port

free carrier abbreviation **FRC** *n* [U] an INCOTERM stating that the seller is responsible for paying for the goods to be taken to a named place where they are given to the buyer or someone named by the buyer, for example a TRANSPORT COMPANY

free on board abbreviation **FOB** *n* [U] an INCOTERM stating that the seller pays for taking the goods to the port where they are placed on a ship for export: *Santos handles about 30 ships a day and 38 million tonnes of cargo a year, worth about $30 billion free on board.*

free on board airport abbreviation **FOB airport** *n* [U] an INCOTERM similar to free on board, except that the seller is responsible for insuring the goods until they are delivered to a CARRIER (=company that moves the goods) at a specified airport

free on rail abbreviation **FOR**, also **free on truck**, abbreviation **FOT** *n* [U] an INCOTERM stating that the seller pays for taking the goods to the place where they are placed on a railway TRUCK of a train which will take them to the buyer: *The sellers had agreed to deliver the machine free on rail.*

in·crease[1] /ɪnˈkriːs/ *v* **1** [I] to become larger in amount, number, or degree: *Manufacturing output increased 0.6% in July, the Fed said.* | *Sales increased to 11.5 million tons from 11 million tons.* + **in**: *The yen is forecast to increase in value over the next year.* | *Two bond offerings were increased in size due to investor demand.* | *The oil that it uses has increased in price to $13 a barrel.*
2 [T] to make something larger in amount, number, or degree: *Southwest increased the number of passengers it carried last year by 14%.* | *He has increased the number of his licensing agreements.* —**increasing** *adj* [only before a noun] *There is increasing difficulty in finding trained staff.*

in·crease[2] /ˈɪŋkriːs/ *n* [C,U] **1** a rise in amount, number, or degree + **in**: *There was an increase in delays of deliveries of supplies.* **be on the increase** (=be increasing): *Demand for low-cost housing is on the increase.*
2 pay/price/tax etc increase an increase in pay etc: *Tobacco use in the state fell mostly because of the rise in the cost of cigarettes as a result of the tax increase.*

in·cre·ment /ˈɪŋkrəmənt/ *n* [C] **1** an amount that is regularly added to someone's pay: *Automatic pay increments based on length of service will be abolished.*
2 the amount by which a number, value etc increases: *The tariff increases by increments of £50.*

in·cre·men·tal /ˌɪŋkrəˈmentl◂/ *adj* **1** an incremental process is one where things happen in small steps: *Kaizen, a Japanese concept of* ***incremental improvements*** *in products through team efforts*
2 an incremental amount, sum etc is small when considered by itself: *The cuts are incremental (2% to 3%), not radical, but they add up.*

incremental cost —see under COST[1]

incubation investment —see under INVESTMENT

incubator space —see under SPACE

in·cum·bent[1] /ɪnˈkʌmbənt/ *n* [C] a person or company in an important or official position, rather than one that is trying to get that position: *The company decided to move the account from the incumbent, Grey Advertising, to another agency.* | *Nine out of ten incumbents who seek re-election win.*

incumbent[2] *adj* **it is incumbent on sb to do sth** *formal* if it is incumbent on you to do something, it is your duty or responsibility to do it: *It is incumbent on us to finalize this transaction so that our shareholders can receive their annual premium.*

in·cum·brance /ɪnˈkʌmbrəns/ *n* [C] another spelling of ENCUMBRANCE

in·cur /ɪnˈkɜː‖-ˈkɜːr/ *v* past tense and past participle **incurred** present participle **incurring** [T] if you incur a cost, a debt, or a fine, you do something that means that you lose money or have to pay money: *The East Moline foundry has been operating at less than 50% capacity and has* ***incurred*** *significant operating* ***losses.*** | *The* ***costs incurred*** *in planning each month run to several thousand dollars.*

in·debt·ed /ɪnˈdetɪ̵d/ *adj* owing money to someone: *Reports indicate that indebted consumers have cut their monthly borrowings by over 25%.*

in·debt·ed·ness /ɪnˈdetɪ̵dnəs/ *n* [U] *written* **1** the amount of money you owe to someone: *My current indebtedness to Citibank is $435.97.*
2 when you owe money to someone: *Sustained economic growth reduces public indebtedness.*

in·dem·ni·fy /ɪnˈdemnɪ̵faɪ/ *v* past tense and past participle **indemnified** [T] **1** to pay for a financial loss that a person or organization has had: *The committee plans to restructure the bank and pledge new capital to indemnify against any losses.*
2 INSURANCE to pay someone money because of loss, injury, or damage that they have suffered: *In accordance with the new policy, the company has agreed to indemnify the directors for any previous losses.* —**indemnification** *n* [C,U] *the indemnification of the firm against liability*

in·dem·ni·ty /ɪnˈdemnɪ̵ti/ *n* plural **indemnities** INSURANCE **1** [U] protection against loss or damage, especially in the form of an official written promise to pay for any losses or damage: *Every full-time employee at our firm receives a policy that gives indemnity against accidental death.*

double indemnity [U] life insurance or personal accident insurance where the amount paid out is twice the normal amount if the insured person dies or is injured in certain types of accident, eg road accidents

2 [C] a payment for the loss of money, goods etc: *The new Civil Service Law states that workers who are fired will get an indemnity equal to a month's salary for each year worked.*

indemnity bond —see under BOND

in·den·ture /ɪnˈdentʃə‖-ər/ *n* [C] **1** FINANCE a legal agreement between an organization that borrows money by ISSUING bonds (=making them available), and the lenders, stating the interest, the date they will be repaid etc: *The homebuilder said it paid the interest due last December in cash, but made the interest payments in stock last June, as allowed by the indentures for the debt.*
2 a legal agreement, especially one in former times between an employer and an APPRENTICE (=a young person who receives training from an employer to do a particular job), stating the terms of the worker's employment

in·den·tured /ɪnˈdentʃəd‖-ərd/ *adj* [only before a noun] **1** FINANCE indentured lenders are ones covered by an indenture agreement when bonds are ISSUED (=made available and sold)

2 an indentured worker is one who is forced to work for an employer for a long period of time with very low wages, bad conditions etc: *legislation banning imports of goods made by forced or indentured child labourers*

indentured labourer —see under LABOURER

independent brewery —see under BREWERY

independent means —see under MEANS

in·dex[1] /ˈɪndeks/ *n* plural **indexes** or **indices** **1** [C] something such as a price, amount, level etc that shows the general level of related prices etc: *The price of gold bullion on the exchange remains a sensitive index of confidence in the international market.*

2 [C] a figure showing the level of something, for example prices, in relation to earlier levels. Indexes often use the figure 100 as the BASE in a particular year and figures for later years are given in relation to this base

benchmark index [C] one of the main indexes for a particular activity or stockmarket: *The S&P 500 is a benchmark index for larger stocks.*

brand development index [C usually singular] a brand's sales in an area in relation to the area's population as a percentage of the country's population

consumer confidence index [C usually singular] in the US, an index of whether people feel the economy will get better or worse: *The consumer confidence index rose to 81 in March from 59.4 in February.*

consumer price index [C usually singular] abbreviation **CPI** [C] an index of prices paid for goods and services by the public in shops etc. The CPI is one measure of inflation: *The nation's consumer price index measures changes in a fixed market basket of goods and services.*

cost of living index [C usually singular] an index that shows the rate by which the cost of living is changing. It works by comparing the current price of particular goods, for example food or clothing, against the cost of the same goods in previous years: *Earnings per employee rose over four times between 1985 and 1992, while the cost of living index rose only three times.*

Dodge index [singular] an index of activity in the CONSTRUCTION INDUSTRY in the US, produced by McGraw Hill, an information services company: *The Dodge Index fell again last month, reflecting continued depression in the construction of new homes.*

industrial output index also **industrial production index** [C] an index of the level of activity in the production of RAW MATERIALS (=materials used in manufacturing) and in manufacturing

Industrial Sentiment index [singular] an index produced in the US by Dun & Bradstreet, a business information services company, showing how people in industry feel about the economic state of their industry, future growth etc

misery index *n* [singular] the rate of unemployment added to the rate of inflation: *The misery index reached new heights.*

order-book index [C] an index showing the general level of orders that have been received by companies in a particular area, industry etc: *The monthly order-books index for the construction industry rose to 151 in February.*

producer price index [C] in Britain, an index of the prices paid by companies for raw materials and of prices charged by producers of goods: *Producer price indices are useful indicators of the likely future trend of inflation.*

Purchasing Managers' index [singular] an index of prices paid by US companies for goods and services, produced by the National Association of Purchasing Managers: *The purchasing managers' index, a measure of manufacturing activity, is expected to rise.*

Retail Price Index abbreviation **RPI** [singular] the official CONSUMER PRICE INDEX in Britain: *Price increases for food, alcohol and petrol helped to drive the retail price index 0.7% higher in October.*

trade-weighted index [C usually singular] an index showing the value of a country's currency in relation to the currencies of a group of countries with which it trades. In the index, each country's currency is given an importance in relation to the amount of trade it does: *The trade-weighted index measures the Australian dollar's value against a basket* (=group) *of 24 currencies; the weights have been set by the Reserve Bank of Australia.*

3 FINANCE also **share index**, **stock index** an official list of the average price of shares in a group of companies on a particular stockmarket: *Milan's Stock Index fell 2% in the year.* | *the Nikkei share index*

FTSE 30 Share Index [singular] the Financial Times-Stock Exchange 30-share index; an average of share prices in 30 large companies on the London Stock Exchange, calculated since 1935, but now less used than some of the other indices

FTSE 100 Share Index [singular] the Financial Times-Stock Exchange 100 share index, an average of share prices in the 100 largest, most actively traded companies on the London Stock Exchange; FOOTSIE: *Banks and insurers were among the worst performers in the FTSE 100.*

FTSE All-Share Index [singular] the Financial Times-Stock Exchange All-Share index; an average of share prices of all companies on the London Stock Exchange, about 1000 companies, often used as a guide to compare the performance of different companies and industries: *ICI's share price* ***outperformed the FTSE All Share Index*** (=performed better than the average) *by 7% during the week.*

FTSE Eurotop 100 Index [singular] an average of the share prices of 100 of the largest, most actively traded companies on European stock markets

FTSE Eurotop 300 Index [singular] an average of the share prices of 300 of the largest, most actively traded companies on European stock markets

FTSE Fledgling Index [singular] an average of the share prices of very small British companies on the London Stock Exchange

FTSE Mid 250 Index [singular] an average of the share prices of 250 middle-size companies on the London Stock Exchange: *Companies in the FTSE Mid 250 Index are less export-oriented and therefore represent a more concentrated investment in the UK.*

FTSE SmallCap Index [singular] an average of the share prices of fairly small companies on the London stockmarket

Hang Seng Index also **Hang Seng** [singular] an index of the shares of Hong Kong's 100 largest companies: *The Hang Seng Index closed 315.29 points down.*

Nikkei index also **Nikkei average** the main share index of shares in companies on the Tokyo stockmarket: *The Nikkei index fell by 40% during the year.*

Standard & Poor's Index also **Standard & Poor's 500 stock index**, abbreviation **S&P 500** [singular] a measure of changes on the stockmarket, based on the performance of shares in 500 large US companies: *The Standard & Poor's index of 500 stocks was down 0.17 point to 396.47.*

weighted index [C] a share index in which certain important shares have value added to them so that when they are compared, their true effect on prices is shown: *Dow Jones's* ***market-weighted index*** (=values added to allow for changes in the stockmarket) *of aerospace stocks surged 2.3%.* —see also CAC 40, DAX, DOW JONES AVERAGES

index² *v* [T] **1** to arrange for the level of payments such as wages or PENSIONS to go up at the same rate as something else, usually prices **index sth to**: *With inflation at 20% a year, tax exemptions should be indexed to the purchasing power of the pound.*
2 if an investment is indexed to something, for example a currency or a STOCK INDEX, its value rises and falls in relation to the currency etc: *The yield of Ukrainian treasury bills is indexed to the value of the local currency, the hryvnia, in terms of the dollar.* —**indexation** *n* [U] *The government has so far resisted claims for a return to wage-price indexation despite a wave of strikes.*

index cards —see CARD INDEX SYSTEM

indexed bond —see under BOND

index fund —see under FUND[1]

index futures —see under FUTURES

index-linked *adj* index-linked loans, PENSIONS etc are those whose value follows the level of prices in the RETAIL PRICE INDEX: *For investors still concerned about inflation, Britannia Building Society's index-linked account is well worth considering.*

index-linked gilts —see under GILTS

index of coincident indicators —see under INDICATOR

index of leading indicator —see under INDICATOR

index option —see under OPTION

in·di·ca·tor /ˈɪndəkeɪtə‖-ər/ *n* [C] a sign of the level of activity in the economy or in a particular company or financial market: *All the main indicators suggest that trade is improving.* + **of**: *Orders for machine tools are considered an indicator of manufacturers' optimism.* —see also BAROMETER

coincident indicator one showing current economic activity, rather than what is going to happen: *The number of people registering at employment agencies is more of a coincident indicator.*

economic indicator a figure showing the performance of a particular part of the economy, for example employment, prices, production etc: *The Fed may move to cut rates if economic indicators released by the government continue to show a stagnant economy.*

financial indicator one showing the state of a company's finances or of a financial market: *By almost any financial indicator their companies were leaders in their industries.*

index of coincident indicators in the US, a combination of indexes that give early signs about what is happening in the economy now rather than what will happen later: *The Commerce Department's index of coincident indicators fell 0.8% in November because of declines in employment, personal income and industrial production.*

index of leading indicators in the US, a combination of indexes that give early signs about what is going to happen in the economy later, including stock prices, orders for machinery etc: *The index of leading indicators fell 1.2% in November, yet another sign of economic weakness.*

key indicator a very important one, giving information about the state of the economy as a whole: *Strong bank profits are key indicators of economic recovery.*

lagging indicator one that only follows what has happened earlier in the economy: *Employment is a lagging indicator of economic strength because many companies don't cut their work forces until they are certain that conditions require it.*

leading indicator one that gives early signs of what is going to happen in the economy later: *Corporate profits are considered a leading indicator, usually rising in advance of the economy.*

sentiment indicator one that gives information about how people feel about the state and the future of a financial market or of the economy: *ISI's bullish/bearish sentiment indicator was 5.98 last Wednesday.*

technical indicator one that shows the direction of a financial market: *The main technical indicator was gold's inability to rise above $375 earlier in the week.*

in·di·ces /ˈɪndəsiːz/ the plural of INDEX

in·dict /ɪnˈdaɪt/ *v* [I,T] LAW *especially AmE* to officially charge someone with a criminal offence **indict sb for sth**: *21 currency traders have been indicted for illegal trading practices.* —**indictable** *adj*: *It is debatable whether he committed an indictable offense.*

in·dict·ment /ɪnˈdaɪtmənt/ *n* LAW *especially AmE*
1 [C] an official written statement charging someone with a criminal offence: *The indictment alleged that he diverted clients' money to unauthorized uses.*
2 [U] the act of charging someone with a criminal offence: *At the time of his indictment, the government's case rested on one key witness.*

in·die /ˈɪndi/ *n* [C] a small, independent company, especially one that produces records of popular music, television programmes, or films

indifference curve —see under CURVE

in·di·ge·nous /ɪnˈdɪdʒənəs/ *adj* indigenous companies, goods etc are found or made in the local area, rather than abroad: *Previous local governments have pursued a policy of attracting in high-tech firms at the expense of developing indigenous firms.*

in·di·gent /ˈɪndɪdʒənt/ *adj formal* not having any money or possessions: *Hospitals continue to provide uncompensated care for the indigent.*

indirect cost —see under COST[1]

indirect exchange —see under EXCHANGE[1]

indirect expense —see under EXPENSE

indirect exporting —see under EXPORTING

indirect labour —see under LABOUR

indirect tax —see under TAX[1]

indirect taxation —see under TAXATION

individual income tax —see under INCOME TAX

individual retirement account —see under ACCOUNT[1]

individual savings account —see ISA

in·dorse /ɪnˈdɔːs‖-ɔːrs/ another spelling of ENDORSE

in·dor·see /ˌɪndɔːˈsiː, ɪnˈdɔːsiː‖-ɔːr-/ *n* [C] another spelling of ENDORSEE

in·duce /ɪnˈdjuːs‖ɪnˈduːs/ *v* [T] to make someone decide to do something, perhaps something that seems unwise **induce sb to do sth**: *Lower interest rates would induce customers to borrow more.*

in·duce·ment /ɪnˈdjuːsmənt‖ɪnˈduːs-/ *n* [C,U] something such as money or a gift that you are offered to persuade you to do something: *There has to be a good inducement for investors to commit money to risky but socially worthwhile ventures.*

in·duct /ɪnˈdʌkt/ *v* [T] to officially introduce someone into a position in a job, company, organization etc, usually through a special ceremony + **into**: *Mr Clay will be inducted into the company as president at a benefit dinner on Sunday.*

in·duc·tion /ɪnˈdʌkʃən/ *n* **1** [C,U] *BrE* the introduction and training of someone into a new job, company, official position etc: *departmental* ***induction courses*** | *A team from personnel will conduct the inductions.*
2 [C] a ceremony in which someone is officially introduced into a position in a job, company, organization etc: *Lauffer gave a 30 minute speech at his induction yesterday.*

I

in•dus•tri•al /ɪn'dʌstriəl/ *adj* **1** connected with industry: *big **industrial companies** such as Fiat S.p.A* | *The **industrial sector** remained weak at the end of the first quarter.* | *China's **industrial output** dropped sharply after floods stopped production in many factories.*
2 having many industries, or industries that are well developed: *The **industrial nations** are less dependent on oil than they were a decade ago.* | *the **industrial heartland*** (=the part where there is most industry) *of Southern California*
3 of the type used in industry: *a company that sells industrial fire alarms.* | *companies with big interests in **industrial chemicals*** | ***industrial products** such as cooling and heating equipment* —see also INDUSTRIALS

industrial action —see under ACTION

industrial co-operative —see under CO-OPERATIVE

industrial design —see under DESIGN[1]

industrial designer —see under DESIGNER[1]

industrial dispute —see under DISPUTE

industrial economics —see under ECONOMICS

industrial efficiency —see under EFFICIENCY

industrial electronics —see under ELECTRONICS

industrial goods —see under GOODS

industrial hygiene —see under HYGIENE

industrial injuries insurance —see under INSURANCE

industrial injury —see under INJURY

in•dus•tri•al•is•m /ɪn'dʌstriəlɪzəm/ *n* [U] the system by which a society gets its wealth through industry: *Does industrialism raise or lower the living standards of the working class?*

in•dus•tri•al•ist /ɪn'dʌstriəlɨst/ *n* [C] a powerful businessman or businesswoman who is the owner or leader of a large industrial company: *A group of Ukrainian ministers and industrialists asked for 6 million euros for technical training.*

in•dus•tri•al•ize also **industrialise** *BrE* /ɪn'dʌstriəlaɪz/ *v* [I,T] if a country or area industrializes or is industrialized, it develops a lot of industry for the first time: *Argentina was one of the first Latin American countries to industrialize.* | *Nasser's efforts to modernise Egypt and industrialise its economy* —**industrialization** also **industrialisation** *BrE n* [U] *the rapid industrialization of Japan*

in•dus•tri•a•lized also **industrialised** *BrE* /ɪn'dʌstriəlaɪzd/ *adj* having a lot of factories, industrial companies etc: *The chemical DDT is banned in all **industrialized countries**.* | *There has been an economic slowdown across the whole of **the industrialized world**.*

industrial output index —see under INDEX[1]

industrial product —see under PRODUCT

industrial production —see under PRODUCTION

industrial production index —see ***industrial output index*** under INDEX[1]

industrial property —see under PROPERTY

industrial psychology *n* [U] the study of how people behave at work, and the relationships between workers, managers, and TRADE UNIONS; OCCUPATIONAL PSYCHOLOGY

industrial relations —see under RELATIONS

industrial revenue bond —see under BOND

Industrial Revolution *n* [singular] the period in the 18th and 19th centuries when machines were first used to produce goods on a large scale: *The Industrial Revolution created a great demand for urban housing.*

in•dus•trials /ɪn'dʌstriəlz/ *n* [plural] FINANCE shares in industrial companies: *On Tuesday, the industrials fell 27.48 points.*

Dow Jones industrials also **Dow industrials** *trademark* another name for the DOW JONES INDUSTRIAL AVERAGE: *The Dow Jones industrials advanced 24.01 points.*

Industrial Sentiment index —see under INDEX[1]

industrial tribunal —see under TRIBUNAL

in•dus•tri•ous /ɪn'dʌstriəs/ *adj* always working very hard: *Mexico has an industrious labour force and enormous natural resources.* —**industriousness** *n* [U] *Hong Kong workers are known for their industriousness.*

in•dus•try /'ɪndəstri/ *n* plural **industries** **1** [U] the production of RAW MATERIALS (=basic materials used in manufacturing) and of goods: *Growth in productivity has dropped, and the competitiveness of industry has declined.*
2 [singular] the people and organizations that work in industry: *The Manpower Services Commission contains representatives from **both sides of industry*** (=employers and workers).
3 [C] a particular type of industry or service: *He joined ICI after working in the **retailing** and **banking industries**.* | *the **aircraft industry*** | *the **oil industry***

basic industry [C] an industry that many other industries in an economy depend on: *companies in basic industries, such as chemicals, oil, or steel*

capital-intensive industry [C] an industry which needs a lot of money for equipment, machinery etc: *large, capital-intensive industries such as steel and mining*

cottage industry ◆ [C] an industry consisting of people who work from home, making things such as toys or clothes
◆ [C] *informal* an industry consisting of small businesses operating from home: *There is a huge cottage industry of proprietors running nursing homes for elderly people.*

declining industry [C] an industry that is gradually getting smaller and less important: *labour lay-offs in declining industries such as textiles and coal*

essential industry [C] an industry that a country considers is very important to its economy and may support with government money, taxes on imports etc: *The continent's biggest, most essential industries – electronics and cars – need tariff protection and aid money.*

extractive industry [C] an industry where materials, such as oil and coal, are obtained from under the ground in DRILLING, MINING, and QUARRYING: *The biggest extractive industry in Cornwall today is the mining of china clay.*

growth industry [C] an industry, service, or activity that is growing fast: *They moved away from steel to tourism, which is a growth industry.*

heavy industry [C,U] an industrial activity involving heavy machinery, large factories, etc or these activities considered as a whole: *heavy industry, including coal mining, mechanical engineering and ship building*

heritage industry [U] the business activity of managing places that are related to a country's past and bringing tourists to them: *The heritage industry brings large numbers of foreign tourists to old centres of attraction like country houses and towns in Stratford, York, or Bath.*

high-tech industry also **hi-tech industry** [C] an industry using or involving advanced methods and the most modern equipment: *such important high-tech industries as chemicals, drugs and aircraft*

infant industry [C] an industry in its early stages of development in a particular country.: *The insurance industry here is an infant industry, and we should try to protect it.*

knowledge industry [C] an industry where success depends on obtaining, managing, and using knowledge

I

in a particular area: *knowledge industries such as computer software*

labour-intensive industry *BrE*, **labor-intensive industry** *AmE* [C] an industry needing a lot of people to operate, usually MANUAL WORKERS: *Many manufacturers in labor-intensive industries in Taiwan have moved operations to China.*

leisure industry [C,U] an industry that provides goods or services for activities that people do for entertainment and enjoyment: *The leisure industry soaks up approximately 12% of the average American's income.*

light industry [C,U] an industry needing only light machinery, small factories etc, for example electronics, or these industries viewed as a whole: *Light industries grew at 12.1% last year, fuelled by rising demand for televisions and washing machines.*

low-tech industry [C] an industry not using very advanced methods or very advanced equipment: *The mining industry has gone from being a low-tech industry to a high-tech industry, and that means more production with fewer people.*

manufacturing industry [C,U] the activity of making goods, rather than providing services, or these activities considered as a whole: *Manufacturing industries, particularly aerospace firms, are reasonably healthy.* | *Orders to Germany's manufacturing industry have been declining and industrial output has fallen.*

mature industry [C] an industry which is not new and with little growth or no growth, and little chance of further growth in the future: *Insurance broking is a mature industry, where revenue growth is slow.*

primary industry [C,U] an industry involved in the production of RAW MATERIALS, FUEL etc, or these industries considered as a whole: *primary industries like mining, quarrying and oil and gas production*

regulated industry [C] an industry that is closely controlled by the government: *regulated industries such as trucking and airlines*

secondary industry [C,U] an industry that makes goods, rather than producing RAW MATERIALS (=basic materials used to make goods) or providing services, or these industries considered as a whole: *They wanted to develop a series of secondary industries: sawmilling, building, textiles and cider-making.*

service industry [C,U] a business such as banking or tourism that provides services, or these activities considered as a whole: *A large part of the workforce switched from manufacturing to service industries in the 1980s.* | *Most of the recently created jobs have been in the service industry and the retail sector.*

smokestack industry [C] a HEAVY INDUSTRY, often in an old industrial area: *China's steel mills, auto plants and other smokestack industries are gathered in the industrial belt.*

strategic industry [C] an industry that a country considers very important for its economic development: *No one in France wanted to see such a strategic industry as nuclear power pass out of the public sector.*

sunrise industry [C] an industry based on new TECHNOLOGY (=the most advanced equipment and methods) often in an area without an industrial past: *sunrise industries including biotechnology, computer technology and robotics*

sunset industry [C] an industry based on an old TECHNOLOGY (=methods and equipment), often in an old industrial area, and often one which is getting smaller: *The EU has often been engaged in protecting sunset industries such as the steel industry.*

tertiary industry [C,U] an industry providing services, rather than producing raw materials or goods, or these industries considered as a whole: *Tertiary industry already accounts for half of Shanghai's output, and its mayor wants to further develop financial services and tourism.*

industry analysis —see under ANALYSIS

industry analyst —see under ANALYST

industry association —see under ASSOCIATION

industry leader —see under LEADER

in·dus·try·wide /ˈɪndəstriˌwaɪd/ *adj* throughout industry or throughout a particular industry: *Internet auctions of flights are part of an industrywide effort to cut distribution costs.* —**industrywide** *adv*: *Sony is estimating sales of a half-million machines industrywide.*

in·elas·tic /ˌɪnɪˈlæstɪk◂/ *adj* ECONOMICS used to say that a change in one thing, for example, the price of a product, makes another thing, for example the demand for it, change by a smaller amount: *Coffee is a fairly inelastic commodity, which means lower prices don't significantly increase consumption.*

price inelastic price inelastic goods, markets etc are those where the price of something does not change very much when the supply or demand for it increases or decreases: *the highly price-inelastic world market for food grains* —**inelasticity** *n* [U] *Price inelasticity was once one of the qualities of cigarettes.*

inelastic demand —see under DEMAND

inelastic supply —see under SUPPLY[2]

in·er·tia /ɪˈnɜːʃə‖-ɜːr-/ *n* [U] a tendency for a situation to stay the same for a long time: *He believes that suppressed demand after years of inertia will lead to a housing recovery this year.*

inertia selling —see under SELLING

infant industry —see under INDUSTRY

in·fect /ɪnˈfekt/ *v* [T] COMPUTING if a computer VIRUS (=a program put secretly into your computer that can destroy the information on it) infects your computer, the programs on the computer stop working properly: *Once write-protected, a disk can't be infected by a virus.*

in·fill /ˈɪnfɪl/ *n* [U] *especially AmE* PROPERTY when new homes and other buildings are built in between the buildings that are already there, rather than around their edge: *Infill is encouraged in areas like Tuscon, which has vast amounts of vacant land within the city limits.*

in·flate /ɪnˈfleɪt/ *v* [I,T] if the cost or level of something inflates or is inflated, it increases, often above what is reasonable or normal: *Overseas sales were inflated by the depreciation of the yen.* | *Costs of bringing crops to market are likely to inflate due to the high price of oil.*

in·flat·ed /ɪnˈfleɪtɪ̈d/ *adj* [only before a noun] inflated prices, sums etc are unreasonably high: *These company directors are paid **grossly inflated** salaries.*

in·fla·tion /ɪnˈfleɪʃən/ *n* [U] **1** a continuing increase in the prices of goods and services: *The Fed views inflation as the most serious worry in the economy.* | *The German central bank pledged to maintain a strong mark as a means to help **contain inflation*** (=control it).
2 the rate at which prices are increasing at a particular time or over a particular period of time + **of**: *Portugal had annual average inflation of 11.4% last year.* | *Gold does well only during periods of **high inflation**.* | *Britain's **inflation rate** rose to 4.5% last month.* | ***Adjusted for inflation*** (=after taking inflation into account) *real growth is estimated to be 1.8%.*

asset inflation when the price of land, shares etc rises more quickly than the rate of economic growth: *The Bank of Japan started worrying that asset inflation could affect consumer price inflation.*

consumer price inflation the increase in prices paid by people buying goods and services: *Consumer price inflation, excluding energy and food, fell to 2.6% in the 12 months to June.*

core inflation inflation calculated without taking into account prices that change a lot such as those for food: *Core inflation, which does not include volatile fuel or food prices, has stopped falling, despite a sharp fall in headline inflation.*

cost inflation also **cost-push inflation** when prices of goods and services increase because of the increased cost of wages, RAW MATERIALS (=materials used to produce goods) etc: *Usually cost-push inflation is strongest when the economy has been expanding for a long time.*

creeping inflation when inflation is rising slowly, but beginning to increase more quickly than people realize: *Data on May retail sales show new signs of life in the economy and creeping inflation.*

demand inflation also **demand-pull inflation** when an economy is growing, and prices rise because the amount of goods and services being produced does not keep up with the amount of money available to buy them or the demand for them: *Delivery times lengthen when demand exceeds supply, and often reflect the development of demand-pull inflation.*

double-digit inflation when prices rise at between 10 and 99 per cent per year: *The US experienced double-digit inflation: in 1974, 1979 and 1980.*

galloping inflation also **runaway inflation** very high inflation that is out of control; HYPERINFLATION: *the galloping inflation of the late 1980s | a plan to rid Brazil of its runaway inflation, which exceeded 4,800% in the preceding 12 months*

headline inflation inflation calculated including prices that change a lot such as those for food and FUEL and, in Britain, MORTGAGE PAYMENTS (=the money that people repay on loans to buy houses): *a headline inflation rate of 5.5%*

hyperinflation also **hyper-inflation** a rapid rise in prices that seriously damages a country's economy; GALLOPING INFLATION: *The aim of the strict budget was to prevent hyperinflation.*

structural inflation inflation that is part of a particular economic system, so that a complete change in economic policy would be needed to get rid of it.

underlying inflation the general TREND (=the general pattern in which something is changing) of inflation, not including prices of things that are untypical of the trend: *Underlying inflation, excluding food and energy costs, edged up to 0.6% from 0.5%.*

wage inflation increase in people's pay: *There has been a modest decline in average hourly earnings of workers, suggesting there is little reason to fear wage inflation.*

wage-push inflation a situation in which wages rise but workers do not produce any more goods than before, so that goods cost more to make and buy

zero inflation when prices are not rising at all: *Canada set a series of inflation-reduction targets, with the aim of achieving zero inflation.*

inflation accounting —see under ACCOUNTING

inflation-adjusted *adj* [only before a noun] inflation-adjusted prices and INDICATORS such as spending, growth etc take inflation into account: *Real, or inflation-adjusted, fares remain lower today than they were 10 years ago. | An annual* ***inflation-adjusted growth rate*** *for GNP of 6% is not bad.*

inflation-adjusted gross domestic product —see under GROSS DOMESTIC PRODUCT

inflation-adjusted price —see under PRICE[1]

in·fla·tion·a·ry /ɪnˈfleɪʃənəri‖-ʃəneri/ *adj* relating to or causing price increases: *The Bundesbank will defend the mark and fight the* ***inflationary effects*** *associated with a falling currency. | Employment costs are one of the best indicators of* ***inflationary pressures*** *in the economy.*

inflation-proof *adj* an inflation-proof investment is not affected by rising prices, or rises in value faster than prices do: *Real estate values have surged 5% to 10%, fueled by investors who are looking for inflation-proof places to put funds.*

inflation risk —see under RISK[1]

in-flight[1] *adj* [only before a noun] provided during a plane journey: *an in-flight movie*

in-flight[2] *n* [C] a magazine provided by an AIRLINE for passengers to read during a plane journey

in·flow /ˈɪnfləʊ‖-floʊ/ *n* [C] a steady movement of something such as money or goods into a place, economy, activity etc: *A stable dollar and a strong economy would encourage an inflow of foreign investment. | He hasn't recently had any big cash inflows into his fund.*

in·flu·ence[1] /ˈɪnfluəns/ *n* [C,U] power to have an effect on the way something happens or the way someone does something: *The car magazines have been* ***gaining influence*** *in recent years. | The banks' directors say they have little influence over their presidents' actions.* —see also UNDUE INFLUENCE

influence[2] *v* [T] to have an effect on the way something happens or the way someone does something: *Children are heavily influenced by advertising.* + **what/where/how etc**: *The number of training centres will influence what training is available and who will receive it.*

in·flux /ˈɪnflʌks/ *n* [C usually singular] the arrival of large numbers of people, or large amounts of money, goods etc, especially suddenly: *Everyone agrees that the flight of the Venetians needs to be halted and the influx of tourists controlled. | In Frankfurt, stocks rose* ***on an influx*** *of foreign funds.*

in·fo /ˈɪnfəʊ‖-foʊ/ *informal n* [U] information

in·fo·mer·cial /ˈɪnfəʊmɜːʃəl‖-foʊmɜːr-/ *n* [C] a television or radio advertisement made to look and sound like a real programme, often a financial news report or an advice show

in·form /ɪnˈfɔːm‖-ɔːrm/ *v* [T] to formally or officially tell someone about something or give them information **inform sb (that)**: *We regret to inform you that your application has been unsuccessful.* **inform sb of/about**: *The firm's US partners were informed of the planned cuts last week.*

in·for·mat·ics /ˌɪnfəˈmætɪks‖-fər-/ *n* [U] *especially BrE* the science of processing information electronically; INFORMATION SCIENCE

in·for·ma·tion /ˌɪnfəˈmeɪʃən‖-fər-/ *n* [U] **1** facts or details that tell you about something or someone: *This is highly* ***confidential information.*** *| Corporations are making more* ***financial information*** *available to investors.*

credit information information about a company's ability to pay its suppliers: *A supplier of credit information to the clothing industry advised manufacturers against shipping new merchandise to this retailer except on a cash basis.*

inside information also **insider information** secret information that is only available to people who are part of a particular organization or group: *He was accused of* ***trading on inside information.*** (=using inside information to make trading decisions)

2 for information only written on copies of letters and documents that are sent to someone who needs to know about them but does not need to deal with them

3 for your information written abbreviation **FYI** written on the front or at the top of a letter when you want a particular person to read it or deal with it

4 *AmE* the telephone service that provides telephone numbers to people who ask for them; DIRECTORY ENQUIRIES *BrE*

information exchange —see under EXCHANGE[1]

information science *n* [U] the science of collecting, arranging, storing, and sending out information

information superhighway *n* [singular] *informal* the various systems that can be used to send or obtain information, pictures, films etc by electronic means, for example from a computer in one place to a computer in a different place: *Ordinary people now have access to the information superhighway.*

information system —see under SYSTEM

information technology —see under TECHNOLOGY

in·fo·tain·ment /ˌɪnfəʊˈteɪnmənt‖-foʊ-/ *n* [U] information presented on television and in computer programs with pictures and sound, that deals with important subjects in a way that people can enjoy

in·frac·tion /ɪnˈfrækʃən/ *n* [C,U] when someone breaks a rule or law: *We would like more detailed records of airlines' safety infractions.* | *The next incident or infraction will result in dismissal.*

in·fra·struc·ture /ˈɪnfrəˌstrʌktʃə‖-ər/ *n* [C,U] **1** the basic systems and structures that a country needs to make economic activity possible, for example transport, communications, and power supplies: *Work is urgently needed to repair our **decaying infrastructure**.* | *The government invested $65 billion in infrastructure.*
2 the basic systems and equipment needed for an industry or business to operate successfully or for an activity to happen: *Countries in Eastern Europe were struggling to improve their phone infrastructures.* | *No retail infrastructure exists to channel these new products to the customers.*
3 COMPUTING the computers, communications networks, and software needed for computer systems to operate or to communicate with other systems: *On-line services are a major part of the Internet infrastructure.*

in·fringe /ɪnˈfrɪndʒ/ also **infringe on** *v* [T] to do something that is against a law or someone's legal rights: *There was no evidence that Apple's work was infringing Xerox copyrights.* | *We'll be watching closely to see whether they infringe on our patents.* —**infringement** *n* [C,U] *The company doesn't believe its promotional material is a **trademark infringement**.*

in·fu·sion /ɪnˈfjuːʒən/ *n* [C,U] the act of putting a lot of money or something else that is needed into a company, organization etc + **of**: *Most Japanese acquisitions have been followed by an infusion of capital or technology.* | *Despite a $65 billion government **cash infusion**, the big banks are not expected to turn decent profits for several years.*

in·got /ˈɪŋgət/ *n* [C,U] a piece of pure metal, for example gold, in the shape of a brick: *a solid 24 kt gold ingot* | *the average price per pound of aluminum ingot*

in·her·it /ɪnˈherɪ̵t/ *v* [T] **1** to receive money or property from someone after they have died: *She will inherit her father's entire fortune when he dies.* **inherit sth from sb**: *We built the house on land inherited from our uncle.*—**inheritor** *n* [C] *How will the inheritors invest their money?*
2 to start being in charge of a situation that was previously controlled by another person: *The incoming president inherited a healthy economy.* **inherit sth from sb**: *Problems he inherited from his predecessor led to the bank's later troubles.*

in·her·i·tance /ɪnˈherɪ̵təns/ *n* [C,U] money, property, or other things that become yours after someone has died: *people who suddenly have large lump sums to invest, perhaps from an inheritance*

inheritance tax —see under TAX[1]

in·hib·it /ɪnˈhɪbɪ̵t/ *v* [T] to prevent something from growing or developing in the way that it could or being as good as it should be: *Air fares tend to be higher at airports where certain factors inhibit competition among airlines.*

in-house *adv* if a job is done in-house, it is done within an organization, especially by the organization's own staff: *Most of Macy's $170 million in advertising continues to be handled in-house.* | *Government agencies discover they can pay less by contracting out jobs instead of doing them in-house.* —**in-house** *adj*: *Many businesses are introducing **in-house training**.* | *the top **in-house lawyer** of General Electric Co*

inhouse magazine —see under MAGAZINE

i·ni·tial[1] /ɪˈnɪʃəl/ *adj* [only before a noun] happening first or at the beginning of an event or process: *Each portfolio has a minimum **initial investment** of $3,000.* | *the **initial capital** required for the project* (=the money needed to start it) | *Somatogen sold two million shares in its **initial public offering*** (=when its shares were made available to the public for the first time).

initial[2] *v* **initialled initialling** *BrE*, **initialed initialing** *AmE* [T] **1** to write your initials on an official document to show that you agree with it: *I would be grateful if you could complete and initial clause two, and return the documents to us.*
2 to make an official agreement or arrangement with someone: *Seoul and Beijing initialed a trade agreement in a move to expand economic exchanges between the two nations.*

initial[3] *n* [C usually plural] **1** the first letter of someone's first name: *I need a list of names, with initials.*
2 initials [plural] the first letters of the words in the name of a company or organization: *Yves Saint Laurent's famous initials, YSL*

i·ni·tial·ize also **initialise** *BrE* /ɪˈnɪʃəlaɪz/ *v* [I,T] COMPUTING **1** if a computer initializes or is initialized, certain important programs are prepared so that it can start running
2 if you initialize a disk or if a disk initializes, you divide it into parts so that it can store information; FORMAT

initial offer —see under OFFER[2]

initial price —see under PRICE[1]

initial public offer —see under OFFER[2]

initial public offering —see under OFFERING

initial yield —see under YIELD[1]

i·ni·tia·tive /ɪˈnɪʃətɪv/ *n* **1** [U] the ability to make decisions and take action without waiting for someone to tell you what to do: *He encourages initiative and new ideas.* | *You must be prepared to work **on your own initiative**.*
2 [C] an important new plan or process, done to achieve a particular aim or to solve a particular problem: *The **cost-cutting initiatives** are expected to result in savings of $300 million.* | *an initiative to attract new customers*

in·ject /ɪnˈdʒekt/ *v* [T] to provide money, ideas, skills etc for an organization or an activity, to make it perform better or to stop it from failing **inject sth into sth**: *This was an opportunity to inject some life into the campaign.* | *The tax cut would inject about FFr5 billion into the French car market.* —**injection** *n* [C] *Investors provided a much-needed **cash injection** of 79.5 million Irish pounds.*

in·junc·tion /ɪnˈdʒʌŋkʃən/ *n* [C] LAW an court order, usually stating that someone must not do something. Sometimes an injunction orders someone to do something + **against**: *A state judge **issued an injunction** against implementing the new system.* | *The SEC was **seeking an injunction** asking a court to make an injunction against Mr Kurtz.*

interim injunction *BrE*, **preliminary injunction** *AmE* an injunction made by a court that prevents someone from doing something until there is a full trial to solve the disagreement: *Kraft was awarded a preliminary injunction against Friendship Dairies Inc. over sour cream packaging that Kraft charged copied its own package designs.*

I

interlocutory injunction *BrE* an injunction made during the course of a trial, that lasts only until the end of the trial

mandatory injunction an injunction stating that someone must do something

permanent injunction an injunction where a court gives a final decision on a disagreement, rather than an interim injunction: *A federal judge issued a permanent injunction barring Wilkinson Sword from making the claim in its ads.*

restrictive injunction an injunction stating that someone must not do something

in•jure /ˈɪndʒə‖-ər/ *v* [T] **1** to cause physical harm to someone or to yourself, for example in an accident: *He sought compensation after being injured by a defective product.*

2 to make an industry, economy, company, or investor lose money or suffer in some other way: *The US steel industry was being injured by imports of subsidized steel.* | *a fund for injured investors*

in•ju•ry /ˈɪndʒəri/ *n* plural **injuries** [C,U] **1** physical harm to a person, for example in an accident: *Mr. Lewis was awarded $75,000 as compensation for injuries suffered in the accident.* | *absence from work due to illness or injury*

criminal injury LAW *BrE* injury to a person caused by another person's criminal activities: *The tribunal awards criminal injuries compensation to the victims of violent crime.*

industrial injury injury that is the result of an accident at work or that is the result of the work that you do there; WORK-RELATED INJURY *AmE*: *The frequency of industrial injuries in small firms is twelve times the rate in large firms.*

personal injury LAW injury that is the fault of a person or organization, for example an employer who does not follow the correct safety standards, a producer of faulty goods, or a driver involved in a car accident: *He is seeking damages for personal injuries.* | *defendants in person injury cases*

repetitive strain injury abbreviation **RSI** pains in your hands, arms, etc caused by doing the same hand movements many times and sometimes experienced by people who work at computers: *Escape Ergonomics sells software for preventing repetitive strain injuries by prompting users to take breaks at regular intervals.*

work-related injury *AmE* injury that is the result of an accident at work or that is the result of the work that you do there; INDUSTRIAL INJURY

2 when a person or organization is made to suffer in some way + **to**: *Donovan claimed he suffered serious injury to his professional and personal reputation.*

inkjet printer also **inkjet** —see under PRINTER

in•land /ˈɪnlənd/ *adj* [only before a noun] **1** inland mail or TRANSPORT services are those used for letters or goods being sent within a country, not abroad: *The letter was lost in the* ***inland post.*** | *inland cargo transport*

2 an inland area, city, point etc is away from the coast: *Loading starts not at the port, but at inland depots.* | *ships that operate on inland waterways* —**inland** *adv*: *An elaborate system of canals was built, enabling goods to be transported inland.*

Inland Revenue written abbreviation **IR** *n* the government department that collects income taxes in Britain: *I have not yet received a tax bill from* ***the Inland Revenue.*** —see also BOARD OF INLAND REVENUE, INTERNAL REVENUE SERVICE

inner city *n* plural **inner cities** [C] the part near the centre of a city where the buildings are often in a bad condition and the people are poor: *The inner cities are covered with dilapidated and dangerous housing.* | *poor, inner-city neighborhoods*

inner city renewal —see under RENEWAL

in•no•vate /ˈɪnəveɪt/ *v* [I] to design and develop new and original products: *He accused Toyota of being conservative and reluctant to innovate.* —**innovator** *n* [C] *Portman became famous in the 1960s as an innovator in hotel design.*

in•no•va•tion /ˌɪnəˈveɪʃən/ *n* **1** [C] a new idea, method, or invention: *It is a fairly* ***recent innovation*** *for rent to be paid in advance.* | ***Financial innovations*** *such as money-market accounts made it even harder to measure the money supply.*

2 [U] the introduction of new ideas or methods: *We encourage creativity and innovation.* | *Mr. Bohn planned to accelerate the pace of* ***technological innovation*** *at Porsche.*

product innovation [C,U] when new or better products are designed and developed, or the new or better product itself: *Many economists blame South Korea's economic problems on its lack of product innovation.*

in•nov•at•ive /ˈɪnəˌveɪtɪv/ *adj* **1** an innovative product, method, process etc is new, different, and better than those that existed before: *Kodak has developed some innovative products in electronic imaging.* | *We supply goods to customers who want innovative design.* | *an innovative approach to problem solving*

2 using or developing new and original ideas and methods: *VW became one of the West's most innovative auto makers.* —**innovatively** *adv*: *innovatively designed and well-engineered cars*

Inns of Court also **Inns** *n* [plural] LAW four societies in London whose members have the right to act as BARRISTERS (=lawyers who can argue cases in the higher courts)

in•op•e•ra•tive /ɪnˈɒpərətɪv‖ɪnˈɑː-/ *adj formal* **1** a machine or piece of equipment that is inoperative is not working or is not in a good enough condition to work: *A power cut* ***rendered*** *1000 ATMs* ***inoperative.*** | *If the water freezes, the cables may become inoperative.*

2 a law, rule etc is inoperative, it is no longer used, or it is not used in a situation when normally it would be used: *If the amount concerned is $50 or less, this clause will be inoperative.*

in-plant *adj* involving or relating to something in a particular factory: *The Newspaper Mail and Deliverers' Union performs a number of in-plant functions at the New York Times in addition to distributing the newspaper.*

in•put[1] /ˈɪnpʊt/ *n* **1** [U] ideas, advice, effort, or money that you put into something to help it succeed **input from sb**: *Geoff works out the designs with a lot of input from Alice.* | *an operation with an annual government input of £12 million* | *Please give us your views as we value our customers' input.*

2 also **factor input** [C usually plural] ECONOMICS a FACTOR OF PRODUCTION (=land, labour, or capital) put into a business in order for it to create wealth: *the value of the product as compared with the cost of the inputs* | *Costs of all factor inputs could be reduced.*

3 [U] COMPUTING when information is put into a computer: *The machines used for* ***data input*** *should be upgraded.*

4 [U] COMPUTING information that is put into a computer system: *the rate of information transfer from input to output*

input[2] *v* past tense and past participle **input** or **inputted** present participle **inputting** [T] to put information into a computer: *Users are responsible for inputting their own data.*

input/output written abbreviation **I/O** *adj* [only before a noun] concerned with putting information into a computer system or getting information from it: *With this new software, input/output processing speeds would be increased by 300%.* | *input/output devices*

I

input tax —see under TAX[1]

in·quire also **enquire** /ɪn'kwaɪə‖-ər/ *v* [I] **1** to ask someone for information + **about**: *Hundreds of prospective buyers have inquired about the auction.* + **whether/when/why etc**: *Employers may not inquire whether an applicant has a disability.* —**inquirer** *n* [C] *Make sure you get the inquirer's name and address.*
2 inquire within used on notices, especially in shop windows, to mean that you can find out more about something inside: *Vacancies – inquire within.*

in·quir·y /ɪn'kwaɪəri‖ɪn'kwaɪri, 'ɪŋkwəri/ *n* plural **inquiries** **1** [C] a question you ask in order to get information: *He has received a flood of* ***telephone inquiries*** *from small investors.* | *customers who call in just to* ***make inquiries***
2 [U] when you ask questions in order to get information: *Mr. Gilberd agreed to this transaction without further inquiry.*
3 [C] an official process, in the form of a series of meetings, intended to find out why something happened + **into**: *The Commission* ***conducted an inquiry*** *into allegations of unfair business practices.*

in rem /ɪn 'rem/ *adv* LAW a legal case that is brought in rem is brought against property or land rather than against a person

ins. written abbreviation for INCHES

IN.SECTS /'ɪnsekts/ *n* [plural] FINANCE Pan European Sector Indices; lists of European prices that show a general tendency in one part of the stockmarket: *The IN.SECTS contain only those liquid stocks that show strong sectoral behaviour in their price-movements.*

in·sert[1] /ɪn'sɜːt‖-ɜːrt/ *v* [T] **1** to put something inside or into something else **insert sth in/into/between**: *He inserted a sheet of paper into the printer.*
2 to add something new to a piece of writing **insert sth into sth**: *Several amendments were inserted into the constitution.*

in·sert[2] /'ɪnsɜːt‖-ɜːrt/ *n* [C] a sheet containing information or an advertisement that is put inside a newspaper or magazine: *an advertising insert* | *This year the company plans to spend $17.9 million on ads, including* ***newspaper inserts.***

in·ser·tion /ɪn'sɜːʃən‖-ɜːr-/ *n* **1** [C,U] when you add something new to a piece of writing or the words that you add: *What effect will the insertion of this clause have?* | *Any editorial insertions to a quotation should be enclosed within square brackets.*
2 [C] another name for INSERT: *The group plans to put its views across through lectures and insertions in the daily press.*
3 [C] an occasion when an advertisement appears in a newspaper: *The Guitarist's Readers' Ads service averages over five hundred separate insertions per month.*

in-service *adj* **in-service training/courses etc** training etc that you do while you are working in a job

in·side[1] /ɪn'saɪd, 'ɪnsaɪd/ *prep* someone who is inside a company or organization works for it and so has information about it that is not available to other people: *He had obviously been helped by someone inside the company.* | *She made enemies both inside and outside the industry.*

inside[2] *adj* [only before a noun] **1** inside information or knowledge is information that comes from people working for a company or organization: *He had obtained* ***inside information*** *about the pending merger.* | *someone who trades on an inside stock tip*
2 already employed by a company: *The leading* ***inside candidate*** *for the post is Robert A. Lutz.*

inside information —see under INFORMATION

in·sid·er /ɪn'saɪdə‖-ər/ *n* [C] someone who works for a company or an organization and so has information about it that is not available to other people: ***Company insiders*** *have expressed their reservations about the deal.* | *Some* ***industry insiders*** *are very critical of the government.*

insider dealing —see under DEALING

insider trade —see under TRADE[1]

insider trading —see under TRADING

inside track *n* [singular] *AmE* if someone has the inside track, they have a position in which they have an advantage and are very likely to be successful: *The consortium now has the inside track for a project valued at more than $1 billion.*

in·sol·ven·cy /ɪn'sɒlvənsi‖-'sɑːl-/ *n* plural **insolvencies** [C,U] a situation in which a person or a company is insolvent: *Higher payments could force some banks into insolvency.* | *The number of insolvencies in the real estate sector more than tripled last year.*

insolvency practitioner *n* [C] in Britain, a person or organization that can by law act for a company that is declaring itself to be INSOLVENT (=unable to pay its debts): *The company consulted an insolvency practitioner and ceased trading three weeks later.*

in·sol·vent /ɪn'sɒlvənt‖ɪn'sɑːl-/ *adj* a person or company that is insolvent does not have enough money or ASSETS to pay their debts: *The company has now been* ***declared insolvent.*** | *The bank could be* ***rendered insolvent*** *by such a large payment.*

in·spect /ɪn'spekt/ *v* [T] **1** to check something officially to see whether it is of the right standard or quality, or whether it is safe to use: *Marquest allowed the agency to inspect its products.* | *The engines are all inspected before they leave the factory.*
2 to visit a factory or other building to check that everything is satisfactory and all the rules are being obeyed: *Petrochemical plants have to be inspected regularly by the Labor Department.* —**inspector** *n* [C] *a quality control inspector* | *FDA inspectors visit seafood processors only once every four years, on average.*

in·spec·tion /ɪn'spekʃən/ *n* [C,U] **1** a visit to a factory or other building to check that everything is satisfactory and all rules are being obeyed: *The factory has regular inspections by the Health and Safety Executive.* | *They refused to allow full inspection of their nuclear facilities.*
2 an official check done on something to see that it is of the right standard or quality, or whether it is safe to use: *The Federal Aviation Administration has ordered inspections of the propeller shafts on all similar planes.*

inspector of taxes *n* [singular] *BrE* a government official responsible for making sure that people and companies pay the correct amount of tax

in·stall also **instal** /ɪn'stɔːl‖-'stɒːl/ *v* past tense and past participle **installed** present participle **installing** [T] **1** to put equipment into a place and connect it so that it is ready to use: *They help install and operate big computer systems.*
2 COMPUTING to copy a program onto a computer so that it is ready to use: *I've installed some new games on my PC.*
3 to give someone an important job or position: *United Technologies installed senior environmental officers in each division.*

in·stal·la·tion /ˌɪnstə'leɪʃən/ *n* **1** [C] a building containing industrial or military equipment and machines: *large industrial installations* | *They targeted their attacks on government installations.*
2 [U] when a new piece of equipment is installed somewhere: *They had allowed $2.7 million for installation of a new computer system.*

in·stal·ler /ɪn'stɔːlə‖-'stɒːlər/ *n* [C] someone whose job is to put equipment into a place and connect it so that it is ready to use: *Your satellite TV system will be installed quickly and professionally by our skilled installers.*

I

installment plan *n* [C] *AmE* a way of buying something by making small, regular payments over an agreed period of time; HIRE PURCHASE *BrE*: *Shares can be purchased on the two-part installment plan.*

in•stal•ment *BrE*, **installment** *AmE* /ɪnˈstɔːlmənt/ *n* [C] one of a series of regular payments that are made until all of an agreed amount has been paid: *Some customers prefer to* ***pay by instalments****.* | *This would be the first installment of the $645 million in aid pledged to the region.*

instalment payment —see under PAYMENT

in•stant /ˈɪnstənt/ *adj* happening or available immediately: *We do not expect instant profits.* | *The agreement will offer subscribers* ***instant access*** *to overseas databases.*

instant access account —see under ACCOUNT[1]

In•sti•net /ˈɪnstɪnet/ *n* [U] *trademark* an electronic network run by Reuters PLC, on which people using a computer that is able to connect to the network can buy and sell shares when a STOCK EXCHANGE is closed: *The stock was trading actively on Instinet.* | *In afterhours* ***Instinet trading****, the stock was quoted at about 69.*

in•sti•tute[1] /ˈɪnstɪtjuːt‖-tuːt/ *n* [C] **1** an official organization that represents people of a particular profession: *the American Institute of Certified Public Accountants* | *the British Institute of Bankers*

2 an official organization concerned with research or education: *California Institute of Technology*

institute[2] *v* [T] to introduce a new system or rule: *The bank instituted a number of cost-cutting measures.* | *The firm instituted a program to provide retirement benefits for its staff.*

Institute Clauses *n* [plural] INSURANCE standard conditions, approved by the Institute of Underwriters, that are used in MARINE and AIR CARGO insurance contracts

Institute of Actuaries *n* a British professional organization for ACTUARIES (=people whose job is to calculate risks, in order to advise insurance companies etc)

Institute of Directors *n* a British organization for company DIRECTORS that puts forward the opinions of people involved in business to politicians and the public: *The Institute of Directors is worried about the long-term effects of high interest rates.*

Institute of London Underwriters *n* INSURANCE an organization of British insurance companies that work with each other to provide MARINE and AVIATION insurance. The Institute of London Underwriters also works closely with LLOYDS OF LONDON

in•sti•tu•tion /ˌɪnstɪˈtjuːʃən‖-ˈtuː-/ *n* **1** [C] a large important organization: *Japanese institutions are steadily increasing their presence in Europe.* | *the Royal Institution of Chartered Surveyors*

depository institution [C] FINANCE a bank or other financial institution into which people can pay money so that it can be held there and earn interest: *Inflation often kept market interest rates above the level that depository institutions were allowed to pay.*

financial institution [C] an organization such as a bank or insurance company where people, companies, or governments put their money, which it invests to produce a profit: *There was some buying of shares by investment funds and financial institutions.*

2 [U] the introduction of a new system or rule: *Most companies are in favour of the institution of a common economic policy.*

3 [C] LAW an established system or custom that is accepted in law: *the institution of private property*

in•sti•tu•tion•al /ˌɪnstɪˈtjuːʃənəl◂‖-ˈtuː-/ *adj* **1** involving an institution or institutions: *economic and monetary union and related institutional reform of the EU*

2 relating to activities of financial institutions, rather than other organizations or members of the public: *Most of the investment was from institutional money.* | *Dealers reported a fair degree of* ***institutional buying*** *of the shares.* | *institutional investors*

institutional advertising —see under ADVERTISING

institutional demand —see under DEMAND

institutional fund —see under FUND[1]

institutional investment —see under INVESTMENT

institutional investor —see under INVESTOR

in•struct /ɪnˈstrʌkt/ *v* [T] **1** to order someone to do something **instruct sb to do sth**: *The government has instructed banks to limit real estate lending growth to 2% this year.*

2 LAW to employ a lawyer to deal with a legal case: *The firm has instructed an attorney.*

in•struc•tion /ɪnˈstrʌkʃən/ *n* **1** [C] a statement telling someone what they must do: *The government has* ***issued instructions*** *to retailers on how to implement the new rules.* | *He claimed that brokers had failed to* ***carry out*** *his* ***instructions*** *to sell the stocks.*

shipping instructions [plural] a document sent by an exporter giving details of how goods are to be shipped and delivered: *Several major customers now send shipping instructions electronically.*

2 [C] COMPUTING a command given to a computer to carry out a particular operation: *The chip has a peak speed of 400 million instructions a second.*

in•stru•ment /ˈɪnstrʊmənt/ *n* [C] **1** FINANCE also **credit instrument**, **financial instrument** any form of borrowing such as a bond, a CERTIFICATE OF DEPOSIT,; COMMERCIAL PAPER etc, and the document showing the amount borrowed. Shares are also sometimes described as instruments: *Latin American companies are selling bonds or other financial instruments on international markets.*

debt instrument any form of borrowing in the form of debt, rather than shares, or the document showing the amount borrowed: *Atlantic Richfield may offer the securities from time to time as long-term debentures, medium-term notes and other debt instruments.*

equity instrument a share or similar form of borrowing by a company

hedging instrument an instrument used by investors to balance any risk of losing money with other investments they hold: *You can protect yourself against future rises in interest rates by a hedging instrument known as a forward rate agreement.*

money-market instrument a bond, a CERTIFICATE OF DEPOSIT,; COMMERCIAL PAPER etc rather than shares: *Treasury bills and other money-market instruments*

negotiable instrument an instrument that can be traded on a financial market: *Debt instruments in the Euromarkets are negotiable instruments.*

2 also **statutory instrument** *BrE* an instruction given by a British minister that has the force of a law: *The Secretary of State may, by order made by statutory instrument, determine the fees payable by any applicant to a licensing board.*

in•su•bor•di•na•tion /ˌɪnsəbɔːdɪˈneɪʃən‖-ɔːr-/ *n* [U] when you refuse to obey someone of a higher rank: *He was fired for insubordination.* —**insubordinate** *adj*: *an insubordinate new recruit*

in•su•late /ˈɪnsjʊleɪt‖ˈɪnsə-, ˈɪnʃə-/ *v* [T] to keep something safe from the harmful effects of something **insulate sth from/against sth**: *Such a strategy helps insulate the portfolio from the stock market's volatility.* —**insulation** *n* [U] *The region's insulation from oil price rises is now set to end.*

in·sur·a·ble /ɪnˈʃʊərəbəl‖-ˈʃʊr-/ *adj* if something is insurable, it is possible to obtain insurance for it: *Almost everything is insurable provided the premium is adequate.*

insurable risk —see under RISK[1]

in·sur·ance /ɪnˈʃʊərəns‖-ˈʃʊr-/ *n* **1** [U] an arrangement in which a company collects money regularly, PREMIUMS, from a person or organization and in return agrees to pay them a sum of money if they are involved in an accident, have something stolen, or cause harm or injury to others. The four main classes of insurance are ACCIDENT, LIFE, FIRE, and MARINE INSURANCE: *Insurance is the only major financial service regulated by states, rather than the federal government.*

2 [C,U] an insurance contract relating to a particular risk + **against**: *Insurance against stealing by employees is a multi-billion dollar expense.* | *The* ***insurance covers*** *you against injury to visitors while on your property.* | *The company has* ***taken out insurance*** *to indemnify its directors against liability when acting for the Group.* | *Can you* ***claim on*** *your household* ***insurance*** *if your bike is stolen?*

3 [U] the money paid regularly to an insurance company; INSURANCE PREMIUM: *We have paid home insurance for the last 25 years and have never made a claim.*

4 insurances [plural] used to talk about the performance of shares in insurance companies on a stockmarket: *Mining stocks advanced and insurances also did well.*

accident insurance [U] insurance against loss or damage to property, against injury or sickness to people, or against LIABILITY through NEGLIGENCE: *Aon, a health, life and accident insurance company*

agreed-value insurance [U] insurance against total loss of property or CARGOES where the amount insured is agreed at the start of the period of insurance, rather than calculated after a claim: *All Pleasurecraft Policies will be based on agreed value insurance, and in the event of a total loss we would pay the sum insured -- not the current market value as in motor insurance.*

all-risks insurance also **all-loss insurance** [U] insurance against all risks except ones particularly EXCLUDED (=specifically stated as not insured) in the insurance policy

annuity insurance [U] insurance bought with a LUMP SUM (=one large payment) for which you receive a series of payments for a particular period of time or for the rest of your life. PENSIONS are a form of annuity insurance —see also ANNUITY

automobile insurance *AmE* [U] another name for CAR INSURANCE: *Only 40% of personal automobile insurance covers car-rental damage.*

aviation insurance [U] insurance for aircraft, their passengers and CARGOES

blanket insurance [U] insurance for different items of property and buildings, perhaps in more than one place

block insurance [U] insurance in which one contract covers several different loads of goods that are being sent somewhere, up to a particular value

buildings and contents insurance *BrE* [U] another name for HOUSEHOLD INSURANCE: *When you borrow to buy a house, it may be compulsory to take out buildings and contents insurance with the lender.*

business interruption insurance [U] insurance against financial loss caused by a business not being able to continue its normal activities after an accident, fire etc

business liability insurance [U] insurance against damage or injury caused by NEGLIGENCE. Companies take it out to cover injury caused by their products, or negligence by people who work for them: *Small companies may be unable to obtain liability insurance.*

business life and health insurance [U] insurance taken out to protect a business against the cost of losing an important employee, partner, owner etc

car insurance [U] insurance against a car being stolen, or damage to it and other cars in an accident: *Neither of them had a driving licence or car insurance, the court was told.*

casualty insurance [U] insurance against damage to property, NEGLIGENCE by someone employed by a company and damage caused by a company's products

comprehensive insurance *BrE* [U] car insurance that covers damage to your own car in an accident, as well as damage and injury to others: *It may not be worth getting comprehensive insurance for an old car.*

contingency insurance [U] insurance against unusual risks not covered by one of the four main classes of insurance: accident, fire, life, and marine

credit insurance [U] insurance taken out by borrowers paying back loans that covers illness, losing their job and other events that may prevent them making the regular payments: *He started the idea of credit insurance for car buyers making installment payments.*

declaration insurance [U] insurance against loss or damage to goods, where the insured informs the insurer of the value of these goods every month, and the cost of insuring them is based on their average value during the year

deposit insurance [U] insurance that protects people with money held in a bank account against the risk of the bank going BANKRUPT. The money for deposit insurance is paid by banks to a central organization, in the US the FEDERAL DEPOSIT INSURANCE CORPORATION

disability insurance [U] insurance against someone not being able to work through illness or an accident, often taken out by employers to cover their workers, especially in the US

double insurance [U] when the same thing is insured with two different insurers, and where, if there is a CLAIM, each insurer pays a part

engineering insurance [U] insurance against failure of industrial machinery

export insurance [U] insurance against an importer not paying for goods etc they have received

fidelity insurance [U] insurance against the results of dishonest acts or mistakes by people who work for a company, or against BREACH OF CONTRACT

fire insurance [U] insurance against loss or damage caused by fire

floating insurance [U] insurance covering goods being sent somewhere up to a particular value, a form of DECLARATION INSURANCE; OPEN COVER

flood insurance [U] insurance against damage to property by flooding from a river or a sea storm

group insurance [U] when a group of people, for example people who work for a company, are covered by one insurance contract: *the sale of group insurance to organizations of doctors and other professionals*

health insurance [U] insurance that will pay for someone's medical treatment if they are ill or injured, often taken out by employers for people who work for them, especially in the US: *These measures would protect people with health problems from losing their health insurance if they change jobs.*

homeowner's insurance *AmE* [U] the US name for HOUSEHOLD INSURANCE: *Buying a home identifies a person as a good candidate for life insurance, homeowner's insurance and banking services.*

household insurance *BrE* [U] insurance against damage to a building and against damage or loss of things they contain; BUILDINGS AND CONTENTS INSURANCE: *Will your household insurance pay for the damage if you spill a can of paint over your carpet?*

income insurance also **income protection**

insurance [U] insurance that pays out when someone is not working, for example because they are ill or unemployed: *While some types of income insurance schemes do exist, eg pensions, the government may be a superior provider.*

industrial injuries insurance [U] in Britain, government insurance for people injured or made seriously ill at work

liability insurance [U] insurance against damage or injury caused by NEGLIGENCE. Professional people take out liability insurance to cover claims made against them by clients, and companies take it out to cover injury caused by their products, or negligence by people who work for them: *Liability insurance can be hard to obtain for small companies.*

life insurance [U] insurance that pays out an amount when someone dies, or, with an ENDOWMENT POLICY, when someone reaches a particular age or dies before they reach that age; LIFE ASSURANCE: *Life insurers will pay a total of $20 billion in AIDS death claims under individual life insurance policies by the year 2005.*

marine insurance [U] insurance for ships and their CARGOES: *The pollution cleanup from the Exxon Valdez was the largest single claim ever paid by the London marine insurance market.*

medical insurance [U] another name for HEALTH INSURANCE

mortgage protection insurance *BrE*, **mortgage insurance** *AmE* [U] insurance against not being able to make repayments on a MORTGAGE (=a loan to buy a house): *The building society requires clients to take out its mortgage protection insurance.*

motor insurance *BrE* [U] another name for CAR INSURANCE: *We will insure you for any vehicle which your certificate of motor insurance allows you to drive or use.*

national insurance also **National Insurance**, written abbreviation **NI** [U] the British system of social insurance: *Many part-time workers will not have been earning enough to pay national insurance, so will not qualify for unemployment benefit.*

property and liability insurance [U] another name for CASUALTY INSURANCE

reinsurance —separate entry

social insurance a system of insurance managed by a government where employers and people who work for them make regular payments, so that workers can receive money when they are ill, unemployed etc: *In 1930 a scheme for social insurance was implemented in France, covering pensions, sickness and family allowances.*

term insurance [U] life insurance where the insurer only pays out if the insured person dies during the period of the insurance

third party, fire and theft insurance *BrE* [U] a type of car insurance that only covers injury to other people and damage to other cars in an accident, damage to your own car by fire, and theft of your own car: *If you only have third party, fire and theft insurance, taking out additional cover is recommended if you travel abroad.*

travel insurance [U] insurance for travellers against illness, accidents, loss of bags etc: *20 million holidaymakers took out travel insurance policies last year.*

under-insurance [U] when the SUM INSURED (=the maximum amount that can be paid out) is not enough to cover real costs if you make a claim: *In the event of a serious loss, considerable financial difficulty can be caused by under-insurance.*

unemployment insurance [U] in the US, insurance for people who lose their jobs: *The percentage of jobless people getting unemployment insurance payments has fallen over the years.*

valued insurance [U] another name for AGREED VALUE INSURANCE

whole-life insurance [U] life insurance where the insurer pays out only when the insured dies —compare ENDOWMENT POLICY under INSURANCE POLICY

insurance adjuster —see under ADJUSTER

insurance agent —see under AGENT

insurance broker —see under BROKER[1]

insurance certificate —see under CERTIFICATE

insurance claim —see under CLAIM[1]

insurance company —see under COMPANY

insurance market —see under MARKET[1]

insurance policy *n* plural **insurance policies** [C] an insurance contract covering a particular risk, and the document giving details of this: *If the watch is stolen, your insurance policy might reimburse only $5,000.* | *Corporate liability insurance policies cover companies for causing environmental pollution.*

annuity policy an insurance policy where in return for a payment or series of payments by the insured person, the insurer makes regular payments for a specific period of time in the future

business interruption policy an insurance policy that protects a business against loss of profit if it is not able to continue its normal activities after an accident, fire etc

business owner's insurance policy an insurance policy for small businesses, taken out to protect them against the cost of damage to their property, or against an employee harming another person or their property

cash-in-transit policy an insurance policy in which the insurance company will pay if money is stolen or lost when it is being moved between two places, for example between a shop and a bank

collective policy an insurance policy that exists when there is CO-INSURANCE (=more than one insurer for a particular risk)

endowment policy an insurance policy where in return for a series of regular payments by the insured person, the insurer pays out a sum of money at the end of a specific period of time or when the insured person dies, if sooner: *He took out an endowment policy ten years ago to mature when he reached the age of sixty.*

fire policy a policy that insures the things contained in a building used for business purposes against fire

household policy *BrE* a policy that insures the things contained in a private house against fire, flood, storm, explosion, theft, damage by thieves, and sometimes accidental damage: *My household policy covers me against accidentally breaking any electrical equipment.*

mortgage protection policy *BrE*, **mortgage policy** *AmE* an insurance policy that protects you against the risk of not being able to make payments on a MORTGAGE (=a loan to buy property), for example because you are ill or out of work: *To ensure that the loan will be repaid if you should die before the term is up, it is essential to take out a mortgage protection policy.*

non-profits policy another name for WITHOUT-PROFITS POLICY

profits policy another name for WITH-PROFITS POLICY

standard fire policy ◆ in Britain, an insurance policy that covers the cost of damage caused by fire, a gas explosion, or LIGHTNING (=flash of light in the sky caused by electricity): *Damage to commercial buildings caused by terrorism was covered by the insured's standard fire policy.*

◆ in the US, the standard type of fire insurance policy used in most states

survivorship policy also **survivorship contract** an insurance agreement that is owned by more than one person and will only be paid when both have died

with-profits policy LIFE INSURANCE taken out in

Britain where the insured person shares in the profits of the insurance company. The share of the profits is added to the sum insured at the end of each year; PROFITS POLICY

without-profits policy a life insurance policy in Britain in which the sum insured is fixed from the start of the contract and the policy holder has no share in the profits of the life insurance company; NON-PROFITS POLICY

insurance premium —see under PREMIUM[1]

insurance product —see under PRODUCT

insurance risk —see under RISK[1]

insurance underwriter —see under UNDERWRITER

in•sure /ɪnˈʃʊə‖-ˈʃʊr/ *v* [I,T] **1** to buy insurance to protect yourself, your family, your business etc against something bad happening, for example accidents, damage to property, or injury caused to others: *Many companies insure executives' lives with the companies as beneficiaries.* **insure (sb/sth) against sth**: *It is advisable to insure all oriental carpets against theft and damage.* **insure sth for £1000/$2000 etc**: *Airlines insure their aircraft for their replacement value.*

2 to provide insurance for something or someone **insure (sb/sth) against sth**: *The company insured against earthquakes and accidents at sea.*

in•sured[1] /ɪnˈʃʊəd‖-ˈʃʊrd/ *n* **the insured** used in insurance contracts to talk about the person, organization etc that is insured: *This section also covers cancellation of a holiday where the insured decides to cancel.*

insured[2] *adj* having insurance: *The Swiss remain the world's most insured people, outspending Japanese and Americans on premiums.* **insured to do sth**: *There were few pilots at that time who were insured to undertake such a flight.* **+ against**: *We insist that you are insured against accidents.* —see also SUM INSURED

in•sur•er /ɪnˈʃʊərə‖-ˈʃʊrər/ *n* [C] **1** an insurance company: *If an insurer failed, the industry organization would pay 90% of all claims.*

2 the insurer/insurers in a particular insurance contract or legal CASE, used to talk about the insurance company providing insurance. You can talk about the insurers even if there is only one: *When he tried to recover his loss, the insurers denied liability.*

intangible asset —see under ASSET

in•te•grate /ˈɪntəgreɪt/ *v* [T] to combine two or more organizations, activities etc so that they become more effective, make better profits etc: *a major study of ways to integrate corporate and personal income taxes* | *Grace aims to better integrate its existing businesses, many of which were acquired.* **integrate sth with sth**: *funding to integrate the Italian railway network with those of other European countries.*

in•te•grat•ed /ˈɪntəgreɪtəd/ *adj* **1** an integrated system, organization etc combines two or more different parts, activities etc in a way that works well: *Labour promised an integrated transport system to cover the whole country.* | *Europe continues its effort to build an integrated market with uniform tax and business regulation.*

2 an integrated part of a product is not separate from the rest of the product: *The videophone contains an integrated camera and video screen.*

3 an integrated company performs all the activities related to producing and selling its products, rather than just some of these activities: *It's an integrated oil company, with production activity as well as refining and marketing operations.*

integrated circuit *n* [C] a very small set of electrical connections printed on a single piece of SEMICONDUCTOR material, such as a CHIP

Integrated Services Digital Network —see ISDN

in•te•gra•tion /ˌɪntəˈgreɪʃən/ *n* [U] **1** the combining of two or more units, organizations etc so that they work closely together and become more effective, make better profits etc: *The important achievement of the European Union is economic integration, but political integration is doubtful.*

2 when a company obtains control of its suppliers, customers, or competitors, resulting in fewer companies in an industry: *Following the merger, further integration of the European packaging industry is inevitable.*

backward integration when a company obtains control of its suppliers, or starts performing the same business activities as them: *Horizon Tours are taking backward integration even further by not only operating their own airline but also developing hotels in the Mediterranean.*

forward integration when a company obtains control of its customers, or starts performing the same business activities as them: *Television is booming in India, and there is potential for forward integration by film companies.*

horizontal integration when a company obtains control of its competitors: *The Federal Communications Commission will rule soon on horizontal integration by cable TV operators.*

vertical integration when a company controls all the different stages in making and selling a particular product: *Critics say TCI's vertical integration gives it an unfair advantage.*

in•teg•ri•ty /ɪnˈtegrəti/ *n* [U] **1** the state of being united or kept together as one whole and strong unit: *He believes that such a move could be detrimental to the financial integrity of the firm.* | *A major difficulty was how to protect the integrity of the welfare and pension funds.*

2 complete honesty: *Regulators questioned the good character and integrity of certain company officials.*

intellectual property —see under PROPERTY

intelligent terminal —see under TERMINAL

intensive agriculture —see under AGRICULTURE

intensive farming —see under FARMING

in•tent[1] /ɪnˈtent/ *n* [U] **1** an intention **intent to do sth**: *Newell Co. announced its intent to acquire a 15% to 25% stake in Stanley.* —see also DECLARATION OF INTENT

2 LAW the intention to do something illegal **intent to do sth**: *The company denied any intent to mislead the Inland Revenue.* | *He pleaded guilty to charges of possessing unauthorized computer access codes* ***with intent*** *to defraud.*

intent[2] *adj* **be intent on doing sth** to be determined to do or achieve something: *Westcoast is intent on expanding its oil and gas production business.*

in•ter•act•ive /ˌɪntərˈæktɪv◂/ *adj* interactive television, computer software etc allows the person using it to affect what happens on the screen: *A handful of small entertainment companies has been exploring the field of* ***interactive television.*** | *Acclaim Entertainment is a world-wide publisher of* ***interactive*** *entertainment* ***software.*** —**interactivity** *n* [U] *The most noticeable feature of the Internet is its two-way interactivity.*

interactive service —see under SERVICE[1]

in•ter a•li•a /ˌɪntər ˈeɪliə, -ˈɑːliə/ *adv formal* among other things: *The latest resolution calls, inter alia, for changes to the tax system.*

in•ter•bank /ˈɪntəbæŋk‖-tər-/ *adj* [only before a noun] interbank lending, borrowing, etc happens or is agreed between banks: ***Interbank lending*** *has declined radically.* | *The US central bank allowed* ***interbank interest rates*** *to decline.*

interbank offered rate —see under RATE[1]

inter-company also **intercompany** *AmE* —*adj* [only before a noun] involving two or more companies: *Many Japanese concerns have close links to suppliers and distributors and these intercompany relationships help keep costs down.*

in·terest /ˈɪntrɪ̈st/ *n* **1** [U] an amount paid by a borrower to a lender, for example to a bank by someone borrowing money for a loan or by a bank to a DEPOSITOR (=someone keeping money in an account there): *Any spare cash is best put in a savings account where it will* ***earn interest***. + **on**: *Chrysler might run out of money to* ***pay interest*** *on its bonds.* | *Amex's main credit cards don't* ***charge interest*** *on unpaid balances.*
2 [U] the rate of interest at which a particular sum of money is borrowed and lent + **at**: *US savings bonds will* ***pay interest*** *at 7.01% from May 1 through Oct. 31.*
accrued interest [U] interest earned during a period of time, whether it has been paid and received or not: *After five years the original loan has to be paid in full, plus all the accrued interest.*
add-on interest [U] interest calculated only on the PRINCIPAL (=the original amount borrowed) of a loan —compare APR
bank interest [U] interest paid by a bank on DEPOSITS and to a bank on loans: *You must declare bank interest you receive to the tax authorities.*
beneficial interest [U] LAW, FINANCE the profit made by someone who benefits from a TRUST: *The shares sold yesterday were held by a number of charitable trusts in which Sir David had a beneficial interest.*
bond interest [U] interest payable or paid to lenders on bonds: *Mr Trump's Taj Mahal Casino might have trouble paying its junk bond interest.*
building society interest [U] the interest a BUILDING SOCIETY pays to investors who have savings accounts: *Building society interest is taxed under a special arrangement, and basic-rate tax does not have to be paid on it.*
compound interest [U] interest calculated on both a sum of money lent or borrowed and on the unpaid interest already earned or charged on that money —compare SIMPLE INTEREST
cum interest —see under CUM
debenture interest [U] interest payable or paid to lenders on DEBENTURES (=a type of bond): *The company also said it can't pay debenture interest of $5.3 million due this month.*
ex interest —see under EX[1]
gross interest [U] interest before tax is taken away: *Only non-taxpayers should be registered for gross interest.*
imputed interest [U] interest on a loan which is based on the difference between the market rates of interest, and the actual interest paid on the loan: *Investors don't have to pay tax on imputed interest every year.*
net interest ◆ [U] interest from a bank account or an investment after tax is taken away: *This cheque account pays net interest of 3.25%.*
◆ [U] the difference between interest that a person or organization receives from investments and interest that they pay for borrowing: *HongkongBank's net interest income increased by 19% last year.*
simple interest [U] interest calculated only on the PRINCIPAL (=the original amount invested), not on any accrued interest: *I charged him 5% simple interest on the principal per week.*
true interest [U] the interest that a particular sum of money would earn at a particular rate of interest to bring it to a known sum at the end of a particular period of time: *The true interest cost on the Series A bonds is 6.262%.*
3 [C] shares that you own in a company, or a part of a company that a person or organization owns; HOLDING; STAKE + **in**: *Highlands Gold Ltd* ***holds a 30% interest*** *in the Porgera gold mine.*
controlling interest [C] where one shareholder owns enough shares to control a company: *Dow bought a controlling interest in Marion Laboratories.*
majority interest [C] where one shareholder has more than half of the shares, or enough shares to control the company: *Roche acquired a majority interest in Genetech.*
minority interest [C] where one shareholder owns less than half of the shares, or fewer shares than the biggest shareholder: *Sun Electric has agreed to buy a minority interest of 25% in Edge Diagnostic Systems.*
short interest [U] the number of shares which have been sold by people who do not yet own them, in the belief that their price will fall before they have to be delivered. This can be a sign that people expect a company's shares or shares in general to fall: *Intel Corp. had one of the largest decreases in short interest last month.*
working interest [C] an interest held by a company in a particular activity, especially the oil industry: *Amoco, an energy concern, is the operator of the project with a 43.75% working interest.* —see also CONFLICT OF INTEREST
4 vested interest [usually plural] *disapproving* the groups of people with strong reasons for wanting something to happen because they will gain an advantage from it: *He is determined to prevent* ***powerful vested interests*** *from blocking the reform.*
5 [C] LAW the possession of rights, especially to land, property etc: *The husband can release his interest in the legal estate to his wife.* —see also OPEN INTEREST

interest cover —see under COVER[1]

interest expense —see under EXPENSE

interest-free *adj* if a loan is interest-free, the borrower does not pay interest on it: *the World Bank's* ***interest-free loan*** *facility for poor countries* | ***interest-free credit***

interest-free loan —see under LOAN[1]

interest payment —see under PAYMENT

interest rate *n* [C] the percentage rate used for calculating interest over a particular period of time, usually one year + **of**: *Citicorp offers a Choice card, which has an interest rate of 14.8%.* | *The plan will* ***increase interest rates*** *and hurt the economy.* | *The fear of* ***higher interest rates*** *is driving down the stockmarket.* | *The* ***fall in interest rates*** *should lead to additional business investment.*
interbank rate the amount banks charge for lending to each other: *Interbank rates, or the fees banks charge each other for funds, have declined.* —see also ***annual percentage rate*** under RATE[1]

interest-rate futures —see under FUTURES

interest-rate risk —see under RISK[1]

interest rate swap —see under SWAP[2]

interface[1] *n* [C] **1** the point at which two subjects, events etc are connected with each other or have an effect on one another + **between**: *The next chapter discusses the interface between accountancy and the law.*
2 COMPUTING the way that a particular computer program shows information on the screen to the user: *the Windows* ***user interface***
graphical user interface also **graphical interface**, **GUI** a computer interface (=way of showing and organizing information on the screen) that is easy to use and understand
3 COMPUTING the part of a computer system that connects two different machines or systems: *the interface between the computer and the printer* | *The purpose of multimedia is to combine the interactivity of a* ***user-friendly interface*** *with mutiple forms of content.*

I

in·ter·face² /ˈɪntəfeɪs‖-ər-/ *v* **1** [I] if two people or companies interface, they work together on a particular problem, each one using their own specialist knowledge + **between/with**: *We're attempting to build a permanent American staff here that can interface with the Japanese.* | *a consultancy service that interfaces between a lawyer and various clients*
2 [I,T] COMPUTING to connect a piece of computer equipment or a computer system with another piece of equipment or another system + **with**: *The e-mail software interfaces with any PABX telephone system.*

in·ter·im /ˈɪntərɪm/ *adj* [only before a noun] **1** used or accepted temporarily until a final or complete one is made: *an* ***interim payment*** *of £15,000* | *an interim pay offer* | *Shareholders will receive an* ***interim dividend*** *of 5.03p per share*
2 prepared after only part of a full financial year has been completed, often after half a year: ***Interim figures*** *announced yesterday show a 16% leap in pre-tax profits to £95 million.* | *Eurotunnel presents its* ***interim results*** *next Monday.*

interim accounts —see under ACCOUNT¹

interim dividend —see under DIVIDEND

interim injunction —see under INJUNCTION

interim payment —see under PAYMENT

interlocutory injunction —see under INJUNCTION

in·ter·mar·ket /ˈɪntəˌmɑːkət‖-tərˌmɑːr-/ *adj* [only before a noun] involving two or more financial markets: *intermarket spreads where the two futures in the spread are traded on different exchanges*

in·ter·me·di·a·ry /ˌɪntəˈmiːdiəri‖ˌɪntərˈmiːdieri/ *n* plural **intermediaries** [C] a person or organization that helps to arrange agreements or business deals between other people or organizations + **between**: *Financial institutions* ***act as intermediaries*** *between lenders and borrowers.* | *Negotiations had taken place* ***through an intermediary***. —**intermediary** *adj* only before a noun *an intermediary role in the negotiations*

financial intermediary a financial institution such as a bank, insurance company etc that uses the money of investors to lend to borrowers: *Personal pensions are available through financial intermediaries such as insurance companies, friendly societies, banks and building societies.*

intermediate goods —see under GOODS

intermediate technology —see under TECHNOLOGY

in·ter·me·di·a·tion /ˌɪntəmiːdiˈeɪʃən‖-tər-/ *n* [U] the financial activity of using money from INVESTORS to lend to borrowers: *Argentina discouraged investors with taxes on the intermediation of credit by banks.* —compare DISINTERMEDIATION

in·ter·mer·cial /ˈɪntəˌmɜːʃəl‖-tərˌmɜːr-/ *n* [C] advertisements that appear on the INTERNET: *Internet shoppers in the experiment reported that some intermercials were misleading or that their orders simply did not arrive.*

in·ter·nal /ɪnˈtɜːnl‖-ɜːr-/ *adj* **1** within a company or organization, rather than outside it: *The bank is holding an* ***internal inquiry*** *into the incident.* | *an* ***internal audit*** | *We have decided to make an* ***internal appointment*** (=give a particular job to someone who already works for the company). | *This tray is for* ***internal mail***.
2 within a particular country or area, rather than involving other countries: *internal trade* | *the European* ***internal market*** | *an internal flight*

in·ter·nal·ize also **internalise** *BrE* /ɪnˈtɜːnəlaɪz‖-ɜːr-/ *v* [T] to include a particular cost in the manufacture of something so that the cost will not need to be paid by someone else later: *We want to encourage manufacturers to produce things that are as safe as they can be, so* ***internalizing the cost*** *of injury prevention.*

internal rate of return —see under RETURN²

Internal Revenue Code —see under CODE

Internal Revenue Service abbreviation **IRS** *n* the government department that collects national taxes in the US: *He was convicted of cheating the Internal Revenue Service of $1.7 million.* —see also INLAND REVENUE

International Accounting Standards Committee abbreviation **IASC** *n* an organization with the aim of making ACCOUNTING RULE*s* the same all over the world

international airport —see under AIRPORT

International Air Transport Association abbreviation **IATA** *n* an organization that most international AIRLINE*s* (=companies that carry people and goods by plane) belong to: *The International Air Transport Association has warned that airport capacity must be increased in western Europe.*

International Bank for Reconstruction and Development abbreviation **IBRD**, also **World Bank** *n* an organization that makes loans to countries in order to encourage economic development

International Chamber of Commerce abbreviation **ICC** *n* an organization whose purpose is to establish rules for international trade and to support the interests of business in international affairs

International Civil Aviation Organization abbreviation **ICAO** *n* an organization whose purpose is to establish safety standards in air travel and provide information and advice to AIRLINE*s* (=companies that carry people and goods by plane)

international commerce —see under COMMERCE

International Court of Justice *n* the court of law of the United Nations that decides how legal disagreements between countries should be settled. It is formed by 15 judges from different countries

International Development Association abbreviation **IDA** *n* an organization that is run by the International Bank for Reconstruction and Development. It provides low-interest loans to poorer countries to encourage economic growth

International Finance Corporation abbreviation **IFC** *n* an organization that provides money for private businesses in poorer countries. It is part of the International Bank for Reconstruction and Development

International Labour Organization also **International Labour Organisation** *BrE*, **International Labor Organization** *AmE* abbreviation **ILO** *n* an organization that is part of the United Nations. Governments, employers, and workers are represented. It works on industrial relations and the pay and employment conditions of workers

international law —see under LAW

International Monetary Fund abbreviation **IMF** *n* an international organization that lends money to countries having difficulties with their BALANCE OF PAYMENTS (=the difference between amounts of money coming into and going out of a country). If a country's difficulties are severe, the IMF has the right to tell it to change its economic policies as a condition for more lending

International Money Market abbreviation **IMM** *n* the part of the CHICAGO MERCANTILE EXCHANGE that trades currency and interest rate FUTURES

international money order abbreviation **IMO** *n* [C] a method of making small payments to a person in another country: *Payment can be by cheque, cash or international money order.*

International Organization for Standardization —see ISO

International Organization of Securities Commissions —see IOSCO

international reply coupon also **international postal reply coupon** *n* [C] a piece of paper that you can send when you write to someone in a foreign country and which they can use to buy stamps to pay for the POSTAGE needed to reply: *I enclose an international reply coupon.*

International Securities Exchange abbreviation **ISE** *n* FINANCE a system that allows people to trade OPTIONS (=the right to buy or sell shares, bonds, currencies etc) at a particular price using a computer: *The International Securities Exchange will be an electronic exchange trading options on the 600 leading US stocks.*

International Standard Book Number —see ISBN

International Standards Organization —see ISO

International Stock Exchange abbreviation **ISE** *n* the official name of the LONDON STOCK EXCHANGE

international trade —see under TRADE[1]

In•ter•net /ˈɪntənet‖-tər-/ *n* the network of computer systems that allows computer users around the world to exchange information: *These regulations have been published **on the Internet**.* | *Do you have access to the Internet?* —compare EXTRANET, INTRANET

Internet commerce —see under COMMERCE

Internet Service Provider —see under PROVIDER

in•ter•pret•er /ɪnˈtɜːprətə‖-ˈtɜːrprətər/ *n* [C] **1** someone who translates what someone says from one language into another, especially as their job: *Speaking through an interpreter, the Foreign Minister explained how impressed he had been with his visit to the new factory.*

2 COMPUTING a computer program that changes an instruction into a form that can be understood directly by the computer: *the PostScript interpreter*

in•ter•state /ˌɪntəˈsteɪt◂‖-tər-/ *adj* [only before a noun] involving more than one state, especially in the US: *efforts to limit interstate shipments of industrial waste* | ***interstate banking*** (=when a bank has activities in more than one state) —compare INTRASTATE

interstate commerce —see under COMMERCE

Interstate Commerce Commission abbreviation **ICC** *n* a US government organization that controls business between people or companies in different states

in•ter•vene /ˌɪntəˈviːn‖-tər-/ *v* [I] to become involved in a situation in order to help deal with a problem: *The Federal Reserve Bank had to intervene to support the dollar* (=buy the currency to keep it from falling). + **in**: *The government may be forced to intervene in the pay dispute.*

in•ter•ven•tion /ˌɪntəˈvenʃən‖-tər-/ *n* [C,U] the act of becoming involved in a situation in order to help deal with a problem: *Smart's financial intervention six years ago saved the firm from liquidation.* + **in**: *the degree of **government intervention** in the economy*

in•ter•ven•tion•ist /ˌɪntəˈvenʃənɪst‖-tər-/ *adj* believing that a government should try to influence trade by spending government money: ***Interventionist policies** in the car industry produced British Leyland.* | *We favour an **interventionist role** for government in the economy.* —**interventionist** *n* [C] —**interventionism** *n* [U]

intervention price —see under PRICE[1]

intervention rate —see under EXCHANGE RATE

in•ter•view[1] /ˈɪntəvjuː‖-ər-/ *n* **1** [C,U] a formal meeting at which someone is asked questions to find out whether they are suitable for a job: *a **job interview*** | *Applicants will be **called for interview** next month.*

exit interview [C] an interview between someone leaving a company or organization and their employer: *The personnel department should hold an exit interview to establish why the employee is leaving.*

2 [C] an occasion when someone, especially a politician, is asked questions about their views or actions on television, for a newspaper etc: *In a radio interview this morning, the Chancellor ruled out a rise in interest rates.*

3 [C] an occasion when someone is asked questions about a product or service, to find out how it can be improved or the best way to advertise it: *a market research interview*

depth interview [C] MARKETING an interview to find out what products someone buys and why, done in the person's home or place of work rather than in the interviewer's office. It may be done in several separate meetings over a long period of time. —**depth-interviewing** *n* [U] *large amounts of time are normally required for depth-interviewing*

interview[2] *v* [I,T] **1** to ask someone questions, especially in a formal meeting, in order to find out if they are suitable for a job: *She was appointed without any other candidates being interviewed.* | *I've been interviewing all afternoon.* **interview sb for sth**: *We interviewed twelve people for the job.*

2 to ask someone, for example a politician, questions about their views or actions on television, for a newspaper etc: *The chairman refused to be interviewed.*

3 to ask someone questions about a product or service, to find out how it can be improved or the best way to advertise it: *A sample of 200 women were interviewed.* —**interviewer** *n* [C] *The interviewer should not ask about your marital status.* | *her reputation as a tough political interviewer*

in•ter•view•ee /ˌɪntəvjuˈiː‖-tər-/ *n* [C] the person who is asked questions in an interview: *Provide the interviewee with a written job description.*

in•ter vi•vos /ˌɪntə viːvɒs‖-tər ˈviːvoʊs, -ˈvaɪ-/ *adv* LAW from one living person to another living person: *A joint tenancy is severed if a joint tenant disposes of his interest inter vivos.* —**inter vivos** *adj*: *an **inter vivos gift***

in•tes•ta•cy /ɪnˈtestəsi/ *n* [U] LAW when someone dies without having made a proper WILL (=an official document, stating who will have your money, property etc after you die): *The shares will normally pass by will or intestacy to the spouse.* | ***intestacy laws***

in•tes•tate /ɪnˈtesteɪt, -stət/ *adv* LAW **die intestate** to die without having made a proper WILL (=an official document, stating who will have your money, property etc after you die): *You need someone to administer the estate of a relative who dies intestate.*

in-the-money option —see under OPTION

in•tra•day /ˈɪntrədeɪ/ *adj* FINANCE happening within one day: *The Nikkei 225 fell at one stage more than 4 per cent – its biggest intraday fall of the year.* | *In Tokyo, stocks closed lower but above **intraday lows** in active trading.*

intraday high —see under HIGH[1]

in•tra•net /ˈɪntrənet/ *n* [C] a computer network used for exchanging or seeing information within a company, that works in the same way as the INTERNET: *We take photographs of the new recruits for posting on the intranet.* —compare EXTRANET

in•tra•pre•neur /ˌɪntrəprəˈnɜː‖-ˈnɜːr/ *n* [C] HUMAN RESOURCES someone who works for an organization, but outside the usual management structure, and who develops new products and activities. If successful, a new activity may be developed into an independent company: *an intrapreneur within the bank who pioneered* *telephone selling of insurance* —compare ENTREPRENEUR —**intrapreneurial** *adj* —**intrapreneurship** *n* [U]

in·tra·state /ˌɪntrəˈsteɪt◂/ *adj* [only before a noun] *AmE* within one state, especially in the US: ***intrastate commerce*** | ***intrastate telecommunications services*** —compare INTERSTATE

in-tray *n* [C] *BrE* a flat container used to hold letters, papers etc that need to be dealt with; IN-BASKET *AmE*: *Open all the incoming mail and place it in the appropriate person's in-tray.* —compare OUT-TRAY

intrinsic value —see under VALUE[1]

in·tro·duce /ˌɪntrəˈdjuːs‖-ˈduːs/ *v* [T] **1** to make a new product or service available for the first time: *Hewlett-Packard introduced a new line of desktop computer workstations.* | *McDonald's grilled steak sandwich will be introduced in selected US markets.*

2 FINANCE to make stocks, shares etc available on the stock exchange for the first time: *The Chicago Mercantile Exchange is to introduce futures and options on the Nikkei Index of 225 Tokyo stocks.*

3 to make a system, plan etc effective for the first time: *Saatchi has introduced a new pay system for senior executives.* | *Since the legislation was introduced, 430 people in the area have received reduced rates of social security.* | *the difficulties of introducing a new currency*

4 to help someone get to know a new person or product + **introduce sb/sth to sb/sth**: *The company has been introducing clients to private banks for several years.* | *It is not always easy to introduce customers to new and unusual varieties of food.*

5 LAW to formally present a new law so that it can be discussed and voted on by a parliament, CONGRESS etc: *The Democratic candidate vowed to introduce a bill to restore the windfall-profits tax.*

in·tro·duc·tion /ˌɪntrəˈdʌkʃən/ *n* [C,U] **1** the act of making something or selling something for the first time + **of**: *the introduction of a new range of designer wear* | *The Pacific Stock Exchange plans to delay the introduction of new share options.*

2 when a particular system, law, method of doing something etc is used for the first time + **of**: *the introduction of value-for-money auditing*

in·trust /ɪnˈtrʌst/ another spelling of ENTRUST

inv. written abbreviation for INVOICE(S)

in·val·id /ɪnˈvælɪ̈d/ *adj* **1** LAW an invalid contract, agreement, document etc is not legally or officially acceptable: *Wellcome's patent to the drug was **ruled invalid** because the company didn't invent the compound.* | *evidence obtained using invalid warrants*

2 invalid information, figures etc are not based on true facts and therefore cannot be used: *The results of the referendum were **declared invalid**.* | *The promotions lacked balance and made **invalid comparisons** between rival products.* —**invalidity** *n* [U] *The bonds are perforated with small holes to show their invalidity.*

in·val·i·date /ɪnˈvælɪ̈deɪt/ *v* [T] LAW to make a contract, agreement, document etc invalid: *Failure to follow the instructions correctly could invalidate the guarantee.* | *The Judge's ruling invalidated the company's patent.* —**invalidation** *n* [U] *The Court of Appeals refused to reconsider its previous invalidation of the contract.*

in·val·u·a·ble /ɪnˈvæljuəbəl, -jᵊbəl‖-ˈvæljᵊbəl/ *adj* very useful indeed: *The skills of executives are invaluable in dispute resolution.* | *The reservation service is invaluable to overseas visitors with a limited knowledge of the area.*

in·vent /ɪnˈvent/ *v* [T] **1** to make, design or produce something new or a new way of doing something: *Researchers have invented a computer that can accurately scan as many as 500 connected railcars.* | *Mr. Monaghan virtually invented the modern pizza delivery business when he founded Domino's.*

2 to tell people something that is not true in order to deceive them: *He told investors the firm had monthly returns of between 10% and 25% but those returns were invented.* | *Perhaps the most popular fraud is to inflate or invent business expenses.* —see also NOT-INVENTED-HERE SYNDROME

in·ven·tion /ɪnˈvenʃən/ *n* **1** [C] a new product that was not available before: *Do you realise that the paint roller is a Canadian invention?* | *There were displays of **new inventions** in the exhibition halls.*

2 [U] when something is made or designed for the first time: *Cars have been made in Birmingham since their invention.* + **of**: *the invention by Citibank of certificates of deposit*

in·ven·tor /ɪnˈventə‖-ər/ *n* [C] a person who makes or designs something for the first time: *The pocket calculator and home computer made Clive Sinclair Britain's best-known inventor.*

in·ven·tory /ˈɪnvəntri‖-tɔːri/ *n* plural **inventories** *AmE* **1** [C,U] ACCOUNTING the amount of stock, including RAW MATERIALS, supplies and finished goods, that a company has at a particular time; STOCK *BrE*: *Companies have **cut inventories** sharply since the downturn began.* | *Cash-and-carry outlets rely on a rapid turnover of stock to keep down **inventory levels**.*

2 [C] a list of the goods and property owned by a particular person, organization, or country + **of**: *a full inventory of the country's nuclear weapons*

continuous inventory also **perpetual inventory** [C] an inventory in which records are changed whenever new items are received or old items are used up or sold, so that it always contains the most recent information

3 take (an) inventory to make a list of goods that a company or a person has at a particular time: *Newmark & Lewis were closed Sunday to take inventory.* —see also FIRST IN, FIRST OUT, LAST IN, FIRST OUT

inventory control —see under CONTROL[1]

inventory risk —see under RISK[1]

inventory-to-sales ratio —see under RATIO

inventory valuation —see under VALUATION

in·verse /ˌɪnˈvɜːs◂‖-ɜːrs◂/ *adj* **in inverse proportion/relation to sth** where one thing increases at the same rate as another related thing gets smaller: *Stocks moved in inverse relation to oil prices throughout the day.*

in·vest /ɪnˈvest/ *v* [I,T] **1** to buy stocks, shares, property etc in order to make a profit: *People are so pessimistic about the future that they won't invest at the moment.* | *The Singapore government is interested in investing abroad.* + **in/into**: *The fund had **invested heavily** in risky assets like junk bonds.*

2 to save money in a high interest bank account or to buy an insurance policy that pays BONUSES: *Before investing, investors should ask about the financial soundness of the company that issues the annuity.*

3 to spend money on something that will be useful: *Cifra is investing some $60 million to maintain its edge in technology.* + **in/into**: *Kellogg has been investing hundreds of millions of dollars in new production facilities.*

investable *adj* another spelling of INVESTIBLE

in·vest·i·ble *BrE*, **investable** *AmE* /ɪnˈvestəbəl/ *adj* an investible income, fund etc is available to invest: *Companies expect their pool of **investable funds** to grow from the current $2 trillion to $3 trillion by the turn of the century.* | *A typical private banking customer has at least $250,000 in annual income and $1 million in **investible assets**.*

in·ves·ti·gate /ɪnˈvestɪ̈geɪt/ *v* [I,T] to try to discover the truth about a crime, accident etc: *The fraud office is **investigating allegations** of insider trading by a former employee of the firm.* —**investigation** *n* [C,U] *a banker **under criminal investigation*** | ***a federal investiga-***

I

tion into junk bond trading —**investigator** *n* [C] *a government investigator*

in·ves·ti·ga·tive /ɪnˈvestɨgətɪv‖-geɪtɪv/ *adj* investigative work or activity involves discovering the truth about a crime, accident etc: *The Office of Fair Trading will be given stronger* ***investigative powers.*** | *investigative journalism*

in·vest·ment /ɪnˈvestmənt/ *n* **1** [C,U] the money that people or organizations put into a business activity, company, or financial institution in order to make a profit + **in**: *The largest Korean investment in China is a $17.7 million factory that will make piano and guitar parts.* | *The Postal Service has* ***made an*** *extremely large* ***investment*** *in automated technology.* | *Mr Olsen founded Digital with a $70,000 investment in 1957.*

2 [C] shares, bonds, COMMODITIES, property etc, or money put into a financial institution to invest for you in order to make a profit: *The Hunt brothers were hit by heavy losses from their investments in silver and oil.*

3 [C] an amount of money that is invested + **of**: *Some international funds demand a minimum initial investment of only $1,000 or even less.*

4 [U] when money is put into business ASSETS (=buildings, machinery etc) in order to produce goods or services and make a profit; CAPITAL INVESTMENT, FIXED INVESTMENT: *The US economy has been expanding for 44 consecutive months, fueled by high* ***corporate investment*** *and personal consumption.*

alternative investment ◆ [C] an investment in an unusual asset or place: *the emergence of alternative investment sites such as Mexico, China and Eastern Europe*

◆ [C] an investment in a non-financial asset such as a work of art; COLLECTIBLE

capital investment [C,U] investment in buildings, machinery, equipment etc needed to produce goods or services: *The coal industry here is suffering from a lack of modern equipment and needs huge amounts of capital investment.*

community investment [U] investment for the general public rather than for financial gain, in things such as schools and roads

corporate investment [U] investment by businesses, rather than by the government: *Japan's corporate investment in plant and equipment will increase by only 0.6% next year.*

direct investment [U] investment by companies in business activities abroad, for example in their SUBSIDIARIES (=companies they own): *US companies had $50.7 billion in direct investment in Brazil at the end of last year.*

domestic investment [U] investment in your own country rather than abroad: *Beijing's strategy is to expand economic development zones and improve the domestic investment climate.*

ethical investment [C,U] an investment in an activity that the investor considers is morally acceptable, or these investments considered together: *Ethical investment funds typically avoid military manufacturers, oil companies and tobacco producers.*

equity investment [U] money invested in a business in the form of shares, or all the money invested in this way in a particular period of time: *They agreed to provide a 10% equity investment to Cedetel to install a cellular telephone system.*

financial investment [C,U] putting money into a business rather than another form of involvement in the business: *A future partnership with Olivetti won't necessarily involve an equity stake or financial investment.*

fixed-income investment [C] an investment that pays regular interest, for example bonds: *Government bond markets are likely to remain the fixed-income investment of choice.*

fixed investment [U] when money is put into business assets: *Fixed investment by both manufacturers and non-manufacturers continues to be strong.*

foreign investment [U] investment in a country other than your own: *Foreign investment is flowing into the US, but capital also is flowing out rapidly.*

government investment [C,U] investment by a government, for example in roads, schools etc, or these investments considered as a whole: *massive government investment in infrastructure, such as transportation*

gross investment [U] the value of investment in buildings, machinery etc before taking away DEPRECIATION (=the fall in value of something over time): *A part of gross investment is needed simply to replace assets used up in the course of production.*

incubation investment [C,U] investment in new companies which are failing to achieve their expected targets: *Parkers received a $355,000 incubation investment during the first few months of opening.*

institutional investment [C,U] an investment by a financial institution, rather than by a business, or these investments considered as a whole: *The report on institutional investment shows the level of investment activity among pension funds, insurance companies and investment trusts.*

inward investment [U] investment in an area, country etc from another area or country: *Inward investment into Wales had been the success story of the Welsh economy throughout the 1980s and 1990s.*

legal investment [C] one that is considered correct for someone with legal responsibility for the money of others, for example under a TRUST: *Investment-grade bonds qualify as legal investments.*

net investment [U] the value of investment in buildings, machinery, supplies etc after taking away amounts for DEPRECIATION (=the fall in value of something over time): *If we subtract this replacement investment from gross investment, then we are left with net investment.*

outward investment [U] investment from one area, country etc into another: *outward investment from the UK into other member states of the EU*

overseas investment [U] another name for FOREIGN INVESTMENT: *An economic slowdown in Japan leads to reductions in overseas investment.*

personal investment [C,U] a financial investment by a person, rather than by a business or a financial institution, or these investments considered as a whole: *Each board member should be required to make a substantial personal investment in the company's stock.*

private investment [C,U] investment by businesses and financial institutions rather than by a government: *Higher government borrowing requirements could discourage private investment.*

property investment [C,U] an investment in land, buildings etc or these investments considered as a whole: *Shuwa Corp., a big Japanese property investment company*

public investment [C,U] another name for GOVERNMENT INVESTMENT: *New public investment could be financed partly by selective taxes, partly by government borrowing.*

real estate investment *AmE* [C,U] a US phrase for PROPERTY INVESTMENT

speculative investment [C,U] an investment with a high degree of risk, or these investments considered as a whole: *Speculative investment in property has encouraged doubtful lending practices by banks.*

investment allowance *n* [C] another name for CAPITAL ALLOWANCE: *a temporary 15% first-year investment allowance for purchases of new equipment*

investment analyst —see under ANALYST

investment bank —see under BANK[1]

investment banker —see under BANKER

investment banking —see under BANKING

investment club *n* [C] a group of investors who meet regularly to decide which investments to buy and sell: *The basic philosophy of investment clubs is long-term investing.*

investment company —see under COMPANY

investment fund —see under FUND[1]

investment goods —see under GOODS

investment-grade *adj* investment-grade SECURITIES (=shares, bonds etc) are a fairly safe investment because they are quite likely to be repaid: *Philadelphia was able to get* ***investment-grade ratings*** *for the issue because money to repay the bonds will be set aside in a special fund.*

below-investment-grade below-investment-grade SECURITIES have a high risk of not being repaid: *below-investment-grade junk bonds*

investment-grade debt —see under DEBT

investment-grade market —see under MARKET[1]

investment grant —see under GRANT[1]

investment income —see under INCOME

investment management —see under MANAGEMENT

investment manager —see under MANAGER

investment mix —see under MIX

investment product —see under PRODUCT

investment research —see under RESEARCH

investment software —see under SOFTWARE

investment trust —see ***investment company*** under COMPANY

investment trust company —see under COMPANY

investment turnover —see under TURNOVER

in•vest•or /ɪnˈvestə‖-ər/ *n* [C] a person or organization that invests money in order to make a profit: *Investors are confused about where to put their money in stocks.* | ***Investor confidence*** *in the market is growing.* + **in**: *Britain is the second largest foreign investor in Mexico.*

institutional investor a financial institution such as a bank or insurance company that invests in something: *The bonds were allocated to institutional investors, rather than individual investors.*

personal investor a person who invests their own money in financial markets, and is not working for a financial institution or as a professional investor: *The system is designed to deal separately with professional market operators and personal investors.*

private investor a person or a PRIVATE COMPANY (=one whose shares are privately held and not traded on a stockmarket) that makes investments, rather than a PUBLIC COMPANY (=one whose shares are traded on a stockmarket): *Orient-Express agreed in principle to sell a beach resort in the Bahamas to a private investor for $4.2 million.*

professional investor someone whose job is investing, either for themselves or for a financial organization: *bond fund managers and other professional investors*

retail investor a person or organization that invests, but that is not a FINANCIAL INTERMEDIARY (=financial institution that deals in bonds, shares etc): *Demand for the notes from retail investors and commercial banks was weaker than expected.*

risk-averse investor someone who prefers to invest in shares etc that carry the lowest risk: *He finds the bonds appealing for risk-averse investors because, as long as you don't cash them in for five years, you collect a minimum interest rate of 6%.*

small investor someone who invests relatively small amounts of money for themselves, in addition to their usual job: *The British Gas sale attracted 4.5 million applications from small investors.*

value investor someone who invests in stocks, shares etc that are considered to be selling at less than their real worth: *Professional value investors have noticed some stocks in their portfolios moving into the selling range.*

vulture investor a person or organization that invests in companies etc that are in financial difficulty, for example by buying their debt or shares very cheaply: *Many vulture investors see more big gains ahead for the bonds, now that the stores show signs of a sales upturn and are restructuring their debts in bankruptcy court.*

investor grouping *n* [C] a number of investors working together, often to take control of a company or part of a company: *An investor group with a 9.89% stake in NuMed said it is seeking seats on its board.*

investor protection —see under PROTECTION

investor resistance —see under RESISTANCE

invisible exports —see under EXPORT[1]

in•vis•i•bles /ɪnˈvɪzəbəlz/ *n* [plural] things that can be used or sold but cannot be seen or touched, for example banking services, advertising or customer GOODWILL: *Officials hope that invisibles such as tourism will improve the country's balance of payments.*

invisible trade —see under TRADE[1]

in•vi•ta•tion /ˌɪnvəˈteɪʃən/ *n* [C] a request to someone to do something, or an offer of the opportunity for them to do something + **to**: *Mr. Greenspan* ***extended an invitation*** *to banks to borrow more freely from the Federal Reserve.* | *Afghanistan's government* ***accepted an invitation*** *to a conference this month.* | *She* ***turned down an invitation*** *to serve on the company's board.*

invitation to subscribe plural **invitations to subscribe** [C] an occasion when a company offers shares for sale: *This document is not a prospectus and does not constitute or form any part of an invitation to subscribe for, underwrite or purchase securities.*

invitation to tender also **invitation to bid** [C usually singular] an occasion when an organization asks companies to say how much they will charge to perform particular work. The company with the lowest price usually gets the work: *Pearl's invitation to tender set out several important objectives. The company required a fully-integrated mainframe-based solution from a single supplier.*

in•vite /ɪnˈvaɪt/ *v* [T] **1** to request that someone do something or offer them the opportunity to do something **invite sb to do sth**: *Barclays de Zoete Wedd Ltd is inviting retailers to acquire 51% of the shares in a new company.* | ***Applications are invited*** *from suitably qualified candidates.* | *Lebanon has* ***invited bids*** *from foreign firms to explore for oil and natural gas.*
2 to ask someone to come for a particular meal, occasion etc **invite sb to sth**: *The president invited a group of architects to a White House breakfast recently.*

in•voice[1] /ˈɪnvɔɪs/ *n* [C] **1** a document sent by a seller to a customer with details of goods or services that have been provided, their price, and the payment date: *We require suppliers to submit invoices with services clearly categorized.*

consignment invoice an export invoice used when goods are sent to someone who is acting for the owner, and who must either sell them or return them to the owner

electronic invoice an invoice held on computer, not on paper: *How do you validate an electronic invoice that lacks an individual's signature?*

export invoice an official invoice used when exporting goods, giving details of goods in a form acceptable to CUSTOMS authorities

false invoice an invoice that does not relate to a real sale and is used to DEFRAUD (=cheat someone): *An accountant has been dismissed after the discovery of £109,000 in false invoices.*

final invoice an invoice giving details of the exact price remaining to be paid: *About ten weeks before departure, you will receive a final invoice showing the total cost of your holiday.*

original invoice the first copy where there are one or more copies of the same invoice: *The original invoice will be processed through the financial accounts and the copy invoice through the cost accounts.*

outstanding invoice an invoice that has not been paid: *The overspend last year was due to payment of outstanding invoices before the end of the financial year.*

pro-forma invoice ◆ an invoice sent to a customer asking for payment before goods are sent, often done when the buyer is a new customer: *The supplier may issue a payment request note or a pro forma invoice.*
◆ an invoice sent to a possible buyer as an example of prices etc of different goods: *Dealer inquiries welcome – discount rates and pro forma invoices on request.*

purchase invoice the name given to an invoice by the buyer of the related goods or services: *Any purchase invoices should be checked and entered into the purchases day book.*

sales invoice the name given to an invoice by the seller of the related goods or services: *The builder prepares the final account and sales invoice for the client.*

tax invoice in Britain, an invoice giving details of VAT (=a form of sales tax) to be paid: *The seller will issue a tax invoice, accounting for tax on the full selling price.*

2 issue/raise an invoice to prepare and send an invoice or to arrange for one to be prepared and sent: *An invoice raised in April related to the first stage of the contract payment.*

3 chase up an invoice *informal* to try to persuade someone to pay an unpaid invoice: *On completion of a job I give a report to the client, raise invoices and if necessary chase them up.*

invoice² *v* [T] to prepare an invoice and send it to a customer **invoice sb for sth**: *We'll invoice you for any damage to the rented car.* —**invoicing** *n* [U] *We handle the whole process, from the receipt of the customer's order to invoicing.*

invoice discounting —see under DISCOUNTING

invoice factoring —see under FACTORING

invoice price —see under PRICE¹

in•voke /ɪn'vəʊk‖-'voʊk/ *v* [T] LAW to use a law, principle or particular authority to support a view or decision: *During the investigation he repeatedly invoked the Fifth Amendment.* | *The Board of Trade was forced to invoke its emergency powers.*

involuntary bankruptcy —see under BANKRUPTCY

involuntary unemployment —see under UNEMPLOYMENT

in•ward /'ɪnwəd‖-wərd/ *adj* [only before a noun] **1** coming into the country or the place where you are, rather than going out of it: *Financial deregulation may encourage* ***inward investment****.* | *systems for handling* ***inward mail***

2 freight inwards ACCOUNTING used in a set of accounts to show that payments are for the cost of TRANSPORTING goods a company has bought; CARRIAGE INWARDS —compare OUTWARD

inward investment —see under INVESTMENT

IOSCO *n* International Organization of Securities Commissions; an association of the organizations that REGULATE the buying and selling of bonds, shares etc in different countries, making sure that rules are followed, laws are obeyed etc

IOU *n* [C] *informal* something, usually a note, that you give to someone to show that you owe them a particular sum of money: *Commercial paper is a kind of* ***corporate IOU****.*

IPO *n* [singular] FINANCE initial public offering; an occasion when a company ISSUES (=makes available) shares on a stockmarket for the first time: *Even after the IPO, KKR still controlled about 68% of the stock.* | *The trend is another sign that the* ***IPO market*** *is becoming even more risky for investors.*

IPO 100 Index FINANCE a measurement of the change in the share prices of companies that have recently made IPOs: *The collapse led to a 9.1% drop in the IPO 100 Index.*

IQ test —see under TEST¹

IR abbreviation for INLAND REVENUE

IRA /ˌaɪrə/ *n* [C] *AmE* individual retirement account; a savings account which SELF-EMPLOYED people or someone working for a company can open if their employer does not offer a PENSION PLAN: *A 35 year-old with $15,000 in* ***IRA accounts*** *would be eligible to withdraw about $453 a year.* | ***IRA investors***

IRR written abbreviation for INTERNAL RATE OF RETURN

ir•re•cov•er•a•ble /ˌɪrɪ'kʌvərəbəl◂/ *adj* irrecoverable debts, fees etc cannot or will not be paid to the person who is owed them: *TI's statistics are based on* ***irrecoverable bad debts*** *and business failures.*

irrecoverable loan —see under LOAN¹

ir•re•deem•a•ble /ˌɪrɪ'diːməbəl◂/ *adj* an irredeemable bond pays interest but has no MATURITY DATE (=date at which the borrower will repay the lender): *There are nine British government stocks outstanding which have no final maturity; they are irredeemable bonds.* —**irredeemable** *n* [C] *Bonds with no redemption date are known as irredeemables, perpetuals or consols.*

irredeemable gilts —see under GILTS

irredeemable stock —see under STOCK¹

ir•reg•u•lar /ɪ'regjələ‖-ər/ *adj* not obeying the usually accepted legal or moral rules: *There were some warning signals that something irregular was going on.* | ***highly irregular*** *trading activities* —**irregularity** *n* [C,U] *A customer's call alerted a bank clerk to* ***accounting irregularities****.* | *In the legal profession, the smallest hint of irregularity cannot pass unnoticed.*

ir•rev•o•ca•ble /ɪ'revəkəbəl/ *adj* impossible to change or stop: *The harm he had caused was substantial and irrevocable.*

irrevocable letter of credit —see under LETTER OF CREDIT

IRS abbreviation for INTERNAL REVENUE SERVICE: *The IRS is taking a closer look at the deal.* | *an IRS assessment*

ISA /'aɪsə/ *n* [C] individual savings account; a savings arrangement in Britain on which you do not have to pay tax. ISAs replaced PEPs in 1999, and were designed to encourage more people to save: *The government says ISAs will encourage people to leave their savings in the account on a long-term basis.*

cash ISA an ISA in a FUND that invests in the MONEY MARKETS rather than in shares etc

equity ISA an ISA in a FUND that invests in shares

maxi-ISA an arrangement where you put money into an ISA at only one financial institution, up to a limit set for a particular year

mini-ISA an arrangement where you can put money into ISAs at several different financial institutions, up to a limit set for a particular year

ISBN *n* [C] International Standard Book Number; a code number that all copies of a particular book have, and

I

which is used especially when ordering copies of the book

ISDN *n* [U] COMPUTING Integrated Services Digital Network; a system that allows computer information to be sent at extremely high speeds along an electronic wire similar to a telephone line: *These companies have made big capital investments in ISDN.* | *an ISDN telephone line*

ISE abbreviation for INTERNATIONAL SECURITIES EXCHANGE

ISO /ˌaɪ es ˈəʊ, ˈaɪsəʊ‖-oʊ/ *n* **1** the name used internationally for the International Organization for Standardization, whose purpose is to establish international standards for services, goods and industrial methods

2 ISO 9000 the ISO's quality standard for companies producing goods: *The process of qualifying for ISO 9000 will improve organizations' quality systems.*

3 ISO 9001/9002 the ISO's quality standards for companies providing services: *The bank's clearing system was the first in the world to be awarded an ISO 9002 certificate.*

4 ISO 14000 the ISO's quality standard for subjects relating to the environment and RECYCLING (=using materials more than once)

i·so·late /ˈaɪsəleɪt/ *v* [T] **1** to prevent a country or company from getting support or business from other countries or companies, so that it becomes weaker: *They attempted to isolate China through trade sanctions.*

2 to separate something so that it can be dealt with by itself, rather than affecting the whole of a business, market etc: *After isolating the problem, investigate it as quickly as possible and resolve it.* —**isolation** *n* [U] *Inflation cannot be addressed* ***in isolation from*** *other economic problems.* —**isolated** *adj*: *The regime has become increasingly isolated.*

i·so·la·tion·is·m /ˌaɪsəˈleɪʃənɪzəm/ *n* [U] the belief that your country should not be involved in the affairs of other countries: *1853 saw the end of Japanese isolationism.* —**isolationist** *adj*: *isolationist policies* —**isolationist** *n* [C]

ISP *n* [C] the abbreviation for INTERNET SERVICE PROVIDER

is·su·ance /ˈɪʃuəns, ˈɪsjuəns‖ˈɪʃuəns/ *n* [C,U] FINANCE another name for ISSUE[2]: *He is effectively able to stop the issuance of any export licenses.* | *Several stock issuances have also been made on the Big Board the past several days.*

is·sue¹ /ˈɪʃuː, ˈɪsjuː‖ˈɪʃuː/ *v* [T] **1** to make something available to someone **issue sb with sth**: *Northwest Airlines issued fliers with discount coupons.* | *Visa USA licenses US financial institutions to issue Visa cards.*

2 FINANCE if an organization issues SECURITIES such as bonds and shares, it makes them available for people to buy: *RJR Nabisco recently* ***issued bonds*** *with yields under 10%.* | *In January, AMR* ***issued*** *5 million new* ***shares*** *at $51.50 a share.*

3 BANKING if a bank issues coins or BANKNOTES (=paper money), it makes them available and puts them into CIRCULATION: *The European Central Bank will issue the euro banknotes by 2002 at the latest.*

issue² *n* [C] **1** FINANCE the act of making SECURITIES such as bonds, shares etc available for sale, and the securities themselves + **of**: *USX shareholders are expected to approve two issues of common stock.* | *Earnings per share slipped to 9.9 pence from 10.1 pence because of the larger number of shares* ***in issue*** (=existing).

authorized issue also **authorised issue** *BrE* the largest amount of capital a company is allowed to have in the form of shares; AUTHORIZED CAPITAL, AUTHORIZED STOCK: *To finance the expansion programme, PAL doubled its authorised capital from 5 billion to 10 billion pesos.*

bonus issue ♦ when a company changes part of its RESERVES (=past profits that have not yet been paid out to shareholders) into share capital. This increases the number of shares held by each shareholder and reduces the value of each share, making them easier to buy and sell; SCRIP ISSUE: *In addition to its regular dividend, Heineken will make a bonus issue of one share for each four shares investors hold* | *the board has proposed a bonus issue of one new share for each 10 shares held.*

capitalization issue also **capitalisation issue** *BrE* another name for BONUS ISSUE

cash issue an offer by a company to people who hold shares in it allowing them to buy new shares that are being made available for the first time; RIGHTS ISSUE: *Your directors would consult the appropriate investor protection bodies before making any cash issue in excess of the guidelines.*

euro-equity issue when a company's shares are made available internationally, rather than just in the country where the company is based

new issue ♦ when new shares are issued in companies that are already on the stockmarket, or when new bonds are issued: *During the first quarter, new issues of bank equity rose to $1.575 billion.*

♦ when shares are issued on a stockmarket for a company that was not LISTED on it before: *Sphinx Pharmaceuticals, a new issue yesterday, was the most active stock.*

public issue when shares, bonds etc are made available for anyone to buy: *Sherrit Gordon plans to raise about C$36.8 million through a public issue of 5.2 million common shares.*

rights issue an occasion when a company makes new shares available to existing shareholders. The new shares are usually cheaper than the current value of the existing shares. Rights to these new shares can be sold on the stockmarket. After a rights issue, the company's share price may go down because of DILUTION: *Nickless plans to raise A$322 million through a 1-for-5 rights issue.*

scrip issue *BrE* another name for BONUS ISSUE: *Scottish Television plans to repeat June's 1-for-1 scrip issue after seeing its shares double in nine months.*

share issue also **share offer** when new shares in a company are made available for sale to the public: *The company has announced it will be* ***launching*** *a £3.25 million* ***share issue***. | *Black Sheep Brewery started production in the summer, having raised £850,000 through a share issue.*

tender issue also **issue by tender** ♦ a share issue in which offers above a particular price are invited for the shares: *Some of the early privatization issues such as Britoil and Cable and Wireless were tender issues.*

♦ in Britain, an ISSUE of TREASURY BILLS that is made every week by the Bank of England: *Discount houses underwrite the weekly tender issue of Treasury bills by bidding competitively for those not sold.*

2 an occasion when a bank or government makes new paper money or coins available to be used + **of**: *Before Christmas the issue of banknotes is increased to meet the extra demand.*

note issue ♦ an occasion when BANKNOTES (=paper money) are made available

♦ the total value of BANKNOTES that are available for use at a particular time: *For 200 years, the Bank of England maintained an adequate gold stock to back the note issue.*

issue advertising —see under ADVERTISING

issue broker —see under BROKER[1]

issued capital —see under CAPITAL

Issue Department *n* BANKING the part of the BANK OF ENGLAND that arranges the printing of paper money and makes it available to be used —compare BANKING DEPARTMENT

issue flop *n* [C] FINANCE a situation when shares are

issued and there are not enough buyers: *There have been two major rights issue flops lately.* —see also UNDERSUBSCRIBED

issue price —see under PRICE[1]

is·su·er /ˈɪʃuə, ˈɪsjuə‖ˈɪʃuər/ *n* [C] **1** a person or organization that makes something available: *The* ***credit card issuers'*** *battle for market share doesn't necessarily mean that credit card customers are getting a better deal.*
2 FINANCE a company that makes its SECURITIES (=bonds, shares etc) available for sale: *Among the issuers yesterday were Kmart Corp., which sold $200 million of 15-year bonds.*
corporate issuer an issuer that is a company rather than a government organization: *Among the biggest corporate issuers was El Paso Natural Gas Co., which offered $575 million of debt securities.*
municipal issuer an issuer that is a local government organization: *State and local governments, as well as other municipal issuers, are offering higher yields to attract investors.*
3 BANKING a bank or government that issues currency in the form of BANKNOTES (=paper money) and coins, making them officially available: *The Bank's function as the issuer of currency notes is separate from its banking activities.*

issuing house —see under HOUSE

IT abbreviation for INFORMATION TECHNOLOGY: *IT has had a dramatic affect on the telecoms infrastructure.* | *the firm's IT department*

ITC abbreviation for INVESTMENT TAX CREDIT

i·tem /ˈaɪtəm/ *n* **1** [C] a single thing, especially something that is for sale: *The CD used to be considered a* ***luxury item***. | *stores selling non-food items*
2 [C] a piece of information written in a set of accounts: *Carry costs can include such items as insurance and storage.*
extraordinary item also **exceptional item** [C usually plural] an amount in a set of accounts that is unlikely to be repeated, for example an amount relating to the sale of assets. Extraordinary items are not included when calculating OPERATING PROFIT: *Profit before extraordinary items totaled 14.4 billion kroner.*
3 [C] one of the subjects that is to be discussed in a meeting, written on a list called an AGENDA: *What's the first item on the agenda?*

i·tem·ize also **itemise** *BrE* /ˈaɪtəmaɪz/ *v* [I,T] to present information in the form of a list, giving details about each item on the list: *The report itemized several areas of concern.* | *Taxpayers who don't itemize* (=don't give a detailed list of all their expenses) *receive a standard deduction.* —**itemized** also **itemised** *BrE adj*: *an itemized phone bill*

itemized billing also **itemised billing** *BrE* —see under BILLING

i·tin·e·ra·ry /aɪˈtɪnərəri‖-nəreri/ *n* plural **itineraries** [C] a list of the places you plan to visit on a trip: *Mr Baker's itinerary will include stops in Saudi Arabia and Egypt.*

Ivy League *adj* connected with a group of old and respected universities in the eastern US: *an* ***Ivy League college***

J

jack•pot /ˈdʒækpɒt‖-pɑːt/ *n* [C] **1** a large prize you can win in a LOTTERY (=a game of chance in which people buy tickets with numbers on): *this week's £3 million jackpot in the National Lottery*
2 a large amount of profit: *General Dynamics sees a potential jackpot in these new aircraft.*
3 hit the jackpot if a person or organization hits the jackpot, they make a lot of money, or have a big success: *Du Pont chemists have hit the jackpot with this new fiber.*

Jan. written abbreviation for JANUARY

jan•i•tor /ˈdʒænətə‖-ər/ *n* [C] *AmE* someone who looks after an office block or other large building; CARETAKER *BrE*

Ja•va /ˈdʒɑːvə/ *n* [U] *trademark* COMPUTING a computer language used mainly to write small programs called APPLETS for the INTERNET (=the computer system that can be used by people all around the world): *You will need a Java compatible internet browser.*

J-curve *n* [C] ECONOMICS a line on a GRAPH (=a drawing with a line showing two related measurements) in the shape of a letter J, that represents a slight fall in the level of something followed by an increase: *Analysts are talking about a J-curve effect, with a slight downturn in share prices followed by a recovery later.*

jeop•ar•dize also **jeopardise** *BrE* /ˈdʒepədaɪz‖-ər-/ *v* [T] to risk losing or harming something: *There are fears that cost cuts might jeopardize safety.* | *The company's financial position is being jeopardized by continuing losses.*

jeop•ar•dy /ˈdʒepədi‖-ər-/ *n* **in jeopardy** in danger of being lost or harmed: *We will not do anything that will **put** our business **in jeopardy**.*

jet•ti•son /ˈdʒetəsən, -zən/ *v* [T] to get rid of something quickly or completely because it is not good enough: *Some Wall Street firms will jettison unprofitable businesses.*

jew•el•ler *BrE*, **jeweler** *AmE* /ˈdʒuːələ‖-ər/ *n* [C] a person, company, or shop that makes or sells jewellery

Jiffy bag *n* [C] *trademark* a thick soft envelope, used for posting things that might break

jin•gle /ˈdʒɪŋgəl/ *n* [C] a short song or tune used in advertisements: *He earned a living writing **advertising jingles**.*

JIT abbreviation for JUST-IN-TIME

Jnr *BrE* written abbreviation for JUNIOR; JR. *AmE*

job[1] /dʒɒb‖dʒɑːb/ *n* **1** [C] the regular paid work that you do for an employer: *What job do you do?* | *I've **applied for a job** with the BBC.* | *1,200 employees could **lose their jobs**.* | *He has been **job hunting*** (=looking for a job) *since last September.* | *tests to measure employees' levels of **job satisfaction*** (=how satisfied they are with their jobs)
desk job [C] a job that you do sitting at a desk in an office: *She has a desk job with the police force.*
2 on the job while doing a particular job: *Workers are not allowed to drink on the job.* | *on-the-job training*
3 jobs for the boys [plural] *BrE* jobs that a powerful person has given to their friends
4 [C] a particular project or piece of work being done or planned to be done: *The company lost out on several jobs because of the newspaper article.* | *Some firms charge by the hour, others by the job.*
5 [C] an operation performed by a computer: *You can cancel any **print job** in the queue.*

job[2] *v* past tense and past participle **jobbed** present participle **jobbing**
job sth ↔ **out** *phr v* [T] to give work to a number of businesses, rather than doing it yourself; contract out: *Even important tasks were jobbed out to contractors.*

job action —see under ACTION

job advertisement —see under ADVERTISEMENT

job analysis —see under ANALYSIS

job application —see under APPLICATION

job bank —see under BANK[1]

job•ber /ˈdʒɒbə‖ˈdʒɑːbər/ *n* [C] **1** *BrE* in Britain before BIG BANG, someone whose job was to buy stocks and shares in a particular area of the market, dealing only with BROKERS or with other jobbers, not directly with investors; STOCKJOBBER. Now any dealer can deal with investors or other dealers: *The distinction between brokers and jobbers has disappeared.*
2 someone who buys a product from a company and then sells it to a customer at a higher price: *The distribution system includes the oil companies, middlemen known as jobbers and the gas stations themselves.* —see also RACK JOBBER

job•bing /ˈdʒɒbɪŋ‖ˈdʒɑː-/ *adj* [only before a noun] **jobbing builder/gardener/printer etc** someone who does small pieces of work for different people

jobbing production —see under PRODUCTION

job centre —see under CENTRE

job costing —see under COSTING

job cycle —see under CYCLE

job description also **job specification** *n* [C] an official list of the work and responsibilities you have in your job: *Photocopying isn't part of my job description.*

job design —see under DESIGN[1]

job enrichment —see under ENRICHMENT

job-hopping *n* [U] when someone changes their job very often: *Executive job-hopping is very common in the US, but rare in Japan.* —**job hopper** *n* [C]

job-hunter *n* [C] someone who is looking for a job; JOB SEEKER: *Slowdowns in several big industries had made New York a 'desert' for job-hunters.* —**job-hunt** *n* [C] *She had just embarked on a job hunt in Chicago, where she has relocated with her husband.* —**job-hunt** *v* [I] *More fired financial and other executives are job-hunting these days.* —**job-hunting** *n* [U] *In a year of job-hunting, I didn't come across one trainee program.*

job•less[1] /ˈdʒɒbləs‖ˈdʒɑːb-/ *adj* without a job; UNEMPLOYED: *1000 jobless workers have still not received their cheques.* | *Britain's **jobless total*** (=the number of people without a job) *rose to three million.* —**joblessness** *n* [U] *Joblessness is steadily rising.*

jobless[2] *n* [plural] people without a job considered as a group: *The prospects for the country's jobless are not good.*

job loss —see under LOSS

job lot —see under LOT

job market —see under MARKET[1]

job order —see under ORDER[1]

job placement —see under PLACEMENT

job protection —see under PROTECTION

job quota —see under QUOTA

job rotation —see under ROTATION

job security —see under SECURITY

job-seeker *n* [C] someone who is looking for a job; JOB HUNTER: *The latest job data shows 147 job offers for every 100 job seekers.*

job-seeker's allowance —see under ALLOWANCE

job sharing *n* [U] when two people share one full-time job, dividing the hours and work between them: *What is your company's policy on job sharing?* | *a job-sharing scheme* —**job share** *v* [I] *We have job shared for two years now.* —**job share** *n* [C] *women working in job shares*

job shop —see under SHOP[1]

job specification *n* [C] another name for JOB DESCRIPTION

join /dʒɔɪn/ *v* [T] **1** [I,T] to become a member of a group, team, or organization: *She was invited to join the company's board.* | *Austria was not a member of the EC, but wanted to join.*

2 [I,T] to start working for a company or an organization: *He first joined Allianz as a salesman.* | *She left in 1995, the year I joined.*

3 join forces to take action together in order to achieve something: *AT&T and NEC agreed to join forces to develop a new mobile telephone system.* + **with**: *Many small insurance companies are joining forces with other insurers.*

4 join together to do something with another person, company, or organization: *Eight Japanese and two American companies are joining together to design communications equipment.*

join in sth *phr v* [T] to take part in something with another group, company, or organization: *We would be eager to join in projects of that sort.*

join with sb/sth *phr v* [T] to do something with another person, company, or organization: *He is joining with a Virginia firm to invest $450 million in real estate assets.*

joint /dʒɔɪnt/ *adj* [only before a noun] shared by, owned by, or involving two or more people, organizations, or countries: *The companies made a **joint statement** last night.* | *The two men were appointed joint managing directors in June.* | *The two groups are **joint owners** of the hotel.* —**jointly** *adv*: *They have set up a jointly owned company.*

joint account —see under ACCOUNT[1]

joint and several liability —see under LIABILITY

joint annuity —see under ANNUITY

joint ownership —see under OWNERSHIP

joint-stock bank —see under BANK[1]

joint venture —see under VENTURE[1]

jolt[1] /dʒəʊlt‖dʒoʊlt/ *n* [C] a shock that causes prices and markets to change suddenly: *Many companies **got a jolt** from the attempted coup.* | *The crisis **gave a jolt** to the world energy markets.*

jolt[2] *v* [T] to give a sudden shock to a person, company, or market: *Traders were jolted yesterday by reports warning of recession.* | *The eruption of war in the Middle East jolted the world's financial markets.*

joule /dʒuːl‖dʒuːl, dʒaʊl/ written abbreviation **J** *n* [C] a unit of energy, work done, or quantity of heat

jour•nal /ˈdʒɜːnl‖-ɜːr-/ *n* [C] **1** a serious magazine or newspaper produced for professional people or those with a particular interest: *the Wall Street Journal* | *the Journal of Political Economy*

2 ACCOUNTING a book containing details of TRANSACTIONS (=acts of buying and selling) of a business in the order that they happen

jour•nal•is•m /ˈdʒɜːnəl-ɪzəm‖-ɜːr-/ *n* [U] the job or activity of writing news reports for newspapers, magazines, television, or radio: *Two Wall Street Journal reporters won awards for distinguished business and **financial journalism**.*

Jr. *AmE* written abbreviation for JUNIOR; JNR *BrE*

judge[1] /dʒʌdʒ/ *n* [C] the official in control of a court who decides how criminals should be punished, or makes decisions about disagreements that the court has been asked to solve: *The case is scheduled for trial today before Judge Robert Parker.* | *a County Court judge*

bankruptcy judge a judge in the US who makes decisions in a BANKRUPTCY COURT when a company is being made BANKRUPT (=officially said to be unable to pay its debts): *A bankruptcy judge appointed a trustee to take control of the firm's assets.*

circuit judge a judge who travels to several small courts in a particular area

district judge a judge in a DISTRICT COURT in the US —see under COURT[1]

federal judge a judge in a FEDERAL COURT in the US —see under COURT[1]

judge[2] *v* [T] to form or give an opinion about how good or bad something is **judge sth on**: *The company will be judged on its quarterly reports.* **judge sth against**: *Analysts' recommendations are judged against a performance index for the industry they follow.*

judgement call —see under CALL[2]

judgement debt —see under DEBT

judgement debtor —see under DEBTOR

judgement sample —see under SAMPLE[1]

judge's order —see under ORDER[1]

judg•ment also **judgement** *BrE* /ˈdʒʌdʒmənt/ *n* **1** [C] an opinion formed or a decision made after careful thought: *Traders said they would wait to see more economic data before **making a judgment** about the economy.* | *Mr Overs has said he is **reserving judgment*** (=not forming an opinion until all the facts are available) *on the deal.*

value judgment [C] a decision or judgment about how good something is, based on opinions rather than facts: *Someone has got to **make a value judgment** about whether the benefits of the deal are worth the cost.*

2 [U] the ability to make good decisions: *There is no substitute for common sense and **good** business **judgment**.* | *The company has shown **poor judgment** in its investment strategy.*

3 [C] LAW a decision made by a court of law: *The former president of the company now faces a $2.2 million federal court judgment against him.* | *Marx sued his employer and **won a judgment** for £25,000.* | *The court **upheld a judgment*** (=said that another court's judgment was correct) *in the firm's favor.*

default judgment also **judgement in/by default** *BrE* [C] a legal judgment made in favour of someone because the other person involved in the case has failed to do something they should have done: *A default judgment was entered against Mr. Antar after he repeatedly failed to appear in court.*

deficiency judgment [C] LAW a decision by a court that a borrower still owes money after the SECURITY for a loan is sold for less than the amount owed

judgment creditor —see under CREDITOR

ju•di•cial /dʒuːˈdɪʃəl/ *adj* [only before a noun] connected with a court of law or the legal system: *All citizens must have confidence in the **judicial system**.* | *This legislation represented an effort by Congress to interfere with the **judicial process**.* | *a new law which limits **judicial power***

ju•di•cia•ry /dʒuːˈdɪʃəri‖-ʃieri, -ʃəri/ *n* [singular] all the judges in a country who are responsible for making decisions about legal matters: *It is important to preserve an independent judiciary.* | *the Federal judiciary*

jug•ger•naut /ˈdʒʌgənɔːt‖-ərnɒːt/ *n* [C] **1** a very large company: *The software juggernaut Microsoft will continue to lead the industry with its Windows operating system.*

2 something large and powerful that could be harmful to smaller things: *They saw a united Germany as an economic juggernaut in the centre of Europe.*

3 *BrE* a very large LORRY (=vehicle for carrying goods by road)

jug•gle /ˈdʒʌɡəl/ *v* [I,T] **1** to buy and sell different investments frequently in order to make as much profit as possible: *Traders juggle stock and options to maximize profits from temporary price differences.* | *Some investors juggle between stocks, bonds and cash in search of high returns with moderate risks.*
2 if you juggle numbers or figures, you present them in a different way so that they show different things or have a different effect: *After juggling the figures, the Commerce Department now says GNP rose by only 1.4% in the third quarter.*
3 if you juggle two jobs or activities, you try to fit them both into your life: *Many women successfully juggle career and family.*

Jul. written abbreviation for JULY

jum•bo /ˈdʒʌmbəʊ‖-boʊ/ *adj* [only before a noun] larger than the usual size: *Jumbo loans carry higher interest rates than smaller loans.*

jump¹ /dʒʌmp/ *v* **1** [I] to increase suddenly by a large amount: *Share prices jumped by almost 8% yesterday.* | *Imports jumped 12% to $5.6 billion.*
2 jump ship to leave a company or organization, especially because it is not very good or very successful: *Their chairman jumped ship for a similar position with a German firm.*
jump in *phr v* [I] to do something quickly, often without thinking about it carefully: *He counseled caution to clients wanting to jump in and buy stocks.*
jump into sth *phr v* [T] to begin investing in, producing, or trading in a particular type of goods or services: *Milacron jumped into robots a few years ago.*

jump² *n* **1** [C] a sudden large increase + **in**: *The company reported an 11% jump in sales last year.* | *another **big jump** in crude oil prices*
2 have/get a jump on sb *AmE* to have or get an advantage over another person or company: *AT&T is trying to get a jump on its rivals in the videophone market.*

jump•start /ˈdʒʌmpstɑːt‖-stɑːrt/ *v* [T] to do something that will help the economy become more active or successful: *The government is hoping that a cut in interest rates will **jumpstart the economy**.* | *The country is in desperate need of foreign capital to jumpstart industrial growth.* —**jumpstart** *n* [singular] *Economists are relying on consumers for a jumpstart to get the economy going again.*

Jun. written abbreviation for JUNE

jun•gle /ˈdʒʌŋɡəl/ *n* [singular] a situation in which a lot of people or businesses are competing with each other in a very determined way: *Without the free publicity, the firm would be lost in the jungle of TV advertising.*

Ju•ni•or¹ /ˈdʒuːniə‖-ər/ written abbreviation **Jr** *AmE*, **Jnr** *BrE* used after the name of a man who has the same name as his father, especially in the US: *John J. Wallace Jr*

junior² *adj* **1** having a low rank in an organization or a profession **be junior to** (=lower in rank than): *Barron had refused to talk to anyone junior to Wickham.* | *Some junior employees might lack the courage to approach the boss.*
2 FINANCE a junior bond, debt etc will be repaid later or have a smaller part repaid than other bonds, debts etc, if the borrower is unable to repay everything **be junior to**: *The new bonds offered by Trump Plaza Associates were junior to the old ones.* | *senior and **junior debt holders*** —compare SENIOR²

junior³ *n* [C] someone who has a low rank in an organization or profession: *They treated her like a junior.*
office junior *BrE* someone who works in an office at the lowest rank: *Even without qualifications, you should be able to find work as a shop assistant or an office junior.*

junior bondholder —see under BONDHOLDER

junior creditor —see under CREDITOR

junior debenture —see under DEBENTURE

junior debt —see under DEBT

junior management —see under MANAGEMENT

junior partner —see under PARTNER

junior staff —see under STAFF¹

junk¹ /dʒʌŋk/ *n* [U] another name for JUNK BONDS (=bonds with a high RETURN but a big risk of not being repaid): *one of the top five firms in junk*

junk² *adj informal, disapproving* **junk email/fax/mail** email etc sent to someone who has not requested it, usually to advertise something: *The system allows the user only to receive filtered messages, a benefit in dealing with junk email.*

junk bond —see under BOND

jun•ket /ˈdʒʌŋkɪ̈t/ *n* [C] *informal* a free trip that is paid for by a company or by the government: *These funds should not have been used to pay for junkets abroad.*

junk mail —see under MAIL¹

jur•is•dic•tion /ˌdʒʊərɪ̈sˈdɪkʃən‖ˌdʒʊr-/ *n* [U] the official right and power to make decisions about something + **over**: *The bankruptcy court now **has jurisdiction** over the company's assets.* | *This matter is **outside my jurisdiction**.* + **of**: *The firm has now become a joint stock company **under the jurisdiction** of the Russian republic.* | *This matter is now **within the jurisdiction** of the US courts.*

ju•rist /ˈdʒʊərɪ̈st‖ˈdʒʊr-/ *n* [C] a person with very detailed knowledge of the law, especially one who writes on matters of law

ju•ror /ˈdʒʊərə‖ˈdʒʊrər/ *n* [C] a member of a jury: *The jurors failed to agree on a verdict.*

ju•ry /ˈdʒʊəri‖ˈdʒʊri/ *n* plural **juries** [C] a group of ordinary people, often 12 in number, who listen to details of a case in court and decide whether someone is innocent or guilty: *The jury has not yet returned its verdict.* | *The case will **go before a jury** next week.* | *The state guarantees the right to a **jury trial** in all civil disputes.*
grand jury a jury in the US that looks at a case that could be brought against someone and decides whether it is strong enough to continue with: *A grand jury last month indicted the former director of the firm on two counts of perjury.*

jus•tice /ˈdʒʌstɪ̈s/ *n* **1** [U] the system by which people are judged in courts of law and criminals are punished: *There are many problems with our criminal justice system.*
2 [C] *AmE* a judge in a law court: *Justice Sandra O'Connor* | *The justices ruled that the company had acted illegally.*
3 [C] *BrE* the title of a judge in the HIGH COURT: *Mr Justice Saville ruled in favour of Lloyd's.*

Justice of the Peace abbreviation **JP** *BrE*, **justice of the peace** *AmE n* plural **Justices of the Peace** [C] a MAGISTRATE (=type of judge) in Britain and in some US states who judges less serious cases in lower law courts: *He gave evidence before the Justice of the Peace.*

just-in-time written abbreviation **JIT** *adj* [only before a noun] if goods are produced or bought using a just-in-time system, they are produced or bought just before they are needed, reducing the cost to the firm of keeping goods for long periods of time: *The firm is worried that delays could cause problems with their **just-in-time manufacturing** methods.* | *Many companies are now moving to **just-in-time delivery** of supplies.*

just-in-time production —see under PRODUCTION

K

K **1** written abbreviation for ONE THOUSAND: *a salary of 59K a year*
2 COMPUTING written abbreviation for KILOBYTE(S)

kai•zen /ˈkaɪzen/ *n* [U] a method of running a company which tries to encourage continuous improvement in its products, staff, management etc: *Every team has goals that give meaning and substance to the principle of kaizen.*

kan•ban /ˈkænbæn/ *adj* [only before a noun] involving the system used in JUST-IN-TIME production, where parts are ordered just before they are needed: *In the* ***kanban system****, metal tickets act as an order from a workstation to the one before it, saying make x number of y parts*

kar•at /ˈkærət/ *n* [C] an American spelling of CARAT

kb COMPUTING written abbreviation for KILOBYTE(S)

keel /kiːl/ *n* **on an even keel** working smoothly without any sudden changes: *The recent flotation of Computervision Corp has helped to* ***put*** *the company* ***back on an even keel.***

keen /kiːn/ *adj* **1** if competition is keen, people are trying very hard to get an advantage over others doing the same thing: *Business has become scarcer, competition keener and profit margins slimmer.* | *These properties are likely to attract* ***keen bidding*** *in a buoyant property market.* —**keenly** *adv*: *the keenly-competitive pasta sauce market*
2 *BrE* keen prices, rates etc are low when compared to competitors' prices etc: *London's present system provides* ***keen prices*** *for actively traded stocks.* | *the opportunity to achieve the* ***keenest interest rates***
3 if someone is keen, they are very eager or interested in doing something: *Investors already have shown* ***keen interest in*** *the $100 million issue.* **be keen on sth**: *Japanese investors are keen on obtaining more foreign assets.* **be keen to do sth**: *Iberia is keen to buy a stake in Pluna, Uruguay's state airline.* —**keenly** *adv*: *Lord Hanson said his company is* ***keenly interested in*** *seeing ICI's performance improve.*

keep /kiːp/ *v* past tense and past participle **kept** **1** [T] to store something that will be useful: *The Credit Reference Agency* ***keeps files on*** *individual's debt records.* | *You should* ***keep a supply of*** *forms.*
2 keep a record/log/account etc to regularly record written information somewhere
keep to sth *phr v* [T] to do what you have promised or agreed to do: *Members of TI will promote standards of conduct and will try to keep to them.*
keep up *phr v* **1** [T] **keep** sth ↔ **up** to prevent something from falling to a lower level + **with**: *The high demand for cereals was responsible for keeping agricultural wages up with prices.*
2 [T] **keep** sth ↔ **up** to continue to make payments such as rent etc on time: *Your home is at risk if you do not* ***keep up repayments*** *on a mortgage.*
3 [I] to remain competitive by trying to do things as well as other people, organizations etc: *Some firms have used technical agreements with foreign enterprises to keep up technologically.* + **with**: *We have to move fast to keep up with changing laws.*

keep•er /ˈkiːpə‖-ər/ *n* [C] **1** someone whose job is to look after a particular place or area of work: *The EC requires each member state to maintain a list of registered traders and authorised* ***warehouse keepers.*** | *The service is provided by New York entrepreneur and* ***store keeper*** (=someone who owns a shop or store), *Jim Goldman.*
2 MARKETING *informal* a product that a company decides to continue selling: *In the new ABC schedules, the keepers are Twin Peaks and two video shows, Coach and Father Dowling Mysteries.*

kei•ret•su /keɪˈretsuː/ *n* plural **keiretsu** [C,U] a group of companies in Japan that decide to work together so that they can control or influence prices within a particular industry: *The study found that ties are loosening within the six major keiretsu.* | *Keiretsu eliminates inefficient competition among fellow members.*

Keogh /ˈkiːəʊ‖-oʊ/ also **Keogh plan** *n* [C] *AmE* a savings plan in the US, used mainly by people who work for themselves rather for an employer. Keoghs provide the person with a PENSION (=income after they have stopped working altogether): *You can put money in a Keogh even if you are already covered by a corporate pension or profit-sharing plan.* | *These days, Keogh plans are of increased interest for executives who have lost their jobs.*

key[1] /kiː/ *n* **1** a part of a computer with letters, numbers etc on it that you press with your fingers to make it work: *Press any key to continue.*
alt key a key that is used together with other keys to give commands, obtain special characters etc: *Many commands require the Ctrl, Shift, or Alt keys to be held down while another key is tapped.*
control key written abbreviation **ctl-key** a key that is used together with other keys to give commands, obtain special characters etc: *The control key must be held down while the R or W key on the keyboard is pressed.*
hot key one or more computer keys that have been programmed to make your computer do a particular thing when you press them: *Use the mouse or a hot key to move to a different window.*
shift key the key that is held down while pressing another key in order to obtain a capital letter
2 a/the key to sth the part of a plan, arrangement etc that is the most important and which everything else depends on: *The key to customer satisfaction is quick access to those best placed to resolve issues quickly.* | *If managers are free to concentrate on the core business, this could be* ***a key to*** *economic* ***success*** *in the difficult times ahead.*

key[2] *adj* **1** very important or necessary: *the impact of foreign investment on* ***key industries*** | *The* ***key elements of*** *Japanese management methods can be applied to Western organisations.* | *A* ***key factor in*** *these companies' success is knowing their customers' preferences.* **be key to sth**: *Technical alliances between companies are key to putting pressure on other cable competitors.*
2 key actor/player/mover a person or company who is very important and influential: *The key players involved in the change must be identified and their commitment to the change obtained.* | *Employers are key actors within industrial relations.*

key[3] *v* **be keyed to sth** if the level, price, value etc of something is keyed to something else, it is related to it and rises and falls with it: *In many cases, brokers' commissions are keyed to share prices.* | *The agreement requires banks to hold a certain amount of capital, keyed to the riskiness of loans.*
key sth ↔ **in** *phr v* [T] to put information into a computer or other machine, using a keyboard or keypad: *They took it to the computer room and keyed in the text in sections.*

key•board[1] /ˈkiːbɔːd‖-bɔːrd/ *n* [C] a board with buttons marked with different letters which are pressed to put information into a computer or other machine: *Sun will demonstrate a Cyrillic keyboard at the Moscow ComTech show.* | *the F2 key on your* ***computer keyboard***

keyboard² *v* [T] to put information into a computer, using a keyboard: *The best way would be to* ***keyboard*** *the entries* ***into*** *the correct places in the document.* —**keyboarding** *n* [U] *an estimate of the keyboarding costs*

key·board·er /ˈkiːbɔːdə‖-bɔːrdər/ *n* [C] someone whose job is to enter information into a computer using a keyboard

key·hold·er /ˈkiːˌhəʊldə‖-ˌhoʊldər/ *n* [C] someone who officially has the key to a particular house, factory, office etc: *Office cleaning is often carried out when the keyholders to the store are not available.*

key indicator —see under INDICATOR

key money —see under MONEY

Keynes·i·an /ˈkeɪnziən/ *adj* ECONOMICS Keynesian actions follow the teaching of John Maynard Keynes. Keynes believed that, in a RECESSION, the economy can be made to grow and unemployment reduced by increasing government spending, even if this causes a BUDGET DEFICIT (=a situation where the government spends more than it receives), and by making reductions in INTEREST RATES (=the cost of borrowing): *In the* ***Keynesian model****, a fall in aggregate demand leads to a fall in real income and reduces employment.* —**Keynesian** *n* [C] *the long-running debate between monetarists and Keynesians as to the precise influence of money on the economy* —**Keynesianism** *n* [U] *the current decline in Keynesianism*

key·note /ˈkiːnəʊt‖-noʊt/ *adj* **keynote address/speech** the most important speech at a large meeting: *A question-and-answer session followed Mr Lamont's keynote speech at the CBI conference.*

key·pad /ˈkiːpæd/ *n* [C] a small box with buttons on it which you can use to put information into a computer, telephone etc: *The calculator, patented by ADDvantage Media, consists of a keypad which lets customers add up costs as they shop.*

kg written abbreviation for KILOGRAM

kick /kɪk/ *v*

kick in *phr v* **1** [I] *informal* if a system, arrangement, event etc kicks in, it begins to have an effect: *Many lawyers are hurrying to arrange settlements before the new tax rules kick in.* | *Huge pension cost increases are expected to kick in around 2010 as the baby-boom generation reaches retirement.*
2 [I,T] **kick** sth **in** *AmE* to join with others in investing or making money for something, especially in order to help people: *In eight years, companies have kicked in $300,000 towards community improvements.* | *Sales per employee – one measure of how the staff may or may not be kicking in for a company – rose by 8%.*

kick sth ↔ **off** *phr v* **1** *AmE* [T] if an investment kicks off payments, it produces those payments for the investor: *Single-state muni funds* ***kick off income*** *that is exempt not only from federal taxes but from state taxes as well.*
2 [I,T] if a meeting, event etc kicks off or you kick it off, it starts: *The conference was scheduled to kick off at noon.* | *Euro Disney will kick off a pre-launch advertising campaign in the UK next week.*

kick sb ↔ **out** *phr v* [T] *informal* to dismiss someone from a job or to try to make them leave a place + **of**: *Some of his fellow attorneys tried to kick him out of the profession.* | *He is among Britain's 100 richest men – and one of the first to be kicked out of Lloyd's.*

K

kick·back /ˈkɪkbæk/ *n* [C] *informal* money that is paid secretly and dishonestly to obtain someone's help; BRIBE: *He is on trial for corruption and allegedly* ***accepting kickbacks from*** *businesses.* | *He and his partner were charged with* ***taking*** *$300,000* ***in kickbacks*** *in exchange for their political influence.*

kick-start *v* [T] to do something to make a process or activity develop more quickly: *Software companies are using their development skills to* ***kick-start the market*** *for radically new information products.* —**kick-start** *n* [singular] *a new initiative which will* ***provide a kick-start for*** *the manufacturing sector.* | *South Korea and Taiwan both got a kick-start to economic growth from their access to the US market.*

kid·vid /ˈkɪdvɪd/ *n* [C] *AmE informal* a television programme or film aimed at children: *Other networks have run down the kidvid block on daytime TV.*

kill /kɪl/ *v* [T] if someone kills an idea, product etc, they decide to stop developing it, selling it etc: *They have killed plans for a weekly regional magazine in Los Angeles.* —see also FILL OR KILL

killer app also **killer ap** /ˈkɪlər ˌæp/ *n* [singular] COMPUTING a MEDIUM (=way of communicating entertainment and information) that everyone wants to have and that will be very profitable for companies involved in it: *Intel put together a $2 million presentation showing that the PC, not TV, was the killer ap.*

kil·ling /ˈkɪlɪŋ/ *n* **make a killing** *informal* to make a lot of money in a very short time: *He made a killing by buying shares in Mercedes shortly before they were exchanged for shares in Daimler-Benz.*

ki·lo /ˈkiːləʊ‖-loʊ/ *n* [C] a KILOGRAM

kilo- /kɪlə/ *prefix* 1000 times a particular unit. For example, a KILOGRAM is 1000 GRAMS and a KILOMETRE is 1000 metres

kil·o·byte /ˈkɪləbaɪt/ *n* [C] COMPUTING a unit of 1,024 BYTES, used for measuring the amount of information a computer can hold

kil·o·gram /ˈkɪləgræm/ *n* [C] a measurement of weight equal to 1000 GRAMS

kil·o·me·tre *BrE*, **kilometer** *AmE* /ˈkɪləˌmiːtə, kɪˈlɒmɪ̈tə‖kɪˈlɑːmɪ̈tər/, written abbreviation **km** *n* [C] a measurement of length equal to 1000 METRES

kind /kaɪnd/ *n* **(a) payment/benefit in kind** a method of paying someone or providing something extra by giving goods or services instead of money: *The company agreed that the loan should be settled* ***by payment in kind.*** | *A workplace nursery is not regarded as a benefit in kind, and is not counted in your income tax assessment.*

kin·dred /ˈkɪndrɪ̈d/ *adj* [only before a noun] *formal* belonging to the same group of things: *Mining stocks made the running as gold and* ***kindred*** *metal* ***prices*** *increased.*

king /kɪŋ/ *n* **1** [U] if something is king, it is the most important thing and has a strong influence on people's decisions: *We were convinced of the superiority of our product, but ultimately* ***the customer is king*** *and it was rejected.* | *Mr Smith suggests that* ***cash is king*** *and that readers should look to the health of a company's cash flow.*
2 [C] someone who is very influential or successful in a particular area; MOGUL: *the conviction of former junk bond king Michael Milken* | *Even the supermarket kings were nervous about the recession.*

king·mak·er /ˈkɪŋˌmeɪkə‖-ər/ *n* [C] *journalism* someone who influences the choice of person for an important job or position: *He will not run for office if he thinks he might lose; instead he will seek to be a kingmaker.*

king-size also **king-sized** *adj* [only before a noun] the largest available size of a particular product: *The duty system greatly favours the king-size brands.* | *The Bronx zoo has ordered a king-sized operating table with hydraulic lifts.*

ki·osk /ˈkiːɒsk‖-ɑːsk/ *n* [C] a small, moveable building in the street where cigarettes, newspapers etc are sold: *Many of the new businesses are small, one-person outfits, snack kiosks and the like.*

KISS /kɪs/ *informal* keep it simple, stupid, or keep it short and simple. Used to say that a method for doing something should be kept simple, in order to avoid mistakes: *The best franchising acronym is KISS: 'Keep it simple, stupid,' says one franchising specialist.*

kit /kɪt/ *n* [C] a set of equipment, materials etc, used for a particular purpose: *1500 public* ***information kits*** *were produced and mailed directly to social service agencies.* | *The company also markets Sound System, a £200* ***upgrade kit*** (=something which brings existing equipment up-to-date).

press kit *AmE* a set of prepared materials and documents about a particular product, sent by a company to people working for the newspapers, radio, or television: *S.C. Johnson & Son Inc. recently press kits promoting its cleaning products as environmentally friendly.*

kite[1] /kaɪt/ *n* **fly a kite** to make a suggestion, often an unusual one, to find out what people think of it: *The kite that Lord Hanson has flown is bobbing around in the political and financial winds.*

kite[2] *v* [I,T] *informal* **1 kite checks** to write cheques for more than the amount in the related account: *Members of the society had kited more than 8,000 checks in a single year.*

2 kite checks to use stolen cheques: *drug-related crimes, like kiting checks to buy drugs*

Kite·mark /ˈkaɪtˌmɑːk‖-ˌmɑːrk/ *n* [C] *BrE* a special triangular-shaped label, used in Britain to show that a product has been tested and approved by the BSI: *Approved child restraints must carry the* ***BSI Kitemark.***

kit·ty /ˈkɪti/ *n* [singular] *informal* an amount of money that is shared by several people: *The result of the EC's policy is a big change in who gets what from the EC kitty.*

KM abbreviation for KNOWLEDGE MANAGEMENT

km written abbreviation for KILOMETRE

km/h written abbreviation for KILOMETRES PER HOUR

knock[1] /nɒk‖nɑːk/ *v* **1** [T] FINANCE if something knocks the price of shares, stocks etc, the price changes very quickly and unexpectedly: *Talk of easing the US credit policy knocked prices higher in light trade.* | *Midlands shares were knocked by the Kuwait Investment's Office's decision to sell 10% of its stake.*

2 knock on/at the door to make it clear that you want to join something or want help from someone: *Eastern Europe is knocking at the European Community's door.* | *You could knock on the door of the Agriculture Committee to discuss farm price support.*

knock sth ↔ **down** *phr v* [T] **1** *informal* to reduce the price of something so that it is very cheap: *Sun has knocked down the prices of its multi-processing servers by 7%.* | *Shirts that left Comme des Garcons with a £100 price tag will be knocked down for a bargain price.* —see also KNOCKDOWN

2 be knocked down to sb to be sold at an auction (=a sale where something is sold to the person willing to pay most): *The item was finally knocked down for £790 to a bidder in the saleroom.*

knock sth **off** *phr v* [T] *informal* to reduce the price, value etc of something by a particular amount: *Profit-taking knocked 13p off Clinton Cards to 95p.* | *Regional Railways have promised they will knock 16 minutes off the journey between Redditch and Lichfield.*

knock sth ↔ **out** *phr v* [T] *informal* **1** to produce a lot of something: *Price's Patent Candle Company has been knocking out candles at its London factory since 1831.* | *A change in the rules would allow them to knock out more US patent applications.*

2 if something knocks out a system, machine etc it stops it working: *Fluctuations in the mains power supply knocked out the computer which normally logs all changes in operations.*

knock[2] *n* [C] something which suddenly makes a product fail or makes prices fall: *The US is likely to* ***take a series of knocks*** *from discounting in the car market.* | *a 612-point knock to the FTSE-index*

knockdown price —see under PRICE[1]

knock·out /ˈnɒk-aʊt‖ˈnɑːk-/ *n* [C] an agreement between people who are trying to buy the same thing not to compete against each other on the price: *It appears to be doubtful whether a knockout was arranged.* | *a* ***knockout agreement***

knot /nɒt‖nɑːt/ *n* **1 tie the knot** *journalism* if two companies tie the knot, they join and become one company; MERGE: *Once BNP and Dresdner have tied the knot, they will reconsider their relationship with Kleinwort Benson.* | *Banks across the country tied the knot as a way to cut costs and boost earnings.*

2 [C] a measurement of the speed at which ships travel, equal to about 1853 metres an hour

know-how *n* [U] practical ability, knowledge and skill in a technical area: *Innovations plc are an unusual and energetic company with considerable in-house* ***technical know-how.*** | *the acquisition of know-how or patent rights*

knowl·edge /ˈnɒlɪdʒ‖ˈnɑː-/ *n* [U] **1** facts, skills and understanding gained through learning or experience: *Given its* ***market knowledge,*** *Price Waterhouse was able to provide a useful insight into each supplier.* + **of**: *Auditors' knowledge of their client company means they are well-placed to judge the likelihood of company survival.*

2 all the information that a company and its employees possess about the TECHNOLOGY (=advanced processes and methods) it uses: *Today the* ***knowledge industry*** (=one where knowledge is the most important thing) *is regarded as the source of most new jobs – while well-paid blue-collar jobs disappear.*

knowledge-based software —see under SOFTWARE

knowledge industry —see under INDUSTRY

knowledge-intensive *adj* a knowledge-intensive job or industry is one where the workers need a lot of education, skills, and experience in order to work effectively: *The growth of knowledge-intensive industries means that many jobs are no longer linked to areas with natural resources.*

knowledge management —see under MANAGEMENT

knowledge officer —see under OFFICER

Kon·dra·ti·ev cycle /kɒnˈdrætiev ˌsaɪkəl‖kɑːn-/ or **Kondratiev wave**, also spelled **Kondratieff** *n* [C] ECONOMICS the idea that in a CAPITALIST economy, periods of fast growth are followed by periods of slower growth or no growth, and that this pattern is repeated every 50 to 60 years: *Kondratieff waves of growth and decline*

kru·ger·rand also **Krugerrand** /ˈkruːgəˌrænd/ *n* [C] a South African coin containing one OUNCE (=28.35 grams) of gold, often bought as an investment

L

L **1** written abbreviation for LIRA; LIRE; POUND(S)
2 *AmE* a unit used by the FEDERAL RESERVE BOARD to measure the total amount of LIQUID ASSETS in the US —see also M

l written abbreviation for LITRE(S)

la•bel[1] /ˈleɪbəl/ *n* [C] **1** a piece of paper or cloth that is attached to something and gives information about it: ***price labels** on goods in a supermarket* | *Read the label carefully and follow the instructions exactly.*
2 a name representing the company that is selling a product: *These products are manufactured by other reputable companies to a standard approved by Marks and Spencer and **sold under the St. Michael label**.* —see also OWN-BRAND, OWN-LABEL, PRIVATE LABEL, STORE LABEL
designer label a company that makes fashionable expensive clothes with its own well-known name on them: *a designer label such as Chanel*
3 the name of a record company: *Phillips' Polygram record company bought the Island label.*
4 the name of a wine-making company: *This wine from the Napa Ridge label is one of the great bargains of all time.*

label[2] *v* **labelled labelling** *BrE*, **labeled labeling** *AmE* [T] **1** to fix a label onto something or write information on something: *Beef producers must obey certain rules in labeling their new low-fat products.* | *All charts, diagrams and tables should be labelled.* | *The government forced six companies to stop labeling their processed pastas, juices and pickles as 'fresh.'*
2 to use a word or phrase to describe someone or something, but often unfairly or incorrectly: *One of the things we tend to do in organizations, unfortunately, is label people.* **label sb/sth (as) sth**: *Plastics aren't perceived as recyclable and so are labelled as environmentally unfriendly.*

la•bel•ling *BrE*, **labeling** *AmE* /ˈleɪbəlɪŋ/ *n* [U] when a label is put on something: *The federal government wants to standardize labeling on all packaged food sold in the United States.*

labelling laws —see under LAW

labor the American spelling of LABOUR

labor contract —see under CONTRACT[1]

labor federation —see under FEDERATION

labor u•nion —see under UNION

la•bour *BrE*, **labor** *AmE* /ˈleɪbə‖-ər/ *n* [U] **1** work involving a lot of physical or mental effort: *The garage charges £30 an hour for labour.* | *Robots are replacing all the **manual labor*** (=work that involves using your hands) *on the factory floor.*
2 withdraw your labour *BrE* to stop working at your job for a period of time as a protest: *Nalgo has called a general meeting when members will be balloted on whether to withdraw their labour.*
3 all the people who work for a company or in a country: *a shortage of **skilled labor*** | *Some US companies relocate to Mexico in search of **cheap labour*** (=people who are paid very low wages). | *The airline's **labor costs*** (=the cost of employing people) *are amongst the lowest in the industry.*
casual labour *BrE*, **casual labor** *AmE* HUMAN RESOURCES workers that a company employs on a temporary basis: *Casual labour is widely used within the hotel and catering industries.*
contract labour *BrE*, **contract labor** *AmE* employees who do not work directly for an organization, but are employed by a firm that has a contract to do particular work for the organization: *One hospital used contract labor for 30,000 or 40,000 hours annually.*
direct labour *BrE*, **direct labor** *AmE* ◆ workers such as those who operate machines, who are directly involved in the production of goods or services, rather than those involved in organizing or managing: *The direct labor work force is up by 60% over last year's levels.*
◆ the cost of employing workers to make a particular product or provide a particular service. This does not include other costs such as the amount spent on materials etc: *A batch of this product requires four **direct-labor hours**.* | ***Direct labour costs** have decreased.*
◆ in Britain, workers who are employed directly by an organization such as a local government authority, rather than being employed through a separate company: *Braintree District Council's former direct labour organisation has put in a bid to reroof 27 houses.*
◆ ACCOUNTING the costs of the workers who make a particular product or perform a particular service: *The introduction of machines halved the direct labour requirement.*
forced labour *BrE*, **forced labor** *AmE* people who are forced to do hard physical work in bad conditions, or the work itself: *the replacement of forced labour by wage labour* | *Thousands suffered imprisonment or forced labour.*
indirect labour *BrE*, **indirect labor** *AmE* workers such as those involved in organizing or managing, who are not directly involved in the production of goods or services: *Under the contract with ISS, Philips pay them a fixed monthly sum to cover ISS's direct and indirect labour costs.*
organized labor *AmE n* all the people in different industries who belong to a UNION (=an organization that protects workers' rights): *KKR and Safeway blame organized labor for the fall of the Dallas division.*
sweated labour *BrE*, **sweat labor** *AmE disapproving* people who work very hard for very low pay: *Working from home is no longer associated with sweated labour.*

labour agreement —see under AGREEMENT

labour dispute —see under DISPUTE

la•bour•er *BrE*, **laborer** *AmE* /ˈleɪbərə‖-ər/ *n* [C] someone whose job involves a lot of heavy physical work: *Nick found work as a laborer at a construction site.* | *a **day laborer*** (=a worker who is hired for a day at a time)
indentured labourer *BrE*, **indentured laborer** *AmE* a poor person in former times, who agreed to work for an employer for a specific number of years. During this period of time, they learnt a skill or job, but had to pay their employer for their travelling and living costs

labour force —see under FORCE[1]

labour-intensive *BrE*, **labor-intensive** *AmE* —*adj* needing a lot of workers in order to produce something: *The company was using old, labour-intensive production methods.* | *Whereas goods production can be automated, the production of services is labor-intensive.* —compare CAPITAL-INTENSIVE

labour-intensive industry —see under INDUSTRY

labour market —see under MARKET[1]

labour mobility *BrE*, **labor mobility** *AmE*, *n* [U] another name for MOBILITY OF LABOUR

labour relations —see under RELATIONS

lack•lus•tre *BrE*, **lackluster** *AmE* /ˈlækˌlʌstə‖-ər/ *adj* **1** lacklustre activity on a financial market is a period of time when there is little buying and selling and prices do not change much: *Tokyo stocks ended mixed after* ***lackluster trading*** *and prices moved mostly in a narrow range.*

2 if a company's or an economy's performance is lacklustre, it is poor, with no increase in profits or low economic growth: *SRS is reporting* ***lackluster results****, with a widened net loss of $3.2 million.* | *The economy remains lacklustre with production and employment in the manufacturing sector either steady or declining.*

la•den /ˈleɪdn/ *adj* **1** loaded with a particular material or substance: *No laden tanker over 10,000 gross tonnes is permitted to pass through the area.* | *an oil-laden truck* + **with**: *a lorry laden with 4 tonnes of waste paper*

2 laden in bulk a ship that is laden in bulk is one with a load, for example of coal, that is loose and not stored in containers

3 having or containing a lot of a particular thing or quality: *an increase in bankruptcies among* ***debt-laden*** *corporations* + **with**: *The new version of the software is laden with useful features.*

laden draught —see under DRAUGHT

Laf•fer curve /ˈlæfə ˌkɜːv‖-fər ˌkɜːrv/ *n* ECONOMICS the idea developed by the US economist Arthur Laffer that money that the government gets from taxes will increase if higher rates of tax are reduced, because there will be more investment and activity in the economy

lag[1] /læg/ past tense and past participle **lagged** present participle **lagging** *v* [I] **1** to move, develop, or improve more slowly than others: *The sales team are lagging in their progress towards this quarter's performance goals.* + **behind**: *US firms lag behind nations such as Germany in training their staff.*

2 to change in amount or level at a later time than something else: *Even after the economy begins growing, hiring new employees tends to lag.* | *When crude-oil prices fell from $30 a barrel to $12 a barrel, retail gasoline prices lagged behind by six months.*

3 if prices of shares, traded goods, etc lag, they do not increase: *While silver has lagged, it hasn't been as weak as platinum.*

lag[2] *n* [C] **1** a delay in a change or improvement in something: *More problematic over the long term is a lag in attitudes. The country was the least reform-minded in East Europe.*

2 a period of time that passes before an amount or level changes: *There's usually a lag between an upturn in manufacturing activity and increased shipments of factory machinery.* | *When taxes drop, the Massachusetts economy typically responds after a short lag, which used to be three years and now is half that.*

time lag a delay between an event and another event that is caused by it or connected with it: *There is a considerable time lag between orders and shipments.*

lagging indicator —see under INDICATOR

lais•ser-faire also **laissez-faire** /ˌleseɪ ˈfeə, ˌleɪ-‖-ˈfer/ *n* [U] ECONOMICS the idea that governments should do as little to the economy as possible and allow private business to develop without the state controlling or influencing it: *a balance between laisser-faire and old style statism* | *The computer industry is almost entirely unregulated, governed only by the Darwinian laws of* ***laissez-faire economics****.*

lame duck *n* [C] *informal* **1** a politician or a government that no longer has any real power or authority: *A bad defeat for his party in October risks making him a lame duck for the remaining two years of his presidency.*

2 a company that is losing a lot of money: *We don't have time to fix broken companies and we won't be buying any lame ducks.*

LAN /læn/ *n* [C] COMPUTING local area network; a way of connecting computers to each other within a particular building or organization so that users can use and work on the same information —compare WAN

land[1] /lænd/ *n* [U] **1** ground, especially ground used for building or farming on: *Land has always been a good investment.*

2 the land ground in the country used for growing food, animals etc: *Many farmers have given up* ***working the land*** *because of low rates of return.*

arable land land that is used for growing crops: *Because of China's limited arable land, food production on the nation's farms isn't increasing as fast as the country's population.*

developed land land that houses etc have been built on or land used for industrial purposes: *They urged the government to raise the amount of new housing on previously developed land.*

development land land where permission has been given for building or industrial activities: *The new road will open up development land for port operations.*

farm land land used for farming: *The county's farm land has gone to development at a rate of about 7,000 acres a year.*

marginal land land where it is only just possible to farm, for example land that is high up or next to a desert: *Newly cultivated areas will be on marginal land, often on steep slopes.*

prime land land of the best quality for farming or building on: *White planters lay claim to virtually all prime land and natural resources.*

raw land land that has never been built on and where no work has been done to prepare for building: *Our priority is to improve raw land so Hawaiians can build homes on it.*

reclaimed land land that was previously under the sea, or that was unusable, made suitable for building: *Sanyo's giant trading floor, erected on reclaimed land along the Tokyo waterfront*

undeveloped land land that has not been built on or used for industrial purposes: *Irvine's holdings include undeveloped land, industrial parks, retail centers and apartment units.*

vacant land land where no one is living or that is not being used: *To the north is a mile-long stretch of vacant land on which factories once stood.*

3 also **lands** an area of land that a person or organization owns: *These lands belong to all of us who like to hike, camp, fish, hunt and enjoy nature.*

federal land also **federal lands** the name for land belonging to the central government of some countries, for example the US: *privatization of federal lands*

private land also **private lands** land not owned by the government: *As the spring is on private land he had to obtain the permission of the owner to visit it.*

public land also **public lands** land belonging to the local or central government: *The oil industry wins greater access to public lands such as the Arctic National Wildlife Refuge.*

land[2] *v* **1** [I,T] if a plane lands, or if a pilot lands it, it moves down on to the ground in a controlled way

2 [T] to put someone or something on land from an aircraft or boat: *He landed his load of illegal immigrants on the Kent coast at midnight.*

3 [T] *informal* if you land a job or a contract, you manage to get it: *Aydin landed a big contract to install a defense communications system for Turkey.*

land agent —see under AGENT

land bank —see under BANK[1]

Land Certificate —see under CERTIFICATE

Land Charges Register —see under REGISTER[1]

landed cost —see under COST[1]

land•fill /ˈlændfɪl/ *n* **1** [U] the practice of burying waste from industry and homes in large holes in the ground, or the waste buried in this way: *The chemicals*

were trucked and used as landfill. —**landfilling** *n* [U] *Recycling programs across the US typically cost far more than landfilling.*
2 also **landfill site** [C] a place where waste is buried: *Typically, used oil is dumped into landfills.* | *It costs £36 a ton to take waste to a landfill site.*

land·ing /ˈlændɪŋ/ *n* [C,U] **1** when a plane lands: *Takeoffs and landings at 40 airports will be restricted, the agency says.*
2 when goods are taken off an aircraft or boat and put onto land: *Commercial landings of fish and shellfish along the southeast Atlantic coast have dropped 42% in the last ten years.*
3 hard landing ECONOMICS when an economy slows down after a period of fast growth and goes into RECESSION (=a period of time with no growth or negative growth): *Governments will also have to use tightened monetary policies and fiscal restraint to avoid a hard landing for their economies.*
4 soft landing ECONOMICS when an economy slows down after a period of fast growth but does not go into RECESSION: *The Fed attempted to manage an economic soft landing by gradually lowering interest rates.*

landing fees —see under FEE

land·less /ˈlændləs/ *adj* not owning land: *The Nicaraguan government redistributed more land to previously* ***landless peasants.***

land·locked /ˈlændlɒkt‖-lɑːkt/ *adj* **1** a landlocked country is surrounded by other countries and has no sea coast
2 *AmE* PROPERTY a landlocked piece of land is not on a public road, and to reach it you have to cross land owned by other people

land·lord /ˈlændlɔːd‖-lɔːrd/ *n* [C] a person or organization that owns land or buildings: *The paper is negotiating with its landlord, LaSalle Partners, to reduce its rent at the Daily News building in Manhattan.*
absentee landlord the owner of land or a building who does not live there: *Legislation was introduced to take land from absentee landlords and give it to peasants.*

landlord and tenant *n* [singular] LAW the area of law that deals with relations between landlords and people who use their land or buildings: *The government has introduced the landlord and tenant legislation that it promised.*

land·mark /ˈlændmɑːk‖-mɑːrk/ *adj* [only before a noun] a landmark agreement, decision, settlement etc is one that is very important and influences how other things develop: *The company won* ***landmark settlements*** *against several competitors from Japan and South Korea, forcing them to pay royalties that have totaled $574 million to date.*

land office —see under OFFICE

land registry —see under REGISTRY

Lan·drum-Grif·fin Act /ˌlændrəm ˈɡrɪfɪn ˌækt/ *n* LAW a law passed in 1959 designed to prevent criminal activities in US LABOR UNIONS, saying how they should organize voting in elections etc

lan·guage /ˈlæŋɡwɪdʒ/ *n* **1** [C,U] a system of speaking and writing used by people in one country or area: *the French language* | *Do you speak any foreign languages?* | *Trading in Europe means communicating in more than one language.*
official language [C] the language that is approved by the government of a country, taught in schools, and used in legal and official documents: *Croatian is the official language of Croatia.*
world language [C] a language such as English that is used in many different parts of the world
2 [U] the kind of words and style used in one kind of writing or by people in a particular job or activity: *technical language*
3 also **computer language** [C,U] COMPUTING a system of commands and instructions used for operating a computer: *Internet Protocol (IP) is a computer language that allows more than 20 million e-mail users to communicate with one another.* | *the business-oriented Cobol computer language*
assembly language [U] a computer language that uses ordinary words and numbers. The computer changes assembly language into the MACHINE LANGUAGE in which it operates. Assembly language is easier to learn than machine language because instructions are not written in BINARY numbers, but include ordinary words and numbers: *Early versions of the software were written in assembly language.* —see also ALGOL, BASIC, COBOL
high-level language [C,U] a computer language used to write computer programs that includes ordinary words and numbers, and is designed to be easy to use. High-level languages include BASIC, C, COBOL, and FORTRAN
machine language [C,U] a computer language used to write computer programs that uses instructions written in BINARY numbers (=combinations of the numbers 0 and 1) that can be understood directly by the computer. Machine language programs run very quickly, but are difficult to write because ordinary words and numbers are not used: *Anything that is input into the computer will in the end be translated into machine language.*
object language a computer language that uses standard blocks of instructions that have already been written. Object language allows programmers to work more quickly
programming language [C,U] a computer language for writing computer programs that contain instructions telling a computer to do different jobs: *HTML is the programming language of the Internet's World Wide Web.*

lapse[1] /læps/ *v* [I] **1** if a contract, agreement, or offer lapses, it ends because an agreed time limit has passed: *American Airlines may allow options to purchase new airplanes to lapse.* | *There are many films on which the copyright has lapsed and hasn't been renewed.*
2 if an INSURANCE POLICY lapses, it ends because the regular payments required have not been made: *Kimble let his fire insurance lapse when he couldn't afford the premiums.*
lapse into sth *phr v* [T] to begin to suffer something: ***The economy lapsed*** *deeper* ***into recession.*** | *The stock market lapsed into a broad decline today.*

lapse[2] *n* [C] **1** a period of time between two events: *There is a four-day lapse between the time a patron buys a ticket and the money is deposited in the bank.*
2 a failure to do something you should do: *The customer complained about a lapse in service.* | *The audit uncovered accounting lapses.*

lapse of time *n* [U] LAW when a contract is ended because both groups involved do not finish what they stated they would do before an agreed time limit

lap·top /ˈlæptɒp‖-tɑːp/ also **laptop computer** *n* [C] a small computer that you can carry with you and use when you are travelling: *Sharp is the leading producer of the ultra-thin video screens which are used in laptop computers.* —see also NOTEBOOK, PALMTOP

lar·ce·ny /ˈlɑːsəni‖ˈlɑːr-/ *n* plural **larcenies** [C,U] LAW the crime of stealing; THEFT: *He was charged with* ***grand*** *(=very serious)* ***larceny*** *and tax evasion.*

large-cap *n* [C] FINANCE a share in a company with a large amount of SHARE CAPITAL —**large-cap** *adj* [only before a noun] *I think secondary stocks will continue to outperform large-cap stocks.* —compare SMALL-CAP

large-cap share —see under SHARE
large-cap stock —see under STOCK[1]
large-scale *adj* [only before a noun] **1** using or involving a lot of people, effort, money, or supplies: *The government hopes to attract large-scale foreign investment.* | *Large-scale changes to the organizational structure of the company are needed.* —**large-scale** *adv*: *We will have to test the new pesticide large-scale.*
2 large-scale production producing goods in large quantities: *Large-scale oil production did not begin in Saudi Arabia until after World War II.*
laser printer —see under PRINTER
last in, first out abbreviation **LIFO** *n* [U] **1** ACCOUNTING a method of calculating the value of goods or materials held in stock, based on the principle that those put in stock last are the first ones sold or used. Any stock that is left at the end of the year is valued at the cost of the first goods bought: *Stocks were valued according to the last in, first out principle.* —compare FIRST IN, FIRST OUT
2 a system used by companies who are reducing the number of people working for them, in which the people who joined the company most recently lose their jobs first: *The company were firing people on the last in, first out basis.*
last sale —see under SALE
latent defect —see under DEFECT[1]
lat·i·tude /ˈlætətjuːd‖-tuːd/ *n* [U] *journalism* freedom to choose what you do or say + **in**: *The new guidelines give banks more latitude in making loans.* | *States generally have wide latitude in setting tax policies.*
launch[1] /lɔːntʃ‖lɒːntʃ/ *v* [I,T] **1** to show or make a new product available for sale for the first time: *The company is launching a new range of hair products.* | *National Westminster Bank has launched a commercial insurance service for small businesses.* | *Our internet service will launch next year.*
2 to start a new company: *Conran launched a business empire that was eventually to employ 83,000 people.*
3 to start a new activity or profession, usually after planning it carefully: *Daihatsu America has* ***launched a*** *new advertising* ***campaign****.* | *Luke took advantage of a Youth Training Scheme to* ***launch a*** *successful* ***career****.*
4 launch a bid if one company launches a bid for another, it makes an offer to buy it: *Swiss food giant Nestle SA has launched a bid for a French mineral-water company.*
launch[2] *n* [C] **1** an occasion at which a new product is shown or made available for sale or use for the first time: *Savings are needed to finance new* ***product launches****.* | *Since its launch two years ago, sales of the software have grown to only about 300,000 a year.*
2 the start of a new activity or plan: *the launch on New Year's day of a set of economic reforms*
laun·der /ˈlɔːndə‖ˈlɒːndər/ *v* [T] BANKING **launder money/profits** to put money which has been obtained illegally into legal businesses and bank accounts in order to hide where it was obtained: *The bank had allegedly laundered money for drug dealers and other criminals.* —**laundering** *n* [U] *Velasquez was convicted of* ***money laundering****.* | *the laundering of drug profits through Panamanian banks and front companies*
laun·dry /ˈlɔːndri‖ˈlɒːn-/ *n* plural **laundries** [C] BANKING a financial organization, such as a bank, used as a place to put money obtained from illegal activities
law /lɔː‖lɒː/ *n* **1** [singular, U] the whole system of rules that citizens of a country must obey: *It is* ***against the law*** (=illegal) *for children to work before they are fifteen.* | *There were easy profits for businessmen who were prepared to* ***break the law*** (=do something illegal). | *The inheritance tax changes announced in the Budget* ***became law*** (=was officially made a law). | ***By law*** (=according to the law) *a company like British Gas has to hold a meeting of its shareholders once a year.* | *They make tough business deals, but are always careful to* ***operate within the law*** (=make sure what you do is legal). | *She's a partner in a major New York* ***law firm****.*
case law [U] law that is based on decisions that judges have made in the past: *In some respects European law is based more on case law than on statute.*
civil law [U] ◆ the laws of a country dealing with the affairs of private citizens, rather than with crime and criminals: *The purpose of the civil law is to compensate; it is the function of the criminal law to punish.*
◆ also **Roman Law** the law of ancient Rome, which is still used as the basis for the legal system in some countries, especially the countries of continental Europe or countries formerly governed by them.
common law [U] law that has been developed from common customs and the decisions of judges rather than being decided by an act of Parliament or an act of Congress: *Judges may have to develop a common law right to privacy, providing guidance for media regulators.*
company law [U] the laws relating to the way in which companies are formed, managed, and run
criminal law [U] law dealing with crime and people who commit crime: *A solicitor offers advice on individual problems in civil or criminal law.*
international law [U] the laws that concern relations between countries: *Trade in Brazilian rosewood is banned* ***under international law****.* | *a breach of international law*
private law [U] the area of law that deals with disagreements between people and organizations, rather than with criminal activity: *Even if the deal is cleared by the authorities, it could still be blocked by a* ***private law suit****.*
public law [U] the area of law deals with relations between citizens, organizations and the state: *Public law provides an effective structure for the implementation of the public good.*
statute law [U] law that has been decided and voted for by a parliament: *A wide range of powers are already available under statute law to combat this crime*
substantive law [U] the part of the law that describes and controls people's rights and duties, rather than the part that describes and controls legal processes: *This is a matter of substantive law, and not merely a procedural matter.*
2 [C] a rule that people in a particular country, city, or local area must obey: *a new* ***state law****, limiting insurance companies' junk-bond holdings to 20% of assets* + **on**: *laws on the distribution of tobacco products* —see also BYLAW
blue laws [plural] laws in some US states preventing shops from opening on Sundays: *The ending of North Dakota's blue laws is expected to raise $15 million in sales taxes over two years.*
blue-sky laws [plural] US state laws designed to protect investors by stating that when shares, bonds etc are offered for sale, certain information must be made publicly available: *The government could reduce the cost of capital by getting rid of the blue-sky laws.*
labelling laws [plural] the part of the law that describes and controls people's rights and duties, rather than the part that describes and controls legal processes
3 rule of law when the people in a country obey the laws: *The state was too weak to impose the rule of law.*
4 [U] law as a subject of study, for example at university: *Peter is a* ***law student****.* | *Jackson* ***studied law*** *at Oxford University.*
5 [C] a way in which things happen in an activity such as business, which is thought of as a rule because it seems impossible to change: *the law of supply and demand* —see also PARETO'S LAW

law-abiding *adj* **law-abiding people/citizens etc** a person or organization that does not break the law: *Hong Kong society is renowned for being law-abiding and stable.* | *law-abiding citizens*

law•ful /ˈlɔːfəl‖ˈlɒː-/ *adj* LAW allowed by law; LEGAL: *The owner has the right to use the property for any lawful purpose.* —**lawfully** *adv*: *a product that has been lawfully produced in a member state of the European Union* —**lawfulness** *n* [U] *Morrison is challenging the lawfulness of the tax demand.*

law of diminishing returns —see under DIMINISHING RETURNS

law report —see under REPORT[1]

Law Society *n* the professional organization in England and Wales that deals with the education and interests of SOLICITORS, and also makes sure that they act within the law and treat their clients fairly

law•suit /ˈlɔːsuːt, -sjuːt‖ˈlɒːsuːt/ *n* [C] a charge, claim, or complaint against someone that is made in a court of law by a private person or company, not by the police or state + **against**: *Local people **filed a** private **lawsuit** over water contamination.* | *Bradley paid a $20,000 fine to **settle the lawsuit** and end the disagreement.*

law•yer /ˈlɔːjə‖ˈlɒːjər/ *n* [C] someone whose job is to give advice, write formal agreements, and represent people in courts —compare BARRISTER, SOLICITOR

lay /leɪ/ *v* past tense and past participle **laid**

lay sb ↔ **off** *phr v* [T] to stop employing a worker, usually when there is not enough work for them to do: *Apple Computer Inc. will lay off 10 % of its workforce.* | *Seagate Technology Inc. **laid off** 1,200 **workers** in a cost-cutting move.* —see also LAY-OFF

lay sth ↔ **out** *phr v* [T] *informal* to spend a lot of money on something **lay out sth for/on sth**: *Some people are willing to lay out huge amounts of money for electronic equipment.*

lay•a•way /ˈleɪəweɪ/ *n* [U] *AmE* a method of buying goods in which the buyer makes a first payment that is a percentage of a larger sum and the goods are kept by the seller until the full price is paid: *Jerry bought some furniture on a **layaway plan**.* | *I **put** a sofa bed **on layaway** at the K Mart in Santa Clara.*

lay•er /ˈleɪə‖-ər/ *n*

marzipan layer [singular] *BrE informal* HUMAN RESOURCES people in a company or organization who have important jobs but who are just below the highest position: *If partners received fewer shares, the surplus could be distributed to the so-called marzipan layer of key managing directors just below partnership level* —compare ***middle management*** under MANAGEMENT

lay-off *n* [C] **1** the act of stopping a worker's employment because there is not enough work for them to do: *a layoff affecting more than 500 workers*

2 layoff announcement/notice a message from your employer saying that you will lose your job because there is not enough work for you to do: *Some employees at United Technologies Corp. are getting **layoff notices**.*

lay•out /ˈleɪaʊt/ *n* [C] **1** the way in which things are arranged in a particular place: *the layout of the building* | *The new laptop uses the same keyboard layout as IBM's desk-top computers.*

2 the way in which writing and pictures are arranged on a page: *Design, layout and typography give the publication a stylish, orderly look.* | *Desktop publishing does not have to involve high powered **page layout** software.*

lb. plural **lbs.** or **lb.** written abbreviation for POUND, a unit of weight equal to 0.454 kilograms: *Coffee prices have fallen by around 25% per lb.*

LBO written abbreviation for LEVERAGED BUYOUT —see under BUYOUT

LCD *n* [C] COMPUTING liquid crystal display; a type of screen where an electric current is passed through a liquid chemical in order to show the numbers and letters. LCDs are used especially on small computers, scientific instruments, and watches

LCE written abbreviation for LONDON COMMODITY EXCHANGE

LCH abbreviation for LONDON CLEARING HOUSE

LDC *n* [C] less-developed country; a poor country whose economy is developing slowly and less successfully than most other countries: *billions of dollars of **LDC loans*** | *the problem of **LDC debts*** | *Many of the LDCs are important producers of raw materials.*

lead[1] /liːd/ *v* past participle and past tense **led** [T] **1** to be in charge of something such as an important activity, a group of people, or an organization: *The manager had led a series of projects that improved productivity in his region.* | *a new management team led by Roger Shute*

2 market-led/demand-led/service-led etc when the market, customer demand etc is the most important influence on the way something happens: *Today's Post Office is an energetic group of market-led businesses serving the community.* | *Social security and other demand-led expenditures placed upward pressure on public spending.*

3 to be more successful than other people, companies, or countries in a particular activity or area of business: *Printing banknotes is one area where Britain leads the world.* | *a company that **leads the field** in software applications*

4 to happen before something else: *Typically, stockmarkets lead the recovery of the real economy by four to six months.*

5 lead the way to be the first to do something, especially something good or successful, which is likely to encourage others to do the same thing: *Large grocery multiples and the oil companies have led the way in retail modelling.*

lead[2] *n* **1** [C] a piece of information such as a list of telephone numbers that may help someone selling something to find customers: *The in-house sales team deals with all telephone **sales leads**.*

2 [singular] when you are in front of or better than everyone else in a competition: *Last year Toyota's financial profit lengthened its lead over Honda and Nissan, both of which made financial losses.*

lead bank —see under BANK[1]

lead•er /ˈliːdə‖-ər/ *n* [C] **1** the person who directs or controls a team, organization, country etc: *He was accompanied on the trip by the chairmen of the three major US-auto makers and 18 other **business leaders**.*

2 a product, service, or company that is the most important or successful of its type

brand leader the brand with the most sales in a particular market: *Boeing is the brand leader in China, with 85 planes flying and 60 on order.*

cost leader the company, product etc with the lowest costs in its industry or market compared with its competitors: *The problem in wanting to become the cost leader is that you may produce the cheapest typewriters, but everyone is moving to PCs.*

industry leader ♦ a company that is important in a particular industry, because it has the highest, or one of the highest, level of sales, the best products etc: *General Mills has gradually been stealing market share from industry leader Kellogg.*

♦ a person who has a very important job in a company in a particular industry, or in industry in general: *Industry leaders said the revised proposal would do little to soften the economic blow to the Northwest.*

loss leader ♦ a product or service that is sold at a loss, but that is intended to encourage people to buy other, profitable products etc: *Supermarkets sometimes sell bread as a loss leader to bring in customers for other, more expensive goods.*

◆ an activity that loses money but that is hoped to make a profit later: *Most law firms view Moscow offices as loss leaders that will eventually bring great profits.*

market leader the company, product, or service with more sales than any other company, product etc in its market: *Opel is the market leader in the eastern region, with a 25% share.*

price leader the competitor that is usually the first in its market to increase or reduce its prices, with other competitors following: *NationsBank will be in a strong position to be a price leader on loans.*

lead•er•ship /ˈliːdəʃɪp‖-ər-/ *n* [U] **1** the position of being the leader of a team, organization, country etc: *GE has changed the leadership of one of its business groups.* | *The company did well* ***under the leadership of*** *its founder, Haruo Suzuki.*

2 the qualities needed in order to be a good leader: *a chairman with vision and leadership*

3 being the most important or most successful product, service or company of a particular type + **in**: *US leadership in the aerospace industry*

market leadership also **industry leadership** when one company or product that has the highest sales in its market or industry: *P&G is famous for gaining market leadership by introducing innovative products.* | *Tesco is the UK's largest supermarket, having taken industry leadership from Sainsbury's.*

price leadership when one competitor is usually the first in its industry to increase or reduce its prices, with other competitors following: *PictureTel has taken price leadership in this fast-growing market by driving prices down.*

lead•ing /ˈliːdɪŋ/ *adj* [only before a noun] best, most important, or most successful: *the leading software provider in the domestic PC markets* | *Compaq, the nation's leading seller of personal computers*

leading case —see under CASE

leading edge *n* [singular] the area of activity where the most modern and advanced equipment and methods are used: *Software companies* ***are on the leading edge of*** *technology in very competitive markets.* —**leading-edge** *adj*: ***leading-edge companies*** *ranging from Apple to Walt Disney* | *Some US companies were unable to get* ***leading-edge technology*** *that was readily available in Japan.*

leading indicator —see under INDICATOR

lead-manage *v* [T] to organize a SYNDICATED LOAN (=a loan to one borrower by many lenders) or a SECURITIES ISSUE (= the sale of new bonds, shares etc): *The 50 billion yen bond issue by NT&T Corp. was lead-managed by Nomura Securities.* —**lead manager** *n* [C] *Elsevier named Swiss Bank Corp. as the lead manager for its bond offering.*

lead partner —see under PARTNER

lead time —see under TIME

leaf•let /ˈliːflɪt/ *n* [C] a small piece of printed paper that gives information or advertises something: *An* ***explanatory leaflet*** *is available from tax offices.* | ***information leaflets*** *about mail services* —see also BROCHURE

leaflet drop *n* [C] *BrE* an occasion when copies of the same leaflet are sent or delivered to many addresses in order to advertise something: *The distributor selects the postal sectors in which to aim a leaflet drop using the UK Post Office Household Delivery Service.*

League of Arab States —see ARAB LEAGUE

leak•age /ˈliːkɪdʒ/ *n* [C,U] **1** when liquid or gas escapes from a container: *leakage from a 275-gallon oil waste tank*

2 when information is deliberately told to others that should be kept secret: *We must ensure that shared knowledge remains internal to the enterprise and that leakage is minimal.* | *A news leakage during negotiations can have a dramatic effect on share prices.*

lean /liːn/ *adj* **1** using the most effective methods and the fewest employees possible: *In the struggle to turn the company into a lean commercial outfit, some lines have been discontinued altogether.*

2 lean manufacturing/production lean manufacturing uses methods and techniques to produce goods as cheaply as possible, for example by using as few workers as possible and using JUST-IN-TIME methods, where parts are delivered only when they are needed: *American companies are learning the tricks of lean manufacture.* | *Toyota's system of lean production cut down on waste because components were used as soon as they were delivered.*

3 a lean period is a very difficult time because there is not enough money, business etc: *a* ***lean year*** *for business* | *Many Welsh tourist attractions are having a very* ***lean time.*** —**leanness** *n* [U] *To achieve the necessary leanness, many more jobs will have to be lost in the defence industry across Europe.*

lean production —see under PRODUCTION

leap[1] /liːp/ *v* past tense and past participle **leapt** *especially BrE*, **leaped** *especially AmE* [I] to increase quickly and by a large amount: *Shares leapt about 5% to $32.375.*

leap[2] *n* [C] a sudden large increase in the number or amount of something: *Sales and earnings* ***took a*** *huge* ***leap.*** + **in**: *Gold shares gained following a leap in the price of gold.*

quantum leap *BrE*, **quantum jump** *AmE* a very large and important improvement: *Quantum leaps in information technologies have revolutionized how people work.*

learning curve *n* [C usually singular] the idea that when you learn something new there is a lot to learn at the beginning, so you work very slowly, but it becomes easier and you work faster as you continue: *The program has everything a trained operator will need, but for others it* ***has a*** *very* ***steep learning curve,*** *especially if you've only used Windows.*

lease[1] /liːs/ *v* [T] **1** if you lease something to someone, you give them the right to use it for a particular period of time in return for payment **lease sb sth**: *The local authority leased him the property.* **lease sth to sb**: *AT&T leased the building to Sony and said it would find cheaper space elsewhere.* **lease out sth (to sb)/lease sth out (to sb)**: *We lease the land out to the forestry people.*

2 if you lease something from someone, you pay them to use it for a particular period of time in return for payment **lease sth from sb**: *Cathay flies the routes with a Boeing 737 leased from Dragonair.* —see also SUBLEASE

lease[2] *n* [C] a legal contract that allows a person or organization to make payments to use something for a particular period of time in return for payment: *She had* ***signed a lease*** *with Texaco to drill for oil on property she owns.* | *The initial* ***term of the lease*** (=the time that it lasts) *is 10 years, with three additional 10-year renewal options.* | *PHH Fleet America leases cars to corporate fleets and then sells them when* ***the leases expire*** (=end).

aircraft lease a lease of planes by an AIRLINE: *The largest portion of the airline's debt load was from off-balance-sheet aircraft leases.*

building lease in Britain, a lease on land where the person or organization leasing it builds buildings and pays rent for the land

car lease also **auto lease** *AmE* a lease allowing someone to use a car: *NFC sold its car lease business for £120 million.*

derivative lease PROPERTY an arrangement in which a person renting a property with a lease arranges another lease on the same property, allowing another person to rent the property from them —compare SUBLEASE, SUBLET

dry lease a lease where an AIRLINE leases aircraft directly from their maker or from a leasing company, rather than from another airline: *The deal between Croatian Airlines and Airbus includes the dry lease of an A320 model.*

equipment lease a lease for machinery, vehicles etc used by a business: *The mining company may be unable to pay its rental obligations on $3.8 million in equipment leases.*

finance lease also **financial lease** a lease in which a company obtains land or equipment with a bank buying the assets and leasing them back to the company: *Newco has the opportunity to finance these assets by way of rental payments under finance leases rather than by direct acquisition.*

operating lease a lease allowing a company to use particular equipment: *The communications program requires a $5,000 minimum leasing expenditure, and offers operating leases of two, three, four or five years.*

repairing lease in Britain an arrangement in which the person renting a building is responsible for paying for repairs to it

store lease a lease allowing a person or organization to run and operate a shop: *BizMart agreed to acquire five store leases in Minneapolis from Highland Superstores.*

wet lease a lease in which an AIRLINE flies between two countries leasing aircraft from an airline in a third country

lease•back /'li:sbæk/ *n* FINANCE [C,U] an arrangement in which you sell something to someone, but then you continue to use it, paying them rent: *The recent sale and partial leaseback of our corporate headquarters complex produced an after-tax gain of $90 million.*

sale and leaseback [U] when a business sells something it owns, for example a building or equipment, and immediately rents it from the buyer, especially in order to raise money quickly or in order to pay less tax: *the profits that Century received from the sale and leaseback of a power plant*

lease•hold /'li:shəʊld‖-hoʊld/ *adj* LAW leasehold land, buildings etc are owned only for as long as is stated in a LEASE: *Due to internal reorganization, the company has recently vacated one of its leasehold buildings.* —**leasehold** *n* [U] *The profits also reflect the $2 million gain on the sale of a leasehold.*—compare FREEHOLD

lease•hold•er /'li:shəʊldə‖-hoʊldər/ *n* [C] someone who lives in a leasehold house, apartment etc, or who uses leasehold land: *The owner may sell the land or property subject to the leaseholder's interest being maintained.*

leasehold estate —see under ESTATE

leasehold possession —see under POSSESSION

leasehold property —see under PROPERTY

leas•ing /'li:sɪŋ/ *n* [U] the financial activity of arranging for people and organizations to lease buildings, machinery etc. Leasing may have tax advantages compared to buying, and the things that are leased do not appear as assets in the business's accounts

employee leasing when a company has people working for it who are not its employees, employing them through an AGENCY: *He contracted with an employee-leasing company for them to provide extra staff over the Christmas period.*

equipment leasing when a company pays to use equipment such as computers, cars, and office furniture rather than buying it: *AT&T Co's equipment leasing and finance subsidiary, AT&T Capital Corp*

leave /li:v/ *n* [U] time that you are allowed to be absent from your work: *Harltons offers attractive benefits, including five weeks' leave per year.* | *The Los Gatos School District has hired 21 new teachers to replace those who are* ***on leave***.

annual leave time with pay that you are allowed to be absent from your work each year: *The manager provides staff with the opportunity to make requests for annual leave.*

compassionate leave time with pay that you are allowed to be absent from your work because of a personal problem, such as the death of a relative: *When a close relative dies, anyone in a full-time job is usually entitled to a few days compassionate leave.*

maternity leave time with pay that a woman is allowed to be absent from work because she has had a baby: *The share of first-time mothers receiving maternity leave has nearly tripled in recent years.*

paternity leave time that a father of a new baby is allowed to be absent from work: *Lost Arrow, a company with only 25 employees, provides up to eight weeks of paid paternity leave.*

sabbatical leave a period of time when someone, especially someone in a university job, stops doing their usual work in order to study or travel

sick leave time with pay that you are allowed to be absent from work because you are ill: *Werner never used a day of sick leave during his first 10 years as a firefighter.*

special leave time that you are allowed to be absent from work, usually because of a personal problem. Special leave is sometimes but not always without pay: *Line managers have discretion to give people time off as special leave.*

leave of absence —see under ABSENCE

-led /led/ *suffix* **1** if something is market-led, consumer-led etc, the market etc is the main force behind the way that it behaves or changes: *The US economy will start a* ***consumer-led*** *recovery by midyear.* | *A union-led group is seeking to acquire United Air Lines' parent company in a $4.38 billion buy-out.* —compare -DRIVEN, -ORIENTED

2 used after the name of a company, organization etc to say that the company etc is leading a particular project or activity: *The Agnelli-led bidding group declined to say whether negotiations have begun.* | *UN-led efforts to put down global conflicts*

led•ger /'ledʒə‖-ər/ *n* [C usually plural] one of the books or computer records showing the totals of items shown separately in the BOOKS OF FIRST ENTRY or DAY BOOKS; BOOK OF FINAL ENTRY: *Gone are the days of ledgers and filing cabinets. In the information age, most information is held on computers and networks.*

bought ledger also **purchase ledger** a ledger showing amounts owed to suppliers

general ledger also **nominal ledger** a ledger showing interest costs, DEPRECIATION (=amounts relating to the loss of value of assets over time) etc

personal ledger a ledger showing amounts owed to or by particular people

real ledger a ledger showing amounts relating to property and equipment

sales ledger a ledger showing amounts owed by customers

ledger clerk —see under CLERK

leg•a•cy /'legəsi/ *n* plural **legacies** [C] **1** a situation that exists as a result of things that happened at an earlier time: *Hotels are in oversupply, a legacy of the last building boom.*

2 LAW money or property that you receive from someone after they die: *His death would secure her a legacy.* | *Many people want to* ***leave a legacy*** *to a charity they have supported all their lives.*

demonstrative legacy money or an object left in a legacy that comes from a particular source

general legacy money or objects left in a legacy that does not come from a particular source

residuary legacy money and property remaining in

a legacy after other particular amounts of money or pieces of property have been given to others

legacy system —see under SYSTEM

le•gal /ˈliːgəl/ *adj* **1** [only before a noun] relating to or involving the law: *It would be impossible to get control of the company without a long legal fight.* | *the country's* ***legal system*** (=courts, lawyers, judges etc) | *reliable* ***legal advice***
2 allowed, ordered, or approved by the law: *The legal speed limit is 30 mph.* | *The court decided that the transfer of pension funds is legal, but ex-workers are launching an appeal.*

legal action —see under ACTION

legal aid —see under AID

legal capacity —see under CAPACITY

legal charge —see under CHARGE[1]

legal entity —see under ENTITY

le•gal•ese /ˌliːgəlˈiːz/ *n* [U] *informal* language used by lawyers that most people find difficult to understand: *The statement will be read by the witness and the client, and should not be written in legalese.*

legal estate —see under ESTATE

legal executive —see under EXECUTIVE[1]

legal investment —see under INVESTMENT

le•gal•i•ty /lɪˈgælɪ̈ti/ *n* plural **legalities** **1** [U] the fact of being allowed by the law: *a judgment ending a lengthy dispute over the legality of Davis's leases*
2 legalities [plural] the things that you have to do by law before something can happen: *He wasn't one to always let legalities stand in his way.*

le•gal•i•za•tion also **legalisation** *BrE* /ˌliːgəlaɪˈzeɪʃən‖-lə-/ *n* [U] making something legal that was previously against the law: *the legalization of trade unions, which had been outlawed*

le•gal•ize also **legalise** *BrE* /ˈliːgəlaɪz/ *v* [T] to make something legal that was previously against the law: *Casino gambling was legalized as a way to rebuild Atlantic City.*

legal liability —see under LIABILITY

le•gal•ly /ˈliːgəli/ *adv* **1** according to the law, or obeying the law: *A pilot can legally fly up to eight hours in a 16-hour duty day.* | *The new law would hold manufacturers, importers and dealers of certain firearms* ***legally responsible*** *for any injuries they inflict.*
2 legally binding an agreement or document that is legally binding must be obeyed by law: *Some of the new rules aren't legally binding unless adopted by individual states.*

legal monopoly —see under MONOPOLY

legal mortgage —see under MORTGAGE[1]

legal pad —see under PAD

legal person *n* [C] an organization considered as a person for legal purposes: *In Scotland a firm is a legal person distinct from the partners of whom it is composed.*

legal remedy —see under REMEDY

legal-size *adj AmE* legal-size paper is 14 inches long and 8 inches wide (35.6×20.3 cm), and mostly used in the US

legal system —see under SYSTEM

legal tender *n* [U] coins and bank notes that are officially allowed to be used as money in a particular place: *the taler, legal tender in Germany between the 15th and 19th centuries*

leg•a•tee /ˌlegəˈtiː/ *n* [C] LAW someone who receives money or property from someone who has died: *Marjorie was his* ***sole legatee*** (=the only one).

leg•a•tor /ˌlegəˈtɔː‖lɪˈgeɪtər/ *n* [C] LAW someone who leaves money or property to someone when they die

le•gi•ble /ˈledʒɪ̈bəl/ *adj* written or printed clearly, and easy to read: *The handwriting is so small it's barely legible.* —opposite ILLEGIBLE

le•gis•la•tion /ˌledʒɪ̈ˈsleɪʃən/ *n* [U] **1** a law or set of laws: *Under the new legislation, employers will be required to offer up to 12 weeks of paid sick-leave per year.* | *Legislation has been introduced in Congress to authorize the sale of two Alaska power projects.*
delegated legislation in Britain, rules and laws which are not made by Parliament but by government ministers who have been given authority by Parliament: *The use of delegated legislation saves Parliamentary time.*
2 the act of making laws: *The purpose of legislation is to support and protect international policy.*

le•gis•la•ture /ˈledʒɪ̈sleɪtʃə, -lətʃə‖-ər/ *n* [C] LAW an institution that has the power to make or change laws, for example a PARLIAMENT: *the Iowa state legislature*

le•git /lɪˈdʒɪt/ *adj spoken* **1** legal or official: *If your business is legit, then you have nothing to fear from the taxman.* | *I borrowed from legit sources so far as I could.*
2 go legit to start working in a legal way after working in a criminal or unofficial way: *a former bootlegger recently gone legit*

le•git•i•mate[1] /lɪˈdʒɪtɪ̈mɪ̈t/ *adj* **1** operating according to the law: *Although most of these shows are legitimate, a growing number are frauds.*
2 reasonable or understandable: *There's a lot of legitimate concern about where the economy is going.*

le•git•i•mate[2] /lɪˈdʒɪtɪ̈meɪt/ *v* [T] another form of LEGITIMIZE: *Corporate power cannot be legitimated merely by reference to the rights of shareholders.*

le•git•i•mize also **legitimise** *BrE* /lɪˈdʒɪtɪ̈maɪz/ *v* [T] **1** to make something legal or official that had not been before: *He hopes to legitimize private ownership of toll roads in California.*
2 to make something acceptable or popular: *Those scandals have legitimized selfishness.*

lei•sure /ˈleʒə‖ˈliːʒər/ *n* [U] time when you are not working and can relax and do things you enjoy: *The recession and worries about unemployment have hurt spending on* ***leisure activities***.

leisure industry —see under INDUSTRY

lend /lend/ *v* past tense and past participle **lent** **1** [T] to let someone borrow money from you or use something that you own, which they will give back to you later **lend sb sth**: *I've never lent him my car.* | *Can you lend me $20 till Friday?* **lend sth to sb**: *Neighbouring countries agreed to lend some ships and airplanes to the country to help in the rescue work.*
2 [I,T] if a bank or financial institution lends money, it lets a person or organization borrow it on condition that they pay it back, with an additional amount as interest, usually gradually over an agreed period of time: *Once again, the government is encouraging banks to lend.* **lend sth to sb**: *Last year, financial institutions lent over $30 billion to new businesses.* —see also OVERLEND
3 lend strength/support to support or help someone or something: *The bond market rally yesterday also lent some strength to the stock market.* | *The dollar's weakness has lent support to precious metals prices.*

lend•er /ˈlendə‖-ər/ *n* [C] a person or organization that lends people money on the condition that they pay it back: *Newspaper ads can be helpful in finding the lender with the most favorable interest rates.* —see also MONEY-LENDER

lender of last resort *n* plural **lenders of last resort** [C] the central bank of a country which is responsible for controlling the banking system. It is considered as a lender for other banks only when there is no other source to borrow from: *The Federal Reserve is a lender of last resort, and banks generally avoid borrowing from it except in extraordinary circumstances.*

less /les/ *prep* taking away or not counting a particular amount: *$150 less what you owe in taxes is $102.*

less-developed country —see LDC

les•see /le'siː/ *n* [C] LAW someone who is legally allowed to use a house, building, land etc in agreement for a fixed period of time in return for payment to the owner: *The lessee occupying 37 San Madras Road is scheduled to open for business on July 15.*

les•sor /le'sɔː‖-'sɔːr/ *n* [C] LAW someone who allows someone else to use their house, building, land etc for a period of time and in return receives payment: *By renting property out to local businesses, the lessor benefits by obtaining tax deductions that would otherwise be unavailable.*

let /let/ past tense and past participle **let** present participle **letting** *v* [T] *BrE* to allow someone to use a room or building in return for rent: *She let the studio to artists.* | *Springtown residents are pushing to increase the total number of houses available* ***for let.*** —**let** *n* [C] *Stein employed a landlord to manage the Browning Street let.*

let sth ↔ **out** *phr v* [T] another name for let: *Once tourist season begins, we should be able to let out the rest of our properties.* —compare LEASE[1], RENT[1]

let•ter /'letə‖-ər/ *n* [C] **1** a written or printed message that is usually put in an envelope and sent by mail: *Please sign the letter and mail it back within two weeks.*

allocation letter also **allotment letter** a letter telling someone how many shares they will receive when new shares are first made available; LETTER OF ALLOCATION: *Qualifying members will get their allocation letters by early April.*

appointment letter a letter from an organization to someone to say that they have been given a job; LETTER OF APPOINTMENT: *Your entitlement to pay will be as set out in your letter of appointment.*

comfort letter FINANCE a letter from a company to a bank in support of a SUBSIDIARY of the company that is asking for a loan; LETTER OF COMFORT: *A parent company will give, if not a formal guarantee, then a comfort letter relating to its subsidiary's indebtedness to banks and others.*

covering letter *BrE*, **cover letter** *AmE* a letter that you send with other documents or a package, explaining why the package has been sent or giving extra information about it: *Copies of the questionnaire and covering letter were sent to heads of department individually.*

engagement letter a letter in which the conditions under which someone is employed are stated; employment contract. In the US, engagement letters are usually given to a CONTRACTOR who has been employed to carry out a particular service or job; LETTER OF ENGAGEMENT: *If you deviate from the conditions laid down in this letter of engagement, we will be free to terminate the engagement at any time.*

form letter a standard letter that is sent to a number of people with just the name and address changed for each different person: *We wrote to quite a large number of companies, but many sent back only form letters.*

2 any of the signs in writing or printing that represent a speech sound: *the letter 'A'*

3 do sth to the letter to pay exact attention to the details of an agreement, rule, set of instructions etc: *In order for the plan to work, you need to follow the instructions to the letter.*

4 the letter of the law the exact words of a law or agreement rather than the intended or general meaning: *The legal process of adopting a child must be followed to the letter of the law.*

let•ter•head /'letəhed‖-ər-/ *n* **1** [C] the name and address of a person or business printed at the top of paper used for writing letters: *An elegant letterhead is a sign of success.*

2 also **headed paper** *BrE* [U] paper with the name and address of a person or business printed on it: *Would you please print out the memo on letterhead?*

letter of allocation *n* plural **letters of allocation** [C] a letter telling someone how many shares they have been allocated when new shares are first made available; ALLOCATION LETTER: *Qualifying members will get their allocation letters by early April.*

letter of allotment *n* plural **letters of allotment** [C] a letter from a company to a person who has asked to buy shares in that company, telling them how many shares they have been given and if they owe any more money: *After you obtain a letter of allotment, you must sign it and return a copy to the company registrar.*

letter of application *n* plural **letters of application** [C] a letter to a company from a person who is looking for a job, usually in response to a job advertisement: *We have received hundreds of letters of application.*

letter of appointment *n* plural **letters of appointment** [C] a letter from an organization to someone to say that they have been given a job; APPOINTMENT LETTER: *Your entitlement to pay will be as set out in your letter of appointment.*

letter of comfort *n* plural **letters of comfort** [C] FINANCE a letter from a company to a bank in support of a SUBSIDIARY of the company that is asking for a loan; COMFORT LETTER: *A parent company will give, if not a formal guarantee, then a comfort letter relating to its subsidiary's indebtedness to banks and others.*

letter of credit written abbreviation **l/c** *n* plural **letters of credit** [C] **1** in foreign trade, a written promise by an importer's bank to pay the exporter's bank on a particular date or at a particular time after the goods are sent by the exporter: *Coffee buyers in Central America are required to have proof of financing, such as a letter of credit.*

2 when bonds are sold, a written promise by a bank that it will repay the bonds to lenders if the borrower is unable to repay them: *The notes are* ***backed by a letter of credit*** *from Morgan Guaranty Trust Co.*

confirmed letter of credit a letter of credit that a bank promises to pay, even if the bank that made it available does not. This gives exporters more confidence that they will receive payment

irrevocable letter of credit a letter of credit that the importer's bank cannot refuse to pay, even if, for example, the importer says there is a problem with the goods: *The irrevocable letter of credit confirmed on a US bank surely saved us from a very bad debt situation.*

revocable letter of credit a letter of credit that the importer's bank can refuse to pay, if, for example, there is a problem with the goods

standby letter of credit a loan that a bank makes available but that is not used unless the borrower needs it

letter of engagement *n* plural **letters of engagement** [C] a letter in which the conditions under which someone is employed are stated; employment contract. In the US, letters of engagement are usually given to a CONTRACTOR who has been employed to carry out a particular service or job; ENGAGEMENT LETTER: *If you deviate from the conditions laid down in this letter of engagement, we will be free to terminate the engagement at any time.*

letter of intent *n* plural **letters of intent** [C] a formal letter stating what someone intends to do. A letter of intent is not a promise or a contract, but does show a serious intention to do something: *Mercedes has* ***signed***

a letter of intent *to form a joint venture with a Czech maker of light trucks.* | *The firm had signed a* ***binding letter of intent*** (=one that counts in law as a formal agreement) *to buy the chain of stores.* | *They had only signed a* ***non-binding letter of intent*** (=one that does not count in law as a formal agreement)

letters of administration *n* [plural] LAW in Britain, a document giving someone the authority to make sure that the property of a dead person is given to the people who have the legal right to receive it, for example those that are named in a WILL (=a document saying who should get your money and property when you die)

let•ting /'letɪŋ/ *n BrE* LAW **1** [C] a house or apartment that can be rented: *short-term property letting*
2 [U] the activity of making houses etc available for rent: *letting agents*

lev•el[1] /'levəl/ *n* [C] **1** the measured amount of something that exists at a particular time or in a particular place: *The longer poor performance continues, the more comfortable employees become with their lower level of productivity.*
2 all the people or jobs within an organization, industry etc that have similar importance and responsibility: *Due to the importance of the issue, negotiations will have to be held at a more senior level.* | *We need to recruit more employees at the management level.*
entry level the level at which someone who has little or no experience of working enters a company or organization at the start of their career: *a training course for communicators at senior and intermediate entry levels of broadcasting and print journalism*

level[2] *v* **levelled levelling** *BrE*, **leveled leveling** *AmE*
level off/out *phr v* [I] to stop climbing or growing and become steady or continue at a fixed level: *Lower mortgage rates should help the market to level out.* | *Short-term interest rates will level off later this year.*

level playing field *n* [singular] *informal* a situation in which different companies, countries etc can all compete fairly with each other because no one has special advantages: *Banks should be able to compete on a level playing field with other financial firms.*

le•ver•age[1] /'liːvərɪdʒ‖'le-, 'liː-/ *n* [U] **1** the influence that one person or organization has on another: *Cleveland companies are using their* ***economic leverage*** *to persuade doctors and hospitals to help in attacking poor medical care.*
2 FINANCE the amount of borrowing that a company has in relation to its SHARE CAPITAL (=the amount lent by shareholders). If the company makes more profit by investing this borrowed money in its business activities than it pays in interest, the company's shareholders will obtain higher payments from their shares than they would without the use of borrowed money. But if the company makes less profit than it pays in interest, shareholders will receive less money. High leverage involves a high degree of risk: *Illinois Tool has* ***reduced its leverage*** (=reduced the amount of borrowing) *since making two large acquisitions, primarily through asset sales.* | *a warning to investors about the risks of* ***high leverage*** | ***Heavy leverage*** *and aggressive expansion made for a weak balance sheet.*
debt leverage another name for LEVERAGE: *Reducing capital spending should allow the company to reduce its debt leverage to about 40% and give it more financial flexibility.*
financial leverage another name for LEVERAGE: *Given Sotheby's strong earnings and cash flow, S&P believes that lower financial leverage will be quickly restored.*
loan leverage the amount that a bank has lent in relation to its SHARE CAPITAL (=the amount lent by shareholders): *In 1945 the American banking system had a loan leverage ratio of 2.8. In other words, in 1945 banks had only $2.80 in loans for each dollar of equity. By 1988, this had risen to $10 of loans for each dollar of equity.* —see also DEBT-EQUITY RATIO

leverage[2] *v* [T] to use borrowed money to buy a particular company or investment: *Their capacity to leverage private capital support of these projects has been variable.* —**leveraging** *n* [U] *He has been a long-time critic of the leveraging of America.*
leverage sth ↔ **up** *phr v* [I,T] if a company leverages up, or if the management leverages it up, the amount of borrowing it has is increased: *American and Delta have kept their debt levels low while other airlines leveraged up.*

lev•er•aged /'liːvərɪdʒd‖'le-, 'liː-/ *adj* FINANCE **1** a leveraged company is financed by a high level of borrowing in relation to its SHARE CAPITAL (=the amount lent by shareholders): *Brandon is profitable even though it is leveraged much more than most small businesses.* | *Arco has carried a more heavily* ***leveraged balance sheet*** *than most other oil companies, with debt making up about 47% of its overall capital.* | *The company is so* ***over-leveraged*** (=has borrowed so much) *that it's likely to face a bankruptcy reorganization.*
2 leveraged deal/purchase/transaction etc a deal etc in which borrowed money is used by the buyer to pay for something: *The market for bank loans for leveraged transactions has grown weak, with many heavily indebted companies suffering financial problems.*

leveraged buyout —see under BUYOUT

leveraged takeover —see under TAKEOVER

lev•y[1] /'levi/ *v* past tense and past participle **levied levy a tax/charge/fine etc** to officially make someone pay a tax etc **levy sth on**: *The city will levy a tax of $68 a year on each piece of property in the Oak Creek district.* | *The penalty is among the largest fines ever levied for environmental crimes.*

levy[2] *n* plural **levies** [C] **1** a tax: *The minister announced higher levies on heating oil and gasoline.*
2 a charge paid by members of a professional association or TRADE UNION: *Henderson is planning a new levy of 15 cents a month from each union member.*
3 *AmE* an occasion when the authorities take a person's or organization's assets because they have not paid tax that they owe: *The IRS now uses two million levies a year to seize wages, bank accounts, and other funds of delinquent taxpayers.*
capital levy ◆ a tax paid by someone on the value of their property and assets: *There will be a 2% capital levy increase beginning April 1.*
◆ a special tax on wealth, for example when a country is at war or in a dangerous situation: *He resisted the idea of a capital levy, and Britain paid a high proportion of the costs of the war out of general taxation.*
import levy a tax on goods coming into a country from abroad, often used by governments as a way of reducing imports and protecting local industries; IMPORT DUTY, IMPORT TARIFF, IMPORT SURCHARGE: *The imposition of a 9% across-the-board import levy has slowed imports and helped to produce a small budget surplus.*

li•a•bil•i•ty /ˌlaɪə'bɪlɨti/ *n* plural **liabilities** **1** [singular] ACCOUNTING, FINANCE an amount of money owed by a business to a supplier, lender etc: *The business has a liability as it owes money to the mortgage provider.*
2 liabilities [plural] ACCOUNTING, FINANCE the amounts of money owed by a business considered together: *In its bankruptcy filing, the company listed liabilities of $363.7 million and assets of $141.3 million.*
assumed liabilities [plural] the debts that a company agrees to be responsible for paying when it buys another company: *Southern Union Gas Co. sold its northern Arizona gas utility operations to Citizens Utilities for $46 million, $39 million in cash and $7 million in assumed liabilities.*

contingent liabilities [plural] debts that may have to be paid later, and that are included in a report on a company's financial situation: *As a result of the legal settlement over royalty rights, it will remove $3.4 million in contingent liabilities from its balance sheet.*
current liabilities [plural] debts that must be paid within one year, for example to suppliers and the tax authorities: *Pacific had long-term debt of $1.71 billion and current liabilities of $1.38 billion.*
deferred liabilities [plural] debts relating to activity in one period of time that will or may be paid in a later period of time: *The company's reserves included $756 million for unspecified deferred liabilities.*
deposit liabilities [plural] money that people and companies have put into banks, and that the banks will have to pay back at some time in the future: *Banks should ensure that their assets are worth enough to meet the deposit liabilities.*
external liabilities [plural] debts to lenders and suppliers, as compared to money owed to shareholders: *The balance sheet should summarize the sources of finance which are the external liabilities of the business, and the interests of the owners.*
fixed liabilities also **long-term liabilities** [plural] debts to be paid in more than one year, for example to lenders such as banks, rather than to suppliers: *Kaiser had long-term debts of $626 million, plus $311 million of other long-term liabilities, such as pension obligations.*
secured liabilities [plural] debts to lenders, for example in the form of bonds, that are SECURED on particular assets of the company. These assets can be sold if necessary to pay the debts: *The thrift's liabilities included about $2.5 billion in deposits in 184,000 accounts and $803 million in secured liabilities.*
tax liability [C,U] when a person or organization must pay tax, or the amount of tax they must pay: *They may have an unexpected $100 million tax liability because of Internal Revenue Service interpretations affecting the sale of its assets.*
3 [U] LAW the responsibility that a person or organization has for loss, damage, or injury caused to others, or for payment of debts + **for**: *The new law would double airlines' liability for lost luggage to $2,500.* | *The company **admitted liability** and said that it was responsible for its negligence from the start.* | *The firm has **denied liability**, said that it was not responsible and isn't discussing settlement terms.* —see also ADMISSION OF LIABILITY, LIMITATION OF LIABILITY
civil liability [U] responsibility for injury or damage that is not serious enough to be covered by criminal law: *The laboratories were subject to civil liability for side effects of any drugs they might approve.*
criminal liability [U] responsibility for injury or damage that is serious enough to be covered by criminal law: *The proposed legislation would remove the threat of criminal liability for some copyright violations of software.*
employer liability also **employer's liability** [U] responsibility by employers for their employees' actions while working or at work: *Employer liability for a worker's driving could reach far.*
joint and several liability [U] when a number of different people or organizations are responsible both as a group and individually for harm or injury they have caused: *In a couple, the woman can be charged her partner's tax if he does not pay, and the man can be charged the woman's tax if she does not pay. This is known as joint and several liability.*
legal liability [U] responsibility for an action covered by the law: *The airline should bear all legal liability for the crash.*
limited liability [U] when the owners of a limited liability company are only responsible for their company's debts up to a certain amount if it goes out of business, and do not have to sell their personal assets to repay these debts: *When he founded the company, he chose limited liability status because of the personal protection it gave him.*
personal liability [U] when someone's personal assets must be sold to pay the debts of the company they own: *If he is forced to sell his major assets, and the proceeds don't cover the debt, he could be left not only with a collapsed empire but with a huge personal liability.*
product liability [U] when the maker of a product is responsible for any damage or injury that the product causes: *She is suing the company for negligence and product liability, alleging that a defect in her car caused the accident.*
professional liability [U] the responsibility of a professional person such as a doctor or lawyer for damage or loss caused by the services or advice that they give
sequential liability [U] a rule stating that a company only has to pay money it owes after it has received payment from its customers: *The board is recommending that members oppose sequential liability.*
strict liability [U] when an organization is not directly responsible for damage or injury to someone, but must still pay DAMAGES (=money for the damage or injury caused): *Recognizing how difficult it is to prove fault in an air accident, airlines agreed to strict liability – automatic compensation of passengers or their relatives.*
unlimited liability [U] when a person or organization is considered responsible for paying the complete cost of any damage or injury they cause, or for paying all of their debts, with no upper limit: *Individual states are free to set unlimited liability for shippers responsible for oil pollution.*
vicarious liability [U] when someone is considered legally responsible for damage or injury caused by someone else: *gun manufacturers' vicarious liability for injuries caused by their guns*

liability insurance —see under INSURANCE

li•a•ble /ˈlaɪəbəl/ *adj* [not before a noun] LAW **1** legally responsible for the cost of something + **for**: *The troubled company will be liable for about $52 million in back taxes and penalties.*
2 likely to be legally punished or forced to do something by law **liable to sb**: *The Firm admitted no wrongdoing and therefore, they were not liable to anyone for the losses that had occurred.* **liable for sth**: *The appeals court ruled that it would hold tobacco companies liable for illnesses related to smoking.*

LIBA /ˈliːbə; ˌel aɪ biː ˈeɪ/ *n* London Investment Banking Association; a professional organization of banks in London, formerly the ACCEPTING HOUSES COMMITTEE, that represents the views of members to the government and other authorities

lib•e•ral /ˈlɪbərəl/ *adj* **1** believing that people should be free to behave as they like, and supporting gradual political and social change: *She has liberal views on such issues as equal education and job opportunities for black and white.* | *the battle between conservative and liberal opinion* —**liberal** *n* [C] *He remains a social liberal on gay rights.*—**liberalism** *n* [U] *He combined social liberalism with a determination to keep firm control of government spending.*
2 ECONOMICS supporting the idea that most economic activity should be run by private business rather than by the government: *Because of the spread of liberal economic ideas, about three to four billion people will be returning to the market economy.* —**liberal** *n* [C] *Economic liberals believe that low taxation encourages wealth creation.*—**liberalism** *n* [U] *The goal of nineteenth-century economic liberalism was based on the individual pursuit of self-interest.*
3 liberal rules, systems etc are generous to the people

L

they affect: *the state's new family-leave law, one of the most liberal in the nation* | *Texas and Florida have the most liberal rules on opening company files for inspection during litigation.*

4 given in large amounts: *a liberal supply of taxpayers' money*

lib·e·ral·ize also **liberalise** *BrE* /ˈlɪbərəlaɪz/ *v* [T] to make a system, law, or moral attitude less strict: *The President promised to push ahead with his commitment to liberalize the economy.* —**liberalizer** also **liberaliser** *BrE n* [C] *a dispute between protectionists and liberalizers* —**liberalization** also **liberalisation** *BrE n* [U] *The economy is expected to deteriorate for a period of six months after the liberalization of prices.*

LIBOR /ˈliːbɔː, ˈlaɪ-‖-ɔːr/ *n* London Interbank Offered Rate; the rate of interest at which London banks offer loans between one another. Other rates of interest are often based on this rate

li·cence *BrE*, **license** *AmE* /ˈlaɪsəns/ *n* [C] LAW **1** an official document giving you permission to own or do something for a period of time: *The charity organization has applied for a city* ***business license*** *to operate weekly bingo games.* | *The factory's* ***operating license*** *will not be granted until after the inspection.* —compare PERMIT

export licence *BrE*, **export license** *AmE* also **export permit** an official document, giving permission to send goods for sale in another country

import licence *BrE*, **import license** *AmE* also **import permit** a government document needed before importing certain types of goods. Import licences can be used, for example, to limit imports if there is a BALANCE OF PAYMENTS DEFICIT, or to stop trade in rare plants and animals: *The duty on cars was 65%, and importers also had to get an import license, which was almost never granted.*

2 *disapproving* official permission to do something, which seems wrong + **for**: *State Governments are concerned that the revised tax laws will provide a license for tax evasion.*

3 licence to print money *disapproving* used in order to say that a situation gives someone a chance to make a lot of money very easily, without much work: *Franchising isn't always a licence to print money. It can take a lot of hard work and personal effort.*

4 under licence if something is sold, made etc under licence, it is sold etc with the permission of the company or organization who owns the PATENT (=an idea or design protected by law) or the COPYRIGHT (=the legal right to be the only producer or seller of a book, play, film, or record): *Appoint a foreign company to manufacture your product under licence.*

licence fee *BrE*, **license fee** *AmE* —see under FEE

licencing fee *BrE*, **licensing fee** *AmE* —see under FEE

li·cense /ˈlaɪsəns/ *v* [T] LAW **1** to give official permission for someone to do something or for an activity to take place: *The building contractors we hired were licensed by the General Service Administration.* | *The company is confident that it will be licensed to do business in California after the start of the new year.*

2 to give someone permission to make something, using a PATENT (=an idea or design protected by law) that you own, or to publish a book, record etc, using COPYRIGHT that you own, usually in return for a payment: *Sandoz has licensed certain manufacturing and marketing rights for the drug.* **licence sth to sb**: *He has licensed the device to a farm equipment manufacturer.*

3 to receive permission to make something using a PATENT (=an idea or design protected by law) owned by another company, or to publish a book, record etc, using COPYRIGHT that they own, usually in return for a payment **licence sth from sb**: *Franklin has licensed electronic publishing rights for the Chinese dictionary from a British publisher.* —**licensed** *adj* [only before a noun] *licensed operators of nuclear power plants* —**licensing** *n* [U] *EDS has* ***licensing agreements*** *that allow it to use some of Computer Associates' software.*

li·cen·see /ˌlaɪsənˈsiː/ *n* [C] LAW **1** someone who has official permission to do something, especially to sell alcohol: *The full licence enables the licensee to sell liquor for consumption either on or off the premises.*

2 an organization that has permission to use the PATENT (=an idea or design protected by law) of another organization: *Pierre Cardin's US licensees*

li·cen·sor /ˈlaɪsənsə‖ˌlaɪsənˈsɔːr/ also **li·cen·ser** /ˈlaɪsənsə‖-ər/ *BrE* —*n* [C] LAW **1** someone who gives official permission to someone to do something: *The general licensor has unlimited time within which to issue a license.*

2 an organization that gives permission to another organization to use a PATENT (=an idea or design protected by law) that it owns in order to make something: *Competition rules protect the licenser as well as the licensee.*

li·en /ˈliːən, liːn/ *n* [C] LAW **1** a person's or organization's right to another's property, usually the right of a lender to take a borrower's property if they fail to repay a loan, or the right of people owed money by a company to take the assets of that company if it goes out of business: *It currently owes about $225 million to its lenders, who* ***hold liens on*** *all of the company's real estate assets.*

2 exercise/file/place a lien to ask a law court to recognize that someone owes you money and to give you the right to take their assets to pay the debt: *The city will file liens and judgments against properties that are one year behind in payment.* | *The carrier may exercise a lien on the cargo for the unpaid freight.*

broker's lien INSURANCE the right of a broker to keep possession of an insurance policy until the client makes the payment for it

carrier's lien the right of a carrier to keep the goods they are delivering if the buyer does not pay the CARRIAGE costs that are due

federal tax lien a lien where the national US tax authorities have the right to take a person's or organization's assets because they have not paid tax

first lien a lien that gives one particular lender the right to take the assets of a person or organization that owes them money before anyone else receives payment: *Southwest would provide Midway with a $20 million loan, which would give Southwest first lien on additional assets at Midway Airport.*

general lien a lien where the person or organization that is owed money has the right to take any of the assets of the person or organization that owes them money, even assets that are not related to that particular debt: *The Carrier shall have a general lien against the owner of the goods for any monies whatever due from the Trader.*

priority lien another name for FIRST LIEN: *A priority lien for Aetna will give it priority over other MMR debts.*

second lien a lien where the assets can be taken to pay debts only after other people and organizations that are owed money have been repaid: *EA said that it had first lien on the company's receivables and that Manufacturers Hanover had the second lien.*

seller's lien a lien where a seller can take back goods sold to a buyer who has not paid for them

tax lien a lien where the tax authorities have the right to take a person's or organization's assets because they have not paid tax: *The bank was trying to cope with a $1.8 million Internal Revenue Service tax lien at the time of its collapse.*

li·e·nee /ˌliːəˈniː, ˌliːˈniː/ *n* [C] LAW a person or organization that owns property on which there is a lien

li·en·or /ˈliːənɔː, ˈliːˈnɔː‖-ɔːr/ *n* [C] LAW a person or organization that has a lien on another's property

life /laɪf/ *n* plural **lives** [C] **1** the period of time during which something takes place or exists: *industrial products used during the life of a mining operation* | *The rate of interest is often subsidized and fixed for the life of the loan.*
2 the period of time during which something is still good enough to use, fresh enough to eat etc + **of**: *Our general purpose machinery has an estimated* ***useful life*** *of 80,000 running hours.* | *Castrol GTX2 oil has been specially formulated to prolong the life of catalytic converters.*
depreciable life ◆ the expected length of time that a FIXED ASSET will last
◆ TAX the number of years over which the cost of something that goes down in value, especially a FIXED ASSET, can be claimed against tax
economic life the length of time that an asset such as a building or machine produces more money than it costs to operate, or before it costs so much to repair that it should no longer be kept: *Almost 15% of buses in service in the county are more than 15 years old, the limit of their economic life.*
shelf life ◆ the length of time that a product, especially food, can be kept in a shop before it becomes too old to sell or use: *Chocolate bars usually have a shelf life of just nine months.* | *the use of additives to lengthen shelf life*
◆ the length of time that a particular product is popular before people no longer want to buy it: *The difference between the book trade and other retail trades is that there are some half million new product lines each year and many of those only have a shelf life of six months.*
useful life the period of time during which something can be used, before it becomes too old or in too bad condition. The useful life of an asset is important in calculating DEPRECIATION (=the amount it falls in value over time): *The average recommended useful life for such small appliances is six to seven years.*
3 service/working life the period of time during which a person works: *The average remaining service life of employees in the scheme at 31 March 2000 was 10 years.* | *Managers may spend as much as 50% of their working lives engaged in meetings.*
4 for life the period of time lasting until a person's death, or until the end of their working life: *The balance of the pension fund is used for an annuity giving a guaranteed* ***income for life****.* | *Few people can count on having* ***a job for life****.* —see also WORKING LIFE

life assurance —see under ASSURANCE

life assured —see under ASSURED[1]

life•blood /ˈlaɪfblʌd/ *n* [singular] the most important thing needed by an organization, country etc to allow to continue or develop successfully: *Cash flow is the lifeblood of any company.* | *Private clients are the lifeblood of options markets overseas.*

life•boat /ˈlaɪfbəʊt‖-boʊt/ *n* [C] *informal journalism* a system or plan used to rescue companies or investors who are losing money: *Officials of National Home Loans emphasized that the lifeboat facility was a precautionary measure they hoped wouldn't be needed.*

life•cy•cle /ˈlaɪfˌsaɪkəl-/ also **life cycle** *n* [C] MARKETING the length of time that people continue to buy a particular type of product
family lifecycle the different stages in people's lives that influence what they buy, used as a way of dividing the consumer market into different groups. Single people, young married people without children, and married people with children are three of these groups: *Advertisers need to be aware of the stage reached by individuals within the family lifecycle.*
product lifecycle the four stages in the existence of a product: INTRODUCTION, when development costs and therefore prices are high, and sales are low; GROWTH, when sales rise fast and profits increase; MATURITY, when sales rise more slowly and weaker competitors leave the market; and DECLINE, when sales and profits fall. The product may eventually be removed from the market: *Shorter product lifecycles mean that investment in innovation is critical in global competition.*

lifecycle analysis —see under ANALYSIS

lifecycle cost —see under COST[1]

life estate —see under ESTATE

life expectancy *n* plural **life expectancies** [C] **1** INSURANCE the age someone will probably live to, used by insurance companies when working out the risk of insuring them: *Sixty-year old men who still smoke have a life expectancy of less than 12 years.*
2 the average number of years that something such as an electrical product will last

life insurance —see under INSURANCE

life•line /ˈlaɪflaɪn/ *n* [C] something a country, organization etc depends on completely: *Hawaii has always been able to count on tourism, its* ***economic lifeline****.*

life-of-contract high —see under HIGH[1]

life•span /ˈlaɪfspæn/ *n* [C] the period of time during which something will continue to be useful: *The new water distribution system could save hundreds of millions of pounds* ***over its 150-year lifespan****.*

life•style /ˈlaɪfstaɪl/ *n* [C] the way someone lives, including where they live, their job and the sort of things they spend money on: *Market segmentation looks at how people differ in their lifestyles and attitudes towards products and purchases.* | *Virgin had long ago ceased to be simply in the music business; it was now in the* ***lifestyle business*** (=buying things based on a particular way of living).

life table —see under TABLE[1]

life tenant —see under TENANT

LIFFE /laɪf/ *n* London International Financial Futures and Options Exchange; a market for FUTURES (=contracts to buy something at a fixed price for delivery on a fixed date), for example in bonds, and OPTIONS (=the right to buy shares, currencies etc at a fixed price during a particular period of time)

LIFO /ˈlaɪfəʊ‖-foʊ/ abbreviation for LAST IN, FIRST OUT

lift /lɪft/ *v* [T] **1** to make prices, profits etc rise: *Political tensions in Côte d'Ivoire briefly lifted cocoa prices above £900 a tonne.* | *The interim dividend to shareholders has been lifted from 2.7p to 3.02p.*
2 to remove a law or rule: *After the exchange controls were lifted in 1989, Swedes rushed to invest abroad.* | *The judge granted an injunction, but the appeals court lifted it.* | *The administration has lifted the trade sanctions it imposed on China.* —**lifting** *n* [U] *The number of Israelis travelling abroad is expected to increase following the lifting of a $100 travel tax.*

light[1] /laɪt/ *adj* **1** light equipment, materials, machines etc are easily moved and used for fairly small tasks: *the* ***light aircraft*** *company, Cessna* | *BP Canada plans to use its revenue from the production of a lighter crude oil.* | *The empty space will be converted for* ***light industrial use****.*
2 light food products contain less fat than similar products. The word 'light' is often used after the name of the product; LITE: *Le Roulé Light has all the flavour of original Le Roulé but only half the fat.*
3 FINANCE when buying and selling of shares etc is light, very little business is being done on a financial market: *Interest-rate concerns and the weakness of US issues combined to send stocks lower in light trading.*
4 light touch if someone in authority uses a light touch, they trust the people or organizations they are in charge of and often let them make their own decisions:

L

He ruled his staff with a light touch and a delightful sense of humour.

light² *n* **1 in a good/bad/positive etc light** if you see something in a particular light, you think about it in a particular way: *As long as the customer perceives the price and the product in a positive light, the extra price will be viable.* | *As rates rise in the money markets, equities may be seen in a less favourable light.*
2 in the light of *BrE* **in light of** *AmE* if something is decided in the light of something else, it is decided after taking that thing into consideration: *Companies need to be satisfied that the contract is suitable in the light of their circumstances and financial position.*
3 give sth the green light to approve a project, plan etc so that it can begin: *The removal of investment controls gave the green light to financial institutions to invest in property.*

light draught —see under DRAUGHT

light-duty *adj* [only before a noun] light-duty products, equipment, vehicles etc are designed to be used for normal work by ordinary users, rather than heavy work in difficult conditions: *Until now, Toyota has produced only jeeps and light-duty trucks here.* —compare HEAVY DUTY, MEDIUM-DUTY

light engineering —see under ENGINEERING

light industry —see under INDUSTRY

lightning strike —see under STRIKE¹

light pen *n* [C] a special piece of equipment shaped like a pen, used to read printed computer codes on product labels: *The TX-2 uses a light pen to enter data straight on to the system.*

light·weight¹ /ˈlaɪt-weɪt/ *n* [C] someone or something that has very little influence or importance: *The furniture division had long been an industry lightweight.*

lightweight² *adj* **1** weighing less than similar products: *a lightweight sports car* | *a lightweight computer*
2 lightweight books, television programmes etc are not serious and are made mainly to entertain people: *The magazines contain a mix of editorial innovation and **lightweight entertainment**.*

lim·bo /ˈlɪmbəʊ‖-boʊ/ *n* **be in limbo** to be in an uncertain situation in which it is not clear what will happen next: *Investors in the shares have been left in limbo since the market tailed off.*

lim·it¹ /ˈlɪmɨt/ *n* [C] the greatest amount, size, number etc that is possible or allowed: *The contract specifies various **time limits** and penalty clauses.* | *Insurance cover for deep-freeze goods is free of charge up to a limit of £500.*
credit limit the maximum amount you can borrow, for example on a CREDIT CARD: *The advantage of this card is that there is a very high credit limit.*
floor limit ◆ the greatest amount of money that can be borrowed or taken out of a bank account at any one time: *A charge is made for all withdrawals above a mutually agreed floor limit.*
◆ *AmE* the greatest amount of money that someone can charge on their credit card at a particular type of store before the store needs to obtain approval from the credit card company

limit² *v* [T] **1** to stop something going beyond a particular point: *The costs of limiting air pollution are difficult to determine.*
2 to reduce the amount, number etc of something a person or organization may have **limit sb/sth to sth**: *Deutsche Bank limits any one shareholder to 5% of the votes.* | *Contributions to political parties are limited by law to $20,000*

lim·i·ta·tion /ˌlɪmɨˈteɪʃən/ *n* [C,U] when only a certain amount, number etc of something is allowed: *Subject to income limitations and other restrictions, investors may be able to avoid paying any tax at all on the interest.*

limitation of liability *n* plural **limitations of liability** [C] LAW when someone is responsible for only part of a debt, loss etc: *In a recent case, it was held that the defendants' limitation of liability was unreasonable and could not be upheld.*

Lim·i·ted /ˈlɪmɨtɨd/ *adj* written abbreviation **Ltd** used after the name of a company to show that it is a LIMITED LIABILITY COMPANY: *Perkins Slade Limited, a highly regarded insurance broking business*

limited (liability) company —see under COMPANY

limited carrier —see under CARRIER

limited edition —see under EDITION

limited liability —see under LIABILITY

limited partnership —see under PARTNERSHIP

limit order —see ***buy limit order*** under ORDER¹

linch·pin also **lynchpin** /ˈlɪntʃˌpɪn/ *n* [singular] the most important thing or person in a system, plan etc, which everything else depends on: *The consumer is the linchpin of the economy.*

line /laɪn/ *n* [C] **1** also **product line** MARKETING a type of product that a company makes or sells, often with several different sizes, models etc; RANGE: *It continues to get about two-thirds of its revenue from this one product, despite repeated efforts to **diversify** its **product line**.* (=develop new products) | *Hasbro, the maker of the G.I. Joe line of dolls* | *The two-engine, wide-body jet that will fill one of the only gaps in Boeing's product line.*
full line a complete range of products, with a product for each type of use or user: *Ziba designed a full line of heaters, from floorstanding to wall-mounted.*
2 MANUFACTURING a team of people who work together, each doing a different job but working to achieve the same thing
assembly line also **production line** MANUFACTURING a method of making goods, especially cars of other machines, in a factory. It involves the product moving down a line of workers who each add a different part or do a different job: *Most blue-collar workers will not easily regain jobs on the assembly line.* | *a **highly automated production line*** (=one with advanced equipment, computers etc) | *The philosophy of the assembly line was to break down the work into simple elements that required no special training.*
3 someone's line of work, business etc is the work that they do: *A corporation may get into a certain line of business as a short-term objective to generate cash-flow.*
4 a company providing a system for moving goods or people by sea, air, road etc: *Denmark's Maersk line* | *a cartel that shut out rival shipping lines*
5 a telephone connection. The word 'line' is also often used for the name of a special telephone number which is used to deal with a particular kind of enquiry: *Our lines are open 7 days a week.* | *For a straightforward professional service, call Mercantile Action Line.*
6 hold the line if you ask someone you are speaking to on the telephone to hold the line, you are asking them politely to wait for a short time: *If you will please hold the line a moment I will see if Mr Wyatt is available.*
7 on the line if someone is on the line, they have called you on the telephone: *Can't it wait? I've got a client on the line.*
8 on the line if your job, home etc is on the line, you risk losing it: *A brave team led by marketing director Stephen Roberts have put their homes on the line to do this deal.* | *If they fail, their reputations are on the line.*
9 in line with if something changes in line with something else, it changes at the same rate and at the same time: *The value of these stocks is uprated each year in line with changes in the retail price index.*
10 in line for likely to get something: *If Burgmans delivers the goods, he should be in line for a job on the committee.* | *Investors in mature bonds could be **first in***

***line for** payment if the deal with GE Capital goes through.*

11 on/off line COMPUTING if you are on line, you can use a computer to communicate with other computers. If you are off line, the computer is not working or not switched on and you are not able to communicate with other computers: *The swipe machine is on line to the central bank network.*

12 come on line if a system, arrangement or new product comes on line, it becomes available: *After several years in decline, new oil production wells are coming on line.* | *Video servers offering video-on-demand have now come on line.*

13 sign on the dotted line to agree officially to something by writing your name on a document: *Demand that the repairs are done before you sign on the dotted line.*

14 in the firing line/in the line of fire to be in a position where you can be criticized because you are responsible for something, or because you have done something wrong: *Auditors, irrespective of their innocence or guilt, have been put in the firing line by investors trying to recoup their losses.* —see also ABOVE THE LINE, BELOW THE LINE, BOTTOM LINE, CREDIT LINE, DATE LINE, DOTTED LINE, OFF-LINE, ON-LINE, STRAIGHT LINE, TAG LINE, TOP LINE

line extension *n* [C] MARKETING a new product that is added to a company's existing range of products in a way that takes advantage of the popularity of its existing products: *Bacardi denies that Breezer ads push rum. The ads' references to rum, they say, are a simple case of line extension.* —see also BRAND EXTENSION

line management —see under MANAGEMENT

line manager —see under MANAGER

line of credit *n* plural **lines of credit** [C] another name for CREDIT LINE

lin•er /ˈlaɪnə‖-ər/ *n* [C] a large passenger ship: *All sorts of vessels are represented within the P&O Group, from small coastal steamers to majestic liners.*

link[1] /lɪŋk/ *n* [C] **1** something that joins two places and allows easy travel or communication between them: *Mongolia has plans to extend its **road, air** and **rail links** with China and Russia.* | *A pipeline link between the UK and the Netherlands would make the UK part of the European gas grid.*

2 an agreement between two companies, countries etc to work together on a particular project + **with/between**: *For Taiwan Aerospace, a link with McDonnell Douglas would be a much-needed boost.* | *The link between AMP and Westpac is part of a trend for Australian banks and insurance companies to form alliances.*

3 a system which connects computers, telephone NETWORKS etc so that they can exchange messages + **with**: *Customers in France, the Netherlands and Germany can conduct transactions through home **computer links** with a bank in Belgium.* | *Campbell Freight Agencies have computerised links with Customs and Excise.*

link[2] *v* **1** [I,T] to put something such as a road or a phone line between two places, joining them together and making travel and communication easier between them: *a train line linking Dallas, Houston and San Antonio* **link sth with sth**: *the English Channel tunnel project linking Britain with France*

2 [I,T] if two or more companies or countries are linked, they agree to work together on a particular project: *By linking with Germany, the Danes have made their economy dependent on the strength of the German economy.* | *Liechtenstein and neighboring Switzerland are linked by a monetary and currency pact.*

3 [T] FINANCE if investments, exchange rates etc are linked, they change at the same time and at the same rate **be linked (to)**: *The 90,000 term-life policies were sold to many borrowers, but weren't specifically linked to their loans.* | *the system of **inflation-linked** pay raises*

4 [T] to connect computers, telephone NETWORKS etc so that they can exchange messages: *Syncordia has put together a network that currently links 14 business centers.* **be linked to/with**: *The cable systems can carry telephone calls and be linked with cellular phone systems.*

link up *phr v* [I] **1** to make a connection between two things: *Department heads in Tokyo and London linked up by telephone.* | *As more computers link up, competitors will have to think more about making their machines work together.*

2 to agree to work together on a particular project: *A Japanese brewery has linked up with a local beer maker to market Japanese beer abroad.* —see also LINK-UP

link•age /ˈlɪŋkɪdʒ/ *n* **1** [U] a condition or restriction in a political or business agreement in which one country or company will only agree to do something if the other promises to do something in return: *U.S. officials reject linkage as contrary to the WTO's aim of free trade.* | *We will seek a procedural agreement accepting this linkage.*

2 [C,U] something which connects systems so that they work together + **with/between**: *calls for greater linkage with and support for local firms* | *There no longer seems to be a very precise linkage between the two interest rates.*

3 [C] an agreement between two companies, countries etc to work together on a particular project + **with/between**: *ICL's linkage with Fujitsu might also open up the UK market for other producers.* | *Americans are suspicious of linkages between public schools and employers.*

link-up *n* [C] a connection between two organizations, things etc, for example when they work together: *Owners Abroad and Thomas Cook Group announced plans of a possible link-up between the two tour operators.* —see also ***link up*** under LINK[2]

liq•uid /ˈlɪkwɪ̈d/ *adj* FINANCE **1** involving cash, or things that can easily be changed into cash: *In a modern economy, liquid wealth is held in the form of money – bank notes and, more importantly, bank deposits.*

2 involving things that can easily be bought and sold: *Dealings in the investment trust's shares are expected to be more liquid than in the individual shares of many smaller companies.* | *the well developed, **highly liquid** and sophisticated money market in London* —opposite ILLIQUID

liquid asset —see under ASSET

liq•ui•date /ˈlɪkwɪ̈deɪt/ *v* FINANCE **1** [T] to sell something an investment for cash: *Holdings of units can be liquidated quite quickly.*

2 [I,T] if someone liquidates a company, or if the company liquidates, all of its assets are sold in order to pay its debts. Any money left after that is returned to shareholders and the company stops operating: *Rather than trying to reorganize, the airline will liquidate.*

liquidated damages —see under DAMAGE[1]

liq•ui•da•tion /ˌlɪkwɪ̈ˈdeɪʃən/ *n* [C,U] FINANCE **1** the action of selling an investment: *Manila's market dropped 26.08 points following a liquidation of foreign investments.*

2 when a company stops operating because it is in financial difficulty and its assets are sold to pay its debts: *Creditors have taken steps to **force** the studio **into liquidation**.* | *No doubt more firms will **go into liquidation** because they took on too much debt.*

compulsory liquidation also **forced liquidation** when a company in financial difficulty is forced to go into liquidation by the people and organizations to which it owes money: *Any creditor may decide to lodge a court petition for compulsory liquidation.*

voluntary liquidation when a company in financial difficulty decides to go into liquidation, rather than being forced to by the people and organizations to which it owes money: *Creditors have been asked to approve a voluntary liquidation plan for the group. If this fails, a forced liquidation is likely.*

liq·ui·da·tor /ˈlɪkwədeɪtə‖-ər/ *n* [C usually plural] FINANCE a professional person or organization whose job is liquidating companies in financial difficulty; RECEIVER: *The liquidators are unlikely to pay more than 10 cents on every dollar owed by the failed bank.*

liquid crystal display —see LCD

li·quid·i·ty /lɪˈkwɪdəti/ *n* [U] **1** ECONOMICS the amount of money in an economy at a particular time: *The central bank* ***injected liquidity into*** *the economy* (=increased liquidity) *last month when it began repurchasing government bonds.* —see also MONEY SUPPLY

2 FINANCE when investments can easily be bought and sold on a particular financial market: *As investors learned in the last stock market crash, liquidity can disappear quickly when everyone tries to sell at once.*

3 FINANCE, ACCOUNTING the ability of a company to make payments to employees and suppliers, interest payments to banks etc: *Disappointing sales and resulting losses have caused* ***liquidity problems***.

4 BANKING the ability of a bank to pay back people and organizations that have put money in the bank and that want to take their money out: *Customers began withdrawing deposits, causing difficulties for the liquidity of the bank.* —opposite ***illiquidity*** under ILLIQUID

liquidity preference —see under PREFERENCE

liquidity risk —see under RISK[1]

liquid measure —see under MEASURE[1]

liquid ratio test —see under TEST[1]

liquified natural gas —see LNG

LISP /lɪsp/ *n* [U] COMPUTING list processing; a type of computer language used especially in ARTIFICIAL INTELLIGENCE

list[1] /lɪst/ *n* [C] a set of items such as figures, names etc that belong to a particular group, written down one after the other: *The Acorn Fund is on an exclusive list of top funds that are closed to new investors.* | *detailed lists of proposed prices*

focus list FINANCE a group of shares, etc that are likely to interest investors who sell stocks, shares etc quite soon after buying them: *Goldman Sachs removed Intel from the firm's focus list.*

hit list *informal* a list of organizations, people etc against which someone is planning to take action: *Most companies, even small ones, have middle managers on their hit lists.* | *Alcohol and tobacco are at the top of the tax hit list.*

mailing list a large collection of customers' names and addresses, used by companies to send products, advertisements etc to each one: *Please add me to your mailing list for all future events.* | *the new* ***electronic mailing list***

shopping list ◆ a list of things that you want to buy when you go to a shop: *She is careful to stick to a shopping list so she doesn't overspend.*

◆ a list of things that a person or organization wants or thinks are necessary: *His proposal presents a long shopping list of tax cuts.*

watch list FINANCE a list of investments that are being watched very closely, for example because people think their price may be about to change, or because they think they are being traded dishonestly: *Several credit-card securities are on investors' watch lists for an early payout.* | *The market is drawing up its own watch list of troubled issuers.* —see also BLACKLIST, CHECKLIST

list[2] *v* [T] **1** to put items such as figures, names etc together in a group so that they can be considered together: *The SBA plans to increase the number of companies it lists on its computerized program to help smaller firms compete.* —see also BLACKLIST

2 FINANCE to make stocks and shares officially available on a stockmarket: *Sony Corp. plans to list 29% of the stock of Sony Music Entertainment on the Tokyo Stock Exchange.*

listed company —see under COMPANY

listed security —see under SECURITY

listed share —see under SHARE

listed stock —see under STOCK[1]

lis·ten·er /ˈlɪsənə‖-ər/ *n* [C] someone who listens to a particular radio station or programme: *To recruit country music radio listeners, CMT has embarked on some innovative marketing methods.*

lis·ten·ing /ˈlɪsənɪŋ/ *adj* **listening figures** [plural] MARKETING the number of people who listen to a particular radio station or programme: *Overall listening figures climbed 10% and all stations are in profit from local income alone.*

list·ing /ˈlɪstɪŋ/ *n* [C] **1** FINANCE when a company is on an official list of shares which can be bought and sold on a particular stockmarket: *Finmeccanica hopes to obtain a Milan Stock Exchange listing by merging with Societa Immobiliare e Finanziaria.*

2 listings [plural] a list of all the television programmes, plays, films etc that are on over a particular period of time showing the times and places for them: *The TV Guide doesn't usually provide local cable listings the way regional newspapers do.*

3 a list of figures, names etc: *He has started posting monthly listings of how the company's sales figures compare with those of competitors.*

listing paper —see under PAPER

list·less /ˈlɪstləs/ *adj* if an economy, trading etc is listless, there is very little growth or trade: *Every year the rich world pumps in billions of dollars of aid to try to breathe life into Africa's listless economies.*

list price —see under PRICE[1]

list processing —see LISP

Lite also **lite** /laɪt/ *adj* used in the name of some food and drink products have less fat and fewer calories than similar products: *the new commercial for Miller* ***Lite Beer***

literary agent —see under AGENT

literary property —see under PROPERTY

lit·e·ra·ture /ˈlɪtərətʃə‖-tʃʊr/ *n* [U] **1** information about a product, company etc: *The speed quoted in the* ***sales literature*** *is frankly optimistic.* | ***advertising literature***

2 books, articles, etc that give information about a particular subject: ***management literature***

li·tho /ˈlaɪθəʊ‖-oʊ/ also **li·thog·ra·phy** /lɪˈθɒgrəfi‖-ˈθɑː-/ *n* [U] a method of printing in which a design is drawn on a wet surface using a special ink containing oil: *Another key to Private Eye's success was its use of* ***offset litho printing*** (=a system that puts the design or words directly onto the machine that prints it). —**lithographic** *adj*: *conventional lithographic equipment*

lit·i·gant /ˈlɪtəgənt/ *n* [C] LAW someone who is making a claim against a person or company in a court of law: *The firm hopes to reach settlements soon with the eight litigants.*

lit·i·gate /ˈlɪtəgeɪt/ *v* [I,T] LAW to take a claim or complaint against a person or organization to a court of law: *He spent several weeks looking for the right lawyers to* ***litigate*** *the* ***case***. + **against**: *She now plans to litigate against the corporation for unfair dismissal.* —**litigation** *n* [U] *The firm now faces litigation from angry consumers.*

lit·i·ga·tor /ˈlɪtəgeɪtə‖-ər/ *n* [C] LAW someone who takes a claim or complaint against a person or organization to a court of law

li·ti·gious /lɪˈtɪdʒəs/ *adj* LAW too willing to take complaints to a court of law: *Doctors live in fear of litigious*

patients. | *America is regarded as the most litigious nation on earth.*

live•li•hood /ˈlaɪvlihʊd/ *n* [C,U] the way in which you earn money in order to live: *If a commercial beekeeper makes a mistake and his bees die, he has* ***lost his livelihood.*** | *More than one million Americans depend on Japanese companies for their livelihood.*

live•ly /ˈlaɪvli/ *adj* comparative **livelier** superlative **liveliest** if trading on the stock market is lively, people are buying and selling a lot of stocks, shares etc: *In Milan, trading was lively for the first time in weeks.*

live•stock /ˈlaɪvstɒk‖-stɑːk/ *n* [U] animals that are kept as a business, to make profit: *Grain and livestock markets are quite strong at the moment.*

liv•ing¹ /ˈlɪvɪŋ/ *n* [singular] the way in which you earn money in order to live, or the money that you earn: *It is becoming more and more difficult just to* ***earn a living.*** | *He was able to* ***make a living*** *as an actor.* | *I don't know what he does* ***for a living.*** —see also COST OF LIVING, STANDARD OF LIVING

living² *adj* **1 living wage** a wage high enough to allow someone to buy food, clothes, and the other basic things that are necessary in order to live: *Trade Unions are still fighting for a living wage in many industries.*
2 living standard another name for STANDARD OF LIVING

living trust —see under TRUST

living wage —see under WAGE

living will —see under WILL¹

Lloyd's /lɔɪdz/ *n* an insurance market based in London where MEMBERS (=specialized people and companies) insure the risks of financial, manufacturing, shipping, oil, and other organizations. Each group of members is represented by an UNDERWRITER who calculates the risks of business offered to the members and decides whether to accept it, and if so what the price paid for the insurance should be

Lloyd's Register —see under REGISTER¹

Lloyd's syndicate —see under SYNDICATE¹

LME abbreviation for LONDON METAL EXCHANGE

LNG *n* [U] liquified natural gas; a type of gas used as fuel that is transported in liquid form: *The country's gas reserves offer great possibilities for domestic use, but so far they are being used mainly for LNG exports.*

load¹ /ləʊd‖loʊd/ *n* [C] **1** an amount of goods or people transported on a road vehicle, train, or plane: *Rail cars are used to move the bigger loads.* + **of**: *The lorry returned with a load of Spanish apricots.* | *The plane was carrying a full load of passengers.* | *a lorry-load of gravel* —see also PAYLOAD
2 the amount of something that a person or organization has to do: *The firm's computers are struggling to cope with the increased load.* | *The network has to deal with a* ***heavy load*** *of telephone traffic.*
case load the number of cases that a lawyer or court has to deal with: *The court's case load has become lighter in recent months.*
debt load the amount of debt that a business or country has; DEBT BURDEN: *Even after restructuring, the firm is still carrying a high debt load.*
work load also **workload** the amount of work that a person or organization has to do: *Their work load has increased in the last couple of years.*
3 FINANCE an amount of money charged for managing an INVESTMENT FUND: *Because of the 5% load, only $950 of the $1,000 actually gets invested in your name.* | *The new fund carries a* ***front-end load*** (=an amount paid when the fund is first started) *of 5.5%* | *Harbor is a* ***no-load fund*** *distributed by HCA Securities of Toledo, Ohio.* | *A number of companies now offer* ***low-load*** *insurance policies.*

load² *v* [T] **1** to put goods into a road vehicle, train, boat, or plane to be transported: *The tankers set off as soon as they have been loaded.*
2 COMPUTING to copy a computer program or file onto a computer: *Many buyers don't want to load their machines themselves, so many manufacturers are offering preloaded software.* **load sth onto sth**: *The new software can be loaded easily onto most machines.*
3 FINANCE to include most or all of the charges at a particular period during the time that an insurance policy or INVESTMENT FUND is in use: *A lot of personal pension funds are* ***front-end loaded*** (=make most of their charges when the fund is first started).
load up on sth *phr v* [T] *journalism* to buy a lot of something: *More big investors are loading up on small stocks.*

load draught —see under DRAUGHT

load•ed /ˈləʊdɪ̈d‖ˈloʊ-/ *adj* carrying a load of goods: *a* ***fully loaded*** *truck* + **with**: *a ship loaded with 5,000 tons of South Korean rice*

load•er /ˈləʊdə‖ˈloʊdər/ *n* [C] a machine used for loading goods onto trucks or ships

load factor —see under FACTOR¹

load•ing /ˈləʊdɪŋ‖ˈloʊ-/ *n* [U] **1** an amount of money added to the cost of an insurance policy to pay for the cost of managing the policy
front loading also **front end loading** the money that UNIT TRUSTS, PENSION FUNDS, and some other financial products charge new investors and which is taken from their first few payments, rather than over a longer period of time
2 when goods are put onto a road vehicle, train, boat, or plane to be transported: *The goods are brought here for loading.* | *It is one of the main Black Sea loading ports.*

loan¹ /ləʊn‖loʊn/ *n* [C] **1** money borrowed from a bank, financial institution, person etc on which interest is usually paid to the lender until the loan is repaid: *The couple* ***took out*** *and* ***repaid*** *several* ***loans*** (=obtained them and paid them back) *to build up their business.* | *The bank recently* ***made a loan*** *to the company for a new warehouse.* | *Citibank will* ***provide loans*** *of $50,000 to $250,000 to small contractors.* | *More than 40 financial institutions have* ***extended loans*** (=given loans) *to the real estate firm.*
2 service a loan to make repayments on a loan: *With rising sales, he saw no problem servicing the loans.*
3 service a loan to collect repayments on a loan for another organization: *Many lenders continue to service loans they have sold into the secondary market.*
4 refinance a loan to replace an old loan with a new one: *Homeowners rushed to refinance and prepay their loans at lower interest rates.*
back-to-back loan a loan in one currency backed by a loan in another in order to avoid currency exchange restrictions: *Back-to-back loans are devices that can aid money laundering.*
bad loan a loan where repayments are not being made as originally agreed between the borrower and the lender, and which may never be repaid: *He says bad loans in the UK will wipe out all the earnings the bank might show next year.*
balloon loan a loan where repayments are small until the end of the loan, when there are one or two very large repayments: *Five-year balloon loans are attractive to starter-home buyers and those who plan to stay in a house for less than five years.*
bank loan an amount of money lent by a bank: *Pemberstone is* ***taking out a bank loan*** *of £14.5 million to fund the acquisitions.* | *Thomas sold off his shares in the company to* ***pay off personal bank loans.***
bridge loan also **bridging loan** a loan made for a short period of time while longer-term financing is arranged

bullet loan a loan where only interest is paid during the period of the loan, and the original loan itself is paid back in one payment at the end: *five- to 10-year bullet loans*

call loan a loan where the lender can ask for their money back at any time: *Commercial banks are unwilling to provide short-term credit to investment banks. This has pushed the overnight call loan rate to 14.5%.*

commercial loan a loan made to a business, rather than to a person: *As with any commercial loan, an examiner will continue to thoroughly review the borrower's financial condition, income, and cash flow.*

consumer loan a loan to a person so that they can buy a house, goods for their house, a car etc, rather than to a business: *Consumer loans are enormously profitable for lenders. For credit cards, you can charge 22% or 23%.*

corporate loan a loan to a business so that it can buy buildings, equipment etc, rather than to a person: *Corporate loan demand remains slow, with few corporations increasing debt to expand plant and equipment.*

credit-card loan money owed to a credit card company by the holder of the card at a particular time

debt consolidation loan a loan used to pay back a number of existing loans, so that payments are only made to one lender instead of to several: *If they're applying for debt consolidation loans to pay off their credit cards, we talk to them about what they're doing with the cards.*

delinquent loan another name for a BAD LOAN

foreign loan a loan to a country or organization made by a foreign government or financial institution: *efforts by Central American governments to attract foreign loans and aid*

home equity loan *AmE* an additional loan that a borrower takes out on a particular property, as a way to obtain money; SECOND MORTGAGE

home loan an amount of money that is lent to someone by a bank or BUILDING SOCIETY to allow them to buy a house. The house is used as SECURITY for the loan: *The company has always specialized in making home loans.*

interest-free loan a loan where the borrower does not have to pay interest for a particular period of time: *Peugeot will extend interest-free loans of up to 48 months if the buyer comes up with a downpayment of at least 20%.*

irrecoverable loan also **non-recoverable loan** a loan that will never be paid back: *More than 2% of the assets of China's state banks are irrecoverable loans.*

long-term loan a loan where repayments are made over several years, usually between five and ten years: *Many consumers appear unwilling to lock themselves into a long-term loan or lease agreement.*

medium-term loan a loan where repayments are made over a period of between one and five years

nonperforming loan another name for a BAD LOAN

nonrecourse loan a loan where, if the borrower fails to make repayments, the lender has the right to take the asset that the borrower bought with the loan, but has no rights to the borrower's other assets

overnight loan a loan between banks that lend each other money for very short periods of time

performing loan a loan where repayments are being made normally and on time: *A review by the bank revealed just three weak, though still performing, loans.*

personal loan a loan to a person for their own use rather than to a business: *the fairly high interest rates we pay on credit cards, car, student and other personal loans*

property loan also **real estate loan** *AmE* a loan used to buy land, buildings etc: *All of GE's commercial real-estate loans are to income-producing properties.*

rollover loan ◆ a loan where a bank allows a borrower, after a particular period of time has passed, to continue owing money after the repayment date ◆ a loan where the borrower agrees to pay interest at a particular rate, and to pay back the money at a particular time

secured loan a loan where the borrower has promised to give the lender certain assets if they fail to make repayments: *Bando makes secured loans on real estate rather than riskier equity investments.*

short-term loan a loan for a period of time up to a year: *The city received a $150 million short-term loan to allow it to pay its employees until taxes are collected in February.*

soft loan a loan with very low interest, often given to countries as a form of AID: *Donors pledged $3.3 billion in grants and soft loans to the Philippines.*

syndicated loan a loan where there are many lenders. A syndicated loan is organized and managed by a LEAD BANK: *Twelve international banks are arranging a $3.6 billion syndicated loan for Saudi Arabia.*

term loan a loan that has to be repaid over a fixed period of time: *Its credit line was converted to a term loan that matures Oct. 31.*

underlying loan one of the original loans that support ASSET-BACKED SECURITIES. These loans may be money that people owe on their credit cards, home loans etc. Repayments from these loans provide the money to repay the securities. The securities lender has the right to these repayments if the borrower does not make repayments on the securities

unsecured loan a loan where there are no assets to which the lender has a right if the borrower does not make repayments: *Unsecured loans are generally more expensive because lenders take on more risk.*

loan² *v* [T] *especially AmE* to lend someone something, especially money **loan sb sth/loan sth to sb**: *The European Investment Bank has loaned Algeria $30 million.*

loan capital —see under CAPITAL

loan club *n* [C] a group of people, for example in the place where they work, who save money together so that members can borrow money at lower interest rates than at banks: *loan clubs of people with a common bond, for example, tenants' association, factory employees*

loan guarantee —see under GUARANTEE²

loan leverage —see under LEVERAGE¹

loan loss —see under LOSS

loan-loss allowance —see under ALLOWANCE

loan-loss provision —see under PROVISION

loan-loss reserves —see under RESERVES

loan market —see under MARKET¹

loan shark —see under SHARK

loan stock —see under STOCK¹

loan syndicate —see under SYNDICATE¹

loan-to-value ratio —see under RATIO

lob·by¹ /ˈlɒbi‖ˈlɑːbi/ *n* plural **lobbies** [C] **1** a group of people with similar interests who try to persuade a government that a particular law or situation should be changed: *Opposition to the new law is expected from India's industry lobby.* | *The Prime Minister is still under pressure from the farm lobby.*
2 an attempt by a group of people to persuade members of a government that a particular law or situation should be changed + **of**: *A mass lobby of parliament is planned for next week.*

lobby² *v* past tense and past participle **lobbied** [I,T] to try to persuade a government that a particular law or situation should be changed: *The financial community is expected to continue lobbying Congress to introduce new legislation.* + **against**: *Industrialists are already lobbying against the reforms.* + **for**: *Small firms are lobbying for a change to the law.* —**lobbying** *n* [U] *The decision followed intense lobbying by banks.* | *The industry*

*launched a huge **lobbying campaign** to persuade the government to change its mind.* | *The corporation hired a **lobbying firm** to put its case to government.*

lob·by·ist /ˈlɒbiəst‖ˈlɑː-/ *n* [C] someone who lobbies members of a government to change a law or a situation: *Small-business lobbyists have responded cautiously to the announcement.* + **for**: *a lobbyist for the car industry*

lo·cal[1] /ˈləʊkəl‖ˈloʊ-/ *adj* connected with a particular area, especially the area where something is produced etc: *The firm produces clothing, shoes and other leather goods for local and overseas markets.* | *The company borrowed the money from two local banks.* | *All payments are made in local currency.* | *Protectionist policies have shielded local industry from outside competition.* —**locally** *adv*: *The goods are made and sold locally.* | *Think globally, act locally.* | *a range of locally produced wines*

local[2] *n* [C] *AmE* a small local organization that is part of a TRADE UNION; BRANCH *BrE*

local area network —see LAN

local authority —see under AUTHORITY

local authority stock —see under STOCK[1]

local content —see under CONTENT

local income tax —see under INCOME TAX

lo·cal·ize also **localise** *BrE* /ˈləʊkəlaɪz‖ˈloʊ-/ *v* [T] **1** to organize a business or industry so that things happen at a local level rather than a national one: *Nissan is continuing with its efforts to localize production.*

2 to make changes in advertising etc to make it more suitable for a particular place: *the free weeklies in Los Angeles that localize news and advertising* —**localized** also **localised** *BrE adj*: *Our strategy is to become a fully localized, customer-oriented company.*

local tax —see under TAX[1]

lo·cate /ləʊˈkeɪt‖ˈloʊkeɪt/ *v* [I,T] **1** to start a business or company in a particular place: *United Airlines announced that it will locate a new $1 billion jet maintenance facility in Indianapolis.* + **in**: *A growing number of small factories are finding it pays to locate in cities.*

2 be located to be based in a particular place: *The offices are located in Portland, Oregon.* | *The new firm is to be located in Shropshire.*

lo·ca·tion /ləʊˈkeɪʃən‖loʊ-/ *n* **1** [C] the place where something is: *The company has not disclosed the location of its new warehouse.* | *All the stores are in good locations.*

2 [C,U] PROPERTY the place where a building is, used to calculate a building's value, how much rent can be charged for it etc: *There are three important factors in real estate: location, location and location.*

3 [U] the starting of a business or company in a particular place: *Many local residents are opposed to the location of a fast-food restaurant in the high street.*

lock[1] /lɒk‖lɑːk/ *v* [T] **1 lock horns (with)** if two people or organizations lock horns, they are involved in a serious disagreement or struggle with each other: *Mr. Lorenzo locked horns with union representatives in his efforts to turn around the struggling business.*

2 be locked in a battle/struggle/dispute etc (with) if two people or organizations are locked in a battle, they are involved in a serious disagreement or struggle against each other: *The two networks are locked in a close ratings battle.* | *New York newspaper unions are locked in difficult negotiations with Tribune Co.'s Daily News.*

lock sth ↔ **away** *phr v* [T] to invest money in such a way that it is not available to be used; lock up: *He didn't want to lock the money away in a ten-year Treasury note.*

lock in *phr v* **1** [T] **lock sth in** to gain something and be certain to keep it: *Investors can lock in an 8.4% yield on a 30-year Treasury Bond.* | *Venezuela, which holds the world's fifth largest oil reserves, is seeking to lock in buyers for its oil.* | *Institutional traders try to lock in profits and protect against losses.*

2 [I] to come to a firm agreement that will last for some time and cannot be broken: *Many homeowners are keen to lock in at current low interest rates.*

lock into sth *phr v* [T] **1** to come to a firm agreement that will last for some time and cannot be broken: *A company is often forced to lock into a pricing schedule before it is sure about the cost of developing and producing a new technology.*

2 to be in a position where you have agreed to do something and so have to do it **be/become locked into**: *Columbia has become locked into long-term contracts.*

lock out *phr v* [T] **1 lock** sb ↔ **out** to prevent people from entering their place of work until they have agreed to accept conditions set down by their employers: *The company responded to the strike by locking out over 5,000 workers.* —see also LOCK-OUT

2 lock sb/sth ↔ **out** to prevent a person or organization from taking part in a business activity or being involved in it: *Smaller firms have been locked out of the US market.*

lock sth ↔ **up** *phr v* [T] to invest money or keep it in such a way that it not available to be used; lock away: *Mutual funds are an appropriate vehicle for income-seeking investors who don't want to lock their money up.* —see also LOCK-UP

lock[2] *n* **1 have a lock on sth** to have complete control of something: *The firm now has an 85% lock on the market.* | *Between them the two airlines have a virtual lock on domestic air traffic.*

2 put a lock on sth to limit or control something: *These currency controls have for decades put a lock on Pakistan's dealings with the larger world.*

lock-out *n* [C] a situation in which people are prevented from entering their place of work until they have agreed to accept conditions set down by their employers —see also ***lock out*** under LOCK[1]

lock·step /ˈlɒkstep‖ˈlɑːk-/ *n* **in lockstep (with)** if two amounts, levels etc rise and fall in lockstep with each other, they rise and fall at the same time: *Because most managers are unwilling to make distinctions among their employees, pay in most organizations still moves in lockstep.* | *MCI's rates should rise in lockstep with those of AT&T.*

lock-up *adj* **1 lock-up agreement/pact** an agreement by which money is invested in such a way that it cannot be used for a period of time

2 lock-up period a period of time during which money is invested in such a way that it cannot be used

lodge /lɒdʒ‖lɑːdʒ/ *v* **1 lodge a complaint/protest/appeal etc** to make a formal or official complaint, protest etc: *An appeal must be lodged within 28 days.* | *Thirty-eight objections have been lodged to the proposals.* | *Unions representing 12,000 Ford salaried employees have already lodged a claim for a substantial rise.*

2 [T] *BrE* to formally give information or documents which have to be given by law to an official authority; file *AmE*: *Two companies failed to lodge printed copies of their annual reports by the opening of trading yesterday.* | *Opening bids will have to be lodged by December 11.* | *To retain copyright you'll have to lodge a patent application.*

3 [T] to put money or something valuable in an official place so that it is safe: *The money was lodged in an account in Hamburg.* **lodge sth with sb**: *Be sure to lodge a copy of the contract with your solicitor.*

lodg·ment also **lodgement** /ˈlɒdʒmənt‖ˈlɑːdʒ-/ *n* [C,U] *BrE* BANKING an amount of money that is paid into a bank account, or the act of paying money into a bank account; DEPOSIT: *Interest can be earned from the lodgement of part of the working capital in a bank deposit account.*

log[1] /lɒg‖lɒːg, lɑːg/ *v* past tense and past participle **logged** present participle **logging** [T] **1** to make a record of each time that something happens: *The new system **logs** every **call** that a customer makes to the company.*

L

2 to change by a particular amount: *The Consumer Price Index could* ***log a gain*** *of 0.5% in August.*

log off also **log out** *phr v* [I] to do the actions that are necessary when you finish using a computer system: *Make sure all users have logged off before shutting the system down.*

log on also **log in** *phr v* [I] to do the necessary actions on a computer system that will allow you to begin using it + **to**: *If you have a modem you can log on to a bulletin board and download it.*

log[2] *n* [C] an official detailed record of something: *Keep a detailed log of telephone calls.* | *production logs*

log book —see under BOOK[1]

log file —see under FILE[1]

log·ging /ˈlɒgɪŋ‖ˈlɒː-, ˈlɑː-/ *n* [U] the work of cutting down trees in a forest in order to sell the wood: *Commercial logging is banned in 40 of the country's 73 provinces.* | *a Brazilian* ***logging company***

lo·gic /ˈlɒdʒɪk‖ˈlɑː-/ *n* [U] **1 commercial/economic/industrial logic** a way of thinking and making good judgements that is connected to a particular area of business, the economy etc: *Their takeover bid appears to have no commercial logic.*

2 COMPUTING a set of choices that a computer uses to solve a problem or perform a task: *a logic circuit*

lo·go /ˈləʊgəʊ‖ˈloʊgoʊ/ *n* [C] a design or way of writing its name that a company or organization uses as its official sign on its products, advertising etc: *a redesigned* ***company logo*** | *the new Toyota logo*

lol·ly /ˈlɒli‖ˈlɑːli/ *n* [U] *BrE informal old-fashioned* money: *He must be rolling in lolly.*

Lo·me Con·ven·tion /ˈlæʊmeɪ kənˌvenʃən‖loʊˈmeɪ-/ *n* an agreement between the EC countries and some of the poorer countries of Africa, the Caribbean and the Pacific, made in 1975 at Lome, capital of Togo. Under the agreement the EC countries agreed to help the economies of the other countries, for example by allowing many of their products to be imported into the EC without paying import tax: *The former colonies of EC member states were covered under the Lome Convention agreement.*

London Clearing House abbreviation **LCH** *n* FINANCE an organization that SETTLES trading activities (=makes the necessary payments) between buyers and sellers of FUTURES (=contracts to buy particular shares, bonds etc on a fixed date) and OPTIONS (=rights to buy shares etc during a particular period of time). Trading on LIFFE is settled through the London Clearing House

London Commodity Exchange *n* the most important market in London for trading COMMODITIES such as tea, coffee, sugar etc

London Gazette *n* in Britain, an official newspaper that gives information about companies, especially such matters as BANKRUPTCIES, changes in companies' names etc

London Inter-Bank Offered Rate —see LIBOR

London International Financial Futures and Options Exchange —see LIFFE

London Investment Banking Association —see LIBA

London Metal Exchange abbreviation **LME** *n* in Britain, the main market where metals other than iron are traded, usually as FUTURES (=contracts to buy something at a fixed price for delivery on a fixed date): *A shortage of zinc forced the cash price of zinc to more than $1400 a tonne, and to a premium of $240 over the forward price on the London Metal Exchange.*

London School of Economics abbreviation **LSE** *n* a college that is part of London University, where people study ECONOMICS, politics, and other social sciences

London Stock Exchange *n* another name for the INTERNATIONAL STOCK EXCHANGE, the London stockmarket: *Mitsubishi became the first Japanese general trading company to be* ***listed on the London Stock Exchange.*** | *a public company whose shares are* ***quoted on the London Stock Exchange***

long[1] /lɒŋ‖lɒːŋ/ *adj* **1** possessing shares, bonds, currencies etc because you believe that their value is going to increase + **on**: *Traders don't like going home long on dollars, because it means, in effect, to bet that the dollar will rise.* | *If the stock rises, you make money on your* ***long position*** *the bonds, shares etc you own, expecting their value to rise.*—**long** *n* [C usually plural] *After massive sales recently of US stocks and futures, the fund now has 30% more shorts, or negative bets, than it has longs, or positive ones.*

2 long day/hours etc if you work long hours or a long day, you work for more time than is usual: *Tax specialists often work long hours during assessment time.*

long[2] *adv* **go long (on) sth** to buy or keep bonds, shares, currencies etc because you believe that their value will rise: *He reversed short positions and went long on Hong Kong stocks.* | *Dealers are going long on dollars in expectation of today's release of a strong US trade figures.*

long-dated *adj* **long-dated bonds/stocks/securities** bonds, securities etc that will be repaid a long time in the future, usually ten or fifteen years: *Long-dated bonds were hardest hit, with the 30-year Treasury falling heavily.*

long gilts —see under GILTS

long position —see under POSITION[1]

long-range *adj* [only before a noun] **1** long-range decisions, plans etc are for a period of time far into the future: *the company's* ***long-range strategy*** *for its health care business*

2 a long-range plane can fly long distances without having to stop: *The 767 is a wide-body, long-range plane.*

longs /lɒŋz‖lɒːŋz/ *n* [plural] bonds issued by the British government that are repaid a long time in the future, usually ten or fifteen years

long·shore·man /ˈlɒŋʃɔːmən‖ˈlɒːŋʃɔːr-/ *n* plural **longshoremen** [C] *AmE* someone whose job is to load and unload ships; STEVEDORE, DOCKER *BrE*: *port reorganization that could cause big job cuts for longshoremen*

long-tail *adj* [only before a noun] INSURANCE long-tail business, claims etc happen a long time after the beginning of the insurance contract, or take a long time to decide how much should be paid: ***Long-tail*** *pollution* ***claims*** *in the US may take decades to resolve.*

long-term *adj* [only before a noun] **1** long-term plans, aims etc are related to a long period of time into the future: *Boeing's predictions about long-term jet sales*

2 (the) long-term unemployed people who have not had a job for a long time: *a new law to extend jobless benefits for the long-term unemployed*

long-term credit —see under CREDIT[1]

long-term debt —see under DEBT

long-term funds —see under FUND[1]

long-term liabilities —see ***fixed liabilities*** under LIABILITY

long-term loan —see under LOAN[1]

long-term security —see under SECURITY

long-term unemployment —see under UNEMPLOYMENT

long ton —see under TON

look /lʊk/ *v*

look up *phr v* [I] if a situation is looking up, it is improving: *Things are looking up for High Street retailers.*

loop /luːp/ *n* [C] **1 in the loop** *informal* if a person is in the loop, he or she is one of the group of people who receive information about important subjects or who are involved in making important decisions
2 COMPUTING a set of commands in a computer program that are intended to be repeated again and again

loop·hole /ˈluːphəʊl‖-hoʊl/ *n* [C] a small mistake in a law that makes it possible to do something the law is supposed to prevent you from doing, or to avoid doing something that the law is supposed to make you do: *You can be sure that any **tax loopholes** will be exploited.* | *The Clinton administration moved to **close** the legal **loopholes** exempting government education programs from the requirements of the Bill.*

loose-leaf *adj* having loose pages that can be put in and removed easily: *a loose-leaf ledger* | *Filofaxes have a loose-leaf format.*

loot /luːt/ *n* [U] *informal old-fashioned* goods or money that have been stolen

loro account —see under ACCOUNT[1]

lor·ry /ˈlɒri‖ˈlɔːri, ˈlɑːri/ *n* plural **lorries** [C] *BrE* a large motor vehicle for carrying heavy goods; TRUCK: *a strike by **lorry drivers*** | *We now have a fleet of 65 lorries and 85 trailers.*

lose /luːz/ *v* past tense and past participle **lost** present participle **losing** [T] **1** to stop having something any more, or to have less of it: *The industry has lost 60,000 jobs.* | *After a boardroom battle, Dixon lost control of the company.* | *Europe is losing its competitive edge.*
2 to have less money than you had before or to spend more money than you are receiving: *We all **lost money** when the firm collapsed.* | *Small investors lost up to £100 million.* | *The group is estimated to have lost $36 million last year.* | *Her company may be losing $150 million a year in potential sales in Asia.* | *lost revenue* | *The resulting crisis of confidence lost the bank* (=caused the bank to lose) *£30 million in deposits.*
3 to fall to a lower figure or price: *In Tokyo, the Nikkei stock index lost 644.82 to close at 17,791.55.* | *British Aerospace lost 12p later in the day at 561p.*
4 to have something such as a contract or customers taken away by someone or something: *They **lost business** by not giving credit.* | *We started **losing customers** to cheaper rivals.* | *The big national chains were **losing market share** to independent one-person operations.* | *1.2 million man-days were lost to strikes.*
5 lose ground to become less in value or to lose an advantage: *Sterling lost ground against the German mark.* | *When the bid failed to appear, shares lost ground.*
6 lose your shirt to lose a lot of money, especially because of making a bad decision in business: *Lockheed stopped manufacturing commercial aircraft after it lost its shirt in 1981 with the Tristar.*
lose out *phr v* [I] to not get something such as a job, business contract, or profit because someone else gets it instead, or to not have an advantage that other competitors have: *Most shareholders lost out financially.* **+ on**: *British industry risks losing out on business opportunities.* **+ to**: *Lloyd's lost out to Commercial Union on a multi-million-pound contract from Trafalgar House.*

loss /lɒs‖lɔːs/ *n* **1** [C,U] the fact of no longer having something that you used to have
job loss [C,U] when people lose their jobs: *Job loss from the proposed merger could reach 20,000 or more.* | *The store closings will result in job losses for about 2,500 workers.*
2 [C] FINANCE when a business or part of a business spends more money than it receives in a particular period of time, or loses money on a particular deal, problem etc: *It had a loss of $22 million or $4.12 a share, on revenue of $33 million.* | *The toy company blamed the losses on poor retail sales.* | *British banks hit by **heavy losses** on bad loans* | *The bus company has had **huge losses** because of the drivers' strike.* | *There's no reason for us to operate **at a loss**.*
3 book/incur/post/take a loss to lose money and make a record of this in the accounts: *The unit **posted losses** for the past two years, hurt by the economic slump.*
actual loss [C] a real loss of money, not one that was calculated or estimated, nor a PAPER LOSS (=where there is no actual cash loss, for example when an asset falls in value but is not sold): *The bank's capital went to zero, but the actual loss there will be close to 12% of assets, or $2.5 billion.* | *By Dec. 18, it had changed that forecast to $254 million. The actual loss was $326 million.*
after-tax loss [C] a loss made by a company after tax has been calculated: *The bank posted an after-tax loss of A$35.3 million, compared with a year-earlier profit of A$71.8 million.*
annual loss [C] a loss over a whole year's activities, even if some parts of the year were profitable: *Analysts said the company could break its string of five consecutive years of annual losses.*
capital loss [C] a loss when an asset or investment loses value or is sold at a loss, especially in relation to the amount of tax payable: *The sale of Cerus's SGB stake will yield a capital loss of FFr1.2 billion.*
credit loss [C] a loss made by a financial institution on its lending activities; LOAN LOSS: *$40 million of the credit losses came from the devastated Arizona real estate market.*
exceptional loss also **extraordinary loss** [C] a loss relating to an unusual event that is not part of a company's normal operating activities, for example the sale of part of the company: *The sale of the company's printing unit resulted in an exceptional loss of £1.1 million.*
first-half loss [C] a loss relating to the first six months of a company's financial year: *They have announced a first-half loss, and cut their full-year forecast.*
full-year loss [C] a loss relating to the whole of a company's financial year, rather than to a three-month or six-month period: *Analysts are predicting a full-year loss of 100 billion lire this year, reflecting the industry-wide recession.*
loan loss [C] another name for CREDIT LOSS: *It is in the best interests of the company to increase the allowance for loan losses during these uncertain economic times.*
net loss [C] a loss taking account of any EXCEPTIONAL LOSSES: *The oil company reported a fourth-quarter net loss of $2 billion after a $2.05 billion charge related to a massive restructuring.*
one-time loss another name for EXCEPTIONAL LOSS: *The results includes a $48 million pretax charge to cover the cost of cutting 900 jobs, as well as some other one-time losses.*
operating loss [C] a loss relating to a company's normal business operations, rather than to activities such as asset sales that only happen from time to time: *Output at the mine was suspended earlier this year due to operating losses.*
paper loss [C] a loss in the value of an investment or of an asset in a company's accounts. A paper loss does not become an ACTUAL LOSS unless the investment or asset is sold
passive loss [C] TAX a loss made on some types of investment, such as on income from property
pre-tax loss [C] a loss made by a company before tax is calculated: *The network took pretax losses estimated at $275 million, and an after-tax loss of $170 million.*
quarterly loss [C] in the US, where companies announce their results every three months, a loss for a particular three-month period of a company's financial year: *The bank reported five big quarterly losses due to the growing loan problems.*
tax loss [C] a loss made deliberately by a business to avoid paying tax on profits, usually by bringing

forward capital spending to use up profits at the end of the tax year: *Mr. Milken pleaded guilty to helping create fraudulent tax losses.*

trading loss [C] ◆ a loss made on a financial market: *The bank suffered foreign-exchange trading losses of $420 million and the entire board and management were replaced.*

◆ another name for an OPERATING LOSS

underwriting loss [C] a loss by an insurance company on its insurance activities: *an underwriting loss of £187 million – £103 million from two hurricanes, and £84 million from marine losses*

4 [C] INSURANCE an event that causes a person or organization to make a claim on an insurance contract

actual total loss [C,U] a loss where the thing insured is stolen or totally destroyed; WRITE-OFF

constructive total loss [C,U] a loss where the thing insured, for example a ship, is not destroyed, but where the insurer is forced to leave it where it is. The thing insured then becomes the property of the insurer, who may be able to get it back and sell it

fire loss [C,U] a loss where property is destroyed or damaged in a fire: *The US has the worst rate of fire loss in the industrialized world.*

general average loss [C,U] a loss where the cost of damage to a ship or the goods it is carrying is shared by all the insurers, not just the insurer of the things actually damaged

partial loss also **particular average loss** [C,U] a loss where the thing insured is not totally lost or destroyed, and can be repaired

5 [C,U] LAW when a person or organization suffers or loses money because of the mistakes or NEGLIGENCE of another

loss adjuster —see under ADJUSTER

loss leader —see under LEADER

loss-making *adj* a loss-making product or business activity is one that does not make a profit: *Loss-making, state-owned businesses will be sold off.* —**loss-maker** *n* [C] *The plant has long been a loss-maker for Volvo.*

lost days *n* [plural] the number of working days that are lost because of STRIKES (=periods of time when workers stop working because of disagreements with employers): *Spain's figure of 677 lost days is an 11% increase, against the general trend.*

lost time —see under TIME

lot /lɒt‖lɑːt/ *n* [C] **1** something that is sold at an AUCTION, especially a group of things that are sold together: *Allsop's auction was a record sell-out, with all but two of 111 lots sold for a total of £6.3 million.*

2 a group of shares that are sold together

round lot a number of shares used as a standard unit when buying or selling shares on a stockmarket: *Orders must be round lots of at least 100 shares.*

3 a quantity of goods that is produced at the same time or sold together as a group: *Batch production is the production of standardised units in small or large lots.*

job lot a mixed group of things that are sold together: *He bought a job lot of washing machines for £2000.*

4 *especially AmE* PROPERTY an area of land, especially one used for building on: *a car lot*

vacant lot an area of land on which nothing has been built and which may be available to rent, buy, or build on: *The city's vacant lots are cluttered with old trucks and farm machinery.*

lot·te·ry /ˈlɒtəri‖ˈlɑː-/ *n* plural **lotteries** **1** [C] a game of chance in which people buy tickets with numbers on and some people win prizes. Lotteries are often used to raise money for the government or for a CHARITY: *The national lottery generates substantial additional funds for charities and other good causes.* | *a* ***lottery winner***

2 [singular] when what happens depends on chance or luck: *The stock market is too much of a lottery.*

low¹ /ləʊ‖loʊ/ *adj* **1** small, or smaller than usual, in amount or value: *City analysts have said the takeover offer is too low.* | *It is vital to keep your overhead costs as low as possible.* | *people on* ***low incomes*** | *a mortgage at a* ***low rate of interest***

2 below the usual level or degree: *a low-risk venture* | *a policy of low inflation*

3 below an acceptable standard or quality: *Safety standards in the industry are much too low.* | *Cost-cutting has led to a lower quality of service.*

4 a supply of something that is low is nearly finished: *Stocks are getting low.*

low² *n* [C usually singular] a low price or level: *Eurotunnel shares* ***fell to a low*** *of 550p.* | *Against the mark, sterling fell from 2.8505 to 2.8389, after* ***hitting a low*** *of 2.8280 at one stage.* | *Inflation is heading for* ***an all-time low.***

low-end *adj* [only before a noun] low-end products are the cheapest available in a company's range of products, or in a market in general: *the low-end PC market* —**low end** *n* [singular] *This model has been developed for the low end of the workstation market.*

low-end product —see under PRODUCT

lowest common denominator *n* [singular] *disapproving* used to talk about something that is popular with or approved of by the largest possible number of people, being something that is therefore of rather a low standard: *Many advertisements are clearly appealing to the lowest common denominator.*

low-grade *adj* **1** of low quality or poor standard: *Women were forced into part-time* ***low-grade jobs.*** | *low-grade steel*

2 FINANCE low-grade bonds, loans etc have a high risk of not being repaid: *low-grade debt issued by lower-rated companies in the junk bond market*

low-paid *adj* **1** earning only a small amount from your job: *people in* ***low-paid jobs***

2 the low-paid people in low-paid jobs: *We shall continue to reduce tax, especially for the low-paid.*

low-price also **low-priced** *adj* cheap in relation to other things of the same kind: *a series of new machines, ranging from top-of-the-line notebook computers to low-priced models*

low-rise *adj* [only before a noun] a low-rise building does not have many floors: *There is a common belief that* ***low-rise housing*** *will increase the urban sprawl.* —compare HIGH-RISE

low season —see under SEASON

low-tech *adj* not using the most modern machines or methods in business or industry: *Waste management, traditionally a* ***low-tech industry,*** *is being turned by the development of new technologies into something closer to chemical engineering.* —opposite HIGH-TECH

low-tech industry —see under INDUSTRY

loy·al /ˈlɔɪəl/ *adj* MARKETING if customers are loyal to a particular product, they continue to buy it and do not change to other products + **to**: *The chain is trying to appeal to customers loyal to other fast-food companies.*

loy·al·ty /ˈlɔɪəlti/ *n* [U] MARKETING the fact of being loyal to a particular product + **to**: *He has noticed a falloff in loyalty to particular brands of tires.*

brand loyalty the degree to which people regularly buy a particular BRAND of product and refuse to change to other brands: *There's no brand loyalty in car tyres – consumers just buy on price.*

loyalty bonus —see under BONUS

loyalty card —see under CARD

LP abbreviation for LIMITED PARTNERSHIP —see under PARTNERSHIP

LSE abbreviation for LONDON SCHOOL OF ECONOMICS

Ltd written abbreviation for LIMITED

lu•cra•tive /ˈluːkrətɪv/ *adj* an activity, project, job etc that is lucrative makes a lot of money: *a **lucrative contract** to distribute movies for Carolco Pictures Inc.* | *The change in bonus payments would be especially lucrative for top executives.*

lu•cre /ˈluːkə‖-ər/ *n* [U] *informal journalism* money: *She finally gets her chance at earning some **filthy lucre**.*

Lud•dite /ˈlʌdaɪt/ *n* [C] *disapproving* someone who is strongly opposed to using modern machinery and methods: *Luddites who insist on using traditional telephones*

luke•warm /ˌluːkˈwɔːm◂‖-ˈwɔːrm◂/ *adj* not showing much interest or excitement: *The market **reaction** to Tenneco's offering was **lukewarm**.* | *The proposal is expected to get a **lukewarm reception** from small businesses.*

lull¹ /lʌl/ *n* [C usually singular] a period of time during which there is very little buying, selling, spending etc taking place: *The bond market is slipping into a year-end lull.* | *The government's intends to resume privatization sales following a three-year lull.* + **in**: *an expected short-term lull in demand*

lull² *v* [T] to make someone feel confident and trusting so that they can be deceived or are not prepared for what happens: *Mrs. Hutson's clients say they were lulled by her easy-going manner.* **lull sb into sth**: *The markets were lulled last week into believing that a war could be avoided.* | *Some investors were **lulled into a false sense of security** made to feel that things are safe when they are not.*

lum•ber /ˈlʌmbə‖-ər/ *n* [U] wood that has been prepared for sale; TIMBER: *Wolohan operates 50 lumber and building material retail stores.*

lump¹ /lʌmp/ *n* **1 take the lumps** *informal AmE* to manage a difficult situation when things are not going well: *Despite its seemingly smooth expansion, VideoTech has taken a few lumps.*

2 the lump *BrE informal* used to talk about a system of employing workers in the building industry. Workers who are SELF-EMPLOYED are paid a fixed amount of money for each day, often in cash: *Some subcontractors expect to **be paid on the lump**.*

lump² *adj* **lump labour** *BrE* SELF-EMPLOYED workers in the building industry who are paid a fixed amount of money for each day, often in cash: *growth in the amount of lump labour employed in the construction industry*

lump sum —see under SUM¹

lunch /lʌntʃ/ *n* [C] **1** a meal eaten in the middle of the day: *facilities for conferences and private **business lunches*** (=when business people go to lunch to discuss things or entertain customers) | *He has **working lunches*** (=when you discuss business and eat) *with his team to develop their approach.* | *It is important that the office is manned during the **lunch hour*** (=the time when people eat lunch).

2 no free lunch *informal* used to say that something may seem free, but that you have to pay for it in the end: *The relevant issue is not whether taxes are higher in one state than another. The economic principle of 'no free lunch' applies – people get the services they pay for.*

3 three-martini lunch *informal* a lunch that is supposed to be a working lunch, but where people enjoy themselves too much to do any work: *Advertising men did anything their clients wanted them to and suffered an excess of three-martini lunches.*

lunch•break /ˈlʌntʃbreɪk/ *n* [C] the time in the middle of the day when people stop working to eat or have a rest: *We worked through our lunchbreak to get the job finished on time.*

lure /lʊə, ljʊə‖lʊr/ *v* [T] to attract customers, investment etc, especially by making a product or service sound very exciting, profitable etc: *Even with Oscar nominations to lure audiences, the films will face tough competition over the next few weeks from new releases.* **lure sb away**: *The company lured a Japanese executive away from Toshiba Corp. to run its Tokyo operations.* —**lure** *n* [C] *The entertainment lures at the casino include a light-show.*

lux•u•ry /ˈlʌkʃəri/ *n* plural **luxuries** **1** [C] something that is expensive and not really necessary but is pleasing and enjoyable: *luxuries such as a yacht and gold-plated bathroom fixtures*

2 luxury apartment/car/airline etc a very expensive and large apartment, car etc: *plans to build a tower of luxury condominium apartments* | *Hammacher has switched its major focus to luxury gift items.* | *Porsche, Saab and BMW are fierce competitors in the luxury car market.*

3 [U] great pleasure and enjoyment from large, beautiful, and expensive cars, houses etc: *The days when Americans paid any price for luxury are probably over.* —**luxurious** *adj*: *He runs his company, Silver Pictures, from a luxurious villa in Hollywood.* | *a luxurious yacht club in Florida*

luxury goods —see under GOODS

luxury market —see under MARKET¹

luxury tax —see under TAX¹

lynchpin *n* [C] another spelling of LINCHPIN

M

M written abbreviation for MOTORWAY: *junction 3 of the M42*

m written abbreviation for MALE; MARRIED; METRE(S); MILE(S); MILLION; MONTH

M & A abbreviation for MERGERS AND ACQUISITIONS (=when companies combine, or when one company buys another) as a financial activity, or the study of this in business schools

M0, M1, M2, M3, M4 —see under MONEY SUPPLY

Maas·tricht Trea·ty /ˌmɑːstrɪkt ˈtriːti, ˌmɑːstrixt-/ *n* the agreement in 1992 by member countries of the EUROPEAN UNION to prepare for closer economic union and the EURO

ma·chine[1] /məˈʃiːn/ *n* [C] a piece of equipment that uses power such as electricity to do a particular task: *Labour and machines are both at full capacity* (=doing as much work as they can) *in the production department.* | *a floppy disc for use on IBM PCs and compatible machines*

answering machine a machine connected to a telephone which records your telephone messages when you are not able to answer the telephone; ANSWERPHONE: *If I'm not in, leave a message on my answering machine.*

automated teller machine abbreviation **ATM** another name for CASH MACHINE

cancellation machine also **postal cancellation machine** *AmE* a machine that prints a special sign on envelopes to show that the cost of sending them by mail has been paid; franking machine *BrE*

cash machine also **cash dispenser** *especially BrE* a machine used by customers of a bank to take money out of their account, using a special card: *There are around 35,000 Eurocard cash machines in Europe.*

client machine COMPUTING one of several small computers connected to a large computer in a NETWORK: *Data is processed on the server before being delivered to the client machine.*

dictation machine a machine which records what you say so that someone can write it down later: *Sanyo dictation machines make good business sense as you can record letters and memos wherever you are.*

fax machine a machine that sends and receives FAXES

franking machine *BrE* a machine that prints a special sign on envelopes to show that the cost of sending them by mail has been paid; cancellation machine *AmE*

vending machine a machine from which you can get cigarettes, chocolate, drinks etc by putting money in: *Pepsi Co. decided not to invest in vending machines.*

machine[2] *v* [T] to make or shape something with a special machine: *Something like 60 tools may be used to machine a single item.* | *The cylinder covers are waiting to be machined.* —**machining** *n* [U] *Cranfield Precision Engineering are world leaders in diamond machining.*

machine language —see under LANGUAGE

machine readable *adj* machine-readable documents can be put into a special machine which reads and processes the information they contain: *The new passport will be machine-readable.*

ma·chin·e·ry /məˈʃiːnəri/ *n* [U] **1** equipment that uses power such as electricity or petrol: *agricultural machinery*

heavy machinery very large machines used in manufacturing, the building industry etc

office machinery equipment such as telephones, computers etc that are used in offices

2 a system or set of processes for doing something: *the machinery of government*

machine shop —see under SHOP[1]

machine tool —see under TOOL[1]

ma·chin·ist /məˈʃiːnɪ̈st/ *n* [C] someone who operates machines in a factory: *The settlement ends a nine-week strike by machinists.*

mac·ro /ˈmækrəʊ‖-roʊ/ *n* [C] COMPUTING a series of commands written to perform a particular task. Macros can be saved and used again: *Write a macro so that when a button is hit, all the fields appear on the spreadsheet.*

macro- /mækrəʊ‖-roʊ/ *prefix* very large and concerned with a whole system rather than just part of it: *A number of chapters are devoted to fiscal policy in a macro-context.*

mac·ro·ec·o·nom·ics· /ˌmækrəʊekəˈnɒmɪks,-iːkə-‖-kroʊekəˈnɑː-,-iːkə-/ *n* [U] the study of the economy of a whole area, for example a whole country or the whole of a particular industry: *The influence of macroeconomics dominates the policy-making of a majority of the world's governments.* —compare MICROECONOMICS —**macroeconomic** *adj* [only before a noun] *macroeconomic analysis* —**macroeconomist** *n* [C] *Most macroeconomists agree it is foolish to move rapidly between high and low rates of monetary growth.*

Mad·am /ˈmædəm/ *n* **1** a polite way of addressing a woman, such as a customer in a shop: *Can I help you Madam?*

2 Dear Madam used at the beginning of a business letter to a woman whose name you do not know

3 Madam chairman/ambassador/president etc the title used when addressing a woman who has an important position

Mad·i·son Av·e·nue /ˌmædɪ̈sən ˈævenjuː‖-nuː/ *n* the street in New York where many advertising and PUBLIC RELATIONS agencies have offices, used also to talk about the US advertising and public relations industry as a whole: *Lowe & Partners' announcement put an end to months of speculation on Madison Avenue.*

mag /mæg/ *informal n* [C] a magazine

mag·a·log /ˈmægəlɒg‖-lɑːg, -lɒːg/ *n* [C] a magazine used by a company to advertise and sell its products, especially by MAIL ORDER: *fashion magalogs*

mag·a·zine /ˌmægəˈziːn‖ˈmægəziːn/ *n* [C] a large thin book containing news, articles, photographs etc which is produced weekly or monthly: *A Time spokesman said the magazine had a weekly circulation* (=the number of copies sold) *of four million.* | *the success of **magazine advertising***

inhouse magazine also **house magazine** a free magazine produced for the people who work in a particular organization; NEWSLETTER: *The chairman's overseas trips are a regular feature in the in-house magazine.*

trade magazine a magazine that deals with a particular industry or business activity: *the trade magazine 'Corporate Finance'*

ma·gis·trate /ˈmædʒɪ̈streɪt, -strɪ̈t/ *n* [C] someone who judges less serious crimes in a court of law: *District Judge J. Lee Sarokin overturned a magistrate's decision that the documents should remain confidential.* | *He filed a suit* (=brought a case to court) *in the **magistrate's court** seeking damages.*

stipendiary magistrate a magistrate in Britain who is paid by the state

M

ma·glev /ˈmæglev/ *n* [C] an advanced type of train which runs on a special track: *The prototype maglev has notched top speeds of 320 mph.*

mag·nate /ˈmægneɪt, -nət/ *n* [C] a very powerful and rich person who owns a large company or group of companies: *the media magnate Rupert Murdoch*

magnetic ink character recognition —see under RECOGNITION

magnetic media *n* [plural] COMPUTING methods of storing information for computers, using MAGNETIC tapes or disks (=ones made from a material that attract metals): *Prudential has made recent gains in its medical, consumer and magnetic media product lines.*

magnetic tape —see under TAPE

maid·en /ˈmeɪdn/ *adj* [only before a noun] involving something that is being done for the first time: *Maiden bond issues* (=the first occasions when they have sold bonds) *expected this year include Ukraine and Uzbekistan.* | *the maiden launch of the Pegasus rocket*

mail[1] /meɪl/ *n* **1** [singular, U] the system of collecting or delivering letters, packages etc; POST *BrE*: *Your cheque is **in the mail*** (=I have mailed it to you and it is on its way). | *Do not send cash **through the mail**.* | *Dell sells its computers **by mail**.*

2 [U] the letters, packages etc that are sent to a particular person at a particular time: *The first thing he does when he arrives in the office is **check his mail**.* | *My secretary sorts through the **incoming mail*** (=mail being received). | *All **outgoing mail*** (=mail being sent) *must have a stamp on it.* | *a sorting machine that processes **first-class mail*** (=letters sent by the fastest normal mail service) *by ZIP code*

business reply mail [U] *AmE* a system that allows members of the public to return mail to a company without paying. The cost is paid by the company; BUSINESS REPLY SERVICE *BrE*

certified mail [U] *AmE* a postal service which, for an additional payment, provides proof that a letter or package has been posted and delivered; RECORDED DELIVERY *BrE*: *All replies must be sent by certified mail.*

direct mail [U] MARKETING advertisements that are sent to people in the post, often people who have been chosen because they might be interested in the product: *Over 3 billion items of direct mail were sent through the post last year* | *a direct mail campaign aimed at US small businesses*

junk mail [U] *disapproving* letters and advertising material that you receive through the mail without asking for it

registered mail [U] *AmE* a postal service which, for an additional payment, protects the sender of a valuable letter or package against loss and damage; REGISTERED POST *BrE*

snail mail [U] *informal* mail sent through the normal mail service, rather than by E-MAIL

surface mail [U] mail that is sent by ship, train, or road, rather than by air: *If you do not write 'airmail' on the envelope, the letter will **be sent surface mail**.* —compare AIRMAIL

3 [C,U] messages sent by E-MAIL: *Have you **read your mail** yet?* | *I got five mails this morning.*

electronic mail [U] a system that allows people to send messages to each other by computer; E-MAIL: *Staff communicate with each other via electronic mail.*

voice mail [U] an electronic system on your telephone that lets you leave messages for people who phone you when you are not available, and lets them leave messages for you: *With voice mail, if a guest is out, callers can leave recorded messages rather than be put through again to a hotel operator.*

mail[2] *v* [T] **1** *AmE* to send a letter or package to someone; POST *BrE*: *The letter was mailed last Thursday.*

2 to send someone a message by electronic mail: *You can phone, fax, or mail me at the office.*

mail·box /ˈmeɪlbɒks‖-bɑːks/ *n* [C] *AmE* **1** a box, usually outside a house, where someone's mail is delivered or collected

2 a container where you put letters that you want to send; POSTBOX *BrE*

mail drop *n* [C] *AmE* **1** an address where someone's mail is delivered, which is not where they live

2 a box in a post office where your mail can be left

mail·er /ˈmeɪlə‖-ər/ *n* [C] **1** a piece of advertising material designed to be sent by mail: *The marketing plan could include sending mailers to likely purchasers.*

2 a person or organization that sends mail, especially in large quantities: *Big corporate mailers try to get discounts from the U.S. Postal Service.*

3 *especially AmE* a container or envelope used for sending something small by mail; POSTAL PACKET *BrE*

mail·ing /ˈmeɪlɪŋ/ *n* [C] when information or advertising material is sent through the mail to a large number of people at one time, or the information or advertising material sent in this way; MAILSHOT *BrE*: *Tick this box if you do not wish to receive mailings from other companies.* | *She follows up the mailings with phone calls.*

mailing list —see under LIST[1]

mail merge *n* [C] COMPUTING when you use a special computer program to combine information from a list of names and addresses and some other document, so that the document can be printed with the names and addresses from the list: *You can send personalized faxes by **doing a mail merge**.* —**mail merge** *v* [I,T] *You can mail merge your documents with Word.*

mail order *n* [U] a method of buying and selling in which the buyer chooses goods at home, either from a CATALOGUE (=a book containing pictures and descriptions of goods for sale) or from the INTERNET, and has them sent to their home: *I buy most of my software **by mail order**.* | *a **mail-order catalogue*** | *a **mail-order house*** (=a company that sends goods direct from a warehouse to customers) | *Mail order is used mainly for clothing, but also for leather goods and small electrical appliances.* —**mail order** *v* [I,T] *CD ROMs can be mail ordered too.*

mail order catalogue —see under CATALOGUE[1]

mail room —see ***post room*** under ROOM[1]

mail·shot /ˈmeɪlʃɒt‖-ʃɑːt/ *n* [C] *BrE* when information or advertising material is sent through the mail to a large number of people at one time, or the information or advertising material sent in this way; MAILING: *I received a mailshot telling me I had won a free holiday.*

main·frame /ˈmeɪnfreɪm/ *n* [C] a large powerful computer that can do many complicated jobs very fast and that a lot of people can use at the same time. Users are connected to the mainframe through TERMINALS: *a network of computers linked to a mainframe* | *This database will be held in the **mainframe computer** at Cambridge University.*

mainframe computer —see under COMPUTER

main·land /ˈmeɪnlənd, -lænd/ *n* **the mainland** the main area of land that forms a country, rather than the islands near to it that are also part of it: *Continental Airlines serves Hawaii from the mainland.* —**mainland** *adj* [only before a noun] *contract labourers from mainland China*

main market —see under MARKET[1]

main memory —see under MEMORY

main·stay /ˈmeɪnsteɪ/ *n* [C usually singular] the most important part of something, that makes it possible for it to be successful or to continue to exist + **of**: *Northern cod was **the mainstay of** the Newfoundland economy, accounting for 21% of all jobs.* | *Polythene and PVC had*

M

been two of ICI's ***mainstay products*** (=most important products).

main•stream¹ /ˈmeɪnstriːm/ *n* **1 the mainstream of sth** the most usual way of doing something or thinking about something: *Depression-era laws have kept banks out of the mainstream of financial change.*
2 the mainstream the people whose ideas about a subject are shared by most people and regarded as normal: *He told readers he was trying to move the newspaper out of the opposition into the mainstream.*

mainstream² *adj* **1** relating to the most frequent or usual way of doing or thinking about something: *Thorn has been selling interests that it considers to be outside its* ***mainstream businesses.*** | *Compaq won't try to compete with Hewlett in the* ***mainstream market*** *for laser printers.*
2 suitable for normal people, rather than for a particular section of society: *They made AnnTaylor clothes less high-fashion and more mainstream.*

main•tain /meɪnˈteɪn, mən-/ *v* [T] **1** to make something continue in the same way or at the same high standard as before: *It is impossible to maintain exports at past levels.* | *To maintain sales growth, the company plans to unveil a new line of bicycles.*
2 to keep something such as a building or machine in good condition by taking care of it: *The National Rivers Authority is responsible for controlling pollution in coastal waters and maintaining sea walls.*
3 to provide someone with money, food, and the other things they need: *the ever-increasing cost of maintaining children*

main•te•nance /ˈmeɪntənəns/ *n* [U] **1** the repairs, painting etc necessary to keep something in good condition or working as it should: *The line will be re-opened once* ***essential maintenance*** *is completed.* | *Technicians were doing* ***routine maintenance work*** *on the aircraft.*
2 when something is continued in the same way or at the same level as before + **of**: *The maintenance of economic growth is very important.*
resale price maintenance a system in which the price of goods is fixed by the manufacturer and the person selling them is not allowed to reduce the price. Resale-price maintenance is against the law in some countries, including the US, because it limits competition: *lawsuits alleging resale-price maintenance*
3 money paid by a DIVORCED person (=someone who has legally ended their marriage) to their former wife or husband, especially towards the cost of keeping their children; CHILD SUPPORT *BrE*, ALIMONY *AmE*: *He has to* ***pay*** *£500 per week* ***maintenance*** *to his ex-wife.*

ma•jor¹ /ˈmeɪdʒə‖-ər/ *adj* **1** [only before a noun] very large or important when compared with other companies, countries, activities etc of a similar kind: *a* ***major*** *New York* ***bank*** | *a meeting of the seven* ***major industrialized nations*** | *The company is currently undergoing a major restructuring.*
2 very serious: *Ford's* ***major problem*** *was its reliance on the big UK market.* | *There are no major safety concerns with this product.*

major² *n* [C usually plural] a very important company in a particular industry: *The majors are taking market share away from smaller companies.* | *the* ***Hollywood majors*** | *the* ***Japanese oil majors***

ma•jor•i•ty¹ /məˈdʒɒrəti‖məˈdʒɔː-, məˈdʒɑː-/ *n* plural **majorities 1** [singular] most of the people or things in a particular group: *Some franchisees quit, but* ***the majority*** *are still hanging on.* + **of**: *The majority of successful entrepreneurs have a clear mission statement.* | *The* ***vast majority*** *of new radio shows fail in their first season on the air.*
2 [C] the difference between the number of votes gained by the winning party or person in an election and the number of votes gained by the other parties or people: *No single party is likely to* ***win a majority.*** | *The resolution was passed* ***by a majority*** *of votes.*
absolute majority [singular] when a party or person wins more than half of the total votes in an election: *If the candidate obtains an absolute majority, he is appointed Chancellor by the Federal President.*
3 [U] LAW the age at which someone legally becomes a responsible adult: *The Family Law Reform Act 1969 reduced* ***the age of majority*** *to 18.*

majority² *adj* [only before a noun] used to say that a someone owns more than half the shares in a company: *Apax will hold a* ***majority stake*** *in the new company.* | *Vernes and Gardini teamed up to* ***take majority control*** *of French portfolio investment company Société Centrale d'Investissements.* | *the bank's* ***majority shareholder***

majority interest —see under INTEREST

majority ownership —see under OWNERSHIP

majority shareholding —see under SHAREHOLDING

majority stake —see under STAKE¹

major-league *adj* [only before a noun] important or influential: *Mr. Lawrence was a major-league market professional.*

make¹ /meɪk/ *v* past tense and past participle **made** present participle **making** [T] **1** to produce something by working or by using industrial processes: *Robbins & Myers makes and sells pumps and motors.* | *a label on the toy read '****made in*** *Taiwan'*
2 to earn or get money: *The purpose of this business is to* ***make money.*** | *He expects to make $100,000 this year.*
3 make a living (doing sth) to earn the money you need to live: *He makes a good living selling used cars.*
4 make a profit/loss to make more or less money than you spend: *The company made a pretax profit of £309,000.*
5 make a market FINANCE if a financial institution makes a market in particular shares etc, it has them available for people and organizations to buy at all times: *Security Pacific Corp. said it would no longer make a market in government securities.* —see also MARKET-MAKER
6 make good if you make good on a promise or loan, you do what you promised or give back money that you owed: *How does Honda plan to make good its pledge?* + **on**: *Pirelli intends to make good on any trading losses by its allies.*
7 make it (big) to be successful in a particular activity or business: *This is a tough business, but I hope you make it.* | *Mr. Bonds failed in efforts to* ***make it big*** *in Los Angeles.*
8 make or break to cause either great success or complete failure: *In a small country such as the Netherlands, exports can make or break a recession.* | *This is a make-or-break year for us.*
make out *phr v* **1 make out a cheque/bill etc** to write a cheque, bill etc so that it can be paid to someone: *Can you make the cheque out to me?*
2 [I] *AmE* to succeed or progress in a particular way: *How did you make out at the interview?*
make sth ↔ **over** *phr v* [T] to officially and legally give money or property to someone: *He made over his share in the estate in return for $10,000 cash.*
make up sth *phr v* [T] **1** to combine together to form a particular total or result: *Plastic bags now make up 60% of all bags used in grocery stores.*
2 to prepare something: *Your accountant will make up your accounts and prepare your tax return.*

make² *n* [C] **1** a particular name for a product, made by a particular company; BRAND: *The goods were the manufacturer's* ***own make.*** + **of**: *Array's devices can work with many different makes of computer.*
2 be on the make *informal* to be always trying to get an advantage for yourself

M

make·good /ˈmeɪkgʊd/ *n* [C usually plural] MARKETING an occasion when a television company has to broadcast an advertisement without payment, because it has not been seen by the number of people originally promised: *If CBS fails to deliver the guaranteed numbers, it would be forced to provide so-called makegoods, giving free spots to sponsors on later programs.*

make-or-buy *adj* a make-or-buy decision involves deciding whether to make a product yourself or to have it made for you by a supplier: *Employers are making tough make-or-buy decisions about nearly everything they do.*

make·o·ver /ˈmeɪkəʊvə‖-oʊvər/ *n* [C] *journalism* a process of making big changes to a product or company to improve its image and encourage more people to buy the product or invest in the company: *As part of a makeover this year, Waterford Wedgwood appointed a new chairman.* | *Analysts have pointed to the sliding sales of the brand and say it needs a complete* ***marketing makeover***. | *India's* ***economic makeover***.

mak·er /ˈmeɪkə‖-ər/ *n* [C] also **makers** a company that makes products: *Sony, one of the world's biggest makers of portable audio equipment* | *Japanese* ***car makers*** *are rushing to make themselves more competitive.*

mal·ad·min·i·stra·tion /ˌmælədmɪnəˈstreɪʃən/ *n* [U] *BrE formal* careless or dishonest management: *Accusations of waste, maladministration and inefficiency have been made.*

mal·a fi·de /ˌmælə ˈfaɪdi‖ˌmeɪlə-/ *adv* LAW used to describe an action that is intended to deceive: *We need to ensure that decisions are not made mala fide.* —**mala fide** *adj*: *mala fide abuse of position* —opposite BONA FIDE

mal·feas·ance /mælˈfiːzəns/ *n* [U] *formal especially AmE* illegal activity: *The Association of Certified Fraud Examiners teaches accountants how to detect financial malfeasance.*

ma·li·cious /məˈlɪʃəs/ *adj* LAW intended to harm or hurt someone: *Time Warner sued Pathé Communications for $100 million, charging 'willful, wanton and malicious' breach of contract.* | *You may not be insured for* ***malicious damage*** (=deliberate damage) *by a lodger.* —**maliciously** *adv*: *Jones was charged with maliciously wounding his wife.*

ma·lin·ger /məˈlɪŋgə‖-ər/ *v* [I] to avoid work by pretending to be ill: *We need to discourage employees from malingering but provide help for those who are genuinely sick.* —**malingerer** *n* [C] *strict screening of applicants to keep out malingerers and criminals*

mall /mɔːl, mæl‖mɒːl/ *n* [C] *especially AmE* also **shopping mall** a large area where there are lots of shops, usually a covered area where cars cannot go

strip mall *AmE* a group of shops and other businesses along a main road, where customers can get to each shop directly from the road: *Many older retailers are in deteriorating strip malls, and cannot afford space in newer, more fashionable malls.*

mal·prac·tice /ˌmælˈpræktəs/ *n* [C,U] when someone breaks the rules of their profession or breaks the law in order to gain some advantage for themselves: *Edelman accused the attorneys of legal malpractice.* | *Insider trading is one of the many malpractices that needs to be stopped.*

man /mæn/ *v* past tense and past participle **manned** present participle **manning** [T] if a person or group mans a vehicle, place, or system, they work there or operate the system: *He has opened an office manned by two of his sons.* | *Can you man the phones* (=answer any telephone calls) *for an hour?* —see also MANNING, FRONT MAN, HALF-COMMISSION MAN, HATCHET MAN, REPO MAN, RIGHT-HAND MAN, VAT MAN

man·age /ˈmænɪdʒ/ *v* **1** [I,T] to direct or control a business, part of a business, or the people who work in it: *He will be managing a staff of about 1,500.* | *The unions had undermined the employers' ability to manage.*
2 [T] FINANCE if a financial institution manages someone's money, it decides when and where to invest it: *investors who use trading advisers to manage their money in futures markets* | *professionally managed pension funds*

managed fund —see under FUND[1]

man·age·ment /ˈmænɪdʒmənt/ *n* [U] **1** the activity or skill of directing and controlling the work of a company or organization: *In banking as in every other business,* ***good management*** *is essential.* | *She blames the industry's difficulties on* ***bad management***. | *He hasn't been on the job long enough to establish his own distinct* ***management style*** (=way of managing).

facilities management the activity of running particular business or industrial processes, factories etc: *A* ***facilities management contract*** *with Picard Surgeles will automate distribution.*

human resource management abbreviation **HRM** the work of employing, training, and helping the people who work in an organization: *The human resource management policies of Japanese firms created well-trained workforces committed to the company's aims.*

line management the direct management of workers in manufacturing or service operations: *Her only experience in line management at Kodak was as general manager of the instant photography unit.*

participative management a style of management where employees take part in management decisions: *Participative management is preferred: nearly 60% of companies said improving employee participation is a priority.*

quality management also **total quality management**, abbreviation **TQM** the management of systems in a company to make sure that each department is working in the most effective way and in order to improve the quality of the goods produced or services provided: *We need to look at improving our quality management systems.*

2 the people who are in charge of a particular company or organization at different levels, rather than ordinary employees: *Management is finding ways to cut costs and improve revenue.* | *The entire* ***management team*** *will be restructured, as six senior vice president positions will be cut.* | *The management are blaming workers for the decision.*

high-level management another name for TOP MANAGEMENT: *Mr Huston's appointment as president is the latest in a series of high-level management changes at the chain.*

junior management managers at the lowest level: *In a large organisation, many of the tasks of junior management are routine and boring.*

middle management managers between senior management and junior management: *Eliminating a layer of middle management, will move the decision-making process closer to the customer.* —compare ***marzipan layer*** under LAYER

senior management the most important managers in an organization: *Glaxo reorganized its senior management to help focus responsibility for operations.*

top management also **top-level management** the person or people in charge of an organization: *Shell announced several top-level management changes, including the retirement of the president.*

3 the people who are in charge of a particular activity in a company or organization and the skills and knowledge needed for their particular job: *Should* ***marketing management*** *be involved in specifying detailed advertising copy?* | *With* ***personnel management*** *more accepted,* *it is easier for managers to leave recruitment to specialists.* | *The principle of **human resource management** is seeing people as an asset.* | *Mr Hanna spent 14 years with IBM in sales, marketing and **general management*** (=not connected to any particular activity).

4 the activity of controlling and dealing with something: *the management of resources, including fish stocks and oil*

asset management ◆ the managing of money for investment so that it makes as much profit as possible, for a financial institution or for another person or organization: *US Trust Corp. specializes in asset management and private banking.*

◆ the managing of a company's property so that it is used in a way that makes as much profit as possible: *As part of its plan to increase its ability to manage properties, Citicorp has already opened new asset management offices.*

brand management the way in which a company tries to control its brands and the way people think about them: *The Persil Power controversy showed up weaknesses in Unilever's brand management skills.*

cash management ◆ the activity of managing how a company deals with its cash, how quickly it gets paid by customers, pays its suppliers etc: *There has been improved efficiency with more strict cash management practices.*

◆ services offered by a bank to its customers for managing their money in a way that makes as much profit as possible: *a cash management account for individual investors*

crisis management the skill or process of dealing with an unusually difficult or dangerous situation: *He is terrific at crisis management, but he is no good when it comes to running a settled organization.*

database management the way an organization manages the information held on its computers, and the software that does this: *a software program used to link database management systems to the company's desktop publishing package*

event management ◆ the organizing of large events such as conferences and concerts: *She joins the company from Wembley, having spent 13 years in event management.*

◆ MARKETING the organizing of a special event as part of a programme of marketing activities

investment management another name for ASSET MANAGEMENT

knowledge management abbreviation **KM** the way a company organizes and makes available to its employees the information it uses in order to function efficiently: *The bank will invest in a knowledge management system, using an intranet to share information in the organisation.*

money management another name for CASH MANAGEMENT or INVESTMENT MANAGEMENT: *The bank will now have all its investment management activities under one executive.*

portfolio management the managing of a group of different types of investments, paying attention to the risk and profits of each in relation to the rest

property management also **real estate management** *AmE* the managing of property such as land and buildings as investments so that they produce as much profit as possible

risk management ◆ INSURANCE the managing of the risks related to a company's activities in a way that limits possible financial losses, for example by obtaining the best types of insurance for the risks involved: *Talk to our risk management department about your company's current management of illnesses and accidents.*

◆ FINANCE the managing of investments in ways that produce as much profit as possible while limiting the danger of losses

time management the activity or skill of controlling the way you spend your time in order to work as effectively as possible: *I was sent on a time management course.*

treasury management another name for CASH MANAGEMENT: *Companies should review treasury management to seek lower borrowing costs.*

management accounting —see under ACCOUNTING

management board —see under BOARD[1]

management buy-in —see under BUY-IN

management buyout —see under BUYOUT

management by objectives abbreviation **MBO** *n* [U] the activity of controlling an activity and measuring performance in relation to particular aims: *Management by objectives works well at lower levels of the organization where tasks are well defined.*

management by walking about also **management by wandering about**, abbreviation **MBWA** *n* [U] *informal* the idea that managers can manage in the best way by visiting the places where operations are carried out and by talking to employees: *You have to see things first hand* (=for yourself). *I suppose it's called management by walking about.*

management charge —see under CHARGE[1]

management committee —see under COMMITTEE

management company —see under COMPANY

management control —see under CONTROL[1]

management development —see under DEVELOPMENT

management fee —see under FEE

management game —see under GAME

management guru —see under GURU

management information system —see under SYSTEM

management science *n* [U] the name for studies in management at some universities and business schools: *He is professor of management science at the University of British Columbia.*

management share —see under SHARE

management training —see under TRAINING

man·ag·er /ˈmænɪdʒə‖-ər/ *n* [C] someone whose job is to manage all or part of a company or organization, or a particular activity: *The life of a manager is a lot more difficult now than 10 years ago.* | *a restructuring designed to give **top managers** more control over operations* | *a cost-cutting program in which more than 20 **middle managers** and **senior managers** have been fired*

account manager someone who deals with a particular client or group of clients, especially in a bank or ADVERTISING AGENCY: *Ask how many customers each account manager is responsible for.*

assistant manager someone who helps another manager, does their work when they are not there etc: *Once the assistant manager proves he's adept at training others, he may advance to store manager.*

bank manager ◆ someone in charge of a bank BRANCH (=office where customers can go that is not its main office): *My bank manager is very understanding.*

◆ someone who works in the central management of a bank: *Most international bank managers looked for ways to reduce their Latin American exposure in the 1980s.*

branch manager someone in charge of a particular place that is not the main office of a bank, shop in a CHAIN of shops etc: *He joined nine years ago as a teller and worked his way up to branch manager.*

brand manager someone in a company responsible for developing and selling one particular brand of product: *He joined British Airways as brand manager for Club Europe.*

M

business manager ♦ a person whose job is to manage and control the financial activities of a company, organization, or part of an organization: *Most of these orders come from business managers in the industrial towns of the Midlands.*
♦ a person whose job is to manage the business affairs of an actor, musician etc: *After the success of Midnight Cowboy, Dustin hired a business manager.*
commercial manager a manager involved with business activities of a company, especially dealing with customers, rather than with other activities
file manager COMPUTING a computer program that lists all the files and DIRECTORIES on a system and shows you where they can be found: *You can flip back to the File Manager using Alt+Esc.*
fund manager someone whose job is to manage a particular type of investment for a financial institution or its clients; investment manager: *A fund manager who holds lots of equities may want to sell right now.*
general manager a manager who has a wide range of management skills, rather than one special skill: *He is general manager of Panasonic's VHS division.*
human resources manager another name for PERSONNEL MANAGER: *The human resources manager said, "Every effort is being made to help find alternative employment for those affected by the layoffs."*
investment manager someone whose job is to manage investments for a financial institution or its clients; fund manager: *If the investment manager picks the right mix of bonds, his total return should rise quickly.*
line manager a manager who is directly in charge of producing goods or providing services, and who works most closely with ordinary employees: *We must give more authority to line managers to make operations more responsive to customers.*
money manager another name for INVESTMENT MANAGER
personnel manager a manager who is in charge of taking care of a company's employees, organizing recruitment, training etc: *Personnel managers say that Europe has a shortage of good senior executives who are willing to move.*
plant manager a manager who is in charge of a particular factory: *Plant managers are in the best position to set safety standards at each plant.*
portfolio manager an INVESTMENT MANAGER with a group of different types of investments, who tries to balance the risks and profits of each in relation to the rest
product manager a manager in a company who is responsible for the development and marketing of a particular product: *Microsoft's product manager for advanced operating systems*
production manager a manager who is in charge of making materials or goods: *a production manager at the company's Paul Masson vineyard*
project manager a person or organization responsible for a particular piece of work that will create something new or improve a situation
property manager also **real estate manager** *AmE* someone whose job is to manage property such as land and buildings as investments so that they produce as much profit as possible: *Real-estate managers are in the best position of anyone to accurately estimate a property's value.*
research manager ♦ in a manufacturing company, a manager whose job is to develop new products: *Hammacher's research manager said its new cordless telephone defeated 10 others in tests for sound quality and range.*
♦ in a financial institution, a manager whose job is to study the profitability of investments: *Oil remains the main influence in stocks, said Ted Eggert, equity research manager at the bank.*
sales manager someone in charge of a company's selling activities, and the people whose job is to sell its products
trading manager a manager who is in charge of the people who buy and sell investments at a financial institution —see also ***lead manager*** under LEAD-MANAGE

man·ag·er·ess /ˌmænɪdʒəˈres‖ˈmænɪdʒərəs/ *n* [C] *BrE old-fashioned* a woman who is in charge of a business such as a shop or restaurant

man·a·ge·ri·al /ˌmænəˈdʒɪəriəl‖-ˈdʒɪr-/ *adj* connected with the job of being a manager: *She lacked **managerial experience** and didn't get the job.* | *It was a clear case of **managerial incompetence*** (=bad management). | *a **managerial position** with a top law firm*

managing agent —see under AGENT

managing director —see under DIRECTOR

managing partner —see under PARTNER

management ratio —see under RATIO

man·date[1] /ˈmændeɪt/ *n* [C] **1** the right and the power to carry out certain actions that is given to a government or elected official **mandate to do sth**: *The re-election of the present board of directors gives them a clear mandate to go forward with current corporate plans.* | *States are under a **federal mandate*** (=a right given by the central US government) *to increase fines for violation of worker safety and health rules.* | *The board has acted with a clear **shareholder mandate*** (=authority given by shareholders).
2 the right and power to carry out certain policies, received by a government or elected official after winning an election + **for**: *The election result was a mandate for all our policies.* **mandate to do sth**: *Mrs Thatcher was elected in 1979 with a mandate to cut public spending.*
3 the period of time that a politician or elected official has their position: *the day President Mobutu's mandate came to an end*

man·date[2] /mænˈdeɪt/ *v* [T] **1** to give an official order that something must be done: *The German system shows that it is possible to mandate universal health insurance through a variety of individual plans.* **mandate sb to do sth**: *economists mandated to produce periodic reports on the state of the economy*
2 to give someone the right or power to do something: *The SEC is mandated by Congress to set accounting rules for US corporations.*
3 *AmE* to make something mandatory **mandate sb to do sth**: *legislation that mandates employers to provide time off* **mandate that**: *Amendments to the Fair Housing Law mandated that all new housing must be accessible to the handicapped.* —**mandator** *n* [C] *Federal mandators and state governments seemed to be competing to see who could increase the cost of car ownership faster.*

man·da·to·ry /ˈmændətəri‖-tɔːri/ *adj* something that is mandatory must be done, usually because the law or an official rule says so; COMPULSORY; OBLIGATORY: *They face mandatory retirement at age 65 under Tenneco's policy.* | *mandatory testing of car-exhaust systems*

mandatory injunction —see under INJUNCTION

maneuver the US spelling of MANOEUVRE

man-hour *n* [C] the amount of work done by one person in one hour: *General Motors budgets for 30.3 man-hours to build a car.*

man·i·fest /ˈmænəfest/ *n* [C] an official list of the goods being carried on a ship or aircraft: *computerized cargo manifests* | *Before each international flight, computers scan the **passenger manifest*** (=the list of passengers travelling on a ship or aircraft).

ma·nip·u·late /məˈnɪpjəleɪt/ *v* [T] **1** to make someone or something behave in the way you want, using skilful and often dishonest methods **manipulate sb to do sth**:

Companies manipulate consumers to buy their products through advertising. | *This was a deliberate attempt to* ***manipulate the market*** (=buy and sell shares to make the market seem active when it is not) | *activities designed to* ***manipulate*** (=change **the price of**) *soybean contracts*

2 to process or operate something that needs a lot of skill, for example technical information or a complicated piece of equipment: *Computer analysis allows researchers to manipulate data in many different ways.* | *software for storing and manipulating images*

ma·nip·u·la·tion /məˌnɪpjəˈleɪʃən/ *n* [C,U] when someone makes someone or something behave in the way they want, using skilful and often dishonest methods: *Regulators work to prevent financial fraud and manipulation of accounting rules.* | *insider trading and other market manipulations*

share manipulation also **stock manipulation** [U] FINANCE when someone tries to influence the price of a company's shares in an illegal or unfair way for their own advantage: *In the stock manipulation scheme, he caused the price of the stock to close at a certain level, so the company could sell its stake at a more advantageous price.*

man·ning /ˈmænɪŋ/ *adj* relating to the number of workers in a particular industry or company, or that do a particular job: ***Manning levels*** *are decided by chief executives.* | *an analysis of manning requirements* —**manning** *n* [U] *a trade union dispute about manning*

ma·noeu·vre[1] *BrE*, **maneuver** *AmE* /məˈnuːvə‖-ər/ *v* [I,T] to use clever and often dishonest methods to make something happen or to make someone do what you want **manoeuvre to do sth**: *The Agnellis had not maneuvered to block Nestlé's bid.* **manoeuvre sb into (doing) sth**: *Not everyone quits jobs voluntarily – some are manoeuvered into it.* —**manoeuvring** *n* [U] *The general's resignation will be the result of months of* ***political manoeuvring****.*

manoeuvre[2] *BrE*, **maneuver** *AmE* —*n* [C,U] a skilful or carefully planned action, often a dishonest one, to achieve a particular result: *Whatever maneuvers the big soda pop companies make affect the smaller companies as well.* | *You will have more* ***room for manoeuvre*** (=possible courses of action) *if you have avoided agreeing to specific restraints.*

man·pow·er /ˈmænˌpaʊə‖-ˌpaʊr/ *n* [U] all the workers available for a particular kind of work in a particular area: *Economic expansion has created serious* ***manpower shortages*** *in the country.* | *We don't have the manpower to open up any more offices.*

man·u·al[1] /ˈmænjuəl/ *adj* **1** using your hands and your physical strength or abilities, rather than your mind: *He did all kinds of* ***manual work****.* | *A shortage of* ***manual labor*** (=people who do manual work) *is keeping wages and inflation high.* | *a low-paid* ***manual worker***

2 operated or done by hand or without the help of power in the form of electricity etc: *The new system will automate many manual tasks.* | *a* ***manual typewriter***

manual[2] *n* [C] a book giving instructions on how to operate a machine, piece of equipment etc: *Consult the manufacturer's* ***instruction manual****.* | *a two-inch-thick* ***training manual***

manual worker —see under WORKER

man·u·fac·ture[1] /ˌmænjəˈfæktʃə‖-ər/ *v* [T] to produce large quantities of goods to be sold, using machinery: *Nike started as a small company manufacturing running shoes.* **manufacture sth from sth**: *Drawers are manufactured from solid beech hardwood.* | *Imports of* ***manufactured goods*** *are increasing.* —**manufacturer** *n* [C] *The contracts allow retailers to sell equipment at below the manufacturer's price.* | *a pharmaceutical* (=drugs) *manufacturer*

manufacture[2] *n* **1** [U] when large quantities of goods are produced to be sold, using machinery: *Cigarettes become stale from one to three months after the* ***date of manufacture****.* + **of**: *machine tools used in the manufacture of aircraft engines*

computer-aided design also **computer-aided manufacture**, abbreviation **CAD/CAM** the use of computers to help design and make industrial products and buildings

computer integrated manufacture also **computer integrated manufacturing**, abbreviation **CIM** when computers are used to plan, design, and make products

2 manufactures [plural] *formal* MANUFACTURING goods produced in large quantities using machinery: *changes in exports and imports of manufactures*

manufactured goods —see under GOODS

manufacturer's recommended price —see under PRICE[1]

man·u·fac·tur·ing /ˌmænjəˈfæktʃərɪŋ/ *n* [U] **1** the process or business of producing goods in factories: *IBM is the world leader in software for manufacturing.* | *The aircraft industry has been one of the few strong spots in US manufacturing.* —**manufacturing** *adj* [only before a noun] ***Manufacturing costs*** *increased at a slower rate than sales growth.* | *Few companies are likely to set up* ***manufacturing plants*** *here.*

2 the part of a company that is concerned with making goods, rather than designing or selling them: *vice president of manufacturing at Compaq*

manufacturing base —see under BASE[1]

manufacturing industry —see under INDUSTRY

manufacturing plant —see under PLANT

ma·qui·la·do·ra /ˌmækiləˈdɔːrə‖ˌmɑːkiːlɑːˈdɔːrɑː/ *n* [C] MANUFACTURING an ASSEMBLY PLANT in Mexico where parts are imported without having to pay tax, put together to make products, and then exported, usually to the US. Workers are cheaper to employ than in the US, environmental laws less strict etc: *Juarez is a fast-growing city on the US border whose economy depends almost solely on maquiladoras.*

Mar. written abbreviation for MARCH

mar·gin /ˈmɑːdʒən‖ˈmɑːr-/ *n* **1** [C,U] the difference between the price that something is sold for and the cost of producing it. A margin is usually calculated as a percentage of the price that something is sold for, unlike a MARK-UP which is calculated as a percentage of the cost of producing it: *Prices and margins were down as a result of the recession.* | *A store that sells for $1 an item costing it 90 cents has a 10% margin.* + **on**: *The margin on canned soup is 15% to 20%.* | *Even small numbers could produce healthy profits. It's a* ***high-margin*** *product.* | *The car division, suffering from weak sales and* ***tight margins*** *very small ones, made an operating loss.* | *Like futures contracts, options require cash guarantees in the form of margin.*

gross margin also **gross profit margin** [C] the difference between the price that a product or service is sold for and the cost of producing it, without including OVERHEADS (=general costs not related to particular products or services): *Selling, general and administrative expenses were more than 30%, so IBM needed a gross margin of around 40% just to make any reasonable profit.*

net interest margin [C] BANKING the difference between the interest that a bank pays to those putting money in the bank and what it gets from those taking out loans; SPREAD: *Thanks largely to the widened net interest margin, profitability at many banks jumped in the latest quarter.*

net margin also **net profit margin** [C] the difference between the price that a product or service is sold for

M

and the cost of producing it, including OVERHEADS (=general costs not related to particular products or services): *The company's net margin neared 28%, making it one of the nation's most profitable industrial companies.*

operating margin also **operating profit margin** [C] the difference between the price of a product or service and the cost of producing it. Operating margins are calculated by different companies in different ways, but are often similar to GROSS MARGINS: *Phone usage by business customers offers carriers the highest operating margins, as much as 18% versus 10% on residential calls.*

profit margin [C,U] the difference between the price of a product or service and the cost of producing it, or between the cost of producing all of a company's products or services and the total sum they are sold for: *Slow sales have cut profit margins in the industry.*

2 on margin FINANCE if you buy shares or other investments on margin, you buy them with borrowed money: *Individuals trading on margin sustained heavy losses during last year's stock price declines.* | *Mr Icahn says that buying on margin – using borrowed funds to finance half the purchase – has boosted his return to 23%.*

margin account —see under ACCOUNT[1]

mar·gin·al /ˈmɑːdʒɪ̇nəl‖ˈmɑːr-/ *adj* **1** a marginal change, increase, fall etc is very small, and not enough to make an important difference: *Canada's unemployment rate declined to 7.5% in June from 7.6% in May, as a result of a marginal increase in employment.* —**marginally** *adv*: *The oil company has closed the refinery, which was only marginally profitable.* | *The US dollar gained marginally on the yen and Canadian dollar.*

2 marginal products, activities, buildings etc are not considered to be the main part of a business or industry, but may still be important: *There will be the same number of hit movies, but an increased number of marginal films will perform poorly.* | *Improvements in the retail group's results come mainly from the closure of marginal stores.*

3 relating to a change in a cost, value etc when one more thing is produced, one more dollar is earned etc: *The marginal return is the added output resulting from employing one more farmer.*

marginal cost —see under COST[1]

marginal costing —see under COSTING

marginal land —see under LAND[1]

marginal producer —see under PRODUCER

marginal rate —see under RATE[1]

marginal revenue —see under REVENUE

margin buying *n* [U] the buying of shares and other investments with borrowed money: *It will take a much healthier stock market to finally bring increased margin buying by investors.*

margin call —see under CALL[2]

ma·rine /məˈriːn/ *adj* [only before a noun] connected with ships or the sea: *marine cargo* | *marine insurance* | *a marine construction company*

marine insurance —see under INSURANCE

marine insurance broker —see under BROKER[1]

marine insurance survey —see under SURVEY[1]

marine underwriter —see under UNDERWRITER

marital status —see under STATUS

mar·i·time /ˈmærɪ̇taɪm/ *adj* connected with the sea or ships: *maritime trade* | *The port of San Francisco has lost virtually all its **maritime industry**.*

mark[1] /mɑːk‖mɑːrk/ *n* [C] **1** the standard unit of money in Germany; DEUTSCHMARK: *The pound has fallen 10% against the mark.* | *In late New York trading, the dollar **closed at** 1.4915 **marks**.*

2 the £20/$1000 etc mark 20 pounds, 1000 dollars etc: *There is usually a fee to be paid, generally around the £100 mark plus VAT.*

mark[2] *v* [T] to put a sign on something: *You must mark all hazardous goods with international danger symbols.*

mark sth ↔ **down** *phr v* [T] **1** to reduce the price of something that is being sold: *The basic machine was marked down at Christmas from $799 to $399.*

2 FINANCE to reduce an estimate of the value of something, for example a particular asset or investment: *He had been projecting per-share earnings in the range of $3–$3.25, but now expects to mark down his forecast to around $2 a share.* —**marked-down** *adj: marked-down merchandise* | *marked-down shares*

mark sth ↔ **up** *phr v* [T] **1** to increase the price of something so that you sell it for more than it cost to produce, or for more than you paid for it: *Resellers and distributors then marked up the price of the parts when selling them to end-users.*

2 FINANCE to increase an estimate of the value of something, for example a particular asset or investment: *Citicorp has realized some of the value of its stake in Reliance by marking up its investment in the company.* —**marked-up** *adj*: *marked-up prices* —see also MARKUP

mark·down /ˈmɑːkdaʊn‖ˈmɑːrk-/ also **mark-down** *n* [C] **1** the act of reducing the price of something, or the amount by which the price is reduced: *The retailer's losses come from clearance markdowns of goods.*

2 a fall in the price of bonds, shares etc: *a $200 million markdown of a high-risk portfolio of shares of start-up companies* | *Creditors will have to **take big markdowns*** (=accept them) *from the face value of their bonds.*

3 a reduction in the RATING of bonds etc (=estimate of the risk that they will not be repaid): *Moody's markdown of the company's commercial paper* —compare MARKUP

mar·ket[1] /ˈmɑːkɪ̇t‖ˈmɑːr-/ *n* [C] **1** the activity of buying and selling goods or services, or the value of the goods or services sold + **in/for**: *the market in consumer electronics* | *The Japanese market for digital communications networks is estimated at $3 billion during the next five years.* | ***the booming market*** (=a profitable one with lots of activity) *for mobile communications* | *heavy losses on apartment loans in states with **depressed markets*** (=ones with falling prices and not much activity) | *Kmart Corp. is **entering** the Hawaiian **market** as part of its nationwide expansion.* | *Import rules could make it hard for foreign van suppliers to **penetrate** that **market*** (=to manage to enter it). | *Harley has **captured*** (=obtained) *about 60% of **the market** for the biggest bikes.* | *Fast food is certainly a **growth market*** (=one that is increasing in size) *with some of the main names developing their brands with great success.*

2 on the market available to buy: *companies with drugs on the market or in the final stages of product-testing* | *The company will repurchase its stock **on the open market*** (=where it can be bought by everyone) *or through private transactions.* | *They **put** their apartment **on the market*** (=offered it for sale) *for $300,000.*

3 the activity of buying and selling particular goods or services: *General Motors is making various efforts to expand in the rapidly growing Asian **car market**.* | *Apple computer really created the **personal computer market**.*

4 the market the economic system in which prices, jobs, wages etc depend on what people want to buy, how much they are willing to pay etc: *We should not leave credit card interest rates to the market – Congress should act.*

5 corner the market if a seller corners the market, they own or produce most of the goods on sale, and can therefore set prices: *In order to prevent one firm from cornering the market on a new Treasury bill issue, the law limits any dealer from purchasing more than 35% of the securities sold.*

6 price yourself out of the market to try to sell at a

price that is so high that no one wants to buy: *As supermodels price themselves out of the market, actresses are open to negotiation – a far better investment.*

7 also **financial market** the buying and selling of bonds, shares, COMMODITIES etc, or a place where this happens. Some markets are in a particular building, while trading on others takes place on computers and over the telephone, with no central building: ***The markets*** (=financial markets in general) *here have improved and the economy is strong.* | *Fear of war shook financial markets around the world.*

8 buck the market if a price bucks the market, it goes in the opposite direction to most of the other prices in the market: *Among shares that bucked the market's downward trend, Thorn EMI finished 4p higher.*

9 buck the market if someone cannot buck the market, they cannot avoid the existing effects of the market as a whole, for example by making money when everyone else is losing it: *Mrs Thatcher was right when she said that governments can't buck the market.*

10 play the market to risk money on a financial market: *One way to play the European markets is through publicly traded mutual funds.*

11 a place where things are bought and sold, especially an open area or large building: *Market day at Bodrum is a lively occasion.*

bear market a financial market in which prices are falling, especially over a long period of time: *We've had a bear market for a couple of months now, but I think it's at or near bottom.*

black market ◆ the illegal buying and selling of goods that are usually impossible to get in a particular city or country: *A pack of foreign cigarettes on the black market goes for the equivalent of at least $17.*
◆ the buying of foreign currency at an unofficial rate: *The official exchange rate is about 5.6 kyat to the dollar, or more than 10 times its current value on the black market.*

bond market the buying and selling of bonds: *Profit-taking dominated the bond market.*

bull market a financial market where prices are rising, especially over a long period of time: *Even badly managed companies do well in a bull market.*

buyer's market ECONOMICS when prices are low because there is more supply than demand, so buyers have an advantage: *The Dordogne is still a buyer's market, with the stock of unsold property keeping prices down.*

capital market a market where companies can get capital in the form of shares or bonds etc: *We have sufficient liquidity and cash and don't need access to public capital markets.*

captive market a market in which buyers have no choice about which product to buy or which seller to buy from: *The company has gained a captive market with its baby-food contract and exclusive access to 107,000 infants in the state.*

cash market a market where COMMODITIES (=oil, metals, farm products etc) are bought for immediate delivery, rather than a FUTURES market; SPOT MARKET: *He specializes in trading financial instruments in both futures and cash markets.*

closed market a market where foreign competitors are not allowed in: *In the Philippines, banking has moved from being a closed market to one where foreign banks can compete freely.*

commodity market a market where COMMODITIES (=oil, metals, farm products etc) are bought and sold: *In the commodity markets yesterday, copper futures prices rose.*

credit market a market for borrowing money in the form of bank loans, bonds etc: *In the credit markets, Treasury bond prices held steady.*

curb market another spelling of KERB MARKET

currency market also **exchange market** other names for FOREIGN EXCHANGE MARKET: *The pound rose and the yen fell as the currency markets reacted to a jump in oil prices.* | *Further international economic cooperation is needed to promote stable exchange markets.*

discount market the discount market in Britain, the MONEY MARKET between the Bank of England, money MARKETMAKERS (until recently discount houses) and COMMERCIAL BANKS: *We accept these bills of exchange and arrange for them to be discounted on the discount market.*

domestic market goods and services sold in the country where they are produced, or where the company producing them has its base: *It will now be difficult to keep foreign airlines out of domestic markets.*

efficient market [singular] ECONOMICS the belief that prices on the stockmarket show not only how much a company is actually worth but also show what investors expect from the company. Those who believe in the efficient market believe that it is not possible to find shares priced below their true value and make a quick profit: *The efficient market hypothesis strongly supports index funds over mutual funds.*

equity market the buying and selling of shares generally, rather than the trade in shares on a particular stockmarket

eurodollar market the buying and selling of eurodollars or bonds etc in eurodollars. London is one of the main centres for this: *The notes will be offered simultaneously in the US domestic and the Eurodollar markets.*

export market goods and services sold outside the country where they are produced: *The US is by far Canada's biggest export market.*

foreign exchange market also **forex market** the buying and selling of currencies by governments, financial institutions etc in a particular FINANCIAL CENTRE (=a place with a lot of financial activities and markets) or in the world as a whole: *The rising yen has become one of the fastest moving currencies in the foreign exchange market.*

forward market the buying and selling of currencies or COMMODITIES (=oil, metals, farm products etc) at fixed prices for delivery on fixed dates in the future: *The Russians have sold gold, but they've also been buying it in the forward market for future delivery.*

free market *approving* a system of buying and selling that is not under the control of the government, and where people can buy and sell freely, or an economy where free markets exist, and most companies and property are not owned by the state: *The tasks included creating free markets for labor and goods, and transferring ownership of thousands of companies from the state to the private sector.*

futures market a market where FUTURES CONTRACTS (=agreements to buy currencies, etc at a particular price in the future) are bought and sold; FUTURES EXCHANGE: *Futures markets suggest oil prices may be headed down.*

gilt-edged market also **gilts market** the market for British government bonds

graveyard market a BEAR MARKET (=a financial market where a lot of shares etc are being sold and the prices are falling) in which investors are likely to lose a lot of money, because buyers do not want to buy until the market gets better

grey market *BrE*, **gray market** *AmE* the buying and selling of shares just before they are officially ISSUED (=made available and sold for the first time): *Thai investors who want to get a piece of what will be Thailand's largest public listing are bidding up the share price in gray market trading.*

high-yield market a market for JUNK BONDS (=bonds that pay a high level of interest but have a high risk of not being repaid)

M

housing market the number and type of houses and flats that are available in a particular area, how much they cost etc: *The Canadian housing market is generally weak. Housing starts declined 14% last year.*

imperfect market ECONOMICS a market in which buyers and sellers do not have complete information about a particular product, where it is difficult to compare prices of products because they are different from each other etc: *What theory says should happen in a state of perfect competition may not occur in real, imperfect markets.*

insurance market the buying and selling of insurance: *The London insurance market paid $344.5 million in settlement of the pollution cleanup from the Exxon Valdez oil spill.*

investment-grade market also **high-grade market** a market for bonds that have a low risk of not being repaid

job market also **labour market** *BrE*, **labor market** *AmE* the number and type of jobs that are available in a particular place: *The labor market has been particularly weak for unskilled workers.*

kerb market also **curb market** ◆ FINANCE an unofficial market in shares etc that operates when the official market is closed, with buying and selling done over the telephone

◆ an unofficial market for shares in some countries. A kerb market takes place in the street outside the stockmarket: *Kerb market traders, angry over the continuing fall in share prices, attempted to block the bourse's main entrance.*

loan market the market for loans made by banks and other financial institutions: *South Korean banks are returning to the commercial-bank loan market.*

luxury market a market for goods that give great comfort and pleasure, such as expensive clothes and food: *There are two new cars for the luxury market from BMW and Mercedes.*

main market a company's most important product, or the place where it sells most: *Duracell's main market, alkaline consumer batteries* | *Brazil is the company's main market in that region.*

mass market a market for a product that is bought, or meant to be bought, by a lot of people: *We sell these clothes to the mass market in department stores and to high earners in boutiques.*

middle market a market for goods and services that are of standard, average, or medium quality, size, or price: *The company lacked the resources to develop both luxury models and the two middle-market cars.*

money market a market for borrowing money over short periods of time in the form of COMMERCIAL PAPER; TREASURY BILLs etc

mortgage market ◆ a market for loans to people and organizations buying property

◆ a market for mortgages that have been bought by financial institutions and are then traded as ASSET-BACKED SECURITIES

new issue market a market for bonds, shares etc when they are first sold, rather than when they are traded later

niche market a market for a product or service, perhaps an expensive or unusual one, that does not have many buyers, but that may make good profits for companies that sell it: *MGI Pharma, a relatively tiny player in the pharmaceuticals market, has targeted specialty cancer treatments as its niche market.*

open market a market where foreign competitors are allowed: *The main aim of the World Trade Organisation is to promote open markets worldwide.*

options market a place where OPTIONS (=rights to buy shares, currencies etc at a specified price in the future) are bought and sold; OPTIONS EXCHANGE: *the Chicago Board Options Exchange, the largest options market in the US*

over-the-counter market abbreviation **OTC market** a stockmarket where shares in newer and smaller companies are traded. On an OTC market, buyers and sellers are connected by computer, rather than trading in a particular building: *There were sharp gains among smaller stocks, particularly in the over-the-counter market.*

parallel market also **parallel money market** a market which trades foreign currencies, stocks, shares etc, and which runs at the same time as a country's own market. Parallel markets mean that a country has less control over its economy: *The government wants to keep control of raw materials while pursuing a* ***parallel market economy****.* | *The growth of parallel markets has created easier lending and borrowing.*

perfect market ECONOMICS a market in which buyers and sellers have complete information about a particular product and it is easy to compare prices of products because they are the same as each other etc: *A perfect market in equilibrium will not allow two prices for identical assets.*

primary market another name for NEW ISSUE MARKET: *In the primary market, no new issues were announced.*

property market the buying, selling, and renting of land or buildings: *a major downturn in the Japanese property market* | *Commercial rents are once more on the increase, returning confidence to the property market.*

secondary market a market for bonds, shares etc that are being traded after they are ISSUED (=first sold)

securities market a market in bonds, shares, or other SECURITIES; SECURITIES EXCHANGE: *The US Treasury bond market is by far the single biggest securities market in the world.*

seller's market a time that is good for sellers because prices are high: *Demand for property in Houston is so good that it's turning into a seller's market.*

shadow market business activities that are difficult for the authorities to find out about, sometimes because they are against the law; SHADOW ECONOMY: *The lack of reliable statistics comes from the growing shadow economies that have escaped accurate analysis.* | *There's a shadow market for new stocks that is doing well.*

single market a group of countries that do not charge tax on the goods and services that they trade with each other, so forming one market. The phrase is often used when talking about the EUROPEAN UNION and the EUROPEAN ECONOMIC AREA: *Even in Europe, independently of a single market, cultural barriers are likely to continue for some time.*

spot market another name for CASH MARKET: *Buyers are chosing the stability of long-term contracts for oil over purchases from the spot market.*

stock market also **stockmarket**, or **stock exchange** *especially BrE* a place where companies' shares are bought and sold: *If the stock market price of the new shares rises, the return for those original investors will be even richer.*

swaps market also **swops market** a market in which a borrower with one type of loan exchanges it with another borrower with a different type of loan. Each borrower is looking for an advantage that the original loan did not have, for example that the loan is in a particular currency, has a particular interest rate, is for a particular period of time etc: *Foreign funds would be allowed to use the nation's swaps markets to move their money in and out of the otherwise unconvertible local currency.*

terminal market *AmE* a market for farm products or other COMMODITIES: *terminal markets where traders can meet their delivery obligations or use cash to settle contracts*

test market MARKETING ◆ [C] the process of introducing a new product or service to one or more areas in a country to find out whether people are likely to buy it when it becomes more widely available: *Another short-cut is to skip the traditional consumer test market and rely solely on laboratory research.* | *preliminary **test-market results** of Tonka Products' new line of stuffed toys*

◆ [C] a particular area of a country used to test a new product or service: *Grocers in the test markets say they're willing to give the new convenience foods a chance.* | *Test markets in Iowa and Illinois indicated there could be problems with the packaging.* —compare TRIAL, PILOT —see also TEST-MARKET

third market in the US, a market in which LISTED SECURITIES (=stocks, shares etc that are officially available on the stock exchange) are bought and sold privately, without using the stockmarket: *Firms can bypass stock exchanges to deal directly with clients in the third market.*

market² *v* [T] **1** to sell something or make it available for sale, especially in a particular way: *Toshiba's consumer electronics products were previously marketed in Italy through a distributor.*

2 to sell something by considering what customers want or need when buying a product or service, for example how much they are willing to pay, where they will buy it etc: *DC has marketed its services well with a highly visible media campaign.* —see also TEST-MARKET

mar·ket·a·ble /ˈmɑːkətəbəl‖ˈmɑːr-/ *adj* marketable goods, services, skills etc can be sold easily because people and organizations want them: *It's a long, uncertain path from the laboratory to marketable drugs.* | *Because he has no higher education or marketable work skills, he is limited to unskilled jobs.* —**marketability** *n* [U] *The increase in the number of Electro shares outstanding will improve their marketability.*

marketable security —see under SECURITY

marketable title —see under TITLE

market basket the prices of a group of typical products that people buy, used to measure inflation: *The consumer-price index, which measures changes in a fixed market basket of goods and services.* —see also BASKET OF CURRENCIES

market demand —see under DEMAND

market-driven *adj* market-driven activities, developments, products etc are a result of the needs of customers: *Russia's continued moves toward a market-driven economy* | *The pressure for change is market-driven, part of a revolution to slow down the increase in healthcare costs.*

market economy —see under ECONOMY¹

mar·ket·eer /ˌmɑːkəˈtɪə‖ˌmɑːrkəˈtɪr/ *n* [C] **1** someone who believes in or is involved in a particular type of market

black marketeer someone who illegally sells goods that are usually impossible to get in a particular place, or who sells foreign currency at an unofficial rate: *The authorities started rationing gasoline last week, and black marketeers were very active.* —**black-marketeering** *n* [U] *drug trafficking, prostitution and black marketeering*

free marketeer someone who believes that the economy or particular activities should not be under the control of the government: *Free marketeers don't like heavily protected, nationalized energy industries.* —**free-marketeering** *n* [U] *The plan combines free marketeering and authoritarian intervention in a strange mix.*

2 another name for MARKETER: *Japanese researchers interact more with product designers, marketeers, and manufacturing engineers.*

market equilibrium —see under EQUILIBRIUM

mar·ket·er /ˈmɑːkətə‖ˈmɑːrkətər/ also **marketeer** *n* [C] **1** an organization that sells a product or service: *Dun & Bradstreet, a marketer of business information and related services*

2 someone in a company who is responsible for marketing: *"The whole new premise of the campaign is to make the Pepsi generation bigger and broader," says a Pepsi marketer.*

direct-mail marketer a marketer that sells directly to buyers through MAILINGS (=information sent by post): *Direct-mail marketers are hungry for information about consumers' life styles, because it helps target expensive mail campaigns.*

direct marketer a marketer that sells directly to buyers through MAILINGS (=advertising sent by post), telephone selling etc: *This direct marketer of consumer products plans to hire 500 telemarketing workers.*

mass marketer a marketer that sells products that a lot of people want: *inexpensive mass marketers like K Mart and Wal-Mart*

niche marketer a marketer that specializes in products that do not have many buyers, but that may produce good profits for companies that sell them: *Niche marketers have to develop an international outlook because their domestic market is comparatively small.* —see also TELEMARKETER

market failure —see under FAILURE

market fluctuations —see under FLUCTUATION

market forces —see under FORCE¹

market garden *n* [C] *BrE* an area for growing fruit and vegetables for sale; TRUCK FARM

mar·ket·ing /ˈmɑːkətɪŋ‖ˈmɑːr-/ *n* [U] activities to design and sell a product or service by considering buyers' wants or needs, for example where and how they will buy it, how much they will be willing to pay etc: *They're going to have to spend even more on **sales and marketing** to win customers back.* | *Successful innovations need to couple R&D, manufacturing, and marketing activities.*

co-operative marketing when two or more producers work together to sell their products, for example by selling one of each of their products as part of a set

corporate marketing ◆ the marketing activities of a company. The phrase is often used in job titles: *The director of corporate marketing said they want to establish the company's presence in low-cost PCs.*

◆ also **business-to-business marketing** marketing in order to sell products or services to other organizations, rather than to the public

direct marketing any form of marketing where possible customers are contacted directly by the seller, for example by telephone or post: *Direct marketing is the fastest growing sector of advertising.*

event marketing marketing using events such as concerts, sporting events etc, for example through SPONSORSHIP (=when a company pays part of the costs of the event in return for advertising)

global marketing marketing activities designed to cover the world as a whole: *global marketing strategies such as using the same advertising in all European countries*

image marketing marketing that uses famous people to help sell a product, for example by getting them to say that they use it: *Athletic shoe manufacturers use image marketing to promote the majority of their products.*

mass marketing the marketing of products that are bought by a lot of people, by using methods designed to reach large numbers of people: *The days of mass marketing are over. Instead, we use a number of different tactics to sell more efficiently.*

M

M

niche marketing the marketing of a special product or service that does not have many buyers, but that may provide good profits for companies that sell it, or the marketing of a product or service in a particular way that is suitable for a small group of customers: *Forget about mass marketing, or even niche marketing. For a growing number of advertisers, the only segment small enough is the segment of one.*

social marketing marketing involved with ideas that are considered to be good for society, for example advertising that teaches people about the importance of protecting the environment: *The policy of moving people from hospitals into the community was the focus of a social marketing process.*

strategic marketing marketing that is designed to make the future position of a company stronger: *We have a strategic marketing alliance with our Japanese and European partners.*

marketing board —see under BOARD[1]

marketing concept —see under CONCEPT

marketing co-operative —see under CO-OPERATIVE

marketing expenditure —see under EXPENDITURE

marketing expense —see under EXPENSE

marketing mix —see under MIX

marketing research —see under RESEARCH

market leader —see under LEADER

market leadership —see under LEADERSHIP

market-led *adj* another name for MARKET-DRIVEN: *The Football League needs to become more market-led in a way that best serves the needs of our customers.*

mar•ket•mak•er /ˈmɑːkɪ̵tˌmeɪkə‖ˈmɑːrkɪ̵tˌmeɪkər/ also **market-maker** *n* [C] FINANCE a financial institution that always has supplies of shares available for buyers: *the continued shortage of stock in the hands of market-makers* | *Each Big Board stock is entrusted to a single marketmaker, or specialist, who constantly matches buy and sell orders and uses his firm's own money to smooth out imbalances.*

market order —see under ORDER[1]

market orientation —see under ORIENTATION

market-oriented *adj* **1** a market-oriented economy, society, system etc is one with FREE MARKETS where people can buy and sell freely and where most companies are not owned by the state: *He plans to replace the rigid planned economy with a more market-oriented one.*

2 market-oriented activities are designed to lead to a more market-oriented economy: *Hungary and Poland were ahead of their neighbors in adopting **market-oriented policies**.* | *Mr Deng's **market-oriented reforms*** —**market orientation** *n* [U] *R&D staff are often perceived to lack market orientation.*

mar•ket•place /ˈmɑːkɪ̵tpleɪs‖ˈmɑːr-/ *n* [C usually singular] the people and activities involved in buying and selling a particular type of goods or services: *Developments in **the marketplace** require that we reduce our costs to remain competitive.* | *Excessive pay is hurting America's ability to compete in the **international marketplace**.* + **for**: *the rapidly changing marketplace for toys*

market player —see under PLAYER

market power —see under POWER[1]

market price —see under PRICE[1]

market rate —see under RATE[1]

market report —see under REPORT[1]

market research —see under RESEARCH

market rigging —see under RIGGING

market risk —see under RISK[1]

market sector —see under SECTOR

market segment —see under SEGMENT[1]

market sentiment —see under SENTIMENT

market share —see under SHARE

market study —see under STUDY[1]

market survey —see under SURVEY[1]

market value —see under VALUE[1]

mark•up /ˈmɑːkʌp‖ˈmɑːrk-/ also **mark-up** *n* [C] the act of increasing the price of something, for example in relation to its cost so as to make a profit, or the amount of this increase: *A dealer's markup for securities shouldn't be greater than 5% above the prevailing market price.* —see also ***mark up*** under MARK[2]

Marl•bo•ro Fri•day /ˌmɑːlbərə ˈfraɪdi‖ˌmɑːrlbəroʊ-/ *n* MARKETING April 2, 1993, when the price of Marlboro cigarettes, which had been more expensive than other brands, was reduced in an attempt to increase sales. This led investors to believe that brands of CONSUMER PRODUCTS (=products bought by people) in general were no longer as valuable as before

mart /mɑːt‖mɑːrt/ *n* [C] **1** *AmE* a shop: *a mini-mart* | *a convenience mart*

2 *BrE* a market, especially one where animals are sold: *a cattle mart* | *a sheep auction mart*

marzipan layer —see under LAYER

Mas•low's hie•rar•chy of needs /ˌmæzləʊz ˌhaɪrɑːki əv ˈniːdz‖-loʊz ˌhaɪrɑːr-/ *n* [U] a THEORY (=set of ideas) about MOTIVATION that was invented by Abraham Maslow, and has sometimes been used to explain the reasons why consumers decide to buy things, and what encourages people who work within an organization. Maslow suggested that there are five levels of human needs. The needs on one level must be satisfied before the next level can be reached, and only unsatisfied needs influence human behaviour

mass advertising —see under ADVERTISING

mass market —see under MARKET[1]

mass marketer —see under MARKETER

mass marketing —see under MARKETING

mass merchant —see under MERCHANT

mass-produce *v* [T] to produce something in large amounts using machinery, so that each object is the same and can be sold cheaply: *Thorn EMI invested £12 million in its factories in Enfield and Gosport to mass-produce a daring new TV design.* —**mass-produced** *adj*: *mass-produced furniture* | *mass-produced goods*

mass production —see also PRODUCTION

mas•ter[1] /ˈmɑːstə‖ˈmæstər/ *n* [C] a document, record etc from which copies are made: *I gave him the master to copy.*

master[2] *adj* [only before a noun] **1 master copy/file/list etc** the original thing from which copies are made: *When a large number of copies of the same document are required, they can be photocopied from a **master copy**.*

2 master craftsman/builder/chef etc someone who is very skilled at a job done with their hands and can teach it to other people: *The company now uses semi-skilled operators instead of master bakers.*

3 the most important or main thing: *Mr Bond's master company, Bond Corporation*

Master of Business Administration —see MBA

ma•te•ri•al /məˈtɪəriəl‖-ˈtɪr-/ *n* [C usually plural] something you need to make or do something: *the **building materials** group, Tarmac*

raw material a substance that is used to make a product: *Crude oil is the basic raw material for styrene.* | *They are short of cash to pay for raw materials.*

material fact *n* **1** [C] INSURANCE any fact which, by law, you must tell an insurance company when you buy insurance from them
2 [C] FINANCE any fact which, by law, a company must tell people when a document giving information about a new SHARE ISSUE is produced: *The company failed to disclose* (=make known) *material facts about its operations and financial position.*
3 [C,U] LAW any information provided by a WITNESS during a COURT CASE that could affect the decision of the court: *The defendants failed to disclose* (=make known) *that material fact to the plaintiff.* | *It is a crime to falsify or hide a material fact.*

materials buyer —see under BUYER

materials control —see under CONTROL[1]

materials handling —see under HANDLING

materials, repair, operation —see MRO

materials requirement planning —see MRP

maternity benefit —see under BENEFIT[1]

maternity leave —see under LEAVE

mathematical economics —see under ECONOMICS

matrix structure —see under STRUCTURE

ma•ture[1] /məˈtʃʊə‖-ˈtʊr/ *v* [I] **1** FINANCE if a financial arrangement such as a bond or an INSURANCE POLICY matures, it becomes ready to be paid: *The debentures will mature in five years' time.*
2 to become fully developed: *The Japanese economy has matured and become more open to competition.*
3 if an industry or market matures, it stops growing as fast as before, and the number of competitors decreases: *The video market has matured, making film purchases even riskier for distributors.*

mature[2] *adj* a mature industry or market is one where growth is relatively low and there are fewer competitors than before: *Many emerging markets have outpaced* (=developed more quickly than) *more mature markets such as the U.S. and Japan.*

mature industry —see under INDUSTRY

ma•tu•ri•ty /məˈtʃʊərəti‖-ˈtʊr-/ *n* plural **maturities** FINANCE **1** [C,U] the time when a financial arrangement such as a bond or an INSURANCE POLICY becomes ready to be paid: *With an individual Treasury bond you are guaranteed to get all your money back* ***at maturity.*** | *money-market instruments of very short maturities* —see also YIELD TO MATURITY
2 [U] when an industry or market has stopped growing as fast as before, and there are fewer competitors etc: *Western economies have* ***reached maturity*** *for insurance cover for goods and property.*

maturity date —see under DATE[1]

maturity yield —see under YIELD[1]

ma•ven /ˈmeɪvən/ *n* [C] *AmE* someone who knows a lot about a particular subject; EXPERT: *Stockmarket mavens say such a pattern usually signals more gains ahead.*

max /mæks/ abbreviation for MAXIMUM

maxi-ISA —see under ISA

max•i•mize also **maximise** *BrE* /ˈmæksəmaɪz/ *v* [T] **1** to increase something such as profit or income as much as possible: *The company's main function is to maximize profit.* —**maximization** also **maximisation** *BrE n* [U] *The maximization of profit is not the only aim of business.*
2 to increase the size of a WINDOW on a computer screen as much as possible when you are using a particular program: *This menu allows you to maximize the window to full screen.* —opposite MINIMIZE

max•i•mum[1] /ˈmæksəməm/ *adj* [only before a noun] the maximum amount, quantity etc is the largest that is possible or allowed: *The* ***maximum cost*** *of the plan would be $9.7 million.* | *Capital gains now are taxed at a* ***maximum rate*** *of 28%.*

maximum[2] abbreviation **max** *n* plural **maxima** or **maximums** [C] the largest number or amount that is possible or is allowed **+ of**: *The company could be fined a maximum of $10,000.*

MB written abbreviation for MEGABYTE

MBA *n* [C] Master of Business Administration; a university degree that teaches you the skills you need to manage a business or part of a business: *Smith* ***received an MBA*** *from the Harvard Business School.*

MBO abbreviation for MANAGEMENT BY OBJECTIVES; MANAGEMENT BUYOUT

MBWA abbreviation for MANAGEMENT BY WALKING AROUND

MD *n* [C] *BrE informal* the MANAGING DIRECTOR of a company: *We all laughed at the MD's jokes, or got fired.*

mea•gre *BrE*, **meager** *AmE* /ˈmiːgə‖-ər/ *adj* very small in amount: *Sales rose a meager 2.5% in January.* | *The chairman predicts very* ***meagre growth*** *this year.*

mean[1] /miːn/ *adj* [only before a noun] average: *Analysts'* ***mean estimate*** *is for earnings of 33 cents a share.*

mean[2] *n* **the mean** the average: *The GDP of this state was 32% below the mean for the country as a whole.*

arithmetic mean [U] STATISTICS a simple average obtained by adding together a series of figures and dividing the result by the number of figures in the series: *Initial price represents the arithmetic mean of Pernod's share price on the 1st, 5th, and 6th November.*

mean price —see under PRICE[1]

means /miːnz/ *n* [plural] the money and resources that a person or organization has available **means to do sth**: *Large corporations* ***have the means*** *to pay large fines without suffering hardship.* | *The group* ***has limited means.*** | *young families and people* ***of modest means*** | *Improving the lot of the poor was* ***beyond*** *the city's financial* ***means.***

independent means a private income that comes from property, investments etc: *Many tropical countries welcome retirees or others* ***of independent means*** *as long-term residents.*

means-test *n* [C] an official check in order to find out if someone is poor enough to receive WELFARE BENEFITS (=payments from the state when you are ill, without work etc): *He has made proposals for means-tests for wealthy Social Security recipients.* —**means-tested** *adj*: *spending on 'means-tested' programs for low income Americans* —**means-testing** *n* [U] *We will ensure that the basic state pension is paid as of right and end means-testing for our poorest senior citizens.*

meas•ly /ˈmiːzli/ *adj disapproving* very small in amount: *Revenue rose a measly 1.8% in the last quarter.* | *Some investments give a very measly yield.*

mea•sure[1] /ˈmeʒə‖-ər/ *n* **1** [C] an official action, taken to deal with a particular problem: *The company has had to* ***take*** *cost-cutting* ***measures,*** *including reducing spending on certain marketing programs.*

austerity measure [C usually plural] official actions taken by a government in order to reduce the amount of money that it spends or the amount that people spend: *The government introduced austerity measures including a freeze on public sector pay.*

2 a measure of sth a way of measuring or calculating something: *Gross domestic product is the Commerce Department's main measure of U.S. economic output.* | *Car sales are often seen as a measure of consumer confidence.*
3 [C,U] an amount or unit in a measuring system: *A centimetre is a measure of length.*

corn and dry measure [U] a measure of volume used in Britain for substances that are not liquid

M

dry measure [U] a system of units for measuring goods such as tobacco and sugar that are not liquids
liquid measure [C,U] an amount or unit for measuring a liquid

measure² *v* [T] to calculate the amount or importance of something: *Many economists estimate that inflation this year, as measured by the rise in consumer prices, will be only about 3%.* **measure sth against**: *All currencies historically have been measured against gold.* **measure sth in**: *Overseas sales, measured in dollars, rose 18% last year.*
measure up *phr v* [I] to be good enough, or as good as expected: *None of the products measured up.* + **to**: *Their performance in recent years hasn't measured up to their longer-term record.*

mec•ca /ˈmekə/ *n* [C] a place that is very popular for a particular reason, attracting a lot of people to go there + **for**: *Georgetown has become a mecca for job-seekers.* | *The city is being promoted as a shopping mecca.*

mechanical engineering —see under ENGINEERING

mech•a•nis•m /ˈmekənɪzəm/ *n* [C] a system used to achieve something or deal with a problem: *The increased lending can be done through existing lending mechanisms.* | *There is a move to introduce free-market mechanisms in the airline sector.* + **for**: *At present there is no satisfactory mechanism for settling disputes.*

me•di•a /ˈmiːdiə/ *n* **the (mass) media** all the different ways of entertaining and giving information to the public and advertising goods, for example television, radio, and newspapers: *The Japanese media have carried detailed reports of the scandal.* | *The company is keen to get its views across **in the media**.* | ***mass media** advertising campaigns* | *The group owns newspapers, TV stations and other **media companies**.* —see also ELECTRONIC MEDIA, MAGNETIC MEDIA

media baron —see under BARON

media buyer —see under BUYER

media buying *n* [U] the business of buying advertising space in newspapers and magazines and on the television and radio: *A New York media buying firm handles all their major promotions.*

me•di•an /ˈmiːdiən/ *adj* [only before a noun] the middle value in a series of values: *The median sales price fell 1.4% from October.* | *Median household income fell by 1.9% last year.* —see also DECILE, QUARTILE, PERCENTILE

median price —see under PRICE¹

media planning —see under PLANNING

me•di•ate /ˈmiːdieɪt/ *v* [I,T] to try to end an argument between two people or groups by talking to both sides and encouraging them to reach an agreement: *He was asked to mediate a labor dispute.* + **between**: *They have proved their ability to mediate between manufacturers and potential customers worldwide.* —**mediation** *n* [U] *As litigation costs soar, mediation is becoming a more popular option.* —**mediator** *n* [C] *An agreement was reached last week with the help of a federal mediator.*

Med•i•caid /ˈmedɪkeɪd/ *n* a system in the US by which the government helps to pay the cost of medical treatment for poor people: *The number of people who qualify for Medicaid has been rising steadily.* —compare MEDICARE

med•i•cal /ˈmedɪkəl/ *adj* connected with medicine and the treatment of illness and injury: *Medicare doesn't cover all **medical expenses**.* | *He has been absent from work for six weeks on **medical leave**.* | *a manufacturer of medical supplies*

medical certificate —see under CERTIFICATE

medical insurance —see under INSURANCE

Med•i•care /ˈmedɪkeə‖-ker/ *n* [U] a system in the US by which the government helps to pay the cost of medical treatment for old people: *There has been talk of cutting the Medicare budget further next year.* —compare MEDICAID

medi•cine /ˈmedsən‖ˈmedɨsən/ *n* **industrial/occupational medicine** the study of the conditions under which people work and the effects of these conditions on their health and safety: *It is known from occupational medicine that exposure to these chemicals can cause health problems.*

Med•i•gap /ˈmedigæp/ *n* a type of private medical insurance in the US that covers costs not paid by Medicare: *Congress has now enacted legislation to standardize Medigap policies.*

me•di•o•cre /ˌmiːdiˈəʊkə◂‖-ˈoʊkər◂/ *adj* not very good: *The business is now riding high, shaking off years of mediocre earnings.* | *Shares have had a mediocre year.*

me•di•um¹ /ˈmiːdiəm/ *adj* of middle size, between small and large: *Disposable nappies come in small, medium and large sizes.* | *Small and medium firms will benefit most from the new rules.*

medium² *n* plural **mediums** or **media** [C] a way or means of communicating or trading: *Television is still the favourite medium for advertisers.* | *The US currency often serves as a medium for transactions in other currencies.*

medium-dated *adj* **medium-dated bonds/stock/securities** bonds etc that are repaid between two and ten years; MEDIUMS —compare LONG-DATED, SHORT-DATED

medium-duty *adj* [only before a noun] medium-duty products, equipment etc are designed for use in average to difficult conditions, rather than for normal use in easy conditions: *medium-duty trucks*

medium of exchange *n* [singular] something that can be used to buy goods or to measure someone's wealth. Money is the usual medium of exchange in most countries: *US currency is widely used as a medium of exchange here.*

me•di•ums /ˈmiːdiəmz/ *n* [plural] bonds issued by the British government that are repaid usually in two to ten years

medium-sized also **medium-size** *adj* between small and large in size: *The bank specializes in loans to small and **medium-sized businesses**.*

medium-term *adj* [only before a noun] not happening or making a profit immediately, but not over a very long period of time: *a medium-term loan* | *It is possible to get some quite good yields on medium-term bonds.* —compare LONG-TERM, SHORT-TERM

medium-term credit —see under CREDIT¹

medium-term debt —see under DEBT

medium-term gilts —see under GILTS

medium-term loan —see under LOAN¹

medium-term security —see under SECURITY

meet¹ /miːt/ *n* [C usually singular] *informal BrE* a meeting: *Let's see if we can fix up a meet sometime next week.*

meet² *v* past tense and past participle **met** **1** [I,T] to get together with another person to discuss something: *The directors met again yesterday evening to discuss the crisis.* | *The committee meets once a month.* | *She spends a lot of time travelling to meet clients.* + **with**: *Bank officials will meet with company representatives later this week.*
2 meet a debt/cost/payment/expense to pay a debt or payment, or to be able to pay it: *The firm is having trouble meeting its debt payments.*
3 meet a target/expectation/projection/standard to achieve a level that has been set or expected: *The car has failed to meet company sales targets.* | *The company has not met its growth projections.*

4 meet a demand to produce enough goods to satisfy the demand for them: *The company is operating both its plants at 100% capacity to meet the increased demand.*

5 meet a deadline to finish something at or before the time it was meant to be finished: *The firm failed to meet the 31 March deadline for submitting the report.*

6 meet a requirement/condition/obligation to succeed in doing something that you have to do: *Although Rax has failed to meet certain financial requirements, the company believes it can meet the conditions in the future.*

7 meet sb halfway to agree to some of the things that someone is demanding in an effort to reach an agreement with them: *The company has offered to meet the unions halfway in their pay demands.*

meet·ing /ˈmiːtɪŋ/ *n* [C] an event at which people meet to talk and decide things: *We **had a meeting** yesterday to discuss progress.* | *It was decided to **hold a shareholders meeting** later this month.* | *Two of the directors refused to **attend the board meeting**.* | *I've been **in a meeting** all afternoon.* | *The preliminary findings will be presented **at a meeting** next week.* + **with**: *Representatives of Middle Eastern banks were due in London this morning for a meeting with Bank of England officials.* + **between**: *a meeting between unions and management*

annual general meeting abbreviation **AGM** *BrE* **annual meeting** *AmE* ◆ an official yearly meeting of the shareholders and directors of a company, at which the company's ACCOUNTS are presented, the AUDITORS are chosen, and the amount of DIVIDEND is decided, as required by law: *A resolution to reappoint Coopers & Lybrand as the company auditors will be proposed at the annual general meeting.*

◆ a yearly meeting of the members of an organization such as a club, TRADE UNION, association etc to discuss matters relating to their organization

company meeting a formal meeting of the shareholders and directors of a company: *Some shareholders criticised the chairman's statement at a recent company meeting.*

creditors' meeting a meeting where creditors of a bankrupt company are told how much each of them will be repaid: *It would take several months to organize the creditors' meeting and asset sale.*

extraordinary meeting also **extraordinary general meeting** abbreviation **EGM** a meeting of the shareholders and directors of a company to discuss subjects that cannot wait until the next annual general meeting: *Shareholders will attend an extraordinary general meeting to vote on the recent management changes.*

statutory meeting in Britain, a meeting that must, by law, be held between one and three months after a company starts doing business and in which shareholders discuss matters relating to the forming of the company: *They had adjourned* (=delayed) *their statutory meeting beyond the limit time.*

mega- /megə/ *prefix journalism* a word put in front of another word to indicate that something is very big or very important: *Three bank mega-mergers have been announced in the last two months.* | *We are not looking for huge mega-returns on our investment.* | *That's the mega-decision the president has to make.*

meg·a·bucks /ˈmegəbʌks/ *n* [plural] *informal AmE* a very large amount of money: *It also means your land is worthless, your credit dries up, and you may owe megabucks.* —**megabucks** *adj* [only before a noun] *a megabucks deal*

meg·a·byte /ˈmegəbaɪt/ *n* [C] a million BYTES (=units of computer information, each holding one number or letter), used to talk about the amount of processing space on a computer: *a floppy disk that holds 4 megabytes of data* | *a 200 megabyte hard disk*

melt·down /ˈmeltdaʊn/ *n* [singular] a situation in which prices fall by a very large amount or an industry or economy becomes much weaker: *A near meltdown in overseas stock markets sent U.S. prices plunging for the third consecutive day.* | *The situation is serious, but new measures have been introduced aimed at preventing a **financial meltdown**.*

melt-up *n* [singular] a situation in which prices rise by a large amount or an industry or the economy becomes much stronger: *What we are witnessing here is an end-of-quarter melt-up of share prices.*

mem·ber /ˈmembə‖-ər/ *n* [C] a person, group, or country that has joined a club or an organization: *Trade between the two countries has increased since Spain became a member of the European Community.* | *The consortium will have 11 member companies.*

Member of Parliament —see MP

Member of the European Parliament —see MEP

mem·ber·ship /ˈmembəʃɪp‖-ər-/ *n* [U] **1** the fact of being a member of a club or an organization: *Both countries are now applying for membership of the European Union.*

2 the number of people who belong to a club or an organization: *Trade Union membership declined by 5% over the last five years.*

members register —see under REGISTER[1]

mem·o /ˈmeməʊ‖-moʊ/ *n* [C] a short official note, usually from one person to another person or group of people in the same company or organization: *A memo was sent to all employees informing them of the merger deal.*

reply memo a document sent in response to a question or statement in an earlier document

mem·o·ran·dum /ˌmeməˈrændəm/ *n* plural **memoranda** or **memorandums** [C] **1** *formal* a MEMO: *The accusations were first set out in an internal memorandum to the chairman.*

2 LAW a legal document recording the important details of an agreement

memorandum of agreement *n* plural **memoranda of agreement** or **memorandums of agreement** [C] LAW another name for MEMORANDUM OF UNDERSTANDING: *Boeing has signed a memorandum of agreement with Thomson-CSF to jointly compete for new business in defense.*

memorandum of association *n* plural **memoranda of association** or **memorandums of association** [C] LAW in Britain, one of the documents needed when a company starts doing business, giving details about its activities, capital etc: *The company's memorandum of association sets out the activities for which the company has been formed.*

memorandum of deposit *n* plural **memoranda of deposit** or **memorandums of deposit** [C] LAW, FINANCE a document showing an agreement with a bank when shares and other investments are left as SECURITY for a loan. It gives details about the bank's right to these investments if the loan is not repaid: *The shares were subject to a memorandum of deposit in favor of the bank, which had effective control of them.*

memorandum of understanding *n* plural **memoranda of understanding** or **memorandums of understanding** [C] LAW a document signed by two organizations to say that they are willing to work together, perhaps before a more detailed contract is signed: *Kobe Steel and Alcoa signed a memorandum of understanding to explore cooperation in recycling and technology transfer.*

mem·o·ry /ˈmeməri/ *n* [U] the part of a computer in which information is stored: *Storing and retrieving video*

M

images requires vast amounts of computer memory. | *a machine with 4 gigabyes of memory* | *Both companies have sought other partners to make* ***memory chips*** *for them in Japan and South Korea.*

main memory also **primary memory** the most important unit of a computer's memory: *It is the first machine capable of running an entire database out of main memory.*

random access memory abbreviation **RAM** the memory in a computer system that is used for running software: *The program requires 512,000 bytes of random access memory.*

read only memory abbreviation **ROM** the memory in a computer system where permanent instructions and information are stored —see also CD-ROM

virtual memory the memory in a computer system that is stored and moved automatically as it is needed so that it appears to be in the main memory

memory address —see under ADDRESS[1]

men•ace /ˈmenɨs/ *n* [C] something that is dangerous: *Many people think that overseas competition is the biggest menace to the industry.*

mend /mend/ *n* **on the mend** improving again after being weak: *The economy is now on the mend.*

mental health day *n* [C usually singular] *AmE informal* a day when you do not go to work, in order to rest

men•tor /ˈmentɔː‖-tɔːr/ *n* [C] an experienced person who gives advice to less experienced people to help them in their work: *He now runs his own company and is a mentor to other young entrepreneurs.* —**mentoring** *n* [U] *She believes that companies should create programs to encourage mentoring and career development.*

men•u /ˈmenjuː/ *n* [C] a list of choices that appears on a computer screen, allowing you to choose certain operations or run particular processes, using a MOUSE: *Go to the menu at the top of your screen and select 'File'.*

help menu a list on a computer screen that you look at to find out how to do something: *Press the 'Control' key to pop up the help menu.*

MEP *n* [C] Member of the European Parliament; someone who has been elected as a member of the parliament of the EUROPEAN UNION: *This idea was first put forward by North Wales MEP Joe Wilson.*

Merc /mɜːk‖mɜːrk/ *n* another name for MERCANTILE EXCHANGE: *On the New York Merc, gasoline jumped 5.15 cents.*

me•rcan•tile /ˈmɜːkəntaɪl‖ˈmɜːrkəntiːl, -taɪl/ *adj* [only before a noun] concerned with trade: *Tree crops such as coconuts became increasingly important in the mercantile economy into which the islanders were drawn.* | *In some countries* ***mercantile law*** *is quite separate from the ordinary law.*

mercantile court —see under COURT[1]

mercantile exchange *n* [C] a place where people meet to buy and sell things, often COMMODITIES (=oil, metals, farm products etc): *the Chicago Mercantile Exchange*

mer•can•til•is•m /ˈmɜːkəntaɪlɪzəm‖ˈmɜːrkəntiːlɪzəm, -tl-/ *n* [U] the idea that trade produces wealth, especially for countries that export goods. Under mercantilism, exports are encouraged but imports are restricted by the government: *A rise of mercantilism in the producer-oriented West helped European trading companies.* —**mercantilist** *adj*: *The country still has some traces of the mercantilist mentality.*

mer•chan•dise[1] /ˈmɜːtʃəndaɪz, -daɪs‖ˈmɜːr-/ *n* [U] goods that are produced in order to be sold, especially goods that are sold in a store: *Even though retailers ordered merchandise carefully this year, they are getting ready for huge after-Christmas sales.*

merchandise[2] *v* [T] to try to sell goods or services using advertising, PROMOTIONS etc: *Retail stores try to merchandise products in a way that will attract customers.*

merchandise mix —see under MIX

mer•chan•dis•er /ˈmɜːtʃəndaɪzə‖ˈmɜːrtʃəndaɪzər/ *n* [C] **1** a person or company that sells goods in a store: *The recession has affected most U.S. toy and clothing merchandisers.* | *Cosmetics are generally sold through drugstores, supermarkets and other* ***mass merchandisers*** (=large stores that sells more than one kind of product).
2 *AmE* a person or company that arranges the way goods are placed in a store: *Outside merchandisers are usually brought in to create shelf displays and manage in-store advertising.*

mer•chan•dis•ing /ˈmɜːtʃəndaɪzɪŋ‖ˈmɜːr-/ *n* [U] **1** toys, clothes, and other products based on a popular film, TV show, etc and sold to make additional profits: *Even before the movie came out, the markets were flooded with the typical forms of merchandising.*
2 *AmE* the way in which goods are arranged and placed in a store: *For the third year in a row, analysts say that Morgans is the best in the industry for creative merchandising.*

cross merchandising when products that are related to each other are placed next to each other in a SUPERMARKET, to encourage customers to buy both products

scrambled merchandising when a shop sells goods that are usually sold by another type of shop, in order to increase profits or attract new customers. For example, a food shop might start to sell some types of clothing

mer•chant /ˈmɜːtʃənt‖ˈmɜːr-/ *n* [C] **1** a person or organization that buys and sells goods or a particular type of goods: *US* ***tobacco merchants*** *are depending more and more on international sales.* | ***wine merchants*** *and distributors*

mass merchant a merchant selling to large numbers of buyers: *low-cost, high-volume products sold by mass merchants and superstores*

retail merchant someone who owns a shop, or the shop itself: *Retail merchants often cannot afford expensive advertising.*

2 used by CREDIT CARD companies to talk about the shops etc that accept their cards: *Visa is planning a direct-mail package to 250,000 merchants.*

mer•chant•a•ble /ˈmɜːtʃəntəbəl‖ˈmɜːr-/ *adj* LAW good enough to be sold: *The furniture is badly scratched, and thus not* ***of merchantable quality****.*

merchant bank —see under BANK[1]

merchant developer —see under DEVELOPER

mer•chant•ing /ˈmɜːtʃəntɪŋ‖ˈmɜːr-/ *n* [U] *BrE* the business activity of buying and selling something, usually as a WHOLESALER (=an organization that sells to other distributors or shops): *manufacturing and merchanting of timber and wood products*

merchant ship —see under SHIP[1]

merchant shipping —see under SHIPPING

Mer•co•sur /ˈmɜːkəusjuə‖ˈmɜːrkousur/ *n* a trade association consisting of Argentina, Brazil, Paraguay, and Uruguay, founded in 1991 to encourage trade, reduce import taxes between them etc —see also ANDEAN PACT

merge /mɜːdʒ‖mɜːrdʒ/ *v* [I,T] **1** if two or more companies, organizations etc merge, or if they are merged, they join together: *The companies will merge their cellular phone operations, forming one of the nation's largest regional systems.* + **with**: *Sanford shares jumped 10½ to 35¾ after the company agreed to merge with Newell Co. in a stock swap.*
2 to combine lists of information so that only one list

remains. This process also includes PURGING information (=throwing away what is no longer needed) which happens while the information is being merged: *Before the company moved into the new location, we were responsible for merging and purging as much information as possible.* —see also MAIL MERGE

merg•er /ˈmɜːdʒə‖ˈmɜːrdʒər/ *n* [C] an occasion when two or more companies, organizations etc join together to form a larger company etc + **between**: *A merger between similar banks in the same area should enable them to eliminate 40% of the expenses of one of the banks.* | *British Air and KLM ended* ***merger talks*** *discussions about the possibility of merging after failing to agree on how much of the combined company each side would own.* | *The* ***merger proposal*** *plan calls for the three companies to be combined into a new entity.* | *Under the* ***merger agreement****, Comerica and Manufacturers will pool their interests.* | *The* ***merger frenzy*** (=when a lot of mergers are taking place) *has helped push up cable valuations to record highs on Wall Street.*

conglomerate merger the joining together of two or more companies that are completely different in the type of work they do: *Since conglomerate mergers involve companies with completely independent products, there are few opportunities for a reduction in production costs.*

cross-border merger a merger between organizations in different countries: *Cross-border mergers in the arms business have proved much harder to realize than once was expected.*

defensive merger a merger where a company joins with another to avoid being TAKEN OVER (=bought and controlled) by a third company: *Elsevier made a hostile takeover bid for Kluwer, and Kluwer responded by rushing into a defensive merger with Wolters Samsom.*

friendly merger a merger that the shareholders of both companies agree should happen: *What started as a friendly merger agreement deteriorated as the banks argued what price Bank of New York would pay for Northeast.*

full merger a merger where two organizations combine completely, rather than working together in looser ways, for example in JOINT VENTURES: *Siemens decided against a full merger of the two companies because of their conflicting corporate strategies and structures.*

horizontal merger a merger where a company combines with another that makes the same products, provides the same services etc: *horizontal mergers that put two regional electricity companies together*

stock merger also **stock-swap merger** a merger where shareholders in one company receive shares in the other: *In the stock-swap merger, Louisiana General shareholders will receive one share of Citizens Utilities for each Louisiana General common share held.*

vertical merger a merger where a company combines with one of its suppliers or customers in the same industry, or with a company that makes the same products or provides the same services as its suppliers or customers: *the vertical merger of British Telecom with Mitel, an equipment maker*

merger partner —see under PARTNER

merit bonus —see under BONUS

mer•i•toc•ra•cy /ˌmerəˈtɒkrəsi‖-ˈtɑː-/ *n* plural **meritocracies** [C] a social system that gives the greatest power and highest social positions to people with the most ability: *It is only in a meritocracy that people with equivalent levels of education and skill may be paid widely differing amounts.*

merit pay —see ***performance-related pay*** under PAY[1]

Messrs /ˈmesəz‖-ərz/ the plural of MR, used in the names of companies: *Messrs. Albrecht and Herzig*

metal-bashing *n* [U] *informal BrE* companies that are involved in metal bashing manufacture parts made of metal, usually in old-fashioned ways without the use of advanced machinery: *The Midlands region's metal-bashing image is outdated, and there are now many high-tech companies based there.* | *The group has businesses ranging from sophisticated electronics to basic metal-bashing.*

me•ter[1] /ˈmiːtə‖-ər/ *n* **1** [C] a machine that measures and shows the amount of something you have used or the amount of money that you must pay: *A new* ***gas meter*** *had to be installed before the building permit would be granted.* | *The revenue from* ***parking meters*** *in downtown Santa Cruz fell 40% in the last fiscal year.*

people meter [C] MARKETING a small electronic machine used for measuring the number and type of people that watch a particular television programme, usually to collect information for advertisers

2 [C,U] the US spelling of METRE

meter[2] *v* [T] to measure the supply of gas, electricity etc being provided, using a meter: *The San Jose Water Co. meters the water use of the entire county.*

meth•od /ˈmeθəd/ *n* [C] **1** a planned way of doing something, especially one that a lot of people use + **of**: *It is best to consider all methods of figuring your annual income tax before deciding on any one option.* + **for**: *A buy-and-try policy is a suitable method for examining new convenience products.*

2 the ABC method ACCOUNTING a method of keeping a record of materials and stock that a company has, in which more time and attention is given to high-value items considered to be in class A, less to mid-value items in class B, and the least to class C, the low-value items

depreciation method ACCOUNTING one of several methods used to calculate the cost of an asset over its expected life. The cost appears in the DEPRECIATION ACCOUNT and is used to calculate the DEPRECIATION ALLOWANCE

declining balance method also **reducing balance method** ACCOUNTING a method of calculating the DEPRECIATION of an asset, in which the value of the asset is reduced by the same percentage each year and the amount is charged to the PROFIT AND LOSS ACCOUNT

method study —see under STUDY[1]

mét•i•er /ˈmetieɪ,ˈmeɪ-‖meˈtjeɪ,ˈmetjeɪ/ *n* [C usually singular] *formal* a kind of work or activity that you enjoy doing because you have a natural ability to do it well: *Ability to create successful advertising campaigns has been the métier of this company for the past decade.*

me-too *adj* [only before a noun] a me-too product is introduced by a company after it has seen that other companies are successful with the same type of product: *The bill would cancel funding for companies which produce me-too copies of existing drugs rather than discovering totally new ones.*

me-too product —see under PRODUCT

me•tre *BrE*, **meter** *AmE* /ˈmiːtə‖-ər/ *n* [C] the basic unit for measuring length in the METRIC SYSTEM: *This material is sold by the metre.*

met•ri•ca•tion /ˌmetrɪˈkeɪʃən/ *n* [U] the change to using the metric system of weights and measures

metric system *n* [singular] the system of weights and measures that is based on the metre and the KILOGRAM: *The metric system is in use in most of the industrial countries.*

metric ton —see under TON

me•trop•o•lis /məˈtrɒpələs‖məˈtrɑː-/ *n* [C] a very large city with a lot of industrial and economic activity that is usually the most important city in a country or area, but not always its capital: *Twenty-five years ago Las Vegas was not the metropolis it is today.*

mezzanine debt —see under DEBT

M

mfg written abbreviation for MANUFACTURING

MICR abbreviation for MAGNETIC INK CHARACTER RECOGNITION

micro- /maɪkrəʊ, -krə‖-kroʊ, -krə/ *prefix* used at the beginning of words to show that something is extremely small: *microcomputer* | *microprocessor*

mi•cro•chip /ˈmaɪkrəʊˌtʃɪp‖-kroʊ-/ *n* [C] a very small piece of SILICON containing a set of electronic parts which is used in computers and other machines; CHIP; MICROCHIP: *Intel plans to introduce a new personal-computer microchip by the end of the year.*

mi•cro•com•put•er /ˈmaɪkrəʊkəmˌpjuːtə‖-kroʊkəmˈpjuːtər/ *n* [C] *old-fashioned* another name for a PC

mi•cro•ec•o•nom•ics /ˌmaɪkrəʊiːkəˈnɒmɪks, -ekə‖-kroʊiːkəˈnɑː-/ *n* [U] the study of a part of the economy, such as the operations of one company or person: *The issue of minimum-wage rates provides constant debate for advocates of microeconomics.* —compare MACROECONOMICS —**microeconomic** *adj*: *a microeconomic analysis*

mi•cro•pro•ces•sor /ˈmaɪkrəʊˌprəʊsesə‖-kroʊˈprɑːsesər/ *n* [C] the central CHIP in a computer, which controls most of its operations: *The development of increasingly powerful and inexpensive microprocessors has led to the high popularity of personal computers.*

Microsoft Disk Operating System —see MS-DOS

mid-cap *n* [C] FINANCE a share in a company with a medium amount of SHARE CAPITAL: *The day's winners were led by mid-caps, with Deutz leaping 24.6%.* —**mid-cap** *adj* [only before a noun] *A lot of growth will be seen in mid-cap stocks with between $500 million and $2 billion in market value.*

mid-cap share —see under SHARE

mid-cap stock —see under STOCK[1]

mid•dle•man /ˈmɪdlmæn/ *n* plural **middlemen** [C] a person, business, organization etc that buys things in order to sell them to someone else, or that helps to arrange business deals for other people, for example BROKERS and WHOLESALERS: *Investors will get better prices by avoiding companies that go through a middleman.*

middle management —see under MANAGEMENT

middle market —see under MARKET[1]

mid-market also **midmarket** *AmE* —*adj* [only before a noun] in the middle of the range of similar companies or products in the market as a whole: *Burton, the mid-market British retailer*

mid-price also **mid-priced** *adj* [only before a noun] neither very expensive nor very cheap in relation to similar things: *He stays in mid-priced hotels and rents economy cars when he's traveling.*

mid-range also **midrange** *AmE* —*adj* a product that is in the middle of the range of similar products available from the same company or in the market as a whole: *IBM will also be announcing some midrange and high-end workstations.*

mi•grant /ˈmaɪɡrənt/ *n* [C] someone who goes to another area or country, especially in order to find work: *Growing rice is usually performed by low-paid* ***migrant workers.*** | *The FSA administered a system to regulate* ***migrant labor*** *in California.*

mi•grate /maɪˈɡreɪt‖ˈmaɪɡreɪt/ *v* [I] to go to another area or country, especially in order to find work: *In the years ahead, tens of thousands of workers looking for high-paid, technical jobs could migrate abroad.* —**migratory** *adj*: *Among the 17,000 workers in Southern New Mexico, approximately half are* ***migratory workers*** *who follow the seasonal jobs.* —compare EMIGRATE, IMMIGRATE

mile /maɪl/ *n* [C] also **geographical mile** a unit for measuring distance or length, equal to 5280 feet or 1609 metres

nautical mile also **sea mile** a unit for measuring distance at sea, equal to 6076 feet or 1852 metres

mile•age /ˈmaɪlɪdʒ/ *n* [U] **1** an amount of money paid for each mile that is travelled by someone using a car for work: *The* ***mileage allowance*** *for use of a personal car for business is up to 24 cents a mile.*

2 the amount of use or advantage that you get from something: *Managers are working furiously on ways to get the most mileage out of the plan.*

miles per gallon —see MPG

miles per hour —see MPH

milk /mɪlk/ *v* [T] *informal* to get as much money or as many advantages as you can from a situation, in a very determined and sometimes dishonest way **milk sb/sth for sth**: *As the only computer technician in the company, Blackwell can milk the latest systems crash for all it's worth.*

milk round *n BrE* **the milk round** a series of visits to universities made each year by large companies in order to find people they may want to employ: *Over 50% of Jackson's new employees were recruited on the milk round.*

mill[1] /mɪl/ *n* [C] MANUFACTURING **1** a building containing a large machine for crushing grain into flour, or the machine itself

2 a factory that produces materials such as cotton, cloth, or steel: *The* ***textile mill*** *is full of modern Japanese machinery.* | *a big pulp and* ***newsprint mill*** (=one for making paper for newspapers) | *Pittsburgh's* ***steel mills***

paper mill a factory where paper is made

mill[2] *v* [T] MANUFACTURING **1** to produce flour by crushing grain in a mill

2 to press, roll, or shape metal in a machine

3 to mark the edge of a coin with regular lines —**milled** *adj* [only before a noun] *milled corn*

Millennium bug —see under BUG

milli- /mɪlə/ *prefix* used at the beginning of words to describe a 1000th part of a particular unit: *a millimetre*

mil•lion /ˈmɪljən/ *number* plural **million** or **millions** written abbreviation **m** 1,000,000

mil•lion•aire /ˌmɪljəˈneə‖-ˈner/ *n* [C] someone who has assets worth at least a million pounds, dollars etc: *Executives at the TV company can expect to become millionaires through a 15% holding.* | *a dollar millionaire*

paper millionaire a person who owns investments which would be worth a million pounds or dollars if they were sold: *As soon as the company was launched on the stock exchange, the three founding directors became paper millionaires overnight.*

min. written abbreviation for MINIMUM; MINUTE; MINUTES

mind /maɪnd/ *n* MARKETING **front of mind/share of mind** if a brand or company is front of mind or has share of mind, people think about it as a possible choice when buying a particular type of product: *Pirelli is trying to establish itself as a front-of-mind brand when it comes to buying tyres. You will not forget their latest ad.* | *Our objective is to keep a high level of awareness of the brand, something often described as 'share of mind'.*

mine[1] /maɪn/ *n* [C] a deep hole or series of holes that are dug in the ground in order to find gold, coal, diamonds etc

mine[2] *v* [I,T] to dig holes or passages under the ground in order to obtain gold, coal, diamonds etc

min•i- /mɪni/ *prefix* used at the beginning of words to show that something is very small compared with the standard size: *minidisk* | *minibus* —compare MICRO-

mini-budget *n* [C] an extra budget prepared by a government, usually because there are specific economic problems that need to be dealt with: *Richardson presented a mini-budget which contained cuts in government spending on health, education, and defence.*

min•i•com•put•er /ˈmɪnikəmˌpjuːtə‖-ər/ *n* [C] a computer that is larger than a PERSONAL COMPUTER and smaller than a MAINFRAME, used by businesses and other large organizations

mini-ISA —see under ISA

min•i•mize also **minimise** *BrE* /ˈmɪnəmaɪz/ *v* [T] **1** to make something as small as possible: *Investing in unit trusts* ***minimises the risks*** *if stock markets fall.* | *We need to* ***minimize*** *our transport* ***costs.***

2 COMPUTING to make a WINDOW on a computer screen as small as possible: *Click on the small square to minimise the window.* —opposite MAXIMIZE

min•i•mum¹ /ˈmɪnəməm/ *adj* [only before a noun] the smallest or least that is possible, allowed, or needed: ***Minimum investment*** *in each fund is £2000.* | *There is a* ***minimum charge*** *of £30.* | *The minimum requirements for the job are a degree and a teaching qualification.* —compare MAXIMUM¹

minimum² written abbreviation **min** *n* [singular] **1** the smallest amount or number of something that is possible, allowed, or needed + **of**: *Applicants should have a minimum of five years' professional experience.* | *Ferranti needed to raise a minimum of £150 million in new equity.*

2 keep/reduce something to a minimum to limit something to the smallest amount or degree possible: *It is essential that we keep costs to a minimum.* | *Risks must be reduced to the* ***absolute minimum.***

minimum lending rate —see ***base rate*** under RATE¹

minimum wage —see under WAGE

min•ing /ˈmaɪnɪŋ/ *n* [U] the action or industry of getting minerals out of the earth by digging: *a* ***mining company***

opencast mining mining in which minerals, especially coal, are dug from an open hole in the ground and not from a deep passage —see also DATA MINING

min•is•ter /ˈmɪnəstə‖-ər/ *n* [C] in Britain and some other countries, a politician who is a member of the government and is either in charge of or has an important job in a government department + **of/for**: *a meeting of EU finance ministers* | *Colombia's trade minister, Juan Manuel Santos* | *the minister of tourism* | *the minister for industry*

mi•nor¹ /ˈmaɪnə‖-ər/ *n* [C] LAW someone who is below the age at which they become legally responsible for their actions: *The bank does not normally lend to minors.*

minor² *adj* less important than other things in a group of things it is related to: *The cost of the bid will have only a minor impact on full-year results.* | *minor currencies*

minority interest —see under INTEREST

minority ownership —see under OWNERSHIP

minority shareholder —see under SHAREHOLDER

minority shareholding —see under SHAREHOLDING

minority stake —see under STAKE¹

minority stockholder —see under STOCKHOLDER

minor-league *adj* [only before a noun] not important or influential: *U.S. companies got only 1.3% of the market here last year, minor-league stuff compared with Japan's 28% of U.S. car and truck sales.*

mint¹ /mɪnt/ *n* **1** [C] a place where a country's coins are officially manufactured: *the Royal Mint*

2 a mint *informal* a very large amount of money: *When she eventually sold the business she* ***made a mint.*** | *As the major shareholder he must be* ***worth a mint.***

mint² *v* [T] to manufacture coins: *the right of a country to mint its own coins*

mint•age /ˈmɪntɪdʒ/ *n* [U] the process of minting coins, or coins made in a mint

mi•nus /ˈmaɪnəs/ *prep* used to show that you are taking one number or quantity from another; LESS: *Net income is gross income minus income tax and National Insurance.*

min•ute¹ /ˈmɪnət/ *n* **1 minutes** [plural] an official written record of what is said and decided at a meeting: *The minutes of the last AGM were read.* | *Will someone* ***take the minutes?*** (=write down what is said) | ***Board minutes*** *and other records should show that events took place in the correct order.*

2 [C] a short official note that gives authority for something or that records a decision: *a Treasury minute dated 2nd December* | *We attach a certified copy of a* ***Board minute*** *authorising the signature of this letter.*

minute² *v* [T] to make a written record of something in the minutes of a meeting: *The board's decision was formally minuted.* | *You'd better minute that point.*

minute book —see under BOOK¹

MIRAS also **Miras** /ˈmaɪræs/ *n* [U] TAX mortgage interest tax relief at source; a system in the UK where people with a MORTGAGE (=loan to buy property) were able to get money back from the tax system. MIRAS stopped from April 2000

mis•ap•pro•pri•ate /ˌmɪsəˈprəʊprieɪt‖-ˈproʊ-/ *v* [T] to dishonestly take something, especially money, that you have been trusted to keep safe, and to use it for your own advantage: *He was accused of* ***misappropriating funds*** *amounting to £4 million.* | *Building materials had been misappropriated for private use.* —**misappropriation** *n* [U] *allegations of gross* ***misappropriation of funds*** | *the misappropriation of a £20 million loan*

misc. written abbreviation for MISCELLANEOUS

miscarriage of justice *n* plural **miscarriages of justice** [C] a situation in which someone is wrongly punished by a court of law for something they did not do

mis•cel•la•ne•ous /ˌmɪsəˈleɪniəs◂/ *adj* [only before a noun] made up of many different things or people that are not connected with each other: *I attach a list of other* ***miscellaneous expenses.*** | *Put a copy of the letter in the* ***miscellaneous file.***

mis•con•duct /ˌmɪsˈkɒndʌkt‖-ˈkɑːn-/ *n* [U] *formal* bad or dishonest behaviour by a professional person: *the penalties for such misconduct as fraudulent trading or theft*

gross misconduct HUMAN RESOURCES, LAW extremely bad behaviour or performance by an employee that may lead to DISMISSAL (=being told to leave their job): *examples of gross misconduct, such as theft, damage to property, or drunkenness during working hours*

mis•count /ˌmɪsˈkaʊnt/ *v* [T] to count something wrongly: *allegations that the vote was deliberately miscounted*

mis•de•mea•nour *BrE*, **misdemeanor** *AmE* /ˌmɪsdɪˈmiːnə‖-ər/ *n* [C] **1** a bad or unacceptable action that is not very serious, at least from a legal point of view

2 LAW *AmE* a crime that is not as serious as a FELONY (=very serious crime such as robbery or murder): *He pleaded guilty to lying on a loan application, which is a misdemeanor in this state.*

mi•ser /ˈmaɪzə‖-ər/ *n* [C] a person, organization, country etc that hates spending money: *The US is a miser when it comes to research and development spending in engineering.* —**miserly** *adj*: *Teachers complain they already work long hours for miserly pay.*

misery index —see under INDEX¹

mis•fea•sance /ˌmɪsˈfiːzəns/ *n* [U] LAW when someone fails to perform something for which they are

M

responsible by law: *If there is any suggestion of misfeasance here concerned with the transfer of the assets, then the Insolvency Act 1986 may apply.* —compare MALFEASANCE, NONFEASANCE

mis·gov·ern /mɪsˈɡʌvən‖-ərn/ *v* [I,T] if a country or organization is misgoverned, it is not being run or managed well, the wrong decisions are being taken etc: *There is no doubt that the country has been terribly misgoverned in recent decades, and that a change is welcome.* —**misgovernment** *n* [U] *the pattern of misgovernment symbolized by Watergate*

mis·man·age /ˌmɪsˈmænɪdʒ/ *v* [T] to manage a company, economy etc badly: *The project has been mismanaged from start to finish.* | *British firms squander billions each year by mismanaging corporate overheads.* —**mismanagement** *n* [U] *Shareholders may sue the directors for mismanagement.* | *The government has been accused of* ***economic mismanagement****.*

mis·rep·re·sent /ˌmɪsreprɪˈzent/ *v* [T] LAW to deliberately give false information to someone, especially in order to persuade them to enter into a contract: *He was found guilty of misrepresenting the true position of his accounts.*

mis·rep·re·sen·ta·tion /ˌmɪsreprɪzenˈteɪʃən/ *n* [C,U] LAW the act of deliberately giving false information to someone, especially in order to persuade them to enter into a contract, or a statement giving false information; MISSTATEMENT: *He was found guilty of misrepresentation and undue influence.* | *A* ***fraudulent misrepresentation*** *is one made without believing in its truth or caring whether it is true or false.*

mis-sale *n* [C,U] the sale of something that is unsuitable for the person buying it

mis-sell also **missell** *v* [T] to sell something that is unsuitable for the person buying it: *Half a million people were missold a personal pension, many being wrongly advised to leave occupational schemes.* —**mis-selling** *n* [U] *the mis-selling of time-share apartments*

mis·sion /ˈmɪʃən/ *n* [C] **1** an important job that someone is given to do: *He is a man on a mission: to overhaul the way Chrysler develops new cars.*

2 used by organizations to talk about their purpose and aims: *Our mission is to provide quality long-term care to the maximum number of patients.*

3 a group of important people who are sent by their government to another country to discuss something or collect information: *Congress has sent a team of observers on a* ***fact-finding mission*** *to the country.*

trade mission a group of politicians and businesspeople who visit a country in order to encourage trade with that country: *He welcomed members of the US Chamber of Commerce to Hong Kong, the first American trade mission to visit for some time.*

mission-critical *adj* mission-critical computer software and NETWORKS (=system of connected computers) are extremely important, allowing a business to be able to operate: *Without mission-critical networks, virtually every aspect of the company's international trade and commerce grinds to a halt.*

mission statement —see under STATEMENT

mis·state·ment /ˌmɪsˈsteɪtmənt/ *n* [C] LAW the act of deliberately giving false information to someone, especially in order to persuade them to enter into a contract, or a statement giving false information; MISREPRESENTATION

Mis·ter /ˈmɪstə‖-ər/ *n* the full form of MR

mis·use /ˌmɪsˈjuːs/ *n* [C,U] the dishonest or wrong use of something: *a misuse of public funds* —**misuse** /mɪsˈjuːz/ *v* [T] *A Florida businessman was arrested for misusing JTPA funds.*

mix /mɪks/ *n* [C usually singular] a group of different things combined together for a particular purpose: *If the investment manager picks the right mix of bonds, his total return should rise quickly.*

asset mix a mix of different investments designed to be the most profitable possible: *The firm's recommended asset mix was 45% stocks, 35% bonds and 20% cash.*

business mix the mix of a business's different types of activities or customers: *The contract would shift the company's business mix from 70% government contracts and 30% commercial business to about 50–50.*

investment mix another name for ASSET MIX: *You don't have to change your investment mix all the time to get good results.*

marketing mix the mix of marketing actions, usually product, price, place, and PROMOTION. A company should find the right combination of products for each market it is in, price them correctly in relation to each other and to competitors' products, use the best ways to deliver them, and support this with suitable communication with customers: *The group is struggling to find a marketing mix that is cost-effective and appeals to its customer base.*

merchandise mix the combination of goods that a store sells: *The store is changing its image with a merchandise mix that places greater emphasis on fashion and color.*

portfolio mix another name for ASSET MIX

product mix the combination of products that a company has to offer: *The company blamed the drop in profits on its product mix, with increased sales of lower-priced, less profitable shoes and lower sales of its more expensive ones.*

sales mix how each of a company's products contributes to its sales: *Their sales mix is moving away from household products, into higher-margin personal care products.*

mixed trading —see under TRADING

mkt. written abbreviation for MARKET

ml written abbreviation for MILLILITRE

MLR abbreviation for MINIMUM LENDING RATE

mm written abbreviation for MILLIMETRE

MMC abbreviation for MONOPOLIES AND MERGERS COMMISSION

MNC abbreviation for MULTINATIONAL CORPORATION

MNE abbreviation for MULTINATIONAL ENTERPRISE

mngmt. written abbreviation for MANAGEMENT

mngr. written abbreviation for MANAGER

MO written abbreviation for MAIL ORDER; MONEY ORDER

mobile shop —see under SHOP[1]

mobile worker —see under WORKER

mobility of labour *BrE*, **mobility of labor** *AmE*, also **labour mobility** *BrE*, **labor mobility** *AmE* — *n* [U] HUMAN RESOURCES the degree to which workers are able and willing to move from one place to another in order to get a job or to change jobs: *The mobility of labour between firms happens especially in the earlier and later years of working careers.* | *The government should invest in housing to encourage labour mobility.*

mobility premium —see under PREMIUM[1]

mode /məʊd‖moʊd/ *n* [C] **1** STATISTICS the figure or value that appears most often in a set of values. For example, the mode is calculated when shops need to know which sizes of a product such as shoes or clothing are selling more than others

2 a way of behaving: *The market has been in an up mode* (=prices have been increasing).

3 the way in which a machine operates when it is doing a particular job: *running Windows in standard mode*

M

mode of payment plural **modes of payment** a particular way of paying for something; METHOD OF PAYMENT

mod•el /ˈmɒdl‖ˈmɑːdl/ *n* **1** [C] a particular type or design of a vehicle or machine: *the cheapest model in the Volkswagen range* | *Our photocopier is the* ***latest model***. —see also BRAND[1], MAKE[2]

2 [C] a simple description or structure that is used to help people understand similar systems or structures: *a theoretical model* | *a computer model of the main factors determining a company's market share*

Black-Scholes pricing model [singular] FINANCE a mathematical way of finding if an OPTION (=the right to buy shares in the future at a particular price) has a fair price, taking into account the price of the related shares, the amount that this price has changed over time, interest rates, the risk of the agreement failing etc: *He is taking the ideas that underpin the Black-Scholes pricing model and applying them to corporate bonds.*

capital asset pricing model [singular] FINANCE the theory that the risk related to a share, bond etc is related to the payments it produces: *The key insight of the capital asset pricing model is that investors can expect a reward for an investment's contribution to the risk of a portfolio.*

option pricing model abbreviation **OPM** [C] FINANCE a way of calculating if the price of an options contract is fair in relation to the price of the shares etc that it relates to, their probably future profitability, general interest rates etc. One of the best-known is the Black-Scholes option pricing model

3 [C] the way in which something is done by a particular country, person etc that can be copied by others who want similar results: *the American model of airline deregulation*

mo•dem /ˈməʊdəm, -dem‖ˈmoʊ-/ *n* [C] COMPUTING a piece of electronic equipment that allows information from one computer to be sent along telephone wires to another computer —see also E-MAIL[1], INTERNET

mode of payment —see under MODE

moderate trading —see under TRADING

mod•i•fy /ˈmɒdəfaɪ‖ˈmɑː-/ *v* past tense and past participle **modified** [T] to make changes, especially small changes, to something in order to improve it and make it more suitable or effective: *The* ***plan*** *has been slightly* ***modified***. | *Banks have modified their traditional role and now offer mortgages, pensions, and other financial services.* | *Vehicles with internal combustion engines will have to be modified for greater energy efficiency.*

mod•ule /ˈmɒdjuːl‖ˈmɑːdʒuːl/ *n* [C] **1** one of several separate parts that can be combined to form a larger thing: *Software is often written in modules by teams of programmers.*

2 *BrE* one of the units that a course of study has been divided into, each of which can be studied separately: *Each video contains* ***training modules*** *from ATV's Business Account programmes.* —**modular** *adj*: *a* ***modular course*** *in business studies*

mo•gul /ˈməʊgəl‖ˈmoʊ-/ *n* [C] **movie/media/oil etc mogul** *journalism* someone who has great power and influence in a particular industry or activity: *Steve Ross, the media mogul who merged Time and Warner in 1989*

mom-and-pop *adj AmE* **mom-and-pop business/store etc** a shop or small business that is owned and operated by members of the same family, and has a very limited amount of capital: *Most wineries in California are mom-and-pop operations with practically no paid help other than your own family.*

mo•men•tum /məʊˈmentəm, mə-‖moʊ-, mə-/ *n* [U] the ability to keep increasing, developing, or being more successful: *A movement to remove government restrictions on business operations* ***gained momentum***. | *Economists warned the economy was* ***losing momentum*** *rapidly and that growth could slip as low as 1.5% next year.*

mon•e•ta•ris•m /ˈmʌnətərɪzəm‖ˈmɑː-/ *n* [U] ECONOMICS the idea that an economy can be controlled by its CENTRAL BANK influencing the MONEY SUPPLY (=amount of money in the economy at a particular time.) For example, the central bank can influence the amount of bank lending by increasing or lowering interest rates

mon•e•ta•rist[1] /ˈmʌnətərəst‖ˈmɑː-/ *n* [C] someone, usually an economist or a politician, who believes in monetarism and who thinks that the economy should be managed using these ideas: *She isn't a pure monetarist who would concentrate only on money-supply measures.*

monetarist[2] *adj* relating to or involving monetarism: *A senior finance ministry official is to resign over moves to drop* ***monetarist policy***. | *a group of* ***monetarist economists*** *who monitor the Fed's actions* | *Economists of the* ***monetarist school*** (=believers in monetarism) *are optimistic because the money supply has been growing at its slowest rate in more than 20 years.*

mon•e•ta•ry /ˈmʌnətəri‖ˈmɑːnəteri/ *adj* relating to or involving money, especially the MONEY SUPPLY (=the amount of money in the economy): *The bond market rallied* (=prices rose) *as the Federal Reserve eased monetary conditions.*

monetary aggregate —see under AGGREGATE[1]

monetary deflation —see under DEFLATION

monetary growth —see under GROWTH

monetary policy —see under POLICY

monetary standard —see under STANDARD[1]

monetary stimulus —see under STIMULUS

monetary system —see under SYSTEM

monetary theory —see under THEORY

mon•ey /ˈmʌni/ *n* [U] **1** coins, BANKNOTES and BANK DEPOSITS (=money held in banks) used to buy things and to show their value: *People are eating out less to* ***save money***. | *Americans* ***spent*** *more* ***money*** *even though they earned less.* | *You should* ***borrow money*** *from the bank to pay for your course.* | *As an estate agent, he* ***made*** (=earned) *a lot of* ***money*** *buying houses cheaply and reselling them.* | *He has picked a difficult time to* ***raise money*** (=obtain it for a particular purpose) *from outside investors.* | *foreigners who wanted to* ***put money into*** (=to invest in) *US stocks*

conduct money LAW money paid to someone when they are a WITNESS in a legal case, to pay for food, travel, hotel rooms; EXPENSES

danger money extra money paid by an employer to a worker, usually one working in the building industry, who is doing an especially dangerous job

easy money ◆ money that you earn very easily, without having to work hard: *People were tempted into the trade by the thought of easy money.*

fall money *AmE informal* money used by criminals to pay legal costs

funny money *informal* ◆ money that is worthless outside the country where it is used: *Who wants to be paid in funny money that is forever being devalued by inflation?*

◆ money that has been printed illegally: *Police issued a warning about funny money after a motorist paid for petrol with a forged £20 note.*

hush money money paid to someone to prevent them from telling other people about something embarrassing or dishonest: *It was the start of an elaborate plan to get hush money from his employer.*

paper money money in the form of BANKNOTES, rather than coins or gold: *He argues that paper money is being printed so rapidly it is worthless.*

M

plastic money CREDIT CARDS (=plastic cards used to buy things)
spending money money that you have available to spend on small personal expenses: *The winner will receive a holiday for two in Thailand, plus £1000 spending money.*
2 all the money that a country, organization, or person owns: *The business collapsed and we lost all our money.*
new money money belonging to people who have only recently become rich, also used to talk about the people themselves: *In the United States there is more new money, and the social structure is different.*
old money money belonging to families that have been rich for a very long time, also used to talk about the families themselves: *the traditional architectural styles associated with old money*
3 money used for investment; capital: *a plan to inject money into Thomson, the defense and electronics concern*
fresh money new money for investment, rather than existing capital: *VW plans to raise DM6 billion in a rare share issue, but the company is unlikely to use the fresh money to buy other carmakers.*
hot money ◆ money that is moved quickly from place to place in order to be invested in the most profitable things in different places: *If interest rates go lower, some of the hot money will start to leave.*
◆ money obtained from illegal activities that is invested in ways which hide its source: *the hot money generated by the cocaine industry*
idle money *BrE* money that is not earning interest: *Speculators prefer to hold idle money in the knowledge that, if they wait, the rate of interest will go up again.*
seed money also **front money** the money needed to start a new business idea or PROJECT: *How much front money will be needed to pay for the new factory?*
4 used to talk about what it costs to borrow money
cheap money also **easy money** money that can be borrowed cheaply because interest rates are low: *With economic expansion and cheap money, many Mexican companies are jumping into the real estate business.*
dear money also **tight money** money that costs a lot to borrow because interest rates are high: *He says that the days of dear money aren't over, despite the interest rate cut.*
easy money when there is easy money, banks and other organizations are willing to lend money, and interest rates are low: *Interest rates tumbled, and easy money financed both growth and inflation.*
one-month money money lent for one month on the money markets: *High short-term interest rates – 40% for one-month money – were needed to defend the currency.*
one-year money money lent for one year on the money markets: *Rates for one-year money jumped from 9% to 10.75%.*
5 ECONOMICS a measure of the MONEY SUPPLY (=the amount of money in the economy at a particular time) —see ***M0/M1/M2 etc*** under MONEY SUPPLY
bank money ECONOMICS money that is held by banks, a part of MONEY SUPPLY: *Central bank money has been allowed to grow beyond the target of 1%.*
broad money ◆ cash and all the forms of money that cannot easily be turned into cash: *Broad money refers to money held both for transactions purposes and as a form of saving.*
◆ ECONOMICS a measure of how much money is available in an economy; M3: *The strong expansion of broad money is causing worries about inflation.*
narrow money cash and the forms of money that can most easily be turned into cash: *Narrow money refers to money balances which are easily available to finance day-to-day spending, that is, for transactions purposes.*
near money something that can easily be turned into cash, for example some types of BANK DEPOSIT (=money held in banks): *near money assets such as short-dated bonds*
6 money paid by someone to prove that they are serious about buying something or about doing business
caution money *BrE* ◆ an amount of money left with a person or organization to pay for damage that might be done or for some other thing that might cost them money; DEPOSIT
◆ money paid by someone who has a contract with someone else, to make certain that they do what the contract says they must do; DEPOSIT
◆ money paid by someone who is about to buy something that is expensive and complicated to buy, for example a house, to prove that they intend to complete the deal; DEPOSIT
deposit money also **earnest money** money that a buyer gives to a seller as a first payment to prove that they intend to complete a deal: *The completion date, when money for the house is handed over, is usually 28 days after the exchange of contracts. So you will be without your deposit money for a month at least.*
good faith money FINANCE the money that you must pay as a DEPOSIT in order to be able to trade on a FUTURES MARKET: *The two markets raised requirements for good-faith money that investors must put up to initiate trades.*
key money *BrE* PROPERTY money someone renting a house or flat gives to the owner as a DEPOSIT (=money paid in advance)
7 at the money/in the money/out of the money FINANCE in OPTIONS TRADING (=buying and selling the right to buy shares etc at a later date for a particular price), an option is at the money when the EXERCISE PRICE (=the price at which the shares etc can be bought using the option) is the same as the MARKET PRICE (=the current price of the shares on the stockmarket). A CALL OPTION (=the right to buy particular shares) is in the money when the exercise price is below the market price and out of the money when it is above it

money at call —see under AT CALL

money broker —see under BROKER[1]

money center —see under CENTRE

money-changer *n* [C] someone whose business is exchanging currencies, usually outside the official banking system: *the alleys where money-changers deal the dollars and deutschemarks*

money damages —see under DAMAGE[1]

mon·eyed also **monied** /ˈmʌnid/ *adj* [only before a noun] *formal* monied people are rich and powerful: *the monied elite who have traditionally run Mexico's banks and conglomerates*

money fund —see under FUND[1]

money-grabbing also **money-grubbing** *adj disapproving* determined to get money, even by unfair or illegal methods: *I haven't turned into a nasty, cynical, money-grubbing old man.* **—money-grabber —money-grubber** *n* [C]

money income —see under INCOME

mon·ey·lend·er /ˈmʌniˌlendə‖-ər/ *n* [C] a person or organization that lends money, usually outside the official banking system: *For poor people in Bangladesh, the local moneylender is the only source of finance.*

money-loser *n* [C] a product, service, or business that makes a loss; LOSS-MAKER: *The recession has turned the once-profitable chain into a money-loser.*

money-maker *n* [C] a product, service, or business that makes a profit; MONEY-SPINNER: *The drug may become Merck's next big money-maker. | Big hostile takeovers are huge money-makers for Wall Street.*

money management —see under MANAGEMENT

money manager —see under MANAGER

money market —see under MARKET[1]

money market deposits —see under DEPOSIT[1]

money-market fund —see under FUND[1]

money-market instrument —see under INSTRUMENT

money of account *n* [C usually singular] the currency used in business and finance in a particular place: *Since 1999, the Euro has been the money of account in most EU countries.*

money order *n* [C] a document you can buy at a bank or post office when you want to send money through the post safely

money-spin•ner *n* [C] another name for MONEYMAKER: *The pet food business is a real money-spinner. The European market is worth £5 billion a year and growing.*

money stock —see under STOCK[1]

money supply also **money stock** *n* [singular] ECONOMICS **1** the amount of money in an economy at a particular time, and the speed with which it is used: *The Fed should aim at a faster growth of the money supply this year.*

2 M0/M1/M2 etc different measures of a country's money supply depending on the types of money they include, such as cash, BANK DEPOSITS (=money held by banks), COMMERCIAL PAPER (=borrowing for short periods of time by organizations) etc: *The Fed said its narrow M1 measure of the money supply fell $400 million in the week ended Sept. 9, while the broader M3 measure fell $500 million.* | *M1 grew more than 8%, reflecting a $20 billion increase in currency and a $47 billion jump in demand deposits.*

money wages —see under WAGE

mon•i•tor[1] /ˈmɒnɨtə‖ˈmɑːnɨtər/ *v* [T] to carefully watch and check a situation in order to see how it changes or progresses over a period of time: *The company constantly monitors its performance against those of its competitors.* | *Our standards of service are rigorously monitored.*

monitor[2] *n* [C] **1** COMPUTING the part of a computer that looks like a television and shows information; VDU: *a color monitor*

2 an independent person whose job is to make sure that an activity, situation etc is fair or legal: *The monitor will assure that the union's members use their own names and social security numbers and that no paychecks are issued for fictitious services.*

Monopolies and Mergers Commission abbreviation **MMC** *n* a British government organization whose job is to examine cases where two companies plan to join together to form one company, and to decide whether this would be bad for other businesses because there will be less competition. There is a similar organization in the US called the FEDERAL TRADE COMMISSION

mo•nop•o•list /məˈnɒpəlɨst‖məˈnɑː-/ *n* [C] ECONOMICS a person or business that is the only supplier of a particular product or service: *A monopolist can earn enormous profits.*

mo•nop•o•lis•tic /məˌnɒpəˈlɪstɪk◂‖məˌnɑː-/ *adj* ECONOMICS controlling or trying to control an industry or business activity completely by not allowing other companies to compete fairly: *monopolistic market conditions* | *Unfair* ***monopolistic practices*** *are prohibited by the Treaty of Rome.*

mo•nop•o•lize also **monopolise** *BrE* /məˈnɒpəlaɪz‖məˈnɑː-/ *v* [T] ECONOMICS if a single company or a government monopolizes an industry, it gets control of all or most of it so that there is little or no competition from other companies or countries: *The company sold below cost in order to drive out competition and monopolize the Los Angeles-area market.*

mo•nop•o•ly /məˈnɒpəli‖məˈnɑː-/ *n* plural **monopolies** **1** [C,U] a situation where a business activity is controlled by only one company or by the government, and other companies do not compete with it: *Turkish Airlines is no longer a monopoly. At least 10 new charter, scheduled and commuter airlines compete against it.* + **on**: *For years, YPF enjoyed a monopoly on oil exploration and production in Argentina.* | *TAV has been* ***granted a monopoly*** *over Italian high-speed train lines.* | *There remains the threat of monopoly.*

legal monopoly [C,U] a monopoly allowed by the law of a particular country

natural monopoly [C,U] an industry where there is only one producer because of the nature of the activity: *Natural monopoly leads to socially inefficient outcomes: too little output and too high a price.*

state monopoly [C,U] also **public monopoly** a monopoly that is owned and managed by a government: *For a long time in Europe, broadcasting was a state monopoly, with public service obligations.* | *The statutory public monopoly of electricity supply has been ended.*

2 have/hold a monopoly on sth if one person, group, or organization has a monopoly on something, they have something that others do not share: *This bank does not* ***have a monopoly*** *on bad loans.*

mo•nop•so•ny /məˈnɒpsəni‖-ˈnɑː-/ *n* [U] ECONOMICS a situation where there are many sellers but only one buyer for a product or service: *Many government bureaux are in the position of monopsony in buying labour, such as firemen, army officers and policemen.* —**monopsonist** *n* [C]

Moody's Investors Service Inc. *n* a US RATINGS AGENCY (=an organization that researches and sells information about borrowers' ability to repay bonds, loans etc)

moon•light /ˈmuːnlaɪt/ *v* [I] if you moonlight, you have a second job in addition to your main job, without the knowledge of your main employer or the tax authorities: *She's been moonlighting as a waitress in the evenings.* —**moonlighter** *n* [C] *If you hire a moonlighter, you're taking a chance.* —**moonlighting** *n* [U] *He's been* ***doing some moonlighting*** *for another company.*

Moore's Law /ˌmʊəz ˈlɔː‖ˌmʊrz ˈlɒː/ *n* COMPUTING the statement that the cost of a particular amount of computer power falls by half every 18 or 24 months

mo•rale /məˈrɑːl‖məˈræl/ *n* [U] HUMAN RESOURCES the level of confidence and positive feelings among a group of people who work together: *On-site child care, increase workers' job satisfaction and morale.*

moral hazard —see under HAZARD

mor•a•to•ri•um /ˌmɒrəˈtɔːriəm‖ˌmɔː-/ *n* plural **moratoria** or **moratoriums** [C usually singular] **1** a period of time when a particular activity is officially stopped: *the lifting* (=ending) *of a trade moratorium* + **on**: *the US moratorium on the production and export of landmines*

2 also **debt moratorium** FINANCE a law or an agreement that gives countries, organizations etc more time to pay their debts: *Banks have helped out several big property concerns on the verge of insolvency by offering debt moratoriums or other refinancing options.* + **on**: *When a business finds itself seriously short of cash, it can ask its creditors for a moratorium on debt payments.*

mortality rate —see under RATE[1]

mortality tables —see under TABLE[1]

mort•gage[1] /ˈmɔːgɪdʒ‖ˈmɔːr-/ *n* [C] a legal arrangement where you borrow money from a financial institution in order to buy land or a house, and you pay back the money over a period of years. If you do not make your regular payments, the lender normally has the right to take the property and sell it in order to get back their money: *He arranged a 30-year mortgage at 7% for the five-bedroom house.* | *They* ***took out a $100,000 mortgage*** (=obtained one) *to pay for the property.* | *He recently* ***paid***

M

off his mortgage (=paid back all the money borrowed) *because he fears that interest rates will rise.*

adjustable-rate mortgage abbreviation **ARM** a mortgage where the interest rate on the loan changes over time, following the general level of interest rates

balloon mortgage in the US, a mortgage where the borrower repays only the interest on the loan for the period of the loan, and then repays the PRINCIPAL (=the amount originally borrowed) at the end of the period of time

capped-rate mortgage a mortgage in which the interest rate can change, but cannot go above a certain value that is fixed at the time when the loan was taken out

direct-reduction mortgage a mortgage in which part of the interest and part of the amount borrowed is paid off with each payment

endowment mortgage a mortgage where the borrower pays only the interest on the loan, and repays the loan itself in one payment at the end of the period of the loan with a sum built up in a LIFE INSURANCE policy. If the borrower dies during the period of the loan, the life insurance policy can be used to pay off the whole loan: *An endowment mortgage gives life cover automatically, whereas repayment loans need separate cover.*

equitable mortgage in Britain, a mortgage that does not give the lender complete control of the property if the loan is not repaid. The lender has to use the legal system to get control of the property

first mortgage lenders that have the first mortgage on property are the first ones to be repaid if the borrower DEFAULTS (=fails to make repayments on the loan): *The casino bondholders hold first mortgages on all his properties.*

fixed-rate mortgage a mortgage where the interest rate on the loan is fixed when the loan is taken out and does not change over the period of the loan

legal mortgage in Britain, a mortgage where the lender gets control of the property if the loan is not repaid, as the property is used as SECURITY on the loan: *The security is by way of specific legal mortgage or charge on the company's land.*

repayment mortgage in Britain, a mortgage where the loan is repaid in the normal way, without using an ENDOWMENT to pay off the loan

second mortgage an additional mortgage that a borrower takes out on a particular property, as a way to obtain money; HOME EQUITY LOAN *AmE*, REMORTGAGE *BrE*: *Some small retailers finance their expansion plans by taking out second mortgages on their homes.*

variable-rate mortgage another name for ADJUSTABLE RATE MORTGAGE

mortgage² *v* [T] **1** to give a financial institution the right to own your house, property, or land if you do not pay back the money they lent you within the agreed time: *They mortgaged their home for $65,000 to a life insurance company and gave the cash to their children.*

2 be mortgaged to the hilt to owe large amounts of money in relation to the value of the property you own: *John was mortgaged to the hilt with the flat in Kensington.*

mortgage-backed security —see under SECURITY

mort·ga·gee /ˌmɔːgɪˈdʒiː‖ˌmɔːr-/ *n* [C] LAW a financial institution that lends money in the form of a mortgage

mortgage finance —see under FINANCE¹

mortgage interest tax relief at source —see MIRAS

mortgage market —see under MARKET¹

mortgage protection insurance —see under INSURANCE

mortgage protection policy —see under INSURANCE POLICY

mortgage relief —see under RELIEF

mort·gag·or /ˈmɔːrgɪdʒɔː‖ˈmɔːrgɪˈdʒɔːr, ˈmɔːrgɪdʒər/ *n* [C] a person or organization that borrows money to buy property: *295,000 mortgagors, 4.6% of the total, were two months or more behind in their payments.*

most-favored nation —see under NATION

moth·ball¹ /ˈmɒθbɔːl‖ˈmɒːθbɒːl-/ *v* [T] **1** if an organization mothballs a factory, building etc, it closes it or does not use it for a long time but may open it or use it again in the future: *The oil company plans to close or sell a third of its retail gas stations and mothball one of its five refineries.*

2 if an organization mothballs plans, it decides not to use them for the moment but may possibly use them later: *No decisions have been made to mothball the project.*

mothball² *n* **put sth in mothballs/take sth out of mothballs** if a building, factory etc or a plan is put in mothballs, it is no longer used but may be used later. If is taken out of mothballs, it is used again: *Mr Reichmann is planning to revive three ambitious projects in Mexico City. 'We're taking them out of mothballs,' he said.*

mo·tion /ˈməʊʃən‖ˈmoʊ-/ *n* [C] a suggestion that is made formally at a meeting and then decided on by voting: ***The motion was carried*** (=accepted) *by 15 votes to 10.* | *I'd like to* ***propose a motion*** *to move the weekly meetings to Thursdays* —see also PROPOSAL, RESOLUTION

motion study —see ***time and motion study*** under STUDY¹

mo·ti·vate /ˈməʊtəveɪt‖ˈmoʊ-/ *v* [T] **1** to encourage someone and make them want to achieve something and be willing to work hard in order to do it: *The profit-sharing plan is designed to motivate the staff.* **motivate sb to do sth**: *The project manager may have problems in motivating people to work for him.*

2 to provide the reason why someone does something: *What motivates a customer to buy a small green apple as opposed to a large red one?* | *Investors are primarily motivated to invest in a company's shares on the basis of the company's likely profitability.* —**motivating** *adj*: *A significant motivating factor for managers is the right to have authority over a particular area of work.*

mo·ti·va·ted /ˈməʊtəveɪtəd‖ˈmoʊ-/ *adj* **1** very keen to do something or achieve something, especially because you find it interesting or exciting: *a* ***highly motivated*** *workforce*

2 financially/commercially etc motivated done for financial etc reasons: *The decision not to renew the player's contract was financially motivated; by releasing him now, the Royals must pay only one-sixth of his $2.4 million salary.*

mo·ti·va·tion /ˌməʊtəˈveɪʃən‖ˌmoʊ-/ *n* **1** [U] eagerness and willingness to do something without needing to be told or forced to do it: *Some of the workers seem to* ***lack motivation***.

2 [C] the reason why you want to do something + **for**: *What was your motivation for becoming a salesman?*

motivational research —see under RESEARCH

motor insurance —see under INSURANCE

motor pool *n* [C] *AmE* a group of cars owned by a company or other organization that its members can use; CAR POOL *BrE*

moun·tain /ˈmaʊntən‖ˈmaʊntn/ *n* [C] **butter/beef/grain etc mountain** a very large amount of food that is stored, especially by the EUROPEAN UNION, in order to prevent prices from becoming lower: *There are frequent butter, grain, wine and beef mountains which are stored at great cost or sold off cheaply to other countries.* —see also CASH MOUNTAIN

mouse /maʊs/ *n* plural **mouses** or **mice** [C] COMPUTING a small object connected to a computer by a wire, which you move around on a flat surface using your hand. You press the buttons to make the computer do certain tasks: *You* ***click*** *on the icons* ***with the mouse*** *to go from one program to another.*

mouse mat *BrE*, **mouse pad** *AmE* —*n* [C] COMPUTING the thing on which you place a computer's mouse, and which allows you to move it easily

mouse potato *n* plural **mouse potatoes** [C] *informal* someone who spends a lot of time playing on a computer, especially using the INTERNET: *My 14-year old son has become a mouse potato ever since he was given his own PC for his birthday.*

mov•a•ble also **moveable** /ˈmuːvəbəl/ *adj* if something is movable, it is not fixed and can move, be moved, or change: *Governments may use movable exchange-rates to keep their economies competitive.* | *movable property*

movable property —see under PROPERTY

move /muːv/ *v* [I,T] **1** *informal* if a product moves, or if a shop, dealer etc moves it, it sells very quickly: *These computer games are moving very fast. The kids love them.* | *PC World are really moving these new computers.*
2 to change to a different job, department etc, or to make someone change to a different job, department etc **move to/from**: *She's just moved from the sales department.*
3 *formal* to officially make a suggestion at a meeting + **that**: *The chairman moved that the meeting be adjourned.*
4 to go to live or work in a different place + **to**: *When are you moving to Memphis?* + **into**: *They've moved into a bigger office.* —see also CAREER MOVE

mover and shaker *n* [C] a powerful and influential person: *The movers and shakers in the stock market predicted a rise in share-dealing.*

move-up buyers —see under BUYER

moving average —see under AVERAGE[1]

MP *n* [C] Member of Parliament; someone who has been elected to represent the people in the HOUSE OF COMMONS, the lower part of the parliament of Britain and Canada: *a Labour MP* | *A significant number of MPs have second careers in City boardrooms.*

mpg miles per gallon; used to describe the amount of petrol a vehicle uses: *More people are buying trucks, which average only 20.8 mpg.*

mph miles per hour; used to describe the speed of a vehicle: *GM claims its car reaches 60 mph in eight seconds.*

Mr. **1** a title used before a man's family name when being polite: *Please can I speak to Mr Shultz?* | *Mr. Rupert Murdoch*
2 a title used when addressing a man in an official position: *May I speak, Mr Chairman?* | *Welcome home, Mr. President.*

MRO *n* [U] MANUFACTURING materials, repair, operation; used to describe things such as office supplies and machine repair parts that are used when something is produced but do not form part of the final product: *MRO supplies*

MRP *n* [U] **1** materials requirement planning; when the materials needed to produce something are ordered at the right times so that they are available to be used when they are needed
2 abbreviation for MANUFACTURER'S RECOMMENDED PRICE

Mrs. /ˈmɪsəz/ a title used before a married woman's family name when being polite: *Mrs Bell is out of the office at the moment.* | *Mrs. Hillary Clinton*

Ms. /məz, mɪz/ a title used before a married or an unmarried woman's family name when being polite: *Is that Mrs or Ms?* (=used when asking how someone likes to be addressed) | *Ms. Anita Roddick*

MSC *n* Multimedia Super Corridor; an area of Malaysia providing offices, telephone, and computer links, and other things that are needed by IT companies: *The types of companies invited to the MSC are hardware and software vendors, R&D organisations and relevant high-tech service providers.*

MSc *n* [C] Master of Science; a university degree in science that you can do after your first degree; MS *AmE*: *Chris Jones MSc*

MS-DOS /ˌem es ˈdɒs‖-ˈdɑːs/ *n* [U] *trademark* COMPUTING Microsoft Disk Operating System; one of the most common OPERATING SYSTEMS for computers: *MS-DOS based computer games*

multi- /mʌltə/ *prefix* used to show that something has many different parts, uses, effects etc: *We are trying to build the company into a multi-industry concern.* | *a multifunction machine*

mul•ti•lat•e•ral /ˌmʌltɪˈlætərəl◂/ *adj* involving several different countries: *a multilateral trade agreement* | *the World Bank and other* ***multilateral*** *development* ***banks*** —**multilaterally** *adv*: *Consultations took place both multilaterally and bilaterally.* —compare BILATERAL, UNILATERAL

mul•ti•lat•e•ral•is•m /ˌmʌltɪˈlætərəlɪzəm/ *n* [U] ECONOMICS when there is complete freedom of trade and exchange between countries: *By 1947, multilateralism within Europe had collapsed. Country A was willing to export to country B only if it could immediately import like-value goods from B.*

mul•ti•lin•gual /ˌmʌltɪˈlɪŋgwəl◂/ *adj* **1** able to speak more than two languages: *More multilingual flight attendants are being recruited.*
2 written or spoken in more than one language: *a 24-hour, multilingual help line for visitors*

mul•ti•me•di•a /ˌmʌltiˈmiːdiə◂/ *adj* **1** COMPUTING using a mixture of sound, pictures, film, and writing to communicate, educate, or entertain: ***Multimedia computers*** *have attracted a new group of buyers.* | *a PC that can run* ***multimedia software*** | *Encarta, a multimedia encyclopedia*
2 using several different methods of presenting or advertising information, for example television, newspapers, books, and computers: *a multimedia public education campaign about the dangers of smoking* —**multimedia** *n* [U] *Soon all teachers will be using multimedia in the classroom.*

Multimedia Super Corridor —see MSC

mul•ti•mil•lion /ˌmʌltɪˈmɪljən◂/ *adj* **multimillion-pound/multimillion-dollar etc** worth or costing many millions of pounds, dollars etc: *MCI launched a multimillion-dollar advertising campaign.* | *a multimillion pound contract*

mul•ti•mil•lio•naire /ˌmʌltɪˌmɪljəˈneə‖-ˈner/ *n* [C] someone who has many millions of pounds, dollars etc: *The former Warner executives are all multimillionaires.*

mul•ti•na•tion•al[1] /ˌmʌltɪˈnæʃənəl◂/ *adj* **1** a multinational organization has offices, factories, activities etc in many different countries: *Big* ***multinational companies*** *can earn huge profits.* | *Immuno is a* ***multinational concern*** *based in Vienna.* | *the rules for dealing with multinational banks*
2 involving companies or people from several different countries: *His access to world oil markets has been closed by a multinational embargo.*

multinational[2] *n* [C] a large company that has offices, factories, and business activities in many different countries: *It can be very hard to compete with the multinationals.* | *a marketing manager with a major Dutch multinational*

multinational corporation —see under CORPORATION

multi-pack *n* [C] a package containing a large number of a particular product: *multi-packs of beer at bargain prices*

M

mul·ti·ple[1] /ˈmʌltəpəl/ *adj* including or involving many things, people, events etc: *They are investigating the company for multiple violations of trade-practices law.* | *the ability for a CD player to handle multiple disks*

multiple[2] *n* [C] **1** a number by which another number is multiplied: *The shares are sold* ***in multiples*** (=groups) ***of*** *200.* | *BNP will offer high income multiples of up to four times your income* (=will lend you up to four times the amount of your yearly income).

2 also **earnings multiple, price-earnings multiple** FINANCE the price of a share divided by its EARNINGS (=share of a company's profits for a year); P/E RATIO: *Russell shares trade at more than 18 times this year's estimated per share earnings of $2.05, a multiple too high for some analysts.* | *stocks selling at* ***high price/earnings multiples*** *because of expectations they will perform well even under bad economic conditions*

forward multiple a multiple that a share is expected to earn for the coming year: *They are forecasting pre-tax profits this year of £7.3 million, putting the shares on a forward multiple of 6.4,*

3 also **multiple of rent** PROPERTY the rent that a property produces as an investment in relation to the price paid for it

4 also **multiple shop, multiple store** *BrE* a company that owns shops trading under the same name in many cities, or one of these shops; CHAIN STORE: *We are taking trade from large multiples where service is poor.*

multiple (share) application —see under APPLICATION

multiple applications —see under APPLICATION

multiple sales tax —see under TAX[1]

multiple store —see under STORE[1]

multiple tariff —see under TARIFF

multiple taxation —see under TAXATION

mul·ti·plex /ˈmʌltɪpleks/ *n* [C] a cinema that shows a large number of films at the same time: *a 10-screen multiplex*

mul·ti·plex·er /ˈmʌltɪˌpleksə‖-ər/ *n* [C] COMPUTING a piece of equipment used to send several electrical signals using only one connection, used especially with MODEMS

mul·ti·plex·ing /ˈmʌltɪˌpleksɪŋ/ *n* [U] a method used to send several electrical signals using only one connection, used especially with MODEMS: *Multiplexing is used to control such vehicle functions as lighting, automatic windows, and door locks.*

mul·ti·pli·er /ˈmʌltəplaɪə‖-ər/ *n* [singular] the idea that increased investment in an economy causes an even bigger increase in total income, as the spending has results that spread through the economy. KEYNESIANS say that this is why governments should increase spending when the economy is growing too slowly, even if it produces a DEFICIT (=when the government spends more than it receives in taxes): *You could argue that this kind of tax cut will boost demand through the multiplier.*

mul·ti·ply /ˈmʌltəplaɪ/ *v* past tense and past participle multiplied [I,T] **1** to increase greatly or to make something increase greatly: *Program-length commercials are multiplying nationwide.* | *This year we hope to multiply exports to about $1.7 million.*

2 to add a number to itself a particular number of times + **by**: *If figures are given in gallons, multiply by 4.5 to obtain litres.* | *Multiply your salary by three to get your maximum loan.*

mul·ti·pro·ces·sing /ˌmʌltiˈprəʊsesɪŋ‖-ˈprɑː-/ *n* [U] another name for MULTITASKING

multi-skilling *n* [U] when employees learn and use a number of different skills in their work: *Their 'people policies' include job enrichment, multi-skilling, and teamwork.*

mul·ti·task·ing /ˈmʌltɪˌtɑːskɪŋ‖-ˌtæs-/ also **multi-tasking** *n* [U] **1** COMPUTING when a computer runs more than one program at the same time on a single PROCESSOR (=the central most important part of the computer); MULTIPROCESSING: *a powerful operating system that allows for multitasking* | *a multitasking program*

2 when someone does more than one job at the same time: *A lot of emphasis is put on supervisory skills and multi-tasking.*

muni —see ***municipal bond*** under BOND

mu·ni·ci·pal /mjuːˈnɪsəpəl‖mjʊ-/ *adj* belonging to or connected with the government of a town or city: ***Municiple budgets*** *are under great strain.* | *a strike by* ***municipal employees*** —**municipally** *adv*: *a municipally owned hospital*

municipal bond —see under BOND

municipal issuer —see under ISSUER

mu·ni·ci·pals /mjuːˈnɪsəpəlz‖mjʊ-/ *n* [plural] FINANCE bonds ISSUED (=made available and sold) by local government authorities; MUNICIPAL BONDS: *In trading, prices of most municipals ended as much as 3/8 point higher.*

mu·nis /ˈmjuːniz/ *n* [plural] *AmE* an informal name for MUNICIPAL BONDS: *We think it's a smart idea to buy munis right now.*

mush·room /ˈmʌʃruːm, -rʊm/ *v* [I] to develop very quickly: *Cable has mushroomed into a giant industry.* —**mushrooming** *adj*: *the mushrooming private business sector*

mu·tu·al /ˈmjuːtʃuəl/ *adj* [only before a noun] FINANCE relating to financial institutions, for example some insurance companies and, in Britain, BUILDING SOCIETIES, where there are no shareholders but where investors receive their share of profits in other forms: *Norwich Union dropped its* ***mutual status*** *to become a public company* —**mutual** *n* [C] *In insurance, two forms of companies coexist in the UK, mutuals and public liability companies.* —see also DEMUTUALIZE

mutual company —see under COMPANY

mutual fund —see under FUND[1]

mutual insurance company —see under COMPANY

mutual savings bank —see under BANK[1]

N

N/A written abbreviation for the words NOT APPLICABLE, used on forms to show that you are not answering a question because it is not designed for people in your situation

NAFTA /ˈnæftə/ *n* North American Free Trade Agreement; an arrangement by Canada, Mexico, and the US to encourage trade between them by reducing import taxes etc

nag•ware /ˈnægweə‖-wer/ *n* [U] computer software which is offered free to customers for a period of time, after which the supplier sends frequent messages to the customer, asking them to buy the program

nail[1] /neɪl/ *v* [T] *informal* to catch someone and prove that they are guilty of a crime or of doing something bad: *The government spent vast resources in an unsuccessful effort to nail him on felony charges.*

nail down *phr v* [T] **1 nail sb down** *informal* to force someone to say exactly what they want or what they intend to do **nail sb down to sth**: *Before they repair the car, nail them down to a price.*

2 nail sth down *AmE journalism* to reach a final and definite decision about something: *The US wants to **nail down an agreement** on anti-subsidy rules.*

3 nail sth down *AmE journalism* to make certain that you will get something: *The prospect of a shortage has U.S. companies rushing to nail down long-term supplies of critical parts.* | *He sold the shares just because he thought it prudent to **nail down a profit**.*

nail[2] *n* **on the nail** *BrE informal* if you pay for something on the nail, you pay for it immediately: *Not paying on the nail could be extremely expensive.*

NAIRU /ˈnaɪruː/ *n* ECONOMICS non-accelerating inflation rate of unemployment; the number of people without work that some economists say is necessary at a particular time in order to prevent prices rising too fast: *Once inflation has levelled out at an acceptable rate demand can be expanded, with the result that the unemployment rate will fall back towards NAIRU.*

naked contract —see under CONTRACT[1]

naked writer —see under WRITER

names /neɪmz/ *n* [plural] at LLOYD'S, the investors who use their own money as a GUARANTEE for contracts against insurance risks

naming and shaming *n* [U] when companies break the law or the rules for a particular activity, and the authorities bring attention to this by saying which companies have been guilty of this: *the naming and shaming of food manufacturers which fail to comply with legislation on safety and quality* —**name and shame** *v* [T] *plans to name and shame individual directors for slow progress in clearing up the pensions mis-selling scandal*

nan•o•sec•ond /ˈnænəʊˌsekənd‖-noʊ-/ *n* [C] COMPUTING one BILLIONTH (=one thousand millionth) of a second. Nanoseconds are used to talk about the speed at which computer CHIPS do calculations: *They will produce a bit of data in 30 nanoseconds, compared with the 50 nanoseconds required for the previous version.*

nan•o•tech•nol•o•gy /ˌnænəʊtekˈnɑːlədʒi‖-noʊtekˌnɑː-/ *n* [U] a science that combines computer technology and chemistry to build things from ATOMS (=the smallest parts of a substance that can exist alone): *Nanotechnology could allow us to invent devices that manufacture at almost no cost, by replicating atoms the way that computers reproduce bits of information.*

nar•ra•tion /nəˈreɪʃən‖næ-, nə-/ also **nar•ra•tive** /ˈnærətɪv/ *n* [C] ACCOUNTING a note explaining the reason for an entry in an account

nar•row[1] /ˈnærəʊ‖-roʊ/ *adj* **1** used to describe something that is small, or that only just exists or is only just achieved: *The polls give Mr. Edwards a **narrow lead**.* | *Analysts had expected a narrow decline in pretax earnings.* | *The Senate rejected the bid **by a narrow margin*** (=it was almost accepted).

2 including only a small number of parts or things: *Iraq's weak and narrow economic base* | *Even in Safeguard's **narrow niche*** (=producing a product for a very small market), *its competition is heavy.*

3 in a narrow range FINANCE if shares, currencies etc trade in a narrow range, their price does not go up or down very much: *The dollar had been trading in a narrow range against the yen.* | *Trading was light and contracts continued to trade in a narrow price range.*

4 FINANCE used to describe a market in which the buying or selling of shares has a great effect on their price, for example because there are only a small number of them available: *Cobalt is traded in a **narrow market** which means speculators can drive prices up or down rapidly.*

narrow[2] *v* [I,T] also **narrow down** to become less or to make something less in range, difference etc: *Growing competition for contracts will narrow profit margins.* | *The gap between Hasbro and Mattel is clearly narrowing.* | *The choice was quickly narrowed down to Luxembourg or Dublin.* —**narrowing** *n* [singular] *There has been a narrowing of differences between the parties.* —**narrowing** *adj*: *the narrowing price gap between domestic and imported vehicles*

narrow money —see under MONEY

NASD *n trademark* National Association of Securities Dealers; the professional association for dealers that trade on Nasdaq, that sets standards, represents dealers' views to the government and investors etc: *The NASD found that the firm charged excessive prices for securities.*

Nas•daq /ˈnæzdæk/ *n trademark* National Association of Securities Dealers Automated Quotations; a system giving the prices of shares in smaller and newer companies that are traded OVER THE COUNTER (=directly between dealers on a national computer network rather than on a stockmarket) in the US. Nasdaq is officially known as the Nasdaq Stock Exchange

na•tion /ˈneɪʃən/ *n* [C] a country, considered especially in relation to its people and its social or economic structure: *The treaty was signed by 22 nations.* | *the **developing nations** of Southeast Asia* | *Annual exports of coffee-producing nations fell to $6.5 billion.* | *Citicorp, the nation's largest bank*

creditor nation in international trade, a country that is owed more by other countries than it owes to them: *Japan had record net overseas assets of $293.2 billion last year, making it the world's largest creditor nation.*

most-favored nation abbreviation **MFN** *AmE* in international trade, a country that is given the same advantages, such as reduced import taxes and higher QUOTAS (=numbers of goods it is allowed to export), as the best ones given to other countries, putting it on the same level as these other countries: *The US will continue its most-favored-nation treatment for imports of Chinese-made goods.*

National Audit Office abbreviation **NAO** *n* in Britain, a government organization that checks that government departments spend money correctly: *A National Audit Office study found that the taxpayer could be losing £1 billion a year in housing benefit fraud.*

national bank —see under BANK[1]

national debt —see under DEBT

national executive —see under EXECUTIVE[1]

National Giro —see under GIRO

national income —see under INCOME

national insurance —see under INSURANCE

N

na·tion·al·i·za·tion /ˌnæʃənəlaɪˈzeɪʃən‖-nələ-/ also **nationalisation** *BrE n* [C,U] the act of bringing a company or industry under the control of a government: *Blair forced the Labour Party to drop its commitment to nationalization.* | *The left accuses Chirac of reversing the nationalisations which de Gaulle oversaw after the second world war.* —compare PRIVATIZATION

na·tion·al·ize also **nationalise** *BrE* /ˈnæʃənəlaɪz/ *v* [T] if a government nationalizes a company or industry, it brings it under state control: *Zulfikar Ali Bhutto nationalized everything from banks to steel plants.* | *The British government nationalised the railways in 1948.* —**nationalized** *adj*: *the nationalised water industry* —compare PRIVATIZE

National Market System abbreviation **NMS** *n* FINANCE a US computer network for trading shares on NASDAQ and some of the shares traded on the NEW YORK STOCK EXCHANGE: *National Market System volume totaled a moderately active 256,750,000 shares.*

national product —see GROSS NATIONAL PRODUCT

National Savings Bank *n* a SAVINGS BANK owned and managed by the British government. Investors use post offices to pay in and take out money: *Tax-free National Savings certificates have always been attractive to higher rate taxpayers.*

National Savings Stock Register abbreviation **NSSR** *n* FINANCE a system for buying GILTS (=British government bonds) through post offices: *Most private investors can only get gilt interest gross if they buy through the National Savings Stock Register.*

National Union of Journalists —see NUJ

national wealth —see under WEALTH

nat·u·ral /ˈnætʃərəl/ *adj* **1** not caused, made, or controlled by human beings: *A series of* ***natural disasters*** *created huge losses for the insurance market.* | *All our hair-care products are made from* ***natural ingredients****.*
2 happening as a normal part of a process or situation: *There is a natural career progression through the police force.* | *Proctor and Gamble termed the organizational changes a 'natural evolution' of its global business.*

natural gas —see under GAS

nat·u·ral·ize also **naturalise** *BrE* /ˈnætʃərəlaɪz/ *v* **be naturalized** if someone who was born outside the country they now live in is naturalized, they become a citizen of the country they are living in: *Only about 1,000 of the 1.8 million Turks in Germany are naturalised each year.* —**naturalized**: *a naturalized American* —**naturalization** *n* [U] *a certificate of naturalization*

natural monopoly —see under MONOPOLY

natural person —see under PERSON

natural resources —see under RESOURCE[1]

natural wastage —see under WASTAGE

nau·ti·cal /ˈnɔːtɪkəl‖ˈnɒː-/ *adj* connected with ships or sailing: *a nautical information database used for making charts*

nautical mile —see under MILE

NAV written abbreviation for NET ASSET VALUE

na·val /ˈneɪvəl/ *adj* [only before a noun] connected with or used by a navy: *We have a contract to build naval aircraft.* | *the Philadelphia naval shipyard*

NB also **nb** *BrE* written abbreviation for NOTE (NOTA BENE), used to make a reader pay attention to an important piece of information: *The net cost of materials may be excluded from the gross payment before tax deduction is calculated (NB The current deduction rate is 27%).*

NBV written abbreviation for NET BOOK VALUE

NCV *n* [U] abbreviation for NO COMMERCIAL VALUE; written on packages sent abroad to show that they contain nothing on which import taxes can be charged

NDPB *n* [C] non-departmental public body. An independent organization in Britain, started by the government but with its own legal powers; QUANGO

near money —see under MONEY

neg·a·tive /ˈnegətɪv/ *adj* **1** bad or harmful: *The Bank's refusal to cut interest rates is having a* ***negative effect*** *on the economy.*
2 saying or meaning 'no': *a* ***negative response***
3 considering only the bad qualities of a situation, person etc and not the good ones + **about**: *Stock analysts are growing increasingly negative about general insurance stocks.*
4 less than zero: *The difference between a positive growth rate of 0.5% and a negative rate of 0.5% is so small the average businessman would be unlikely to feel it.* —**negatively** *adv*: *Financial markets reacted negatively to the Fed's announcement.*

negative cash flow —see under CASH FLOW

negative equity —see under EQUITY

negative income tax —see under INCOME TAX

negative interest rate —see under RATE[1]

negative net worth —see under NET WORTH

neg·li·gence /ˈneglɪdʒəns/ *n* [U] LAW failure to take enough care over something that you are responsible for, for which you may have to pay DAMAGES: *The captain of the ship was* ***accused of negligence*** *in carrying out safety procedures.* | *The jury found the company guilty of* ***gross*** (=very serious) ***negligence*** *and awarded the dead man's family $10 million.*

contributory negligence when the injuries suffered by someone were partly caused by their own carelessness. A court can reduce the amount of DAMAGES which an injured person receives if the accident involved contributory negligence: *The plaintiff's damages were reduced for his contributory negligence in riding with a drunken driver and failing to wear a seat belt.*

neg·li·gent /ˈneglɪdʒənt/ *adj* LAW not taking enough care over something that you are responsible for: *The products were defective due to the manufacturer's negligent workmanship.* + **in**: *TWA was negligent in allowing a known terrorist to board one of its jets in Egypt.*

ne·go·ti·a·ble /nɪˈgəʊʃiəbəl, -ʃə-‖-ˈgoʊ-/ *adj* **1** BANKING a negotiable document, such as a BANKNOTE or a BILL OF EXCHANGE, can be exchanged for money or goods
2 an offer, price etc that is negotiable can be discussed and changed before being finally agreed on: *The terms of the contract are not negotiable.* —opposite NON-NEGOTIABLE —**negotiability** *n* [U] *the negotiability of international bills of exchange*

negotiable instrument —see under INSTRUMENT

negotiable security —see under SECURITY

ne·go·ti·ate /nɪˈgəʊʃieɪt‖-ˈgoʊ-/ *v* **1** [I,T] to discuss something in order to reach an agreement: *Union leaders have* ***negotiated an agreement*** *for a shorter working week.* | *The Procter & Gamble Co. was* ***negotiating a*** *multimillion-dollar* ***contract*** *to advertise on the MTV cable network.* + **with**: *Siemens was negotiating with SGS-Thomson to develop semi-conductors.*—**negotiator** *n* [C] *Clyde Prestowitz, a former U.S.* ***trade negotiator***
2 negotiate a loan to discuss with a bank or other

organization that lends money the amount they will lend you, the rate of interest they will charge etc
3 [T] BANKING to exchange money or goods by using a document such as BILL OF EXCHANGE that allows you to do this

ne·go·ti·a·tion /nɪˌɡəʊʃiˈeɪʃən‖-ˌɡoʊ-/ *n* [C usually plural, U] official discussions between groups who are trying to reach an agreement: *The company* ***entered into negotiations*** *for the purchase of a site in Penge.* | *The terms of the contract are still* ***open to negotiation*** (=can be negotiated and changed).

nep·o·tis·m /ˈnepətɪzəm/ *n* [U] *disapproving* the practice of giving jobs to members of your family when you are in a position of power: *Allegations of corruption and nepotism in the government are growing.*

nerd /nɜːd‖nɜːrd/ *n* [C] *informal* someone who knows a lot about a technical subject, usually computers, but who is not good at communicating with people; GEEK: *Just a few years ago, internet telephony was little more than a hobby for nerds. Now it is set to enter the mainstream.* —**nerdish** *adj*: *nerdish hackers* —**nerdy** *adj*

nest egg *n* [C] *informal* an amount of money that you save to use later, especially for your RETIREMENT (=after you stop working): *Life insurance endowment policies are a great way to build up a family nest egg for the future.*

net[1] also **nett** *BrE* /net/ *adj* [only before a noun] **1** a net amount of money is one that remains after things such as costs and tax have been taken away: ***Net income*** *after higher taxes, provisions and depreciation jumped more than 25%.* | *Dexter reported a* ***net loss*** *for the period after a charge related to reorganization costs.*
2 in buying, exporting etc, concerning a situation where the amount bought etc by one side is more than the amount bought etc by the other: *Because of its oil fields in the North Sea, Britain is a* ***net exporter*** (=a country that exports more than it imports) *of oil, though a small one.* | *Canadian investors were* ***net purchasers*** *of US equities for the third straight quarter.* (=the value of US shares bought by Canadians was more than the value of Canadian shares bought by people in the US)

net[2] *n* **1 the net** also **the Net** the INTERNET, the system that allows computer users all over the world to communicate with each other: *Most users do not aimlessly* ***surf the net*** (=look at information in different places as a form of entertainment). *They always or usually go back to the same sites.*
2 [U] *AmE* a company's profit after tax has been taken away; NET PROFIT: *The supermarket chain said net for the quarter was $40.3 million, or 33 cents a share.*
3 safety/welfare etc net used to talk about actions to prevent people from suffering financial problems if they become ill, unemployed etc: *safety net programs, including unemployment compensation and retraining of workers during the current effort to restructure industry* | *The social welfare net is essential; a social partnership exists between employers and the employed.*

net[3] *v* past tense and past participle **netted** present participle **netting** [T] *especially AmE* **1** if something nets a company or a person a particular amount of money, it gives them that amount, perhaps after costs are taken away: *Its public stock offering netted the company $72 million.* | *charges involving a fraud scheme that netted him $12 million*
2 if a person or a company nets a certain amount in a year, they earn that amount as income or as profit after tax is taken away: *The farm – nearly 20 square miles – netted as much as $1.5 million a year.* | *After the capital-gains tax was paid, we only netted about $3.25 per hour.*

net out *phr v* [I] if profit nets out at a particular amount, it is that amount after taxes etc are taken away: *The trading for the world-wide group on its own account netted out as income of DM200 million.*

net sth ↔ **down** *phr v* [I,T] if a quantity nets down to another quantity, or if you net it down to that quantity, you take off things such as tax or expenses from the total amount to find the net amount + **to**: *The employer's contribution is £4,524. This is fully tax deductible for the employer, so the liability nets down to £3,393 for the employer.* —opposite ***gross sth up*** under GROSS[3]

net 10/eom *adv AmE* ACCOUNTING net 10 days end of month; written on an invoice to show that it should be paid within 10 days of the beginning of the following month and that there is no DISCOUNT (=price reduction)

net 30 *adv AmE* ACCOUNTING net 30 days; written on an invoice to show that it should be paid within 30 days and that there is no DISCOUNT (=price reduction)

net annual value —see under VALUE[1]

net asset backing —see under BACKING

net assets —see under ASSET

net asset value —see under VALUE[1]

net book value —see under VALUE[1]

net borrowings —see under BORROWING

net current assets —see under ASSET

net emigration —see under EMIGRATION

net exporter —see under EXPORTER

net immigration —see under IMMIGRATION

net importer —see under IMPORTER

net income —see under INCOME

net interest —see under INTEREST

net interest margin —see under MARGIN

net investment —see under INVESTMENT

net·i·quette /ˈnetɪket/ *n* [U] *informal* the correct behaviour to use when communicating with people on the Internet, for example not being rude or using bad language

net loss —see under LOSS

net margin —see under MARGIN

net output —see under OUTPUT[1]

net PE ratio —see under RATIO

net player —see under PLAYER

net present value —see under VALUE[1]

net price —see under PRICE[1]

net proceeds —see under PROCEEDS

net profit —see under PROFIT[1]

net quick assets ratio —see under RATIO

net realizable value —see under VALUE[1]

net receipts —see under RECEIPT[1]

net registered tonnage —see under TONNAGE

net rent —see under RENT[2]

net return —see under RETURN[2]

net salary —see under SALARY

net sales —see under SALE

net seller —see under SELLER

nett *adj* [only before a noun] a British spelling of NET[1]

net ton —see under TON

net wages —see under WAGE

net weight —see under WEIGHT[1]

net·work[1] /ˈnetwɜːk‖-wɜːrk/ *n* [C] **1** a group of people or organizations that are connected or that work together + **of**: *It's important to build up a network of professional contacts.*
2 COMPUTING a set of computers which are connected to each other and operate as part of the same system, able to exchange information and messages: *network software* | *The vendor automatically orders new deliveries from the retailer through its* ***computer network.***

wide area network abbreviation **WAN** an arrangement in which computers in different areas or buildings are connected to each other and users in different places can look at and work on the same information: *Sumitomi uses a WAN to link all three of its global sites.*

3 a group of radio or television stations that broadcast many of the same programmes, but at different times in different places: *the Fox Television Network*

4 road/rail/telecommunications network the system of roads, railways, or communication systems such as telephones used in a country: *a cellular phone network | Britain's network of motorways*

5 a group consisting of many things that are connected, but are in different places: *the Post Office's network of shops across the country*

network[2] *v* **1** [I] to make use of meetings with people or organizations involved in the same kind of work, in order to share information, help each other etc: *He spent a couple of evenings a month networking at business functions.*

2 [T] COMPUTING to connect several computers together so that they operate as part of the same system, able to exchange information and messages: *This software will allow us to network our computers.*

network analysis *n* [U] another name for CRITICAL PATH ANALYSIS

net·work·ing /ˈnetwɜːkɪŋ‖-wɜːr-/ *n* [U] **1** making use of meetings with other people involved in the same kind of work, in order to share information, help each other etc: *The Conference Board is an organization that aids networking among top executives.*

2 COMPUTING when several computers are connected together so that they operate as part of the same system, able to exchange information and messages: *networking software | 3Com Corp. is a* ***computer networking company****.*

net worth *n* [U] ACCOUNTING, FINANCE the value of a company calculated by taking its total liabilities away from its total assets: *At that time, Fairfield-Noble had assets of $5.9 million and a net worth of $11,000.*

negative net worth the amount by which a company's liabilities are greater than its assets: *It was not unusual for cable television companies to have negative net worth because of high start-up costs.*

positive net worth the amount by which a company's assets are greater than its liabilities: *He couldn't say whether Y&A will have a positive net worth after the audit is completed.*

tangible net worth net worth that is calculated without considering assets that do not have clear and easily measured financial value, such as GOODWILL: *Tangible net worth is a key measure of a company's financial health.*

net wt. written abbreviation for NET WEIGHT

net yield —see under YIELD[1]

New Deal *n* ECONOMICS **1** an employment and training programme introduced in Britain by the Labour government in 1998, in order to help people without jobs, especially people who have been unemployed for a long time

2 a programme of economic and social changes introduced in the US by President Franklin D. Roosevelt in 1933 in order to help people who had lost their jobs or their property as a result of the GREAT DEPRESSION: *New Deal economic legislation*

new issue —see under ISSUE[2]

new issue market —see under MARKET[1]

newly industrialized country —see NIC

new money —see under MONEY

news·group /ˈnjuːzˌgruːp‖ˈnuːz-/ *n* [C] COMPUTING a place on the INTERNET where people with a shared interest can exchange messages; USENET

new share —see under SHARE

Newspaper Publishers' Association —see NPA

new stock —see under STOCK[1]

new time —see under TIME

New York Mercantile Exchange —see NYMEX

New York Stock Exchange written abbreviation **NYSE** *n* FINANCE one of the main stockmarkets in the US, where shares in companies in the largest companies are bought and sold. Its building is on WALL STREET; BIG BOARD *informal*: *Citicorp's stock closed at $9.75 per share on the New York Stock Exchange.*

NI written abbreviation for NATIONAL INSURANCE: *Employees'* ***NI contributions*** *are paid on earnings up to a certain limit.*

NIC *n* [C] **1** newly industrialized country; a country where the economy has recently changed from one based mainly on agriculture to one based on industry: *Asia's first generation of newly industrialized countries, or NICs – South Korea, Taiwan, Hong Kong and Singapore*

2 National Insurance Contributions; money paid by employers and employees in Britain so that employees receive BENEFITS when they are ill, unemployed etc

niche /niːʃ/ *n* [C] MARKETING a group of customers with particular needs. The group is usually small but may be profitable for companies that sell to it: *In the US market for shoes, Clark's occupies an upmarket niche where it can trade on its English image.*

niche market —see under MARKET[1]

niche marketer —see under MARKETER

niche marketing —see under MARKETING

nich·er /ˈniːʃə‖-ər/ *n* [C] **1** a company that sells a product or service in a niche or the product or service itself

2 a product or service sold in a NICHE MARKET (=a market for a product or service, perhaps an expensive or unusual one, that does not have many buyers) or the company that sells it

nich·ist /ˈniːʃɪst/ *n* [C] MARKETING a company that sells a product or service in a niche

nick·el /ˈnɪkəl/ *n* **1** [U] a coin in the US or Canada that is worth five cents: *Gasoline rose more than a nickel a gallon.*

2 [U] a hard silver-white metal used in manufacturing and traded on COMMODITY MARKETS: *Nickel rose nearly as strongly as zinc on the London Metal Exchange yesterday.*

Niel·sen Rat·ings /ˈniːlsən ˌreɪtɪŋz/ also **Nielsens** *n* [plural] *trademark* a system used to show how many people watch particular television programmes in the US. The Nielsen Ratings were developed by Nielsen Media Research, an important MARKET RESEARCH COMPANY, and are used by television companies to decide how much to charge for advertising during particular programmes, and also to decide on whether to continue making or broadcasting a particular programme: *"60 Minutes" was one of the top three ranked TV shows in the Nielsen ratings last week.*

NIESR *n* **the NIESR** the National Institute of Economic and Social Research; an organization in Britain that produces reports on what is likely to happen in the economy, based on the information that is available: *Economic forecasts are produced by the NIESR, the Bank of England, and the London Business School.*

NIF written abbreviation for NOTE ISSUANCE FACILITY

night depository —see under DEPOSITORY

night safe —see under SAFE[2]

night shift —see under SHIFT[1]

NIH syndrome —see NOT-INVENTED-HERE SYNDROME

Nik·kei av·e·rage /ˌnɪkeɪ ˈævərɪdʒ/ —see under AVERAGE[2]

Nikkei index —see under INDEX[1]

nil /nɪl/ *n* [U] nothing: *The new machine reduced labour costs to almost nil.*

nil PE ratio —see under RATIO

nim·by /ˈnɪmbi/ *n* plural **nimbys** [C] *informal* not in my backyard; used to talk about someone who does not want a particular activity or building near their home —**nimby** *adj*: *The Green Party opposes the new road; but rather than adopting a negative nimby position, it proposes improvements to the existing road.*

NMS —see NATIONAL MARKET SYSTEM

No. plural **Nos.** written abbreviation for NUMBER

No 10 /ˌnʌmbə ˈten‖-bər-/ *n journalism* Number 10 Downing Street in London; the official home of the British prime minister, and used to talk generally about his or her decisions and activities: *economic movements with which No.10 has yet to come to grips*

no-claims discount —see under DISCOUNT[1]

no-frills *adj* [only before a noun] no-frills companies, products, or services are very basic and cheap. They cover the main or most necessary part of something with no extras: *a bill requiring banks in the state to offer low-cost, no-frills checking accounts* | *Midway Metrolink went from being a no-frills discount carrier to a single-class, first-class airline.*

no-load fund —see under FUND[1]

no·lo con·ten·de·re /ˌnəʊləʊ kɒnˈtendəri‖ˌnoʊloʊ kən-/ *n* [U] LAW a PLEA (=when someone accused of a crime says if they are guilty or not guilty) where the accused says that they will not make a defence: *Of those prosecuted on this charge, about 80% were convicted, the majority of these entering pleas of nolo contendere.*

nomadic worker —see under WORKER

nom·i·nal /ˈnɒmɪnəl‖ˈnɑː-/ *adj* **1 nominal head/leader etc** someone who has the title of head, leader etc but does not have the normal qualities, responsibilities etc of that job: *Longo was the real power in the party, while Togliatti was merely the nominal head.*
2 a nominal sum of money is very small, compared to the usual amount that would be paid or charged for something: *He charges a nominal amount for his software, enough to cover expenses.*
3 a nominal figure, level etc is not the real one because it has not been ADJUSTED (=changed to take other things into account): *While the Fed can peg the nominal federal funds rate, it cannot control the real rate (i.e. the nominal rate minus the rate of inflation).*

nominal accounts —see under ACCOUNT[1]

nominal damages —see under DAMAGE[1]

nominal interest rate —see under RATE[1]

nominal ledger another name for GENERAL LEDGER —see under LEDGER

nominal price —see under PRICE[1]

nominal value —see under VALUE[1]

nominal wages —see under WAGE

nominal yield —see under YIELD[1]

nom·i·nate /ˈnɒmɪneɪt‖ˈnɑː-/ *v* [T] **1** to officially suggest that someone should have an important position, job, or prize **nominate sb for sth**: *The president has nominated economist Lawrence Lindsey for one of the vacancies.* **nominate sb as**: *John S. Tamagni was nominated as vice chairman.* **nominate sb to do sth**: *I nominate Jane to represent us at the meeting.*
2 to officially choose someone to do a particular job **nominate sb as sth**: *They are seeking to have themselves nominated as directors.* **nominate sb to sth**: *Each country can nominate two members to the committee.* **nominate sb to do sth**: *Unilever have nominated Michael Perry to succeed Sir Michael Angus as chairman.*

nom·i·na·tion /ˌnɒmɪˈneɪʃən‖ˌnɑː-/ *n* **1** [C,U] the act of officially suggesting someone for a position or prize, or the fact of being suggested for it + **for**: *All the committee's nominations were approved.*
2 [C] the name of a book, film, actor etc that people have formally suggested should receive an honour or prize: *'Titanic' was an obvious nomination for best picture.*
3 [C,U] the act of choosing someone for a particular job, or the fact of being chosen + **as**: *O'Neil's nomination as chief executive*

nom·i·nee /ˌnɒmɪˈniː‖ˌnɑː-/ *n* [C] **1** someone who has been suggested for a job, position, or prize: *Board nominees must be approved by shareholders.* | *16 winners were chosen from 500 nominees.*
2 FINANCE a person or organization that holds shares, bonds etc for someone: *What is there to prevent a taxpayer from putting his shares in the name of a nominee?*
3 INSURANCE in LIFE INSURANCE, the name of the person who will get money if the insured person dies

non-accelerating inflation rate of unemployment —see NAIRU

non-callable debenture —see under DEBENTURE

non-callable notes —see under NOTE[1]

non-contributory pension plan —see under PENSION PLAN

non-contributory pension scheme —see under SCHEME

non-convertible currency —see under CURRENCY

non-disclosure agreement —see under AGREEMENT

non-durable goods —see under GOODS

non-durables *n* [plural] ECONOMICS products that are not intended to have a life of more than three years from when they are made or bought; NON-DURABLE GOODS: *Spending on nondurables was up 0.5% in November.*
consumer non-durables products that people buy regularly and often: *Cyclical shares performed better than those in companies producing consumer non-durables.* —compare CONSUMER DURABLES

non-economic damages —see under DAMAGE[1]

non-executive director —see under DIRECTOR

non·fea·sance /nɒnˈfiːzəns‖nɑːn-/ *n* [U] LAW when someone does not do what they have to do by law —compare MALFEASANCE, MISFEASANCE

non-insurable risk —see under RISK[1]

non-marketable *adj* if bonds, shares etc are non-marketable, selling them to other people is not allowed: *TJ will issue $15 million of non-marketable, convertible preferred stock to its employee stock ownership plan.*

non-negotiable *adj* **1** if a financial document such as a cheque is non-negotiable, it cannot be used by the person or organization receiving it to pay a third person or organization. CROSSED CHEQUES are non-negotiable
2 if someone says that a demand, condition etc is non-negotiable, they mean that they are not willing to accept other suggestions, conditions etc: *To think we can compromise on raising the fuel tax is wrong; it's non-negotiable.* —opposite NEGOTIABLE

non-participating shares —see under SHARE

non-pay·ment *n* [C,U] when a person or organization does not make a payment that should be made: *They were sued for alleged non-payment of bills and loans.*

non-performing loan —see under LOAN[1]

non-prime bill —see under BILL[1]

non-profit also **non profit-making** *BrE* —*adj* [only before a noun] a non-profit organization is one with aims that are not related to business or making a profit. These organizations usually work in education, health etc; NOT-FOR-PROFIT *AmE*: *a non-profit low-income-housing organization* | *Consumer's Union, the non-profit organization that publishes Consumer Reports magazine* —**nonprofit** *n* [C usually plural] *Grants for Asian nonprofits were extremely low in grants from government contributions.*

non-profit policy —see under INSURANCE POLICY

nonrecourse loan —see under LOAN[1]

non-recoverable *adj* if an amount of money is non-recoverable, you cannot get it back, for example by claiming it against tax

non-recurring *adj* ACCOUNTING, FINANCE a non-recurring item, charge etc is one that only relates to a particular period of time, and will not be repeated in later periods of time: *The loss was reduced by a non-recurring $17.8 million tax benefit from an accounting change.*

non-renewable *adj* non-renewable types of energy such as coal or oil cannot be replaced once they have been used: *Half the tax will be levied on all forms of **non-renewable energy**.* | *These regulations will only encourage a massive waste of valuable and **non-renewable natural resources**.*

non-resident *n* [C] TAX someone who for tax purposes is not considered as living permanently in a particular country: *real estate bought through offshore companies under a system used by non-residents* —**non-resident** *adj*: *Italy moved to exempt non-resident investors in government securities from a 12.5% withholding tax.*

non-standard *adj* not the usual size or type: *McDonnell Douglas is to introduce a non-standard week, which would make Saturday and Sunday regular work days.*

non-union *adj* non-union workers do not belong to a TRADE UNION (=an organization that protects workers' rights): *The union is seeking a better wage-and-benefits package and protection against use of non-union labor at the plant.*

non-voting share —see under SHARE

non-voting stock —see under STOCK[1]

no-par stock —see under STOCK[1]

no-par-value share —see under SHARE

norm /nɔːm‖nɔːrm/ *n* [singular] the usual and expected situation, way of doing something etc: *Private businesses award an average of 0.35% commission compared with the industry's norm of 0.5%.* | *Budget surpluses are now the norm and the emphasis is on repaying government debt rather than borrowing.*

north /nɔːθ‖nɔːrθ/ *adj informal AmE* if an amount is north of another amount, it is more than that amount: *To be a big player, a company must spend somewhere north of $500 million a year.*

North American Free Trade Agreement —see NAFTA

Nos. written abbreviation for NUMBERS

nose•dive /ˈnəʊzdaɪv‖ˈnoʊz-/ *v* [I,T] if sales, exports, shares etc nosedive, their value or number falls suddenly and by a large amount: *In Hong Kong, stocks nosedived in active trading.* | *The corporate banking unit's **profit nosedived** 74%, to $20 million.* —**nosedive** *n* [C] *The U.S. currency began its nosedive late in the morning.*

no-show *n* [C] someone who is expected at a restaurant to eat or at an airport to take a plane but does not arrive, or an occasion when this happens: *No-shows are destroying the restaurant-client relationship.* | *Most airlines guard against the threat of no-shows by overbooking flights.*

nostro account —see under ACCOUNT[1]

no•ta•rize also **notarise** *BrE* /ˈnəʊtəraɪz‖ˈnoʊ-/ *v* [T] LAW to make a document, statement etc official: *Spain's agentes de cambio are responsible for notarizing all security transactions.* | *The defendant had forged a customer's signature, notarized the papers and submitted them to court.*

no•ta•ry /ˈnəʊtəri‖ˈnoʊ-/ *n* plural **notaries** also **notary public** plural **notaries public** [C] someone such as a lawyer with the legal power to make a document official: *Most of the centers offer secretarial and notary services.* | *the procedure that verifies* (=makes official) *certificates issued by notaries* —**notarial** *adj*: *Concerns about notarial abuse led Governor Martinez to commission a study.*

notch[1] /nɒtʃ‖nɑːtʃ/ *n* [C] a degree or level on a scale that measures achievement, price etc: *The Federal Reserve's credit policy committee is expected to reduce interest rates another notch.* | *The 500-stock index gained 0.43 to 358.43, a notch below the record close of 359.80.*

notch[2] also **notch up** *v* [T] *journalism* to obtain or achieve something important or something that gives you an advantage over other people: *Boeing launched the twin-engine plane late last year, quickly notching 49 firm orders.* | *Mutual funds that hold stocks in smaller companies have **notched up** huge **gains**.*

note[1] /nəʊt‖noʊt/ *n* **1** [C] *BrE* a piece of printed paper that is used as money; BANKNOTE; BILL *AmE*: *In Hungary the highest-denominated note now has a face value of* (=is worth) *1000 forints.*

currency notes [plural] banknotes in a particular currency: *There is nothing of an economic nature to prevent a private bank from issuing currency notes denominated in ECUs, though there may be legal restrictions.*

2 [C] a short document, or part of a book containing extra information: *Please read the **explanatory notes** below.* | *I enclose notes from our meeting for your information.*

advice note also **dispatch note** [C] a document showing that goods have been sent to a customer

bond note [C] an official document allowing imported goods to be removed from a building where they have been kept because no import tax has been paid on them yet

bought note [C] a note from a STOCKBROKER to a client, giving details of a deal in which they have bought shares for their client

consignment note [C] written abbreviation **C/N** a document sent with goods that are being delivered, that acts as a RECEIPT for the goods and also shows the agreement with the company delivering the goods

contract note [C] FINANCE a document given to someone buying or selling shares showing the price, number of shares bought etc: *Our instant dealing branches offer immediate settlement with a contract note and cheque on the spot.*

cover note [C] *BrE* INSURANCE a temporary document sent to you by your insurance company or dealer, proving that an insurance contract exists. A cover note is usually sent to you when you take out insurance, while the complete contract is being prepared: *To tax the vehicle, you must show a Certificate of Motor Insurance or cover note.*

credit note [C] *BrE* a document sent to a customer who is owed money, for example because they have returned goods; CREDIT RECEIPT *AmE*: *We've introduced electronic debit and credit notes which go straight to a client's account.*

debit note [C] *BrE* a written record showing that a customer owes money, for example because the INVOICE (=document showing the price to be paid) was not correct; DEBIT RECEIPT *AmE*: *Many larger companies adopt* *the procedure of raising a debit note for any errors on invoices.*

delivery note [C] a document showing that goods have been delivered: *The delivery note should be used for checking purposes against the goods.*

demand note [C] ◆ a written request for payment, for example of taxes: *Birmingham City Council has now set its community charge and the basic amount payable is shown on the enclosed demand note.*

◆ a loan which the lender can ask to be repaid at any time: *APM loaned Stotler Group $1 million in the form of a demand note.*

shipping note [C] a document that gives details of goods being shipped somewhere

sold note [C] a note from a STOCKBROKER to a client, giving details of a sale of the client's shares

3 notes [plural] FINANCE used in the names of bonds ISSUED (=made available and sold by governments and companies) or COMMERCIAL PAPER (=borrowing for less than a year by companies): *The government has auctioned $15 billion of* ***three-year notes*** (=borrowing that will be repaid after three years).

convertible notes [plural] notes that can later be exchanged for shares: *Mr Manning, OIS Optical's largest shareholder, converted his convertible notes of OIS Optical into common stock.*

Euro medium-term note [C] an arrangement for borrowing several times on the EUROBOND market without needing the official documents each time: *Coca-Cola Enterprises will issue the first tranche of bonds under a $2.5 billion euro-medium term note programme.*

floating rate note [C] a type of bond sold on the EUROMARKET with VARIABLE RATE interest (=a rate that can change over time): *a $50 million issue of floating-rate notes due in 2004*

non-callable notes [plural] notes that cannot be repaid to lenders before the date originally fixed

promissory note also **P Note** [C] a document stating that someone promises to pay a particular sum of money on a certain date: *Promissory notes and bills of exchange are often guaranteed or endorsed by a third party.*

revenue anticipation notes also **tax anticipation notes** [plural] notes sold by local authorities in the US that are repaid with income received later from taxes: *the annual New York state sale of tax and revenue anticipation notes*

secured notes [plural] notes where, if the borrower gets into financial difficulty and is unable to repay them, lenders have the right to take and sell particular assets of the borrower in order to get their money back: *the airline's 15% senior secured notes, for which the same landing slots* (=rights to use airports at particular times) *were serving as collateral*

senior notes [plural] notes where, if the borrower gets into financial difficulty, lenders will be repaid before other lenders, or will get back a larger percentage of the amount they have lent

subordinated notes [plural] notes where, if the borrower gets into financial difficulty, lenders will be repaid only after other lenders, or will get back a smaller percentage of the amount they have lent

Treasury notes [plural] notes ISSUED (=made available and sold) by the US government: *Comments by Federal Reserve Chairman Alan Greenspan caused prices of short-term Treasury notes to fall and long-term Treasury bonds to rise.*

unsecured notes [plural] notes where, if the borrower gets into financial difficulty and is unable to repay them, lenders have no rights to take and sell particular assets of the borrower in order to get their money back —see also SICK NOTE

note² *v* [T] **1** to mention something important or interesting so that people will notice it: *Futures are attractive to brokerage houses trading for their own accounts, noted Mr. O'Keefe.* **note that**: *Analysts note that unless the discount rate is lowered, a substantial stock market recovery isn't likely.*

2 to notice or pay careful attention to something: ***Please note*** *the following amendments to the guidelines.* **note that**: *Investors should note that these new long-term options are currently quite a risk.* | *It's* ***worth noting*** *that almost all the oil that could be delivered by pipeline.*

note·book /ˈnəʊtbʊk‖ˈnoʊt-/ *n* [C] COMPUTING a small personal computer which is easy to carry somewhere with you: *Toshiba says it is offering the industry's most advanced notebooks at competitive prices.* | *These screens add about $2,000 to the price of a* ***notebook computer***. —compare LAPTOP

note·hold·er /ˈnəʊtˌhəʊldə‖ˈnoʊtˌhoʊldər/ *n* [C] *AmE* a person or organization that owns notes in a company: *$180 million is owed to noteholders.* | *The noteholders are blocking completion of the sale.*

note issuance facility —see under FACILITY

note issue —see under ISSUE²

note payable —see under PAYABLE

note receivable —see under RECEIVABLE

note to the accounts *n* plural **notes to the accounts** [C] ACCOUNTING an explanation of a particular item in a company's accounts: *The note to the accounts on investment properties says they have been valued at their current market value.*

not-for-profit *adj* [only before a noun] *AmE* a not-for-profit organization is one with aims that are not related to business or to make a profit. These organizations usually work in education, health etc; NON-PROFIT-MAKING; NON-PROFIT *AmE*: *the not-for-profit sectors dealing with museums, art galleries and universities*

no·tice /ˈnəʊtɪ̈s‖ˈnoʊ-/ *n* **1** [U] information or a warning about something that is going to happen: *These rules are subject to change* ***without notice*** (=no notice needs to be given). | *Either party may terminate the contract* ***with three months' notice.***

2 serve notice to officially warn someone that something is going to happen: *The tenant has the right to serve notice on the landlord if they fail to carry out the rent review.*

3 [C] a formal document warning someone about something or asking them to do something

deficiency notice also **notice of deficiency** [C] TAX in the US, a document from the tax authorities informing someone that they owe more tax than they have paid

renewal notice [C] an official document reminding someone that they must make an insurance policy continue for a further period of time. Renewal notices show all the details of the policy, and must be signed and returned: *Your new premium is shown on your renewal notice.*

4 [U] HUMAN RESOURCES the period of time that someone works after they said that they are going to leave their job, or after they have been told to leave their job: *She would ring the agency and* ***give in her notice***. | *The employee need not* ***work out*** *the period of* ***notice*** *if he prefers not to.*

5 [U] PROPERTY also **notice to quit**, **notice of eviction** if a property owner gives someone notice to quit, or notice of eviction, they tell them to leave the property by a particular date: *Once a Notice to Quit has been served upon you, and has expired, your landlord has the legal right to order you to leave your accommodation.*

notice account —see under ACCOUNT¹

no·tice·board /ˈnəʊtɪ̈sˌbɔːd‖ˈnoʊtɪ̈sˌbɔːrd/ *n* [C] *BrE* a large board fixed to a wall where people can put notes and messages for other people to read; BULLETIN BOARD

AmE: The names, telephone numbers and locations of trained staff are shown on the company's noticeboards.

no·ti·fy /ˈnəʊtəfaɪ‖ˈnoʊ-/ *v* past tense and past participle **notified** [T] to tell someone something officially or formally, usually by writing to them: *Fisher-Price notified about 110 employees they would lose their jobs because of the planned closure.* **notify sb of sth**: *Under the new contracts, dealers can sell foreign cars but must notify Nissan in advance.* —**notification** *n* [C,U] *You can ask for notification in writing if you wish.* | *The goods may be assembled in the UK, provided the above notification is sent to Customs.*

not-invented-here syndrome abbreviation **NIH syndrome** *n* [singular] *disapproving* when people in a company department consider new products or ideas from other departments as threats, rather than trying to take advantage of them for the benefit of the whole company: *Board rooms are under pressure to avoid the not-invented-here syndrome and accelerate product introduction.*

no·tion·al /ˈnəʊʃənəl‖ˈnoʊ-/ *adj* a notional amount, price, rent etc is not real but is used as a basis for making calculations, for example about tax: *Its original notional £10,000 investment in the Stock Exchange is now 'worth' £10,719.*

Nov. written abbreviation for NOVEMBER

no·va·tion /nəʊˈveɪʃən‖noʊ-/ *n* [C,U] LAW when there is a change of one or more of the people or organizations that have agreed to a contract, with the permission of the other PARTIES (=people and organizations involved): *The suit is based on the contract-law principle of novation: duties and obligations of a contract can't be transferred without the consent of both parties.*

nov·el·ty /ˈnɒvəlti‖ˈnɑː-/ *n* plural **novelties** [C usually plural] a new, unusual product which is cheap to produce and will probably only be popular with customers for a short time: *Waterbury, maker of premium ice cream and novelties, reported net profits of $1.2 million.* | *novelty sweatshirts and sweaters*

NOW account —see under ACCOUNT[1]

no-win *adj* **no-win situation/issue/task etc** a situation, issue etc which will end badly whatever people decide to do: *The decision could put companies in a no-win situation.* | *He undertook what many regarded as a no-win task: streamlining the company's data processing.*

no win no fee *n* [U] a phrase used in advertising a lawyer's services, showing that if a customer loses their legal case, they will not have to pay the lawyer —**no win no fee** *adj* [only before a noun] *'no win, no fee' agreements between lawyers and clients*

NPA *n* Newspaper Publishers' Association; an organization in Britain whose members work in the newspaper PUBLISHING industry. The NPA is responsible for making sure its members obey the law and represents their views and opinions to government

NPV written abbreviation for NET PRESENT VALUE

NTA written abbreviation for NET TANGIBLE ASSETS

nt wt written abbreviation for NET WEIGHT

nude contract *n* [C] another name for NAKED CONTRACT —see under CONTRACT

nudge /nʌdʒ/ *v* [T] to increase the value or position of something on a scale by a small amount **nudge sth to/up/over etc**: *Investors bought blue chips again, nudging the Dow Jones Industrial Average to another all-time high.* | *Honda increased its share of the car market even though its sales nudged up only slightly.* —**nudge** *n* [C usually singular] *The interest rate cuts will give the economy an upward nudge.*

nu·dum pac·tum /ˌnjuːdʊm ˈpæktʊm‖ˌnuː-/ —see ***naked contract*** under CONTRACT[1]

nui·sance /ˈnjuːsəns‖ˈnuː-/ *n* [C,U] LAW someone or something that causes public annoyance: *After a local jury found the noise was a nuisance, a judge ruled that the bell can no longer ring at night.* | *movement of vehicles creating **public nuisance***

NUJ *n* National Union of Journalists; an organization in Britain whose members work mainly in newspaper and magazine PUBLISHING and which passes their views to the government and to their managers: *The union was informed that the agreement between the company and the NUJ was to be terminated.*

null /nʌl/ *adj* [only before a noun] **1** STATISTICS a null effect, result etc is one that is zero or nothing
2 LAW another name for NULL AND VOID: *Their suit also asks the court to declare null the buyer's shareholder-rights plan.*

null and void *adj* [not before a noun] LAW a contract, agreement etc that is null and void has no effect because it is against the law: *Judge Reasoner decided that the RTC overstepped its authority in adopting the regulation and declared it unlawful, null and void.*

null hypothesis —see under HYPOTHESIS

nul·li·fy /ˈnʌləfaɪ/ *v* past tense and past participle **nullified** [T] LAW **1** to state officially that something does not have any legal force and is therefore considered not to exist: *The Illinois Supreme Court reversed the decision of two lower courts and nullified the publisher's contract.*
2 to make something lose its effect or value: *The surtax nullifies the benefit these taxpayers get from the lower, 15% tax rate.* —**nullification** *n* [U] *Juries are being encouraged to exercise their nullification power more frequently.*

nul·li·ty /ˈnʌləti/ *n* [C usually singular] plural **nullities** LAW a document, statement, contract etc that has no legal force and is therefore considered not to have existed: *The appellant's case was supported, and the decision by the FCC was therefore ruled a nullity.*

number[1] /ˈnʌmbə‖-bər/ *n* **1** a series of numbers used to identify someone or something: *What's your office **telephone number**?* | *Our Freephone number is in the phone book.* —see also TELEPHONE NUMBER

box number also **post office box number** [C] an address used by a firm for receiving letters at a POST OFFICE instead of its own address: *It is usually best to avoid box numbers in advertisements as they tend to put people off replying.*

PIN number also **PIN** [C] personal identification number; a secret number given to you by your bank that you use when getting money from an ATM (=machine that distributes cash) with a BANK CARD: *You can use your card, together with your PIN at most NatWest self-service banking machines.* | *Never tell anyone your PIN number.*

serial number [C] a number used on things that are produced in large quantities, making it possible to identify each one: *The illegal software makes it possible to change the phone's unique **electronic serial number**.*

2 account/card number the series of numbers used to show who a bank or credit account belongs to: *Please quote your credit card number in all correspondence.*
3 numbers [plural] how many people there are in a particular situation, activity etc: *Airline passenger numbers in America have more than doubled.* | *An increase in membership numbers was helped by a recruitment drive.*
4 numbers [plural] figures or amounts, for example those in a company's accounts or in statistics: *The field staff knew what the numbers should have been, but the computer numbers didn't agree with what we knew was there.* | *If you **run the numbers*** (=do the necessary calculations), *there is no way you can make money renting the space at $30 a square foot.*
5 [singular] the total amount of something + **of**: *Another service attracting **a growing number** of sub-*

scribers is Commercial Payment Profile. | *The number of companies created in the first half of this year was 3.1% lower than last year.*

6 number one/two etc *informal* the most important person or thing, the second most important person etc in an organization or group: *Mr Steed is number two to the group chief executive.* | *Grand Metropolitan, the hotel and retailing giant ranking number 10 in The Times 1000 Index* —see also DUN'S NUMBER, OPPOSITE NUMBER

number[2] *v* [T] **1** to be a particular amount or quantity: *Locations accepting Visa cards now number more than nine million.* | *Sales numbered 8.1% fewer than a year before.*

2 to give a number to things that are part of a set or list of things: *Each doll is individually numbered and comes with a certificate of authenticity.*

number-cruncher *n* [C] *informal* **1** someone whose job involves doing very large calculations using a computer: *The number-crunchers at the National Association of Manufacturers maintain that the U.S. can keep pace with the 7.6% gain in exports.*

2 COMPUTING a powerful computer that is used for calculations —**number-crunching** *n* [U] *the fastest number-crunching machines in the world*

numbered account —see under ACCOUNT[1]

nu·mer·i·cal /njuːˈmerɪkəl‖nuː-/ also **nu·mer·ic** /njuːˈmerɪk‖nuː-/ *adj* [only before a noun] expressed or considered in numbers: *Computerized numerical control systems accounted for 70% of overall sales.* | *The software will allow you to transfer* ***numeric data*** *from a spreadsheet to a business letter.*

NYMEX /ˈnaɪmeks/ *n* New York Mercantile Exchange; a COMMODITY MARKET for dealing in oil and oil-related products

NYSE abbreviation for NEW YORK STOCK EXCHANGE

N

O

OAP *n* [C] *BrE* Old Age Pensioner; a person who is old enough to receive a PENSION from the government

oath /əʊθ‖oʊθ/ *n* **1** [C] a formal promise to do something: *The president **has taken an oath to** support and defend the Constitution.* | *Yeltsin **took the oath of office** as the Russian republic's first-ever popularly elected president.*
2 be under oath LAW also **be on oath** *BrE* to have made a formal promise to tell the truth in a court of law: *Mr. Boesky acknowledged that he lied under oath.* | *The witnesses should be examined on oath.*
3 take the oath to make a formal promise to tell the truth in a court of law

o/b written abbreviation for on or before, used before a date that is the latest possible date that a bill can be paid or goods can be delivered

ob•ject[1] /əb'dʒekt/ *v* [I] to complain or protest about something, or to feel that you oppose it or disapprove of it: *Regulators objected when Columbia paid Mr. Spiegel a $3 million bonus.* + **to**: *The banks objected to the proposal fiercely.* —**objection** *n* [C,U] *The creditors **raised no objection** to the deadline extension.* —**objector** *n* [C] *There are few objectors to the proposal amongst private investors.*

ob•ject[2] /'ɒbdʒekt‖'ɑːb-/ *n* [C] **1** a solid thing, especially something you can hold or touch: *The firms sell products ranging from art objects to vintage cars.*
2 the intended result of a plan, action, activity, or document; aim, OBJECTIVE: *Our object is to keep costs down.* + **of**: *The object of a contract of sale is to transfer the property from the seller to the buyer.* | *Applying for extra amounts in loans **defeats the object*** (=does not have the result you intended)*, because the students then get themselves further into debt.*
3 objects [plural] the things that a company has been formed to do and the types of goods or services that it has been formed to deal in: *The objects of a business dictate what sort of organisation structure it needs.*
4 be the object of sth to be the cause of a particular activity or situation: *The banking bill is currently the object of intense negotiations in Congress.*
5 money/expense is no object used to say that you do not care how much money is spent on something: *It would appear that money is no object for the people behind this offer.*
6 COMPUTING a combination of DATA (=written information) and instructions acting on the data, for example in the form of a document or a picture: ***object orientated** programming* | *multimedia data objects*

ob•jec•tive[1] /əb'dʒektɪv/ *n* [C] something that you are trying to achieve; aim: *Our objective is to grow earnings at about 6% a year.* | *An estimated 86% of products failed to reach their **business objectives**.* | *a client's **investment objectives***

objective[2] *adj* not influenced by your own needs, wishes, or situation: *An analyst's role is to provide an informed, objective opinion regarding the future of a company.* —**objectively** *adv*: *The Bank will do all it can to investigate your complaint objectively.* —**objectivity** *n* [U] *Some members of the board questioned the auditor's objectivity.*

object language —see under LANGUAGE

object-oriented *adj* [only before a noun] COMPUTING object-oriented programs and software are built up from different parts, rather than being supplied as a single package: *a new operating system based on object-oriented software*

objects clause —see under CLAUSE

ob•li•gate /'ɒblɪgeɪt‖'ɑːb-/ *v* [T] *especially AmE* **1** to make it necessary for someone to do something: *A new law will obligate all companies engaging in banking business to get approval from the finance ministry.*
2 if an authority obligates an amount of money for something, it officially says it will spend that amount on it: *The Pentagon has obligated $987.9 million to overhaul and improve the aircraft.*

ob•li•gat•ed /'ɒblɪgeɪtɪd‖'ɑːb-/ *adj especially AmE* **1 be obligated (to do sth)** to have to do something or have a duty to do it: *The insurer is obligated by contract to compensate the policyholder for the damage.*
2 be/feel obligated to sb to owe someone loyalty, thanks, or money because they have done something for you: *Congressmen whose terms are limited would not be obligated to a president.*

ob•li•ga•tion /ˌɒblɪ'geɪʃən‖ˌɑːb-/ *n* **1** [C,U] a legal or moral duty to do something **obligation to do sth**: *It's our obligation to provide telephone service at the lowest possible cost.* | *We've **fulfilled our obligation** performed it to the creditors and shareholders.* | *The county has a **legal obligation** to return stolen guns to their owners.* | *Russia has failed to **honor contractual obligations*** (=perform ones in a contract) *to supply the Ukraine with oil.*
financial obligations [plural] payments that a person or organization must make: *The company may fail to **meet financial obligations** and suggest a bankruptcy-law filing as an alternative.*
2 be under an obligation to have to do something because it is a legal or moral duty: *The water company is under an obligation to enhance drinking water standards.* **be under no obligation to do sth**: *The government **is under no obligation** to finance art.*
3 without obligation if you are invited to look at a product or service without obligation, you can look at it without having to buy it: *This mortgage advice is completely free and without obligation.*

o•blig•a•to•ry /ə'blɪgətəri‖-tɔːri/ *adj formal* something that is obligatory must be done because of a law, rule etc; COMPULSORY,; MANDATORY: *The Housing and Town Planning Act made it obligatory for local authorities to prepare surveys of their housing needs.*

o•blige /ə'blaɪdʒ/ *v* **1** [T] to make it necessary for someone to do something **be obliged to do sth**: *As a result of falling profits, we were obliged to close the factory.*
2 [I,T] to do something that someone has asked you to do: *Many sellers ask Satra to keep their payments abroad until they can open foreign bank accounts, and Satra is only too happy to oblige.* | *They wanted more direct information than we were giving, and we've obliged them.*

ob•so•les•cence /ˌɒbsə'lesəns‖ˌɑːb-/ *n* [U] when a product, system etc is becoming no longer useful because something better is available, possible etc: *Now markets are subject to the faster obsolescence of products due to greater competition.* —**obsolescent** *adj*: *a region tied to an obsolescent industrial base*
planned obsolescence also **built-in obsolescence** when a product is deliberately made to be old-fashioned or impossible to use after a short period of time, so that people have to replace it

ob•so•lete /'ɒbsəliːt‖ˌɑːbsə'liːt/ *adj* if something is obsolete, it is old-fashioned and no longer useful, because something newer or better has been invented:

ISDN could make modems obsolete. | *companies burdened with* ***obsolete equipment***

oc·cu·pan·cy /ˈɒkjəpənsi‖ˈɑːk-/ *n* [U] *formal* **1** when someone uses a building or piece of land for living or working in: *The facility will be ready for occupancy on Feb. 20.*

2 used to talk about how many beds or rooms in a hotel, hospital etc are being used by guests, patients etc: *Marriott said occupancy was up throughout its lodging divisions.* | *Hospital* ***occupancy rates*** *are declining nationwide.*

oc·cu·pant /ˈɒkjəpənt‖ˈɑːk-/ *n* [C] someone who lives in a building or an organization that has offices in a building, especially a building owned by someone else: *There are many empty offices seeking new occupants.*

oc·cu·pa·tion /ˌɒkjəˈpeɪʃən‖ˌɑːk-/ *n* [C] a job or profession, used especially on official forms or for writing about the jobs people do: *Please state your name, age, and occupation.* | *The least stressful occupations in our study were museum and library work.*

service occupation a job that involves providing a service for a person or company, rather than producing a product, for example a cleaner, sales person, or lawyer: *Service occupations are present in all sectors of the economy.*

oc·cu·pa·tion·al /ˌɒkjəˈpeɪʃənəl◂‖ˌɑːk-/ *adj* [only before a noun] related to someone's job: *questions about credit card applicants'* ***occupational backgrounds*** | *She is moving steadily up* ***the occupational ladder***. | *Specific* ***occupational skills*** *should be combined with general education.*

occupational hazard —see under HAZARD

occupational pension —see under PENSION[1]

occupational psychology *n* [U] the study of how people behave at work, including the relationships between workers, managers, and TRADE UNIONS; INDUSTRIAL PSYCHOLOGY —**occupational psychologist** *n* [C] *He had a two-hour interview with an occupational psychologist.*

Occupational Safety and Health Administration abbreviation **OSHA** *n* the government organization in the US that controls the risks to people's health and safety at work —compare HEALTH AND SAFETY EXECUTIVE

oc·cu·py /ˈɒkjəpaɪ‖ˈɑːk-/ *v* past tense and past participle **occupied** **1** [T] to use a particular building to live or work in: *a large computer company that occupies a building of some 60,000 sq ft* —**occupier** *n* [C] *Texaco became one of the big-name occupiers of Canary Wharf.*

2 [T] to have an official position or job: *He occupies an important position in government.* | *The group chief executive job was occupied by Philip Charlton.*

3 [I,T] if something is occupying you, you are busy doing it: *As PA to the chief executive, there is plenty to* ***keep you occupied***. | *Mr Ball* ***is occupied with*** *a customer at the moment.*

4 [T] to use a particular amount of space or time: *Computer files occupy much less storage space than paper ones.* | *Our fees are based on the time spent occupied on the work.*

5 [T] to enter a place in large numbers and take control of it: *He expects that sacked workers will occupy their factory, sooner or later.*

ocean bill of lading —see under BILL OF LADING

OCR *n* COMPUTING optical character recognition; a computer system for automatically recognizing letters and numbers that have been printed or written by hand on paper: *the scanner's built-in OCR software*

Oct. written abbreviation for OCTOBER

o/d written abbreviation for OVERDRAFT; OVERDRAWN

odd·ment /ˈɒdmənt‖ˈɑːd-/ *n* [C usually plural] an object or piece of something that is left over from a larger set or piece, especially one that is being sold cheaply: *They were selling oddments of china from around £2.*

odds /ɒdz‖ɑːdz/ *n* [plural] **1** the odds of something happening is how likely it is to happen: *The odds of us achieving our sales targets are very poor.* | *The odds are* (=it is likely that) *selling will continue.*

2 difficulties that make a good result seem very unlikely: *The small company battled its way, despite* ***enormous odds***, *into a success.* | *Successful entrepreneurs have a will to succeed* ***against all odds*** (=even when there are great difficulties).

3 be at odds (with) if two people or groups are at odds, they disagree about something or they often disagree about things: *The head cook and head porter are constantly at odds.*

4 be at odds (with) if two statements, descriptions, actions etc are at odds with each other, they are different although they should be the same: *Sometimes trade union negotiators set targets which are at odds with the targets set by management.*

5 pay/charge over the odds *BrE informal* to pay or charge a higher price than is usual or reasonable: *Are supermarket customers paying over the odds for fruit and vegetables?*

OECD *n* Organization for Economic Cooperation and Development; an international organization based in Paris that helps its member states to develop economically by producing studies, statistics etc

oeic abbreviation for OPEN-ENDED INVESTMENT COMPANY

Of·ex /ˈɒfeks‖ˈɔː-/ *n* a stockmarket based in London for new, growing British companies, in which a computer network is used to buy and sell shares —compare EASDAQ, NASDAQ

off-balance sheet —see under BALANCE SHEET

off-board trading —see under TRADING

of·fence *BrE*, **offense** *AmE* /əˈfens/ *n* **1** [C] an illegal action or a crime: *The company was not aware that it* ***was committing an offence***. | ***It is an offence to*** *drive when your eyesight is not up to the required standard.* | *You may be guilty of a* ***criminal offence***.

2 [U] behaviour which makes someone angry or upset: *As a manager, you must know how to handle a difficult customer without* ***giving offence***.

of·fend /əˈfend/ *v* **1** [I] to do something that is a crime: *What can be done to stop criminals offending again?*

2 [I,T] to make someone angry or upset: *The advertisement was never intended to offend anyone.* | *hard-sell tactics that offended many customers* —**offended** *adj*: *Many sales personnel would be offended if sales forecasts were made without their input.*

of·fend·er /əˈfendə‖-ər/ *n* [C] **1** someone who is guilty of a crime: ***Repeat offenders*** (=people who do something illegal several times) *will face higher fines.* | *the sentencing of* ***first-time offenders*** | *a school for* ***young offenders***

2 someone or something that is the cause of something bad: *Discrimination specialists say small businesses are the* ***worst offenders***.

of·fend·ing /əˈfendɪŋ/ *adj* **the offending...** the thing that is causing a problem: *He demanded that the offending paragraph be deleted.* | *SmithKline told the judge that the offending ads would no longer be used.*

offense *n* [C] the US spelling of OFFENCE

of·fer[1] /ˈɒfə‖ˈɔːfər, ˈɑː-/ *v* [T] **1** to say that you are willing to give someone something, or to give them it **offer sb sth**: *They offered him a very good job, but he turned it down.* **offer sth to sb**: *The magazine offered discounts to advertisers.*

2 to say that you are willing to pay a particular amount of money for something **offer (sb) sth for**: *They've offered us $200,000 for the house.*

3 to make an investment available for sale: *Associates Corp. offered $300 million of five-year notes priced to yield 6.965%.* | *Sony Music offered about 18 million shares to investors on the Tokyo Stock Exchange at 6,800 yen each.*

4 to provide a product or service: *Citicorp offers six credit cards with varying rates.*

5 if a product or service offers particular advantages or features, it has those features or advantages: *The little phone also offers only a small display and keypad that make dialing difficult.*

O

offer[2] *n* [C] **1** a statement that you are willing to give someone something or do something for them + **of**: *Before the offers of early retirement, Northeast had about 8,000 employees.* **offer to do sth**: *Pirelli's offer to merge its tire division with Continental* | *They approached him with the new **job offer** and, within hours, he accepted the post.*

2 an amount of money that you are willing to pay for something **make (sb) an offer (for)**: *Penney said QVC has made an offer for its JC Penney Television Shopping Channel.* | *1,200 workers **accepted** an early-retirement **offer**.* | *Businessland **declined*** (=refused) ***the** $1-a-share **offer** from JWP because it wanted $3 a share.* | *BP's **offer price** for Gerland's shares is about 23% higher than the average traded price over the past month.*

firm offer a definite offer to buy or sell something at a particular price: *The land will be sold off, but as yet no firm offers have been received for the site.*

initial offer an offer when it is first made, or the amount involved: *The company and its creditors rejected Chiquita's initial offer.*

initial public offer abbreviation **IPO** an occasion when a company offers shares on a stockmarket for the first time; INITIAL PUBLIC OFFERING: *the sale of part of the government-owned Orbis hotel chain through an initial public offer of 40% of the company's equity*

open offer a type of RIGHTS ISSUE where existing shareholders have the right to buy new shares in a company, and financial institutions buy the shares that they do not buy

self-tender offer an offer by a company to buy its own shares from investors, to try and prevent the company from being bought by someone else: *The company plans to spend more than $800 million on a self-tender offer.*

settlement offer an amount of money, property etc that one person offers to another in order to end a disagreement: *The risk that the other party might appeal the court's decision made the settlement offer attractive.*

share exchange offer in a TAKEOVER, an occasion when a company offers its own shares in exchange for shares in the company that it wants to control; PAPER OFFER: *Vereinsbank owns 45% of Hypo-Bank after a share exchange offer.*

share offer also **stock offer** *AmE* ◆ an occasion when particular shares in a company are made available for sale for the first time, and the number of shares involved; SHARE ISSUE; STOCK ISSUE: *Liberty Life said it expected the new share offer to raise 444 million rand.*

◆ an occasion when a company offers to buy another's shares in a takeover: *BTR's cash and share offer values Hawker Siddeley at £1.5 billion.*

takeover offer an occasion when one company offers to buy another company, or the amount of money involved: *Tootal fought a **hostile takeover offer*** (=one that it did not want) *by a rival textile concern, Coats Viyella.*

tender offer ◆ an occasion when an investor offers to buy a particular quantity of existing shares or bonds at a particular price. The sale occurs only if all the existing owners agree to sell at this price: *Generali will make a tender offer for AMB at DM210 a share.*

◆ a type of new share offer, when investors say how many shares they are willing to buy and at what price. Only investors who make offers at or above the STRIKING PRICE (=the actual price fixed after offers have been received) obtain shares

◆ in the US, an offer to SHAREHOLDERS of a company to buy a particular number of shares from them at a particular price, which can be done as a way of gaining control of the company: *LIN has been the object of a hostile tender offer by McCaw.*

unsolicited offer an offer to buy a company, property etc that the owner did not ask for: *Crystalate called for Vishay's aid in **fending off*** (=defending itself against) *an unsolicited offer by TT Group PLC.*

3 be open to offers to be ready to consider different offers of money or other things people are willing to give you: *We have no definite plans to sell but we are certainly open to offers.*

4 on offer to be available to be bought or used: *It's still a seller's market because of the shortage of property on offer.*

5 on offer *BrE* available for a short time at a reduced price; ON SALE *AmE*: *Olive oil is on offer this week.*

6 a reduction in the price of something for a short time: *Take advantage of our 'buy six for the price of five' offer.*

7 be under offer *BrE* PROPERTY if property that is for sale is under offer, someone has offered an amount of money for it: *We can confirm the club is under offer, but that's as much as we can say at this stage.*

8 a free product or service that is added to something in order to encourage you to buy it

free offer something that is available without cost for a particular period of time, for example so that you can try it: *More than 90% of the free offers on cosmetics are for women.*

special offer ◆ a reduction in the price of something for a short time, made in order to encourage you to buy it: *The ferry company is **running a special offer**: a day trip to France for only £7.* | *the kind of watches you see **on special offer** at petrol stations*

◆ a product or service that is added to something in order to encourage you to buy it: *Special offer: all guests of Amsterdam Travel Service are offered a free sauna during their stay.*

trial offer [C] a new product or service offered free to customers so that they can see what it is like before they decide whether to buy it: *American Express is promising new cardholders a free trial offer for three months.*

offer document —see under DOCUMENT[1]

offered price —see under PRICE[1]

of·fe·ree /ˌɒfəˈriː‖ˌɒː-, ˌɑː-/ *n* [C] LAW a person or organization to whom something is offered for sale: *The revocation did not come to the notice of the offeree, so the offeree's acceptance of the offer was valid.* —compare OFFEROR

offer for sale *n* plural **offers for sale** [C usually singular] FINANCE an occasion when a company offers shares for sale at a fixed price directly to the public, for example in newspaper advertisements: *When companies sell securities, they need to decide between a fixed-price offer for sale, and an auction.*

of·fer·ing /ˈɒfərɪŋ‖ˈɒː-, ˈɑː-/ *n* [C usually singular] **1** a product or service sold by a company, or a number of these considered as a group: *Like most new high-tech products when they first hit the market, Sony's **latest offering*** (=its most recent product) *won't be cheap.* | *Invacare **broadened its offering*** (=made more products available) *of home health-care products.*

2 FINANCE an occasion when shares, bonds etc are made available for sale, or the amount involved: *$248.4 million of 8.30% securities will be offered through First Boston Corp. and the underwriters expect the offering to be rated triple-A by Moody's.* | *Nomura Securities **underwrote*** (=arranged to sell) ***the** Aeromexico **offering**.* | *Kober **placed*** (=sold) *90% of Fox's **offering** with its own* *clients.* | *The bank plans to raise $1.25 billion in a* ***stock offering*** *later this month.* | *Proceeds of the* ***share offering*** *will be used to reduce Cameco's debt.*

blank check offering *AmE* an occasion when people are asked to invest money without knowing exactly what businesses their money will be invested in

initial public offering abbreviation **IPO** an occasion when a company offers shares on a stockmarket for the first time, and the amount of shares involved; INITIAL PUBLIC OFFER: *Bizmart went public at $10 a share in an initial public offering led by Alex. Brown & Sons.*

private offering when shares or bonds are sold directly to a small group of investors, rather than on the open market

public offering an occasion when shares are offered to all interested investors, and the amount of shares involved

shelf offering in the US, an occasion when a company sells a specific number of new shares or bonds from a larger number which the authorities have given them permission to sell: *Boeing Co. registered for a shelf offering of up to $1.25 billion of debt securities.*

of·fer·or /ˈɒfərə‖ˈɒːfərər, ˈɑː-/ *n* [C] LAW a person or organization that offers to buy something: *When an offeror successfully completes a takeover bid for a target company it acquires control of the target with all its assets and liabilities.* —compare OFFEREE

offer price —see under PRICE[1]

of·fice /ˈɒfɪ̆s‖ˈɒː-, ˈɑː-/ *n* **1** [C] a room or building where people work at desks, often belonging to an organization: *The agency recently closed its Houston office.* | *I applied for the job of* ***office manager***. | *There is a shortage of low-cost* ***office space***. | *I'd like to see you in my office.* | *I work in a large* ***open-plan*** *office (=an office without any walls dividing it into separate rooms).*

assay office [C] an office in Britain where gold and silver objects are officially marked to show how pure the metal they are made of is

back office [singular] FINANCE the department of a financial institution that does work connected with managing and organizing the work of the institution, rather than actual work of trading, working with clients etc: *Back office problems led to a suspension of trading.*

branch office [C] a local office of a company, usually in a different town or city to the company's main office: *Stadtbank opened 13 branch offices in East Berlin.*

exchange office [C] a place where you can change currencies, but which does not offer other banking services: *The decision allows commercial banks and tourism companies to set up exchange offices.*

front office [C] the department in companies, especially financial institutions, that deals directly with clients rather than administrative activities: *He has been appointed to the front office staff as a senior consultant, with responsibility for foreign exchange trading and sales.*

head office also **main office** ◆ [C,U] the main office of a company: *There is a customer liaison department at head office.* | *New York used to house the main offices of hundreds of top companies.*

◆ [U] the managers who work at the main office of a company: *Most of the important decisions are made by head office.*

land office PROPERTY a government office in the US that records sales of public land: *the Texas General Land Office*

receiving office the part of a company where goods are received and checked

registered office [C] in Britain, the official address of a company where all letters and notices must be sent. By law, every British company must have a registered office and the REGISTRAR OF COMPANIES must be given the address: *The address of our registered office is printed at the head of this letter.*

satellite office [C] an office that is part of a larger organization and is some distance away from the main office which controls it: *Captions Inc., based in Los Angeles, recently opened up satellite offices in New York and Dallas.*

small office/home office written abbreviation **SOHO** [C] a room in someone's home with electronic equipment such as a computer and a fax machine, that is used as a place in which to work

sorting office [C] *BrE* a place where letters and packages that have been collected from post boxes are put into groups according to where they have to be delivered

statistical office [C] an organization responsible for collecting detailed information about a country's economy and arranging it in tables of numbers: *the French statistical office INSEE*

2 do a land office business *informal AmE* to do a lot of business and make a lot of money: *The conference organizers did a land office business at first, but now watch people go to competitors' events.*

3 [C] a room or building where people can go to buy tickets, get information, or for some other service: *Information leaflets are available from the* ***enquiry office***. | *The woman in the* ***ticket office*** *said there would be a train in 5 minutes.* | *the Opera House* ***booking office***

box office also **box-office** ◆ [C] the place at a cinema or theatre where people can buy tickets

◆ [singular] if a film or show does well at the box office, it sells a lot of tickets and so makes a lot of money: *Box-office sales for the film continue to rise.* | *The group is suffering after a series of box-office flops.* | *the type of film that will do well at the box office*

4 [U] an important job or position, especially in a government: *He is determined to stay* ***in office*** *until the end of the year.* | *When Mr. Collor* ***took office***, *inflation was running at 84%.*

5 Office used in the names of some British government departments and organizations: *the Foreign Office* | *the Office of Fair Trading*

office copy —see under COPY[1]

Office for National Statistics abbreviation **ONS** *n* the British government organization responsible for collecting information about the economy: *The number of tourists from North America increased by 11% compared with the same period last year, according to the Office for National Statistics.*

office hours *n* [plural] the time when people in companies are working. In the English-speaking world this is usually between about 9am and 5pm or 6pm: *No one is allowed in the building outside office hours.*

office junior —see under JUNIOR[3]

office machinery —see under MACHINERY

Office of Fair Trading abbreviation **OFT** *n* a British government organization whose job is to make sure that the laws protecting people from being cheated by shops and other businesses are not broken, and to help customers who have been cheated or treated unfairly

Office of Management and Budget abbreviation **OMB** *n* a US government organization that provides help for the President in organizing the work of government departments, especially preparing the BUDGET

Office of Thrift Supervision —see OTS

office park —see under PARK[1]

of·fi·cer /ˈɒfɪ̆sə‖ˈɒːfɪ̆sər, ˈɑː-/ *n* [C] HUMAN RESOURCES someone who has an important position in an organization. 'Officer' is often used in job titles: *a local government officer* | *a personnel officer*

Chief Executive Officer abbreviation **CEO** the manager with the most authority in the normal, everyday management of a company. The job of Chief

Executive Officer is sometimes combined with other jobs, such as that of PRESIDENT: *Michael J Spector, Margo's chairman, president and chief executive officer*

chief financial officer abbreviation **CFO** the finance manager with the most authority in a company: *Mr Liberati, the chief financial officer, says the company has decided on the assets it wishes to sell.*

chief information officer abbreviation **CIO** ♦ a manager who is responsible for giving information to people inside or outside a company

♦ a manager who is responsible for managing information technology

chief operating officer the person with responsibility for normal, everyday management of the operations or activities of a company: *He has no experience in the large-scale management a chief operating officer will perform.*

company officer LAW someone with legal responsibility for a company: *some person such as a director, company secretary or similar company officer*

compliance officer LAW someone in an organization, especially a financial institution, whose job is to make sure that the institution is obeying the law: *The company agreed to appoint a compliance officer to monitor its transactions.*

knowledge officer the person in a company whose job is to gather and manage all the information that a company and its employees possess about the TECHNOLOGY (=methods and processes) that it uses, and about its markets, competitors etc: *Titles such as 'chief knowledge officer' reflect the change in the role of the head of information technology.*

press officer the person in an organization whose job is to deal with questions from people working for the newspapers, radio, or television; PRESS SECRETARY: *Some governing bodies appoint a press officer.*

procurement officer also **purchasing officer** someone whose job involves buying equipment, supplies, services etc for a company or organization: *Procurement officers prefer to deal face-to-face with suppliers.* —see also CAREERS OFFICER

of•fi•cial[1] /ə'fɪʃəl/ *adj* **1** approved of or done by someone in authority, especially the government: *You have to get **official permission** to build a new house.* | *the **official inquiry** into the Bombay securities scandal* | *Impatient with the slow progress made through the **official channels**, local lawyers and community workers set up a law centre in North Kensington.* | ***Official documents** indicated that Hunter and managing-director Paul Thomas were sole trustees of the pension fund.*

2 done as part of your job and not for your own private purposes: *Are you here **in your official capacity**?* | *If you have to go away from the office on **official business**, ES will pay for the cost of travel.* | *The agreement was signed during an **official visit** to France by the Prime Minister.* | *a damaging two-week **official strike***

3 chosen to represent someone or an organization, or do something for them: *The role of trade unions as workers' official representatives comes into play during strikes and other kinds of industrial action.*

official[2] *n* [C] someone who has a responsible position in an organization: *trade union officials* | *a government official*

official exchange rate —see under EXCHANGE RATE

official language —see under LANGUAGE

official price —see under PRICE[1]

official receiver —see under RECEIVER

official strike —see under STRIKE[1]

off-line *adj* COMPUTING not directly connected to a computer or directly controlled by it: *an off-line terminal* | *off-line storage of data* —compare ON-LINE —**off-line** *adv*: *The information is stored off-line in the computer's hard drive.*

off•load /ˌɒf'ləʊd‖ˌɒːf'loʊd/ *v* [T] to get rid of something you do not want by giving or selling it to someone: *Most high street chains managed to offload last season's stock by offering discounts of up to 50%.* **offload sth onto sb**: *A dealer offloaded 5,000 of the shares onto a client.*

off-market *adj* [only before a noun] FINANCE an off-market deal involves buying or selling shares, but not on an official stockmarket: *an off-market dealer* | *The commodities traders were accused of cheating customers through pre-arranged and **off-market trades** that prevented orders from being offered in the open, competitive market.*

off-message *adj, adv* a politician who is off-message says things that do not agree with the ideas and policies of the political party they belong to

off-peak *adj* [only before a noun] **1** off-peak travel, electricity etc is cheaper than normal because fewer people are travelling, using electricity etc at that time: ***Off-peak fares** will be cut as much as $31.*

2 off-peak hours or periods are the times when fewer people want to do or use something, and when it is usually cheaper: *Telephone charges are lower during **off-peak periods**.* —compare PEAK[2] —**off-peak** *adv*: *It is much cheaper to travel off-peak.*

off-peak fare —see under FARE

off-price *adj AmE* **off-price store/shop/retailer** a store etc that sells goods at lower prices than other shops. The goods are bought from businesses that have gone out of business or from manufacturers that have produced more goods than they need: *an off-price department store* | *Ross Stores Inc. operates a national chain of **off-price retail stores**.*

off-sale date —see under DATE[1]

off season —see under SEASON

off•set[1] /'ɒfset, ˌɒf'set‖'ɒːfset, ˌɒːf'set/ past tense and past participle **offset** present participle **offsetting** *v* [T] if something such as a cost or sum of money offsets another cost etc, it has the effect of reducing or balancing it, so that the situation remains the same: *He expects the fourth quarter to be profitable, though not profitable enough to offset losses earlier in the year.* | *The cost of the flight **was offset by** the cheapness of the hotel.* **offset sth against sth**: *He was able to offset his travel expenses against tax.*

off•set[2] /'ɒfset‖'ɒːf-/ *n* **1** [U] BANKING the legal right of a bank to take money from a customer's bank account if a loan has not been paid

2 [C] ACCOUNTING an amount of money recorded on one side of a LEDGER (=financial record) that is equal to an amount on the opposite side of the same ledger, or is equal to an amount recorded in the ledger for a different account

3 [C] in international trade, a quantity of goods that is exported in exchange for a quantity of goods that has been imported: *Israel has followed the general rule that all government purchases – including, of course, arms – should be paid for by offsets.* —see also BARTER[2]

off•shore /ˌɒf'ʃɔː◂‖ˌɒːf'ʃɔːr◂/ *adj* **1** involving an activity performed outside a particular country, rather than inside it: *Taiwanese regulators have been unhappy with offshore trading in its stock futures.*

2 offshore bank/company/investment etc TAX a bank etc that is based in a country where taxes are lower, laws are less strict etc: *offshore centres like the Cayman Islands* | ***offshore banking** in places such as Switzerland*

3 connected with oil and gas production that is done on or under the sea: *offshore oil drilling* —**offshore** *adv*: *There have been complaints about capital being invested offshore.* | *He worked offshore on an oil rig.*

offshore banking —see under BANKING

O

offshore company —see under COMPANY

off-the-books *adj* [only before a noun] off-the-books payments are those made or received without being officially recorded, so that the tax authorities do not know about them: *Officials used to give off-the-books bonuses to senior executives.* —**off the books** *adv*: *The workers often are paid off the books, well below the minimum wage.*

off-the-peg *BrE*, **off-the-rack** *AmE* —*adj* an off-the-peg arrangement, product etc is a standard one, rather than one designed for a particular person, situation etc: *With travel insurance, you can get an off-the-peg policy for a single trip, or one tailor-made for the places you are likely to visit during a whole year.* —compare TAILOR-MADE

off-the-shelf *adj* an off-the-shelf product is made to a standard design and can be bought in the shops: *off-the-shelf database software* | *Standard off-the-shelf systems are displacing the custom products that were IBM's mainstay.* —compare TAILOR-MADE —**off the shelf** *adv*: *Anybody can* ***buy*** *software programs like FontStudio* ***off the shelf*** *and create new typefaces.*

off-the-shelf company —see under COMPANY

OFT —see OFFICE OF FAIR TRADING

oil•field /ˈɔɪlfiːld/ *n* [C] an area of land or sea under which there is oil: *The oilfield began producing in 1997, and last year reached its peak at 1.6 million barrels a day.*

oil•man /ˈɔɪlmæn/ *n* plural **oilmen** [C] someone who owns an oil company or who works in the oil industry

oil platform —see under PLATFORM

oil rig *n* [C] a large structure with equipment for getting oil from under the sea bottom or under the ground

oil well also **well** *n* [C] a hole that is dug in the ground or under the sea in order to get oil

old age pension —see under PENSION[1]

Old Age Pensioner —see OAP

old money —see under MONEY

ol•i•gar•chy /ˈɒləgɑːki‖ˈɑːləgɑːrki, ˈoʊ-/ *n* plural **oligarchies** **1** [U] when a country is ruled or controlled by a small group of people, usually from the same social class: *Oligarchy took over from democracy.*
2 [C] a country, organization, industry etc controlled by a small group of people, or the group who control it: *The industry is dominated by an oligarchy of three oil companies.* —**oligarch** *n* [C] *the changing alliances of Russia's corporate oligarchs* —**oligarchic** —**oligarchical** *adj*: *The Party still owns 95% of the means of production and we must change this oligarchical system.*

om•buds•man /ˈɒmbʊdzmən‖ˈɑːm-/ *n* plural **ombudsmen** [C] someone who deals with complaints made by the public against government departments, banks, insurance companies etc. In Britain, the main government ombudsman is called the Parliamentary Commissioner for Administration: *You can apply to the* ***Banking Ombudsman*** *for arbitration.* | *Customers have the right to ask the* ***Insurance Ombudsman*** *to review their complaint.*

o•mis•sion /əʊˈmɪʃən, ə-‖oʊ-, ə-/ —see ERROR OF OMISSION

on account —see under ACCOUNT[1]

on approval —see APPROVAL

on call —see AT CALL

on-cost *n* [C] a cost in producing a product, that does not change with the amount produced; FIXED COST: *When price competition is at its keenest, the extra on-cost that is entailed in the payment of an employee training tax can be unwelcome.*

on demand *adv AmE* FINANCE if money is lent on demand, it must be repaid immediately if the lender asks for it; AT CALL, ON CALL *BrE*: *Money at call is the main reserve that banks draw on if they are short of cash.*

one-man business —see under BUSINESS

one-month money —see under MONEY

one-off cost —see under COST[1]

onerous contract —see under CONTRACT[1]

one-stop *adj* [only before a noun] a one-stop shop, service etc brings together and provides information or services that are usually only available from several different places: *Some building societies are offering home-buyers a 'one-stop' service, including legal advice and insurance.* | *The new helpline has been set up as a 'one-stop shop' for all travel enquiries.*

one-time also **one-off** *BrE* —*adj* [only before a noun] a one-time event, payment etc happens once and is not part of a regular series of such events: *Nacco expects to* ***take a one-time charge*** (=show one in its accounts) *of $10.3 million due primarily to restructuring and plant closings.* | *Lawyers face a one-off tax hit as a result of the tax changes.*

one-time loss —see under LOSS

one-time-only *adj* [only before a noun] used to describe something that is available or done only once: *The fast-food company has used the magazine space for a one-time-only campaign.*

one-way fare —see under FARE

one-way ticket —see under TICKET

one-year money —see under MONEY

on-lending *n* [U] when an organization lends money that they have borrowed from another organization or person: *Heavy borrowing by central government for on-lending to the local authorities and public corporations is increasing.*

on-like brokerage —see under BROKERAGE

on-line *adj* COMPUTING directly connected to a central computer or a DATABASE (=written information stored on a computer): *an on-line financial news service* | *Each terminal has on-line access to the database.* —**on-line** *adv*: *These procedures can be carried out on-line.*

on-line brokerage —see under BROKERAGE

online catalogue —see under CATALOGUE[1]

on-line updating *n* [U] COMPUTING a system in which information that is put into a computer TERMINAL is recorded by the central computer and so is immediately available at any other terminal

on-message *adj, adv* a politician who is on-message says things that are in agreement with the ideas and policies of the political party they belong to

ono *BrE* written abbreviation for OR NEAREST OFFER, used in advertisements to show that you may be willing to sell something for slightly less money than the actual amount stated: *Computer for sale: £300 ono.*

on•shore /ˌɒnˈʃɔː◂‖ˌɑːnˈʃɔːr◂, ˌɒːn-/ *adj* **1** involving an activity performed in a particular country, rather than outside it: *The Thai baht reached new lows in onshore trading in Bangkok.*
2 onshore bank/company/investment etc TAX a bank etc that is based in a country where taxes are at normal levels, laws are strict etc: *The bank now wants to expand in onshore business centres such as London, New York and Tokyo.*
3 connected with oil and gas production that is done on land: *There was only one onshore discovery last year out of seven exploration wells drilled.* —**onshore** *adv*: *the point where Mobile Bay gas comes onshore*

on tap —see under TAP

on-the-job training —see under TRAINING

OPEC /ˈəʊpek‖ˈoʊ-/ *n* Organization of Petroleum Exporting Countries; an organization of nations that produce and sell oil and which tries to influence the price of the oil: *Practically all payments to **OPEC countries** are made in dollars.* | *the reduction in demand for OPEC oil*

open[1] /ˈəʊpən‖ˈoʊ-/ *adj* **1** [not before a noun] if a shop etc is open, it is allowing customers to enter and is ready to serve them: *The bank is open till 12.00 on Saturdays.* | *What she liked about the shop was that it was **open for business** on every day of the year.*
2 if a financial market is open, buying and selling on it are possible: *Among Asian and Pacific markets that were open, stocks overall had a mixed performance.*
3 if a country is open to foreign products, they can be sold there without restrictions such as high import taxes: *Many people think the country is far less open to foreign products than Europe or the US.*
4 on the open market if something is sold on the open market, it is available for anyone to buy: *The shares would be purchased on the open market or in privately negotiated transactions.*
5 be open to offers to be ready to consider people's offers of how much they are willing to pay for something you are selling: *The company said it was open to offers from potential buyers.*
6 be open to discussion/negotiation if something is open to discussion, you can discuss it and suggest changes: *The number of board seats they will have, like all other terms of the proposal, is open to negotiation.*
7 in open court in a court of law where everything is public: *I am giving this judgment in open court at the request of all parties.*

open[2] *v* **1** [I] if a shop, office, financial market etc opens at a particular time, it starts business at that time: *What time do the banks open?* | *Oil prices softened $1 a barrel as European and Asian markets opened yesterday.*
2 [I,T] if a new business opens or is opened, someone starts it: *She plans to open a chain of restaurants.*
3 [I] if shares, bonds etc open at a particular price, they have that price when the financial market on which they are traded opens for business: *Platinum opened lower following Japanese sales of platinum overnight.*
4 open your markets if a country opens its markets to foreign goods, it allows them to be sold there, or it reduces restrictions on them: *The US and Europe would open their markets in agriculture and textiles to developing nations by cutting quotas and subsidies.*
5 open an account to start a new account at a financial institution, for example by putting money into it: *Private clients are asked to produce an initial deposit of at least 250,000 marks to open an account.*
open up *phr v* **1** [I,T] **open sth up** if a shop, business etc opens up or is opened up, someone starts it: *More than a dozen US law firms have opened up in the city.*
2 [I,T] **open sth up** if a shop, business etc opens up or is opened up at a particular time, it starts business at that time
3 [I,T] **open sth up** if a country or market opens up, or someone opens it up, it becomes possible or easier to invest there or sell foreign goods there: *Algeria opened up its big oil and natural gas industry to foreign investment.* | *When China opened up, over-optimistic Americans were full of ideas of selling to one billion Chinese.*
4 [I] if a job opens up, it becomes available: *When the job she expected at the university opened up, it went to a professor's wife.*
5 [I,T] **open sth up** if a disagreement opens up or is opened up between people, it starts to divide them: *A rift has opened up, splitting the committee down the middle.*

open[3] *n* [singular] FINANCE the beginning of a trading session on a financial market: *The dollar was quoted at 143.77 yen, down from 143.80 yen at the open.* | *US wheat prices might slip **at the open of trading** today.*

open bid —see under BID[1]

opencast mining —see under MINING

open cheque —see under CHEQUE

open-cry auction —see under AUCTION[1]

open-door policy —see under POLICY

open-end *adj* [only before a noun] a CLOSED-END fund or trust invests in an UNLIMITED number of shares: *an **open-end mutual fund***

open-end·ed *adj* if someone's involvement in something is open-ended, it has no limit or end: *The White House asked Congress for open-ended authority to cover the Pentagon's costs.* | *Our commitment to the project is totally open-ended, and we will pay all expenses.*

open-end fund —see under FUND[1]

open-end investment company also **open-ended investment company** —see under COMPANY

o·pen·ing /ˈəʊpənɪŋ‖ˈoʊ-/ *n* **1** [C,U] FINANCE the beginning of a trading day on a financial market: *After a **weak opening**,* (=one with falling prices) *Stockholm equities recovered to close mostly higher.* | *Oil and gasoline prices ended higher in moderate trading after a **strong opening*** (=one with rising prices.)
2 [U] also **opening up** when a country allows types of imports or foreign investment that it did not allow before, or when it allows more of these + **of**: *last year's opening of the capital market to foreigners* | *a gradual opening up of the EU market to Japanese car makers*
3 [C] a job or position that is available: *With markets declining, banks have fewer openings for merger specialists.*

opening balance —see under BALANCE[1]

opening price —see under PRICE[1]

opening stock —see under STOCK[1]

open insurance —see ***floating insurance*** under INSURANCE

open interest *n* [U] FINANCE in FUTURES (=buying a quantity of something for delivery at a fixed date in the future), the number of contracts that are active and have not been cancelled out by contracts in the other direction: *Open interest in platinum contracts is now fluctuating at record levels.*

open-jaw fare —see under FARE

open market —see under MARKET[1]

open-market *adj* [only before a noun] FINANCE in an open market action, operation etc, a CENTRAL BANK increases or reduces the MONEY SUPPLY (=the amount of money in the economy): *a Federal Reserve **open-market operation** that injected $1 billion of cash into the banking system* | *a tightening of the Bundesbank's **open-market policy***

open offer —see under OFFER[2]

open outcry *n* [U] FINANCE when trading on a financial market takes place directly between dealers on a trading floor, rather than using computers and the telephone: *While electronic trading is cheaper, supporters of open outcry say it offers better liquidity.*

open-plan *adj* open-plan offices, work areas etc do not have walls dividing them into separate rooms: *Financial institutions want large, open-plan floors.*

open skies *n* **open skies talks/agreements etc** discussions, agreements etc between governments to allow airlines to operate more freely in each other's countries: *The open-skies deal would give US airlines greater freedom to land in Japan and take passengers on to third countries in Asia.*

open system —see under SYSTEM

open systems interconnection —see OSI

op•e•rate /ˈɒpəreɪt‖ˈɑː-/ *v* **1** [T] to use and control a machine or equipment: *the software necessary to operate the machine*

2 [I] if a machine, factory etc operates in a particular way, it works in that way + **in/at**: *The factory will operate at half capacity for about two months.*

3 [I] if a business, system etc operates in a particular way, it works in that way: *differences between the way the two countries' economies operate* + **as**: *Goodby will operate as an independent Omnicom unit.*

4 [I] if a business, system etc operates in or from a particular place, it is based there or offers goods or services from there + **in/from/out of**: *Jamesway Corp., a discount chain operating in the Mid-Atlantic region* | *a new airline operating out of St Petersburg*

5 [T] if a person or organization operates a business, system etc, they manage it and make it work: *Under the contract, EDS will supply and operate all of the computer systems needed to process claims.*

operating assets —see under ASSET

operating expense —see under EXPENSE

operating income —see under INCOME

operating lease —see under LEASE[2]

operating loss —see under LOSS

operating margin —see under MARGIN

operating profit —see under PROFIT[1]

operating strategy —see under STRATEGY

operating system —see under SYSTEM

op•e•ra•tion /ˌɒpəˈreɪʃən‖ˌɑː-/ *n* **1** [U] the way the parts of a machine, system, or organization work together: *the design and operation of specialized equipment*

2 in/into operation if something is in operation, or is put into operation, it is working or is made to start working: *The nuclear plants **in operation** produce 400,000 megawatts.* | *The new subway lines are scheduled to **go into operation** at the end of the year.* | *The manufacturer **put** a $120 million joint venture in Hungary **into operation** last March.*

3 [C] a business activity or company: *Network SouthEast claimed to be the only European commuter rail operation not supported by public money.*

4 [C] a part of a large business or company that does a particular activity or type of work: *GM's West European operations have emerged as the biggest profit earners in the entire group.* | *The business has been able to shed its loss-making operations.* | *This move strengthens CRH's **retailing operations** in the Netherlands.*

5 [C,U] the process of operating as a business: *Many small businesses fail in the first year of operation.* | *The publishing house ceased operations in 1998.* | *How many coal mines are currently **in operation**?*

6 operations [plural] FINANCE a company's normal activities related to providing services or producing goods, rather than other actions with financial effects, such as selling assets: *Knight-Ridder reported earnings from operations of about 88 cents a share.*

7 [C] FINANCE the action of buying or selling something; TRANSACTION: *As part of the operation, Apax are buying the brands and assets of Worth Parfums.*

8 come into operation/put sth into operation to make a law, system, or rule have an effect or be used: *The new rule comes into operation on 1 February.* | *We hope to put the new regulations into operation immediately.*

9 [C] an action done by a computer or a machine: *Several **operations** can be **carried out** by the programme at the same time.*

10 [C] a set of actions, usually involving a large number of people, that are planned to achieve a particular purpose: *a salvage operation* | *The construction and administration of questionnaires is a highly skilled operation.*

op•e•ra•tion•al /ˌɒpəˈreɪʃənəl◂‖ˌɑː-/ *adj* **1** working and ready to be used: *Even when the new system is **fully operational** it will be subject to important conditions.* | *The power station will **become operational** next year.* | *These vehicles have an operational life of five years.*

2 [only before a noun] related to the running of a business, government etc: *You will be in charge of day-to-day operational matters.* | *Our **operational budget** is over £1,100 million.* | *We need to cut our **operational costs** in half.*

operational research —see under RESEARCH

operations research —see under RESEARCH

op•e•ra•tive[1] /ˈɒpərətɪv‖ˈɑːpərə-, ˈɑːpəreɪ-/ *adj* working and able to be used: *When does the plant **become operative**?* | *If the bond is currently trading below par, its operative life is likely to be the number of years to maturity.*

operative[2] *n* [C] a worker, especially one who works in a factory: *a machine operative* | *the recruitment and training of skilled operatives*

operative mistake *n* [C] LAW a mistake in a contract that is so serious that it means that the contract has no legal effect

op•e•ra•tor /ˈɒpəreɪtə‖ˈɑːpəreɪtər/ *n* [C] **1** someone who works a machine or piece of equipment: *a **computer operator*** | *This machine requires a skilled operator.*

2 a person or company that operates a particular business: *the ferry operator Stena*

tour operator *BrE* a company that arranges holidays for people, including their travel arrangements, hotels etc: *There is likely to be a battle between the major tour operators this summer.*

3 someone who works on a telephone SWITCHBOARD, who you can call for help when you have problems: *I tried calling the operator.*

OPM abbreviation for OPTION PRICING MODEL

op•por•tun•ist /ˌɒpəˈtjuːnɪ̈st‖ˌɑːpərˈtuː-/ *n* [C] a person or organization willing to use every chance to gain power or an advantage over others: *These companies represent a growing band of economic opportunists – they plan for every conceivable contingency, and can move with lightning speed whenever an opportunity opens.* —**opportunistic** *adj*: *We're a very opportunistic company, continually looking to strengthen ourselves strategically in individual market segments.* | *A spokesman confirmed that the company is examining 'opportunistic acquisitions', but declined to be more specific.* —**opportunistically** *adv*: *We're learning how to sell much more opportunistically.*

opportunities to see *n* [plural] MARKETING the number of times that a person is likely to see a particular advertisement, used as a measure in advertising

op•por•tu•ni•ty /ˌɒpəˈtjuːnɪ̈ti‖ˌɑːpərˈtuː-/ *n* plural **opportunities** [C] a chance for you to do something successfully: *This is an excellent **career opportunity** for a recent graduate.* | *In order to make money, you will need to identify **market opportunities**.* | *an **investment opportunity*** | *a significant business opportunity*

opportunity cost —see under COST[1]

op•pose /əˈpəʊz‖əˈpoʊz/ *v* [T] to disagree with a plan or idea and try to prevent it from happening: *Three members of the board opposed the motion.* | *Several leading City investors had opposed the Bank of England's proposals.*

opposed bid —see under BID[1]

opposite number *n* [C] someone who has a similar job to yours in another organization: *Selling is sometimes performed by a sales team, with each member of the team* *working with his or her opposite number in the buying team.*

opt /ɒpt‖ɑːpt/ *v* [I] to choose one thing rather than another + **for**: *Faced with voluntary redundancy, nearly half the managers opted instead for early retirement.* + **against**: *TWA opted against a cut in fares because such a move is almost always matched quickly by rivals.* **opt to do sth**: *Policyholders opting to get out early would be entitled to about 48 cents on the dollar.*

opt out *phr v* [I] to choose not to do something or not to remain in a particular arrangement: *The board of directors may opt out and choose to have a fixed board with all members elected annually.* + **of**: *A key question for employees opting out of a medical plan is how well they would be covered in the case of an accident.*—see also OPT-OUT

optical character recognition —see under RECOGNITION

op·ti·mal /ˈɒptɪməl‖ˈɑːp-/ *adj* **1** another name for OPTIMUM

2 the best or most suitable: *An increased corn crop is expected, based on optimal growing conditions across much of the Corn Belt.* | *This stock level is considerably higher than the 65-to-70 day range usually regarded as optimal.* —see also PARETO OPTIMAL

op·ti·mis·m /ˈɒptɪmɪzəm‖ˈɑːp-/ *n* [U] a feeling or belief that things will get better or be more successful in the future: *There is an air of optimism now in Taiwan.* | *Shares gained from renewed optimism about interest-rate cuts.*

op·ti·mist /ˈɒptɪmɪst‖ˈɑːp-/ *n* [C] someone who believes things will get better or be more successful in the future: *As giants such as Businessland Inc. and the Computer Factory Inc. continue to show poor results, even optimists are getting worried.* —compare PESSIMIST —**optimistic** *adj*: *Mr. Gordon remains optimistic about Amgen's long-term prospects.* | *The government's **over-optimistic** economic forecasts have encouraged manufacturers to put too many products into their inventories.*

op·ti·mize also **optimise** *BrE* /ˈɒptɪmaɪz‖ˈɑːp-/ *v* [T] to make the best possible use of something or to do something in the best possible way: *technical specifications designed to **optimize the performance** of Windows software* | *Cash flow should be managed to **optimize the return** from cash received and to minimize the cost of finance.*

op·ti·mum /ˈɒptɪməm‖ˈɑːp-/ *adj* [only before a noun] the best amount, size, number etc that is possible: *The **optimum size** for a bank may be much smaller than previously supposed.* | *An early sale would allow Berisford to realize optimum value for its remaining assets.*

op·tion /ˈɒpʃən‖ˈɑːp-/ *n* [C] **1** a choice between two or more possible types in something you are buying: *Choosing between the available options in mobile phones is very confusing.*

2 something that is offered in addition to the standard equipment when you buy something, especially a car: *Passenger airbags are available as standard or as an option on all of its cars.*

3 COMPUTING one of the possible choices you can make when using a computer program: *the split-screen option*

4 also **option to purchase** when an organization buys something, the possibility that it will buy more later; OPTION TO PURCHASE + **for/on**: *The Spanish air force is due to take 87 of the aircraft, with an option for a further 16.* | *Shanghai Aviation agreed to buy 26 MD-80s and **took options** on 15 others.*

5 FINANCE the right to buy or sell shares, bonds, currencies, or COMMODITIES (=oil, metals, farm products etc) at a particular price within a particular period of time or on a particular date in the future: *Options allow an investor to bet on moves in large amounts of currencies using relatively small stakes.* | *Each crude-oil **options contract** entitles its holder to buy or sell the equivalent of 1,000 barrels of oil at a predetermined price.* | *The stock price fell and the option **expired*** (=came to the end of the period of time when it could be used).

American option an option that allows you to buy or sell particular shares etc at any moment during its life, rather than on a specific date

call option an option that gives you the right to buy shares etc at a particular price in the future. Investors who buy call options think the market will rise above that price: *Many speculators have been buying $4.50 call options on silver for March delivery, which gain value as the price of silver approaches the $4.50-an-ounce level.*

covered option an option where the seller has the shares etc available to give to the buyer if the share price rises and the buyer EXERCISES (=uses) the option: *BZ Bank Zurich, a small bank that pioneered covered options on Swiss shares*

currency option an option to buy or sell a particular amount of a currency at a particular price in the future

double option also **put and call option** an option that gives the holder the right either to buy or to sell the related shares etc

employee stock option an opportunity for employees to buy shares in the company that they work for at below their normal price: *Delta placed 14% of its shares in an employee stock option plan.*

European option an option that you can use to buy or sell shares etc on a specific date, rather than during a whole period of time

index option an option in the value of a SHARE INDEX (=the average value of a group of shares on a particular stockmarket): *trading in Standard & Poor's 100 stock index options contract*

in-the-money option an option that has value, because it allows you to buy shares etc for less than their present price, or to sell them for more than their present price

out-of-the-money option an option that EXPIRES (=comes to the end of its life), or looks as though it will expire, with no value because it only allows you to buy shares etc above their present price, or to sell them for less than their present price: *Out-of-the-money options are worthless unless there is a sudden, dramatic change in the value of the underlying investment.*

put option an option that allows you to sell shares etc at a specific price in the future, that you buy because you think prices will fall below that price

share option the right given by a company to its workers to buy shares in the company at a fixed price: *We have introduced an employee **share option scheme**.*

stock-index option an option related to a particular group of shares on a stockmarket: *Many small investors now trade the Chicago Board Option's Exchange's Standard & Poor's 100-Stock Index.*

stock option an option to buy shares at a particular price. The pay of a company's top managers often includes stock options in the company they work for: *a stock option plan for key employees that gives Mr O'Reilly options to buy four million shares of Heinz stock*

traded option an option that is bought and sold on an OPTIONS EXCHANGE (=a financial market where options are traded) —see also ***option premium*** under PREMIUM[1]

op·tion·al /ˈɒpʃənəl‖ˈɑːp-/ *adj* if something is optional, you can choose whether or not you have it, do it, or use it: *Chrysler is making some previously **optional equipment** – such as power mirrors – standard.* | *You can have a 17 inch monitor as an **optional extra*** (=something in addition to the basic type) —compare STANDARD[2]

option premium —see under PREMIUM[1]

option pricing model —see under MODEL

options contract —see under CONTRACT[1]

options market —see under MARKET[1]

opt-out *n* [singular] when a country or organization decides not to join a group or system: *The government has promised to end Britain's opt-out from the European agreement.* | *The company secured an* ***opt-out clause*** *in the proposed law.* —see also ***opt out*** under OPT

OR abbreviation for OFFICIAL RECEIVER; OPERATIONAL RESEARCH; OWNER'S RISK

o•ral /ˈɔːrəl/ *adj* spoken, rather than written: *The debtor may attend court to give* ***oral evidence*** *as to his financial situation.* | *The firm argued that it had an* ***oral contract*** *to use the television characters.*

oral contract —see under CONTRACT[1]

or•ches•trate /ˈɔːkəstreɪt‖ˈɔːr-/ *v* [T] to organize an important or complicated event, plan etc, often secretly: *Kellogg orchestrated a big public-relations effort to promote their new cereal.* | *Not all of Japan's energy management has been orchestrated by bureaucrats.*

ord written abbreviation for ORDINARY SHARES

or•der[1] /ˈɔːdə‖ˈɔːrdər/ *n* **1** [C] a request by a customer for goods or services: *The recession has prompted advertisers to plan their spending a month in advance, instead of* ***placing orders*** *a year ahead.* + **for**: *The company* ***has received an order*** *for 1,500 machines.* | *Polaris Aircraft Leasing has three* ***firm orders*** (=definite ones) *for MD-83 twin-jet aircraft.*

back order [C] an order from an earlier period of time for goods that have not yet been produced or that have not been delivered: *The improvement was due to larger inventories, which led to fewer lost sales, and lower back orders for out-of-stock items.*

buy order also **buying order** [C] FINANCE a request to a dealer to buy shares etc on a financial market: *The City's mood improved yesterday after a big buying order for sterling gave the currency an early boost.*

buy limit order [C] FINANCE a request to a dealer to buy shares etc on a financial market within a particular price range: *You should never put in a market order. Instead, put in a buy limit order at a price slightly below the current market price.*

copy order [C] a document that states the items being supplied to a buyer together with their prices and the conditions of sale; INVOICE, PURCHASE SALES ORDER: *You should keep a copy order and make a note of due dates so that you can plan for the arrival of the stock.*

delivery order written abbreviation **DO** [C] a written instruction from the owner of goods to someone who is storing or keeping them to give or take them to another person: *The sellers got the rice ready for collection and were asked by the buyer for a delivery order enabling him to collect the rice.*

job order [C] ♦ an order to produce a particular number of goods or to provide a particular service for a customer: *The factory will close down in January, when the final job order is finished.*

♦ an order that a company places with an EMPLOYMENT AGENCY (=a company that finds new staff for companies) when it is looking for someone to do a particular job

market order [C] FINANCE a request to a dealer to buy or sell shares etc on a financial market at the best price available at that time: *Work with your broker to establish a realistic price relative to the spread, rather than simply putting in a market order to buy or sell at the prevailing – but undetermined – price.*

part order [C] an order that has only been partly produced, delivered etc

purchase order [C] an official document stating that someone wants to buy something and giving details of size, cost etc. Purchase orders are often used by different departments within companies: *Provide a separate invoice for each purchase order.*

repeat order [C] a supply of the same product or services to a customer who has ordered them before: *The quality of those machines brought us repeat orders.*

sell order also **selling order** [C] FINANCE a request from an investor to a dealer to sell shares etc on a financial market: *A badly handled sell order had market makers scrambling to cut prices.*

stop order also **stop-loss order** [C] FINANCE a request to a dealer to buy or sell shares etc when they reach an agreed level: *To protect your profit, you might set a stop order at, say, $20.*

2 advance orders [plural] the number of requests by customers to buy a new product, book, or record before it has been put on sale: *His new album had been released to advance orders in the UK of 100,000.*

3 on order if goods are on order, a customer has asked for them but has not yet received them: *America's airlines alone have more than $130 billion-worth of aircraft on order.*

4 to order if something is made or supplied to order, it is made or supplied especially for a particular customer who has asked for it: *Alumasc Systems offer powder coatings in ten standard colours or other shades to order.* | *Our exclusive conservatories are still handmade to order, using traditional skills.*

5 [C] LAW an official statement from a court of law or other authority stating that something must be done: *The decision removed a temporary* ***restraining order*** *that prevented the New York Department of Insurance from releasing the reports.*

administration order [C] an order from a court that a company in financial difficulty should be put into ADMINISTRATION (=be reorganized by an outside specialist): *The board decided to seek an administration order to facilitate the reconstruction of the company.*

bankruptcy order [C] when a court recognizes a business as bankrupt, so that its assets can be sold and those that it owes money can be paid: *The company's financial services subsidiary isn't included in the proposed bankruptcy order.*

compulsory purchase order abbreviation **CPO** [C] PROPERTY in Britain, an instruction from a court of law that allows the local government to buy a property that is very old and in a dangerous condition: *London Transport received a compulsory purchase order for the bridge.*

court order [C] an order from a court of law, telling someone to do something or to act in a particular way: *The owners of the building said they would seek a court order to evict the squatters.*

gagging order *BrE* **gag order** *AmE* [C] *journalism* an agreement not to discuss something with people working for the newspapers, television etc: *His former wife agreed to a gagging order over their marriage as part of her divorce settlement.* | *Federal Judge Tom S. Lee immediately issued a gag order forbidding discussion of the case.*

judge's order [C] an official instruction given by a judge, ordering someone to do or not to do something: *Officials in Long Beach* ***complied with a judge's order*** (=obeyed it) *and canceled the contract.*

receiving order [C] an order from a court in Britain, putting the RECEIVER in charge of a business that may be going bankrupt: *On May 23 a receiving order was made and on November 11 he was adjudicated bankrupt.*

6 [U] the condition of goods or property when they are bought or sold: *The documents state the quantity of goods and their apparent order and condition when received.* | *The property benefits from a wealth of period features and is* ***in good decorative order.***

7 be in (good) working/running order if equipment, a machine etc is in good working order, it is working well: *Our standards ensure a BMW bought from us is in perfect running order.*

8 be out of order if equipment or a machine is out of order, it is not working: *Stamford's executives couldn't be contacted to comment because the company's phones were out of order.*

9 [singular, U] the way that several things are arranged, showing which comes first, second etc: *Place the proposals in order of priority.*

pecking order [C usually singular] the way that people or companies are ranked according to how important, successful etc they are: *The IMF ranking is used to measure the pecking order of the world's leading economic powers.* | *He remained at Chrysler as president, with Bidwell as chairman, largely as a way of establishing an executive pecking order.*

O

10 the order of business the arrangement of different subjects for discussion at a meeting: *As clerk to the committee, your main task is to establish the order of business.*

11 the first/top order of business *AmE* the most important thing to be discussed at a meeting or dealt with: *House Democratic leaders plan to make the surtax on millionaires the top order of business when Congress returns.* —see also BANKER'S ORDER, INTERNATIONAL MONEY ORDER, MAIL ORDER, MONEY ORDER, POINT OF ORDER, POSTAL ORDER, STANDING ORDER

order[2] *v* [T] **1** to ask a company to supply goods or services: *Dealers have been reluctant to order new cars in the face of weak sales.* | *Shoppers use a handheld scanning device to order video titles that aren't in stock.*

2 to tell someone to do something, using your authority or power over them: *A federal appeals court in Philadelphia overturned the verdict and ordered a new trial.* **order sb to do sth**: *Congress has ordered businesses to comply with the new regulations.*

order-book *n* [C] a book listing all the orders for goods or services a company has received; also used to talk about the orders themselves: *Boeing said its order-book now lists 742 planes.* | *The Flat Rock facility isn't the only one that can't keep its order-books filled.*

order-book index —see under INDEX[1]

order-driven *adj* FINANCE an order-driven financial market is one where prices change in relation to orders from brokers and dealers in AUCTIONS (=occasions when something is sold to the person willing to pay most for it): *Many foreign exchanges are order-driven and still maintain trading floors.* | *SelectNet has recently introduced order-driven features into Nasdaq's trading capability.* —compare QUOTE-DRIVEN

order-point *n* [singular] the point at which it is time for a company to order more goods or materials: *An order-point system saves time and money – and dissatisfied customers.*

order-taker *n* [C] someone whose job is to take customers' orders for goods over the telephone: *The nation's biggest discount broker has boosted its staff of telephone order-takers by 15%.*

or·di·nance /ˈɔːdɪnəns‖ˈɔːrdənəns/ *n* [C] a law of a city or town that forbids or restricts an activity: ***zoning ordinances** that prohibit certain businesses from operating near churches*

ordinary capital —see under CAPITAL

ordinary dividend —see under DIVIDEND

ordinary interest —see under INTEREST

ordinary share —see under SHARE

ordinary stock —see under STOCK[1]

or·gan /ˈɔːgən‖ˈɔːr-/ *n* [C] *formal* **1** a large organization that represents a particular group of people or a particular industry: *There are 4,000 mainland **government organs** and state companies with offices in Hainan.* | *A number of additional cases are being handled by China's judicial organs.*

2 a magazine or newspaper which presents the ideas and opinions of a political party or other organization: *These newspapers were essentially **house organs** for political factions.* | *a copy of the McDonald's Corp. **in-house organ*** (=magazine that it produces for its own employees)

or·gan·i·za·tion also **organisation** *BrE* /ˌɔːgənaɪˈzeɪʃən‖ˌɔːrgənə-/ *n* **1** [C] a company, business, group etc that has been formed for a particular purpose: *Cultural Survival, a not-for-profit organization* | *Federal officials making the grants consider such factors as an organization's ability to raise other funds.*

employers' organization also **employers' organisation** *BrE* [C] an organization of employers who work together when discussing wages and working conditions with trade unions, and represent employers in discussions with public organizations and government; TRADE ASSOCIATION: *Negotiations were going on between the TUC and the Confederation of Employers Organizations and the Federation of British Industries.*

2 [U] the planning and arranging of work of a particular business, company, group etc: *new management methods that challenge classical ideas about organisation* | *Mr Hampel's group looked at organisation, Mr Hutchison's at strategy.*

3 organization Man/Woman *disapproving* HUMAN RESOURCES someone working for a company who never takes risks and always agrees with the people in authority: *Entrepreneurial types are more creative and experimental – without them organization Man and Woman will suffer.*

or·gan·i·za·tion·al also **organisational** *BrE* /ˌɔːgənaɪˈzeɪʃənəl‖ˌɔːrgənə-/ *adj* relating to the way an organization and its activities are planned and arranged: *Approaches now being implemented offer significant opportunities for improved organizational performance.* | *the stimulus for **organizational change** at Pilkingtons* | *changes in the management and **organizational structure***

organizational behaviour —see under BEHAVIOUR

organization and methods also **organisation and methods** *BrE*, abbreviation **O&M** *n* [U] the process of examining how the work is done in a business, industry etc and finding ways of doing it more effectively: *In the future, an exercise will be undertaken by the organization and methods section to examine the feasibility of using one document to produce the information.*

organization chart —see under CHART[1]

Organization for Economic Cooperation and Development —see OECD

Organization of Petroleum Exporting Countries —see OPEC

or·gan·ize also **organise** *BrE* /ˈɔːgənaɪz‖ˈɔːr-/ *v* **1** [T] to plan and arrange an event or other activity: *Publishers, writers and booksellers are joining forces to organize alternative distribution networks.*

2 [T] to arrange work, information, a group etc so that it works correctly and is useful: *Accountants say that organizing paperwork first can reduce errors and cut the costs of tax preparation.* | *a major change in the way banks are organized and regulated*

3 [I,T] *AmE* to form a UNION (=an organization that protects workers' rights) or to persuade people to join one: *The talk helped AFSCME organize 2,300 clerical workers at the University of Illinois.* | *Lechmere had violated federal labor law by denying workers **the right to organize**.*

or·gan·ized also **organised** *BrE* /ˈɔːgənaɪzd‖ˈɔːr-/ *adj* made to work in a effective, ordered, and sensible way: *There isn't an organized market data system for U.S. stocks traded on the London exchange.* | *Motorola has built a $500 million factory to make the chip, which even rivals praise as **well-organized**.*

organized labour —see under LABOUR

or·gan·i·zer also **organiser** *BrE* /ˈɔːgənaɪzə‖ˈɔːrgənaɪzər/ *n* [C] **1** someone whose work involves planning and arranging events, activities, work etc: *The regional organizer has negotiated a company agreement with the Board.* | *What information would a* ***conference organiser*** *need?*

2 a small book or computer in which important dates, telephone numbers etc can be written: *Fullerton, Calif., a maker of* ***electronic personal organizers***

organizing business —see under BUSINESS

o·ri·en·ta·tion /ˌɔːriənˈteɪʃən,ˌɒ-‖ˌɔː-/ *n* [U] MARKETING used to talk about the way that a business thinks of its products or services

market orientation also **marketing orientation** when a business concentrates on designing and selling products that satisfy customer needs in order to be profitable: *Organizations which have a market orientation need to respond quickly to changes in the way people live and work.*

product orientation when a business bases its ability to make profits on the high technical quality of its products, rather than on customer needs

sales orientation when a business bases its ability to make profits on using powerful selling techniques to persuade people to buy its products, rather than on customer needs

-o·ri·ent·ed /ˈɔːrientəd, ˈɒ-‖ˈɔː-/ also **-o·ri·en·tat·ed** /ɔːriənteɪtəd, ɑ-‖ɔː-/ *suffix* if something is market-oriented, customer-oriented etc, it is developed or done to meet the market's or the customer's needs: *Mexico is moving toward a market-oriented economic model.* | ***Consumer-oriented*** *stocks have done well.* | *NCNB and Banc One are trying to bring aggressive* ***consumer-oriented*** *retail banking to Texas.* —compare -DRIVEN, -LED

or·i·gin /ˈɒrədʒən‖ˈɔː-, ˈɑː-/ also **origins** *n* [C,U] **1** the situation, place, or substance something comes from + **of**: *Swiss authorities were doubtful about the origins of his financing.* | *products of petroleum origin* | *The software helps you trace the origin of any piece of data.*

2 country/nation/point of origin the country or place that goods have come from: *lists showing U.S. imports of crude oil and other products by country of origin* | *The shipper assumes full responsibility for the cargo from the point of origin to point of destination.* —see also CERTIFICATE OF ORIGIN

o·rig·i·nal /əˈrɪdʒənəl, -dʒənəl/ *adj* [only before a noun] happening or existing first: *Keep a copy of the* ***original invoice***. | *The index-linked certificates were paying indexation plus 4% of the* ***original investment***. —**original** *n* [C] *Send us a signed copy of the invoice and keep the original.*

original invoice —see under INVOICE[1]

o·rig·i·nate /əˈrɪdʒəneɪt/ *v* **1** [T] FINANCE to arrange and supply a loan, especially a MORTGAGE (=loan for buying a house): *Commercial banks originated 42% of all mortgages last year compared with 32% the previous year.* | *ISB has reached an agreement with the banking regulator on the types of loans it may originate.*

2 [I] to start in or come from a particular place or situation **originate in/from/with**: *It will be possible to fly between Boston and Paris, with the service originating in Minneapolis.* | *the country from which the currency originates*

originating application —see under APPLICATION

originating summons —see under SUMMONS[1]

o·rig·i·na·tion /əˌrɪdʒəˈneɪʃən/ *n* [U] **1** FINANCE the process of arranging and supplying a loan, especially a MORTGAGE (=loan for buying a house): *Sallie Mae will also provide* ***loan origination*** *to Chase in Tampa.* | *An* ***origination fee*** *is generally charged.*

2 the work involved in making something from the beginning through to the finished product: *How efficiently can our organization implement an idea from origination to commercialization?* | *The group incurred heavy* ***origination costs*** *in developing its video catalogue.*

o·rig·i·nat·or /əˈrɪdʒəneɪtə‖-ər/ *n* [C] **1** someone who has an original idea, starts an activity etc: *Xerox, the originator of many innovations, which it then failed to exploit*

2 a financial institution that makes a loan, rather than one that buys the loan, collects interest payments on it etc: *Many banks have been large originators of business loans, but resell the loans to other lenders.*

OS also **O/S** abbreviation for OPERATING SYSTEM; OUT OF STOCK; OUTSIZE; OUTSTANDING

os·cil·late /ˈɒsəleɪt‖ˈɑː-/ *v* [I] to move regularly between two limits: *The currency could oscillate noticeably within the exchange rate band even as a result of insignificant daily transactions.* —**oscillation** *n* [C, U]

OSHA *n* Occupational Safety and Health Administration; an organization in the US that is responsible for making sure companies and other employers obey the rules about health and safety for the people who work in their factories, offices etc

OSI *n* [singular] COMPUTING open systems interconnection; a system developed in the 1980s to try to connect computer networks anywhere in the world: *Boeing and General Motors were also supporters of OSI.*

OTC written abbreviation for OVER THE COUNTER

OTE *BrE* HUMAN RESOURCES overall total earnings; an abbreviation used in job advertisements to show the total amount someone would earn in a job that is being advertised: *£32K OTE, pension scheme and company car*

OTO written abbreviation for ONE-TIME-ONLY

OTS *n* Office of Thrift Supervision; a government organization in the US that is responsible for making sure that SAVINGS AND LOAN ASSOCIATIONS (=banks where people save money and that give loans to people buying houses) obey banking rules and laws

ounce /aʊns/ written abbreviation **oz.** *n* [C] a measurement of weight equal to 28.35 grams

oust /aʊst/ *v* [T] *journalism* **1** to force someone to leave a job or important position: *Profit margins collapsed and Martinez was ousted as chairman.* **oust sb from**: *two top executives who had been ousted from the NCR board*

2 if one company or product ousts another from its market position, it becomes more successful **oust sth from**: *Warburg ousted Morgan Stanley & Co. from second place in the league table of the total value of bids.* | *Will the Macintosh ever oust the PC from the corporate market?*

ous·ter /ˈaʊstə‖-ər/ *n* [C] *AmE* an act of moving someone from a powerful job, position etc in order to take their place: *The board faced an ouster by shareholders after it rejected a $55-a-share offer by Carey Energy Corp.*

out /aʊt/ *adj* [not before a noun] *informal* **1** *BrE* if the workers in a company, factory etc are out, they are refusing to work; ON STRIKE: *If I lost my job, or was* ***out on strike***, *there would be money in the medical care account to continue my insurance.*

2 *AmE* if a worker is out or out sick, they are not at work because they are sick; OFF SICK *BrE*: *Ralph's been out sick four times this month already.*

3 *AmE* if a machine is out, it is not working; OUT OF ORDER *BrE*

4 if you or your accounts, calculations etc are out by a particular amount of money, you have lost that amount of money: *Ms. Hardwick is out $1,100 in premiums and has had to pay $8,000 in medical bills.*

out-basket *n* [C] *AmE* a container used to hold letters, papers etc that have been dealt with; OUT-TRAY *BrE* —compare IN-BASKET

out•bid /aʊtˈbɪd/ *v* past tense and past participle **outbid** present participle **outbidding** [T] to succeed in obtaining a product, contract etc by making a better offer than anyone else: *Midland still has a chance of outbidding Hongkong if it can make savings through rationalisation.* | *AT&T outbid two of Mexico's largest suppliers to win the right to build 60% of the network.*

out•bound /ˈaʊtbaʊnd/ *adj* [only before a noun] outbound traffic, goods, flights etc are ones leaving a country: *The outbound tourist flow from Taiwan rose 14% last year.*

out•cry /ˈaʊtkraɪ/ —see OPEN OUTCRY

O

out•fit[1] /ˈaʊtfɪt/ *n* [C] *informal* a small company or organization, especially one that not many people know about: *The Romanian government sponsored the meeting with an American outfit, the Project on Ethnic Relations.* | *These outfits are solo lawyers or small law firms that advertise themselves as experts.*

outfit[2] *v* past tense and past participle **outfitted** present participle **outfitting** [T] to prepare a vehicle, building, piece of equipment etc for a particular purpose: *Rolls-Royce PLC won an order to outfit the Boeing 777 aircraft.* | *Mr. Hull's job is to outfit a cafeteria so that volunteers can start work.* **outfit sth with**: *Best Foods Baking Group has outfitted its delivery trucks with Grid Systems computers.* —**outfitting** *adj* [only before a noun] *the ship outfitting division of Yarrow Shipbuilders*

out•fit•ter /ˈaʊtfɪtə‖-ər/ *n* [C] **1** also plural **outfitters** *BrE old-fashioned* a shop that sells men's clothes: *Austin Reed, the* ***men's outfitters***
2 *AmE* a shop selling equipment for outdoor activities such as camping: *More outfitters are diversifying into organizing expeditions on top of their retail activities.*

out•flank /aʊtˈflæŋk/ *v* [T] if one company, country etc outflanks another, it is more successful than it: *For cheaper products, the Japanese have outflanked Taiwan and Korea by building factories in Southeast Asia.* | *KKR considered making a bid for SeaFirst Corp. but was outflanked by BankAmerica.*

out•flow /ˈaʊtfləʊ‖-floʊ/ *n* [C,U] money which is being taken out of a company, country etc: *First Executive paid over $1.33 billion to policyholders, creating a vast* ***cash outflow***. | *The Bundesbank's primary task is keeping the currency stable, and* ***capital outflow*** *to a minimum.* | *Some fund groups even report outflows from their junk-bond funds.*

out•go•ing /ˈaʊtˌgəʊɪŋ‖-ˈgoʊ-/ *adj* [only before a noun]
1 outgoing telephone calls, mail etc are made or sent by someone rather than being received by them: *This telephone can only be used to make* ***outgoing calls***. | *outgoing facsimile and data transmission traffic* | *You will need to log all* ***outgoing invoices***.
2 the outgoing chairman/president etc someone who is leaving their job as chairman, president etc: *Charlotte Beers, the outgoing chief executive officer of Chicago's Tatham RSCG* —compare INCOMING

out•go•ings /ˈaʊtˌgəʊɪŋz‖-ˌgoʊ-/ *n* [plural] an amount of money that is spent regularly: *We are keeping our outgoings down until our new production facilities come on stream.* | *Exclude outgoings payable by the landlord when considering the amount of rent charged for a property.*

out•lay /ˈaʊtleɪ/ *n* [C,U] an amount of money that has to be spent, especially at the start of a new business, project etc: *BP's* ***initial outlay*** *would be about 20.7 billion pesetas.*
capital outlay FINANCE money spent on capital equipment; CAPITAL EXPENDITURE: *Higher profits enable companies to raise capital outlays and productivity.*

out•let /ˈaʊtlet, -lɪ̈t/ *n* [C] a shop, company, or organization through which products are sold: *Ratner's outlets trade under a variety of names.* | *Manweb managed to improve margins in its high street* ***retail outlets*** (=shops that are open to members of the public). | *an agreement to sell 21 of its* ***factory outlet stores*** (=shops selling damaged or out-of-date products that have come directly from the factory)
captive outlet a shop that sells the products of one company only: *Alberto-Culver doesn't use Sally as a captive outlet – its products represent only 5% of sales.* —compare FRANCHISE[1]

out•look /ˈaʊtlʊk/ *n* [singular] the way things are expected to develop in the future: *Given the current* ***economic outlook***, *Tribune expects its media businesses to generate increased earnings over the next five years.* **+ for**: *The company blamed its weak performance on the recession and said the outlook for the rest of the year is brighter.*

out of court —see under COURT[1]

out-of-date *adj* things that are out-of-date are old, and therefore cannot be used or are not correct, fashionable etc: *complaints about out-of-date information used by credit bureaus* | *These regulations are totally out-of-date in today's worldwide marketplace.*

out-of-house *adv* people who work out-of-house work at their own home or for another company, rather than in the company building —compare IN-HOUSE

out of order —see under ORDER[1]

out-of-pocket *adj* [only before a noun] out-of-pocket costs, fees etc are those you have to pay yourself, because they are not covered by insurance, paid by your employer etc: *The other* ***out-of-pocket expenses*** *you will have to pay include legal fees, and the land registry fee.*

out of print —see under PRINT[2]

out of stock —see under STOCK

out-of-the-money option —see under OPTION

out•place•ment /ˈaʊtˌpleɪsmənt/ *n* [C,U] HUMAN RESOURCES a service provided by a company to help its professional employees find new jobs when the company is no longer able to employ them: *firms specializing in relocation and outplacement* | *Employees were provided with an extensive package of* ***outplacement services***.

out•port /ˈaʊtpɔːt‖-pɔːrt/ *n* [C] a small port that is used mainly for exporting goods to a larger port some distance away: *The cod fishery is the only source of jobs in many of the province's tiny outports.*

out•post /ˈaʊtpəʊst‖-poʊst/ *n* [C] *AmE* a shop, office etc in a particular area that is part of a large organization; BRANCH: *The Hard Rock Cafe empire has outposts all over the world.*

out•put[1] /ˈaʊtpʊt/ *n* **1** [C,U] the amount of goods or services produced by a person, machine, factory, company etc: *The plant employs around 7,000 staff and has* ***annual output*** *of around three million metric tons of steel.* | *The outputs of the production system need to be accounted for, invoiced and delivered to the customer.*
net output [U] ECONOMICS the difference between the cost of producing something and the price it is sold for; VALUE ADDED: *The car producer has a value added or net output of £3000 per car.*
2 [U] ECONOMICS the total amount of goods and services produced in the economy or a part of the economy during a particular period of time: *Global* ***economic output*** *grew by 3.1% last year.* | *Farmers could suffer from declining commodity prices as world* ***agricultural output*** *rises.* | ***Manufacturing output*** *in Scotland has risen, and the number of firms operating below full capacity has fallen.*
3 [U] COMPUTING the information produced by a computer, either on screen or printed out on paper: *high quality text output*

output² *v* past tense and past participle **output** present participle **outputting** [T] COMPUTING if a computer outputs information, it produces it + **to**: *These software packages are ideal for outputting to colour printers.*

output tax —see under TAX¹

out·sell /aʊt'sel/ *v* past tense and past participle **outsold** [T] **1** to be sold in larger quantities than another product of the same type: *Chardonnay outsells other white wines by a huge margin.*
2 to sell more products than a competitor: *Toyota had its best sales month ever, outselling Chrysler Corp. by about 31,000 cars.*

outside shareholder —see under SHAREHOLDER

out·size /'aʊtsaɪz/ also **outsized** *adj* larger than normal: *She has done more to promote the manufacture of* ***outsize clothes*** *at modest prices than any other designer.*

out·source /'aʊtsɔːs‖-sɔːrs/ *v* [T] if a company, organization etc outsources its work, it employs another company to do it; SUBCONTRACT: *As more companies outsource design skills and expertise, the sector is likely to expand.* | *It is highly desirable to outsource a portion of our production needs.* —**outsourcing** *n* [U] *Workers affected by outsourcing will have the right to take the issue to a tribunal.* | *Kodak's highly praised outsourcing strategy*

out·stand·ing /aʊt'stændɪŋ/ *adj* **1** FINANCE a company's outstanding shares are all the shares that it has sold and that are held by its shareholders: *Morrison Knudsen Corp. will have 14.4 million shares outstanding after the offering.* | *Memorex wants to raise the $5 million from employees purchasing some of its outstanding junk bonds.*
2 outstanding loans, debts etc are ones that have not been paid yet: *Proceeds from the sale are expected to pay the company's* ***outstanding debts***. | *The landlord took out a warrant in respect of the outstanding rent.* —compare OVERDUE
3 not solved, done, or dealt with: *Only queries still outstanding after this stage should be referred to the Help Desk.* | *The committee reached broad agreement on all outstanding issues.*

outstanding invoice —see under INVOICE¹

outstanding shares —see under SHARE

outstanding stock —see under STOCK¹

out-tray *n* [C] *BrE* a container used to hold letters, papers etc that have been dealt with; OUT-BASKET *AmE* —compare IN-TRAY

out·turn /'aʊtˌtɜːn‖-ˌtɜːrn/ *n* [C usually singular] *BrE* the actual amounts, results etc at the end of a period of activity, rather than those that were expected or calculated earlier; ACTUALS: *Current expenditure is forecast to increase by 6% over last year's outturn.* | *Social security spending will be lower than expected due to lower recent outturns for unemployment.*

out·vote /aʊt'vəʊt‖-'voʊt/ *v* [T] to defeat a person or their ideas, proposals etc by voting against them: *If this Bill is outvoted, we are faced with dire* (=very bad) *consequences.* | *Some of the smaller EU countries could combine to outvote the UK, France and Germany.*

out·ward /'aʊtwəd‖-wərd/ *adj* [only before a noun]
1 leaving a place, rather than arriving in it: *The* ***outward flow of investment*** *by British multinationals is high in manufacturing industry.* | *We use the following methods of despatching* ***outward mail***. | ***outward-bound*** *shipments of aid*
2 freight outwards ACCOUNTING used in a set of accounts to show that payments are for the cost of TRANSPORTING goods a company has sold; CARRIAGE OUTWARDS —compare INWARD

outward investment —see under INVESTMENT

out·work /'aʊtwɜːk‖-wɜːrk/ *n* [U] *BrE* work which is done for a business by people working at home: *Workers engaged in domestic outwork, seasonal working or subcontracting will secure none of the benefits.* —**outworker** *n* [C]

o·ver·age /'əʊvərɪdʒ‖'oʊ-/ *n* [C] *AmE* a situation in which there is too much of a particular product; OVERSUPPLY: *The decreasing demand for copper is catching up with supply, and an overage is building up.*

o·ver·al·lot·ment /'əʊvərə'lɒtmənt‖'oʊvərəˌlɑːt-/ *n* [C,U] FINANCE when a financial institution sells all the available shares in a company's SHARE ISSUE or SECONDARY OFFERING and then sells more, or the number of shares sold in this way; GREENSHOE: *Merrill Lynch also sold its 15%* ***overallotment allowance*** (=the new amount it is authorized to sell), *which increased the size of the Duracell offering to 34.5 million shares.* | *Delta, which this month issued 3.6 million common shares, said it will* ***exercise its overallotment option*** (=use it) *and sell an additional 540,000 shares.*

overall total earnings —see OTE

o·ver·banked /'əʊvə'bæŋkt◂‖'oʊvər-/ *adj* BANKING if a city, area, country etc is overbanked, there are too many banks in relation to the number of customers: *Lebanon is a hugely overbanked country – there are 80 banks for a population of 3.5 million.* —**overbanking** *n* [U] *The authorities could help solve the overbanking in the region by agreeing to the merger of these banks.*

o·ver·bid /ˌəʊvə'bɪd‖ˌoʊvər-/ past tense and past participle **overbid** present participle **overbidding** *v* [I] to offer or pay too high a price for something + **for**: *Several TV companies who may have overbid for licences are now in financial trouble.* —**overbid** /'əʊvəbɪd‖'oʊvər-/ *n* [C] *They inflated customer orders when they bought the debt and then filed false reports based on those overbids.*

o·ver·bill /ˌəʊvə'bɪl‖ˌoʊvər-/ *v* [I,T] to send an INVOICE (=a document showing how much is owed for goods) to a customer for a higher amount than what they really owe: *He is alleged to have overbilled NASA for many years for production and repair work on the space shuttle.* —**overbilling** *n* [C,U] *Money from the overbillings went to pay for his lavish life style.*

o·ver·book /ˌəʊvə'bʊk‖ˌoʊvər-/ *v* [I,T] to sell more tickets for a plane, hotel etc than there are places available: *The airline offers cash as compensation for passengers when flights are overbooked.* —**overbooking** *n* [U] *the right to sue airlines for overbooking*

o·ver·bor·row /ˌəʊvə'bɒrəʊ‖ˌoʊvər'bɑː-, -'bɔː-/ *v* [T] FINANCE to borrow too much money in relation to your ability to make payments on the debt: *Egypt may find it has overborrowed in the international capital markets.* —**over-borrowed** *adj* [not before a noun] *The increase in lending to stimulate the economy has not worked as Japanese companies and individuals are already so overborrowed.* —**over-borrowing** *n* [U] *The state encouraged overborrowing by firms and overlending by banks because of its commitment to higher growth.*

o·ver·bought /ˌəʊvə'bɔːt‖ˌoʊvər'bɒːt/ *adj* FINANCE if a financial market is overbought, prices are higher than many people think they should be, and will probably come down: *He thinks the gold market is overbought and there will be a correction in two to three months.*

o·ver·buy /ˌəʊvə'baɪ‖ˌoʊvər-/ past tense and past participle **overbought** *v* [I,T] to buy more than you need or more than you can pay for

o·ver·ca·pa·ci·ty /ˌəʊvəkə'pæsəti‖ˌoʊvər-/ *n* [U] MANUFACTURING when there are more factories, buildings, equipment etc that are able to produce a particular product or service than there is demand for it: *The banks are hurt by the industry's overcapacity, and fear that there will be too many banks chasing too few customers.* —compare ***spare capacity*** under CAPACITY

o•ver•cap•i•tal•ized also **overcapitalised** *BrE* /ˌəʊvəˈkæpɪtl-aɪzd◂‖ˌoʊvər-/ *adj* FINANCE if a company is overcapitalized, it has more capital than it needs for its activities and investment plans: *ICI is already overcapitalised, so it hardly needs more cash for its expansion.* —**overcapitalization** *n* [U] *Government farm programs have led to the overcapitalization of agriculture.*

o•ver•charge /ˌəʊvəˈtʃɑːdʒ‖ˌoʊvərˈtʃɑːrdʒ/ *v* [I,T] to charge someone too much money for something + **for**: *Divorce lawyers often overcharge women clients.* | *The company overcharged the government for labor and materials.* —**overcharging** *n* [U] *fraud involving the overcharging of corporate clients* —**overcharge** *n* [C] *Federal law doesn't require lenders to reimburse consumers for any overcharges.*

O

o•ver•class /ˈəʊvəˌklɑːs‖ˈoʊvərˌklæs/ *n* [C,U] *journalism* a group of people who are very powerful, rich, or have a lot of influence

o•ver•draft /ˈəʊvədrɑːft‖ˈoʊvərdræft/ *n* [C] *especially BrE* BANKING an arrangement between a bank and a customer, allowing them to take out more money from their CURRENT ACCOUNT than they had in it, or the amount involved: *We can offer current accounts with* ***overdraft facilities.*** | ***Authorised overdraft*** (=one that the bank agreed to give) *interest rate is normally cheaper than bank personal loan rates.* | *You will find that you will be charged more for an* ***unauthorised overdraft.*** | *We often reached our* ***overdraft limit*** *because of cashflow problems.*

bank overdraft an amount by which a bank account is in debt

o•ver•drawn /ˌəʊvəˈdrɔːn◂‖ˌoʊvərˈdrɒːn◂/ *adj* **be/go overdrawn** to be in or to get into a situation where you owe the bank money on an overdraft: *You are entitled to free banking, even when your account is overdrawn.* —**overdraw** *v* [I,T] *There's a monthly usage fee of £6 if you overdraw by more than £50.*

o•ver•due /ˌəʊvəˈdjuː◂‖ˌoʊvərˈduː◂/ *adj* a payment that is overdue should have been made earlier: *The share of auto loans more than 30 days overdue remains significantly higher than average.* | *Interest on* ***overdue taxes*** *will stay at 11%.*

o•ver•ex•ten•ded /ˌəʊvərɪkˈstendɪ̈d◂‖ˌoʊ-/ *adj* **1** an overextended organization is involved in more activities than it can manage, or it does not have enough money to do what it wants, for example because it has borrowed or spent too much: *Overextended private borrowers, unlike the government, can't print money or raise taxes to pay bills.* —**overextend** *v* [T] *There are still some big companies with major problems because they overextended themselves in real estate.*

2 in an overextended financial market, prices are too high and will probably fall: *Stocks are nowhere near the overextended prices he expects to see at the top of the bull market.*

o•ver•fund•ed /ˌəʊvəˈfʌndɪ̈d◂‖ˌoʊvər-/ *adj* [not before a noun] if an organization is overfunded, it receives too much money in relation to its needs: *The reduction in the Agricultural Research Council's subsidy is acknowledgement that agricultural research is overfunded.*

o•ver•fund•ing /ˌəʊvəˈfʌndɪŋ‖ˌoʊvər-/ *n* [U] **1** when an organization receives too much money in relation to its needs: *Some departments may, through overfunding, be absorbing resources unfairly.*

2 BANKING when a CENTRAL BANK borrows more money from financial institutions in order to take money out of the economy and reduce the MONEY SUPPLY (=the amount of money in the economy): *The government engaged in overfunding, making a net issue of bonds to the private sector in excess of the total government borrowing requirement.*

over•geared *adj BrE* FINANCE if a company or country is overgeared, it has borrowed too much and cannot make payments on the debt; OVERBORROWED; OVERLEVERAGED: *Much of the money invested went into overpriced or over-geared companies.* —**overgearing** *n* [U] *The most common mistakes in failed businesses are over-optimism and overgearing.*

o•ver•hang¹ /ˌəʊvəˈhæŋ‖ˌoʊvər-/ *v* past tense and past participle **overhung** [T] **1** to have a bad influence on something: *Currency worries overhung many engineering stocks. Rolls-Royce lost 9 to close at 232p.*

2 overhang the market FINANCE if a large quantity of something overhangs the market, it has not been sold when it should have been and therefore has a negative influence on prices. For example, shares that overhang the stockmarket are often those held by UNDERWRITERS that they have not succeeded in selling them to investors: *The stock fell on one poorly placed trade, leaving a large amount of stock overhanging the market.*

o•ver•hang² /ˈəʊvəhæŋ‖ˈoʊvər-/ *n* [C,U] FINANCE an unsold quantity of something that has a bad influence on prices, markets etc: *The huge overhang of world-wide crude oil inventories further depressed energy prices.* | *As long as there is a* ***supply overhang*** *silver will do poorly.* —see also DEBT OVERHANG

o•ver•haul /ˌəʊvəˈhɔːl‖ˌoʊvərˈhɒːl/ *v* [T] to repair or change all the parts of a machine or system that is not working correctly: *a proposal to overhaul the health-care system* —**overhaul** *n* [C] *an overhaul of civil court procedures to speed up cases*

o•ver•head /ˈəʊvəhed‖ˈoʊvər-/ *n* [C,U] a company's general costs for activities not related to particular products: *Such costs count as an overhead of the business, and VAT on them is deductible.* | *Because* ***overhead costs*** *won't increase, profit margins at the hospital should expand.* | *It spends about 17 cents to sell $1 of its goods, among the highest overheads in the tire industry.* | *Firms have centralized buying to reduce both cost of goods and* ***administrative overheads.***

direct overhead a cost such as rent or electricity that is included in the total cost of making a particular product when calculating costs

overhead cost —see under COST¹

overhead expense —see under EXPENSE

o•ver•heat /ˌəʊvəˈhiːt‖ˌoʊvər-/ *v* [I,T] ECONOMICS if an economy overheats, demand rises too fast, causing prices and imports to rise, a situation that governments may try to correct by raising taxes and interest rates: *Germany* ***overheated its economy*** *as it poured money into rebuilding the east.* | *Lifting economies out of recession is easy compared with deciding when to re-apply the brakes so the economy does not overheat later.* —**overheating** *n* [U] *Economic growth is modest, with little fear of overheating.*

o•ver•is•sue /ˈəʊvərˌɪʃuː, -ˌɪsjuː‖-ˌɪʃuː/ *n* [U] FINANCE when a company sells more shares than it is allowed to

o•ver•lend /ˌəʊvəˈlend‖ˌoʊvər-/ *v* past tense and past participle **overlent** [I] BANKING if a financial institution overlends, it lends more than it should, for example to borrowers that are unable to make repayments —**overlending** *n* [U] *Overlending in the mid-1980s increased banks' risk exposure.*

o•ver•le•ver•aged /ˌəʊvəˈliːvərɪdʒ◂‖ˌoʊvərˈle-, -ˈliː-/ *adj* FINANCE if a company or country is overleveraged, it has borrowed too much money and cannot make payments on the debt; OVERBORROWED; OVERGEARED *BrE*: *The banks are taking over more real estate from overleveraged developers and putting it on the market.* —**overleverage** *n* [U] *Overleverage and the economic slump have combined to depress the industry.* —**overleveraging** *n* [U] *the overleveraging of corporate America*

o•ver•load /ˌəʊvəˈləʊd‖ˌoʊvərˈloʊd/ past participle **overloaded** or **overladen** *v* [T] **1** to give someone more work, information etc than they can deal with **overload sb with sth**: *Don't scare your buyer, don't overload him with too much information.*

2 be overloaded with sth if something is overloaded with a particular problem, it is badly affected by that problem: *The economy was overloaded with so much debt that a real depression was possible.* —**overload** *n* [C,U] *Opening up another channel of information will add to the* ***information overload*** *suffered by managers.* | ***traffic overload***

o•ver•manned /ˌəʊvəˈmænd◂‖ˌoʊvər-/ *adj* having more workers than are needed for a job, activity etc; OVERSTAFFED: *The police department was severely overmanned, and they called for the elimination of 1,605 police positions.* —**overmanning** *n* [U] *It was the world's most inefficient port, due to overmanning and rigid labour laws.*

o•ver•night[1] /ˌəʊvəˈnaɪt◂‖ˌoʊvər-/ *adj* [only before a noun] **1** done in one night: *Much of what is shipped via overnight express delivery is not really needed the next day.*

2 continuing for all or most of the night: *an overnight flight*

3 happening last night: *London stocks ended higher, fueled by* ***overnight gains*** *on Wall Street.*

4 used to talk about money that is lent for one night and must be paid back the next day: *Credit was tightened and the cost of overnight money touched 10%.* | *overnight commercial paper*

overnight[2] *v* [T] *AmE* to send something overnight: *We were told on Thursday that our check would be overnighted to us on Friday.*

overnight loan —see under LOAN[1]

o•ver•paid /ˌəʊvəˈpeɪd◂‖ˌoʊvər-/ *adj* if someone is overpaid, they are paid too much for the job they do: *Many CEOs are overpaid and underworked bureaucrats.*

o•ver•pay /ˌəʊvəˈpeɪ‖ˌoʊvər-/ *v* past tense and past participle **overpaid** **1** [I,T] to pay someone too much, or to pay too much for something: *The effect of the tax change is that a lot of people will overpay and will then have to claim refunds.* + **by**: *The Pentagon claims the two defense firms were overpaid by more than $1.3 billion over the years.*—**overpayment** *n* [U] *alleged overpayment of taxes* | *There has been an overpayment of $170,000 on this contract.*

2 [I] to pay too much for something in relation to its real value + **for**: *Did Hasbro overpay for Tonka? The price was probably on the high side.*

o•ver•pro•duce /ˌəʊvəprəˈdjuːs‖ˌoʊvərprəˈduːs/ *v* [I,T] to produce too much of something, either more than is needed or more than was planned: *Originally, malls just sold merchandise that was overproduced or sent back unsold by retailers.* —**overproducer** *n* [C] *Pressure for output reductions fell most heavily on big overproducers such as Saudi Arabia.* —**overproduction** *n* [U] *Cereal producers have complained of low prices because of overproduction.*

o•ver•ride /ˌəʊvəˈraɪd‖ˌoʊ-/ *v* past tense **overrode** past participle **overridden** [T] to ignore a decision, rule, law etc made by a person or organization with less authority: *Resolution Trust Corp. has the power to override state banking laws to sell insolvent thrifts.*

o•ver•run[1] /ˌəʊvəˈrʌn/ *n* [C] an occasion when something costs more to develop and produce than was originally planned, or the amount of money involved in this: *The Pentagon is expecting overruns of as much as $2.6 billion on its cargo plane program.*

cost overrun when it costs more to build or make something than was originally planned, or the amount by which this happens: *Eurotunnel said the contractors were responsible for the* ***cost overrun****, but the contractors rejected that claim.*

o•ver•run[2] /ˌəʊvəˈrʌn‖ˌoʊ-/ *v* past tense **overran** past participle **overrun** [I,T] to cost more or continue longer than expected or intended: *The health service ended up subsidising the venture because the costs overran.* | *Businesses refused to commit themselves in case the project's costs overran its budget.*

o•ver•seas[1] /ˌəʊvəˈsiːz◂‖ˌoʊvər-/ *adv* to, in, or from a foreign country across the sea: *Most applications came from overseas.*

o•ver•seas[2] /ˈəʊvəsiːz‖ˈoʊvər-/ *adj* [only before a noun] coming from, existing, or happening abroad: *Overseas trusts are being made subject UK income taxation.* | *exchange control requirements applying to overseas shareholders* | *The law made it possible for overseas companies to hold a stake in Russian companies.*

overseas agent —see under AGENT

overseas aid —see under AID

overseas investment —see under INVESTMENT

overseas trade —see under TRADE[1]

o•ver•see /ˌəʊvəˈsiː‖ˌoʊvər-/ *v* past tense **oversaw** past participle **overseen** [T] **1** to organize and control an activity or the work that people or an organization do; MANAGE: *The bank has hired Mary B. Lehman to oversee domestic private banking.*

2 FINANCE to be responsible for making investments: *Mr Cook oversaw $80 billion in assets at Fidelity.*

3 to check that an activity is being performed honestly and legally; REGULATE: *While CPAs check the company's financial results, they cannot oversee the company's overall financial operations.*

o•ver•seer /ˈəʊvəsɪə‖ˈoʊvərsɪr/ *n* [C] **1** a person or organization whose job is to check that an activity is being performed honestly and legally; REGULATOR: *The State Property Fund is the overseer of the privatisation process.*

2 *journalism* a person or organization appointed by a court to deal with the affairs of a bankrupt company: *the court-appointed overseers of Maxwell Communication Corp.'s bankruptcy-protection proceedings*

3 *old-fashioned* someone in charge of a group of workers, who checks their work is done properly: *The overseers had exactly twice the labourers' pay.*

o•ver•sell /ˌəʊvəˈsel‖ˌoʊvər-/ also **over-sell** *v* past tense and past participle **oversold** or **over-sold** [T] to say that something you are selling is better, more useful etc than it really is: *Vendors tend to oversell the software. That gives people more confidence to work with it than they should have.* —**overselling** *n* [U] *He's investigating the possible overselling of time-share resorts*

o•ver•shoot /ˌəʊvəˈʃuːt‖ˌoʊvər-/ *v* past tense and past participle **overshot** [T] to go past a figure or level that was set as a limit or target: *Money supply grew at a rapid rate in January, and overshot the German central bank's 5.5% limit.* —opposite UNDERSHOOT —**overshooting** *n* [U] *There would be a continuing problem of overshooting or undershooting.*

oversight board —see under BOARD[1]

o•ver•sold /ˌəʊvəˈsəʊld‖ˌoʊvərˈsoʊld/ also **over-sold** *adj* FINANCE an oversold financial market has prices that have fallen too far: *"The market is oversold," he said. "It's time to buy low-priced blue chips."*

o•ver•spend /ˌəʊvəˈspend‖ˌoʊvər-/ *v* past tense and past participle **overspent** [I] to spend more than you can afford or more than you intended + **by**: *Health authorities, which overspent by more than £300 million last year, must balance their books this year.* —**overspend** /ˈəʊvəspend‖ˈoʊvər-/ *n* [C usually singular] *They have moved from a £21 million surplus to a £6 million overspend.* —**overspending** *n* [U] *years of overspending on public programs*

O

o·ver·staffed /ˌəʊvəˈstɑːft◂‖ˌoʊvərˈstæft◂/ *adj* an overstaffed company, organization etc has more people working for it than it needs; OVERMANNED: *We were overstaffed in some areas and not as competitive as we should have been.* —opposite UNDERSTAFFED —**overstaffing** *n* [U] *He cut the workforce sharply to eliminate overstaffing.*

o·ver·stock /ˌəʊvəˈstɒk‖ˌoʊvərˈstɑːk/ *v* [I,T] if a business or shop overstocks, or overstocks a part or product, it has more in stock than it needs for production or more than it is likely to sell: *The temptation is always to overstock, and this means that the land is asked to produce more than its true potential.* —**overstock** *n* [C,U] *Smithmark publishes garden and art books and resells other publishers' overstock.* —**overstocking** *n* [U] *The new order processing system cuts costs by avoiding overproduction and overstocking.*

o·ver·sub·scribed /ˌəʊvəsəbˈskraɪbd◂‖ˌoʊvər-/ *adj* FINANCE, an oversubscribed SECURITIES ISSUE (=an occasion when they are made available for sale) has more people asking for more shares etc than are available. If this happens, each buyer receives fewer shares than they asked for, or there is a BALLOT to decide who will receive them: *The bonds were oversubscribed, and there will be no unsold balance remaining, the underwriter said.* —**oversubscription** *n* [U] *Analysts expect them to receive only about 2.5% of the shares they ordered because of massive oversubscription.*

oversubscription allowance also **oversubscription option** *n* [C] FINANCE when additional shares are made available if there is oversubscription; GREENSHOE; OVERALLOTMENT ALLOWANCE: *Billiton raised £825 million from the placing and this will rise to £949 million if the* ***oversubscription allowance is exercised*** (=the additional shares are bought) *in full.*

over-the-counter dealing —see under DEALING

over-the-counter drug —see under DRUG

over-the-counter market —see under MARKET[1]

over-the-counter pharmaceuticals —see under PHARMACEUTICALS

over-the-counter share —see under SHARE

over-the-counter stock —see under STOCK[1]

over-the-counter trading —see under TRADING

o·ver·time /ˈəʊvətaɪm‖ˈoʊvər-/ *n* [U] **1** time that you spend working in your job in addition to your normal working hours: *Is there any limit on your ability to* ***work overtime?*** | *Staff at the bank will begin* ***an overtime ban*** (=refuse to work overtime) *tomorrow in a protest over pay.*
2 time that a factory, office etc is operating in addition to its normal hours: *The plant has* ***worked overtime*** *in some recent weeks because those models are selling well.* | *They agreed to Saturday* ***overtime shifts*** (=working periods of time) *to meet rising demand.*
3 the money that you are paid for working more hours than usual: *Police officers who do this extra work are* ***paid overtime.*** | *They need paid holidays and vacations, as well as* ***overtime pay*** *for extra hours.*

o·ver·trade /ˌəʊvəˈtreɪd‖ˌoʊvər-/ *v* [I] **1** if a business overtrades, it does not have enough WORKING CAPITAL (=available cash) to pay its CREDITORS (=people and organizations it owes money to) and employees: *Directors of a tour operating company have to give financial guarantees which will be used if the company overtrades and then fails.*
2 if a BROKER overtrades, they buy and sell investments for customers more often than they should, in order to increase the amount of COMMISSION they earn; CHURN —**overtrading** *n* [U] *Before expanding, arrangements must be made for the higher cash requirements needed for this. If not, there is a risk of overtrading.* | *The securities house imposed fines for overtrading habits that in fact were encouraged.*

o·ver·val·ue /ˌəʊvəˈvæljuː‖ˈoʊvər-/ *v* [T] if you overvalue something, you give it a value that is too high: *The accounting firm wrongly permitted Columbia to overvalue its junk bonds.*

o·ver·val·ued /ˌəʊvəˈvæljuːd◂‖ˌoʊvər-/ *adj* a currency, group of shares etc that is overvalued has a higher value than it should have and will probably fall: *Equities are overvalued relative to the economic outlook around the world.* + **by**: *At present interest rates I think bonds are overvalued by about 7%.*

o·ver·weight /ˌəʊvəˈweɪt◂‖ˌoʊvər-/ *adj* **1** an overweight organization has too many people working for it: *this overweight monopoly, the Postal Service* | *Railtrack is considered to be overweight and overbureaucratic*
2 FINANCE if someone is overweight in a particular type of investment in relation to other investments they hold, they have more of it than is usual, or more of it than they should have: *He suggested portfolio managers be overweight in shares in electronics, machine tool makers and utilities.* | *Most people were overweight in the dollar because they believed in a US economic recovery.* —opposite UNDERWEIGHT —**overweight** *v* [T] *Economists at Merrill Lynch are advising clients to overweight their holdings of US, Canadian, and Australian dollars.*

o·ver·work /ˌəʊvəˈwɜːk‖ˌoʊvərˈwɜːrk/ *n* [U] when someone works too much or too hard: *What kinds of health problems accompany the stress from overwork?* —**overworked** *adj*: *Workers here feel underpaid and overworked.*

ovno *n* [singular] written abbreviation for 'or very near offer'; used in private advertisements to say that the seller will accept a slightly lower price than the one stated in the advertisement: *Rickenbacker 330, excellent condition, £550 ovno*

owe /əʊ‖oʊ/ *v* [T] to have to pay someone for goods or services they have sold to you, or to have to repay money someone has lent you **owe sb sth**: *The Russians owe Finnish paper exporters about $22 million.* **owe sb for sth**: *We still owe the builder for the work on the roof.* **owe sth**: *She owes taxes for the past three years.*

ow·ing /ˈəʊɪŋ‖ˈoʊ-/ *adj* [only after a noun] *BrE* an amount of money owing has not been paid yet: *We will send an estimate of the amount owing for the goods or services provided.* | *The brewery settled the £149 debt owing to him.* —compare OUTSTANDING

own /əʊn‖oʊn/ *v* [T] to have or possess something that is legally yours: *Mr. Gerstel owns 200,000 shares of Alza stock.* | *Mexico has auctioned 11 of the 18* ***state-owned*** *banks.* | *IDS Life Insurance Co. is a large Minneapolis life insurer owned by American Express.*

own-brand *adj* [only before a noun] *BrE* own-brand products have the name of the shop that is selling them, rather than the name given to them by the producer; OWN-LABEL *AmE*: *The regional breweries found it hard to promote their own-brand lagers in an image-conscious market.* —compare GENERIC

-owned /əʊnd‖oʊnd/ *suffix* added to other words in order to say who owns something or how much of it they own: *It has 55* ***company-owned*** *stores and 130 franchised stores in 21 states.* | *The* ***family-owned*** *concern is proudly independent.* | *SAS is the* ***jointly-owned*** (=owned by more than one owner) *airline of Denmark, Norway and Sweden.*

government-owned also **publicly-owned**, or **state-owned** adjowned by a country's government: *NTT was a government-owned company that was still being privatized.*

privately-owned ◆ *adj* not owned by the government: *municipal cable TV systems that compete against privately owned concerns*
◆ owned by shareholders whose shares are not

available for sale to outside investors: *This privately owned firm doesn't disclose its revenues and profits.*

own·er /ˈəʊnə‖ˈoʊnər/ *n* [C] **1** a person or organization that owns something: *Legally, the buyer becomes the owner at the instant the contract is made.* | *The Bank's new fixed-rate mortgage is proving popular with* ***home owners.*** + **of**: *The publisher is the owner of the trademark 'Oxford'.*

beneficial owner ◆ LAW the person or organization that has the advantages of ownership of a property ◆ FINANCE, LAW the real owner of an investment, rather than an organization holding the investment for them: *Swiss law now says that the beneficial owner of deposits must be identified; a Panama company name will not do.*

part owner a person or organization that owns part of something, at the same time as one or more other owners: *Hong Kong billionaire Robert Miller is part-owner of the world's largest chain of airport shops.*

2 at (the) owner's risk if something is bought or taken somewhere at the owner's risk, the owner, not the person selling it or taking it, is responsible if it is damaged or lost: *Luggage is carried at the owner's risk.*

owner-occupier *n* [C] PROPERTY someone who owns the house, flat etc that they live in: *The property tax is paid by tenants and owner-occupiers.*

owner-operator *n* [C] *AmE* PROPERTY someone who owns a small business and runs it

owner's equity —see under EQUITY

own·er·ship /ˈəʊnəʃɪp‖ˈoʊnər-/ *n* [U] **1** the state of owning something: ***Car ownership*** *by teenagers tripled during the decade.* | ***Home ownership*** *is more common in Britain than Europe generally.*

2 LAW the legal state of owning something: *Limited partnerships give holders an* ***ownership interest*** (=partial ownership) *in assets such as office buildings or oil fields.*

absolute ownership when someone owns something completely, without restrictions: *To develop the area for housing required the absolute ownership of the site by one man or corporation.*

beneficial ownership when someone really owns an investment, rather than when another organization holds the investment for the real owner: *Regulators should have the right to look into the beneficial ownership of suspicious or nominee shareholdings.*

common ownership also **ownership in common** ◆ when ownership is shared by two or more people or organizations ◆ FINANCE the ownership of companies

cross-ownership when a company in one industry owns a company in another related industry: *Italy limits cross-ownership of television stations and newspapers.*

employee ownership when the people who work for a company or part of a company own it: *He believes in employee ownership and said all employees will have a chance to buy equity in the company.*

foreign ownership when a company is owned by a foreign company: *Federal law bars foreign ownership of a US airline of more than 25%.*

full ownership when one person or organization owns all of a company, property etc, rather than just part of it: *It took over full ownership of Parenting magazine, where it initially had a half-interest.*

government ownership also **public ownership**, **state ownership** when a company is owned by the government: *The party traditionally has supported government ownership of some companies.*

joint ownership when a company, property etc has two or more owners: *Under the joint ownership arrangement, most decisions required approval of both partners.*

majority ownership when one person or group owns more than 50 per cent of the shares of a company

minority ownership when one person or group owns less than 50 per cent of the shares of a company: *Subordinated debt investors generally receive minority ownership in the acquired company in return for purchasing debt.*

part ownership also **part-ownership**, **partial ownership** when an investor owns part of a company's shares: *Desperate for cash, they signed an agreement giving part ownership and control of the operation to Homestake.*

private ownership when a company is owned by people or organizations that are not part of the government of a country: *The Chinese government wants to transfer these companies into private ownership.*

owner's risk —see under RISK[1]

own-label *adj* [only before a noun] *AmE* own-label products have the brand name of the shop that is selling them, rather than the name given to them by the producer; OWN-BRAND *BrE*: *Adidas already sells own-label shoes in Budapest and is planning franchises in Warsaw and Prague.* —compare GENERIC

oz. written abbreviation for OUNCE(S)

P

P *prefix* in Britain, the letter used to describe different documents used by the INLAND REVENUE, for example a P45 is a document given to a worker who is changing their job —see also FOUR PS

p **1** *BrE* written abbreviation for PENNY; PENCE: *Shares opened at 47.12p but soon rose to 56p.*
2 p. written abbreviation for PAGE

P&L written abbreviation for PROFIT AND LOSS

p & p written abbreviation for POSTAGE AND PACKING

P45 *n* [C usually singular] in Britain, an official document given to a person when they leave their job, showing how much money they have earned, and how much tax and NATIONAL INSURANCE they have paid during the period of time when they were employed

PA **1** written abbreviation for PER ANNUM; PERSONAL ASSISTANT
2 *AmE* written abbreviation for PUBLIC ACCOUNTANT

pace /peɪs/ *n* [singular] **1** the rate or speed at which something happens: *Canada's consumer price index rose at an annual pace of 4.8%.* | *The average price of a new car began to soar at a faster pace than household incomes.*
2 keep pace (with) to change at the same rate as someone or something else: *Next year's spending may not even keep pace with inflation.* | *Demand continues to keep pace, with shipments rising about 2.5%.*
3 set the pace to establish the speed at which your competitors try to do something, or the standard of quality they try to achieve: *The BNFL contract has continued to set the pace for all other sections of business.*

pace·set·ter /ˈpeɪsˌsetə‖-ər/ *n* [C] a company that is more successful than its competitors because it develops new products, methods etc before they do: *Sega Inc is fighting an uphill battle against pacesetter Nintendo Co. in the electronic-game business.* | *the pacesetter for the airline industry*

Pacific Rim *n* **Pacific Rim countries/nations/markets** the countries and states that border the Pacific Ocean, such as Japan, Australia, and the west coast of the US, considered as an economic group

Pacific Stock Exchange abbreviation **PSE** *n* FINANCE one of the most important stockmarkets in the US, based in Los Angeles and San Francisco

pack¹ /pæk/ *n* **1** [C] a small container with a set of things in it; PACKET, PACKAGE: *Five million tickets to Disney films will be placed in specially-marked packs.* + **of**: *a pack of Marlboro cigarettes*
2 6-pack/12-pack etc a pack that contains six, twelve etc items: *Corona Extra Lite Beer is now available in 12-packs.*
blister pack also **bubble pack** [C] a type of wrapping used for small items sold in shops, such as TABLETS which separates and protects each item with a small plastic cover attached to a piece of card: *Blister packs are difficult to recycle because the blisters are made of a different material from their backing.*
display pack [C] a specially made box, used to show goods that are on sale in shops: *Aqua Soil Ltd have distributed a new shop display pack for the coming season.*
gift pack [C] a small, decorated container, used to make the product inside it look more attractive: *The group faces heavy additional costs for assembling and transporting the gift packs.* —see also MULTI-PACK
3 lead/be ahead of the pack to be more successful than your competitors: *The Saatchi Agency has fallen to seventh place in the ad-agency rankings, after leading the pack for three years.* | *With Adidas in difficulties, Nike has been able to shoot ahead of the pack.*
4 [singular] a group of people who all work in the same industry, especially in films, the press, or the theatre, that you do not like or approve of: *The whole **media pack** is closing in on him.* | *a typical **brat pack*** (=young people who are just starting to become well-known) *movie*

pack² *v* [T] **1** to put products in boxes, a vehicle etc so they can be taken somewhere: *At sixteen, Brian went to work packing freight on the shipping docks.* **pack sth in sth**: *The video equipment is packed in aluminum trunks and air freighted to the site.* | *fish packed in fresh-water ice* —see also PACKAGING, PACKING
2 COMPUTING to put a lot of information on to the part of a computer or other piece of ELECTRONIC equipment that stores DATA (=information stored on a computer) **pack sth on/onto/into sth**: *The disks are engineered to pack at least twice as much data onto their recording surface.*
3 to arrive in large numbers into a space that is not big enough, or to make people or things do this: *Because moviegoers haven't been packing the theaters this fall, they haven't seen the trailers for our new releases.* **pack sth with sth**: *Matsushita has opened a 60-store shopping mall packed with clothes, stationery and food.* **pack sth into sth**: *CBS has infuriated viewers by packing an extra 3 minutes of commercials into popular hour-long programs.*
4 pack a board/committee/jury etc to secretly and dishonestly arrange for most of the people on a committee etc to support someone: *He packed the company's board with his relatives.*

pack up *phr v* [I] *BrE informal* **1** if a machine or piece of equipment packs up, it stops working: *The heating thermostat packed up on one of the coldest days this year.*
2 to stop working, trading etc: *The market collapsed and the company packed up and moved into something else.*

pack·age¹ /ˈpækɪdʒ/ *n* [C] **1** an amount of something or a number of things, packed together and wrapped up ready to be sent somewhere; PARCEL¹: *UPS delivers 300,000 packages overnight.* | *The machines were rejecting packages with wire fragments attached.*
2 a small container with a set of things in it; PACKET
3 a set of related things, services, or proposals that are sold or presented together: *the best-selling **desktop publishing package** on the market* + **of**: *Interco is urging bondholders to accept a package of new securities.* | *Gulf Canada Resources Ltd. announced a **package** of cost-cutting **measures**.*
4 HUMAN RESOURCES the pay and things such as holidays, pensions etc that you get with a particular job: *an attractive financial package*
benefits package the total amount of pay and all the other advantages that an employee may receive such as bonuses, health insurance, a company car etc: *The benefits package includes bonuses tied to the company's performance.*
compensation package *AmE* the total amount of pay and all the other advantages such as STOCK OPTIONS (=the right to buy the company's shares cheaply) that are offered to a company's important managers: *The compensation package includes bonuses tied to the company's performance.*
remuneration package also **salary package** *BrE* HUMAN RESOURCES the pay offered to employees, along with any other advantages such as long holidays or a car: *an excellent **remuneration package** and a profit-sharing scheme* | *The position is generously rewarded, with a **salary package** that includes a company car, pension scheme and mortgage subsidy.*
severance package an amount of money, and

other advantages such as advice on finding a new job, that are offered to an employee when a company tells them to leave. Severance packages are often offered when companies are RESTRUCTURING (=reorganizing): *20 full-time employees will be offered a severance package or other job opportunities at Chevron.*

package[2] *v* [T] **1** also **package up** to wrap or pack something so that it is ready to be sent somewhere: *Many firms send components overseas to be packaged.* | *materials for packaging food and consumer products* —**packaged** *adj*: *nutritional labeling on **packaged food*** | *the Anglo-Dutch **packaged goods** giant Unilever.*

2 to prepare something for sale, especially by adding something to it or by making it more attractive to buyers: *Ms. Fonda built a video empire by packaging her own fitness routines and selling them to millions of Americans.*

3 FINANCE if a financial institution packages loans, it buys the loans from lenders such as banks and uses the loans as BACKING for bonds. The financial institution uses the repayments on these loans to make payments to investors who buy the bonds. Money that the lenders get from the financial institution when it sells the bonds is used to make more loans to customers: *As seller of the mortgages, American Mortage forwarded repayments to the Federal Home Loan Mortgage Corporation, which had bought the loans and packaged them into securities.* —see also ***asset-backed security*** under SECURITY

package deal —see under DEAL[2]

packaged goods —see under GOODS

package price —see under PRICE[1]

pack·ag·er /ˈpækɪdʒə‖-ər/ *n* [C] **1** a company that prepares goods to be sent somewhere by wrapping or packing them: *In November, the company acquired Jimbo's Jumbos Inc., a processor and packager of peanuts.* | *Manufacturers and packagers have arranged to pick up transport wrappings from retailers for recycling.*

2 a company that puts together products, information, or other services and prepares them to so they can be sold together: *Credit-card issuers are major packagers of financial information, often telling merchants how much customers spend in their stores, and how often they shop there.* | *a television sports packager*

3 FINANCE a financial institution that puts together and sells investments offered by other companies and financial institutions: *John Nuveen & Co. is one of the largest packagers of tax-exempt unit investment trusts.*

4 FINANCE a financial institution that packages loans that it has bought from lenders and sells as bonds: *Student Loan Marketing Association, or Sallie Mae, lost 5/8 to 59. The student loan packager's growth prospects may be limited.* —see PACKAGE[2]

pack·ag·ing /ˈpækɪdʒɪŋ/ *n* [U] **1** material, boxes etc, used for wrapping goods to protect them, for example because they are being taken somewhere; PACKING: *recyclable plastic foam packaging*

2 the process of wrapping or packing goods so they are ready to be sent somewhere; PACKING: *the world leader in **food packaging** and distribution* | *The company has 15% of the $5 billion packaging business.*

3 the process of putting together products, information, or other services and offering them for sale together: *the packaging by cable companies of telephone and television services*

4 a way of presenting a plan, proposal etc so that it is more likely to be accepted: *the imaginative packaging of this unpopular tax*

packed /pækt/ *adj* extremely full of people or things: *President Yoh Kurosawa addressed a **packed press conference** yesterday.*

pack·er /ˈpækə‖-ər/ *n* [C] **1** another name for PACKAGER

2 someone whose work involves preparing goods and putting them in containers: *Glass items must be packaged by professional packers.*

pack·et /ˈpækɪ̈t/ *n* [C] **1** a small container, usually made of paper, with a set of things in it; PACK[1]: *United Biscuits produces 5 billion packets a year.* + **of**: *Supermarkets withdrew thousands of packets of chocolates after discovering a production error.* | *Under a direct-marketing promotion, Quaker Oats sent out packets of coupons to 18 million homes.*

postal packet *BrE* a container made of paper or card, used for sending goods through the post; MAILER *especially AmE*: *enquiries about a lost or damaged postal packet*

2 a set of related things or services which are offered or sold together; PACKAGE[1] + **of**: *He advised the firm to buy a packet of Jacobs Suchard shares to facilitate the takeover.* | *We are putting together a packet of services from various parts of the bank.*

3 another name for PACKAGE[1]

packet-switch·ing *n* [U] COMPUTING a way of sending a large amount of DATA (=information stored on a computer) between computers by dividing it into small pieces which are each sent separately and put together again when they are received: *Canada's Northern Telecom Ltd. will equip the Czech Republic with data packet-switching equipment for a public network.* —**packet-switched** *adj*: *45% of Transpac's packet-switched computer traffic comes from its Minitel terminals.*

pack·ing /ˈpækɪŋ/ *n* [U] **1** the process of wrapping goods or putting them in boxes, ready to be sent somewhere: *Tetra Pak have ruled out any interest in packing or distributing non-foods.*

2 packing note/list/slip a list of goods that have been packed and are ready to send: *The packing list read 'Parts for a Dairy Plant', but the contents were high-quality steel components more suited to weapons.*

3 materials such as paper, card, plastic etc, used for packing things: *Farmingdale, N.Y., the maker of paperboard packing* —see also ***postage and packing*** under POSTAGE

packing plant also **packing station** —see under PLANT

pack shot *n* [C] MARKETING a picture of a product or the packet it comes in, used in advertising to sell the product: *The consumer press will not be interested in any kind of pack shot, so brand and company names should be removed.*

Pac·Man defense /ˈpækmæn dɪˌfens/ —see under DEFENCE

pact /pækt/ *n* [C] a formal agreement between two countries, companies, groups of people etc, promising to do something for each other or help each other in some way: *Workers at Mazda ratified* (=made official) *a three-year pact that boosts their pay.* + **with**: *The National Institute of Health **signed a pact** with a Japanese drug company to develop and test a new anti-AIDS drug.* | *Mexico is in its fourth month of negotiations on a **free-trade pact** with the US and Canada.*

pad /pæd/ *n* [C] several sheets of paper fastened together, used for making notes: *Always have a pad and pen next to your telephone.*

legal pad a pad of yellow paper with lines, available mainly in the US

page[1] /peɪdʒ/ written abbreviation **p** *BrE*, **p.** *AmE* — *n* [C] **1 ad/advertising pages** [plural] the pages in magazines, newspapers etc that are used to advertise goods and services: *Fortune magazine will show a 13% increase in ad pages for the first quarter.*

2 business/sports etc pages [plural] the pages in magazines, newspapers etc that deal with business, sport etc: *The format could make The Wall Street Journal's financial-markets pages easier to read.* | *the outspoken columnists on the* ***op-ed pages*** (=where writers for the newspaper give their opinions on events)

3 front page the first page at the front of a newspaper, where the most important news is: *New York Newsday carried the item on its front page.* | *Mr. Guerin was profiled in* ***a front-page*** *Wall Street Journal* ***story***.

4 a piece of writing or pictures on a computer screen that will fill one side of a piece of paper when printed: *It is possible to build in a feature that will create a blank page where needed.* | *The system offered little control over* ***page breaks*** (=places where a new page starts). —see also FULL-PAGE, WHITE PAGES, YELLOW PAGES

page² *v* [T] to contact someone, using a pager: *The customer is paged automatically every time a new fax or email arrives.* —**paging** *n* [U] *Mtel will introduce nationwide paging.*

pag•er /ˈpeɪdʒə‖-ər/ *n* [C] a small device which makes a sharp sound to tell the person carrying it to contact someone by telephone: *The Japanese are developing pagers the size of credit cards.*

page traffic *n* [U] MARKETING a measure of the number of people who read a particular page in a magazine, newspaper etc: *In European countries, page traffic figures show higher noting of items on right-hand than left-hand pages.*

paid-in capital —see under CAPITAL

paint shop —see under SHOP¹

pair /peə‖per/ *v* [T] **1** if two companies, people, or things are paired, they are put into groups of two because they are connected in some way or will work together: *He claims his compasses led to the success of the Mobil Road Atlas when the two items were paired last year.* + **with**: *Chrysler paired with Hilton Hotels for a promotion giving frequent hotel guests free Chrysler cars.* | *Any cut in capital gains taxes would be paired with increases in other taxes.*

2 FINANCE if the shares in two companies are paired, they are considered to be shares in one company when they are bought or sold, even though the companies have separate management arrangements: *The companies are managed separately, but their* ***shares are paired for trading*** *in the market.*

pair sb/sth ↔ **up** *phr v* [I,T] if two people or companies pair up, or are paired up, they work together: *Six months ago Oeschli created a 'buddy system' which paired up employees.* + **with**: *To avoid losing his company, Mr. Ross paired up with Chris-Craft Industries Inc.*

pal•at•a•ble /ˈpælətəbəl/ *adj* if a suggestion, offer, proposal etc is made palatable, it is changed so that people will accept it and approve of it: *The proposal was engineered as a more palatable alternative to PacifiCorp's offer.* + **to**: *The offer will have to be made at a larger discount to be palatable to existing shareholders.*

pal•let /ˈpælɨt/ *n* [C] a large, flat wooden frame, used for lifting, storing, and moving very heavy things; SKID *AmE*

palm /pɑːm‖pɑːm, pɑːlm/ *v*

palm sb/sth ↔ **off** *phr v* [T] to persuade someone to accept something, especially by making them think it is better or more valuable than it really is: *Some suppliers have tried to palm off cheap telephones or outdated fax machines.* + **on**: *a worthless ring which he palmed off on an unwary buyer*

palm-sized *adj* palm-sized computers or other electronic devices are very small and can be carried easily: *a palm-sized electronic spreadsheet.* | *IBM plans to unveil a palm-sized hard disk drive that is likely to become the next generation of computer storage systems.*

palm•top /ˈpɑːmtɒp‖ˈpɑːmtɑːp, ˈpɑːlm-/ also **palmtop computer** *n* [C] a very small computer which can be carried in your pocket or a small bag; LAPTOP; NOTEBOOK: *These products include personal computers, printers, and a hot-selling palmtop.*

pal•try /ˈpɔːltri‖ˈpɒːl-/ *adj* very small in number or amount and therefore not useful, important, or valuable: *As interest rates fell, returns on fixed-income investments looked paltry compared with the stock market gains.* | *Squeezed by paltry ratings, broadcasting companies have canceled their newscasts in favor of entertainment shows.*

pam•phlet¹ /ˈpæmflɨt/ *n* [C] a thin book with paper covers, giving information about something: *The transfer is explained in a* ***glossy pamphlet*** *sent to the bank's customers.*

pamphlet² *v* [T] to deliver pamphlets in a particular area: *Estate agents have been pamphleting Clifton, looking for houses and flats to sell.*

pan•a•cea /ˌpænəˈsɪə/ *n* [C] something that people think will make everything better: *Further rate cuts, while helpful, are no* ***economic panacea***. + **for**: *Industry analysts quickly dismissed the idea that the international market is a panacea for profits.*

pan•el /ˈpænl/ *n* [C] **1** a group of people chosen to give advice or decide something: *An* ***advisory panel*** *will review new data on the safety of the products.*

consumer panel *BrE* MARKETING a group of people organized by a company or an organization doing MARKET RESEARCH to give their opinions about products: FOCUS GROUP *AmE*: *Using the findings of consumer panels across the country, we redesigned over 1,000 existing products.*

takeover panel FINANCE in Britain and some other countries, an official body that makes sure that TAKEOVERS (=occasions when one company buys another) are performed according to the rules it has established: *The takeover panel criticised the bank for failing to tell the panel that a client company's shares were rising rapidly while it was in takeover talks.*

2 MARKETING in market research, a group of people chosen to discuss particular products so that changes can be made to them or to the way they are sold: *These findings are backed up by the* ***panel research*** *I mentioned earlier.*

Pan European Sector Indices —see INDICES

pan•ic¹ /ˈpænɪk/ *n* [C,U] **1** a feeling of great fear and anxiety that makes you act without thinking: *The stock market crash left an air of panic from which many individual investors still haven't recovered.* | *By announcing future price increases, the administration touched off a consumer panic.*

2 panic buying/selling/trading when people are so anxious or worried about the future that they buy or sell goods, shares etc without thinking carefully first: *Manila shares plunged 10.9% in panic selling.* | *At a supermarket in Brussels, panic buying got so furious that the managers stopped trying to put sugar, coffee and mineral water on the shelves.*

panic² *v* past tense and past participle **panicked** present participle **panicking** [I,T] to suddenly become so frightened and anxious that you do things without thinking clearly, or to make someone do this: *Financial markets panicked, causing a run on the currency* (=causing the currency to lose a lot of its value). | *Crowds of depositors, many panicked by fears they would lose their life savings, formed outside the banks.*

pa•per /ˈpeɪpə‖-ər/ *n* **1** [U] material in the form of thin sheets used for writing things on, wrapping things etc: *plants that make chemicals for the* ***paper industry***

listing paper *BrE* **continuous paper** *AmE* [U] paper made for use on computer printers, where the sheets are joined together and can be separated later

2 [C] a newspaper: *Many* ***daily papers*** *have a financial section.* | *The Hollywood Reporter is a* ***trade paper*** (=one that reports on a particular industry) *for the film industry.*

3 [U] also **financial paper** FINANCE SECURITIES (=bonds etc) that can be traded on financial markets, rather than cash, and the CERTIFICATES (=documents) relating to them: *Mitsubishi is to **issue** (=make available and sell) as much as 200 billion yen of **paper**.* | *There are times when people are doubtful of the viability of the financial paper they hold.*

bank paper [U] BILLS OF EXCHANGE that can be traded on financial markets

bearer paper [U] any type of bond, share etc where the owner's name is not officially recorded, but the owner is considered to be the person who has it in their possession

commercial paper [U] a type of borrowing by companies and institutions in the form of loans where lenders do not have the right to take the assets of the borrower if they fail to repay. These loans are given for a period of a year or less: *Knight-Ridder recently refinanced from intermediate bonds to short-term commercial paper.* | *It is harder to tap international markets for short-term capital, though not impossible: **Eurocommercial paper** provides a way.* | *The rate on 90-day **prime commercial paper** (=one with the lowest risk of not being repaid) was 7.57%.*

fine paper [U] commercial paper with only a small risk that the borrower will not repay the loan and where, therefore, the seller of the paper gives a smaller DISCOUNT (=reduction in relation to its value) than usual when it is traded

4 papers [plural] documents used by a person or organization in their work: *The hotel **filed papers** (=officially sent them to the authorities) three weeks ago, seeking various building permits.* | *According to **court papers**, the judge's decision was based on the bank's failure to comply with banking laws.*

ship's papers documents that every ship must always have ready for officials to look at, including the CERTIFICATE OF REGISTRY, the LOG, and documents relating to any goods or passengers that are being carried

5 official document you need in order to do something: *Once all the necessary papers have been signed, the house is yours.*

working papers [plural] an official document you need in the US in order to get a job if you are young or were born outside the US: *Migrants lined up each morning to apply for working papers.*

paper bid —see under BID[1]

pa·per·chase /ˈpeɪpəˌtʃeɪs‖-pər-/ *n* [C usually singular] *disapproving* **1** an administrative process that takes more time and uses more documents than seem reasonable: *It is possible to claim back the tax, but this involves something of a paperchase.*

2 FINANCE an occasion when a company sells a lot of new shares to finance a series of takeovers; WALLPAPER

paper currency —see under CURRENCY

pa·per·less /ˈpeɪpələs‖-pər-/ *adj* a paperless system, process etc is one where information is held on and communicated by computers, without the use of paper: *Most of the information held by companies is still transferred to paper, despite promises long ago of the **paperless office**.* | *paperless ordering systems*

paper loss —see under LOSS

paper mill —see under MILL[1]

paper millionaire —see under MILLIONAIRE

paper money —see under MONEY

paper profit —see under PROFIT[1]

paper pusher *n* [C] *informal disapproving* someone whose job is doing unimportant office work; PEN-PUSHER: *unnecessary regulations that turn would-be entrepreneurs into paper pushers*

paper title —see under TITLE

par /pɑː‖pɑːr/ *adj* **1** [only before a noun] FINANCE the par value of a bond, share etc is its stated value when it is ISSUED (=sold for the first time). This is not necessarily the actual price paid for it. Bonds, for example, may be sold slightly above or below this value. The par value of bonds is used to calculate YIELD (=their profitability to the investor); FACE AMOUNT; FACE VALUE; NOMINAL VALUE

+ **at/above/below/under**: *The notes are trading at 10% above par, or $1,100 for each $1,000 face amount.* | *If the bond is trading below par, the issuer is likely to repurchase the bond in the market.* | *The bonds, which carry a coupon of 5.5%, were trading at about 97% of their **par value**.*

2 below/under par also **not up to par** to be less good than usual or below the proper standard; SUBPAR: *The casinos are not performing up to par because the entire economy is suffering.*

3 be on a par (with) to be at the same level, value, or standard: *The free trade agreement between the US and Turkey would be on a par with the one the US has signed with Canada.*

para written abbreviation for PARAGRAPH

par·a·chute[1] /ˈpærəʃuːt/ *n* —see GOLDEN PARACHUTE

parachute[2] *v* [I] *informal* if someone parachutes or is parachuted into a job, they are brought in from outside the organization and may not have much preparation or experience + **into**: *Mr. Iger needed all the help he could get when he parachuted into the job.*

par·a·digm /ˈpærədaɪm/ *n* [C] *formal* a good example of how a particular product, system etc can work or be produced + **of/for**: *J.J's success in building Tylenol into a best-seller has become a paradigm of consumer drug marketing.* | *IBM hope the Enterprise Alliance will be a paradigm for the twenty-first century.*

economic paradigm ECONOMICS the basic way that an economy works: *Moderate growth and low inflation are a new economic paradigm; the traditional business cycle no longer exists.*

paradigm shift —see under SHIFT[1]

par·a·graph /ˈpærəgrɑːf‖-græf/ *n* [C] a group of several related sentences in a piece of writing, with the first sentence beginning on a new line

par·a·le·gal /ˌpærəˈliːgəl/ *n* [C] *AmE* someone whose job is to help a lawyer; LEGAL EXECUTIVE *BrE*: *In corporate law departments, the number of paralegals increased by nearly 10%.*

par·al·lel /ˈpærəlel/ *adj* [only before a noun] parallel goods, imports etc are sold avoiding the DISTRIBUTION CHANNELS (=ways of making goods available to the public) approved by the makers: *Luxury brands manufacturers are angry about the sale of parallel goods in supermarkets.*

parallel data query —see under QUERY[1]

parallel imports —see under IMPORT[1]

parallel market also **parallel money market** —see under MARKET[1]

parallel port —see under PORT[1]

parallel processing —see under PROCESSING

pa·ram·e·ter /pəˈræmɨtə‖-ər/ *n* [C usually plural] a set of fixed limits that control the way something is done: *Business lawyers advise clients on the **legal parameters** within which economic activity must operate.* | *The agency now plans to propose a rule that would **set parameters** for exchange markets.*

par·cel[1] /ˈpɑːsəl‖ˈpɑːr-/ *n* [C] **1** an object or objects, packed together and wrapped up ready to be sent somewhere; PACKAGE[1]: *The next lot of parcels is being collected by TNT and delivered the next day.* | *the closure of BR's **parcel service**.* | ***parcel post** (=a mail service for collecting and delivering parcels)*

P

2 a piece of land that is one of several parts of a larger area of land: *UPS Properties owns 76 parcels of industrial land in 23 states.* | *HTV is redeveloping a 21-acre parcel of land close to its studios.*

3 FINANCE a set of related shares etc that are all sold or bought at the same time: *Disney boss Michael Eisner sold a big parcel of shares last week for £82.6 million.*

parcel[2] *v* **parcelled parcelling** *BrE*, **parceled parceling** *AmE*

parcel sth ↔ **out** *phr v* [T] to divide something into several parts, especially in order to share it between several people: *Farmers argue that parcelling out commercial farmland into small plots will reduce productivity.* | *Savers may withdraw up to $600 from their accounts and any balances will be parceled out in 12 monthly instalments.*

parcel sth ↔ **up** *phr v* [T] *BrE* to make something into a parcel by wrapping it, usually to send it somewhere

P

pare /peə‖per/ also **pare down** *v* [T] to gradually reduce a number or amount: *The company has been paring its regional accounting staff.* | *Both companies have pared down their operations in order to survive.*

par·ent /ˈpeərənt‖ˈper-/ also **parent company** *n* [C] if one company is the parent of another, it owns at least half the shares in the other company, and has control over it: *The Minneapolis-based parent of investment firm Piper announced record revenue and earnings.* | *Hibernia is exploring opportunities to improve the capital position of both the* ***parent company*** *and its subsidiaries.*

parent company —see under COMPANY

Pa·re·to-op·ti·mal /pəˌriːtəʊ ˈɒptɪ̈məl‖pəˌreɪtoʊ ˈɑːp-/ *adj* ECONOMICS if available RESOURCES (=things that you need to make or do something) have been given to people in a Pareto-optimal way, this is the most effective way of using them. In this situation, it is impossible to put one person in a better position by giving them more resources, without putting someone else in a worse position. In practice, resources are rarely given out in a Pareto-optimal way: *The government thinks that the distribution of financial resources is Pareto-optimal because different departments compete for resources.*

Pareto's law also **Pareto's principle**, **Pareto's rule** *n* ECONOMICS the idea that a small part of something is responsible for a large part of its value. For example, 20% of the work people do produces 80% of the rewards. It is also sometimes called the 80/20 rule

par·i pas·su /ˌpæri ˈpæsuː/ *adv formal* equally: *The Dollar Preference Shares will* ***rank pari passu*** *with the existing Redeemable Preference Shares.*

Paris Bourse —see under BOURSE

Par·is Club /ˈpærɪ̈s ˌklʌb/ *n* another name for the GROUP OF TEN

par·i·ty /ˈpærɪ̈ti/ *n* plural **parities** **1** [U] the state of being the same as or equal to something else + **with**: *The nations of Eastern Europe are hoping to move toward* ***economic parity*** *with* (=having the same wealth as) *the West.* | *The price cuts bring Sprint's prices into parity with those charged by AT&T.* | *The members have had voting parity with the governors in recent weeks.*

product parity [U] MARKETING the similarity that people think exists between all the different kinds of a particular product: *Perceptions of product parity are highest in markets like the US, where 220 different brands of breakfast cereal are available.*

2 [U] COMPUTING a system for finding mistakes in the sending of information from one computer or another

3 [U] FINANCE when one unit of a currency or COMMODITY (=oil, metal, farm product etc) is worth the same as one unit of another: *Platinum prices could decline further, perhaps reaching parity with gold.*

swap parity [C] the rate at which an investment can be exchanged for another investment of the same kind: *The swap parity was set at 85 Redland shares for every 100 Steetley shares.*

4 [C] ECONOMICS a figure representing what a particular currency is worth in another currency at a particular time: *One of the parities they will be checking is the dollar/yen rate.*

fixed parity [C] the official value of one currency in relation to another, in a system where currencies are fixed against each other: *The pound and the peseta were allowed to rise or fall by 6% from their central fixed parities against other member currencies of the Exchange Rate Mechanism.*

purchasing power parity abbreviation **PPP** [U] if two currencies have purchasing power parity, an amount of one country's currency needed to buy particular goods there will buy the same amount of goods in another country when exchanged into the currency of that country. This is used to see if currencies are correctly valued against each other on the CURRENCY EXCHANGE markets: *On the basis of purchasing power parity, the dollar was 'really' worth between DM1.80 and DM2.10 and between 160 and 180 yen, well above the current rates.* | *Most developing countries keep the exchange rates of their currencies low compared to purchasing power parity rate. This allows them to limit imports and stimulate exports.*

park[1] /pɑːk‖pɑːrk/ *n* [C] **industrial/science/business/retail park** also **office park** *AmE* an area of land where there are several small businesses or factories. The buildings there are often rented from local government: *Stapleton Airport became an industrial park after the opening of Denver's new airport.* | *Several large corporations have their regional headquarters in the office park.*

park[2] *v* [T] FINANCE if someone parks money, shares etc they leave them with another person or organization. If an investor does this to hide the fact that they own the money, shares etc, they are breaking the law: *Fund assets are parked to avoid exposing too large a portion to the risk of loss in the markets.* | *He was accused of helping investors park stock to conceal their true ownership.* —**parking** *n* [U] *He pleaded guilty to one count of engaging in a stock parking arrangement with a speculator.*

Par·kin·son's Law /ˌpɑːkɪnsənz ˈlɔː‖ˌpɑːrkɪnsənz ˈlɒː/ *n* a humorous theory which states that the amount of work that needs doing increases to fill the time available to do it in

par·lay /ˈpɑːli‖ˈpɑːrleɪ/ *v* [T] *AmE* to increase the value of something you have, especially your abilities, money, or success, by using your opportunities well **parlay sth into sth**: *She parlayed $2,500 and the contacts she made on vacation into a successful business.*

par·lia·ment /ˈpɑːləmənt‖ˈpɑːr-/ *n* [C] the group of people elected to make a country's laws and discuss important national issues: *The Dutch parliament voted to begin lifting economic sanctions.*

par·si·mo·ny /ˈpɑːsɪməni‖ˈpɑːrsɪ̈ˌmoʊni/ *n* [U] *formal* extreme unwillingness to spend money: *The gap between government parsimony and the needs of sport is filled by commercial sponsorship.* —**parsimonious** *adj*: *Republicans are claiming the budget plans are too parsimonious to protect the environment.* —**parsimoniously** *adv*

part /pɑːt‖pɑːrt/ *n* **1** [C,U] a piece of something such as an object, area, or group + **of**: *He will have to repay all or part of the money.* | *part of the trend towards globalisation*

2 [C] one of the separate pieces that a machine, vehicle etc is made of; COMPONENT: *Demand for* ***replacement parts*** *is increasing as consumers repair aging cars.* | *a supplier of engines, equipment and* ***spare parts*** (=parts used to replace original parts that are broken) *for commercial aircraft*

3 [U] some but not all of a particular thing or group of things: *Only part of the company is being sold.*

part delivery —see under DELIVERY

part-exchange *n* [C,U] *BrE* a way of buying a new car, television etc in which you give the seller your old car etc as part of the payment, or a car etc given as part of the payment for something new; TRADE-IN *AmE*: *He sold the car in part-exchange for another vehicle.* —**part-exchange** *v* [T] *I part-exchanged my old golf clubs for a new set.*

partial acceptance —see under ACCEPTANCE

partial equilibrium —see under EQUILIBRIUM

partial loss —see under LOSS

partial ownership —see ***part ownership*** under OWNERSHIP

par·tic·i·pate /pɑːˈtɪsəpeɪt‖pɑːr-/ *v* [I] **1** if someone participates in the management of a company, they help make important decisions, for example by being on the BOARD OF DIRECTORS + **in**: *Investors can participate in the management of the company they invest in, but must keep ownership at less than 50%.* | *If you've got good people, allow them to participate in factory management.*

2 HUMAN RESOURCES if employees of a company participate in its profits, they receive part of them + **in**: *Portland's workers have a stake in the corporation's success and they participate in its growth and profits.*

3 FINANCE if investors who are members of MUTUALS (=financial institutions such as some insurance companies, without shareholders) participate in their profits, they receive a share of the profits in addition to the normal payments from their investments —**participation** *n* [U] ***Employee participation*** *in corporate decisions helps reduce absenteeism.* | *Members also benefit from their participation in the profits of the mutual company.* | *the impact of worker participation schemes on enterprise performance*

participating preference share —see under SHARE

participating preferred stock —see under STOCK

par·ti·ci·pa·tive /pɑːˈtɪsəpətɪv‖pɑːrˈtɪsəˌpeɪtɪv/ *adj* a participative activity is one where many people work together in order to reach a result, decision etc: *Given the non-union culture of many US companies, why don't employers make their enterprises more participative?*

participative management —see under MANAGEMENT

particular average —see under AVERAGE[2]

par·tic·u·lars /pəˈtɪkjələz‖pərˈtɪkjələrz/ *n* [plural] facts and details about a person, event etc: *The company couldn't comment on particulars because it hadn't seen all the documents.* + **of**: *Judge Ward immersed himself in the particulars of the case.*

par·ti·tion /pɑːˈtɪʃən‖pər-, pɑːr-/ *n* **1** [C] a thin wall that divides one part of a large room from another, for example in an OPEN-PLAN office: *glass partitions*

2 [U] the act of dividing something —**partition** *v* [T] *The office was partitioned to contain the noise of the new computers.* | *The bidders intended to break up Perrier and partition the assets between Nestlé and BSN.*

partly-owned subsidiary —see under SUBSIDIARY[1]

partly-paid share —see under SHARE

partly-paid stock —see under STOCK[1]

part·ner /ˈpɑːtnə‖ˈpɑːrtnər/ *n* [C] **1** a company that works with another company in a particular activity, or invests in the same activity: *British Airways is actively seeking partners for joint ventures.* | *Air Products and its* ***equity partners*** *have invested in six energy projects.* | *foreign investors and their Russian joint-venture partners*

lead partner the most important partner in a partnership between two or more companies, for example the one that invests the most money: *Schal and its Japanese associates – including lead partner Ohbayashi Corp. – will build a control tower for the planned airport.*

merger partner a company that MERGES (=combines) with another company: *The company is seeking a merger partner as a way to raise its capital levels.*

strategic partner a company that another company works with because doing so is important for its development

2 someone who starts a new business with someone else by investing in it: *Like all new* ***business partners****, the three founders of the company hoped for smooth teamwork.*

sleeping partner *BrE* also **silent partner** a partner who invests in a business but does not take an active part in managing it; SILENT PARTNER

working partner also **active partner** a partner who takes an active part in the running of a business; ACTIVE PARTNER: *Our proposal is that we do business together as working partners with a common interest.*

3 a member of certain types of business or professional groups, for example partnerships of lawyers, architects etc: *Donald Andres, a tax partner at accountants Ernst & Young*

general partner a full member of a partnership: *Kohlberg Kravis Roberts & Co. is adding two general partners, further expanding its leadership.*

junior partner a partner in a partnership who is less important than a senior partner, but may become a senior partner later

lead partner another name for SENIOR PARTNER

managing partner a very important partner who makes management decisions in a partnership: *Mr Hielscher, formerly a senior partner, was promoted to chief operating officer and managing partner.*

senior partner an important partner in a partnership: *deals arranged by senior partners*

4 also **economic partner**, **trade partner**, **trading partner** a country that invests in another or is invested in by another, or that trades with another: *China is an important economic partner and provider of oil for North Korea.* | *Exports won't boom this year because so many of America's major trading partners are going through tough times, too.*

part·ner·ship /ˈpɑːtnəʃɪp‖ˈpɑːrtnər-/ *n* **1** [C] a relationship between two people, organizations, or countries that work together + **between**: *the partnership between US capital and Mexican labor*

public-private partnership [C] a partnership where investment comes from the government and from companies: *a public-private partnership between IT companies and the Department of Energy to develop new computer chips*

2 [U] the situation of working together in business: *Biogen developed the drug, which is marketed* ***in partnership with*** *Schering-Plough.* | *He* ***went into partnership with*** *Greek cement mogul George Tsatsos.*

3 [C] LAW, FINANCE a business organization made up of a group of accountants, lawyers etc who work together, or of a group of investors: *the Canadian partnership of the accounting firm PriceWaterhouseCooper* | *Prime sold a 65% stake in Howard Johnson to an* ***investment partnership*** *for $200 million.*

general partnership [C] in the US, a partnership where partners are responsible for the partnership's debts without limit up to the value of its assets: *A general partnership is the most suitable form of organization for many small businesses.*

limited partnership [C] written abbreviation **LP** in the US, a partnership where partners are responsible for the partnership's debts only up to the amount they originally invested: *The company has converted to a corporation from a limited partnership.*

private limited partnership [C] a private partnership with LIMITED LIABILITY (=where investors do not have to sell their own assets to repay debts if the organization goes BANKRUPT (=fails financially and has to close)

private partnership [C] a type of investment organization in the US, often one investing in property: *Horizon Healthcare Corp. has agreed to lease and manage four nursing homes owned by private partnerships.*

public partnership [C] in the US, a partnership open to outside investors: *One in five public partnerships is in financial trouble.* —see also DEED OF PARTNERSHIP

part order —see under ORDER[1]

part owner also **part-owner** —see under OWNER

part ownership also **part-ownership** —see under OWNERSHIP

part-paid share also **partly-paid share** —see under SHARE

part-payment also **partial payment** *n* [C,U] a payment that is part of the total payment for something; PAYMENT ON ACCOUNT: *Nothing at all has been paid. There has been no payment on account.*

parts per million —see PPM

part-time *adj* someone who has a part-time job only works for part of the week: *The forestry projects will generate part-time and seasonal employment.* | *He provides scientific expertise* ***on a part-time basis.*** —compare FULL-TIME, FLEXITIME —**part-time** *adv: 31% of women* ***work part-time***

par·ty /ˈpɑːti‖ˈpɑːrti/ *n* plural **parties** [C] **1** LAW the people or group of people involved in a legal case, argument, agreement etc: *It is difficult to obtain a ruling from the court if the other party contests* (=officially disagrees with) *the decision.* | *copies of relevant correspondence between the parties*

2 third party LAW when two people are involved in a legal case, a third party is anyone who is not directly involved but might be affected by it: *Touche Ross was criticised for not allowing third parties to see their report.* | *Switch from comprehensive to* ***third party insurance*** (=insurance covering anyone affected by an accident, as well as the person who takes out the insurance) *if your car's value has fallen.*

3 an organization whose members share the same political beliefs and aims and which tries to get elected to government. The word 'party' is often used in the name of the organization: *India's Bharatiya Janata Party* —see also CONCERT PARTY, WORKING PARTY

party wall *n* [C] PROPERTY, LAW a dividing wall between two house, apartments etc which belongs to both owners

par value —see under VALUE[1]

PASCAL /ˈpæskæl‖pæˈskæl/ *n* [singular] COMPUTING a type of computer language, often used for teaching people to program computers —compare COBOL

pass[1] /pɑːs‖pæs/ *v* **1** [T] if an official group passes a law, proposal etc, or it passes that group, it is accepted by them, especially by voting: *Shareholders of Fibreboard Corp. narrowly* ***passed a measure*** *doubling the shares in the company's employee stock option plan.* | *Congress this year will* ***pass a bill*** *giving banks permission to open branches nationwide.* | *Legislation similar to the anti-price-fixing bill passed the Senate last month.*

2 [I,T] to succeed in an examination, test etc: *Policyholders must pass a medical to qualify for lower insurance rates.* | *How could faulty valves have passed the inspections?*

3 [T] to give someone a piece of information, knowledge, a message etc that has been received from someone else **pass sth to/onto etc**: *Firms can't pass information to third parties until it is released by the stockmarket's own news service.* | *The transmitters pass phone calls to and from cellular phones.* **pass sth on/along**: *employees suspected of passing on confidential documents*

4 [I] LAW to go officially from one person's control or ownership to someone else's: *Sales will be recognised when title* (=ownership) *passes or when the contract is signed* + **to**: *The property had passed to him after his father's death.*

5 pass a dividend FINANCE to fail to pay the DIVIDEND on a share (=the part of the profit paid to shareholders) in a particular period of time, usually because of financial difficulties: *The steelwork group is passing its final dividend after profits plunged last year.*

6 [I,T] if a particular date or time passes, or you pass it, it goes by and is in the past: *After the* ***deadline has passed*** *the bids are brought upstairs for processing.*

7 pass 500/pass the $2,000 mark etc to go above a particular amount, number or level, as a total gradually increases: *Aluminum prices passed $1 a pound last week, a rise of 43% since March.* | *Israel's population passed the six million mark in 1999.*

pass sth ↔ **on** also **pass** sth ↔**along** *AmE phr v* [T] if a company passes on increased costs of providing products or services to its customers, it increases the prices of its products or services to pay for these costs. If the company passes on lower costs, it makes the prices of its products or services lower | **pass sth on/along to sb**: *Cable companies should pass on cost reductions to customers rather than earn fatter profit margins.*

pass sth ↔ **off** *phr v* [T] to pretend that something is more valuable than it really is in order to deceive people | **pass sth off as sth**: *The company had passed off brand-name drugs as its own.*

pass sb ↔ **over** *phr v* [T] if a person in an organization is passed over for a job, someone else is given a job they were expecting to get: *She was* ***passed over for*** *a key* ***promotion*** *after a reorganization of the London agency.*

pass sth ↔ **through** sth *phr v* [T] if money passes through a bank account or someone passes it through the account, it is put in the account for only a short time before being moved to another account. Sometimes this is done as a way of hiding where money comes from: *evidence suggesting $400 million in drug money passed through Ecuadorean financial institutions last year*

pass up *phr v* [T] **pass up a chance/opportunity/offer etc** to not use the chance etc to do or have something when it is offered: *You wonder, when you pass up a deal like that, whether you'll ever get one again.* | *Even careful consumers are finding these bargains too good to pass up.*

pass[2] *n* [C] a special document containing a person's name and often their photograph, showing that they are allowed to enter a particular building, travel somewhere etc: *Simply present your Executive Club card and* ***boarding pass*** (=one that allows you to get on a plane) *to receive a complimentary drink.*

pas·sage /ˈpæsɪdʒ/ *n* [U] LAW the progress of a law, bill etc through parliament before it takes effect: *A month after its passage, Italy's insider-trading law is continuing to stir debate.* + **of**: *One result of the oil crisis could be a slowdown in the passage of a tougher Clean Air Act.*

pass-book *n* [C] a book showing all the money going in and out of someone's bank account: *Auditors must examine bank statements and pass-books if these explain movements on the accounts.*

passing trade —see under TRADE[1]

pas·sive /ˈpæsɪv/ *adj* **1** [only before a noun] FINANCE passive investment activities are those in which the investor does not take part in making management decisions in the company they invest in, for example by being on its BOARD: *The New Jersey Casino Control Commission is considering changing its rule limiting passive institutional investing.*

2 passive electronic equipment, machines etc do not contain electrical power and are therefore only able to receive signals, not send them: *The invention improves the video capability of* ***passive liquid crystal displays.***

P

passive commerce —see under COMMERCE

passive loss —see under LOSS

pass·port /ˈpɑːspɔːt‖ˈpæspɔːrt/ *n* [C] a small book containing a person's name and photograph, given by a government to a citizen. It proves who the person is and allows them to leave or enter countries

pass-through *n* [U] *AmE* FINANCE an arrangement where payments on particular home loans are sent by the lender to a financial institution that has sold MORTGAGE-BACKED SECURITIES based on these loans. Mortgage-backed securities are bonds where interest payments on loans are used to pay interest to investors who have bought the bonds, and to repay the bonds when they MATURE (=reach the time when they must be repaid): *$200 million of* ***mortgage pass-through certificates*** (=bonds) *was underwritten by Shearson Lehman Hutton Inc.*

pass·word /ˈpɑːswɜːd‖ˈpæswɜːrd/ *n* [C] a series of secret letters or numbers that must be put into a computer before it can be used: *Some hackers even change the company password, making the system inaccessible to employees.*

past due *adv* past the time when a debt or payment should have been paid: *Nationwide, companies paid their bills an average of nine days past due.*

past due bill —see under BILL[1]

pa·tent[1] /ˈpeɪtnt, ˈpæ-‖ˈpæ-/ *n* **1** [C] an legal document giving a person or company the right to make or sell a new invention, product, or method of doing something and stating that no other person or company is allowed to do this: *We believe our patent covers the actual commercial process used in making the new drug.* | *alleged* ***patent infringement*** (=breaking the law by using a product, idea etc without permission) | *He said that Texas Instruments had beat Intel in* ***filing a patent*** (=making it official) *and it would be difficult to overturn it.*
2 patent pending a phrase used to say that someone has asked for a patent: *Although the company has a patent pending on its product, it doesn't plan on keeping it.*

patent[2] *v* [T] to obtain a patent, protecting the rights to make or sell a new invention, product, or method of doing something: *The drug is owned and patented by Hoffmann-La Roche.* —**patented** *adj* [only before a noun] *patented heat-transfer technology*

patent agent —see under AGENT

pat·en·tee /ˌpeɪtnˈtiː, ˌpæ-‖ˌpæ-/ *n* [C] a person or company who owns the patent for an invention, product, or method of doing something: *The patentee normally has up to 12 months to apply for patents in other countries.*

Patent Office *n* [C] a government department that deals with and approves patents

patent protection —see under PROTECTION

pa·ter·ni·ty /pəˈtɜːnɨti‖-ɜːr-/ *n* [U] LAW the fact of being the father of a particular child, or the question of who the child's father is: *The court was unable to act in instances where paternity couldn't be established.*

paternity leave —see under LEAVE

pat·ri·mo·ny /ˈpætrɨməni‖-mouni/ *n* [U] LAW property, goods etc that are passed through a family or nation over a very long period of time; INHERITANCE: *Under the service contract, any oil found remains the exclusive patrimony of the nation.*

pa·tron /ˈpeɪtrən/ *n* [C] **1** *formal* someone who regularly uses a particular shop, restaurant, hotel etc; CUSTOMER: *The library sought to ban Mr. Kreimer on the grounds that he disturbed other patrons.*
2 someone who supports the activities of a public organization, CHARITY etc, especially by giving money; BENEFACTOR: *It has been left to a small group of art historians, patrons and restorers to do something about the lost art treasures.*

pat·ron·age /ˈpætrənɪdʒ/ *n* [U] **1** *AmE* the support a customer gives a shop, restaurant etc by spending money there: *What will prevent the customer from shifting his patronage to someone else?*
2 the support given to an organization, CHARITY etc by a patron, especially financial support: *We hope that the new law will encourage* ***private patronage*** *of the arts.*
3 *disapproving* a system in which someone in authority helps people get important positions, jobs etc in return for their support: *The study found that promotions were based on patronage.*

pat·ron·ize also **patronise** *BrE* /ˈpætrənaɪz‖ˈpeɪ-, ˈpæ-/ *v* [T] **1** *AmE* to use or visit a particular shop, restaurant, hotel etc: *Many homosexuals patronize gay-owned companies simply because they feel more comfortable there.*
2 to speak to someone in a way that suggests that they are not as intelligent as you: *The agency has a reputation for patronizing clients who don't agree with its creative ideas.* —**patronizing** also **patronising** *BrE adj*: *It's patronizing not to expect women to fulfill a contract just because she has childcare responsibilities.*

pat·tern[1] /ˈpætən‖ˈpætərn/ *n* [C] **1** the regular way in which something happens, changes, or is done: *The standards are expected to* ***set a pattern*** *for cleaner, more expensive fuels.* + **of**: *a survey on the* ***spending patterns*** *of various nationalities*
2 pattern agreement/settlement/contract etc *AmE* an agreement etc between a company and a union based on other agreements with similar companies: *He disputed that the contract was a pattern settlement because it doesn't match contracts at foreign steel plants.* | *Some executives are grumbling that* ***pattern bargaining*** *is making competition with Japanese auto makers very difficult.*
3 be in a holding pattern to be in a period of time when very little trading, spending etc is taking place because people are not sure what to do next: *Investors are in a holding pattern waiting for clear signals about the economy's direction.*

pattern[2] *v* [T] **be patterned on/after** if one thing is patterned on another, it is very similar to it because it has been copied from it: *Credit Mobilier of America, a finance company patterned after a French venture* | *a model of economic development patterned on Japan's*

pau·per /ˈpɔːpə‖ˈpɒːpər/ *n* [C] LAW a person who has no money at all and has to depend on other people for support: *The court will refuse to grant* ***pauper status*** *to 'frivolous'* (=not serious or sensible) *petitions.*

pawn /pɔːn‖pɒːn/ *v* [T] to leave a valuable item with a pawnbroker in order to borrow money from them. If the person borrowing the money does not pay it back, the pawnbroker can sell the item to get back the debt, and any interest that is owed: *As credit has gotten tighter for many people, the number willing to pawn their cars has increased.*

pawn·bro·ker /ˈpɔːnˌbrəʊkə‖ˈpɒːnˌbroukər/ also **pawnbrokers** *n* [C] someone whose business is to lend people money in exchange for valuable objects: *Pawnbrokers are now allowed to charge any interest rate on loans above $2,500.*

pawn·shop /ˈpɔːnʃɒp‖ˈpɒːnʃɑːp/ *n* [C] a pawnbroker's shop

pay[1] /peɪ/ *n* [U] the money someone receives for the job they do: *She got the job, but it meant a big* ***pay cut.*** |

P

an **increase** *in* **hourly pay** | *All I want is a full day's work for a full day's pay.* | *The* **basic pay** (=the usual amount, without any extra) *is so low you end up putting in overtime.* —see also EQUAL PAY

back pay money an employer owes to workers, for example because a wage increase was late or because workers have not taken their holiday: *The system will calculate back pay, including overtime allowances.* | *The agency was ordered to restore $60 million* **in back pay** *that was saved by the cutbacks in hours worked.*

differential pay a system of pay that is supposed to show the relative importance of two jobs by paying different amounts for each job

free pay TAX the part of someone's income that is not taxed

holiday pay money employers pay to workers who are on holiday

performance-related pay also **merit pay** pay that increases when your work improves or becomes more productive and goes down if the opposite happens: *Performance related pay and individual performance review has been introduced for general managers.* | *For teachers, the Government intends to link merit pay and promotion to an appraisal scheme.*

premium pay additional pay for working outside normal working hours; OVERTIME PAY: *The company proposed a reduction in premium pay on weekends.*

sick pay money employers pay to workers who are not well enough to work: *the likelihood of some cut in sick pay*

strike pay money paid by a union to workers who are on strike

take-home pay the amount of money workers receive, after taxes, insurance etc have been taken off: *One policy that nearly all sides favor is an increase in families' take-home pay.*

vacation pay pay given to workers while they are on holiday: *Workers get 30% of their compensation in vacation pay and bonuses.*

pay² past tense and past participle **paid** *v* **1** [I,T] to give a person or company money for a product or service they have supplied: *How much can you afford to pay?* | *GM won't pay a Christmas bonus to salaried employees next year.* + **for**: *Farmers desperately need hard credit to pay for seed and fertilizer.* | *The proportion of shoppers willing to* ***pay more*** *for special brands has fallen sharply.* **pay sb for sth**: *United has agreed to pay Pan Am $290 million for its London routes.*

2 [T] to give a person or company money you owe them: *Celutel has been trying to raise cash to* ***pay debt***. | *The association has set up the loan fund to help its members* ***pay fines***. | *Shoppers in Newfoundland* ***pay*** *19%* ***tax*** *on purchases of goods and services.*

3 [I,T] to give someone money for the job they do: *Cane cutters here are paid about $1.50 per ton.* | *attempts by management not to pay employees overtime*

4 [T] FINANCE if investments pay a particular amount of money or rate of interest, the investors who own them will receive that amount of profit: *Our Gold Account is currently paying a 5.3%* ***interest rate***. | *All the current junk bonds pay cash interest.* | *Under the current deal, BBDO stock is paying about 10 times last year's earnings.*

5 [I] if a shop or business pays, it makes a profit: *If the Chinese can ship this equipment 12,000 miles, how is it that British industry cannot make it pay?*

pay sb/sth **back** *phr v* [T] to give someone the money you owe them; REPAY: *The salespeople working there made more than $40,000 before paying back over-claimed expenses.* **pay sb back (sth)**: *Some investors say that if McCaw falters, it can sell assets to pay them back.* | *Orion expects to pay Mr. Kluge back his original investment plus a return of 13% a year.* **pay sth back**: *guarantees on loans to foreign countries that are paid back in full*

pay down sth *phr v* [T] *AmE* to pay a person or company part of the money you owe them, reducing the total owed: *Americans paid down their installment credit balances last month by $1 billion.* | *The money will be used primarily to* ***pay down*** *short-term* ***debt***.

pay off *phr v* **1** [T] **pay sb/sth off** to pay all the money you owe a person or company: *BHC also has* ***paid off*** *all its long-term* ***debt***. | *$1.2 billion in funds was originally earmarked to* ***pay off creditors***. | *The money left to her by her father made it possible to* ***pay off*** *the* ***loan***.

2 [I] if a plan, idea etc pays off, it is successful: *He predicted the company's modernization program would result in higher sales. So far, it has paid off.* | *Investors shouldn't expect NCR's more aggressive strategy to pay off right away.*

pay sth **out** *phr v* [T] to give a person or company money you owe, especially when it is a large amount: *Mutual funds are required to pay out a quarterly cash dividend.* | *The price increase was based on an analysis of the revenue that Chase receives and the fees it pays out.*

pay·a·ble /ˈpeɪəbəl/ *adj* [not before a noun] **1** a bill, debt etc that is payable must be paid, often by a certain date: *Shareholders will receive a final dividend of 0.75p, payable on July 1.* | *Sanders' donation was $450,000, payable over three years.*

2 accounts payable *AmE* ACCOUNTING money that a company owes; CREDITORS *BrE*: *The company's liabilities include accounts payable totaling $29.1 million.*

3 dividends payable ACCOUNTING a figure included in a company's accounts showing the amount that has been or will be paid in dividends for a particular period of time: *Surprisingly, the profit and loss account reveals in the latest year that dividends payable were greater than profits for the year.*

4 note payable ACCOUNTING a note relating to money that a company owes: *Proceeds from the share offering will be used to repay a portion of the company's current notes payable.* —see also ***bills payable*** under BILL OF EXCHANGE

5 payable to sb a cheque that is payable to someone has that person's name written on it and must be paid only to them: *Send a postal order or cheque for £2.50* ***made payable to*** *Dent & Reuss Ltd.*

pay·a·bles /ˈpeɪəbəlz/ *n* [plural] ACCOUNTING loans, debts etc owed by a company, especially those which are expected to be paid within the financial year: *Against total assets of NZ$42.2 billion, the company has borrowings of NZ$46.7 billion and payables of NZ$3.4 billion.* —compare RECEIVABLES

pay and file *n* [singular] TAX, ACCOUNTING a system used in Britain since 1993 for paying CORPORATION TAX (=a tax paid by companies on their profits). The company calculates how much tax it owes and pays that amount when it sends the tax forms to the INLAND REVENUE (=the tax authority), where the calculations are checked

pay as you earn —see PAYE

pay-as-you-go *adj* [only before a noun] a pay-as-you-go arrangement is one in which a customer pays for a product or service as they use it, rather than paying the whole amount before or after receiving it: *PTI Environmental Service will conduct the study, which will be funded on a* ***pay-as-you-go basis***.

pay·back /ˈpeɪbæk/ *n* [C,U] **1** the money or rewards gained from a new business, project etc: *One hurdle that often trips new entrepreneurs is the amount of time invested in a start-up before realizing any payback.* | *It is a solid project that will generate hard currency with a fairly short* ***payback period*** (=the period of time needed to get back the cost of an investment)

2 FINANCE an illegal payment by a financial institution to an investor to replace money they have lost: *Executives were worried that the credit transfer would look like payback.* | *The* ***payback deals*** *might never have come to light had local tax officials not leaked the schemes to the press.*

P

pay bargaining —see *wage bargaining* under BARGAINING

pay·cheque *BrE*, **paycheck** *AmE* /ˈpeɪ-tʃek/ *n* [C] **1** a cheque that pays someone's wages: *At the end of the month, stretching your money until the next paycheque arrives often becomes difficult.*
2 *AmE* the amount of money someone earns: *The new management has been willing to slash employees' paychecks to increase earnings.*

pay claim —see under CLAIM[1]

pay day *n* [C] the day on which workers receive their wages: *Pay day always fell on a Thursday, but now workers are paid monthly.*

pay·dirt /ˈpeɪdɜːt‖-dɜːrt/ *n AmE* **hit/strike paydirt** *informal* to make a useful or valuable discovery that will make a lot of money; STRIKE GOLD *BrE*: *Sales have been flat, and manufacturers can only hope they'll strike paydirt with the new toy.*

PAYE *n* TAX pay as you earn; a system for paying tax used in Britain and some other countries in which tax is taken off workers' wages and paid directly to the government: *Employees whose tax is deducted at source under PAYE are not sent an income tax return.*

pay·ee /peɪˈiː/ *n* [C] **1** BANKING the person or organization to whom money, especially a cheque, must be paid: *The Eurocheque is free of charge to its payee.* | *Reports can show transactions by date, amount or payee.* —compare PAYER
2 **account payee (only)** written abbreviation **a/c payee (only)** *BrE* BANKING a phrase written on a cheque to show it can only be paid into the account held by the person whose name is written on the cheque

pay envelope *n* [C] *AmE* another name for PAY PACKET

pay·er also **payor** /ˈpeɪə‖-ər/ *n* [C] a person or organization that pays a particular bill, debt etc: *Further tax relief is given to* ***mortgage payers****.* | *Credit agencies always check whether someone has been a* ***bad payer*** (=does not pay their bills) *in the past.* —compare PAYEE

pay freeze also **wage freeze** —see under FREEZE[2]

paying agent —see under AGENT

paying bank —see under BANK[1]

paying-in *adj* **paying-in book/slip** *BrE* a special book or piece of paper that a customer fills in when they put money in their bank account; DEPOSIT BOOK; DEPOSIT SLIP: *When you want to pay cash or cheques into your account, complete one of the paying-in slips provided.*

pay-in-kind debenture —see under DEBENTURE

pay·load /ˈpeɪləʊd‖-loʊd/ *n* [C] the amount of goods or passengers that are carried by a vehicle or aircraft, measured by their weight, and for which payment is received: *The Federal Express freighters will carry a* ***gross payload*** *of 187,500 pounds.*

pay·mas·ter /ˈpeɪˌmɑːstə‖-ˌmæstər/ *n* [C] **1** a person or organization responsible for giving people their wages or the money they are owed: *As trusted paymasters, banks will continue to be asked to pay letters of credit after examining bills of lading.*
2 *journalism* someone powerful who pays other people to do something illegal or dangerous for them: *his trade union paymasters*

Paymaster General *n* **the Paymaster General** in Britain, the member of government responsible for making payments by government departments: *The Comptroller is charged with authorizing the amounts paid out by the Paymaster General.*

pay·ment /ˈpeɪmənt/ *n* **1** [C,U] an amount of money that must be or has been paid, or the act of paying it: *Some suppliers to the company had tightened credit terms, allowing the company only 30 days to* ***make payments****.* | *$900 million of loans to help the country* ***meet payments*** (=make them on time) *for energy imports* | *Cash discount is an allowance off a debt given to encourage* ***prompt payment*** (=payment on time). | *I enclose a cheque* ***in payment of*** *my account.* | *The plan also calls for* ***payment in full*** *to creditors by 31 Dec.*
2 [C,U] one of the methods of paying for something, and the act of using one of these methods: *Buyers made the first payment by letter of credit instead of cash.* | *Discounts are given for* ***cash payment****.* | ***quarterly payments*** | ***direct-debit payments***

credit card payment also **card payment** ◆ [C,U] a payment made to buy something using a CREDIT CARD: *Some states allow card payments for certain taxes.*
◆ [C,U] a regular payment made by the user of a CREDIT CARD to a credit card company to pay for what they have bought using the card, and any interest: *High finance charges are made if customers fail to meet their monthly card payments*

3 [C,U] amounts of money paid at the different stages of buying something or being paid for something

advance payment [C] a payment made before a product is delivered or a piece of work is completed: *Many export contracts contain provisions for advance payments to meet the exporter's costs.*

down payment [C] the first payment made in the repayment of a large debt, such as a mortgage: *Canada Mortgage reduced to 5% the minimum down payment that first-time homebuyers must make.* | *Unsecured creditors should agree to accept a down payment of around 35p in the pound.*

final payment [C,U] the last of a series of payments: *They decided his services were no longer necessary and in May he was given a final payment.* | *The airline has received final payment for the sale of its trans-Atlantic routes.*

goodwill payment ◆ [C] a payment made to senior members of a business as a reward for hard work: *Goodwill payments can benefit from tax relief.*
◆ [C] a payment made for the GOODWILL of a business when it is bought: *A purchaser will only be able to recover its goodwill payment if the business is a going concern without too many problems.*
◆ [C] a payment made by a supplier to a customer because of a problem the customer has had, for example with quality or late delivery of goods

instalment payment *BrE* **installment payment** *AmE* [C,U] one of a series of payments for a debt, loan etc: *repayment in eight installment payments at six-month intervals*

interim payment [C] a payment made while waiting for other payments, or the size of other payments, to be decided: *The chemical company has made interim payments in some cases while damages are negotiated.*

progress payment [C] a payment made for an amount of work already done on something. Sometimes progress payments are made in the form of a loan: *The Air Force has halted all progress payments on the C-17, pending a cost-performance review.*

4 **payment on account** a payment that is part of the total payment for something; PART-PAYMENT: *Nothing at all has been paid. There has been no payment on account.*
5 **payment in kind** a way of paying for something using goods or services rather than money
6 **payment on delivery** abbreviation **POD**, also **payment on receipt of goods** payment that is made at the time when goods are delivered, often made to the person delivering them: *Sellers prefer payment on delivery, but buyers have a different view.*
7 **payment on invoice** payment that is made when a buyer receives an INVOICE (=document giving details of goods ordered, their cost, the time allowed for payment etc)
8 **payment on statement** payment that is made when a

P

buyer receives a statement saying how much is owed on an account at an agreed later date

9 [C] money paid to people for the work they do

bonus payment [C] a payment made for doing your job better than normal, for example producing or selling more goods than usual: *GM changed its management bonus payments to stock from cash.*

royalty payment ◆ [C] a payment made to a writer, musician etc that depends on how many of their books, records etc have been sold, played etc: *a dispute over royalty payments between a publisher and one of its authors*

◆ [C] a payment made to a company or person that has invented or developed a product by the company that sells it: *Wyeth will have the rights to manufacture and market the drugs and Oncogene will receive royalty payments based on product sales.*

salary payment [C] a payment made to an employee for the work they have done, especially one who is paid monthly: *Employees' contributions will be deducted from salary payments by employers.*

wage payment [C] a payment made to an employee for the work they have done, especially one who is paid weekly: *A freeze was imposed on wage payments in a large part of the public sector.*

10 [C] money paid to people who are ill, unemployed etc

disability payment [C] a payment made to people who are ill, injured etc: *He hasn't received a penny in disability payments since his accident.*

social security payment [C] money taken by the British government from people's wages to pay for the system of payments to people who are unemployed, ill etc: *high social security payments to finance the state pension system*

transfer payment [C] *AmE* in the US, money given to people by the government which is neither wages, nor payment for goods or services. For example, SOCIAL SECURITY payments are transfer payments: *The recession means consumers have been forced to rely more on government transfer payments and interest income.*

welfare payment [C] *AmE* a payment made by the US government to people who are unemployed, ill etc: *Placing limits on welfare payments has an appeal to taxpayers.*

11 [C,U] FINANCE money paid to SHAREHOLDERS, or the repayments of loans, bonds etc to lenders: *Brazil hasn't made payments on its bank debt in recent months.* | *Creditors have also agreed to* ***reschedule payments*** (=accept later payment) *of senior debt initially due next month.*

accelerated payment [C,U] a payment made when a borrower is forced to pay back a loan more quickly than originally planned, usually because of the danger of DEFAULT (=failure to repay): *Failure to restructure its debt led its bankers to demand accelerated payments of their loans.*

balloon payment [C] a large final repayment on a BALLOON LOAN (=a loan where there are small repayments during the life of the loan, followed by one or two large repayments): *News Corp.'s next big debt hurdle is a $2.4 billion balloon payment.*

debt payment [C,U] a repayment of a loan, bond etc: *The company is* ***current on its debt payments*** (=has made all repayments on time).

dividend payment [C] a payment of a part of a company's profits to its SHAREHOLDERS (=the people who own shares in it): *Weak dividend payments may be one indication that profits are in a downturn.*

interest payment [C] a payment that repays interest on a loan, bond etc, rather than paying off any of the original amount: *The company lacks cash to make interest payments on its junk bonds.*

principal payment [C] a payment that pays off part or all of the original amount of a loan, bond etc rather than any interest payment: *The restructuring eliminates all principal payments for 10 years.*

12 [C] money paid to someone to settle a claim, dispute etc: *Lawyers say that this move is likely to delay the payment of damages to many victims.*

compensation payment [C] a payment made to someone who has suffered because of someone else's mistake: *Workers' compensation payments have no limit under most state funds.*

ex gratia payment [C] a payment made to help someone or as a gift, not because you have a legal duty to make it: *The government would make ex gratia payments to all investors who had suffered loss, while stressing that it had no legal liability to pay compensation.* —see also BALANCE OF PAYMENTS, PART-PAYMENT

payment-by-results *n* [U] a system of paying people according to how much they produce or sell: *Wages in the clothing industry are based on a payment-by-results system.*

payment terms —see under TERM[1]

pay·off /ˈpeɪɒf‖-ɒːf/ *n* [C] **1** a good result from a particular plan, project etc: *Are you looking for a low-risk strategy that promises a payoff regardless of what the stockmarket does?* | *The biggest payoff came in May, when Salomon estimates it made as much as $18.4 million.*

2 a payment made to someone in order to stop them causing trouble: *The company refused to* ***make the payoff*** *and complained to the authorities.*

pay·o·la /peɪˈəʊlə‖-ˈoʊlə/ *n* [U] *informal* the practice of making secret payments to someone so they will use their influence, especially on television or radio, to help sell a particular product: *a four-year investigation into payola in the record industry* —compare BRIBE[1]

pay·or /ˈpeɪə‖-ər/ *n* [C] another spelling of PAYER

pay·out /ˈpeɪ-aʊt/ *n* [C] **1** a large sum of money, given to someone for the work they have done: *an increase in commission payouts for some top-producing brokers*

2 INSURANCE a payment made to someone who has made an insurance claim: *Allianz's profit fell 13% because of big payouts related to a series of hurricanes.*

3 FINANCE a DIVIDEND payment (=part of a company's profits for a particular period of time paid to people who own shares in it): *The board voted to cut the payouts in response to current operating results.*

payout ratio —see under RATIO

pay packet also **pay envelope** *AmE*, **wage packet** *BrE* — *n* [C] an envelope containing a worker's pay and a PAY SLIP. In Britain, the phrase 'pay packet' is often used to talk about the amount of money workers receive: *Workers earning £115 a week or more will receive just over £3 extra in their weekly pay packets.* | *Hitting the pay packet in increased taxes always affects the housing market.*

pay-per- *adj* **pay-per-view/pay-per-call** a system in which customers pay for the particular television programmes they watch or the number of minutes they use a phone: *Cable subscribers have been reluctant to pay $4 or $5 to see a movie on a* ***pay-per-view channel***. | *The bill requires pay-per-call services to disclose costs before consumers begin ringing up charges.* —compare PAY-AS-YOU-GO

pay period —see under PERIOD

pay rise —see under RISE[2]

pay·roll /ˈpeɪrəʊl‖-roʊl/ *n* **1** [C,U] the total amount of wages paid to all the people working in a particular company or industry: *Hanover Corp. have cut their total payroll by 7% since the merger.* | *More than half the state budget goes to payroll and only 11% to public works.*

2 [U] HUMAN RESOURCES the activity of managing wage and SALARY payments for employees: *all the jobs normally performed by a corporate bureaucracy – everything from facilities management to payroll to hiring and firing*

be on the payroll (=be employed by a particular company): *Under the plan, every employee on the payroll can buy 100 shares at $127.25 each.*—**payrolled** *adj* [only before a noun] *the hospital's payrolled doctors*

payroll tax —see under TAX[1]

pay scale —see under SCALE

pay settlement —see under SETTLEMENT

pay slip —see under SLIP[2]

pay spine *n* [C] —see ***payscale*** under SCALE

pay talks —see under TALKS

pay TV *n* [singular] a system in which customers pay for the length of time they watch a particular television programme or CHANNEL: *Pay TV will be delivered on at least four channels.* | *Time Warner dominates the pay TV market with more than 20 million subscribers.*

PBX *n* [singular] private branch exchange; a telephone system which makes it possible to send calls between the different telephone numbers used in an office: *R&B will offer complete telephone services via a PBX, installed in its buildings.*

PC *n* [C] **1** personal computer; a small computer that can be used by one person, or connected to a NETWORK; MICROCOMPUTER: *IBM compatible PCs* | *Although US companies dominate the world PC business, they have less than 10% of the Japanese market.*
2 written abbreviation for PER CENT

PCC *n* Press Complaints Commission; an organization in Britain whose job is to make sure writers of newspapers, magazines etc obey all the rules

pcm *adv* per calendar month; used to show often something has to be paid, especially rent: *The overhead costs include $350 pcm.*

PCN *n* personal communications network; a system for connecting MOBILE PHONES; GSM: *Later this year, Mercury will be launching its* ***digital PCN****.*

pct. written abbreviation for PER CENT

PDA *n* [C] COMPUTING personal digital assistant; a very small, light computer that you can carry with you; NOTEPAD; PALMTOP; PERSONAL ORGANIZER

PDF *adj* COMPUTING portable document format; a PDF computer file is one that can be read using many different types of software: *PDF files can describe documents containing any combination of text, graphics and images.*

PDQ *n* COMPUTING parallel data query; a system on a computer that can deal with several problems, tasks etc at the same time: *Barclay's PDQ terminals can read Visa, Access, American Express and Diner's Club cards as well as some store and fuel cards.*

PDR FINANCE written abbreviation for PRICE-DIVIDEND RATIO

peak[1] /piːk/ *n* [C] the time when prices, shares etc have reached their highest point or level: *Even Microsoft, which is expected to sustain its brisk growth, is 15% below its peak.* | *The company's share of overseas assets* ***reached a peak*** *in 1999.* + **of**: *Rents have fallen as much as 50% from their peak of three years ago.* | *The FTSE 100 climbed to 2577.1, just below the* ***intraday peak*** *the highest point on a particular trading day of 2580.1.*

peak[2] *adj* **1 peak level/price/rate etc** the highest level etc something reaches: *Many Japanese investors bought property at peak prices just before values began to slump.* | *The company expects to hit* ***peak production*** *by 2004.*
2 peak time/period/hours/season the time etc when the greatest number of people in a country are doing the same thing, using the same service, etc: *Our manufacturing process needs to reduce the electric power it uses at peak periods.* | ***off-peak travel*** (=travel that is not at the peak time)

peak[3] *v* [I] to reach the highest point or level: *The Bundesbank President declined to say whether German interest rates had peaked.* + **at**: *Sources estimate that output from the oilfield will peak at about 25,000 barrels a day.* | *Cascade's stock peaked at $11.50.* + **out**: *European metal dealers have been buying copper only as needed while waiting for prices to peak outreach the highest expected level.*

peak fare —see under FARE

peak season fare —see under FARE

pea•nuts /ˈpiːnʌts/ *n* [U] *informal* an amount of money so small it is hardly worth mentioning: *Some of the best investments are made for peanuts.* | *The estimated surplus of more than 3 million tons is peanuts in the context of total production.*

pecking order —see under ORDER[1]

pec•u•la•tion /ˌpekjᵘ̈ˈleɪʃən/ *n* [U] *formal* the act of obtaining or using money dishonestly; EMBEZZLEMENT

pe•cu•ni•a•ry /pɪˈkjuːniəri‖-nieri/ *adj formal* LAW connected with or consisting of money: *Mr Wallach did not cause the company to* ***suffer any pecuniary loss****.*

peer group —see under GROUP

peg /peg/ *v* past tense and past participle **pegged** present participle **pegging** [T] **1** to fix something such as prices or wages at a particular level, or fix them in relation to something else **peg sth to sth**: *The Swedish krona has been pegged to the European Currency Unit.* **peg sth at**: *Florida orange production was pegged at 139 million boxes.*—**peg** *n* [C usually singular] *Banks use the base rate as a peg to set interest rates on loans.*
2 *AmE* to state what you believe an amount to be or what you believe will happen **peg sth at**: *Some analysts peg the losses at $125 million.* **peg sb as sth**: *Opinion polls peg him as her likely successor.* —see also CRAWLING PEG, OFF-THE-PEG

pegged currency —see under CURRENCY

pen•al•ty /ˈpenlti/ *n* plural **penalties** [C] **1** a punishment for breaking a law or rule + **for**: *Maximum penalties for insider trading will be raised to 50 million yen.* | *The* ***stiff*** *severe* ***penalties*** *facing the eight racketeers are likely to act as a strong deterrent.* | *Drexel agreed to* ***pay penalties of*** *$650 million in connection with the plea.*
2 an amount of money someone has to pay if they do not keep to a legal agreement, especially an agreement with a bank + **for**: *There is a 10% penalty for withdrawing funds in the first 3 years.*

surrender penalty also **surrender charge** INSURANCE an amount of money someone owning an insurance policy has to pay if they stop the policy before it MATURES (=becomes due for payment): *Most annuities have steep surrender charges in the first seven years.* | *Investors should always compare surrender penalties.*

penalty clause —see under CLAUSE

pence /pens/ abbreviation **p** *BrE* the plural of PENNY

pencil pusher *n* [C] *AmE* a PEN PUSHER

pend•ing[1] /ˈpendɪŋ/ *prep formal* while waiting for something, or until something happens: *A decision has been delayed pending further inquiries.*

pending[2] *adj* **1** [not before a noun] *formal* not yet decided or settled: *Two lawsuits remain pending against the company.* | *Although the company has a* ***patent pending*** *on its product, it doesn't plan on keeping it.*
2 *formal* something that is pending is going to happen soon: *The bank said its poor performance would not affect its pending merger with BankAmerica.*
3 pending file/tray a place for putting papers, letters etc that have not yet been dealt with: *The messages have all been placed in his pending file.*

P

pen•e•trate /'penətreɪt/ *v* [T] if a company penetrates a particular market or area, it starts selling goods or services in a new market etc: *Sanofi has been struggling to* ***penetrate the US market.***

pen•e•tra•tion /ˌpenə'treɪʃən/ *n* [U] MARKETING **1** when a product starts to be sold in a new area or to a new group of people: *The workstation is becoming cheaper and portable, continuing its* ***penetration of the*** *PC* ***market.***
2 how much of a particular market one company's sales or one product's sales cover. This can be shown as a percentage of the possible sales in that market: *Camcorders are found in only 14% of US homes. In Japan, penetration has reached 20%.*

penetration pricing —see under PRICING

pen•ni•less /'penɪləs/ *adj* having no money: *Many of the migrants arrive penniless.*

P

pen•ny /'peni/ *n* [C] **1** *BrE* abbreviation **p** plural **pence** a unit of money used in Britain since 1971. There are 100 pence in one pound: *It only costs a few pence.* | ***a 20 pence piece*** (=coin worth 20 pence)
2 *BrE* plural **pennies** a small coin, used in Britain since 1971, worth one hundredth (1/100th) of a pound: *a bag of pennies*
3 *AmE* plural **pennies** a small coin worth one CENT (1/100th of a dollar) in the US and Canada

penny-pincher *n* [C] someone who does not like to spend money: *In spite of his reputation as a penny-pincher, he has some expensive tastes.* —**penny-pinching** *adj*: *discounts aimed at penny-pinching consumers*

penny share —see under SHARE

penny stock —see under STOCK[1]

pen pusher *n* [C] *BrE* someone who has a boring and unimportant job in an office; PENCIL PUSHER *AmE*

pen•sion[1] /'penʃən/ *n* [C] an amount of money paid regularly by a government, company, or financial institution to someone who is officially considered to be too old or too ill to earn money by working; RETIREMENT PLAN *AmE*: *If you retire at 55 you can expect your pension to be half the size it would be at age 65.* | *He lives in a modest house* ***on a*** *small* ***pension.*** | ***Pension contributions*** (=money that you give or an employer gives to pay for the pension that you will get) *attract no tax.*

disability pension also **disablement pension** a pension paid to someone who cannot work any more because they are ill or injured: *He retired from the force with a disability pension.*

occupational pension a pension from a past employer, rather from the government: *Members of* ***occupational pension schemes*** *should think carefully before transferring to private personal pension plans.*

old age pension *informal* a RETIREMENT PENSION

personal pension a pension that someone arranges for themselves with an insurance company, or that is arranged for them by a BROKER: *The law changed in 1998 to allow individuals to opt out of their company plans and start a personal pension.*

portable pension a pension that can be moved if you change your employer, without you losing any money

private pension a PERSONAL PENSION

retirement pension a pension paid to someone who has reached the official age when you retire, especially one paid by the government: *The state retirement pension was £52 per week.*

self-administered pension a pension arranged and controlled by the employer, not through an insurance company. This is usually part of a small pension plan, which may cover only one employee

stakeholder pension in Britain, a pension in addition to the basic state pension. Employees pay into stakeholder pensions through their company, TRADE UNION, or other collective organization, and the state also contributes to it: *Stakeholder pensions are at the heart of the British government's proposals for pension reform.*

state pension a pension paid by the government: *people wholly dependent on the state pension*

top-hat pension an extra pension offered to the managers of the highest rank in a company, in addition to the normal company pension

top-up pension *BrE* a pension in addition to the normal state pension, provided by the state or a financial institution: *Public sector employees in France have schemes for top-up pensions from the state.*

pension[2] *v*
pension off [T] *BrE informal* **1 pension** sb ↔ **off** to make someone who is old or ill leave their job and pay them a pension: *He had worked hard all his life, and in three years they would pension him off.*
2 pension sth ↔ **off** to get rid of something because it is too old or not useful any more: *Old coal-fired power stations will be pensioned off.*

pen•sion•a•ble /'penʃənəbəl/ *adj* **1** having the right to receive a pension: *We wish to encourage people to go on working after* ***pensionable age*** (=the age at which they would normally receive a pension). | *Donald retired at 56, after attaining the* ***maximum pensionable service*** (=working enough years to get the highest possible pension) *with an insurance company.* | *The Civil Service came to be thought of as a secure, pensionable occupation.*
2 pensionable pay/salary pay from which money is regularly taken to pay for a pension: *The employee's contribution is 5% of pensionable salary.*

pen•sion•er /'penʃənə‖-ər/ *n* [C] *BrE* someone who is receiving a RETIREMENT PENSION: *The increase will particularly affect pensioners and those on low incomes.*

pension fund —see under FUND[1]

pension plan also **retirement plan** *AmE* — *n* [C] a system by which an employer, insurance company etc provides workers with a pension after they have made regular payments to them over many years: *individuals covered by a* ***company pension plan*** | *Congress has changed the laws governing* ***private pension plans.***

contributory pension plan a pension plan into which the employee and the employer both make payments

non-contributory pension plan a pension plan into which only the employer makes payments, not the employee

pension rights —see under RIGHT

pension scheme —see under SCHEME

Pen•ti•um /'pentiəm/ also **Pentium chip** *n* [C] *trademark* a type of PROCESSOR (=central CHIP that controls most of a computer's operations) that allows a computer to process and store information very quickly: *The Pentium is about five times as fast as the 486 chip.*

people-intensive *adj* a people-intensive business or organization needs a lot of people to make it run correctly: *Schools are people-intensive. They need pupils and they need staff.*

people meter —see under METER[1]

PEP /pep/ *n* [C] Personal Equity Plan; an investment plan introduced by the British government in 1987 to encourage ordinary people to own shares and invest in industry by allowing them to not pay any tax on the money made. In April 1999 PEPs were replaced by ISAS

peppercorn rent —see under RENT[2]

PER abbreviation for PRICE-EARNINGS RATIO

per /pə, pɜː‖pər, pɜːr/ *prep* **1** for each: *an average beef cattle price of $74.20* ***per hundred pounds*** | *The price tag is $1500* ***per square foot*** *of retail space.* | *Earnings* ***per***

***share** rose 12% to 31.3 pence.* | *The Japanese have in recent years reported a higher income **per person** than the Americans.*

2 per hour/day/week etc during each hour etc: *How many calls do you make per day?* | *a train travelling at 150 **miles per hour*** —see also AS PER

per an·num /pər 'ænəm/ abbreviation **PA, pa** *adv* for or in each year; PER YEAR: *The economy grew at an average rate of 6% per annum.* | *a salary of $30,000 pa*

PE ratio —see under RATIO

per calendar month —see PCM

per cap·i·ta /pə 'kæpɨtə‖pər-/ *adv* for or by each person: *Japanese visitors' **spending per capita** was much higher than average spending by tourists from other countries.* | *The US uses twice as much oil per capita as European competitors.* **—per-capita** *adj* [only before a noun] *Israel's **per-capita income** is comparable to that of Spain.*

per capita gross domestic product —see under GROSS DOMESTIC PRODUCT

per-capita income —see under INCOME

per capital gross national product —see under GROSS NATIONAL PRODUCT

per·cent[1] /pə'sent‖pər-/ also **per cent** *BrE* — *adj, adv* **5 percent (5%)/10 percent (10%) etc** equal to 5, 10 etc parts out of every 100 parts: *a one percent* (=1%) *cut in interest rates* | *a 15 percent* (=15%) *tip*

percent[2] also **per cent** *BrE*, abbreviation **PC** *n* **1 5 percent (5%)/10 percent (10%) etc** an amount equal to 5, 10 etc parts out of every 100 parts: *Some of the lenders charge as much as 35 percent.* + **of**: *40 percent of the survey participants expect business to slow down in the next six months.* | *Annual revenue grew **by 6 percent**.*

2 [C] another name for PERCENTAGE: *our marketing spending as a **percent of** sales*

per·cen·tage /pə'sentɪdʒ‖pər-/ *n* **1** [C,U] an amount considered as part of a larger amount, especially as if it is part of a total which is 100 + **of**: *What **percentage of** sales are generated abroad?* | *Rental companies bought a **high percentage** of the vehicles sold.* | *Spending on research and development **as a percentage** of profits is low.*

2 percentage increase/decrease/rise etc the increase, decrease etc considered as part of a total which is 100: *The **percentage increase** in the construction sector was much higher than in manufacturing.*

percentage point —see under POINT[1]

per·cen·tile /pə'sentaɪl‖pər-/ *n* [C] **the 60th/70th etc percentile** the level, amount etc that is reached by the highest 60, 70 etc percent of people or things in a group: *Our employees' pay is at the 90th percentile of that offered by similar companies* (=only 10% of similar companies pay more). —see also DECILE, MEDIAN, PERCENTILE

per·cep·tion /pə'sepʃən‖pər-/ *n* [C] the way that people feel about a company, product, or market and what they think it is like: *There is a perception among investors that an economic recovery is beginning.* | *Consumers buy perfume because it is French and leather because it is Italian. National stereotypes do play a role in **product perceptions**.* | *After he took over, Mr. Buffet changed **public perceptions*** (=what people thought) *of Salomon Inc.*

per di·em /pə 'diːəm‖pər-/ *adj formal* for each day: *Our consultants earn a **per diem rate** of $1,600.* **—per diem** *adv*

perfect competition —see under COMPETITION

perfect market —see under MARKET[1]

per·form /pə'fɔːm‖pər'fɔːrm/ *v* **1** [T] to do work, carry out a duty, task etc: *These chips are designed to perform very specific functions, such as controlling computer disk drives.* | *It takes a highly skilled mechanic to perform repairs on a Daf 55.* | *Symbols across the top of the screen let a user click a mouse button to **perform** common **operations** such as adding up a column of figures.*

2 [I] to do something in a way that is expected or wanted: *She looked good during the interview, but will she perform once she's in the job?* | *The company's three divisions all **performed well**, despite the recession.*

per·form·ance /pə'fɔːməns‖pər'fɔːr-/ *n* **1** [C,U] the degree to which a company, investment, financial market etc is profitable: *The company is showing **strong performance** and doing considerably better than the retail industry as a whole.* | *They will report a $500 million loss, one of the **worst performances** ever by a US brokerage firm.*

2 [U] how well a machine, vehicle etc works: *Consumers believed the car's price was relatively expensive for its performance.*

3 [U] the way that someone does their job, and how well they do it: *Some people were critical of her performance as a manager.*

4 [U] LAW the act of doing the things mentioned in a contract in the way that they should be done: *the seller's performance of his part of the contract*

specific performance [U] LAW when a court orders someone to do what they had agreed to do in a contract etc rather than ordering them to pay DAMAGES (=money) as a punishment for not doing these things: *An order for specific performance is one which requires the seller to deliver the goods and does not give him the option of paying damages instead.* | *a specific performance claim*

performance appraisal —see under APPRAISAL

performance assessment *n* [C] another name for PERFORMANCE APPRAISAL

performance bond —see under BOND

performance bonus —see under BONUS

performance contract —see under CONTRACT[1]

performance evaluation *n* [C] another name for PERFORMANCE APPRAISAL

performance fund —see under FUND[1]

performance guarantee —see under GUARANTEE[2]

performance-related *adj* performance-related pay, BENEFITS etc are ones that increase when your work improves or becomes more productive and decrease if the opposite happens: *Workers at most gold mines will receive an average 6% increase, plus performance-related bonuses.*

performance-related pay —see under PAY[1]

performance review *n* [C] another name for PERFORMANCE APPRAISAL

performing loan —see under LOAN[1]

performing rights —see under RIGHT

pe·ri·od /'pɪəriəd‖'pɪr-/ *n* [C] a particular length of time: *She has been taken on for a 6-month **trial period**.*

accounting period ACCOUNTING a period of time to which a particular payment is related for accounting or tax purposes: *The company has sold the property during the current accounting period, and tax is payable on the gain realised.*

cooling-off period ◆ a period of time, usually between 10 and 20 days, in which you can think about certain types of contract you have just signed and change your mind about entering into it: *The new Timeshare Act gives you a 14-day cooling off period, so you can pull out of buying.*

◆ HUMAN RESOURCES in a disagreement between employers and employees, a period of time during which workers are not allowed to strike or during which employers are not allowed to prevent workers from working: *a 90-day cooling off period before strike action started*

control period ACCOUNTING a period of time during which budgeted amounts are compared with actual amounts

deferment period INSURANCE in health insurance taken out in Britain, a period of time that the insured person agrees to let pass when they are ill before they claim money from the insurance company: *Varying between four and 104 weeks, the longer the deferment period, the cheaper private health insurance becomes.*

earn-out period FINANCE a period of time after a company is sold, when, if the company makes more than a certain amount of profit, some of the profit will be paid to the seller if this has been agreed

pay period the length of time someone works, such as a month, before they receive their wages

recovery period TAX the number of years over which you are allowed to DEPRECIATE an asset (=get back the money it cost by paying less tax)

reporting period ACCOUNTING the period of time covered by a particular set of results, usually the financial year, or part of that year: *Overseas sales during the last reporting period came to 104.96 billion yen.*

P

pe•ri•od•i•cal /ˌpɪəriˈɒdɪkəl‖ˌpɪriˈɑː-/ *n* [C] a magazine, especially one about a technical or serious subject, that comes out regularly: *The company's publishing operations include business and consumer periodicals.*

pe•riph•e•ral /pəˈrɪfərəl/ *adj* **1 peripheral activity/business etc** an activity, business etc that is not the most important one that a company is involved in: *The firm is neglecting profitable core businesses to develop peripheral activities.*

2 peripheral equipment/product COMPUTING equipment that is connected to a computer and used with it: *Tech Data focused on supplying peripheral products such as printers.* —**peripheral** *n* [C] *a maker of **computer peripherals**, particularly disk drives*

perishable goods —see under GOODS

per•ish•a•bles /ˈperɪʃəbəlz/ *n* [plural] food products that are likely to decay if they are not kept in the proper conditions: *Prices of consumer goods, except for perishables, are 3.4% above last year's levels.* —**perishable** *adj*: *Never leave **perishable food** out of the refrigerator.*

per•ju•ry /ˈpɜːdʒəri‖ˈpɜːr-/ *n* [U] the crime of telling a lie after promising to tell the truth in a court of law: *A company official **committed perjury** during the trial.*

perk /pɜːk‖pɜːrk/ *n* [C] something in addition to money that you get for doing your job, such as a car: *bonuses, housing allowances and other perks* | *Employees must pay tax on anything regarded as a perk.*

executive perk something that an executive gets in addition to their salary, for example extra money based on company profits, the right to buy company shares cheaply, or the use of an expensive car: *In most firms, top management incentives are thinly disguised executive perks.*

per•ma•nent /ˈpɜːmənənt‖ˈpɜːr-/ *adj* **1 permanent contract/job/employment** a contract, job etc that is intended to continue for a long time or for ever: *The company has created 650 permanent jobs.* | *He is acting chief executive, and under consideration for a permanent appointment.*

2 permanent employee/worker/staff an employee, worker etc whom a company intends to employ for a long time or for ever: *Hyundai said some of the plant's 900 permanent employees would be reassigned.* —compare TEMPORARY

permanent injunction —see under INJUNCTION

per mille also **per mil.** /pə ˈmɪl‖pər-/ *adj, adv* **35/175 etc per mille** equal to 35, 175 etc parts in every thousand: *Foreign holidays are now deemed to account for 30 per mille (3 per cent) of the cost of living.*

per•mis•sion /pəˈmɪʃən‖pər-/ *n* [U] when someone is officially told that they are allowed to do something **permission to do sth**: *The Board denied TransCanada Pipelines Ltd permission to build the pipeline.* | *The officer approved $4.5 million in loans without **getting the bank's permission**.* + **for**: *Airlines need their own government's permission for internal flights.*

planning permission *BrE* also **permission to build** [U] PROPERTY when a local government authority gives someone the right to build a house etc, or to change an existing building: *The company **applied for planning permission** to build a factory on the site.* + **for**: *The committee voted to refuse planning permission for the petrol station.*

permission to build —see ***planning permission*** under PERMISSION

permission to deal *n* [U] FINANCE in Britain, official permission from a stockmarket for people to start buying and selling a new set of shares

per•mit /ˈpɜːmɪt‖ˈpɜːr-/ *n* [C] an official document stating that someone is allowed to do something: *The governor would **issue a permit for** construction to proceed.* **permit to do sth**: *The company requested a permit to operate a hazardous-waste treatment plant.*

building permit also **construction permit** *AmE* an official document that allows someone to build on a piece of land: *McDonald's applied for a building permit for a new franchise restaurant.*

export permit an official document that you need to export certain types of goods

import permit an official document that you need to import certain types of goods

residence permit an official document that allows someone to live in another country: *Immigrants had to live in Denmark for five years before their spouses* (=husband or wife) *could acquire a residence permit.*

work permit an official document that allows someone to work in another country, usually for a specific length of time: *He is only in Britain for three months **on a work permit**, and fears being deported afterwards.*

per•pe•tu•i•ty /ˌpɜːpəˈtjuːəti‖ˌpɜːrpəˈtuː-/ *n* **in perpetuity** LAW for all future time: *The contract allows them to use the photographs in perpetuity.*

per pro —see PP.[2]

per•qui•site /ˈpɜːkwəzɪt‖ˈpɜːr-/ *n* [C] *formal* another name for a PERK

per-share *adj* **per-share earnings/profit/gain etc** the amount of profit made by a company for each of its shares: *a 42% decline in **per-share earnings***

per•son /ˈpɜːsən‖ˈpɜːr-/ also **legal person** *n* plural **persons** [C] LAW a person or group of people who have certain rights and duties: *In Scotland, a firm is a legal person distinct from the partners of the firm.*

artificial person also **fictitious person** a group of people who, in law, are considered as one person: *For this purpose, 'person' includes an artificial person.*

natural person one single person: *A corporation does not have all the rights of a natural person to sue for defamation.* —see also DETAIL PERSON

personal assistant —see under ASSISTANT

personal cheque —see under CHEQUE

personal communications network —see PCN

personal computer —see PC

personal credit —see under CREDIT[1]

personal day *n* [C] HUMAN RESOURCES time that you are allowed to be absent from work, usually because of a personal problem: *Mazda has added four paid personal days a year to the contracts of all employees.*

personal digital assistant —see PDA

personal effects —see under EFFECT

Personal Equity Plan —see PEP

personal finance —see under FINANCE[1]

personal identification number —see PIN

personal income —see under INCOME

personal income tax —see under INCOME TAX

personal injury —see under INJURY

personal investment —see under INVESTMENT

Personal Investment Authority abbreviation **PIA** *n* an organization in Britain that makes sure that institutions selling investments to the public obey the law, and which is part of the FINANCIAL SERVICES AUTHORITY

personal investor —see under INVESTOR

per·son·al·i·ty /ˌpɜːsəˈnæləti‖ˌpɜːr-/ *n* plural **personalities** [C] **1** LAW an organization that from a legal point of view is separate from the people who own it or manage it: *A company has a separate legal personality, and its members are not liable for its debts.*

2 MARKETING a product's personality is the qualities that people think it has, considered as a whole: *Gasoline has always been a tough sell, without much product personality.*

personal leave —see under LEAVE

personal ledger —see under LEDGER

personal liability —see under LIABILITY

personal loan —see under LOAN[1]

personal organizer —see under ORGANIZER

personal pension —see under PENSION[1]

personal property —see under PROPERTY

personal representative —see under REPRESENTATIVE[1]

personal saving —see under SAVING

personal selling —see under SELLING

per·son·al·ty /ˈpɜːsənəlti/ *n* [U] LAW personal property

personnel manager —see under MANAGER

per subscriber price —see under PRICE[1]

PERT abbreviation for PROJECT EVALUATION AND REVIEW TECHNIQUE

pes·si·mist /ˈpesəmɪst/ *n* [C] someone who always expects that things will get worse or that bad things will happen in the future —opposite OPTIMIST —**pessimistic** *adj*

pe·ti·tion /pəˈtɪʃən/ *n* [C] LAW an official letter to a law court, asking for a legal case to be considered: *She is threatening to file a petition for divorce.*

bankruptcy petition when a person or business that is owed money asks a court to recognize that a business is bankrupt so that they can obtain the money, or part of the money, that they are owed: *If an individual appears unable to pay his debts or has no reasonable prospect of paying he may also face a bankruptcy petition.*

pet·ro·chem·i·cals /ˌpetrəʊˈkemɪkəlz‖-troʊ-/ *n* [plural] the industrial activity of making products from oil, and the products themselves: *They are diversifying into electronics, petrochemicals, telecommunications and biotechnology.* | *plastic bottles made from petrochemicals*

petty cashier —see under CASHIER

Pfand·brief /ˈfændˌbriːf, ˈpfænt-/ *n* plural **Pfandbriefe** [C] FINANCE a type of bond issued in Germany which is BACKED by (=supported by income from) MORTGAGES (=loans for buying property) and debt from industries and services owned by the government; FAND: *Pfandbriefe are starting to feature more in the portfolios of European fund managers.*

phar·ma·ceu·ti·cal /ˌfɑːməˈsjuːtɪkəl◂‖ˌfɑːrməˈsuː-/ *adj* [only before a noun] concerned with the development and production of drugs and medicines: *Bayer, a chemical and* ***pharmaceutical company*** | *Wellcome, the* ***pharmaceutical giant***

phar·ma·ceu·ti·cals /ˌfɑːməˈsjuːtɪkəlz‖ˌfɑːrməˈsuː-/ *n* [plural] **1** drugs and medicines, and the industry that develops and makes them; DRUGS: *McKesson's distributes pharmaceuticals and health and beauty products.* | *This country is a world leader in telecommunications and pharmaceuticals.*

2 shares in pharmaceutical companies: *In London, pharmaceuticals fell after the FDA report on the new drug was leaked to The Times.*

generic pharmaceuticals pharmaceuticals that do not have BRAND NAMES: *a company that makes generic pharmaceuticals as an alternative to more expensive brand names*

over-the-counter pharmaceuticals pharmaceuticals that can be obtained without a PRESCRIPTION (=a written order) from a doctor; OVER-THE-COUNTER DRUGS

prescription pharmaceuticals pharmaceuticals that can only be obtained with a written order from a doctor; PRESCRIPTION DRUGS

phar·ma·cy /ˈfɑːməsi‖ˈfɑːr-/ *n* plural **pharmacies** [C] *especially AmE* a shop where there are specially trained staff who can sell or give out medicines as ordered by a doctor; DISPENSING CHEMIST *BrE*

phase[1] /feɪz/ *n* [C] **1** a part of a process of development or growth: *Pfizer is conducting phase 1 and phase 2 clinical trials with the drug.* | *The consortium will pay $92 million for insurance to cover the construction phase of the project.*

2 in phase/out of phase (with sth) working together in a way that produces the right effect, or not working together in this way: *Britain's economic cycle is out of phase with the Continent.*

phase[2] *v* [T] to make something happen in a planned way: *By phasing the dollar purchases over time, the change will not be misunderstood by the market.* | *British Commonwealth foreign ministers will hold a special meeting to consider a phased lifting of sanctions.*

phase sth ↔ **down** *phr v* [T] *AmE* to gradually reduce something or to stop producing something; scale down: *Litton Industries plans to phase down the operations at its automation division*

phase sth ↔ **in** *phr v* [T] to introduce something gradually: *His promised 60% increase in the minimum wage will be phased in over four years.*

phase sth ↔ **out** *phr v* [T] to gradually stop using or providing something: *The Great Valley facility had about 700 workers at one point and now employs 100. The plant is expected to be phased out by the end of this year.*

phone /fəʊn‖foʊn/ *n* [C] a piece of equipment you use to talk to someone who is in another place; TELEPHONE

cellular phone also **cell phone** *AmE*, **mobile phone** *BrE* a phone that you can carry with you, that works by using a network of radio stations to pass on signals —see also ANSWERPHONE

phone rage —see under RAGE

pho·to·cop·i·er /ˈfəʊtəʊˌkɒpiə‖ˈfoʊtəˌkɑːpiər/ *n* [C] a machine that quickly makes photographic copies of documents: *an expensive colour photocopier*

pho·to·cop·y /ˈfəʊtəʊˌkɒpi‖ˈfoʊtəˌkɑːpi/ *n* plural **photocopies** [C] a photographic copy of a document etc, made using a photocopier: *He* ***made a photocopy of*** *the letter which he sent to a solicitor.* —**photocopy** *v* [T] *You should always photocopy original documents in case they are lost in the post.* | ***Photocopying facilities*** *are available.*

P

phys·i·cal /ˈfɪzɪkəl/ *adj* **1** real and actual, rather than calculated: *the physical counting of goods in stock*
2 ACCOUNTING related to assets that can be seen and touched, such as machines and buildings; TANGIBLE: *They had a physical plant valued at $3,455,050 and cash reserves of $729,886.*
3 FINANCE involving shares, bonds etc where there are CERTIFICATES (=documents showing ownership), rather than shares etc where ownership is recorded on a computer: *It's hard to imagine that many investors would prefer having physical certificates when a computer entry seems at least as reliable.*
4 FINANCE involving COMMODITIES (=oil, metals, farm products etc) for actual or immediate delivery, rather than FUTURES (=contracts for delivery at a later date): *Traders of agricultural futures contracts usually don't take physical delivery of the underlying commodity.*

physical commodity —see under COMMODITY

physical price —see under PRICE[1]

phy·si·cals /ˈfɪzɪkəlz/ *n* [plural] COMMODITIES (=oil, metals, farm products etc) for actual or immediate delivery, rather than FUTURES (=contracts for delivery at a later date): *physicals-based trading*

PIA —see PERSONAL INVESTMENT AUTHORITY

pick /pɪk/ *v*
pick up *phr v* [I] if business or trade picks up, it improves

pick·et /ˈpɪkɪ̇t/ *n* [C] **1** also **picket line** a group of people who stand in front of a shop, factory, or other building to protest about something or to stop people from going to work during a STRIKE: *a picket on the steps of the Federal court building* | *Workers refused to* ***cross a picket line*** *to unload the fish.*
2 also **picketer** *AmE* one person in a picket line: *The pickets persuaded some drivers not to enter the factory.* —**picket** *v* [I,T] *Labor unions picketed the plant, protesting at the use of non-union workers.* | *250 students will be picketing at the college.*

pick·ing /ˈpɪkɪŋ/ also **order picking** *n* [U] the process of collecting goods together in a WAREHOUSE (=large building where goods are stored) in the right order, so that they can be packed and sent to a customer

piece /piːs/ *n* [C] **1 ten pence/fifty-cent etc piece** a coin of a particular value: *Does anyone have change for a 50 pence piece?*
2 a single thing of a particular type: *Apples were $1 a piece.*
3 supply/sell sth by the piece to supply or sell something as a single article rather than in a pair or a set
4 pay sb/work by the piece if people work or are paid by the piece, they are paid for each item they produce, not for the amount of time it takes to produce it

piece goods —see under GOODS

piece rate —see under RATE[1]

piece work also **piecework** /ˈpiːswɜːk‖-wɜːrk/ *n* [U] work that is paid according to the number of items that are completed rather than the number of hours worked: *The management and the workers are bargaining over* ***piecework rates****.* | *You can do freelance work, or part-time work, or piecework in your home.* —see also ***piece rate*** under RATE[1]

pie chart —see under CHART[1]

pi·geon·hole¹ /ˈpɪdʒɪ̇nhəʊl‖-hoʊl/ *v* [T] to consider a person, activity etc as belonging to a particular type or group, in a way that is too simple and therefore unfair; LABEL: *People tend to pigeonhole her just because she's a feminist.* | *Electronic books and multimedia had originally been pigeonholed as a small, exclusive market.*

pigeonhole² *n* [C] one of a set of small boxes built into a desk or into a frame on a wall, in which letters or papers can be put, usually so that they can be collected by the people you work with: *I left a copy of the report in* ***your pigeonhole****.*

pig·gy·back /ˈpɪgibæk/ *v* **1** [I] to use a situation that already exists in order to do or get what you want + **on/onto**: *Tesco's supermarket is launching a credit card with the Royal Bank of Scotland, initially piggybacking on the Royal Bank's banking licence.* | *The Stockholm Stock Exchange is working on the idea of piggybacking its new trading system onto the trade agreement.*
2 [T] to move goods from one place to another, using containers that can be carried both by train and by road

pil·fer /ˈpɪlfə‖-ər/ *v* [T] to steal small amounts of things, or things that are not worth much, especially from an office, factory etc: *A UPS employee has been* ***charged with pilfering*** *a set of automobile wheels.* —**pilfering** *n* [U] *Stationery stocks are running 15% below last year's levels, mostly due to pilfering.* —**pilferage** *n* [U] *Losses from employee pilferage are estimated at $8 billion.*

pi·lot /ˈpaɪlət/ *n* [C] a test that is done to see if an idea, product etc will be successful: *If the pilots are successful, Mr Lees hopes to go into full production in 2003.* | *GM Corp. has no plans to participate in a* ***pilot project*** *to produce electric cars.* —**pilot** *v* [T] *They are piloting parts of the book in language schools.*

PIMS /pɪmz; ˌpiː aɪ em ˈes/ *n* Profit Impact of Market Strategy; a study of the things that influence the profitability of companies in different industries, performed by the STRATEGIC PLANNING INSTITUTE: *A PIMS study concludes that return on investment increases significantly as market share increases.*

PIN /pɪn/also **PIN number** *n* [C usually singular] personal identification number; a secret number given to you by your bank that you use when getting money from an ATM (=machine that distributes cash) with a BANK CARD: *You can use your card, together with your PIN at most HSBC self-service banking machines.* | *Never tell anyone your PIN number.*

pink-collar *adj* [only before a noun] *AmE* HUMAN RESOURCES relating to or involving women in low-paid office jobs: *women in pink-collar, undervalued jobs* —compare BLUE-COLLAR, WHITE-COLLAR

pink-collar worker —see under WORKER

Pink Pages *n* **The Pink Pages** a book for HOMOSEXUALS (=people who are sexually attracted to people of the same sex) in which businesses advertise, giving their addresses and telephone numbers

pink pound —see under POUND

Pink Sheets also **pink sheets** *n* [plural] FINANCE in the US, information on shares in very small companies that are not traded on a stockmarket or OVER THE COUNTER (=directly between dealers using a computer system): *The company's shares have been* ***trading on the pink sheets*** (=bought and sold using them) *and it will now apply to have the shares listed over the counter.*

pink slip —see under SLIP[2]

PIN number —see under NUMBER[1]

pi·o·neer /ˌpaɪəˈnɪə‖-ˈnɪr/ *n* [C] the first person or organization to do something that other people and organizations later develop or continue to do: *pioneers willing to try a new software product and lead others to it* + **of**: *Victor Co. of Japan, pioneer of the VHS videocassette recorder* + **in**: *Kentucky Fried Chicken, one of the pioneers in the fast-food business* —**pioneer** *v* [T] *Unlike Sony, which pioneered such products as the Walkman, Matsushita has virtually no innovations of its own.* | *Surgeons are pioneering techniques to get patients back to work sooner.* —**pioneering** *adj*: *Seagate, a pioneering disk-drive maker*

pipe·line /ˈpaɪp-laɪn/ *n* [C] **1** a line of connecting pipes, often under the ground or sea, used for taking gas, oil etc over long distances: *a plan to build a 250-kilometer pipeline to supply the city of Bulawayo with water from the Zambezi river*

2 be in the pipeline if a plan, idea, or event is in the pipeline, it is still being prepared, but it will happen or be completed soon: *Goldmine has other distribution deals in the pipeline to be announced over the next few weeks.*

pi·ra·cy /ˈpaɪərəsi‖ˈpaɪrə-/ *n* [U] LAW **1** the illegal copying of books, TAPES, VIDEOS etc: ***software piracy***
2 the crime of stealing from a ship at sea: *piracy in the Malacca Straits*

pi·rate /ˈpaɪərət‖ˈpaɪrət/ *n* [C] LAW **1** a person or organization that dishonestly copies and sells films, tapes etc for which the COPYRIGHT (=legal ownership) belongs to others: *Manufacturers fear that Seoul may emerge as a new centre for the **software pirates**.* —**pirate** *v* [T] *Microsoft Corp. charged that a Shanghai-based company pirated the game programs.* | ***pirated videotapes***
2 pirate radio/TV (station) illegal radio or television broadcasts, or the station sending them out: *About 80 pirate cable systems have brought US network news into thousands of homes.*
3 a person who steals from a ship at sea

pit /pɪt/ *n* [C] *AmE* **1** FINANCE an area of the floor of a financial market where buying and selling takes place and dealers speak directly to each other; FLOOR; TRADING FLOOR: *the currency pit of the Chicago Commodity Exchange* | *Mr. Baldwin is the most active trader in the world's most active futures-trading pit – the T-bond pit at the Board of Trade.*
2 a mine, especially a coal mine: *We have no choice but to close unprofitable pits.*

pitch¹ /pɪtʃ/ *n* [C] **1** MARKETING also **sales pitch** *informal* what a sales person says about a product to persuade people to buy it
2 MARKETING an attempt by an ADVERTISING AGENCY to persuade a company to use its services to advertise a product: *The company has handed its £500,000 account to the Hansett Group, after a four-way pitch with Lewis Broadbent Advertising, the Tenet Group, and Archminster.*
3 *BrE* a place in a public area where a street trader goes to sell things

pitch² *v* **1** [T] to set prices at a particular level: *Prices for the new trucks are pitched very competitively.* | *To pitch franchise bids correctly, firms need to be expert market-forecasters.*
2 [I,T] *informal* to try to make a business agreement, or to sell something in a particular way: *sales reps pitching the latest gadgets* | *Orange juice is to be pitched as a sportsman's drink in a new marketing strategy adopted by the Florida Citrus Commission.* + **for**: *Luxury clothing retailer Burberrys has invited a number of agencies to pitch for its estimated £1.5 million international business.*

pit·tance /ˈpɪtəns/ *n* [singular] a very small or unfairly small amount of money: *She gets **paid a pittance**.*

pix·el /ˈpɪksəl/ *n* [C] COMPUTING the smallest unit making up an image on a computer screen

PL written abbreviation for PROGRAMMING LANGUAGE

place¹ /pleɪs/ *v* [T] **1 place an order (with sb)** to ask a shop or business to provide goods: *Lufthansa has placed a large order for jets with Boeing.*
2 place an order (with sb) to ask a BROKER to buy shares, bonds etc for you: *A speculator placed a large order for stock but couldn't afford to pay for it.*
3 FINANCE if a financial institution acting for a company places its shares, bonds etc, they manage to sell them to investors: *Hoare Govett easily placed the 16 million shares in Southern Glass.* + **with**: *25% of the firm's shares will be placed with institutional investors.*
4 place sb in a job HUMAN RESOURCES if an organization such as an EMPLOYMENT AGENCY places someone in a job, they find a job for them: *The agency is not paid until the individual is placed in a job and holds it for a set amount of time.*
5 place an ad/advertisement to arrange for an advertisement to appear in a newspaper: *He wanted to sell his car, so he placed an ad in the 'Auto Trader'.*
6 place a (telephone) call (to sb) to give the number of a person you want to speak to a telephone OPERATOR so that they can connect you: *He went to the hotel to place two telephone calls, one local and one to London.*
7 place a business in/under receivership to ask a court of law to declare that a company cannot continue to operate normally because of its financial difficulties: *Creditor banks are considering cutting off assistance and forcing the company to be placed under receivership.*

place² *n* [C] **1 place of work/employment** *formal* the office, factory etc where you work: *Our place of work provides us with a base for social interaction.*
2 take place to happen, especially after being planned or arranged: *The sale of VASP took place in an auction at the Sao Paulo Stock Exchange.*
3 in sb's place if you do something in someone's place, you do it instead of them because they cannot do it: *Mr Nakayama will be visiting the five countries this week in Mr. Kaifu's place.*
4 be going places *informal* to start becoming successful: *The market had just started to look as if it was going places when the crash came along.*
5 in high places in positions of power or authority: *corruption in high places*

place·ment /ˈpleɪsmənt/ *n* **1** [C,U] FINANCE the sale by a financial institution of shares, bonds etc, for a company, or a particular quantity of shares sold in this way; OFFERING
2 [C] *BrE* a job, usually as part of a course of study, which gives you experience of a particular type of work: ***work placement schemes*** | *The placement involves a programme of meetings and activities.*
job placement [C,U] HUMAN RESOURCES when someone, especially a student or an unemployed person, is put into a job that is suitable to their skills and interests, usually for a temporary period: *The University's Careers Service offers careers guidance and job placement facilities to all students.*
3 [U] the act of finding a place for someone to live or work: *There are currently 500 young people on the scheme awaiting placement with an employer.*
product placement [C,U] MARKETING when the maker of a product arranges for it to appear or be used in a film or television programme as a form of advertising: *Product placement has reached new heights. In one recent movie, more than a dozen brands were strategically worked into the action.*

plac·ing /ˈpleɪsɪŋ/ *n* [C,U] FINANCE the sale by a financial institution of shares, bonds etc for a company, or a particular quantity of shares etc sold in this way; OFFERING; PLACEMENT: *The share issue will be through placings in the UK and internationally.* | *the placing of 54 million British Gas shares*
private placing also **private placement** [C] the act of selling shares etc to a group of investors directly without offering them openly on a financial market: *Some 45 companies raised $4 billion in London and Luxembourg and through private placings.*
vendor placing *BrE* [C] a sale of shares by a company, done in order to provide the finance which will allow it to buy all or part of another company: *Capita is raising £11.8 million in a vendor placing to finance its acquisition of Hartshead.*

plaint /pleɪnt/ *n* [C] *BrE* LAW the reason why a plaintiff has brought a LEGAL ACTION (=use of the legal system to settle a disagreement) against someone, or a written statement giving these reasons; COMPLAINT *AmE* —see also COMPLAINT, PLEA

P

plain•tiff /ˈpleɪntɪf/ *n* [C] LAW someone who brings a LEGAL ACTION (=use of the legal system to settle an argument) against someone in a court of law; COMPLAINANT: *Plaintiffs in the Korean Airlines disaster are seeking damages from the airline.*

plan¹ /plæn/ *v* past tense and past participle **planned** present participle **planning** **1** [I,T] to think carefully about something you want to do in the future, and decide exactly how you will do it: *We've been planning this visit for months – you can't cancel now.* | *The whole operation went exactly as planned* | *A business must **plan ahead*** (=make plans for a long time in the future), *making use of sales and market forecasts.*

2 [T] to intend to something, especially when you have definite plans for how you will do it: *The company is planning a major investment programme.* **plan to do sth**: *The company plans to spend $739.9 million on capital improvements next year.*

plan² *n* [C] **1** a set of actions for achieving something in the future, especially one that has been considered carefully and in detail: *the government's five-year **economic plan*** +**for**: *The company's plans for growth are threatened by their inability to find, keep, and manage key staff.* **plan to do sth**: *The President is working on a plan to turn around the economy make the economy successful again.* | *Boeing and McDonnell had considered merging some years earlier, but the **plan fell through*** (=the plan was not completed). | *If everything **goes according to plan*** (=happens in the way that was expected or arranged), *the first stage of the project will be completed by December.*

business plan FINANCE a document produced by a company, especially a new company, giving details of expected sales and costs, how the business can be financed and showing why the plan will make money: *To raise the cash they need, managers will be required to give their bankers a three-year business plan.*

contingency plan a plan for dealing with a future event or situation that might cause problems: *We tried to ensure that the company prepared an adequate oil spill contingency plan.*

2 plan B your second plan, which you will use if things do not happen as you expect: *Always have a plan B in case your original choice becomes impractical for any reason.*

3 something you have decided to do or achieve: *His plan is to get a degree in economics and then work abroad for a year.* | *She'd have to have a long-term **career plan** if she wanted to fulfill her dream of becoming an international trade consultant.* | *There's been a **change of plan**. The meeting's on Monday instead of this afternoon.* | *Robinhood Homes **has plans for** 625 homes* (=intends to build 625 homes) *northwest of the airport.*

4 a drawing of a building, room, or machine as it would be seen from above, showing the shape, measurements, position of the walls etc: *a floor-by-floor plan of the three-storey building.*

plot plan PROPERTY a plan showing how a piece of land is being used or is going to be used

5 a drawing that shows exactly how something will be arranged —see also 401(K) PLAN, DIVIDEND REINVESTMENT PLAN, HEALTH PLAN, INSTALLMENT PLAN, PENSION PLAN

planned obsolescence —see under OBSOLESCENCE

plan•ning /ˈplænɪŋ/ *n* [U] when you think carefully about something you want to do in the future, and decide exactly how you will do it: *If you want to ensure a trouble-free retirement, it's never too early to start **financial planning**.* | *The main planning focus for suppliers will be **business planning** to enable them to secure and fulfil contracts.*

corporate planning when a company plans what it will do in the future. This involves deciding which products it should be making, which markets it should be in, and how profits can be increased; STRATEGIC PLANNING: *Global inflation is of great importance to corporate planning.*

economic planning ECONOMICS ◆ when the government of a country plans how it will control or influence the national economy: *Poor economic planning has led to high inflation.* | *The Russian leadership hesitated on moving his country from central economic planning to a market-based system.*

◆ when you plan the best way of using the different things involved in producing goods, such as capital, land, and labour, in order to achieve an economic aim

estate planning planning before someone dies for how their money and property will be dealt with after they die, especially so that as little INHERITANCE TAX as possible is paid: *Owners of smaller companies who begin estate planning early can transfer much of their equity to children tax-free.*

media planning the process of planning the advertising for a product, using different methods such as television, newspapers, and magazines: *The firms operate separately, with no centralized media planning or buying.*

strategic planning another name for CORPORATE PLANNING

planning application —see under APPLICATION

planning permission —see under PERMISSION

plant /plɑːnt‖plænt/ *n* **1** [U] industrial machinery: *There is a desperate need to rebuild the stock of productive **plant and equipment** in this country.*

2 [C] MANUFACTURING a factory or building where an industrial process takes place or a product is made: *a **chemical plant*** | *Nissan plans to spend $600 million on a new **engine plant**.* | *a **nuclear power plant***

assembly plant [C] a factory where products are put together from all the different parts: *the Volvo car assembly plant at Kalmar in Sweden*

fabrication plant also **fab plant** [C] other names for a MANUFACTURING PLANT, especially for making advanced products: *a semiconductor fabrication plant*

manufacturing plant [C] a factory where products are made or put together: *a big television manufacturing plant*

packing plant also **packing station** [C] a large building where goods are packed, ready to be sent somewhere: *the tin-roofed packing stations of the Echeverri farm* | *Inspection is proposed for the beef industry's 80 largest packing plants.*

plant manager —see under MANAGER

plant utilization also **plant utilisation** *BrE* — *n* [U] MANUFACTURING the time when a factory is being used to produce goods, as a percentage of the total time it could be used or the number of machines being used as a percentage of the total number that could be used: *Levels of plant utilisation have fallen again.*

plas•tic /ˈplæstɪk/ *n* [singular, U] *informal* used to talk about buying things with a CREDIT CARD, or the card itself: *I'm going to have to pay for this with plastic.* | *When I go out, I depend on the plastic I have in my wallet. I carry very little cash.*

plastic card —see under CARD

plastic money —see under MONEY

plat book —see under BOOK¹

plat•form /ˈplætfɔːm‖-fɔːrm/ *n* [C] **1** the raised place beside a railway track where you get on and off the train

2 a system used to broadcast television or radio programmes

3 a tall structure built so that people can work around the surrounding area

oil platform also **production platform** a platform for producing oil; OIL RIG: *Explosions on a Shell production platform further limited North Sea oil output.*

4 also **computer platform** a particular type of computer system or software: *a company's IT infrastructure for different computer platforms and networks*

plat•i•num /ˈplætɪnəm/ *n* [U] a silver-grey metal used in manufacturing and traded on COMMODITIES MARKETS: *Platinum, used mainly for car catalysts that remove pollutants* (=substances that harm the environment) *from automotive engines and in jewellery, fell to $339 an ounce.*

play[1] /pleɪ/ *v* [T] **1 play the market(s)** FINANCE if you play the market, you buy and sell shares on the stockmarket, especially to make a quick profit rather than as an investment for the future: *"I tried to be as cautious as I could," she says. "I never played the equity market."*
2 play the system to use the rules of a system in a clever way, to gain an advantage: *These accountants know how to play the tax system.*
3 have money to play with to have extra money which you can use for a particular purpose: *If you do get a severance check* (=money you get from your employer when you lose your job) *and land a job immediately, you'll have some extra money to play with.*

play[2] *n* [C] **1** FINANCE an occasion when someone risks money on a financial market: *In stock options, the biggest play of the day was in BP, where 500 of the January 850p calls were bought for 94p.*
2 *journalism* **in play** if a company is in play, it may be bought in a TAKEOVER: *The company has strongly denied it's in play.*

play•er /ˈpleɪə‖-ər/ *n* [C] one of the important people, companies etc involved in a particular industry, market, situation etc + **in**: *Murdoch is one of the* ***major players*** *in the multimedia industry.* | *Ericsson is a* ***world player*** *in telecommunications equipment exporting.*
gross player in the film industry, a director, actor, writer etc who is paid a percentage of the RECEIPTS (=money that people pay to see the film) before production, distribution, and other costs are taken away
market player *journalism* a company or financial institution involved in a particular market: *London market players pushed prices down early in the day.*
net player in the film industry, a director, actor, writer etc who is paid a percentage of the profits of a film after all production, distribution, and other costs are taken away —see also TEAM PLAYER

play time —see under TIME

PLC 1 also **plc** abbreviation for PUBLIC LIMITED COMPANY
2 abbreviation for PRODUCT LIFE CYCLE

plea /pliː/ *n* [C usually singular] LAW a statement by someone in a court of law, saying whether they are guilty of a crime or not: *Your honor, we* ***enter*** (=make) ***a plea*** *of 'not guilty'.*

plead /pliːd/ *v* past tense and past participle **pleaded** or **pled** [I,T] to state in a court of law whether you are guilty of a crime or not: *Charged with fraud for selling the fakes, they agreed to* ***plead guilty*** (=to admit that they did the crime). | *He* ***pleaded no contest to*** (=said that he would not defend himself against) *two assault charges and resigned his office in disgrace.*

plead•ings /ˈpliːdɪŋz/ *n* [plural] LAW the arguments used by lawyers and others involved in a CASE in a court of law: *Bankruptcy lawyers are wondering how they will handle the pleadings of the roughly 21,000 creditors in the case.*

pledge[1] /pledʒ/ *n* [C] **1** *journalism* a formal, usually public, promise that you will do something: *the French government's pledge to invest FFr2 billion in Air France*
2 FINANCE something that you offer as SECURITY (=an asset that lenders can take if you do not repay) when you borrow money: *The loan was secured on the basis of a pledge to offer Japanese equities as collateral.*

pledge[2] *v* [T] **1** *journalism* to make a formal, usually public, promise that you will do something: *At the meeting, Western industrial nations didn't* ***pledge*** *any* ***money*** *to help Moscow.* | *Beijing will continue to* ***pledge support*** *for the special economic zones.*
2 FINANCE when you borrow money, to offer something you own as SECURITY (=something that lenders have a right to take and sell if you do not repay): *He will pledge virtually all of his assets – including his personal residences – to secure his borrowings.*

pledg•ee /ˌpleˈdʒiː/ *n* [C] LAW a lender that accepts a pledge for a loan

pledg•er also **pledgor** /ˈpledʒə‖-ər/ *n* [C] a borrower who offers a pledge for a loan: *The pledgor gives the pledgee some rights but does not part with all rights of ownership.*

plot[1] /plɒt‖plɑːt/ *n* [C] PROPERTY a small piece of land for building or growing things on: *a* ***vacant plot*** (=empty piece of land) | *a plot of land*

plot[2] *v* past tense and past participle **plotted** present participle **plotting** [T] to draw a line or curve that shows facts or figures: *We* ***plotted a graph*** *to show the increase in sales figures this year.*

plot plan —see under PLAN[2]

plough *BrE*, also **plow** *AmE* /plaʊ/ *v*
plough sth ↔ **back into** sth *phr v* [T] to put money that you have earned back into a business, in order to make the business bigger and more successful, rather than giving it to shareholders: *Companies can* ***plow*** *their* ***profits back into*** *plant and equipment.* | *The group has ploughed back £31 million into the business over the last six months which should lead to further improvements in services.*

plug[1] /plʌg/ *n* [C] **1** MARKETING *informal* an attempt to persuade people to buy a book, see a film etc, by talking about it publicly, especially on television or radio: *She appeared on all the talk shows to* ***give*** *her new show* ***a plug***. + **for**: *The author* ***put in a plug*** *for his new book.*
2 pull the plug (on sth) to prevent a plan or business from being able to continue, especially by not giving it any more money: *We were doing fine until the bank pulled the plug on us.*

plug[2] *v* past tense and past participle **plugged** present participle **plugging** [T] *informal* MARKETING to try to persuade people to buy a book, see a film etc, by talking about it publicly, especially on television or radio: *Arnold Schwarzenegger was only on the show to plug his new movie.* | *The insurance company Laurentian Life is plugging the advantages of mortgage protection insurance.*

plug-and-play *adj* COMPUTING plug-and-play computer equipment is able to start working as soon as it is connected to a computer: ***Plug and Play technology*** *makes computer peripherals, such as modems and printers, easy to install.*

plum•met /ˈplʌmɪt/ *v* [I,T] to suddenly and quickly go down in value or amount; PLUNGE: *House prices have plummeted.* | *The Nikkei index of 225 leading shares plummeted by 577.38 points yesterday.* | *CyberCash Inc.'s stock plummeted 19% after an investment analyst said the company has had trouble selling its Internet commerce technology.* —**plummet** *n* [C] *Reacting to Friday's plummet, prices firmed up again as traders regained their optimism.*

plun•der[1] /ˈplʌndə‖-ər/ *v* [T] to steal large amounts of money or property from somewhere: *a corrupt tycoon who plundered his companies' pension funds* | *Government funds are being plundered by the party.* —**plunderer** *n* [C] *The first plunderer of Zaire's immense wealth was Belgium's King Leopold II.*

plunder² *n* [U] **1** large amounts of money or property that have been stolen: *Denon filled the Louvre with plunder from churches and palaces all over Europe.*
2 the act of plundering: *The dictator's fortune was amassed during three decades of plunder of his own country.*

plunge¹ /plʌndʒ/ *v* [I,T] *journalism* if a price, value, or rate plunges, it suddenly goes down by a large amount; PLUMMET: *Stock prices plunged again yesterday.* | *The company's shares plunged 33% in a single day.*
plunge into *phr v* [T] **1 plunge into sth** to begin to do something suddenly, without thinking about the possible results: *Investors are plunging into the world of international bonds.*
2 plunge (sb/sth) into sth to start to experience a difficult or unpleasant situation, or to make someone or something start to experience it: *After the war, Europe plunged into recession.* | *Various disasters plunged Lloyd's into deficit.*

P

plunge² *n journalism* **1** [C usually singular] a sudden large fall in a price, value, or rate; PLUMMET + **in**: *The plunge in oil prices lead to losses of about $50 million.*
2 take the plunge to finally decide to take a risk, especially after delaying it for a long time: *Advertisers are studying the new technology with interest, but most have yet to take the plunge.*

plus¹ /plʌs/ *prep* **1** used when one amount or number is added to another: *Weekend calls cost a $1 base fee, plus $1 a minute.* | *His salary is £30,000 a year, plus bonuses.*
2 used when giving the second reason for something: *Cost-cutting, plus strong sales, enabled Cummins to break even.*

plus² *n* [C] an advantage or good feature of something: *One of the pluses of the job is having really supportive colleagues.* | *A huge* ***plus factor*** *is the central location of the hotel.*

plus³ *adj* **1 50/100 etc plus** more than 50, 100 etc: *Some waterside apartments are selling at £100,000 plus.* | *the 80-plus employees of Mr Murphy's television company*
2 plus tick FINANCE on a stockmarket, if shares are sold on a plus tick, they are sold at a higher price than their previous one: *He traded near the close of the day on either a plus tick or a zero-plus tick* (=where the price is unchanged.)

ply /plaɪ/ past tense and past participle **plied** *v journalism* **1** [T] to sell something: *60 retailers were plying their products on the radio.*
2 ply your trade to work at your job or business + **in**: *the people within IBM that ply their trade in software*
3 [I,T] if a vehicle or boat plies between two places, it makes the journey regularly + **between**: *ferries plying between Dover and Calais* | *Australian government policy prohibits Qantas from* ***plying*** *domestic* ***routes.***
ply sb **with** sth *phr v* [T] to keep giving someone something in order to persuade them to do something: *The sales force plied doctors with free samples.*

PO /ˌpiː ˈəʊ‖-ˈoʊ/ written abbreviation for POST OFFICE and POSTAL ORDER

poach /pəʊtʃ‖poʊtʃ/ *v* [I,T] **1** to persuade someone to leave an organization and come and work for you: *Wall Street firms have always poached each other's star brokers.* + **from**: *We prefer not to poach from other firms.*
2 to unfairly or illegally use someone else's ideas: *They were accused of poaching Coca Cola's ideas.* + **from**: *a concept poached from their main rival* —**poaching** *n* [U] *There is still some poaching between the major executive search firms.*

PO Box /ˌpiː əʊ ˈbɒks◂‖-oʊ ˈbɑːks◂/ *n* [C] a numbered box in a post office to which someone's mail can be sent and from which they can collect it: *For further information write to PO Box 714, Key Largo, Florida.* —see also BOX NUMBER

pock·et¹ /ˈpɒkɪ̈t‖ˈpɑːkɪ̈t/ *n* [C] **1** *journalism* used to refer to the amount of money people have available to spend: *We need to find a way to* ***put*** *more* ***money in people's pockets.*** | *a savings scheme* ***to suit all pockets*** (=suitable however much money you have) | *a company with* ***deep pockets*** (=a lot of money)
2 a small area or part of something where a situation is very different from other areas or parts + **of**: *Certain pockets of the aircraft market already have shown themselves to be vulnerable.*
3 be out of pocket *informal* to have less money than you should have after a business deal: *All expenses will be paid. You won't be out of pocket.*
4 put your hand in your pocket *informal* to give money to someone who needs it
5 line your pockets *disapproving* to earn a lot of money, especially by using unfair methods: *Banks are lining their pockets by charging their customers sky-high interest rates.*

pocket² *adj* **pocket calculator/dictionary etc** a calculator, dictionary etc that is small enough to carry in your pocket: *You can now buy pocket televisions.* | *a pocket computer*

pocket³ *v* [T] *informal* **1** to get money, used especially when you think someone does not deserve the money or when they get it in a slightly dishonest way: *For operating the network, Jefferies pockets about $60,000 a day.* | *He sold her car for more than she asked for, and* ***pocketed the difference*** (=kept the extra money for himself).
2 to steal money, especially money you are responsible for: *The insurer had no record of the policy because the agent had pocketed the premiums.*

POD payment on delivery; used to show that something must be paid for when it is delivered to the buyer

point¹ /pɔɪnt/ *n* [C] **1** a single idea, opinion, or fact, especially one that is part of a plan, argument, or discussion: *That's a very interesting point.* | *I agree with your point about the importance of safety.* | *Mr Clark* ***made the point that*** *economic growth would create the wealth necessary to protect the environment.*
2 the point the main idea in something that is said or done which gives meaning to all of it: ***The point is*** *that staff are not allowed to smoke in the building.* | *Have I completely* ***missed the point*** (=failed to understand the main meaning of something)*?*
3 one of a series of parts into which a meeting, plan etc is divided: *What's the first point on the agenda?* | *Citicorp announced* ***a five-point plan*** *for overhauling its businesses.*
action point something that you decide must be done, especially after a meeting or after studying something carefully: *We drew up a list of action points arising from the interview.*
4 FINANCE a unit of measure used in INDEXES (=series of figures giving the general level of financial markets, economic activity etc): *The Financial Times 30 Share Index closed up 11 points at 1659.5.*
basis point FINANCE a measurement of the interest rate on bonds. One basis point is one hundredth of one percent: *The price of New York City bonds should go up by no more than about 10 basis points in next Wednesday's sale.*
percentage point a unit of measure used for changes in interest rates. If one loan has an interest rate of 10% and another 12%, the difference between them is two percentage points: *The Bank of Japan cut the rate by half a percentage point, to 4% from 4.5% to 4.0%.*
5 a place or position: *Your luggage will be searched at the* ***point of departure.*** | *Visas cannot be issued at the* ***entry points*** *along the border.*
6 an exact moment, time, or stage in the development of something: *Creativity is the* ***starting point*** *for any*

innovation. | *It is too early to tell whether last month's increase marks a* ***turning point*** (=a time when a situation changes) *for McDonalds.* | *The economy seems to be moving to* ***the point of no return*** (=the point where it becomes so bad it cannot recover).

break-even point the level of sales at which the income from goods sold is just enough to cover the costs of production so that neither a profit or loss is being made: *Cognito's break-even point is around 3,500 subscribers.*

reorder point MANUFACTURING the point when it is necessary to order more of a product, taking into account the demand for the product, and the time it takes to deliver it

trigger point ◆ FINANCE the number of shares in a company above which a shareholder is forced to take a particular course of action. For example, if the shareholder has 30% of the shares in a company, it is forced to make an offer for the remaining shares: *We can accumulate more Avon shares up to the trigger point.*
◆ the price below which an imported product must fall before trade restrictions are put on it

7 a unit used to measure how good someone or something is or how suitable they are for something: *The details you give are assessed according to* ***a points system.***

8 a particular quality or feature that something or someone has: *Finance has never been his* ***strong point.*** | *Every system has its* ***good points*** *and drawbacks.*

selling point a feature of a product that makes it sell well: *A selling point for houses around here is the amazing lake view.*

unique selling point also **unique selling proposition**, abbreviation **USP** a feature of a product that no other similar products have, used in advertising etc to try to persuade people to buy it: *Finding a unique selling point for banking services is not easy.*

9 *spoken* a sign (.) used to separate a whole number from any DECIMALS that follow it —see also BULLET POINT

point[2] *v* **1 point the finger (at sb)** to blame someone for something: *To minimise his sentence, Boesky pointed the finger at people he had dealt with.*

2 point the way to show how something could change or develop successfully: *The article summarises the current law and* ***points the way forward.***

point sth ↔ **out** *phr v* [T] to tell someone something they did not already know or had not thought about: *Few courts, Ms Lord pointed out, have enforced the rights of fathers regarding child care.*

point to sth *phr v* [T] to mention something because you think it is important: *He pointed to widespread reports that the plane crash was due to faulty repair work.*

point to/towards sth *phr v* [T] if something points to a fact, it makes it seem very likely that it is true: *The economy's performance in April pointed toward a recovery in the manufacturing sector.*

point sth ↔ **up** *phr v* [T] to make something seem more important or noticeable: *The latest economic figures point up the failure of the government's policies.*

point·er /ˈpɔɪntə‖-ər/ *n* [C] **1** a useful piece of advice or information, that helps you do or understand something: *He occasionally gets pointers on public speaking from media consultants.*

2 something that shows how a situation is developing or is a sign to what might happen in the future + **to**: *Local election results traditionally are not a very good pointer to a government's national support.*

point of law *n* plural **points of law** [C] a particular legal rule, especially one that ordinary people find difficult to understand: *The judge may be able to clarify certain points of law.*

point of order *n* plural **points of order** [C] in a meeting or parliament, a question about whether its rules are being followed properly: *The South Carolina Democrat* ***raised a point of order*** *against the planned change.*

point of purchase *n* plural **points of purchase** [C] MARKETING the place where a product is bought: *Refunds can be obtained from the point of purchase.* | *point-of-purchase displays*

point of purchase advertising —see under ADVERTISING

point of sale written abbreviation **POS** *n* plural **points of sale** [C] the place where a product is sold: *The general sales tax is imposed only at the point of sale.* | *point-of-sale credit card scanners*

point-of-sale *adj* [only before a noun] MARKETING relating to the place where customers pay for something in a shop, hotel etc: *point-of-sale terminals that automate credit-card payment transactions* | ***point-of-sale advertising*** —**point of sale** *n* [C usually singular] *The general sales tax is imposed only at the point of sale to the consumer.*

poison pill *n* [C] FINANCE *journalism* something in a company's financial or legal structure that is meant to make it difficult for another company to buy it in a TAKEOVER: *Eljer's poison-pill anti-takeover measure prevents a group from purchasing more than 10% of the company's stock.* | *ITT may sell some of its hotels and manage them under contracts with their new owners. The contracts would become void if ITT were taken over – a form of* ***poison pill defence*** *against Hilton's bid.* —see also SHARK REPELLENT

po·lar·i·za·tion also **polarisation** *BrE* /ˌpəʊləraɪˈzeɪʃən‖-rə-/ *n* [U] FINANCE a system under which financial advisors in Britain are divided into those who sell the products of a particular organization and those who sell a range of products from different organizations

po·lice /pəˈliːs/ *v* [T] to control a particular activity or industry by making sure that people follow the correct rules; REGULATE: *The agency was set up to police the nuclear power industry.*

pol·i·cy /ˈpɒl̩si‖ˈpɑː-/ *n* plural **policies** [C,U] **1** [C] an INSURANCE POLICY; a contract with an insurance company, or an official written statement giving all the details of such a contract: *She did not realize that her policy had expired.* | *Your account number is printed on the top of your* ***policy document.*** —see also separate entry at INSURANCE POLICY

2 a course of action that has been officially agreed and chosen by a political party, business, or other organization: *The decision marks a distinct change of policy.* | *It's* ***company policy*** *not to give interviews to the press.* | *The two ministers disagreed on certain aspects of* ***economic policy.***

credit policy ◆ a company's policy on when its customers should pay for goods or services they have ordered: *Reinforce your credit policy with a reputable debt collector.*
◆ a government's policy at a particular time on how easy or difficult it should be for people and businesses to borrow and how much it should cost. The government influences this through changes in interest rates: *the constraints of a tight credit policy and high interest rates*

dear money policy ECONOMICS a policy in which a government reduces the amount of money being spent in an economy by raising INTEREST RATES, making it more expensive to borrow money

domestic policy government policy concerned with education, health, and other issues that affect its own country: *There have been complaints about a lack of direction in domestic policy.*

fiscal policy also **budgetary policy** government policy concerned with raising money, especially through TAXATION, and how this money is spent: *"Tax increases* *cannot remain the only instrument of fiscal policy,' said the Bundesbank.*

foreign policy government policy concerned with the country's relations with other countries, especially in trade and DEFENCE: *Business interests strongly affect American foreign policy.*

incomes policy government policy concerned with keeping inflation at a low level by controlling wages and prices: *Some argue that government control of the economy must include an effective incomes policy.*

monetary policy ECONOMICS the way a CENTRAL BANK controls the amount of money in the economy at a particular time, for example by changing interest rates: *Unless the Bank of Japan* ***relaxes monetary policy*** (=makes it easier to borrow), *for example by lowering interest rates the stock market is unlikely to improve.* | *The program is aimed at maintaining the exchange rate against other currencies by* ***tightening monetary policies*** (=making them more strict) *for example by raising interest rates.*

P

open-door policy ◆ when a country encourages businesses from other countries to invest in it and to trade with it: *'We are trying to follow an open-door policy,' said the finance minister to an angry foreign investor, 'but there have been problems.'*

◆ HUMAN RESOURCES an official system where the top managers of a company deal with employees' complaints: *IBM has an open door policy that allows employees to pursue complaints against their supervisor all the way to the chairman's office.*

pol·i·cy·hold·er /ˈpɒləsi ˌhəʊldə‖ˈpɑːləsi ˌhoʊldər/ also **policy holder** *n* [C] LAW someone who has an insurance policy: *The policyholder must inform the insurance company of any change of address.*

political action committee —see under COMMITTEE

political economy —see under ECONOMY[1]

political risk —see under RISK[1]

poll[1] /pəʊl‖poʊl/ *n* [C] **1** an occasion when a large number of people are asked questions, to find out about the public's opinions or behaviour: *MORI* ***conducted a poll*** *among senior managers to get their views on taxation.* | *A recent* ***opinion poll*** *put him in third place.* | *According to our poll, Scandinavians buy shares more than other Europeans.*

exit poll a poll in which people are asked how they have voted in an election. The poll is taken before the result of the election is known, in order to discover its likely result: *Early exit polls suggested he was the clear winner.*

Gallup poll *trademark* a poll in which a REPRESENTATIVE group of people (=one that is typical of a particular group in society) are asked questions about a specific issue, done to find out the public's opinion on it

straw poll one in which people are asked their opinion about something, in an informal and unofficial way: *A quick straw poll of delegates revealed that most would prefer a longer conference.*

2 the polls [plural] an election to choose a government or a political representative: *The ruling Social Democrats suffered the worst defeat* ***at the polls*** *in 60 years.* | *In Oklahoma, voters may* ***go to the polls*** (=vote in an election) *as early as September.*

3 an occasion when the members of a company vote for or against something in a meeting: *Both directors were elected after a poll of shareholders.*

4 the poll the number of votes recorded at an election: *The winning party must gain at least 50% of the poll.*

poll[2] *v* [T] to try to find out about the public's behaviour or opinions by questioning a large number of people: *47% of office workers polled by Louis Harris said that eye strain was a serious concern.*

poll·ster /ˈpəʊlstə‖ˈpoʊlstər/ *n* [C] *journalism* a person or organization that carries out polls

poll tax —see under TAX[1]

pollution credit —see under CREDIT[1]

po·ny /ˈpəʊni‖ˈpoʊ-/ *v* past tense and past participle **ponied**

pony sth ↔ **up** *phr v* [I,T] *AmE informal* to pay a sum of money: *Voters were in no mood to pony up more taxes.*

Pon·zi scheme /ˈpɒnzi skiːm‖ˈpɑːn-/ —see under SCHEME

pool[1] /puːl/ *n* [C] **1** an amount of money or a number of things shared by a group of people: *Both partners put money into a common pool, and both may spend this money.*

blind pool a FUND where investors do not know exactly what businesses their money will be invested in: *a $60 million blind pool from which he hopes to start a number of high-technology companies*

2 a group of people who are available to do a particular job, if they are needed: *Taiwan offered a pool of cheap labour.* | *There is a considerable pool of experience within our own organization.*

3 INSURANCE an association of insurance companies organized to UNDERWRITE (=be responsible for) a particular risk, each member sharing any costs or losses: *the state-run pool for high-risk drivers.* —see also CAR POOL[1], MOTOR POOL

pool[2] *v* [T] to combine your money, ideas, skills etc with those of other people so that you can all use them: *Sharing problems and* ***pooling ideas*** *have all proved helpful.* | *More and more firms are* ***pooling their resources*** *and going into joint ventures.* —**pooling** *n* [U] *the pooling of information*

pooling of interests *n* [singular] FINANCE in a MERGER (=when two firms become one), a method of accounting in which the accounts of each firm are added together, item by item: *The acquisition will be accounted for as a pooling of interests.*

popular capitalism —see under CAPITALISM

pop·u·la·tion /ˌpɒpjəˈleɪʃən‖ˌpɑː-/ *n* **1** [C,U] the number of people who live in a particular country or area: *a city with a population of over 2 million* | *Hong Kong's rapid growth in population*

2 [C usually singular] all the people who live in a particular area: *12% of the population now has private health insurance.*

active population also **economically active population, working population** [C,U] all the people who normally work in an area, country etc: *Even by 1930, 46% of the active population of Italy was still directly involved in agriculture.* | *Unemployment has risen to 4.1% of the working population.*

pork barrel *n* [U] *AmE informal disapproving* a government plan to increase the amount of money spent in a particular area in order to gain a political advantage: *One person's pork barrel is another's essential local courthouse or dam.*

pork bellies *n* [plural] FINANCE meat from pigs that is used to make BACON (= a type of salted meat). Pork bellies are one of the COMMODITIES (=farm products, metals etc) bought and sold on the CHICAGO MERCANTILE EXCHANGE: *Larger-than-expected storage of pork bellies typically causes futures prices to fall.*

port[1] /pɔːt‖pɔːrt/ *n* **1** [C,U] a place where ships can load and unload people or things, or a town or city that has one of these places: *Inspectors were holding up grain exports at Canadian ports.* | ***Port officials*** *reported huge losses on port operations last year.* | *The cargo can* ***leave port*** *immediately.* | *the Jordanian port of Aqaba*

Channel port [C] a port along the south coast of England or the north coast of France, especially one where ships carrying people and goods between England and France arrive and leave: *the transfer of money away from the channel ports to the Eurotunnel*

container port [C] a port with special machines for loading and unloading large containers
free port [C] a port where CUSTOMS DUTY (=a tax paid on imported goods) does not have to be paid on imports that are to be sent to another country to be sold, or used to manufacture goods that will be sold abroad
home port [C] the port where a ship is found most of the time when it is not travelling
port of registry plural **ports of registry** [C] a ship's home port is where it is REGISTERED (=the place given as its base in official records for purposes of taxation etc). This may or may not be its home port
port of entry plural **ports of entry** [C] a port or airport where people or goods can enter a country: *The animals must be removed from the port of entry in a registered vehicle.*
2 [C] COMPUTING a part of a computer where you can connect another piece of equipment such as a PRINTER: *The unit plugs into the printer port of your PC.*
comm port [C] part of a computer where you can connect a piece of equipment used to communicate with other computers, such as a MODEM: *Installation is simple, although you may have to reset the comm port.*
parallel port [C] part of a computer that sends or receives information through more than one wire, connected to something such as a printer
serial port [C] part of a computer that sends or receives information through one wire in a series of stages

port² *v* [T] COMPUTING to run SOFTWARE on another computer system without changing it in any way **port sth to sth**: *Can Windows applications be ported to Unix?*

por•ta•ble¹ /ˈpɔːtəbəl‖ˈpɔːr-/ *adj* **1** light and able to be carried or moved easily: *a portable computer* | *portable phones*
2 FINANCE the money from a PENSION PLAN (=saving for when you no longer work) that is portable can be taken from one company to another when you change jobs: *One idea is to allow payroll deductions into a portable accounts for each employee.*
3 COMPUTING portable SOFTWARE (=computer programs) can be run on another computer system without changing it in any way: *The applications will be portable across different graphical user interfaces.* —**portability** *n* [U] *the portability of a VSAM file from one device to another*

portable² *n* [C] a computer that is light enough to be carried around: *He set his portable to automatically check his electronic mail boxes.*

portable document format —see PDF

portable pension —see under PENSION¹

por•tal /ˈpɔːtl‖ˈpɔːrtl/ *n* [C] COMPUTING a system for connecting a computer to another NETWORK (=a set of connected computers), especially the INTERNET; GATEWAY: *Portals attract millions of Internet users and consequently lots of lucrative advertising.*

port authority —see under AUTHORITY

por•ter /ˈpɔːtə‖ˈpɔːrtər/ *n* [C] **1** someone whose job is to carry people's bags, for example at railway stations, airports etc
2 *BrE* someone whose job is to help guests arriving at a hotel

por•ter•age /ˈpɔːtərɪdʒ‖ˈpɔːr-/ *n* [U] when someone helps you carry bags that you are travelling with: *The cost of the trip includes round-trip air fare, transfers, and porterage.*

port•fo•li•o /pɔːtˈfəʊliəʊ‖pɔːrtˈfoʊlioʊ/ *n* **1** [C] a collection of shares owned by a person or company: *European stocks make up 50% of his* ***investment portfolio.*** | *a measure of portfolio performance*
2 [C] all the products or services offered by a particular business: *The company has struck a deal with a biotechnology company of similar size and* ***product portfolio.***
3 [C,U] the area of responsibility of a particular government minister in Britain or cabinet member in the US government: *Nick Brown was given the Agriculture portfolio.* | *the* ***Minister Without Portfolio*** (=with general responsibilities)
4 [C] a large flat case, used especially for carrying drawings and documents

portfolio management —see under MANAGEMENT

portfolio manager —see under MANAGER

portfolio mix —see under MIX

portfolio worker —see under WORKER

port of embarkation —see under EMBARKATION

port of entry —see under PORT¹

port of registry —see under PORT¹

POS written abbreviation for POINT OF SALE

P

po•si•tion¹ /pəˈzɪʃən/ *n* [C] **1** the situation that a person or organization is in, or the situation concerning a particular subject: *What's the present position with regard to import restrictions?* | *The new legislation puts the unions in a* ***difficult position.*** —see also BARGAINING POSITION
2 how much money a person or organization has or how successful it is: *The investment would weaken Wilkinson Sword's* ***competitive position*** *while strengthening Gillette's.*
cash position the amount of cash, shares etc that can quickly be turned into cash, that a company has at a particular time: *The company's cash position from trading activities appears to be healthy.*
technical position FINANCE whether the price of a share, bond, currency etc is gradually rising or falling
3 be in a position to do sth to be able to do something because you have the ability, money, or power to do it: *We will refund your money when we are in a position to do so.*
4 jockey/manoeuvre/jostle for position to try to get an advantage over other people who are all trying to succeed in the same activity: *US advertising agencies are jostling for position in Eastern Europe.*
5 also **financial position** a person's or company's financial situation: *Newhall's* ***strong financial position*** *with more than $7 million in cash and no short-term debt* | *RSCG's* ***weak financial position*** *forced it to merge with Eurocom.*
6 the level or rank someone or something has in a society or organization + **in**: *He was a doctor with a respectable position in society.* | *We need more women in* ***positions of authority*** *and* ***influence*** *in television.* | *Financial institutions are in a unique* ***position of trust*** *when handling funds belonging to the public.* | *He did not want to be accused of* ***abusing his position*** *using his authority wrongly.*
7 *formal* a job, especially an important one: + **as** *He has been offered a* ***management position*** *in Cairo.* | *Twelve people* ***applied for the position*** (=asked to have the job). | *He* ***is filling a position*** (=taking a job) *that has been vacant since July.* | *The highest* ***entry-level position*** *job on joining an organization in the department is assistant manager.* | *He is older than most executives in their first* ***senior position*** (=important job) *abroad.*
8 someone's opinion or judgement on something + **on**: *What's your position on using freelance staff?* | *The administration hadn't reviewed the compromise and didn't yet have a position on it.*
9 FINANCE an investment in something, or the amount invested: *The family has a recent history of buying positions of over 5% in public companies.* | *The fund's largest* ***bond position*** (=investment in the form of bonds) *is in Gulf Resources.* | *Nynex said it will* ***take a 10% equity***

position (=buy 10% of the shares) *in TelecomAsia.* | *After we have earned a modest profit, we will simply **cash** our **position out*** (=sell our investment).

long position also **bull position** when you possess particular bonds, shares, currencies, etc, believing that their value will rise: *To **hold a long position** in silver futures is, in effect, to bet that silver prices will rise.*

short position also **bear position** a situation in which someone sells shares that they have borrowed and not paid for, believing the price will fall before the shares have to be delivered and they can profit from the difference between the price at which they are selling the shares and the price they will pay for them: *They built up a short position of five contracts in the Japanese yen, anticipating a decline relative to the dollar.* | *He sold the stock for more than $23 a share. After the company's announced loss, he bought back the shares at $21 to **cover** his **short position** to be able to deliver shares that he had already sold but did not own.*

P

position[2] *v* [T] **1** to put something in a particular position: *Position the cursor before the letter you want to delete.*

2 if you position yourself in a particular way, or if something positions you in that way, you are prepared for a situation that you want to happen or think is going to happen: *The company's restructuring has positioned Fuqua to compete more effectively.* | *Cigna has been working to position itself as a seller of group health insurance to major corporations.*

3 MARKETING if a company positions a product in a particular way, it tries to get people to think about it in that way in relation to the company's other products and to competing products: *The trend over the past decade has been to position pizza as a health food.* | *We're trying to position the product toward younger buyers.* —**positioned** *adj*: *Hyundai said its newest entry is positioned between its subcompact Excel and the upscale Sonata.* | *Chase Chemical is **well positioned** in the market-place.*

po•si•tion•ing /pəˈzɪʃənɪŋ/ also **product positioning** *n* [U] MARKETING the way that people think about a product in relation to the company's other products and to competing products, or the way that the company would like them to think about it: *A price reduction may have the effect of damaging the brand's image and positioning.* | *The teams will develop and manage global plans for branding and product positioning.* | *the positioning of Seven-Up as a cola alternative*

positive discrimination —see under DISCRIMINATION

positive net worth —see under NET WORTH

pos•sess /pəˈzes/ *v* [T] *formal* **1** to own or have something, especially something valuable or important, or something illegal: *The US is the only country that possesses global economic, military and political power.* | *Judges rarely send people to jail for possessing illegal drugs, but they jail people for selling them.*

2 to have a characteristic or ability: *He possesses the qualities required to manage the organization's varied commercial interests.*

pos•ses•sion /pəˈzeʃən/ *n* **1** [C] something that someone owns: *All his possessions fit into two suitcases.*

2 [U] the state of having or owning something: *Japan will not give aid until a quarrel with Russia over possession of the Kuril Islands is settled.* | *What happens if the buyer **has possession** of a work, but has not completely paid for it when it is stolen?* | *The creditors will **take possession** of* (=obtain) *assets worth the $85 million owed to them.* | *Healthcare said it refused to **relinquish possession** of* (=give up) *of the 68-bed hospital.*

freehold possession [U] *BrE* PROPERTY when you own land, a house, a flat etc, rather than rent it

immediate possession [U] PROPERTY the legal right to move into a house or other property immediately after buying it

leasehold possession [U] *BrE* PROPERTY when you rent land, a house, a flat etc rather than own it

private possession [U] when something is owned by a person for their own use rather than by an organization or government: *a federal law that bans the private possession of automatic weapons*

quiet possession [U] LAW the legal right of being able to use your own property or goods without other people causing problems, for example by claiming that they own them: *They had the right to sell the goods and also of the warranty of quiet possession.*

vacant possession *BrE* [U] PROPERTY when land, a house etc is for sale with no one living there: *the huge difference in price between land with and land without vacant possession*

3 [U] LAW the crime of having illegal drugs or a gun when it is illegal to do so: *He was sentenced to 16 months in prison for cocaine possession.*

pos•ses•sor /pəˈzesə‖-ər/ *n* [C] *formal* the owner of something: *Saudi Arabia is the possessor of the largest oil reserves in the world.*

post- /pəʊst‖poʊst/ *prefix* later than, after: *developing a post-acquisition strategy* | *Helical Bar's share price rocketed from its post-crash low.* —compare PRE-

post[1] /pəʊst‖poʊst/ *n* **1 the post** *especially BrE* the official system for sending and receiving letters, parcels etc; MAIL: *items that are lost or damaged in the **inland post*** | ***Letter post** items* (=letters rather than parcels) *must not exceed 610mm in length.* **by post**: *Winners will be notified by post.* **in the post**: *A copy of the document should be sent in the post.* **through the post**: *Only 2% of those questioned would choose to buy a policy through the post.* —see also FREEPOST, TRADING POST

2 [U] *especially BrE* the time when letters are collected or delivered: *Place items in the out-tray by 4.45 to meet the last post.*

3 by return (of) post if you reply to a letter by return of post, you reply almost immediately: *Send payment by return of post.*

4 [U] *BrE* letters, parcels etc; MAIL *AmE*: *paying for salaries, administration, post and telephones* | *We've cut our costs by using **first class post** only for urgent items.*

registered post also **special delivery** [U] a service to insure items sent through the post in case they are lost or damaged; REGISTERED MAIL; CERTIFIED MAIL *AmE*: *Bank notes should not be sent unless by registered post.*

5 [C,U] a job, especially an important or well paid one; POSITION: *He is special adviser to the DTI, a **post** he has **held** since 1998.* | *The bank chief plans to **resign** his **post*** (=leave it) *later this year.* **in post**: *Most of the executives interviewed had already been in post for 12 months.*

post[2] *v* [T] **1** *especially BrE* to send a letter, parcel etc using the official service; MAIL *AmE*: *the correct way to pack and protect the items you post* | *Shareholders will be sent details in a newsletter due to be posted today.*

2 FINANCE to offically record and announce results for a company or information about the economy: *Golden West Financial Corp **posted** a 25% **gain** in second-quarter net income.* | *JLG Industries shed a ¾ pt after **posting** a second-quarter **loss** of 35 cents a share.* | *Shares closed lower as the government posted worse inflation figures than the City expected.*

3 ACCOUNTING to enter a figure in a LEDGER (=a book used by a company to record money received or spent) **post sth to**: *The billing office will check that all charges have been posted to the guest's account.*

4 post bail —see under BAIL[1]

post•age /ˈpəʊstɪdʒ‖ˈpoʊs-/ *n* **1** [U] the money charged for delivering letters, parcels etc: *The industry's biggest cost variables are postage, paper and printing.* | *The annual subscription is $60, plus $2 postage and handling.*

2 postage paid envelope a phrase written on an envelope, showing that the cost of sending it has already been paid and there is no need to use a stamp; REPLY-PAID ENVELOPE *BrE*, BUSINESS REPLY ENVELOPE *AmE*: *Changing to a different credit card issuer is as easy as mailing back a postage-paid, direct mailshot.* | *a* ***postage paid envelope***
3 postage and packing written abbreviation **p&p** *BrE* a charge made for the cost of packing and sending something you have bought: *All books are offered at 20% below publishers' prices (plus post and packing).*

postage stamp —see STAMP[1]

post·al /ˈpəʊstl‖ˈpoʊs-/ *adj* [only before a noun] connected with the official system of sending and receiving letters, parcels etc: *strikes by* ***postal workers*** | *The* ***Postal Service*** (=official system for delivering letters, parcels etc in the United States) *has seen a significantly better financial performance.*

postal account —see under ACCOUNT[1]

postal order abbreviation **PO** *n* [C] *BrE* an official document bought at a post office, used to send money through the post safely; MONEY ORDER *AmE*: *Send a cheque or postal order for £13.99, payable to Dent and Reuss.*

postal packet —see under PACKET

post·bag /ˈpəʊstbæg‖ˈpoʊst-/ *n* [singular] *BrE* all the letters received by a public person, television programme etc: *The series did not please everyone, and the ZBS postbag was full of complaints.*

post·card /ˈpəʊstkɑːd‖ˈpoʊstkɑːrd/ *n* [C] a small card that can be sent through the post without an envelope: *The airmail postage for postcards is 34p to EU countries.*

post·code /ˈpəʊstkəʊd‖ˈpoʊstkoʊd/ also **postal code** *n* [C] *BrE* a series of letters and numbers showing exactly where a building is. Postcodes are used so that post can be delivered more quickly. Insurance companies also use postcodes to calculate insurance rates in different areas; ZIP CODE *AmE*: *A specialist agency will add postcodes to addresses where customer records are incomplete.*

post·date /ˌpəʊstˈdeɪt‖ˌpoʊst-/ *v* [T] to write a date on a cheque that is later than the date it was actually signed, and does not become effective until then

post-dated *adj* [only before a noun] a post-dated cheque has a date on it that is later than the date the cheque was actually signed, and cannot be cashed until that date: *From time to time, hard-pressed debtors will offer you* ***postdated cheques*** —compare ANTE-DATED, UNDATED

post-dated cheque —see under CHEQUE

post·er /ˈpəʊstə‖ˈpoʊstər/ *n* [C] a large printed notice, used to advertise something: *country-wide campaigns through posters and literature*

poste res·tante /ˌpəʊst ˈrestɒnt‖ˌpoʊst reˈstɑːnt/ *n* [U] *BrE* a post office department which keeps letters for people who are travelling; GENERAL DELIVERY *AmE*: *You'll find full details of the poste restante facility in the booklet 'UK Letter Rates'.*

post-free *adv* a letter sent post-free has no charge for the person who sends it; POST-PAID *AmE*

post·hu·mous /ˈpɒstjʊməs‖ˈpɑːstʃə-/ *adj* used to describe something that is produced or happens after a person's death: *the recent publication of a posthumous work by Gilles Barbedette* —**posthumously** *adv*: *The award will be granted posthumously.*

post·ing /ˈpəʊstɪŋ‖ˈpoʊs-/ *n* **1** [U] *especially BrE* the act of sending a letter, parcel etc through the official delivery system: *The insured service gives you evidence of posting.* | *If you do not obtain a* ***certificate of posting*** *we are not legally liable to pay compensation.*
2 [U] ACCOUNTING the work of entering figures in a LEDGER (=a book or computer record used by a company to record money received or spent): *A posting error can be corrected using the correction key.* —see also ERROR OF POSTING
3 [C] an occasion when an employee is sent to another country by their employer to do a particular job + **to**: *Mr Gardiner requested, and was granted, a posting to Japan.*

Post-it *n* [C] *trademark* a small piece of sticky coloured paper, used for leaving notes for people or marking pages in a book: *GM's* ***Post-it notes*** *are a classic case of marketing ingenuity.*

post·mark /ˈpəʊstmɑːk‖ˈpoʊstmɑːrk/ *n* [C] an official mark made on a letter, showing when and where it was sent: *Despite the crackdown, the documents are still sweeping the continent,* ***bearing postmarks*** *from Poland.* —**postmarked** *adj*: *Applications must be postmarked by midnight the day before the auction.*

post·mas·ter /ˈpəʊstˌmɑːstə‖ˈpoʊstˌmæstər/ *n* [C] *BrE* the person in charge of a POST OFFICE, often used in titles: *If you are not satisfied take up the matter with your District Head Postmaster who will try to help.*

post office *n* **1** [C] a place where you can buy stamps, send parcels etc: *Customers have complained about the length of time spent queuing at their* ***local post office.***
2 the Post Office the national organization in several countries, including Britain, responsible for collecting and delivering letters, parcels etc: *The Canadian Post Office has only a 4% market share for international deliveries.* | *Today's Post Office is an energetic group of market-led businesses serving the community.*

post office box —see under PO BOX

post office box number —see ***box number*** under NUMBER[1]

post-paid *adv AmE* a letter sent post-paid has no charge for the person who sends it; POST-FREE *BrE*

post room —see under ROOM[1]

Post·Script /ˈpəʊsˌskrɪpt‖ˈpoʊs-/ *n* [U] *trademark* COMPUTING a high level computer language used to produce photographs, drawings etc on a printed page; PAGE DESCRIPTION LANGUAGE: *Adobe's monopoly on PostScript has been broken.*

post·script /ˈpəʊsˌskrɪpt‖ˈpoʊs-/ *n* [C] **1** something added to the end of a report, account etc: *A limitation of liability should be explained in a postscript to the clause explaining its purpose.* | *The company didn't admit any wrongdoing but there's a postscript – complaints are still flooding in.*
2 —see PS

PostScript file —see under FILE[1]

po·ten·tial[1] /pəˈtenʃəl/ *adj* [only before a noun] a potential customer, market, buyer etc is not yet a customer, market etc, but may become one in the future: *American Express declined to confirm the names of the two* ***potential bidders.*** | *When the deal was circulated to* ***potential investors,*** *Citicorp was offering a 10% dividend.* | *The executives fear merger will expose FDC to new potential losses.*

potential[2] *n* [U] **1** the possibility that something will develop in a certain way: *The market isn't giving the company credit for any upside* (=successful) *potential.* | *weighing the likely* ***commercial potential*** *against the long research and development process* + **for/of**: *San Diego's potential for expanding its local television market* | *the labor-saving potential of information technology*
brand potential the possible future success in a particular market of a particular BRAND of product: *Heinz are determined to maximise brand potential by introducing more new products.*
2 a natural ability or quality that shows someone or something will be successful: *companies which are as yet unproven but* ***have potential*** —**potentially** *adv*: *Potentially, the market is huge.* | *A dispute that potentially involves tens of millions of dollars.*

P

POTS /pɒts‖pɑːts/ *n* [singular] *informal* plain old telephone service; traditional voice telephone services, rather than newer services such as the INTERNET

pound /paʊnd/ *n* [C] **1** written abbreviation **£** the standard unit of currency in Britain, which is divided into 100 pence: *The Perfect Pizza chain has total sales of £25 million to £30 million.* | *Rolls-Royce PLC has a 75 million-pound contract to supply turbine generators.*

2 the (British) pound the value of British currency compared with that of other countries: *Annual interest rates were 11.37% for the British pound and 8.21% for the Canadian dollar.* | *The pound and the peseta are allowed to rise or fall by 6% against other currencies.*

grey pound used to talk about the amount of money that older people have available to spend, or the things on which they choose to spend it

pink pound used to talk about the amount of money that HOMOSEXUAL people have available to spend, or the things on which they choose to spend it

3 the unit of currency in a number of countries, including Cyprus, Ireland, Malta, Sudan, Egypt, Syria, and Lebanon: *Waterford Wedgwood is expected to report an operating loss of about 20 million Irish pounds.*

4 written abbreviation **lb** a unit of weight equal to 16 OUNCES or 0.454 KILOGRAMS: *Apple prices averaged 24.9 cents a pound, down 4.2 cents.*

pound·age /ˈpaʊndɪdʒ/ *n* [U] a charge or tax made on each pound in money or in weight: *If the house was valued at £30,000 and the local poundage was 2p in the pound, the tax would be £30,000* × 0.02 or £600 a year. | *The measurements indicate the poundage of textile products that different clothing imports contain.*

pov·er·ty /ˈpɒvəti‖ˈpɑːvərti/ *n* [U] **1** the situation or experience of being poor: *86% of the population* ***lives in poverty***. | *a major anti-poverty initiative*

2 the poverty line the income below which people are officially considered to be very poor and needing help + **above/below**: *families* ***living above*** *the* ***poverty line***. | *The number of Americans* ***below the poverty line*** *has increased by two million.*

3 the poverty trap a situation in which a poor person without a job cannot afford to take a low paying job because they would lose the money they receive from the government

pow·er¹ /ˈpaʊə‖paʊr/ *n* **1** [U] the ability or right to control people, organizations, events etc: *I'm against giving too much power to one man.* + **over**: *Congress's power over federal spending* | *He plans to resign after losing a* ***power struggle*** *when people try to defeat each other to get control within the firm.*

2 [C,U] the right or authority to do something: *The lawmakers approved the President's demands for* ***special powers*** *to implement change.* | *The Board of Trade* ***invoked emergency powers*** (=special powers used to deal with an unusual, dangerous situation) *to stop an attempt to limit the soybean market.* | *Pirelli's chairman has decided to hand over his* ***executive powers*** (=powers to manage an organization) *to Mr Provera.* | *While not having direct* ***legislative power*** (=power to make laws), *the Bundesrat can block legislation.*

banking power [C] the legal right given to banks to perform certain activities that other types of business organization cannot perform: *The Fed favors capital-strong institutions in awarding increased banking powers.*

borrowing powers [plural] powers that are given to the directors of a company by its shareholders to borrow money: *Hanson shareholders have recently agreed to extend its borrowing powers.*

underwriting power [U] FINANCE the legal right of some financial institutions to UNDERWRITE (=arrange to sell) bonds, shares etc: *With underwriting power, we get a large share of the profits.*

3 [C] a country or organization that is strong and has a lot of influence: *The US is still the world's leading* ***economic power***. | *The Euro will strengthen Europe's position as a* ***financial power***. | *a war between film producers and some of cable TV's biggest powers*

4 [C] an ability to do something, influence a situation etc: *the incredible power of advertising* | *the job-generating power of small firms*

bargaining power [singular] *AmE* power that one person or group has during discussions about work matters to get an agreement in their favour: *This new law gives management tremendous bargaining power.*

buyer power [U] the relative strength of buyers in relation to sellers: *Centralised buying by different departments means that the industrial marketer may be faced with an increase in buyer power.*

buying power ◆ [U] the ability of a person or organization to buy things, depending on the amount of money they have available; PURCHASING POWER

◆ [U] the amount that a unit of a particular currency buys at a particular time; PURCHASING POWER, SPENDING POWER

earning power [U] the ability of a person to earn money, or of a business or an investment to make a profit: *the market for men 25 to 45 years old, with high earning power* | *This year's results aren't typical of the company's true earning power.*

grey power also **gray power** *AmE* [U] *journalism* the political and economic power of older people: *Politicians are only just becoming aware of the impact that grey power might have on the next election.* | *3,000 pensioners joined a grey power conference yesterday where speakers attacked government policies on pensions, invalidity benefits and supported housing.*

market power [U] the relative strength that a seller in a market has to set prices etc: *We prevent abuse of market power through anti-trust and anti-monopoly laws.*

purchasing power ◆ [U] the amount of money that a person, company etc has available to spend on goods and services: *Inflation is also caused by too much purchasing power in the economy.*

◆ [U] another name for BUYING POWER: *The purchasing power of the dollar has declined.*

spending power [U] another name for BUYING POWER: *The lowering of interest rates increased consumer spending power.*

5 [U] energy that is used to make electricity, electricity itself, and the industries that produce it: *Turn the power on with the switch.* | *Italians voted after Chernobyl to drop* ***nuclear power*** *development.* | *renewable energy, such as* ***wind*** *and* ***solar power*** (=power from the sun's energy)

6 [U] the ability of a machine to perform work: *Supercomputers use multiple processors to vastly increase* ***computing power*** *and speed.*

power² *v* **1** [T] to supply power to a vehicle or machine: *One of the two Swatch car models will be powered by electricity.* | *a PC powered by Intel's Pentium chip*

2 gas-powered/nuclear-powered etc working by means of gas, NUCLEAR ENERGY etc: *gas-powered turbines*

power sth ↔ **up** *phr v* **1** [I,T] FINANCE *journalism* if the price of shares etc powers up, or is powered up by something, it rises very fast: *The three-month price for zinc powered up to $1675 a tonne, a seven-year peak.*

2 [T] if you power up a computer, you start it

power³ *adj* [only before a noun] **1** driven by a motor: *power tools*

2 *informal* showing that you are an important person in a business organization: *If you think you can have a* ***power career*** *and a fulfilling family life, you're crazy.* | *the director's* ***power lunches*** *with movie moguls in trendy restaurants* | *a* ***power nap*** (=a short sleep during the day that allows you to work more effectively later)

P

pow·er·house /ˈpaʊəhaʊs‖ˈpaʊr-/ *n* [C] an organization that produces a lot of ideas or activity, and has a lot of power or influence in its field: *He wanted to turn the securities firm into a Wall Street powerhouse.*

power of attorney abbreviation **POA** *n* plural **powers of attorney** LAW **1** [U] legal permission to act for another person, for example because they are too ill to do something themselves: *Laws governing power of attorney can vary significantly from state to state.*
2 [C] a document giving someone this permission: *A power of attorney is never a substitute for a will.*

power-sharing *n* [U] when a political group or organization that holds power agrees to share it with other groups: *Greater power sharing is promised by the ruling People's Democratic Party of Afghanistan.* | *The* ***power-sharing negotiations*** *are at a critical stage in their development.*

pp. **1** written abbreviation for PAGES
2 per pro; written on a document before someone's name to show they have it signed for someone else

ppd. written abbreviation for PRE-PAID

ppi written abbreviation for PRODUCER PRICE INDEX

ppm *n* [U] parts per million; a measurement showing how much of a particular substance something contains: *employees exposed to formaldehyde concentrations of 1 ppm or more*

PPP written abbreviation for PURCHASING POWER PARITY

PPS —see under PS

PR *n* [U] public relations; the work of persuading people to have a good opinion of an organization, company etc: *Janney Montgomery Scott Inc. has hired a* ***PR firm*** *to promote its media image.* | *Nabisco says it is delighted with the extra PR generated by the popular evening show.*

prac·tice /ˈpræktɨs/ *n* **1** [U] the work done by a particular profession, especially lawyers or doctors who are working for themselves rather than a public organization: *Mr. Barr returned to private law practice in the mid-1990s.* | *Patricia Gillman, formerly staff attorney with CTFC and now* ***in practice*** (=working) *in Washington*
2 [C] the place where doctors, lawyers etc work, especially those who work for themselves: *what the future holds for small accountancy practices* | *They were partners in a general medical practice in central London.* | *He left to go into* ***private practice.***
3 [C,U] the way people do a particular task, activity etc, especially one which is done often: *Japanese management practices* | *It was* ***normal practice*** *for hotels to require confirmation in writing.* + **of**: *Toshiba will continue its practice of exporting the screens to California.*
custom and practice [U] HUMAN RESOURCES the way that something has always been done in the past, which can be used in discussions between workers and managers, even if it is not written down in any formal or legal document: *According to custom and practice my job description formed part of my contract.*
sharp practice [U] behaviour that is dishonest but not illegal: *Some of the rival bus companies have been accused of sharp practice.*
4 good/best practice a good example of how a regular task or activity in a particular profession should be done: *The Code reflects what the City considers to be best practice in the conduct of takeovers.*

prac·tise *BrE*, **practice** *AmE* /ˈpræktɨs/ *v* [I,T] **1** to work in a particular profession, especially medicine or law: *He joins the company from Gibson, Dunn and Crutcher, where he practised law for 15 years.* | *Firms are adopting the system of practicing in larger partnerships and teams.* + **as**: *Students must reach the highest standards to allow them to practise as actuaries.*
2 to use a particular method for doing a job, or a regular task or activity: *an application for entitlement to practise* | *chartered accountants who practise taxation*

prac·tis·ing *BrE*, **practicing** *AmE* /ˈpræktɨsɪŋ/ *adj* a practising lawyer, doctor etc is working as a lawyer, doctor etc: *The team comprised two practising barristers, a QC and a Circuit judge.*

practising certificate —see under CERTIFICATE

pre- /priː/ *prefix* coming before something: *the difference between the pre- and post-crash results* | ***Pre-tax profits*** (=profit before tax has been taken off) *were up 7.5%.*

pre·cau·tion /prɪˈkɔːʃən‖-ˈkɒː-/ *n* [C] something done to prevent something unpleasant or dangerous happening: *All companies with limited resources must* ***take precautions*** *to limit their liability.* | ***As a precaution,*** *the company advised consumers to examine any jar before it is opened.*

pre·ce·dent /ˈpresɨdənt/ *n* [C] LAW an official action or decision which can be used later to support another legal decision: *The injunction on imports could* ***set a precedent*** *for other patent-infringement cases.* | *Solicitors are aiming to* ***follow a precedent established*** *several years ago.* —see also CONDITION PRECEDENT

pre·cinct /ˈpriːsɪŋkt/ *n* [C] **1** *BrE* an area of a city with many different shops, and where cars are not allowed: *The hotel is within 5 minutes of the main* ***shopping precinct.***
2 *AmE* an area in a city with its own local government, police force etc: *working-class black precincts*

pré·cis /ˈpreɪsiː‖preɪˈsiː/ *n* plural **précis** [C] *formal* a statement giving the main ideas in a report, speech etc; SUMMARY: *Please provide a 1-2 page précis of your report.*

precision engineering —see under ENGINEERING

pred·a·tor /ˈpredətə‖-ər/ *n* [C] *journalism* a company which takes advantage of another company weaker than itself, for example by trying to buy it: *The takeover threat cooled, and would-be predators decided to wait and see how new management performs.* | *Speculation mounted that the brewery was the focus of a predator.*

pred·a·to·ry /ˈpredətəri‖-tɔːri/ *adj* trying to use someone's weaknesses to get an advantage: *Goldman was accused of acting in a hostile and predatory fashion to other bondholders.*

predatory pricing —see under PRICING

pre·de·ces·sor /ˈpriːdɨsesə‖ˈpredɨsesər/ *n* [C] *formal* **1** a person who was in a particular post or job before the person who is doing it now: *Problems he inherited from his predecessor led to the bank's later troubles.*
2 a machine, system, etc that existed before another one that has developed from it: *The Civic sedan will have a more aerodynamic shape than its popular predecessor.*

pre·empt /priːˈempt/ also **pre-empt** *v* [T] **1** LAW to officially make something that has been planned or agreed no longer effective: *The court ruled that the ordinance was unconstitutional and preempted by federal labor laws.* | *The federal law requiring health warnings on cigarette packs preempts lawsuits against manufacturers for their failure to warn of the dangers.*
2 to make what someone else has planned to do not worth doing by doing or saying something first: *Powerful cable operators were trying to preempt competition from satellite services by offering a similar service.* —**preemption** *n* [U] *Administration officials advocate food labeling uniformity and preemption of state laws if necessary.*

pref written abbreviation for PREFERENCE; PREFERRED (SHARES)

pref·e·rence /ˈprefərəns/ *n* **1** [C,U] the state of liking something more than something else, or something you like more than another thing: *People were twice as likely to change their* ***brand preference*** *if they liked an*

P

advertisement. | *a change in* ***consumer preference*** *from adjustable-rate to fixed-rate mortgages*

liquidity preference [U] ECONOMICS the degree to which people and organizations like to hold their assets and investments in different forms, some of which can be bought and sold more easily than others. This influences the demand for money and a country's control of the amount of money in the economy: *The phenomenon of liquidity preference can find no place in a model that contains only one asset, cash.*

2 [U] when a country treats some countries more favourably than others in international trade, for example through lower import taxes: *Britain must take a strong line with its trading partners, but without damaging* ***Community preference*** (=treating goods from the European Union more favourably than others.)

preference capital —see under CAPITAL

preference dividend —see under DIVIDEND

preference share —see under SHARE

preference stock —see under STOCK[1]

P

pref·e·ren·tial /ˌprefəˈrenʃəl◂/ *adj* [only before a noun] preferential treatment, rates etc are deliberately more favourable than others in order to give an advantage to particular people, organizations etc: *Norway develops domestic oil companies by giving them* ***preferential treatment*** *in awarding oil-field licenses.* | *If you find you need to borrow more, we'll charge you a special* ***preferential rate.***

preferential creditor —see under CREDITOR

preferential terms —see under TERM[1]

pre·fer·ment /prɪˈfɜːmənt‖-ɜːr-/ *n* [U] *formal* when someone is given a more important job: *the appointments and preferment policies of the Prime Minister*

pre·ferred /prɪˈfɜːd‖-ɜːrd/ *adj* [only before a noun] **1** FINANCE used to talk about a company's most important investors. If the company is in financial difficulty, preferred investors may receive payment of dividends, debts etc even if others do not receive them, or full payment if others receive less: *Divi Hotels filed a reorganization plan negotiated with its secured lenders and* ***preferred stockholders.*** | *The new company would be 95%-owned by unsecured and* ***preferred creditors.***

2 preferred investments are those held by a company's most important investors, or the payments that they receive on these investments: *It has a controlling interest in Neiman and annually receives $22.5 million in* ***preferred dividends.*** | *Standard & Poor lowered its ratings on the engine maker's* ***preferred debt.***

prej·u·dice[1] /ˈpredʒədəs/ *n* **1** [C,U] an unreasonable dislike of people because they are different from you in some way, especially because of their race, sex, or religious beliefs: *prejudice in the workplace* | *The new laws are challenging old anti-business prejudices.*

2 an unreasonable opinion about something or dislike of it + **against**: *There's still a great deal of prejudice against direct marketing.*

3 with/without prejudice LAW if a legal case is settled with prejudice, it will not be possible to open the case again. If it is settled without prejudice, it will be possible to bring the case to court at a later date: *All pending lawsuits between the two companies will* ***be dismissed with prejudice.*** | *The findings were accepted without prejudice.*

prejudice[2] *v* [T] **1** to influence someone so they have an unfair opinion about someone or something, and therefore does not treat them equally: *She argued that the publicity will endanger her client's right to a fair trial by prejudicing future jurors.* **prejudice sb against sb/sth**: *Her domineering managerial techniques must have prejudiced employees against her still more.*

2 to have a bad effect on someone's chances or opportunities to do something: *Fees to nominate someone to stand for election would prejudice poor candidates.* —**prejudiced** *adj*: *Far from being prejudiced against women, we have tried hard to advance promising women staff.* | *Prejudiced behavior can be directed against a racial or a national origin group.*

pre·lease /ˌpriːˈliːs/ *v* [T] PROPERTY to obtain agreements in advance from companies to rent part of a building: *Most of HRO's properties were in prime locations; many were preleased.*

pre·lim·i·na·ry /prɪˈlɪmənəri‖-neri/ *adj* [only before a noun] coming before something in order to prepare it or agree what it will finally be: ***Preliminary estimates*** *indicate that earnings will decline substantially from a year ago.* | *The Lehman Brothers group will set the* ***preliminary pricing*** *for $235 million revenue bonds.* | *Kraft General Foods was awarded a* ***preliminary injunction*** (=a legal ruling, stopping someone doing something) *against Friendship Dairies Inc. over its packaging.*

prem·i·er /ˈpremiə‖prɪˈmɪr/ *adj* [only before a noun] the most successful or important: *Salomon Brothers Inc., the premier bond-trading firm on Wall Street* | *an agreement to buy some of America's premier golf resorts*

prem·i·ere /ˈpremieə‖prɪˈmɪr/ *n* [C] the first time a product, especially a film or television show, is seen by the public: *In its premiere episode, the half-hour show had 7.4 million viewers.* —**premiere** *v* [I,T] *When premiered at the Automotive Parts and Accessories Association trade show, the car created a minor sensation.* | *The series is scheduled to premiere in March.*

prem·is·es /ˈpreməsəz/ *n* [plural] the buildings and land used by a shop, business, hotel etc: *establishments serving beers and ales brewed on the premises* | ***business premises***

pre·mi·um[1] /ˈpriːmiəm/ *n* [C] **1** INSURANCE the amount paid for insurance during a particular period of time: *Some insurance companies offer small sum policies, with* ***monthly*** *or* ***annual premiums.*** | ***single premium*** *life insurance policies* | *Annual* ***insurance premiums*** *for physical damage to oil rigs range from 1% to 1.5% of a platform's replacement cost.*

renewal premium INSURANCE a sum of money charged for making an insurance policy continue for a further period of time: *Fill in the tear-off slip and send it with your renewal premium to the address below.*

2 an additional amount of money, above a standard amount or rate: *H-P will buy 1.2 million Convex shares at $14.875 a share, representing a $1.25-a-share premium over the price of Convex stock.* | *The company's earnings will grow by about 25% a year and investors will be willing to* ***pay a premium*** (=pay more than usual) *for that growth.* | *As long as there is a threat of war in the Middle Eastern oil fields, oil prices will* ***command a premium*** (=buyers will have to pay more than usual).

bond premium FINANCE the amount by which the price paid for a bond is more than its actual value

conversion premium FINANCE an increase in value to an investor when one form of investment in a company is exchanged for another: *The debentures are convertible into common stock at $18.14 a share, representing an 18% conversion premium over yesterday's closing price.*

mobility premium HUMAN RESOURCES money paid to important international businessmen when they have to move from one country to another because of their jobs

option premium FINANCE the price paid for an OPTION (=the right to buy shares, bonds etc at a particular price in the future): *Commissions on option trades run about 2% to 5% of the option premium.*

3 at a premium if something is at a premium, there is little of it available or it is difficult to obtain: *With parking space at a premium in Japanese cities, the microcar is a popular form of transport.*

4 at a premium (to sth) if one thing is sold at a premium to another, it costs more: *Platinum usually trades at a premium to gold.*
5 put/place a premium on sth if you put a premium on something, you consider it to be especially valuable: *Employers today put a premium on reasoning skills and willingness to learn.*

premium² *adj* [only before a noun] premium products, goods etc are of higher quality than usual: ***Premium brands** of beer such as Grolsch will grow faster, in line with the trend toward people demanding better quality.*

Premium Bond *n* [C usually plural] a type of LOTTERY in Britain. People buy numbered Premium Bonds for £1 each. Every week, a computer chooses numbers AT RANDOM (=by chance) and holders of these numbers win prizes

premium income —see under INCOME

premium pay —see under PAY¹

premium price —see under PRICE¹

pre-owned *adj AmE* if something for sale is pre-owned, it has been owned and used by someone before; SECOND-HAND: *With Mercedes' 'pre-owned' car warranty program, dealers offer warranties on most second-hand models.*

pre•pack•aged /ˌpriːˈpækɪdʒd◂/ also **pre-packaged** *adj* **1** if a product is prepackaged, it is prepared and wrapped before it is sold: *Imperial Foods Inc. operates a prepackaged sandwich and vending business.* | *prepackaged software*
2 FINANCE, LAW a prepackaged arrangement for a company in financial difficulty has been agreed to by CREDITORS (=people and organizations to whom it owes money) before the company goes to a BANKRUPTCY COURT. Prepackaged arrangements are used so that creditors can be paid, or so that the company can continue in another form, more quickly: *The company can seek bankruptcy court approval for a prepackaged reorganization plan if it receives approval from at least half of the bondholders.*

pre•paid /ˌpriːˈpeɪd◂/ also **pre-paid** *adj* **1** prepaid amounts are payments for things that you have not yet received: *The pay phones are designed for phone cards and generate more than $2 billion in **prepaid revenues**.* —see also FREIGHT PREPAID
2 FINANCE a prepaid loan is repaid to the lender before the normal time: *The loan for the dam was prepaid after criticisms of the way the project was financed.*
3 a prepaid letter, envelope etc is one where the sender does not have to use a stamp; POSTAGE-PAID: *prepaid postcards and toll-free numbers*
4 INSURANCE prepaid insurance contracts are to pay for services that may be needed by the insured person in the future: *Everyone has legal needs and the latest option is a prepaid package from Midwest Legal Services.* —**prepay** *v* [I,T] *Don't pre-pay for vacations that carry heavy penalties if canceled.*

pre•pay•ment /ˌpriːˈpeɪmənt/ *n* [C,U] **1** the act of paying for something that you have not yet received, or the amount involved: *Hall-Houston Offshore received $20 million in prepayments for natural gas production in the Gulf of Mexico.*
2 FINANCE the act of repaying a loan to the lender before the normal time, or the amount involved: *TW Holdings Inc. is making two prepayments totaling $70 million on senior debt.* | *We'd like to get out of the loan, but it carries expensive **prepayment penalties*** (=additional costs for repaying early).
3 TAX the act of paying tax in an earlier TAX YEAR than the time it needs to be paid, in order to avoid paying more tax later, or the amount involved

pre•quel /ˈpriːkwəl/ *n* [C] a book, film, play etc that tells an earlier part of the story in a book etc that already exists: *the new prequel movies to 'Star Wars'* —compare SEQUEL

pre•sale /ˌpriːˈseɪl◂/ *n* **1** [C,U] FINANCE an agreement to sell a product before it has been completed: *The picture will at worst break even, based on presales of the film for various territories.*
2 presale estimate/price the price someone expects to get for a product, especially one sold at an AUCTION (=an occasion when something is sold to the person willing to pay most for it): *It fetched $24,200 against a presale estimate of $700 to $900.*

prescription drug —see under DRUG

prescription pharmaceuticals —see under PHARMACEUTICALS

pre•sent /prɪˈzent/ *v* [T] **1** to make a speech introducing an idea, plan etc to be considered: *a lack of evidence presented by prosecutors* **present sth to sb**: *The company has until July to restructure its debt and present an operating plan to its creditors.*
2 to produce a document, such as a ticket or pass, for an official to check: *When a shopper presents a supermarket ID card, the purchases can be linked to his or her name and address.* **present sth to sb**: *To receive care, every patient will need to present a health insurance card to the hospital or doctor.*
3 if something presents an opportunity, advantage, problem etc, it creates it: *With interest rates slightly above 8%, the securities present an attractive alternative to stocks.* | *Microsoft's Windows presents the most formidable technical challenge ever to the Macintosh.*

pre•sen•ta•tion /ˌprezənˈteɪʃən‖ˌpriːzen-, -zən-/ *n* [C] **1** an event at which a new product, idea, plan etc is described and explained: *a slick multimedia presentation*
2 the way in which something is said, shown, or explained to others: *The group has taken the opportunity to overhaul the presentation of its annual report.*

pres•en•tee•is•m /ˌprezənˈtiːɪzəm/ *n* [U] *informal* when employees spend more time at their place of work than is necessary, often because they want to make people think that they are working harder than they really are: *Presenteeism is not natural. People should spend as little time at their jobs as possible.*

pres•i•dent /ˈprezɪdənt/ *n* [C] **1** *AmE* the person in charge of a large company, bank etc: *Itel's president said the proceeds will be used to reduce debt.*
vice president also **vice-president** *AmE* the title given in some organizations to the person directly below the president in rank: *After three years as **vice-president**, he became chief executive officer.*
2 the official leader of a country that does not have a king or queen

press¹ /pres/ *v* **1** [I,T] to try hard to persuade someone to do something: *Investor Harold Simmons is pressing to have the company's annual meeting delayed.* **press sb to do sth**: *Finance Ministry officials are pressing the brokerage houses to eliminate the problem.* | *The extension will give the union more time to press Chrysler to keep the plant open.*
2 [T] if someone presses a claim, demand etc, they continue trying to get it accepted: *China is pressing its claim to the scattered territories, some of which have oil-drilling potential.* | *We will continue to press our case vigorously in the courts.*
3 press charges press an action *AmE* LAW to say officially that someone has done something illegal and must go to court: *A Citicorp official said the bank would not be pressing charges.* | *The government is pressing a civil action to get the money from investors.*
press (sb) **for** sth *phr v* [T] to try hard to achieve something, especially by persuading someone to accept a plan, suggestion etc: *The U.S. and French oil companies*

P

are said to be pressing for production-sharing arrangements. | *Shareholders may* ***press for changes*** *that would make the company more profitable.* | *Bulk buyers are increasingly pressing drug makers for price discounts.*

press on also **press ahead** *phr v* [I] to continue doing something difficult in a determined way: *The company has vowed to press ahead, despite the threat of a global boycott.* + **with**: *Internatio pledged to press on with its new strategy.*

press[2] *n* **1 the press** the people writing for the newspapers, radio, or television: *The judgement reflected badly on the press, including his own newspaper.* | *a meeting with the financial press*

2 [singular, U] reports in the newspapers and on radio and television: *Real-estate agents have enough trouble with the economy without getting* ***bad press.*** | *a savage attack on the banking sector in* ***the local press reports.*** | *Criticism from the investigation committee could lead to some unpleasant* ***press coverage*** (=reports in the newspapers, on television etc).

3 [C] a business that prints and sometimes sells books: *a small independent press* | *the University of Chicago Press*

P

press baron —see under BARON

Press Complaints Commission —see PCC

press conference also **press briefing** —see under CONFERENCE

press kit —see under KIT

press officer —see under OFFICER

press release —see under RELEASE[2]

press secretary —see under SECRETARY

pres•tige /preˈstiːʒ/ *n* [U] the respect and importance a person, organization, profession, or product has because of their success and high quality: *The bank lost both money and prestige as a result of the transaction.* | *Revlon launched a comprehensive marketing program for its* ***prestige brands.***

pre•sump•tion /prɪˈzʌmpʃən/ *n* [C,U] LAW the act of thinking that something is true because it seems very likely, although there is no proof: *The amendment would create a legal presumption.* + **of**: *The claims against the company will be dismissed without any presumption of liability by the defendants.*

pre-tax also **pretax** *adj* [only before a noun] a company's pre-tax profit, loss etc is calculated before tax is taken away: *Latest quarter net loss of $256.7 million includes $400 million pretax restructuring charge.*

pre-tax earnings —see under EARNINGS

pre-tax loss —see under LOSS

pre-tax profit —see under PROFIT[1]

pre•ten•ces *BrE*, **pretenses** *AmE* /prɪˈtensɨz‖ˈpriːtensɨz/ *n* LAW **by/under false pretences** if someone does something under false pretences, they do it by pretending that something is true when it is not: *Obtaining by false pretences is ordinarily thought of as different from theft.* | *obtaining information under false pretences*

pre•vail /prɪˈveɪl/ *v* [I] *formal* **1** if someone or their arguments, views etc prevail, they finally win an argument after a long period of time: *The company is hoping to prevail in a court challenge to the water board ruling.* + **over**: *Kimberly-Clark is asking for a ruling that its patent should prevail over the one issued to P&G.*

2 if an attitude or belief prevails, it continues to exist in a particular situation: *Pessimism and gloom have continued to prevail about Britain's economic expectations.* + **in/among**: *Slow holiday trading prevailed in the Treasury market yesterday.* | *the new spirit of caution that now prevails among Japan's car makers*

pre•vail•ing /prɪˈveɪlɪŋ/ *adj* [only before a noun] existing at a particular time or in a particular situation; CURRENT: *The prevailing* ***economic conditions*** *have had a serious impact on our operations.* | *The shares will be bought at* ***prevailing market prices.***

prev•a•lent /ˈprevələnt/ *adj* frequent or common at a particular time or in a particular situation: *Sexual harassment is prevalent in the workplace.* | *the most prevalent mistakes made by individual investors*

pre•vent /prɪˈvent/ *v* [T] to stop something happening, or someone doing something: *government regulators working to prevent fraud* **prevent sb/sth (from) doing sth**: *The region's huge economic problems will prevent it from realizing its potential.*

pre•ven•tive /prɪˈventɪv/ also **pre•ven•ta•tive** /prɪˈventətɪv/ *adj* [only before a noun] intended to stop something happening: *improvements in auto safety and other* ***preventive measures.***

prey[1] /preɪ/ *v*

prey on/upon sb/sth phr v [T] to take advantage of people who are weak or easily deceived: *fake charities that prey on small businesses for contributions*

prey[2] *n* **1** [U] *journalism* FINANCE the TARGET COMPANY (=the company that another company wants to buy) in a takeover: *MIN would prefer to be predator* (=a company that buys another company) *rather than prey, but it was outbid in its last attempt to buy a regional newspaper.*

2 be/fall prey to sth to be unable to avoid a harmful or difficult situation: *After opening higher, the OTC market fell prey to profit-taking.* | *The once-soaring South Korean economy has fallen prey to steep wage increases and high inflation.*

price[1] /praɪs/ *n* **1** [C,U] the amount of money for which something is bought, sold, or offered: *They agreed on a price of $10,000 for the car.* | *Some mines may close because of gold's current* ***low price.*** | *The bonds continued to* ***fall in price.*** | *Buy one shirt and get a second at* ***half price.*** | *People today are attracted to discount stores because they don't want to pay* ***full price.*** —see also CUT-PRICE

actual price ◆ [C] a price that is really paid, rather than one that was stated or calculated earlier: *A $1.1 billion buy-out would in principle equal $40 a share, but the actual price could well be higher.*

◆ [C] FINANCE another name for SPOT PRICE

adjusted share price [C] FINANCE the price of a company's shares after a new SHARE ISSUE (=an occasion when new shares are sold)

all-in price [C] a price for a product or service that includes everything, with no additional charges; PACKAGE PRICE *AmE*

asking price also **asked price** *AmE* [C] on a financial market, the price at which an investor can buy shares, bonds etc from a dealer: *It is trading with a buying, or 'bid,' price of $32.75, and a selling, or 'asked,' price of $33.* —compare ***bid price*** under PRICE[1]

bargain-basement price [C] *journalism* a very low price that is particularly good for the buyer: *This Wal-Mart store has the same bargain-basement prices found in all its outlets.*

bargain price [C] a low price that is good for the buyer: *Consumers want top quality paints, but they want them at bargain prices.*

basic price also **base price** *AmE* [C] the price for the cheapest product in a range, without additional features, ACCESSORIES etc: *The company raised base prices on most of its cars and light trucks.*

below-cost price [C] a price for something that is less than the cost of producing it: *Chrysler claimed that Japanese manufacturers were dumping minivans in the US at below-cost prices.*

best price [C] the lowest price a buyer can obtain something for or the highest price a seller can sell something for: *Farmers will take a commodity like grain wherever they can get the best price.*

bid price [C] on a financial market, the price at which an investor can sell shares, bonds etc back to a dealer: *It* *is trading with a buying, or 'bid,' price of $32.75, and a selling, or 'asked,' price of $33.* —compare ASKING PRICE

buying price [C] ◆ the price at which someone buys or can buy something: *Add lawyers' fees and the cost of buying property can rise to 10% of the buying price.*
◆ the price at which a dealer will buy shares, bonds etc, rather than the price at which they are willing to sell them: *For investors, the new trading system could bring a narrower spread between buying and selling prices.*

cash price [C] ◆ the price paid when you pay the full cost of something immediately in cash or by cheque, rather than the full cost of something bought using CREDIT: *Ibanez guitar urgently wanted, any condition, genuine private buyer, good cash price paid or part exchange*
◆ in a takeover or MERGER (=when two companies combine), an amount paid to investors in cash rather than in shares: *American International's $32.50-a-share cash price for International Lease*
◆ the price for immediate delivery of a COMMODITY (=oil, metal, farm product etc); SPOT PRICE: *In copper, the premium of the cash price over the three-months' contract* (=the amount by which the cash price is more than the futures price) *continued to narrow.*

catalogue price also **catalog price** *AmE* [C] the usual or official price for something, before any reductions; LIST PRICE: *Federal Express will probably pay as much as 30% less than the A300's catalog price, which is about $85 million a plane.*

ceiling price [C] the highest possible price for something; PRICE CEILING: *When MNC first proposed a public stock offering of the unit, it cited a ceiling price of $25 a share.*

closing price [C] the price of shares etc at the end of a trading day on a financial market: *Bond prices ended above Friday's closing prices.*

consumer price [C] the price paid by the public for goods and services, rather than by businesses: *Excluding energy, consumer prices actually declined 0.3% this year, reflecting lower housing costs.*

cost price [C,U] the price of something that is sold for what it cost to produce, without any profit for the producer: *Copies of the video will be made available to course participants* ***at cost price.***

current prices [plural] prices measured after INFLATION (=the rise in prices) has been taken off, used to compare real present values with earlier ones: *Retail sales value in current prices in October was 6% higher than a year earlier.*

delivered price [C] a price that includes all charges, for example packing and TRANSPORT costs, up to the place of delivery

demand price [C usually singular] ECONOMICS the price which buyers of a particular product will pay when a particular amount of it is made available for sale: *When the demand price is equal to the supply price, the amount produced has no tendency either to be increased or to be reduced; it is in equilibrium.*

discount price [C] a price which is particularly cheap, or lower than the normal price: *S&K Famous Brands buys excess inventories of men's suits from retailers and resells them at discount prices.*

exercise price [C] in OPTIONS (=the right to buy particular shares etc at a fixed price during a particular period of time), the price at which you can buy the related shares if you buy a CALL OPTION and the price at which you can sell if you buy a PUT OPTION; STRIKE PRICE: *Call options become almost useless if the stock is below the exercise price.*

factor price [C] ECONOMICS the price of something that is used or needed to produce something: *Current factor prices – wages, rents, interest – tell producers about the likely cost of producing the product.*

factory-gate price also **factory price, factory cost, producer price** [C] a price paid by distributors to producers of a product: *Recent figures show relatively firm retail sales and rises in factory-gate prices.*

fair price [singular] FINANCE the amount of money that it is reasonable to pay for something: *This measures the ratio of the* ***fair price of the share*** *to the book price taken from the balance sheet.* | *The long-gilt futures price was 91–21, which is slightly overpriced compared with the fair price.* —compare MARKET PRICE

firesale price *journalism* [C] a very cheap price for something that the seller has to sell because they need the money: *Bankrupt firms are falling into foreign hands at firesale prices.*

firm price ◆ [C] a price that is fixed and definite: *Sony was the first to announce a firm price and shipping date for DAT recorders.*
◆ [C] FINANCE a price that is not falling: *Also helping raw sugar prices has been firm prices of refined white sugar.*

fixed price ◆ [C] a price that is definite and that cannot be reduced or increased; GUARANTEED PRICE: *Over the first five years of the contract, most of the gas will be sold at a fixed price.*
◆ [C] an official price for a product or service, set by a government. When the amount has been set, it is illegal to sell the item above this price; GUARANTEED PRICE: *The taxis charge a fixed price and are regulated by the city government.*

floor price [C] the lowest price a particular product can be sold for: *The Australian Wool Corporation lowered its floor price by 20% because of falling demand.* | *The contract has* ***a floor price of*** *$5.50 per million BTUs – the equivalent of about $32 a barrel.*

forward price [C] the fixed price offered for buying a currency or COMMODITY (=oil, metal, farm product etc) for delivery on a fixed date in the future: *Most of the activity in aluminium has been in nearby prices and gains in further forward prices have been restricted by continued producer selling.* —compare SPOT PRICE

futures price [C] the price for a FUTURES CONTRACT (=an arrangement to buy a particular currency, metal, farm product etc for a fixed price for delivery on a fixed date): *Coffee futures prices rose on concerns over available supplies.*

guaranteed price ◆ [C] another name for FIXED PRICE
◆ [C] another name for SUPPORT PRICE: *The agriculture commissioner wants to lower milk quotas and to cut guaranteed prices for dairy products.*

guide price [C] PROPERTY in selling property, a price that gives buyers a general idea of how much the seller wants, but which may be reduced: *The old plantation house is for sale, with a guide price of $5 million.*

inflation-adjusted price [C] a price that takes INFLATION (=a continuing increase in prices in an economy) into account: *Inflation-adjusted prices for tin products decreased over the past decade.*

initial price ◆ [C] another name for ISSUE PRICE
◆ [C] the price at which something is sold when it is first available: *Critics complain that the initial price for interactive TV equipment may be too high.*

intervention price [C] the price paid by the European Union to farmers who are not able to sell their produce, in order to stop prices falling too low: *For cereals, he wants to cut the EU's intervention price by 40%.*

invoice price [C] the price of something as shown on the INVOICE (=document sent by a seller to a customer with details of goods or services that have been provided and the payment date), rather than a price that may have been given earlier

issue price [C] the price at which new shares, bonds etc are sold. The issue price of bonds is usually given as a figure in relation to a NOMINAL PRICE of 100; INITIAL PRICE: *By late afternoon in London, the bonds had risen by about 1.5 from their issue price of 99.161.*

P

knockdown price *informal* [C] a very cheap price: *Banks repossessing property face a problem – sell it at a knockdown price or hold it, hoping for a higher price if the market recovers.*

list price [C] another name for CATALOGUE PRICE

manufacturer's recommended price abbreviation **MRP** [C] another name for RECOMMENDED RETAIL PRICE: *Pharmacies halved the price of the drug, but when legal action followed, they were forced to charge the manufacturer's recommended price.*

market price ◆ [C] the price of something on a market at a particular time: *The price of A$6.75 for the new shares compares with Thursday's closing market price of A$7.88.*
◆ [C] used to talk about the real price or cost of something that a market decides, rather than one calculated or fixed, for example by a government: *OPEC self-interest will ensure us of oil at market prices.*
◆ [C] the price of something calculated in relation to what buyers are willing to pay at a particular time, rather than in some other way: *measures forcing banks to value assets at market prices – rather than at their original cost*

P

mean price [C] the average price of a number of things

median price [C] the most typical, common, or frequent price of a number of things: *The mean price of a yacht listed by BUC now is about $610,000, while the median price is $405,000.*

net price ◆ [C] the price actually received by a seller after any costs are taken away: *The selling price of $78.1 million includes both the buyer's and the seller's commission, so the net price to the seller is approximately $64.5 million.*
◆ [C] the price actually paid by a buyer after any reductions: *We don't want promotions. We just want net prices.*

nominal price ◆ [C] a price that does not take account of INFLATION (=a continued rise in prices in an economy): *Whereas oil's nominal price remained stable, its real price fell during this period.*
◆ [C] a price that does not represent the real cost or value of something: *Meals were available to the unemployed at a nominal price.*
◆ [C] the stated price that appears on a bond etc. Bonds are often sold slightly above or below a nominal price of 100; FACE AMOUNT; NOMINAL AMOUNT; PAR VALUE

offer price also **offered price**, **offering price** ◆ [C] in a takeover, the price offered by the buyer for existing SHAREHOLDERS' shares, or the total value of all the shares at this price: *Hutchinson's offer price values Cavendish at about HK$11.8 billion.*
◆ [C] the price at which a share, bond etc is offered for sale; ASKING PRICE: *$300 million of 7½% eurobonds due Feb. 27, 2007 at an initially fixed offer price of 98.91*
◆ [C] the price of shares when they are bought and sold for the first time: *Shares in Newsquest rose from their opening price of 250p to close at 252p yesterday as the company floated.*

official price [C] the price of a product that is fixed by the government of certain countries, for example in the former Soviet Union. It is usually illegal to sell goods for more than the official price: *Luxury items are regularly sold for much more than the official price by corrupt sales clerks.*

opening price [C] the price of a share, bond etc at the beginning of a particular day's trading on a financial market: *The dollar was trading at 159.62 yen, unchanged from the opening price.*

package price *AmE* [C] a price for a product or service that includes everything, with no additional charges; ALL-IN PRICE *BrE*

per subscriber price [C] the money paid regularly by someone to receive a broadcasting or telephone service

physical price [C] another name for CASH PRICE

premium price [C] a high price for something special or unusual: *A strategic buyer is often willing to pay a premium price to gain control of an entire company.*

producer price [C] another name for FACTORY-GATE PRICE: *Producer prices rose 0.2%, or 0.3% after food and energy were excluded.*

pump price [C] a price paid by car users for petrol: *a 16-cent-a-gallon increase in gasoline pump prices*

purchase price [C] the price it costs to buy something: *The reason for the high purchase price is to encourage consumers to rent the video, rather than buy it.*

recommended retail price abbreviation **RRP** [C] *BrE* a price that the producer or WHOLESALER (=a seller that sells to businesses rather than to the public) of a product suggests that it should be sold for in shops; MANUFACTURER'S RECOMMENDED PRICE; SUGGESTED RETAIL PRICE *AmE*: *The government has banned manufacturers from setting recommended retail prices for some electrical goods.*

reserve price [C] a minimum price that a seller will accept, usually in an AUCTION (=an occasion when something is sold to the person who will pay most for it): *Land valued up to $2 million can be auctioned with extremely low reserve prices, with acceptable bids as low as 50% of appraised value.*

retail price [C] the price of something in a shop, rather than to a WHOLESALER (=a seller that sells to shops etc rather than to the public); STREET PRICE *AmE*: *Record high retail prices of pork are cooling consumer demand.*

rock bottom price *informal* [C usually plural] the lowest price possible: *The company said it could continue to prosper through lean overhead, tight cost controls and rock-bottom prices.*

sale price ◆ [C] the price at which something is offered for sale: *He declined to estimate the sale price or how long it might take to sell the division.*
◆ [C] the price for which something is actually sold: *The investor's return is the difference between the purchase price and the sale price of the bonds.*
◆ [C] the price of something sold in a SALE (=a period of time when a seller offers goods or services at prices that are lower than usual): *The fare cuts are substantial, but the sale prices still may strike some customers as high.*
◆ [C] the price of something sold in an AUCTION (=an event when something is sold to the buyer willing to pay most for it): *This was a record for a baseball card, with a sale price of $451,000 at Sotheby's.*

selling price [C] the price at which something can be bought, or at which it has been sold: *Union Carbide's earnings are likely to be cut in half by lower selling prices for polyethylene.*

share price [C] the price of a particular company's shares at a particular time: *Share prices of construction and property investment companies were particularly hard hit during the recession.*

soft price [C] a price on a financial market that is steady or falling gradually over a period of time: *Demand for precious metals will rise during the year and current soft prices will firm.*

spot price [C] the price for immediate delivery of a COMMODITY (=oil, metal, farm product etc); CASH PRICE: *Physical supplies of gold are extremely scarce. The result has been upward pressure on the spot price.* —compare FORWARD PRICE

sticker price [C] *AmE* the basic published price of something, especially a car, before any DISCOUNT has been taken from it; LIST PRICE: *Cherokees in Japan carry a sticker price of 5.2 million yen.*

stock price [C] the price of a company's shares: *He is trying to help the company operate more efficiently and raise its stock price.* | *Stock prices won't keep rising forever.*

street price [C] *AmE* another name for RETAIL PRICE: *Hewlett-Packard expects its new laser printer to sell for a street price of under $800.*

strike price also **striking price** [C] another name for EXERCISE PRICE

subsidized price also **subsidised price** *BrE* [C] a price that is less than it would normally be because a government pays the producer part of the costs of producing something: *For a long time, oil came to Cuba at a subsidized price from the Soviet Union.*

suggested retail price *AmE* [C] a US name for RECOMMENDED RETAIL PRICE: *It's offering consumers a $3 rebate from the suggested retail price of $26.99.*

supply price also **supplier price** [C] a price paid to suppliers by shops and WHOLESALERS (=a seller that sells to businesses rather than to the public): *The price is good through next March: Sears* ***locks in its supply prices*** (=fixes them) *early on with suppliers.*

support price [C] a price for food products promised to farmers by a government. For example, governments who are members of the European Union pay farmers the difference between market prices and support prices whenever market prices are lower; GUARANTEED PRICE: *Farmers are looking for alternative crops in the face of expected cutbacks in EU farm support prices.*

trade price ◆ [C] a price paid by a business when buying from another business, rather than one paid by the public: *Trade prices or discounts depend on order volume.*

◆ [C] FINANCE a price at which an investment is bought and sold: *He altered some reported trade prices for customers during the stock market crash.*

transfer price [C] the price for something that is sold by one part of an organization to another part, rather than to a final buyer: *an agreement with the IRS on transfer prices of products passing between US and foreign affiliates*

wholesale price [C] a price paid by a WHOLESALER (=a seller who sells to businesses rather than to the public): *Some big wholesale price increases still remain to be passed on to consumers.*

wide price [C] on a stockmarket, a situation in which the difference between the selling and buying price of a share is larger than usual

2 at a price used to say that you can obtain something, but only if you pay a lot of money for it, or if the cost is very high in other unpleasant ways: *The track was designed to allow higher train speeds at a price, and that price was safety.*

3 at any price if you are prepared to do something at any price, you are determined to do it, even if it is very difficult and the cost is very high: *His only will is to preserve his power at any price.* | *Sorry, that painting's not for sale, not at any price* (=no price could be high enough).

4 put a price on sth to say how much something costs, or to give something a financial value: *The government hasn't put a price on the stake it wants to sell.*

price² *v* [T] **1** to fix the price of something that is for sale **be priced at**: *If the stock is priced at about C$24 a share, it probably will be well received by the market.* | *She priced her T-shirts at $22 only to find a competitor moving faster at $20.* | *Today's* ***moderately priced*** *clothes look almost as good as* ***high priced*** *designer clothes.*

2 to fix the price of bonds, shares etc: *The notes were priced to yield 6.88%.* + **off** (=in relation to): *Many commercial loans are priced off Fed funds, which currently are around 4%.*

3 to compare the prices of things: *We spent the morning pricing microwaves.*

4 to put the price on goods, showing how much they cost

5 price sb out of the market if you have been priced out of the market, you can no longer afford to buy something because prices have become too high: *Younger people with jobs need homes but they have been priced out of the housing market.*

6 price yourself out of the market to demand too much money for the goods or services you are offering, so that people are no longer willing to buy them: *The hotels have priced themselves out of the market with typical cost at one chain of $100 to $120 a night – compared with our average room cost of $50.*

price ceiling —see under CEILING

price competition —see under COMPETITION

price control —see under CONTROL¹

price-cutting *n* [U] when sellers reduce prices, usually several times over a relatively short period of time: *Many of its older product lines saw poor profit margins as a result of severe price cutting.* | *an aggressive* ***price-cutting campaign*** (=series of reductions carried out for a particular purpose)

price differential —see under DIFFERENTIAL¹

price discrimination —see under DISCRIMINATION

price-earnings ratio —see ***PE ratio*** under RATIO

price effect —see under EFFECT

price elasticity —see under ELASTICITY OF DEMAND

price-fixing *n* [U] **1** when companies in an industry agree on the prices they will charge for something. This form of price-fixing is done so that companies avoid competing with each other, and is normally illegal: *The EU investigated international telephone agreements to see if there was price fixing in violation of EU competition rules.* | *Japan's Fair Trade Commission ordered 13 ink makers to break up a* ***price-fixing cartel*** (=arrangement between a group of companies).

2 when a company tells the shops etc that sell its products how much they must charge for them. This form of price-fixing is sometimes illegal; RETAIL PRICE MAINTENANCE *BrE*: *The UK's last* ***price-fixing arrangement*** *was retail price maintenance for non-prescription medicines.*

3 when a government decides the price at which something should be sold: *government price-fixing for the sale of drugs to the National Health Service*

price floor —see under FLOOR

price fluctuation —see under FLUCTUATION

price freeze —see under FREEZE²

price inelastic —see under INELASTIC

price leader —see under LEADER

price leadership —see under LEADERSHIP

price·less /ˈpraɪsləs/ *adj* **1** so valuable that it is impossible to give a financial value: *priceless works of art*

2 if a quality, skill, or improvement is priceless, it is extremely important or useful: *The ability to motivate people is a priceless asset.*

price·list /ˈpraɪsˌlɪst/ *n* [C] a list of prices for things being sold by a producer, provider of services, or shop: *GM has mailed detailed pricelists for this year's models to dealers.*

price restraint —see under RESTRAINT

price ring —see under RING¹

price scanner —see under SCANNER

price sensitivity —see under SENSITIVITY

price support —see under SUPPORT²

price tag *n* [C] **1** a small ticket showing the price of something: *There's no price tag on this printer.*

2 used to talk about the price of something, especially when this is very high: *a project that could have a price tag in excess of $100 million* | *The government* ***put a price tag of*** (=said the price would be) *more than £2 billion on the shares it is privatizing in National Power PLC.*

price terms —see under TERM[1]

price theory —see under THEORY

price war —see under WAR

pric•ey also **pricy** /ˈpraɪsi/ *adj* comparative **pricier** superlative **priciest** *informal* expensive: *Skiing is a pricey sport, between equipment, travel and ski-area costs.* | *Some money managers think that stocks are getting too pricey.*

pric•ing /ˈpraɪsɪŋ/ *n* [U] **1** the prices of a company's products or services in relation to each other and in relation to those of their competitors, and the activity of setting them: ***Aggressive pricing*** (=cheaper prices than its competitors') *helped increase the airline's passenger traffic by 10% for the year.* | *Weak demand for chemical products has led to* ***competitive pricing*** *and poor sales margins.* | *the gas industry's new* ***pricing agreement*** (=arrangement between sellers and buyers) | *The drug company's* ***pricing policies*** *have been the subject of inquiries by a federal grand jury.* | *Apple's new, sharply lower* ***pricing strategy*** *fueled an enormous increase in unit sales.* | *Pontiac plans to launch a revised ad campaign and* ***pricing structure*** (=prices in relation to each other) *for next year's models.*

common pricing LAW when companies agree to charge the same prices as each other, often illegally: *Bus operators are prevented from establishing common pricing under legislation that deregulated the bus industry.* —see also PRICE-FIXING

discount pricing when prices of a company's products are lower than normal: *Discount pricing that began last summer requires heavy marketing expenditures.*

penetration pricing the practice of offering a product at a very low price in order to start selling in a new market so that a MARKET SHARE can be built up

predatory pricing ◆ the practice of selling something for less than it costs to produce. This is often done to increase MARKET SHARE (=a company's proportion of a market) and to drive competitors out of the market: *They argue that the 10% discount on long-distance calls amounts to predatory pricing against other telecommunications companies.*

◆ when competitors illegally agree to charge the same price for something; PRICE-FIXING

pri•ma fa•cie /ˌpraɪmə ˈfeɪʃi‖-ʃə/ *adj* [only before a noun] LAW based on facts that appear to be true, although they may later be proved not to be: ***prima facie evidence*** *of fraud*

pri•ma•ry /ˈpraɪməri‖-meri/ *adj* **1** main or most important: *Its* ***primary business*** *is developing and marketing new software.* | *The* ***primary problem*** *for the airlines is the recession.* | *It uses coal as its* ***primary source*** *of fuel.*

2 FINANCE relating to shares, bonds etc when they are ISSUED (=sold for the first time), and the markets where they are sold, rather than shares etc that are traded later: *the primary bond market*

primary data —see under DATA

primary dealer —see under DEALER

primary industry —see under INDUSTRY

primary market —see under MARKET[1]

primary memory —see under MEMORY

primary production —see under PRODUCTION

primary residence —see under RESIDENCE

primary share —see under SHARE

prime[1] /praɪm/ *adj* **1** of the best quality: *acres of prime real estate right by an international airport* | *prime cuts of beef*

2 main or most important: *Martin Marietta Corp., the prime contractor in the rocket-engine development program*

prime[2] *v* **prime the (economic) pump** *journalism* to make the economy grow faster by increasing government spending, hoping that this will encourage business to invest more: *Direct investments in job creation are essential to prime the pump and get the economy up and running again.* —see also PUMP-PRIMING

prime[3] *n* **above prime** FINANCE used to talk about how much higher an interest rate is than the PRIME RATE (=the interest rate charged by banks to their best borrowers): *The working-capital loan carried an interest rate of 3½ points above prime.*

prime-1 *n* [singular] FINANCE a RATING given by some CREDIT AGENCIES showing that the risk of non-payment of a loan etc is very low. Prime-1 is the best rating, followed by prime-2 and prime-3: *Moody's assigned their top ratings – prime-1 and A-1-plus, respectively – to the government agency's planned offering of commercial paper.*

prime commercial paper —see under COMMERCIAL PAPER

prime land —see under LAND[1]

prime rate —see under RATE[1]

prime tenant —see under TENANT

prime time —see under TIME

prime-time *adj* [only before a noun] relating to the time in the evening when most people are watching television, and the cost of advertising is at its most expensive: *The three major networks' combined share of the* ***prime-time audience*** *has fallen to a new low.* | *Warner will have about 20 series on* ***prime-time television*** *in the fall.* —**prime time** *n* [U] *The President will address the nation with a televised speech in prime time.*

prin•ci•pal[1] /ˈprɪnsəpəl/ *n* **1** [singular] FINANCE the original amount of a loan, not including any of the interest that is paid: *The loan amounts outstanding totaled about $32.2 million in principal and $2.2 million in interest.* | *No principal is due for repayment until next year.*

2 [C] an important person, manager etc in some types of organization, who may be legally responsible for its actions: *Mr O'Brien is a principal of the Law and Economics Consulting Group.*

3 [C] LAW the actual buyer and the seller in a business deal, rather than the people who represent them, or BROKERS who buy and sell for them: *None of the principals would comment on the purchase price.*

principal[2] *adj* **1** most important; MAIN: *Portland is one of the principal unloading points for Japanese automobiles.* | *Gulf's strategy of concentrating on its* ***principal business*** *of oil and gas production* | *As* ***principal shareholders*** *in the company, no one has a greater interest in its management.* | *Baxter Healthcare is the* ***principal subsidiary*** *of Baxter International Inc* (=the largest company owned by them).

2 FINANCE relating to the original amount of a loan, rather than any interest: *The total* ***principal amount*** *of debentures being sold was increased to $75 million.* | *A new government may be unwilling to repay interest on the* ***principal sum*** *loaned.*

principal payment —see under PAYMENT

principal trading —see under TRADING

prin•ci•ple /ˈprɪnsəpəl/ *n* **1** [C,U] a moral rule or set of ideas that makes you behave in a particular way: *The single European market works on market principles.* | ***As a matter of principle*** (=a rule that is very important and that should not be broken), *disabled people should have the right to work.* —see also ERROR OF PRINCIPLE

2 [C] a rule that explains how something works, or an idea that something is based on: *The* ***basic principle*** *is that all information collected for one purpose is confidential.* | *The US market* ***is built on the principle*** *that a*

marketplace should be available to everyone. | *accounting practice based on the accruals principle*

accounting principle [C] a rule or idea used for preparing accounts in a particular company or place: *The accounting principles adopted must be objective in the sense that any accountant would produce an acceptable set of accounts from the same data.* —see also GENERALLY ACCEPTED ACCOUNTING PRINCIPLES

benefit principle [singular] *BrE* the idea that the people who use a particular public service should pay for it through taxes: *There are two principles behind taxation: ability to pay and the benefit principle.*

3 in principle if something is possible in principle, there is no reason why it should not happen, but it has not actually happened yet: *In principle, we pay all our freelance staff within one month.*

4 in principle if something happens in principle, decisions, rules etc say that it should happen, even if in practice it does not always happen: *In principle, a hostile takeover is possible, but we want to discourage it.*

5 in principle if you agree to do something in principle, you agree in a general way to the idea or plan, without agreeing to any details: *North and South Korea agreed in principle to link their separate air-traffic control systems.*

print[1] /prɪnt/ *v* **1** [I,T] to produce words, numbers, pictures etc on paper, using a machine that puts ink onto the surface: *The system prints each transaction on the customer's passbook.* | *Kodak's new desktop machine prints16 pages a minute.* **print sth on sth**: *The electronic sorters can only read bar codes printed on the lower right-hand corner of letters.*

2 [T] to produce many copies of a document, newspaper, book etc in printed form: *His company lost a contract to print 20,000 temporary auto license tags for Tennessee.* | *Estonia hired a foreign firm to print banknotes to replace the ruble.*

3 [T] to put a letter, speech, article etc in a book, newspaper etc; PUBLISH: *Newsday printed the story on Dec. 8.* | *An apology was printed in yesterday's edition.*

4 [I,T] if a computer prints words on a screen, they appear on the screen: *After a delay of four seconds, the translated sentence is printed on a computer screen.*

5 [T] to write words or letters by hand without joining the letters together, so that they look like the letters in a book: *Print your name at the top and sign the declaration at the bottom of page 2.*

print sth **out/off** *phr v* [T] to produce a printed copy of a document from a computer: *a machine that prints out airline tickets* | *You can read faxes on the screen, or print them off.* —see also PRINT-OUT

print sth **up** *phr v* [T] to produce something in print, especially in a short period of time: *As an afterthought, marketing and sales printed up a brochure of the property.*

print[2] *n* [U] **1** information and news in books, newspapers etc, rather than in other MEDIA: *European services concentrate on print, while in the U.S. the emphasis is on television.* | *We send information to clients using both print and electronic media.*

2 in print if a book is in print, it is available to be bought. If it is out of print, it is no longer available: *He hopes to see the biography in print soon.* | *'Diary of a Nobody' was published in 1892, and has never been out of print.*

3 be in print/out of print if a book is in print, new copies of it are still being printed and it is easily available. If it is out of print, it is no longer being printed: *His small publishing firm has kept classics by American writers in print.*

4 the fine/small print the details in a legal document, contract etc that many people do not take the time to read, but that may have serious effects: *Even cardholders who pay their bills in full are advised to read the small print carefully.* | *advertisements that display low ticket prices but hide surcharges in the fine print*

print ad —see under ADVERTISEMENT

print advertisement —see under ADVERTISEMENT

print•er /ˈprɪntə‖-ər/ *n* [C] **1** COMPUTING a machine connected to a computer, used for printing documents: *high demand for* ***colour printers***

bubblejet printer also **bubblejet** a printer that works by sending out a stream of small drops of ink onto the paper

dot-matrix printer also **dot-matrix** an inexpensive, low-quality printer that prints each letter as a group of small dots: *Dot matrix printers can, at best, manage 240 dots per inch and are both slow and noisy.*

inkjet printer also **inkjet** a printer that prints documents by forcing very small amounts of ink onto the paper

laser printer also **laser** a high-quality printer that works by using LASER light (=a powerful narrow beam of light): *Eastman Kodak Co. has introduced a laser printer for desktop users of IBM personal computers.*

2 a company which prints books, newspapers etc, or the person running such a company: *The world's largest* ***commercial printer*** | *She found a printer in Iowa who was willing to print her next book.*

security printer a company which prints secret or very valuable things, such as paper money or financial information: *The mailing facilities of the security printers are the most efficient way of sending documents to shareholders.*

print•ing /ˈprɪntɪŋ/ *n* **1** [U] the work of producing books, newspapers etc on a machine that puts words, numbers, pictures etc onto the surface of paper: *Thomson is a printing and publishing concern.* | *The firm has access to printing and typesetting facilities throughout the UK.*

2 [C] the act of printing a number of copies of a book: *Houghton Mifflin, responding to bookseller demand, has ordered a fourth printing.*

print-out *n* [C] a sheet of paper with printed information on it, produced by a computer: *print-outs of all long-distance telephone calls* —see also ***print out*** under PRINT[1]

print run *n* [C] the number of copies of a book, newspaper etc that are printed at any one time: *Publishers aren't publishing fewer titles, but they are doing smaller* ***initial print runs*** (=first ones).

print space —see under SPACE

pri•or /ˈpraɪə‖praɪr/ *adj* [only before a noun] coming before something is finally decided, agreed etc: *Most firms require* ***prior approval*** *of analysts' personal trades before selling stock to them.* | *Sales are expected to be $62 million, up slightly from $60 million in the prior year.* + **to**: *Those calculations are based on AT&T's average stock price prior to a shareholder meeting.*

pri•o•ri•tize also **prioritise** *BrE* /praɪˈɒrɪ̈taɪz‖-ˈɔːr-/ *v* [I,T] to put several tasks, problems etc in order of importance so that the most important ones are done first: *We are going to have to prioritize because of the very severe cutbacks in staff.* | *Those cars were critical to Nissan's image, so they prioritized them in the product cycle.*

pri•or•i•ty /praɪˈɒrɪ̈ti‖-ˈɔːr-/ *n* plural **priorities** [C] **1** the thing that is more important than anything else, and that needs attention first: *Cost-cutting measures continue to be the* ***first priority*** *at the company.* | *The measures dominated Finland's economic priorities.* + **for**: *A free-trade pact with Mexico should be a* ***top priority***.

2 be given/have/get/take/ priority to be considered more important or needing more attention than anything else and therefore dealt with first: *Workers accepting redundancy will have priority for jobs elsewhere at G.M.* | *American Express cardholders will be given priority booking at Forte hotels.* + **over**: *Criminal cases take priority over civil suits.*

priority claim —see under CLAIM[1]

priority lien —see under LIEN

pri•vate /ˈpraɪvɨt/ *adj* **1** [only before a noun] private property, businesses, activities etc are owned or paid for by people and companies, rather than the government: *They transferred ownership of thousands of companies from the state to the **private sector*** (=the part of the economy not owned by the government). | *Investment bankers say that **private money** should be used for new municipal projects.* | ***private property*** | ***private pensions*** —**privately** *adv*: *Joe Sims, a former Justice Department lawyer who now practices privately* | *a privately run prison* | *privately operated toll roads*

2 FINANCE involving something that is sold directly to people or organizations, without being offered openly for anyone to buy: *The company has raised $50 million in a **private placement** arranged by Kemper Financial Services.* | *Goldman will seek new sources of capital through a **private investment offering**.* | *a **private sale** of 70 million shares, to be offered to investment institutions at A$2.55 each* —**privately** *adv*: *The banks will privately place the shares with individual investors.* | *He will decide which works will be sold privately and which works will be sold at auction.*

3 in private hands not belonging to the government: *Slovak officials approved proposals to put 200 companies in private hands.*

4 in private hands belonging to a member of the public rather than to an organization: *There are more than 100 million handguns in private hands in the US.*

5 go private also **turn private** if a government-owned organization goes or turns private, it is sold to investors: *Iberia Airlines will be ready to go private next year.* | *Poland's remaining state enterprises have put forward plans to turn private.*

6 go private *BrE* to pay for medical treatment instead of getting it free at a public hospital

7 a private company does not make its shares available for anyone to buy on a stockmarket: *Cargill, the largest **private company** in the US, wants to stay that way. Says Mr West, a vice president: 'We'll go public* (=sell shares on the stockmarket) *the week after snowballs form in hell.'* —**privately** *adv*: *Cortisol Medical Research Inc., a **privately held** owned drug manufacturer*

8 go private if a company with shares on the stockmarket goes private, its owners buy back those shares from existing shareholders so that it becomes privately owned: *The majority of companies that went private in the last few years will become public again by reselling stock.*

9 take a company private if a company's owners take it private, they buy back all shares from existing shareholders: *The company's chairman plans to take the company private through a buy-out of the 74% of shares he doesn't already own.*

10 only for use by one particular person or group, not for everyone: *a private road* | *private accommodation*

11 a private meeting, agreement, conversation etc involves only a small number of people and is kept secret: *Mr. Miscio rose to protest, saying 'This is a private meeting'.* | *The visit was preceded by a private audience* (=a meeting with someone important) *for the chairmen.* —**privately** *adv*: *He and his lawyers will be permitted to meet privately at the Oakland jail.*

private bank —see under BANK[1]

private branch exchange —see PBX

private carrier —see under CARRIER

private company —see under COMPANY

private corporation —see under CORPORATION

private enterprise —see under ENTERPRISE

private income —see under INCOME

private investment —see under INVESTMENT

private investor —see under INVESTOR

private label *adj* [only before a noun] *AmE* MARKETING private-label products have the name of the shop that sells them, rather than the name given to it by the producer; OWN-LABEL, OWN-BRAND *BrE*: *The company makes and distributes private-label products for supermarket retailers.*

private land —see under LAND[1]

private law —see under LAW

private limited company —see under COMPANY

private limited partnership —see under PARTNERSHIP

privately-owned —see under -OWNED

private offering —see under OFFERING

private ownership —see under OWNERSHIP

private partnership —see under PARTNERSHIP

private pension —see under PENSION[1]

private placing also **private placement** —see under PLACING

private possession —see under POSSESSION

private property —see under PROPERTY

private sale —see under SALE

private secretary —see under SECRETARY

private sector —see under SECTOR

private treaty —see under TREATY

private trust —see under TRUST

pri•vat•i•za•tion also **privatisation** *BrE* /ˌpraɪvət-aɪˈzeɪʃən‖-tə-/ *n* [U] the act selling a company or activity controlled by the government to private investors: *The Labour party was opposed to the privatisation of water and electricity.* —compare NATIONALIZATION

pri•vat•ize also **privatise** *BrE* /ˈpraɪvətaɪz/ *v* [T] if the government privatizes a company or activity that it owns or operates, it sells the company etc to a business or to members of the public, who become its new SHAREHOLDERS: *the Argentine government's drive to privatize a number of businesses* | *When it privatized agriculture two years ago, Vietnam went from rice-importer to exporter in one growing season.* —**privatized** also **privatised** *BrE*, *the privatised gas industry*—compare NATIONALIZE

priv•i•lege /ˈprɪvɨlɪdʒ/ *n* **1** [C] a special advantage given to a small group of people, organizations, countries etc: *The new **trade privileges** will enhance Vienna's effort to attract US companies.* | *The Treasury will allow dealers to bid on government securities, a privilege previously restricted to only 39 firms.*

2 [C,U] LAW a right in law that protects a person, for example by not forcing them to discuss something, or allowing them freedom to say things that would not normally be acceptable; IMMUNITY: *Ms. Backiel asserted the **attorney-client privilege** and refused to discuss the case.* | *Committee members expressed concern that case could threaten Parliament's traditional privileges.* —**privileged** *adj*: *The information will remain privileged because it is the result of Westinghouse's relationship with its lawyers.*

priv•i•ty /ˈprɪvɨti/ *n* [U] LAW the legal relationship existing between the people who have signed a contract, agreement etc: *A successful legal action for insider trading is unlikely, since privity would be virtually impossible to prove.*

prize[1] /praɪz/ *n* [C] something that is very valuable or important to have: *With a portfolio of $1 billion, Amerco is an attractive prize.* | *The administration has worked behind the scenes to help Turkey win the big prize – EU membership.*

prize[2] *adj* [only before a noun] the best, most valuable or important: *In recent weeks, a number of* ***prize assets*** *have been sold.* | *the agency's* ***prize client****, Coca Cola.*

prized /praɪzd/ *adj* considered very valuable, important etc: *BMW is producing some of the most prized and expensive cars in the world.* | *Orinoco's oil is not highly prized because it is hard to refine.*

PRO *n* [C] public relations officer; someone whose job is to supply information about a company or organization in a way that makes people have a good opinion of it

pro- /prəʊ‖proʊ/ *prefix* in favour of or supporting something: *He proved you can be pro-management, pro-labor, and pro-health and safety at the same time.*

pro•ac•tive /prəʊˈæktɪv‖proʊ-/ *adj* being ready for changes and doing something to influence or effect them before they happen: *For our guarantee to be effective, our employees had to adopt a more* ***proactive attitude*** *toward service.* | *Can we realistically expect auditors to be proactive in assessing business risk?* —compare REACTIVE —**proactively** *adv*: *Management will deal with all suggestions as proactively as possible, regardless of their source.*

prob•a•bil•i•ty /ˌprɒbəˈbɪləti‖ˌprɑː-/ *n* plural **probabilities** [C,U] STATISTICS the chance that something will happen, calculated mathematically: *Companies may collaborate* (=work together) *in working out loss probabilities.* | *the influence of significant variables, including probability*

pro•bate /ˈprəʊbeɪt, -bət‖ˈproʊbeɪt/ *n* [U] LAW the process used to establish that a WILL (=a statement saying who you want to have your money and property when you die) has been properly made out, according to the law: *All joint-owned property goes to the named beneficiaries without passing through probate.* —**probate** *adj*: *a probate court*

pro•ba•tion /prəˈbeɪʃən‖proʊ-/ *n* [U] **1** HUMAN RESOURCES a period of time during which a new employee is tested to make sure they are suitable for a job: *At the end of the year I can pass or fail or have my probation extended.* | *After a three-month* ***probation period****, a Maruwa Orimono recruit is entitled to a car.* **on probation**: *The chief executive hired me on probation for three months.*
2 a fixed period of time during which a person or company must improve their performance if they are to continue working, trading etc **place sb on probation**: *Calpers said it was placing Salomon on probation, meaning it could sever all its business ties with the firm.*
3 LAW a system of dealing with criminals which allows them not to go to prison, if they behave well and see an official adviser regularly, for a fixed period of time: *Two of the accused were sentenced to prison terms, and the third received 10 months' probation.* **on probation**: *The disgraced former regional director was* ***placed on probation*** *for three years.*

pro•ba•tion•a•ry /prəˈbeɪʃənəri‖proʊˈbeɪʃəneri/ *adj* [only before a noun] relating to the period of time during which a new employee is tested to make sure they are suitable for a job: *Applicants hired should work a suitable* ***probationary period*** *of between one and six months.* | ***probationary employees***

probe[1] /prəʊb‖proʊb/ *n* [C] *journalism* a very thorough examination of something that has happened; INQUIRY: *The probe focuses on an unauthorized bid placed by the company two months ago.* + **into/of**: *The agency is conducting a wide-ranging probe into possible collusion and fraud.* | *federal probes of trading practices at the Chicago exchanges*

probe[2] *v* [I,T] to ask very detailed questions to find something out, especially things people do not want you to know: *To probe further, I called economist John Mueller.* | *The scale of losses is prompting regulators to probe the portfolios of US banks.*

pro•bi•ty /ˈprəʊbəti‖ˈproʊ-/ *n* [U] *formal* honesty and correctness: *An accountant provides assurance of fiscal probity to businesses.* | *The people managing these large pension funds are models of probity.*

problem child *n* plural **problem children** [C usually singular] **1** a product or business that has financial problems, often one that its makers or owners do not know what to do with: *The troubled company is widely regarded as the problem child in the group's portfolio.*
2 MARKETING a product with a low percentage of the total sales in a market that is growing quickly. Problem children are one of the four types of product in the GROWTH/SHARE MATRIX

pro bono /prəʊ ˌbəʊnəʊ‖proʊ ˌboʊnoʊ/ also **pro bono publico** /-ˈpʊblɪkəʊ‖-koʊ/ *adj, adv formal* used to describe work done by a lawyer or other professional for which they do not charge a payment: *42% of attorneys surveyed reported doing some pro bono work last year.* | *Mr. Kunstler is handling the case pro bono.*

P

pro•ce•dure /prəˈsiːdʒə‖-ər/ *n* **1** [C] the correct way of doing something, especially something that is done often: *We have hired an accounting firm to evaluate our audit procedures.* + **for**: *The bank must review its procedure for maintaining adequate loan-loss reserves.*
2 [U] the accepted method and order of doing something in a formal situation, such as a law case or official meeting: *The recent argument between the directors concerned procedure, not policy.* | *a* ***lapse in procedure*** (=an occasion when the normal procedure is not followed) | *The police* ***complaints procedure*** *provides a formal mechanism for citizens to lodge complaints about instances of police misconduct.* —**procedural** *adj*: *The case was overturned* ***on procedural grounds****.*

pro•ceed /prəˈsiːd/ *v* [I] *formal* to continue to do something that has been started: *The discussions between the two firms are proceeding slowly but satisfactorily.* | *In order to proceed, Millicom needs a radio frequency to test the network.* + **with**: *The banks are proceeding with preparations for the merger.*
proceed against sb *phr v* [T] LAW to begin a legal case against someone: *The court will allow the plaintiff to proceed against the partners.*
proceed to sth *phr v* [T] to move to the next stage of a plan, meeting etc: *We will conduct a cost-benefit analysis before proceeding to a full hearing.*

pro•ceed•ings /prəˈsiːdɪŋz/ *n* [plural] LAW actions taken in a law court or legal case: *The company's creditors asked an Ontario court to begin formal proceedings against the company.*
bankruptcy proceedings a legal case taken against someone who is unable to pay their debts, in order to share their assets among the people and businesses that they owe money to —see also STAY OF PROCEEDINGS

pro•ceeds /ˈprəʊsiːdz‖ˈproʊ-/ *n* [plural] FINANCE **1** the money gained from selling something: *Allied-Signal was planning to use the proceeds from the sale of Union Texas to reduce debt.* | *cocaine-trafficking proceeds*
2 the money that a business gets from ISSUING (=selling) bonds, shares etc: *San Diego will use the proceeds from the bond issue to acquire and install new police facilities.*
net proceeds ◆ the profit from selling assets after costs are taken away: *PWA said net proceeds from the sale of the five aircraft will be about C$150 million.*
◆ the money obtained from a share or bond ISSUE, after costs are taken away: *UDR will use the $15.4 million net proceeds from the stock sale to reduce outstanding borrowings.*

pro•cess¹ /ˈprəʊses‖ˈprɑː-/ *n* **1** [C] a series of actions taken to perform a particular task or achieve a particular result: *simpler design and manufacturing processes* | *Industry executives said ABC's plans would slow down the process.* | *the union's disciplinary and electoral processes*

due process [U] LAW the correct way to deal with a legal case: *a violation of the company's* ***right to due process***

2 be in the process of doing sth to have started doing something that is not yet finished: *General Motors is in the process of beginning discussions with potential partners.*

process² *v* [T] **1** MANUFACTURING to change a substance as part of the manufacture of a product: *The refineries are processing 1.4 million barrels of crude oil a day.* | *The paper will be processed from pineapple and banana leaves.*

2 to deal with a document in the usual way: *The service was started to help process copyright permissions more rapidly.* | *The Securities Industry Automation Corp. processes stock quotations from the major exchanges.*

3 COMPUTING if a computer processes information, figures etc, it uses them to produce a particular result: *the accounts are processed by the Systems Union Sun Account system.* | *facilities for changing, deleting and* ***processing data*** —**processing** *n* [U] *a new initiative in materials processing* | *Fire broke out at a* ***food processing plant*** *in Hamlet, N.C.* | *T/Maker will demonstrate a prototype of its* ***word-processing software*** *software for preparing written documents*—see also CENTRAL PROCESSING UNIT

pro•cessed /ˈprəʊsest‖ˈprɑː-/ *adj* **processed food/meat/cheese etc** food that has been treated or changed to colour it, keep it fresh etc: *the manufacture and marketing of processed potato products*

pro•ces•sing /ˈprəʊsesɪŋ‖ˈprɑː-/ *n* [U] **1** MANUFACTURING when a substance is changed as part of the manufacture of a product: *Fire broke out at a* ***food processing plant*** *in Hamlet, N.C.*

2 COMPUTING the use of information, figures etc to produce a particular result

batch processing when a computer system processes different BATCHES (=groups) of data (=information) or different jobs one after the other

data processing also **electronic data processing**, abbreviation **EDP** the use of computers to store and organize data: *computers designed for commercial and business data processing* | *Invoicing is precisely the kind of function that can be taken over by electronic data processing.*

distributed processing when a computer system processes DATA (=information) at various places, instead of using one central computer

parallel processing a system in some types of computer that can work on several problems, calculations etc at the same time, making it much faster: *NCR systems range from notepad computers to systems with parallel processing.* | *parallel-processing research and development projects*

pro•ces•sor /ˈprəʊsesə‖ˈprɑːsesər/ *n* [C] **1** COMPUTING the central part of a computer that does the calculations on the information put into it: *an Intel Pentium III processor* | *systems that need a big expensive* ***central processor*** *to work* —see also CENTRAL PROCESSING UNIT, WORD PROCESSOR

2 a company that prepares substances, especially food, for sale or as part of another product: *Georgia officials blocked sales by an Atlanta milk processor after detecting contamination in its milk.*

pro•cure /prəˈkjʊə‖proʊˈkjʊr/ *v* [T] *formal* to obtain something that is needed for a particular task: *Companies in the industry reported difficulty in procuring raw materials.* | *Investors showed faith in Pathé's ability to procure the $900 million required to close the deal.*

pro•cure•ment /prəˈkjʊəmənt‖proʊˈkjʊr-/ *n* [C,U] *formal* the act of ordering and buying the equipment, supplies, services etc needed by a company or other organization: *Uncertainty in government procurements hit Sutherland's results in the first quarter.* | *The order is equivalent to only 4% of the company's total procurement of $8.75 billion.* | *alleged* ***procurement fraud***

procurement officer —see under OFFICER

prod•uce¹ /ˈprɒdjuːs‖ˈproʊduːs/ *n* [U] food that has been grown on the land or produced in large quantities, using farming methods: *Where it once offered 125 items of produce, A&P now sells 300 fruits and vegetables.* | ***fresh produce***

pro•duce² /prəˈdjuːs‖-ˈduːs/ *v* **1** [I,T] to make or grow something in large quantities to be sold: *The plant in Leningrad will produce parts used in building construction.* | *The British assembly plants still don't produce as efficiently as those in Germany.* | *Colombia produced a bumper* (=very large) *coffee crop this year.* —see also MASS-PRODUCE

2 [T] to make something happen or to have a particular result or effect: *A strong market could mean sales will produce substantial profit gains.* | *The planning sessions have not yet produced a coherent strategy.*

3 [T] to control the preparation of a film, television programme etc, especially the amount of money spent making it: *Disney's computer-animated film will be produced by Pixar.*

4 [I,T] to show an official document when it is needed, for example as proof of something: *The judge ordered officials to produce financial records within three days.*

pro•duc•er /prəˈdjuːsə‖-ˈduːsər/ *n* [C] **1** a person or organization that manages and finds the finance for films, plays etc: *Westwood One Inc., a Los Angeles-based producer and distributor of radio programs*

2 a company or country that makes goods or grows foods: *Drummond Co. is the largest coal producer in Alabama.* | *Hong Kong imports of textiles are hurting US producers.*

marginal producer a producer with producing only a small number of a certain type of product, meaning their costs are high for each unit produced, and their profits are low: *At prices below $4 an ounce for silver, marginal producers are squeezed from the market.*

producer price —see under PRICE¹

producer price index —see under INDEX¹

prod•uct /ˈprɒdʌkt‖ˈprɑː-/ *n* **1** [C] something useful and intended to be sold that comes from nature or is made in a factory: *Distributors for Amway* ***sell*** *numerous* ***products****, including cleaning and personal-care products.* | *Companies must be able to* ***launch new products*** (=introduce them) *quickly and alter existing ones.* | *SL Industries designs, manufactures and distributes engineered products.* | *There were thought to be no safety problems, but the company decided to* ***withdraw the product*** (=no longer make it available) *so the incidents could be investigated.*

2 milk/steel/tobacco/wood etc products products made from milk etc: *Corning produces glass fiber and other specialty glass products.* | *petroleum products*

3 [C] a service: *The bank offers products such as cash management and short-term loans.*

4 [U] products in general: *He needed $6,000 more a month to invest in inventory, but didn't have it. As a result he couldn't keep enough product on the shelf.*

commercial product ♦ [C] a product that can be sold, rather than one still being developed: *They had trouble converting promising research in drugs into commercial products.*

♦ [C] another name for CONSUMER PRODUCT

commodity product ♦ [C] a product such as a metal, farm product, oil etc: *Canadian paper companies*

concentrate on commodity products such as pulp and newsprint, while US companies often concentrate on products with higher value added.
◆ [C] a product that is hard to DIFFERENTIATE (=make seem different) from other products of the same kind: *PCs are becoming commodity products, with consumers just buying on price.*

consumer product [C] a product for use by people rather than businesses: *the food and consumer products manufacturer Unilever*

copycat product [C] a product that copies a competitor's idea for a product: *There has been a surge of copycat products, but we expected many companies to copy our approach to desktop video conferencing.*

core product [C] a main product that a company makes or sells, and which is very important to it: *The company is withdrawing from software and refocusing on its core products in hardware.*

derivative product [C] a financial product such as a FUTURE or OPTION rather than the actual shares, currencies etc that they relate to. Options give the buyer the right to buy shares etc at a fixed price within a particular period of time, and futures allow the buyer to buy a fixed amount of a currency, farm product etc at a fixed price for delivery later: *The unit was formed last year to trade interest-rate swaps, currency swaps and other derivative products.*

entry-level product [C] a version of a product designed for someone buying this type of product for the first time. Entry-level products are usually the cheapest in a company's product range: *On some entry level products the company is also including simplified software for first-time users.*

financial product [C] a particular type of investment: *Investors often find financial products increasingly complex and seek advice on how to buy and sell them.*

generic product [C] a product that is sold under the general name for a type of product, rather than a brand name. Many medicines and drugs that you can buy are generic products: *Although R&D spending is soaring, generic products are reducing the profitable life of brand-name drugs.*

gross product [C] ECONOMICS the total value of goods and services produced in a particular place: *In California, farmers produce about 10% of the state's gross product.*

high-end product [C] a product that is one of the most expensive or advanced in a company's product range, or in the market as a whole: *The company blamed the loss on higher costs and lower sales of high-end products.*

high-tech product also **hi-tech product** [C] a product that is made using the most modern technical knowledge and methods: *demand for new computers and other high-tech products*

home product ◆ [C] a product used in people's homes, such as furniture etc: *Cosmetics account for 8%, accessories 9% and home products, including bed and bath items, 10%.*
◆ [C] another name for HOUSEHOLD PRODUCT

household product [C] a cleaning product used in people's homes etc: *household products such as Ajax cleanser and Palmolive dishwashing liquid*

industrial product [C] a product for use in industry and business, rather than by people for their own use: *power transmission parts and other industrial products*

insurance product [C] a particular type of insurance contract: *An insurance product called an immediate annuity pays a fixed sum each month for life or some other period.*

investment product [C] another name for FINANCIAL PRODUCT: *Purchasers of insurance and investment products are concerned about the financial strength of providers of these products.*

low-end product [C] a product that is one of the cheapest in the range of products made by a company, or generally: *Polo shirts are increasingly a low-end product: 30% of them are now sold through discount outlets.*

me-too product [C] *informal* a product introduced by a company after it has seen that other companies are successful with the same type of product: *In vodka, the shelves were full of me-too products that lacked taste or marketing support.*

proprietary product [C] a product sold under a brand name owned by a company, rather than a GENERIC name (=a general name for a type of product): *a proprietary product, called Danafate, that treats stomach ulcers*

value-added product [C] a product with special benefits for which buyers are willing to pay more. Producers are able to charge more for these products and therefore make more profit from them: *The food service market includes both commodity and value-added products.* | *The company's strong performance is due to its continued push into* ***high-value-added products*** *such as its Formula Shell high octane gas.* —see also BY-PRODUCT, END-PRODUCT, GROSS DOMESTIC PRODUCT, GROSS NATIONAL PRODUCT

product advertising —see under ADVERTISING

product differentiation —see under DIFFERENTIATION

product endorsement —see under ENDORSEMENT

product innovation —see under INNOVATION

pro·duc·tion /prəˈdʌkʃən/ *n* **1** [U] the process of making or growing things to be sold as products, usually in large quantities: *Toshiba is increasing production of its popular line of laptop computers.* | *They have plans to design a smaller submarine that could* ***go into production*** (=start being produced) *by the end of the decade.* | *a new plant with an annual* ***production capacity*** *of* (=the ability to produce) *500,000 disk drives* | *Germany's high* ***production costs*** | *a magnesium metal* ***production facility*** (=factory) | *He was a* ***production manager*** *for Lockheed Corp.* | *By adjusting the* ***production process****, they were able to reduce the plant's waste by two-thirds.* | *Bonuses were introduced for employees meeting* ***production targets*** (=aims). | ***production workers*** *assembling pianos* —see also FACTOR OF PRODUCTION

2 [U] an amount of something that is produced: *In August, production of passenger cars climbed 12% from a year earlier.*

batch production [U] when a factory makes a quantity of one form of a product or part, followed by a quantity of another different form: *small batch production on a flexible manufacturing system*

continuous production also **flow production, process production** [U] when a finished product is produced from basic materials in one production process: *Assembly line operation is an important feature of flow production.*

direct production [U] when someone produces all the things they need using their own efforts and skills, without the advantages of SPECIALIZATION (=concentrating on producing only one product) or the DIVISION OF LABOUR (=using different people to do different jobs). Direct production is more an economic model than a real production method

industrial production [U] used to talk about the total production from all industrial activities in a particular period of time: *Industrial production figures due today are likely to show that the UK manufacturing sector remains depressed.*

jobbing production [U] when a single product is made, rather than large quantities of goods: *Jobbing production is used to produce prototype models, spare parts, and countless other tailor-made pieces.*

just-in-time production [U] when parts are delivered just before they are needed in the process of producing something: *Just-in-time production dictates that parts be delivered to a factory at the last minute. That cuts inventories and finance costs.*

lean production [U] when things are manufactured using just-in-time production methods, with the aim of ZERO DEFECTS (=no faults), no REWORKING (=working again on things that were done wrong) etc: *He wants to bring in lean production, with fewer workers and more components being subcontracted.*

mass production [U] when products are made in large numbers by machines, so that they can be produced cheaply: *The new model will become cheaper with mass production.* | *The technique developed by Matsushita brings the* ***mass-production cost*** *down to under £3.00 per watt.*

primary production ◆ [U] activities such as agriculture, fishing, and MINING, rather than manufacturing: *The proportion of jobs coming from primary production is much greater in the Highlands than in the rest of Scotland.*

◆ [U] the first stage in producing oil, metals etc, rather than producing other things from oil etc: *Aluminum producers have announced cuts in primary production of 900,000 metric tons.*

3 [C,U] the process of making films, television, and radio broadcasts, or plays, or a particular film etc: *a* ***film production*** *company* | *CBS has been discussing possible* ***co-productions*** *with the BBC.*

production control —see under CONTROL[1]

production manager —see under MANAGER

pro•duc•tive /prəˈdʌktɪv/ *adj* **1** producing or achieving something: *We want to turn welfare recipients into productive, working members of society.* | *The program is designed to help business users be more productive.* | *The plant has the newest and most productive steel-making technology.*

2 producing crops, goods, or wealth: *The strike is cutting deeper into the company's* ***productive capacity*** (=ability to produce things). **—productively** *adv*: *Email allows people to use their time more productively.* **—productiveness** *n* [U]

pro•duc•tiv•i•ty /ˌprɒdʌkˈtɪvəti, -dək-‖ˌprɑː-/ *n* [U] the rate at which goods are produced, and the amount produced in relation to the work, time, and money needed to produce them: *Declines in factory jobs and hours worked mean that only more productivity per worker could have raised output in May.* | *Strong manufacturing* ***productivity growth*** *reduced the number of manufacturing workers by one million in the 1980s.*

productivity bonus —see under BONUS

prod•uct•ize also **productise** *BrE* /ˈprɒdʌktaɪz‖ˈprɑː-/ *v* [T] MARKETING to make something that previously only existed as an idea, or in a version used in research etc into a product that can be sold

product launch —see under LAUNCH[2]

product liability —see under LIABILITY

product lifecycle —see under LIFECYCLE

product line —see under LINE

product manager —see under MANAGER

product mix —see under MIX

product orientation —see under ORIENTATION

product parity —see under PARITY

product placement —see under PLACEMENT

product range —see under RANGE[1]

product research —see under RESEARCH

product substitution —see under SUBSTITUTION

product withdrawal —see under WITHDRAWAL

pro•fes•sion /prəˈfeʃən/ *n* [C] **1** a job that needs advanced education and special training: *realtors, a profession with an established record of service to the public* | *People assume that money management is a* ***well-paid profession.***

2 by profession if someone is a doctor, teacher etc by profession, that is what they do as their work. The phase is usually used when talking about the fact that someone is doing different work for a period of time: *He's a landscape gardener by profession.*

3 the legal/medical/teaching etc profession used to talk about the people working in a particular job, considered as separate groups: *In the bankruptcy field you find some of the* ***legal profession's*** *most forceful personalities.*

4 the professions [plural] accountants, doctors, lawyers, teachers etc considered as one group: *During this century, the professions have been one of the fastest growing sectors of the occupational structure.*

pro•fes•sion•al[1] /prəˈfeʃənəl/ *adj* **1** [only before a noun] connected with a job requiring special education and training: ***professional qualifications*** | *professional trade associations* | *providers of business and* ***professional services***

2 (continuing) professional development HUMAN RESOURCES abbreviation **CPD** training offered to people working in professions as part of their job: *the Law Society's continuing professional development scheme*

3 *approving* very well trained and showing high standards of work: *The women made an excellent showing – they were every bit as professional as their male colleagues.* | *If you build your business and run it in a professional way, you'll be around to pick up the rewards.*

4 doing an activity, sport etc to earn money, rather than for pleasure: *a professional footballer* | *The weather could put a third of the nation's professional beekeepers out of business.*

professional[2] *n* [C] **1** someone who does a job requiring special education and training: *A number of market professionals are recommending cyclical stocks.* | *Business Risks employs 225 professionals, many of them former law-enforcement officers.*

2 someone who is very experienced, has a lot of knowledge, and does things very skilfully: *The successful applicant will be a decisive professional, capable of making hard decisions.*

3 someone who earns money doing a job, sport etc that other people do for pleasure: *Nike say the shoe is designed for professionals and advanced amateurs* (=people who do a sport for pleasure).

professional investor —see under INVESTOR

professional liability —see under LIABILITY

pro•fi•cien•cy /prəˈfɪʃənsi/ *n* [U] a high standard of skill in a particular job or knowledge of a particular subject: *One corporation spends $2,000 a quarter bringing its employees up to* ***technical proficiency.*** + **in**: *Foreign medical graduates must pass a rigorous series of tests, showing proficiency in English.*

pro•fi•cient /prəˈfɪʃənt/ *adj* able to do something skilfully and well: *As standards rise, less proficient pilots won't be hired.* + **in/at**: *To do a multimedia presentation you need to be proficient in public speaking.*

pro•file[1] /ˈprəʊfaɪl‖ˈproʊ-/ *n* [C] **1** a short description of someone or something, giving the most important details about them + **of**: *A profile of the company in the latest edition of Barron's contributed to interest in the stock.* | *expectations that the company's* ***financial profile*** *will begin to strengthen*

2 used to talk about how much things are noticed and the degree to which they are given attention: *The bank*

P

wants to ***raise its profile*** (=become better known) *as an asset manager for wealthier individuals.* | *Mr Dershowitz, a* ***high-profile*** *defense attorney* | *Despite his broad influence in the world's second-largest computer company, Mr. Smith* ***has a low profile*** *in the industry as a whole.* | *He asked Mr Curry to* ***keep a low profile*** (=not to draw attention to himself) *until the nomination was confirmed.*

age profile the number of people of different ages in a country or organization or who buy a particular product or service. Age profiles are important in RECRUITING new employees, marketing a product etc: *The age profile of Internet users shows that more than 40% are over 40.*

customer profile also **consumer profile** MARKETING a description of the typical customer likely to be interested in a particular product: *Jack Daniels' consumer profile is significantly younger than those of other bourbons.* | *We have more than one asset-allocation model for different investor profiles.*

demographic profile a study of the population in each place, how much they earn, spend etc: *a demographic profile of cheese buyers with data showing which supermarkets drew most of those shoppers*

risk profile FINANCE the degree of probability that a company will make payments on its debt: *Moody's Investors Service Inc. downgraded the long-term ratings of Credit Lyonnais, citing its increased risk profile.*

profile² *v* [T] to give a short description of someone or something in a newspaper, television programme etc: *The stock was favorably profiled in Friday's edition of Investor's Daily.* | *Dewar's ad campaign profiling interesting individuals*

prof•it¹ /ˈprɒfɪ̈t‖ˈprɑː-/ *n* [C,U] **1** money that you gain from selling something, or from doing business in a particular period of time, after taking away costs: *A business has to* ***make a profit.*** | *Nemacolin so far hasn't* ***earned a profit*** *but could break even this year.* | *Coca-Cola, Boeing and McDonald's all* ***reported*** *strong* ***profits*** *in the latest quarter.* | *They will have to produce and sell more than 300,000 cars a year to* ***turn*** (=make) ***a profit*** *on the model.* | *We've got to see the economy recover, and we've got to see* ***corporate profits*** (=those of companies in general) *increase.* | *They controlled the market for the stock and drove it up to artificially high prices, netting themselves and others* ***excess profits*** (=profits that people think are too high). | *60% of the perfume price is simply* ***pure profit*** (=actual profit) *for the retailer.* | *The company said that* ***sales and profits*** *increased in four of its major divisions.*

2 first-quarter/second-half/etc profit profits for the first three-month period, second six-month period etc of the financial year: *The insurer recorded fourth-quarter profit of 86 cents a share, compared with year-earlier net income of 82 cents.*

accumulated profit the profits a company has made in previous years and held in its RESERVES: *The available reserves of its accumulated profit were reduced by workers' demands so that there was little money for capital investment.*

after-tax profit a company's profit after tax has been taken away: *NatWest said the decline in after-tax profit was the result of significantly higher tax charges.*

book profit ◆ a profit as shown in a company's accounts: *Philips will report a book profit of about Fl1,800 million on its sale of shares in TSM.*

◆ a profit not in actual money, but from the increase in the value of an asset; PAPER PROFIT: *If the land was revalued and stated in the balance sheet at its current price, this would result in the company making a book profit.*

consolidated profit in a group of companies, the total profit from all the companies in a group for a particular period of time: *Solvay's consolidated profit fell 20% because of lower margins in its plastics sector.*

distributable profit also **distributed profit** profit earned during a particular period of time that a company pays to shareholders: *Preference dividends can be accumulated if there are not sufficient distributable profits to pay them in a particular financial year.* | *There was a further reduction of corporation tax on reinvested income, while distributed profits remained taxable at 42%.*

gross profit a company's profit before certain costs and taxes are taken away: *The insurer reported that gross profit, before taxes and losses on equity and foreign-exchange operations, edged down 1%.*

net profit the profit from a deal, or from business activity for a particular period of time, after all costs and taxes are taken away; NET: *Their contract stipulated that they were entitled to a fee of 41% of the film's net profit.* | *Profit after tax, or net profit payable to shareholders, rose to £20.1 million.*

operating profit profit relating to a company's normal activities of providing goods or services: *Air Methods had $3.9 million in operating profit before interest, cash and depreciation, on revenue of $15.3 million.*

paper profit an increase in the value of an investment, but which is not an actual amount of money unless the investment is sold: *Many investors are sitting on fat paper profits from the rally, and are worried about losing those profits if the market has peaked.*

pre-tax profit also **pretax profit** *AmE* profit for a particular period of time before tax is taken away: *The company reported retax profit of 175 billion yen, net of 94 billion yen on sales of 3.228 trillion yen.*

pure profit [U] real profit, with no costs to be taken away: *Sponsorship income is pure profit for the club because there are no costs associated with it.*

retained profit net profit for a particular period of time, or for several periods of time, that are not paid to shareholders in DIVIDENDS; UNDISTRIBUTED EARNINGS: *Furr's wants to use retained profits for expansion and renovation.*

taxable profit profits that can be legally taxed: *Corporations can deduct their interest expenses from taxable profits.*

trading profit ◆ the profit made by a financial institution from buying and selling investments: *Both foreign-exchange trading profit and gains from the sales of securities were lower in the quarter.*

◆ another name for OPERATING PROFIT: *BAT said trading profit from its commercial activities rose 28%.*

undistributed profit profit from a particular period of time, that is not paid to shareholders: *Undistributed profits should be allowed to accumulate free of tax.*

windfall profit a profit gained from an unusual or unexpected event; WINDFALL: *Should the Automobile Association sell its commercial activities and distribute a windfall profit to its members?*

profit² *v* [I] to gain money from an event, selling something etc **profit by/from sth**: *Tiger profited by anticipating the fall in the Tokyo stock market.* | *Coca-Cola profited from a weaker dollar and higher sales overseas.*

prof•it•a•bil•i•ty /ˌprɒfɪ̈təˈbɪlɪ̈ti‖ˌprɑː-/ *n* [U] the state of producing a profit, or the degree to which an activity, company etc is profitable: *restructuring proposals to help* ***boost profitability*** (=increase it) | *K-mart's earnings were helped by* ***improved profitability*** *in its fashions division.* | *S&P said the lower ratings reflect the bank's* ***declining*** (=falling) ***profitability.*** | *the company's effort to* ***return*** *its credit card operation* ***to profitability*** (=make it profitable again)

prof•it•a•ble /ˈprɒfɪ̈təbəl‖ˈprɑː-/ *adj* **1** producing a useful result: *I thought the meeting was very profitable.*
2 producing a profit: *Sheffield is profitable, but will earn less than a year ago.* | *Innovation has made Sidek one of Mexico's most* ***profitable companies.*** | *Mutual Benefit's group health business has been its most* ***profitable line*** (=activity).

profit and loss account also **profit and loss statement** —see under ACCOUNT[1]

profit centre —see under CENTRE

prof·i·teer /ˌprɒfɪ̊ˈtɪə‖ˌprɑːfɪ̊ˈtɪr/ *n* [C] *disapproving* a person or organization that makes unfairly large profits, for example by selling things that are hard to get at very high prices: *A handful of profiteers are using the legally protected monopoly to charge absurdly high prices for these drugs.* | *black market profiteers* —**profiteering** *n* [U] *Airlines need fare increases of 2% to 3% to recover the added fuel costs. Anything beyond that is pure profiteering.*

profit forecast —see under FORECAST[1]

Profit Impact of Market Strategy —see PIMS

profit-making *adj* a profit-making product, activity, organization etc is one that makes money, or one that exists in order to make money: *We concentrate on being a profit-making company rather than on just chasing sales.* | *He plans to set up hundreds of profit-making schools in every state of the union.* —**profit-maker** *n* [C] *Heinz's ketchup is one of its biggest profit-makers.*—compare LOSS-MAKING

P

profit margin —see under MARGIN

profit motive *n* [singular] ECONOMICS the act of doing something in order to make money: *The social aspects of German economic policy have always been as important as the profit motive.*

profit sharing *n* [U] **1** when a company gives part of its profits to its employees: *He has long believed in employee profit-sharing or employee ownership.* | *Bethlehem Steel Corp. will make **profit-sharing payments** of $9.4 million.*
2 when a MUTUAL (=an insurance company or other financial institution without shareholders) pays out part of its profits to its members

profits policy —see under INSURANCE POLICY

profit squeeze —see under SQUEEZE[2]

profits warning *n* [C usually singular] *especially BrE* FINANCE an occasion when a company announces that its profit for a particular period of time will be less than expected: *Waste Management International **issued a profits warning**, citing restructuring charges and the loss of a large contract.*

profit-taking *n* [U] FINANCE when investors on a financial market sell investments in order to profit from a rise in prices: *Prices settled lower after profit-taking late in the session by commodity fund managers.*

pro-for·ma /prəʊ ˈfɔːmə‖proʊ ˈfɔːrmə/ *adj* [only before a noun] FINANCE pro-forma figures, results etc are not complete or final, but show what is expected to happen: *York International reported **pro-forma earnings** of 32 cents a share for the fourth quarter.* | *Saatchi's loss compares with pro-forma pretax profit of $14.6 millions.*

pro-forma invoice —see under INVOICE[1]

pro·gram[1] /ˈprəʊgræm‖ˈproʊ-/ *n* [C] **1** COMPUTING also **computer program** a set of instructions used to make a computer perform a particular task; SOFTWARE: *Ashton-Tate, the maker of database programs* | *Sharp discovered two viruses in programs for its computer game.*
application program a piece of SOFTWARE for a particular job or use: *Can your application programs use files created on another type of computer?*
2 *AmE* an important plan that will be continued over a period of time; PROGRAMME *BrE*: *The commission is in favour of the auto investment programs.*
employee assistance program abbreviation **EAP** *AmE* HUMAN RESOURCES ◆ a set of organized actions by employers in the US to help employees with personal or family problems: *More than two thirds of major firms now support employee assistance programs for drug abusers.*
◆ actions by an employer to help people find new jobs when they are dismissed: *Disney said it would provide employment assistance programs for the 1,000 workers affected by the closure of its Long Beach attractions.*
wellness program HUMAN RESOURCES *AmE* a program for a company's employees, intended to help them learn how to keep healthy and offering them free medical examinations: *The goals of our wellness program are pretty basic: Stop smoking, eat more fruit, and get some exercise.*

program[2] *v* past tense and past participle **programmed** present participle **programming** [T] **1** to put a set of instructions into a computer or other machine to make it perform a particular task **program sth to do sth**: *The computer is programmed to calculate the likely loss of revenue in various imaginary situations.*
2 the American spelling of PROGRAMME

program file —see under FILE[1]

programmable read only memory —see PROM

pro·gramme[1] *BrE*, **program** *AmE* /ˈprəʊgræm‖ˈproʊ-/ *n* [C] **1** an important plan that will be continued over a period of time: *Lufthansa is halfway through an expansion programme.* | *The commission is in favour of the auto investment programs.*
2 a television or radio show: *the main satellite used to broadcast programmes into Latin America*

programme[2] *BrE*, **program** *AmE* — *v* past tense and past participle **programmed** present participle **programming** [T] **1** to set a machine to work in a particular way: *The system can be programmed to shut off the engine or stop it from restarting once the car is parked.*
2 to arrange for something to happen as part of a series of planned events or activities: *Cable TV operators generally agree that a well-programmed comedy network is an attractive asset.*

pro·gram·mer /ˈprəʊgræmə‖ˈproʊgræmər/ *n* [C] **1** COMPUTING someone whose job involves writing instructions for computers to perform particular tasks: *a labor shortage, particularly in trained **computer programmers***
systems programmer a person whose job involves writing instructions for computers
2 a person or company involved in producing television or radio shows: *Turner Broadcasts marketed the cable programmer's entertainment shows in Japan.* | *Paramount offered the series to ABC's chief programmer.*

programme trading —see under TRADING

pro·gram·ming /ˈprəʊgræmɪŋ‖ˈproʊ-/ *n* [U] **1** COMPUTING the work of writing instructions for computers to perform particular tasks: *an expert in computer programming*
2 television or radio programmes, or the work involved in producing them: *The network will broadcast eight hours of programming a day.* | *The company's move into programming began in 1997.*

programming language —see under LANGUAGE

program trading —see under TRADING

pro·gress[1] /prəˈgres/ *v* [I] **1** to develop over a period of time, becoming better or more complete: *The joint venture is progressing faster than expected.* + **to**: *We haven't yet progressed to the negotiating table with any US companies.*
2 if a situation progresses, it continues to happen: *As the afternoon progressed, prices nosed upward in light trading.*

pro·gress[2] /ˈprəʊgres‖ˈprɑː-/ *n* **1** [U] the process of improving something, or getting closer to finishing it: *He has convinced the board of Amtrak's financial progress.* + **in/of/towards**: *Allied-Signal has **made little progress** in its patent dispute.* | *The company is pleased with the progress of the capital-raising effort.* | *He e-mails a **progress report** back to head office each month.*

2 in progress if a plan, project etc is in progress, it has started but is not finished yet: *There are only faint signs that an economic recovery is in progress.* | *Gaston & Snow claims about $37 million in accounts receivable and **work in progress**.*

pro•gres•sion /prəˈgreʃən/ *n* [U] gradual development and improvement over a period of time: *The typical career progression includes two years of technical training.*

pro•gres•sive /prəˈgresɪv/ *adj* **1** happening or changing over a period of time, and often becoming worse: *The results reflect the progressive collapse of sales of the company's high-end computers.*
2 *approving* supporting new or modern ideas, methods etc: *Albania named a young progressive economist, Fatos Nano, to be general secretary.*

progressive tax —see under TAX[1]

progress payment —see under PAYMENT

pro•hib•it /prəˈhɪbɪt‖proʊ-/ *v* [T] to officially stop someone doing something by making it illegal or against the rules: *The firm's own internal rules now prohibit that type of loan.* **prohibit sb from doing sth**: *regulations prohibiting companies from promoting their shares immediately after an offering* —**prohibition** *n* [C,U] *the prohibition of cigarette advertising on television*

pro•hib•i•tive /prəˈhɪbɪtɪv‖proʊ-/ *adj* prohibitive costs, prices etc are very high, and people cannot afford them: *Given the resources of small companies, marketing **costs** can be **prohibitive**.* | *Disney started its own record label rather than pay a prohibitive price for an existing independent.*

proj•ect[1] /ˈprɒdʒekt‖ˈprɑː-/ *n* [C] **1** an important and carefully planned piece of work that will create something new or improve a situation: *the country's largest ever **construction project*** | *San Miguel plans to finance the project 42% from equity and 58% from loans.* | *a joint copper-mining **research project*** | *British Aerospace don't expect the project to be completed before 2005.*
capital project a plan to build a large building, factory etc that will be paid for by loans and investments: *Declining interest rates make some companies less reluctant to borrow for capital projects.* —see also GREENFIELD PROJECT
2 project finance/financing money needed for a large building project, usually in the form of investment loans: *Olympia & York Developments Ltd. is negotiating long-term project financing for its Canary Wharf development in London.*

pro•ject[2] /prəˈdʒekt/ *v* [T] to calculate the size, amount, or rate of something will be in the future: *California Microwave dropped 2 points after it **projected earnings** of 19 cents a share for the third quarter.* | *Sources said that privately the company is projecting a bigger decline.* —**projected** *adj*: *New Jersey's projected rates of return are in line with assumptions made by other corporations.* | *a $17 billion cut in projected spending* —**projection** *n* [C,U] *The company twice revised its projection downward* (=changed its opinion to make it less hopeful) *before yesterday's disclosure.* | *The Agriculture Department's projection for planted corn acreage is bigger than private estimates.* | *pessimistic projections*

projected growth rate —see under GROWTH RATE

Project Evaluation and Review Technique abbreviation **PERT** *n* [singular] a method of measuring the progress made on a large project, using a special diagram showing how long each stage will take, which stages need to be completed before others can begin etc; CRITICAL PATH ANALYSIS

project manager —see under MANAGER

PROLOG /ˈprəʊlɒg‖ˈproʊlɔːg, -lɑːg/ *n* [U] *trademark* COMPUTING a type of computer language, similar in form to human language

PROM /prɒm‖prɑːm/ *n* [singular] COMPUTING programmable read only memory; a type of memory on a computer that will only record material once. The material cannot easily be removed from the computer

promissory note —see under NOTE[1]

pro•mo /ˈprəʊməʊ‖ˈproʊmoʊ/ *n* [C] *informal* a PROMOTION: *a **movie promo***

pro•mote /prəˈməʊt‖-ˈmoʊt/ *v* [T] **1** to help something develop, grow, become more successful etc, or encourage something to happen: *The CBI is in favour of promoting alliances between small businesses.* | *Oftel favors firm controls on pricing to help **promote competition**.* | *Capital spending enables companies to reduce costs, increase employment and generally **promote economic growth**.*
2 to try hard to sell a product or service by advertising it widely, reducing its price etc: *The book will be heavily promoted by publisher Random House.* | *We need a credible strategy for promoting high-definition television.*
3 to give someone a better paid, more responsible job in a company or organization: *He turned increasingly to Mr. Barr for help and eventually promoted him to deputy attorney general.* **promote sb to sth**: *Univision Holdings Inc. has promoted four executives to new posts as part of a reorganization.*
4 to be responsible for arranging a large public entertainment event, especially a musical or sports event: *The athletics events are promoted jointly by industrial and commercial sponsors.*

pro•mo•tion /prəˈməʊʃən‖-ˈmoʊ-/ *n* [C] also **sales promotion** an activity such as special advertisements or free gifts intended to sell a product or service: *ABC has announced a joint promotion with Miller Lite.* | *Penney has increased its sales promotion with direct mail.* | *A **special promotion** in January produced a spectacular rise in profits.*
cross promotion [C] MARKETING an advertising campaign involving two companies selling their products together: *The video is supported by a $20 million marketing campaign and a cross-promotion with PepsiCo's Pizza Hut restaurants.* —**promotional** *adj* [only before a noun] *the use by cigarette companies of promotional giveaways free gifts*

prompt[1] /prɒmpt‖prɑːmpt/ *adj* done quickly, immediately, or at the right time: *We guarantee **prompt delivery** of your purchases.* | *Many customers are taking advantage of a 2.5% discount for prompt payment.* —**promptly** *adv*: *Answer the telephone promptly – within three rings if possible.* | *The prices of certain goods such as agricultural produce respond very promptly to changes in supply and demand.* —**promptness** *n* [U] *BT responded with great promptness and had two telephone lines and a fax line installed within three days.*

prompt[2] *n* [C] COMPUTING a sign on a computer screen which shows that the computer has finished one operation and is ready to begin the next: *When you see the 'C' prompt, type 'WP'.*

prompt date —see under DATE[1]

proof copy —see under COPY[1]

proof of title —see under TITLE

prop. written abbreviation for PROPRIETOR

pro•pen•si•ty /prəˈpensɪti/ *n* plural **propensities** [C] **1** a tendency to behave in a particular way: *The plastic-bodied car's propensity to catch fire killed demand.*
2 marginal propensity to consume ECONOMICS the relationship between a change in people's income and the change in the amount that they spend on goods: *The marginal propensity to consume is 0.8, because for every £10 million rise in income, consumption rises by £8 million, and the marginal propensity to save is 0.2.*

P

3 marginal propensity to import ECONOMICS the relationship between a change in people's income in a country, and the change in the amount that the country imports: *The marginal propensity to import is 0.2, so that for every £10 million rise in income, spending on imports rises by £2 million.*

4 marginal propensity to save ECONOMICS when there is a change in people's income, the change in the amount that they save in relation to the amount they spend

prop•er•ty /ˈprɒpəti‖ˈprɑːpər-/ *n* plural **properties**
1 [U] all the things that someone owns: *Some of the stolen property was found in Mason's house.* | *The President supports a tax cut on profits from sales of property such as stocks and real estate.*

artistic property [U] LAW an artistic work for which someone owns the COPYRIGHT (=legal right to be the only producer or seller of something): *The Copyright Act of 1976 states that the owner of a copyright can sue anyone who infringes his or her exclusive right to control the distribution of literary or artistic property.*

industrial property [U] PATENTS and TRADEMARKS

intellectual property [C,U] LAW an idea, design, or artistic work which a person or organization has invented or created and on which they have obtained a COPYRIGHT, TRADEMARK, or PATENT (=legal rights to be the only producer or seller): *The country's indifference to* (=lack of caring about) *copyright protection not only hurts foreign creators of intellectual property, such as software makers, but it discourages home-grown creativity too.* | *Microsoft's regional manager for* ***intellectual property rights***

literary property [C,U] LAW a literary work on which someone owns the COPYRIGHT (=legal right to be the only producer or seller): *Rawlings' will states that the university has the right to his published and unpublished manuscripts and literary property.*

movable property also **moveable property** [U] LAW personal property which can be moved, rather than a building or land that stays in the same place —compare ***immovable property***

personal property [U] things such as money or shares, but not buildings or land, which you own; PERSONALTY

2 [U] land and buildings, and the activity of buying, selling, and renting them; REAL ESTATE: *Property prices have shot up* (=quickly increased) *recently.* | *Homeowners around Miramar, site of a planned new airport, are worried about noise and property values.* | *The tax increase amounts to an extra $3 a month for the average* ***property owner***.

commercial property [U] land and buildings for use by businesses, such as offices, factories, hotels etc: *They are involved in shopping mall and commercial property development.* | *HK Land Holdings Ltd, owner of a large proportion of Hong Kong's* ***prime*** (=best and most profitable) ***commercial property***.

distressed property [U] property bought with a loan on which repayments are no longer being made: *Mr Zell is an investor renowned for his skills in buying distressed property at rock-bottom prices.*

immovable property also **immoveable property** [U] LAW buildings or land, rather than personal property: *the law relating to the mortgage of immovable property* —compare ***movable property***

private property [U] property, especially land, that belongs to a private owner rather than to the public: *The law would allow for prosecution of those trespassing* (=going into a building or onto land without the owner's permission) *on any city property or private property.*

public property [C,U] land or buildings owned by a local or national government: *The storms caused $60 million of damage to public property.*

real property [U] LAW land, buildings etc: *people whose wealth consists mainly of real property*

3 [C] a building, especially a house, and the land that surrounds it: *Several properties on this street are for sale.*

freehold property [C,U] *especially BrE* property which you own completely and for an unlimited time: *increases in the value of freehold properties*

leasehold property [C,U] *especially BrE* property that is owned only for as long as is stated in a LEASE (=a legal agreement that allows you to use a building for a period of time in return for rent): *The Woolwich Building Society is offering a special 4.99% two-year mortgage on leasehold properties that have been on its books for more than six months.*

4 [U] ownership of land, goods etc: *a belief in the idea of communal property*

property and liability insurance —see under INSURANCE

property bond —see under BOND

property company —see under COMPANY

property development —see under DEVELOPMENT

property investment —see under INVESTMENT

property loan —see under LOAN[1]

property management —see under MANAGEMENT

property manager —see under MANAGER

property market —see under MARKET[1]

property register —see under REGISTER[1]

property rights —see under RIGHT

property tax —see under TAX[1]

proportional tax —see under TAX[1]

pro•pos•al /prəˈpəʊzəl‖-ˈpoʊ-/ *n* **1** [C,U] a plan or idea which is suggested formally to an official person, or when this is done: *The President is facing a battle to get Congress to accept his* ***budget proposals***. | ***I made a proposal*** *for opening an office in Seoul, complete with projected costings.* **proposal to do sth**: *The Senate* ***rejected a proposal*** *to limit the program to two years.* + **that**: *The company had to* ***put forward a proposal*** *that layoffs be considered.* —compare MOTION

2 [C] INSURANCE an official document in which you give details about yourself or your property when you are buying an INSURANCE POLICY —see also ACCEPTANCE OF PROPOSAL

pro•pose /prəˈpəʊz‖-ˈpoʊz/ *v* [T] **1** to suggest something such as a plan or course of action: *Lyle proposed large cuts in the training budget.* **propose that**: *Hansen has proposed that I become his business partner.* **—proposed** *adj* [only before a noun] *the financial and legal consequences of* ***proposed changes*** *to the agreement*

2 to formally suggest a course of action at a meeting and ask people to vote on it: *The chairman proposed a scheme to save both the company and investors' funds.* | *He will* ***propose a motion*** *at Monday's special meeting, calling on the committee to reverse its decision.* | *Continental's managers urged shareholders to vote against several of the resolutions proposed by Mr Vicari.*

3 *formal* to intend to do something **propose to do sth**: *Which of his assets is he proposing to sell?* | *The Sales Director is proposing to boost sales by spending an additional £3,000 per month on advertising.*

pro•pos•er /prəˈpəʊzə‖-ˈpoʊzər/ *n* [C] **1** someone who makes a proposal at a formal meeting —compare ***seconder*** under SECOND[2]

2 INSURANCE someone who is buying an INSURANCE POLICY

prop•o•si•tion /ˌprɒpəˈzɪʃən‖ˌprɑː-/ *n* [C] **1** a business idea, offer, or suggestion, for example a possible business deal: *I'll consider your proposition and let you know my decision next week.* | *We have a proposition to make.* | *The newest software makes computerized recruitment an* ***attractive proposition***.

2 also **Proposition** LAW in the US, a suggested change to the law of a state, which citizens vote on: *Proposition 13, passed by California voters in 1978, requires that any new special taxes be approved by at least two-thirds of the voters.*

3 a statement that consists of a carefully considered opinion or judgement: *Kondratiev's basic proposition was that the advanced capitalist economies go through cycles of booms and slumps* (=ups and downs) *in a regular pattern.* + **that**: *The proposition that the world economy is a system means that all parts are in one way or another dependent on each other.*

pro·pri·e·ta·ry /prəˈpraɪətəri‖-teri/ *adj* **1** based on ideas, information etc belonging to one particular company, rather than on ideas etc that any company can use: *The process we use to review what we market is proprietary, and therefore it's our policy not to discuss it.* | ***Proprietary information** about a company's commodity buying plans could influence the markets if it were publicly known.* | *The computer uses a **proprietary operating system** rather than Microsoft's Windows.*

2 MARKETING a proprietary product is sold under a company's brand name, rather than a GENERIC name (=a general name for a type of product): *Award's contact lenses are sold both under its own name and under retailers' proprietary brands.* | ***proprietary drugs***

proprietary company —see under COMPANY

proprietary product —see under PRODUCT

proprietary rights —see under RIGHT

proprietary trading —see under TRADING

pro·pri·e·tor /prəˈpraɪətə‖-ər/ written abbreviation **prop** *n* [C] **1** someone who owns a business + **of**: *Echenard was the proprietor of the famous Hotel du Louvre.* | *Horace Greeley was a powerful **newspaper proprietor**.*

sole proprietor someone who owns and runs a business on his or her own rather than with another person: *Carvel was the typical sole proprietor. He was responsible for his debts and entitled to any profits.*

2 someone who owns land or buildings

registered proprietor in Britain, someone who owns property when the legal right to do so has been recorded at the LAND REGISTRY

3 LAW someone who owns a legal right such as a PATENT or a COPYRIGHT (=rights to be the only maker, producer, or seller of something for a specific period of time): *The proprietor of a trademark has the exclusive right to use the mark in relation to the class of goods or services against which it is registered.*

proprietorship register —see under REGISTER[1]

pro ra·ta /prəʊ ˈrɑːtə‖proʊ ˈreɪtə/ *adj* [only before a noun] a pro rata payment or share in something is calculated according to exactly how much of something is used, how much work is done etc: *The residents here pay more than their pro-rata share of taxes.* | *Fees for longer or shorter courses are calculated **on a pro rata basis**.* —**pro rata** *adv*: *The company directors are required to allot the shares to existing shareholders pro rata to the number of shares owned.*

pro·rate /prəʊˈreɪt‖proʊ-/ *v* [T] *AmE* to calculate a charge, price etc according to the actual amount of service received rather than by a standard sum: *I moved in on the 23rd of the month so the landlord prorated my rent.*

pros·e·cute /ˈprɒsɪkjuːt‖ˈprɑː-/ *v* [I,T] LAW **1** if the state authorities prosecute someone, they officially say that person must be judged by a court of law for a particular crime: *Shoplifters* (=people who steal things from shops) *will be prosecuted.* **prosecute sb for sth**: *Johnson is being prosecuted for an offence under the Trade Descriptions Act.*

2 if a lawyer prosecutes a case, he or she tries to prove that the person charged with a crime is guilty: *Peter Lieb, the assistant U.S. attorney **prosecuting the case**, refused to comment on the trial.* —compare DEFEND

pros·e·cu·tion /ˌprɒsɪˈkjuːʃən‖ˌprɑː-/ *n* LAW **1** [C,U] the process or act of bringing a charge against someone for a crime, or of being judged for a crime in a court of law: *The evidence is now sufficient to **bring a prosecution against** him.* | *Making false statements in adverts may lead to criminal prosecution.*

2 the prosecution the lawyers in a court of law who try to prove that someone is guilty of a crime: *the chief witness for the prosecution* | *The prosecution asked for costs to be awarded against the defendants.* —compare DEFENCE

pros·e·cu·tor /ˈprɒsɪkjuːtə‖ˈprɑːsɪkjuːtər/ *n* [C] **1** a lawyer who represents the authorities in bringing a criminal charge against someone

2 a lawyer representing the government in a court of law: *The agreement between the two companies is being challenged in court by a public prosecutor.*

public prosecutor an important official in the legal system in a particular area who decides which cases should be tried: *The public prosecutor's office in Munich has begun the investigation of aircraft makers for violations of export-control laws.*

pros·pect[1] /ˈprɒspekt‖ˈprɑː-/ *n* **1** [C,U] a possibility that something which you hope for will happen soon + **of**: *There is little real prospect of significant economic growth.*

2 prospects [plural] chances of future success + **for**: *firms offering the best prospects for increasing productivity, profitability, and expansion* | *In Singapore, investors remain optimistic about prospects for the economy.*

3 [singular] something that is possible or is likely to happen in the future + **of**: *The prospect of still higher unemployment as growth slows is causing great concern.*

4 [C] a person, job, plan etc that has a good chance of success in the future: *Radio is an exciting prospect; the forthcoming deregulation of the industry and an expected boom in advertising revenues, is finally making the City take notice.*

5 [C] someone who is not a customer yet, but may become one in the future: *Mercedes-Benz has kept its reputation by reminding prospects that its vehicles are 'engineered like no other car in the world.'*

pro·spect[2] /prəˈspekt‖ˈprɑːspekt/ *v* [I] to examine an area of land or water, in order to find gold, silver, oil etc + **for**: *Anglo-United was prospecting for gold in the area in the early eighties.* —**prospector** *n* [C] *The government has given **gold prospectors** access to more than a million acres of forest land.*

pro·spec·tive /prəˈspektɪv/ *adj* [only before a noun] **1** likely to do a particular thing or achieve a particular position: *I'm meeting a **prospective buyer** for the house today.* | *All **prospective employees** are required to undergo a medical examination.*

2 likely to happen: *What are the **prospective returns** from an investment of $10,000 over five years?*

prospective yield —see under YIELD[1]

pro·spec·tus /prəˈspektəs/ *n* [C] **1** FINANCE a document produced by a company when inviting the public to buy its shares. By law, the company must include certain information in a prospectus, such as how the money is going to be used, what the chances of future success are etc: *The full prospectus for the share sale will be out next Thursday.*

2 a small book that advertises a school, college, new business etc: *Each year the college publishes a postgraduate prospectus which contains details of the degree courses offered.*

pros·per /ˈprɒspə‖ˈprɑːspər/ *v* [I] to be successful and become rich: *As families prosper, consumer demand for meat increases.* | *With hard work and long hours, our **business prospered**.*

pro·sper·i·ty /prɒˈsperəti‖prɑː-/ *n* [U] the condition of having money and being successful: *a time of **economic***

P

prosperity | *The country hopes to achieve prosperity through increased trade and investment.*

pros·per·ous /ˈprɒspərəs‖ˈprɑː-/ *adj* successful and rich: *a prosperous businessman* | *a prosperous commercial district* | *As Mexico becomes more prosperous, it will need even more of the goods that the US is best at producing – computers, manufacturing equipment, high-tech and high-value products.*

pro·tect /prəˈtekt/ *v* [T] **1** to keep someone or something safe from harm, damage, bad influences etc: *laws protecting the rights of disabled people* **protect sb/sth from sth**: *P&G wants to protect its $180 million investment by obtaining a 10-year extension of three patents.* **protect (sb/sth) against**: *The wage index system protects workers against inflation.* | *traders trying to lock in profits and protect against losses*

2 to try to help an industry in your own country by taxing foreign goods that are competing with it, so limiting the number that can be imported: *For decades, the Mexican government protected its domestic growers by regulating corn imports.* —**protected** *adj* [only before a noun] *Global banking has changed from being a* ***protected industry*** *to a deregulated one.* | *Tight import quotas in five protected markets will be gradually reduced.*

P

pro·tec·tion /prəˈtekʃən/ *n* [U] **1** the act of protecting something, or the state of being protected: *Milk testing will add another layer of protection for consumers.* + **against**: *Many people buy insurance as protection against an unexpected illness.* | ***legal protection*** *for workers' rights*

bankrutpcy protection also **bankruptcy-law protection** laws to protect companies that are in financial difficulty, limiting payments they have to make to CREDITORS (=organizations they owe money to): *If the company doesn't* ***file for bankruptcy protection*** (=ask the authorities to give it protection from creditors) *it faces a major problem on June 15, when $42.2 million of payments on senior debt are due.* | *The building company emerged from bankruptcy protection under a reorganization plan.*

Chapter 11 bankruptcy protection in the US, the part of the law that gives protection to companies in financial difficulty: *The trust operates under Chapter 11 bankruptcy protection.*

consumer protection laws to protect people when they have bought goods or services, covering things such as price, quality, or safety: *Meat inspectors say that the plan to reduce checks will undercut consumer protection against filthy food.*

data protection LAW laws and rules relating to information about a person stored on computer. These laws and rules say how the information can be obtained, how long it can be kept, whether other people or organizations are allowed to see it, and whether the person involved must be allowed to see it: *an EU directive on data protection* | *the Data Protection Act*

investor protection ◆ actions to encourage honest advertising of financial products, and to prevent FRAUD: *The New York Stock Exchange's market regulation is a proactive form of investor protection against fraud and other illicit stock-market activity.*

◆ actions to make sure that investors do not lose money if their investments DEFAULT (=are not repaid): *These securities often come with investor protection, such as bond insurance and letters of credit.*

job protection also **employment protection** the legal right of employees to keep their jobs if, for example, they STRIKE (=stop working to protest about something), or if the company they work for gets into financial difficulty: *The auto maker may offer the job protection its union wants, in return for increased quality and productivity.*

patent protection laws protecting a person or organization that has developed a new product or way of doing something, preventing it from being copied by competitors for a particular length of time: *Cutting the time it takes to get a drug approved also increases the duration of effective patent protection.*

2 when a government tries to help an industry in its country by taxing foreign goods that compete with it, so limiting the number that can be imported: *The lowering of protection faces resistance from the region's industrialists.*

pro·tec·tion·is·m /prəˈtekʃənɪzəm/ *n* [U] when a government tries to help industry, farming etc in its own country by taxing foreign goods that compete with it, so limiting the number that can be imported: *Economists know that protectionism promotes inefficiency and waste.* | *protectionism and trade wars* —**protectionist** *n* [C] *His reluctance to fight the trade issue politically will only help the protectionists succeed.* —**protectionist** *adj*: ***protectionist laws*** *that shield the nation's computer industry from foreign competition*

protection racket —see under RACKET

pro·tec·tive /prəˈtektɪv/ *adj* [only before a noun] **1** protective actions, measures, laws etc are designed to keep someone or something safe from harm, damage, negative influences etc: *The company has armed itself with* ***protective barriers****, making a hostile takeover virtually impossible.*

2 protective taxes and other measures are designed to protect an industry from foreign competition: ***Protective tariffs*** (=import taxes) *are a means whereby nations attempt to protect their own industries.*

protective tariff —see under TARIFF

pro tem /ˌprəʊ ˈtem‖ˌproʊ-/ also **pro tem·po·re** /-ˈtempəreɪ/ *adj, adv formal* happening now, but only for a short time; TEMPORARY: *a pro tem committee* | *I have identified a printer which Marisa could use pro tem.*

pro·test¹ /ˈprəʊtest‖ˈproʊ-/ *n* **1** [C,U] an angry complaint that shows you disagree with something, or when you state publicly that you think something is wrong or unfair: *The union is making a* ***formal protest*** *to the government about the matter.* + **against/at**: *Miners staged a two-hour strike in protest against the effects of the economic reforms.* | *Health workers marched on Nov. 17 in protest at government restrictions on health service expenditure.*

2 [C] an occasion when people meet together in public to express disapproval or opposition to something: *17,000 demonstrators took part in a* ***student protest*** *against education loans.* | *Later this month,* ***protest marches*** *are planned by farmers' groups.* —**protester** *n* [C] *More than 2,000 protesters demonstrated outside Parliament today.*

3 under protest unwillingly, and with the feeling that you have been unfairly treated: *I only* ***signed*** *the document* ***under protest.*** | *The tax demand was disputed by the company, and the* ***payments were made under protest.***

pro·test² /prəˈtest/ *v* **1** [I] *BrE* to show publicly that you disagree with something you think is wrong or unfair: + **against/at/about**: *People always protest against new forms of taxation.*

2 [I,T] *AmE* to say or do something publicly to show that you disagree with something you think is wrong or unfair **protest sth**: *About 40,000 angry Connecticut residents gathered outside the Capitol in Hartford to protest a new income tax.*

3 [T] to state very firmly that something is true, especially when other people do not believe you **protest that**: *The AFL-CIO's Richard Sawyer protested that thousands of local jobs may be lost to Mexico if the trade agreement is approved.*

pro·to·col /ˈprəʊtəkɒl‖ˈproʊtəkɒːl, -kɑːl/ *n* **1** [C] COMPUTING an established method for connecting computers so that they can exchange information: *You have to use a different protocol with this new modem.* | *HTTP is an Internet protocol.*

2 [U] the system of rules on the correct and acceptable way to behave on official occasions: *Protocol demands that we meet the company chairman at the airport.* | *a breach of* (=failure to follow) ***diplomatic protocol***

pro•to•type /ˈprəʊtətaɪp‖ˈproʊ-/ *n* [C] MANUFACTURING the first form that a newly designed car, machine etc has + **of/for**: *a complete working prototype of the new model*

proven reserves —see under RESERVES

pro•vide /prəˈvaɪd/ *v* [T] **1** to give someone what they need, or to make sure they get it: *The World Bank is providing funding for the project.* **provide sb with sth**: *Our computerised information service can provide busy managers with all the information they need.* | *The deal will provide Rolls-Royce with work for the next five years.* **provide sth for/to sb**: *The agreement provided guarantees for union members when layoffs are considered.*

2 to produce a useful result, opportunity etc: *We are hoping the enquiry will provide an explanation for the accident.*

3 provide that *formal* if a law or rule provides that something must happen, it states that it must happen: *The Companies Act provides that the consent of shareholders is required for the sale of assets valued at £100,000 or more to a director of the company.*

provide against sth *phr v* [T] *formal* to make plans in order to deal with something that might happen: *Health insurance can provide against loss of income through illness or accident.*

provide for sb/sth *phr v* [T] **1** to give someone the things they need, such as money, food etc: *Without work, how can I provide for my children?* | *There will be an increasing number of retired and elderly people to be provided for by a progressively smaller number of workers.*

2 *formal* to make plans in order to deal with something that might happen in the future: *The calculations must provide for the increase in inflation.* | *If you suffer serious injury as the result of an accident, insurance cover can provide for this eventuality* (=possible event).

3 if a law, contract, rule etc provides for something, it makes doing that thing possible: *Recent legislation provides for a tribunal to hear the complainant's case.* | *The new contract provides for the purchase of 25 systems over four years.*

provident society —see under SOCIETY

pro•vid•er /prəˈvaɪdə‖-ər/ *n* [C] **1** an organization that provides goods or services: *a provider of engineering and design services* | *hospitals, nursing homes and other* ***health-care providers*** | *the long-distance* ***telephone services provider***

Internet Service Provider abbreviation **ISP** COMPUTING a company that provides the technical services that allow people to use the INTERNET: *Hooking up a connection through a local Internet Service Provider is easy.*

2 an adult who supports their family with his or her income: *A widow, she is the* ***sole provider*** (=the only one) *for her family.*

pro•vi•sion /prəˈvɪʒən/ *n* **1** [U] the act of providing something that someone needs: *the provision of childcare facilities at work* | *provision for people with disabilities*

2 make provision(s) to make plans for future needs + **for**: *People should be encouraged to make provision for themselves and their families; state support should only provide a safety net for the very poor.*

3 [C,U] LAW a part of a law, contract, agreement etc that relates to a particular subject: *Under the document, there was provision for the improvement of hospital standards.*

grandfather provision [C] when new rules are introduced, the right for existing organizations etc to continue to use the old rules: *The SEC prohibited public firms from issuing multiple classes of stock with unequal voting rights, but there was a grandfather provision allowing companies with two classes of stock already in place to keep them.*

4 [C] ACCOUNTING an amount set aside by a company in its accounts to protect it against something bad that has happened or that might happen in the future. This amount has to be taken away in calculating profit for a particular period of time: + **to**: *The company* ***made a provision*** *to cover the costs of 4000 job cuts.* | *The bank* ***took*** (=made) ***provisions*** *to comply with tougher regulatory standards.*

bad debt provision [C] ACCOUNTING amounts in a company's accounts showing the likely level of bad debts in a particular period of time that will have to be taken away when calculating profits; BAD DEBT RESERVES *AmE*: *Phoenix Technologies said its loss widened in the third quarter, partly because of an increase in bad debt provisions.*

loan-loss provision also **bad loan provision** [C] BANKING a provision made by a bank for loans that will probably not be repaid: *The bank set a loan-loss provision of $56 million, primarily for bad commercial real estate loans.*

restructuring provision [C] ACCOUNTING a provision to take account the probable cost of reorganizing a company, reducing the number of employees etc: *Trinova set a restructuring provision to cover the sale of some assets.*

tax provision [C] ACCOUNTING a provision for tax that a company will probably have to pay: *C&W expects taxes to be higher both in the UK and Hong Kong, so the tax provision was raised to £74 million from £57 million.*

provision for depletion —see under DEPLETION

pro•vi•so /prəˈvaɪzəʊ‖-zoʊ/ *n* [C] **1** LAW a part of a contract that covers a particular subject: *Landlords frequently include a proviso stating that nothing contained in the lease shall prevent them from carrying out work on their property.*

2 *formal* something that must happen before you will agree to something + **that**: *The only proviso is that you should let the office manager know well in advance if you decide to take a day off.* | *Some companies are happy to invest in community projects,* ***with the proviso*** *that the government does not neglect its own duty.*

proximate cause —see under CAUSE

prox•y /ˈprɒksi‖ˈprɑːksi/ *n* plural **proxies** [C] **1** someone whom you choose to act for you. For example, if a person owning shares in a company cannot come to a company meeting, someone else can be given the power to vote for him or her: *If you have consulted the proxy and confirmed that he or she is able and willing to vote for you, they do not have to sign any forms.* | *The poll showed 68% (mainly* ***proxy votes*** *from institutional shareholders) in favour of the idea.*

2 a document that gives one person the power to speak, vote, or make decisions for someone else, especially at a meeting

3 by proxy if you do something by proxy, you arrange for someone else to do it for you: *You will need to say on the application form whether you want to attend the meeting or* ***vote by proxy***.

proxy fight *n* [C] a method used by a company when it is trying to get control of another one in a TAKEOVER. It involves persuading people owning shares in the TARGET COMPANY (=company which the takeover attempt is aimed at) to vote for new members of the board who approve of the takeover: *Kerkorian will* ***launch a*** *threatened* ***proxy fight*** *and ask for shareholder votes to elect York to the board at Chrysler's annual shareholders meeting in May.*

P

pru·dence /ˈpruːdəns/ *n* [U] **1** when you are sensible and careful to avoid unnecessary risks; CONSERVATISM: *The financial reserves of Abbey National have been built up over many years through a combination of prudence and innovation.*
2 ACCOUNTING the rule that a business should not state an asset value, possible profit etc to be bigger, or a possible loss to be smaller, than it actually might be

pru·dent /ˈpruːdənt/ *adj* **1** sensible and careful, especially by trying to avoid unnecessary risks: *These must be prudent loans requiring the buyer to put in significant capital.*
2 ACCOUNTING following the rule that a business should not state an asset value, possible profit etc to be bigger, or a possible loss to be smaller, than it actually might be; CONSERVATIVE

PS *n* [C] written abbreviation for POSTSCRIPT; written at the end of a letter when you want to add more information. You can add PPS if more information comes after the PS: *She added a PS asking me to send her some money.* | *Best wishes, Julie. PS If Thursday is not convenient, let me know. PPS You can reach me on email at the address below.*

P

PSBR *n* [singular] ECONOMICS public sector borrowing requirement; the amount that a government has to borrow in a particular period of time to cover the difference between the money it gets from taxes and the amount it spends: *In Britain in recent years, the PSBR has been lower than the financial deficit because of the proceeds from privatisation* (=the income from the sale of previously government-owned companies).

PSE written abbreviation for PACIFIC STOCK EXCHANGE

PSL written abbreviation for PUBLIC SECTOR LOAN(S)

psychic income —see under INCOME

psy·cho·graph·ics /ˌsaɪkəʊˈgræfɪks‖-koʊ-/ *n* [plural] MARKETING a way of dividing consumers into different groups according to qualities such as a person's character, the way they live, and how important price, quality etc is to them, rather than dividing them according to their age, job etc

PTO /ˌpiː tiː ˈəʊ‖-ˈoʊ/ written abbreviation for PLEASE TURN OVER; written at the bottom of a page

pub *BrE* written abbreviation for PUBLIC

pub. *AmE* written abbreviation for PUBLICATION

pub·lic[1] /ˈpʌblɪk/ *n* **the public** ordinary people who do not belong to the government or have any special position in society: *An offer for the sale of shares to **the general public** was planned for early next year.* | *The privatisation was carried out against the wishes of the public.* | *Companies that take significant sums of money from **members of the public** before providing goods are in a special position of trust.*

public[2] *adj* **1** connected with all the ordinary people in a country, who are not members of the government or do not have important jobs: *The law was changed as the result of public pressure.*
2 available for anyone to use: *a public telephone*
3 connected with the government and with the services it provides for people: *55% of university funding in Britain comes from **public money**.* | *We do not believe he is fit for **public office*** (=the job of being part of a government).
4 known about by most people: *The report will be **made public*** (=told to everyone) *in mid-January.* | *The membership of the Board was **public knowledge**.*
5 intended for anyone to know, see, or hear: *Demands for a public investigation have been ignored.* —**publicly** *adv*: *It is time for multinational companies publicly to acknowledge that they have not always acted properly.*
6 go public to become a PUBLIC COMPANY (=a company that has shares owned by the public): *David Systems Inc. has filed to go public with an initial offer of 2.5 million new shares at $7.75 a share.*

public account —see under ACCOUNT[1]

Public Accounts Committee abbreviation **PAC** *n* a committee set up by the British parliament to check that money is being spent correctly by the government, without waste, CORRUPTION etc —compare NATIONAL AUDIT OFFICE

pub·li·ca·tion /ˌpʌbləˈkeɪʃən/ *n* **1** [U] the act of making a book, magazine etc available for sale, or the time at which this is done: *the publication of books with titles like 'The Great American Collapse'* | *This novel began attracting attention well before its **publication date**.*
2 [C] a book, magazine etc: *The ads will run in publications like the New York Times and The Wall Street Journal.* | *Media Industry Newsletter, a **trade publication*** (=a newspaper for people in a particular profession or industry)
3 [U] the act of making something known to the public: *the publication of large share deals on the Stock Exchange Automated Quotation system*

public carrier —see under CARRIER

public company —see under COMPANY

public corporation —see under CORPORATION

public debt —see under DEBT

public deposits —see under DEPOSIT[1]

public domain —see under DOMAIN

public employee —see under EMPLOYEE

public enterprise —see under ENTERPRISE

public examination —see under EXAMINATION

public expenditure —see under EXPENDITURE

public finance —see under FINANCE[1]

public funds —see under FUND[1]

public hearing —see under HEARING

public housing —see under HOUSING

public investment —see under INVESTMENT

public issue —see under ISSUE[2]

pub·li·cist /ˈpʌbləsəst/ *n* [C] a person or organization whose job is to make sure that people know about an event or a new product, book, film etc: *She got a letter from the magazine promising every publicist's dream: guaranteed favorable coverage in its pages.*

pub·lic·i·ty /pʌˈblɪsəti/ *n* [U] **1** the attention that someone or something gets from newspapers, television etc: *The case has received massive publicity.* | *Sales of the drug are falling due to **adverse*** (=negative) ***publicity** about side-effects.* | *The fashion show was organized as a **publicity stunt*** (=an event whose purpose is to get publicity), *with women prisoners modeling fur coats.*
2 the business activity of making sure that people know about a new product, film etc: *The company plans a major **publicity campaign*** (=a series of events, advertisements etc designed to give something publicity) *for the new technology.*

pub·li·cize also **publicise** *BrE* /ˈpʌbləsaɪz/ *v* [T] **1** to give information about something to the public, so that they know about it: *Emissions have been reduced significantly and car makers have publicized these advances in their advertising.*
2 well-/widely/highly publicized receiving a lot of attention: *The company's well-publicized financial problems have forced it to spend time reassuring customers about its future.*

public land —see under LAND[1]

public law —see under LAW

public liability policy —see under INSURANCE POLICY

public limited company —see under COMPANY

publ·ic·ly /ˈpʌblɪkli/ *adv* FINANCE if a company is publicly held or publicly owned, or its shares are publicly traded, its shares are available to be bought and sold by investors: *the annual reports that publicly held companies send to their shareholders* | *Abbey National converted from a building society into a publicly listed company.*

public monopoly —see under MONOPOLY

public nuisance —see under NUISANCE

public offering —see under OFFERING

public ownership —see under OWNERSHIP

public partnership —see under PARTNERSHIP

public-private *adj* [only before a noun] in public-private arrangements, there is investment from the government as well as investment from commercial organizations: *a public-private insurance program where private brokers assume 20% of the risk, and the federal government is responsible for the remainder*

public-private partnership —see under PARTNERSHIP

public property —see under PROPERTY

public prosecutor —see under PROSECUTOR

public relations abbreviation **PR** *n* [plural] the activity of telling the public about an organization, person, product etc so that people think of them in a good way: *They've **launched a public-relations campaign*** (=started a series of public relations activities), *including newspaper ads and subway posters.* | *The company hired a **public relations company**.*

public relations officer —see PRO

public sale —see under SALE

public sector —see under SECTOR

public sector borrowing requirement —see under REQUIREMENT

public servant *n* [C] *formal* an elected government official, or someone whose job is working for the government: *a 41-year-old **career public servant*** (=someone who spends their whole working life in a government job, usually at a high level)

public service —see under SERVICE[1]

public service vehicle —see under VEHICLE

public-service vehicle —see under VEHICLE

public spending —see under SPENDING

public trust —see under TRUST

public utility —see under UTILITY

public works *n* [plural] buildings such as hospitals, roads, ports etc. that are built and paid for by the government

pub·lish /ˈpʌblɪʃ/ *v* **1** [I,T] to arrange the writing, production, and sale of a book, magazine etc: *Her second novel was published in July.* | *We publish education books.*
2 [T] to make official information such as a report available for everyone to read: *The latest unemployment figures will be published tomorrow.* | *Public companies have to publish an annual report and accounts.*

pub·lish·er /ˈpʌblɪʃə‖-ər/ written abbreviation **pub** *n* [C] **1** a person or company whose business is to arrange the writing, production, and sale of books, newspapers etc: *NTC Publishing Group, a publisher of textbooks and tapes for language learners* | *Microsoft Corp. is the world's biggest **software publisher**.*
2 *AmE* the owner of a newspaper

pub·lish·ing /ˈpʌblɪʃɪŋ/ *n* [U] the business of producing books, newspapers etc: *Tony wants to get a job in publishing.* | *Viking-Penguin, the New York-based **publishing house**, announced a book deal with Clark worth $4.2 million.*

desktop publishing abbreviation **DTP** the work of arranging the writing and pictures for a magazine, small book etc, using a computer and special software: *looking for a job in desktop publishing* | *This issue of Action Newsletter is the first to be designed and laid out on desktop publishing equipment.*

pubn *BrE* written abbreviation for PUBLICATION; PUB. *AmE*

puff /pʌf/ *n* [C] *informal* an advertisement or other piece of writing in a newspaper etc that strongly praises a product

pull /pʊl/ *v*

pull in *phr v* [T] **1 pull** sth ↔ **in** *informal* if you pull in a lot of money you earn it: *She must be pulling in £80,000 a year.* | *The government expects to pull in around £1 billion from adding on VAT at 17.5%.*
2 pull sb/sth ↔ **in** if an event pulls in a lot of people, they go to it: *Les Miserables has been pulling in huge crowds in New York.*

pull sth ↔ **off** *phr v* [T] *informal* to succeed in doing something difficult: *Applix Inc. **pulled off** an exclusive $15 million **deal** with K K Ashisuto.* | *Sun Microsystems Inc. **pulled off** another recruiting **coup** last week.*

pull out *phr v* [I] to get out of an agreement, deal, or difficult situation so that you are no longer taking part in it: *If the project costs continue to rise, we may be forced to pull out.* + **of**: *Catalogue shopping group Argos is pulling out of its furniture store venture because it sees no prospect of improved trading conditions.*

pull together *phr v* **1** [I] if a group of people pull together, they all work hard to achieve something: *If we all pull together, we'll finish on time.*
2 [T] **pull** sth **together** to improve something by organizing it more effectively: *We need an experienced manager to pull the department together.*

pull strategy —see under STRATEGY

pump /pʌmp/ *v* [T] **pump money/millions etc into sth** to put a lot of money into a business, plan etc: *The government has already pumped a huge amount of money into the project.*

pump price —see under PRICES

pump-priming *n* [U] encouraging a business, industry, or economy to develop by putting money into it. For example, a government may increase its spending in order to increase economic activity during a RECESSION: *With Training Agency Compacts, the funding has to be seen as pump-priming.* | *the fiscal tools of tax cuts and pump-priming* —**pump-prime** *v* [I,T] *Some states and cities will resort to pump-priming their economies with spending on roads, airports and waste-management.*

punitive damages —see under DAMAGE[1]

pu·ni·tives /ˈpjuːnətɪvz/ *n* [plural] *AmE* another name for PUNITIVE DAMAGES: *This 25 to 1 ratio of punitives to actual damages is a sign that the legal system is out of control.*

punitive tariff —see under TARIFF

punt·er /ˈpʌntə‖-ər/ *n* [C] *BrE informal* **1** a person who tries to make money buying and selling shares etc on a financial market: *Such privatisations are aimed more at the general punter than the industrial investor.* | *punters on the commodities and futures markets*
2 a customer or client: *We try to give the punters what they want.* | *For the average punter the most important thing is the price.*

pur·chase[1] /ˈpɜːtʃəs‖ˈpɜːr-/ *n* **1** [U] the act of buying something: *Keep the receipt as your **proof of purchase**.* | *the **date of purchase*** | *The $2 billion purchase of the Holiday Inn chain makes Bass the world's largest hotelier.* | ***House purchase** is the biggest decision that most people make.* | *the purchase of shares in Manpower Incorporated*
2 make a purchase to buy something: *According to our*

P

records she made a number of purchases from our Oxford Street store.

3 [C] something that has been bought: *If you are not satisfied with your purchase, we will give you a full refund.* | *We offer discounts on multiple purchases.* —see also COMPULSORY PURCHASE, HIRE PURCHASE

purchase[2] *v* [T] *formal* to buy something, especially something big or expensive: *a loan to purchase a new car* | *The property was purchased for investment purposes.* | *A public company cannot purchase its own shares out of capital.*

purchase (day) book —see under BOOK[1]

purchase invoice —see under INVOICE[1]

purchase journal *n* [C] ACCOUNTING another name for PURCHASE BOOK

purchase ledger *n* [C] —see ***bought ledger*** under LEDGER

purchase order —see under ORDER[1]

purchase price —see under PRICE[1]

P

pur•chas•er /ˈpɜːtʃəsə‖ˈpɜːrtʃəsər/ *n* [C] *formal* the person who buys something: *He has been unable to* ***find a purchaser*** *for the business.* | *Many* ***potential purchasers*** *can be identified with minimum cost using research.*

purchases account —see under ACCOUNT[1]

purchase tax —see under TAX[1]

pur•chas•ing /ˈpɜːtʃəsɪŋ‖ˈpɜːr-/ *n* [U] the activity of buying the materials, stock, equipment etc that a company needs to produce goods: *She is the company's purchasing manager.* | *The purchasing of consulting services has changed and is affected by the economy.*

Purchasing Managers' index —see under INDEX[1]

purchasing officer —see under OFFICER

purchasing power —see under POWER[1]

purchasing power parity —see under PARITY

pure profit —see under PROFIT[1]

purge /pɜːdʒ‖pɜːrdʒ/ *v* [T] to get rid of information that is no longer needed, especially when combining lists of information

purse /pɜːs‖pɜːrs/ *n* **1** [singular] the amount of money that a person, organization, or country has available to spend: *We offer holidays to* ***suit every purse.*** | *There are so many demands on the rich world's purse from Eastern Europe.*

2 the public purse the money controlled by a government: *The project is a continuing drain on the public purse.* | *These payments should be met out of the public purse.*

3 hold/control the purse strings to control how money in a company, family etc is spent

4 tighten/loosen the purse strings to increase or reduce the control you have over spending: *The government has decided that it must now tighten the purse strings.*

purs•er /ˈpɜːsə‖ˈpɜːrsər/ *n* [C] an officer who is responsible for the money on a ship and is also in charge of the passengers' rooms, comfort etc

pur•vey•or /pɜːˈveɪə‖pɜːrˈveɪər/ *n* [C] a person or company that supplies goods or services to people, especially food or drink: *Taunton Cider, purveyor of cider brands Red Rock, Diamond White and Dry Blackthorn* —**purvey** *v* [T]

push[1] /pʊʃ/ *v* [T] **1** to work hard to persuade people to buy more of a product, for example by advertising it a lot: *Our sales staff will be pushing the new model hard.* | *IBM will use its huge sales force to push this product.*

2 to try to get people to accept an idea, proposal etc: *Manufacturing groups are pushing a federal products liability law to limit punitive damages.*

push ahead *phr v* [I] **1** if prices on a financial market push ahead, they rise: *The Composite Index pushed ahead 3.77 to 466.56.*

2 to continue with a plan or activity, especially in a determined way + **with**: *Japanese companies are pushing ahead with plans to expand production facilities elsewhere in Asia.* | *The government is determined to push ahead with its economic reforms.*

push (sb) **for** sth *phr v* [T] to keep asking for something or trying to persuade people to do something, because you feel it is important or necessary: *The unions are now pushing for wage increases.* | *Marketing people will push for anyone with a good sales technique to be hired.* | *I'll have to push you for a decision.*

push sth ↔ **down** *phr v* [T] to make the price or value of something decrease: *The surplus has helped to push prices down.*

push sth ↔ **through** *phr v* [T] to succeed in getting a new law or change officially accepted: *the President's attempts to push through his ambitious programme of reform*

push sth ↔ **up** *phr v* [T] to make the price or value of something increase: *News of the bid has pushed up the group's share price.* | *There are fears that import price rises will push up inflation.* | *Housing starts increased 2.6% in December, pushed up by falling interest rates.*

push[2] *n* **1** [singular] a period of determined effort in business, especially one in which you gain an advantage over your opponents + **into**: *Mattel acquired International Games, a leading maker of card games, as part of the toy maker's push into the game business.* | *We have recently made a big push into the Japanese market*: *a* ***sales push***

2 give sb the push *BrE informal* to make someone leave their job, especially because they have done something wrong: *So they gave you the push, did they? You're so lazy, I'm not surprised!*

push[3] *adj* [only before a noun] COMPUTING on the INTERNET, push systems deliver information, advertising etc to your computer without you having to ask for it to be DOWNLOADED: *push technologies*

put[1] /pʊt/ *v* past tense and past participle **put** present perfect **putting** **1 put a proposal/case etc to sb** to offer a proposal, plan etc to a group of people which they can accept or reject: *The latest offer will be put to the negotiating committee this afternoon.*

2 put your name to sth to sign a letter, document etc saying that you agree with what is written in it

put sth ↔ **across** *phr v* [T] **1** to explain your ideas, beliefs, policies etc in a way that people can understand: *The finance director put her argument across very effectively.*

2 put yourself across to communicate effectively, so that people have a clear idea of your character, ideas etc: *advice on putting yourself across at interviews*

put sth ↔ **aside** *phr v* [T] to save money regularly, usually for a particular purpose: *Like many people, you may be* ***putting money aside*** *in one of the deposit-based savings accounts now available.*

put sth **at** sth *phr v* [T] to calculate and state an amount, without trying to be very exact: *Official estimates put the storm damage at over $10 million.* | *Net assets are put at about £225 million.* | *Analysts put the break-up value of the company at £3 billion more than its current £6.5 billion capitalization.*

put sth ↔ **away** *phr v* [T] to save money to spend later: *He has a few thousand put away for his retirement.*

put sth ↔ **back** *phr v* [T] **1** to arrange for an event to start at a later time or date: *This afternoon's meeting has been put back to next Thursday.*

2 to cause something to be delayed: *The strike could put back the completion date by several weeks.*

put sth ↔ **by** *phr v* [T] to save money regularly in order to use it later

put sth ↔ **down** *phr v* [T] **1** to pay part of the total cost of something as a deposit: *You will be required to put down a 25% deposit.* | *How much could you afford to put down on a house?*
2 put down a motion/an amendment to suggest a subject, plan, change in the law etc for a parliament or committee to consider
put sth ↔ **forward** *phr v* [T] to suggest a plan, proposal etc, especially in order to start discussions about something that needs to be decided: *The UK accountancy bodies have put forward the idea of a European accounting standards body.* | *The working party has put forward a number of interesting proposals.*
put in *phr v* [T] **put in a claim/request/bid etc** to officially make a claim, request etc to buy something, do something etc: *Other unions immediately put in similar wage claims.* | *Various companies have put in bids for the business.*
put sth ↔ **in/into** (sth) *phr v* [T] **1** if you put money in or into a business, a particular activity etc, you invest it there: *Daewoo wanted GM expand the joint-venture car plant. The plan called for each company to put in $100 million.*
2 if you put money in or into a bank, you leave money in an account there: *Why invest in stocks, which can be dangerous, when you can put money in a bank without any risk?* | *small investors who **put their money** into building society savings accounts*
put in for sth *phr v* [T] to make a formal request for something: *I'm putting in for a pay increase.*
put sth **on** sth *phr v* [T] **1** to add an amount of money onto the price or cost of something: *The new tax could put another ten cents on the price of gas.* | *At the close of trading, Sears put on 2 to 92p.* | *Turnover put on almost £70 million to £337.5 million.*
2 to risk an amount of money on the result of a game, race etc: *We put £50 on Brazil to win the Cup.*
put sth ↔ **out** *phr v* [T] **1** to produce something for sale: *A great many people are involved in putting out a newspaper.*
2 if a company puts out a piece of work, it sends the work to be done by someone who does not work for the company + **to**: *These days we put out a lot of work to freelancers.*
put sth ↔ **through** *phr v* [T] to do what is necessary in order to get a plan or suggestion accepted or approved: *Production will start up again when these changes have been put through.*
put sth ↔ **up** *phr v* [T] **1** to increase the price, cost, or value of something: *The Bundesbank put up its rate by 1%.* | *My landlord is putting the rent up.*
2 put up money/£50/$3 million etc to provide an amount of money for a particular purpose, especially to start a business: *He has agreed to put up $750 million for a 15% stake in the buyout consortium.* | *Nearly £5 billion has been put up by private investors.*
3 put sth up for sale/auction etc: *Freeport put up for sale all its oil and gas reserves, but the company didn't receive any realistic offers.* | *They put up the silver for auction* (=an event when something is sold to the person who is willing to pay the most for it) *at Sotheby's last year.*
4 if you put up an asset as collateral for a loan, you obtain the loan on condition that the lender has the right to take and sell this asset if you fail to repay the loan: *The bank refused to give him a loan until he put his home up as collateral.*

put[2] *n* [C] FINANCE another name for PUT OPTION (=the right to sell shares etc at a particular price within a specific period of time): ***In-the-money puts*** *are options where the price at which the holder can sell the stock is well above the current market price of the shares.* | *Japanese players are holding a large amount of **dollar puts** at 132.4 yen.*

put and call option *n* [C] another name for DOUBLE OPTION

put option —see under OPTION

pw written abbreviation for per week: *Rent is £95 pw.*

pyr·a·mid /ˈpɪrəmɪd/ *n* [C] an organization with only a few people at the top, who have a lot of power and influence over those below them

pyramid scheme —see under SCHEME

pyramid selling —see under SELLING

P

Q

QC *n* [C] Queen's Counsel; a BARRISTER (=a type of lawyer) of high rank in the British legal system

qtr. written abbreviation for quarter: *sales for last qtr*

quad•ru•ple /ˈkwɒdrʊpəl, kwɒˈdruː-‖kwɑːˈdruː-/ *v* [I,T] to increase or make something increase by four times: *Pre-tax profits have more than quadrupled from £5 million to over £20 million.* | *OPEC quadrupled the price of oil between 1973 and 1974.* | *We hope to quadruple production in two years.*

qua•dru•pli•cate /kwɒˈdruːplɪkɪt‖kwɑː-/ *n* **in quadruplicate** with four copies: *Please print out the contract in quadruplicate.*

qual•i•fi•ca•tion /ˌkwɒlɪfɪˈkeɪʃən‖ˌkwɑː-/ *n* **1** [C usually plural] an examination that you have passed at school, university, or in your profession: *The government is determined to reduce the number of young people leaving school with no qualifications.* | *Even without* ***paper qualifications*** (=official qualifications rather than experience or personal qualities), *a well-motivated young girl should be able to find work as a shop assistant or a waitress.*
2 [C] a skill, personal quality, or type of experience that makes you suitable for a particular job: *Mr. Burkett has all the qualifications for a big-time fund-raiser: a limitless capacity for talking on the phone, and a lot of rich personal contacts.* | *Isobel has all the right qualifications to become a good manager.*

qual•i•fied /ˈkwɒlɪfaɪd‖ˈkwɑː-/ *adj* **1** having suitable knowledge, experience, or qualifications, especially for a particular job: *highly qualified engineering staff*
2 qualified agreement, approval etc is limited in some way, because you do not completely agree or approve: *The Gann Report received qualified approval from the colleges.*
3 having reached a particular stage in the process of competing for something: *The Florida Lottery named the agencies qualified to bid for its $27 million ad account.*

qualified opinion also **qualified report** *n* [C usually singular] a comment by an AUDITOR (=specialized outside accountant) that the accounts of a company give a TRUE AND FAIR VIEW of its finances except in specified ways, for example that they show some things in a way that the auditor does not approve

qual•i•fy /ˈkwɒlɪfaɪ‖ˈkwɑː-/ *v* past tense and past participle **qualified** **1** [I] to gain the qualifications needed for a particular profession etc + **as**: *Olga recently qualified as a pilot.*
2 [I] to have the right to claim something + **for**: *You may be able to qualify for unemployment benefit.*
3 [T] if your knowledge or ability qualifies you to do something, it makes you a suitable person to do it: *Our three-week course will qualify you to teach English overseas.*
4 [I] to reach a particular stage in the process of competing for the right to do something, for example in a BID (=an occasion when someone offers to buy something, or build or make something): *Three multinational groups have qualified to bid for Emetel, the Ecuadorean telephone company.*

qualitative research —see under RESEARCH

qual•i•ty[1] /ˈkwɒlɪti‖ˈkwɑː-/ *n* plural **qualities** **1** [C] something such as courage, intelligence, or loyalty that people may have as part of their character: *You need special personal qualities to work as a nurse.*
2 [C] something such as size, colour, feel, or weight that makes one thing look different from other things: *The analysis looks at the physical and chemical qualities of the sample.*
3 [U] used to talk about how good or bad something is: *Because of the* ***high quality*** *of its crudes, Indonesia's oil prices usually are above the average.* | *She was shocked by the* ***low quality*** *of the country's hospitals.*
4 [U] used to talk about how likely an investment is to be profitable: *The bond issues carried triple-A ratings and appealed individuals looking for* ***high-quality*** *securities.*
5 [U] a high standard: *Remember it's quality we're looking for, so don't rush the job.* | *Veuve Clicquot has the most potential because of the company's commitment to quality.*
6 flight to quality when people stop buying low-quality products, investments etc and start buying high-quality products etc: *The company saw a flight to quality among whisky drinkers and worked to improve the image of its whisky brands.* | *The fear of war has provoked a flight to quality for the dollar.*

quality[2] *adj* [only before a noun] **1** a word meaning very good, used especially in advertising products: *We provide quality rented accommodation for professional people.* | *quality child-care at prices people can afford*
2 quality newspapers/press/journalism *BrE* newspapers etc aimed at educated readers

quality assurance *n* [U] the management of the quality of production of goods or services so that they remain at a high standard: *Are we maintaining adequate quality assurance procedures?* | *a quality assurance manager*

quality circle *n* [C] a small group of factory workers who meet regularly to discuss ways to improve working methods and to solve problems: *Quality circles were introduced into Ford UK to form the communications basis for these organizational changes.* | *a Quality Circle leader*

quality control —see under CONTROL[1]

quality management —see under MANAGEMENT

quality time —see under TIME

quan•go /ˈkwæŋgəʊ‖-goʊ/ *n* plural **quangos** or **quangoes** [C] an independent organization in Britain, formed by the government but with its own legal powers. Quangos are responsible for controlling and supporting particular activities, for example by deciding who should receive money given by the government. The new name for quangos is NDPBS: *Unelected quangos have replaced elected boards in much of the administration of government.* | *quangos such as the Arts Council*

quan•ti•fy /ˈkwɒntɪfaɪ‖ˈkwɑːn-/ *v* past tense and past participle **quantified** [T] to measure something and express it as a number, especially something that is difficult to measure: *Quantifying the effect of advertising on sales is difficult.* —**quantifiable** *adj*: *Can the project offer a quantifiable payback?* —**quantification** *n* [U] *the quantification of future loss*

quan•ti•ta•tive /ˈkwɒntɪtətɪv‖ˈkwɑːntɪteɪ-/ *adj* connected with amounts rather than with the quality or nature of something: *the introduction of new quantitative import restrictions*

quantitative research —see under RESEARCH

quan•ti•ty /ˈkwɒntɪti‖ˈkwɑːn-/ *n* plural **quantities** **1** [C] an amount of something that can be counted or measured: *A* ***small quantity*** *of our oil is sold to France.* | *Stock managers have raised* ***huge quantities*** *of cash.* | *Citrus fruits are grown but not in* ***commercial quantities*** (=amounts large enough to be sold).
economic order quantity [U] the best amount of goods to order at one time, when considering all the

costs involved, including costs of sending the order, storing the goods etc

2 [U] used to talk about how much of something there is: *The **quantity and quality** of personnel is inadequate.*

3 [U] a large amount of something: *US lumber, which the Japanese buy **in quantity***

4 a known/an unknown quantity someone or something that people know something about or know very little about: *The new director is a known quantity, having served as finance administrator to the company from 1986–90.* | *The administration of an annuity is an unknown quantity and the charge may rise from the current 1%.*

quantity surveyor —see under SURVEYOR

quantum leap —see under LEAP²

quar•an•tine /ˈkwɒrəntiːn‖ˈkwɔː-/ *n* [U] when an animal or food product is kept apart from others in case it is carrying a disease, especially when it has just entered a country: *The exotic species will be kept **in quarantine** until health requirements are met.* | *the relaxing of Britain's tough **quarantine laws***

quar•ry /ˈkwɒri‖ˈkwɔː-, ˈkwɑː-/ *n* plural **quarries** [C] a place where large amounts of stone, sand etc are dug out of the ground: *a granite quarry* —**quarry** *v* [T] *granite that is quarried in Brazil*

quart /kwɔːt‖kwɔːrt/ *n* [C] **1** *BrE* a unit of measure for liquids and some dry goods such as grain or coffee, equal to 1.136 litres

2 *AmE* a unit of measure for liquids and some dry goods, equal to 0.946 litres

quar•ter¹ /ˈkwɔːtə‖ˈkwɔːrtər/ *n* [C] **1** one of four equal parts into which something can be divided: *They're firing almost a quarter of the workforce.* | *A quarter of the project's income comes from government grants.*

2 a period of three months, especially in connection with bills, payments, and income: *We will send you a bill every quarter.* | *Sales in **the fourth quarter** rose 28% to $1.2 million* | *The sales director of the SMMT expects sales **in the final quarter** to be below those in 1999.* | *At the end of each **financial quarter**, the chief executive provides information on performance against targets.* —see also QUARTERLIES

3 a coin in the US and Canada, worth 25 cents

quarter² *v* [I,T] if something quarters or is quartered, it decreases to a quarter of what it was: *Mergers and acquisitions fees have quartered in the past year.*

quar•ter•back /ˈkwɔːtəbæk‖ˈkwɔːrtər-/ *v* [T] *AmE informal* to organize or be in charge of an activity or event: *JPMS quarterbacked the selling effort of a Wall Street syndicate.*

quarter day *n* [C] *BrE* a day that officially begins a three-month period of the year, and on which payments are made: *Rent is payable in advance on the usual quarter days.*

quar•ter•lies /ˈkwɔːtəliz‖ˈkwɔːrtər-/ *n* [plural] the financial results of large companies in the US that are announced every three months: *UDC declared quarterlies of 93.75 cents a share.*

quar•ter•ly /ˈkwɔːtəli‖ˈkwɔːrtər-/ *adv* happening or produced once every three months: *Interest will be paid quarterly.* | *a magazine that comes out quarterly* —**quarterly** *adj*: *Occidental had a quarterly profit of $45 million.* | *a quarterly newsletter*

quarterly dividend —see under DIVIDEND

quarterly loss —see under LOSS

quar•tile /ˈkwɔːtaɪl‖ˈkwɔːr-/ *n* [C] STATISTICS one quarter of a set of things or people, arranged in order of value, amount, wealth etc: *the three funds in the **top quartile** of their sectors* —see also DECILE, MEDIAN, PERCENTILE

quash /kwɒʃ‖kwɑːʃ, kwɒːʃ/ *v* [T] **1** to officially state that a judgement or decision is no longer legal or correct: *He was found guilty but had his conviction quashed later on appeal.*

2 to stop something from starting or developing: *Car-rental companies say they quashed a state government plan to double Florida's car rental surcharge.* | *A hospital chief executive has **quashed rumours** that nursing staff will lose jobs.*

quasi- /kwɑːzi, kweɪzaɪ/ *prefix* used to say that something acts, works, or operates partly like something else, but is not the actual thing: *a quasi-judicial agency that conducts investigations and makes recommendations to Congress on international trade issues*

quay /kiː‖keɪ/ *n* [C] a place where boats can be tied up and can stop to load and unload

Queen's Counsel —see QC

que•ry¹ /ˈkwɪəri‖ˈkwɪri/ *n* plural **queries** [C] **1** a question you ask to get information, or to check that something is true or correct: *A team of telephone operators are here to **answer your queries**.*

2 COMPUTING one or more words or signs that you put into a computer in order to get a particular piece of information from a store of information held on the computer: *You can make complex queries by setting up a set of conditions that check the date every time you run the program.*

parallel data query abbreviation **PDQ** a system on a computer that can deal with several problems, tasks etc at the same time: *Barclay's PDQ terminals can read Visa, MasterCard, American Express and Diner's Club cards as well as some store and fuel cards.*

query² *v* past simple and past participle **queried** [T] **1** to express doubt that something is legal, true, or correct: *A VAT officer queried the VAT returns of the business.* + **whether**: *I'd query whether these figures are reliable.*

2 to ask someone questions: *The survey queries 5,000 households about their perception of present business conditions.*

ques•tion¹ /ˈkwestʃən/ *n* [C] **1** a sentence or phrase that asks for information: *They **asked** me a lot of **questions** about my work experience.* | *Don't hesitate to contact me if you have any questions.*

2 a subject or problem that needs to be settled, discussed, or dealt with: *The real question is whether the employee has any power over customers.* + **of**: *This whole question of measuring risk has became a mess.*

3 a feeling of doubt about something: *This incident **raises** further **questions** about airport security.* | *He is by far the best candidate. There **is no question** about it.* | *The wisdom of this policy is **open to question*** (=it will be doubted by some people).

4 in question the things, people etc in question are the ones that are being discussed or talked about: *Is the information in question really a business secret?*

5 out of the question not possible or allowed: *The idea of merging with another company was now out of the question.*

question² *v* [T] **1** to ask someone questions to find out what they know about something: *None of the defendants were questioned by the police before their arrest.* **question sb about sth**: *We have questioned many of our customers about the new services.*

2 to have doubts about whether something is true or if it is the right thing to do: *The report questioned ISC's heavy reliance on three international customers.*

ques•tion•a•ble /ˈkwestʃənəbəl/ *adj* **1** not definitely correct or true: *Looking back, we did make some questionable decisions.*

2 behaviour or actions that are questionable seem likely to be dishonest or wrong: *business deals of a rather questionable kind*

Q

question mark *n* [C] **a question mark over** if there is a question mark over something, there is a possibility that it will not be successful or will not continue to exist: *There is a big question mark over the bank's long-term future.*

ques•tion•naire /ˌkwestʃəˈneə, ˌkes-‖-ˈner/ *n* [C] a written set of questions which you give to a large number of people in order to collect information: *Consumers **filled out a** detailed **questionnaire** about their smoking habits.*

queue[1] /kjuː/ *n* [C] **1** *BrE* a line of people waiting to enter a building, buy something etc; LINE *AmE*: *There may be **long queues** outside stores at sale times.*

dole queue *BrE* used to refer to the number of people who are unemployed; UNEMPLOYMENT LINE *AmE*: *Another 21,300 people joined the dole queue in May.*

2 *BrE* used to refer to a group of people who are very eager to do something: *Chrysler had a queue of people wanting to put down their deposits on the new two-wheel drive truck.*

3 COMPUTING a list of jobs that a computer has to do in a particular order: *the number of jobs in the batch queue*

queue[2] *v* past tense and past participle **queued** present participle **queuing** or **queueing** *BrE* **1** [I] also **queue up** to form or join a line of people or vehicles waiting to do something or go somewhere: *Customers queued for hours to buy the new toy.* | *I queued up at the travel centre to pick up my tickets.*

2 [T] COMPUTING if a computer queues a job, it puts it in a list of jobs that are to be done in a particular order: *Input or output requests to a file are queued by the operating system.*

queuing theory —see under THEORY

quick /kwɪk/ *adj* **quick and dirty** quick and dirty methods or solutions are simple ones that can be used quickly, especially until something better and more permanent can be decided: *We need a quick and dirty way to cut fuel costs.*

quid /kwɪd/ *n* plural **quid** [C] *BrE informal* **1** one pound in British money

2 be quids in to make a profit, especially a large one: *We'll be quids in if we get this contract.*

quid pro quo /ˌkwɪd prəʊ ˈkwəʊ‖-proʊ ˈkwoʊ/ *n* [C] something that you give or do in exchange for something else, especially when this arrangement is not official: *There should be a quid pro quo arrangement whereby we all cooperate.*

qui•et /ˈkwaɪət/ *adj* **1** if business, a market etc is quiet, there are not many customers or there is not much activity: *August is a quite time of year for the retail trade.* | *The market has been quiet this morning.*

2 quiet enjoyment LAW the right to use property or land without any interference: *The purchaser shall have quiet enjoyment of the land.*

3 quiet possession LAW the right to use goods you have bought or hired without interference: *warranties promising no disturbance of quiet possession by the seller*

quiet possession —see under POSSESSION

quit /kwɪt/ *v* past tense and past participle **quit** also **quitted** *BrE* present participle **quitting** [I,T] **1** *informal* to leave your job, especially because you are annoyed or unhappy with it: *I was grossly underpaid, so I quit.* | *He quit a management training job at Sears.*

2 to close a computer program when you have finished using it: *To shut the machine down, quit Windows and then switch off the machine.*

quo•rate /ˈkwɔːrɪ̈t/ *adj formal* a meeting that is quorate has a quorum present: *If the company had only two members, the death of one may mean that no quorate meetings can be held.*

quo•rum /ˈkwɔːrəm/ *n* [singular] the smallest number of people who must be present at a meeting for official decisions to be made: *Not enough members turned up to **achieve a quorum**.*

quo•ta /ˈkwəʊtə‖ˈkwoʊ-/ *n* [C] an amount of something that is officially allowed or expected in a particular period of time: *The U.S. has for years **imposed quotas on** Chinese garment imports.* | *France enforces an **import quota** of 3% of total car sales.* | *a meeting of OPEC to discuss **production quotas*** | *Salesmen selling over their quota receive a $1000 bonus.*

disabled quota HUMAN RESOURCES the minimum percentage of jobs that an organization must give to people who have a disability: *An employer who fails to meet the disabled quota will be prosecuted.*

IMF quota ECONOMICS money that a country which is a member of the International Monetary Fund (IMF) has to give the fund so that it can lend money to countries needing help: *Without major support, the IMF quota increase cannot go into effect.*

job quota HUMAN RESOURCES, LAW in the US, a minimum number of jobs that must be given by organizations to members of particular groups, such as women, African Americans etc: *He has put forward a measure that declares job quotas to be 'an unlawful employment practice' but permits other forms of affirmative action consistent with the law.*

quota sample —see under SAMPLE[1]

quo•ta•tion /kwəʊˈteɪʃən‖kwoʊ-/ *n* [C] **1** a written statement of how much something will cost, for example some building work; QUOTE: *Could you give us a quotation for fixing the roof?* | *an insurance quotation*

2 FINANCE the price of a share on a stockmarket, either its selling price or its buying price: *The company processes the **stock quotations** from all of the nation's major exchanges.* | *the day's listing of mutual fund quotations*

quote[1] /kwəʊt‖kwoʊt/ *v* [T] **1** to tell a customer the price you will charge them for a service or product: *Hotels often quote a special rate for groups who use the hotel on a regular basis.*

2 FINANCE to give the price of a share or currency **be quoted at**: *ConAgra shares were quoted at $35.375, down 12.5 cents.* | *The dollar was quoted at 124.85 yen.*

quote[2] *n* [C] a written statement of how much something will cost, for example some building work; QUOTATION: *Always get a quote before proceeding with work.*

quot•ed /ˈkwəʊtɪ̈d‖ˈkwoʊ-/ *adj* **1 quoted company** a company whose shares are bought and sold on the Stock Exchange: *the best-paid executives of a British quoted company*

2 quoted shares shares that are bought and sold on a stockmarket: *money earned from the sale of quoted shares*

quote-driven *adj* FINANCE a quote-driven financial market is one in which prices are given by dealers. Investors buy or sell at these prices if they want to, and dealers change their prices according to demand from investors: *Because London's stock market works on the basis of a quote-driven system, rather than an orders-driven system, market-makers can find themselves needing to hold large amounts of stock.* —compare ORDER-DRIVEN

quoted share —see under SHARE

quoted stock —see under STOCK[1]

qwert•y /ˈkwɜːti‖ˈkwɜːrti/ *adj* a qwerty KEYBOARD on a computer or TYPEWRITER has keys with the letters Q-W-E-R-T-Y on at the beginning of the top row of letters

R

R&D —see R AND D

race discrimination —see under DISCRIMINATION

ra•cial /ˈreɪʃəl/ *adj* to do with a person's race or colour: *The firm was accused of racial discrimination in its recruitment procedures.*

racial equality —see under EQUALITY

racial harassment —see under HARASSMENT

rack•et /ˈrækɪt/ *n* [C] a dishonest or illegal way of obtaining money: *He had used his position to set up a **cocaine racket**.* + **in**: *a racket in stolen goods*

extortion racket a situation in which criminals get money from someone by threatening them: *He was the victim of an extortion racket.*

protection racket a situation in which criminals demand money from someone by threatening to damage their business or property if they do not pay: *The gang was **running a protection racket** in East London.*

rack•e•teer /ˌrækɪˈtɪə‖-ˈtɪr/ *n* [C] someone who is part of an organization involved in getting money illegally: *a convicted racketeer* —**racketeering** *n* [U] *He has admitted fraud and racketeering.*

rack jobber *n* [C] a manufacturer that supplies goods for RACKS (=special shelves) in some shops, sharing the profit with the shop owner. The rack jobber, rather than the store owner, is responsible for keeping the shelves filled

rack rent —see under RENT[2]

rage /reɪdʒ/ *n* [C,U] a feeling of extreme, uncontrollable anger

air rage [U] violent and angry behaviour by air passengers towards AIRLINE employees: *In another air rage incident, a flight to Spain was forced to land after a passenger threatened cabin staff when they refused to serve him more alcohol.*

phone rage [U] violent and angry behaviour on the telephone by people who are not satisfied with the service they are receiving: *Phone rage has increased dramatically, with an insincere tone of voice at the other end of the line the main reason that people lose their temper.*

rag trade —see under TRADE[1]

raid /reɪd/ *n* [C] FINANCE an occasion when someone suddenly buys a lot of shares in a company, usually as part of an attempt to take control of it + **on**: *In a successful raid on Emhart Corp., the Fisher-Getty partnership earned a $50 million investment profit.*

bear raid an occasion when someone suddenly sells a lot of shares in a particular company in order to bring down prices: *a bear raid by Saudi traders, who hoped to buy the gold back cheaply after depressing the price*

dawn raid an occasion when someone buys a lot of shares in a company in the first few minutes of the day's trading, in an attempt to get control of it: *A dawn raid allows the build-up of a significant stake in a target company within a matter of hours, giving the board of the target company little time to react or advise its shareholders.*

rail /reɪl/ *n* [U] travel or transport by train: *What percentage of goods are sent **by rail**? | rail travel*

rail•head /ˈreɪlhed/ *n* [C] the place where a railway line ends: *The barges pull up to a railhead.*

rail•road[1] /ˈreɪlrəʊd‖-roʊd/ *n* [C] *AmE* **1** a railway: *a railroad company*

2 the railroad all the work, equipment etc connected with a train system: *He had taken a job as a ticket agent on the railroad.*

railroad[2] *v* [T] to force or persuade someone to do something without giving them enough time to think about it **railroad sb into doing sth**: *The workers were railroaded into signing the agreement.*

rail•way /ˈreɪlweɪ/ *n* [C] *BrE* **1** a method of travelling or moving goods by train; RAILROAD *AmE*: *Britain's railways | railway workers*

2 the railway/the railways all the work, equipment etc connected with a train system; RAILROAD *AmE*: *He worked on the railways.*

rain•mak•er /ˈreɪnˌmeɪkə‖-ər/ *n* [C] *informal* someone who makes a lot of money for a company, for example by attracting rich clients: *His law firm almost lost its key rainmaker to another firm.*

raise[1] /reɪz/ *v* [T] **1** to increase an amount, number, or level: *We can cut the state budget or raise taxes. | The bank raised interest rates to 15%.*

2 raise a question/objection/point etc to make people consider a question etc, for example by beginning to talk or write about it: *I tried to raise several points at the meeting. | The Guinness affair raised the question of abolishing trial by jury in complicated fraud cases.*

3 raise money/capital/funds etc to collect the money, capital etc that is needed to do something: *Hammond Co. will need to raise $2 million to finance the offer.*

4 raise a loan/mortgage to succeed in getting a loan or mortgage: *He raised a loan of $20 million from commercial banks.*

5 raise an invoice to write out or print out an INVOICE (=document stating how much has to be paid for work or goods), or to ask someone to do this: *Where goods move between VAT registered traders, a tax invoice has to be raised.*

raise[2] *n* [C] *AmE* an increase in the money you earn; RISE *BrE*: *The Senate voted itself a 23% **pay raise**.*

rake /reɪk/ *v*

rake sth ↔ **in** *phr v* [T] to obtain money, profits etc in large amounts: *Batman merchandise raked in an estimated $500 million in retail sales while it was hot.*

rake sth ↔ **off** *phr v* [T] to take a share of someone's profits, sometimes secretly or dishonestly: *The owners of the pub chain hope to rake off a large cut of the bigger discounts it negotiates with beer suppliers.*

rake-off *n* [C] *informal* a share of profits, sometimes one that is obtained secretly or dishonestly: *Corrupt officials may expect a rake-off when expensive goods are imported.*

ral•ly /ˈræli/ *v* past tense and past participle **rallied** present participle **rallying** [I] if prices of shares, currencies etc rally, they rise again after falling: *Stock prices rallied this afternoon after earlier falls. | Volvo B shares rallied 5 Swedish kronor to 398 kronor.* —**rally** *n* [C] *a powerful stock market rally*

RAM /ræm/ *n* [C,U] Random Access Memory; the memory in a computer system that is used to store information for a short time. The more RAM a computer has, the more software can be used on it at the same time: *Programs are getting bigger, requiring more RAM. | The Marixx DS comes with 64 Megabytes of RAM.*

ramp /ræmp/ *v*

ramp sth ↔ **up** *phr v* [T] **1** FINANCE if someone ramps up a company's shares, they try to persuade people that they are worth more than they really are: *To ramp up a share price during a takeover bid is unacceptable.*

2 if a company ramps up an activity, it increases it: *Producers can quickly ramp up production to prevent any shortages. | The company spent millions of pounds ramping up its marketing in the US.*

3 to increase prices, costs etc: *The strength of the pound sterling has ramped up the cost of imported materials.*

ramp·ing /ˈræmpɪŋ/ *n* [U] FINANCE when someone tries to persuade people that shares etc are worth more than they really are. Ramping may happen when investors want to sell shares etc at an increased price and make a quick profit: *Ramping played a major role in the Taipei stock market's volatility.*

R and D also written **R&D** *n* [U] **1** research and development; the part of a business concerned with studying new ideas and planning new products: *We attempt to relate expenditure on R and D to performance.* | *Dunlop's R and D manager Bob Haines*
2 research and development; the department in a company responsible for developing new products, improving existing products etc: *She works in R and D.*

ran·dom /ˈrændəm/ *adj* **1 random sample/check/test etc** a sample, check etc in which things or people are chosen without any particular reason or pattern so that they will include a typical mixture of the larger group they represent: *The group polled a random sample of US manufacturers.* | *Pennsylvania conducts random checks on trucks to see that they are properly maintained.* | *a rule requiring random drug testing of airline employees* —compare ***quota sample*** under SAMPLE[1]
2 random error/effect etc an error etc that happens without any pattern, so it is difficult to say when it will happen again or why it happens: *Random errors in the survey will not matter greatly; what is of concern is the possibility of bias.*
3 at random without any particular reason or pattern: *Pollsters interviewed 1000 adults picked at random in 50 states.*

R

random access memory —see RAM

random walk *n* [singular] STATISTICS, FINANCE the idea that an amount, level etc changes without any pattern, so that it is not possible to say what future amounts etc will be. Some people think, for example, that prices on financial markets follow a random walk, and that it is impossible to calculate what prices will be in the future by looking at price movements in the past: *Some recent research has shown persistent exceptions to the random walk model.*

range[1] /reɪndʒ/ *n* [C] **1** the limits within which amounts, quantities etc can vary: *We are looking at properties within a certain* ***price range****.* | *People in the 35 to 44* ***age range*** *are most likely to hold more than one job.* | *Brokers typically charge commissions* ***in the*** *4%* ***to*** *8%* ***range****.* + **of**: *Sales will rise to a range of $12 million to $13 million.*
2 FINANCE the highest and lowest prices reached by a SECURITY (=bond, share etc) or market over a period of time: *GM shares traded in the $37 to $42 range for most of last year.* | *Oil remains in a $26-to-$30-a-barrel range.*
3 also **product range** a set of similar products made by a particular company or available in a particular shop: *a new range of kitchenware* | *a* ***wide range*** *of products and systems* | *the* ***top of the range*** (=best sold by a company or shop) *Rucanor shoe*
4 the area of power, responsibility, or activities that a person or organization has: *These issues fall* ***outside the range of*** *the enquiry.*

range[2] *v* [I] if prices, levels etc range from one amount to another, they include both those amounts and anything in between + **from/to/between etc**: *The judges' salaries range from $82,000 to $99,000.* | *The population of these cities ranges between 3 and 5 million inhabitants.* | *The mainframe systems* ***range in price*** *from $1.3 million to $3.6 million.*

rank[1] /ræŋk/ *n* [C] **1** a particular level of job in an organization, especially a government organization or the army: *His father retired with the rank of major.* | *Knight-Ridder named Maxwell King, 46, to succeed Mr. Roberts, but at a* ***lower rank****.* | *The companies have been trying to reduce the number of management ranks in a bid to be more cost-efficient.*
2 a particular position in a list that has been put in order of quality or importance: *No US airline broke the top 10 rank* (=no US airline was higher than 10th) *in an airline survey released yesterday.*

rank[2] *v* **1** [I] to have a particular position in a list that has been put in order of quality or importance: *It ranks in the top 3% of all mutual funds.*
2 [T] to decide the position of something or someone in a list in order of quality or importance: *The firm was ranked the number five underwriter of US bond and stock issues.* **rank sth as sth**: *The real estate executives ranked the Northeast as the least attractive area for development.*

rank and file *n* **the rank and file** the ordinary members of a union, who are not union officials: *So far, leaders are maintaining discipline among the rank and file.* —**rank-and-file** *adj* [only before a noun] *rank-and-file union members*

rank·ing /ˈræŋkɪŋ/ *n* [C] **1** the position of something or someone in a list that has been arranged in order of quality or importance: *The US recaptured from Germany the* ***number one ranking*** *among exporters.*
2 a list of things or people in order of quality or importance: *a ranking of the 30 largest US cities on the basis of finance and management*

rat·a·ble also **rateable** *BrE* /ˈreɪtəbəl/ *adj* **1** a ratable share of something such as a payment is calculated according to the amount someone owes or is owed, relative to the amounts other people owe or are owed: *the collection and* ***ratable distribution*** *of the bankrupt's available assets* | *Each insurer is only liable to contribute its* ***rateable proportion****.*
2 something that is ratable can have tax charged on it: *a ratable estate*

ratch·et[1] /ˈrætʃɪt/ *n* [C] an arrangement in which the value of someone's share in a company depends on how well the company performs. This is often done where company managers own a share in the company: *A ratchet is a mechanism by which investors provide management with an incentive.*

ratchet[2] *v*
ratchet sth ↔ **down** *phr v* [I,T] to decrease, or make something decrease: *She expects inflation to ratchet down by one percentage point.* | *Their chief analyst is ratcheting down expectations for the third quarter because of the weak employment data.*
ratchet sth ↔ **up** *phr v* [I,T] to increase, or make something increase: *Environmental standards were ratcheted up to meet public demands for clean water.*

ratch·et·ing /ˈrætʃətɪŋ/ *adj* [only before a noun] ratcheting levels, amounts etc are increasing: *Film studios are becoming increasingly alarmed at ratcheting costs.* | *Vons is doing a fine job, but you've got a weak economy and ratcheting competition.*

rate[1] /reɪt/ *n* [C] **1** a charge or payment fixed according to a standard scale: *We have advised* (=informed) *our client of your* ***hourly rate****.* | *The councils have powers to set minimum* ***rates of pay****.* | *I'm told $25 an hour is* ***the going rate*** (=the usual amount paid) *for private tuition.*
cheque rate [singular] BANKING the rate of COMMISSION charged, for example by a bank for writing or cashing a cheque in a foreign currency
day rate the amount paid for someone to do a day's work: *JPF Clarke builders in North London work out their day rates by a range of set charges for various craftsmen.*
market rate ◆ the real price or cost of something, decided by a market rather than calculated or fixed, for

example by a government: *Restrictive gas contracts required the company to purchase its gas at prices far* ***above market rates.***

◆ a typical rate for something on a market at a particular time: *This measure will force credit card issuers to change from fixed to flexible rates, which would rise and fall with market rates.*

◆ the price of something calculated in relation to what buyers are willing to pay at a particular time: *The spread between the official and the market rate has remained at less than 1% for the past five years.*

piece rate also **piecework rate** an amount of money that is paid for each item a worker produces, rather than for the time taken to make it: *The workers* ***are paid on a piece rate.***

2 the number of examples of something or the number of times something happens, often expressed as a percentage: *Canada's* ***unemployment rate*** *rose to 8.3% of the working population in August.* | *The pension finding service has an 87%* ***success rate.*** | *The* ***failure rate*** *of small businesses is notoriously high.*

conversion rate ◆ MARKETING the number of sales in relation to the number of sales visits, phone calls etc: *The key to direct marketing is whether you open the envelope, and our conversion rates should be three times higher than our rivals'.*

◆ the figure showing how much of one thing you get in exchange for another thing: *Foreign banks generally offer a better conversion rate for travellers' cheques than for cash.* | *The new debentures are convertible into Kroger common stock at a conversion rate of $26.70 a share.*

mortality rate also **death rate** INSURANCE the number of people who die every year in a particular area, country etc as a proportion of the population as a whole; DEATH RATE: *The mortality rate for male hotel, restaurant and food service workers is double that for teachers.*

3 the speed at which something happens: *Companies have been going out of business* ***at an incredible rate*** (=very fast).

absorption rate PROPERTY the speed at which new houses, offices etc are sold or rented: *The city has a negative absorption rate right now – more space is being vacated than rented.*

4 also **tax rate** the part of your income or the part of the price of something that you pay in tax: *Those who earn $180,000 to $280,000 will see their tax rates drop to 31% from 33% this year.*

basic rate *BrE* the percentage of income that most people pay in tax. The basic rate is paid on income up to a particular level, after which a higher rate is paid: *The Conservatives cut the basic rate of income tax by nearly a quarter, from 33p to 25p in the pound.*

effective tax rate *BrE* the average rate at which someone pays tax on their total income, calculated from the income on which they pay no tax and the income on which they pay tax at a particular rate: *American Home Products Corp. reported a 12% gain in its earnings as the company benefited from a lower effective tax rate.*

marginal rate also **marginal tax rate** TAX the rate of income tax that someone pays on the part of their income that is taxed the most: *This year's top marginal rate, the rate at which your last dollar of income is taxed, is actually higher than 31% for many high-income taxpayers.*

standard rate *BrE* ◆ the rate of income tax paid by most people who earn enough to pay tax but not enough to pay a high rate of tax: *The government has cut the standard rate of income tax to 25p in the pound.*

◆ the normal rate of VALUE ADDED TAX paid on goods: *The cost of the building work would attract Value Added Tax at the standard rate.*

uniform business rate abbreviation **UBR** a tax on land and buildings used for business which is the same rate for the whole country: *Small firms benefited from a reform of the uniform business rate.*

5 also **interest rate** BANKING, FINANCE the percentage charged for borrowing money, or a percentage you receive when you put money in a bank, make an investment etc: *Interest rates are falling and now is the time to buy property.* | *The rate on Chemical's standard credit cards will be 18.9%.* | *Mortgage rates will fall; corporate bond rates will fall; municipal bonds rates will also fall.* | *the most recent changes in the* ***short and long rates*** (=the rates for borrowing over short and long periods of time)

annual percentage rate abbreviation **APR** the COMPOUND RATE that you must pay when you borrow money, including all charges. In many countries, the APR must be shown in advertisements for loans to give the true cost of borrowing

Bank of England minimum lending rate another name for BASE RATE

bank rate another name for BASE RATE

base rate the basic rate of interest charged by the BANK OF ENGLAND, that replaced the BANK RATE and the MINIMUM LENDING RATE. The rates charged by all banks on their lending rise and fall with the base rate, and this has an important influence on the economy as a whole. Bank rate and minimum lending rate are still used in Britain and other countries to talk about the base rate: *You will pay 2% below the base rate for the first two years of your mortgage.*

bill rate FINANCE the interest rate for TREASURY BILLS (=government bonds): *money attracted to Kenya by high bill rates*

capitalization rate also **capitalisation rate** *BrE* the interest rate used to calculate the present value of a series of future payments

capped rate an interest rate on a loan that can change, but cannot go above a certain value that is fixed at the time when the loan is taken out

compound rate an interest rate based on the PRINICIPAL (=the original amount invested or borrowed) and on the interest payments received earlier on an investment, or the amount remaining to be repaid on a loan: *Left untouched for five years, an investment of £100 in the Series A bond is guaranteed to grow to £176.24, a compound rate of 12% per year.*

coupon rate the rate of interest paid on a bond: *debentures issued at coupon rates which reflect current rates of inflation*

discount rate ◆ the rate charged by a CENTRAL BANK for lending to other banks. Changes in this rate will influence interest rates in the economy as a whole: *The central bank increased its discount rate to discourage borrowing.*

◆ the rate charged by a bank to DISCOUNT a BILL OF EXCHANGE

◆ the interest rate used to calculate the DISCOUNTED CASH FLOW from an investment: *At a discount rate of 20%, which project should be accepted?*

effective rate ◆ the rate of interest paid on a loan or received from money held in a bank account

◆ the amount of profit from a bond, calculated from the purchase price and the interest that is paid until the bond becomes due for payment

European interbank offered rate abbreviation **Euribor** BANKING the interest rate for lending between banks in EUROS

fixed rate an interest rate on a loan that is fixed at the time when the loan is taken out and does not change

flat rate a rate of interest charged on a loan from the moment it is taken out. The loan is paid back in INSTALMENTS (=a series of payments)

floating rate also **variable rate** an interest rate that can change during the life of the loan: *CB is trying to substitute floating rate for fixed rate mortgages in France.*

interbank offered rate an interest rate at which

R

banks lend to each other, often used as a reference point for other rates: *DM6 billion of floating-rate notes at the six-month Frankfurt interbank offered rate plus 0.05 points*

minimum lending rate another name for BASE RATE

negative interest rate the difference between the inflation rate and interest rates when prices are rising more quickly than interest rates: *The government's measures have caused negative interest rates in real, inflation-adjusted terms.*

nominal interest rate ♦ an interest rate on bonds which does not take account of the real price at which they are sold: *The convertible bonds will carry a nominal interest rate of 8% and expire in 9.5 years.*

♦ an interest rate that is considered by itself, without referring to INFLATION (=the speed at which prices are rising): *All a country gets from higher monetary growth is higher inflation, higher nominal interest rates and a less productive economy.*

prime rate also **prime lending rate** the most favourable interest rate for borrowing by a bank's best customers, those companies with the least risk that they will not repay the loan: *The prime rate is the base for various bank lending charges.*

teaser rate a low interest rate charged at the beginning of a loan to encourage people to borrow money: *Although thrifts offer initial teaser rates on adjustable mortgages that are lower than the current fixed rates, many consumers seem to prefer the security of a fixed rate.*

variable rate another name for FLOATING RATE

6 also **insurance rate** the amount you have to pay for insurance: *Women drivers get cheaper insurance rates because their accident records are better.*

average rate the average of several rates for different kinds of insurance risk

short-period rate a rate charged on an insurance contract that lasts for less than a year

7 a payment for a public service, usually based on the value of the property owned by the person who uses the service: *a non-domestic **water rate** of 3.4 pence in the pound*

8 rates [plural] in Britain before 1990, a tax paid to local government for public services, based on the value of the property owned by the tax payer. Rates have now been replaced with the COUNCIL TAX —see also EXCHANGE RATE, CURRENCY RATE, GROWTH RATE

rate² *v* **1** [T] to think that someone or something has a particular quality, value, or standard **be rated (as) sth**: *The Salzburg Sheraton is rated as one of the city's best hotels.* | *I **rate** this agreement **highly** as an achievement by the two governments.*

2 [I,T] to be considered as having a particular quality, value, or standard **+ as**: *It rates as one of the most comfortable PC keyboards I've tried.* | *The SLR can hardly be rated as a precision piece of equipment.*

3 [T] FINANCE to measure the risk of investing in or lending to a company, local authority etc: *Moody's Investors Service Inc. has rated the bonds single-A-1.* | *Richard Simon of Goldman Sachs has rated Paramount stock a 'hold' for the past year.* —**rated** *adj* [not before a noun] *The bonds are insured and triple-A-rated.*

4 [T] to measure the performance of a ship or machine so it can be put in a particular class —**rated** *adj*: *Each machine has a **rated capacity of*** (=ability to produce) *600 tonnes per hour.*

rateable *adj* a British spelling of RATABLE

rateable value —see under VALUE¹

rate card *n* [C] a document which shows how much it costs to advertise in a particular magazine, newspaper etc, depending on how much space is used, when the advert appears etc: *According to USA Today's rate card, the insert costs $181,000.*

rate of exchange —see EXCHANGE RATE

rate of interest —see under INTEREST RATE

rate of return —see under RETURN²

rate relief —see under RELIEF

rat·i·fy /ˈrætəfaɪ/ *v* past tense and past participle **ratified** present participle **ratifying** [T] to make a written agreement official by signing it: *The government delayed ratifying the treaty.*

rat·ing /ˈreɪtɪŋ/ *n* **1** [C] a level on a scale that shows how good, important, or popular something or someone is: *The President's **popularity rating** has never been higher.*

average audience rating abbreviation **AA rating** [C] a measure of the average number of people watching or listening to a TV or radio programme at a particular time

2 [C] FINANCE a measurement of the risk of lending to a company etc, calculated by an independent organization called a RATINGS AGENCY: *Standard and Poor's **downgraded*** (=reduced) ***the rating** on Pacific's commercial paper to single-A-3 from single-A-2.* | *Moodys' **upgraded*** (=improved) *its **rating** on Disney's senior debt to double-A-3 from single-A-2.*

AAA rating [C] a credit rating that can be given to a share, bond, or bank by US credit rating agencies such as Standard and Poor's or Moody's, indicating that it is considered to be a very safe investment: *The bank had AAA debt ratings from both Standard & Poor's and Moody's.*

Best rating [C] in the US, a measurement of what an insurance company's financial strength is. The top rating is A+: *20% of life insurers hold the top Best rating.*

credit rating [C] a calculation of a company's or government's financial strength and the risk of it not being able to repay loans or pay suppliers when it should: *Chrysler's credit rating dropped to junk-bond levels when the company was virtually bankrupt.* | *Some analysts believe that Mexico's **credit rating** will be **upgraded** increased to investment grade in the near future.* | *Standard & Poor is **downgrading*** (=decreasing) ***the credit rating** for Sun Alliance Group to double-A-plus from triple-A.*

debt rating [C] a calculation of the ability of a company or government to pay interest on its debts and to repay them: *Following the missed payment, Moody's **downgraded its debt rating**.* | *Standard & Poor's has **upgraded the debt ratings** of Penn Traffic to single-B-minus from triple-C-plus because of improved operating performance.*

Standard & Poor's rating [U] the class in which bonds are placed according to the risk involved in investing in them

3 FINANCE an estimate of the future profitability of investing in a particular company: *Kidder Peabody recommended Texas Instruments stock, which carries the firm's highest **investment rating**.*

bond rating [C] the level of risk of a particular bond not being repaid, or of interest payments not being made: *If the state continues to overspend, its bond rating could drop to single-A.*

buy rating [C] a dealer's advice that investors should buy a particular company's shares, and that those who already own some should buy more: *Medtronic jumped 3¾ to 115 after Dean Witter Reynolds repeated a 'buy' rating on the stock.*

hold rating [C] a dealer's advice to holders of a particular company's shares telling them not to sell the shares they have, nor to buy any more shares in that company: *Some believe Goodyear's situation will improve. Morgan Stanley's Mr Merlis, for example, changed his 'hold' rating on Goodyear to a 'buy'.*

security rating [C] FINANCE a measurement of the risk of investing in a particular company: *Analysts* *gave the company a security rating indicating 'questionable financial security'.*

sell rating [C] a dealer's advice to holders of a particular company's shares to sell them: *The stock came under pressure last week after Goldman Sachs downgraded its rating on the stock while First Boston reiterated repeated its 'sell' rating.*

4 also **insurance rating** [C] a measurement of the risk of loss, used to calculate how much will be charged for insurance

fleet rating [C] a special low rate charged by an insurance company for insuring a group of vehicles or ships owned by one company

5 the ratings [plural] a measurement of how many people watch a television programme or listen to a radio programme: *CBS Evening News slipped to second place in the ratings.* | *NBC's ratings dropped 3% in November.*

6 [C] the class in which a ship or machine is placed, according to its size

rating agency —see under AGENCY

ra·ti·o /ˈreɪʃiəʊ‖ˈreɪʃoʊ/ *n* [C] a relationship between two amounts that is represented by a pair of numbers showing how much greater one amount is than the other: *The company's* ***ratio of*** *current assets* ***to*** *current liabilities is 5 to 1.*

acid ratio also **acid test ratio**, **current ratio**, **liquid ratio test** ACCOUNTING the relationship between the total amount that a business has in cash, in its bank accounts, and owed by customers, and the total amount that it owes to suppliers. By checking this relationship it is possible to see whether the business is SOLVENT (=able to pay immediately the money it owes)

book-to-bill ratio *AmE* ACCOUNTING an amount showing the number of new orders received by a company compared to the number of products sold by the company: *Its book-to-bill ratio rose to 1.08, which means that for every $100 of microchip orders that are shipped, manufacturers received $108 of new orders.*

capital ratio also **capital adequacy ratio** *BrE* BANKING a bank's capital as a percentage of what it lends, an important measure in calculating if it is likely to fail; SOLVENCY RATIO *AmE*: *Among the commercial banks, capital adequacy ratios are very poor and new capital may be necessary.*

cash ratio BANKING money that a bank must have in cash as a percentage of money customers have put into the bank, to be sure that the bank has enough to pay people wanting to take money out of the bank and as a control on MONEY SUPPLY: *Banks hope the rate for cash ratio deposits will drop from 0.35% of their sterling deposits to 0.2%.*

collection ratio *AmE* ACCOUNTING the average number of days it takes for money owing to a company to be paid, a measure of the company's effectiveness in collecting payment and customers' ability to pay

debt-equity ratio FINANCE the amount of a company's debt in relation to the amount of share capital it has; DEBT RATIO: *Colgate raised $460 million in equity to retire debt and lower its debt/equity ratio from 50/50 to about 30/70.*

debt ratio ◆ FINANCE the amount of a company's debt in relation to the amount of share capital it has; DEBT-EQUITY RATIO: *Japan's corporate debt ratio increased four times faster than that of the U.S. in the 1980s.*

◆ a country's debt in relation to the value of all the goods and services it produces: *Rising government spending including interest payments will move the debt ratio to about 55% of GDP.*

debt service ratio the amount of a country's interest payments on its foreign debt as a percentage of its exports: *Large early debt repayments using receipts from privatisation have helped Hungary cut its debt service ratio to 24% this year from 41% two years ago.*

dividend payout ratio FINANCE the amount that a company pays out to shareholders in dividends as a percentage of its profits. This calculation is used especially in the US: *German firms tend to have much lower dividend payout ratios than companies in the English-speaking world.*

dividend-price ratio FINANCE a company's DIVIDEND (=the amount of profit it pays to shareholders in a particular period of time) as a percentage of its share price

expense ratio ◆ the costs of operating a company shown as a percentage of sales: *K-mart's expense ratio is 23% for its discount stores, compared with only 15% for Wal-Mart's discount stores.*

◆ FINANCE the costs of operating an INVESTMENT FUND shown as a percentage of the amount the fund earns from its investments: *This imaginary fund owns bonds yielding 10% but the fund also has a 1% annual expense ratio; the portfolio is only returning 9% after expenses.*

◆ INSURANCE the costs of operating an insurance company shown as a percentage of the money it receives from people paying for insurance policies: *Equitable is one of the lowest cost operators in the industry, with an expense ratio – expenses to premiums – of 4.3%.*

financial ratio ACCOUNTING a comparison of one figure from a company's FINANCIAL STATEMENT with another in order to measure its performance or to see if it can pay its debts: *All our financial ratios are fine except for research and development spending, where we are still below revenue.*

inventory-to-sales ratio the amount of stock that a company has compared with the amount of goods that they have sold in a particular period of time: *In September, U.S. retailers' inventory-to-sales ratio was 1.57.*

loan-to-value ratio abbreviation **LVR** PROPERTY the value of a house, land etc in relation to the value of the loan used to buy it: *In order to refinance, they'll have to pay down their first mortgage so that the loan-to-value ratio meets the requirements.*

management ratio one of the ratios that the people in charge of a company use to see how it is performing

net PE ratio FINANCE a PE ratio calculated on the base of how much profit is actually distributed to shareholders in a particular period of time

net quick assets ratio FINANCE a calculation of whether a business could pay its debts if sales stopped or slowed down. It takes into account money owed to suppliers, tax authorities etc, things such as bonds that can be easily sold and turned into cash, and money owed by customers etc. Supplies of materials, work in progress, and finished goods are not included as they might not be easily turned into cash

nil PE ratio FINANCE a PE ratio calculated on the base of how much profit a company makes in a particular 12-month period, whether it is actually distributed to shareholders in that period of time or not

payout ratio FINANCE the percentage of a company's profits paid to shareholders in DIVIDENDS in a particular period of time: *Beware of very high payout ratios. If a company is paying out 80% to 90% of its earnings in dividends, it's a danger sign.*

PE ratio or **P-E ratio**, also **price-earnings ratio**, written abbreviation **PE** FINANCE a company's share price divided by the amount of profits it makes for each share in a 12-month period. PE ratios are normally calculated on the base of all the profit made in the period, whether or not the profit is paid out to shareholders in that period: *Statistics on earnings growth and P-E ratios are useful to money managers in determining which markets and individual stocks to trade.* | *She recently began selling growth stocks with* ***high PE ratios*** *but knew that these could really suffer if the market turned down.* | *We buy cheap shares with* ***low P-E ratios*** *that are out of favour with other investors.*

reserve ratio BANKING the amount of money a

R

financial institution possesses in relation to the amount of money it has lent: *the insurance fund's thinnest reserve ratio in its history*

solvency ratio *AmE* BANKING a bank's capital as a percentage of what it lends, an important measure in calculating if it is likely to fail; CAPITAL ADEQUACY RATIO *BrE* —see also BASLE RATIOS

ratio analysis —see under ANALYSIS

ra•tion[1] /ˈræʃən‖ˈræ-, ˈreɪ-/ *n* [C] a fixed amount of something such as food or petrol that you are allowed to have when there is not much available: *Food is in short supply and the country has apparently tightened rations* (=made less available to each person).

ration[2] *v* [T] **1** to control the supply of something such as food or petrol by allowing people to have only a fixed amount of it: *Cuba has rationed food for four decades, largely because of the U.S.-imposed embargo.*

2 to allow someone to have only a small amount of something, or less than they would like, because there is not enough: *Its new refrigerator was such a hit that Maytag had to ration supplies of it.* | *The government sets budgets for hospitals and area health authorities and forces the providers to ration health care.*

ration sth ↔ **out** *phr v* [T] to give out supplies of something in small amounts: *They had to ration out supplies of the best-seller to one per customer.*

ra•tion•al•ize also **rationalise** *BrE* /ˈræʃənəlaɪz/ *v* [I,T] to make a business or organization more effective by getting rid of unnecessary staff, equipment etc, or reorganizing its structure: *The company has been taking steps to rationalize its printing operations.* —**rationalization** also **rationalisation** *BrE n* [C,U] *We shall press ahead with our rationalization and cost-reduction program.*

rat race *n* **the rat race** the unpleasant situation in business or in life in which people are always struggling to compete against each other for success: *A vacation is a chance to escape the corporate rat race for two weeks.*

raw /rɔː‖rɒː/ *adj* [only before a noun] **1** raw metals or other substances are in their natural state and have not been prepared or used to make anything: *German companies produced 6.1% less raw iron in March.* | *the export of raw logs*

2 raw data/statistics etc information that has not been arranged, checked, or prepared in any way: *Carpenter examined the study's raw data to tease out factors such as turnover rates.*

raw land —see under LAND[1]

raw material —see under MATERIAL

R/D written abbreviation for REFER TO DRAWER —see under DRAWER

Rd. also **Rd** the written abbreviation for Road, used in addresses: *150 London Rd, Liverpool*

Re *n* [U] INSURANCE abbreviation for REINSURANCE (=when an insurance company arranges to share a large insurance risk with other companies, that pay their part of any losses), often used in the names of reinsurance companies: *Munich Re, the world's biggest reinsurer*

re /riː/ *prep* concerning; used in business letters and notes to introduce the subject that you are writing about: *Dear Sirs, re Blackacre: We act for the buyer of the above property.*

reach[1] /riːtʃ/ *v* [T] **1** to increase or improve to a particular level or amount: *Sales are expected to reach 1.2 billion francs this year.*

2 to succeed in making someone see an advertisement, hear about a product etc: *Sponsors want to reach 18-to-34-year olds.* | *The company has an opportunity to reach new customers.*

3 to succeed in speaking to someone or giving them a message by telephone: *He tried three times to reach Mr. Gumbel at his hotel.*

4 reach an agreement/decision/settlement etc to succeed in making an agreement, decision etc: *The company failed to reach a labor agreement with the United Steelworkers Union.*

reach[2] *n* [singular, U] **1** MARKETING the number of people that see or hear an advertisement, television programme etc: *Courtroom Television Network starts today with a reach of about 4 million homes.*

2 within/beyond someone's reach within or beyond what someone can afford: *The price of high-powered PCs has been brought within the reach of average users.*

re•act /riˈækt/ *v* [I] FINANCE to start rising or falling in price, level etc because of something that has happened or that has been said + **to**: *The market reacted favorably to the announcement.* | *Oil prices reacted only mildly to news of the cut in Saudi production.*

re•ac•tive /riˈæktɪv/ *adj* not being ready for changes that effect you, and having to do something unplanned when they happen —compare PROACTIVE

read•er•ship /ˈriːdəʃɪp‖-ər-/ *n* [C,U] the people who read a particular newspaper or magazine: *The magazine has a largely male readership.* | *Readership of the 'Birmingham Evening Mail' fell about 10.6% last year.*

read only memory —see ROM

read•y /ˈredi/ *adj* **ready money/cash/source/supply** money etc that is easily available to be used at any time: *a government initiative to ensure a ready supply of skilled software graduates*

ready-made *adj* [only before a noun] **1** already prepared, and ready to be used immediately: *The company produces canned soup and ready-made meals.*

2 ready-made clothes/shoes etc clothes etc that have been manufactured in large quantities, rather than made for a particular customer: *a range of ready-made knitwear*

Rea•gan•om•ics /ˌreɪgəˈnɒmɪks‖-ˈnɑː-/ *n* [U] the economic policies followed in the 1980s by the US under President Reagan. These included support for the free market, cutting taxes and public spending, and reducing government control of business and industry

real /rɪəl/ *adj* **real earnings/profits/value etc** earnings etc that are calculated after including in the calculation the effects of inflation: *Their data show that average real earnings of men aged 20–40 in 1987 were lower than in 1974.* —see also CHATTELS REAL

real accounts —see under ACCOUNT[1]

real cost —see under COST[1]

real estate *n* **1** [U] land or buildings; REAL PROPERTY; REALTY *AmE*: *Pension funds often invest in real estate.* | *a piece of real estate*

2 [U] *AmE* the business of selling land or buildings: *those who make a living in real estate*

real estate agency —see under AGENCY

real estate agent —see under AGENT

real estate broker —see under BROKER[1]

real estate investment —see under INVESTMENT

real estate investment trust abbreviation **REIT** *n* [C] in the US, an investment company that invests in real estate, usually for a large number of small investors: *A real estate investment trust acquired the apartment complex for $2.3 million.*

real estate mortgage investment conduit —see REMIC

real estate tax —see under TAX[1]

re•a•lign /ˌriːəˈlaɪn/ *v* [T] **1** if a government realigns its currency, it changes the currency's value in relation to other currencies **realign sth against sth**: *The government insists that it won't consider realigning the pound against the mark.*

R

2 to change the way that a company is organized: *Genicom Corp. will realign its marketing and sales activities.*

re•a•lign•ment /ˌriːəˈlaɪnmənt/ *n* [C,U] **1** a change in the exchange rate, especially between currencies that are fixed in relation to each other: *a realignment of sterling within the EMS*

2 a change in the way that a company is organized: *The corporate realignment involved moving senior managers to the company headquarters in Santa Monica.*

real income —see under INCOME

reality software —see under SOFTWARE

rea•liz•a•ble also **realisable** *BrE* /ˈrɪəlaɪzəbəl/ *adj* **realizable assets/investments** assets or investments that can be sold quickly to provide money that is needed: *BCCI had realizable assets of only $1.16 billion against liabilities of $10.64 billion.* —see also ***net realizable value*** under VALUE[1]

rea•li•za•tion also **realisation** *BrE* /ˌrɪəlaɪˈzeɪʃən‖-lə-/ *n* [singular, U] the act of changing something into money by selling it: *The sale will result in the realization of over £325 million.*

realization concept also **realisation concept** *BrE* — *n* [singular] ACCOUNTING the principle that a profit is made at the time when goods are actually given to the customer, not when the customer orders the goods or pays for them

rea•lize also **realise** *BrE* /ˈrɪəlaɪz/ *v* [T] **1 realize money/profits etc** to make money from something: *He estimated they could realize $115 million on the sale before taxes.* | *The company was able to realize a 35% increase in operating profit.*

2 realize a gain/loss to sell something that has increased in value or lost value: *People rushed to realize gains because the capital gains tax rate was about to rise to 28% the following year.* | *The bank will realize losses from sales of certain parts of its investment portfolio.*

3 realize assets to sell assets that you own in order to make money: *They have three years to realize the firm's assets and pay back as much of the debt as possible.*

4 realize an ambition/a goal etc to achieve something that you were hoping to achieve: *She realized a lifelong ambition to fly a plane.*

real ledger —see under LEDGER

real property *n* [U] another name for REAL ESTATE

real-time *adj* COMPUTING a real-time computer system deals with information as fast as it receives it, so that it can produce information about changes as soon as they happen: *Telerate Inc. supplies real-time financial information.* —**real time** *n* [U] *Airline booking systems need to work in real time.*

Real•tor /ˈrɪəltə, -tɔː‖-tər, -tɔːr/ *n* [C] *AmE trademark* a member of the National Association of Realtors; a person whose job is to sell houses of land for other people; REAL ESTATE AGENT; REAL ESTATE BROKER —see also BOARD OF REALTORS

real•ty /ˈrɪəlti/ *n* [U] *AmE* land or buildings; REAL ESTATE

real wages —see under WAGE

ream /riːm/ *n* [C] **1 reams** [plural] a large amount of writing or information, usually on paper: *She found her boss reading reams of e-mail printouts.*

2 a pack containing 500 pieces of paper

rea•son•a•ble /ˈriːzənəbəl/ *adj* fair and sensible: *Robin Kaplan, who had sued Senoret for non-payment, maintained that its bills were reasonable.* | *The law requires the employer to take 'reasonable' steps to accommodate disability.*

re•bate[1] /ˈriːbeɪt/ *n* [C] **1** an amount of money that is paid back to you when you have paid too much: *a **tax rebate** relating to prior years' tax paid* | *1.6 million tenants claimed a **rent rebate**.* + **on**: *You may get a rebate on your car insurance, if your car is off the road for at least 28 days.*

2 part of the price that is paid back to customers when they buy something + **on**: *Buyers can now get a $2000 rebate on a Ford Festiva.*

re•bate[2] /rɪˈbeɪt‖rɪˈbeɪt, ˈriːbeɪt/ *v* [T] **1** to pay part of the price of something back to customers when they buy it. In some places it can be illegal to do this **rebate sth to sb**: *the agency's practice of rebating to its clients part of the commission it receives from the sale of securities* —**rebating** *n* [U] *Insurance companies say rebating hurts insurers, agents, and ultimately consumers.*

2 to pay an amount of money back to someone when they have paid too much **rebate sth to sb**: *Council members want to rebate half the city's $21 million surplus to taxpayers.*

re•bound /rɪˈbaʊnd/ *v* [I] to increase or grow again after decreasing: *signs that the economy will rebound next year* | *Stock prices rebounded from Wednesday's steep slide.* —**rebound** *n* [C] *He forecasts a strong rebound in oil prices.*

re•brand /ˌriːˈbrænd/ also **re-brand** *v* [T] MARKETING if a company rebrands a product or service, it tries to change the way that people think about it, often by changing its name or the way it is advertised: *The agreement will allow Hilton Hotels to rebrand Sheraton hotels outside the US as Hiltons.* —**rebranding** *n* [singular, U] *Cowie said the rebranding would unite its 140 existing brands.*

re•but /rɪˈbʌt/ *v* past tense and past participle **rebutted** present participle **rebutting** [T] *formal* to prove that a statement or a charge made against you is false: *This clause could be used to rebut the suggestion made by the landlord's insurers.* —**rebuttal** *n* [C] *a point-by-point rebuttal of the accusations*

re•call /rɪˈkɔːl‖-ˈkɒːl/ *v* [T] **1** if a company recalls one of its products, it asks customers to return it because there may be something wrong with it: *Source Perrier S.A. was forced to recall its mineral water after health authorities found traces of benzene.* —**recall** *n* [C] *the recall of 13 million defective radial tyres*

2 to officially tell someone to come back: *The U.S. recalled its ambassador from Haiti in protest.* | *Some 30,000 auto workers were recalled from layoffs.*

3 to remember something that you have seen or heard, such as an advertisement: *Consumers' ability to recall TV commercials has dropped steadily.* —**recall** *n* [U] *Interviewers tested consumers' recall of a selection of advertisements.*

re•cap•i•tal•ize also **recapitalise** *BrE* /riːˌkæpɪtl-aɪz/ *v* [I,T] **1** to increase the amount of capital that a company has: *The nine airlines want $436.1 million in short-term loans to recapitalize the industry and allow them to keep carrying out investments.*

2 to change the way a company's capital is organized, for example by exchanging bonds for shares. This is often done after a company goes bankrupt: *The company has been negotiating with lenders to restructure debt and recapitalize.* —**recapitalization** also **recapitalisation** *BrE n* [C,U] *Shareholders approved a recapitalization plan that will exchange about £4 million of bank debt for newly issued stock.*

re•cap•tion /riːˈkæpʃən/ *n* [U] LAW when goods etc that have been taken by someone are taken back by their owner, either because they were taken illegally or because of certain conditions in a contract: *What financial relief does a hirer get under a consumer hire agreement following the owner's recaption of the goods?*

recd. written abbreviation for RECEIVED

re•cede /rɪˈsiːd/ *v* [I] if prices, interest rates etc recede, they decrease: *Growth was expected to recede throughout the year.* | *The domestic market is receding.*

R

re•ceipt[1] /rɪ'siːt/ *n* **1** [U] the act of receiving something: *The money has to be re-invested within 60 days of receipt, otherwise it will be taxed.* + **of**: *The customer acknowledged receipt of a shipment.* | *a list of those* ***in receipt of*** *receiving unemployment benefits*
2 [C] a written statement showing that you have received money, goods, or services: *Keep all your receipts for work-related expenses.* | *a credit card receipt*
credit receipt [C] *AmE* a document sent to a customer who is owed money, for example because they have returned goods; CREDIT NOTE *BrE*
debit receipt [C] *AmE* a written record showing that a customer owes money, for example because the INVOICE (=document showing the price to be paid) was not correct; DEBIT NOTE *BrE*
delivery receipt ◆ [C] a delivery note that has been signed by the person receiving the goods
◆ [C] *AmE* a document sent by the POST OFFICE, telling someone who has been sent a letter by RECORDED DELIVERY that it has been delivered; DELIVERY CONFIRMATION; ADVICE OF DELIVERY *BrE*
deposit receipt also **deposit slip** [C] a document showing an amount of money that has been put into a bank account: *Desperate savers pressed against the windows waving deposit slips.*
dock receipt [C] a document giving details of goods left at a port for loading
trust receipt [C] BANKING a document given to a bank by an importer who has accepted a delivery of goods, but who cannot pay for them until they are sold. The bank pays for the goods and, by giving the bank a trust receipt, the importer promises to pay it back when it has sold the goods
warehouse receipt [C] a list of all the goods that are stored in a warehouse. It can be sold to someone, who then legally owns all the items on the list: *The company was prosecuted after it issued warehouse receipts for tanks of oil that turned out to be mostly water.*
3 receipts [plural] money that has been received: *Export receipts in January totalled £626 million.*
gross receipts [plural] the profit from a deal, activity etc before costs such as tax are taken away: *Dustin Hoffman is said to be receiving $7 million, plus as much as 25% of gross receipts from the film.*
net receipts [plural] the profit from a deal, activity etc after taking away certain costs such as tax: *Each company will share equally in net receipts from the new TV shows.*

receipt[2] *v* [T] to write 'paid' and the date on a bill or invoice and sign it: *One copy of the notice is receipted and returned to you.* | *a receipted hotel bill*

re•ceiv•a•ble /rɪ'siːvəbəl/ *adj* [only after noun] **1** due to be received: *Pretax profit including net interest receivable was up 42%.*
2 accounts receivable *especially AmE* ACCOUNTING money owed to a business by its clients and shown in its accounts as an asset; RECEIVABLES; DEBTORS *BrE*: *Xyvision had more than $10 million in cash and $10 million in accounts receivable.*
3 note receivable ACCOUNTING a note relating to money that a company is owed: *Prime said the estimated adjustments are for write-downs on the carrying value of its assets – primarily notes receivable.* —see also ***bills receivable*** under BILL OF EXCHANGE

re•ceiv•a•bles /rɪ'siːvəbəlz/ *n* [plural] amounts of money due to be paid to a company; ACCOUNTS RECEIVABLE: *The company recently collected more than £30 million in overdue foreign receivables.*

re•ceiv•er /rɪ'siːvə‖-ər/ *n* [C] **1** also **official receiver** *BrE* someone who is chosen by a court to be in charge of a business or property for someone else. This is done when a business is bankrupt, when a PARTNERSHIP ends, or when people disagree about who owns something: *A 1.5 billion franc bid for the bankrupt supermarket company was accepted by the receiver.* | *The company is now* ***in the hands of the receivers.***
2 someone who buys and sells stolen property: *a known receiver of stolen goods*

re•ceiv•er•ship /rɪ'siːvəʃɪp‖-vər-/ *n* [U] when a business is put under the control of a receiver, especially because it is bankrupt: *The company is owed for parts supplied before Leyland Daf* ***went into receivership.*** | *The business is now threatened with receivership.*

receiving office —see under OFFICE

receiving order —see under ORDER[1]

re•cep•tion /rɪ'sepʃən/ *n* **1** [U] the desk or office where visitors who arrive in a hotel or large organization go first: *Please leave your key at the* ***reception desk.***
2 [U] the area around or in front of a reception desk or office: *I'll meet you in reception in half an hour.*
3 [C] a large formal party to celebrate an event or to welcome someone: *a champagne reception to launch his new book*

re•ces•sion /rɪ'seʃən/ *n* [C,U] a period of time when an economy or industry is doing badly, and business activity and employment decrease. Many economists consider that there is a recession when industrial production decreases for six months in a row: *The economy is heading into a recession.* | *Analysts concluded that the US would get out of recession and interest rates would rise.* —compare DEPRESSION
double-dip recession a recession in which the economy begins to grow after a recession but then falls into a second recession before growing again

re•cip•i•ent /rɪ'sɪpiənt/ *n* [C] *formal* someone who receives something: *The international money orders can be cashed by the recipient at any Amex travel office.* | *The scheme is placing more than 300* ***welfare recipients*** *a year in jobs.*

re•cip•ro•cal /rɪ'sɪprəkəl/ *adj* a reciprocal arrangement or relationship is one in which two people, countries etc do or give the same things to each other, usually so that each is helped in some way

re•ci•pro•ci•ty /ˌresɪ'prɒsɪti‖-'prɑː-/ *n* [U] **1** when two people, countries etc agree to give each other similar kinds of help or the same rights: *Because of reciprocity between Germany and the US, Mr Bauer's license will be valid.*
2 agreement between two countries to charge low rates of tax on imports of each other's goods: *legislation that calls for sanctions against nations that don't provide reciprocity to US companies*

reck•less /'rekləs/ *adj* not thinking or caring about the possible bad or dangerous results of your actions. In some cases someone's actions may be illegal if a court decides they have been reckless: *He was fined £80 for* ***reckless driving.*** | *The firm's failure to detect* ***reckless trading*** *led to a $450 million trading loss.*

reck•on /'rekən/ *v* [T] **1** to guess a number or amount that you know something about but have not calculated exactly **reckon sth to be sth**: *The deal is reckoned to be worth over $1.3 billion.*
2 *formal* to calculate an amount: *The time in which the proceedings for the recovery of money may take place is reckoned from the date of the demand.*

re•claim /rɪ'kleɪm/ *v* [T] **1** to get back something that has been taken from you, or to officially ask for something to be given back to you: *If a delivery date is not met, the buyer can reject the goods and reclaim any money paid.* | *Tax deducted on the dividends can be reclaimed.*
2 to make an area of very wet or very dry land suitable for building or farming: *The drainage canal is designed to reclaim 1.5 million square kilometres of salt marsh.* | *The new airport is to be located on reclaimed land.*
3 to obtain useful products from waste material: *The*

R

new recycling plant can reclaim 27,000 tons a year of discarded plastic. —**reclamation** *n* [U] *land reclamation* | *recycling and reclamation*

reclaimed fund —see under LAND[1]

rec·og·ni·tion /ˌrekəgˈnɪʃən/ *n* [U] **1** MARKETING when people know who a person is or what something is, or know something about them as soon as they see them or hear their name: *Nintendo is up there with Coca-Cola and Xerox in* ***name recognition***. | *Working with Avis Inc. we are able to take advantage of their* ***brand recognition***.
2 when a machine can recognize something
magnetic ink character recognition abbreviation **MICR** a system that recognises printed letters, for example on a cheque or official document
optical character recognition abbreviation **OCR** a computer system for automatically recognizing letters and numbers that have been printed or written by hand on paper
voice recognition a system in which a computer understands and obeys instructions spoken by a human voice: *Many phone operators will be replaced by voice recognition technology that responds to a caller's verbal prompts.*

re·cog·ni·zance also **recognisance** /rɪˈkɒgnɪzəns‖-ˈkɑːg-/ *n* [C] LAW a promise that someone makes in a court of law. If they do not keep this promise, they have to pay money to the court: *The two men were released* ***on their own recognizance*** (=after they had promised to return) *to appear in court next month.*

rec·og·nize also **recognise** *BrE* /ˈrekəgnaɪz, ˈrekən-/ *v* [T] **1** to know who a person is or what something is, or to know something about them as soon as you see them or hear their name: *How will investors recognize the bottom of the market when it comes?*
2 to accept officially that an organization, government etc has legal or official authority: *The US has not recognised the Cuban government since 1961.*
3 to accept and admit that something is true: *The plan simply fails to recognize the difficulty and the time required to increase production.*
4 ACCOUNTING to show something at a particular amount, in a particular way etc in a company's accounts: *Perini said it will recognize a pretax gain of about $23 million, or $6 a share, from the sale of the subsidiary.*

rec·om·mend /ˌrekəˈmend/ *v* [T] **1** to advise someone to do something, especially because you have special knowledge of a situation or subject: *Most brokers are recommending that investors take some cash out of money funds.*
2 to praise something or someone, or suggest them for a particular purpose: *Can you recommend a good lawyer?* **recommend sb for**: *I would recommend Mr Bryant for the position of Assistant Manager.*

rec·om·men·da·tion /ˌrekəmenˈdeɪʃən/ *n* [C,U] **1** official advice given to someone about what to do: *His office will review the proposal and* ***make a recommendation*** *to the commission.* | *The plant was closed* ***on the recommendation of*** *regulators.*
2 a suggestion that someone should choose a particular thing or person that you think is very good or suitable: *He was offered the job* ***on Johnson's recommendation***.

recommended retail price —see under PRICE[1]

rec·om·pense[1] /ˈrekəmpens/ *v* [T] **1** to give someone a payment for trouble or losses that you have caused them: *The dividend was increased to recompense the company's shareholders, who had endured considerable financial uncertainty.* **recompense sb for sth**: *The service charge recompenses the bank for the costs involved in exchanging cheques with other banks.*
2 to give someone a payment or a reward for doing something: *It is important that authors should be properly recompensed.*

recompense[2] *n* [singular, U] a payment given to someone because they have done something for you or you have caused them trouble or losses + **for**: *We don't think £200 is proper recompense for the use of our name.* | *Substantial damages were paid* ***in recompense***.

rec·on·cile /ˈrekənsaɪl/ *v* [T] to make two accounts or statements agree or add up to the same total: *This hurried attempt to reconcile the books was a mistake.*

reconciliation statement —see under STATEMENT

re·con·struct /ˌriːkənˈstrʌkt/ *v* [I,T] to build something again or repair it after it has been destroyed or damaged: *Iran's $120 billion plan to reconstruct its economy, shattered by eight years of war*

re·con·struc·tion /ˌriːkənˈstrʌkʃən/ *n* **1** [U] the work that is done after a war or other event such as an EARTHQUAKE, to repair the damage that was caused to buildings, industry etc: *contracts won by British firms in the reconstruction of Kuwait*
2 [C,U] FINANCE when a company changes the way its capital is organized, usually because of financial difficulties. This may be done, for example, by joining with another company or by forming a new company: *Garuda Indonesia will not invest in any reconstruction of failed Australian domestic airline Compass Holdings Ltd.* —see also EUROPEAN BANK FOR RECONSTRUCTION AND DEVELOPMENT, INTERNATIONAL BANK FOR RECONSTRUCTION AND DEVELOPMENT

rec·ord[1] /ˈrekɔːd‖-ərd/ *n* **1** [C] a piece of information that is written down or stored on computer, film etc so that it can be looked at in the future: *The exchange checked its employment records but found no trace of the individual involved.* + **of**: *There's no record of what was said at any private meetings between Weaver and Landis.*
2 on record written down or stored in a record: *The Italian market had one of its most depressing years on record* (=that has ever been recorded).
3 [C] the best or highest level that has ever been reached: *Total volume of new US stock and bond issues hit $587 billion, more than double the previous record.*
4 [singular] the known facts about the past behaviour and success of a person or company: *The company had a solid record of sales growth for several years.* | *Mr. Clifford strongly defended his record at First American.* | *Mr Shute has had an impressive* ***track record*** (=record) *with BM.*

record[2] *adj* **a record high/low/amount etc** the highest, lowest etc amount or level that has ever been recorded: *The Dow Jones Industrial Average was left at a record high.* | *Corporations issued a record $200 billion in bonds.* —see also STOCK OF RECORD, STOCKHOLDER OF RECORD, TRACK RECORD

re·cord[3] /rɪˈkɔːd‖-ˈkɔːrd/ *v* **1** to write information down or store it in a computer etc so that it can be looked at in the future: *The $55 million mortgage was never recorded in the County records.* + **that**: *In 1985 it was recorded that the top 6% of the population now received 25% of national income.*
2 record gains/losses/sales etc if a company, share etc records gains or losses of a particular amount, it makes those gains, losses etc: *Shares recorded sharp gains as market worries lessened.*

record-breaking *adj* [only before a noun] higher, faster etc than anything similar ever achieved: *The company announced record-breaking profits.*

record date —see under DATE[1]

recorded delivery —see under DELIVERY

record high —see under HIGH[1]

record-keeping *n* [U] the work involved in storing files, papers, information etc in an office: *The investigation showed that the company lacked internal controls and that its record-keeping was inadequate.*

R

re•coup /rɪˈkuːp/ *v* [T] to get back an amount of money you have lost or spent: *Finance companies have managed to recoup some of the losses they made during the recession.* | *The institute hopes to recoup its investment through a 5% royalty.*

re•course /rɪˈkɔːs‖ˈriːkɔːrs/ *n* [U] **1** something that you can use to help you in a difficult situation: *Partnership holders often find they* ***have little recourse*** (=not much can be done to help them) *when the value of their investment plummets.* | *Individuals should* ***have recourse to*** *the same bankruptcy-law protection as businesses.*
2 the right of someone who has made a loan to take assets belonging to the borrower if the loan is not repaid, in addition to the asset on which the loan is SECURED: *The finance company will often require the dealer to enter into a recourse agreement.* | *Pertamina plans to obtain financing on a* ***non-recourse basis****, meaning the lenders won't have the rights to seize assets if the loans aren't paid.*
3 the right of someone who holds a BILL OF EXCHANGE that is not paid when it becomes due to claim payment from people who have signed the bill, unless the words 'without recourse' have been written next to the signatures

re•cov•er /rɪˈkʌvə‖-ər/ *v* **1** [I] to increase or improve after falling in value or getting worse: *Lonrho shares plunged at the start of trading, but recovered to close only slightly down.*
2 [T] to get back money that you have spent or lost: *The firm sued Mr Yasutomi and has recovered about one-third of its loss.*
3 [T] to get back something that was stolen, lost, or almost destroyed: *The FBI recovered over 100 stolen items from his apartment.*
4 recover damages/costs LAW to be paid money by order of a court of law: *She failed to recover damages since she had not informed the hairdresser of her allergy.*
5 [T] if someone recovers oil, gold etc, they take it from under the ground or sea: *They plan to recover 35 million barrels of oil from the two fields over six years.*

re•cov•er•a•ble /rɪˈkʌvərəbəl/ *adj* **1** if something such as money is recoverable, you can get it back after it has been lost or spent: *Some of the funds may be recoverable, or their loss may be covered by insurance.*
2 LAW if damages or costs are recoverable, a court can order them to be paid to someone: *In this case punitive damages are recoverable.*
3 recoverable oil, gold etc can be taken from under the ground or sea: *There might be as much as a billion barrels of recoverable oil in their Yemeni field.*

re•cov•er•y /rɪˈkʌvəri/ *n* plural **recoveries** **1** [C,U] when prices increase or the economy grows again after a difficult period of time: *Share prices staged a slight recovery yesterday.* | *Hopes for an* ***economic recovery*** *evaporated.*
2 [U] when you get something back, such as money that you are owed: *Masco Industries said it will pursue recovery of its investment.*
bad debt recovery [U] ACCOUNTING payment of debts that had been considered unlikely to be paid, or forcing someone, for example in a court of law, to pay a debt they should already have paid: *Italian banks have been handicapped by the extremely slow legal process for bad debt recovery.*
3 [U] ACCOUNTING when you gradually get back an amount of money that you have spent on an asset by paying less tax. This reduction in tax is allowed to make up for DEPRECIATION (=the asset's loss of value over time)
4 [U] INSURANCE anything that an insurance company is able to get back that reduces the total amount of a loss, such as damaged property, stolen goods that are found by the police etc

recovery period —see under PERIOD

re•cruit¹ /rɪˈkruːt/ *v* [I,T] to find new people to work for an organization, do a job etc: *So far, they have recruited 10 new sales representatives.* | *He was recruited by the new chairman to increase production.* | *It is difficult to recruit in this industry.*

recruit² *n* [C] someone who has recently joined a company or organization: *a* ***new recruit***

re•crui•ter /rɪˈkruːtə‖-ər/ *n* [C] **1** someone who helps companies and organizations to find new people to work for them: *Advertising recruiter Judy Cunningham used to receive a lot of job orders involving freelance work.*
2 someone in a company who is involved in recruiting new employees: *interviewers and recruiters for major companies*

re•cruit•ment /rɪˈkruːtmənt/ *n* **1** [U] the process or the business of recruiting new people: *Recruitment is difficult at the moment.* | *the recruitment of new sales people*
graduate recruitment [U] *BrE* when large companies offer jobs each year to a certain number of university GRADUATES: *Ernst and Young has cut its annual graduate recruitment over the last two years.*
2 [C] an occasion when someone is recruited: *They are engaged on a temporary basis until permanent recruitments can be made.*

recruitment agency —see under AGENCY

recruitment firm *n* [C] another name for RECRUITMENT AGENCY

rec•ti•fy /ˈrektɪfaɪ/ *v* past tense and past participle **rectified** [T] to correct something that is wrong: *We apologise for the delay and are doing everything we can to rectify the situation.*

rec•to /ˈrektəʊ‖-toʊ/ *n* [C] **1** the page on the right-hand side of a book: *The verso always carries the even page number and the recto the odd number.*
2 the front of a document —opposite VERSO

re•cu•pe•rate /rɪˈkjuːpəreɪt, -ˈkuː-/ *v* **1** [I] to increase or improve after falling in value or getting worse: *International bond markets continued to recuperate after Monday's severe losses.*
2 [T] to get back money that you have lost or spent: *He hopes to recuperate at least part of the FF30 million.*

re•cy•cle /ˌriːˈsaɪkəl/ *v* [I,T] to put used objects or materials through a special process, so that they can be used again: *We recycle all our cans and bottles.* | *Environmentalists have attacked the material because it doesn't recycle as well as steel.* —**recyclable** *adj*: *recyclable materials* —**recycled** *adj*: *recycled paper* —**recycling** *n* [U] *a metals recycling plant.*

red /red/ *n* **be in the red** to owe more money than you have, or to make a loss in a particular period of time: *Analysts expect the company will be in the red for the full year.* | *A long recession could drive the fund $5 billion into the red.* —compare ***in the black*** under BLACK³

red chip —see under CHIP

red chip share —see under SHARE

red chip stock —see under STOCK¹

re•deem /rɪˈdiːm/ *v* [T] **1** to pay off a loan or debt: *He intends to* ***redeem*** *the* ***mortgage*** *at the earliest opportunity.* | *When do you expect to* ***redeem*** *this* ***debt****?*
2 to exchange shares, bonds etc for cash: *A company will not normally be allowed to* ***redeem*** *its* ***shares*** *during the offer period if its board believes that a takeover offer is imminent.* —**redeemable** *adj*: *The 12% unsecured loan stock is redeemable at par on 31 May 2010.*

redeemable share —see under SHARE

redeemable stock —see under STOCK¹

re•demp•tion /rɪˈdempʃən/ *n* [C,U] FINANCE **1** an occasion when shares, bonds etc are exchanged for cash from the organization that sold them and made them

available: *The table sets out the amount payable* ***on redemption.*** | *the redemption value of a security* | *Analysts expect another large volume of* ***early redemptions****, of municipal bonds issued when interest rates were much higher than they are now.*
2 the act of paying off a loan or debt: *the redemption of a mortgage* —see also EQUITY OF REDEMPTION, YIELD TO REDEMPTION

redemption date —see under DATE[1]

redemption yield —see under YIELD[2]

re•de•ploy /ˌriːdɪˈplɔɪ/ *v* [T] **1** to move workers to a different place or job: *Redeployed staff should be given consideration for vacancies occurring within any area of the Group.*
2 to use assets in a different way: *Those planes are to be redeployed into more profitable areas of the company, such as charter activities and international operations* —**redeployment** *n* [C,U] *proposals regarding retraining and redeployment of staff*

re•de•vel•op /ˌriːdɪˈveləp/ *v* [T] to improve an area by removing the buildings that are there and building new ones: *National Westminster Bank is about to apply for planning permission to redevelop a 114-acre site it owns.*

re•de•vel•op•ment /ˌriːdɪˈveləpmənt/ *n* [C,U] when an area is improved by removing the buildings that are there and building new ones: *proposals for inner-city redevelopment*

red-eye *n* [C usually singular] *informal AmE* a night flight

red goods —see under GOODS

red ink *n* [U] *journalism* used to talk about companies in financial difficulty: *The latest financial results from US computer companies are* ***swimming in red ink****, due to a slowdown in US sales.* | *Amsterdam analysts are bracing themselves for a* ***flood of red ink.***

re•di•rect /ˌriːdaɪˈrekt, -dɪ̇-/ *v* [T] **1** to use money, effort etc for a different purpose **redirect sth into/to sth**: *We are redirecting funds to other departments.* | *Management effort needs to be redirected into strategy and decision-making.*
2 *BrE* to send someone's letters to their new address from an address that they have left; FORWARD: *All mail will be redirected to our new offices.*

re•dis•count•ing /riːˈdɪskaʊntɪŋ/ *n* [U] BANKING the act of DISCOUNTING a BILL OF EXCHANGE (=buying it before its normal payment date for less than it will be worth on that date) that has already been discounted once for someone else

re•dis•tri•bu•tion /ˌriːdɪstrɪ̇ˈbjuːʃən/ *n* [U] when a country's wealth and income are shared out more equally among people, especially as a deliberate effect of a government's tax system: *This government is committed to a* ***redistribution of income and wealth.***

redistributive tax —see under TAX[1]

red•lin•ing /ˈredˌlaɪnɪŋ/ *n* [U] *AmE* PROPERTY the practice of refusing to give MORTGAGE loans or insure properties in certain areas because of the race of the people living there: *The Consumers Union sued the state insurance commissioner for not enforcing regulations against redlining.* —**redline** *v* [T] *The banks had redlined the neighborhood, denying loans and forcing the district to go downhill.*

re•draft /ˌriːˈdrɑːft‖-ˈdræft/ *v* [T] to make changes to a letter, report, agreement etc: *We will need to redraft the contract.*

red tape *n* [U] official rules that seem complicated and unnecessary and prevent things from being done quickly and easily: *The only way to get this project off the ground is to* ***cut through the red tape.*** | *Planning permission is* ***tied up in red tape.***

red-top *n* [C] *BrE* a popular newspaper with a large number of readers

re•duce /rɪˈdjuːs‖rɪˈduːs/ *v* [T] to make something less or smaller in price, amount, or size: *Jobs have been cut in order to* ***reduce costs.*** | ***Prices*** *have been* ***reduced*** *by 20%.* | *All these calculators have been reduced (from £30) to £10.* —**reduced** *adj*: *Sales have been hit by* ***reduced demand.***

reducing balance method *n* [singular] ACCOUNTING a method of calculating the DEPRECIATION of an asset, in which the value of the asset is reduced by the same percentage each year and the amount is charged to the PROFIT AND LOSS ACCOUNT

re•duc•tion /rɪˈdʌkʃən/ *n* **1** [C,U] when prices, costs etc become lower or are made lower: *Our winter sale includes many* ***price reductions.*** | *We can* ***make a reduction*** (=sell something more cheaply) *if you buy in bulk.* | *a reduction of 40%* + **in**: *a 1% reduction in interest rates* | *the reduction in VAT from 22% to 18.6%*
2 [C] the amount by which something is reduced in price: *They are selling their computers at a huge reduction.*

re•dun•dan•cy /rɪˈdʌndənsi/ *n* plural **redundancies** [C,U] *especially BrE* when someone loses their job in a company because the job is no longer needed: *Over 2000 car workers now* ***face redundancy.*** | *Several members of staff have taken* ***voluntary redundancy*** (=they have agreed to be made redundant, usually in return for a cash payment). | *a generous* ***redundancy package*** (=all the payments and other benefits that someone receives from their company when they are made redundant) | *The closure of the export department resulted in over 100 staff redundancies.* | *Because of low export sales, Jaguar was forced to* ***make 700 redundancies.***

re•dun•dant /rɪˈdʌndənt/ *adj especially BrE* if you are made redundant, you lose your job because your employer no longer has a job for you: *The bank expects to make 15,000 staff redundant over the next three years.*

re•en•gi•neer /ˌriːendʒɪ̇ˈnɪə‖-ˈnɪr/ also **re-engineer** *v* **1** [T] to improve the design of a product: *The components were re-engineered to fit with less variation from one engine to another.*
2 [I,T] to change the structure of an activity, organization etc so that it performs better: *Businesses continue to re-engineer and lose administrative staff.* | *American Express said it was re-engineering its global electronic system for processing credit-card transactions.* —**re-engineering** *n* [U] *the current reengineering of business processes occurring at many firms* —see also BUSINESS PROCESS RE-ENGINEERING

re-examination —see under EXAMINATION

re-exports *n* [plural] goods that have been imported into a country and are then exported without being changed at all: *Nearly 58% of Hong Kong's total exports consisted of re-exports from China.*

ref /ref/ written abbreviation for REFERENCE: *your ref 4122*

re•fer /rɪˈfɜː‖-ɜːr/ *v* past tense and past participle **referred** present participle **referring**
refer to *phr v* [T] **1 refer to sth** to mention or be about something: *I refer to your letter of 22 March.* | *These figures refer to first quarter sales.*
2 refer to drawer written abbreviation **R/D** BANKING the words 'refer to drawer' are written on a cheque by a bank when the bank refuses to pay the cheque, usually because there is not enough money in the account
3 refer sth to sb/sth to send a problem to another place so that a decision can be made: *The merger is likely to be referred to the Monopolies and Mergers Commission.* | *Disputes can be referred to arbitration.*

ref•er•ee /ˌrefəˈriː/ *n* [C] **1** *BrE* a person who provides information about your character, abilities, or qualifications when you are trying to get a job: *Applications should be in the form of a CV, to include the names of three referees.* | *His former manager agreed to* ***act as his referee.***

2 BANKING a person or organization named on a BILL OF EXCHANGE as a 'referee in case of need' and from whom the person holding the bill may demand payment if the bill is not paid or accepted

ref·er·ence /ˈrefərəns/ *n* [C] **1 with reference to** *formal* used to say what you are writing or talking about, especially in business letters: *With reference to your recent advertisement, I am writing to apply for the post of sales manager.*

2 also **reference number**, abbreviation **ref** a group of numbers and letters that identify a document or letter. A reference is often put at the top of a business letter: *Thank you for your letter (reference JC/216).* | *Please quote the reference number above in all correspondence.*

3 a letter written by someone who knows you well, usually to a new employer, giving information about your character, abilities, or qualifications: *We will be* ***taking up*** (=getting) ***references*** *from your former employers.* | *No employee can insist upon being* ***given a reference*** *when he leaves a job.*

4 a person who provides information about your character, abilities, or qualifications when you are trying to get a job: *Could I ask you to act as one of my references?*

5 a report giving information on a company's business reputation and financial situation: ***Bank references*** *are sought by companies to ensure that those with whom they are trading are solvent and can pay for the goods supplied to them.* | *We always ask for* ***trade references*** (=from members of the customer's own trade) *from our customers.*

banker's reference also **banker's enquiry** a statement given by a bank about the financial position of a business, given to another business, for example a supplier, who wants to decide whether or not to allow the business credit

6 terms of reference [plural] the agreed limits of what an official committee or report has been asked to deal with: *The matter of compensation is not within the committee's terms of reference.*

R

re·fi·nance /ˌriːˈfaɪnæns, -fɪˈnæns/ *v* [T] FINANCE to replace one loan with another one, usually at a lower rate of interest: *Many fixed-rate mortgages are now being refinanced at interest rates of around 8%.* —**refinancing** *n* [C,U] *The troubled DIY group has been in talks with its bankers* ***arranging a refinancing*** *of the £553 million loan taken out at the time of the management buy-out.*

re·fit /ˌriːˈfɪt/ *v* past tense and past participle **refitted** present participle **refitting** [T] to put a shop, factory etc in good condition by doing repairs and adding new equipment: *We refitted the plant last year.* —**refit** /ˈriːfɪt/ *n* [C] *The factory has undergone a complete refit.*

re·flate /riːˈfleɪt/ *v* [I,T] FINANCE if a government reflates the economy, it increases government spending, reduces interest rates etc in order to increase demand and encourage economic activity: *measures to reflate the economy* | *The Chancellor was unwilling to reflate, fearing inflation.* —compare DEFLATE —**reflation** *n* [U] *Governments can play a positive role in stimulating demand through reflation of the economy.* —**reflationary** *adj*: *reflationary measures*

re·form¹ /rɪˈfɔːm‖-ɔːrm/ *v* [T] to change a system, law, organization etc so that it operates in a fairer or more effective way: *The government has announced its plans to reform the tax system.* —**reformer** *n* [C] *The reformers will have to keep public support on their side if their bold economic experiments are to succeed.*

reform² *n* [C,U] a change made to a system, law, organization etc so that it operates in a fairer or more effective way: *radical reforms of the company taxation system* | *There is an urgent need for* ***economic reform.***

refresher course —see under COURSE

re·fund¹ /ˈriːfʌnd/ *n* [C] a sum of money that is given back to you: *If the goods are faulty in any way you will be entitled to a* ***full refund.*** | *We don't* ***give refunds.*** | *You can expect to receive a* ***tax refund*** *of £4000.*

re·fund² /rɪˈfʌnd/ *v* [T] to give someone their money back, for example because they are not satisfied with the goods or services they have paid for: *We guarantee to refund your money if you are not entirely satisfied.* | *Postal costs will be* ***refunded in full.*** | *I enclose a cheque refunding the difference.*

re·fund·a·ble /rɪˈfʌndəbəl/ *adj* if a charge, deposit etc is refundable, it can be paid back: *You are required to pay a* ***refundable deposit*** *of £100 when booking.*

re·fund·ing /riːˈfʌndɪŋ/ *n* [C,U] FINANCE the act of replacing one loan with another one, usually at a lower rate of interest; REFINANCING

re·fus·al /rɪˈfjuːzəl/ *n* [U] **give/offer someone first refusal** to let someone be the first to decide whether they want to buy something you are selling before you offer it to other people: *If you ever sell the business I'd like to be offered first refusal.*

reg. written abbreviation for REGISTRATION; REGISTERED

re·gain /rɪˈgeɪn/ *v* [T] **regain (lost) ground** to start to be more successful again after a difficult period of time: *The dollar regained some of its lost ground today.* | *He stressed that the company was on budget and was confident of regaining lost ground thanks to new product promotions.*

regd. written abbreviation for REGISTERED

re·gion /ˈriːdʒən/ *n* **1** [C] a fairly large area of a country or of the world: *The north-east region has been suffering high employment.* | *There are already over 200 people teleworking in the region.* | *the unequal availability of venture capital between regions*

2 in the region of used to describe an amount of money etc without being exact: *Their annual sales are somewhere in the region of £300 million.*

re·gion·al /ˈriːdʒənəl/ *adj* connected with a particular region: *one of the largest regional building societies in the UK* | *a tour of the regional offices* | *regional transport services*

regional aid —see under AID

regional airport —see under AIRPORT

Regional Stock Exchange *n* FINANCE in the US, a national stockmarket that is made up of the US stockmarkets outside New York, including, for example, those in Boston, Chicago, Los Angeles, and Philadelphia

re·gis·ter¹ /ˈredʒəstə‖-ər/ *n* [C] an official list containing the names of all the people, organizations etc of a particular type: *The Compliance unit in the London office* ***maintains*** *a central* ***register*** *of corporate finance engagement letters obtained by the firm.*

charges register also **register of charges** LAW in Britain, a record of all the CHARGES on a company's assets (=the money that it owes on loans for property etc), kept at the company's registered office

companies register also **register of companies** LAW the official list of the companies in a country, with names of their directors, records of their accounts, and any CHARGES on their assets

directors register also **register of directors** LAW, FINANCE in Britain, the official list of the DIRECTORS of a company which must by law be sent to the REGISTRAR OF COMPANIES

Land Charges Register also **Charges Register** PROPERTY LAW in Britain, a record kept by the LAND REGISTRY of the CHARGES on a property such as an unpaid loan, or of any restrictions to the DEEDs of the property

Lloyd's Register also **Lloyd's Register of Shipping** a list, produced every year, which puts all non-military ships into groups according to their type and size and gives other information about them

members register also **register of members** another name for SHARE REGISTER

property register also **Property Register** the property register in Britain, a document in which details are recorded about a property which has been REGISTERED (=entered in an official list) with the LAND REGISTRY

proprietorship register also **Proprietorship Register** the proprietorship register in Britain, a document in which details are recorded about the owner of a property and the price paid for it which has been REGISTERED (=entered in an official list) with the LAND REGISTRY

share register also **shareholders' register, members register** an official list of the shareholders in a company, held at the company's main office

transfer register also **register of transfers** FINANCE a book in which changes in who owns a company's shares are recorded —see also CASH REGISTER

register² *v* [T] **1** to record a name or details about someone or something in an official list: *Transfers of shares will not normally be registered after the close of business on the record date.* **be registered (as)**: *people who are registered as unemployed* **register sb/sth for sth**: *Are you registered for VAT?* **register sb/sth with sth**: *Each of our advisors is registered with Fimbra.* | *A new share issue must be registered with the Securities and Exchange Commission.*

2 to show or record an amount: *Hays Allen registered a 2.7% drop in fee income to £6.8 million for the year to 30 April.* | *Japan was the only industrialized nation to register an increase in the number of patents received per scientist and engineer.*

re·gis·tered /ˈredʒəstəd‖-ərd/ *adj* included in an official register: *The AAPA has 554 registered members and firms.* | *a* ***registered charity*** | *Freight Train is a* ***registered trademark****.*

registered bond —see under BOND

registered company —see under COMPANY

registered design —see under DESIGN¹

registered mail —see under MAIL¹

registered office —see under OFFICE

registered post —see under POST¹

registered proprietor —see under PROPRIETOR

registered security —see under SECURITY

registered share —see under SHARE

registered stock —see under STOCK¹

registered title —see under TITLE

re·gis·trar /ˌredʒəˈstrɑː◂‖ˈredʒəstrɑːr/ *n* [C] the person whose duty is to record changes in the people who own the shares of a company. The registrar is usually someone who works for the company: *The Companies Act provides for registrars to give complete shareholder lists to persons on payment of a fee.*

Registrar of Companies also **Companies' Registrar** *n* plural **registrars of companies** [C usually singular] in Britain, a government official whose job is to keep detailed records about all LIMITED COMPANIES (=those whose owners only have to pay a limited amount if the company gets into debt)

re·gis·tra·tion /ˌredʒəˈstreɪʃən/ *n* [U] **1** the act of recording names and details on an official list: *the registration of a trademark*

2 FINANCE in the US, the process of a company officially informing the SECURITIES AND EXCHANGE COMMISSION that it wishes to sell bonds, shares etc on a financial market, and getting its agreement to do this: *companies registered with the SEC or seeking SEC registration to sell securities to the public*

shelf registration *AmE* FINANCE when shares, bonds etc are REGISTERED by a company but are not ISSUED (=made available) immediately. They can be issued later at times when it is possible to take advantage of market opportunities —see also CERTIFICATE OF REGISTRATION

registration statement —see under STATEMENT

re·gis·try /ˈredʒəstri/ *n* plural **registries** [C] a place where official records are kept and can be examined by members of the public: *the Trade Marks Registry*

companies registry [C usually plural] LAW the official list of the companies in Britain and other countries, with names of their directors, records of their accounts etc: *According to the Hong Kong companies registry, City Horse Trading did not exist.*

land registry [singular] LAW, PROPERTY in Britain and many other countries, a central organization that keeps records of who owns land in different places: *She will apply to the land registry for a copy of the title deeds of the property.*

regression analysis —see under ANALYSIS

regressive tax —see under TAX¹

regs /regz/ *n* **rules and regs** [plural] rules and regulations; all the rules that have to be followed when doing something

reg·u·lar¹ /ˈregjələ‖-ər/ *adj* **1** happening often and at the same time each day, month, year etc: *At least the job guarantees you a* ***regular income****.* | *Payments should be made* ***at regular intervals****, preferably weekly.* | *Make sure you back up the data* ***on a regular basis****.*

2 [only before a noun] *especially AmE* of a normal or standard size or amount: *We offer three sizes: small, regular and large.* | *Save 30% off the regular price.*

3 regular customer/client a customer who always goes to the same shop or uses the same service: *A discount is available to our regular customers.*

4 regular staff/employees people who work for a company for the whole of the working day or week, not for just some of the time: *union fears that casual workers (temporary workers) were replacing regular staff*

regular² *n* [C] *BrE informal* a customer who goes to the same shop etc very often: *She's one of our regulars.*

reg·u·late /ˈregjəleɪt/ *v* [T] to check that an industry, business activity etc is obeying the law, operating fairly etc: *The Personal Investment Authority regulates the selling of ISAs to the public.* | *Many futures exchanges are closely regulated.* | *The City has so far failed to* ***regulate itself*** *effectively.* —compare DEREGULATE

regulated industry —see under INDUSTRY

reg·u·la·tion /ˌregjəˈleɪʃən/ *n* **1** [C] an official rule or order: *The company was found to be in breach of* (=to be breaking) ***health and safety regulations****.* | *Tighter regulations are being introduced to protect the environment from car exhaust emissions.*

building regulation [C usually plural] *BrE* one of a set of rules about how buildings should be built, for safety and appearance: *All structures must* ***comply with*** *obey the current* ***building regulations****.*

2 [singular, U] control over something, especially by rules: *the regulation of public spending* | *City regulation has failed to deal with insider-dealing and market manipulation.* | *There needs to be tighter regulation of advertisements for drugs.*

statutory regulation [U] when a financial market or industry is controlled by a government organization, such as the Securities and Exchange Commission in the US, rather than being allowed to control itself

R

reg·u·la·tor /ˈregjᵊleɪtə‖-ər/ *n* [C] a person or organization who is chosen by the government to be responsible for making sure that an industry or system works legally, and fairly: *Oftel, the official telecommunications regulator*

reg·u·la·to·ry /ˌregjᵊˈleɪtəri‖ˈregjᵊlətɔːri/ *adj* having the purpose of controlling an activity, system or industry, especially by rules: *The industry has set up a number of* ***regulatory bodies****. | Lautro, the* ***regulatory authority*** *for the marketing of life assurance and unit trusts*

regulatory examination —see under EXAMINATION

re·im·burse /ˌriːɪmˈbɜːs‖-ɜːrs/ *v* [T] *formal* to pay money back to someone that they have spent because of their work: *Will your employer reimburse you? | Any* ***expenses*** *will* ***be reimbursed****.* **reimburse sb for sth**: *We will reimburse you for any expenses incurred.* —**reimbursement** *n* [C,U] *the reimbursement of expenses*

re·im·port /ˌriːɪmˈpɔːt‖-ɔːrt/ also **re-import** *v* [T] to import goods back into a country that have previously been exported from the same country: *US firms can gain tariff exemptions for products exported from the USA, processed abroad and reimported to the USA.* —**reimport** /riːˈɪmpɔːt‖-ɔːrt/ *n* [C] *France's right to exclude reimports of books bought cheaply in Spain disappeared with the Single Market.*

rein[1] /reɪn/ *n* [C] **1 keep a tight rein on sth** to control something strictly: *The finance director keeps a tight rein on spending.*

2 take/hand over the reins to take or give someone control over an organization or country: *I only took over the financial reins three weeks before the end of the financial year.*

rein[2] *v*

rein sth ↔ **in** also **rein back** *phr v* [T] to start to control something more strictly and stop it from increasing: *The government is reining in public expenditure. | Surely the Treasury will want to rein back inflation.*

re·in·state /ˌriːɪnˈsteɪt/ *v* [T] **1** to put someone back into a job or position of authority that they had previously been removed from: *His claim of unfair dismissal was upheld and he was later reinstated.* **reinstate sb as sth**: *She was cleared by the investigation and immediately reinstated as Finance Director.*—**reinstatement** *n* [C,U] *The sacked workers are fighting for reinstatement.*

2 to put something back into a document, agreement etc that had previously been taken out: *We agreed to reinstate this clause into the contract.*

3 INSURANCE to bring back into effect an insurance POLICY that has not been in effect for some time, for example because the regular payments for it have not been made —**reinstatement** *n* [U]

re·in·sur·ance /ˌriːɪnˈʃʊərəns‖-ˈʃʊr-/ *n* [U] INSURANCE when an insurance company arranges to share a large insurance risk with other companies. All companies then pay their part of any losses

re·in·sure /ˌriːɪnˈʃʊə‖-ˈʃʊr/ *v* [T] INSURANCE to share the insurance of something between two or more insurance companies, so that there is less risk for each

re·in·sur·er /ˌriːɪnˈʃʊərə‖-ˈʃʊrər/ *n* [C] INSURANCE an insurance company that agrees to share a large insurance risk with another company and to pay part of any loss: *Swiss RE, the world's largest reinsurer*

re·is·sue /ˌriːˈɪʃuː, -ˈɪsjuː‖-ˈɪʃuː/ *v* [T] to make something available again: *They had to reissue their annual report, with a revised financial statement.*

REIT *n* [C] FINANCE real estate investment trust; in the US, a MUTUAL FUND that invests in land and buildings. REITs have special tax advantages for investors: *five shopping centers currently owned and operated by Price Co. REIT*

re·ject[1] /rɪˈdʒekt/ *v* [T] **1** to refuse to accept a request, suggestion, or offer: *The Commerce Department* ***rejected applications*** *for 39 export licenses. | The* ***proposals*** *were* ***rejected*** *by a large majority. | The Bank does not reject applicants for loans without good reason.*

2 HUMAN RESOURCES to refuse to accept someone for a job, course of study etc: *He was rejected for the job because of his age.*

3 to throw away or refuse to accept something that has been made because its quality is not good enough: *A buyer may reject goods which do not conform to the sample.* —**rejection** *n* [C,U] *The miners reversed their earlier rejection of the company proposals. | After the job interview, the company sent her a* ***rejection letter*** *wishing her luck in her search for work.*

re·ject[2] /ˈriːdʒekt/ *n* [C] a product which is not good enough and will be thrown away or sold cheaply: *If the number of rejects exceeds this level, the batch is returned.*

re·jig·ger /riːˈdʒɪgə‖-ər/ *AmE*, **re·jig** /riːˈdʒɪg/ *BrE* — *v* past tense and past participle **rejigged** present participle **rejigging** [T] *informal* to change something to make it more effective: *We rejiggered the accounting system so that the value of equipment is updated automatically. | Many strategists want to radically rejig the whole financial structure.*

re·ju·ve·nate /rɪˈdʒuːvəneɪt/ *v* [T] to make a company, product, market etc successful again, for example by changing it or by introducing something new: *This new engine might rejuvenate Honda's image as a trendsetter. | Even lower rates won't be enough to* ***rejuvenate the economy****.*

re·lapse /rɪˈlæps/ *v* [I] to start to get worse again after things had seemed to improve + **into**: *The U.S., after a brief recovery mid-year, is relapsing into a second slump.* —**relapse** /rɪˈlæps‖ˈriːlæps/ *n* [singular] *Industrial output rose, lessening fears of a relapse.*

re·late /rɪˈleɪt/ *v*

relate to sth *phr v* [T] to be directly connected with something or affected by it: *expenses relating to the company's trading activities | The drop in sales was related to the end of a tax break on new cars.*

re·lat·ed /rɪˈleɪtᵻd/ *adj* directly connected with or affected by something: *Stocks were hit by earnings-related selling. | Robert-Mark Inc. agreed to sell its real estate business and other related assets.*

related company —see under COMPANY

re·la·tions /rɪˈleɪʃənz/ *n* [plural] **1** official connections between countries, companies etc: *Sara Lee and Bic have retained* ***good relations*** *since Sara Lee bought a controlling stake in Bic.* + **with/between**: *a bid to improve* ***diplomatic relations*** *with Beijing | developing* ***economic relations*** *between Romania and the West*

2 FINANCE the way people behave towards each other + **with/between/among**: *We are pleased to resolve the matter on a basis that restores good relations with a valued customer. | Relations between management and Chartwell remain frosty.*

industrial relations also **labour relations** *BrE*, **labor relations** *AmE n* the behaviour of workers and management towards each other: *Bieber's removal will damage Chrysler's labor relations.* —see also PUBLIC RELATIONS

re·la·tion·ship /rɪˈleɪʃənʃɪp/ *n* [C] the way in which people, companies, countries etc that are working together behave towards each other + **with/between/among**: *Fox made the first move by building a sound relationship with cable operator TeleCommunications Inc. | Good personal relationships among office members are important.*

rel·a·tive /ˈrelətɪv/ *adj* having a particular value or quality when compared with similar things: *the* ***relative***

strength of the dollar | *IBM was a relative latecomer to the laptop market.*

re•launch /ˈriːlɔːntʃ‖-lɒːntʃ/ *n* [C] a new effort to sell a product that is already available, often involving a change in advertising, packaging etc: *If the relaunch goes smoothly, sales should increase by at least 5%.* —**relaunch** /riːˈlɔːntʃ‖-ˈlɒːnt/ *v* [T] *Apax Partners aim to relaunch both brands.*

re•lax /rɪˈlæks/ *v* [T] **relax rules/laws/restrictions etc** to make rules etc less strict: *Madrid is* ***relaxing curbs*** *on Spanish banks' lending.* | *Many employers are taking steps toward relaxed dress codes* (=being allowed to dress informally at work).

re•lease[1] /rɪˈliːs/ *v* [T] **1** to make information, figures etc publicly available: *Peugeot is scheduled to release 2000 earnings figures on Wednesday.*
2 to make a new product, especially a film, book, or record, available for people to buy or see: *Intel initially released the i860 XP as a rival to Sun Microsystem chips.* | *The court barred the publisher from releasing the book.*

release[2] *n* **1** [C] an official statement, making information publicly available: *In a joint* ***news release****, the companies said no agreement had been reached.*
press release [C] an official statement giving information to the newspapers, radio, or television: *The company didn't comment on the charges, but will be issuing a press release today.*
2 [C,U] a new product, especially a film, book, or record, or the fact that it is available: *Apple is hoping to keep ahead of the market by bringing out a* ***new release*** *of its operating system.* | *The movie has taken $5.1 million since its release.* | *The film will be* ***on general release*** (=available in most places) *on August 3.*
day release [U] *BrE* HUMAN RESOURCES an arrangement in which a worker is allowed time away from work to go to college: *time off for study on day release*

re•li•a•ble /rɪˈlaɪəbəl/ *adj* someone or something that is reliable can be trusted or depended on: *The system will significantly improve communications and be more reliable than the current equipment.* —**reliability** *n* [U] *The design delivers reliability and performance.*

re•lief /rɪˈliːf/ *n* [U] **1** a feeling of comfort when something difficult, painful etc ends: *Any sign of relief from price pressures will be welcome news for the economy.*
2 money, food, clothes etc given to people who are poor or hungry: *a relief fund for refugees*
3 *AmE* money given by the government to people who are poor, hungry, unemployed etc; BENEFIT *BrE*: *In the future, the system simply won't provide enough relief for low-income people.* | *rising relief spending as unemployment spreads* | *Farmers will receive* ***federal relief*** *for crops damaged by drought.*
4 money or special tax arrangements etc given to countries or companies which owe money or have other problems: *The committee will petition the bankruptcy court for appropriate relief.*
debt relief when poor countries no longer have to pay back loans or interest on loans from foreign governments and banks: *Commonwealth finance ministers backed a debt relief plan for the world's poorest nations.*
double-income tax relief an arrangement between two countries so that someone does not pay tax twice, for example in the country where they work and in the country where they normally live
mortgage relief *BrE* an amount of income that is not taxed because the taxpayer has a loan to buy a house: *Mortgage relief on interest payments to banks is worth some 15% of the gross monthly payments.* —compare MIRAS
rate relief a lower rate of income tax paid for a limited period of time by companies with financial problems: *Delmarva will need additional financing and rate relief.*
taper relief a form of tax relief in Britain on the profit investors make buying and selling shares (=when a share is worth more than it cost). The amount of tax is reduced depending on how long you have owned the share, to allow for the effects of INFLATION (=price increases over time)
tax relief the right not to have to pay tax on part of a sum of money that is earned or received. Sometimes the tax is paid first, and then given back by the authorities: *The Democrats' bill would give tax relief to middle-income individuals.* | *Borrowers can* ***claim tax relief*** *on their pension contributions.*

re•lieve /rɪˈliːv/ *v* [T] to make a difficult or unpleasant situation less severe: *The Japanese parent company is expected to inject capital into Bridgestone to relieve its crushing $3 billion debt.*
relieve sb **of** sth *phr v* [T] **1** to help someone by taking something from them that they find difficult or unpleasant: *MarCor said the transaction will relieve it of $19.4 million in debt.*
2 relieve sb of their job/post etc to take away someone's job because they have done it badly or done something wrong: *Columbia has suspended production of the movie and relieved the director of his job.*

re•lo•cate /ˌriːləʊˈkeɪt‖riːˈloʊkeɪt/ *v* [I,T] if a company or workers relocate or they are relocated, they move to a different place: *Many workers are unwilling to relocate.* **relocate (sth/sb) to**: *Inspiration Resources Corp. plans to relocate its corporate headquarters to Iowa.* —**relocation** *n* [C,U] *Half the workers will be offered relocation, and the remaining jobs will be eliminated.* | *Profits fell 18% following Phibro's restructuring and office relocations.*

re•main•der[1] /rɪˈmeɪndə‖-ər/ *n* **1 the remainder** the part of something left after the other parts have gone or been dealt with: *The company will pay £316 million to the pension fund this year, and the remainder over 30 years.*
2 [C] a book sold cheaply because it has not been successful: *The quantity of remainders has increased greatly in the last decade.*

remainder[2] *v* [T] to sell books cheaply because they have not been successful **be remaindered**: *The original price was £15.50, but it did not sell well and was remaindered at £4.50 a copy.* —**remaindered** *adj* [only before a noun] *American-style methods in retailing remaindered books*

re•mar•ket /riːˈmɑːkɪt‖-ɑːr-/ *v* [T] **1** to sell new or used goods made by other companies: *RD Trading recycles and remarkets computer products.*
2 to sell bonds, shares etc ISSUED (=sold and made available) by borrowers: *Dealers typically compare bids to see who won the issue. The dealer with the highest bid then begins to remarket the securities to investors.* —**remarketer** *n* [C] *IBM said it would reduce its discount to computer remarketers, reducing their profit margins.* —**remarketing** *n* [U] *Shearson acts as remarketing agent for 12 of the Mutual Benefit bond issues.*

rem•e•dy /ˈremɪdi/ *n* plural **remedies** [C] a way of dealing with a problem: *The company will vigorously pursue all* ***legal remedies*** *against anyone interfering with its rights.* | *The loan agreement allows the bank to declare a default and seek remedies.* —**remedy** *v* [T] *The industry tried to remedy some of its financial problems by raising domestic fares 2%.*

REMIC *n* [C] FINANCE real estate mortgage investment conduit; in the US, a type of MORTGAGE-BACKED SECURITY

re•mind•er /rɪˈmaɪndə‖-ər/ *n* [C] a letter telling someone that they have not paid a bill, and must do so: *Prodigy's computers send electronic reminders to members' personal computers.*
final reminder also **final demand** a last request to someone to pay a bill before legal action is taken to make them pay it

R

re•mis•sion /rɪˈmɪʃən/ *n* **1** [C,U] a period of time when the economy, interest rates, or share prices improve, although they are expected to get worse again in the future: *Interest rate futures gave little sign of a remission.*
2 [C] LAW the right not to have to pay money that is owed: *policies for controlling legitimate capital transfers and the remission of dividends*

re•mit[1] /rɪˈmɪt/ *v* past tense and past participle **remitted** present participle **remitting** [T] *BrE formal* **1** to send money somewhere by post: *a ban preventing companies from remitting profits, dividends or capital abroad* **remit sth to**: *Our overseas branches remit a small proportion of their profits to the parent company.*
2 LAW to send a legal case from a high court to a court that deals with less important cases **remit sth to**: *The appeal was remitted to the Employment Tribunal for a fresh hearing.*

re•mit[2] /ˈriːmɪt‖rɪˈmɪt, ˈriːmɪt/ *n* [singular, U] *formal* the area of a particular subject that a group, committee etc has the authority or responsibility for dealing with: *Our remit was to make the newsletter brighter and livelier, to appeal to as many employees as possible.*

re•mit•tance /rɪˈmɪtəns/ *n formal* **1** [C] an amount of money sent somewhere by post or the banking system: *Lower oil prices and improved remittances from overseas workers have eased pressure on foreign reserves.* | *Our Finance Department cannot trace your remittance.*
2 [U] the sending of money by post: *There have been no restrictions on the remittance of profits abroad.*

R

rem•nant /ˈremnənt/ *n* [C usually plural] part of something that is left after most of it has been removed, used, sold etc: *Prospective buyers continued to come forward for the remnants of the Maxwell empire.* | *Carpet-makers often buy remnant batches of the materials.*

re•mort•gage[1] /ˌriːˈmɔːgɪdʒ‖-ɔːr-/ *v* [I,T] *BrE* to borrow money by having a second or bigger MORTGAGE (=loan) on your property, especially a house: *He advised me to remortgage with a lender with a lower interest rate.* | *Millions of homeowners have remortgaged their homes to take advantage of lower interest deals.* —**remortgaging** *n* [U] *There are costs involved in remortgaging which you should weigh up against the savings you will make.*

remortgage[2] *n* [C] *BrE* a second or bigger MORTGAGE on your property, especially a house; HOME EQUITY LOAN *AmE*; SECOND MORTGAGE: *A remortgage is one of the cheapest ways of borrowing money.*

re•mote /rɪˈməʊt‖-ˈmoʊt/ *adj* **1** [only before a noun] remote systems or equipment are used to control a machine, computer system etc from a distance: *All the data is stored on a single computer in New York, with **remote access** from London and Hong Kong.*
2 if a possibility, risk, danger etc is remote, there is only a small chance it will happen: *A 7% cut in production is in the air, although 10% is also a **remote possibility**.* | *The likelihood of the company paying this debt is remote.*

remote working *n* [U] HUMAN RESOURCES when people working for a company work from their homes, using a computer which is connected to the computer system in an office: *What personnel departments did not anticipate were the problems of isolation suffered by people engaged in remote working.*

re•mov•al /rɪˈmuːvəl/ *n* [C,U] **1** the act of taking something away: *the removal by Mexico of barriers to direct U.S. investment*
2 when someone is forced to leave their job or position: *a meeting to consider the removal of a majority of the board* | *These executive removals aren't due to fraud, but simple incompetence.*
3 *BrE* the act of moving from one office, house etc to another: *the removal of its editorial offices to London*
4 removals [plural] *BrE* the business of packing equipment, furniture etc and moving it from one place to another: *The booklet covers buying a property, arranging removals, insurance cover and legal costs.*

re•move /rɪˈmuːv/ *v* [T] **1** to take something away: *We need to consider the trade implications before border controls are removed.* **remove sth from**: *an injunction removing the vote from 80,000 shareholders* | *The committee is recommending that the drug be removed from the market altogether.*
2 to force someone to leave an important job or position: *The new directors intend to meet on Monday to remove the company's chief executive.* | *The governor was **removed from office** following allegations of misconduct.*

re•mu•ne•rate /rɪˈmjuːnəreɪt/ *v* [T] *formal* to pay someone for their work: *The shareholders agree to remunerate the directors with an undisclosed sum.* | *Stockbrokers should not be remunerated on the basis of stocks sold or bought.*

re•mu•ne•ra•tion /rɪˌmjuːnəˈreɪʃən/ *n* [U] *formal* payment for work, especially in the form of a SALARY and additional benefits such as a car: *Employees have agreed to cut back their hours and corresponding remuneration by 6%.* | *We are offering an attractive **remuneration package** including a company car and other benefits.*

remuneration package —see under PACKAGE[1]

re•mu•ne•ra•tive /rɪˈmjuːnərətɪv‖-nəreɪtɪv/ *adj formal* making a lot of money: *Ross takes on the most difficult assignments, but they are also the most remunerative.* | *They are not allowed to hold another remunerative position while teaching at the university.*

ren•der /ˈrendə‖-ər/ *v* [T] *formal* **1** to cause something to change in a particular way: *He was denied building permission for his property, effectively rendering it worthless.* | *In some cases, companies were rendered insolvent when they took on big debts in the buy-outs.*
2 render accounts ACCOUNTING to officially present a company's accounts showing its profits and losses to people who own shares in it or have another interest in seeing the accounts: *The petition claims the company failed to render proper accounts and make timely payments.*
3 render a decision/verdict/judgement etc LAW to officially make a decision, etc about something: *The union hopes the board will render a verdict on the dispute this summer.*
4 services rendered work that has been done, and that is due for payment: *Employees who left were barred from collecting payment for services rendered before they withdrew.*

re•nege /rɪˈniːg, rɪˈneɪg‖rɪˈnɪg, rɪˈniːg/ *v formal* **renege on an agreement/deal/contract etc** to fail to do something you had promised or agreed to do: *Some clients reneged on their agreements to sell when the price climbed.* | *The agency reneged on an out-of-court settlement to pay tradesmen for work on the hotel site.*

re•new /rɪˈnjuː‖rɪˈnuː/ *v* **1** [I,T] to arrange for an existing contract, agreement, deal etc to continue: *Most airlines **renew** their **insurance policies** between July and October.* | *The original contract had a term of three years, with an option to renew for two more.*
2 [T] to begin to do something again, after a period of time: *If oil prices remain high, U.S. industry will renew efforts to conserve energy.* | *McDonald's Corp. is renewing its focus on customer satisfaction.*

re•new•a•ble /rɪˈnjuːəbəl‖rɪˈnuː-/ *adj* **1** renewable materials, energy etc will continue to exist or will grow again and are therefore never used up: *investments in renewable energy projects such as solar power*
2 a contract, agreement, deal etc that is renewable can be continued: *Make sure the policy is annually renewable with reasonable rate increases.* | *renewable lease payments*

re·new·al /rɪˈnjuːəl‖-ˈnuː-/ *n* [C,U] when people agree that a contract, agreement, deal etc will continue: *Gilliam County will get a second chance when the contract* ***comes up for renewal****.* | *The government can deny license renewals if a station doesn't carry adequate programming for children.* | *a six-month* ***renewal option***

inner city renewal also **urban renewal** [U] the process of bringing new jobs, industry, homes etc to the poor areas of large cities: *The new mayor has made urban renewal his priority.*

renewal notice *n* [C] an official document reminding someone that they must make an insurance policy continue for a further period of time. Renewal notices show all the details of the policy, and must be signed and returned: *Your new premium is shown on your renewal notice.*

renewal premium —see under PREMIUM[1]

re·newed /rɪˈnjuːd‖-ˈnuːd/ *adj* [only before a noun] happening or increasing again after a period of time: *The dollar is riding higher on renewed optimism about the U.S. economy.* | *fears of a renewed slump in consumer spending*

ren·o·vate /ˈrenəveɪt/ *v* [T] to repair and improve a building so it is in good condition again: *Mellon Stuart Construction was awarded a $72 million contract to renovate a train terminal.* —**renovation** *n* [C,U] *The hotel chain has spent $700 million on expansion and renovation.* | *The chain will have more funds with which to invest in store renovations and newer computer systems.*

rent[1] /rent/ *v* **1** [I,T] to pay a regular amount of money for the use of something such as a house, office etc: *Arrowhead had been renting for seven years before buying a 13,000-square-foot headquarters.* | *Businesses can rent PCs to alleviate peak workloads.* **rent sth from sb**: *The New York Futures Exchange rents space from the Cotton Exchange.*

2 [T] also **rent** sth ↔ **out** to allow someone to use something in return for payment: *video stores that rent Nintendo games* | *the lucrative business of renting out trailers and trucks* **rent** sth ↔ **(out) to** sb: *A New York dealer rented an Avis car to an unauthorized driver.* | *Many people trying to sell their second homes have decided to rent them out to tourists instead.*

3 [T] *AmE* to pay money for the use of something owned by someone else for a short period of time; HIRE *BrE*: *AT&T will rent the phone to customers at a rate of $30 a day.* | *Travelers prefer to rent cars with low mileage.*

4 [I] if a house, office etc rents at or rents for a particular amount of money, that is how much it costs to use it: *The new units are renting for £350 a month or less.* —**rented** *adj* [only before a noun] *living in* ***rented accommodation***

rent[2] *n* [C,U] PROPERTY money paid for the use of a house, office etc: *Commercial rents have decreased significantly since their peak in 1997.* | *In Florida, there are 41 million square feet of office space* ***for rent****.*

fair rent [C] *BrE* the amount of rent thought to be fair or reasonable for someone to pay to live somewhere. In Britain, if the LANDLORD (=property owner) and TENANT (=person renting) cannot agree on an amount, this can be officially fixed by a RENT OFFICER: *You can apply to the Rent Office to fix a fair rent.*

ground rent [C,U] a sum of money, paid to the person who owns the land on which a rented building stands: *a ground rent of £15 per annum*

net rent [C,U] the amount received by the owner of a rented property after taking off costs such as taxes, insurance, electricity etc: *Her client has signed a 20-year lease yielding $170,000 in net rent a year.*

peppercorn rent [C] a very small amount of money, paid to show that there is an official contract between the owner and the person using a building, piece of land etc: *Croydon Corporation will lease part of the new station to London Transport at a peppercorn rent.*

rack rent [C] an amount of money for renting a house, office etc that is not fixed or controlled by law, but is agreed between the person owning the property and the person renting it. In the US, this expression is used to talk about unfairly high rent charged for a property: *The property was sub-let to tenants at rack rents.*

rent·al /ˈrentl/ *n* **1** [singular] payment made for the use of a car, equipment etc for a period of time: *The first month's rental on every pager is free of charge.*

2 [C,U] the arrangement by which something is rented for a period of time: *expenses such as air fares, hotels, car rental and upkeep* | *The rates for computer rentals drop swiftly as the equipment ages.* | *We have reduced our equipment* ***rental costs*** *by 14%.*

fleet rental [C,U] an arrangement in which a company rents all the cars it uses from the same company at a special rate

rent control —see under CONTROL[1]

rent·er /ˈrentə‖-ər/ *n* [C] *AmE* someone who makes regular payments for the use of a house, car, equipment etc: *Lower mortgage rates are attracting renters into the housing market.*

re·nun·ci·a·tion /rɪˌnʌnsiˈeɪʃən/ *n* [U] FINANCE when an investor returns shares they have been offered to the company offering them: *The share certificate carries a form for renunciation on the reverse.*

re·o·pen /riˈəʊpən‖-ˈoʊpən/ *v* [I,T] **1** if a company, factory, business etc reopens, or someone reopens it, it starts to do business again after being closed: *Heritage's 13 offices will* ***reopen for business*** *today.* | *The stock market reopened on Friday after the six-day holiday.*

2 if discussions or talks reopen, or someone reopens them, they begin again after they had stopped: *The Amalgamated Transit Union is seeking to* ***reopen talks*** *aimed at settling the strike.* | ***Bidding reopens*** *this week for the sale of QVC's assets.*

3 if the police or court of law reopen a legal case, the facts of the case are considered again in order to decide whether the decision that was made was the right one

re·or·der /riˈɔːdə‖-ˈɔːrdər/ *v* [I,T] to order more of a product, usually because there is none left: *Buyers in the clothing trade are reordering the most popular items heavily.* | *Ingram Video initially ordered 80,000 copies, but reordered three times to keep pace with demand.* —**reorder** *n* [C] *Net income fell, as reorders of jewelry were weaker than expected.*

reorder point —see under POINT[1]

re·or·gan·i·za·tion also **reorganisation** *BrE* /riːˌɔːgənaɪˈzeɪʃən‖-ˌɔːrgənə-/ *n* **1** [C,U] a new or different way of arranging the work in a company, organization etc, for example by changing people's jobs or tasks: *the latest in a long string of corporate reorganizations* | *Three new posts were created in the reorganization of Pfizer's business groups.*

2 [U] *AmE* FINANCE the act of officially organizing a company and its finances in a new way because it has become bankrupt: *The company has until 3 March to file a* ***reorganization plan****.* | *They may seek protection from creditors in a* ***Chapter 11*** (=the part of US bankruptcy law dealing with reorganizations) ***reorganization***.

re·or·gan·ize also **reorganise** *BrE* /riːˈɔːgənaɪz‖-ˈɔːr-/ *v* **1** [I,T] if a company reorganizes, or someone reorganizes it, the working arrangements, jobs are arranged in a new or different way: *Management decided to reorganise the business, and 10 offices were closed.* | *It's in our economic interest to focus, reorganize, compete and improve.*

2 [T] to arrange or deal with things in a new and often better way: *Campbell Soup Co. has* ***reorganized*** *its*

R

*global business **operations**. | The cost-cutting program will find various tasks that can be reorganized.*

rep /rep/ *n* [C] *informal* **1** someone employed to sell a company's products or services by meeting customers or talking to them on the phone; REPRESENTATIVE: *We needed more **sales reps** on the road to compete with the big boys. | We rely on our reps to handle each account's day-to-day needs.*

2 someone who speaks officially for a group of people, company etc; REPRESENTATIVE: *He'd had a chat with his union rep and was told not to worry.*

re·pair[1] /rɪˈpeə‖-ˈper/ *v* [T] **1** to fix something that is damaged, broken, or not working properly: *All the cranes were inspected and repaired before federal safety officials arrived.*

2 to try to remove the damage a mistake or wrong action has caused: *Gates is talking with IBM executives about ways to repair the relationship between the companies.*

repair[2] *n* **1** [C,U] the act of fixing something that is damaged, broken, or not working properly: *Mainframe computers typically need repairs after 7,000 hours. | Much of the drilling equipment is **in need of repair**. | Many of the vehicles are **beyond repair*** (=so badly damaged they cannot be repaired). | *The bridge is **under repair*** (=being repaired) *and a 5 mph restriction is in force.*

credit repair [U] *AmE* FINANCE a service offered to people or companies with debts in which a finance company charges for arranging payment of the debts over a period of time: *20 states have enacted legislation to regulate credit repair. | Hundreds of **credit repair clinics** have sprung up in recent years.*

home repair [C,U] *AmE* the activity of making and repairing things yourself, rather than paying someone to do it; DIY *BrE*: *Home Depot has become the largest home-repair chain in the business.*

2 in good/bad/poor etc repair something in good, bad etc repair is in good, bad etc condition: *The equipment was considered to be in sufficiently good repair to be useable.*

repairing lease —see under LEASE[2]

rep·a·ra·tion /ˌrepəˈreɪʃən/ *n* [C,U] *formal* payment made to someone for loss, damage etc that someone has caused them in the past; COMPENSATION: *A commission will gather demands for reparations from companies and individuals. | The company has few resources to finance **reparation payments**.*

re·pat·ri·ate /riːˈpætrieɪt‖riːˈpeɪ-/ *v* [T] to send money, profits etc back to your own country: *Capital gains on investments may be repatriated only once a year. | Japanese companies continue to **repatriate** some overseas **assets**.* —**repatriation** *n* [U] *an increase in foreign investment and capital repatriation*

re·pay /rɪˈpeɪ/ *v* past tense and past participle **repaid** [T] to pay back money that has been borrowed: *The funds will be used to **repay** short-term **debt**.* **repay sb sth**: *Pergament will repay creditors $25 million over 10 months.* —**repayable** *adj* [not before a noun] *The loan is repayable over 12 months.*

re·pay·ment /rɪˈpeɪmənt/ *n* **1** [U] when money that has been borrowed is paid back: *The government is to call for **early repayment** of $1.8 billion of Treasury bonds. | a schedule for **debt repayment***

2 [C] an amount of money that is paid back: *Only two repayments have been made in the last six months.*

repayment mortgage —see under MORTGAGE[1]

repayment risk —see under RISK[1]

repayment supplement —see under SUPPLEMENT[2]

re·peal /rɪˈpiːl/ *v* [T] to officially end a law, rule, restriction etc: *The bill would repeal a 10% luxury tax on yachts and private planes. | Attempts by the producers to have the tariffs repealed have failed.* —**repeal** *n* [C] *The mutual-fund and securities industries strongly back the repeal.*

re·peat[1] /rɪˈpiːt/ *v* [T] to achieve the same results, level of performance etc: *The policy would avoid the risk of repeating the inflationary explosion of the 1970s. | The Honda Accord was the best-selling car last year and may well repeat that success this year.* —**repeated** *adj* [only before a noun] *repeated efforts to boost prices*

repeat[2] *n* [C] an event, situation etc that is very similar to one that has happened before + **of**: *I don't think 2001 will see a repeat of 2000 earnings.*

repeat business *n* [U] if a company gets repeat business, customers return to it to buy more of its products or services: *Cruise lines are hoping the revised routes will attract new passengers as well as bringing repeat business by offering previous customers a new experience.*

repeat order —see under ORDER[1]

re·per·cus·sions /ˌriːpəˈkʌʃənz‖-pər-/ *n* [plural] the bad effects that are the results of an action or event, and which last a long time: *The collapse of the group could have severe **economic repercussions**.*

repetitive strain injury —see under INJURY

re·place /rɪˈpleɪs/ *v* [T] **1** to use one product, piece of equipment, system etc instead of the one currently being used: *The tax replaces a levy of 13.5% on manufactured goods. | Steel and shipbuilding have been replaced by low energy industries.* **replace sth with sth**: *Annual wage increases will be replaced with a bonus system.*

2 to give someone a product instead of one that they bought which was damaged or not perfect: *The shop offered to replace the television for me.*

3 to remove someone from their job, position etc and give the job to a different person: *The executive team was replaced by a Japanese-style management committee.*

re·place·ment /rɪˈpleɪsmənt/ *n* **1** [C] a product, piece of equipment etc that takes the place of the one currently being used: *Johnson & Johnson will produce and market the sugar replacement under a licensing agreement with Tate & Lyle.*

2 [C] someone who takes the place of another person in a job, position etc: *Clark Oil will seek a replacement for its chief finance officer.*

3 [U] when a company gives someone a product instead of one that they bought that was damaged or not perfect: *We provide a services for the replacement of damaged goods.*

replacement cost —see under COST[1]

replacement value —see under VALUE[1]

re·plen·ish /rɪˈplenɪʃ/ *v* [T] *formal* to make something full again by adding new supplies to replace those that have been used: *Manufacturers are scheduling overtime work to replenish low inventories. | Many banks rely on profits from credit cards to help **replenish** their **capital**.*

re·ply[1] /rɪˈplaɪ/ *v* past tense and past participle **replied** [I,T] to answer someone, in writing or in speech **reply that**: *Asked about the bank's operations, the chairman replied that the record speaks for itself.* **reply to**: *Our aim is to reply to all letters within 10 working days.*

reply[2] *n* plural **replies** [C] **1** a written or spoken answer: *The Exchange said it had received a satisfactory reply from the bank. | We await your reply.*

letter of reply plural **letters of reply** a letter answering one that has been received: *I received the standard letter of reply in response to my complaints.*

2 in reply to *formal* a way of starting a letter that answers one that has been received: *In reply to your letter of 24 Jan, I am sorry to hear our product has not met our usual high standards.*

3 reply paid envelope *BrE* an envelope for which the cost of posting has already been paid POSTAGE PAID ENVELOPE; BUSINESS REPLY ENVELOPE *AmE*: *Use the enclosed reply-paid envelope (no stamp needed).*

reply memo also **reply memorandum** *n* [C] a document sent in response to a question or statement in an earlier document

re·po[1] /ˈriːpəʊ‖-poʊ/ *n* [C] FINANCE **1** *informal* an occasion when a lender takes property from a person or company that has borrowed money to buy a house, flat etc, but that they have not paid back; REPOSSESSION: *There are* ***repo bargains*** *among the thousands of properties on the market that have been repossessed by banks.*

2 *informal* an occasion when the holder of particular bonds sells them and agrees to buy them back on a specific date in the future at a fixed price. CENTRAL BANK*s* use repos to control the MONEY SUPPLY (=the amount of money in the economy) by buying back government bonds for specific periods of time; REPO AGREEMENT; REPURCHASE AGREEMENT; SALE AND REPURCHASE AGREEMENT: *Repos are a cheap way of raising money. Because the securities act as collateral, the rate at which money is borrowed is cheaper than for unsecured loans.*

reverse repo an occasion when a borrower returns money to a lender for a specified time and at an agreed price; REVERSE REPURCHASE AGREEMENT; REVERSE SALE AND REPURCHASE AGREEMENT: *To drain cash from the market, a central bank can execute reverse repos: it takes money from commercial banks and gives them government securities as collateral.*

repo[2] *v*

repo sth ↔ **out** *phr v* [T] to sell bonds in a repo: *By repoing out their securities, fund managers can earn revenues equivalent to several percentage points on the value of their portfolio.*

repo man *n* plural **repo men** [C] *informal* someone whose job is repossessing property: *Some repo men have a violent reputation.*

re·port[1] /rɪˈpɔːt‖-ɔːrt/ *n* [C] **1** a written or spoken description of a situation or event: *a favorable first quarter earnings report* | *an interim financial* ***progress report***

auditor's report ACCOUNTING an official document written by an auditor, stating whether the accounts that have been examined have been kept properly and if there is anything the auditor is not happy with: *Some criticisms of the firm's accounting methods were made in the auditor's report.*

Custom-House report a document containing details of the passengers and goods carried on a ship, that is given to the CUSTOMS officials when the ship arrives in a port

directors' report a statement by a company's directors in its annual accounts giving the directors' opinion of the state of the company, and how much should be paid to people owning shares in the company: *If the information in the directors' report is not consistent with the accounts, the auditors must state that fact in their report.*

employment report the part of a company's ANNUAL REPORT that gives details of the company's employees and their rates of pay, the benefits they receive etc

2 a report presented by the directors to the members and shareholders of the company, containing financial information about a company's trading activities and the documents the company must produce by law, namely the BALANCE SHEET, the PROFIT AND LOSS ACCOUNT, and the AUDITORS' AND DIRECTORS' REPORT: *The company's annual report revealed a rise of 3.8% in overall passenger income to £7.2 million.* | *Copies of the Annual Report of the Pensions Ombudsman are available from The Stationery Office.*

law report an official record of legal cases, used to help lawyers decide on a particular course of action: *The law reports contain a number of examples where this behaviour has led to a successful claim.*

market report news about a particular financial market: *The first-quarter bond market report held some encouraging news for the long-suffering junk market.*

3 an official document produced by a group of people, examining a particular subject. People often use the name of the committee producing the report to talk about it: *the Cadbury report on the financial aspects of corporate governance*

4 a newspaper article or part of television or radio programme about a particular situation or event: *The Daily Mirror's report focused on the variation in evidence.*

report[2] *v* **1** [T] if a company reports a profit, loss etc, it announces publicly how much profit etc it has made: *Coors* ***reported second-quarter earnings*** *of $25.1 million.* | *Kolmar is expected to report a 6% increase in sales.*

2 [I,T] to give people information about an event, situation etc: *His remarks were first reported in yesterday's Chicago Tribune.* + **on**: *Head office will report on outgoings each month.* **report that**: *The newspaper reported that the multi-millionaire brothers had a 3% stake in Williams.*

3 [I] to officially state you have arrived in an office, factory etc, usually by signing your name + **to**: *All delivery vehicles please report to the site office.*

report back *phr v* [I] to find out about something as part of your job, and then to tell your employer about it: *She reported back to management with bold restructuring proposals.*

report to sb *phr v* [T] to work under someone's authority, and to be managed by them: *Following his promotion, Mr London will* ***report directly to*** *the Paramount chairman.*

re·port·ing /rɪˈpɔːtɪŋ‖-ɔːr-/ *n* [U] **1** the work of providing an explanation or account of something, especially a company's financial position: *Sundstrand Corp. will accelerate the* ***financial reporting*** *of its Brazilian operation.* | *guidelines on accounting and* ***reporting standards***

financial reporting the financial information that companies give about their activities, and the ways that they prepare and show it: *Financial reporting helps to satisfy the needs of users who cannot obtain information from other sources.*

2 credit reporting business/company/agency etc a company providing financial information about people who apply to borrow money: *Currently, the law allows credit reporting agencies to gather and sell personal financial information.*

reporting lines *n* [plural] the way the people in a company, organization etc are organized, showing which people have authority, who they manage and who is in charge of checking their work: *The creation of new reporting lines eliminated thousands of desk jobs.*

reporting period —see under PERIOD

re·po·si·tion /ˌriːpəˈzɪʃən/ *v* [T] MARKETING if a company repositions a brand, product etc, it tries to get people to think about it in a new and different way in relation to the company's other products and to competing products: *It tried to reposition Safeguard, which has long been viewed as a male soap.* —**repositioning** *n* [C,U] *R.J. Reynolds is talking to advertising agencies about a major repositioning of its Winston cigarette brand.*

re·pos·sess /ˌriːpəˈzes/ *v* [T] to take back goods or property from a person or company that has borrowed money to buy them but has not paid it back: *Creditors are seeking to repossess 10 jets and 62 additional engines.*

re·pos·ses·sion /ˌriːpəˈzeʃən/ *n* [C,U] the act of taking back goods, property etc from someone who does not pay their debts: *The court order allows Mercantile to proceed with the repossession.* | *an increase in* ***car repossessions.***

rep·re·sent /ˌreprɪˈzent/ *v* [T] **1** to speak or go somewhere officially in order to state the views, opinions etc of another person or group of people: *Speaking to publishers representing 1,300 magazines, Mr. Brack called for an industry-wide campaign.* | *Workers hired during the strike are opposed to being represented by the union.* | *A Baltimore law firm will represent Drexcel in the case.*

2 if something represents a proportion of something else, it is equal to it: *The sale represents only 1.6% of Shell's average daily production.* | *Russia represented 85% of the market for Czech exports.*

re-pre-sent /ˌriː prɪˈzent/ *v* [T] to give, offer, or send an official document again: *Cheques that have failed to clear should be re-presented within five days.*

rep•re•sen•ta•tion /ˌreprɪzenˈteɪʃən/ *n* [U] when someone else speaks on your behalf: *The union has expanded its representation among office, hospital and food workers.*

board representation when the heads of particular departments or groups within a company are on the BOARD OF DIRECTORS and so help to influence decisions made about the company: *Board representation for employees is only one of three options we intend considering.*

employee representation HUMAN RESOURCES the system in a company for managers to take into account employees' opinions, wishes etc in managing the company: *Unions are calling for better employee representation.* —see also FALSE REPRESENTATION

rep•re•sen•ta•tive[1] /ˌreprɪˈzentətɪv/ *n* [C] **1** a person who sells a company's products or services by speaking to customers on the phone or travelling to meet them; REP: *The work of a* ***sales representative*** *includes after-sales service.* | *Your local Tupperware representative will be more than happy to lay on a display.*

2 someone chosen to speak or make decisions for another person or group of people: *Make sure your employees' representatives are involved.* | *A stockmarket representative was sceptical of the outcome.*

personal representative *n* LAW someone put in charge of the affairs of a person who has died

representative[2] *adj* like other members of the same group, and therefore showing what they are all like: *Unfortunately, your sample is not statistically representative of the population.* | *the most extensive and representative information currently available on temporary labour*

rep•ri•mand /ˈreprɪ̈mɑːnd‖-mænd/ *n* [C] **1** an occasion when you tell someone officially that they have done something very wrong: *He is likely to receive some kind of reprimand for trying to influence the regulators unfairly.*

2 HUMAN RESOURCES an occasion when an employer officially informs an employee that something they have done is very wrong —**reprimand** *v* [T] *The judge reprimanded the company for having 'abused and manipulated' the bankruptcy process.*

re•print /ˌriːˈprɪnt/ *v* [I,T] if a book, document etc is reprinted, or it reprints, more copies are printed: *the costs of redesigning and reprinting stationery* | *Gollancz is reprinting 20,000 copies with corrections.* —**reprint** /ˈriːprɪnt/ *n* [C] *Book publishing has soared to more than 55,000 new titles and reprints.*

re•pro•cess /riːˈprəʊses‖-ˈprɑː-/ *v* [T] to treat a waste substance so that it is safe or can be used again: *Germany has the capacity to reprocess at most 6,000 tonnes of plastic.* —**reprocessing** *n* [U] *a controversial thermal oxide* ***reprocessing plant***

re•pro•duc•tion /ˌriːprəˈdʌkʃən/ *n* [U] the work of copying documents, books etc or preparing them for printing: *Bulk reproduction is performed by high-speed photocopiers.*

re•pu•di•ate /rɪˈpjuːdieɪt/ *v* [T] LAW to officially state that a contract, agreement, sale etc is no longer effective: *The RTC has the power to repudiate bonds issued or secured by insolvent companies.*

repurchase agreement —see under AGREEMENT

rep•u•ta•ble /ˈrepjətəbəl/ *adj* respected for honesty and good work: *Consumers should buy only from reputable dealers offering unconditional guarantees.*

rep•u•ta•tion /ˌrepjəˈteɪʃən/ *n* [C] the opinion people have of something or someone, based on what has happened in the past: *A lengthy legal battle would* ***damage the reputation*** *of both sides.* | *The firm has a very* ***good reputation*** *and track record in equal opportunities.* + **for/as**: *Warner has a reputation for being a tough negotiator.* | *Chairman Q.T. Wiles has built a reputation as a financial wizard.*

re•quest[1] /rɪˈkwest/ *n* [T] to officially or formally ask for something: *The rate increase was less than Potomac Electric had requested.* | *The state has requested that the companies provide data on lead levels in their products.*

request[2] *n* [C] an official or formal demand for something + **for**: *The fund group received 150,000 requests for its prospectus.* | *Bank officials meet today to consider a request for further credit from the troubled newspaper concern.* | *A free sample copy will be provided* ***on request***.

re•quire /rɪˈkwaɪə‖-ˈkwaɪr/ *v* [T] *formal* **1** to officially demand that people do something, because of a law or rule: *The takeover requires a majority vote by preferred shareholders.* **require sb to do sth**: *the ruling requiring companies to disclose the value of stock* **require that**: *Accounting rules require that corporate financial statements disclose the updated value of assets.*

2 to need something: *At first, CD-ROMs required a special disk drive that costs around $700.*

re•quire•ment /rɪˈkwaɪəmənt‖-ˈkwaɪr-/ *n* **1** [C] something that an official organization says a company or person must have or do: *There are deed restrictions, including a requirement that the buyer live in the property.*

2 something that is needed for a particular activity, task etc: *We're off to a good start to* ***meet*** *our* ***customer requirements*** *for 2001.* | *Nuclear power plants generate 19.1% of U.S. electricity requirements.*

capital requirement FINANCE ◆ [C] the capital needed by a company to operate, grow etc: *The equity from shares that they have sold has gone to reinforcing the company's capital requirements in anticipation of the merger.*

◆ [C] the capital that a government says that a financial institution must have in relation to the amount that it lends, so that it can operate safely: *The Fed believes higher capital requirements are needed to deter unusually risky lending by banks.*

central government borrowing requirement abbreviation **CGBR** [singular] ECONOMICS the amount of money that a government needs to borrow in a particular period of time: *improvements in public sector finances that have greatly reduced the central government borrowing requirement*

public sector borrowing requirement abbreviation **PSBR** [singular] ECONOMICS public sector borrowing requirement; the amount that a government has to borrow in a particular period of time to cover the difference between the money it gets from taxes and the amount it spends: *In Britain in recent years, the public sector borrowing requirement has been lower than the financial deficit because of the proceeds from privatisation, the income from the sale of previously government-owned companies.*

reserve requirement [C] *AmE* FINANCE an amount of money the government says that banks must possess, or leave with the CENTRAL BANK, calculated in relation to the amount of the loans that it makes: *Reducing reserve requirements eases credit conditions, so its effect on the economy is similar to that of reducing interest rates.*

req•ui•site /ˈrekwɪ̈zɪ̈t/ *adj* [only before a noun] *formal* needed for a particular purpose: *The financiers may be willing to step in and provide the requisite guarantees.*

req·ui·sites /ˈrekwəzəts/ *n* [plural] *formal* things needed for a particular purpose: *pens, paperclips and other small office requisites*

req·ui·si·tion[1] /ˌrekwəˈzɪʃən/ *n* [C] an official written order for something: *government aircraft requisitions* | *The department must receive a **purchase requisition** before the items can be supplied.*

requisition[2] *v* [T] to officially ask for something in writing: *Australian stakeholder AustMin Gold has requisitioned an extraordinary general meeting.*

re·quit·al /rɪˈkwaɪtl/ *n* [U] *formal* payment for something done or given: *an obligation which demands requital*

re·sale /ˈriːseɪl/ *n* **1** [U] the selling of goods that you have bought from someone else: *BASF began buying computer peripherals from Hitachi **for resale to** its European customers.* | *comparing **resale prices** to the original* | *the computer **resale market***

2 resales [plural] goods, property etc bought with the purpose of selling them to someone else: *The California Association of Realtors predicted house resales would increase 4%.*

resale-price maintenance —see under MAINTENANCE

re·sched·ule /ˌriːˈʃedjuːl‖-ˈskedʒʊl, -dʒəl/ *v* [T] **1** to make new arrangements for the payment of a debt, loan etc, often because the person, company, or country owing the money cannot pay it back in the time agreed earlier: *Faced with mounting losses, Iberia Air Lines **rescheduled payments** for new aircraft from Airbus Industries.* | *Magna reached an agreement with its bankers to reschedule C$560 million in debt.*

2 to arrange a new time or date for a meeting or event: *The shareholders meeting has been postponed several times, and is now rescheduled for June 4.*

re·scind /rɪˈsɪnd/ *v* [T] to officially end a law, agreement, or decision made earlier: *Westport Bancorp rescinded its agreement.*

re·scis·sion /rɪˈsɪʒən/ *n* [C,U] the official stopping of a law, agreement, or decision: *The lawsuit seeks the rescission of the acquisition of Citizens Federal Savings Bank.*

res·cue[1] /ˈreskjuː/ *v* [T] to save a company, country, or economic system that is in danger of failing, for example because of financial problems: *The fund is aimed at rescuing financially troubled companies.* | *DataMart has slipped so far against its rivals that even good products may not rescue it.* | *efforts to **rescue the economy** by lowering interest rates*

rescue[2] *n* [C] **1** an occasion when a company, country, or economic system is saved from failing: *Harcourt faces bankruptcy unless a rescue can be negotiated.* | *The Morgan-Belmont banking syndicate **came to the rescue** and protected the country's gold reserves.*

2 rescue attempt/effort/plan etc an attempt, effort etc to save a company, country, or economic system from failing: *It's an ambitious rescue effort, and some marketing experts question whether the strategy will be effective.* | *a last-ditch financial rescue package*

re·search /rɪˈsɜːtʃ, ˈriːsɜːtʃ‖-ɜːr-/ *n* [U] **1** serious study of a subject to find out new things about it or to test new ideas, products etc: *Chugai Pharmaceutical Co. will finance the research and receive commercialization rights.* | *What sets us apart from the rest of the industry is that we **do research on** our products to prove our claims.*

audience research MARKETING a study of the number and kinds of people who saw a particular film, television programme, advertisement etc: *the vice president of audience research at NBC*

customer research also **consumer research** MARKETING work done to find out why people buy certain products or services: *Concerned officials began consumer research to determine to what extent the brand's image was damaged by the bad publicity.*

field research MARKETING work that involves travelling to meet possible customers in order to get their opinions on products or services

investment research work done to study the performance of stocks, shares etc, usually as a guide to investments to make: *Salomon Inc. is a reliable source of impartial investment research.*

market research also **marketing research**, abbreviation **MR** MARKETING the activities involved in obtaining information about a particular market, including how much of a product is being sold, who is buying it, why they are buying it etc, or information about what they might buy: *Market research showed 'good potential' for marketing the aftershave to Hispanic men.* | *Performance Research, a sports **marketing research company***

motivational research MARKETING a type of MARKET RESEARCH that involves collecting information about the reasons why people decide to buy one product or BRAND (=type of product made by a particular company) rather than another. This helps companies to decide which new products to develop and how they should advertise their products: *Expert skill is involved in motivational research because this is investigation into the psychology of why individuals behave as they do.*

operations research also **operational research**, abbreviation **OR** work done to find out the best way of organizing the work and making decisions in a company, organization etc

qualitative research MARKETING a type of market research, especially in the form of interviews or group discussions, that aims to find out people's attitudes or opinions about something, where the results cannot be shown in numbers: *We regularly carry out qualitative research to generate ideas for new products.* —compare ***quantitative research***

quantitative research MARKETING a type of market research where the results can be shown in the form of numbers, percentages etc, for example sales volumes or market share —compare ***qualitative research***

2 research centre/institute etc an organization or department where new ideas and products are developed, tested etc: *a research centre to test US-made Honda parts* | *These studies were conducted in more than 160 independent universities and research institutions in 23 countries.*

research and development —see R AND D

re·search·er /rɪˈsɜːtʃə‖-ˈsɜːrtʃər/ *n* [C] a person whose job is to study a particular subject to find out new things about it

research grant —see under GRANT[1]

research manager —see under MANAGER

re·sell /ˌriːˈsel/ past tense and past participle **resold** *v* [I,T] to sell something that has been bought: *Some firms buy units for investment funds with the intention of reselling at a higher price.* **resell sth to sb**: *Harpener's aim in purchasing Hudson was to resell it quickly to another travel firm.*

re·sel·ler /riːˈselə‖-ər/ *n* [C] a company that sells goods made by another company, especially in the computer industry: *a major reseller of personal computer software*

value-added reseller abbreviation **VAR** a company selling the products or services of another company, especially computers, and which adds something to it or combines it with other products etc in order to make it worth more: *Storage Technology eventually hopes to have as many as 3,000 value-added resellers.*

R

res·er·va·tion /ˌrezəˈveɪʃən‖-zər-/ *n* [C] an arrangement in which a place on a plane, in a hotel, restaurant etc is kept for a customer who will arrive later; BOOKING *BrE*: *Every passenger is guaranteed a seat without a reservation and departures are hourly.*

re·serve /rɪˈzɜːv‖-ɜːrv/ *v* [T] **1** to arrange for a place on a plane, in a hotel, restaurant etc to be kept for a customer who will arrive later; BOOK *BrE*: *the convenience of reserving tickets in advance with credit cards | The airline reserved hotel rooms for the stranded crew.*
2 to keep something so that it can be used by a particular person or for a particular purpose at a later time: *High-speed lines required for video conferences have to be reserved well in advance.* **reserve sth for sth/sb**: *Of the total capital, 19% is expected to be reserved for strategic investors. | We reserve 50% of our restaurant tables for nonsmokers.*
3 reserve the right (to do sth) to state in an agreement, contract etc that you want the opportunity to do something or change something: *Warner reserved the right to invest directly in some of the movies.*
4 all rights reserved a statement put onto printed, recorded, or electronic material to show it is illegal to copy it without special permission: *Copyright 1999 James B. Stewart. All rights reserved*
5 reserve judgement to delay a decision or opinion about something until a later date: *The five-judge panel will reserve judgement until they see further evidence.* —see also RESERVES

reserve currency —see under CURRENCY

reserve price —see under PRICE[1]

reserve ratio —see under RATIO

reserve requirement —see under REQUIREMENT

re·serves /rɪˈzɜːvz‖-ɜːr-/ *n* [plural] **1** a company's profits from previous periods of time that have not been paid to shareholders: *Midland's insurance units have invested their reserves very conservatively. | CBS may* ***dip into*** (=use part of) *its* ***cash reserves*** *of $800 million to pay Midwest in cash.*
2 *AmE* amounts kept aside by a company in its accounts to be used if needed. The amount a company has in reserves has to be taken away when calculating profit for a particular period of time: *The company had a loss of $15.2 million, or 74 cents a share, after setting up reserves to reflect property depreciation.* (=falls in the value of property it owned)
3 also **bank reserves** money held by a bank and used to pay out money to customers when they ask for it. The amount that must be kept in this way is decided by government: *The Bank of Japan slashed by 40% the reserves banks must keep at the central bank.*

bad debt reserves *AmE* amounts shown in a company's accounts that are owed by customers etc and will probably never be paid. These are taken away when calculating profits; BAD DEBT PROVISIONS *BrE*: *The increase in bad debt reserves results from financial problems at one of the company's major customers.*

capital redemption reserves a part of a company's RESERVES and capital from money invested in shares that is not allowed to be given to shareholders in the form of DIVIDENDS

capital reserves money that a company, financial institution, or government has available for future spending: *Germany has built up great capital reserves – the Germans have one of the highest savings rates in the world.*

currency reserves also **foreign reserves** money in foreign currency held by a country and used to support its own currency and to pay for imports and foreign debts: *a sharp drop in Japan's foreign reserves | Currency reserves dropped $1.42 billion, while gold reserves were unchanged at $11.06 billion.*

draining reserves actions that the FEDERAL RESERVE SYSTEM takes to reduce the amount of money in the country's economy by restricting the amount of money banks have available to lend

gold reserves stocks of gold, usually those held by a country's CENTRAL BANK: *The nation's holdings of foreign currencies dropped $1.22 billion in January to $44.72 billion, while its gold reserves rose $1 billion to $11.058 billion.*

hidden reserves amounts of money which are difficult to find in a company's accounts because they are not stated openly: *The bank maintains hidden reserves, which can be used to boost disclosed* (=made known publicly) *profit figures. | HK$13 billion in hidden reserves*

loan-loss reserves money kept by a bank and used to cover loans it has made that will probably not be paid back: *DG Bank hopes to boost loan-loss reserves to around 55% of its unsecured loans.*

revaluation reserves amounts in a company's accounts showing increases in the value of land, buildings etc. These amounts may be increased following a re-calculation of a company's property, showing that it is worth more than before: *The investment property was valued at open market value during the year, resulting in a surplus of £40,000 which has been credited to the revaluation reserve.*

4 an amount of something valuable such as oil, gas etc: *Petroleum reserves now amount to the equivalent of 142 days' supply. | The company needs to focus on building its coal and copper reserves.*

proven reserves the amount of oil or natural gas known to exist in a particular place: *There are some 257 billion barrels of proven reserves in the Ghawar field, 25% of the world's supply.* —see also CAPITALIZATION OF RESERVES

re·shuf·fle /riːˈʃʌfəl/ *v* [T] to move people in a large organization, especially a government, from one job to another: *Shearson has reshuffled senior management and plans to cut its workforce to restore its finances.* —**reshuffle** *n* [C] *a* ***Cabinet reshuffle*** (=an occasion when government ministers change jobs)

res·i·dence /ˈrezədəns/ *n formal* **1** [U] the fact of living in a particular place: *Insurance companies use* ***place of residence*** *to calculate automobile insurance rates.*
2 [U] permission to live in a particular country permanently: *an application for* ***permanent residence*** *| Without a residence permit, immigrants are easily exploited.*
3 [C] a house where people live: *Florida law protects personal residences against seizure in bankruptcy-law.*

primary residence [C] LAW the house in which someone lives most of the time, even though they own other houses: *The property is no longer occupied as a primary residence.*

residence permit —see under PERMIT

res·i·den·tial /ˌrezəˈdenʃəl◂/ *adj* residential property or a residential area is one consisting of private houses where people live, rather than offices or factories: *NTT plans to provide cable television to business and residential customers.* —compare COMMERCIAL[1]

re·sid·u·al /rɪˈzɪdʒuəl/ *adj* **residual income/revenue/assets** FINANCE the amount of money left after all taxes or other necessary payments have been made: *the right to any residual assets on the liquidation of the company*

residual value —see under VALUE[1]

residuary legacy —see under LEGACY

re·sign /rɪˈzaɪn/ *v* [I,T] to officially leave a job, position etc through your own choice, rather than being told to leave: *The vice-president will* ***resign*** *his* ***post*** *and join BPI as chairman.* **+ as/from**: *One director recently resigned as trustee of the fund. | He has resigned from the board for personal reasons.*

res·ig·na·tion /ˌrezɪgˈneɪʃən/ *n* [C,U] when someone

officially states that they want to leave their job, position etc: *The board accepted their resignations, along with that of the vice-chairman.* | *The finance minister* ***offered*** *his* ***resignation*** *following a series of scandals involving brokerage firms.*

re·sil·i·ent /rɪˈzɪliənt/ *adj* a resilient country, economy, currency etc is strong and performs well, even under difficult conditions: *The dollar proved resilient against the yen in trading yesterday.* —**resilience** *n* [U] *Unilever's resilience in the face of economic recession and weak demand*

re·sist /rɪˈzɪst/ *v* [I,T] to try to prevent something happening or changing: *United Artists Entertainment Co. resisted a bid by the Denver company to acquire a 46% stake.* | *The board voted to file for bankruptcy, even though two directors resisted.*

re·sist·ance /rɪˈzɪstəns/ *n* [U] a refusal to accept change or new ideas, methods etc: *The company faces resistance from middle managers, who fear the changes will put them out of jobs.*

consumer resistance also **customer resistance** MARKETING dislike of or lack of interest in a new product or service by people + **to**: *Coca-Cola has been increasing promotional spending to lessen consumer resistance to higher soft-drink prices.*

investor resistance FINANCE when investors dislike particular types of investment: *overcoming investor resistance to riskier shares*

re·skill /ˌriːˈskɪl/ *v* [I,T] *BrE* to teach people new work skills, especially people who are unemployed: *The college aims to reskill workers to help them into alternative employment.* —**reskilling** *n* [U] *a major provider of high-quality training and reskilling for international industry*

res·o·lu·tion /ˌrezəˈluːʃən/ *n* **1** [C] an official decision or statement agreed on by two or more people or groups of people, often after a vote: *a* ***shareholder resolution*** *calling for a review of the company's policy* | *The directors were asked to* ***adopt a resolution*** *giving Girard control of the board.*

special resolution [C] FINANCE a resolution that has to be passed by 75% or more of shareholders, in a meeting that they were told about 21 days or more in advance

2 [C,U] when a particular dispute, legal case etc has been settled: *Occidental wants a* ***speedy resolution*** *of the matter to limit its losses.*

3 [U] COMPUTING a measurement of the number of PIXELS a computer screen can show. The measurement, called DPI, is the number of dots over an inch of the screen. Screens with high resolution (=lots of dots) are clearer than those with low resolution: *The chip makes PC screen resolution almost as good as that of a $10,000 workstation.*

re·solve /rɪˈzɒlv‖rɪˈzɑːlv, rɪˈzɒːlv/ *v* **1** [T] to find a satisfactory way of settling a disagreement, dispute etc: *China plans to use share issues to help resolve the difficult question of business ownership in a socialist economy.* | *Most pension* ***disputes*** *will be* ***resolved*** *within a year.*

2 [I] to make an official decision, especially by voting **resolve to do sth**: *The directors have resolved to ask Westpac to appoint a receiver.*

re·sort /rɪˈzɔːt‖-ɔːrt/ *v*

resort to sth *phr v* [T] to take a bad or unpleasant course of action because everything else has failed: *The company may resort to a temporary closure of its only plant.* | *We regret we must resort to legal action.* —see also LENDER OF LAST RESORT

re·source¹ /rɪˈzɔːs, -ˈsɔːs‖ˈriːsɔːrs/ *n* **1** [C usually plural] something such as money, property, skill, labour etc that a company has available: *We have the necessary* ***financial resources*** *to respond to these problems.* | *The fall in industrial production will free up resources to create a consumer economy.*

2 [C usually plural] something such as oil, land, or natural energy that exists in a country and can be used to increase its wealth: *Namibia has substantial coal resources and diamond deposits.* | *Natural gas is an environmentally clean* ***natural resource****.*

re·source² /rɪˈzɔːs, -ˈsɔːs‖-ˈsɔːrs/ *v* [T] **be resourced** to have enough money or people to carry out a particular job, project etc: *The government must ensure the department is properly staffed and resourced for its increased responsibilities.* —**resourcing** *n* [U] *The initiative failed because of* ***inadequate resourcing****.*

resource allocation —see under ALLOCATION

re·spect /rɪˈspekt/ *n formal* **1 in respect of** a phrase used in formal business letters meaning in payment for: *Tesco's auditors also received £1.2 million in respect of audit work.*

2 with respect to about or concerning: *The new rules apply with respect to a transfer of property occurring after 9 March 2005.*

re·spond /rɪˈspɒnd‖rɪˈspɑːnd/ *v* [I] **1** to react to something that has happened: *Mutual Benefit responded aggressively by selling market-rate investments.* + **to**: *Overseas exchanges can't respond as quickly as Wall Street to new product ideas.* | *Consumers will respond to any recession by buying less.*

2 to reply to a letter, telephone call etc: *Thousands of readers saw the ad and responded.* + **to**: *We are committed to responding to all customer complaints within 10 days.*

re·spon·dent /rɪˈspɒndənt‖rɪˈspɑːn-/ *n* [C] *formal* **1** someone who replies to an advertisement or set of questions: *Only 2.7% of the* ***survey respondents*** *said they had plans to buy a home in the next six months.*

2 LAW someone who defends themselves in a law case: *Without admitting the allegations, the respondents agreed with the court's finding that the firm failed to maintain the minimum capital required.*

re·sponse /rɪˈspɒns‖rɪˈspɑːns/ *n* **1** [C,U] something done as a reaction to something that has happened: *Macy's difficulties have touched off widely differing responses among its five largest shareholders.* + **to**: *Dell's moves are a response to price slashing by Zeos International Ltd.* | ***In response to*** *the offering, Warnaco's junk bonds went up.*

2 [C] a reply to a letter, telephone call, advertisement etc: *Shearson Lehman Brothers Inc. ran a series of radio ads and got 10,000 responses from investors.*

3 response time the time it takes to react to something: *a 24-hour response time on all customer enquiries* | *The additional load has slowed the computers' response times.*

re·spon·si·bil·i·ty /rɪˌspɒnsəˈbɪləti‖rɪˌspɑːn-/ *n* **1** [U] when someone is officially in charge of something and has to make decisions about it + **for**: *A corporate executive was given additional responsibility for Saatchi & Saatchi Advertising.* | *In his new post, he will* ***assume responsibility*** *for Great America's radio and TV operations.*

2 responsibilities [plural] all the things someone is in charge of in a particular job, position etc: *My workload and responsibilities have increased more than my salary.*

3 blame for something bad that has happened + **for**: *As chief executive, I* ***accept responsibility*** *for certain administrative problems.* | *Lawyers for Chiquita's subsidiary* ***denied*** *any* ***responsibility*** *for the incident.*

re·spon·si·ble /rɪˈspɒnsəbəl‖rɪˈspɑːn-/ *adj* **1 be responsible for sth** to be officially in charge of something as part of your job, meaning you must accept the blame if something goes wrong: *Partners are officially responsible for all the firm's financial obligations.* | *IMRO, the City watchdog responsible for regulating fund managers*

2 be responsible to sb if you are responsible to someone in your job, you have to report your actions, progress etc to them: *The Computer Group Manager is responsible to the Head of Computer Development.*

3 responsible job/position etc a job, position etc in which the ability to make good judgements and decisions is important: *Bank assistants carry out a responsible range of duties.*

re•spon•sive /rɪˈspɒnsɪv‖rɪˈspɑːn-/ *adj* if a company, organization etc is responsive, it is ready to react in a useful or helpful way to problems, complaints, market changes etc: *Telecom's drive to become a more flexible,* ***customer-responsive*** *organization* + **to**: *Companies have become more responsive to shareholder demands.*

rest /rest/ *v*

rest with sb *phr v* [T] *formal* if a decision, responsibility etc rests with someone, they are in charge of it: *The committee is of an advisory nature, and authority rests with individual banks.*

res•ti•tu•tion /ˌrestɪ̇ˈtjuːʃən‖-ˈtuːʃən/ *n* [U] *formal* the act of giving back something that was stolen, or paying for damage done to something: *He was ordered to pay £1 million in restitution after his guilty plea.*

re•stock /ˌriːˈstɒk‖ˌriːˈstɑːk/ *v* [I,T] to replace supplies of something that has been used with new supplies: *Wholesalers and retailers aren't restocking on the same scale as in previous years.* | *The gift shop closes down several times a year to restock its inventory with new merchandise.*

R

re•store /rɪˈstɔː‖-ɔːr/ *v* [T] **1** to make something return to its former level or condition: *Without fundamental reforms, the profitability of the banking system will not be restored.* | *Many analysts see the new plane as the key to restoring McDonnell Douglas's financial health.*

2 restore confidence/credibility/prestige etc to make people have confidence etc in something again after they have been worried or unsure about it: *Hoping to restore investor confidence, the company replaced the head of its credit unit.* | *He is credited with saving the whiskey industry by raising prices, and restoring the drink's prestige.*

3 to give something back, especially money that is owed: *The government agreed to restore an estimated $120 million that had been cut from the Energy Department budget.*

re•strain /rɪˈstreɪn/ *v* [T] to control or limit something that is starting to increase: *tough rules to restrain the creation of monopolies* | *A cut in consumer credit would restrain an economic recovery.*

re•straint /rɪˈstreɪnt/ *n* [C,U] a rule or principle limiting what countries, companies etc can sell, advertise, buy etc: *Beijing promised to ease* ***import restraints*** *and buy more U.S. products.* | *The regulations were ruled to be an unreasonable restraint of trade.* + **on**: *regulations* ***imposing restraints*** *on competition*

price restraint when a government asks companies not to raise prices by more than a certain amount: *The senator's proposal on limiting drug prices was part of a price restraint bill introduced last month.*

wage restraint also **pay restraint** an agreement not to demand or pay large wage increases: *The economic crisis led to three years of wage restraint.*

re•strict /rɪˈstrɪkt/ *v* [T] to limit or put controls on the amount, size, or range of something **restrict sth to sth**: *The bank imposed a ruling, restricting credit increases to 2.5%.* | *laws that restrict public employee pension funds to making only certain types of investment* —**restricted** *adj*: *Japanese consumers pay higher prices for goods because of* ***restricted competition***.

re•stric•tion /rɪˈstrɪkʃən/ *n* [C] an official rule that limits or controls what people can do or what is allowed to happen: *Construction lending has been badly hit by restrictions on loans.* | *India will relax the tough* ***import restrictions*** *it imposed in March.* | *US* ***trade restrictions***

re•stric•tive /rɪˈstrɪktɪv/ *adj* **1** tending to limit or control what is allowed to happen by more than is necessary: *The rest of Europe kept interest rates high to match the Bundesbank's restrictive* ***monetary policies***. | *Environmentalists have drafted another proposal that is far more restrictive than last year's initiative.*

2 restrictive (trade/business) practice an unfair method by a company, country etc that limits trade, competition etc: *The U.S. suspects that China's restrictive trade practices are partly to blame for the rising trade deficit.*

3 restrictive practices *BrE* unreasonable limits that one TRADE UNION puts on the kind of work the members of other trade unions are allowed to do: *The restrictive practices of stubborn unions kept the new printing presses idle.*

restrictive covenant —see under COVENANT

restrictive injunction —see under INJUNCTION

re•struc•ture /ˌriːˈstrʌktʃə‖-ər/ *v* **1** [I,T] if a company restructures, or someone restructures it, it changes the way it is organized or financed: *The iron ore company has restructured its operations, and began the year with a strong balance sheet.* | *McDonnell Douglas's helicopter unit will restructure, reducing the workforce by as much as 19%.* —see also DOWNSIZE

2 [T] FINANCE if a company restructures its debts, it makes an agreement with lenders to pay the debts in a different way to the one agreed before: *Interco's lenders agreed to restructure $1.9 billion in financing.* | *The troubled department store failed to make scheduled interest payments and faces bank demands that it restructure its debt.*

restructuring provision —see under PROVISION

re•sults /rɪˈzʌlts/ *n* [plural] **1** FINANCE the profit or loss made by a company in a particular period of time: *Two British banks announced management changes after announcing poor* ***financial results***. | *Merrill Dow's first full-year results showed sales of $2.46 billion.* | *The bank's strong* ***operating results*** *boosted its stock price.*

2 things that happen successfully because of someone's efforts, plans etc: *I knew I could* ***achieve results*** *despite the difficulties.* | *A wide range of financial incentives is likely to* ***produce*** *the best* ***results***. —see also PAYMENT-BY-RESULTS

re•sume /rɪˈzjuːm‖rɪˈzuːm/ *v* [I,T] to start to do something again after a period of rest or an interruption: *Profit-taking resumed as the yen began to lose ground.* | *Asamera said it won't* ***resume efforts*** *to sell assets until gold prices rise.*

ré•su•mé also **resume** /ˈrezjʊmeɪ ˈreɪ-‖ˌrezʊˈmeɪ/ *n* [C] *AmE* a short written account of your education and previous jobs that you send to an employer when you are looking for a new job; CV *BrE*: *Like hundreds of his peers, he had a good resume: Harvard Business School and the First Boston Corp. class of 1999.*

re•sur•gence /rɪˈsɜːdʒəns‖-ɜːr-/ *n* [singular] the return of an activity or success after a period of rest: *The car looks almost exactly like the Taurus, which led to Ford's resurgence during the mid-1980s.* | *If we* ***see*** *a* ***resurgence*** *in demand, we are likely to experience shortages.* —**resurgent** *adj*: *Fears of resurgent inflation sent long-term interest rates climbing.*

re•tail[1] /ˈriːteɪl/ *n* **1** [U] the sale of goods to customers for their own use, rather than to shops etc: *His experience in retail includes managing a number of shopping centres in New Zealand.* | *The Potato Marketing Board determines the size range of potatoes which can be offered for retail.* —compare WHOLESALE[1]

2 retail trade/market/business etc companies involved in selling goods or services to members of the public: *Levi's attributed the increased sales of jeans to a stronger retail market for denim.* | *Japan's traditional retail chains such as Seibu and Mitsukoshi, are big players in the luxury goods field.*

3 retail shop/outlet/store etc a shop etc that is open to members of the public: *The business is to direct its selling efforts away from retail outlets and toward more direct marketing.* | *The Taiyo Kobe bank has 700 retail branches.*

4 retail banking/brokerage banking or investment services available to members of the public, rather than to companies, businesses etc: *NCNB and Banc One are trying to bring consumer-oriented retail banking to Texas.* | *First Boston doesn't have any aspirations to be a major force in retail brokerage.*

5 retail customer/investor/consumer an individual customer, investor etc, rather than a business or company: *strong demand from a mix of institutional and retail investors*

re·tail² /ˈriːteɪl, ˈriːteɪl/ *v* [I,T] to sell goods in small quantities to members of the public, usually in a shop + **for/at**: *The Rollerblade doll, which will retail for about £36, furthers the toy maker's push into the large doll category.* | *Both cars will retail at $40,000, challenging a market dominated by European luxury imports.* —**retailing** *n* [U] *The losses reflect the company's continuing problems in retailing.* | *a weak period for the* ***retailing sector***

retail bank —see under BANK¹

retail banking —see under BANKING

retail co-operative —see under CO-OPERATIVE

retail deposits —see under DEPOSIT¹

re·tail·er /ˈriːteɪlə‖-ər/ *n* [C] **1** a business that sells goods to members of the public, rather than to shops etc: *Heilig-Meyers Co., a home furnishings retailer, said December sales rose 18% to $75.1 million.* | *Among retailers, Toys 'R' Us is expected to report flat earnings.*

2 someone who owns or runs a shop selling goods to members of the public; SHOPKEEPER

retail investor —see under INVESTOR

retail merchant —see under MERCHANT

retail price —see under PRICE¹

Retail Price Index —see under INDEX¹

retail sales —see under SALE

retail therapy *n* [U] when people go shopping in order to feel better, rather than because they really need to buy things: *Window-shopping is a painless form of retail therapy.*

re·tain /rɪˈteɪn/ *v* [T] **1** to keep something or to continue to have it: *A duplicate copy of the invoice will be retained for record purposes.* | *Following the merger, the Cross family will* ***retain*** *a 1.9%* ***stake*** *in Wiley.* —**retention** *n* [U] *Sales to new clients are ahead of a year ago, while client retention remained flat.*

2 HUMAN RESOURCES to continue to employ people after a company has changed ownership, reduced in size etc: *The new company retained all the staff employed at the time of the takeover.*

3 if a company retains a lawyer or other specialist, it pays them to do work for it, now or in the future: *Quorum will retain an auditing firm for six months to review its business practices.* | *First Boston Corp. has been retained by Mary Kay as an adviser.*

re·tained /rɪˈteɪnd/ *adj* FINANCE a company's retained profit, income etc is the money that is left after shareholders in the company have received DIVIDENDS for a particular period of time. Retained profits are considered to be part of a company's CAPITAL: *Health-care costs for its current employees could wipe out Chrysler's retained earnings of $5.2 billion.*

retained earnings —see under EARNINGS

retained profit —see under PROFIT¹

re·tain·er /rɪˈteɪnə‖-ər/ *n* [C] money paid now to a specialist, such as a lawyer for work they are expected to do in the future: *Directors received £550 for each board meeting and an annual retainer of £10,000.* | *Mr. Young is* ***on retainer to*** (=receiving a retainer from) *an international engineering firm.*

retaliatory tariff —see under TARIFF

re·ten·tion /rɪˈtenʃən/ *n* [U] HUMAN RESOURCES when workers stay with a company rather than taking a job with another employer: *We have detected a definite improvement in* ***employee retention.*** | *The assisted vacation scheme is an effective recruitment and retention tool in the competitive Silicon Valley job market.*

re·think /ˌriːˈθɪŋk/ *v* past tense and past participle **rethought** [I,T] to consider a plan or idea again carefully because it might need to be changed: *If things get worse, Porsche may have to* ***rethink*** *its* ***strategy.*** —**rethink** /ˈriːθɪŋk/ *n* [C] *a complete rethink of the company's product line*

re·tire /rɪˈtaɪə‖-ˈtaɪr/ *v* **1** [I] to stop work at the end of your working life: *In this country, women can retire at 60 and men at 65.* | *Jaguar plans to eliminate 1,000 jobs by offering workers money to quit or* ***retire early*** (=before the usual age). + **as/from**: *Goldman Sachs's No. 3 executive abruptly retired as a general partner, citing personal reasons.* | *Johan Veldman, 62, will retire from his post on the management board in April.*—**retired** *adj* [only before a noun] *Miller Lite's new advertising campaign stars retired athletes.*

2 [T] to dismiss someone who is near the end of their working life: *I took over the office when Mr Hargreaves was retired due to ill health.*

3 [T] FINANCE if a company retires bonds, shares etc, it buys them back from investors and takes them off the market; RETRACT: *The group has purchased and retired $5.1 million of its Series B shares.* | *Bally is trying to* ***retire*** *its* ***junk bond issue*** *at a discount.* | *Campeau Corp. agreed to pay C$80 million to* ***retire*** *C$153 million in personal* ***loans.***

4 [I] LAW if the jury in a court case retires, it goes to a separate room to decide its VERDICT (=whether someone is guilty or not)

re·tir·ee /rɪˌtaɪəˈriː‖-ˌtaɪˈriː/ *n* [C] *AmE* someone who has retired from work: *Our target market is retirees of 75 years and over with an annual income of at least $45,000.*

re·tire·ment /rɪˈtaɪəmənt‖-ˈtaɪr-/ *n* **1** [U] the act of leaving a job because you have reached the end of your working life, or the period of your life after you do this: *290 employees are eligible to* ***take early retirement*** (=before the usual age). | *Mr. Baker turns 65 next month, the usual* ***retirement age*** *for Air Products officers.* | *a* ***quiet retirement*** *in Bournemouth*

compulsory retirement when you have to stop working because you have reached the age your employer or your TRADE UNION has set as the age when you have to stop, usually 60 or 65: *The Sex Discrimination Act makes it unlawful for employers to have different compulsory retirement ages for men and women.*

2 retirement income/benefits/pension income etc paid to someone at the end of their working life: *IBM decided to give full retirement benefits to employees with 30 years of service, regardless of their age.* —see also ***individual retirement account***

3 [U] FINANCE the act of paying loans, bonds etc before the normal time + **of**: *The remaining £21 million in charges will cover the* ***retirement of debt.***

debt retirement [C,U] when a borrower completely pays back a particular type of debt that they owe, usually before the time originally planned, perhaps to replace it with a new form of debt

retirement pension —see under PENSION¹

R

re·tir·ing /rɪˈtaɪərɪŋ‖-ˈtaɪrɪŋ/ *adj* **the retiring manager/president/chairman etc** a manager etc who is about to leave their job, usually because they have reached the end of their working life: *Milacron developed under the leadership of the retiring chief executive, who has headed the company since 1980.*

re·tool /ˌriːˈtuːl/ *v* **1** [I,T] MANUFACTURING to change or replace the production equipment used in a factory: *Sony will spend $300 million retooling a plant to produce televisions.* + **for**: *The company plans to shut two plants for a month to retool for the redesigned Chrysler minivans.*
2 [T] *AmE informal* to change the way in which something is done: *Two big auction houses are* ***retooling*** *their sales* ***strategies*** *in hopes of succeeding in a difficult market.* —**retooling** *n* [U] *the high costs of retooling and operating a small-scale production facility*

re·tract /rɪˈtrækt/ *v* [T] **1** FINANCE if a company retracts bonds, shares etc, it takes them off the market by buying them back from investors; RETIRE: *Corona will use its credit line to retract C$53.3 million in preferred shares.*
2 to make an official statement saying that something you said earlier is not true; REVOKE: *A key witness has* ***retracted*** *his* ***testimony*** (=a statement in a law court) *a year after the conviction.* —**retraction** *n* [C,U] *The retraction of Ivaco's preferred shares will be completed as scheduled.* | *Some newspapers ran retractions of stories they had printed.*

re·train /ˌriːˈtreɪn/ *v* [I,T] to learn new skills or to teach someone the skills needed to do a different job: *We bought new software and had to retrain everyone to use the database.* —**retraining** *n* [U] *He undertook eight weeks of retraining and was offered a position as a hazardous-materials specialist.*

re·treat¹ /rɪˈtriːt/ *v* [I] **1** FINANCE *journalism* if shares etc retreat, their value falls to a lower level: *In Frankfurt, share prices retreated as the market consolidated recent gains.* | *The Dow Jones Industrial Average retreated 10.07 points to 11,199.46.*
2 to decide not to continue with a plan, idea, agreement etc because it is too difficult or no longer worth doing: *Japanese buyers have retreated after paying huge prices for U.S. properties in the past.* + **from**: *Chartwell became the latest corporate raider to retreat from a takeover contest.*

retreat² *n* **1** [singular, U] FINANCE *journalism* a situation in which the value of shares etc falls to a lower level: *The stock market retreat came just as crop prices were starting to recover.*
2 in retreat if a company, industry, market etc is in retreat, its performance is less good than before: *With the Tokyo* ***stockmarket in retreat***, *the central bank is likely to be even more cautious about agreeing corporate loans.*
3 [singular, U] when someone decides not to carry out a plan, idea, agreement etc because it is too difficult or no longer worth doing + **from**: *The decision to return American Airlines to profitability* ***marks a retreat*** *from its fast-growth strategy.*

re·trench /rɪˈtrentʃ/ *v* [I] *formal* if a company, industry, or government retrenches, it spends less money on new products, developments etc because there is not enough money available: *The larger U.S. carriers need the opportunity to retrench and consolidate their operations.* | *Defense companies and computer makers are retrenching and have scaled back orders.* —**retrenchment** *n* [U] *No sooner had Mr. Collor taken office when he announced a savage program of retrenchment and deflation.* | *a drastic* ***retrenchment plan***

re·tri·al /ˌriːˈtraɪəl,ˈriːtraɪəl‖ˌriːˈtraɪəl/ *n* [C,U] the process of bringing a legal case back to court so that it can be decided again: *Mr. Rutland's request for a retrial was dismissed.* | *The judge reversed the verdict and sent the case back for retrial.*

R

re·trieve /rɪˈtriːv/ *v* [T] **1** COMPUTING to get information or a particular document from a computer: *The application stores and* ***retrieves data*** *according to the user's requirements.* | *To* ***retrieve a file***, *double click on it using the mouse.*
2 if a company retrieves money, costs, or losses, it succeeds in obtaining an amount of money from investors equal to the amount it spent or lost; RECOUP: *The bank will have trouble retrieving anything like the value of its loans.*

ret·ro·ac·tive /ˌretrəʊˈæktɪv◂‖-troʊ-/ *adj formal* a law or decision that is retroactive is effective from a particular date in the past; RETROSPECTIVE + **to**: *Pennzoil said it will adopt the new accounting method retroactive to Jan. 1.* —**retroactively** *adv*: *The pension benefits* ***apply retroactively*** *to employees who retired on or after last Dec. 31.*

ret·ro·spec·tive /ˌretrəˈspektɪv◂/ *adj* a law or decision that is retrospective is effective from a particular date in the past; RETROACTIVE: *The bank tried to persuade the government to enact* ***retrospective legislation*** *to legalize the contracts.* —**retrospectively** *adv*

re·turn¹ /rɪˈtɜːn‖-ɜːrn/ *v* **1** [T] FINANCE if an investment returns a particular amount of money, that is the amount of profit it makes: *High-performing Janus Fund has returned 20.8% a year on average over the past decade.*
2 [T] to take a product back to the shop you bought it from to get your money back, or to get other goods in exchange for it: *Any product purchased from Milo may be returned for a full refund.*
3 [I] to go back to an activity or condition that was being done or existed before + **to**: *The mine returned to production in November.* | *Striking Canadian mint workers* ***returned to work***, *ending a four-month stoppage.*
4 [T] if you return a telephone call, you telephone someone because they have telephoned you: *Mr Burkitt didn't return a call asking for comments on the crisis.*
5 return a cheque if a bank returns a cheque, it refuses to pay it because there is not enough money in the account to do so; BOUNCE: *If we have to return a cheque, a charge of £15 will be made.* —compare STOP[1]
6 return a verdict LAW if a JURY in a law case returns its VERDICT, it says whether it thinks someone is guilty or not

return² *n* **1** [U] also **returns** the amount of profit made from an investment: *British government bonds have produced a total return of 8.52% so far this month.* | *Executive Life have predicted initial returns to policyholders as high as 90 cents on the dollar.* | *This investment promises a high* ***rate of return*** (=level of profitability).

accounting rate of return abbreviation **ARR** plural **accounting rates of return** [C,U] ACCOUNTING the amount of profit made from an investment, measured as a percentage of the value of the assets used in the investment: *Analysts are still using some less secure approaches, such as the accounting rate of return and payback.*

gross return [C,U] the amount an investment produces before tax is taken off: *Interest is taxable, so the bond's 7% gross return would be worth 5.6% or 4.2%, depending on the tax rate.*

internal rate of return plural **internal rates of return** abbreviation **IRR** [C,U] a measure of the value of an investment, expressed as a percentage and calculated by comparing the profit in a year with the amount that was originally invested: *The average internal rate of return for the industry is 6.6%.*

net return [C,U] the amount received from a company's activities, an investment etc, after costs have been taken away: *The higher the total expenses of the fund, the lower the net return to investors.*

rate of return plural **rates of return** [C] the amount of profit that a particular investment will make, expressed as a percentage: *Merrill Lynch Ready Assets Trust showed an annual rate of return of 5.42%.*

2 [singular, U] when someone or something goes back to an activity or condition that was being done or existed before: *Favorable government rates have aided Meralco Corp's return to profitability.* | *the return of petroleum prices to the highest levels since mid-February*

3 [C] TAX an official form that is filled in and sent to the tax authorities so they can calculate how much tax is owed: *Over 12.2 million taxpayers **filed federal returns** electronically this year.* | *allegations that the company had falsified its corporate **tax return***

annual return [C] LAW an official statement signed by the directors and secretary of a LIMITED COMPANY in Britain made, by law, once a year to the REGISTRAR OF COMPANIES, and containing details of the company's shares and assets shown on the BALANCE SHEET: *Annual returns should be filed within 14 days of the AGM, rather than the current 60 days.*

4 [U] COMPUTING the button that is pressed on a computer KEYBOARD when you have finished typing an instruction; ENTER: *Wordwise is accessed by typing 'W' and pressing Return.* —see also COMPOUND ANNUAL RATE OF RETURN, SALE OR RETURN, TAX RETURN

return[3] *adj* **return ticket/fare etc** *BrE* a ticket etc that allows you to travel to a place and back again; ROUND-TRIP TICKET/FARE *AmE*: *The package includes the return air fare from the UK and accommodation.*

re•turn•a•ble /rɪ'tɜːnəbəl‖-ɜːr-/ *adj* something that is returnable can or should be sent back to the place or person it came from: *a returnable plastic bottle* | *Applications are returnable by 7 March.*

re•turn•er /rɪ'tɜːnə‖-'tɜːrnər/ *n* [C] *BrE* someone who comes back to work or education after being away for a long time: *a one-year certificate course for women returners*

return fare —see under FARE

return on assets abbreviation **ROA** *n* [singular, U] FINANCE a company's profit in a particular period of time in relation to the value of its assets, used to judge how well it is using its assets compared to other companies in the same industry: *It has an **annualized return** (=for a complete year) **on assets** of 1.46%, well below the 3.04% achieved by Spain's most profitable bank.*

return on capital abbreviation **ROC** *n* [singular, U] FINANCE **1** the profit on an investment in relation to the amount invested; RETURN ON INVESTMENT: *US companies have invested more than $7 billion in Chile with an annual return on capital of more than 40%.*

2 also **return on capital employed**, abbreviation **ROCE** a company's profit in a particular period of time in relation to its CAPITAL (=money from shareholders and lenders): *Heinz's return on capital invested was 31%, putting it in the same league as other big food companies.*

return on equity abbreviation **ROE** *n* [singular, U] FINANCE a company's profit in a particular period of time in relation to its SHARE CAPITAL (=money from shareholders): *He sets his standards high, seeking a 20% return on equity for firms he invests in.* —compare ***equity yield*** under YIELD[1]

return on investment abbreviation **ROI** *n* [singular, U] FINANCE **1** the profit on an investment in relation to the amount invested; RETURN ON CAPITAL: *You could buy municipal bond mutual funds, but the return on investment is unpredictable.*

2 a company's profit from one or more of its activities in a particular period of time in relation to the amount it has invested in the activities: *Continuing strong sales and earnings gains enabled the company to increase its shareholders' total return on investment.*

return on sales abbreviation **ROS** *n* [U] FINANCE the profit that one or more companies have obtained from selling their products or services in a particular period of time, in relation to their sales for the period: *Ten years ago EMI had a return on sales of less than 6% and only a 10% world-wide market share. Since then, sales have doubled and profits have quadrupled.*

return ticket —see under TICKET

revaluation reserves —see under RESERVES

re•val•ue /riː'væljuː/ *v* [T] **1** to examine something again in order to calculate its current value in relation to other similar things: *Some properties need to be revalued.* | *MMC recommended that we should **revalue our assets** once every five years.*

2 to increase the value of a country's money in relation to that of other countries: *The central bank wanted to revalue the mark.* —**revaluation** *n* [C,U] *From that date there were no revaluations of property.* | *revaluation of the pound within the ERM* —see also REVALUATION RESERVES

re•vamp /riː'væmp/ *v* [T] to organize something in a new and more modern way so that it operates more effectively: *General Motors revamped its biggest US car-making operation to make it function more like Japanese companies.* —**revamp** *n* [C] *a revamp of the banking sector* —**revamping** *n* [C] *The revamping has made little difference to the company's profits.*

rev•e•nue /'revənjuː‖-nuː/ *n* [U] **1** also **revenues** money that a business or organization receives over a period of time, especially from selling goods or services: *B&L has an **annual revenue** of about $8 million.* | *We earn about £3000 a month in **advertising revenue**.* | *a 10% fall in revenue from sales*

average revenue the amount of money received from selling goods divided by the total number of goods or products sold

marginal revenue ECONOMICS the additional revenue received when selling one more product or item: *This excess of price over both marginal revenue and marginal cost is a convenient measure of the firm's monopoly power.*

2 also **revenues** money that a government receives from tax: *a government plan to help boost revenue* | *The pensions are a good source of **income tax revenue**.*

3 the Revenue another name for the Inland Revenue, the government organization in Britain that collects taxes: *The Revenue will not regard a backlog of work as a reasonable excuse for the late delivery of a tax return.* —see also INLAND REVENUE, INTERNAL REVENUE SERVICE

revenue account —see under ACCOUNT[1]

revenue anticipation notes —see under NOTE[1]

revenue bond —see under BOND

revenue reserve —see under RESERVES

revenue stamp —see under STAMP[1]

revenue tariff —see under TARIFF

revenue tax —see under TAX[1]

re•vers•al /rɪ'vɜːsəl‖-ɜːr-/ *n* **1** [C] a change to an opposite arrangement, process, or course of action + **of**: *The move was a reversal of Kodak's previous policy.* + **in**: *Money managers predict a reversal in the industry's rising share values.*

2 [C] a failure or other problem that prevents you from being able to do what you want: *In spite of setbacks and reversals, his business was at last making money.*

reversal of entries plural **reversals of entries** [C] ACCOUNTING when a credit is accidentally added to the debit side of a set of accounts and a debit is added to the credit side, but the error does not affect the final BALANCE because the amounts are the same

re•verse[1] /rɪ'vɜːs‖-ɜːrs/ *v* [T] **1** to change something such as a decision, judgement, or process so that it is the opposite of what it was before: *Will the government **reverse its decision** to lower oil prices?* | *The California*

R

*Supreme Court **reversed a** lower **court ruling** that blocked a resort hotel from being built.* | *Prime had been struggling to **reverse huge losses**.*

2 reverse direction/course to develop or do something in the opposite way to before: *Bond prices abruptly reversed direction and fell.* | *The President reversed course and cut a deal with Congress.*

3 reverse the charges *BrE* to make a telephone call which is paid for by the person you are telephoning; CALL COLLECT *AmE*

reverse[2] *n* **1 the reverse** the exact opposite of something: *U.S. law on this matter is virtually the reverse of British law.*

2 [C] *formal* a defeat or problem that delays your plans: *Losing the Senate vote was a serious reverse for the President.*

reverse[3] *adj* [only before a noun] used to describe something that is the opposite of something else: *In 1996, we had a lot of supply and not much demand. But in 1997, we had the reverse situation.*

reverse discrimination —see under DISCRIMINATION

reverse engineering —see under ENGINEERING

reverse repo —see under REPO[1]

reverse share split —see under SPLIT[2]

reverse takeover —see under TAKEOVER

re·ver·sion /rɪˈvɜːʃən‖rɪˈvɜːrʒən/ *n* [U] LAW the return of property to a former owner, for example at the end of a period of time when someone else has had the right to use it: *the reversion of Hong Kong to Chinese rule*

re·ver·sion·er /rɪˈvɜːʃənə‖-ˈvɜːrʒənər/ *n* [C] LAW the person to whom property will be returned, for example at the end of a LEASE

re·view[1] /rɪˈvjuː/ *n* **1** [C,U] when a situation or process is examined and considered carefully to see if it can be improved, or an occasion when this is done + **of**: *Nomura is conducting an **internal review** done by employees of the company of company activities.* | ***performance reviews** of hospitals* | *The plant is still **under review** for possible closure.*

2 [C,U] FINANCE when a RATINGS AGENCY examines particular bonds to see if there has been a change in the level of risk that they will not be repaid: *Moody's has **placed** $2.5 billion of Illinois Power's debt **under review** for possible upgrading.*

3 [C] an article in a newspaper or magazine that gives an opinion about a new restaurant, product, film etc: *Despite **good reviews** from food critics, the restaurant hasn't made a profit in two years.*

review[2] *v* [T] **1** to examine or consider a situation or process carefully to see if it can be improved: *We hired an outside consultant to review our pricing policies.* | *The situation is being reviewed on a day-to-day basis.*

2 FINANCE to examine particular bonds, debt etc to see if there has been a change in the level of risk that they will not be repaid: *Chrysler's debt is being reviewed by Moody's for possible downgrading.*

3 to write an article saying how good you think a new restaurant, product, film etc is: *He reviews new models for a car magazine.* —**reviewer** *n* [C] *a reviewer for the Detroit News*

4 *AmE* to look at a document such as a report in detail: *I need more time to review your report.*

re·vise /rɪˈvaɪz/ *v* [T] **1** to change a plan or your figures for something because of new information: *He already has revised the plan to please shareholders.* | *Minolta **revised downward** its group sales forecast.* | *a **revised estimate** of costs*

2 to change a piece of writing by adding new information, making improvements, or correcting mistakes: *a **revised edition** of the encyclopedia* —**revision** *n* [C,U] *The policy appears headed for revision.* | *a revision of a 1989 technical manual*

re·vi·tal·ize also **revitalise** *BrE* /riːˈvaɪtəlaɪz/ *v* [T] to make a place, company, economy etc interesting or active again: *Managers have revitalized Disney's theme park.* | *Sears was struggling to revitalize its sagging retail business.* —**revitalization** also **revitalisation** *BrE n* [U] *the revitalization of New York City's paralyzed economy*

re·vi·val /rɪˈvaɪvəl/ *n* [C,U] **1** when something becomes active or strong again: *the first signs of **economic revival*** + **in**: *Various surveys show a revival in consumer confidence.* + **of**: *Some people feared a revival of inflation.*

2 when something becomes popular again + **in**: *A revival in local radio means increased profits for GWR.* | *American fashion designers are beginning to **enjoy a revival**.*

re·vive /rɪˈvaɪv/ *v* **1** [I,T] if a company, the economy etc revives, or if something revives it, it becomes stronger or more active: *Some regions, such as the Northeast, will revive much more slowly than the national economy.* | *To revive sales, BMW has cut prices by as much as 9%.*

2 [T] to bring something back into existence or popularity again: *The dog that listens for 'his master's voice,' is being revived in a series of new TV spots for the RCA brand.*

revocable letter of credit —see under LETTER OF CREDIT

re·voke /rɪˈvəʊk‖-ˈvoʊk/ *v* [T] to officially state that a law, official document, agreement etc is no longer effective: *We had no alternative but to revoke the contract.* —**revocable** *adj*: *Four events are mentioned that make the agreement revocable.* —**revocation** *n* [C,U] *She faces revocation of her licence.*

rev·o·lu·tion /ˌrevəˈluːʃən/ *n* [C] a complete change in ways of thinking, methods of working etc + **in**: *Computer technology has caused a revolution in working practices.* —**revolutionary** *adj*: *revolutionary advances in aircraft design*—see also INDUSTRIAL REVOLUTION

rev·o·lu·tion·ize also **revolutionise** *BrE* /ˌrevəˈluːʃənaɪz/ *v* [T] to completely change the way people think about something or the way something is done: *Swatch revolutionized the market for watches in the early 1980s, with its inexpensive watches aimed at the youth market.*

re·volve /rɪˈvɒlv‖rɪˈvɑːlv/ *v* [T] BANKING to make loan repayments of less than the full amount due each month: *Banks make money on the interest rates they charge cardholders who revolve their balances.*

revolving credit —see under CREDIT[1]

revolving fund —see under FUND[1]

re·ward[1] /rɪˈwɔːd‖-ˈwɔːrd/ *n* **1** [C] something that you receive because you have done something good or helpful + **for**: *Officials often were posted abroad as a reward for loyal service.*

2 [C,U] money that you earn for doing a job or providing a service: *Working as a lawyer can bring big **financial rewards**.* | *Her success has brought her little **commercial reward**.* | *the **economic rewards** that come with tourism*

3 [C,U] money earned by an investment: *Investors are hoping for **big rewards**.* | *Allied-Signal has **reaped huge rewards*** (=gained them) *in the stock market.*

4 [C] an amount of money offered to someone in return for some information about something: *The Mirror is offering a £100,000 reward for information.*

reward[2] *v* [T] to give someone something such as money because they have done something good or helpful: *a bonus system that rewards workers who meet targets* **reward sb with sth**: *The best managers are rewarded with greater responsibility.*

reward system —see under SYSTEM

re·work /ˌriːˈwɜːk‖-ˈwɜːrk/ *v* [T] **1** to make changes to something so that it can be used again or is more suitable for a particular use: *The reworked commercial was much more successful than the original one.*

2 MANUFACTURING to correct mistakes or faults in something: *10% of the engines had to be reworked when they came off the production line.*

3 to do a calculation again: *The first-half figures had been reworked to reflect the fact that Imetal's holding in mining unit Minimet S.A. is no longer wholly consolidated.* —**rework** *n* [C,U] *The manufacturer will pay the costs of rework.* —**reworking** *n* [C,U] *The proposals were sent back for reworking.*

ride[1] /raɪd/ *v* past tense **rode** past participle **ridden** *journalism* **1 be riding high** to be very successful or confident: *The Agnelli family, which owns almost 40% of Fiat, was riding high.*

2 be riding for a fall to be doing something unwise that could result in failure: *Are junk bond buyers riding for a fall?*

3 free ride to get an advantage for yourself without doing anything to earn it + **on**: *Rival firms sometimes free ride on each others' research and development.*

ride sth ↔ **out** *phr v* [T] if you ride out a difficult situation, you are not badly harmed by it: *Do they have the financial resources to* ***ride out the recession****?*

ride[2] *n* **1** [C usually singular] *journalism* used to say how easy or difficult a process or period of time is for someone: *It won't be an* ***easy ride*** *for Alcatel.* | *Hungarian investors have been having a* ***bumpy ride*** (=a difficult time) *recently.*

2 free ride if someone gets a free ride, they get an advantage without having to work for it: *They're* ***getting a free ride*** *at the taxpayer's expense.*

3 take sb for a ride to trick someone, often in order to get money from them: *Some auto dealers are taking car buyers for a ride by charging inflated prices on extended warranties.*

rid•er /ˈraɪdə‖-ər/ *n* [C] **1** a statement that is added to an official decision or judgement

2 INSURANCE a statement added to an insurance policy that gives extra information about the insurance, for example a list of things that are not covered by it

rig[1] /rɪg/ *n* [C] **1** a large structure used to get oil from under the ground: *an offshore* ***oil rig*** | *Norton owns and operates 13* ***drilling rigs*** *in the Southwest USA.*

2 a large TRUCK: *Truckers say the bigger rigs will reduce their costs by a third.*

rig[2] *v* past tense and past participle **rigged** present participle **rigging** [T] **1** to arrange or influence a business deal or election in a dishonest way so you get the result you want: *There were claims that the election was rigged.*

2 if companies, groups of investors etc rig prices or rig the market, they work together illegally or unfairly to influence prices, conditions etc to their advantage: *Exxon and Conoco were accused of rigging oil prices.* | *Investors who believe that the* ***market*** *is* ***rigged*** *are likely to withhold their investment.*

rig•ging /ˈrɪgɪŋ/ *n* [U] when companies, groups of investors work together illegally or unfairly to influence prices, conditions etc to their advantage

market rigging when some of the companies in a market act together to stop a market working as it should in order to gain an unfair advantage: *Market rigging devices rarely hold up for ever.*

right /raɪt/ *n* **1** [C usually singular] if you have the right to do something, you are morally, legally, or officially allowed to do it: *Like other businesses, we have a right to set competitive prices.* | *Do regions such as Champagne have the* ***exclusive right*** (=a right that only it has) *to the use of their names in wine labeling?* | *Employers have the* ***legal right*** *to hire replacement workers for striking unionists.*

inalienable right LAW a right that cannot be taken away from you: *the inalienable right to own property* | *People are being* ***denied their inalienable rights****.*

2 rights [plural] the freedom and advantages that everyone should be allowed to have: *New legislation is gradually taking away* ***worker's rights****.* | *Your* ***legal rights*** *are the same when you buy mail order as from a shop.*

pension rights *especially BrE* the right that someone has to receive a pension from a company or from the government, especially when they stop work at a particular age: *Britain is required to equalize pension rights between men and women.*

voting rights the right of someone who has shares in a company to attend and vote at the company's GENERAL MEETING: *A new French law removes the voting rights of shares a company holds in itself.*

3 rights also **stock rights** [plural] rights offered to existing shareholders to buy more shares in a company, perhaps at a reduced price: *The board approved a plan to raise $30 million through a* ***stock rights offering****. Each shareholder will receive rights to subscribe to 1.25 shares for each share held.* —see also ***rights issue*** under ISSUE[2]

4 rights [plural] if a person or company has the rights to something, they are legally allowed to use it to make money: *They were granted the movie rights to Diana's life story.* | *Warner will have all* ***distribution rights*** *in the U.S. and Canada.*

performing rights the rights of the person who has the legal ownership of a piece of music, a play etc to control where and when it can be performed, and to charge money for performing it: *Broadcast Music Inc., a performing rights organization, licensed the Family Channel to play its music.*

property rights the right to own and make a profit from capital, land etc

proprietary rights the rights of a company to sell a product based on particular ideas and designs, or to sell or allow others to use those rights for payment: *Collagen still has all proprietary rights to the substance, called TGFb2.*

right first time *adv* MANUFACTURING used to say that, in making a product, it is better to perform an operation correctly the first time, rather than have to work on it again in order to correct mistakes: *Quality efforts ensure that 96% of products are now going out right first time.*

right-hand man *n* [singular] the person who supports and helps you most in your job: *Robert Wussler was Mr. Turner's right-hand man for 10 years.*

right of action *n* plural **rights of action** [C,U] LAW the right to take legal action against someone in a court of law: *The investor had no right of action against the solicitors.*

right of way *n* plural **rights of way** [C,U] LAW the legal right to pass across land that does not belong to you: *The court said California must pay compensation in exchange for a* ***public right of way*** *over beachfront property.*

rights issue —see under ISSUE[2]

right•siz•ing /ˈraɪtˌsaɪzɪŋ/ *n* [U] *journalism* **1** when a company becomes a more suitable size, especially by employing fewer people: *Many aerospace workers lost their jobs as a result of rightsizing.*

2 when an organization starts using smaller, more modern, and less expensive computers: *Rightsizing may be good news for users, but it is bad news for many big IT firms.* —**rightsize** *v* [T] *They have been given one year to rightsize their workforce.*

ring[1] /rɪŋ/ *n* [C] **1** also **price ring** a group of manufacturers or suppliers who have agreed to fix prices, often illegally, so that there is no competition between them and they can make large profits

2 also **auction ring** or **bidders' ring** a group of dealers who work together illegally to buy things at an AUCTION (=an event where something is sold to the person who is willing to pay most) at low prices, then sell them later at higher prices and share the profit

3 LAW a group of people who illegally control a business or criminal activity: *Police suspect a **drug ring** may be operating in the area.*

4 FINANCE the area of a COMMODITY EXCHANGE where trading takes place

5 give sb a ring *especially BrE* to make a telephone call to someone: *Give me a ring if you want to discuss the proposal.*

ring² *v* past tense **rang** past participle **rung** **1** [I,T] *especially BrE* to make a telephone call to someone; CALL: *I rang you yesterday but you weren't in.* | *Ring 192 for information.*

2 [I] If a telephone rings, it makes a sound to show that someone is phoning you: *The phone hasn't stopped ringing all day.*

ring sb **back** *phr v* [I,T] *BrE* to telephone someone again, for example because they were not available when you telephoned them: *John rang, and he wants you to ring him back.*

ring in *phr v* [I] *BrE* **1** to telephone the place where you work: *Jane's rung in to say she'll be late.*

2 ring in sick *BrE* to telephone the place where you work to say that you are too ill to work

ring off *phr v* [I] *BrE* to end a telephone call; hang up: *He rang off without giving his name.*

ring round sth *phr v* [I,T] *BrE* to make telephone calls to a group of people, in order to organize something, find out information etc: *I'll ring round to see whether anyone's interested in coming with us.*

ring up *phr v* **1** [I,T] **ring** sb/sth ↔ **up** *BrE* to telephone someone: *I'll ring the manager up tomorrow.*

2 [T] **ring sth up** to press buttons on a cash register to record how much money is being put inside: *The cashier rang up $300 by mistake.*

R

rip /rɪp/ *v* past tense and past participle **ripped** present participle **ripping**

rip sb ↔ **off** *phr v* [T] *informal* to charge someone too much money for something, or sell someone a product that is faulty: *The average customer simply can't tell if he's being ripped off by hidden charges.*

rip-off *n* [C] *informal* something that is unreasonably expensive, or a faulty product which has been sold as perfect: *Consumer Reports surveyed 95,000 American dieters, and found that most thought diet programs were a big rip-off.*

rise¹ /raɪz/ *v* past tense **rose** past participle **risen** [I]
1 to increase in number, amount, or value: *House prices are likely to rise towards the end of this year.* + **by**: *Sales rose by 20% over the Christmas period.* | *As more foreign banks have arrived in Singapore, wages for experienced staff have **risen sharply*** (=increased quickly) *and by a large amount.* | *Their salaries will continue to **rise steadily** until they reach the top of their professions.* | *Information technology has been blamed for **rising unemployment**.* | ***Rising prices** are seen as a threat to living standards.*

2 rise through the ranks to start working for an organization in a low-paid job, and to gradually improve your position, until you get a very important, well-paid job: *She had risen through the ranks, having joined the company as a secretary after she graduated from high school.*

3 rise to the top to be very successful and reach a top position in your job or the type of business you are involved in etc: *his rise to the top of the industry* | *An agency is where you will have the biggest chance of rising to the top in the advertising business.*

rise² *n* **1** [C] an increase in number, amount, or value: *We have sold 120,000 cars this year, a 20% rise on last year.* | *Tenants face a 20% rent rise.* + **in**: *BAA reported a 46% rise in first half profits before tax to £220 million.* | *A rise in taxes will be necessary if we are to improve our education system.*

2 [C] *BrE* an increase in wages; RAISE *AmE*: *After you've worked here for one year you get a rise.* | *The railworkers were offered a 3% **pay rise**.*

3 [singular] the process of becoming more important, successful, or powerful + **of**: *One important consequence of the mass production of goods has been the rise of extensive media advertising by manufacturers.* | *the **rise of capitalism** in the country*

risk¹ /rɪsk/ *n* **1** [C,U] the possibility that something may be lost, harmed, or damaged, or that something bad, unpleasant, or dangerous may happen: *If you're considering starting a business, think carefully about the risks involved.* + **of**: *If your cheque book is lost or stolen, let your bank know immediately in order to **reduce the risk** of fraud on your account.* | *Satellites seemed to offer Britain a useful area, high in technology and science and fairly low in **financial risk**.* + **that**: *There is always a risk that the supplier will go out of business before the order is delivered.*

downside risk [C] FINANCE the greatest amount of money that might be lost in a particular business or project, if it goes wrong: *You can reduce the downside risk considerably by using futures and options.* | *This advice is particularly geared to contested bids or where the downside risks are high.*

2 [C,U] FINANCE the possibility that the value of an asset may go up or down on the stockmarket: *There is always some risk with any kind of investment.* | *Fund managers have the resources and time to make judgments on which non-rated bonds are worth the risk.*

currency risk [C,U] the danger that changes in a currency's value may affect the value of investments or of a company's exports: *These countries don't take a currency risk when buying US securities because their major export, oil, is priced in US dollars.* | *There is a range of futures, swaps and currency options to **hedge against*** (=try not to be affected by) *currency risk.*

exchange risk also **foreign exchange risk** *n* [C,U] FINANCE the possibility of making a loss on a sale, deal etc because of changes in the value of one currency in relation to another: *Most exporters would like to avoid exchange risk by invoicing in their own currency, but they are now finding that markets will set the price and the currency of payment.*

inflation risk [C,U] the risk that inflation will increase: *Some analysts believe the inflation risk is worth taking in an effort to jump-start the economy.*

interest-rate risk [C,U] the possibility that an increase in the rate of interest will cause the price of stocks, shares etc to decrease: *Investors must also worry about interest-rate risk. If interest rates shoot up, stocks and bonds usually fall in price.*

inventory risk [C,U] the possibility that something such as a price change will cause the value of an INVENTORY (=the materials and goods in factories and shops) to decrease

liquidity risk [C,U] ◆ the risk that you will have to pay a charge or fee if you sell an investment to raise money

◆ the risk that an investor will not be able to buy or sell a SECURITY fast enough or in large enough quantities

market risk [C,U] another name for SYSTEMATIC RISK

political risk [C,U] the risk that the value of an investment may be affected by something that a government does, for example changing a tax law: *People associate greater political risk with offshore deposits.*

systematic risk [C,U] ◆ the risk of investing in a specific type of investment such as shares, bonds etc: *These shares have low systematic risks and are expected to earn a return of 10%.*

◆ a risk that affects the whole of an industry, rather than just one company

underwriting risk [C,U] when an INVESTMENT BANKER buys all of the new of shares that a company is selling, the risk that the price will go down before they are sold, or that investors will not want to buy them
unsystematic risk [C,U] ◆ a risk caused by something that affects only one or a few assets, not the whole of the market: *Unsystematic risk can be avoided by holding a well-diversified* ***portfolio*** *variety of investments.*
◆ a risk that affects just one company or industry

3 [C] BANKING the possibility that a person or business will not pay back a loan: *Many banks will not lend to high-risk borrowers*
country risk *n* [C,U] another name for SOVEREIGN RISK
credit risk [C,U] the risk that a person or company will not pay back a loan or debt: *Ford Credit's program ranks customers on a scale from level one, the best credit risk, to level four, the worst risk.*
political risk [C,U] another name for SOVEREIGN RISK
repayment risk [C,U] another name for CREDIT RISK
sovereign risk [C,U] the risk that a foreign government will not pay back a loan or keep a promise to enter into a business deal; COUNTRY RISK; POLITICAL RISK

4 [C] the possibility of a particular type of damage against which you are insured: *Check in detail the risks that are covered by your policy.*

5 [C] also **insurance risk** INSURANCE a person or business judged according to the danger involved in providing them with insurance: *Drivers under 21 are regarded as* ***poor risks*** *by insurance companies.* | *People with previous heart attacks are considered a higher insurance risk.*
actuarial risk [C,U] the possibility that something that is covered by an insurance agreement will actually happen. Insurance companies have to calculate actuarial risks carefully in order to be sure of making a profit
buyer's risk also **buyer risk** ◆ [U] if goods are moved from one place to another at buyer's risk, the buyer must insure the goods while they are being moved: *As soon as the goods are delivered to the buyer, they are at buyer's risk.*
◆ [U] LAW the risk run by someone buying something, for example that the goods are not good quality: *Goods are offered at buyer's risk.*
carrier's risk [U] if goods are moved from one place to another at the carrier's risk, any loss or damage must be paid for by the company that moves them
catastrophe risk [C,U] the possibility that insurance companies will suffer very large losses if there is a CATASTROPHE (=a terrible event that causes a lot of destruction)
insurable risk [C,U] a normal risk such as an accident or a fire for which an insurance company will provide insurance because it can calculate the chance of it happening
non-insurable risk another name for UNINSURABLE RISK
owner's risk [U] *BrE* if goods are moved from one place to another at the owner's risk, the owner must insure the goods while they are being moved: *The seller made a contract for the goods to be carried at 'owner's risk.'*
underwriting risk [C,U] the risk that an insurance company will have to give a customer money to cover loss or damage
uninsurable risk [C,U] a risk for which an insurance company will not provide cover because it cannot calculate the chance of it happening

6 take a risk to decide to do something even though you know it may have bad results: *The choice facing the Government is whether or not to take a risk with inflation by reducing interest rates.*

7 run a/the risk to be in a situation where there is a risk of something bad happening to you: *Building societies must begin to return more of their profits to members or else run the risk of being taken over.*

8 at risk if something is at risk, it is in a situation where it may be damaged or lost: *We have to stop these rumours; the firm's reputation is at risk.* | *Older workers are most at risk of experiencing long-term unemployment.* | *Your home is at risk* (=you might lose it) *if you do not keep up repayments on the loan.*

risk² *v* [T] **1** to put something in a situation in which it could be lost, destroyed, or harmed: *Dexter and Birdie Yager risked their financial future on a brand-new business.* **risk sth on sth**: *You'd be crazy to risk your money on an investment like that!*
2 to get into a situation where something unpleasant may happen to you: *The workers* ***risked dismissal*** *without compensation if the strike continued.*
3 to do something that you know may have dangerous or unpleasant results **risk doing sth**: *Workers who broke the strike risked being attacked when they left the factory.*

risk analysis —see under ANALYSIS

risk arbitrage —see under ARBITRAGE

risk assessment —see under ASSESSMENT

risk-averse *adj* not willing to take risks: *Financial institutions might be so risk-averse that they will not lend money.*

risk-averse investor —see under INVESTOR

risk capital —see under CAPITAL

risk management —see under MANAGEMENT

risk profile —see under PROFILE¹

ri·val¹ /ˈraɪvəl/ *n* [C] **1** a person, group, or organization that you compete with: *Jack left his job and went to work for a* ***rival company***. | *The car was a success because it met the needs of car buyers better than most of its rivals.* | *Japanese suppliers assume they will lose new orders to American rivals for political reasons.* + **for**: *The two men had been rivals for the top job three years ago.*
2 rival bid/offer a BID etc that is competing with another: *General Dynamics' bid was $400 million more expensive than the rival bid from Boeing.* | *L'Oreal significantly increased its bid for the U.S. cosmetics giant Maybelline Inc. to $720 million in an attempt to stop a rival offer from a German firm.*

rival² *v* **rivalled rivalling** *BrE* **rivaled rivaling** *AmE* [T] to be as good or important as someone or something else: *The NCR 3125 notebook computer rivals the power of some desk-top models.*

ri·val·ry /ˈraɪvəlri/ *n* plural **rivalries** [C,U] competition between people, companies, organizations etc who are in the same business or selling similar goods or services in the same market: *Retailers have been pressing manufacturers to keep prices from rising as they face heavy store-versus-store rivalry.*

ROA abbreviation for RETURN ON ASSETS

road·show /ˈrəʊdʃəʊ‖ˈroʊdʃoʊ/ *n* [C] FINANCE a series of meetings in different places organized by a company trying to raise money for investment in order to show its plans to possible investors: *During the roadshow we visited 40 cities and talked to about 900 international investors.*

road tax —see under TAX¹

roar /rɔː‖rɔːr/ *v*
roar ahead *phr v* [I] also **roar up** if sales of a product, prices on a financial market etc roar ahead, they increase very quickly: *Share prices roared ahead last year on falling interest rates.* | *Hong Kong roared up to a record close.*

roar·ing /ˈrɔːrɪŋ/ *adj* **do a roaring trade (in sth)** *informal* to sell a lot of something very quickly: *The food-sellers were doing a roaring trade in spiced sausages.*

ro·bot /ˈrəʊbɒt‖ˈroʊbɑːt, -bət/ *n* [C] a machine used in a manufacturing process: *Robots fulfil many dull and* *tedious jobs on the production line.* | *While half of all American robots are making cars or trucks, Japan's robots are performing a much wider variety of jobs.* —**robotics** *n* [U] *Robotics play a large part in the manufacturing process.*

ROC abbreviation for RETURN ON CAPITAL

ROCE abbreviation for RETURN ON CAPITAL EMPLOYED

rock-bottom *adj* **rock-bottom price/rate/level** a price etc that is as low as it can possibly be: *The declining economies in many countries were the result of rock-bottom prices for export commodities.* | *Interest rates in Japan are already at rock-bottom levels.* —**rock bottom** *n* [U] *The beef business* ***hit rock bottom*** *after the European Commission imposed a global ban on British beef.*

rock bottom price —see under PRICE[1]

rock•et /ˈrɒkɪ̈t‖ˈrɑː-/ also **rocket up** *v* [I] if a price or amount rockets, it increases quickly and suddenly: *Interest rates rocketed.* | *Mexican shares rocketed up 5.4% yesterday.*

rocket scientist *n* [C] *informal* FINANCE someone employed by a financial institution who uses advanced mathematics to calculate what investments to make, to design new financial products etc: *Rocket scientists have compared the movement of stockmarket prices with the movement of particles.*

rocks /rɒks‖rɑːks/ *n* **be on the rocks** *informal* a business or business activity that is on the rocks is having a lot of problems and is likely to fail soon: *Losses from the Thames estuary land deal have put the Ingard group on the rocks.*

ROI abbreviation for RETURN ON INVESTMENT

roll /rəʊl‖roʊl/ *v*

roll sth ↔ **back** *phr v* [T] *AmE* to reduce the price of something to a previous level: *the administration's promise to roll back taxes*

roll in *phr v* [I] *AmE* if money or orders are rolling in, they are arriving in large quantities: *Orders are rolling in from all over Europe.*

roll sth ↔ **out** *phr v* [T] to supply a new product to shops and companies in a region or country after it has been successfully tested and marketed in a small area: *Their aim is to roll out a lot of products. They've got 26 in development.*

roll sth ↔ **over** *phr v* [T] FINANCE if you roll over a loan or investment, you obtain a new loan or investment to replace one that has MATURED (=reached the end of its life): *Balances on bank credit cards can be rolled over into next month's payment, incurring interest.* | *Certificates of deposit are automatically rolled over at current interest rates for another period of the same duration unless the bank is given other instructions.*

roll sth ↔ **up** *phr v* [T] FINANCE if a company or financial institution rolls up the regular payments that would normally be made on an investment, it adds them to the value of the investment and pays them out when the investment MATURES (=reaches the end of its life): *zero-dividend preference shares in which the interest is rolled up over the life of the security and paid out when it is redeemed*

roll•back /ˈrəʊlbæk‖ˈroʊl-/ *n* [C] ECONOMICS when prices, taxes etc are changed back to a previous level as the result of government action: *The President is opposed to a rollback in Social Security taxes.*

roller coaster *n* [singular] when there are large up and down movements in the prices of shares, currencies etc within a short period of time: *Different economic forces turned the market into a buy-sell rollercoaster.* | *After a roller-coaster day, the dollar was down against the mark but up moderately against the yen.*

rolling contract —see under CONTRACT[1]

rolling settlement —see under SETTLEMENT

rolling stock *n* [U] all the trains, carriages etc that are used on a railway: *Amtrak is upgrading* (=improving) *its rolling stock and selling off its old cars.*

roll-on roll-off abbreviation **RORO** *adj BrE* **roll-on roll-off ferry/ship/vessel etc** a roll-on roll-off ferry, ship etc is one that vehicles can drive straight on and off: *a roll-on roll-off car ferry*

roll•out /ˈrəʊlaʊt‖ˈroʊl-/ *n* [C,U] when a new product or service is made available in a region or country after it has been successfully tested and marketed locally: *Pac Bell has been testing its Internet service for rollout sometime this summer.* | *a nationwide* ***product rollout***

roll-over *n* [C] FINANCE **1** *AmE* an occasion when an investment is moved from one financial institution to another without being taxed: *a direct rollover of retirement funds from your former employer to a new pension or IRA*

2 FINANCE when a loan etc that ends in one period of time is replaced by a similar loan etc in the following period: *continued rollover of maturing commercial paper*

3 an occasion when a company changes the products that it sells: *The new series of machines comes just 10 months after the last rollover of the product line.*

rollover loan —see under LOAN[1]

ROM /rɒm‖rɑːm/ *n* COMPUTING read only memory; the part of a computer's memory where permanent instructions and information are stored

rook•ie /ˈrʊki/ *n* [C] *AmE* someone who has just started doing a job and has little experience: *He's just a rookie. That's why he lost the case.*

room[1] /ruːm, rʊm/ *n* **1** [C] a part of the inside of a building: ***conference room*** *facilities* | *the college* ***staff room***

post room also **mail room** [C] the room in a building where letters, parcels etc are sorted and delivered to different people in an organization

2 [U] the possibility that something might happen, or the chance to do things you want to do + **for**: *The U.S. cellular phone industry still has room for growth over the long haul.* | *There is little room for expansion in Softbank's existing businesses.*

3 room for improvement when someone's work or performance is not perfect and needs to be improved: *The report shows that there is room for improvement.*

4 rooms [plural] two or more rooms that you rent in a building —see also BOARDROOM, BOILER ROOM, CHAT ROOM, SALE ROOM

room[2] *v* [I] *AmE* **room with sb** to share a rented room, apartment, or house with someone: *Debra roomed with Pamela and Gregg in an apartment near Florida State University.*

root of title —see under TITLE

RORO /ˈrəʊrəʊ‖ˈroʊroʊ/ abbreviation for ROLL-ON ROLL-OFF

ROS abbreviation for RETURN ON SALES

ro•tate /rəʊˈteɪt‖ˈroʊteɪt/ *v* [I,T] if a job rotates, or if people rotate jobs, they each do the jobs for a fixed period of time, one after the other: *Within each section of the company, workers are now rotated from job to job regularly.* | *The chairmanship of the committee rotates annually.*

ro•ta•tion /rəʊˈteɪʃən‖roʊ-/ *n* **1 by/in rotation** if a group of people do something in rotation, they do it one after the other in a regular order: *The four were Area Board chairmen, serving in rotation.* | *The Director who retires by rotation is Mr F. Cox who, being eligible, offers himself for re-election.*

2 [C,U] the practice of changing regularly from one thing to another, or regularly changing the person who does a particular job: *There are opportunities for **job rotation** throughout the team.*

rou•ble also **ruble** /ˈruːbəl/ *n* [C] the standard unit of money in Russia

rough /rʌf/ *adj* **1** a rough figure or amount is not exact: *It is possible to give here only very **rough figures**. | I can only give you a **rough estimate** at this stage.*
2 not finished: *a **rough draft** of the report*
3 a rough period, time etc is one in which you have a lot of problems or difficulties: *IBM may have a **rough time** marketing the computers as consumer spending is declining due to economic uncertainty. | The group's general insurance business suffered a **rough ride*** (=a very difficult time) *in the early 1990s.*

round¹ /raʊnd/ *adj* **1** a round number or sum is a whole number, often ending in 0: *Let's make it a round £50 I owe you.*
2 in round figures when an amount is not expressed as an exact number, but as the nearest 10, 100, 1000 etc: *In round figures, the expected profit is about £600 million.*

round² *n* [C] a number or set of things that are connected such as a series of meetings or discussions + **of**: *The current round of bargaining began on Oct. 23. | Canadian retailers are facing a round of bankruptcies after being hit by one of the worst holiday sales seasons ever.* —see also BUYING ROUND, MILK ROUND

round³ *v*
round sth ↔ **down** *phr v* [T] to reduce an exact figure to the nearest whole number: *Exact amounts of half a penny or less are rounded down. | The committee rounded down the $6.5 billion result to get $6 billion.*
round sth ↔ **up** *phr v* [T] to increase an exact figure to the next highest whole number: *The IRS allows you, when calculating a partial deduction, to round up to the next $10. Thus, $301 becomes $310.*

round•ing /ˈraʊndɪŋ/ *n* [U] when you express an amount not as an exact number, but as the nearest whole number: *Percentages may not add up to 100% because of rounding. | In fact the sum is 0.99 not 1, the error being due to rounding to two decimal places.*

round lot —see under LOT

round-trip *adj AmE* **round-trip ticket/fare etc** a ticket etc that allows you to travel to a place and back again; RETURN TICKET/FARE *BrE*: *The cheaper fares will apply only to round-trip tickets with a Saturday overnight stay.*

route¹ /ruːt‖ruːt, raʊt/ *n* [C] **1** the way from one place to another, especially a way that is regularly used and can be shown on a map: *What's the best route to Cambridge? | We weren't sure which route we should take.*
2 a road, railway etc along which vehicles often travel: *The London–New York route is the busiest. | Is your office on a **bus route**? | There are plans for a Turkish **shipping route** to Tripoli.*
3 en route (from/to/for) on the way somewhere: *We remained in Belgrade for a few hours en route to Montenegro.*
4 a way of doing something or achieving a particular result: *Free enterprise is the only sure route to financial independence.*
5 Route 54, 66 etc used to show the number of a main road in the US: *Take Route 95 through Connecticut.*

route² *v* [T] to send something or someone using a particular route **route sb/sth through/by**: *They had to route goods through Germany.*

Route 128 *n* COMPUTING an area outside Boston, Massachusetts, where many computer research companies are situated: *the Route 128 region, the East Coast's answer to California's booming Silicon Valley*

rout•er /ˈruːtə‖ˈruːtər, ˈraʊ-/ *n* [C] COMPUTING a device on a computer that makes it possible to connect it to another computer of a different type or on a different NETWORK; GATEWAY: *communications products called routers, which transfer information between computer networks in different locales | Cisco Systems Inc. of Menlo Park makes multimedia and multiprotocol routers.*

rou•tine¹ /ruːˈtiːn/ *n* **1** [C,U] the usual, normal, or fixed way in which you do things: *John's departure had upset their **daily routine**. | the usual office routine*
2 [C] COMPUTING a set of instructions given to a computer so that it will do a particular job: *You can use machine code routines in a number of these programs.*

routine² *adj* **1** regular and usual: *New software will make it possible for employees to make many **routine decisions** that previously had to be referred to managers. | John had been in Pakistan on **routine** company **business**.* —**routinely** *adv*: *Every organization routinely communicates with its employees about a variety of topics.*
2 ordinary and boring: *Much **routine work** has vanished from factories thanks to modern technology. | the drudgery* (=hard boring work) *of routine paperwork*

Royal Charter *n* [C,U] a signed document from a king or queen which allows an organization or university to officially exist and have special rights: *The BBC was established under Royal Charter and is financed by licence fees. | A Royal Charter was granted to the Royal Institution of Chartered Surveyors over a hundred years ago.*

Royal Mint *n* **the Royal Mint** BANKING a British government department which is responsible for producing paper money and coins

roy•al•ty /ˈrɔɪəlti/ *n* plural **royalties** [C] **1** a payment made to someone who owns a COPYRIGHT or a PATENT (=legal right to be the only producer or seller of something), for example an inventor or the writer of a book. The amount depends on the number of products or copies of the work which are sold: *The writer gets a 10% royalty on each copy of his book. | Gingrich was paid $1.2 million in royalties for his best-selling book, 'To Renew America'.*
2 a payment made to someone for the right to remove minerals from their land: *Chevron Corp. yesterday disputed a report that it owed the federal government millions of dollars in royalties and interest on undervalued crude oil produced in California.*

royalty payment —see under PAYMENT

RPI written abbreviation for RETAIL PRICE INDEX

RPM abbreviation for RETAIL PRICE MAINTENANCE

RRP written abbreviation for RECOMMENDED RETAIL PRICE

RSI abbreviation for REPETITIVE STRAIN INJURY

RSVP used on invitations to ask someone to reply

rubber check —see under CHECK¹

rubber chicken circuit *n* [singular] *informal AmE* used to talk about the activity of going to talk as a speaker at dinners where people are encouraged to give money to political parties, NON-PROFIT ORGANIZATIONS (=ones whose aim is to give help in health, education etc) etc: *Dr. Berger may have second thoughts about a book tour. He has probably lost his taste for the rubber chicken circuit.*

rubber stamp —see under STAMP¹

rubber-stamp *v* [T] to give official approval to something without really thinking about it: *Consultants getting a company pay cheque are likely to rubber-stamp all management decisions without question.*

ruble another spelling of ROUBLE

ru•in¹ /ˈruːɪ̇n/ *n* **1** [U] when you have lost all your money, your social position, or the good opinion that people had of you: *The war plunged Yugoslavia into*

economic ruin. | *a company* ***on the brink of financial ruin*** (=about to lose all its money)
2 in ruins if something is in ruins, it has great problems and cannot continue: *countries whose economies are in ruins*

ruin² *v* [T] **1** to spoil or destroy something completely: *The airport's radar failed, ruining travel plans for 30,000 people.* | *a scandal that ruined his reputation*
2 to make someone lose all their money: *A series of bad investment decisions threatened to ruin him.* | *a ruined economy*

ru•in•ous /ˈruːɪ̇nəs/ *adj* **1** causing great damage to something: *Poland is recovering from decades of ruinous central planning.*
2 costing a lot more than you can afford: *the prospect of ruinous legal costs* —**ruinously** *adv*: *ruinously high interest rates*

rule¹ /ruːl/ *n* **1** [C] an official instruction that says how things should be done or what is allowed: *The company had violated accounting rules.* | *The phone companies are working under new rules now.* | *The Customs Service found that Honda* ***broke the rules*** *of the U.S.-Canada free-trade pact.* | *company* ***rules and regulations*** *regarding sexual harrassment* —see also HAGUE RULES

accounting rule also **accounting standard** an official instruction on how something must be treated and presented in accounts: *Accounting rules required us to recognize the costs as an expense.*

earnings rule [singular] in Britain, a rule which until 1979 limited how much people with a state PENSION could earn by working, for example in a part-time job: *By abolishing that hated earnings rule we have enabled pensioners to keep their retirement pension, even if they take a job in retirement.*

2 [U] the government of a country by a particular group of people or using a particular system: *a constitution that formally ended one-party rule*
3 work to rule to work less quickly or effectively than usual, but without breaking your employer's rules, as a protest: *The customs men are prohibited from striking, but some have worked to rule out of sympathy with the government workers.*
4 be the rule to be the normal or usual thing to happen in a situation: *Monopoly business practices in Mexico are the rule and not the exception.*

rule² *v* [I,T] **1** to have the official power to control a country or organization: *Nicaragua is no longer ruled by a Marxist-Leninist government.* | *Each bank would be ruled by a mix of outside directors.*
2 to make an official decision about something, especially a legal problem + **(that)**: *The board ruled that the contract was valid and should be honored.* + **against**: *The court had ruled against the use of any unpublished works.* | *a court decision to* ***rule in favour of*** *the Bell companies* —see also ***work to rule*** under WORK¹

rule sth ↔ **out** *phr v* [T] **1** to decide that something is not possible or suitable: *Management has not ruled out further redundancies.*
2 to make it impossible for something to happen: *The mountainous terrain rules out most forms of agriculture.*

rule book —see under BOOK¹

rul•ing¹ /ˈruːlɪŋ/ *n* [C] an official decision, especially one made by a court + **that**: *a district court ruling that the plaintiff's medical evidence was unreliable* | *The ITC must* ***issue a final ruling*** *by October.*

ruling² *adj* [only before a noun] the ruling group in a country or organization is the group that controls it: *the ruling party's economic policies*

ru•mour *BrE*, also **rumor** *AmE* /ˈruːmə‖-ər/ *n* [C,U] information that is passed from one person to another and which may or may not be true: *A Porsche spokesman* ***denied rumours*** *that the company was considering abandoning the U.S. market.*

ru•moured *BrE*, also **rumored** *AmE* /ˈruːməd‖-ərd/ *adj* if something is rumoured to be true, people are saying secretly or unofficially that it is true: *Several companies were rumoured to be among the bidders for Alpo.* | *a rumored reorganization of the company*

run¹ /rʌn/ *v* past simple **ran** past perfect **run** present participle **running** **1** [T] to control or be in charge of an organization, company, or system: *I've always wanted to* ***run*** *my own* ***business.*** | *For a while, she ran a restaurant in Boston.* | *A* ***well-run*** *company should not have problems of this kind.* | *a* ***state-run*** *airline*
2 [T] COMPUTING to be able to use a particular kind of operating system or computer program: *The RS8 system runs both Unix and MPX-32.*
3 up and running working fully and correctly: *The new system won't be up and running until next week.*
4 [I] to continue to be VALID (legally or officially acceptable) for a particular period of time: *The contract runs for a year.* | *My car insurance only has another year to run.*
5 [I] to happen or take place, especially in the way that was intended: *So far, it had all* ***run according to plan*** (=happened in the way you planned). | *Her job is to ensure university catering* ***runs smoothly*** (=happens with no unexpected problems).
6 [T] to operate a bus, train, or plane service: *They're running special trains to and from the exhibition.*
7 be running at to currently be at a particular level: *Inflation at that time was running at 10%.*
8 be running short of sth to have very little of something left: *The insurance fund was running short of cash.*
9 be running late to be doing everything later than planned or expected: *They were running late, so I didn't get interviewed until nearly 4 o'clock.*
10 run a check/test on to arrange for something or someone to be checked or tested: *Car-rental companies are running background checks on drivers who rent for long periods.* | *She worked for a company* ***running credit checks*** *on people.*
11 [I] to try to be elected in an election + **for**: *He has yet to decided whether to run for chairman.* + **against**: *Liberal Democrats are running against conservative Republicans.*
12 run an advertisement/a story/a feature etc to print an advertisement, a story etc in a newspaper or magazine: *magazines that don't run tobacco ads* | *The paper still runs articles that anger dealers.*

run sth ↔ **down** *phr v* [T] **1** to let an organization gradually become smaller or stop working: *The coal industry is being slowly run down.*
2 to use something without replacing it: *The Saudis have been running down their financial reserves.* | *They have let their sugar stocks run down to extremely low levels.*

run into sth *phr v* **1 run into difficulties/ problems/debt** to start to experience difficulties: *shareholders who sue when institutions run into financial difficulties*
2 run into hundreds/thousands etc to reach an amount of several hundred, several thousand etc: *Attorneys' fees can run into tens of millions of dollars in business litigation.*
3 run sth into the ground to harm or destroy a company by using too much of its money: *I got tired of seeing guys run banks into the ground and then leave with a massive fortune.*

run sth ↔ **off** *phr v* [T] **1** to quickly print several copies of something: *Can you run off a couple of copies of this report?*
2 be run off your feet to be very busy: *It was just before Christmas and all the sales staff were rushed off their feet.*

R

run out *phr v* [I] **1** to use all of something and not have any of it left + **of**: *Indonesia is worried about running out of oil some day.*
2 if something runs out, there is none of it left: *Regulators close a bank when its capital runs out.*
3 if an agreement or other official document runs out, it reaches the end of a period of time when it is officially allowed to continue: *My contract runs out in September.*
run to sth *phr v* [T] to reach a particular amount: *The damages awarded by the court could run to one billion pounds.*
run up *phr v* [I] FINANCE **1** if share prices run up, they increase: *The stock price had run up just before the deal was announced.*
2 run up a bill/expenses/debts to use a lot of something or borrow a lot of money, so that you owe a lot of money: *He ran up thousands of pounds worth of debts using other people's credit cards.*
run up against sb/sth *phr v* [T] to have to deal with unexpected problems or a difficult opponent: *We ran up against some unexpected opposition.*

run² *n* **1** [C] a period of time when something is done or something happens:
bear run [C] a period of falling prices on a financial market: *Seoul's bear run continued for its third week, as prices continued to plunge.*
bull run [C] a period of time when prices are rising on a financial market: *The stock market was on a spectacular bull run in which almost any investment paid off.*
2 a run on sth when a lot of people suddenly buy a particular product: *Controls were necessary to prevent a run on inexpensive Czech goods.*
3 a run on a/the bank also **bank run** when a lot of people all take their money out of a bank at the same time: *A run on any bank could spread to other banks and threaten the entire system.* | *Even a minor bank run could bring down the system.*
4 a run on the dollar/pound etc when a lot of people sell dollars, pounds etc and their value goes down: *Financial markets panicked, causing a run on the Brazilian currency.*
5 in the long run at a later time in the future or over a longer period of time: *Companies such as Microsoft do benefit in the long-run from copying, because it is a form of free advertising.*
6 in the short run in the near future: *The plan does provide some help in the short run.*
7 a run of failures/wins/strikes etc a series of failures, wins etc: *The company has had a run of spectacularly successful years.* —see also PRINT RUN

run•a•way /ˈrʌnəweɪ/ *adj* **1 runaway costs/prices/inflation etc** costs, prices etc that are increasing uncontrollably: *the runaway costs of workers' compensation* | *Bolivia was experiencing runaway inflation and foreign debt.*
2 a runaway success/hit/bestseller etc an extremely successful product, book, film etc: *The latest version of Windows has been a runaway bestseller.*

run•down /ˈrʌndaʊn/ *n* [singular] **1** a quick report or explanation of an idea, situation etc + **of**: *Can you* ***give me a rundown*** *of everything you discussed in the meeting?*
2 when a business or industry is made smaller and less important: *The rundown continued and hospitals continued to close.*

run-down *adj* a building or area that is run-down is in very bad condition: *We have a contract to renovate 5 run-down apartment buildings.*

rung /rʌŋ/ *n* [C usually singular] a particular level or position in an organization or system: *She is already on the* ***highest rung*** *of the salary scale.*

run•ning¹ /ˈrʌnɪŋ/ *n* **1 the running of** the way in which an organization or system is managed or organized: *He has little say in the running of the company.*
2 be in the running/out of the running to have some hope or no hope of achieving something + **for**: *Two European aircraft builders are in the running for the contract.*

running² *adj* **1 running argument/battle/debate etc** an argument etc that continues or is repeated over a long period of time: *the running debate over taxes and growth*
2 running total a total that is continually increased as new costs, amounts etc are added: *We have been* ***keeping a running total of*** *layoff announcements by major corporations.*
3 in running order a machine that is in running order is working correctly: *They had failed to keep the crane in running order.*
4 the running order the order in which the different parts of an event have been arranged to take place: *The running order had to be changed at the last minute.*
5 three years/five times etc running for three years, five times etc without a change or interruption: *We have made a profit two years running.*
6 running repairs small repairs that you do to a machine to keep it working

running cost —see under COST¹

running yield —see under YIELD¹

run•up /ˈrʌnʌp/ *n* [C] FINANCE if there is a runup in the stockmarket, prices rise: *Chrysler's stock has enjoyed a rapid runup in recent weeks.*

run-up *n* **1 the run-up to** the period of time just before an important event: *the run-up to the general election*
2 [C usually singular] FINANCE when prices increase, especially suddenly and quickly + **in**: *the recent run-up in share prices*

ru•ral /ˈrʊərəl‖ˈrʊr-/ *adj* happening in or connected with the countryside, not the city: *a rural development program*

rur•ban /ˈrɜːbən‖ˈrɜːr-/ *adj* happening or connected with areas on the edge of cities that are being developed and may soon become part of the city: *What changes are happening on the* ***rurban fringe*** *of towns and cities?*

rush¹ /rʌʃ/ *v* **1** [I] to move or go somewhere very quickly and in large amounts + **into**: *Foreign capital is rushing into Asia at an incredible rate.*
2 [I,T] to do something too quickly, especially so that you do not have time to do it carefully or well: *There's plenty of time – we don't need to rush.* | *GM chose not to rush development of the powerful 32-valve V-8 engine.*
3 rush to do sth to do something eagerly and without delay: *Investors are rushing to buy bonds.*
4 [T] to take or send something somewhere very quickly, especially because of an unexpected problem: *We had to rush the backup disk to the office.* | *Volkswagen rushed in its bid early.*
5 [T] to try to make someone do something more quickly than they want to: *I'm sorry to rush you, but we need a decision by Friday.* **rush sb into doing sth**: *Don't let them rush you into signing the contract.*
rush into sth *phr v* [T] to get involved in something without taking enough time to think carefully about it: *Some firms rushed blindly into unsuitable mergers.*
rush sth ↔ **out** *phr v* [T] to make a new product, book etc available for sale very quickly: *We had to rush out extra copies of the manual.*
rush sth ↔ **through** *phr v* [T] to deal with official or government business more quickly than usual: *The Senate rushed through a $28 billion transportation bill.*

rush² *n* **1** [singular, U] a situation in which you need to hurry: *We don't see any rush or urgency to buy right now.* | *They are* **in no rush** *to make a deal.* | *The army placed a* **rush order** *for a special tape.*
2 [singular] when a lot of people suddenly try to do or get something + **for**: *We're going to see a big rush for Western goods.* + **on**: *a rush on swimsuits in the hot weather* **rush to do sth**: *The rush to buy shares did not last long.*
3 [singular] the time in the day, month, year etc when a place or group of people are particularly busy: *The cafe is quiet until* **the lunchtime rush**. | **the Christmas rush** —see also GOLD-RUSH

rush hour *n* [U] the time of day when the roads, buses, trains etc are most crowded, because people are travelling to or from work: *I try not to travel at rush hour.* | *heavy rush-hour traffic*

rust·belt /ˈrʌstbelt/ also **rust·bowl** /-bəʊl‖boʊl/ *n* [C] an old industrial area where the factories are old or have closed down: *The Midwest continued to lose its image of the nation's rustbelt.* | *Rustbelt cities like St. Paul and Indianapolis*

R

S

S & L abbreviation for SAVINGS AND LOAN ASSOCIATION

SA used in the names of a type of LIMITED COMPANY in French-, Portuguese-, and Spanish-speaking countries, and Italy: *Peugeot SA* —see also SARL

sab•bat•i•cal /sə'bætɪkəl/ *n* [C,U] a period of time when someone, especially someone in a university teaching job, stops doing their usual work in order to work in business, study, or travel: *He spent his sabbatical from Stanford University at Salomon Brothers, studying computer applications in finance.* —**sabbatical** *adj*: *She's on* ***sabbatical leave.***

sabbatical leave —see under LEAVE

sab•o•tage /'sæbətɑːʒ/ *v* [T] **1** to secretly damage or destroy equipment, vehicles etc that belong to an enemy or opponent, so that they cannot be used: *There are fears that striking workers may try to sabotage the plant.*
2 to deliberately spoil someone's plans because you do not want them to succeed: *He's trying to sabotage my career.* | *Why would anyone want to sabotage the deal?* —**sabotage** *n* [U] *Boeing was investigating an apparent case of* ***industrial sabotage*** *after a jetliner in the final stages of production failed certain tests because of "highly irregular" wire cuts.*

SACD *n* [C] super audio compact disk; a very high quality CD

sach•et /'sæʃeɪ‖sæ'ʃeɪ/ *n* [C] a small plastic or paper package containing a product in liquid or powder form

sack¹ /sæk/ *n BrE informal* **get the sack/give sb the sack** to be dismissed from your job or to dismiss someone from their job + **for**: *He got the sack for stealing.* | *They've never actually given anyone the sack.*

sack² *v* [T] *informal* to dismiss someone from their job; fire: *I was given a choice – resign or be sacked.* —**sacking** *n* [C] *the events that led to his sacking*

sac•ri•fice¹ /'sækrɪfaɪs/ *n* [C,U] something valuable that you decide not to have, in order to get something that is more important: *Our group may be willing to* ***make*** *certain* ***sacrifices*** *to make the company financially viable.* | *Polish people faced a hard winter of* ***economic sacrifice.***

sacrifice² *v* [T] to willingly stop having something you want or doing something you like in order to get something more important **sacrifice sth for**: *Nurses working for agencies sacrifice security for the power to regulate their own careers.* **sacrifice sth to do sth**: *Intense competition has forced VW to sacrifice profit margins to stay competitive.*

sad•dle¹ /'sædl/ *n* **be in the saddle** *informal* to be in charge of an organization or system: *Rogers was back in the saddle again at Hardee's Food Systems Inc.*

saddle² *v*
saddle sb **with** sth *phr v* [T] to give someone a difficult or boring job that causes problems for them: *The changes would saddle banks with costly new paper work.*

sae /ˌes eɪ 'iː/ *n* [C] *BrE* **1** stamped addressed envelope; an envelope that you put your name, address, and a stamp on, so that someone can send you something
2 self-addressed envelope; an envelope that you put your own name and address on

safe¹ /seɪf/ *adj* **1** not likely to cause any harm or injury: *Our products are safe when used correctly.* | *Recycling is a safer and cheaper alternative to burning waste.*
2 not in danger of being lost, harmed, or stolen: *How safe is your job?* + **from**: *a technology to keep electronic documents safe from forgery*
3 [only before a noun] not involving any risk and very likely to succeed: *The dollar is usually regarded as a* ***safe investment.*** | *Precious metals stocks are a* ***safe haven*** *for investors in uncertain periods.* (=people who invest in them are unlikely to lose money)
4 play it safe to not take any risks: *The pension funds are playing it safe by going with the large ones.*

safe² *n* [C] a strong metal box or other container with strong locks, where you keep your money and other valuable things
night safe *BrE* a special container built into the outside wall of a bank into which a customer can put money or documents when the bank is closed; NIGHT DEPOSITORY *AmE*

safe custody —see under CUSTODY

safe-deposit box *n* [C] a small box used for storing valuable objects, usually kept in a special room in a bank

safe•guard¹ /'seɪfgɑːd‖-gɑːrd/ *v* [I,T] to protect something from harm or damage: *New regulations were introduced to safeguard the environment.* + **against**: *We will safeguard against future problems by appointing a quality control inspector.*

safeguard² *n* [C] a rule, law etc that is intended to protect someone or something from possible dangers or problems: *The law contains important safeguards to protect housebuyers.* + **against**: *a safeguard against financial abuse*

safe haven *n* [C] a place for business where there are few risks, and where it is safe to invest your money etc: *Switzerland is no longer the safe haven it once was for the world's wealthy.* | *Dealers moved to the dollar – the traditional* ***safe-haven currency*** (=one that is unlikely to lose value).

safe-haven *adj* **safe-haven currency/bond/investment etc** a currency, bond, or investment that has few risks: *the dollar's reputation as a safe-haven currency* | *safe-haven buying triggered by recent tensions in the Middle East*

safe•ty /'seɪfti/ *n* [U] **1** the state of being safe from danger or harm: *The company seemed totally unconcerned about the safety of its workers.*
2 the state of not being dangerous or likely to cause harm or injury: *There were no* ***safety problems*** *with the product.* | *The accident would never have happened if the correct* ***safety procedures*** *had been followed.* | *a long list of* ***safety measures***

safety net *n* [C] FINANCE actions by a government to help companies and financial institutions with financial difficulties: *a regulatory safety net to guard against possible risks in the event of a securities trading firm's collapse*

sag /sæg/ *v* past tense and past participle **sagged** present participle **sagging** [I] to become weaker or to fall in amount: *The airline industry tends to sag during recessions.* | *the* ***sagging demand*** *for steel* —**sag** *n* [singular] *There has been a slight sag in oil production.*

salable *adj* another spelling of SALEABLE

sal•a•ried /'sælərid/ *adj* having a permanent job with an organization and receiving payment for it every month, rather than every week or every hour: *100* ***salaried employees*** *were dismissed.* | *I would prefer to have a* ***salaried job.***

sal•a•ry /'sæləri/ *n* plural **salaries** [C,U] money that you receive as payment from the organization you work for, usually paid to you every month: *She's* ***on a salary of*** *£28,000.* | *This is my first increase in salary.*

S

basic salary your salary before extra money such as BONUSES and COMMISSION (=extra money you get when you make a sale) is added to it: *On top of the basic salary there are numerous other benefits.*

gross salary your salary before tax has been taken from it

net salary your salary after tax has been taken from it

starting salary the salary you get for doing a job, when you first start doing it: *Your starting salary will be in the range of £15,000.*

sal·a·ry·man /ˈsæləriˌmæn/ *n* plural **salarymen** [C] *informal* a man who works in an office and receives a salary as payment, especially in Japan: *Mr. Nishimura, a 48-year-old information-systems manager, is a typical salaryman, Japan's man in the gray suit.*

salary payment —see under PAYMENT

salary scale —see under SCALE

sale /seɪl/ *n* **1** [C,U] the act of selling someone property, food, or other goods + **of**: *Singapore placed a ban on the sale of chewing gum.* | *The house sale was completed in four weeks.* | *Every time we* ***make a sale****, I get $50 commission.* | *Rather than* ***lose a sale****, car salesmen will often bring down the price.* | *Tickets* ***go on sale*** (=become available to buy) *later this week.* —see also BILL OF SALE, CONDITIONS OF SALE, OFFER FOR SALE, POINT OF SALE, TRUST FOR SALE, TRUSTEE FOR SALE

cash sale [C] a sale in which full payment is received immediately, rather than in regular monthly payments: *P&O announced the £360 million cash sale of its industrial services division.*

conditional sale [C,U] *BrE* a sale in which payment will be made in one payment some time in the future or in smaller regular payments over a period of time. The seller remains the owner of the property or goods being sold until full payment is made: *He bought the vehicle under a* ***conditional sale agreement****.*

credit sale [C,U] a sale in which payment will be made in one payment some time in the future or in smaller regular payments over a period of time. The buyer is the owner of the property of goods being sold from the time the arrangement is made: *the distinction between hire purchase, credit sale, and conditional sale*

direct sale [C,U] ◆ a sale made by a manufacturer or importer direct to a shop, rather than through a WHOLESALER or a DISTRIBUTOR: *We rely on local distributors rather than direct sales in Europe.* | *a company's* ***direct sales force***

◆ a sale made by a WHOLESALER or DISTRIBUTOR direct to the public, rather than through shops

direct sales [plural] when a company sells goods directly to shops, rather than using another company to distribute its goods

firm sale ◆ [C,U] when a shop buys a quantity of goods from a supplier, and cannot return any goods it does not sell: *Specialist booksellers usually have a minimum order and offer only firm sales.*

◆ [C] an agreement to buy something, but for which no payment has actually been received: *Are you sure this is a firm sale?*

last sale [C] FINANCE the most recent sale of shares in a particular company on a stockmarket

private sale [C,U] the sale of something in an arrangement directly between the seller and the buyer, rather than openly: *Verit completed the private sale of 61,500 shares of preferred stock to a Liechtenstein investment company.*

public sale [C,U] when something is offered for sale openly, rather than sold in a private arrangement: *Easycall Communications plans to raise 216 million Philippine pesos through the public sale of 12 million common shares.*

short sale [C] FINANCE an occasion when someone sells shares they do not yet own, believing that the price will fall so that the shares can be bought more cheaply before they have to be delivered; BEAR SALE

wash sale FINANCE an occasion when the buyer and seller of shares is the same person or organization. Wash sales are done to give the false impression that investors are interested in the shares, and are illegal: *He told investigators that large blocks of Angeion stock were being traded in wash sales.*

2 for sale available to be bought: *Executives said the firm may be for sale.* | *We don't have a* ***for-sale sign*** *up outside the building.* | *She recently* ***put her house up for sale****.*

3 [C] a period of time when a shop sells its goods at lower prices than usual: *She buys soap in bulk when the drugstore* ***has a sale****.*

clearance sale [C] a sale in which a shop gets rid of all its old stock: *Shoppers returned over the weekend, drawn by clearance sales.*

closing down sale *BrE* [C] ◆ a sale in which a shop gets rid of all its stock before it closes permanently: *a street of boarded-up shops and closing down sales*

◆ **on sale** *AmE* available for a short time at a reduced price: ON OFFER *BrE*: *I bought a set of iron skillets on sale for $8.99.*

end-of-season sale [C] a sale in which a shop sells unsold stock of spring, summer, autumn, or winter clothing at the end of each particular season at a reduced price

4 the sales [plural] *BrE* when shops are selling their goods at a lower prices than usual: *You might be able to get a cheap bed* ***in the sales****.* | *The cost of footwear was reduced by 12%* ***at the January sales****.*

5 [C] an event at which things are sold, especially to the person who offers the highest price + **of**: *a sale of 17th century paintings* | ***Auction sales*** *took place to get rid of properties quickly.*

fire sale also **firesale** [C] an occasion when someone sells something at a very low price because they need the money very quickly: *The insurer lost $7.32 a share amid a fire sale of large parts of its real estate and junk bond portfolios.*

6 sales [plural] the total number of products that a company sells during a particular period of time: *We grossed more than £500,000 in sales last year.* | *The division continues to show* ***sales growth****.* | *They've already reached their* ***sales targets*** *for this year.* | *Do you have this month's* ***sales figures****?*

gross sales [plural] money from sales, without taking costs, tax etc into account; GROSS RECEIPTS: *His contract gave Mr Kroc 1.9% of the gross sales from McDonalds' franchisees.*

net sales [plural] money from a company's sales in a particular period of time, after taking off goods returned by customers, DISCOUNTS (=price reductions given to customers) etc: *The beer company's net sales, that is, sales after excise taxes, climbed to $2.78 billion from $2.48 billion.*

retail sales [plural] sales to members of the public, rather than to a shop or other business: *Retail sales rose 0.6% in January.*

trade sales [plural] sales to shops or businesses, rather than to members of the public: *Trade sales of children's books rose by 25%.* —see also TELESALES

7 sales [U] the part of a company that deals with selling products: *I'd like to work in sales.* | *She is director of* ***sales and marketing****.* | *a* ***sales manager***

sale·a·ble also **salable** /ˈseɪləbəl/ *adj* **1** something that is easy to sell: *Credit cards have become major* ***saleable assets*** *for retailers.*

2 something that can be sold: *turning agricultural commodities into saleable goods* —**saleability** *n* [U] *ideas on how to improve the saleability of the product*

S

sale and leaseback —see under LEASEBACK

sale and repurchase agreement —see under AGREEMENT

sale as seen *n* plural **sales as seen** [C,U] when a seller does not promise that the goods he or she is selling are in good condition or are right for a particular purpose

sale by description *n* plural **sales by description** [C,U] a sale made under the agreed condition that the goods being sold are as they are described by their seller: *Even a sale in a supermarket is a sale by description.*

sale by sample *n* plural **sales by sample** [C,U] a sale made under the agreed condition that most of the goods being sold are as good as one that has been shown to the buyer as a SAMPLE

sale or return *n* [U] *BrE* if a shop buys something on a sale or return basis, it can return the goods it is unable to sell

sale price —see under PRICE[1]

sale room *BrE* also **salesroom** *n* [C] a room where things are sold by AUCTION

sales account —see under ACCOUNT[1]

sales and repurchase agreement —see under AGREEMENT

sales area —see under AREA

sales campaign —see under CAMPAIGN

sales•clerk /ˈseɪlzklɑːk‖-klɜːrk/ *n* [C] *AmE* someone who sells things in a shop; SHOP ASSISTANT *BrE*

sales day book —see under BOOK[1]

sales drive —see under DRIVE[2]

sales expense —see under EXPENSE

sales fee —see under FEE

sales force —see under FORCE[1]

sales invoice —see under INVOICE[1]

sales ledger —see under LEDGER

sales•man /ˈseɪlzmən/ *n* plural **salesmen** [C] a man whose job is to persuade people to buy his company's products: *an insurance salesman*

travelling salesman someone whose job involves going from place to place, selling a company's products; COMMERCIAL TRAVELLER *BrE*

sales manager —see under MANAGER

sales•man•ship /ˈseɪlzmənʃɪp/ *n* [U] the ability to persuade people to buy your company's products: *Mr Ball's salesmanship skills are the reason why he was hired.*

sales mix —see under MIX

sales orientation —see under ORIENTATION

sales•per•son /ˈseɪlzˌpɜːsən‖-ˌpɜːr-/ *n* plural **salespeople** [C] someone whose job is to persuade people to buy his or her company's products

sales pitch —see under PITCH[1]

sales representative —see under REPRESENTATIVE[1]

sales returns account —see under ACCOUNT[1]

sales returns book —see under BOOK[1]

salesroom *n* [C] another name for SALE ROOM

sales slip —see under SLIP[2]

sales tax —see under TAX[1]

sales war —see under WAR

sales•wom•an /ˈseɪlzˌwʊmən/ *n* plural **saleswomen** [C] a woman whose job is to persuade people to buy her company's products

sal•vage /ˈsælvɪdʒ/ *v* [T] to save goods or property from a situation in which things have already been damaged or destroyed: *Unsuccessful attempts were made to salvage the ship immediately after it sank.*

sal•vor /ˈsælvə‖-ər/ *n* [C] INSURANCE someone who organizes or takes part in the rescue of lost or damaged goods or property, especially of a ship: *Claims from salvors can be referred to the Personal Claims Department.*

sam•ple[1] /ˈsɑːmpl‖ˈsæm-/ *n* [C] **1** a group of people who have been chosen to give opinions or information about something + **of**: *Of a sample of executives in 600 companies, 15% had no plans to do business in the EU.* | *The General Accounting Office surveyed a* ***random sample*** (=a group of people chosen without knowing anything about them) *of 9,400 employers.* | *The agency interviewed a* ***representative sample*** (=a specially chosen group including several different types of people) *of 1,003 people in the city.*

quota sample when a market is divided into different groups by age, sex, area etc, and a sample is then taken from each group, to reflect what percentage of each group is in the total market: *The quota sample can avoid the kind of gross errors made by attitude surveys in the past.*

2 a small amount of a product that people can try in order to find out what it is like: *He used the product after receiving a* ***free sample*** *in the mail.* | *'Entertainment Weekly' had thousands of requests for sample issues.*

3 a small part or amount of something that is tested in order to find out something about the whole + **of**: *A sample of the water showed too much sodium for the company to use the term 'sodium free' on the bottle.*

judgement sample also **judgment sample** *AmE* ACCOUNTING a number of items in a company's accounts that an AUDITOR (=an accountant from outside the company) examines in order to decide if the accounts as a whole are correct

sample[2] *v* [T] **1** to ask a group of people chosen from a larger group questions, in order to get information or opinions from them, so as to better understand the larger group: *Four different groups of adults were sampled for the survey.*

2 to try a small amount of a product in order to find out what it is like: *Here's your chance to sample our latest product.*

samp•ling /ˈsɑːmplɪŋ‖ˈsæm-/ *n* [C,U] STATISTICS the activity of checking a small number of products from a larger number, asking questions to people from a larger number etc, so as to understand better the group as a whole: *We use extensive* ***product sampling*** *to guarantee the freshness of our products.* | *The statistics were based on a sampling of 400 people.* | *weekly samplings of mosquito populations at hundreds of locations around the county*

acceptance sampling ◆ MANUFACTURING a way of checking the quality of MASS-PRODUCED goods, in which a small number of the finished items are examined, and the standard of this sample is used as a guide to the quality of the rest: *Inspection is undertaken primarily by process control and acceptance sampling.*
◆ ACCOUNTING when a small number of documents, records etc are checked to see if they are correct, and the standard of this sample is used as guide to whether the rest are correct

Sam•u•rai bond /ˈsæmʊraɪ ˌbɒnd‖-ˌbɑːnd/ —see under BOND

sanc•tion /ˈsæŋkʃən/ *n* [C] **1 sanctions** [plural] official orders or laws stopping trade, communication etc with another country as a way of forcing political changes + **against**: *US sanctions against Cuba* | *Japan lifted* ***economic sanctions*** *against South Africa when Mandela came to power.*

2 a punishment for disobeying a rule or law: *The most severe sanction the panel could recommend is expulsion from the Senate.*

3 official permission or approval: *He indicated they would go ahead without OPEC sanction if necessary.*

S

—**sanction** *v* [T] *Shareholders must sanction donations to political parties before they are made.*

sandwich course —see under COURSE

SARL used in the names of a type of LIMITED COMPANY in French-, Portuguese-, and Spanish-speaking countries, and Italy: *Companhia de Investimentos SARL* —see also SA

sat•el•lite /ˈsætəlaɪt/ *n* **1** [C,U] a machine that has been sent into space and goes around the Earth, used for radio, television, and other electronic communication: *a **satellite communications** company* | *They provide news and live sporting events **by satellite**.* | ***Satellite TV** competes with cable.*
2 [C] a country or organization that is controlled by or is dependent on another larger one: *Deutsche Bank has established ties with the former Russian satellites and with Russia itself.*

satellite office —see under OFFICE

sat•is•fac•tion /ˌsætəsˈfækʃən/ *n* **1** [C,U] a feeling of happiness or pleasure with what you have got or what you have achieved: *A survey of Passat owners showed 97% satisfaction.* | *Now that we are getting more business, we plan to focus on **customer satisfaction**.* | *Financial rewards are important, but so is **job satisfaction**.*
2 [U] the act of providing what is needed, demanded, or desired: *the satisfaction of material needs*

sat•u•rate /ˈsætʃəreɪt/ *v* **saturate the market** to offer so much of a product for sale that there is more than people want to buy: *Seagate and its rivals saturated the market with 3.5 inch hard disk drives, bringing down the price.* | *Smaller banks are struggling to compete in an already saturated market.* —**saturation** *n* [U] *Companies are worried about market saturation.*

save /seɪv/ *v* **1** also **save** sth ↔ **up** [I,T] to keep or collect money to use later, especially when you gradually add more money over a period of time: *She saves £200 a month from her salary.* | *We want to increase incentives to work, save, and invest.* + **for**: *I'm saving up for a new car.* **save to do sth**: *After three years he had saved up enough to fly to Australia.*
2 [T] to use less money, time, energy etc, so that you do not waste any: *The Bank expects to save $1.4 million a year with the job cuts.* | *new energy-saving technology* **save sb sth**: *An experienced tax professional can save you time and trouble.*
3 [I,T] to make a computer keep the work that you have done in its permanent memory: *You transfer information to permanent disk storage by saving your file.* | *Don't forget to save every few minutes.*

save as you earn abbreviation **SAYE** *n* [U] a system in Britain in which money is taken from your wages before you are paid and invested for you in NATIONAL SAVINGS

sav•er /ˈseɪvə‖-ər/ *n* [C] someone who saves money in a bank: *tax breaks for savers* | *Regular savers enjoy high interest rates.*

savi•ng /ˈseɪvɪŋ/ *n* **1** [U] the act of keeping money to use later rather than spending it: *We want to encourage saving and investment.*
forced saving [U] when people spend less than they earn because there are not enough goods available to buy or because goods are too expensive
personal saving [U] when a person rather than a company or organization saves money to spend or invest later: *tax breaks to encourage personal saving*
2 [C usually singular] an amount of something that you have not used or spent, especially compared with a larger amount that you could have used or spent: *This amount represents a considerable saving over last year's expenditure.* + **of**: *Recent pension-plan changes will make a saving of $400 million next year.*
3 savings [plural] money that is kept in a bank to use later or to invest, rather than to spend: *Investors lost their **life savings** (=all the money they had saved during their life) when the bank collapsed.*
4 [U] ECONOMICS when total income in the economy is more than the total amount spent on goods —compare DIS-SAVING, SPENDING

savings account —see under ACCOUNT[1]

Savings and Loan Association also **savings and loan**, abbreviation **S&L** *n* [C] FINANCE in the US, an organization that lends money, usually to build or buy houses, using money from investors who put their savings into it; THRIFT: *His mortgage application was turned down by a savings-and-loan association.* —compare BUILDING SOCIETY

savings bank —see under BANK[1]

savings bond —see under BOND

sav•vy /ˈsævi/ *n* [U] *informal* practical knowledge and experience: *companies with the money and market savvy to manipulate prices* —**savvy** *adj* [only before a noun] *Savvy investors will do more than just go for companies with straight A rankings.*

SAYE abbreviation for SAVE AS YOU EARN

SBA abbreviation for SMALL BUSINESS ADMINISTRATION

SBU abbreviation for STRATEGIC BUSINESS UNIT —see under UNIT

scab /skæb/ *n* [C] an insulting word for someone who works when other people in the same factory, office etc are on strike

scal•a•ble /ˈskeɪləbəl/ *adj* a scalable machine, system etc can be increased in size: *We needed a computer system that was scalable and that could keep up with our growing number of users.*

scale /skeɪl/ *n* **1** [singular, U] the size or level of something, especially when this is large + **of**: *No-one had anticipated the scale of the redundancies* (=that there would be so many). | *There will be losses, but nothing **on the scale** of last year's.* | *We need to recycle plastics **on a** much bigger **scale**.*
2 diseconomies of scale [plural] the disadvantages that a big factory, shop etc has over a smaller one, for example because it is more difficult to run a larger production unit: *Over a period of decades, output becomes less efficient and profitable as diseconomies of scale arise.*
3 economies of scale [plural] the advantages that a big factory, shop etc has over a smaller one because it can spread its FIXED COSTS over a larger number of units and therefore produce or sell things more cheaply: *Toys 'R' Us buys massive quantities directly from manufacturers and has gigantic stores with huge economies of scale.*
4 [C] a list of figures used for measuring and comparing amounts + **of**: *a progressive scale of tax rates for capital gains* | *Managers gave their opinion of the bond markets, ranked **on a scale** of one to ten.* | *the company **pay scale***
salary scale [C] also **payscale, pay spine** *BrE* a scale showing the rates of pay for employees working at each level of an organization. It also shows the increases in pay an employee gets when they spend a certain length of time at a particular level: *Geoff is almost at the top of his salary scale.* | *Their pay scales made it difficult to recruit and keep good salesmen.* | *Japanese companies have focused on seniority-based promotion and **incremental pay spines*** (=salaries that increase in stages).
sliding scale [C] a system for paying tax, wages etc in which the rates that you pay are different, dependent upon changing conditions: *Water rates will be raised **on a sliding scale**.*

scale fee —see under FEE

scalp /skælp/ *v* [I,T] *informal* **1** *AmE* to buy tickets for an event and sell them again at a much higher price: *guys that scalp tickets outside the stadium* —**scalper** *n*

S

[C] *Fans were willing to pay scalpers up to $1,500.* —**scalping** *n* [U] *Super Bowl ticket scalping*
2 FINANCE to buy and quickly sell small quantities of SECURITIES (=bonds, shares etc), in order to make small but fast profits: *Traders try to scalp profits as contract prices rise and fall.*

scam /skæm/ *n* [C] a clever but dishonest plan, usually to get money: *He was jailed for his part in an oil-trading scam.* | *credit-card scams*

scan•ner /'skænə‖-ər/ *n* [C] **1** a machine that passes an electronic BEAM over something in order to read information on it or produce a picture of what is inside: *Customers simply have to wave the product's bar code under a scanner.* | *credit-card scanners*
price scanner a machine that automatically reads BAR CODES showing the price of goods in shops. Price scanners are used for calculating customers' bills and for managing INVENTORY (=supplies of goods to be sold)
2 a piece of computer equipment that copies words or images from paper onto the computer: *color printers and scanners for desk-top publishing*

scarce /skeəs‖skers/ *adj* if something is scarce, there is not enough of it available: *Here, land is a scarce resource and house prices have risen sharply.* | *Jobs are scarce.* —**scarcity** *n* [singular, U] *the present scarcity of labour* | *Reducing the supply of long-term bonds would give them* ***scarcity value*** (=make people want them more because they are more scarce).

scat•ter /'skætə‖-ər/ *n* [U] *AmE* MARKETING used to talk about advertising that is spread over a wide range of television or radio programmes according to what is available, rather than done by selecting particular programmes to SPONSOR: *NBC believes the market for scatter will still be strong.* | *The* ***scatter market*** *is popular among advertisers who don't want to make a long-term commitment.*

scatter diagram —see under DIAGRAM

SCC the written abbreviation for SINGLE COLUMN CENTIMETRE

sce•na•ri•o /sə'nɑːriəʊ‖-'næriou-, -'ne-/ *n* [C] a way in which a situation could possibly develop: *The most likely scenario is that rates will be cut by 0.5%.* | *We need to consider a* ***worst case scenario*** (=the worst situation that could possibly happen). | *With luck the Bank will achieve its* ***golden scenario*** (=best possible situation) *for the value of the pound, reducing consumer demand without damaging exports.*

sched•ule¹ /'ʃedjuːl‖'skedʒʊl, -dʒəl/ *n* [C] **1** a plan of what someone is going to do and when they are going to do it: *I've got a very full* (=busy) *schedule today.* | *Our production schedule is tight and we may need extra staff.* | *We are running several weeks* ***behind schedule***. | *The company is* ***on schedule*** *to bring out its new product in March.*
aging schedule ACCOUNTING a way of listing a business's ACCOUNTS RECEIVABLE by date to show how quickly they are being paid and which ones are in danger of not being paid
2 *AmE* the list of television or radio programmes that are broadcast: *Shows like 'Drug Crackdown' and 'Crime Scene' fill the schedule.* | *NBC's daytime schedule*
3 a formal list of something, for example prices: *a schedule of postal charges*
4 LAW a list added to a law, contract, or other formal document, giving details of things affected by the main document: *The Supplier will supply to the Company the products set out in Schedule 1 to this Agreement.*
5 INSURANCE a list sent with an insurance policy document which gives details of the things that the policy covers: *See the attached schedule of insurance.*
6 also **tax schedule** TAX one of the different classes that incomes are put into under tax law. For example, in Britain there are six schedules from A to F, and income from employment falls into Schedule E: *This amount will be taxed as income under Schedule F.*
7 *AmE* a tax form for one of the different classes of income

schedule² *v* [T] to plan that something will happen at a particular time **schedule sth for**: *I've scheduled a meeting for this afternoon.* **be scheduled to do sth**: *The new airport is scheduled to open just before Christmas.* | *Premier offers direct* ***scheduled flights*** *that fly at the same time every day or every week between Stansted and Florence.*

scheme /skiːm/ *n* [C] **1** *BrE* an official plan or arrangement that is intended to help people in some way: *a government* ***training scheme*** *for the unemployed*
2 *BrE* an arrangement in which the government or an employer provides financial help to people: *a low-interest loan scheme for employees who have been with the company for over two years*
contributory pension scheme *BrE* a pension scheme into which both the employee and the employer both make payments
non-contributory pension scheme *BrE* a pension scheme into which only the employer makes payments, not the employee
pension scheme *BrE* a system by which an employer, insurance company etc provides workers with a pension after they have made regular payments to them over many years; PENSION PLAN: *A good* ***company pension scheme*** *helps to attract and keep staff.* | *The ruling applies to* ***occupational pension schemes*** *but not to the state earnings-related scheme.*
state earnings-related pension scheme abbreviation **SERPS** in Britain, a government arrangement for getting a PENSION (=income after you stop working) that depends on how much you pay while you are working. State earnings-related pension is in addition to the basic pension
3 a clever plan, especially to do something bad or illegal: *a $1.9 billion fraud scheme*
pyramid scheme or **Ponzi scheme** a dishonest way of selling investments, in which the money paid by new investors is used to pay interest and other money owed to existing investors. When new investment brings less than the money owed, new investors lose their money: *a Ponzi scheme, in which investors were paid 'returns' from the funds of later investors*
4 a system used to organize information: *a classification scheme*

SCI the written abbreviation for SINGLE COLUMN INCH

scorched-earth *adj* **scorched-earth policy/tactics** activities in which a company gets rid of its most valuable assets in order to try and avoid a HOSTILE TAKEOVER (=one it does not want): *They accused the company of adopting a scorched-earth policy.*

scrambled merchandising —see under MERCHANDISING

scrap¹ /skræp/ *n* [U] materials or objects that can no longer be used for the purpose they were made for, but that can be used again in another way: *The car was eventually sold for scrap.* | *commodities such as* ***scrap metal*** *and waste paper* | *steel bought from a* ***scrap dealer*** | *All aluminium is recyclable; it has a high* ***scrap value*** (=value when sold as scrap).

scrap² *v* past tense and past participle **scrapped** present participle **scrapping** [T] **1** to decide not to use a plan or system because it is not practical: *The arrangement was scrapped about three years after it was started.*
2 to get rid of an old machine, vehicle etc: *We need cash to replace ancient equipment that had to be scrapped.*

screen¹ /skriːn/ *v* [T] **1** to test people or examine their past history to make sure that they are suitable to do or have something, for example to work for a particular

S

organization: *a personality assessment test to screen security personnel* **screen sb for sth**: *All employees are screened for drugs.*
2 to test or check something such as a product to make sure that it is suitable, does not break the law etc: *The ruling will force all advertisers to screen advertising closely and take out any deceptive statements.*
3 to show a film or television programme: *The ad was screened late at night on Channel 4.* —**screening** *n* [U] *Wells Fargo Guard Services recently launched a pre-employment screening service.* | *routine screening of milk for contaminants*

screen[2] *n* [C] **1** the flat glass part of a computer or television: *The customer's account details are displayed on the screen.* | *the commercials we see on our TV screens*
touch screen a computer screen which allows you to give commands to the computer by touching the screen
2 on screen on a computer screen: *It's easy to change the text on screen before printing it.*

screen•sav•er /ˈskriːnˌseɪvə‖-ər/ *n* [C] COMPUTING a picture that appears on your computer screen when you are not using it but while it is still switched on. You use a screensaver to make the life of the screen longer: *You can download a screensaver from the Internet.*

scrip /skrɪp/ *n* [C,U] **1** a document showing that someone owns shares or bonds: *There is a lack of liquidity in most stocks here, making it difficult for foreign investors to pick up large amounts of scrip.*
2 a document given instead of money, that can be exchanged for money or shares: *To finance his new restaurant chain, Mr Romano thought of giving away scrip to his first few thousand customers, who could use it to buy stock in the company.*

scrip dividend —see under DIVIDEND

scripholder *n* [C] someone who owns scrip

scrip issue —see under ISSUE[2]

scripophily *n* [U] the activity of collecting old share and bond CERTIFICATES, for example because they have an interesting history or design

scroll /skrəʊl‖skroʊl/ *v* [I,T] to move information on a computer screen up or down so that you can read it + **up/down**: *You can scroll up to the top of the document using this bar.*

SCSI /ˈskʌzi/ *n* [singular] COMPUTING Small Computer Systems Interface; a part of a computer where you can connect another piece of equipment such as a printer: *The PC Scan uses a SCSI interface to communicate with the PC.*

SDR *n* [C usually plural] special drawing right; a unit of money created by the IMF. Each member country can borrow SDRs at favourable interest rates from the IMF's RESERVES when they are needed for reasons related to a country's BALANCE OF PAYMENTS (=payments between countries related to trade etc)

seal[1] /siːl/ *n* [C] a mark that has a special design and shows the legal or official authority of a person or organization: *a black book stamped with the Presidential Seal*
common seal LAW a mark pressed into the paper of formal company documents: *The requirement for a company in England and Wales to have a common seal was abolished on 31 July 1990.*
company seal a mark containing the name of a company that is pressed into the paper used by the company for formal or official documents

seal[2] *v* **seal a deal/agreement/promise etc** to do something that makes a deal, agreement etc formal and definite: *A handshake sealed the deal.*

sealed bid —see under BID[1]

sealed-bid auction —see under AUCTION[1]

sealed bid tender —see under TENDER[1]

seal of approval *n* [singular] **1** a mark or sign that shows that an organization has tested a product and it meets their standards: *Green Cross Certification Co. will put its seal of approval on environment-friendly products.*
2 if you give something your seal of approval, you say officially or publicly that you approve of it: *All we need now is the chairman's seal of approval.*

SEAQ /ˈsiːæk/ *n* FINANCE Stock Exchange Automated Quotation System; a computer system showing share prices on the LONDON STOCK EXCHANGE, with dealers using the information to buy and sell over the telephone

search[1] /sɜːtʃ‖sɜːrtʃ/ *n* **1** [C] an attempt to find someone or something, usually one that takes a lot of time + **for**: *Foremost Corp. said it had ended a five-month search for a buyer for the company.* | *Graduates in debt simply can't afford lengthy **job searches**.*
executive search [C,U] HUMAN RESOURCES the business of finding new senior employees for companies. The executive search company finds people working for other companies who have the right skills and experience to do the job, and tries to persuade them to work for their client company; HEADHUNTING: *High-technology businesses, with an open attitude to recruitment, have also been large users of executive search.* | *an executive search consultant*
2 [C] when police or other people with official power look through someone's possessions, business records etc because they think they have done something illegal + **of**: *They found evidence of copyright infringement during a recent search of the company offices.* | *A Customs spokesman confirmed that a **search warrant** document showing legal permission for a search was served at Swissco Development Co.* —see also CERTIFICATE OF SEARCH
3 [C] COMPUTING the action of looking for information in a computer's memory or on the INTERNET + **on**: *I did a search on the company and found out it had a lot of money in real estate in the Northeast.*

search[2] *v* **1** [I,T] to spend time looking for someone or something + **for**: *Mr. Plackett began searching for a merger partner.* | *We searched the whole state for a contractor.*
2 [I,T] COMPUTING to look for information on a computer or on the INTERNET + **for**: *She searched the Internet for financial information.* | *You have to wait a few minutes while the software is searching.*

search firm —see under FIRM[1]

search unemployment —see under UNEMPLOYMENT

sea•son /ˈsiːzən/ *n* [C,U] a period of time in the year when most business is done, or the time of year when something happens: *A full shuttle service is not expected until after the summer **tourist season**.* | *You can get some cheap travel deals **out of season*** (=during the period of time when most people do not travel).
dead season [singular] the time of year when DEMAND for (=the number of people wanting) goods, travel etc is at its lowest
high season [singular] the part of a year when there is a lot of business and prices are usually higher, especially in the TOURIST industry: *a five-day tuition package costing £320 per person in high season*
low season [singular] the time of year when there is the least business for hotels, shops etc; OFF-SEASON: *Some of the resort's facilities will be limited during low season.* | *Many hotels offer discounts, especially in the low season.* —**low-season** *adj*: *Take advantage of these low-season prices.*
off season [singular] the part of a year when there is not as much business as usual, and when prices are usually lower, especially in the TOURIST industry: *In the off season, you do not need to make a reservation.* | *off-season discounts*

S

sea•son•al /ˈsiːzənəl/ *adj* **1 seasonal adjustments/changes/variations etc** adjustments, changes etc caused or done because of things that happen during a particular period of the year and that are not typical of the rest of the year: *The Labor Department's seasonal adjustment of the unemployment figures tries to compensate for the usual January layoffs of temporary holiday workers.* —**seasonally** *adv*: *France's seasonally adjusted foreign trade deficit*

2 seasonal business/employment/workers etc happening or needed only at a particular time of year: *The firm hired seasonal workers to process and pack salmon.*

seasonal unemployment —see under UNEMPLOYMENT

season ticket —see under TICKET

seat /siːt/ *n* [C] **1** a position as a member of a government or a group that makes official decisions: *The appointments give the ruling Progressive Conservatives 54 seats in the Senate.*

2 FINANCE a position as a member of a financial market: *Foreign brokerage houses will be offered more seats on the Stock Exchange of Singapore.*

SEATS /siːts/ *n* FINANCE Stock Exchange Alternative Tracking Service; a computer system run by the LONDON STOCK EXCHANGE giving share prices of smaller companies

SEC abbreviation for SECURITIES AND EXCHANGE COMMISSION

sec. written abbreviation for SECRETARY

sec•ond¹ /ˈsekənd/ *adj* **second half/quarter/period** the second half, quarter etc of the financial year: *Atari expects **second-quarter sales** to be substantially below those of the equivalent period a year ago.*

second² *v* [T] to officially support a suggestion, idea etc made by another person at a formal meeting so that it can be discussed or voted on: *Mr Roberts' nomination, proposed by Mr Ken Lucas, was seconded by Mr Cattle.* —**seconder** *n* [C] *His proposal failed to find a seconder, and was dropped.*

second³ /sɪˈkɒnd‖-ˈkɑːnd/ *v* [T] *BrE* HUMAN RESOURCES to arrange for an employee to work for another organization for a period of time: *Barclays seconds at most 100 people at any one time.* **second sb to**: *We provide the opportunity for you to be seconded to industry to receive additional in-service training.* —**secondment** *n* [C,U] *You can encourage personal contact with suppliers through seminars, site visits and short-term secondments.* | *Two members of the team are **on secondment from** the DTI.*

sec•ond•a•ry /ˈsekəndəri‖-deri/ *adj* **1 secondary shares/bonds etc** FINANCE shares, stocks etc in companies that are not considered to be the biggest or most important; SECOND-TIER: *The market for secondary corporate issues was quiet yesterday.*

2 secondary industry/product an industry or product that has developed from another industry and uses materials from that larger industry: *They hope to restore farming, horticulture and forestry, and to develop secondary industries: sawmilling, building, and cider-making.* | *The distillation produces whisky, and several secondary products such as flavourings are collected from the alcohol.*

3 secondary trading/action/activity/dealings *AmE* FINANCE trading in shares etc that takes place late in the day, usually after the stockmarket is closed; LATE TRADING: *In secondary activity, the New Jersey Turnpike Authority's bonds were unchanged at 97.* | *Aside from the RTC activity, secondary dealings were subdued.*

4 secondary market/trading etc FINANCE trading of investments that have already been ISSUED (=made available and sold for the first time), and which are now available on the market for other investors to buy and sell: *Foreign debt is unloaded by banks in the secondary market, then bought and exchanged for equity.* | *the 300,000 shares in the secondary offering*

secondary action —see under ACTION

secondary boycott —see under BOYCOTT²

secondary data —see under DATA

secondary industry —see under INDUSTRY

secondary market —see under MARKET¹

secondary shares —see under SHARE

second-class *adj* [only before a noun] **1** second-class mail is cheaper to send than FIRST-CLASS mail because it takes slightly longer to arrive: *We aim to deliver 96% of **second-class letters** by the third working day after collection.* | *a **second-class** stamp*

2 second-class travel, fares etc are cheaper than FIRST-CLASS ones because they do not offer such a comfortable journey: *a second-class ticket* —**second class** *adv*: *Only copy documents should be sent second class.* | *Passengers travelling second class can buy two sleeper tickets for the price of one.*

second-hand *adj* not new, and having one or more previous owners; PRE-OWNED *AmE*; USED: *For the first time, car makers are pushing sales of second-hand vehicles.* —**second hand** *adv*: *The solution for small businesses may be to buy their IT equipment second-hand.*

second lien —see under LIEN

second mortgage —see under MORTGAGE¹

sec•onds /ˈsekəndz/ *n* [plural] goods that are sold cheaply because they are damaged or not of the usual quality: *Visit the factory shop, and look out for cheap seconds of new leather riding boots.*

second section —see under SECTION

second-tier also **second-line**, **second-section** *adj* FINANCE **1 second-tier shares/bonds etc** shares, bonds etc in companies that are not considered to be the biggest or most important: *Meeder & Associates has about a quarter of its assets in **second-tier securities**.* | *Some leading and **second-line** building **stocks** benefited from speculation that UK base lending rates will be cut.*

2 second-tier company/firm a company that is not considered to be one of the biggest or most important: *Many second-tier companies are expected to gain as a result of the higher dollar.* | *Portugal's stock exchanges opened **second-tier markets** to provide financing for small and medium-sized companies.* —compare BLUE CHIP, FIRST-TIER —see also ***Tier 2 capital*** under CAPITAL

second-tier share —see under SHARE

second-tier stock —see under STOCK¹

se•cret /ˈsiːkrɪ̆t/ *adj* **1** something that is secret is only known about by a few people and kept hidden from other people, sometimes because it is illegal: *repeated denials of a **secret deal*** | *the acquisition of a **secret interest** in First American Bankshares Inc.* | *The judge has twice insisted that the **ballot** will be **kept secret*** (=no one will know who you have voted for).

2 trade/industrial/business etc secret information about a company or its products which is known only to a few people in the company, and which must not be given to anyone not working for it: *The company has labelled the underlying sales data a trade secret.* | *a law prohibiting employees from divulging* (=telling other people) *corporate secrets*

sec•re•tar•i•al /sekrɪ̆ˈteəriəl‖-ˈter-/ *adj* concerned with the work of a secretary, such as answering the telephone, TYPING, and arranging meetings: *She was only qualified for secretarial and advertising sales positions.* | *secretarial and other clerical staff*

sec•re•tar•i•at /ˌsekrɪ̆ˈteəriət‖-ˈter-/ *n* [C] the office of a government or international organization which runs

S

its daily affairs: *Analysts at WTO's secretariat say Tokyo has made progress in opening its markets.*

sec•re•ta•ry /ˈsekrɪ̵təri‖-teri/ *n* plural **secretaries** [C] **1** someone who works in an office helping to organize the work, answering the telephone, arranging meetings etc: *I want all my communications to go through my secretary.* | *He enjoyed a corner office and had a* ***private secretary*** (=one working for only him).

2 someone who works for a large organization and who is responsible for running its daily affairs: *the general secretary of Britain's GMB union* | *Martin Rice,* ***executive secretary*** (=having particular powers, such as spending money, approving policy etc) *of the Canadian Pork Council*

company secretary also **chartered secretary** *BrE*, **corporate secretary** *AmE* someone with a high position in a company, dealing with legal and administrative matters: *The company secretary has requested a full audit of the budget approval procedures.*

executive secretary someone who has the job of secretary to an executive in an organization or company: *Is there anybody brave enough to take on the post of SAA Executive Secretary?*

press secretary the person in an organization whose job is to deal with questions from people working for the newspapers, radio, or television; PRESS OFFICER

3 a government official in charge of a particular department or area of work: *the* ***Trade Secretary*** | *The ex-governor of Arizona has been appointed interior secretary.*

sec•tion /ˈsekʃən/ *n* **1** [C] one of the parts of an organization or department: *You will need to speak to the manager of the marketing services section.* | *Toyota's biggest drop in profit since its sales and manufacturing sections merged*

2 [C] one of the parts of a document, book, newspaper etc: *The lease qualifies for special protection under section 11 of the Bankruptcy Code.* | *The director disclosed the gifts in the wrong section of his financial statement.*

first section [singular] FINANCE the group of companies listed on a stockmarket that are considered to be the biggest and the most important: *Tokyo stocks on the first section ended flat.*

second section [singular] FINANCE the group of companies listed on a stockmarket that are considered to be smaller and less important: *The* ***second section index*** *was down 8.13 points.*

sec•tor /ˈsektə‖-ər/ *n* [C] all the organizations or companies in a particular area of activity, industry etc: *The electronics sector accounted for revenue of £940.4 million.* | *The performance of the troubled housing sector is being watched very closely.* | *the growth of jobs in the service sector* —**sectoral** *adj*: *A major commitment is required on the part of agricultural and forestry concerns to bridge sectoral barriers.*

corporate sector [singular] the part of the economy made up by companies: *The government is trying to protect the corporate sector by keeping interest rates low.*

market sector [C] a particular part of a market, for example a particular type of activity, product, or customer: *One market sector, banking, remains below its best level of the past year.* | *American multinationals continue to overlook the world's largest market sector – small-scale farmers.*

private sector also **commercial sector** [singular] the industries and services that are not owned by the government: *Import decisions belong to the private sector and the government has no power to interfere.* | ***private sector jobs*** | ***private sector investment***

public sector also **state sector** [singular] the companies, organizations, and activities in an economy that are owned by the government: *Petrobras and the Banco do Brasil commercial bank had to remain in the public sector under the privatization bill.* | *More than 200,000* ***public-sector workers*** *began a two-day strike over the government's proposed wage freeze.*

public sector borrowing requirement —see PSBR

service sector [singular] the companies, organizations, and activities in an economy that provide services such as banking, TRANSPORT, TOURISM etc, rather than manufacturing goods

se•cure¹ /sɪˈkjʊə‖-ˈkjʊr/ *v* [T] **1** to get something you need after a lot of effort: *The airline has* ***secured financing*** *of $150 million from New York-based Bankers Trust Corp.* | *Five companies bid an average of $9.7 million each to secure seats on the Securities Exchange of Thailand.*

2 FINANCE if a company secures a debt or loan, it promises the lender that they can take certain assets, such as property or shares, if the debt or loan is not paid within the agreed time limit: *Three of National Bancshares' most profitable banks were used as collateral to secure the loan.* **secure sth against/on sth**: *Loans on the properties will be secured on cashflow from those properties.*

secure² *adj* **1** investments or companies which are secure are not likely to lose money: *safe investments in a* ***financially secure*** *company* | *Higher yields are considered to be less secure.*

2 feeling confident about a particular situation, especially one which concerns the future: *The frequent announcements of staff cuts are making Americans feel less secure in their jobs.*

3 safe and protected from damage, change, being stolen etc: *customer guarantees that the machines will be secure from theft or unauthorized use* | *The single currency is giving industry more secure operating conditions.* | *secure communications equipment*

se•cured /sɪˈkjʊəd‖-ˈkjʊrd/ *adj* FINANCE **1** a secured loan, debt etc is protected by an agreement that if it is not paid, the company borrowing the money has to give the lender certain assets, such as property or shares: *Secured credit cards are backed by a deposit that a consumer must make with the card issuer.* | *The* ***secured debentures*** *will mature on Jan. 15, 2006.*

2 secured lender/creditor someone who lends money, with an agreement that if the debt is not paid, the company borrowing the money has to give the lender certain assets, such as property or shares: *Secured lenders have provided Greyhound with $50 million in loans.* | *The company owes about $24 million to its major secured creditor Mellon Bank Corp.*

secured credit —see under CREDIT¹

secured creditor —see under CREDITOR

secured debt —see under DEBT

secured liabilities —see under LIABILITY

secured loan —see under LOAN¹

secured notes —see under NOTE¹

Securities and Exchange Commission abbreviation **SEC** *n* in the US, a government organization which controls the way in which bonds, shares etc are traded and makes sure investment arrangements are legal. The organization that does this in Britain is the Securities and Investments Board

Securities and Futures Authority abbreviation **SFA** *n* in Britain, a government organization that makes sure that BROKERS obey the law. It is part of the FINANCIAL SERVICES AUTHORITY

securities house —see under HOUSE

securities market —see under MARKET¹

se•cur•i•tize also **securitise** *BrE* /sɪˈkjʊərɪ̵taɪz‖-ˈkjʊr-/ *v* [T] FINANCE if a financial institution securitizes loans, it buys the loans from lenders such as banks and uses them as BACKING for bonds. The financial institution uses the repayments on these loans to make payments to investors who buy the bonds. Money that the lenders get from the financial institution when it sells the bonds is used to improve its financial situation, make more loans to customers etc: *Fannie Mae purchases home mortgages and securitizes them for sale in the secondary market.* —**securitization** also **securitisation** *BrE n* [U] *Tandy's recent asset securitization sale will improve its liquidity.* | *The company said the securitization of its lease receivables will expand its available funding sources and reduce its financing costs.*

se•cu•ri•ty /sɪˈkjʊərəti‖-ˈkjʊr-/ *n* plural **securities**
1 [U] actions to keep someone or something safe from being damaged, stolen etc: *We spend roughly as much on security as on sales promotion.* | *On April 29th, a* ***security alert*** *shut down the London Stock Exchange.* | *teams of professional* ***security guards***

2 [U] a feeling of being safe and free from worry about what might happen: ***Job security*** (=when you are unlikely to lose your job) *is the main issue in the dispute.* | *Many Koreans like the* ***financial security*** *of working for big companies.*

3 [U] FINANCE property or other assets that you promise to give someone if you cannot pay back the money that you owe them: *We offer flexible borrowing for people with bank accounts, usually without security, and paid off over a few months.* | *His parents have* ***pledged*** (=promised) *their homes* ***as security*** *so that he can obtain finance for his new business.*

4 [C] FINANCE a financial investment such as a bond or share etc, or the related CERTIFICATE showing who owns it: *funds specializing in gold-mining securities* | ***Securities firms*** *outside the EU often operate under different rules.* | *the government's slowness in opening the* ***securities market*** *to foreigners*

asset-backed security [C] if a financial institution sells asset-backed securities, it buys loans from lenders such as banks and uses the loans as BACKING for bonds. The financial institution takes the repayments on these loans and uses them to pay interest to investors who buy the bonds, and to repay the bonds. Lenders sell their loans in this way in order to improve their financial situation and to make more loans

bearer security [C] a security where the person possessing it is considered to be the owner even though their name might not be recorded on an official list —compare ***registered security***

continuing security [C] something a borrower gives to a bank, which the bank can keep if they fail to repay a loan

convertible security [C] one of the bonds, shares etc in a company that may be exchanged later for another type of bond etc under certain conditions

dated security [C] a security that will be repaid on a fixed date, unless it is CALLED (=unless the borrower repays it early). Almost all securities are dated

deferred security [C] a loan where interest is not paid in the normal way, but where the lender obtains one big payment when the loan period ends or receives stocks, shares etc in exchange: *First Boston Corp. said deferred interest securities like zero-coupon bonds outperformed cash paying bonds during April.*

fixed-interest security [C] a type of bond that pays an agreed fixed rate of interest at regular times during the year

gilt-edged security [C] a British government bond

government security [C] one of the bonds sold by a government to finance its BUDGET DEFICIT (=the difference between what it gets in taxes and what it spends). Government bonds are usually considered to be a very safe form of investment; GOVERNMENT STOCK

listed security [C] one of the bonds or shares in the largest companies that are traded on the main financial markets

long-term security [C] a security repayable in more than fifteen years

marketable security [C] a security that can easily be sold. Marketable securities are considered to be nearly as LIQUID (=easily sold) as cash

medium-term security [C] a security repayable in between five and fifteen years

mortgage-backed security [C] a type of ASSET-BACKED SECURITY that is BACKED by loans to people to buy property

negotiable security [C] a security that can be bought and sold for money

registered security [C] a security where the name of the holder is officially recorded by the financial institution that sold it —compare ***bearer security***

short-term security [C] a security repayable in under five years

undated security [C] a security that will never be repaid, and that only pays interest. A few British government securities are undated

unlisted security [C] one of the bonds or shares in smaller companies that are not traded on the main financial markets in a particular place —see also SOCIAL SECURITY

security of tenure *n* [U] *BrE* the legal right to keep a job or keep renting the property you are living in: *University teachers argue that security of tenure protects freedom of opinion.* | *If you are renting from a private landlord, your security of tenure will depend on the type of contract.*

security printer —see under PRINTER

security rating —see under RATING

seed[1] /siːd/ also **seedcorn** *BrE* /ˈsiːdkɔːn‖-ɔːrn/ *n* **seed capital/money/financing etc** FINANCE money used to start a new company, project, activity etc: *Leading Edge is trying to get loans and* ***seed capital*** *to finance in-house manufacturing.* | *Our total computer-related* ***seed investment*** *amounted to $29.1 million.*

seed[2] *v* [T] to provide the money needed to start a company: *In Germany, government funding has helped seed about 300 companies in three years.*

seed money —see under MONEY

seek /siːk/ past tense and past participle **sought** *v* [T] to try to get or achieve something: *Even while takeover talks were in progress, Shawmut sought other potential buyers.* | *Benefit claimants are asked to prove they are actively* ***seeking work***. **seek to do sth**: *GPA is seeking to float the shares in the first half of this year.* —**seeker** *n* [C] *A fall in the number of young* ***job-seekers*** *is expected.* | *speculative shares that attracted short-term profit-seekers*

seg•ment[1] /ˈsegmənt/ *n* [C] **1** a part of the economy of a country or of a company's work: *Litton's shipbuilding segment reported higher earnings.* | *Within the health care segment, pharmaceuticals sales increased 17%.* + **of**: *Commodity funds are the fastest-growing segment of the retail futures business.*
2 also **market segment** a group of customers that share similar characteristics, such as age, income, interests, and social class: *How can a manufacturer target his products successfully on his chosen market segments?* | *Our Healthy Option range is aimed at specific smaller segments, such as the elderly and people on a restricted diet.*
3 also **market segment** the products in a particular part of the market: *the market segment between midsized family cars and high-priced luxury models*

seg•ment[2] /segˈment/ *v* [T] MARKETING to divide a large group of people into smaller groups of people of a similar age or with similar incomes, interests etc, so that products that are most suitable for each group can be sold to it: *Social class is a useful variable for segmenting consumer markets.* —**segmentation** *n* [U] *Product segmentation focuses on how consumers perceive and differentiate between available products.*

seg·ment·ed /seg'mentəd/ *adj* a segmented business activity has many companies involved in it; FRAGMENTED: *Before Mr. Hunt came along, trucking was heavily unionized, segmented and inefficient.*

sei·gnor·age /'seɪnjərɪdʒ/ *n* [U] BANKING the amount that a government earns from printing its own money: *If Argentina fixed its currency to the dollar, one big problem would be the loss of seignorage, worth about $750m a year.*

seize /siːz/ *v* [T] **1** if the police or another official authority seize goods or property, they take them away because they are illegal or because the person owning them owes money: *South Korean authorities seized 186,000 fake products in 1999.* | *A warrant of execution allows a bailiff to seize sufficient goods to pay your debt and costs.*

2 *AmE* if the government or another authority seizes a company, it forces it to stop trading because of debts or illegal activities: *The troubled insurance company was seized by regulators on April 11.*

3 if you seize a chance or opportunity, you take advantage of it when it becomes available: *Everyone in the organization can find and* ***seize initiatives*** *to improve their contribution.* | *Ohio has converted its technology to seize a share of the fast-growth $200 billion polymers industry.*

sei·zure /'siːʒə‖-ər/ *n* [C,U] *formal* **1** the act of taking goods or property because they are illegal, or because the owner has not paid a debt: *a county court judgment allowing seizure and sale of goods*

2 *AmE* the act of forcing a company to stop trading because of debts or illegal activities: *The company's failure, seizure and liquidation cost the state $2.6 billion.*

S

se·lect[1] /sə'lekt/ *v* [T] **1** to choose something from a group of things, after thinking carefully about which is the best, most useful, most profitable etc: *The board hasn't yet set a timetable for selecting a chief executive.* | *Investors shouldn't select a stock fund just because it has low annual costs.*

2 COMPUTING if you select words or pictures on a computer screen, you use the MOUSE to make them change colour, before moving, cutting, or saving them: *The program teaches children to spell by asking them to select each letter of the word.* —**selected** *adj* [only before a noun] *Instead of selling only selected assets, Orlando is trying to sell the entire concern.* | *The most useful editing tool is Magnify, which increases the selected area by up to eight times.*

select[2] *adj* used, visited, or bought only by a small group of people; EXCLUSIVE: *At the Brahman Centre, you'll be one of* ***a select few*** (=a few people) *to be taught these learning techniques.* | *This flat is situated on a small select development.*

select committee —see under COMMITTEE

se·lec·tion /sə'lekʃən/ *n* **1** [U] the careful choice of a particular person or thing from a group: *The Health Authority is not involved in* ***staff selection*** *and recruitment.* | *The selection of a preferred bidder will be made with the client.* | *Our deputy manager can supply details of the job, including our* ***selection criteria*** (=things considered when choosing someone for a job).

selection panel also **selection committee** *n* [C] a group of people who choose something or someone for a particular job, activity etc: *The chief executive officer has a duty to attend meetings of the selection panel.* | *Brokerage firms are judged on an official recommended list drawn up by a* ***stock selection committee***

2 [C] something that has been chosen from a group of similar things: *Over the next year, you make four more selections from over 300 book titles.*

3 [singular] a collection of goods of a particular type that are offered for sale: *Sears has been buying big-name brands to expand its product selection.*

self-addressed envelope —see under ENVELOPE

self-administered pension —see under PENSION[1]

self-assessment —see under ASSESSMENT

self-correcting *adj formal* a self-correcting system, activity etc will, when it is in a bad state, improve without anyone having to take action: *In the West, depressions are often cyclical and essentially self-correcting.* | *Regulatory attacks by legislators can over-ride the* ***self-correcting mechanisms*** *in the market.* —**self-correct** *v* [T] *Given time, commercial real estate values will self-correct.*

self-dealing *n* [U] FINANCE when someone working for a company uses their influence or knowledge illegally to gain a personal advantage: *The director was engaged in self-dealing in a real estate project to the benefit of his private company.*

self-directed *adj* [only before a noun] *AmE* **1** a self-directed PENSION is managed by the employee rather than his or her employer, and allows the employee to sell or move any investments they have in the company they work for: *Employees who change jobs can move their retirement account into their new employer's plan, or into a* ***self-directed IRA*** (=individual retirement account).

2 HUMAN RESOURCES self-directed workers are responsible for organizing and judging their own work, rather than taking instructions from managers; SELF-MANAGED *BrE*: *Mr. Jessup now operates his business from home, helping companies develop* ***self-directed teams***.

self-employed *adj* **1** having your own business, rather than being employed by a company: *Over a quarter of agency-supplied computer staff are self-employed.* | *Many* ***self-employed businessmen*** *are dependent on loans for working capital.*

2 the self-employed people who work for themselves, rather than being employed by a company: *One of the services we offer to the self-employed is a series of free consultations with financial and legal experts.* —compare FREELANCE[1] —**self-employment** *n* [U] *The rise in self-employment is likely to increase the flexibility of earnings*

self-financing also **self-financed** *adj* a self-financing business or system makes enough money for it to be developed further without borrowing money: *Time Warner plans to restructure its operations by creating a new, self-financing TV entertainment partnership.* | *The new projects will be mostly self-financed from cash flow.*

self-healing *adj* [only before a noun] COMPUTING a self-healing computer or other electronic system is designed so that if the energy supply is interrupted, messages can still be received: *US West Inc. will invest about $35 million to develop* ***self-healing*** *telephone* ***networks*** *in five cities.*

self-imposed *adj* [only before a noun] a self-imposed rule, condition, or limit has been set by the people who must obey it, and does not have to be obeyed by anyone else: *Even with the approach of a* ***self-imposed deadline***, *there was no clear sign of an agreement.* | *the banks'* ***self-imposed*** *credit* ***rationing***

self-incrimination *n* [U] LAW when a person says something that makes them seem guilty of a crime: *He had been advised that he risked self-incrimination if he gave information on any of these matters.*

self-insure *v* [I,T] INSURANCE in the US and some other countries, if a company self-insures, it keeps money specially to pay for any accidents to employees, harm caused to others etc, instead of buying insurance from an insurance company: *Intelsat, which had self-insured the project, said that retrieving the satellite would be cheaper* *than launching a new one.* —**self-insurance** *n* [U] *Encouraging self-insurance would force companies to bear the actual costs of their health and safety practices.* —**self-insurer** *n* [C] *More employers are becoming self-insurers for health care.*

self-liquidating *adj* **1** BANKING a self-liquidating loan is for a short period of time and used to complete a particular investment, activity etc. The loan is usually paid back with profit made from the investment: *It was difficult to find outlets for short-term lending which would be self-liquidating at a definite time.*
2 FINANCE if a self-liquidating company pays all its available money to people who own shares in it, rather than paying them a DIVIDEND (=regular payments from profits): *B&H's shareholders recently voted to convert from self-liquidating to continuing dividend status.*

self-made *adj* **self-made man/woman/millionaire etc** someone who has become very successful and rich in business through their own hard work, without any advantages such as a high social position

self-managed *adj* [only before a noun] *BrE* HUMAN RESOURCES self-managed workers are responsible for organizing and judging their own work, rather than taking instructions from managers; SELF-DIRECTED *AmE*: *Sherwood Computer Services has turned its entire organisation into **self-managed** client **teams** that report directly to the board.* —**self-management** *n* [U] *The sense of understanding and involvement that staff have is the key to successful self-management.*

self-regulatory *adj* also **self-regulating**, **self-policing** a self-regulatory organization or industry sets its own standards and makes sure that its members obey the law, rather than being controlled by an independent organization: *One idea that is gaining in popularity is the establishment of a **self-regulatory organization** similar to the National Association of Securities Dealers.* | *The NFA is the **self-regulatory body** for the futures industry.* | *The commodities industry's **self-policing agency** is considering raising its fees to members.* —**self-regulation** *n* [U] *Germany needs more market controls to replace its system of self-regulation based on a voluntary code.*

self-service *adj* a self-service shop, restaurant etc is one in which customers get the goods themselves and then go and pay for them: *a self-service food concern* —**self-service** *n* [U] *The average gas station in the US offers a generous discount for self-service.*

self-starter *n* [C] someone who is eager to succeed and able to work well on their own, without needing help or instructions: *Management is seeking to promote ambitious self-starters.*

self-sufficient *adj* providing all the things that are needed without help from outside: *The creation of a 'yen block' would result in a more self-sufficient region in Asia, better able to provide its own raw materials and markets.* + **in**: *We are trying to make Japan more self-sufficient in energy.* —**self-sufficiency** *n* [U] *Could the UK achieve self-sufficiency in gas without recourse to Norway's Sleipner field?*

self-sustaining also **self-supporting** *adj* continuing to succeed and grow without help or money from outside: *While the newsletter is a good idea, it will be several years before it is self-sustaining.* | *Bonneville has demonstrated the capacity to establish itself as a competitive, **self-supporting enterprise**.*

self-tender offer —see under OFFER[2]

sell[1] /sel/ past tense and past participle **sold** *v* **1** [I,T] to give someone property, assets, goods, services etc in return for money: *Chrysler plans to raise cash by **selling assets**.* | *Investors are selling more aggressively ahead of quarterly earnings reports.* **sell sth to sb**: *Canada's largest oil and gas concern will be sold to the public through a series of share issues.* **sell sth for**: *He was forced to sell the magazine to Reader's Digest Association Inc. for $29.1 million.*
2 [T] to make something available for people to buy: *Dillard sells mostly tried and tested brands like Liz Claiborne in women's clothes.*
3 sell at/for £100/$3,000 etc to be offered for sale at a particular price: *high-priced desktop computers selling for $20,000 and up*
4 [T] to encourage people to buy something: *Reebok hopes the controversial promotion will sell the sportswear range.*
5 [I] to be bought in large quantities: *Corporate bonds issued this year have sold fast.* | *Many companies are developing packaging that both protects the environment and sells.*
6 sell yourself to impress people with your abilities and good qualities: *He believes in his company, and he sells himself, marketing his own beliefs.* —see also CONTRACT TO SELL, HARD SELL

sell sth **forward** *phr v* [T] FINANCE to agree to sell a commodity (=oil, metal, farm product etc) at a fixed price for delivery at a later date: *Kaiser has been selling forward large volumes of its 2002 steel production at fixed prices.*

sell sth ↔ **off** *phr v* [T] to sell all or most of an industry, company, business etc, usually at a low price: *He plans to break the company up and sell it off as several independent businesses.* | *The privatization of state enterprises will be delayed until they can be sold off at a better price.* —see also SELL-OFF

sell on *phr v* [T] **1 sell sb on sth** *AmE* to persuade someone to buy a particular thing or support a particular idea: *Gentex has cut the costs of selling more automakers on its new mirror products.* | *Many consumers are sold on the company's environmental message.*
2 sell sth on to sell something immediately after buying it **sell sth on to sb**: *Bell Resources would not comment on whether the shares had been sold on to another party.* | *Lonhro rescued Shah's 'Today' paper, but quickly sold it on.*

sell out *phr v* **1** [I,T] **sell** sth ↔ **out** if an investor or owner of a company sells out, they sell their investments or the company: *Relations between the directors are strained, and shareholders have said they would like to sell out.* | *By pure luck I sold out my futures contracts at the exact top of the market.* + **to**: *Southland Corp. announced that it was selling out to a Japanese company.*
2 [I] if a shop sells out of a product, it has no more of that particular product left + **of**: *Stores quickly sold out of many CD titles only days after they were released.*
3 [I] if a product, seats at an event, tickets for a journey etc sell out, there are none left: *First-class cabins are starting to sell out on some transcontinental flights.* —see also SELL-OUT

sell up *phr v* [I] *BrE* to sell almost everything you own, especially your home or business: *He resigned his job, sold up and bought air tickets for all the family.*

sell[2] *n* **1 hard sell** when someone uses a lot of pressure to make a customer buy something: *Account executives find the hard sell more difficult.*
2 soft sell when someone tries to encourage and persuade a customer to buy something, rather than using a lot of pressure: *The soft sell works in four out of five cases.*

sell-by date —see under DATE[1]

sell•er /ˈselə‖-ər/ *n* [C] **1** a person or organization that sells something: *Most sellers use an estate agent to set a price and advertise the property.* + **of**: *All-American is a programming distributor and seller of commercial time to advertisers.*
net seller FINANCE a person, organization, country etc that sells more of something than they buy: *It's the first time in 10 years that Japanese investors have been net sellers of US portfolio investments.*
short seller FINANCE someone who makes a profit by

selling borrowed bonds, shares etc. A short seller sells the shares etc immediately after borrowing them, then buys them again later at a lower price to return to the lender, making a profit: *Short sellers target stocks they think are overvalued or even fraudulent.*

2 good/bad/big etc seller a product that sells well or badly etc: *'Pretty Woman', starring Richard Gere, is among the 10 **top sellers** of all time.* | *Frozen yoghurt has been a **big seller** over the past two years.* —see also BEST SELLER, BOOKSELLER

seller's lien —see under LIEN

seller's market —see under MARKET[1]

sell·ing /ˈselɪŋ/ *n* [U] **1** when people sell products, services, shares etc: *The dollar's decline came amid hectic dollar selling in the Japanese currency market.* | *Activity was busiest in London, where dealers reported **heavy selling** by investors from all around the world.* | *Microsoft's **selling costs** amounted to 33% of sales.* —see also CROSS-SELLING

distress selling when a person or company is forced to sell something because they are in need of money

pyramid selling a business activity where the main income is from people who pay to sell products, rather than from sales of products themselves. Pyramid selling is illegal in many places: *In pyramid selling, someone might find it difficult to get back her joining fee if she could not find new members, because she would then find it difficult to sell the goods.*

short selling FINANCE when a trader sells shares immediately after buying them, and then buys them back later, making a profit because the price of the shares has fallen: *Critics of short selling say it can cause huge falls in prices.*

2 the job and skill of persuading people to buy things: *Reader statistics play an important role in supporting their advertisement selling.* | *A keen interest in selling is a requirement of the post.*

direct selling when a company or manufacturer offers its products, services etc directly to customers, rather through shops: *Exhibitions and trade shows are often used for direct selling.*

hard selling when salespeople use a lot of pressure to make people buy things: *Two salesmen were criticized for hard selling to the aged or infirm.*

inertia selling selling to people by sending them goods that they have not asked for and then asking them to pay for them. Inertia selling depends on people not making the effort to send the goods back

personal selling when a company employs salespeople to offers its products, services etc to customers: *Personal selling is carried out mainly by sales representatives and sales assistants.*

telephone selling also **teleselling** the practice of telephoning people in order to try to sell them things, or sales made by telephone; TELESALES: *Our firm is heavily dependent on telephone selling.*

3 best-/top-/biggest-/hot-selling a best-selling, top-selling etc product is very successful and many people have bought it: *It was until a few months ago the best-selling PC in the US.* | *Stephen King is already one of the **top-selling authors** in publishing history.*

4 selling agent/broker a person or company paid to sell property, goods etc for a customer: *viewing by arrangement with the **sole selling agents*** (=the only company involved in the sale of something, especially property)

selling point —see under POINT[1]

selling price —see under PRICE[1]

sell-off *n* [C] **1** FINANCE a situation in which many investors sell their bonds, shares etc, often very quickly: *Equity's shares lost half their value in a sell-off sparked off by the company's low earnings projection.* | *In an otherwise calm market, there were steep sell-offs in shares.*

2 when a business, company etc is sold to another company: *6,000 metal union workers occupied two shipbuilding companies to protest at their planned sell-offs.* —see also ***sell off*** under SELL[1]

sell order —see under ORDER[1]

sell-out *n* [singular] if a product, share offer, event etc is a sell-out, it is very successful and lots of people buy it or go there, and no more products, shares, tickets etc are available: *Nestlé's $200 million five-year bonds were an absolute sell-out.* —see also ***sell out*** under SELL[1] **—sell-out** *adj*: *a sell-out crowd*

sell rating —see under RATING

sell-through *adj* [only before a noun] MARKETING sell-through films on VIDEO are intended for customers to buy rather than rent: *Disney executives have decided to release the film as a sell-through title.* **—sell-through** *n* [C]

semi- /semi/ *prefix* **1** used to show that something happens, appears etc twice in a particular period of time: *We hold a semi-weekly meeting for all team leaders.*

2 used to show that something is partly but not completely done: *Raw materials and **semi-finished** goods rose 0.6%.* | *He describes himself as **semi-retired**, but remains on several boards.*

semi-annual *adj* happening or done twice a year: *Schield Management has postponed its semi-annual preferred dividend.* —see also ANNUAL

sem·i·con·duc·tor /ˌsemikənˈdʌktə‖-ər/ *n* [C] COMPUTING a substance, such as SILCON, used in electronic equipment to pass an electric current from one part of the equipment to another, or a CHIP made using this substance: *Hitachi produces semiconductors, medical instruments and computer parts.* | *Computers account for 40% of the **semiconductor market**.*

sem·i·nar /ˈsemɨnɑː‖-nɑːr/ *n* [C] a fairly informal meeting of a group of people, who share information and ideas, discuss matters relating to their work etc: *Most of the people **attending** the **seminar** were from accountancy firms.* | *The Association is **holding** a **seminar** to highlight opportunities in the Japanese market.*

semi-skilled *adj* semi-skilled workers are not in highly skilled or in professional jobs, but need some special skills to do their job: *It would sometimes take months to fill **semi-skilled** assembly **jobs**.* —compare SKILLED, UNSKILLED

Sen·ate /ˈsenɨt/ *n* [singular] in the US and some other countries, the upper part of the two parts of government with the power to make laws

send /send/ past tense and past participle **sent** *v* [T]

1 to arrange for something to go to another place: *The computer network can **send data** at very high speeds.* **send sth to sb**: *He **sent a memo** to board members criticizing his boss.* **send sb sth**: *The company **sent** her **a letter** apologizing for the oversight.* | *a 10% tax on dividends sent abroad*

2 to tell someone to go somewhere, usually in order to do a particular task **send sb to do sth**: *The Institute sent 43 engineers to work in Japanese laboratories.* | *Mick was sent to Croatia to give a talk on the latest research.*

3 if something sends prices, profits, costs etc to a different level, it makes them go to that level: *The labor dispute at a copper mine in Chile sent futures prices lower.* | *The news **sent** bond **prices tumbling**.*

send away for sth also **send off for** *phr v* [T] to ask for something to be sent by post: *For more information, send away for our free booklet.*

send sth ↔ **back** *phr v* [T] to return something to the place it came from: *If you're not completely satisfied with the goods, send them back for a full refund.*

send in *phr v* [T] **1 send** sth ↔ **in** to send something, usually by mail, to a place where it can be dealt with:

Customers can send in their sales receipts to get the discount coupons.

2 send sb ↔ **in** to tell someone to go somewhere to do a particular task, especially a difficult one: *As the work continues, Continental sends in a team to reassure residents about the company's services.*

send off for sth *phr v* [T] another name for **send away for**

send sth ↔ **on** *phr v* [T] to send something that has been received to another place so that it can be dealt with: *Don't let your paperwork pile up – send it on as soon as possible and work to a deadline.*

send sth ↔ **out** *phr v* [T] to send things from a central place to various other places: *Motorola will be sending out samples to all its customers.* | *Once your business cards are printed, start sending them out as soon as possible.*

send·er /ˈsendə‖-ər/ *n* [C] the person who sends a message, letter, parcel etc: *Each incoming message has a code that identifies the sender.*

se·nes·cent /sɪ̇ˈnesənt/ *adj formal* getting older and showing the effects of this: *His task was to market coal as a developing rather than a senescent industry.*

Se·ni·or /ˈsiːniə‖-ər/ written abbreviation **Snr.** *adj* [only after a noun] *AmE* used after a man's name to show that he is the older of two men with the same name and from the same family: *John Walker, Snr.* —compare JUNIOR[1]

senior *adj* **1** having a high position in an organization, company etc: *a panel of* ***senior*** *corporate* ***executives*** | *He has held several* ***senior management positions*** *at Prudential.* | *Previously, he had been a* ***senior partner*** (=the more important person in a business partnership) *at Coopers & Lybrand.* + **to**: *In advertising, an experienced creative person won't consider that you are senior to him, even if you are in charge.*

2 [only before a noun] FINANCE senior lenders, SHAREHOLDERS etc have to be paid before other lenders etc if the borrower gets into financial difficulty: *Only after* ***senior creditors*** *were paid in full would ordinary shareholders get some cash.* | *The group has agreed a plan with its* ***senior lenders*** *to restructure its credit facilities.*

3 [only before a noun] FINANCE a company's senior shares, bonds etc are considered to be more valuable because investors owning them will be paid before those owning ordinary shares, bonds etc. Those with senior shares etc will also be paid a larger percentage of what they are owed if the company gets into financial difficulty: *Half of the purchase price was paid in cash and the balance in* ***senior stock***. | *an offering of $100 million of medium-term* ***senior notes*** | *Macy's 1999* ***senior debentures*** *are paying 14.5%.* —compare JUNIOR[3]

senior bondholder —see under BONDHOLDER

senior citizen *n* [C] someone over the age of 65, usually someone who has finished their working life

senior creditor —see under CREDITOR

senior debenture —see under DEBENTURE

senior debt —see under DEBT

se·ni·or·i·ty /ˌsiːniˈɒrɪ̇ti‖-ˈɔː-, -ˈɑː-/ *n* [U] **1** the fact of being older or higher in rank than someone else: *Chief judges are chosen by seniority.*

2 the official advantage someone has because they have worked for an organization for a long time: *Workers with longer seniority get up to three years of benefits.*

3 FINANCE the situation in which particular loans etc are paid before other loans etc if a company is in financial difficulty: *privileged creditors that insist on the seniority of their loans*

senior management —see under MANAGEMENT

senior notes —see under NOTE[1]

senior partner —see under PARTNER

senior staff —see under STAFF[1]

sen·si·tive /ˈsensɪ̇tɪv/ *adj* **1** very easily and quickly affected by changes: *Many* ***economically sensitive*** *companies have closed factories and cut their staff.* | *We face fierce competition from imports and* ***price-sensitive consumers*** (=customers who are likely to buy a product if the price goes down, and not buy it if the price rises) + **to**: *A fall in bond prices discouraged investors from buying stocks that are* ***sensitive to interest rates***.

2 something that is sensitive is kept secret because it might be used to gain an advantage: *During the trial, the company argued that the documents contained* ***sensitive trade secrets*** *and should be kept confidential.* | *Modern telecommunications technology means there is a greater risk that* ***sensitive information*** *will be misused or stolen.*

3 able to understand other people's needs, problems, etc: *Local authorities will have to become more* ***customer sensitive***. | *standards for treating waste in an* ***environmentally sensitive*** *way* + **to**: *We're sensitive to consumers' needs and opinions.*

sen·si·tiv·i·ty /ˌsensɪ̇ˈtɪvɪ̇ti/ *n* [U] the degree to which something is likely to be affected by something else: *Because of their sensitivity to aluminum ingot prices, both companies expect a fall in profits.* | *Particular areas of sensitivity include future profits and asset values.* | *Women showed greater sensitivity to company politics than men.*

price sensitivity ECONOMICS the degree to which a change in the price of something leads to a change in the amount sold or that could possibly be sold; PRICE ELASTICITY: *The lengthy recession has increased price sensitivity and pressured profit margins.*

sensitivity analysis —see under ANALYSIS

sensitivity training —see under TRAINING

sen·ti·ment /ˈsentɪ̇mənt/ *n* [U] the feelings and opinions people have about something: *The Dow Jones index rose, reflecting* ***market sentiment*** *that the economy is improving.* | ***Consumer sentiment*** *isn't always useful in trying to predict economic growth.* | *Encouraging economic news reinforced* ***bullish*** (=positive and hopeful) ***sentiment*** *toward the U.S. dollar.*

sentiment indicator —see under INDICATOR

sep·a·rate[1] /ˈsepərɪ̇t/ *adj* **1** things that are separate are not connected or related to each other in any way: *The finance team left to start a* ***separate company***. | *Many advertisers are running ads for two or more separate products.* —**separately** *adv*: *Debt should be stated on the balance sheet separately from other liabilities.*

2 under separate cover if something is sent under separate cover, it is sent through the post in a different envelope from other documents: *The information you requested is being sent under separate cover.*

separate[2] /ˈsepəreit/ *v* [I,T] to divide something into two or more parts, or to cause it to do this: *The decision to* ***separate the business*** *reflects the management's current marketing strategy.* **separate sth from sth**: *Rising competition separates the strong from the weak.*

sep·a·ra·tion /ˌsepəˈreɪʃən/ *n* [C,U] *AmE* the act of leaving your job, because you have been dismissed or have RESIGNED: *Employees whose applications for separation are accepted would each receive a separation allowance.* | *The job reductions will be met through layoffs and* ***voluntary separations*** (=when people leave their jobs willingly rather than being dismissed).

Sept. written abbreviation for SEPTEMBER

se·quel /ˈsiːkwəl/ *n* [C] a book, film, play etc that continues the story of an earlier one: *Warner executives are very optimistic about the sequel.* —compare PREQUEL

se·quen·tial /sɪˈkwenʃəl/ *adj formal* happening in a fixed order, where a series of related actions, events etc lead to a particular result: *The buying process is analysed as a series of* ***sequential steps***. | *The figures will disap-*

S

point investors looking for sequential gains in sales and profits. —**sequentially** *adv*: *Keep a close eye on sequentially numbered invoices to detect any missing ones.*

sequential liability —see under LIABILITY

se·ques·ter[1] /sɪˈkwestə‖-ər/ *v* [T] *formal* **1** to make a group of people, such as a JURY, stay away from other people: *The remaining jurors were sequestered under guard for the remainder of the trial.*
2 another word for SEQUESTRATE

sequester[2] *n* [C] *AmE formal* an order by the US government stating that a government organization or department must reduce the money it spends: *If the projected deficit is more than $74 billion, a sequester will be administered.* | *Education and labor and are among the agencies scheduled for* ***sequester cuts.***

se·ques·trate /sɪˈkwestreɪt, ˈsiːkwə̇-/ also **se·ques·ter** /sɪˈkwestə‖-ər/ *v* [T] LAW to officially take property, goods etc away from someone because they have not paid their debts or have broken some other law: *The* ***shares were sequestered*** *by the Milan district court at the request of the chairman.* | *a private injunction* ***sequestering*** *$796.2 million of company* ***assets*** —**sequestration** *n* [C,U] *the sequestration of trade union funds* | *The court lifted a* ***sequestration order*** *on a key block of AMEF shares.*

se·ri·al /ˈsɪəriəl‖ˈsɪr-/ *adj* [only before a noun]
1 FINANCE serial bonds etc are a set of investments which MATURE (=become due for payment) at regular intervals over a period of time: *All of the issue's* ***serial bonds*** *have split maturities of March 1 and Sept. 1.* | *The Exchange launched* ***serial options*** *in its sugar market yesterday.*
2 appearing or happening in a fixed order, one after the other: *If you use the index facility on your PC, a serial search is not necessary.* | *We are considering* ***serial publication*** (=printing parts of a book at regular intervals, for example in a newspaper or magazine).

serial number —see under NUMBER[1]

serial port —see under PORT[1]

se·ries /ˈsɪəriːz‖ˈsɪr-/ *n* [singular] **1** FINANCE a group of investments that MATURE (=become due for payment) at different times but which are covered by the same agreement between the person offering them and people who buy them. The word series is often used with a letter or date to show when the investments become payable: *The Treasury's mortgage revenue bonds series 1998–99 are due Dec. 1, 2018.* | *The C and D preferred stock series have a face value of $100.*
2 a group of events, actions etc of the same kind that happen one after the other: *Itel has embarked on a series of asset sales.*

Serious Fraud Office *n* abbreviation **SFO** in Britain, the part of the police force responsible for finding out about serious crimes that involve getting money dishonestly —see also FRAUD SQUAD

SERPS /sɜːps‖sɜːrps/ *n* [singular] state earnings-related pension scheme; in Britain, a government arrangement for getting a PENSION (=income after you stop working) that depends on how much you pay while you are working. SERPS is in addition to the basic pension

serve /sɜːv‖sɜːrv/ *v* **1** [T] to supply customers with a particular product or service or with something they need: *The firm plans to open a London office to* ***serve clients*** *with investments and businesses in Europe.* | *Japan's leading international airline serves 63 overseas cities.*
2 [I,T] to give the customers in a shop, restaurant etc the things they want to buy: *Free wine will be served on flights.*
3 [I,T] to spend a period of time doing a particular job, often an important one that helps the organization: *If elected, she will* ***serve*** *the remaining 15 months of Mr. Helmick's four-year* ***term.*** | *He had to* ***serve an apprenticeship*** (=a period of training) *with an accounting firm.* + **as**: *He once served as president of Apple Computer Inc.'s products division.*
4 serve a summons/writ/notice etc LAW to officially send or give someone a written order to appear in a court of law + **on**: *The manufacturing company served a writ on him after he failed to register the patent.*

serv·er /ˈsɜːvə‖ˈsɜːrvər/ also **file server** *n* [C] COMPUTING a powerful computer used to store large amounts of information and to connect other smaller computers in a NETWORK. The smaller computers are sometimes called CLIENTS: *The network kept crashing because it was running on a file server with only 12Mb of memory.*

ser·vice[1] /ˈsɜːvə̇s‖ˈsɜːr-/ *n* **1** [C usually plural] business that involves selling help and advice, or delivering goods etc for customers, rather than manufacturing goods: *He charged a £600,000 fee for* ***consulting services.***

business continuity services [plural] services provided to companies so that they can continue operating if they are affected by a serious event such as a fire, computer failure etc: *Guardian are the largest supplier of business continuity services – disaster recovery is their speciality.*

dealing-only service [C] FINANCE a service offered by a firm of STOCKBROKERS in which they make deals for their customers but do not offer advice

financial services [plural] the business activity of giving advice about investments and selling them to people and organizations: *Banks have been moving into other areas of the* ***financial services industry*** *such as stockbroking, securities underwriting, and insurance.*

interactive service [C usually plural] a service which customers receive through the INTERNET and by telephone line, for example HOME BANKING: *Digital television enables broadcasters to offer interactive services.*

2 [C] the regular work done by a public or other large national organization, or the organization itself: *For many years, the state* ***postal service*** *fell outside the monopoly rules.*

public service ◆ [C] a service that a government provides, such as the police, the health service etc and which is paid for by taxation: *He must show a willingness to spend more on health, education and other public services.*
◆ [U] the government and its departments: *18% of the college's graduates intend to pursue* ***careers in public service.***
◆ [C] a service provided to people because it will help them, and not for profit: *The Postal Service is not a business, but a public service operating in a businesslike manner.*

3 [C] a system of regular flights etc between two places: *Singapore International Airlines has opened a trans-Atlantic service between Toronto and Singapore.* | *a daily* ***air service*** *between London and Paris*
4 [C] an organization or department that provides advice and help, for example on legal or personal problems: *A* ***counselling service*** *can provide employees with appropriate support.*
5 [U] the help given to customers by people working in a shop, restaurant etc: *Our* ***service standards*** *are monitored to ensure they are maintained at a consistently high level.*

after-sales service [U] repairs and advice given to a customer by a company after the customer has bought a product from the company: *A good after-sales service is just as important as the product itself.*

customer service also **customer services** [U] ◆ the department in a large organization that deals with questions and complaints from its customers, gives advice on using the product or service its provides etc: *Just ring 660000 and ask for the Customer Services department.* | *For further information on The*

US market for plastics additives, contact Customer Service, Frost & Sullivan, Sullivan House, London.
◆ when an organization helps its customers by answering their questions and listening to their complaints, giving them advice on using the product or service they provide, providing a good quality product etc.: *The company claims customer service is its number one priority.* | *Competitive rates are only one factor in good customer service.*
6 [plural, U] the work an employee does for a company or organization: *automatic pay increases based on **length of service*** | *amounts payable to the director in respect of the services performed* —see also BUSINESS REPLY SERVICE, CONTRACT OF SERVICE, DEBT SERVICE

service² *adj* [only before a noun] service roads, stairs, lifts etc are for the use of people working in a place or delivering goods to it, rather than the general public: *A new service road and tanker turning area is proposed for the site.*

service³ *v* [T] **1** FINANCE to pay a debt, loan etc: *Cardholders are having trouble **servicing** their **debts** to the lender.*
2 FINANCE if a financial institution services loans, debts etc, it manages them for another company, for example by collecting payments, calculating interest etc: *The underlying loans are being serviced by Chrysler Credit Corp.*
3 to examine a machine or piece of equipment and to mend it if necessary: *Compaq relies heavily on independent dealers to sell and service its computers.*
4 to provide a particular service, such as help, advice, transport etc: *Cigna had previously **serviced** its **customers** in Mexico through a network of independent insurance firms.* | *The travel concern made its name by servicing travelers on the Orient Express.* —**servicing** *n* [U] *We plan to bring the equipment back to the U.S. for servicing.* | *Income from **mortgage servicing** rose sharply.* | *The company has been increasing its **loan servicing** portfolio.*

service agreement —see under AGREEMENT
service charge —see under CHARGE¹
service contract —see under CONTRACT¹
service economy —see under ECONOMY¹
service industry —see under INDUSTRY
service occupation —see under OCCUPATION
service sector —see under SECTOR

ses·sion /ˈseʃən/ *n* **1** [C] FINANCE a period of time, usually a day, when buying and selling takes place on the stockmarket: *The exchange has introduced an evening **trading session** to accommodate demand for Far East currency options.* | *Stock prices sank for the fourth consecutive session.*
2 [C] a meeting used by a group of people for a particular purpose: *After the **opening session** we run a series of workshops.* | *There can be no substitute for thorough preparation before a **negotiation session** with the client.*
3 [C,U] a formal meeting or group of meetings, especially of a court or a parliament: *Morocco and Tunisia are host to the next two sessions of the trade talks.* | *The European parliament is **in session** in Strasbourg.*

session high —see under HIGH¹

set¹ /set/ *v* past tense and past participle **set** present participle **setting** [T] **1** to decide that something should happen on a particular date, cost a particular amount, be done in a particular way etc: *We have **set** a **deadline** of 31 December for the receipt of bids.* | *The initial **price is set at** $6 a share.* | *The OPEC agreement **set** a **production ceiling** (=limit) of 22.5 million barrels of oil a day.*
2 set standards/aims/targets/goals to establish standards, aims etc for doing something: *Mazda's new president will be under pressure to maintain the growth targets set by his predecessor.* | *Twenty-one computer companies met to set a standard for advanced computers.*
3 set sb a goal/challenge/target to decide that someone should try to achieve something, especially something that needs a lot of effort: *The Health Service has set itself the target of recruiting a minimum of 33% of female directors.* | *The sales force was set a challenge – to find three good ideas for improving profit levels.*
set sth **against** sth *phr v* [T] to consider something in relation to another thing, especially when that other thing is more important: *The industry's growth is remarkable when set against the background of the Philippines' poor economic performance.* | *The large supply is set against a backdrop of low demand.*
set sth **(off) against** sth *phr v* [T] ACCOUNTING to balance two amounts of money, so that the income you receive and the money you pay in tax, interest etc are as close to each other as possible: *Trading losses can be set against income from the disposal of assets.* | *The company will be able to set off the tax credit against part of its debt liability.*
set sth ↔ **aside** *phr v* [T] **1** to keep something, especially a particular amount of money, so that it can be used for a special purpose: *Chase is **setting aside reserves** for existing bad debts.*
2 to officially cancel an earlier legal decision or agreement: *The judge **set aside** a jury **verdict** awarding £3.2 million to a private firm in a contract dispute.* —see also SET-ASIDE
set back *phr v* [T] **1 set** sth ↔ **back** to delay the progress or development of a plan, project etc: *The recession in luxury car sales has set back Jaguar's recovery plan.* **set sth back to**: *The schedule was set back to June while auditors review the company's financial condition.*
2 set sb back *informal* if something sets you back a large sum of money, it costs you that much: *The company rescue will set taxpayers back an estimated $111.5 billion.* —see also SETBACK
set sth ↔ **down** *phr v* [T] to establish rules, laws etc about how something should be done: *Banking regulators could set down similar rules for sales practices by banks.*
set out *phr v* **1** [T] **set** sth ↔ **out** to write or talk about something, such as a group of facts, ideas, or reasons in an organized way: *Details of the case are set out in a briefing paper.* | *The performance measurement system sets out what tasks each person is responsible for.*
2 [I] to start a particular kind of job or start doing something in a particular way **set out to do sth**: *The new government set out to manage inflation by using interest rates to control the money supply.*
set sth **up** *phr v* [I,T] **1** to start a company, organization, committee etc: *Japan's largest advertising concern is setting up a branch office in Moscow.* | *The Action Team is keen to support ideas promoting the area with the aim of making it more attractive to firms setting up.*
2 set up shop/in business *informal* to begin operating a business: *There are many tax advantages that encourage foreign banks to set up shop here.* | *He would prefer to set up in business as an independent financial adviser.*
3 to make all the arrangements so that something can happen, such as a meeting, event or a system for doing something: *Several companies set up 24-hour telephone hotlines to deal with enquiries.* | *He recently set up a stress-management class that was attended by about 60 workers.* —see also SET-UP

set² *adj* [only before a noun] **set amount/time/price etc** an amount, time etc that is fixed and cannot be changed: *If your income is above £74.80 a week, 70% of the additional benefit is cut from the **set payments**.* | *The subcontractor employs the workforce for a **set wage**.* —see also COMMERCIAL SET

set-aside *n* [C] **1** an amount of money kept so that it can be used for a special purpose; RESERVE: *The bank*

S

plans to keep increasing its set-aside at the rate of roughly $50 million a quarter.

2 *AmE* an arrangement in which a local government helps small businesses to develop by making loans etc available to them: *In 1976, Connecticut established one of the nation's first* ***set-aside programs.*** —see also ***set aside*** under SET[1]

set·back /'setbæk/ *n* [C] something that delays the progress or development of a plan, activity etc or makes things worse than they were before: *The company* ***suffered a setback*** *when it lost a bid to become the partner in a new venture.* | *After* ***a series of setbacks*** *things are beginning to look up for Britain's second-largest bank.* —see also ***set back*** under SET[1]

SETS /sets/ *n* FINANCE Stock Exchange Trading System; a computer system giving share prices and for trading shares on the LONDON STOCK EXCHANGE, with dealers buying and selling over the system itself, rather than by telephone

set·tle /'setl/ *v* **1** [I,T] to end an argument by agreeing to do something: *The company signed a pact with Amtel,* ***settling*** *a patent* ***suit*** *between the two companies.* | *Before the second phase of the trial, the company* ***settled out of court*** (=ended the argument without having to go to court). **settle sth with sb**: *Diasonics Inc. has* ***settled*** *a* ***dispute*** *with Toshiba over the final sale price of its computing division.*

2 [I] FINANCE if prices on a market settle, they stop rising or falling and stay at a particular level for a period of time: *Crude oil futures prices settled lower in light trading.*

3 [T] to pay money that is owed: *Proceeds from the sale will be used to* ***settle debt*** *to other creditors.* | *Credit cards are one of the best ways of* ***settling bills*** *when you travel abroad.*

settle on/upon *phr v* [T] **1 settle on/upon sth** to decide or agree about something: *Motorola has settled on a Mips computer for its new product line.*

2 settle sth on/upon sb to make a formal arrangement to give money or property to someone: *After he had collected his money, he settled up and left the hotel.*

settle up *phr v* [I] to pay what you owe on an account or bill: *After he had collected his money, he settled up and left the hotel.*

set·tle·ment /'setlmənt/ *n* **1** [C,U] an official agreement or decision that ends an argument between two people or organizations: *The two former executives hope to* ***reach*** *a* ***settlement*** *with Saatchi by the end of July.* | *Under the* ***proposed settlement****, ADP is prohibited from distributing the software.* | *The inflation rate fell, reflecting recent overtime cutbacks and low* ***wage settlements.*** | *increases in public sector* ***pay settlements***

2 [C,U] the payment of money that someone owes: *The company made a* ***full and final settlement*** *of £30 million.* | *Non-US residents are prepared to use the dollar* ***in settlement of debts.***

3 [U] FINANCE the process of making payments relating to cheques, buying investments etc; CLEARING: *the Talisman settlement system on the London Stock Exchange*

cash settlement [C,U] FINANCE when shares etc that are bought on a financial market are paid for with money, rather than with other investments: *The Tokyo and Osaka options markets will use stock, not cash settlement.*

rolling settlement [U] a rule stating that when you buy or sell shares on the London Stock Exchange, the payment must be made within a certain number of days from the time when the contract is made: *Dealings here are for seven-day rolling settlement except in the case of new issues.*

settlement date —see under DATE[1]

settlement offer —see under OFFER[2]

settlement terms —see under TERM[1]

settling day *n* [C] *BrE* another name for SETTLEMENT DATE

set·tlor /'setlə‖-ər/ *n* [C] LAW a person who gives property or goods to someone under a special agreement, especially a WILL (=statement saying who you want to have your property and money after you die): *It is important that settlors can have complete faith in their trustees.*

set-up also **setup** *n* [C] **1** the way something is organized or arranged: *The trust will be managed by a board of directors, although that setup requires regulatory approval.* —see also ***set up*** under SET[1]

2 all the parts that work together in a system, especially a computer system: *Multimedia setups can mix video clips, recorded speech, music, and computer graphics.* | *Before the new setup was installed, only 54% of telephone enquiries got through.*

setup cost —see under COST[1]

sev·er /'sevə‖-ər/ *v* [T] to end a business relationship or connection with someone because of a disagreement: *He has* ***severed*** *all financial* ***ties*** *with his former firm.* | *A business dispute caused Lasorda Foods and its distributor to* ***sever relations.***

sev·e·ral·ly /'sevərəli/ *adv* **jointly and severally** LAW if two companies own or are responsible for something jointly and severally, they have an equal share in it: *In many states, firms are* ***jointly and severally liable*** *for injuries caused at work.*

sev·er·ance /'sevərəns/ *n* [U] LAW the act of officially ending an agreement or contract, especially between an employer and an employee: *Before signing, it is important to know whether severance is available.* | *The company hasn't yet negotiated* ***severance payments*** *for the 70 employees affected by the closure.*

severance package —see under PACKAGE[1]

sew /səʊ‖soʊ/ *v* past tense **sewed** past participle **sewn** also **sewed** *AmE*

sew sth ↔ **up** *phr v* [T] **1** *informal* to agree to a plan or arrangement with someone which will give you both the result you want: *Deutsche Bank and Dresdner Bank have sewn up their plans to divide the retail banking system between them.*

2 *disapproving* to get control of a situation so that you are certain to gain an advantage from it: *They had the market so sewn up that the salesmen hardly had to try to sell the products at all.*

sexual discrimination —see under DISCRIMINATION

sexual harassment —see under HARASSMENT

sgd written abbreviation for SIGNED

SGML *n* [U] standard generalized mark-up language; a computer language for creating files, using a system of codes to label the different parts of a file so that those parts can be grouped together or treated in a similar way to each other: *The SGML data format allows documents to be shared between different publishing systems.* —compare HTML

shad·ow /'ʃædəʊ‖-doʊ/ *v* [T] **1** to watch someone very closely or work with them in order to learn how they do their job: *The managers were shadowed by trainees in the bank's development programme.*

2 to change at the same rate or in the same way as something: *In London, share prices shadowed Wall Street's, to close midway.* | *Gloomy news in the technology sector was shadowed by smaller electronics stocks.*

shadow economy —see under ECONOMY[1]

shadow market —see under MARKET[1]

shady dealings —see under DEALING

shake /ʃeɪk/ *v* past tense **shook** past participle **shaken** [T] if something shakes people's confidence, hopes, belief etc, it makes them feel less confident, hopeful etc:

*Consumer **confidence** has been badly **shaken** by fears of another recession.* | *A series of management changes has shaken staff morale.*

shake down *phr v* **1** [T] **shake** sb ↔ **down** *AmE informal* to get money from someone, using threats: *The former business agent was charged with shaking down contractors.*

2 [I] *informal* if a new situation or arrangement shakes down, people start to get used to it and it becomes more effective: *The restructure has shaken down, and staff are showing a new sense of purpose.*

shake out *phr v* **1** [I] if an organization or industry shakes out, it becomes calmer after a difficult period of time. In a market, this happens when weaker companies are forced out of business or bought by bigger companies, leaving fewer competitors: *He will look for bargains in a year or two, after the real estate **market shakes out.***

2 [T] **shake** sth ↔ **out** to change a situation by removing things about it that are not useful or profitable: *As the airline industry shakes out all but the very fittest, catering companies could face serious troubles.*

shake sth **up** *phr v* [T] to make changes in an organization or system to make it more successful, effective etc: *The move could **shake up** the Japanese PC **market** and boost IBM's share.* | *He shook the firm's bond-trading operations up by hiring four new directors.*

shake·down /ˈʃeɪkdaʊn/ also **shake-down** *n* [C] **1** *AmE* the process of getting money from someone, using threats: *The shakedown ring* (=criminal group) *was smashed and Mafia bosses were sentenced to 100-year prison terms for extortion.*

2 a period of time when people start to get used to a new arrangement and it becomes more effective: *But as we get more cities, our distribution will get better. We are finally coming out of our shakedown.*

3 FINANCE a period of time when prices are falling on a financial market: *The shakedown in engineering shares seems to be nearly over, with only minor declines yesterday.*

shake·out /ˈʃeɪkaʊt/ *n* [C] ECONOMICS a change in market conditions that causes less successful or profitable businesses, investments etc to fail: *The Treasury bond **market** appears to be headed for a **shakeout**.* | *Weaker institutions are not expected to survive the shakeout in the crowded business-school market.*

shake·up /ˈʃeɪkʌp/ *n* [C] a process in which an organization makes lots of changes in a short time in order to become more successful, effective etc: *The shakeup could cost as many as 3,000 of the bank's 41,600 employees their jobs.* | *High-level **management shakeups** were announced at two major Japanese brokerage firms.*

shak·y /ˈʃeɪki/ *adj* comparative **shakier** superlative **shakiest** not definite or firm, and likely to fail: *The market began a shaky recovery.* | *Taiwan's economic success has made things tougher for China's already shaky tourism industry.*

share /ʃeə‖ʃer/ *n* [C] **1** FINANCE one of the parts into which ownership of a company is divided: *Webb **issued*** (=made available and sold) *2.5 million new **shares** of common stock.* | *Friendly companies and banks alone **hold*** (=own) *56% of all **shares** in Germany's listed companies.* | *Goldman, Sachs & Co. sold a **block of** 2.4 million **shares*** (=a large quantity, usually more than 10,000)

2 (Class) A/B/C shares [plural] different classes of a company's shares. Each class has different characteristics, for example the right to vote at shareholders' meetings: *Torstar had 36.5 million Class B shares and 5.1 million voting Class A shares outstanding. The Class A shares aren't publicly traded.*

advancing shares [plural] shares that increase in value on a particular day of trading on a stockmarket; ADVANCERS: *Declining issues outnumbered advancing shares 462 to 441, while 161 others remained unchanged.* —compare DECLINING SHARES

American depositary share also **American depository share** [C] a share that allows investors in the US to trade in the shares of non-US companies without buying or selling the actual shares; ADR

authorized shares also **authorised shares** *BrE* [plural] the maximum number of shares that a company's rules allow it to ISSUE (=make available and sell): *Shareholders will be asked to approve an increase in the number of authorized shares to 175 million from 100 million.*

bearer share [C] a share owned by the person who possesses the related SHARE CERTIFICATE. This name might not be recorded on an official list: *Lufthansa has until now issued its capital in the form of anonymous bearer shares.*

blue chip share also **blue-chip share** [C] a share in a well-managed company with a large amount of PAID-UP CAPITAL and a long record of paying profits to SHAREHOLDERS during good and bad economic conditions; BLUE CHIP STOCK

bonus share [C] one of the shares given to existing shareholders when profits are distributed. Bonus shares are sometimes given in addition to the normal DIVIDEND: *In addition to its regular dividend, Heineken said it will propose issuing a bonus share for each four shares investors hold.*

capital share also **capital growth share** [C] in MUTUAL FUNDS, a share where holders profit from any increase in the value of investments held by the fund: *The income shares get all the dividends produced by the securities in the fund's portfolio, while the capital shares benefit from any appreciation in the portfolio's value.*

common share [C] *especially AmE* another name for ORDINARY SHARE: *Unicorp suspended its dividend on common shares after reporting a big loss for the year.*

convertible share [C] a share that may be exchanged for another share under certain conditions: *Convertible shares would have a preferential right to a fixed payment if the company were liquidated and be convertible into ordinary shares if the firm recovers.*

cumulative preference share also **cumulative preferential share**, or **cumulative preferred share** [C] one of the class of PREFERRED SHARES where, if the company does not pay DIVIDENDS in some years, the amount of these dividends is paid in later years, and is not lost to the shareholder

cyclical share [C] a share in a company whose performance is strongly affected by the rate of growth in the economy as a whole: *cyclical shares, such as auto, bank, insurance and aluminum stocks*

declining shares [plural] shares that fall in value on a particular day of trading on a stockmarket; DECLINERS: *Declining shares overtook advancers, 963 to 858.* —compare ADVANCING SHARES

defensive share [C] one of the shares in a company that people think will still make good profits even if economic growth is low: *For the time being, analysts recommend sticking with traditional defensive shares such as utilities or food retailers.*

deferred share ◆ [C] one of a class of shares where DIVIDENDS are only paid in a particular period of time after dividends have been paid on all other classes of shares: *EDS proposed to pay 45 pence in cash for each of SD-Scicon's ordinary shares, 85 pence for each of its preference shares, and six pence for its deferred shares.*

◆ [C] one of a class of shares which do not pay DIVIDENDS immediately, but pay them later, for example when the company reaches a particular level of sales: *Management may take deferred shares which will convert into ordinary shares when performance targets are reached.*

delta shares [plural] in Britain, shares in small companies that are not often actively traded and are not listed on SEAQ

diluted shares [plural] all the shares of a company considered together, especially after a SHARE ISSUE (=when new shares are made available and sold), and DIVIDENDS are spread over a larger number of shares: *The number of **fully diluted shares** rose 23% to 48.1 million.*

fractional share [C] a part of a share that a shareholder may receive, for example in a SHARE DIVIDEND (=where a payment to shareholders is made in the form of new shares) or STOCK SPLIT (=when shares are divided into smaller units). Shareholders are often offered cash instead of fractional shares

fully-paid share [C] one of a group of shares that has been paid for completely —compare PARTLY-PAID SHARE

fund share [C] one of the shares in an INVESTMENT FUND or MUTUAL FUND: *Instead of receiving their dividends in cash, investors often tell their funds to reinvest those dividends in additional fund shares.*

golden share [C] a government share in a company, usually a company that has been partly PRIVATIZED (=sold to investors), but where the government wants to continue to have influence. The share gives the government the right to decide on how the company is managed, who owns it etc: *The Spanish government is to retain a golden share in Argentaria after it sells its remaining 25 % in the banking group, in a move to prevent hostile takeovers.*

growth share [C] a share that increases in value quickly: *Drug and food issues were among the favored growth shares.*

heavy share [C] one of a company's shares which are considered to have a high price and may therefore be difficult to buy and sell. Different stockmarkets have different ideas about how much shares can be worth before they think they are heavy: *The share price has risen to 800p, a heavy share by UK standards.*

income share ◆ [C] a share that pays good DIVIDENDS in relation to its price, rather than one that increases in value quickly

◆ [C] in MUTUAL FUNDS, a class of share where shareholders get the DIVIDENDS that the fund collects from its investments, rather than a share in any increase in the value of the investments: *Income shares in River & Mercantile – largely invested British blue chips – yield 12%.*

large-cap share also **large-capitalization share**, **large-capitalisation share** *BrE* [C] a share in a company with a large amount of SHARE CAPITAL (=total share value); LARGE-CAP: *large-capitalization shares such as shipbuilding and steel companies*

listed share [C] one of the shares in a company that is traded on a particular stockmarket; QUOTED SHARE: *About 50% of Repsol's listed shares currently trade in New York.*

management share [C] one of a class of shares offered to the managers of a company

mid-cap share or **mid capitalization share**, also **mid capitalisation share** *BrE* [C] a share in a company with a medium amount of SHARE CAPITAL (=total share value); MID-CAP: *In Paris in recent weeks, mid-cap shares have lagged behind the CAC-40 index of major companies.*

new share also **newly-issued share** [C] one of a company's shares that have just been sold for the first time, rather than shares that already exist: *Proceeds from the company's sale of the five million newly issued shares will be used to reduce debt.*

non-participating shares [plural] shares that do not give their owners a right to a share in the profits and that only pay a fixed rate of interest, for example preferred shares

non-voting share [C] one of a class of shares that do not give their holders the right to vote at shareholders meetings: *The rule seemed to protect the one share, one-vote principle. But nonvoting shares are now on the rise.*

no-par-value share [C] a type of share that does not have a PAR VALUE (=a stated value) when it is ISSUED (=made available and sold). No-par-value shares exist in the US and some other countries, but not in Britain

ordinary share [C] *especially BrE* the most frequent type of share in most companies. If the company is in financial difficulty, DIVIDENDS on common shares are paid only after those made on other particular types of share, such as PREFERENCE SHARES: *Operating profit is down and company management is freezing the dividend at last year's level of FFr8.6 for ordinary shares and FFr9.4 for preferred shares.*

outstanding shares [plural] all of a company's shares that currently exist and are held by shareholders

over-the-counter share abbreviation **OTC share** [C] one of the shares in newer and smaller companies that are not bought and sold through dealers on the main stockmarket, but rather on a computer-based market such as NASDAQ: *Continued nervousness about biotechnology stocks helped fuel another decline in over-the-counter shares.*

participating preference share [C] one of a class of PREFERENCE SHARES where the holders also receive DIVIDEND payments like those on ordinary shares, related to the profits of the company during a particular period of time

part-paid share also **partly-paid share** [C] a share that the investor has only paid part of the price: *Shareholders must now decide whether to pay the second instalment on the partly-paid shares or to get out.* —compare FULLY-PAID SHARE

penny share [C] *BrE* a share that is only worth a few pence or cents, for example one of the shares in a company whose performance has been bad recently, but that may improve, or in a new, unknown company: *It amazes me how ready small investors are to buy rubbishy penny shares.*

preference share also **preferential share**, **preferred share** [C] one of a class of shares on which, if a company is in financial difficulty, DIVIDENDS may still be paid even if they are not paid on ordinary shares. Dividends on preference shares are usually paid in the form of fixed interest payments: *By issuing preference shares, GM is effectively borrowing money without adding to the debt load on its balance sheet.*

primary share ◆ [C] one of a company's shares before counting new shares, for example BONUS SHARES, that have been made available

◆ [C] one of a class of a company's shares that has more advantages than other shares, such as voting rights

quoted share [C] *BrE* another name for LISTED SHARE

red chip share or **red-chip share** [C] a share in a Chinese company that is listed on the Hong Kong stockmarket; RED CHIP STOCK

redeemable share [C] one of a class of shares that a company agrees to buy back from their holders under certain conditions

registered share [C] one of a class of shares where ownership is recorded on a list, and which is not always shown on SHARE CERTIFICATES (=documents showing ownership)

second-tier share ◆ [C] one of the shares in companies that are not among the biggest and most profitable on a particular stockmarket: *Blue-chips were affected by profit-taking, second-tier shares posted small gains.*

◆ [C] one of the shares in companies that are not bought and sold on the main stockmarket in a particular place

secondary shares ◆ [plural] shares in companies that are not BLUE-CHIP: *While blue-chip stocks ended mixed, secondary shares were stronger.*

◆ [plural] used to talk about a particular class of shares in a company in relation to another class that has more advantages, such as voting rights: *The public offering involves eight million primary shares and four million secondary shares.*

small cap share also **small capitalization share, small capitalisation share** *BrE* [C] a share in a company with a small amount of SHARE CAPITAL (=total share value)

split share [C] one of a group of a company's shares that has been divided into smaller units. This is done to reduce the share price and make them easier to buy and sell, and does not affect the value of the company to shareholders: *Following the 2-for-1 stock split, the company is increasing its dividend to 15.5 cents on the split shares..*

underlying share [C] one of the actual shares related to OPTIONS (=the right to buy shares at a particular price within a particular period of time) or other DERIVATIVES such as FUTURES

unlisted share also **unquoted share** *BrE* [C] a share in a company that is not traded on a main stockmarket, but rather on the OVER-THE-COUNTER MARKET (=computer-based trading in shares of newer and smaller companies)

voting share [C] one of a class of shares that gives its owner the right to vote at shareholders' meetings

when-issued share [C] *AmE* one of a group of shares that are being traded before they have been officially ISSUED (=made available) —see also DIVIDEND PER SHARE, EARNINGS PER SHARE

3 [singular] the part of something that belongs to a particular person, organization etc: *Corporations are being encouraged to give a share of their profits to social programs.* | *Currently, auto malls account for fewer than 5% of all U.S. car and truck sales. But their share will grow to 12% by the end of the decade.*

brand share [singular] the market share of a particular brand: *Nielsen provides regular data on sales, brand shares and prices in the retail trade.*

unit share [U] the numbers of a particular product that have been sold, in relation to the total number of products that are sold: *Most researchers think that Lotus has remained at the same level in dollar sales but has fallen in terms of unit share.*

market share also **share** [C,U] MARKETING the percentage of sales in a market that a company or product has: *The company foresees improvement in profit this year through* ***increasing*** *its* ***share*** *of the California housing market.* | *If the two companies' market shares are combined, they'll have 28% of the US market.* | *GM spends hundreds of millions of dollars in advertising to try to* ***gain market share*** (=increase it). | *Our strategy through the year was to* ***maintain market share*** *keep it at the same level and control costs.* | *Faced with* ***declining*** *decreasing* ***market share*** *and falling profits, the firm laid off workers, cut prices, replaced its chief executive.*

4 market share by value market share that is measured by SALES REVENUE (=money obtained from sales): *Gillette's current 60% market share by value in the UK would rise to 80% after including Wilkinson's market share*

5 market share by volume market share that is measured by the number of products sold: *Tia Maria is the country's leading traditional liqueur and claims a 46% market share by volume.*

6 to buy market share to increase market share by charging low prices, even if they are not profitable: *People have been competing with silly prices just to buy market share.*

share application —see under APPLICATION

share•bro•ker /ˈʃeəˌbrəʊkə‖ˈʃerˌbroʊkər/ *n* [C] a STOCKBROKER

share capital —see under CAPITAL

share certificate —see under CERTIFICATE

share•crop•per /ˈʃeəˌkrɒpə‖ˈʃerˌkrɑːpər/ *n* [C] *especially AmE* a farmer who uses someone else's land, and gives the owner part of the crop in return

share dividend —see under DIVIDEND

share exchange offer —see under OFFER[2]

share•hold•er /ˈʃeəˌhəʊldə‖ˈʃerˌhoʊldər/ *n* [C] *especially BrE* FINANCE someone who owns shares in a company; STOCKHOLDER *especially AmE*: *The bid was accepted by 90% of the shareholders.* | *Dividends are paid to the shareholders each year if adequate profits are made.* | *We are calling a* ***shareholders' meeting***. | *She is a 45% shareholder in the company.* | ***Institutional shareholders*** (=financial organizations such as banks and insurance companies) *account for the great majority of shareholdings on the Stock Exchange.*

controlling shareholder also **majority shareholder** someone who owns more than half the shares in a company: *The collapse of Friguia is a consequence of a lack of interest and investment by its controlling shareholder.*

minority shareholder someone who owns less than half the shares in a company: *The effect is to increase the stake of the minority shareholders from 20% to 45%.*

outside shareholder one of the minority shareholders in a company that is owned by another company that is the majority shareholder: *Outside shareholders holding the 20% of AEG shares not held by Daimler-Benz will receive a dividend of 2.50 marks a share, paid by Daimler-Benz.*

shareholder equity —see under EQUITY

shareholder rebellion *n* [C] *journalism* an occasion when the shareholders of a company do not agree with decisions made by its directors, and try to change them: *Shares in Storebrand and Christiania fell after a shareholder rebellion at Storebrand stopped a merger between the two companies.*

shareholders' equity —see under EQUITY

shareholders' funds —see under FUND[1]

shareholders' register —see ***share register*** under REGISTER[1]

share•hold•ing /ˈʃeəˌhəʊldɪŋ‖ˈʃerˌhoʊ-/ *n* [C] a quantity of shares in a company held by a particular person or organization; STAKE: *Shareholders can protect themselves from hostile takeovers by not agreeing to* ***sell their shareholdings*** *at a discount.* + **in**: *He has now* ***acquired*** *a 51%* ***shareholding*** *in the group.*

majority shareholding a quantity of shares held by someone in a company, that are more than half the total

minority shareholding a quantity of shares held by someone in a company, that are less than half the total

share index —see under INDEX[1]

share issue —see under ISSUE[2]

share manipulation —see under MANIPULATION

share offer —see under OFFER[2]

share option —see under OPTION

share price —see under PRICE[1]

share register —see under REGISTER[1]

share split —see under SPLIT[2]

share transfer —see under TRANSFER[2]

S

share•ware /ˈʃeəweə‖ˈʃerwer/ *n* [U] computer software that is given away free, or given away free for a particular period of time. After that time, people have to pay for it —compare FREEWARE

share warrant —see under WARRANT[1]

shark /ʃɑːk‖ʃɑːrk/ *n* [C] *informal* someone who cheats other people out of money, especially by giving bad financial advice: *Never do business with these sharks.*

loan shark someone who lends money at very high rates of interest

shark repellent *n* [C] *AmE* an action that is taken by a company to make an unwanted TAKEOVER less likely —see also POISON PILL

shark watcher *n* [C] a company whose business is discovering and giving advice on TAKEOVERs that are likely to be attempted, for example by seeing which people or companies are buying a large number of shares in a particular company

sharp /ʃɑːp‖ʃɑːrp/ *adj* a sharp increase, fall etc is very sudden and very big: *a **sharp rise** in interest rates* | *Unemployment generally brings a **sharp fall** in income.* | *The group reported a **sharp decline** in full-year profits.* —**sharply** *adv*: *During that month, Fidelity's share price **fell sharply**.* | *House prices have **risen sharply** over the past year.*

sharp practice —see under PRACTICE

shed /ʃed/ *v* past tense and past participle **shed** present participle **shedding** [T] **1** to get rid of something that you no longer need, especially workers: *IBM unveiled plans to shed another 10,000 employees.* | *There are companies who are making high levels of profit and who are still **shedding jobs**.* | *Analysts expect the company to shed its large stake in merchant bank Singer & Friedlander.*

2 if shares shed an amount they become less in value by that amount: *News Corporation shares shed 55 cents to close at A$15.9.*

S

shelf company —see under COMPANY

shelf life —see under LIFE

shelf offering —see under OFFERING

shelf registration —see under REGISTRATION

shelf space *n* [U] the amount of space that is available on shelves in shops to hold goods that are on sale: *All these brands are **competing for shelf space**.*

shell /ʃel/ *v*

shell out sth *phr v* [I,T] *informal* to spend a lot of money on something, often when you do not really want to; FORK OUT + **for/on**: *The insurance company refused to shell out for repairs.* | *NFC shelled out £75 million on 16 businesses.*

shell company also **shell corporation** *AmE* —see under COMPANY

shelve /ʃelv/ *v* [T] to decide not to continue with a plan, idea etc, although you might continue with it at a later time: *Plans for the project have been shelved.* | *Sumitomo Metal Industries agreed to shelve its 300 billion warrant-bond issue.*

shift[1] /ʃɪft/ *n* [C] **1** one of the set periods of time during each day and night when a group of workers in a factory etc are at work before being replaced by another group of workers: *She **works** an eight-hour **shift**.* | *Are you on the **day shift** or the **night shift**?*

graveyard shift a regular period of time that people work during the night: *To support his family, Frank found temporary work on the graveyard shift at a local tool company.*

split shift a shift that is divided into two or more parts on the same day: *Catering assistants work split shifts (7–10 am, 4–7 pm) to cover breakfasts and evening meals.*

swing shift *AmE* a shift in a factory from 3 or 4 o'clock in the afternoon until 12 o'clock at night

2 the group of workers who work shifts: *The **night shift** was just about to go off duty.*

3 a change in the way people think about something, in the way something is done etc + **in**: *The best way to measure shifts in a country's exchange rate is to use its trade-weighted exchange rate.* + **from/to**: *the shift from private to institutional shareholders* | *the closure of small outlets and the shift to larger out-of-town sites*

paradigm shift a complete change in your attitude towards the economy or a particular industry, caused by an event or discovery that has changed your way of thinking: *Some say that traditional shopping is going to be replaced by shopping on the Internet, but I don't think that sort of paradigm shift is going to happen.*

4 the KEY on a computer etc that you press to print a capital letter: *the shift key*

shift[2] *v* [T] to move or sell something: *This deal is the key to shifting about A$3 billion of debt off the balance sheet.* | *We shifted 10,000 units last week.*

shift key —see under KEY[1]

shift•work /ˈʃɪftwɜːk‖-wɜːrk/ *n* [U] a system of work in a factory in which different groups of workers work at different times of the day and night: *The factory has recently introduced shiftwork.* | *a report on the effects of shiftwork on sleep patterns*

shin•gle /ˈʃɪŋgəl/ *n* **hang out your shingle** *AmE* to start your own business, especially as a lawyer or doctor

Ship /ʃɪp/ PROPERTY Safe Home Income Plan association; an official organization in Britain that represents and controls companies who provide home income plans: *the Ship code of practice* —see also HIP

ship[1] /ʃɪp/ *n* [C] a large boat used for carrying people or goods across the sea: *The island's waste is taken by ship to the mainland.*

cargo ship a ship built to carry goods rather than people

container ship a large, fast ship built to carry CONTAINERS (=large metal boxes specially designed for moving goods)

dirty ship a TANKER that has not yet been cleaned out and so is not ready to take another load

dry ship a ship carrying goods such as tobacco and sugar that are not in liquid form

factory ship a large fishing boat, carrying all the equipment needed for cleaning, freezing etc the fish that are caught

general ship a cargo ship that has not been CHARTERED, so it can carry goods for anyone

merchant ship a ship used to carry goods or passengers, rather than soldiers, military equipment etc

ship[2] *v* past tense and past participle **shipped** present participle **shipping** [T] **1** to send or carry something by ship **ship sth out/to sb etc**: *I had my car shipped out to me.*

2 to send or deliver something by road, train, or air **ship sth to sb**: *A new computer was shipped to him within two weeks.*

3 to make goods, especially computer software, available for people to buy or use: *The new Windows software was announced in April and they're planning to ship it in October.*

ship•brok•er /ˈʃɪpˌbrəʊkə‖-ˌbroʊkə/ *n* [C] a person or organization that finds customers and arranges insurance for shipowners

ship•build•er /ˈʃɪpˌbɪldə‖-ər/ *n* [C] a company that makes ships —**shipbuilding** *n* [U] *key industries such as steel and shipbuilding*

ship•ment /ˈʃɪpmənt/ *n* **1** [C] a load of goods sent by sea, road, train, or air + **of**: *A shipment of 1700 cars left for Italy.* | *The railroad company's coal shipments rose 15%.*

bulk shipment [C] a delivery of a load of goods such

as grain or oil that are transported loose, not packed in containers

2 [U] the act of sending a load of goods by sea, road, train, or air: *Computer maker Cray's new models are now ready for shipment.* + **of**: *the shipment of cars and parts*

ship·owner /ˈʃɪpˌəʊnə‖-ˌoʊnər/ *n* [C] a person or company that owns a ship or ships: *insurance organizations providing oil pollution coverage for shipowners*

ship·per /ˈʃɪpə‖-ər/ *n* [C] a company that sends something by ship, road, train, or air: *Railroads are trying to attract shippers that are now using trucks.*

ship·ping /ˈʃɪpɪŋ/ *n* [U] **1** when goods are sent or delivered somewhere by ship, road, train, or air: *the shipping of US wheat* | *plastic products used in packaging and shipping*

2 ships considered as a group: *The port is closed to all shipping.*

merchant shipping ships that carry goods or passengers, or the activity of carrying goods or passengers by ship: *Merchant shipping is now becoming increasingly specialized.* | *pollution from merchant shipping*

shipping agent —see under AGENT

shipping documents —see under DOCUMENT[1]

shipping instructions —see under INSTRUCTION

shipping note —see under NOTE[1]

ship's papers —see under PAPER

ship·yard /ˈʃɪp-jɑːd‖-jɑːrd/ *n* [C] a place where ships are built or repaired: *a naval shipyard*

shoot /ʃuːt/ *v* past tense and past participle **shot** [I] to quickly increase in number or amount + **above/from/to**: *Oil prices shot above $40 a barrel.* | *The monthly interest rate shot to 40% in January.*

shoot ahead *phr v* [I,T] to quickly increase in number or amount + **by/from/to**: *The FTSE index shot ahead by 15 points.* | *Thorn's shares shot ahead 20p to 282p.*

shoot sb/sth ↔ **down** *phr v* [T] to reject something such as a suggestion or offer, or stop it from happening: *Union members shot down a four-year contract proposal.*

shoot for sth *phr v* [T] *especially AmE* to try to achieve a particular aim: *Mineaba is shooting for 500 billion yen in sales by next year.*

shoot up *phr v* [I] to quickly increase in number or amount: *Prices have certainly shot up recently.* —see also OVERSHOOT, UNDERSHOOT

shop[1] /ʃɒp‖ʃɑːp/ *n* [C] **1** *BrE* a building or part of a building where goods are sold to the public; STORE *AmE*: *The shops close at 5.30.* | *a clothes shop*

bucket shop ♦ a dishonest STOCKBROKING firm that uses its clients' money to buy high-risk stocks and COMMODITIES

♦ *informal BrE* a business that sells cheap tickets for air travel: *He got the cheap one-way ticket in a bucket shop.*

co-operative shop *BrE* a shop owned and run by a group of people as a co-operative; CO-OPERATIVE STORE or CO-OP *AmE*: *Burton used to work behind the counter at the town's co-operative shop.*

corner shop *BrE* a small shop on a street where people live rather than in a town centre, that sells things that are needed every day such as food and newspapers

factory shop *BrE* a shop where people can buy slightly damaged goods for less money than the goods would cost in normal shops

mobile shop *BrE* a large vehicle that has been changed into a shop and is driven from place to place: *a mobile shop selling groceries and newspapers*

2 MANUFACTURING a place where things are made or repaired: *a* ***repair shop***

job shop a business, for example a small factory, that produces a particular quantity of goods only when it receives an order for them: *the job shops that sell to major manufacturing concerns*

machine shop ♦ also **machine room** the place in a factory where products are made using machines: *One or two grinders in the machine shop have excessive maintenance costs.* | *The new equipment was delivered and located in the East machine room.*

♦ *AmE* a company, often a small one, that makes things using machines: *The new products will target machine shops and manufacturers of electrical equipment.*

paint shop the area in a car factory where cars are painted: *Mazda Motor Corp. lost two production days as the result of a fire in the paint shop.* | *paint-shop employees*

3 set up shop *informal* to start a business: *Firms can get grants to set up shop in the area.*

4 talk shop to talk about things that are connected to your work, especially in a way that other people find boring: *a bunch of pharmacists talking shop* —see also CLOSED SHOP

shop[2] *v* [I] past tense and past participle **shopped** present participle **shopping** **1** to go to one or more shops to buy things + **for**: *She went down town to shop for groceries.* + **at**: *Almost two-thirds of Americans shop at a convenience store at least once a week.*

2 go shopping to go to one or more shops to buy things, usually clothes, for enjoyment: *Young kids don't have the money, but they go shopping with Mom.*

shop around *phr v* [I] to compare the price and quality of different things before you decide what to buy + **for**: *Shop around for the best interest rates.* —see also SHOPPING

shop assistant —see under ASSISTANT

shop·fit·ter /ˈʃɒːpˌfɪtə‖ˈʃɑːpˌfɪtər/ *n* [C] *BrE* a company or person whose business is to supply and put in equipment such as shelves and containers for shops —**shopfitting** *n* [U] *shopfitting costs estimated at £500,000*

shop front *n* [C] *BrE* the outside part of a shop that faces the street, usually with a large window; STOREFRONT *AmE*

shop·keep·er /ˈʃɒpˌkiːpə‖ˈʃɑːpˌkiːpər/ *n* [C] *especially BrE* someone who owns or is in charge of a small shop; STOREKEEPER *AmE*: *Many shopkeepers are facing bankruptcy in the latest recession.*

shop·lift·ing /ˈʃɒpˌlɪftɪŋ‖ˈʃɑːp-/ *n* [U] the crime of taking something out of a shop without paying for it: *Shoplifting and robberies forced the company to spend heavily on security.* —**shoplifter** *n* [C] *measures to deter shoplifters* —**shoplift** *v* [I]

shop·per /ˈʃɒpə‖ˈʃɑːpər/ *n* [C] **1** someone who buys things in shops: *Store managers get blamed when shoppers can't find a particular product.*

2 in the US, a newspaper sold or given free to people in a particular area, that advertises stores, restaurants etc in that area

shop·ping /ˈʃɒpɪŋ‖ˈʃɑː-/ *n* [U] the activity of going to shops to buy things: *Shopping is now a major leisure industry.* | *We always* ***do the shopping*** (=buy food and other things needed regularly) *on Fridays.*

window shopping when you go to look at things in shops, often without intending to buy anything

shopping centre —see under CENTRE

shopping list —see under LIST[1]

shopping mall *n* [C] *AmE* another name for MALL: *a 100-store shopping mall*

shopping pre·cinct —see under PRECINCT

shop·soiled /ˈsɒpsɔɪld‖ˈʃɑːp-/ *adj BrE* shopsoiled goods are slightly damaged or dirty because they have been in a shop for a long time; SHOPWORN *AmE*: *sales of secondhand or shopsoiled goods*

shop steward —see STEWARD

S

shop•worn /ˈʃɒpwɔːn‖ˈʃɑːpwɔːrn/ *adj AmE* shopworn goods are slightly damaged or dirty because they have been in a shop for a long time; SHOPSOILED *BrE*

shore /ʃɔː‖ʃɔːr/ *v*

shore sth ↔ **up** *phr v* [T] to help a system or organization that is likely to fail or is not working well: *The company was shored up by an emergency infusion of cash from its main bank.*

short[1] /ʃɔːt‖ʃɔːrt/ *adj* **1** not having as much of something as there should be or as much as you need: *Have you all paid me? I'm still about £9 short.* + **of**: *The insurance fund was* ***running short*** *of cash.*

2 be short of stock/be short stock FINANCE if someone is short of stock, they have sold shares that they do not yet own, believing that the price will fall before the shares have to be delivered

short[2] *adv* FINANCE **1** if someone sells bonds, shares, currencies etc short, they sell bonds etc that they do not yet own believing that the price will fall so that they can be bought more cheaply before they have to be delivered: *traders who sell short*

2 go short (on) sth to sell bonds, shares, currencies etc that you do not own, believing that their value will fall and that you will be able to buy them more cheaply before they have to be delivered: *These money managers go short, making bets that certain stocks will decline.*

short[3] *v* [I,T] FINANCE to sell shares that you do not yet own, believing that the price will fall so that the shares can be bought more cheaply before they have to be delivered: *Many were actually shorting the market, betting prices would fall.* | *Even after News Corp. hit a 52-week low, the bears kept shorting.* —**shorting** *n* [U] *Chemical Banking had been the subject of shorting.*

short•age /ˈʃɔːtɪdʒ‖ˈʃɔːr-/ *n* [C,U] a situation in which there is not enough of something that people need or want: *We suffer from a* ***labor shortage***. | *The real estate developer is facing an acute* ***cash shortage***. + **of**: *an energy crisis caused by a shortage of imported oil* | *There will be* ***no shortage of*** *applicants* (=there will be a lot).

short-change *v* [T] **1** to treat someone unfairly by cheating them or not giving them what they deserve: *The consumer is tired of being short-changed by cartels.*

2 to give someone too little CHANGE (=money given back to someone when they have paid more than the exact price): *I later discovered I was short-changed by $10 when I went through the Midtown Tunnel.*

short-covering *n* [U] FINANCE when someone who has sold shares that they do not yet own buys shares in order to deliver what they have promised: *Treasury bonds benefited on Monday from short-covering, investors buying securities to cover short positions.*

short-dated *adj* **short-dated bonds/stock/securities** bonds, securities etc that are repaid in a short time, usually less than one year; SHORTS: *Investments in public-sector stock are mainly in short-dated government bonds.* —compare LONG-DATED, MEDIUM-DATED

short•fall /ˈʃɔːtfɔːl‖ˈʃɔːrtfɒːl/ *n* [C] a difference between the amount that you have and the larger amount you need or expect: *a $300 million* ***budget shortfall*** + **in/of**: *a shortfall in staffing levels*

short•hand /ˈʃɔːthænd‖ˈʃɔːrt-/ *n* **1** [U] a fast method of writing using special signs or shorter forms to represent letters, words, and phrases: *Mary was* ***taking shorthand*** (=making notes in shorthand).

2 [singular, U] a shorter but less clear way of saying something: *Jargon uses a shorthand of technical words and phrases.* + **for**: *The term 'one-parent family' is misleading shorthand for a variety of situations.*

short•hand•ed /ˌʃɔːtˈhændɪ̈d◂‖ˌʃɔːrt-/ *adj* having fewer workers or helpers than you need: *We'll be short-handed next month as five of my staff will be on holiday.*

short interest —see under INTEREST

short-period rate —see under RATE[1]

short position —see under POSITION[1]

shorts /ʃɔːts‖ʃɔːrts/ *n* [plural] bonds, etc that are repaid in less than two years

short sale —see under SALE

short seller —see under SELLER

short selling —see under SELLING

short squeeze *n* [C] a situation in which a lot of SHORT SELLERS are trying to buy the shares they need to deliver, causing prices to rise: *A short squeeze forces short sellers to pay escalating prices to replace their borrowed positions.*

short-term *adj* **1** continuing for only a short time, or concerned only with the period of time that is not very far into the future: *Most of the staff are on short-term contracts.* | *We will continue to manufacture products to build our market share, even at the cost of short-term losses.*

2 in the short term in the immediate future, rather than later: *The bank is unlikely to cut interest rates in the short term.*

3 FINANCE short-term lending, borrowing etc is for less than one year: *short term loans in the form of commercial paper* —**short-term** *adv*: *Short-term prospects do not look good.* —**short-termism** *n* [U] *These countries are criticised for lack of planning, lack of strategic thinking and short-termism.* —compare LONG-TERM

short-term credit —see under CREDIT[1]

short-term debt —see under DEBT

short-term funds —see under FUND[1]

short-term gain —see under GAIN[2]

short-term gilts —see under GILTS

short-term loan —see under LOAN[1]

short-term security —see under SECURITY

short-time working *n* [U] *BrE* when workers work less than the usual number of hours or days, because of a lack of orders or materials: *Bosses admit that short-time working at the car plant remains a possibility.* | *Most of the group's factories remain* ***on short-time working***.

short ton —see under TON

show /ʃəʊ‖ʃoʊ/ *n* [C] an occasion when a lot of similar things are brought together in one place so that people can come and look at them or so that they can compete against each other —see also ROADSHOW

agricultural show a public show of farming products and skills: *an agricultural show organized for European farm ministers*

show•biz /ˈʃəʊbɪz‖ˈʃoʊ-/ *n* [U] *informal* another name for SHOW BUSINESS

show busi•ness —see under BUSINESS

show•card /ˈʃəʊkɑːd‖ˈʃoʊkɑːrd/ *n* [C] a card in a shop that attracts attention to a product, supplied to the shop by the maker of the product: *The production department in an ad agency has the job of producing finished brochures, posters, showcards etc.*

show•case /ˈʃəʊkeɪs‖ˈʃoʊ-/ *n* [C] an event or situation that is designed to show the good qualities of a person, organization, or product: *The conference is intended to be a showcase for leading-edge technology.* —**showcase** *v* [T] *The Olympic Games gave the country an opportunity to showcase its economic achievements.*

show of hands *n* [singular] a vote taken by counting the raised hands of people at a meeting: *The resolution was passed on a show of hands.*

show•room /ˈʃəʊrʊm, -ruːm‖ˈʃoʊ-/ *n* [C] a large room where you can look at things that are for sale, especially cars: *When customers walk into the showroom, they are greeted by sales managers.*

shred /ʃred/ *v* [T] to cut documents into small pieces so that no one can read them: *Investigators retrieved documents that had been thrown away and in some cases shredded.*

shred•der /ˈʃredə‖-ər/ *n* [C] a machine that cuts documents into small pieces so that no one can read them

shrink /ʃrɪŋk/ *v* past tense **shrank** past participle **shrunk** **1** [I] to become smaller in amount, size, or value: *The economy is expected to shrink slightly.* | *Midlantic said its number of employees will shrink 30%.* | *Companies are battling for a share of the shrinking market.*

2 [T] to reduce the amount, size, or value of something: *An 11% drop in imports helped shrink the trade deficit.*

shrink•age /ˈʃrɪŋkɪdʒ/ *n* **1** [C,U] the act of shrinking, or the amount that something shrinks: *a further shrinkage in the size of the workforce*

2 [U] when goods intended for sale are damaged, stolen by employees etc: *The manager of the store is allowed only 1% shrinkage.* | *Shrinkage – or theft – is a very real problem for industry.*

shrink-wrap *n* [U] tight plastic wrapping for goods: *The plastic shrink-wrap prevents tampering.* —**shrink-wrap** *v* [T] *The free gift is shrink-wrapped and glued to the magazine page.*

shut /ʃʌt/ *v* [I,T] past tense and past participle **shut** present participle **shutting** **1** also **shut down** if a company, factory etc shuts or is shut, it stops operating permanently; CLOSE DOWN: *The steel company plans to shut two of its factories.* | *The airline shut down at midnight on Friday.* | *Regulators were threatening to shut the bank down.*

2 if a shop or business shuts or is shut, it stops operating at the end of the working day or for the weekend etc; CLOSE: *We shut at 5.30.* | *Do you shut the shop for lunch?*

shut•down /ˈʃʌtdaʊn/ *n* [C] the closing of a factory, business etc: *a nuclear plant shutdown*

shys•ter /ˈʃaɪstə‖-ər/ *n* [C] *AmE informal* a dishonest person, especially a lawyer

SI —see SI UNITS

SIB —see SECURITIES AND INVESTMENTS BOARD

SIBOR /ˈsiːbɔː‖-ɔːr/ *n* BANKING Singapore Inter-Bank Offered Rate; the rate at which banks in Asia lend money to each other, used as a standard for other loans: *City Corp.'s loan to the Vietnamese company is priced at 185 basis points over SIBOR.*

SIC written abbreviation for STANDARD INDUSTRIAL CLASSIFICATION

sick /sɪk/ *adj* **1** a sick company, economy etc is one that has financial or other difficulties such as CORRUPTION (=dishonest, illegal, or immoral behaviour): *The President lost popularity when his reforms failed to revive a sick economy.* | *a terminally sick company* | *By the late '80s, no longer could Britain be described as the "sick man of Europe".*

2 off sick not at work because you have an illness or a disease: *He has been off sick for the last six weeks.*

sick•ie /ˈsɪki/ *n* [C] *informal* **throw a sickie** *BrE* **pull a sickie** *AmE* when you say that you are ill and do not go to work, even though you are not really ill: *He was so fed up that he decided to throw a sickie instead of going into the office.*

sick leave —see under LEAVE

sickness benefit —see under BENEFIT[1]

sick note *n* [C] *BrE* a note written by your doctor saying that you are too ill to work: *Employers can ask workers for a sick note from their doctor, but only if they have been away for more than seven days.*

sick•out /ˈsɪkaʊt/ *n* [C] *AmE* HUMAN RESOURCES an occasion when employees protest against something by taking SICK LEAVE (=not working because they say they are ill) when they are not really ill: *American Airlines pilots are staging a sickout over pay talks, and this has contributed to flight cancellations.*

sick pay —see under PAY[1]

sight /saɪt/ *n* FINANCE **1 at sight** FINANCE words written on a BILL OF EXCHANGE or PROMISSORY NOTE to show that it is payable as soon as it is shown to the ACCEPTOR: *The more usual situation is where payment is at sight, meaning when the paying bank has examined the documents and found them to be in order.*

2 after sight words written on a BILL OF EXCHANGE or PROMISSORY NOTE to show how much later it will be paid after it has been given to the payer, usually 30, 60, or 90 days later

3 payable at sight a financial document that is payable at sight must be paid when it is received by the person who is responsible for paying it

4 payable after sight a financial document that is payable after sight must be paid on a stated number of days after it is received by the person who is responsible for paying it

sight bill —see under BILL OF EXCHANGE

sight deposit —see under DEPOSIT[1]

sign[1] /saɪn/ *v* **1** [I,T] to write your SIGNATURE on a letter, document, or CHEQUE: *The customer must* ***sign*** *the traveller's* ***cheque*** *in front of the cashier.*

2 sign an agreement/contract to show formally that you agree to do something, by signing a legal document: *Biggins has refused to sign a new contract unless he gets an immediate pay rise.*

3 signed and sealed/signed, sealed, and delivered with all the necessary legal documents agreed and signed: *The agreement with IBM Corp. is not signed and sealed yet.*

sign on *phr v* **1** [I] *BrE* to go to your local job centre and sign a form which states officially that you are unemployed, so that you can get money from the government: *Childcare Allowance is available only for married women whose child/children are over four years of age and who have been signing on for the previous six months.*

2 [I,T] **sign** sb ↔ **on** if you sign on, or sign someone on, you sign or persuade someone to sign a document agreeing to do something, for example accepting a job, studying on a course, or becoming involved in a business deal: *Two more members of staff were signed on full-time.* + **as**: *Jacobs signed on as a junior attorney with a Santa Rosa law firm.* + **to**: *The corporation is deciding whether to sign on to a deal to build a new U.S. manufacturing plant to compete with the French.*

3 [I] COMPUTING to start using a computer system, the Internet, or to go to a website: *The Internet has strange economics; individual users are charged for signing on, but can then surf the net for nothing.* | *Lee used Ramsey's password to secretly sign on to the company's computer system.* —compare LOG ON under LOG[1]

sign[2] *n* [C] **1** a piece of paper, metal etc in a public place, with words or drawings on it that give people information, warn them not to do something etc: *a* ***no smoking sign***

2 a picture, shape etc that has a particular meaning: *For some reason the computer can't display the dollar sign.*

sig•na•to•ry /ˈsɪgnətəri‖-tɔːri/ *n* plural **signatories** [C] one of the people or countries that sign an official agreement: *We will accept a copy invoice which bears a company stamp and the signature of an authorised signatory.* + **to/of**: *Most Western countries are signatories to* *this agreement.* | *Experts from 118* ***signatory*** ***countries*** *met in Geneva.*

sig•na•ture /ˈsɪgnətʃə‖-ər/ *n* **1** [C] your name written in the way you usually write it, for example at the end of a letter or on a CHEQUE. It is often used to give official or legal permission for something: *I couldn't read his signature.* | *Most bankers say that the large volume of checks means that most banks only spot-check* (=quickly examine) *a few signatures.*

facsimile signature [C] an exact copy of the way that someone signs their name which is put on a special rubber stamp so that it can be used on a large number of letters, cheques etc: *The most common error by solicitors was using a facsimile signature on application forms.*

specimen signature [C] an example of your signature that you give to a bank when you first open an account so that the bank's employees can use it to check cheques etc which have been signed with your name

2 [U] the act of writing a signature on something: *the date of signature of the present agreement*

sil•i•con /ˈsɪlɪkən/ *n* [U] an ELEMENT (=simple chemical substance) that is often used for making parts for computers and other things such as glass

silicon chip —see CHIP

Silicon Fen *n journalism* companies and research institutions involved in computer development and manufacturing that are based in and around Cambridge, England, considered as a whole

Silicon Glen *n journalism* companies and research institutions involved in computer development and manufacturing that are based in Scotland, considered as a whole: *Hyundai Electronics has selected Silicon Glen for its main semi-conductor plant.*

Silicon Valley *n* the area of California between San Francisco and San Jose, which is known as a centre of the computer industry

SIMM /sɪm/ *n* [C] COMPUTING Single-In-Line Memory Module; a piece of electronic equipment that gives a computer more RAM (=memory used as a temporary store for information): *The manual shows a motherboard with the SIMM chips to the right of the expansion slots.*

simple interest —see under INTEREST

sim•u•la•tion /ˌsɪmjəˈleɪʃən/ *n* [C,U] an activity or situation that produces conditions which are not real, but have the appearance of being real, used especially for testing something: *A* ***computer simulation*** *allows project engineers to study in detail the manufacturing process operations at the factory site.* —**simulate** *v* [T] *computers used by automotive companies to simulate car wrecks* —**simulator** *n* [C] *CAE makes commercial and military aircraft simulators and develops related training sytems.*

sin•cere•ly /sɪnˈsɪəli‖-ˈsɪr-/ *adv* **Yours sincerely** *BrE*, **Sincerely yours** *AmE* an expression used to end a formal letter. You use this expression when you have addressed the person you are writing to by name, rather than Dear Sir or Dear Madam —compare FAITHFULLY

si•ne•cure /ˈsaɪnɪkjʊə,ˈsɪn-‖-kjʊr/ *n* [C] a job which you get paid for even though you do not have to do very much: *The bureaucrats saw their sinecures endangered by the demand for efficiency.*

si•ne di•e /ˌsaɪni ˈdaɪ-iː/ *adv* LAW **adjourn/postpone sth sine die** to stop something and arrange for it to continue later, without actually fixing a date for it: *The meeting was postponed sine die.*

si•ne qua non /ˌsɪni kwɑː ˈnəʊn‖-ˈnɑːn/ *n* [singular] *formal* something that you must have, or which must exist, for something else to be possible + **for/of**: *The control of inflation is a sine qua non for economic stability.*

Singapore Inter-bank Offered Rate —see SIBOR

sin•gle /ˈsɪŋgəl/ *n* [C] *BrE* a ticket for a journey from one place to another but not back again: *A single to Oxford, please.* —compare RETURN[2]

single column centimetre written abbreviation **SCC** *n* [C] the standard unit used in Britain to sell advertising space in newspapers and magazines

single column inch written abbreviation **SCI** *n* [C] the standard unit used in the US to sell advertising space in newspapers and magazines

single currency —see under CURRENCY

single entry book-keeping —see under BOOK-KEEPING

single fare —see under FARE

Single-In-Line Memory Module —see SIMM

single market —see under MARKET[1]

sin•gle•sit /ˈsɪŋgəlsɪt/ *n* [C] MARKETING a house or apartment for a single person living on their own, rather than a couple or a family: *One in three visits to couples ends in a successful sale, while in a singlesit the figure is one in 10.*

single ticket —see under TICKET

single-use *adj* [only before a noun] a single-use product is one that you use once only; DISPOSABLE: *a Kodak Fling 35 single-use camera* | *Environmental activists criticized producers of single-use, throwaway packages for such products as juice and laundry detergent.*

sinking fund —see under FUND[1]

sin tax —see under TAX[1]

si•phon also **syphon** /ˈsaɪfən/ *v* [T] to dishonestly take money from a business, account etc and use it for a purpose for which it was not intended **siphon sth from/off sth**: *I later found she had siphoned thousands of dollars from our bank account.* | *Corrupt officials had been siphoning off public funds for private business ventures.*

sister company —see under COMPANY

sit-down *adj* **sit-down protest/strike** a protest in which people sit down, especially to block a road or other public place, until their demands are listened to: *Workers at the country's second-largest steel factory began a sit-down strike.* | *News reports said investors staged sit-down protests, demanding special government measures to prevent a stock market crash.*

sit-down strike —see under STRIKE[1]

site[1] /saɪt/ *n* [C] an area of ground that is used or is going to be used for a particular purpose: *On any* ***building site****, falling is the most frequent type of accident.* | *The Sunnyvale City Council last week approved a 186-unit apartment complex on the 4.5 acre site.* | *Solectron employs 2,200 people at sites in San Jose and Milpitas.*

brownfield site a site used for building where there has already been building, industrial activity etc, especially in a town or city: *The government wants to raise the proportion of housing built on brownfield sites, rather than on unspoilt countryside.*

greenfield site a site used for building where there has never been building or industrial activity in the past: *As the space requirements of companies changed, they sought more open greenfield sites away from the cities.*

site[2] *v* **be sited in/near etc** be placed or built in a particular place: *The new factory is to be sited in Fort Collins.* | *The Birse Homes' Hutton Grange development is sited three miles from Weston town centre.* —**siting** *n* [singular] *A nuisance is caused by the siting of petrol stations in residential areas.*

sit-in *n* [C] a type of protest in which people refuse to leave the place where they work or study until their demands are agreed to: *Several hundred employees of a national bank ended a two-day sit-in to protest against plans to close branches and cut jobs.*

S

sitting tenant —see under TENANT

sit·u·at·ed /ˈsɪtʃueɪtɪd/ *adj* **1 be situated** to be in a particular place or position: *a small town situated just south of Cleveland* | *All the apartments are beautifully situated overlooking the beach.*

2 be well/badly situated to be in a good or bad situation: *Microsoft is well situated to exploit this new market.*

sit·u·a·tion /ˌsɪtʃuˈeɪʃən/ *n* [C] a combination of all that is happening and all the conditions that exist at a particular time and place: *I'd better go and see the boss and explain the situation.* | *In view of the company's* ***financial situation****, there will be no salary increases this year.* | *We are unlikely to have a full-employment situation this year.*

special situation a company whose shares could rise quickly and suddenly in value if a particular thing happens: *Investors focused on special situations.*

Situations Vacant *n* [U] *BrE* the title of the part of a newspaper in which jobs are advertised

Situations Wanted *n* [U] *BrE* the title of the part of a newspaper where people advertise that they are looking for a job

SI units *n* [plural] an international system of units of measurement that is based on seven METRIC units: the AMPERE, CANDELA, KELVIN, kilogram, metre, MOLE, and second

six sig·ma /ˌsɪks ˈsɪgmə/ *n* [U] STATISTICS when the number of faults in a product or process is reduced to just over three per million: *the unforgiving demands of six sigma quality control*

skid /skɪd/ *n* [C] *AmE* a PALLET

skill /skɪl/ *n* [C,U] an ability to do something well, especially because you have learned and practised it: *You need* ***computing skills*** *for that job.* | *The successful applicant should be able to use their own initiative and have good* ***communication skills****.* | *There are still excellent jobs available for those with the right* ***specialist skills*** *and knowledge.* | *Unfortunately, listening may be the least practiced* ***management skill*** *in today's workplace.* + **at/in**: *The Federal Reserve Chairman has demonstrated skill in adjusting interest rates.*

transferable skill [C usually plural] someone with transferable skills is able to use their skills to do a job for which they have not been formally trained: *There is a high level of temporary working amongst professionals, largely because of their transferable skills.*

skilled /skɪld/ *adj* **1** someone who is skilled has the training and experience that is needed to do something well: ***Skilled craftsmen****, such as carpenters, bricklayers etc, are in great demand.* | *Medical technology companies face a serious shortage of* ***skilled labor*** (=workers with special skills) *in the next decade.* | *Britain is likely to become a more technological society in future years and so it is likely that there will be an increased demand for a* ***skilled workforce****.* + **at/in**: *She's very skilled at dealing with members of the public.*

2 work that is skilled needs special abilities or training in order to do it: *Bricklaying is very skilled work.* —compare SEMI-SKILLED, UNSKILLED

skilled worker —see under WORKER

skill-intensive *adj* a skill-intensive job is one in which workers must be very skilled

skim /skɪm/ *v* past tense and past participle **skimmed** present participle **skimming** [T] also **skim off** *AmE* to take money illegally, for example by not saying that you have made profits so that you do not have to pay tax: *He was accused of skimming profits from junk bond trading.* | *The former Prime Minister is charged with ordering state-owned companies to deposit large sums in the bank and conspiring with the bank's owner to skim off the interest payments.*

skim·ming /ˈskɪmɪŋ/ *n* [U] **1** when a company charges a very high price for a new product in order to make as large a profit as possible before competing products appear on the market and force the company to lower the price

2 TAX when a person or company cheats the tax authorities by not telling them about some of the profit that has been made: *a dispute over alleged profit skimming*

skint /skɪnt/ *adj* [not before a noun] *BrE informal* not having much money, especially for a short time: *I'm skint at the moment.*

skunk works *n* [C] a place where a large company gives a small group of workers the job of trying to develop new products within a shorter period of time than usual: *A few companies have a skunk works where secret projects are funded with the hope that they will lead to products in a couple of years.*

sky·rock·et /ˈskaɪˌrɒkɪt‖-ˌrɑː-/ *v* [I,T] to increase quickly and suddenly; ROCKET: *The stock price of Unisys Corp. on Monday skyrocketed 37%, or $1.38, to close at $5.13.* | *The Middle East crisis caused oil prices to skyrocket.* | *The government's tough market-oriented reforms that have* ***sent prices skyrocketing****.*

slack[1] /slæk/ *adj* **1** a slack period of time is one with less business activity than usual: *Business is slack just now.* | *With one month to go before Christmas, sales are still slack.* | *The workers feared being laid off* (=losing their jobs) *in* ***slack periods****.*

2 if someone is being slack, they are not taking enough care or making enough effort to do things right: *The report criticized airport security as "disgracefully slack".* | *High prices and the absence of competition may make firms slack in their use of resources.* —**slackness** *n* [U] *the slackness of the London market at present* | *The report accuses the government of slackness.*

slack[2] also **slack off** *v* [I] to make less of an effort than usual or be lazy in your work: *He was accused of slacking and taking too many holidays.*

slack[3] *n* [U] money, space, or people that an organization is not using at present, but could use in the future: *There is very little slack in the training budget for this year.*

slack·en /ˈslækən/ also **slacken off** *v* [I,T] to gradually become weaker or less active, or to make something do this: *As business slackens, major accounting firms are reducing their professional staffs and shaking up office leadership.* | *Industrial* ***demand*** *has* ***slackened off*** *because of the worldwide economic slowdown.* | *The ending of a special tax incentive is widely expected to* ***slacken the pace*** *of new car purchases.* —**slackening** *n* [U] *The price cuts may help exporters get through the usual seasonal* ***slackening*** *of oil* ***demand*** *in the second quarter.*

slan·der[1] /ˈslɑːndə‖ˈslændər/ *n* [C,U] a spoken statement about someone that is not true and is intended to damage the good opinion that people have of him or her, or the legal offence of making a statement of this kind: *The company is being* ***sued for slander*** *by four pharmacists who say the retailer fired them and ruined their reputations.*

slander[2] *v* [T] to say untrue things about someone in order to damage other people's good opinion of them: *Smith slandered Wiseman by accusing him of proposing an illegal business deal.*

slash /slæʃ/ *v* [T] *journalism* to greatly reduce an amount, price etc: *Over the last year the workforce has been slashed by 50%.* | *Freeman wants to slash at least $400 million from an annual budget of $2.4 billion.*

sleaze /sliːz/ *n* [U] immoral behaviour, especially involving money or sex: *The killings convinced many that there is a network of sleaze and corruption below the surface of society.* —**sleazy** *adj*: *sleazy dealings with cash payments in brown envelopes*

S

sleep·er /ˈsliːpə‖-ər/ *n* [C] *AmE* a share or a product that is not successful immediately, but then suddenly starts to sell well or be successful: *The film Fried Green Tomatoes turned out to be a sleeper.*

sleeper stock —see under STOCK[1]

sleeping beauty *n* [C] a company, especially one with attractive features such as a large amount of cash, that other companies would like to buy, but that has not yet received any offers

sleeping partner —see under PARTNER

slice /slaɪs/ *n* [C] a part or share of something + **of**: *Sales reps will get a slice of any catalogue sales to customers in their area.*

slick /slɪk/ *adj* **1** a slick person uses clever talk to persuade people to do something, especially in a way that does not seem honest or sincere: *He is uncomfortable in the role of **slick salesman**. | a slick investment banker*
2 cleverly made and attractive, but often not containing any important or interesting ideas: *The agency has a reputation for producing work that is slick and classy. | slick advertising brochures*

slide /slaɪd/ past tense and past participle **slid** *v* [I] to gradually become lower or less: *Some dealers continued to buy silver as the price slid. | The new model didn't stop GM's share of the U.S. car market from sliding.* —**slide** *n* [C] + **in**: *There has been a recent slide in crude oil production. | a series of **price slides***
slide into sth *phr v* [T] to gradually start to experience an unpleasant or difficult situation: *The Australian economy was sliding into recession. | Could he prevent the company from sliding into bankruptcy?*

sliding scale —see under SCALE

slim[1] /slɪm/ *v* past simple and past participle **slimmed** present participle **slimming** [I,T] also **slim down** to reduce the size or number of something, or to become smaller in size or number: *Mitsui Taiyo Kobe slimmed its total assets by 3.2%. | Many large insurers are slimming down* (=employing fewer people). —**slimming** *n* [U] *Despite success in holding down overall costs, further slimming will be needed.*

slim[2] *adj* comparative **slimmer** superlative **slimmest**
1 very small in size or amount: *The **slim increase** in revenues reflected the slowing economy. | Will the Democrats hold on to their **slim majority**?*
2 very little chance of something happening: ***Chances** are **slim** that such bosses will make as much money as they once earned. | There are **slim hopes** of a compromise.*

slip[1] /slɪp/ *v* past tense and past participle **slipped** present participle **slipping** [I] to become worse or less or fall to a lower amount, standard etc than before: *There are fears that consumer confidence may be slipping. | Earnings per share slipped 2% to 9.9 pence.*
slip into sth *phr v* [T] to gradually start to experience an unpleasant or difficult situation: *The economy may be slipping into a recession. | Filofax PLC slipped into the red made a loss for the first time.*
slip up *phr v* [I] to make a mistake: *Where you slipped up was selling to the first bidder.* —see also SLIP-UP

slip[2] *n* **1** [singular] an occasion when something becomes worse or becomes less or lower + **in**: *The slip in demand is seen in other markets besides the U.S.*
2 [C] a small narrow piece of paper: *Always keep your **credit card slips**. | Have you received a **confirmation slip**?*
compliments slip [C] a small piece of paper with a person's or company's name and address on it, sent with goods, documents, or other materials instead of a letter: *His photographs finally come back from The Sunday Times Magazine with a printed compliments slip and no explanation.*
pay slip [C] *BrE* a piece of paper that an employee gets every time they are paid, showing the amount they have been paid and the amount that has been taken away in tax: *You'll find your tax code on the top of your pay slip.*
pink slip [C] *AmE* a piece of paper given to a worker, officially telling them that they no longer have a job: *About 700 employees will **receive pink slips** this week, with another 200 dismissals expected soon.*
sales slip [C] *AmE* a small piece of paper that you are given in a shop as proof that you have paid for something; RECEIPT

slip·page /ˈslɪpɪdʒ/ *n* [U] **1** a reduction in a level of activity, amount etc: *The central bank is prepared to ease interest rates further if the economy shows signs of slippage. | Last week's slippage in bond prices followed a nearly 13-week rise.*
2 when calculations are not exact because some figures can only be guessed: *Opinion poll reliability is affected by slippage. Not all voters bother to respond, for example.*
3 FINANCE when investments are bought at higher prices or sold at lower prices than those wanted: *One way to minimize slippage is to avoid placing orders on the open or the close of a trading session because of volatility* (=fast and frequent price changes).

slip-up *n* [C] a careless mistake that spoils a process or plan: *Slip-ups by the company's management resulted in the launch failure.* —see also ***slip up*** under SLIP[1]

slo·gan /ˈsləʊgən‖ˈsloʊ-/ *n* [C] a short phrase that is easy to remember and is used by an advertiser, organization, or other group: *We need an **advertising slogan** for the new campaign. | Weight Watchers' new slogan was "Total indulgence. Zero guilt."*

slot /slɒt‖slɑːt/ *n* [C] **1** a short period of time allowed for one particular event in a series of other, similar events: ***landing slots** at Tokyo's Narita airport | TV stations running repeats of Oprah's daytime show in the **late-night slot***
2 *AmE* a particular job in an organization: *The board elected a new director to fill one of the slots on Turner's board. | 4,000 slots, mostly white-collar, could be eliminated from the company's Missouri plant alone.* —see also EXPANSION SLOT

slow[1] /sləʊ‖sloʊ/ *v* [I,T] also **slow down** to become slower: *Consumer borrowing has slowed noticeably since Jan. 1. | They're delaying sales reports to the factory to slow down shipments of new cars.*

slow[2] *adj* **1** not happening, being done, or moving with much speed or not as quickly as it should: *Prices are rising, but at a **slower pace** than before. | a period of **slow economic growth** | We expect a slow improvement in sales. | Designing a new car can be a **slow process**.* —**slowly** *adv*: *Disposable income grew slowly.*
2 be slow to do sth *disapproving* to not do something immediately: *The city has been slow to follow through on many of the budget cuts it promised.*
3 if business or trade is slow, there are not many customers or not many things are sold: *Manufacturers say that business remains slow. | Monday is usually the slowest day of the week.*

slow·down /ˈsləʊdaʊn‖ˈsloʊ-/ *n* **1** [C usually singular] when something gets slower + **in**: *a slowdown in domestic demand for automobiles | There are signs of an **economic slowdown**.*
2 [C] *AmE* a period of time when people deliberately work slowly in order to protest about something; GO-SLOW *BrE*: *The unions already have a **work slowdown** under way.*

slug·gish /ˈslʌgɪʃ/ *adj* happening or reacting more slowly than usual: *Trading activity has been sluggish all week. | sluggish consumer demand* —**sluggishly** *adv*: *Economists predict that income will grow only sluggishly.*

—**sluggishness** *n* [U] *sluggishness in the food services industry*

slump /slʌmp/ *n* [C usually singular] **1** a sudden fall in the price, value, or number of something + **in**: *There has been a slump in sales this month.* —**slump** *v* [I] *Securities firms' profits have slumped in recent years.*
2 a period of time when there is a big reduction in economic activity, forcing many companies to close and many people to lose their jobs: *Savings were already extremely low at the beginning of the current slump.*

slush fund —see under FUND[1]

small /smɔːl‖smɒːl/ *adj* **1** not large in size or amount: *Boeing doesn't make a small, 100-seat plane.* | *The recent fare increases are small.* | ***For a small fee****, we can sell your shares for you.*
2 unimportant or easy to deal with: *The company has admitted to small mistakes in billing.* | *It would be a small matter to offer employees interest-free loans for a limited period.*

small ad —see under AD

small business —see under BUSINESS

Small Business Administration abbreviation **SBA** *n* a US government organization that helps small businesses, for example by lending them money at low interest rates: *The Small Business Administration will help each business to develop a sound business plan.*

small business investment company —see under COMPANY

small-cap *n* [C] FINANCE a share in a company with a small amount of SHARE CAPITAL (=total share value); SMALL CAPITALIZATION SHARE; SMALL CAP SHARE: *Midcaps are the real star performers, not the small-caps.* —compare LARGE-CAP

small cap share also **small capitalization share, small capitalisation share** *BrE* —see under SHARE

small claims court —see under COURT[1]

Small Computer Systems Interface —see SCSI

small·hold·ing /ˈsmɔːlˌhəʊldɪŋ‖ˈsmɒːlˌhoʊld-/ *n* [C] *BrE* a piece of land used for farming that is smaller than an ordinary farm: *Middle-sized farms are being split up, with part of the land being taken over by larger farms and part becoming smallholdings.* —**smallholder** *n* [C] *organic foods produced by small-scale farmers and smallholders*

small investor —see under INVESTOR

small office/home office —see under OFFICE

small or medium enterprise —see SME

small print —see under PRINT[2]

small-scale *adj* small in size or limited in degree: *small-scale enterprises* | *small-scale industrial activities*

small stock —see under STOCK[1]

smart card —see under CARD

SME *n* [C usually plural] *BrE* small or medium enterprise; fairly small companies that are usually based in one place and owned by one person or small group of people: *Many SMEs often do not appreciate how they might benefit from technology.* | *seminars to promote business networks, especially for SMEs* —see also SMALL BUSINESS

smear /smɪə‖smɪr/ *n* [C] an attempt to harm someone by spreading untrue stories about them: *Was this just another political smear?* | *The media had launched a* ***smear campaign*** *against him.* —**smear** *v* [T] *Republicans were trying to smear the President.*

smoke·screen /ˈsməʊkskriːn‖ˈsmoʊk-/ *n* [C] something that someone does or says to hide their real plans or actions: *Was TWA's owner using the war as a smokescreen to shrink the airline permanently?*

smokestack industry —see under INDUSTRY

smug·gle /ˈsmʌɡəl/ *v* [T] to take something or someone illegally from one country to another **smuggle sth into/out of**: *They caught her trying to* ***smuggle drugs*** *into France.* | *The silver was found in Yugoslavia and smuggled out.* —**smuggling** *n* [U] *They claimed the government knew about the* ***arms smuggling****.* —**smuggler** *n* [C] *the impossibility of trying to catch smugglers around this enormous coastline*

snail mail —see under MAIL[1]

snap /snæp/ *v* past tense and past participle **snapped** present participle **snapping**
snap up *phr v* [T] **1 snap** sth ↔ **up** to buy something immediately, especially because it is very cheap: *If you see a computer for under £400, you should snap it up.*
2 snap sb ↔ **up** to eagerly take an opportunity to employ someone or have them as part of your team: *He so impressed the Shell executives that they snapped him up immediately.*

snip /snɪp/ *n* **be a snip** *BrE informal* to be surprisingly cheap: *At £20 for twelve, they're a snip!*

snow /snəʊ‖snoʊ/ *v* **be snowed under (with sth)** to have a lot more work than you can deal with: *He's in danger of being snowed under and badly needs an assistant.* | *We're snowed under with paperwork.*

snow·ball /ˈsnəʊbɔːl‖ˈsnoʊbɒːl/ *v* [I] to grow or increase at a faster and faster rate: *Our sales in Europe have snowballed.* + **into**: *'Primary Colors' snowballed into one of the biggest selling books of the year.* —**snowballing** *adj* [only before a noun] *a scheme to cover his snowballing losses*

Snr. written abbreviation for SENIOR, used after a man's name to show he is the older of two men with the same name and from the same family: *James Taylor, Snr.* —compare JNR.

soar /sɔː‖sɔːr/ *v* [I] to increase quickly to a high level: *Demand for home computers has soared in recent years.* —**soaring** *adj* [only before a noun] *Despite soaring prices, business is good.*

Soc. written abbreviation for Society

so·cial /ˈsəʊʃəl‖ˈsoʊ-/ *adj* **1** concerning human society and its organization, or the quality of people's lives: *What is the* ***social cost*** *of economic reform in Eastern Europe?* | *Companies who dump waste are ignoring their* ***social responsibility****.*
2 related to people's position in society, according to their job, family, wealth etc: *British lawyers enjoy a higher* ***social status*** *than French ones.* | *Money management is not, as you might expect, dominated by the upper* ***social classes****.*
3 concerning the relationship between companies and employees, and between companies and society: *This is the first time that institutional investors have challenged a company on environmental and social issues.*
4 related to activities you do to enjoy yourself when you are not at work: *The firm spent thousands of dollars on social gatherings.*
5 related to the way you meet people and form relationships: *We are looking for graduates with a high level of* ***social skills*** (=ability to meet people easily and deal with them well). —see also ***social marketing*** under MARKETING

social accounting —see under ACCOUNTING

social audit —see under AUDIT[1]

social capital —see under CAPITAL

social democracy —see under DEMOCRACY

social engineering —see under ENGINEERING

social insurance —see under INSURANCE

so·cial·is·m /ˈsəʊʃəl-ɪzəm‖ˈsoʊ-/ *n* [U] a system of political beliefs and principles whose main aims are that

S

everyone should have an equal opportunity to share wealth and that industries should be owned by the government: *Is there a way to combine the efficiency of the market with the values of socialism?*

so·cial·ist[1] /ˈsəʊʃəl-ɪ̇st‖ˈsoʊ-/ *adj* **1** based on socialism or connected with a political party that supports socialism: *socialist principles* | *the socialist manifesto*

2 a socialist country or government has a political system based on socialism

socialist[2] *n* [C] someone who believes in socialism: *Not all socialists take a negative view of the market.*

social marketing —see under MARKETING

social security *n* [U] **1** *BrE* government money that is paid to people who are unemployed, old, or ill; WELFARE *AmE*: *Are you receiving **social security benefits**?* | *Cutbacks in **social security payments** were implemented on April 1st.*

2 Social Security abbreviation **SS** a system of insurance run by the US government, into which workers make regular payments, and which provides money when they are unable to work, especially because they are old: *spending on programs such as Social Security and Medicare* | *I need your name, age, and **Social Security number**.*

social security payment —see under PAYMENT

Social Security tax —see under TAX[1]

so·ci·e·ty /səˈsaɪ̇ti/ *n* plural **societies** **1** [U] people in general, considered in relation to the structure of laws, organizations etc that makes it possible for them to live together: *the unequal division of labour in society*

stakeholder society [singular] a society in which companies and their employees share economic successes

2 [C,U] a particular large group of people who share laws, organizations, customs etc: *We have grown up in a materialistic, **capitalist society**.* | *Is greed a product of the **consumer society**?*

3 [C] an professional organization or club with members who share similar aims and interests: *the American Society for Training and Development*

co-operative society also **cooperative society** [C] in Britain, an organization run by a group of people whose aim is to give benefits to its members, rather than to make a profit; CO-OPERATIVE

credit society *BrE* [C] a cooperative society that lends money, collected from its members, at low rates of interest; CREDIT CO-OPERATIVE; CREDIT UNION *AmE*

friendly society [C] an organization whose members pay money into a FUND that is used to help them if they become sick or lose their job, or when they become old. REGISTERED friendly societies are able to borrow money at reduced interest rates or receive a higher rate on money they invest: *The Loyal Standard Association operated as a friendly society for sick, injured and elderly seamen.*

provident society [C] used in the names of some types of MUTUAL COMPANIES (=financial institutions in which people do not own shares) where people can save money, obtain insurance etc: *the Australian Mutual Provident Society, the country's largest insurance concern* —see also BUILDING SOCIETY, CLASSIFICATION SOCIETY

Society for Worldwide Interbank Financial Telecommunications —see SWIFT

so·ci·o·ec·o·nom·ic /ˌsəʊsiəʊekəˈnɒmɪk, ˌsəʊʃiəʊ-, -iːkə-‖ˌsoʊsioʊekəˈnɑː-, ˌsoʊʃioʊ-, -iːkə-/ *adj* based on a combination of social and economic conditions: *Researchers divided respondents into four **socioeconomic groups**.* | *his **socioeconomic status*** —**socioeconomically** *adv*: *Design and marketing are socioeconomically determined.*

soft /sɒft‖sɒːft/ *adj* **1** soft goods are used up soon after they are bought, for example food products: *Ohio's manufacturing base covers a wide range of soft and hard goods.* | *a soft-commodity trader*

2 FINANCE soft loans or soft credit is money that is lent at a lower interest rate than usual, usually because it is for a project that is to be encouraged, for example a new business in an area of high unemployment: *The fund was authorized to help the market by providing soft loans to institutional investors.* | *The mills got $73 million in soft credit to keep their gates open.*

3 a soft market or economy has prices that are falling because supply is greater than demand: *How do you sell your house in a soft market?* | *Our results continue to be adversely affected by a very soft regional economy.*

4 if sales, orders, demand etc are soft, there are not as many sales, orders etc or as much demand as usual: *Many retailers experienced **soft sales** in May and June.* | *Orders from the construction industry are particularly soft.* | *The newspaper industry was suffering from a very **soft demand** for ad space.*

soft currency —see under CURRENCY

soft goods —see under GOODS

soft landing *n* [singular] if an economy has a soft landing, it does not experience high unemployment or a fall in living standards as a result of something that is done to control inflation: *The Fed attempted to engineer an economic soft landing by lowering interest rates.*

soft loan —see under LOAN[1]

soft price —see under PRICE[1]

soft sell —see under SELL[2]

soft·ware /ˈsɒftweə‖ˈsɒːftwer/ *n* [U] the sets of programs that you put into a computer when you want it to do particular jobs: ***Loading the software*** (=putting it on the computer) *should be quick and simple.* | *the giant **software company**, Microsoft*

application software software that is designed for a particular use or user: *We need to ensure that the application software on both the PC and the Macintosh produces compatible files.* | *There is a range of other software application programs on the market.*

database software software that allows you to keep a large amount of information and to search easily for the information you want

desk-top publishing software abbreviation **DTP software** software that allows ordinary users to produce newspapers, magazines etc

graphic software the set of detailed instructions in a computer that allow it to use and produce images and symbols: *Microsoft Corp. recently unveiled its new version of Windows graphic software for PCs.*

investment software software that gives you information about possible investments and lets you see the results of making particular investments

knowledge-based software software that learns while it works and is able to use this knowledge to find more effective ways of doing a particular job

reality software software that allows you to show THREE-DIMENSIONAL (=seeming to have length, depth, and height) images on a cinema screen that give you the experience of seeing or being inside a real place or physical object. It is used especially by designers and engineers to produce models of new products such as cars

speech recognition software software that allows you to operate a computer by speaking to it

spreadsheet software a computer program that shows rows of figures and performs calculations with them. Spreadsheet software is often used to work out sales, taxes, profits, and other financial information

word-processing software software that allows you to write documents, move parts of the document around, checks your spelling etc —see also FIRMWARE, FREEWARE, GROUPWARE, NAGWARE, SHAREWARE

software engineering —see under ENGINEERING

SOHO /ˈsəʊhəʊ‖ˈsoʊhoʊ/ abbreviation for SMALL OFFICE/HOME OFFICE

sold /səʊld‖soʊld/ *v* the past tense and past participle of SELL —see also COST OF GOODS SOLD

sold note —see under NOTE[1]

sole /səʊl‖soʊl/ *adj* [only before a noun] **1** a sole thing or person is the only one: *The company's* ***sole business*** *is the development of TCET technology.* | *the* ***sole owner*** *of CompuAdd*

2 a sole responsibility, duty, right etc is one that is not shared with anyone else: *Derek has* ***sole responsibility*** *for sales in Eire.* | *Whitehead resigned as co-chairman, leaving Mr. Weinberg* ***in sole control****.*

sol•emn /ˈsɒləm‖ˈsɑː-/ *adj* **1 solemn and binding** LAW an agreement that is solemn and binding is recognized in law: *Only on the basis of a* ***solemn and binding undertaking*** *did they allow the purchase to proceed.*

2 solemn oath/promise/pledge etc a promise that is made very seriously and with no intention of breaking it: *He gave his testimony under solemn oath.* | *The President had betrayed a solemn pledge.*

sole proprietor —see under PROPRIETOR

sole trader —see under TRADER

so•li•cit /səˈlɪsᵻt/ *v* [T] **1** *formal* to ask someone for information or help: *She called meetings to solicit the views of her staff.*

2 *disapproving* to ask someone for money **solicit sth from sb**: *He admitted that he solicited $34 million from 1,000 investors.*

3 *AmE* to sell something by taking orders for a product or service, usually by going to people's houses or businesses: *an office products supplier that solicits business in North Dakota* —**solicitation** *n* [C,U] *direct mail solicitations* | *door-to-door solicitation*

so•lic•i•tor /səˈlɪsᵻtə‖-ər/ *n* [C] a type of lawyer in Britain who gives advice, does the necessary work when property is bought and sold, and can defend people in the lower courts: *The matter is being dealt with by my solicitor.* | *a medium-sized firm of solicitors* —compare BARRISTER, LAWYER

solvency ratio —see under RATIO

sol•vent /ˈsɒlvənt‖ˈsɑːl-/ *adj* having enough money to pay your debts at the time they must be paid: *Large companies that you think are solvent may not be.* —opposite INSOLVENT —**solvency** *n* [U] *The solvency of insurance companies is overseen by state insurance regulators.*

sort /sɔːt‖sɔːrt/ *n* [C] if a computer does a sort, it puts things in a particular order: *Change the question numbers, then do a paragraph sort.* —**sort** *v* [I,T] *You can sort these tables and even perform mathematical calculations on them.* | *Press F2 to sort.*

sort code —see under CODE

sorting office —see under OFFICE

sound•card /ˈsaʊndkɑːd‖-kɑːrd/ *n* [C] COMPUTING a part of a computer that makes it able to produce sound

source[1] /sɔːs‖sɔːrs/ *n* **1** [C,U] a thing, place, activity etc that you get something from: *They get their money from* ***various sources****.* **+ of**: *The insurance division is ITT's biggest source of revenue.* | *Is your pension taxed* ***at source*** *before it is paid to you?*

2 [C] the cause of something, especially a problem, or the place where it starts **+ of**: *The cuts are a* ***source of concern*** *to all of us.* | *The* ***source of the problem*** *is the inferior quality of our labour supply.*

3 [C] a person, book, or document that supplies you with information: ***Industry sources*** *say that Chrysler is planning to increase production.* | *We know readers are getting information from other sources than print.*

source[2] *v* [T] if a company sources materials, parts etc from a particular place, it obtains them from there: *Components will be sourced from Polish producers.* —**sourcing** *n* [U] *Local sourcing would be cheaper than importing parts.*—see also OUTSOURCE

source and application of funds *n* [U] also **sources and uses of funds** ACCOUNTING information contained in a company's accounts about the flow of money into and out of the company over a particular period of time, including information on where it came from and how it was used. In many countries, companies have to include this information in their financial reports: *a source and application of funds statement*

source and application of funds statement —see under STATEMENT

sourc•ing /ˈsɔːsɪŋ‖ˈsɔːr-/ *n* [U] MANUFACTURING the job or activity of getting supplies of goods, especially ones that are used to make other goods: *Kodak's director of corporate sourcing* | *The quality of the tomatoes suggested that the restaurant's* ***product sourcing*** *is not ideal.*

dual sourcing when a company has two SUPPLIERS for the same product so as to be sure that the product will always be available and to be able to compare the suppliers' prices etc

sovereign debt —see under DEBT

sovereign risk —see under RISK[1]

SpA abbreviation for SOCIETA PER AZIONI, used in the names of some Italian companies

space /speɪs/ *n* **1** [U] the area or amount of room in a newspaper, magazine etc that is used for a particular subject

advertising space [U] somewhere that advertising is placed or shown: *a company that sells advertising space in journals*

print space [U] MARKETING the amount of space on paper an advertiser pays for when their advertisements appear in a newspaper, magazine etc: *Most studios use big ad agencies to buy TV time or print space.*

2 [C,U] land or an area of land that has not been built upon: *It has an attractive town centre with lots of* ***open spaces****.*

incubator space [C] PROPERTY a cheap space for new businesses to rent. This space is usually near services that help a business to operate, for example, food, computer, and safety services: *Our start-up company was lucky to find an incubator space during its first year of business.* —see also SHELF SPACE

space bar *n* [C] the long key at the bottom of a KEYBOARD that you press to make a space

spam[1] /spæm/ *v* past tense and past participle **spammed** present participle **spamming** [I,T] COMPUTING to send copies of the same information to many different groups on the INTERNET: *As many as 30,000 spammed messages were sent on Usenet.* —**spamming** *n* [U] *MCI will not tolerate the use of its network for spamming.*

spam[2] *n* [U] E-MAIL messages that a computer user has not asked for and does not want to read, for example messages from advertisers: *Net users can filter out spam with software such as Eudora and Zippo.* —see also ANTI-SPAM

spare capacity —see under CAPACITY

-speak /spiːk/ *suffix* added to other words to form nouns that mean the special language of a particular business or activity, especially slang or technical words that are difficult for ordinary people to understand: *I can't understand this* ***computerspeak****.* | ***business-speak***

spec /spek/ *n informal* **1** [C] detailed instructions about how something should be designed or made; SPECIFICATION: *We have made a few alterations to the* ***design spec****.*

2 [C] the spec of a machine, computer etc is the combination of all its special feature; SPECIFICATION: *The most expensive computers have the best specs.* | ***a spec sheet** describing the product*

3 on spec if you do something on spec, you do it without being sure that you will get what you are hoping for: *I sent in an application on spec, but I still haven't heard from them about any jobs.*

spe•cial¹ /ˈspeʃəl/ *adj* **1** not ordinary or usual but different in some way and often better or more important: *They're doing a **special promotion** on digital cameras.* | ***Special bonuses** were paid to top executives.*

2 used to describe someone who has had a position specially created for them: *Mr. Aida accepted an appointment as **special adviser** to Nomura Securities Co.* | *a former **special assistant** to President Clinton*

special² *n* [C,U] *informal* a lower price than usual for a particular product for a short period of time + **on**: *This month, the bar will have a special on wine by the glass.* | *Breyer's ice-cream is **on special** this week.*

special buyer —see under BUYER

special delivery —see under DELIVERY

special dividend —see under DIVIDEND

special drawing right —see SDR

special interest group —see under GROUP

spe•cial•is•m /ˈspeʃəlɪzəm/ *n* [C] an activity or subject that you know a lot about: *graduates with a specialism in Tourism and Leisure* | *A chief officer implements policy in fields relating to his specialism.*

spe•cial•ist /ˈspeʃəlɪst/ *n* [C] **1** a person or business that has a lot of skill or knowledge in a particular subject, and often gives advice to others + **in**: *Ross is a specialist in restructurings.* | *a firm of **marketing specialists*** | *a **bankruptcy specialist***

2 *AmE* a dealer on a stockmarket who buys and sells shares in a small list of companies for investors —**specialist** *adj* [only before a noun] *U.S. Healthcare didn't like the **specialist firm** assigned to handle trading in its shares.*

spe•ci•al•i•ty¹ /ˌspeʃiˈælɪti/ *n* plural **specialities** [C] *BrE* a subject or skill that you know a lot about or have a lot of experience of; SPECIALTY *especially AmE*: *My speciality is international tax law.*

speciality² *adj* [only before a noun] *BrE* **1** speciality products are special or unusual in some way, and are therefore usually expensive: *a range of speciality paints*

2 speciality shop/restaurant a shop or restaurant that sells unusual products or food that are special in some way

spe•cial•ize also **specialise** *BrE* /ˈspeʃəlaɪz/ *v* [I] to limit all or most of your business to a particular activity + **in**: *money managers who specialize in small stocks* | *an accounting firm specializing in helping people who suddenly become rich.* | *the company's push to specialize* —**specialization** also **specialisation** *BrE n* [C,U] *Specialization may be a drawback for those who lose their jobs.*

spe•cial•ized also **specialised** /ˈspeʃəlaɪzd/ *BrE adj* designed or developed for a particular purpose or type of work: *The company sells specialized computer software* | ***highly specialized** steel mills*

special leave —see under LEAVE

special offer —see under OFFER²

special resolution —see under RESOLUTION

special situation —see under SITUATION

spe•cial•ty¹ /ˈspeʃəlti/ *n* plural **specialties** [C] *especially AmE* a subject or skill that you know a lot about or have a lot of experience in; SPECIALITY *BrE*: *ABSS's specialty is combining computer hardware of various sorts into a single operating system.*

specialty² *adj especially AmE* **1** specialty products are special or unusual in some way, and are therefore usually expensive; SPECIALITY *BrE*: *a specialty chemicals business*

2 speciality store/restaurant a shop or restaurant that sells products or food that is special or unusual in some way

spe•cie /ˈspiːʃiː‖-ʃiː, -siː/ *n* [U] money in the form of coins, not bank notes: *The government announced it was prepared to exchange paper money for specie.*

spe•ci•fi•ca•tion /ˌspesɪfɪˈkeɪʃən/ *n* [C usually plural] **1** a detailed description of how something should be designed or made: *the design specifications of the new computer system* | *Each machine is built **to the highest specifications**.*

2 to specification(s) if something is made, working etc to specification, it is doing so according to the description of how it should be designed: *My job is to ensure that the plant is performing exactly **to specification**.*

3 conform with/meet specification(s) to be designed exactly following the specification: *They delivered parts that did not conform with contract specifications.* | *In defense electronics, components must meet especially rigid specifications set by the Pentagon.*

4 an official written description of something, giving details of what it is or what it involves

customs specification an official document needed by customs for goods leaving or coming into a country: *customs specification requirements including delivery terms, weight, method of transport and, for arrivals, the country of origin*

job specification an official list of the work and responsibilities you have in your job; JOB DESCRIPTION

specific duty —see under DUTY

specific performance —see under PERFORMANCE

specific tax —see under TAX¹

spe•ci•fy /ˈspesɪfaɪ/ *v* past tense and past participle **specified** [T] to state something in an exact and detailed way: *It is useful to specify the due date for payment.* | *Repayment within the **specified period** is guaranteed.* | *Agreements often specify market price.* **specify that**: *The contract fixes prices but specifies that output will equal whatever is demanded.*

spe•ci•men /ˈspesɪmɪn/ *adj* [only before a noun] provided as a typical example of something: *a **specimen letter*** | *When you open an account with us you will be asked to provide a **specimen signature**.* | *Specimen contracts are available from the Institute of Purchasing and Supply.* —**specimen** *n* [C] *This specimen sets out the way a formal valuation report must be written.*

specimen signature —see under SIGNATURE

spec•u•late /ˈspekjʊleɪt/ *v* **1** [I] to buy goods, shares, property etc in the hope that their value will increase so that you can sell them at a higher price and make a profit, often quickly + **in**: *Bond raiders speculate in distressed companies that they think may restructure themselves or be taken over.* + **on**: *Many ordinary people have now started to **speculate on the stock market**.* | *News that George Soros was speculating on gold's rise sparked the recent rally.*

2 [I,T] to think or talk about the possible causes or effects of something without knowing all the facts or details + **on/about**: *One can only speculate on the effect of long-term unemployment on the crime rate.* | *He declined to speculate about the likely cost of the project.* **speculate that**: *Analysts now speculate that Hershey, the US chocolate company, is a more likely bidder.*

spec•u•la•tion /ˌspekjʊˈleɪʃən/ *n* **1** [C,U] the act of trying to make a profit by speculating: *He made most of his money through **property speculation**.* | *Inflation encourages consumption, borrowing and speculation.* + **in**: *the bank's efforts to discourage speculation in the Singapore dollar*

2 [U] the act of guessing without knowing all the facts about something, or the guesses that you make: *There is speculation of a revival in the property market.* | *The group is now the focus of* ***takeover speculation****.* | *A Treasury official dismissed the reports as "pure speculation".* + **that**: *Institutions poured into the issue* ***amid speculation*** *that the flotation would start trading at a substantial premium.* | ***Speculation mounted*** (=increased) *that the Bundesbank was set to raise its key interest rates.*

spec·u·la·tive /ˈspekjələtɪv‖-leɪ-/ *adj* **1** bought or done in the hope of making a profit: *Kingfisher's £461 million bid for Dixon's led to a good deal of* ***speculative activity*** *yesterday.* | *The Bank of Mexico is confident it can see off any speculative attack on the peso.* | *Prices fell on heavy speculative selling after the weekend.*
2 based on guessing, not on information or facts: *These figures are, at best, speculative.* | *She dismisses rumours of a boardroom split as "totally speculative".*

speculative builder —see under BUILDER

speculative investment —see under INVESTMENT

spec·u·la·tor /ˈspekjəleɪtə‖-ər/ *n* [C] someone who buys goods, shares, property, or foreign currency in the hope that their value will increase so that they can be sold again at a higher price in order to make a profit: *Speculators who bought the options before the bid and sold 24 hours later showed a 100% profit.* | *a* ***currency speculator*** | *a* ***Wall Street speculator***

speech recognition software —see under SOFTWARE

spell·check·er /ˈspelˌtʃekə‖-ər/ also **spell checker** *n* [C] a computer program that checks spelling in documents written with WORD-PROCESSING SOFTWARE

spend[1] /spend/ *v* past tense and past participle **spent** [I,T] **1** to use your money to buy or pay for things: *How much do we have to spend?* | *Glaxo spent more than S$200 million on a new multi-purpose facility.* | *It is worth spending money on advertising.*
2 to use or pass time: *Effective managers* ***spend time*** *getting to know their workers.* | *I have spent the past seven years working in industry.*

spend[2] *n* [U] *BrE* the amount of money spent by a company on a particular activity in a particular period of time: *They increased the marketing spend needed to launch the new brands.*

spend·ing /ˈspendɪŋ/ *n* [U] the amount of money spent, especially by a government or organization: *The slump in* ***high street spending*** *could reduce imports.* | *a rise in* ***consumer spending*** | ***Spending cuts*** *are being imposed to keep the franc stable.* | *Grumman cut its* ***capital spending*** *to $50 million.* | *the need to control* ***public spending*** (=money spent by the government) + **on**: *Spending on goods and services is down.*

deficit spending ECONOMICS when a government spends more than it receives from taxes and other income: *The Democrats want to stimulate the weak economy, and believe that more deficit spending, rather than less, would do that.*

discretionary spending ◆ spending by consumers on things that they want to buy rather than on things they need such as housing or food: *Jewelry companies, which depend on discretionary spending, are forecasting better times.*
◆ spending by a company or organization that can easily be increased or reduced, for example on advertising or developing new products: *Although the company now is sharply limiting discretionary spending, it is maintaining major projects that other companies might have tried to cancel.*

spending money —see under MONEY

spending power —see under POWER[1]

spend·thrift /ˈspendˌθrɪft/ *n* [C] someone who spends money in a careless and wasteful way, even when they do not have a lot of it

spin /spɪn/ *v* past tense and past participle **spun** present participle **spinning**

spin sth ↔ **off** *phr v* [T] to form a separate, independent organization or unit from part of an existing organization: *Zeneca, the drugs firm spun off by ICI* | *a parent company spinning off its own operating divisions to form separate companies in the same field* | *The profession needs to spin off its regulatory role to an independent agency.*

spin-off *n* [C] **1** an unexpected but useful result of something, that happens in addition to the intended result: *Collaboration will produce cost savings and other spin-offs.* | *a public relations spin-off*
2 *especially AmE* a separate and partly independent company formed from parts of an existing company: *The board is considering creating a spin-off.*

spi·ral[1] /ˈspaɪərəl‖ˈspaɪr-/ *n* [C] a process, usually a harmful one, in which something continuously rises, falls, gets worse etc, often starting off slowly but gradually speeding up until it is out of control: *Sales are on a* ***downward spiral****.* | *The current oil price rise may cause an* ***inflationary spiral*** *and, in the end, a recession.*

wage-price spiral a situation in which rising prices cause wages to rise, which means that goods cost more to make so that prices rise again etc: *There was anxiety that Germany would be drawn into a wage-price spiral.*

spiral[2] *v* **spiralled spiralling** *BrE* **spiraled spiraling** *AmE* [I] if debt or the cost of something spirals, it increases quickly and uncontrollably: ***Spiralling costs*** *may force staff cuts.* | *Inflation is* ***spiralling out of control****.*

split[1] /splɪt/ *v* past tense and past participle **split** present participle **splitting** **1** [T] to divide something into separate parts so that two or more people each get a part: *We agreed to split the fee.* **split sth between**: *Profits will be split between the three companies.* | *The merger forced us to split operations between London and Edinburgh.* **split sth three/four etc ways** (=into three, four etc parts): *All profits will be split three ways.*
2 [I,T] also **split up** to divide or separate something into different parts, or be divided into different parts + **into**: *ICI is proposing to split itself into two companies.* | *They planned to split into three companies to fight the bid.* | *There are fears that he has plans to split the firm up between his two sons.*
3 split shares FINANCE to divide a company's shares into smaller units so that the value of each share is reduced and the number of shares is increased. This may be done to make it easier to buy and sell the shares: *The company is splitting its 5p nominal shares into units of 2.5p to make them more marketable.*
4 split the difference to agree on a price, charge etc that is exactly half way between the one that has been offered and the one that has been asked for

split[2] *n* [C] the act of sharing money between a group of people, organizations etc, or the share that each group gets: *the turnover split between UK and overseas* | *The partners have agreed a* ***three-way split*** (=a share of something that is divided equally between three people).

reverse share split also **reverse stock split** *AmE* FINANCE the act of putting a company's shares into larger units. This is done to increase the share price and make them more attractive to investors, and does not affect the value of the company to shareholders: *The reverse stock split should increase the share price from about $1 to the $9-to-$10 range, and make shares more attractive to institutional investors.*

share split also **stock split** *AmE* FINANCE the act of dividing a company's shares into smaller units. This is done to reduce the share price and make the shares easier to buy and sell, and does not affect the value of the company to shareholders: *Glaxo announced a 2-for-1 share split, after which it will have three billion ordinary shares outstanding.* | *PepsiCo Inc. declared a 3-for-1 stock split. The move followed a doubling of its stock price in the past 19 months.*

split capital —see under CAPITAL

split share —see under SHARE

split shift —see under SHIFT[1]

split stock —see under STOCK[1]

split-up *n* [C] an occasion when an organization is divided into two or more parts: *Cross-border mergers and split-ups remain difficult in many cases because of company law obstacles.*

spokes·per·son /ˈspəʊksˌpɜːsən‖ˈspoʊksˌpɜːr-/ *n* plural **spokespeople** [C] a person who has been chosen to speak officially for a group, organization, or government

spon·sor[1] /ˈspɒnsə‖ˈspɑːnsər/ *v* [T] **1** to give money to pay for a television programme, a sports or arts event, training etc, in exchange for advertising or to get public attention: *Eagle Star Insurance sponsored the charity's first TV campaign.* | *The award was sponsored by National Westminster Bank.* | *Some of the students are sponsored by engineering firms.* | *a government-sponsored scheme*

2 to officially support a proposal or suggestion: *The report was sponsored by 12 top companies.*

sponsor[2] *n* [C] **1** a person or company that pays for a television programme, a sports or arts event, training etc, in exchange for advertising or to get public attention: *The exhibition organizers are now looking for sponsors.*

2 someone who officially introduces or supports a proposal or suggestion

spon·sor·ship /ˈspɒnsəʃɪp‖ˈspɑːnsər-/ *n* [U] **1** also **sponsorships** financial support given to pay for a sports or arts event, training etc, in exchange for advertising or to get public attention: *We are **looking for sponsorship** from local businesses.* | *She plans to **raise £6,000 in sponsorship**.* | *Television coverage attracted lucrative sponsorships* (=for a lot of money) *to the sport.* | *The Olympic committee will raise money from **corporate sponsorships**, television rights, ticket sales and merchandise.*

2 the act of officially supporting a proposal or suggestion: *The project has benefited from the personal sponsorship of the new technical director.*

sporting goods —see under GOODS

spot /spɒt‖spɑːt/ *adj* FINANCE involving delivery now, rather than in the future: *The settlement period for spot transactions is two business days.* | *a spot cash payment* (=for goods that are delivered immediately)

spot check —see under CHECK[1]

spot delivery —see under DELIVERY

spot (exchange) rate —see under EXCHANGE RATE

spot market —see under MARKET[1]

spot price —see under PRICE[1]

spread[1] /spred/ *v* past tense and past participle **spread**

1 [T] to share work, responsibility, or money among several people: *Companies may want to spread their equity widely among stable, long-term shareholders.*

2 [T] also **spread out** to pay for something gradually over a period of time: *Can I spread out the repayments?* **spread sth over sth**: *Spread your premium payments over 12 monthly instalments.* | *The cost is spread out over ten years.*

3 [I] to become widely used or known about: *Deregulation is spreading across the whole of Europe.*

4 spread a risk INSURANCE to reduce the chance of a large loss by sharing the risk of insuring someone or something with other insurance companies

spread[2] *n* **1** [singular] a range of people or things, especially investments + **of**: *Lloyd's is keen to broaden its spread of risks.* | *The assets represent a **wide spread** of fixed interest stocks, UK and overseas equity shares and property.*

2 [C] BANKING the difference between the interest rate a bank pays on DEPOSITS (=money put in the bank) and the interest rate it charges on loans; AGIO + **between**: *Banks must maintain an adequate spread between borrowing and lending rates.*

yield spread ◆ [C] BANKING the difference between the amount it costs banks to borrow money and the price they charge for lending it: *When the economy is sluggish* (=less active) *it's not unusual to see the yield spread at around 2 percentage points.*

◆ [C] FINANCE the difference in the amount of money you get from different types of investments: *The yield spread between two-year notes and 30-year bonds widened 6 basis points today.*

3 [C] FINANCE the difference between two rates of interest. Interest on company bonds is often set in relation to the interest on particular government bonds: *The non-callable notes were priced at a spread of 87.5 basis points* (=0.875%) *over the yield on the Treasury's 10-year note.*

4 [C] FINANCE the difference between the buying price and the selling price of shares, UNIT TRUSTS etc: *The spread between the bid and ask prices for the options is $\frac{1}{8}$ to $\frac{1}{4}$ point – $12.50 to $25 an option.*

5 [C] FINANCE the difference between the buying price and the selling price of a currency, or between two rates for a currency: *The typical spread on the D-Mark is two pips* (=DM 0.2). | *a policy of frequent devaluations of the Nicaraguan currency, designed to eliminate the spread between official and black-market exchange rates*

6 [C] also **underwriting spread** FINANCE the difference between the price a financial institution pays to buy shares from the company that ISSUES them (=makes them available) and the higher price the firm charges to investors who buy them: *The underwriting spread can range from 3.5% to 7% of the offering price.*

bid-offer spread [C] the difference between the prices at which a dealer will buy and sell something

7 [C] in a MONETARY SYSTEM (=an arrangement where the values of currencies move in relation to each other within certain limits), the difference between the highest valued currency and the lowest: *The Irish punt remained the grid's strongest currency, with the spread between it and the weakest, the Italian lira, widening to 11%.*

spread·sheet /ˈspredʃiːt/ *n* [C] a computer program that can show rows of figures and perform calculations with them. Spreadsheets are often used to work out sales, taxes, profits, and other financial information: *Most spreadsheets provide a facility for creating graphs and charts from the information held in the model.* | *spreadsheet and database programs*

spreadsheet software —see under SOFTWARE

spree /spriː/ *n* [C] **spending/buying/takeover etc spree** a short period of time during which someone spends a lot of money: *Consumers **went on a spending spree**.* | *The company embarked on a takeover spree during the 1980s.*

spurt /spɜːt‖spɜːrt/ *n* [C] a short sudden increase of activity: *The stock market **put on a spurt*** (=suddenly increased in activity for a short period of time) *late in the day.* | *Commentators linked the spurt in output to sterling's departure from Europe's exchange-rate mechanism.*

Sq. written abbreviation for SQUARE, used in addresses

squan·der /ˈskwɒndə‖ˈskwɑːndər/ *v* [T] to spend money or use your time carelessly on things that are not useful: *The bank squandered $500 million playing the U.S. bond market.* | *Gorbachev **squandered** his **chance** to create a market economy.* **squander sth on sth**: *He squandered the company's assets on such things as corporate*

S

aircraft, a yacht and very large salaries. —**squandering** *n* [U] *the irresponsible squandering of stockholder's assets*

square[1] /skweə‖skwer/ *adj* **1 square metre/mile etc** an area of measurement equal to a square with sides a metre long, a mile long etc: *office space at a monthly rent of 5,000 yen per square metre*

2 5 feet/2 metres etc square shaped like a square with sides that are 5 feet, 2 metres etc long: *The room is six metres square.*

3 (all) square *informal* if two people are square, they do not owe each other any money: *Here's your £10 back – that makes us all square.*

square[2] *v* [T] *informal* to pay money to someone in an official position, so that they do what you want; BRIBE: *We'll have to square a few government officials, if we're going to get this scheme approved.*

square sth ↔ **away** *phr v* [T] *AmE* to finish something, especially by putting the last details in order: *Get your work squared away before you leave.*

square up *phr v* [I] to pay money that you owe: *I'll pay for the drinks and you can square up later.*

square sth **with** sb *phr v* [T] to arrange something with someone by persuading them to agree to it or allow it: *I'll take the day off if I can square it with my boss.*

Square Mile *n* **the Square Mile** *journalism* another name for THE CITY (=the financial and banking centre of London). It is called this because the area of the City is about one square mile

squat[1] /skɒwt‖skwɑːt/ *v* past tense and past participle **squatted** present participle **squatting** [I] to live in a building or on a piece of land without permission and without paying rent: *There are people squatting in the house next door.*

squat[2] *n* [singular] *BrE* a house that people are living in without permission and without paying rent.

squat·ter /ˈskwɒtə‖ˈskwɑːtər/ *n* [C] **1** someone who lives in an empty building without permission or without paying rent

2 LAW someone who lives on unowned land without permission or without paying rent, but has legal rights over it and may in some cases become its owner: ***squatters' rights*** *over municipal land*

squeeze[1] /skwiːz/ *v* [T] **1** to strictly limit the amount of money that is available to a company or organization: *Health care spending is being squeezed.* | *Roanoke Electric Steel Co. says its* ***profit margin*** *is getting* ***squeezed*** *by rising costs for its primary raw material.* | *Growers are being squeezed by the tobacco companies who have turned to foreign lands as a way to produce cheaper crops.*

2 squeeze sth out of/from sth to get the most you possibly can from something: *Johnson was known to squeeze every dollar out of every contract.* | *Company managers can squeeze more from their capital assets if they choose markets carefully and set clearer goals.*

squeeze sb/sth ↔ **out (of sth)** *phr v* [T] to make it difficult for someone to continue in business, by doing things to attract their customers: *It's the big operators squeezing the independents out of the markets.*

squeeze[2] *n* [singular] a situation in which wages, prices, borrowing money etc are strictly limited, especially by a government in order to control inflation: *The union is protesting against the 1.5%* ***pay squeeze****.* + **on**: *a squeeze on gross margins.*

credit squeeze a period of time when the government strictly limits the amount of lending that banks are allowed to do, leading to businesses and individuals having difficulty getting loans and paying more interest on them: *Consumer demand has collapsed as a result of the credit squeeze.* | *A credit squeeze for smaller companies is just beginning and may translate in the future into fewer capital goods projects and investments.*

profit squeeze a period of time when a company is making less profit than usual: *Dow's chief financial officer warned of a further profit squeeze in chemicals in the fourth quarter if it can't raise prices enough to offset rising raw material costs.* —see also BEAR SQUEEZE, SHORT SQUEEZE

S/R written abbreviation for SALE OR RETURN

Sr. written abbreviation for SENIOR; SNR.: *Frank Lawson Sr.*

SRO written abbreviation for SELF-REGULATORY ORGANIZATION

SRP written abbreviation for SUGGESTED RETAIL PRICE

St. written abbreviation for STREET

st written abbreviation for SHORT TON

sta·bil·i·ty /stəˈbɪləti/ *n* [U] the condition of being strong, steady, and not changing: *The prospects for political and* ***economic stability*** *in the country continue to fade.* | *The EU needs* ***exchange-rate stability*** *to promote intra-regional trade and investment.* | *Lifetime employment gives employees greater* ***career stability****.*

sta·bi·li·za·tion also **stabilisation** *BrE* /ˌsteɪbəlaɪˈzeɪʃən‖-lə-/ *n* [U] **1** the process of becoming firm, steady, or unchanging: *The International Coffee Organization failed to agree on a new* ***price stabilization*** *agreement.*

2 ECONOMICS when a government changes its tax or MONETARY POLICY in order to prevent large or sudden movements in the level of prices, unemployment etc: *The* ***economic stabilization plan*** *resulted in higher interest rates and taxes.* | *Ministers have talked about shifting economic policy from one of stabilization to one of growth.*

3 ECONOMICS when a country buys and sells its own currency on FOREIGN EXCHANGE MARKETS in order to control its value: *Pressure on exchange rates resulted in calls by the leading industrialized countries for* ***currency stabilization****.*

sta·bil·ize also **stabilise** *BrE* /ˈsteɪbəlaɪz/ *v* [I,T] to become firm, steady, or unchanging, or to make something do this: *We want to* ***stabilize*** *consumer* ***prices*** *for sugar and sugar products.* | *the government's plan to* ***stabilize the economy*** | *Intervention can only play a limited role in* ***stabilizing currency exchange rates****.* | *Calm returned to Wall Street as* ***financial markets stabilized*** *around the world.* | *The most immediate benefit of yesterday's deal may be to help* ***stabilize*** *Packard Bell's* ***finances****.*

stabilized bond also **stabilised bond** *BrE* —see ***indexed bond*** under BOND

sta·bil·iz·er also **stabiliser** *BrE* /ˈsteɪbəlaɪzə‖-ər/ *n* [C usually plural] one of the ways in which a government tries to prevent large movements in the level of employment, incomes, prices, and production, for example by controlling interest rates, income tax, and government spending: *the role of taxes and public spending as automatic stabilisers in modern economies*

sta·ble /ˈsteɪbəl/ *adj* steady and not likely to move or change: *Japanese enterprises operate under relatively* ***stable*** *capital market* ***conditions****.* | *The key to growth and* ***stable employment*** *will be through improving the international competitiveness of our companies.* | *The Government is committed to maintaining a* ***stable exchange rate****.* | *Prices for most goods were stable.*

stack[1] /stæk/ *n* [C] COMPUTING a temporary store of information on a computer

stack[2] *v* **1** [T] to put things into neat piles: *The supermarkets failed to stack the shelves during opening hours.*

2 [I,T] to put a group of people, or vehicles or other things in a particular order as they wait to do something: *The two airliners were stacking as they waited to land.* —**stacking** *n* [U] *a machine that prepares huge bags of* *salt for stacking* | *British police have prepared plans for the French ferry strike, including the stacking of lorries in a parking area outside Dover.*

stack up *phr v* [I] *informal* to have a particular performance when compared with something + **against**: *How does their product stack up against our own?*

staff[1] /stɑːf‖stæf/ *n* plural **staff** HUMAN RESOURCES [C] the people who work for an organization or business: *We now employ a staff of 25.* | *Every* ***member of staff*** *has strengths and weaknesses.* | *It's good to have you* ***on the staff.*** | *The company's* ***accounting staff*** *are preparing a financial budget.* | *Most* ***office staff*** *want to project a smart, professional image for their companies.*

clerical staff [plural] people who work in offices: *Computers are replacing thousands of clerical staff and middle managers.*

counter staff [plural] people who work in shops and serve customers

field staff [plural] employees who do not work at a company's or organization's office, but travel to different places in order to do their work: *Residential staff have tended to become isolated from field staff and their pay has fallen behind that of field social workers.*

junior staff [plural] employees who are younger or less important than others working in the same company: *Junior staff were short of money and welcomed the opportunity to earn more through overtime.*

senior staff [plural] employees who are older or more important than others working in the same company: *The Patent Office lacked experienced senior staff to train the new employees.*

staff[2] *v* [T] HUMAN RESOURCES to provide the workers for an organization: *We have an office and a warehouse staffed by 16 employees.* —**staffing** *n* [U] *The company expects to* ***reduce staffing*** *by about 8% next year.* | ***Staffing costs*** *rose 12%.* | *The company recently* ***reduced staffing levels*** *by 14 employees.*

staff agency —see under AGENCY

staff association —see under ASSOCIATION

staf•fer /ˈstɑːfə‖ˈstæfər/ *n* [C] *journalism* someone who works for a particular organization, especially in the computer industry or the MEDIA (=television, radio, and newspapers): *19 of the consortium's 23 full-time staffers had their contracts terminated.* | *The former IBM staffer is now marketing director at the company.*

stag[1] /stæg/ *n* [C] FINANCE *BrE* someone who buys new shares in a company in order to sell them quickly and make a profit, rather than to keep them as an investment

stag[2] *v* past tense and past participle **stagged** present participle **stagging** [T] **stag an issue** *BrE* FINANCE to buy shares in a company in order to sell them quickly and make a profit, rather than to keep them as an investment: *Substantially reducing the pricing of the tender* (=formal statement of the price) *makes it unpopular with those who like to stag new issues.*

stage[1] /steɪdʒ/ *n* **1** [C] one of several points that something reaches as it grows or develops: *The plan is still* ***in its early stages.*** | *It would be unwise to comment* ***at this stage*** *of the negotiations.* | *The equipment can be purchased* ***in stages*** *as funds become available.*

2 [singular] a place where something important happens: *Geneva has been the stage for many such conferences.*

stage[2] *v* [T] **1** to organize an event that people will come to see, or that you hope many people will notice: *The exhibition is the biggest* ***event*** *of its kind to be* ***staged*** *in Britain.* | *Employees* ***staged*** *a one-day* ***strike.***

2 to make something happen, or to start happening: *Glaxo shares* ***staged a recovery*** (=became stronger again after a difficult period of time) *and closed just 4p lower at 664p.*

stag•fla•tion /stægˈfleɪʃən/ *n* [U] an economic condition in which there is inflation but the economy is not growing, so many people do not have jobs and businesses are not doing well. This word is a combination of the words stagnation and inflation: *Most of the downtown stores have been driven out of business by stagflation.*

stag•ger /ˈstægə‖-ər/ *v* [T] **1** to arrange people's working hours, holidays etc so that they do not all begin and end at the same time: *The meetings are staggered throughout the day to give shift workers the opportunity to attend.* | *More could be done to encourage flexible or* ***staggered working hours.***

2 to arrange a series of payments, deliveries etc so that they do not all happen at the same time: *The loan repayments were staggered over a long period.* | *The remaining aircraft will be delivered* ***on a staggered basis*** *by the year 2025.*

stag•nant /ˈstægnənt/ *adj* not changing, developing, or making progress: *Industrial output has remained stagnant.* | *Japan's corporate profits are slumping* (=falling suddenly) *because of a* ***stagnant*** *domestic* ***economy.***

stag•nate /stægˈneɪt‖ˈstægneɪt/ *v* [I] if an economy or industry stagnates, it does not grow, or it grows only very slowly: *The construction industry is stagnating and there has been a steep fall in new orders.* | *a* ***stagnating economy*** —**stagnation** *n* [U] *In Japan in the 1990s, a financial collapse led to* ***economic stagnation*** | *Continuing stagnation in New York's commercial-property market means that property-tax revenues may be about $200 million lower than expected in the coming fiscal year.*

stake[1] /steɪk/ *n* **1** [C usually singular] FINANCE money risked or invested in a business: *Cable & Wireless Plc has* ***cut its stake*** *in Digital Telecommunications Philippines Inc to 25% from 40%.* | *Pearson, which* ***has a*** *major* ***stake in*** *BSkyB, gained 4p to 451p.* | *AT&T Co plans to* ***buy a*** *big* ***stake in*** *McCaw Cellular Communications Inc.*

equity stake [C] when a company owns shares in another company; SHAREHOLDING: *Matsushita has agreed to* ***acquire an equity stake*** *in Loewe Opta.* | *Sabena wants to find a partner that will* ***take an equity stake*** *in the airline.* | *Hershey Foods Corp. signed a definitive agreement to* ***sell*** *its 17%* ***equity stake*** *in Marabou.*

majority stake [C usually singular] if an investor has a majority stake in a company, they own more than half the shares of that company: *Canada, Mexico and South Korea refused to allow foreign companies to* ***hold majority stakes*** *in their main telephone companies.* | *Daimler is also looking to sell a majority stake in regional aircraft maker Dornier GmbH.*

minority stake [C usually singular] if an investor has a minority stake in a company, they own less than half the shares of that company: *AXA bought a minority stake (49%) in Equitable Life, America's fourth-largest life insurer, for $1 billion.* | *The company is negotiating the purchase of a minority stake in the French airline, Transport Aerien Transregional.*

2 be at stake if something that you value very much is at stake, you will lose it if a plan or action is not successful: *If we lose the contract, hundreds of jobs are at stake.*

3 [C] money risked on the result of something, especially a horse race; BET: *a $100 stake*

4 stakes [plural] used to talk about how much risk there is in a particular activity: *He plays the* ***high-stakes game*** (=involving a lot of risk) *of trading on margin, where investors use borrowed money to buy stocks, bonds and mutual funds.*

5 play for high stakes if you play for high stakes, you are in a situation where you gain or lose a lot

stake[2] *v*

stake sth **on** sth *phr v* [T] **1** to risk losing money if a business activity is not successful: *They are* ***staking their money on*** *the chances for a market recovery by next spring.*

2 to risk losing something that is valuable or important to you if a plan or action is not successful: *The President is **staking his reputation on** these trade talks.*

stake·hold·er /ˈsteɪkˌhəʊldə‖-ˌhoʊldər/ *n* [C] **1** a person who is considered to be an important part of an organization or of society because they have responsibility within it and receive advantages from it: *When a company is new and small, it can stay close to its stakeholders – staff, customers and suppliers – and they all share the same values and aims.*

2 *AmE* someone who owns shares in a company; SHAREHOLDER *BrE*: *Algoma Steel Corp. is asking its stakeholders to invest 395 million Canadian dollars in cash, concessions and loan guarantees.*

stakeholder pension —see under PENSION[1]

stakeholder society —see under SOCIETY

stale cheque —see under CHEQUE

stall[1] /stɔːl‖stɒːl/ *n* [C] a table on which goods are placed, found in a public place such as a market: *a **market stall***

stall[2] *v* [I,T] **1** to stop or cause something to stop, usually before continuing again: *Investment in the country has stalled and billions of dollars have been transferred elsewhere.* | *The layoffs could be the start of a widespread job scaleback as the **economy stalls**.* | *Maybe we can stall the sale until the prices go up.* | *When the previous contract expired and bargaining **talks stalled**, the workers went on strike.*

2 to be delayed, or to delay something or someone: *Sales of North American-made cars fell 12.7% in mid-April, further stalling a hoped-for recovery for the industry.*

stall·hold·er /ˈstɔːlˌhəʊldə‖ˈstɒːlˌhoʊldər/ *n* [C] someone who pays rent to have a stall at a market

stamp[1] /stæmp/ *n* [C] **1** also **postage stamp** a small piece of paper that you buy and stick onto an envelope or package before posting it: *a 29-cent stamp* | *Care must be taken that the correct postage stamps for overseas post are used.*

2 *BrE* a small piece of paper that is worth a particular amount of money and bought and collected towards paying for something over a period of time: *television licence stamps*

food stamp *AmE* an official piece of paper that the US government gives to poor people so that they can buy food at a low price: *Only households with a net income at or below the poverty line may qualify for food stamps.*

revenue stamp TAX in Britain, a piece of paper for sticking to some official papers to show that tax has been paid

trading stamp a type of stamp given by a shop to a customer each time the customer spends a certain amount of money, for sticking in a book and which later can be exchanged for goods or money: *Last year about 25% of supermarkets were giving trading stamps.*

3 a tool for pressing or printing a mark or pattern onto a surface, or the mark made by this tool: *a **passport stamp***

date stamp ◆ a stamp that has movable numbers, and is used to print the date on a document or envelope ◆ a printed date that shows when something was done or made, or when it should be eaten, sold, or used by: *According to the date stamp on the report, it was delivered last December.* | *The foods now have a date stamp and are guaranteed to reach British shops within six weeks of production.*

rubber stamp ◆ a small piece of rubber with a handle, used for printing dates or names on documents ◆ the person or thing that provides the official approval for something to happen + **for**: *The legislature is essentially a rubber stamp for the actions of a powerful political executive.*

stamp[2] *v* [T] **1** to put a pattern, sign, or letters on something, using a special tool **stamp sth on sth**: *Stamp the date on all the letters.* **stamp sth with sth**: *Your passport must be stamped with your entry date.*

2 to stick a stamp on a letter, parcel etc

stamp duty —see under DUTY

stamped addressed envelope —see under ENVELOPE

stamp tax —see under TAX[1]

stand[1] /stænd/ *v* past tense and past participle **stood**

1 [I] to be at a particular level or amount + **at**: *Inflation currently stands at 4%.* | *Your bank balance currently stands at £720.92.*

2 [I] to be in, stay in, or get into a particular state: *The law, **as it stood**, favoured the developers.* | *I don't see a serious challenge to London as a financial centre **as things stand** currently.* | *The committee **stands divided*** (=disagrees completely) *on this issue.* | *There are currently 65 industrial premises **standing empty**.*

3 [I] to continue to exist, be correct, or be VALID: *The court of appeal has ruled that the conviction should stand.*

4 stand pat *AmE informal* to refuse to change a decision, plan etc + **on**: *Harry's standing pat on his decision to fire Janice.*

5 where sb stands someone's opinion about something, or the official rule about something + **on**: *The voters want to know where the President stands on taxes.*

6 stand trial LAW to be brought to a court of law to have your case examined and judged + **for**: *Nelson ordered Nudelman to stand trial for allegedly attempting to receive stolen property.*

7 stand bail LAW to pay money as a promise that someone will return to court to be judged

8 stand accused LAW to be the person in a court of law who is being judged for a crime + **of**: *He now stands accused by the city council of serious mismanagement of the museum's financial affairs.*

9 stand to gain/lose/win etc to be likely to do or have something: *We stand to make a lot of money from the merger.*

10 [I] to try to become elected to a parliament, board of directors etc + **for**: *He will not be **standing for election** as Institute vice president this year.* | *Who's standing for the Democrats in the 44th district?*

11 stand or fall by/on to depend on something for success: *A product will stand or fall by its quality.*

stand down *phr v* [I] to agree to leave your position or stop trying to be elected, so that someone else can have a chance: *I'm prepared to stand down in favor of a younger candidate.*

stand in *phr v* [I] to temporarily do someone else's job + **for**: *Can you stand in for Meg while she's on vacation?*

stand[2] *n* **1** [C] a small structure for selling or showing things: *Come by our stand at the exhibition and see the new products.*

exhibition stand [C] a structure used at an exhibition for showing pictures and examples of a company's products, and where sales people can talk to customers about their products: *Make sure there is plenty of space between exhibition stands.*

2 [C usually singular] a position or opinion that you state firmly and publicly: *He did not **take a stand on** the proposed regulations.*

stand-alone *adj* [only before a noun] **1** COMPUTING a stand-alone computer works without being part of a NETWORK (=a set of computers connected to each other): *The Macintosh, a desktop computer, is usually a **stand-alone machine**.*

2 a stand-alone company or business is one that is not part of a large CORPORATION: *It is just too difficult as a **stand-alone company** our size to get to profitability.*

stand-alone brand —see under BRAND[1]

stan•dard¹ /ˈstændəd‖-ərd/ *n* **1** [C,U] a level of quality, skill, ability, or achievement by which someone or something is judged, and that is considered good enough to be acceptable: *The airline has rigorous* (=very strict) ***safety standards***. + **of**: *We take pride in the **high standards** of service offered to clients.* | *The General Accounting Office of the Federal Government has **set standards*** (=decided what people are expected to do) *for federal departments and agencies.* | *Her work was not **up to standard*** (=good enough).
2 [C] something you use to compare one thing with another **by sb's standards**: *By American standards, Rafael's salary is pretty low.*
3 [C] a fixed official measure of weight, purity, value etc: *an official government standard for the purity of silver*

accounting standard —see ***accounting rule*** under RULE¹

CAT standard [singular] FINANCE fair charges, easy access, fair terms; in Britain, a standard set by the government that advertising for investments for members of the public must meet

gold standard [singular] ECONOMICS a system in which the value of the standard unit of currency is equal to a fixed weight of gold of a particular quality. This system was used in the past by many countries and had the result of making the exchange rates between such countries fixed: *The gold standard forced the central bank to exchange currency for gold at a fixed price.*

monetary standard [C] ECONOMICS something on which the value of money is based, for example gold: *the change in the monetary standard from gold to paper*

standard² *adj* **1** accepted as normal or usual: *It's **standard practice*** (=the usual way of doing things) *to employ people on a freelance basis.* | *We paid them the **standard rate** for the job.*
2 regular and usual in shape, size, quality etc: *We make shoes in **standard** and wide **sizes**.* | *All these vans are made to a **standard design**.*

Standard & Poor's Index —see under INDEX¹

Standard & Poor's rating —see under RATING

standard coinage —see under COINAGE

standard cost —see under COST¹

standard deduction —see under DEDUCTION

standard deviation —see under DEVIATION

standard fire policy —see under INSURANCE POLICY

standard generalized mark-up language also **standard generalised mark-up language** *BrE* —see SGML

Standard Industrial Classification written abbreviation **SIC** *n* in Britain, a system in which each industry is given a number, used to describe which group a company belongs to: *To conform with most Government economic statistics, the scope of the survey is defined by the Standard Industrial Classification definition of manufacturing.*

stan•dard•ize also **standardise** *BrE* /ˈstændədaɪz‖-ər-/ *v* [T] to make all the things of one particular type the same as each other: *Computer bulletin boards have become increasingly standardized in recent years.* —**standardization** *n* [U] *Automobiles have been subjected to a good deal of standardization in matters concerning safety and pollution.*

standard of living *n* plural **standards of living** [C usually singular] the amount of wealth or comfort that a person, group, or country has: *Two incomes are generally required to **maintain** a decent middle-class **standard of living**.* | *New businesses have created higher-paying jobs, lifting tens of millions of Chinese to a far higher standard of living.*

standard rate —see under RATE¹

standard spending assessment —see under ASSESSMENT

stand•by¹ /ˈstændbaɪ/ also **stand-by** *n* **1** [C] someone or something that is ready to be used when needed: *Pakistan has received the first $200 million of a **standby loan** approved by the IMF in December.*
2 [U] when you are ready to travel on a plane, but can only do so if there are seats left when it is ready to leave: *The flight is full, but we can put you **on standby**.*

standby² also **stand-by** *adj* [only before a noun] **1** a standby ticket is a cheap ticket for a plane journey that you buy just before the plane leaves —**standby** *adv*: *Most of the carriers would allow people to **fly standby**.*
2 ECONOMICS a standby arrangement or agreement allows a member state of the INTERNATIONAL MONETARY FUND to receive money if it has serious financial problems: *The Bulgarian Finance Minister announced the agreement of a new standby arrangement with the International Monetary Fund.* | *IMF officials **approved** a $1 billion **standby credit agreement** for Yugoslavia.*

standby cost —see under COST¹

standby letter of credit —see under LETTER OF CREDIT

stand•ing /ˈstændɪŋ/ *n* [U] **1** someone's position or rank in a system, organization, or society etc, based on people's opinion
2 the amount of money that a person or organization has: *Marriage to foreign heiresses helps to maintain the **financial standing** of noble families.*

credit standing FINANCE a measure of a lender's willingness to lend money to a particular person or organization, depending on their ability to repay; CREDIT STATUS; CREDIT RATING: *Every time you looked up, another company was refinancing, restructuring or doing something to improve its credit standing.*

standing order *n* **1** [C,U] BANKING an arrangement between a bank and a customer to pay a fixed amount of money regularly from the customer's bank account to another account; BANKER'S ORDER: *Customers would also be charged for paying regular bills by standing order.* | *With a standing order you tell your branch exactly how much is to be paid and when.*
2 [C,U] an arrangement in which goods are sent regularly in agreed amounts, without the customer having to make a new order each time: *They have cancelled their standing order of 12,000 copies a day of the newspaper.*
3 standing orders [plural] an organization's rules about how meetings should be held and organized: *Standing orders allow the chairman to propose the selection of specific amendments and the rejection of others.*

stand•still /ˈstændˌstɪl/ *n* [singular] a situation in which there is no movement or activity: *Strikes **brought** production **to a standstill**.* | *The negotiations are basically **at a standstill**.*

standstill agreement —see under AGREEMENT

sta•ple¹ /ˈsteɪpəl/ *n* [C] **1** a small piece of thin wire that is pushed into sheets of paper and bent over to hold them together
2 a food that is needed and used all the time: *staples like flour and rice*
3 the main product that is produced in a country: *Bananas and sugar are the staples of Jamaica.*
4 a standard or common product: *The Kiwi fruit quickly became a supermarket staple in the expanding section of exotic fruits.*

staple² *v* [T] to fasten things, especially sheets of paper, together with a staple: *He stapled a batch of papers together.*

staple³ *adj* [only before a noun] a staple food, product, activity etc is one that is basic, most important, or standard: *Oil is Nigeria's **staple export**.* | *a collapse of*

S

staple industries in East London | These garments are now becoming a ***staple product*** *of the company.*

sta·pler /ˈsteɪplə‖-ər/ *n* [C] a tool used for putting staples into sheets of paper

star /stɑː‖stɑːr/ *n* [C] in the GROWTH/SHARE MATRIX, a company or product with quite a large share of a market that is growing quickly

start¹ /stɑːt‖stɑːrt/ *v* **1** [I] if prices start at or from a particular figure, that is the lowest figure at which you can buy something, for example for the most basic product, service etc in a range + **at/from**: *Delivery prices start at £10.40.*

2 also **start up** [T] to create a new business or new business activity: *Bruno* ***started*** *his own plumbing* ***business*** *when he was only 24. | On April 5 Manx Airlines, based on the Isle of Man, starts up a Stansted to Waterford daily link.*

3 [I,T] to begin a new job, or to begin going to school, college etc: *How soon can you start? | The sales manager phoned this morning to ask if I could start next week.*

start off *phr v* **1** [I,T] **start** sth ↔ **off** to begin happening or make something begin happening: *The stock market started off Thursday's half-day session with a rush of buying. | Like many young software firms, Dimension X started off consulting for other companies to help pay the bills.*

2 [T] **start** sb ↔ **off** to help someone begin an activity: *His father started him off in the business.*

start² *n* **1** [C usually singular] the beginning of an activity, event, or situation + **of**: *The share price has increased by 22% since the start of the year. | They've had problems* ***right from the start****. | The whole process takes 10 days* ***from start to finish****. | Shops* ***got off to a bad start*** *in the weeks after currency union.*

2 [C usually plural] a job that has just started, a business that has just been created, or someone who has just started a new job: *The number of* ***business starts*** *plummeted 10.5% during the second half from a year earlier. | a training course for new starts*

housing starts [plural] ECONOMICS the number of new houses, apartments etc on which building work has started in a particular period of time. The number of housing starts is an important ECONOMIC INDICATOR (=sign of the level of economic activity): *Canadian housing starts declined 3.4% from November to a seasonally adjusted annual rate of 173,000.*

3 [singular] *BrE informal* the beginning of a new job: *He went to the building site and asked if there was any chance of a start.*

4 [C usually singular] a situation in which you have an advantage over other people: *We've got a real* ***head start*** *on the rest of the industry. The only real competitor for top-line operating system software will be Microsoft Corp.*

starter home *n* [C] a small house or apartment bought by people who are buying their first home: *Much of the demand for new housing is now concentrated in starter homes for single people or married couples.*

starting salary —see under SALARY

start·up also **start-up** /ˈstɑːtʌp‖ˈstɑːrt-/ *n* [C] a new company that has been started fairly recently: *startups that make new types of Internet devices, such as two-year-old Qubit Technology*

start-up *adj* start-up costs, spending etc are connected with beginning and running a new business or new business activity: *a* ***start-up budget*** *of £90,000 | The company saw its profits drop because of the effect of* ***start-up costs*** *at a new plastics molding plant.*

start-up company —see under COMPANY

starved /stɑːvd‖stɑːrvd/ *adj* **cash-/credit-/capital-starved** *journalism* used to describe organizations or industries that have very little cash, credit etc: *Capital-starved businesses can only hope Congress will realize that high taxes on capital give other nations an advantage over domestic producers. | Cash-starved universities are aiming to raise money by running low-cost, high-margin short business courses.*

stash /stæʃ/ *v* [T] *informal* to store something, especially money, in a safe, often secret place **stash sth away**: *He has money stashed away in the Bahamas. | The former president had stashed $6 billion in Swiss banks.* —**stash** *n* [C] *After 20 years, she would have an after-tax stash of $467,000 in her taxable account.*

state /steɪt/ *n* **1** [C] the condition that someone or something is in at a particular time: *The property market is* ***in a poor state****. | I personally think the economy is in a worse state than the Government has been admitting.*

2 [C] also **State** one of the areas with limited law-making powers that some countries, such as the US, are divided into: *New York State has attracted more foreign companies than any other state. | The bank now sells life insurance policies in 380 branches across four states.*

3 [C,U] also **State** a country or its government: *state industries | The government plans to sell off several* ***state companies****. | the* ***state monopoly*** *of radio and television broadcasting*

corporate state [C] a country where most of the economy is owned by the government: *Saudi Arabia remains a protectionist, centrally planned corporate state.*

welfare state [singular] a system by which a government provides help, money, care etc to people who are poor, unemployed, ill etc: *Britain's welfare state needs a complete overhaul.*

4 the States [plural] the United States of America: *Sales of U.S. cars have not boomed* (=increased) *in the States as carmakers had hoped.*

state bank —see under BANK¹

state benefit —see under BENEFIT¹

state capitalism —see under CAPITALISM

state court —see under COURT¹

stated case —see under CASE

state earnings-related pension scheme —see under SCHEME

state expenditure —see under EXPENDITURE

state funding —see under FUNDING

state funds —see under FUND¹

state income tax —see under INCOME TAX

state·ment /ˈsteɪtmənt/ *n* [C] **1** something you say or write publicly or officially to let people know your intentions or opinions, or to record facts: *False statements on your tax form could land you in jail. | The Congressman* ***issued a statement*** *to the press. | The brokers had* ***made*** *misleading* ***statements****.*

chairman's statement the statement that the chairman of a company makes to shareholders once a year, telling them about the company's performance over the past year: *In his chairman's statement, Terry Shand explains why the group has overhauled the presentation of the annual report.*

environmental impact statement abbreviation **EIS** in the US, a document that studies the possible effects to the environment of an intended industrial or commercial activity: *The project is frozen pending an environmental impact statement.*

mission statement a short written statement made by an organization, intended to communicate its aims to customers, employees, shareholders etc: *The bank's mission statement uses language such as "Our personal conduct will reflect the highest professional standards."*

registration statement FINANCE in the US, a document giving information about a company, that the company has to give to the Securities and Exchange Commission before selling its shares to the public: *Brunswick Corp.* ***filed a registration statement*** *with the Securities and Exchange Commission covering a proposed offering of six million new shares.*

2 a list showing amounts of money paid, received, owing etc and their total: *You will receive a monthly statement showing the state of your account.*

average statement INSURANCE a statement saying how much each person or organization must pay when the cost of damage to a ship or the goods it is carrying is shared between the insurers and the owners

bank statement a statement sent regularly by a bank to a customer, showing the money that has gone into and out of their account over a particular period of time

completion statement *BrE* LAW a statement that shows how much money a buyer owes a seller at the end of a contract: *You will not know the precise balance until you have* ***prepared a completion statement****.*

financial statement FINANCE ◆ a statement showing the financial state of a business, at the end of a particular period of time, including its BALANCE SHEET, PROFIT AND LOSS ACCOUNT, and other necessary information: *Benfield's annual financial statement showed that operating profits slipped from £27.9 million to £26.5 million.* | *The company hasn't* ***filed*** (=sent to the authorities) *its* ***financial statement*** *for its fiscal year ended March 31.* | *the consortium's* ***consolidated financial statement*** (=one showing the results of a group of companies)

◆ another name for SOURCE AND APPLICATION OF FUNDS STATEMENT

funds flow statement FINANCE a statement showing money coming into and going out of a business in a particular period of time, where this money came from, and what it was used for. Two types of this statement are the SOURCE AND APPLICATION OF FUNDS STATEMENT and the CASH FLOW STATEMENT: *The funds flow statement explains the change in cash balances over the year.*

income statement also **operating statement** *AmE* FINANCE a statement showing the amount of money earned and spent in a particular period of time by a company; PROFIT AND LOSS ACCOUNT *BrE*: *According to the company's income statement, reported net income of $35 million is down sharply from a record $366 million a year earlier.* | *The challenge was to expand L'Auberge without raising costs unacceptably. The operating statements suggest that this has not been done.*

reconciliation statement a statement that explains a difference between two related sets of accounts

source and application of funds statement *BrE* **sources and applications of funds statement** *AmE* FINANCE a particular form of the FUNDS FLOW STATEMENT: *As the statement of source and application of funds reveals, an increase of £162,000 in the company's cash balances was only made possible by a loan of £350,000.*

statement of account *n* plural **statements of account** [C] a document sent regularly to a buyer who has an account with a particular seller, showing the dates of INVOICES sent to the buyer, the dates and amounts of payments made, and the total that must be paid

statement of affairs *n* plural **statements of affairs** [C] LAW, ACCOUNTING a document showing a company's assets and liabilities at a certain date. A statement of affairs is usually prepared when a company is about to go bankrupt

statement of claim *n* plural **statements of claim** [C] LAW a document in which the person bringing a legal action states the facts of a case and the reasons why the ACCUSED person should be punished: *Paragraph four of the statement of claim contains allegations of breach of contract.*

statement of principles *n* plural **statements of principles** **1** [C] a statement by an organization of the moral or political beliefs which the organization's actions will be based on: *The statement of principles of the Federation was drawn up at the conference and signed by all the organizations present.*

2 the Statement of Principles ACCOUNTING in the UK, a statement by the ACCOUNTING STANDARDS BOARD, giving the ideas and rules that should be followed in accounting: *The first chapter of the ASB's Statement of Principles defines fundamental terms such as asset, liability, and equity.*

state monopoly —see under MONOPOLY

state-of-the-art *adj* using the most modern and recently developed methods, materials, or knowledge: ***state-of-the-art technology*** | *state-of-the art manufacturing methods*

state-owned *adj* a state-owned industry or company is owned by the government of a particular country: *the privatization of* ***state-owned enterprises*** | *the French* ***state-owned airline****, Air France*

state pension —see under PENSION[1]

states·man /ˈsteɪtsmən/ *n* plural **statesmen** [C] a political or government leader, especially one who is respected as being wise, honourable, and fair: *Japanese statesmen talked about Japan's "fulfilling its international role".* —**statesmanlike** *adj*: *the statesmanlike response to protectionist pressures* —**statesmanship** *n* [U] *an act of international statesmanship*

state tax —see under TAX[1]

stat·ic /ˈstætɪk/ *adj* not moving, changing, or developing, especially when movement or change would be good: *Economists predict that house prices will remain static for some time.* | *a* ***static*** *oil* ***market***

sta·tion·ers /ˈsteɪʃənəz‖-ərz/ also **stationer's** *BrE* — *n* [C] a shop where stationery is sold

sta·tion·e·ry /ˈsteɪʃənəri‖-neri/ *n* [U] materials that you use for writing, such as paper, pens, and pencils: *a maker of stationery and school supplies* | *a stationery store*

stat·is·m /ˈsteɪtɪzəm/ *n* [U] when economic power is with central government, rather than with business: *the country had experienced 40 years of anti-competitive statism.* —**statist** *adj*: *statist economic policies*

sta·tis·tic /stəˈtɪstɪk/ *n* **1** [C usually plural] a collection of numbers that represent facts or measurements: *Statistics show that 35% of new businesses fail in their first year.* | *the October* ***employment statistics*** —**statistical** *adj*: *There is no* ***statistical evidence*** *that the economy is recovering.* —**statistically** *adv*: *The results were not* ***statistically significant****.*

2 statistics [plural] the branch of mathematics that studies facts and information represented by a collection of numbers: *The branch of statistics called sampling theory allows calculations about the entire collection to be inferred* (=known) *by checking a small percentage of it.*

3 [singular] a single number that represents a fact or measurement: *Annual sales per employee have jumped about 37% – that's a statistic we feel very good about.*

statistical office —see under OFFICE

stat·is·ti·cian /ˌstætəˈstɪʃən/ *n* [C] someone who works with statistics as part of their job or studies: *Duncan is chief statistician for Dun & Bradstreet.*

stats /stæts/ *n* [plural] *informal* abbreviation for STATISTICS

sta·tus /ˈsteɪtəs‖ˈsteɪtəs, ˈstæ-/ *n* **1** [C,U] the legal position or condition of a company, group, person etc: *What* *is the company's **financial status**?* + **as**: *Salomon Brothers Inc.'s status as a primary dealer of government securities*

credit status FINANCE a measure of a lender's willingness to lend money to a particular person or organization, depending on their ability to repay; CREDIT STANDING; CREDIT RATING: *The country has a good credit status, large hard-currency reserves, a stable currency and manageable debt.*

marital status [U] used to talk about whether or not someone is married, especially on official forms: *Please state your name, age, and marital status.*

2 [U] your social or professional rank or position, considered in relation to other people: ***high status** businessmen* | ***low status** immigrant workers*

3 [U] high social position that makes people recognize and respect you: *Rice-farming has a special status in Japan.* | *Cellular phones were at one time a **status symbol*** (=a sign of someone's important position, wealth etc).

4 [singular] a situation at a particular time, especially in an argument, discussion etc: *What is the status of the trade talks?*

status symbol *n* [C] something you own that you think is a sign of high social status: *BMW, the "Ultimate Driving Machine", became the **ultimate status symbol*** (=the best one) *in many places.*

stat·ute /ˈstætʃuːt/ *n* [C,U] **1** a law passed by a parliament, council etc and formally written down: *He never violated any **criminal statutes**.* | *Protection for the consumer is laid down **by statute**.*

2 the statute book a real or imaginary written collection of the laws in existence: *The government would like to see this new law on the statute book as soon as possible.*

statute barred *adj* LAW *BrE* a statute barred legal action is one which cannot be brought to trial in a civil court because too much time has passed: *The solicitor had allowed the case to become statute barred, by failing to serve on time.*

statute law —see under LAW

statute of limitations *n* plural **statutes of limitations** [C] LAW *AmE* a law that gives the period of time within which action can be taken on a legal question or crime: *Under the current statute of limitations, he has up to three years to take the company to court.*

stat·u·to·ry /ˈstætʃᵊtəri‖-tɔːri/ *adj* fixed or controlled by law: *Germany's Bundesbank has a **statutory obligation** to fight inflation.* | *the **statutory deadline** for changing the nutrition labelling on foods* | *This guarantee does not affect your **statutory rights**.* —**statutorily** *adv*: *spending that is beyond what is statutorily required*

statutory book —see under BOOK[1]

statutory instrument —see under INSTRUMENT

statutory meeting —see under MEETING

statutory regulation —see under REGULATION

statutory tenant —see under TENANT

staunch /stɔːntʃ‖stɔːntʃ, stɑːntʃ/ *adj* giving strong loyal support to a person, organization, or belief: *They are staunch trade unionists.* | *He is a **staunch supporter** of the free market.* —**staunchly** *adv*: *The company has staunchly defended its right to use the name on its new model.*

stave /steɪv/ *v*

stave sth ↔ **off** *phr v* [T] to prevent something bad from happening or affecting you for a short period of time: *The company is restructuring in an attempt to stave off bankruptcy.*

stay of execution *n* plural **stays of execution** [C usually singular] **1** LAW the stopping or delaying of a punishment by a judge: *His attorneys filed a seventh petition, winning a stay of execution.*

2 the stopping or delaying of something unpleasant or difficult to deal with: *They have a stay of execution between now and the next set of trade figures.*

stay of proceedings *n* plural **stays of proceedings** [C usually singular] LAW the stopping or delaying of a legal trial by a judge: *The court granted a stay of proceedings for three weeks.*

STD *n* [U] subscriber trunk dialling; the telephone system in Britain that allows people to connect their own long-distance calls: *What's the **STD code** for Manchester?*

std. written abbreviation for standard

stead·y[1] /ˈstedi/ *adj* comparative **steadier** superlative **steadiest** **1** happening, developing, or moving in a continuous gradual way: *There has been a **steady decline** in demand over the past 12 months.* | *The market has experienced three years of **steady growth**.* | *We continue to make **steady progress** in improving key areas of our business.*

2 staying at about the same level: *the Federal Reserve's policy of maintaining steady interest rates* | *In December, energy prices plunged 1.4% after **holding steady** the month before.*

3 steady job/work/income a job or work that will definitely continue over a long period of time: *For years, the promise of steady work attracted waves of immigrants to Birmingham.* —**steadily** *adv*: *Business has **steadily increased** year by year.* —**steadiness** *n* [U] *sterling's relative steadiness against other currencies*

steady[2] *v* past tense and past participle **steadied** [I,T] to stop increasing or decreasing and stay about the same, or to make something do this: *The dollar has steadied after early losses on the money markets.* | *Some cautious buying by Japanese life insurance companies steadied the market.*

steal[1] /stiːl/ *v* past tense **stole** past participle **stolen** **1** [I,T] to take something that belongs to someone, without their permission + **from**: *They had admitted stealing from clients.* | *He was accused of stealing ideas from a rival studio.*

2 steal a march on sb to secretly or unexpectedly start something that someone else had planned to do, so that you gain an advantage over them: *One of three rival groups planning movies about Robin Hood tried to steal a march on competitors with a change in strategy and an accelerated production timetable.*

steal[2] *n* **be a steal** *informal* to be very cheap: *At 20 bucks the camera was a steal.*

steam·roll·er /ˈstiːmˌrəʊlə‖-ˌroʊlər/ also **steamroll** *AmE* — *v* [T] *informal* to force someone to do what you want them to do, or to make sure something happens by using all your power and influence: *He steamrollered the bill through parliament despite fierce opposition.* | *Even healthy companies can get steamrolled by an acquiring company.*

steel·works /ˈstiːlwɜːks‖-wɜːrks/ *n* plural **steelworks** [C] a factory where steel is made

steep /stiːp/ *adj* **1** steep prices, charges etc are unusually expensive: *Consumers are paying relatively **steep prices** for dairy products.* | *Anyone caught fiddling their expenses will face **steep fines**.*

2 a steep increase or rise in something is a very big increase: *There has been a **steep decline** in oil prices.* | *a **steep drop** in consumer spending* —**steeply** *adv*: *The mark isn't likely to **fall steeply**.*

steer /stɪə‖stɪr/ *v* [T] **1** to guide the way a situation develops, especially in a way no one notices **steer sth to sb**: *He insisted he had no role in steering business to his son.* **steer sb away from sth**: *Women are often steered away from jobs in core areas such as marketing, production and sales.*

2 to be in charge of an organization, team, or process and make decisions that help it be successful, especially

S

during a difficult time: *Rivetti is steering a comprehensive restructuring program that will transform the company.*
3 steer clear (of) *informal* to try to avoid something or someone unpleasant or difficult: *Will the economy steer clear of a recession?*
4 steer a middle course to choose a course of action that is not extreme and that does not favour one side more than another + **between**: *The President will try to steer a middle course between environmentalists, who have pushed for a permanent ban, and the oil industry, which is eager to resume drilling.*

steering committee —see under COMMITTEE

sten·o /ˈstenəʊ‖-noʊ/ *n AmE* **1** [C] a stenographer: *someone from the* ***steno pool*** (=group of stenographers) **2** [U] stenography

ste·nog·ra·pher /steˈnɒgrəfə‖-ˈnɑːgrəfər/ *n* [C] *AmE* someone whose job is to write down what someone is saying, using stenography, and then type a copy of it: *a* ***court stenographer***

ste·nog·ra·phy /stəˈnɒgrəfi‖-ˈnɑː-/ *n* [U] *AmE* a system of writing quickly by using signs or short forms for words and phrases; SHORTHAND

step[1] /step/ *n* [C] **1** one of a series of things that you do to deal with a problem or to succeed: *The changes are only the* ***first step*** *in a long-term plan.* + **towards**: *a step towards full EMS membership* | *Japan* ***took steps*** *to boost confidence in its tumbling stock market.* | *The new computer line will be a big* ***step forward*** *for Digital.*
2 a stage in a process or a position on a scale + **on**: *Every year you go up one step on the salary scale.* | *I've taken the first step on the managerial ladder.* | *Nina's promotion is quite* ***a step up*** *for one so young.*
3 be out of step if people or their ideas are out of step, they are different from the other people in the group + **with**: *Some business leaders are out of step with the trend toward globalization.*
4 be one step ahead (of sb) to be better prepared for something or know more about something: *Adobe's capacity to stay one step ahead of its rivals*

S

step[2] *v* past tense and past participle **stepped** present participle **stepping** **step forward** to come and offer help: *So far, only one potential investor has stepped forward.* **step forward to do sth**: *Many of his colleagues stepped forward to publicly defend him.*
step down also **step aside** *phr v* [I] to leave your job or official position + **as**: *Eve has stepped down as chairperson.Lister is stepping down in favour of a younger man.*
step in *phr v* [I] to become involved in a discussion or disagreement, especially in order to prevent trouble; intervene: *If the dispute continues, the government will have to step in.*
step sth ↔ **up** *phr v* [T] to increase the amount of an activity or the speed of a process in order to improve a situation: *We will be stepping up production to meet increased demand.*

stepping-stone *n* [C] something that helps you to progress towards achieving something, especially in your work: *Think of this job as a stepping-stone to something better.*

ster·ling /ˈstɜːlɪŋ‖ˈstɜːr-/ *n* [U] the system of money in Britain, based on the pound: *Sterling was trading at $1.6490, up from $1.6470.* | *His salary is paid in* ***pounds sterling.***

sterling bond —see under BOND

sterling silver *n* [U] silver that has 925 or more pure silver parts in every 1000 parts

ste·ve·dore /ˈstiːvədɔː‖-dɔːr/ *n* [C] *AmE* someone whose job is loading and unloading ships; LONGSHOREMAN *AmE*; DOCKER *BrE*

ste·ve·dor·ing /ˈstiːvədɔːrɪŋ/ *n* [U] *AmE* the work of loading and unloading ships —**stevedoring** *adj*: *the stevedoring industry*

stew·ard /ˈstjuːəd‖ˈstuːərd/ *n* [C] **1** a man who serves food and drinks to passengers on a plane or ship
2 also **shop steward** a worker who is elected by members of a TRADE UNION in a factory or other business to represent them when dealing with managers: *A meeting of shop stewards from the National Union of Public Employees approved the strike action.*

stew·ard·ess /ˈstjuːədəs‖ˈstuːərd-/ *n* [C] a woman who serves food and drink to passengers on a plane or ship

stew·ard·ship /ˈstjuːədʃɪp‖ˈstuːərd-/ *n* [U] the way in which someone controls and takes care of an organization or event: *Mr. Manzi's stewardship of Lotus came under fire.*

stick·er /ˈstɪkə‖-ər/ *n* [C] a small piece of paper or plastic with a picture or writing on it that you can stick on to something

sticker price —see under PRICE[1]

stick·y /ˈstɪki/ *adj* **1** sticky prices do not change very much and are slow to react to changing market conditions: *prices that tend to be sticky and are unresponsive to shifts in the market*
2 have sticky fingers *informal* to be likely to steal something

stiff /stɪf/ *v* [T] *AmE informal* to not pay someone money that you owe them or that they expect to be given, for example by not leaving a tip in a restaurant —see also WORKING STIFF

stim·u·late /ˈstɪmjəleɪt/ *v* [T] to encourage an activity to begin or develop further: *Banks were urged to lower credit-card interest rates to* ***stimulate consumer spending.*** | *efforts to* ***stimulate demand*** *for new telephone installations* —**stimulative** *adj*: *stimulative fiscal measures* —**stimulation** *n* [U] *short-term economic stimulation*

stim·u·lus /ˈstɪmjələs/ *n* [singular, U] something that helps a process to develop more quickly or strongly + **to**: *The discovery of oil acted as a stimulus to the local economy.*
fiscal stimulus ECONOMICS an attempt to make the economy grow faster by reducing taxes: *'Politicians will have to produce a recovery with fiscal stimulus,' he says.*
monetary stimulus ECONOMICS an attempt by a government to make the economy grow faster by increasing the MONEY SUPPLY (=the amount of money in the economy): *There is a risk that the Fed will provide too little monetary stimulus, causing weak growth or renewed recession.*

sting /stɪŋ/ *v* past tense and past participle **stung**
sting sb **for** sth *phr v* [T] *BrE informal* to charge someone too much for something: *The garage stung him for £300.*

stint /stɪnt/ *n* [C usually singular] a limited or fixed period of time of doing a particular job + **as**: *his two-year stint as managing director* | ***Doing a stint*** *overseas is important to getting ahead in many companies.*

sti·pend /ˈstaɪpend/ *n* [C] an amount of money paid regularly to someone such as a priest or a student as wages or money to live on: *Coaching stipends run to only $1,200 a year for a head football coach.*

stipendiary magistrate —see under MAGISTRATE

stk. written abbreviation for stock

stock[1] /stɒk‖stɑːk/ *n* **1** [C,U] *especially AmE* FINANCE one of the shares into which ownership of a company is divided, or these shares considered together: *The company might* ***issue*** (=make available and sell) ***stock*** *in order to pay down debt.* | *the superior returns that investors are likely to earn if they* ***hold*** (=own) ***stock*** *for five* *years or longer* | *More than 100 companies have filed plans to* ***sell stock*** *to the public for the first time,* | *Chartwell sold a 10 million-share* ***block of*** *Avon* ***stock*** (=a large quantity of shares, usually more than 10,000) *on March 14.* | ***Stock prices*** *were up in heavy trading.*

2 (Class) A/B/C stock different classes of a company's stock. Each class has different characteristics, for example the right to vote at shareholders' meetings: *The Class B stock carries 10 times the votes of the Class A common.*

active stock [C,U] a stock that is being actively bought and sold: *Sun Microsystems was the day's most active stock as more than 5.8 million shares changed hands.*

advancing stocks [plural] stocks that increase in value on a particular day of trading on a stockmarket; ADVANCERS: *Advancing stocks led those retreating 291 to 269.*

authorized stock also **authorised stock** *BrE* [U] the largest amount of capital a company is allowed to have in the form of shares; AUTHORIZED CAPITAL; AUTHORIZED ISSUE: *To finance the expansion programme, PAL doubled its authorised stock from 5 billion to 10 billion pesos.*

barometer stock [C,U] shares in certain important companies whose performance gives an idea of the condition of the stockmarket as a whole

bearer stock [C,U] shares that are owned by the person who possesses the documents related to them, even though their name might not be recorded on an official list: *UBS plans to replace one old share with five new ones, bringing down the price of its bearer stock from around SFr3,790 to SFr758.*

Big Board stock [C,U] stock that is traded on the NEW YORK STOCK EXCHANGE: *The Big Board stock symbol for Jenny Craig Inc. is JC.*

blue chip stock also **blue-chip stock** [C,U] stock in a well-managed company with a large amount of PAID-UP CAPITAL and a long record of paying profits to SHAREHOLDERS during good and bad economic conditions; BLUE-CHIP SHARE: *For more than 50 years, I have bought blue-chip stocks that pay a 5% dividend, and I have done very well.*

bonus stock [C,U] new shares given out instead of money to people already owning shares in a company as their share of the profits made by the company

capital stock [U] ◆ *AmE* the amount of capital a company has from investors who have bought shares; SHARE CAPITAL: *WDLG controls about 12% of Hoesch's capital stock, but hasn't decided what to do with the shares.*

classified common stock [C,U] *AmE* stock that has been divided into classes, usually class A whose holders have no right to vote and class B whose holders have a right to vote

common stock [C,U] the most frequent type of stock in most companies. If the company is in financial difficulty, DIVIDENDS on common stock are made only after those made on some other types of stock, such as PREFERENCE STOCK: *Total corporate pension investments in common stocks has remained constant at about 46%.* | *Corporations issued a record $56 billion of common stock.*

consolidated stock [U] British government bonds or SECURITIES that have no fixed date for repayment and so will continue to pay interest; CONSOLS

convertible loan stock [C,U] a loan to a company in the form of bonds that can later be exchanged for shares under certain conditions

convertible stock [U] one type of a company's stock that may be exchanged for another under certain conditions

cumulative preferred stock [U] a class of PREFERENCE STOCK where if the company does not pay DIVIDENDS in some years, the amount of these dividends is paid in later years, and not lost to the stockholder: *Forest Oil Corp. said that it deferred payment of cash dividends on its $15.75 cumulative preferred stock, due Sept. 1.*

cyclical stock [C] stock in companies whose performance is most affected by the rate of growth, or lack of it, in the economy as a whole: *Cyclical stocks such as the chemical, steel, and machine building sectors continue to suffer from the weak global economy.*

debenture stock [C,U] a type of stock that pays interest rather than DIVIDENDS; DEBENTURE

declining stocks [plural] stocks that fall in value on a particular day of trading on a stockmarket; DECLINERS: *On the Big Board, declining stocks beat advancers by 912 to 585.*

defensive stock [C] stock in companies that people think will still make good profits even if economic growth is low: *Weakening in Japan's industrial output made investors focus on defensive stocks such as pharmaceutical and food companies.*

diluted stock [U] all the stock of a company considered together, especially after a SHARE ISSUE (=when new shares are made available and sold), and DIVIDENDS are spread over a larger number of shares: *The public currently owns about 18% of RJR's* ***fully diluted stock.***

Exchequer stock [C] a British government bond that receives a particular rate of interest paid twice a year, and must be sold back to the borrower on a particular date

glamour stocks also **glamor stocks** *AmE* [plural] stocks in companies that investors are attracted to, for example because of their high growth rate, but that may fall in value quickly: *Glamour stocks have been bid up too high by unrealistic expectations.*

growth stock [C] a stock that increases in value quickly: *She favors the big growth stocks – blue-chip companies in the drugs, beverage and food businesses.*

income stock [C,U] stock that is attractive for the DIVIDENDS it pays, rather than any increase in its value: *IBM became income stock, one that some investors buy as much for its 4.3% dividend yield as for its growth prospects.*

large-cap stock also **large-capitalization stock** [C] a stock in a company with a large amount of SHARE CAPITAL (=total share value); LARGE-CAP: *I think secondary stocks will continue to outperform the large-cap stocks.*

listed stock [C] a stock in a company that is traded on a particular stockmarket, or on a country's main stockmarket: *While the listed stocks fell in the afternoon, OTC stocks eased higher.*

loan stock [U] stock which pays interest rather than DIVIDENDS

mid-cap stock or **mid capitalization stock**, also **mid capitalisation stock** *BrE* [C] a stock in a company with a medium amount of SHARE CAPITAL (=total share value); MID-CAP

new stock also **newly-issued stock** [C,U] a company's stock that has just been made available for sale, or just sold for the first time, rather than stock that already exists: *Fees earned by Wall Street investment banks for underwriting new stocks and bonds jumped to $10 billion last year.* | *It still isn't clear where the firm's newly-issued stock will trade.*

non-voting stock also **nonvoting stock** *AmE* [U] a type of stock that does not give holders the right to vote at shareholders' meetings: *Some investors oppose all nonvoting stock because you end up with nonresponsive management.*

no-par stock also **no-par-value stock** [U] in the US, stock that does not have a particular value attached to it when it is ISSUED (=first sold)

ordinary stock especially *BrE* [C,U] another name for COMMON STOCK

outstanding stock [U] all of a company's stock that

currently exists and is held by shareholders: *The company said it would undertake a share buyback programme, accounting for about 10% of its outstanding stock.*

over-the-counter stock abbreviation **OTC stock** [C,U] stock in a newer or smaller company that is not bought and sold through dealers on the main stockmarket but on a computer-based market such as NASDAQ: *the Nasdaq trading system, where traders buy and sell over-the-counter stocks on electronic screens*

partly-paid stock [C,U] stock that has been partly paid for, rather than a FULLY-PAID STOCK: *The shares have surprised investors since the partly-paid stock was first quoted at 100p a year ago.*

penny stock [C] a stock that is only worth a few cents or pence, perhaps in a company whose performance has been bad recently but that may improve, or in a new, relatively unknown company

preference stock also **preferred stock** [C,U] stock on which, if a company is in financial difficulty, DIVIDENDS may still be paid even if they are not paid on ordinary shares. Dividends on preference stock are usually in the form of fixed interest payments: *Eastland said the preferred stock will pay an initial dividend rate of 6% that will rise to 14% in the fourth year.*

quoted stock *BrE* [C,U] another name for LISTED STOCK: *The Warsaw Stock Exchange now has 88 quoted stocks.*

red chip stock also **red-chip stock** [C] stock in a Chinese company that is listed on the Hong Kong Stock Exchange

redeemable stock [U] a class of stock that a company agrees to buy back from its holders under certain conditions: *Roche has the right to buy all of the redeemable stock at various dates over the next five years.*

registered stock ◆ [C,U] stock where ownership is recorded on a list, and which is not always shown on SHARE CERTIFICATES: *If your stock is held in bearer form, you might find that settlement is quicker if you switch the holding into registered stock.*

◆ [C,U] used to talk about the stockmarket where a particular stock is traded: *HSBC London-registered stock was up 17 1/2 to £14.76.*

second-tier stock [C,U] shares in companies that are not bought and sold on the main stockmarket in a particular place: *The Credit Suisse stock index, measuring mainly second-tier Swiss stocks, was up 0.3%.*

sleeper stock [C,U] a small stock that has not been performing particularly well, but that may do well in the future; SLEEPER: *He looks for sleeper stocks seeming to have little downside risk and prefers stocks that trade at low multiples to their earnings.*

small stock also **small cap stock, small capitalization stock, small capitalisation stock** *BrE* [C,U] a stock in a company with a small amount of SHARE CAPITAL (=total share value); SMALL-CAP: *Small stocks have underperformed larger stocks for the past six years.*

split stock [U] stock that has been divided into smaller units. This is done to reduce the share price and make them easier to buy and sell, and does not affect the value of the company to shareholders: *American Brands declared a 2-for-1 stock split on its common shares.*

underlying stock [C,U] the actual stock related to OPTIONS (=the right to buy shares at a particular price within a particular period of time) or other DERIVATIVES such as FUTURES: *Put options gain in price when the underlying stocks decline in value.*

unlisted stock also **unquoted stock** *BrE* [C,U] one of the stocks that is not traded on a main stockmarket, but rather on the OVER-THE-COUNTER MARKET (=computer-based trading in shares of newer and smaller companies): *Unlisted stocks were unable to match the gains posted by New York Stock Exchange issues yesterday.*

value stock [C,U] a stock that seems cheap in relation to the profits, earnings etc of the company

volatile stock [C,U] stock that moves up and down in value quickly and by large amounts: *The company's volatile stock peaked at $46.50 in July and traded at $5 in December.*

voting stock [U] stock in a company that gives the person who owns it the right to vote at the company's GENERAL MEETING: *The offer must be accepted by shareholders representing at least 90% of Volvo's voting stock.*

watered stock [C,U] stock offered to investors by a company at much higher prices than they are actually worth

when-issued stock [C,U] *AmE* stock that is being traded before it has been officially ISSUED (=made available): *USX rolled out two new when-issued stocks that provide shareholders with a choice of investing in either the company's steel operations or its oil operations.*

widow-and-orphan stock [C,U] stock that is a very safe investment: *Investments in regional brokerages are not 'widow and orphan' stocks, Mr. Athey warns. They are volatile.*

3 [C,U] also **government stock** FINANCE one of the bonds sold by a government to finance its BUDGET DEFICIT (=the difference between what it gets in taxes and what it spends). Government bonds are usually considered to be a very safe form of investment; GOVERNMENT SECURITY

gilt stocks also **gilt-edged stocks** [plural] bonds sold by the British government to raise money; GILTS: *The Bank of England signalled that there would be no drop in UK interest rates, and longer-dated gilt-edged stocks gained as much as £1.*

irredeemable stock also **undated stock** [C,U] government bonds with no MATURITY DATE (=date when they will be bought back from lenders by the government): *These government stocks with no final maturity are a historical survival and no new irredeemable stocks have been issued for many years.*

local authority stock *BrE* [C,U] bonds sold by local government authorities; MUNIS *AmE*: *Local authority stocks provide long-term funding.*

tap stock [C,U] British government stock that is not sold immediately it is ISSUED (=made available). It is sold over a period of time when the government needs to or is able to: *The Bank took advantage of rising bond prices to sell what was left of its tap stocks.*

Treasury stock [C,U] one of the names used by the British government for its stock: *If 5% Treasury stock, originally priced at £100, can be bought on the market at £50, the buyer receives £5 a year from the government.*

4 [C,U] also **stocks** a supply of a COMMODITY (=oil, metal, farm product etc) that has been produced and is kept to be used when needed: ***Global stocks*** (=total stocks in the world) *of cocoa amount to 2 million tons, the equivalent of about eight months usage.*

buffer stock [C,U] a stock of a COMMODITY (=oil, metal, farm product etc) that is used to control the level of its supply in order to influence prices: *the International Natural Rubber Agreement, the global pact which controls buffer stocks*

5 [C,U] *especially BrE* a supply of RAW MATERIALS (=materials for use in manufacturing) or parts before they are used in production, or a supply of FINISHED GOODS; INVENTORY: *Many builders do not consider it financially viable to* ***maintain*** (=keep) *a stock of materials.* | *If an unexpected rise in demand occurs, they meet it partly by producing more and partly by* ***running down*** (=reducing by using) *their* ***stocks*** *of finished goods.* | *It keeps a careful eye on* ***stock control*** *to make sure that inventories are maintained at 'sensible levels'.*

6 [C,U] a supply of goods, kept for sale by a shop or other RETAILER: *Equipment importers had big stocks of last year's skis and boots still on their hands.* | *Heffers Children's Bookshop makes sure they always have these titles* ***in stock.*** | *Kodak ships film and paper overnight to labs* *when dealers are* ***out of stock*** (=have none left). | *Distribution control has cut out two layers from the chain, giving greater control of retail* ***stock levels*** (=quantities in stock).

average stock [C,U] ACCOUNTING the average value of stock during a financial year, calculated by adding together the values of the stock at the beginning and end of the year and dividing by two

closing stock [C,U] the amount in stock at the end of a particular period of time: *The cost of the goods sold is often calculated by taking the opening stock plus purchases less closing stock.*

dead stock [C,U] a stock of something that is not selling very well or at all, and is not profitable to keep

opening stock [C,U] the amount in stock at the beginning of a particular period of time: *Opening stocks of coffee were 32.9 million bags. Rothfos, the German trader, forecast that these would fall to 31.3 million over the coming year.*

7 [C,U] PROPERTY the houses, flats etc available in a particular place: *The list of discounts offered by housebuilders gets longer as the stock of unsold new homes rises.* | *the role of rent control in reducing the* ***housing stock*** *of many cities*

8 [C,U] ECONOMICS an amount of gold, money etc that a country, company etc has available at a particular time: *The US gold stock was down $1 million in November to $11.06 billion.* | *By making goods scarce, high tax policies render the existing stock of money more inflationary.*

capital stock [C,U] ECONOMICS the amount of money invested by a country, company etc at any one time: *Between 1955 and 1970 the capital stock in US manufacturing rose by 74%.*

money stock [U] ECONOMICS the amount of money in an economy at a particular time; MONEY SUPPLY: *Money-supply growth was exceptionally slow and the real money stock actually declined.*

9 [U] farm animals, especially cattle; LIVESTOCK: *He invested in stock, building up a herd of 1000 cattle.* —see also ROLLING STOCK

stock² *v* [T] **1** if a shop stocks a particular product, it keeps a supply of it to be sold: *Independent boutiques that sell expensive clothes are stocking less merchandise as their sales drop.*

2 to have a supply of something so that it is ready be used: *The parts depot in California is* ***well-stocked*** (=has lots of parts in stock). —see also OVERSTOCK

stock up *phr v* [I] to buy a lot of something to use when you want to + **on**: *Wholesalers had been stocking up on juice before cash prices rose.*

stock·bro·ker /ˈstɒkˌbrəʊkə‖ˈstɑːkˌbroʊkər/ *n* [C] FINANCE a person or organization whose job is to buy and sell shares, bonds etc for investors and sometimes for themselves: *The securities can be sold any business day by placing an order with a stockbroker.*

stock·bro·ker·age /ˈstɒkˌbrəʊkərɪdʒ‖ˈstɑːkˌbroʊ-/ *n* [C] FINANCE a financial institution that buys and sells shares, bonds etc: *The shares were sold to Smith New Court, a London stockbrokerage firm, which resold them to institutional investors.*

stock certificate —see under CERTIFICATE

stock control —see under CONTROL¹

stock dividend —see under DIVIDEND

stock exchange —see under EXCHANGE¹

Stock Exchange Alternative Tracking Service —see SEATS

Stock Exchange Automated Quotation System —see SEAQ

Stock Exchange Trading System —see SETS

stock fund —see under FUND¹

stock·hold·er /ˈstɒkˌhəʊldə‖ˈstɑːkˌhoʊldər/ *n* [C] *especially AmE* FINANCE a person or organization that owns shares in a particular company; SHAREHOLDER: *He believed that such a large stockholder is entitled to some board seats.*

controlling stockholder also **majority stockholder** the stockholder with more than half the shares in a company: *He is the company's chairman, chief executive officer and controlling stockholder.*

minority stockholder a stockholder that owns less than half the shares in a company: *The court ruled that the company's dual-class structure is unfair to minority stockholders.*

stockholder equity —see under EQUITY

stockholder of record *n* plural **stockholders of record** [C] the owner of stock on a particular date, in relation to the right to DIVIDEND payments etc: *The stock split will be distributed on June 21 to stockholders of record May 16.*

stock·hold·ing /ˈstɒkˌhəʊldɪŋ‖ˈstɑːkˌhoʊl-/ *n* [C] FINANCE an amount of a company's shares owned by one person or organization: *Itel plans to sell its 15% stake in Santa Fe Pacific through a public offering of the stockholding.* | *Before you call your broker and* ***dump*** (=sell, even at a loss) *all your* ***stockholdings****, consider the data carefully.*

stock index —see under INDEX¹

stock index futures —see under FUTURES

stock-index option —see under OPTION

stock-in-trade *n* [U] **1** words or behaviour that are typical of someone: *politicians whose stock-in-trade is economic populism*

2 a business's normal activity: *After he finished his apprenticeship, kitchens became a part of his stock-in-trade.*

stock·ist /ˈstɒkɪ̈st‖ˈstɑː-/ *n* [C] *BrE* a person, company, or shop that keeps a particular product for sale: *Rodier Hommes is building up a network of approved stockists around the UK.*

stock·job·ber /ˈstɒkˌdʒɒbə‖ˈstɑːkˌdʒɑːbər/ *n* [C] another name for JOBBER

stock·list /ˈstɒklɪst‖ˈstɑːk-/ *n* [C] a list of the goods that a seller, dealer etc has available to sell: *The Amazon Books stocklist runs to 2.5 million titles.*

stock manipulation —see under MANIPULATION

stock market —see under MARKET¹

stock·mar·ket /ˈstɒkˌmɑːkɪ̈t‖ˈstɑːkˌmɑːr-/ also **stock market** *n* [C] FINANCE a market where company shares are traded; STOCK EXCHANGE: *The stock market clearly believes that the economy will turn around next year.* | *The company's shares missed out on the recent* ***stock market rally*** (=increase in share prices). | *the 1987* ***stock market crash*** (=sudden, big fall in prices)

stock merger —see under MERGER

stock of record *n* [U] *AmE* used to talk about the owner of stock on a particular date, in relation to the right to receive DIVIDEND payments etc: *The board declared a dividend of 30 cents a share, payable Sept. 29 to stock of record Sept. 10.*

stock option —see under OPTION

stock·out /ˈstɒkaʊt‖ˈstɑːk-/ *n* [C] *especially AmE* the situation of not having particular goods in stock, because they have all been used or sold: *When stockouts of Christmas trees occurred, the company brought in new supplies, only to be left with a surplus after Christmas.*

stock parking *n* [U] FINANCE when the owner of shares leaves them with another person or organization, usually in order to hide their real ownership: *Regulators charged them with 20 violations of securities laws and rules, including stock parking.*

stock·pile¹ /ˈstɒkpaɪl‖stɑːk-/ *v* [T] to keep adding to a large supply of goods, weapons etc that are being kept for use or possible use in the future: *The US government began stockpiling oil in response to the Arab oil embargo.* **—stockpiler** *n* [C] *We have yet to see one of the big stockpilers of gold announce significant disposals.* **—stockpiling** *n* [U] *the stockpiling of chemical and biological weapons*

stockpile[2] *n* [C] a large supply of goods, weapons etc that are being kept for use in the future, often because they will be difficult to obtain later: *Following poor harvests, stockpiles of grain are expected to fall to their tightest level for 20 years.*

stock price —see under PRICE[1]

stock rights —see under RIGHT

stock•room /ˈstɒkrʊm, -ruːm‖ˈstɑːk-/ *n* [C] a room where stocks of materials or goods are kept, in a shop, office, or factory

stock savings bank —see under BANK[1]

stock split —see under SPLIT[2]

stock•tak•ing /ˈstɒkˌteɪkɪŋ‖ˈstɑːk-/ *n* [C,U] *BrE* an occasion when a company or shop checks the quantities of materials and goods that it has a supply of; INVENTORY *AmE*: *The records must contain a statement of stock held at the end of the financial year and statements of stocktakings from which that was prepared.* | *The group uncovered the loss after* ***year-end stocktaking***. **—stocktake** *n* [C] *The accountants never attended the stocktake or checked the valuation.* **—stocktake** *v* [I] **—stocktaker** *n* [C] *An outside stocktaker was appointed to draw up an annual inventory of all stocks.*

stock-ticker *n* [C] an electronic sign showing share prices

stock turn *n* [U] —see ***stock turnover*** under TURNOVER

stock turnover —see under TURNOVER

stock valuation —see under VALUATION

stock warrant —see under WARRANT[1]

S

stock•yard /ˈstɒkjɑːd‖ˈstɑːkjɑːrd/ *n* [C] a place where cattle etc are delivered so that they can be sold, sent to an ABATTOIR (=place where animals are killed for their meat) etc: *Deliveries of cattle to Argentina's biggest stockyard dropped by about 30% with the start of a two-day strike by farmers.*

stop[1] /stɒp‖stɑːp/ *v* past tense and past participle **stopped** present participle **stopping** [T] **1** to prevent someone from doing something or something from happening: *The government should intervene to stop the takeover.* | *How can we stop the decline in sales?* **stop sb/sth (from) doing sth**: *This latest crisis did not stop the Bank of France cutting its key interest rates.* | *News of the takeover immediately stopped the company's shares from sliding.*

2 to no longer continue to do sth: *What time do you stop work?* | *Lack of funds forced us to stop production.* **stop doing sth**: *Japan's four leading brokerages agreed to stop issuing new shares for a month.* | *You can stop paying premiums at any time.*

3 stop a cheque *BrE* **stop payment on a check** *AmE* to tell a bank not to pay a cheque you have written: *Staff are failing to charge customers for such services as stopping cheques or returning standing orders unpaid.*

4 to prevent money from being paid after you agree to pay it **stop sth from sth**: *Money for breakages will be stopped from your wages.*

stop[2] *n* **1 come to a stop** to stop happening: *Production came to a virtual stop during the two-week strike.*

2 put a stop to sth to prevent something from continuing or happening: *These quotas put a stop to further export growth.*

3 put a stop on a cheque to tell a bank not to pay a cheque you have written

stop-go *adj* **stop-go policy/approach etc** *BrE* ECONOMICS a way of controlling the economy by deliberately restricting government spending for a period of time and then restricting it for a time: *The uncertainty of such stop-go policies reduced business confidence and discouraged investment.* **—stop-go** *n* [U] *The policy of expanding and then contracting demand, 'stop-go', was a result of the direct conflict between the employment and balance of payments objectives.*

stop order also **stop-loss order** —see under ORDER[1]

stop•page /ˈstɒpɪdʒ‖ˈstɑːp-/ *n* **1** [C] a situation in which workers stop working for a short time as a protest: *The* ***stoppage*** *was* ***called*** (=organized) *to protest against the cancellation of wage agreements.*

2 [C,U] the act of stopping something from moving or happening: *complete stoppages of production*

3 stoppages [plural] *BrE* money from your wages that your employer keeps in order to pay your tax, for your PENSION etc; DEDUCTIONS: *I earn £200 a week before stoppages.*

stoppage in transit also **stoppage in transitu** *n* [U] LAW the right of a seller to stop the delivery of goods while they are on their way to the buyer if the seller learns that the buyer has gone bankrupt and so cannot pay for them

stor•age /ˈstɔːrɪdʒ/ *n* [U] **1** the act of keeping or putting something in a place while it is not being used, or the space used for this + **of**: *The premises were previously used for the storage of bank records.* | ***Storage costs*** *often exceed the value of goods stored during the normal turnover period.* | *We do not have much* ***storage capacity*** (=space available for storing things). | *All our office furniture had to be kept* ***in storage***. | *Storage is very limited.* (=there is not much room for storing things).

2 the price you pay for storing goods: *You will have to pay storage.*

3 the means by which information is kept on a computer: *CD-Rom is an ideal system for data storage.* | *disk storage capacity*

storage unit —see under UNIT

store[1] /stɔː‖stɔːr/ *n* [C] **1** a large place that sells many different kinds of goods on several different floors or goods in large quantities: *Most* ***high street stores*** *hold sales in January.* | *The firm has over 800 stores in Britain.* | *the London furniture store, Heals* | *Asda, the stores group*

cash-and-carry store a very large shop where customers representing a business or organization can buy large amounts of goods at cheap prices

chain store one of a group of shops in different towns or cities that are all owned by one organization and sell the same products: *selling clothes for less than half the price charged by leading chain stores*

department store a large shop that is divided into separate departments, each selling a different type of goods: *Department stores tend to be based in city centres and are losing trade to out-of-town sites.* | *Most large department stores now offer in-house credit cards.*

discount store a shop selling goods at much lower prices than elsewhere

multiple store *BrE* another name for a CHAIN STORE

2 *AmE* a place where goods are sold to the public; SHOP: *a liquor store* | *a book store*

co-operative store also **co-op** *AmE* a shop owned and run by a group of people as a co-operative; CO-OPERATIVE SHOP *BrE*

convenience store *AmE* a shop where you can buy food, alcohol, magazines etc, especially one that is open for 24 hours every day: *America's 7-Eleven chain of convenience stores*

dime store *AmE* a shop that sells many different kinds of cheap goods, especially for the house: *Dime stores will always thrive if the location is right and the rent stays reasonable.*

drive-in store also **drive-up store** *AmE* a shop where people can do their shopping without getting out of their cars

general store a shop that sells a wide range of foods and goods, especially one in a small town in the US —see also DRUGSTORE

3 a large building in which goods are stored so they can be used or sold later; WAREHOUSE: *a grain store*

4 a supply of something that you keep to use later + **of**: *A 600-million barrel store of crude oil rests underground in Texas and Louisiana.*

store[2] *v* [T] **1** also **store away** to put things away and keep them until you need them: *Stationery should be stored in a clear and dry cupboard or stockroom.* | *Goods are also stored on the warehouse floor, by high-rise stackings.*

2 to keep information on a computer or DISK: *Standard letters can be stored on floppy disks.* | *All the sales data is stored on a CD-Rom.*

store card —see under CARD

store•front /ˈstɔːfrʌnt‖ˈstɔːr-/ *n* [C] *AmE* the outside part of a shop that faces the street, usually with a large window; SHOP FRONT *BrE*

store•keep•er /ˈstɔːˌkiːpə‖ˈstɔːrˌkiːpər/ *n* [C] *AmE* someone who owns or manages a shop; SHOPKEEPER *BrE*

store label *adj* [only before a noun] *AmE* store label products have the name of the shop that is selling them, rather than the name given to it by the producer; PRIVATE LABEL; OWN BRAND; OWN-LABEL *BrE*

store lease —see under LEASE[2]

store•man /ˈstɔːmən‖ˈstɔːr-/ *n* plural **storemen** [C] a person in charge of a STOREROOM in a factory or shop: *a storeman in a cement works*

store•room /ˈstɔːrʊm, -ruːm/ *n* [C] a room where goods are stored

strad•dle /ˈstrædl/ *n* [C] FINANCE **1** a combination of CALL OPTIONS (=rights to buy particular shares at a fixed price within a certain period of time) and PUT OPTIONS (=rights to sell particular shares at a fixed price within a certain period of time) relating to the same shares and with the same EXERCISE PRICE. The holder of a straddle makes a profit if the share price goes up or down by a large amount during the life of the options: *One investor bought 400 lots of the November 425p puts and calls at 50p each to set up a straddle which would be profitable if the underlying shares move out of a small trading range.*

2 a situation where someone buys FINANCIAL FUTURES or COMMODITIES FUTURES with different delivery dates: *Straddle investments, where an investor reduces risk by buying a contract of one month and selling the contract of another, are popular with producers and consumers of commodities.*

straight /streɪt/ *adj* honest and truthful **be/play straight with sb**: *He always played straight with people, which was why the Government was so respected.*

straight line *adj* ACCOUNTING the straight line method of calculating DEPRECIATION (=fall in value) on an asset involves dividing the original cost of the asset, less its value as SCRAP, by the number of years it is expected to be used. This amount is taken away as a depreciation cost each year of the asset's life: *The* ***straight line method*** *was rejected as it does not reflect the relationship between finance costs and the amount outstanding.* | *Motor vehicles are depreciated* ***on a straight line basis.***

stran•gle /ˈstræŋgəl/ *n* [C] FINANCE another name for STRADDLE: *The strangle would be profitable if the stock price moves out of the 372p–444p range before expiry of the options on Nov 19.*

stran•gle•hold /ˈstræŋgəlˌhəʊld‖-ˌhoʊld/ *n* [C usually singular] *disapproving* complete control over a particular market, industry, or situation + **on/over**: *legislation that will* ***break*** *cable TV's* ***stranglehold*** *on the industry and allow broadcasters to compete on a more even footing* —compare MONOPOLY

strapped /stræpt/ *adj* **strapped (for cash)** *informal* having little or no money at the moment; CASH-STRAPPED: *So many airlines are strapped for cash these days.*

stra•te•gic /strəˈtiːdʒɪk/ *adj* done as part of a plan to gain an advantage or achieve a particular purpose: *There may be strategic advantages in manufacturers remaining separate from retailers.* | *We need to define our* ***strategic goals.*** | ***Strategic decisions*** *are those which determine the long-term policies of the firm.* | *a comprehensive strategic review* —**strategically** *adv*: *This is a strategically important acquisition for the group.* | *We believe that telecoms and computer businesses fit together strategically.*

strategic alliance —see under ALLIANCE

strategic analysis —see under ANALYSIS

strategic business unit —see under UNIT

strategic fit —see under FIT[2]

strategic industry —see under INDUSTRY

strategic marketing —see under MARKETING

strategic partner —see under PARTNER

strategic planning —see under PLANNING

strat•e•gy /ˈstrætɪdʒi/ *n* plural **strategies** **1** [C] a plan or series of plans for achieving an aim, especially success in business or the best way for an organization to develop in the future: *the group's acquisition strategy* | *The Chancellor favours a high interest rate strategy.* + **for**: *We need to* ***develop a strategy*** *for marketing the company's products in each locality.* | *a strategy for growth*

2 [U] the process of skilful planning in general: *Competitive strategy has two weapons: price and differentiation.*

business strategy [C,U] a company's aims in a particular market, and the way it hopes to achieve them: *Investment in research is a key business strategy.*

corporate strategy [C,U] a company's aims in general, and the way it hopes to achieve them: *She has been appointed head of corporate strategy.*

harvesting strategy [C,U] a method for keeping as much profit as possible from a business or activity and investing as little as possible in it

operating strategy [C,U] the way a business is organized and managed in order to produce goods or services: *the effectiveness of the company's cautious operating strategy in containing losses*

pull strategy [C usually singular] MARKETING a method of selling goods in which the manufacturer uses advertising, DIRECT MAIL etc to contact customers directly in order to create demand for the goods. The consumers will ask retailers to stock the goods and the retailers will then ask the manufacturer to supply them with the goods: *Detergent is mainly marketed using a 'pull' strategy of marketing, relying upon consumer advertising to create brand loyalty and pre-sell the product.*

push strategy [C usually singular] MARKETING a method of selling goods in which the manufacturer directs its efforts at the people selling goods, for example by trade DISCOUNTS (=special lower prices). By making the goods widely available the manufacturer hopes to increase sales: *Companies which utilize an aggressive sales policy, based on personal selling, are said to be adopting a push strategy.*

straw poll —see under POLL[1]

stream /striːm/ *n* [C] **1** a long and almost continuous series of things + **of**: *the Federal Reserve's* ***steady stream*** *of interest rate cuts* | *A regular income stream is required to meet these costs.* | *The refinery will* ***come on stream*** (=start producing a stream of oil) *next year.*

2 regular amounts of money coming into a company or organization from a particular activity or source, especially over a long period of time: *The city will get an* ***income stream*** *from property and income taxes paid by the new owners.* | *The new products account for more than 80% of Novell's* ***revenue stream****.*

stream•line /ˈstriːmlaɪn/ *v* [T] to make something such as a business or organization work more simply and effectively: *Much has been done to streamline the production process.* | *The organization has been streamlined to reduce bureaucracy.* | *Over 250 jobs were cut in a* ***streamlining operation****.* —**streamlined** *adj*: *a streamlined accounting system*

street price —see under PRICE[1]

strength /streŋθ, strenθ/ *n* [C] **1** the value of a country's money, especially when this is at a high level + **of**: *the strength of the yen on the international money markets*

2 the power or influence that a person, organization, country etc has + **of**: *the strength of the US economy* | *the relative strength of the bargaining position of the parties*

3 the good qualities or abilities that someone or something has: *One of her management strengths is the ability to delegate.* | *Judging one's own* ***strengths and weaknesses*** *is far from easy.*

strength•en /ˈstreŋθən, ˈstrenθən/ *v* **1** [I,T] if a currency strengthens, or something strengthens it, the currency increases in value: *The Singapore dollar has gradually strengthened against the pound and the US dollar.* | *The G7 industrial nations might act later this month to strengthen the yen.*

2 [T] to improve the financial situation of a country, company etc: *These measures are designed to strengthen the company's market position.*

stress /stres/ *n* [U] continuous feelings of worry about your work or personal life, that prevent you from relaxing: *a* ***stress-related*** *illness* (=one caused by stress) | *She's been* ***under stress*** *at work.* | *a* ***stress management*** *consultant* (=someone who helps people deal with stress) —**stressful** *adj*: *a stressful job* | *stressful working conditions*

S

stretch /stretʃ/ *v* **1** [T] if something stretches an amount of money or a supply of something, it uses it up so you have hardly enough for your needs: *Our finances are* ***stretched to the limit****.* | *We're completely stretched at the moment.*

2 [I,T] to make an amount of money last longer than usual by being careful how it is spent and not wasting it: *All departments are having to stretch their budgets.*

3 [I,T] MARKETING if a company stretches a brand, it starts to use an existing brand name on a different type of product, hoping that people will buy it because they recognize the name: *Following Coca-Cola's decision to market clothes, we ask how far a brand can be stretched.*

strict liability —see under LIABILITY

strike[1] /straɪk/ *n* [C] a period of time when a group of workers deliberately stop working because of a disagreement about pay, working conditions etc: *a one-day postal strike* | *Female staff have* ***gone on strike*** *for equal pay.* | *Staff* ***held a*** *two-hour* ***strike****.* | *Lorry drivers have been* ***on strike*** *for three weeks.*

all-out strike a strike involving all the workers in a company or union

general strike a strike involving most of the workers in a country

lightning strike *BrE* a strike that is held without any warning

official strike a strike organized and approved by the main union in an industry

sit-down strike a strike in which workers come to their place of work but refuse to do any work or to leave

sympathy strike a strike intended to give support to another group of workers who are already on strike

token strike a short strike, usually lasting only a few hours, that is used as a warning that more serious action may follow if the workers' demands are not listened to

unofficial strike a strike which has not been organized or approved by the main union

wildcat strike a strike in which workers suddenly stop working in order to protest about something, but which has not been approved by the union

strike[2] *v* past tense and past participle **struck** **1** [I] to deliberately stop working for a time because of a disagreement about pay, working conditions etc: *the right to strike* + **for**: *Dock workers are striking for more pay.*

2 strike a deal/bargain to make an agreement with someone: *The US and China have recently struck a deal over trade.* | *Salyut struck a $16 million deal with Inmarsat.*

3 strike gold/oil etc to suddenly find gold, oil etc, especially after you have been looking for it for some time

strike off *phr v* **be struck off** *BrE* if a doctor, lawyer etc is struck off, their name is removed from the official list of people who are allowed to work as doctors, lawyers etc

strike out *phr v* **strike out on your own** to start doing something new, without other people's help: *He left the family business and struck out on his own.*

strike action —see under ACTION

strike ballot —see under BALLOT[1]

strike•bound /ˈstraɪkbaʊnd/ *adj* not able to move, work, or operate because of a strike: *a strikebound port* | *strikebound firms*

strike•break•er /ˈstraɪkˌbreɪkə‖-ər/ *n* [C] someone who is paid to do the work of a worker who is on strike: *During the strike, the management successfully employed strikebreakers.* —see also BLACKLEG —**strikebreaking** *n* [U] *Limits on strikebreaking by employers are a top priority for unions.*

strike fund —see under FUND[1]

strike pay —see under PAY[1]

strike price —see under PRICE[1]

strik•er /ˈstraɪkə‖-ər/ *n* [C] a worker who is on strike: *There is considerable public support for the strikers.*

strin•gent /ˈstrɪndʒənt/ *adj* **1 stringent rule/control/test** a rule, control etc that is very strict and must be obeyed: *Stringent air quality standards will be imposed on oil companies.*

2 stringent economic conditions exist when there is a severe lack of money and there are strict controls on the supply of money: *Brazil was suffering some labor unrest in response to stringent economic policies.*

string•er /ˈstrɪŋə‖-ər/ *n* [C] someone who regularly sends news stories to a newspaper, but who is not employed by that newspaper: *The news service may replace its workers with stringers and contract employees.*

strip[1] /strɪp/ *n* [C] **1** FINANCE a SECURITY that has been created by separating a bond into the right to interest payments and the right to the repayment of the PRINCIPAL (=the original capital amount). For example, a 30-year bond would create 61 strips, 60 giving the right to receive interest payments every six months and one giving the right to have the capital repaid after 30 years: *The* ***principal strips*** *yield 8.25% in 2009, and the* ***interest strips*** *mature in February and August of each year.*

2 FINANCE an OPTION contract consisting of two PUT OPTIONS and one CALL OPTION on the same shares and with the same price and date

strip[2] *v* past tense and past participle **stripped** present participle **stripping** [T] to separate a bond into strips: *When a bond is stripped, its corpus, or principal due upon maturity, is sold separately without interest payments.* —**stripping** *n* [U] *the practice of stripping* —see also ASSET-STRIPPING, DIVIDEND-STRIPPING

strip mall —see under MALL

strong /strɒŋ‖strɔːŋ/ *adj* **1** a strong economy or business is financially successful, especially because a lot of money is being earned or received: *They fear a strong economy will lead to higher inflation.* | *products that will help the company maintain a* ***strong cash flow***

2 if a financial market is strong, prices in it are rising: *the recent strong performance by the stock market*

3 strong currency/dollar/pound etc a currency whose value is high compared with other currencies: *He blamed the company's poor exports on the strong pound.*

4 strong demand/growth/sales etc high demand or growth, a high number of sales etc: *Demand will continue to be strong and to outpace production.* | *Prices of some bonds moved up a point after strong buying.*

strong·box /ˈstrɒŋbɒks‖ˈstrɔːŋbɑːks/ *n* [C] a box, usually made of metal, that can be locked and is used for keeping valuable things in, for example in a bank or shop

strong·room /ˈstrɒŋrʊm, -ruːm‖ˈstrɔːŋ-/ *n* [C] a special room in a bank, shop etc where valuable objects can be kept safely: *The property deeds are usually kept with a bank or in a solicitor's strongroom.*

structural analysis —see under ANALYSIS

structural engineering —see under ENGINEERING

structural inflation —see under INFLATION

structural unemployment —see under UNEMPLOYMENT

struc·ture /ˈstrʌktʃə‖-ər/ *n* [C,U] the way an organization, system, market etc is organized or put together: *Mr. Reed has set a course that ultimately will dismantle much of the bank's huge bureaucratic structure.* | *a complex structure of affiliated companies*

capital structure also **financial structure** [C] the way a business is financed, for example the amount of debt it has in relation to SHARE CAPITAL (=total share value): *The refinancing improves the company's financial structure and cash flow.*

cost structure [C] an organization's different costs and the way they are related to each other: *We have too high a cost structure, and it's obvious that we can eliminate more jobs.*

highly leveraged capital structure [C] a capital structure in which there is a lot of debt in relation to the amount of capital invested in shares: *Arkla has a highly leveraged capital structure, with debt representing 73% of the company's $3.3 billion capital.*

matrix structure [C] an arrangement in which some employees are responsible to managers in two or more different departments in an organization: *A matrix structure is more common in organizations with a range of different products, brands, or markets.*

stub /stʌb/ *n* [C] the part of something such as a cheque that you complete and keep as a record; COUNTERFOIL: *I went through my* ***check stubs*** *and other records to try to find where the money had gone.*

stub equity —see under EQUITY

stud·y[1] /ˈstʌdi/ *n* plural **studies** [C] a piece of work that is done to find out more about a particular subject or problem, and usually includes a written report: *According to a new study, home ownership in Europe ranges from 29% in Switzerland to 82% in Ireland.* + **of/into**: *a four-month study of the world's largest debt market*

case study a detailed account of the development of a particular person, group, or situation that is studied as a typical or good example of something: *Hancock's sports marketing is the subject of a Harvard Business School case study.*

feasibility study a careful study of how a planned activity will work, how much it will cost, and what income it is likely to produce. Feasibility studies are carried out to discover whether it is worth investing in a particular project + **into**: *a feasibility study into spreading telecommunications into remote areas*

market study the study of how something is sold, who buys it etc: *World trade in spices now amounts to about 600,000 tons a year, worth $3 billion, according to a market study.*

method study a detailed examination of the way something is done in order to see if it can be done cheaper or quicker: *A method study is essential in the successful operation of a growing corporation.*

time and motion study also **time study**, or **motion study** a study of the time spent on particular activities, in order to find out how effective working methods are: *In a time and motion study the question asked is: why can't all workers produce the output achieved by the best workers?*

study[2] *v* past tense and past participle **studied** **1** [T] to carefully consider a plan, idea, document etc: *I haven't had time to study the proposals yet.* | *We are studying a bonus system based on how long brokers stay at the firm.*

2 [T] to watch or examine something carefully over a period of time in order to discover more about it: *Japanese firms are studying the U.S. market very carefully.* | *Chrysler is studying how other companies treat customers.*

3 [I,T] to spend time reading, going to classes etc in order to learn about a subject: *She was studying economics at Fordham University.* | *My brother's* ***studying to be*** *an accountant.*

stunt /stʌnt/ *n* [C] something that is done to attract people's attention to a product or company: *The companies turned the event into a* ***publicity stunt***. | *They deliberately created a controversial commercial as a stunt to get free publicity.*

style /staɪl/ *n* [C] **1** a particular way of doing something, designing something, or producing something, especially one that is typical of a particular time, place, or group of people + **of**: *the Japanese style of stock investment* | *1980s-style excessive spending* | *American-style shopping malls*

house style a particular style of writing used by a company in all the documents, books etc it produces: *We have a house style for all our reports.*

2 the particular way that someone does something or deals with other people + **of**: *an authoritarian style of leadership* | *His tough* ***management style*** *has upset some executives.*

3 a product with a particular design, shape, and appearance: *Each diaper comes in 'girl' and 'boy' styles.* | *This is one of our new styles, a $135 dress shoe with a rubber sole.*

4 LAW the official name or title of a company: *a company trading under the style of Macron Ltd*

sub[1] /sʌb/ *n* [C] *informal* **1** a SUBSCRIPTION

2 *BrE* part of your wages that you receive earlier than usual because you need money; ADVANCE *AmE*

sub[2] *v* past tense and past participle **subbed** present participle **subbing** [T] *BrE informal* to give someone part of their wages earlier than usual or lend them money: *Can you sub me £20 until pay day?*

sub-agent *n* [C] a person or company who works for or represents an agent: *Wood Group Offshore will collect payments via two sub-agents.*

sub·com·mit·tee /ˈsʌbkəˌmɪti/ *n* [C] a small group formed from a committee to deal with a particular subject in more detail: *The Federation Against Software Theft aims to establish a subcommittee to address the problem of Unix software piracy.*

sub·con·tract /ˌsʌbkənˈtrækt‖-ˈkɑːntrækt/ *v* [I,T] if a company subcontracts work, they pay other people to do part of their work for them **subcontract sth to sb**: *Consultants can give advice and then subcontract the actual engineering work to specialists.* —**subcontract** *n* [C] *a $1.2 million subcontract to build diamond multichip*

S

modules —**subcontracting** *n* [U] *Subcontracting is common in the construction industry.*

sub•con•trac•tor /ˌsʌbkənˈtræktə‖-ˈkɑːntræktər/ *n* [C] a person or company who is paid to do part of the work of another person or company: *Always check whether a contractor is using subcontractors, and who is liable if things go wrong.*

sub•ed•i•tor /ˌsʌbˈedɪtə‖-ər/ *n* [C] someone whose job is to examine other people's writing, for example newspaper articles, and to correct mistakes; COPY EDITOR *AmE*

sub•ject /ˈsʌbdʒɪkt/ *adj* **1 subject to** used to say that something is affected or can be affected by something: *Withdrawals are subject to a withholding tax of between 10% and 30%.* | *Dealers convicted of felony charges will be subject to suspension.*

2 subject to dependent on something else: *The proposed transaction is subject to shareholder approval.* | *A deal has been struck, **subject to contract*** (=it is not final until the contract has been signed).

3 subject to average INSURANCE used in insurance contracts to describe a situation in which a property has been insured for less than its real value, and the insured person has to pay for part of any loss: *In the event of under-insurance, the settlement would be subject to average.*

sub ju•di•ce /ˌsʌbˈdʒuːdɪsi‖ˌsʊb ˈjuːdɪkeɪ/ *adj, adv* LAW if a legal case is sub judice, it is now being dealt with by a court, and therefore people are not allowed to discuss it publicly, for example in newspapers: *The newspaper claimed it did not know the material was sub judice.*

sub•lease /ˈsʌb-liːs‖sʌbˈliːs/ *n* [C] an agreement in which someone who rents property from its owner then rents that property to someone else: *The firm has obtained subleases for its excess office space.* —**sublease** *v* [I,T] *Shrewd investors have subleased their property for as much as eight times their rent.*

sub-lessor *n* [C] someone who sublets a property that they rent from its owner

sub•let /sʌbˈlet/ *v* past tense and past participle **sublet** or **subletted** present participle **subletting** [I,T] to rent property that you rent from its owner to another person: *Efforts by the remaining partners to sublet the building failed.* —**sublet** *n* [C] *The showroom is a short-term sublet.*

subliminal advertising —see under ADVERTISING

sub•mis•sion /səbˈmɪʃən/ *n* **1** [U] the act of giving a plan, piece of writing etc to someone in authority for them to consider or approve: *The deadline for the submission of proposals is May 1st.*

2 [C] a plan, piece of writing etc that is given to someone in authority for them to consider or approve: *In its budget submission, NASA will ask Congress for $40 million.*

3 [C] LAW a request or suggestion that is given to a judge or court for them to consider: *The court heard submissions from two Dutch companies.*

sub•mit /səbˈmɪt/ *v* past tense and past participle **submitted** present participle **submitting** [T] **1** to give a plan, piece of writing etc to someone in authority for them to consider or approve: *All applications must be submitted by Monday.*

2 *formal* to agree to obey a person, group, or set of rules + **to**: *We are willing to submit to arbitration.*

3 *formal* to suggest or say something **submit that**: *I submit that the jury has been influenced by the publicity in this case.*

sub•op•ti•mi•za•tion also **suboptimisation** *BrE* /sʌbˌɒptɪmaɪˈzeɪʃən‖-ˌɑːptɪmə-/ *n* [U] when one part or department of a business operates in a way that prevents the whole business from being as successful as it could

sub•or•di•nate¹ /səˈbɔːdɪnət‖-ˈbɔːr-/ *adj* less important or powerful than something or someone: *a subordinate role on the committee* + **to**: *a commission that is subordinate to the Security Council*

subordinate² *n* [C] someone who has a lower position and less authority than someone else in an organization: *Supervisors are regularly evaluated by their subordinates.*

sub•or•di•nat•ed /səˈbɔːdɪneɪtɪd‖-ɔːr-/ *adj* **subordinated bond/debt/loan etc** a bond, debt etc which will be repaid only after all other debts and loans have been paid if the borrower gets into financial difficulty: *The company has $230 million in bank debt and $285 million in subordinated debt.*

subordinated debenture —see under DEBENTURE

subordinated debt —see under DEBT

subordinated notes —see under NOTE¹

sub•par /ˌsʌbˈpɑː◂‖-ˈpɑːr◂/ *adj* **1** something that is subpar is below the level of quality, performance etc that you would usually expect: *The banks had subpar earnings due to bad loans.*

2 a subpar amount is below normal or average: *Inflation is subpar and still going down.*

3 another name for BELOW PAR —see under PAR

sub•poe•na¹ /səˈpiːnə, səb-/ *v* past tense and past participle **subpoenaed** [T] LAW to order someone to come to court and be a witness, or to order someone to give documents to the court: *Telephone companies' records can be subpoenaed.* **subpoena sb to do sth**: *We will subpoena him to give evidence.*

subpoena² *n* [C] LAW a document ordering someone to come to court and be a witness, or ordering someone to give documents to the court: *The regulators issued a subpoena for documents relating to 23 company audits.*

sub•ro•ga•tion /ˌsʌbrəˈgeɪʃən/ *n* [U] INSURANCE the principle that when an insurance company pays a claim, it has the right to any other money that the insured person can get for the same loss, for example money from the person who caused the loss: *There is a **subrogation clause** in the policy.*

sub•rou•tine /ˌsʌbruːˈtiːn/ *n* [C] COMPUTING a part of a computer program containing a set of instructions that will be followed every time the main program calls for it. This is used when the same small job may need to be done several different times as part of a larger job: *Subroutines can increase productivity by simplifying common programming tasks.*

sub•scribe /səbˈskraɪb/ *v* **1** [I] to pay money regularly in order to have a newspaper or magazine sent to you, or to receive a broadcasting or telephone service + **to**: *Only 1% of Japanese households now subscribe to any cable TV network.*

2 [I] FINANCE to ask or agree to buy shares in a company that has offered shares to investors + **for**: *Each rights holder will be entitled to subscribe for one share of IBP common stock.*

3 subscribe to to pay money regularly to be a member of an organization or to help its work: *Chris subscribes to an environmental action group.*

4 [T] *formal* to sign your name: *Please subscribe your name to the document.*

sub•scribed /səbˈskraɪbd/ *adj* **fully/90%/100% subscribed** used to talk about how many of the shares in a SHARE ISSUE (=when shares are made available for sale) have been bought: *The company has an option to issue as many as five million more shares if the offering is fully subscribed.*

sub•scrib•er /səbˈskraɪbə‖-ər/ *n* [C] **1** someone who pays money regularly to have a newspaper or magazine sent to them, or to receive a broadcasting or telephone service: *Country Music Television currently has 15 million subscribers.* + **to**: *We are longtime subscribers to your paper.*

S

2 FINANCE someone who asks or agrees to buy shares in a company that is offering shares to the public + **for**: *Financial forecasts should be disclosed to intending subscribers for shares in the company.*
3 FINANCE someone who agrees to become one of the first members of a LIMITED COMPANY by signing the company's MEMORANDUM OF ASSOCIATION + **to**: *Subscribers to the memorandum must take at least one share each.*
4 a person or organization that signs a document + **to**: *Britain is not a subscriber to the 1970 UNESCO convention.*

subscriber trunk dialling —see STD

sub•scrip•tion /səbˈskrɪpʃən/ *n* **1** [C] an amount of money you pay regularly to receive a newspaper, magazine, or broadcasting or telephone service + **to**: *A subscription to their quarterly report costs $575 a year.* | *The World Service TV channel is a* ***subscription service*** *available to millions of homes around the world.*
2 [C,U] FINANCE when a company offers shares to the public: *They intend to raise £1.9 million via a share subscription.* | *The* ***subscription price*** *for the new shares was 225p.*
3 [U] FINANCE the act of asking to buy or agreeing to buy shares in a company: *25.2 million shares are available for subscription.* | *Existing shareholders have priority* ***subscription rights*** (=the right to subscribe to shares before they are offered to anyone else).
4 [C] *BrE* an amount of money that you pay regularly to be a member of an organization or to help its work; DUES + **for/to**: *his subscription for the Student Union*

sub•sid•i•a•ry[1] /səbˈsɪdiəri‖-dieri/ *n* plural **subsidiaries** [C] a company that is at least half-owned by another company: *Among Berkshire's holdings is an 80.1%-owned subsidiary, Wesco Financial Corp.* + **of**: *Chase Manhattan Bank is a subsidiary of Chase Manhattan Corp.*
partly-owned subsidiary a company that is partly owned by another company, and also has other owners: *BNP Intercontinentale, a partly-owned subsidiary of Banque Nationale de Paris*
wholly-owned subsidiary a company that is completely owned by another company: *A parent company in the UK will be legally responsible for the debts of its wholly-owned subsidiaries.*

subsidiary[2] *adj* connected with, but less important than, something + **to**: *The issue of responsibility is subsidiary to the pressing need to compensate victims.*

subsidiary company —see under COMPANY

sub•si•dize also **subsidise** *BrE* /ˈsʌbsɪdaɪz/ *v* [T] if a government or organization subsidizes a company, activity etc, it pays part of the cost: *The railroad company is partially subsidized by the federal government.* | *Some companies subsidize high-quality childcare facilities.* —**subsidized** *adj* [only before a noun] *heavily subsidized agricultural exports*

subsidized price —see under PRICE[1]

sub•si•dy /ˈsʌbsɪdi/ *n* plural **subsidies** [C] money that is paid by a government or organization to make something such as a particular food or product cheaper to buy, use, or produce: *Billions of dollars were given out in* ***agricultural subsidies****.*

sub•sis•tence /səbˈsɪstəns/ *n* [U] **1** a small amount of money or food that is just enough to survive: *refugees who are dependent for subsistence on support from aid agencies* | *Unfortunately, these people have become used to living at* ***subsistence levels*** (=with just enough food etc to survive). | *Foreign staff are paid* ***subsistence wages*** *by local standards.*
2 **subsistence agriculture/farming etc** farming in which farmers produce just enough food for their families to live on

subsistence allowance —see under ALLOWANCE

subsistence crop —see under CROP

substance and form *n* [U] ACCOUNTING the principle that what actually happens or is actually done may be different to, and sometimes more important than, the legal or technical way that something is described: *arguments between substance and form in financial reporting and taxation contexts*

sub•stan•tial /səbˈstænʃəl/ *adj* large enough in amount or number to be noticeable or to have an important effect: *The document requires substantial changes.* | *You could make substantial monthly savings on your mortgage.* —**substantially** *adv*: *She claimed that, if she was a man, her pay would be substantially higher.*

substantive law —see under LAW

sub•sti•tute[1] /ˈsʌbstɪtjuːt‖-tuːt/ *n* [C] **1** something new or different that can be used instead of something else: *a sugar substitute used by the soft drinks industry* + **for**: *Money is no substitute for* (=cannot take the place of) *management.*
2 someone who does someone else's job for a limited period of time: *We need to find a substitute while she is sick.* —**substitute** *adj* [only before a noun] *a substitute material for ozone-damaging CFCs* | *a substitute driver*

substitute[2] *v* **1** [T] to use or do something new or different instead of something else **substitute sth for/with sth**: *Corporations have been able to avoid some tax by substituting debt for equity.* | *Byproducts are reduced if a different bleaching agent is substituted for pure chlorine.*
2 [I] to be used or done instead of something else + **for**: *a shift towards hydro-electric power and nuclear power to substitute for oil*
3 [I,T] to do someone's job until the person who usually does it is able to do it again + **for**: *Bill substituted for Larry who was off sick.*

sub•sti•tu•tion /ˌsʌbstɪˈtjuːʃən‖-ˈtuː-/ *n* [C,U] when you use or do something new or different instead of something else, or something new that is used or done like this: *There was a substitution of temporary labour for regular workers.*
product substitution ◆ when a company starts making or selling one product instead of another, for example because it is more profitable
◆ when people start buying one product instead of another, for example because it is better, more effective etc —see also ELASTICITY OF SUBSTITUTION

substitution effect —see under EFFECT

sub•ten•ant /ˌsʌbˈtenənt/ *n* [C] someone who pays rent for an office, apartment etc to the person who is renting it from the owner: *The bank financing the deal demanded the power to approve all future subtenants.*

sub•to•tal /ˈsʌbˌtəʊtl‖-ˌtoʊtl/ *n* [C] the total of a set of numbers that is added to other numbers to form a complete total: *We have grouped the costs under appropriate headings with subtotals for each group.*

sub•tract /səbˈtrækt/ *v* [T] to take a number or an amount from something larger **subtract sth from sth**: *Subtract 34% corporate tax from the total.*

sub•ven•tion /səbˈvenʃən/ *n* [C] a gift of money for a special use, especially money given by a person, organization, or government to help the arts, education etc: *The Fine Arts Museum rejected a half-million dollar subvention from a company trading in arms.*

sue /sjuː‖suː/ *v* [I,T] to make a legal claim against someone, especially for an amount of money, because you have been harmed in some way: *If the builders don't fulfil their side of the contract, we'll sue.* + **for**: *The company was sued for nonpayment by their supplier.* | *The council were sued for £2.2 million because of delays in building the bypass.*

suggested retail price —see under PRICE[1]

suit /suːt, sjuːt‖suːt/ *n* **1** [C] LAW a case brought to a court of law by a private person or company, not by the police or government; LAWSUIT: *Ms. Sobel **filed a suit**, claiming sex discrimination.*

2 [C] a set of clothes made from the same material and including a JACKET (=short coat) and trousers or a skirt

3 [C usually plural] *informal* someone such as a manager working for a company that produces books, advertisements, or films, and who has to wear a suit when they are at work: *He looks more like a copywriter than an account managing 'suit'.* —compare CREATIVE[2]

sum[1] /sʌm/ *n* [C] **1** an amount of money: *trading schemes involving **large sums of money** | The company was sold for a sum estimated at $2.3 billion.*

capital sum ◆ FINANCE a single amount of money paid out to an investor by an investment, rather than a series of payments: *Corporate bonds pay a fixed rate of interest and then a capital sum on the bond's maturity. | Some restaurant owners are accepting generous offers for their sites, capital sums which their restaurants rarely produced.*

◆ INSURANCE a single payment to an insured person if certain conditions are met: *An endowment policy pays a capital sum to the insured at a specified time in the future.*

lump sum an amount of money given in a single payment: *Accident victims can receive compensation payments in installments over time, or as a lump sum. | an early retirement plan offering four week's pay for every year of service, plus a **lump-sum payment***

2 the sum of the total produced when you add two or more numbers together: *The sum of the fraudulently obtained loans was nearly 360 billion yen.*

3 *BrE* a simple calculation done by adding, multiplying, dividing etc: *You will have to **do your sums*** (=calculate all the amounts involved), *because interest-free credit may not be the cheapest way to buy.* —see also SUM OF THE DIGITS

sum[2] *v* past tense and past participle **summed** present participle **summing**

sum up *phr v* **1** [I,T] **sum** sth ↔ **up** to give the main information about a report, speech etc in a short statement: *The report is 260 pages long, but Mr. Barrett sums up its message in three words: "Keep standards high". | **To sum up**, I suggest that if you are investing a sizeable sum for the first time, put it into two or three UK-based funds.*

2 [I] LAW when a judge sums up, he or she makes a statement at the end of a trial giving the main facts of the trial: *Summing up, the coroner praised the police for their investigation.*

sum certain —see under CERTAIN

sum insured also **sum assured** *n* [C] the maximum amount of money that an insurer will have to pay, according to an insurance contract: *Their Policy schedule shows a sum insured of £1,000.*

sum·ma·ry[1] /ˈsʌməri/ *n* plural **summaries** [C] a short statement that gives the main information contained in a document, plan etc or the main things that happened at an event, without giving all the details: *Here is a summary of the Commerce Department's report on business inventories.*

summary[2] *adj* [only before a noun] done immediately, without paying attention to the usual processes, rules etc: *This is classed as gross misconduct, justifying **summary dismissal**, ie without notice.*

summing up *n* plural **summings up** [C usually singular] LAW an occasion when a judge makes a statement at the end of a trial giving the main facts of the trial: *The judge, in his summing up, failed to direct the jury that the defendant's previously good character was relevant.*

sum·mons[1] /ˈsʌmənz/ *n* plural **summonses** [C] LAW an official order to appear in a court of law: *Administrators of his estate have **issued a summons** to get him to return to Australia.*

originating summons *BrE* LAW a document which formally begins a legal case where people agree on the facts, but need a judge to decide on the meaning of a law, contract, or other document: *The Crown struck out the originating summons on the grounds that the case was outside its jurisdiction.* —compare WRIT

witness summons *BrE* an order to someone to come to a MAGISTRATE'S COURT and tell the court what they know about a crime or event; SUBPOENA: *He has been served with a witness summons.*

writ of summons a way of starting a legal action by someone who has a claim against a particular person, that orders that person to come to court unless they admit the claim: *Woolwich issued a writ of summons against the Commissioner of Inland Revenue claiming repayment.*

summons[2] *v* [T] LAW to officially order someone to appear in a court of law: *I was summonsed to appear as a witness.*

sum of the digits also **sum of the years' digits**, abbreviation **SOFTY** *n* [singular] ACCOUNTING one of the ways of calculating the DEPRECIATION (=loss of value over time) of an asset. For example, if an asset has a life of four years, 4+3+2+1=10, so in the company's accounts the asset is depreciated 40% in the first year, 30% in the second year and so on

sun·dries /ˈsʌndriz/ *n* [plural] various small objects, especially ones that are not important enough to be named separately: *The Post Office also sold stationery and sundries. | His weekly expenditure included £28.23 for food, £21.38 for travel, and £22.27 for sundries.*

sundries account —see under ACCOUNT[1]

sundry debtor —see under DEBTOR

sunk cost —see under COST[1]

sun·rise /ˈsʌnraɪz/ *adj* [only before a noun] sunrise industries, companies etc are new and growing very quickly, working in new TECHNOLOGIES. Sunrise industries are often found in areas where there was little industry in the past: *Even **sunrise companies** specialising in new technology have found it necessary to cut their work-force. | It may be possible to subsidize **sunrise industries**.* —see also ***sunrise industry*** under INDUSTRY

sun·set /ˈsʌnset/ *adj* [only before a noun] **1** sunset industries, companies etc are no longer very profitable or important and are based on old TECHNOLOGIES: *The parent company dismissed sewing machines as a **sunset industry**. | The **sunset sectors** of steel and shipbuilding have been undercut by more efficient producers in the Pacific basin.*

2 sunset rules or laws are ones which cancel rules or laws that were made in the past: *The new **sunset law** will eliminate statutes that are more than 10 years old. | The **sunset provisions** will cancel most tax increases since June 30.*

sunset industry —see under INDUSTRY

sun·shine /ˈsʌnʃaɪn/ *adj* [only before a noun] sunshine laws, rules etc are designed to make it easier for people to find out how an organization operates, what profits it makes etc: *Pattison thought expanding **sunshine laws** to include government departments might help. | Open meetings were introduced as part of the **sunshine policy** at the Accountancy Institute.*

su·per /ˈsuːpə, ˈsjuː- ‖ ˈsuːpər/ *n* [C] *informal* spoken abbreviation for SUPERINTENDENT

super- /suːpə, sjuː- ‖ suːpər/ *prefix* used to show that something is bigger or more powerful than other things of the same kind: *The merger could create the first of a new breed of world-class superbanks. | a new super-fast version of Intel's microprocessor | purchase agreements for six supertankers*

su·per·an·nu·a·tion /ˌsuːpərænjuˈeɪʃən, ˌsjuː- ‖ ˌsuː-/

S

n [U] *BrE* HUMAN RESOURCES money paid to someone after they have finished their working life or are too ill to continue working; PENSION: *Financing your retirement through superannuation is no longer considered sufficient.* | *Some authorities operate* ***superannuation funds*** *on behalf of past employees.*

super audio compact disk —see SACD

su·per·cat /'su:pəkæt, 'sju:-‖'su:pər-/ *n* [C] *journalism disapproving* a businessperson who earns a very large amount of money for running a company, especially one that was previously owned by the government before being PRIVATIZED (=sold to the public); FAT CAT: *The fat cats of the 1990s are chicken feed compared with the supercats who run the computer giants such as Microsoft and IBM in this century.*

su·per·com·put·er /'su:pəkəmˌpju:tə, 'sju:-‖'sju:pərkəmˌpju:tər/ *n* [C] a large and powerful computer that can do complex jobs or process a lot of information very quickly

Su·per·fund /'su:pəˌfʌnd, 'sju:-‖'su:pər-/ *n* [singular] in the US, an amount of money kept by the government for cleaning areas damaged by industry: *More than 20,000 sites are expected to require Superfund cleanups.*

su·per·in·tend /ˌsu:pərɪn'tend, ˌsju:-‖ˌsu:-/ *v* [I,T] *formal* to be in charge of something, especially someone's work, and to control how it is done: *He went to Bombay to superintend a large land reclamation scheme.*

su·per·in·tend·ent /ˌsu:pərɪn'tendənt, ˌsju:-‖ˌsu:-/ *n* [C] someone who is officially in charge of a place or area of work: *Things got worse when the superintendent left to start a competing business.*

su·pe·ri·or[1] /su:'pɪəriə, sju:-‖sʊ'pɪrɪər/ *adj* **1** better in quality than other things of the same kind: *Hamptons let superior apartments and houses to substantial international companies.* | *Many participants in the survey did not think round teabags were in any way superior.*

2 having a higher position or rank than someone or something: *Civil servants are accountable for their decisions either to* ***superior officers*** *or to the general public.* | *The case was filed in the Los Angeles* ***superior court****.*

superior[2] *n* [C] someone with a higher position or rank than another person, especially in a job: *Superiors sometimes find it difficult to delegate their authority.* | *You should communicate clearly both to subordinates* (=people of a lower position or rank) *and your superiors.*

su·per·mar·ket /'su:pəˌmɑ:kɪt,'sju:-‖'su:pərˌmɑ:r-/ *n* [C] a large shop selling very many different kinds of food and other products used especially in the home: *Yaohan's supermarket is bigger than almost any in Japan.* | *Delhaize owns about 44% of a US* ***supermarket chain*** (=several shops owned by the same company).

financial supermarket *journalism* a financial institution that offers many different types of investment products and advice: *Prudential-Bache dreamed of forming a financial supermarket selling insurance and stocks.*

su·per·nor·mal /ˌsu:pə'nɔ:məl◂, ˌsju:-‖ˌsu:pər'nɔ:r-/ *adj* [only before a noun] ECONOMICS supernormal profits or growth are unusually high: *The first stage in any company's life-cycle is a period of very fast or supernormal growth.*

su·per·sede /ˌsu:pə'si:d,ˌsju:-‖ˌsu:pər-/ *v* [T] **1** if a law, instruction, rule etc supersedes another, it takes its place: *The* ***agreement supersedes*** *a similar contract made five years ago.* | *The court ruled that the* ***law was superseded*** *by a 1985 statute.*

2 if a product, method, or idea supersedes another one, it is used instead of the old product or idea because it is more modern, effective etc: *The earlier software was later superseded by Lotus Development's spreadsheet.*

su·per·ser·ver /'su:pəˌsɜ:və,'sju:-‖'su:pərˌsɜ:rvər/ *n* [C] a very large, powerful computer used to control other computers in a NETWORK (=group of connected computers): *This is the first in a line of high-powered computers that will culminate next year in IBM's superserver.*

super sinker bond —see under BOND

su·per·store /'su:pəˌstɔ:,'sju:-‖'su:pərˌstɔ:r/ *n* [C] a large shop, often found on the outer part of a town, that sells a very large variety of a particular product such as furniture, computers etc: *The proposals include plans to sell the cheaper models through high-volume, low-cost superstores.* | *The office equipment superstore has closed outlets in four states.*

su·per·tax /'su:pətæks, 'sju:-‖'su:pər-/ *n* [C,U] a special high rate of tax paid by people or companies with a high level of income + **on**: *The government is likely to punish big organizations by introducing a supertax on their profits.* —compare SURTAX

su·per·vise /'su:pəvaɪz,'sju:-‖'su:pər-/ *v* [I,T] to be in charge of a group of people or a particular area of work: *She* ***supervises 26 workers*** *in a business with annual sales of £4 million.* | *As managing director, he is supervising a portfolio of investments.* | *The fund manager pleaded guilty to failing to supervise properly.* —**supervised** *adj* [only before a noun] *The company will qualify for* ***court-supervised*** *debt restructuring.* | *the biggest* ***government-supervised*** *election in U.S. labor history*

su·per·vi·sion /ˌsu:pə'vɪʒən, ˌsju:-‖ˌsu:pər-/ *n* [U] the work of making sure something is done properly and according to all the rules: *The bank chiefs set up a subcommittee to coordinate policies on* ***banking supervision****.* | *He learned to fly* ***under the supervision of*** *special airline instructors.* —see also BOARD OF BANKING SUPERVISION

su·per·vis·or /'su:pəˌvaɪzə, 'sju:-‖'su:pərˌvaɪzər/ *n* [C] someone who is in charge of a group of workers or a particular area of work: *Any holidays not already booked should be cleared with your supervisor.*

su·per·vis·o·ry /ˌsu:pə'vaɪzəri, ˌsju:-‖ˌsu:pər-/ *adj* relating to the work of making sure something is done properly and according to all the rules: *He will fill the vacancy at PolyGram as chairman of the* ***supervisory board****.* | *The plant has been manned by* ***supervisory personnel*** *and replacement workers since the strike.*

supervisory board —see under BOARD[1]

sup·ple·ment[1] /'sʌpləment/ *v* [T] to add something to something to make it more successful, useful, or complete: *The acquisition will supplement British Steel's strategy to produce higher-margin products.* | *As the number of farmers falls, many are seeking new outlets to* ***supplement their incomes****.* **supplement sth with sth**: *The staff handbooks will be supplemented with a series of workshops.*

sup·ple·ment[2] /'sʌpləmənt/ *n* [C] **1** something you add to make something better, more useful, or more complete: *The* ***welfare supplement*** *is payable to employees who retire between Nov. 1 and Dec. 31.* + **to**: *The informal discussion groups are a good supplement to the overall training program.*

2 an additional part of a book, newspaper, report etc: *a 16-page* ***advertising supplement*** + **to**: *The actual amount of commission is only disclosed in a supplement to the firm's prospectus.*

3 a sum of money added to the price of service, such as a hotel room or plane journey: *There is a single room supplement of £10 per night.*

repayment supplement *BrE* TAX an extra sum of money the tax authorities must pay to a company if they fail to repay a sum of money owed to the company on time: *A business is entitled to a repayment supplement if a VAT claim is not processed within 30 days.*

sup·ple·men·ta·ry /ˌsʌplə'mentəri◂/ *adj* provided in addition to what is already there: *If a purchaser wishes to* *obtain **supplementary information**, they should contact a KPMG representative.* | *For most retired people, even those with **supplementary pensions**, state welfare is a financial lifeline.* | *Operation of La Cinq can only continue if they receive heavy **supplementary financing**.*

sup•pli•er /səˈplaɪə‖-ər/ *n* [C] a company that provides a particular type of product + **of**: *Microsoft is the world's largest supplier of PC software.* | *With California's orange crop halved, **local suppliers** have had to find alternative sources.* | *Xerox has reduced its **supplier base** to about 500.*

sup•ply[1] /səˈplaɪ/ *v* past tense and past participle **supplied** [T] **1** to provide goods or services to customers, especially regularly and over a long period of time: *Grolsch will assume responsibility for supplying and distributing Ruddles products.* **supply sth to sb**: *The company supplies products and services to the energy industry.* **supply sb with sth**: *The computer giant has agreed to supply Mitsubishi with mainframe and minicomputers.*
2 to give someone something they want or need: *Several pharmaceutical companies are supplying **additional data** and making recommendations on labeling.* | *Financing was supplied by a syndicate led by Sumitomo Bank.* **supply sb with sth**: *All employees were supplied with protective clothing.*

supply[2] *n* plural **supplies** **1** [C] an amount of something that is available to be sold, bought, used etc: *The quality of the local **labour supply** has helped to keep his company growing.* | *One-quarter of the nation's **oil supply** is shipped via the pipeline.* | *Coal inventories at the end of March were 390,000 metric tons, a 14-day supply.*
inelastic supply [C] ECONOMICS when a large change in the price of something results in only a small change in the supply of it
2 be in short supply if something is in short supply, very little of it is available: *Pricing information is in short supply because computer makers don't like to talk about the latest trends.* | *The building projects are behind schedule and construction materials in desperately short supply.*
3 water/gas/electricity etc supply a system that provides water, gas etc: *The **public water supply** company said the charge was related to its environmental testing laboratory.* —see also MONEY SUPPLY
4 [U] the act of supplying something + **of**: *efforts to control the quality and supply of aspirins*

supply and demand *n* [U] ECONOMICS the relationship between the amount of products and services that are for sale and the amount that people want to buy, especially in the way this affects prices: *the widening gap between supply and demand* | *The **laws of supply and demand** clearly contribute to higher prices.* —compare DEMAND AND SUPPLY

supply chain —see under CHAIN

supply crunch *n* [singular] ECONOMICS a fall in the amount of a particular product that is available to buy which makes it more expensive and difficult to obtain: *Attempts to shelter world petroleum markets from a supply crunch have failed to be effective.*

supply price —see under PRICE[1]

supply-side *adj* [only before a noun] supply-side economic ideas emphasize making the best use of capital. Supply-side economists have persuaded many right-wing governments to introduce lower taxes and to encourage saving, believing that this will make capital more productive over longer periods of time through greater investment, rather than just influence demand immediately —**supply-sider** *n* [C] *Supply-siders among Republicans are hoping for more tax cuts before the end of the year.*—compare DEMAND-SIDE

supply side economics —see under ECONOMICS

sup•port[1] /səˈpɔːt‖-ɔːrt/ *v* [T] **1** to provide enough money for something to begin or continue: *The supermarket had questioned Heileman's ability to **financially support** its brands.*
2 to show you agree with a person or group of people, or their ideas, plans etc: *10 countries indicated they would support a suspension of production quotas.* | *Most lawmakers **strongly support** governmental **policy**.* | *Sony issued a statement supporting the chief executive.*
3 to help a system continue to work properly: *The company will provide equipment to **support** the complex electronics **systems**.* | *A Group of Seven move to support the dollar had been disappointing.*
4 to show or prove that something is true or correct: *We've got a good, solid defense case supported by clinical research.* | *Many economists believe the economic recovery will be slow, and yesterday's **data supported** that view.*

support[2] *n* [U] **1** money or other help given to someone or something: *The young entrepreneur had approached the bank several times for **financial support**.* | *Mr Rolfe will take responsibility for **technical support**.*
price support a system in which a government pays farmers the difference between the real market price for their products and a higher, agreed price: *The strength of the farm lobby prompted the US administration to operate a price support system.*
2 approval and encouragement for a person or group of people, or their ideas, plans etc: *The striking workers have key support from TWA's labor unions.* | *The rate cut found **widespread support** within Japan.* **support for sth**: *Shareholders believe there is adequate **support for** the **proposal**.* **in support of sth**: *Many financial services companies are lobbying in support of the new laws.*

support price —see under PRICE[1]

sup•press /səˈpres/ *v* [T] **1** to prevent something from developing or making progress: *The recession is **suppressing demand** for our products.* | *Tax increases simply made inflation worse by **suppressing economic growth**.* | *We feel the government is attempting to **suppress competition** in favor of large companies.*
2 to deliberately prevent people knowing important information, ideas, opinions etc: *Advertisers use their influence to suppress negative news coverage about their products.* | *attempts to **suppress evidence***

su•pra•na•tion•al /ˌsuːprəˈnæʃənəl, ˌsjuː-‖ˌsuː-/ *adj* involving more than one country: *We will focus on the way supranational economic forces affect us.*

Supreme Court —see under COURT[1]

sur•charge[1] /ˈsɜːtʃɑːdʒ‖ˈsɜːrtʃɑːrdʒ/ *n* [C] money that has to be paid in addition to the normal payment for something: *Taxpayers would be **liable to surcharges** if they failed to send in payments.* + **on**: *Trade has been hampered* (=harmed) *by high Chinese surcharges on South Korean products.* | *Hertz Corp. recently **imposed surcharges** of as much as $56 a day on car rentals in certain areas.*
import surcharge a tax on goods coming into a country from abroad, often used by governments as a way of reducing imports and protecting local industries; IMPORT DUTY; IMPORT LEVY; IMPORT TARIFF: *The Czech budget might impose import surcharges on cars and consumer goods.*

surcharge[2] *v* [T] to make someone pay an additional amount of money: *Retailers will be able to choose whether to surcharge credit card customers or to offer a discount for cash.*

sur•e•ty /ˈʃɔːrəti‖ˈʃʊr-/ *n* [C,U] LAW **1** a person who promises to pay a debt, appear in court etc if someone else fails to do so: *The use of individual sureties grew sharply as contractors found it increasingly difficult to get insurance.* | *He **had acted as surety** for both companies when they borrowed to finance the projects.*
2 an amount of money or other things of value someone

S

gives to make sure someone else will appear in court, pay a debt etc: *He was allowed out of custody with sureties totalling £12,000.* | *a third party entering into a* ***contract of surety***

surety bond —see under BOND

surf /sɜːf‖sɜːrf/ *v* [T] **surf the net/TV channels** to look quickly at information on the Internet or at several different television programmes to find something that interests you: *You can surf 35 home shopping channels and still not find what you want.* —**surfer** *n* [C] *a website popular with Internet surfers*

surface mail —see under MAIL[1]

surface transport —see under TRANSPORT[1]

surge[1] /sɜːdʒ‖sɜːrdʒ/ *v* [I] to increase suddenly: ***Stock prices surged*** *in early trading.* | ***Demand*** *in the market for middle and top range cars* ***surged*** *by over 100%.* | ***Surging*** *global interest* ***rates*** *hurt investors in international stocks.*

surge ahead *phr v* [I] to suddenly start to become more successful, profitable etc than other companies or products of the same type: *Its main competitors Toyota and Honda are surging ahead in the U.S. market.*

surge[2] *n* [C] a sudden increase in something such as demand, profit, price etc + **of/in**: *Nearly two million people applied for shares in a last-minute surge of applications.* | *the huge and largely unpredicted surge in pensions business*

sur•plus[1] /ˈsɜːpləs‖ˈsɜːr-/ *n* **1** [C,U] an amount of something that is more than what is wanted, needed, or used: *Sugar prices fell after revised estimates of the surplus for the current crop year.* + **of**: *There is a current housing surplus of approximately 500,000 properties.*

budget surplus [C] ECONOMICS when spending, usually by a government, is less than the amount of money received in taxes or other income during a particular period: *The government, which is* ***running a healthy budget surplus*** (=is spending much less than it is receiving), *must spend billions of dollars to build apartments, roads, and other infrastructure to improve the quality of life.*

capital surplus ◆ [C] ECONOMICS, FINANCE when a company or country has more money for investment than it needs: *One borrows in the capital surplus countries and lends to the country where capital is relatively scarce.*

◆ [C] INSURANCE the difference between the amount of money received by insurers from customers paying for policies, and the amount paid out for claims: *They must eliminate the deficit and report a $70 million capital surplus next year or face closure by state regulators.*

consumer surplus also **buyers' surplus** [U] ECONOMICS the amount of money someone is willing to pay for something, minus the amount they actually paid for it: *If you would be willing to spend £2,000 on a holiday, and paid £1,200, you would be obtaining £800 of consumer surplus.*

2 [C,U] FINANCE in MUTUALS (=insurance companies etc that do not have shareholders) the profit for a particular period of time, or from several periods of time, that has not been paid out to members: *Executive Life Insurance Co. had capital and surplus totaling $459.2 million.*

3 [C] FINANCE in insurance companies and PENSION FUNDS, the amount by which the money held is more than they have to pay out in claims or pensions: *Consett steelworks pensioners joined the fight to get a share of a £300 million British Steel pension surplus.*

4 [C] also **balance of payments surplus**, or **external surplus** ECONOMICS the amount by which the money coming into a country is more than the money going out in a particular period of time: *A country that has a balance of payments surplus may receive payment from the debtor's foreign exchange reserves.*

trade surplus also **balance of trade surplus** [C,U] ECONOMICS a surplus related to imports and exports, rather than other payments: *A sharp rise in the country's balance of trade surplus to 23.3 billion baht.* | *We must rebuild manufacturing so as to generate a balance of trade surplus.* + **with**: *We were in surplus with a few countries but in deficit, unfortunately, with all the major trading nations of the world.*

surplus[2] *adj* more than is needed or wanted: *Many businesses relocated, surplus space having become available because of the recession.* | *Those employees will become surplus, and costly to retain.*

surplus value —see under VALUE[1]

sur•ren•der[1] /səˈrendə‖-ər/ *v* **1** [T] INSURANCE if you surrender an insurance policy, you stop it before it MATURES (=becomes due for payment) and receive only a part of what it would have been worth if you had kept it: *Many policyholders had held their* ***annuities*** *for years because of heavy penalties for* ***surrendering*** *them.* | *First Executive paid out $1.33 billion in the first quarter to customers* ***surrendering insurance policies.*** —compare REDEEM

2 [I,T] if someone surrenders their power, influence, high position etc, they allow someone else to have it: *Eight months after taking over the day-to-day running of the business, she* ***surrendered*** *that* ***authority*** *to a man who had only just joined.* | *Investor William Farley plans to* ***surrender*** *his majority* ***ownership*** *of the company.*

3 [T] FINANCE *journalism* if shares etc surrender their value, price etc, the value, price etc falls: *After* ***surrendering*** *39% of its* ***value*** *in the early 1990s, the Nikkei average has moved steadily upwards.*

4 [T] LAW to give something to an official authority when it is asked for: *Under the Bankruptcy Code, debtors must* ***surrender*** *most of their* ***assets.*** | *The seven men have been granted bail on condition that their* ***passports be surrendered.***

surrender[2] *n* [C,U] the act of stopping an insurance policy before it MATURES (=becomes due for payment): *Last year's losses follow a flood of* ***policy surrenders.*** | *Any profit arising on surrender or maturity will be taken into account.*

surrender charge —see under CHARGE[1]

surrender penalty —see under PENALTY

surrender value —see under VALUE[1]

sur•tax /ˈsɜːtæks‖ˈsɜːr-/ *n* [C,U] an additional tax paid by people or companies with a high level of income + **on**: *plans to impose a 10% surtax on incomes of more than $100,000*

sur•vey[1] /ˈsɜːveɪ‖ˈsɜːr-/ *n* [C] **1** a set of questions given to a group of people to find out about their opinions or behaviour: *People are becoming more pessimistic about the economy, according to the latest* ***consumer survey.*** + **of**: *A mild economic recovery starts this spring, according to a survey of 42 economists by the Wall Street Journal.*

market survey a study of the state of a particular market, showing competitors' sales, buyers' intentions etc: *The annual market survey, called Emerging Trends in Real Estate, was conducted by Real Estate Research Corp.*

2 PROPERTY an examination of the condition of a building or area of land, done by a specialist for someone who is considering buying it

marine insurance survey an examination of the condition of the CARGO (=goods carried by a ship) in order to decide how much money the insurer must pay when a CLAIM for loss or damage is made. The insurer asks a SURVEYOR to do the examination and produce a report based on it

sur•vey[2] /ˈsɜːveɪ, səˈveɪ‖ˈsɜːr-, sər-/ *v* [T] **1** to ask a group of people a set of questions to find out about their opinions or behaviour: *The agency surveys executives in about 300 companies around the country.* | *Only 15% of*

S

respondents surveyed *would admit to leaving the workplace early.*

2 PROPERTY to examine and report on the size, condition etc of a building or area of land for someone who is considering buying it —**surveying** *n* [U] *It doesn't take a qualification in surveying to see damp patches or loose tiles.* | *a specialist surveying instrument firm*

sur•vey•or /sə'veɪə‖sər'veɪər/ *n* [C] PROPERTY someone whose job involves examining the size, condition etc of buildings or land: *Advice from a professional surveyor will prove invaluable.* | *The Code of Practice covers insurance brokers and* ***chartered surveyors*** (=those who have passed special examinations).

quantity surveyor someone whose job is to calculate the amount of materials, money, time etc needed to build something

sur•viv•al /sə'vaɪvəl‖sər-/ *n* **1** [U] the state of continuing to exist, even though a situation is difficult: *The change of strategy will ensure the firm's* ***economic survival.*** | *For McDonnell Douglas, survival in the commercial business depends on its ability to expand its product line.*

2 survival of the fittest a situation in which only the strongest and most successful people, organizations etc continue to exist: *I enjoyed the intensity, the competition – it was the survival of the fittest.*

sur•vive /sə'vaɪv‖sər-/ *v* [I,T] **1** if a business survives, it manages to continue operating, even though it is in a very difficult situation: *To survive, companies will have to focus on staff development.* | *The retailing company is cutting the number of its stores in an effort to* ***survive*** *its severe recessionary* ***problems.***

2 if you survive, you continue to live. If you survive someone, you continue to live after they have died: *She appointed her husband, provided he survived her by 30 days, to receive the income from her father's estate.* —**surviving** *adj* [only before a noun] *The merger will cost the surviving company $136 million from tax effects.* | *He leaves no* ***surviving children.***

sur•vi•vor /sə'vaɪvə‖sər'vaɪvər/ *n* [C] **1** someone or something that continues to exist through a difficult or dangerous period of time + **of**: *Olivetti will be among the survivors of the current losses in the computer industry.* | *Investors think they are the likely survivors of this economic downturn.*

2 *formal* people in your family who continue to live after you have died: *Give burial instructions; this can save your survivors thousands of dollars.*

survivorship contract —see under INSURANCE POLICY

survivorship policy —see under INSURANCE POLICY

sushi bond /'suːʃi bɑːnd/ —see under BOND

sus•pend /sə'spend/ *v* [T] **1** to officially stop something from continuing or happening for a short time: *The company has* ***suspended production*** *at its Arkansas plant.* | *The troubled computer concern had to* ***suspend*** *dividend* ***payments*** *on its preferred shares.*

2 to make someone leave a job, position, or organization for a short time, especially because they have broken the rules: *The firm suspended two senior accountants after allegations of financial mismanagement.* **suspend sb from sth**: *He was fined £300,000 and* ***suspended from trading*** *for four months.*

suspense account —see under ACCOUNT[1]

sus•pen•sion /sə'spenʃən/ *n* [C,U] **1** the act of officially stopping something from continuing or happening for a short period of time + **of/on**: *The increase was due mainly to the* ***suspensions of*** *interest* ***payments.*** | *The government lifted the suspension on trading yesterday.*

2 the removal of someone from their job, position, or organization because they have broken the rules: *The offence has a minimum penalty of a one-year suspension.* | *He will return to the office after the suspension to resume most of his supervisory duties.*

sus•tain /sə'steɪn/ *v* [T] **1** if a company sustains losses or other difficulties, it has them: *Like other insurance companies, we have* ***sustained*** *heavy* ***losses.*** | *The record industry* ***sustained*** *a sales* ***slump*** *in the first half.*

2 to manage to make something continue to exist over a long period of time: *The Dow Jones broke above the 2935 level in the early afternoon but was unable to* ***sustain the gains.*** | *Officials predict the electronics industry will be able to* ***sustain growth.*** | *We're seeing a healthy fall in inflation, but the question is whether it can be sustained.* —**sustained** *adj*: *a period of* ***sustained economic growth***

sus•tain•a•ble /sə'steɪnəbəl/ *adj* strong enough to continue existing or happening for a long time: *The market wants to see more evidence that price stability is sustainable.*

sustainable growth —see under GROWTH

swal•low /'swɒləʊ‖'swɑːloʊ/ *v* [T] **1** to accept something unpleasant: *Ford dealers are sceptical that customers will* ***swallow*** *the* ***price increases.***

2 if an activity swallows a lot of time or money, it takes that length of time or uses that amount of money: *Development of the new model's engine will have swallowed at least six years and an estimated 6 billion kronor.*

3 also **swallow up** if one organization, company swallows another, it takes control of it: *Sony swallowed two U.S. entertainment giants – CBS Records, then Columbia Pictures Entertainment.* | *Interstate-banking regulations were changed, which led to hundreds of smaller banks being swallowed up.*

swamp /swɒmp‖swɑːmp/ *v* [T] **1** to suddenly give someone a lot of work or things to deal with: *The flood of orders swamped some understaffed trading desks.* **be swamped (with sth)**: *Brokers said they were swamped with calls after the announcement.*

2 if goods or manufacturers swamp an economy, market etc, there are so many of them available that the price of goods becomes very low: *Cheap imports still swamp U.S. sales in electronic appliances.* **swamp sth with sth**: *The moment they see a chance to make money, mining companies* ***swamp the market with*** *new shares.*

swap[1] also **swop** /swɒp‖swɑːp/ *v* past tense and past participle **swapped** present participle **swapping** [T] FINANCE to exchange one investment for another **swap sth for sth**: *Investors have doubled their money after* ***swapping*** *the* ***bonds*** *for a package of cash and shares.* | *Employees were allowed to* ***swap*** *old, effectively worthless* ***stock*** *for new options.*

swap[2] also **swop** *n* [C] FINANCE an exchange of one investment for another: *Bell agreed to acquire the shares in a* ***stock swap*** *valued at $44 a share.* | *The Accounting Standards Board has launched a project to value* ***debt-for-equity swaps*** *more accurately.*

currency swap an exchange of the interest payments when two lenders have made loans in different currencies with the same interest rate. This happens so that each lender receives the interest in the currency of the other loan: *interest-rate swaps, currency swaps and other instruments known as derivatives that allow corporate clients to protect themselves against financial risks*

debt swap also **debt-equity swap**, or **debt/equity swap** when a company gives shares to lenders in exchange for loans they have made: *Citibank has become a shareholder in companies through debt-equity swaps.*

interest rate swap an exchange between a borrower with one type of loan and a borrower with a different type of loan. Each borrower is looking for an advantage that the original loan did not have, for example that the loan is in a particular currency, has a particular interest rate, is for a particular period of time etc: *It entered an interest rate swap transaction where it exchanged its fixed-rate liabilities for floating-rate payments.*

swap parity —see under PARITY

swaps market also **swops market** —see under MARKET[1]

swap·tion /ˈswɒpʃən‖ˈswɑːp-/ *n* [C] FINANCE a loan with a VARIABLE interest rate (=one that changes) that can be exchanged for a loan with a fixed interest rate if rates fall below a certain level: *The swaption mortgage will allow borrowers to switch out of fixed rate if the variable rate falls.*

swatch /swɒtʃ‖swɑːtʃ/ *n* [C] a small piece of cloth used to show customers what the material is like: *swatches of finely woven cloth*

sweat /swet/ *v*

sweat sth ↔ **out** *phr v* [T] to continue doing something that has been started, even though it is very difficult or worrying: *Companies that have taken the plunge to the private sector must sweat out low returns in the hope that they can return to profit.* | *We had a slow start-up in the business, but we were determined to* ***sweat it out****.*

sweated labour —see under LABOUR

sweat·shop /ˈswet-ʃɒp‖-ʃɑːp/ *n* [C] *disapproving* a small business, factory etc where people work very hard in poor conditions for very low pay: *My prices are competitive but I can't compete with the sweatshops.*

sweep·ing /ˈswiːpɪŋ/ *adj* sweeping changes, cuts etc affect many people and make a big difference: *NatWest PLC announced a* ***sweeping reorganization*** *of its trading and investment arm.* | *The firm has taken* ***sweeping steps*** *to tackle its operating problems.*

sweeps /swiːps/ *n* [plural] *AmE informal* a measure of the number of people watching a particular television NETWORK which is used to decide how many programmes a company will be able to put on television in the following year: *The CBS sweeps victory is some much-needed good news.*

sweet·en /ˈswiːtn/ *v* [T] to make an offer, suggestion etc seem more attractive in order to encourage someone to accept it: *United Airlines* ***sweetened*** *its* ***offer*** *for Pan Am's Latin American routes to $235 million.* | *The British auto maker has sweetened its customer incentives by adding credit facilities.*

sweet·ener /ˈswiːtnə‖-ər/ *n* [C] **1** something used to make an offer, suggestion etc more attractive: *Its board accepted a sweetener from Staveley Industries to buy 43% of the company.* | *As a sweetener, managers who retire by Dec. 30 will receive an extra 15% on their pension.*

equity sweetener FINANCE when a company raises money by issuing (ISSUE) debt, with the right for investors in the debt to exchange it at a later date for shares in the company, perhaps with a right to buy shares at a lower price than usual; EQUITY KICKER

2 a BRIBE (=illegal or unfair payment made to someone to persuade them to do something): *its reputation as a country where every transaction required a sweetener*

sweet·heart /ˈswiːthɑːt‖-hɑːrt/ *adj* [only before a noun] a sweetheart deal, contract, agreement etc is unfair because it gives people who know each other well or have a lot of influence an unfair advantage: *Some executives have been taking kickbacks from suppliers and accepting* ***sweetheart deals****.* | *Critics say prosecutors gave him a* ***sweetheart sentence*** (=a very short one) *in return for evidence against his partner.*

SWIFT /swɪft/ *n* Society for Worldwide Interbank Financial Telecommunications; an electronic system that allows banks all over the world to send payments to each other

swin·dle /ˈswɪndl/ *v* [T] to get money from someone dishonestly by deceiving them **swindle sb out of sth**: *He was convicted of charges that he swindled clients and partners out of £3.5 million.* **swindle sth out of sb/ swindle sth from sb**: *criminal schemes designed to swindle more than $250 million from the bank* —**swindle** *n* [C] *a £12 million insurance swindle* —**swindler** *n* [C] *a band of international bank swindlers*

swing¹ /swɪŋ/ *v* past tense and past participle **swung** [I,T] to change from one level, rate, or position to another so that a situation is the opposite of what it was before: *If the economy swings from recession into recovery, the banks' problems will ease significantly.* | *Prices swung over a wide range, dropping in early trading to $1,383 before recovering.*

swing² *n* [C] a sudden and noticeable change in the level, rate, or position of something: *Changes in revenue could produce large* ***earnings swings****.* | *Investor uncertainty is likely to translate into* ***price swings****.*

swing shift —see under SHIFT[1]

swipe /swaɪp/ *v* **swipe a card** to pass a special plastic card such as a CREDIT CARD through a machine that can read the information it contains: *The system allows stores to check a customer's credit account by swiping the card through an electronic device.*

swipe card —see under CARD

switch·board /ˈswɪtʃbɔːd‖-bɔːrd/ *n* [C] a system used to connect telephone calls in an office building, hotel etc: *Calls must pass through the switchboard with the minimum delay.* | *Contact the* ***switchboard operator*** *to arrange an early morning call.*

switch·ing /ˈswɪtʃɪŋ/ *n* [U] COMPUTING a system which allows information to be exchanged between different computer NETWORKS (=groups of connected computers): *Four suppliers were chosen to develop* ***switching*** *and transmission* ***equipment****.* | *The price includes the installation of central switching.* —see also PACKET-SWITCHING

swop another spelling of SWAP

SWOT /swɒt‖swɑːt/ *n* strengths, weaknesses, opportunities, threats; a system for examining the way a company is run or the way someone works, to see what the good and bad points are: *Before producing a business development plan, it may be helpful to carry out a* ***SWOT analysis****.*

sym·bol /ˈsɪmbəl/ *n* [C] **1** a picture, shape, or set of letters that represents a particular meaning: *We need a symbol – a logo – we can put on our service stations.*

2 also **ticker symbol** the letters used to represent a particular company's shares on a stockmarket: *The exchange began options on Dreyer's Grand Ice Cream Inc., trading under the ticker symbol DYQ.* —see also STATUS SYMBOL

sym·pa·thy /ˈsɪmpəθi/ *n* **1 come out in sympathy** if workers come out in sympathy with workers who STRIKE (=refuse to work), they refuse to work as well: *The truck company is on strike, and Autosan's employees have downed tools* (=stopped working) *in sympathy.*

2 be in sympathy with *journalism* if prices, rates, investments etc change in sympathy with other prices etc, they change at the same time or rate: *Wheat futures prices rose in sympathy with corn and soybeans.*

sympathy strike —see under STRIKE[1]

sym·po·si·um /sɪmˈpəʊziəm‖-ˈpoʊ-/ *n* plural **symposiums** or **symposia** [C] a formal meeting in which people involved in a particular business or subject discuss it: *the annual symposium of St. Gallen's business school* + **on**: *a company-sponsored symposium on degradable plastic and the environment*

syn·di·cate¹ /ˈsɪndɪkət/ *n* [C] a group of people or companies that work together to achieve a particular aim; PARTNERSHIP: *The shares will be offered by a* *syndicate led by Lehman Brothers.* | *The publishing group has bought a 45% stake, joining the company's* ***shareholder syndicate.***

Lloyd's syndicate INSURANCE a group of NAMES (=members) at LLOYD'S that provides insurance against particular risks: *Despite losses related to its involvement with a Lloyd's syndicate, London Capital reported a 70% rise in pre-tax profits.*

loan syndicate BANKING a group of banks that act together to provide a particular loan: *The loan syndicate comprises Chase Manhattan, J.P. Morgan, and SBC Warburg.*

underwriting syndicate FINANCE a group of financial institutions that work together to ISSUE (=make available and sell) shares, bonds etc, and agree to buy any that they do not sell to investors: *Bank of America led a 26-member underwriting syndicate in the sale of a $4.1 billion issue of bonds for the state of California.*

syn·di·cate² /ˈsɪndɪkeɪt/ *v* [T] **1** FINANCE if a company, especially a bank or insurance company, syndicates a loan, debt etc, it provides the loan, debt etc with a group of other companies **syndicate sth to**: *Some of the largest loans were syndicated to smaller creditors.* | *Citicorp was lead-lender on the mortgage and syndicated about 75% of it to a consortium of Japanese lenders.*

2 to arrange for articles, photographs, or radio or television programmes to be sold to a number of different newspapers, television stations etc **be syndicated**: *Wisconsin Public Radio asked him to put together a talk show that could be syndicated nationally.* —**syndicated** *adj* [only before a noun] *The sale proceeds will be used to help the firm renegotiate its* ***syndicated debts.*** | *Most stations will seek to fill the 60 minutes with* ***syndicated programming.***

syndicated loan —see under LOAN[1]

syn·di·ca·tion /ˌsɪndɪˈkeɪʃən/ *n* [C,U] **1** FINANCE an arrangement in which a loan is provided by a group of companies, especially banks or insurance companies: *Bank regulators have argued that thrifts will have to begin arranging* ***syndications of loans.***

2 the sale of articles, photographs, or radio or television programmes to several newspapers, television stations etc: *King World distributes three of the most popular television shows in syndication.*

3 FINANCE a method of selling something, especially property, in which a company or group of companies sells shares in it to investors: *Companies that participated in the syndication might be less likely to join in a similar deal next time.*

syn·er·gy /ˈsɪnədʒi‖-ər-/ *n* plural **synergies** [C,U] additional advantages, profits etc that are produced by two people or organizations combining their ideas and RESOURCES (=means to achieve their aims): *The new group has problems with achieving the desired synergy among its varied operations.* | *The companies could benefit from cost savings, as well as synergies from combining their manufacturing activities.* —**synergistic** *adj*: *More and more companies, customers, suppliers, and competitors recognise the need to build synergistic relationships.*

syn·tax /ˈsɪntæks/ *n* [U] COMPUTING the rules describing how words and phrases in a computer language are ordered: *The commands follow a strict syntax, but they are not difficult to learn.*

syn·the·size also **synthesise** *BrE* /ˈsɪnθɪsaɪz/ *v* [T] to produce something by combining different things, especially to create something that is similar to a natural product: *Researchers first synthesized the anti-depressant Prozac in 1972.* | *The technique may allow scientists to synthesize large diamonds more cheaply than they can be mined.* —**synthesized** *adj* [only before a noun] *Callers are already familiar with the* ***synthesised voice*** *that replies to their questions.*

syn·thet·ic /sɪnˈθetɪk/ *adj* produced by combining artificial materials, rather than naturally: *The lightweight shoes are made from synthetic suede and nylon.*

sys·tem /ˈsɪstɪm/ *n* [C] an arrangement or organization of ideas, methods, or ways of working: *Deregulation has created worries about the stability of the country's* ***financial system.*** | *All staff will benefit from a well-run performance appraisal system.*

accelerated cost recovery system abbreviation **ACRS** [singular] ACCOUNTING a way of calculating the value of assets used in the US, in which the value of an asset is taken to decrease quite quickly, over a period of time fixed by the tax authorities, rather than over the period of time in which it actually remains useful to a company

accounting system ◆ [C] the rules used for accounting in a particular company or place: *Overhead changes are reported differently in different accounting systems.*

◆ [C] COMPUTING a computer system used for accounting: *Great American Software, with its 'One-Write Plus' accounting system*

banking system [C] the way banks work together to make payments, make money available etc: *A financial crisis in Asia could affect the world banking system.*

card index system [C] a method of storing information on cards, usually arranged in alphabetical order in drawers: *This computerised index replaced a card index system that had to be updated by hand.*

computer system [C] a group of connected computers in an organization; NETWORK: *IBM has won a $1.6 billion contract with the Army to provide a huge computer system.*

database management system abbreviation **DBMS** [C] COMPUTING a computer program which organizes the information on a database and allows you to find and use it easily

digital nervous system [C] COMPUTING the idea, suggested by Bill Gates, that NETWORKs of computers in companies should act like the human body's NERVOUS SYSTEM (=system that sends brain messages), passing information between them so that companies can work more effectively: *Microsoft seems to have a finely tuned digital nervous system.*

disk operating system abbreviation **DOS** [U] COMPUTING basic software that is loaded onto a computer system to make all the different parts work together: *The operating system became know as MS-DOS (Micro-Soft Disk Operating System).*

economic system [C] the particular way in which the economy of a country is organized, for example whether the economy is controlled by the government or allowed to develop in its own way: *the liberal, open political and economic system that has worked so well*

expert system [C] COMPUTING a computer system that contains a lot of information about a subject and is designed to copy the thought processes of experts in that subject so that it can help someone find an answer to a problem: *Expert systems can improve human expertise and allow it to be used more efficiently in the specific working environment of aircraft maintenance.*

filing system [C] the method of organising and arranging the information that is stored in an office, often on a computer: *All users of the filing systems will be trained in keeping the computer records up to date.* | *a* ***manual filing system*** (=on paper, rather than on a computer)

fixed instalment system [C] *BrE* ACCOUNTING when the recorded value of an asset is reduced by a certain amount each year in a company's accounts. This amount is recorded as a loss until the value of the asset becomes equal to its value at the end of its useful life

Hay system [singular] HUMAN RESOURCES a way of

measuring the responsibilities in a particular job and how well someone is doing in that job: *Hay Management Consultants, who have their own Hay system*

imputation system [singular] TAX a method of taxation in Britain in which the tax that company shareholders pay on their shares is taken into account when calculating the total amount of tax that must be paid: *In most cases the imputation system ensures that nil and net earnings are the same.*

information system [C] COMPUTING a computer system used to communicate information in an organization, for example an INTRANET

legacy system [C] COMPUTING old software that is still used even though newer software is available: *Many companies still rely on so-called legacy systems despite the revolution in the Internet and PCs.*

legal system [C] the laws and the people and institutions that make them work in a particular country: *a legal system that protects the right of all individuals to hold, buy and sell property*

management information system COMPUTING [C] a system that gives the people in charge of a company the information that they need to take decisions: *It has installed a management information system to show branch managers how their operation is doing compared with Banc One's other 750 branches.*

monetary system [C] ECONOMICS the system of money in a particular country or the world as a whole, and the way that it is controlled by governments and CENTRAL BANKS: *the Bretton Woods monetary system that produced world prosperity* | *The most urgent task for the new regime is creating a well-functioning monetary system.*

open system [C] COMPUTING a computer system on which you can use APPLICATIONS (=programs for particular uses) that were designed to work on other systems: *They are moving from mainframes to open systems that can link payroll with other human resources functions.*

operating system [C] COMPUTING the most basic software on a computer that allows it to work and programs to work on it: *the Unix operating system*

reward system [C] HUMAN RESOURCES pay and things such as pensions, health insurance, and a company car that you get from being employed: *A manager must design reward systems which satisfy individuals and the objectives of the organization.* —see also EUROPEAN MONETARY SYSTEM, METRIC SYSTEM

systematic risk —see under RISK[1]

systems analyst —see under ANALYST

systems programmer —see under PROGRAMMER

T

tab /tæb/ *n* [C] **1** a small piece of paper or cloth that is fixed to the edge of something, usually giving information about it
2 a bill for something, especially one that has gradually increased over time: *One out of three credit card holders pays their credit card tab in full every month.* | *the estimated government tab for resolving the S&L crisis*
3 a system used in some bars and restaurants in which they keep a record of what you have bought and you pay for it later: *Can you **put** these drinks **on my tab**?*
4 pick up the tab to pay for something, especially when it is not your responsibility to pay: *Taxpayers are picking up the tab for the government's mistakes.*
5 also **tab stop** a button on a computer or TYPEWRITER that you press to move forward to a particular place on a line of text

ta•ble[1] /ˈteɪbəl/ *n* [C] **1** used to refer to a place where people come together to discuss important matters: *The union has threatened to walk away from **the bargaining table** if a settlement isn't made soon.* | *Miners at another Codelco mine agreed to return to **the negotiating table**.*
2 a list of numbers, facts, or information arranged in rows across and down a page: *Distribution tables should show taxes actually paid.* | *a book's **table of contents***
life table also **mortality table** a set of figures showing how long different types of people are expected to live
3 on the table an offer, idea etc that is on the table has been officially suggested and you are considering it: *The offer on the table at the moment is a 10% wage increase.*
4 on the table *AmE* an offer, idea etc that is on the table is no longer being considered at the moment but will be dealt with in the future
5 under the table money that is paid under the table is paid secretly and illegally to someone in order to get what you want: *payments made under the table to local officials*

table[2] *v* **1 table a proposal/question/demand etc** *BrE* to suggest something for other people to consider: *Two separate proposals were tabled.*
2 table a bill/measure/proposal etc *AmE* to leave something to be dealt with in the future: *He tabled the bills to break up the state monopolies in insurance and telecommunications.*

tab stop *n* [C] another name for a TAB

tab•u•lar /ˈtæbjᵊlə‖-ər/ *adj* arranged in the form of a TABLE (=set of numbers arranged across and down a page): *The figures are presented **in tabular form**.* | *tabular data*

tab•u•late /ˈtæbjᵊleɪt/ *v* [T] to arrange sets of figures or information in a list so they can be easily compared: *The trade association tabulates the monthly figures.* —**tabulation** *n* [C,U] *the tabulation of overhead expenses* | *tabulations of per capita income*

T-account *n* [C] ACCOUNTING an account showing the finances of a business, laid out in the form of two lines in the shape of a T. The title of the account is printed above the top line and debits appear to the left of the other line with credits to the right of it

tac•tic /ˈtæktɪk/ *n* [C usually plural] a method that you use to achieve something: *Aggressive advertising tactics may mislead consumers.* | *The union has used every possible **delaying tactic*** (=something you do to give yourself more time).

tac•tic•al /ˈtæktɪkəl/ *adj* **1** done in order to achieve what you want at a later time, especially in a large plan: *a **tactical move** to avoid the threat of legal action*
2 tactical mistake/error a mistake that will harm your plans in the future: *It was probably a tactical mistake to offer the contract to a new company.*

tag /tæg/ *n* [C] COMPUTING a series of letters or words that are put before and after a piece of electronic text to show that it is to be treated in a particular way: *a list of **HTML tags*** —see also PRICE TAG

tag line *n* [C] the last few words in a television or radio advertisement: *advertisements with the tag line, "Engineered like no other car in the world".*

tai•lor /ˈteɪlə‖-ər/ *v* [T] to make something or put something together so that it is exactly right for someone's needs: *We can tailor the insurance policy to fit your family's needs.* —**tailored** *adj*: *tailored financial advice*

tailor-made *adj* a tailor-made arrangement or product is one that has been designed so that it is exactly right for someone's needs: *Private banking offers tailor-made financial management for the very wealthy.* —compare OFF-THE-PEG

take[1] /teɪk/ *n* [C usually singular] *AmE informal* **1** the amount of money earned by a business in a particular period of time: *About 80% of the band's take is from merchandise.*
tax take *AmE* the amount of money a government or local authority receives from taxes: *Cities that experience a big drop in population can suffer as the tax take shrinks.*
2 be on the take to be willing to do something wrong or illegal in return for money: *I knew he was on the take, but I never had enough evidence to prove it.*

take[2] *v* past tense **took** past participle **taken** [T] **1** also **take away** to subtract one number from another number **take sth from**: *Take three from nine and what do you get?*
2 also **take in** *AmE* if a business takes or takes in a particular amount of money, it earns that money from selling its goods and services: *We usually take around £2000 on a Saturday.*
take sth ↔ **in** *phr v* [T] if a price or cost takes something in, it includes it: *This price takes in the cost of all accommodation and food.*
take off *phr v* **1** [T] **take** sth ↔ **off** to have a holiday from work on a particular day, or for a particular length of time: *I'm taking Thursday off to do some Christmas shopping.*
2 [I] to start being successful: *I hear the business is really taking off.* —see also TAKEOFF
take on *phr v* [T] **1 take** sb ↔ **on** to start to employ someone: *We're taking on 50 new staff this year.*
2 take sth ↔ **on** to agree to do some work or to be responsible for something: *Gibson is taking on the post of vice president.*
take sth ↔ **out** *phr v* [T] to arrange to get something officially, especially from an insurance company or a court of law: *I'm thinking of taking out a life insurance policy.* | *If discounting took place without the publishers' permission, they would take out an injunction asking a court of law to give an orderto prevent it.*
take over sth *phr v* [I,T] **1** to take control of something: *Who will take over when Ewing resigns?* | *Kubota had already taken over distribution of the Titan line in Japan.*
2 to take control of a company by buying more than 50% of its shares: *A consortium of new companies took over the company a year ago.* | *Baby Basics is a family business and it would lose something if it was taken over by a big conglomerate.* —see also TAKEOVER
take sth ↔ **up** *phr v* [T] **1** to start a new job or have a new responsibility: *He is leaving to take up a position with the BBC.*

2 to do something about an idea or suggestion that you have been considering: *I'm going to take this matter up with my lawyer.*

3 to use a particular amount of space or time: *Computer equipment takes up about a quarter of the office space.* | *This problem is taking up too much of my time.*

take sb **up on** sth *phr v* [T] to accept an offer or invitation that someone has made: *2000 managers took Ameritech up on its offer of voluntary retirement.*

take-home pay —see under PAY[1]

take•off /ˈteɪkɒf‖-ɒːf/ *n* [C] the time when an activity, business, industry, or economy starts being successful: *entrepreneurs whose companies enjoy a fast takeoff*

take-or-pay *adj* [only before a noun] a take-or-pay agreement is one in which a customer agrees to buy a particular quantity of goods at a particular price over a particular period of time. If the customer does not buy the goods as agreed, they must still pay the seller: *Under **take-or-pay contracts**, utilities agree to pay for amounts of gas regardless of their ability to accept delivery.*

take-out *n* [C] when investors who provided the capital to start a new business sell shares in the business once it has become successful

take•o•ver /ˈteɪkˌəʊvə‖-ˌoʊvər/ *n* [C] FINANCE the act of getting control of a company by buying over 50% of its shares: *To avoid a takeover, Carbide went deeply in debt to pay a huge special dividend.* | *Thorn EMI announced a **takeover bid*** (=attempt to get control) *for regional television company Thames Television.* | *an **anti-takeover** plan* (=one to try and avoid a takeover)

creeping takeover a takeover which involves gradually buying shares of a company from different shareholders until you have enough to take control of their company, rather than making an offer to all shareholders to buy a fixed number of shares at a fixed price: *Falconbridge was concerned about a creeping takeover by Noranda.*

friendly takeover a takeover that the company being taken over wants or agrees to: *Management described the move as a "friendly takeover" and said Crossair would remain an independent concern.*

hostile takeover a takeover that the company being taken over does not want or agree to; UNFRIENDLY TAKEOVER: *Corporate Partners bought the $300 million of Polaroid preferred stock to help them **fend off a hostile takeover attempt** by Shamrock Holdings Inc.*

leveraged takeover a takeover using borrowed money. The assets of the company being taken over are used as SECURITY for the loans taken out by the buying company and the repayments are made from the CASH FLOW (=money going into the business) of the company taken over, or from selling some of its assets: *the debt that Hillsborough took on when it launched a $2.4 billion leveraged takeover in the building industry*

reverse takeover the takeover of a larger company by a smaller one, or a takeover in which the company that has been taken over controls the new organization: *Under a **reverse takeover offer** for Volvo, Procordia offered nine of its own shares for every four Volvo shares already held.*

unfriendly takeover another name for a HOSTILE TAKEOVER: *methods used to **guard against unfriendly takeovers***

Takeover Code —see under CODE

takeover offer —see under OFFER[2]

takeover panel —see under PANEL

takeover target —see under TARGET[1]

tak•ers /ˈteɪkəz‖-ərz/ *n* **be no/few/not many takers** used to say that no one or very few people accepted or wanted something that was offered: *The house is up for sale, but so far there have been no takers.*

take-up *n* [U] the rate at which people buy or accept something offered by a company, government etc + **of**: *the **high take-up** of unleaded petrol by car manufacturers* | *There has been a 95% **take-up rate**.*

tak•ings /ˈteɪkɪŋz/ *n* [plural] the money that a business such as a shop or bank gets from selling its goods or services in a particular period of time: *He was taking **the day's takings** to the bank.* | *the takings from wines, spirits, and beers*

talks /tɔːks‖tɒːks/ *n* [plural] formal discussions between governments, organizations etc: *Talks are continuing about lifting trade restrictions.*

pay talks discussions between management and workers about the amount the workers should be paid: *The last round of pay talks broke off with the two sides only a percentage point apart on the salary increase.*

tal•ly[1] /ˈtæli/ *v* past tense and past participle **tallied** [I]

1 [I] if numbers or statements tally, they match each other exactly: *If the figures don't quite tally, you might be missing an invoice.* + **with**: *The original estimate did not tally with the final bill.*

2 also **tally up** [T] to calculate the total number of things done, points won etc: *Let's tally up how much we've spent.*

tally[2] *n* plural **tallies** [C] **1** a continuous record of how much a person or organization has spent, obtained, won etc so far + **of**: *Please **keep a tally** of how many books you sell.*

2 the amount or number of something + **of**: *The company has only one-third its usual tally of accountants because so many have taken voluntary redundancy*

tal•on /ˈtælən/ *n* [C] a special piece of paper that comes with some BEARER BONDS, and is used when all the COUPONS have been used and more are needed

tam•per /ˈtæmpə‖-ər/ *v*

tamper with sth *phr v* [T] to touch something or make changes to it without permission, especially in order to deliberately damage it: *Some of the packs may have been tampered with.* | *The government does not want to tamper with an economy that is already healing itself.*

tamper-evident *adj BrE* a package or container that is tamper-evident is made so that you can see if someone has opened it before it is sold in the shops

tamper-proof *adj* **1** a package or container that is tamper-proof is made in a way that prevents people from opening it before it is sold; TAMPER-RESISTANT

2 impossible to change or spoil: *tamper-proof bar code labels*

tamper-resistant *adj* another name for TAMPER-PROOF

tan•gi•ble /ˈtændʒəbəl/ *adj* **1** tangible results, proof, benefits etc are easy to see so there is no doubt that it exists or has happened: *The loan will create **tangible benefits** for Polish people by providing a cleaner, reliable heat source in winter.* | *There is little **tangible evidence** that there will be an economic recovery.* —**tangibly** *adv*: *Can centers of excellence tangibly improve productivity and quality?*

2 able to be felt by touch: *Gold is a tangible commodity that investors can turn to in times of financial instability.*

tangible asset —see under ASSET

tangible net worth —see under NET WORTH

tan•gi•bles /ˈtændʒəbəlz/ *n* [plural] investments such as gold, silver, jewellery, and works of art rather than shares and other financial investments: *At that time, investors preferred cash to tangibles such as precious metals and art.*

tank /tæŋk/ *n AmE* **in the tank** likely to fail and lose money: *With the junk-bond market in the tank, smarter investors are trying to pick up other investments* | *Sales can't keep going up at that rate, but that doesn't mean the industry is going in the tank.*

tank·er /ˈtæŋkə‖-ər/ *n* [C] a vehicle or ship built to carry large quantities of gas or liquid, especially oil: *The **oil-tanker** industry's outlook depends largely on the price of oil.*

tap /tæp/ *n* **on tap** ready for immediate use when you need it: *Foreign currency loans provide you with cash on tap in the appropriate currency.*

tape /teɪp/ also **magnetic tape, mag tape** *n* [C,U] narrow plastic material, usually inside a plastic box, used for storing computer information, sounds, or pictures: *These tapes are held centrally and are accessible to many users.* | *Court proceedings are usually recorded on tape.* —see also RED TAPE, TICKER TAPE

tape drive —see under DRIVE[2]

taper relief —see under RELIEF

tap stock —see under STOCK[1]

tare /teə‖ter/ *n* [C usually singular] **1** the weight of the material in which goods are packed or wrapped
2 the weight of an unloaded goods vehicle, taken away from its loaded weight to calculate the weight of the goods it is carrying: *Truck drivers must keep their own records of **tare weighings** carried out.*

tar·get[1] /ˈtɑːgɪt‖ˈtɑːr-/ *n* [C] **1** an organization, industry, government etc that is deliberately chosen to have something done to it + **of**: *Ellis was the target of a ten-year investigation by the Securities and Exchange Commission.* | *Computers are helping choose targets for direct-mail and telephone campaigns.* | *Europe will be the **main target** for rising South African coal exports.*
2 a result such as a total, an amount, or a time which you aim to achieve: *Dealers are under pressure to **meet sales targets**.* | *Bonuses were introduced for employees who met **production targets**.* | *The federal funds rate slipped to $7\frac{3}{4}$% from its **target level** of 8%.*
3 on target on the way to achieving a result: *The export business is booming and the U.S. business is right **on target**.*
4 target customer/group/area etc MARKETING a limited group of people or area that a plan, idea etc is aimed at: *Who is the **target audience** for this book?* | *These advertisements are aimed mainly at our **target customers**.*
takeover target a company that may be bought or that is being bought by another company: *The drug company has struggled in recent years to develop major new pharmaceutical products, and it long has been rumored to be a takeover target.*

T

target[2] *v* [T] **1** to make something have an effect on a particular limited group or area **target sth on sth**: *We will target funds on areas of research where breakthroughs are imminent.* **target sth at sth**: *Many cassettes are priced at about $100 because they are targeted at video stores, which will rent them out.*
2 to choose someone or something as your target: *Major U.S. law firms have targeted international work as a growth area.* | *Smaller, more vulnerable banks have been targeted.* —**targeted** *adj* [only before a noun] *Investing relatively small amounts in targeted areas can bring big profits.* | *a targeted advertising campaign*

target audience —see under AUDIENCE

tar·iff /ˈtærɪf/ *n* [C usually plural] **1** a tax on goods coming into a country or going out of it: *France and Germany imposed **import tariffs** on grain.* | *Canadian retailers said that higher tariffs in Canada compared with the U.S. were contributing to higher prices on some goods sold in Canada.*
ad valorem tariff a tariff that varies, depending on the value of the goods, rather than one that is a fixed amount
compound tariff a tariff with two parts, one that depends on the value of the goods and one that is a fixed amount
customs tariff a tax on goods brought into a country that is used to raise money for the government and to protect industries in the country from competition from abroad; CUSTOMS DUTY: *High customs tariffs were introduced to prevent a large-scale inflow of consumer goods.*
discriminating tariff another name for MULTIPLE TARIFF
import tariff a tariff on goods coming into a country from abroad, often used by governments as a way of reducing imports and protecting local industries; IMPORT DUTY; IMPORT LEVY; IMPORT SURCHARGE: *In Honduras, we have opened our market dramatically, reducing import tariff rates from 135% to 20%.*
multiple tariff a tariff with different rates that depend on the country the goods are coming from
protective tariff a tariff aimed at controlling the amount of foreign goods coming into a country, protecting home producers from foreign competition: *protective tariffs which limited the expansion of commerce between nations*
punitive tariff an extra tariff charged on goods going into or out of a country, that is introduced because a country has done business in an illegal or unfair way: *The administration issued a list of Chinese products that could be subject to punitive tariffs if Beijing didn't do more to protect U.S. patents and copyrights.*
retaliatory tariff another name for PUNITIVE TARIFF
revenue tariff a tariff that is introduced to earn money for a country, rather than one to protect home businesses
2 a list of fixed prices, especially ones that change, depending on the time, day etc: ***Telephone tariffs** are set by a government model to provide a 12% real rate of return.*

task /tɑːsk‖tæsk/ *n* [C] **1** a piece of work that must be done, especially one that must be done regularly: *Scheduling is a key task for most managers.* | *day-to-day management tasks* | *computers that can do dozens of tasks at the same time*
2 a piece of work that is difficult but very important + **of**: *the Bundesbank's task of keeping the currency stable* | *Mr. Greenwald faced the **daunting task*** (=difficult and slightly frightening) *of leading the largest experiment ever in employee ownership.*
3 take sb to task to tell someone that you strongly disapprove of something they have done: *The tobacco companies have been taken to task for exposing its cigarette brands to kids.*

task force —see under FORCE[1]

Tau·rus /ˈtɔːrəs/ *n* FINANCE a computer system for buying and selling shares that the LONDON STOCK EXCHANGE started to develop, but never completed

tax[1] /tæks/ *n* [C,U] an amount of money that you must pay to the government according to your income, property, goods etc, that is used to pay for public services: *The President said he would **cut taxes** for middle-income America.* | *a government plan to **raise taxes** in order to reduce the budget deficit* + **on**: *a tax on sales of cigarettes* | *Consumer spending declined 0.3% in October, and **after-tax** income rose 0.2%.* —see also separate entry for INCOME TAX
ad valorem tax [C,U] a tax that changes, depending on the value of the goods it is added to, rather than being a fixed amount
capital gains tax written abbreviation **CGT** [U] in Britain, a tax that ordinary people, not companies, pay when they make a large amount of money by selling an asset such as property. In the US, capital gains tax is also paid by companies: *UK pension funds are exempt from both capital gains tax and income tax on their investments.*
capital tax [C,U] a tax on capital, rather than on spending. CAPITAL GAINS TAX, for example, is a type of capital tax

consumption tax [C,U] a tax that a government puts on certain types of goods in order to make people buy fewer of them, for example during a war or difficult economic conditions; EXPENDITURE TAX: *Despite the introduction of a consumption tax as part of the austerity package, sales of cars are still rising.*
corporation tax [U] in Britain, a tax on the profits of companies, both on profits paid as DIVIDENDS (=payments to shareholders) and RESERVES (=profits from a particular period of time not paid to shareholders in that period)
council tax [C,U] in Britain, a tax paid to your local government authority that depends on the value of the house or apartment that you live in
death tax [C,U] another name for ESTATE TAX
deferred tax [U] tax relating to a particular year that the authorities allow to be paid in a later year: *The company also said it will eliminate a deferred-tax asset on its books, because of adoption of new Financial Accounting Standards Board standards.*
degressive tax [C] a tax where people with low incomes pay a smaller percentage of what they earn than those with high incomes
direct tax [C,U] a tax on what you earn, for example INCOME TAX, rather than one paid on goods that you buy: *the distinction between direct taxes levied on households' and enterprises' incomes and indirect taxes levied on expenditure* | *To pay for the direct tax cuts, petrol tax and VAT will be increased.*
discriminatory tax [C,U] ◆ a tax on particular producers intended to make it easier for other producers to compete: *Georgia must provide a tax refund to liquor distillers located in other states who paid a discriminatory tax on alcohol that they sold in Georgia.*
◆ a tax on a particular activity that some people think is unfair: *A reduction in the capital-gains tax would be but a small step in reducing the discriminatory tax burden on risk investment.*
estate tax [C,U] in the US, a tax on the value of someone's property that must be paid when they die; DEATH TAX; ESTATE DUTY
excise tax [C,U] a tax on certain goods produced and sold in a country, for example cigarettes and alcoholic drinks; EXCISE DUTY: *Despite a doubling of the federal excise tax on beer, Anheuser-Busch Cos. reported record sales in the first quarter.*
expenditure tax [C,U] another name for CONSUMPTION TAX
federal tax [C,U] in the US, tax paid to the Inland Revenue Service or to the Bureau of Customs rather than to local tax authorities. INCOME TAX, ESTATE TAX, and EXCISE TAX are all federal taxes: *At the President's order, big employers are taking less money out of their workers' paychecks for federal taxes.*
flat tax [C] a tax at one fixed rate for all levels and types of income, with no TAX ALLOWANCES: *The administration rejected a flat tax because it shifted too much of the tax burden from the rich to the poor.*
gift tax [C,U] in the US, a tax that you must pay when you give money or property above a certain value to someone: *Federal law permits an individual to give $10,000 a year to any one person free of gift tax.*
goods and services tax abbreviation **GST** [C,U] a type of VALUE ADDED TAX charged on goods and services in some countries
graduated tax [C,U] INCOME TAX that rises in stages according to a tax payer's income. For example it may be 20% for the first £4,100 of income, 23% for the next £22,000, and 40% for the rest
head tax [C,U] a tax paid by every person in a country at the same rate, whatever their income; POLL TAX
hypothecated tax [C,U] a tax where the money obtained, or part of the money obtained, is used for a particular purpose, rather than spent on a number of things: *The Party's proposal in the last election for a 1p increase on income tax for education was popular. A similar hypothecated tax for health could be even more attractive.*
indirect tax [C,U] tax on goods or services that are bought, rather than on the income that people and companies earn. VALUE ADDED TAX and EXCISE DUTIES are indirect taxes
inheritance tax [C,U] another name for ESTATE TAX: *Works of art that are able to be viewed by the public are not subject to inheritance tax.*
input tax [U] tax added to a buyer's bill when buying particular goods or services. At regular periods of time the buyer adds up the input tax from all its bills and takes the total away from the tax they have charged buyers of their products or services to arrive at a final VALUE ADDED TAX figure which they must pay to the government: *Registered VAT payers have to present a three-monthly return on which all output tax and input tax is declared for the period and the net tax paid.*
local tax [C,U] tax that is paid to a local government authority, rather than to central government, that helps pay for public services such as education, health, waste collection etc
luxury tax [C,U] tax on special goods that people do not really need but that are pleasant and enjoyable: *a 10% luxury tax on yachts and private planes*
multiple sales tax [C] a tax on the price of goods sold in shops, and also on the prices charged by the producers of those goods and the company that sells the goods to the shops; TRANSACTIONS TAX; TURNOVER TAX
output tax [U] tax that a seller adds to a buyer's bill when they sell particular goods or services. At regular periods of time, the total tax they have paid when buying goods and services themselves is taken away from the total output taxes they have paid to arrive at a VALUE ADDED TAX figure that they must pay to the government
payroll tax [C,U] tax taken from someone's wages, for example INCOME TAX and NATIONAL INSURANCE or SOCIAL SECURITY TAX
poll tax [C] a tax of a particular fixed amount that every person in a country has to pay: *The British government announced details of its plans to abolish the unpopular poll tax as of 1993.*
progressive tax [C] a tax that is charged at an increasing rate as income increases: *a progressive tax that hits higher-income taxpayers at least as hard as lower-income people*
property tax [C,U] a tax on the value of property such as land and buildings and in some countries also on property such as jewellery, furniture, and investments
proportional tax [C] a tax that is charged at a rate that does not change as the amount of income, for example, increases
purchase tax [C,U] a tax that is added to the price of goods sold in shops, but not on basic goods that people need to buy, that the owner of the shop must pay to the government
real estate tax [C,U] *AmE* a tax on property such as land and buildings
redistributive tax [C] a tax that is intended to spread incomes more fairly among people, by taxing rich people more and poor people less
regressive tax [C] a tax where people with low incomes pay a larger percentage of what they earn than those with high incomes: *a regressive tax on the savings and retirement income of millions of Americans*
road tax [U] in Britain, a tax that every car owner must pay
sales tax [C,U] a tax on a wide range of goods or services. Many states in the US charge their own sales tax: *New York state imposes a 4% sales tax on most consumer goods.*

sin tax [C] a tax on goods such as alcohol or cigarettes which the government wants to discourage people from consuming; REPRESSIVE TAX: *Voters in Ohio's Cuyahoga County approved a higher "sin tax" on liquor and cigarettes to finance a new $344 million downtown sports complex.*
Social Security tax [C,U] in the US, a tax paid by employees and employers to provide money for unemployed people and PENSIONS for people who are too old to work. A similar tax in Britain is called NATIONAL INSURANCE: *Farm workers don't pay Social Security tax on non-cash wages such as lodging and farm products.*
specific tax [C] a tax whose rate is based on a particular quantity of a product, rather than on its value
stamp tax [C,U] a tax on certain financial TRANSACTIONS, for example sales of shares; STAMP DUTY: *an effort to persuade the Swiss government to repeal* (=remove) *its stamp tax on securities transactions*
state tax [C] in the US, a tax paid to the government of a state, rather than to central government: *During the next year, he will pay federal government and state taxes of about $600,000.*
transactions tax [C] another name for a MULTIPLE SALES TAX
turnover tax [C] another name for a MULTIPLE SALES TAX
unitary tax [C,U] in the US, a state tax calculated on a company's profits all over the world, not just on activities in that state: *California's unitary tax system bases a company's tax on world-wide earnings.*
value-added tax abbreviation **VAT** [C,U] a tax on some goods and services. Businesses pay value-added tax on most goods and services they buy and if they are VAT REGISTERED, charge value-added tax on the goods and services they sell. At regular periods of time, the total amount of tax paid is taken away from the total amount charged to arrive at an amount that is owed to or by the business. Final customers pay VAT on these goods in shops and on services. VAT is a way of charging tax on the increase in value of goods and services at each stage as they are produced, rather than just on their final selling price to customers: *The government announced a temporary increase in value-added tax on consumer goods.*
wealth tax [C,U] a tax on the value of a person's assets if their value is above a particular amount
windfall tax [C] a tax that must be paid by a company that has suddenly and unexpectedly earned a large amount of money, especially a large company that has recently been PRIVATIZED (=sold by the government)
withholding tax [C,U] ♦ the amount of interest or DIVIDEND (=regular income from shares) that a financial institution must take from someone's investments and give to the government as income tax
♦ in the US, the amount of an employee's income that their employer must keep to give to the government as income tax —see also EARNINGS BEFORE INTEREST AND TAX, SUPERTAX, SURTAX

tax² *v* [T] **1** to make a person or organization pay tax: *Traditionally, state authorities have taxed the rich far more lightly than the federal government.* **get/be taxed on**: *Shareholders get taxed on the dividends they receive.*
2 tax a car/motorcycle *BrE* to pay the sum of money charged each year for using a vehicle on British roads

tax abatement *n* [C] the right to pay a very low rate of tax on something. Tax abatements are often used to encourage businesses to invest in times of difficult economic conditions: *Mr. Trump managed to receive a 99-year tax abatement from New York City and state in 1977, when the city's real estate market was languishing* (=in a bad condition).

tax·a·ble /ˈtæksəbəl/ *adj* if something is taxable, you must pay tax on it: *Money in the account is taxable.* | *taxpayers with **taxable income** in excess of £200,000* | *investors who buy **taxable bond funds***

taxable income —see under INCOME

taxable profit —see under PROFIT[1]

tax-and-spend *adj* [only before a noun] *disapproving* used to describe people who believe that governments should raise money through taxes and spend a lot of money, particularly on WELFARE (=payments to poorer people), or to describe methods of doing this: *He was an orthodox tax-and-spend liberal.* | *the tax-and-spend policies of the Democratic Party*

tax·a·tion /tækˈseɪʃən/ *n* [U] **1** the act or system of charging taxes: *These reforms will occur at the same time as changes in banking and taxation.* | *Reinvested profits would be exempt from taxation* (=would not be taxed).
capital taxation tax on money owned as capital rather than on money earned as income: *There are differences between the parties' policies on capital taxation, namely inheritance tax and capital gains tax.*
deferred taxation taxation using DEFERRED TAXES
direct taxation taxation using DIRECT TAXES
discriminatory taxation taxation using DISCRIMINATORY TAXES
double taxation when a single amount of money is taxed twice. For example, company profits are taxed and then taxed again when they are given to shareholders in the form of DIVIDENDS: *The US taxes corporate profits twice: first when they are earned and later when they are paid to shareholders in the form of dividends; eliminating this double taxation has long been a goal of economists.*
indirect taxation taxation using INDIRECT TAXES
multiple taxation when a single amount of money is taxed more than once, often by two or more different authorities in a way that may be unfair or illegal: *The tax was imposed in a way that would expose the same property to multiple taxation by Florida and other states where the company does business.*
2 money collected from taxes: *We'll have to consider even higher taxation in the next year or two.* —see also EQUITY OF TAXATION

tax avoidance *n* [U] legal ways of paying less tax: *The law has never prevented clever lawyers from finding ways of tax avoidance for their clients.* —compare TAX EVASION

tax base —see under BASE[1]

tax bite *n* [C usually singular] the part of someone's income or other money that is taken in the form of tax: *Mr. Saito was looking for ways of passing his empire on to his children without a big tax bite.*

tax bracket —see under BRACKET

tax break *n* [C] a special reduction in taxes that the government allows for a particular purpose: *a temporary investment tax credit, which would provide a tax break to businesses that invest in equipment*

tax burden —see under BURDEN

tax credit —see under CREDIT[1]

tax declaration —see under DECLARATION

tax-deductible *adj* tax-deductible costs can be taken off your total income before tax is calculated on it: *Charitable donations are tax-deductible.*

tax-deferred *adj AmE* not taxed until a later time: *tax-deferred savings*

tax dodge *n* [C] *informal* an illegal way of paying less tax: *Tax relief on forest ownership was abolished after it was revealed that business corporations were investing in conifer plantations as a tax dodge.* —**tax dodger** *n* [C] *the Inland Revenue's work in seeking out tax dodgers*

tax-efficient *adj* a tax-efficient way of doing something makes it possible for you to pay less tax: *It would be*

T

more tax-efficient to register the holding company in the U.S., rather than in Europe. | *A pension is a tax-efficient way of saving money.* —**tax efficiency** *n* [U] *funds that offer clients high yields and tax efficiency*

tax evasion *n* [U] illegal ways of paying less tax: *He pleaded guilty to charges of bank fraud and tax evasion.* —compare TAX AVOIDANCE —**tax evader** *n* [C] *The IRS is taking steps to catch tax evaders.*

tax-exempt¹ *n* [C] an investment on which you do not have to pay tax: *There is strong investor demand for tax-exempts.*

tax-exempt² *adj* **1** tax-exempt investments, savings, income etc are not taxed: *The Labour government under Mr Blair introduced ISA, a tax-exempt savings account.* | *issuers of* ***tax-exempt bonds***

2 an organization that is tax-exempt does not have to pay tax: *a tax-exempt Friendly Society* | *Some hospitals risk losing their* ***tax exempt status.*** —**tax exemption** *n* [C,U] *The sales tax exemption for newspapers and magazines has been lifted.*

tax-exempt income —see under INCOME

tax exile *n* **1** [C] someone who lives abroad to avoid paying high taxes in their own country: *Hunt lived for a time as a tax exile in Marbella.*

2 [U] when someone lives as a tax exile: *There were rumors that he was preparing to* ***go into tax exile.***

tax-free *adj* tax-free income, investments, activities etc are not taxed: *Most municipal bonds are totally tax free.* | *He retired with a* ***tax-free lump sum*** (=single large amount of money) *of £80,000.* —**tax-free** *adv*: *Earnings can be withdrawn tax-free after seven years.*

tax haven *n* [C] a place where people go to live or to invest money, in order to avoid paying high taxes in their own country: *Luxembourg and the Cayman Islands are tax havens that don't have strong central bank regulators.*

tax holiday —see under HOLIDAY

tax inspect•or *n* [C] someone who works for the government, deciding how much tax people or businesses should pay

tax invoice —see under INVOICE¹

tax liability —see under LIABILITY

tax lien *n* [C] —see under LIEN

tax loss *n* [C] —see under LOSS

tax•man /ˈtæksmæn/ *n* plural **taxmen** [C] **1** a tax inspector: *Taxmen are finding it harder to keep up with clever finance directors.*

2 the taxman *informal* the government department that collects taxes: *They managed to hide part of their profits from the taxman.*

tax•pay•er /ˈtæksˌpeɪə‖-ər/ *n* [C] a person or organization that pays taxes: *The takeover was estimated to have cost taxpayers $1.5 billion.* —**taxpaying** *adj* [only before a noun] *There was a lot of anger on the part of the taxpaying public.*

tax provision —see under PROVISION

tax relief —see under RELIEF

tax return *n* [C] the form on which you have to give information so that your tax can be calculated: *step-by-step instructions on how to* ***fill out a tax return***

tax shelter *n* [C] a plan or arrangement that allows you to legally avoid paying tax: *Many investors used annuities as a tax shelter rather than as a retirement savings program.* —**tax-sheltered** *adj*: *taxpayers with significant tax-sheltered income*

tax take —see under TAKE¹

tax year —see under YEAR

tba written abbreviation for 'to be advised', 'to be agreed', and 'to be announced'

T-bill —see ***Treasury bill*** under BILL¹

T-bond —see ***Treasury bond*** under BOND

team¹ /tiːm/ *n* [C] a group of people who work together to do a particular job: *We have recruited an excellent* ***management team.***

team² *v*

team up *phr v* [I] to join with someone in order to work on something: *The two companies will team up to develop new database software.* + **with**: *Chrysler has announced that it is teaming up with Renault to build a $500 million plant in Europe.*

team player *n* [C] a person who works well as a member of a team: *He was a brilliant businessman, but never a team player.*

team•ster /ˈtiːmstə‖-ər/ *n* [C] *AmE* someone whose job is to drive a TRUCK: *the President of the Teamsters union*

team•work /ˈtiːmwɜːk‖-wɜːrk/ *n* [U] the ability of a group of people to work well together: *Success has come from effective teamwork.* | *There is an emphasis on teamwork in the company.*

teas•er /ˈtiːzə‖-ər/ *n* [C] an advertisement intended to get people's attention for advertisements that will come later or products that will be available later: *Mazda's teasers urged viewers to tune in at a specific time to watch the launch of their advertising campaign.* | *Nintendo has been generating advance interest for the new product by running teasers about it for months in the press.*

teaser ad —see under AD

teaser rate —see under RATE¹

tech•ie /ˈteki/ *n* [C] *informal* a person who works in computing or in some other TECHNOLOGICAL industry: *Most of my colleagues are techies.*

tech•ni•cal /ˈteknɪkəl/ *adj* connected with practical knowledge, skills, or methods, especially in industrial or scientific work: *The manual contains all the* ***technical information*** *on the product.* | *Our staff provide* ***technical support*** *7 days a week.* | *We have appointed a new technical director.* —**technically** *adv*: *Is the project technically feasible?* | *a technically advanced industry*

technical analysis —see under ANALYSIS

technical correction —see under CORRECTION

technical efficiency —see under EFFICIENCY

technical indicator —see under INDICATOR

technical position —see under POSITION¹

tech•ni•cals /ˈteknɪkəlz/ *n* [plural] FINANCE things that influence prices in a financial market that are related to the way the market works, rather than to the nature of the investments being traded: *High on the list of negative technicals is the huge amount of new bills, notes and bonds the Treasury must sell in the coming months.* —compare FUNDAMENTALS

tech•ni•cian /tekˈnɪʃən/ *n* [C] a skilled scientific or industrial worker: *These machines must be installed by trained technicians.* | *a laboratory technician*

tech•noc•racy /tekˈnɒkrəsi‖-ˈnɑː-/ *n* plural **technocracies** [C,U] a social system in which people with a lot of scientific or technical knowledge have a lot of power: *The higher ranks of the civil service were steeped in a tradition of technocracy.*

tech•no•crat /ˈteknəkræt/ *n* [C] a highly skilled scientist who has a lot of power in industry or government: *The liberalization of the economy has helped technocrats to start hundreds of new industries.* —**technocratic** *adj*: *a country run by a small technocratc elite* | *a technocratic outlook*

tech•no•lo•gi•cal /teknəˈlɒdʒɪkəl‖-ˈlɑː-/ *adj* dealing with scientific or industrial methods and the use of

T

these methods in industry, farming etc: *the rapid pace of technological change* —**technologically** *adv: technologically advanced hardware*

tech•nol•o•gy /tek'nɒlədʒi‖-'nɑː-/ *n* plural **technologies** **1** [C,U] knowledge dealing with scientific or industrial methods and the use of these methods in industry, farming etc: *What impact is the **new technology** having on people at work?* | *Getting industry to adopt new technologies has long been a problem.* | *The system uses advanced digital and satellite technologies.*

high technology [U] the use of the most modern technical knowledge and methods: *small and medium-sized enterprises involved in high technology* | *LDI Corp. leases and sells data-processing, telecommunications and other **high-technology equipment**.* | *Not all **high-technology stocks** fell. Microsoft gained a dollar and Oracle Systems also rose.*

information technology abbreviation **IT** [U] the study or use of electronic processes for storing information and making it available

intermediate technology [C,U] practical science which is suitable for use in poorer countries because it is simple and cheap, involving ways of doing things that make use of materials that are available locally, are not difficult to repair etc: *The country relies heavily on modern intermediate technology methods.*

2 [U] machinery and equipment used or developed as a result of scientific and technical knowledge: *We manufacture our products using the very latest technology.*

niche technology [C,U] technological products that are designed for a particular small area of a market: *small companies specialising in niche technologies such as E-commerce and Internet routers* —see also NANOTECHNOLOGY —**technologist** *n* [C] *opportunities for communications technologists*

tel written abbreviation for telephone number

tele- /teli, telə/ *prefix* **1** at or over a long distance: *telecommunications* | *teleshopping* (=using a computer in your home to order goods) | *teleworking* (=working from home using a computer connected to the main office)
2 by or for television: *a telerecording*
3 by telephone: *telesales* | *telemarketing*

T

tel•e•cast /'telikɑːst‖-kæst/ *n* [C] *AmE* a programme on television: *the marketing of college football telecasts* —**telecast** *v* [T] *TNT will telecast five hours of Olympic games coverage each afternooon.*

tel•e•com /'telikɒm‖-kɑːm/ *adj* another name for telecommunications, sometimes used in the name of companies: *The company designs, manufactures and installs telecom equipment.*

tel•e•com•mu•ni•ca•tions /ˌtelikəmjuːnə'keɪʃənz/ *n* [plural] the process or business of sending and receiving information by telephone, television, the INTERNET etc: *the telecommunications industry* | *a telecommunications satellite*

tele•com•mut•er /'telikəˌmjuːtə‖-tər/ *n* [C] someone who works from home using a computer connected to the office of the company they are working for; TELECOMMUTER —**telecommuting** *n* [U]

tel•e•coms /'telikɒmz‖-kɑːmz/ *n* [plural] another name for telecommunications: *Europe's telecoms industry* | *the telecoms market*

tel•e•con•fe•rence /ˌteli'kɒnfərəns‖-'kɑːn-/ —see under CONFERENCE

tel•e•cot•tage /'teliˌkɒtɪdʒ‖-kɑː-/ *n* [C] another name for ELECTRONIC COTTAGE

tel•e•gram /'teləgræm/ *n* [C] a message sent by TELEGRAPH (=by using radio signals or electrical signals along wire)

telegraphic transfer —see under TRANSFER[2]

tel•e•mar•ket•er /'teliˌmɑːkətə‖-ˌmɑːrkətər/ *n* [C] a company which operates its business over the telephone, contacting people to offer them a product or service

tel•e•mar•ket•ing /ˌteli'mɑːkətɪŋ‖-'mɑːr-/ *n* [U] the practice of telephoning people in order to sell things: *the company's telemarketing and direct mail work*

inbound telemarketing selling goods or services by telephone to people who call a number given in an advertisement etc

telephone banking —see under BANKING

telephone exchange *n* [C] a central building or office where telephone calls are connected to other telephones, or the equipment that is used: *the contract to modernize Indonesia's telephone exchange system* | *the installation of a digital telephone exchange*

telephone interviewing *n* [U] MARKETING a method of MARKET RESEARCH in which people are telephoned in order to be asked questions about which products they buy, the reasons they buy them etc: *a study comparing face-to-face interviewing with telephone interviewing*

telephone number written abbreviation **tel** *adj* [only before a noun] *journalism informal* telephone number amounts, especially amounts of money, are very large: *Some of these managers are earning **telephone number salaries** while at the same time laying off staff and cutting training budgets.* | *From a period of depressed growth, the company has turned itself around and is now achieving telephone number sales.*

telephone selling —see under SELLING

te•leph•o•nist /tə'lefənəst/ *n* [C] *BrE* someone whose job is to connect telephone calls at a SWITCHBOARD or telephone exchange

te•leph•o•ny /tə'lefəni/ *n* [U] the activity and business of providing telephone services: *business applications linking computing and telephony*

tel•e•sales /'teliseɪlz/ also **tel•e•sel•ling** /'teliˌselɪŋ/ *n* [U] the practice of telephoning people in order to try to sell them things, or sales made by telephone; TELEPHONE SELLING: *our telesales force* | *Many central heating companies use telesales.*

tel•e•text also **Teletext** /'telitekst/ *n* [U] a system of broadcasting written information with recent news, traffic information etc on television: *the CEEFAX teletext system* | *teletext pages*

Teletext Output of Price Information on Computer —see TOPIC

tel•e•work•er /'teliˌwɜːkə‖-ˌwɜːrkər/ *n* [C] someone who works from home using a computer, FAX etc connected to the office of the company they are working for; TELECOMMUTER

tel•e•work•ing /'teliˌwɜːkɪŋ‖-ˌwɜːr-/ *n* [U] working from home using a computer, FAX etc connected to the office of the company you are working for; TELECOMMUTING: *Teleworking involves managing staff at a distance.* | *the benefits of teleworking* —see also ELECTRONIC COTTAGE, TELECOTTAGE

tel•ex[1] /'teleks/ *n* **1** [U] a system of sending written messages from one business to another along telephone lines or by SATELLITE. This system has been widely replaced by FAX and E-MAIL: *Negotiations were concluded by telex.* | *a telex number*
2 [C] a message sent in this way: *We have just received a telex from our Kenya office.*

telex[2] *v* [I,T] to send a message, piece of information etc to someone using a telex: *Money can be telexed abroad.* | *Can you telex the details of the new contract?*

tell•er /'telə‖-ər/ *n* [C] *especially AmE* someone whose job is to receive and pay out money in a bank; CASHIER *BrE*: *Tellers are now using on-line real time systems to access customers' accounts.*

temp¹ /temp/ *n* [C] a person, especially a secretary, who is employed to work in an office for only a short or limited period of time while someone is absent or while there is a lot of work to do: *There is a shortage of good temps in London.* | *We've got a temp in this week.* | *a **temp agency*** (=a business that supplies temps, especially secretaries)

temp² *v* [I] *especially BrE* to work as a temp: *He has been temping for an accountancy firm.*

tem•po•ra•ry /ˈtempərəri, -pəri‖-pəreri/ *adj* **1 temporary contract/job/employment** a contract, job etc that is only intended to continue for a short time, for example until a particular piece of work is finished
2 temporary employee/worker/staff an employee who is only employed for a short time, for example to do a particular piece of work —compare PERMANENT

temporary help —see under HELP

ten•a•ble /ˈtenəbəl/ *adj* **be tenable for** a job or position that is tenable for a particular length of time can be held by a person for that length of time: *How long is the post tenable for?*

ten•an•cy /ˈtenənsi/ *n* plural **tenancies 1** [C,U] an agreement which gives someone the right to use a building, land etc for which they have paid rent: *The amount of rent you have to pay will depend on the type of tenancy you have.* | *a tenancy agreement* | *We are applying for a new tenancy of the premises.*
assured tenancy [C,U] an arrangement between a LANDLORD and a TENANT in which the tenant agrees to rent the landlord's property until a particular date, and the landlord agrees not to make them leave before that date
2 [C] the period of time that someone rents a building, land etc: *a six-month tenancy* | *When does the tenancy expire?*

ten•ant /ˈtenənt/ *n* [C] a person or organization that pays rent in order to live or work in a house, room, office etc: *The building is mainly occupied by large commercial tenants.*
anchor tenant one of the most important tenants in a particular building, SHOPPING MALL etc; prime tenant: *At present, Canadian bankers won't lend to a shopping mall development until anchor tenants have been found.*
life tenant LAW another name for a TENANT FOR LIFE: *a trustee holding investments on trust for a life tenant*
prime tenant ◆ another name for ANCHOR TENANT
◆ a business tenant of the best quality for example because their name is famous: *We would be able to attract prime tenants if we could show them a nearly completed top-quality building.*
sitting tenant a tenant that cannot be forced to move if a building is sold
statutory tenant a tenant who has the right to stay in a property even after their tenancy agreement with the LANDLORD has come to an end —see also SUBTENANT

tenant at sufferance *n* plural **tenants at sufferance** [C] LAW a tenant who continues to remain in a building, on land etc after the LEASE (=legal agreement to rent the property) has ended and without the owner's agreement

tenant at will *n* plural **tenants at will** [C] LAW a tenant who holds land that is owned by someone else, with the owner's agreement, when either the tenant or the owner may end the TENANCY at any time

tenant farmer —see under FARMER

tenant for years *n* plural **tenants for years** [C] LAW a tenant who has a LEASE (=legal agreement to rent a property) for a fixed number of years

tenant in common *n* plural **tenants in common** [C] LAW a person who shares the ownership of land or property with two or more other people

ten•der¹ /ˈtendə‖-ər/ *n* [C] **1** an offer to do a job or provide goods or services for a particular price, usually as part of a competition between several companies for the same work: *Their bid was £150,000 more than the lowest tender.* | *Councillors agreed that the contract to build the homes should be **put out to*** (=offered for) ***tender**.* —**tenderer** *n* [C] *It is preferable for tenders to be opened publicly with the tenderers present.*
sealed bid tender a system in which several companies make tenders for a job without anyone knowing what the other tenders are. The offers are then all opened at the same time and the work given to the company who makes the best offer —see also ***sealed bid*** under TENDER¹
2 FINANCE an offer to buy shares, which will be sold to the investor who offers the highest amount: *The tender offered 225 marks a share for Siemens stock.*
3 LAW an offer of the exact amount of money in CASH (=coins and notes) needed to pay for something —see also LEGAL TENDER

tender² *v* **1** [I] to make a formal offer to do a job or provide goods or services at a particular price + **for**: *The company said it is unable to tender competitively for contracts unless it has the flexibility of Sunday working.*
2 [I] FINANCE to make a formal offer to buy shares at a particular price + **for**: *The company has agreed to tender for two million of the shares at $4 a share.*
3 [T] *formal* to offer or show something to someone: *She will tender a proposal at the meeting.* | *The company vice-president had **tendered his resignation*** (=officially said he wanted to leave his job).
4 [T] *formal* to give money as payment: *She tendered a £10 note.*

ten•der•ing /ˈtendərɪŋ/ *n* [U] the act or practice of making offers in the form of tenders: *The Government is introducing **competitive tendering*** (=when several companies make tenders to try and get work) *for local leisure facilities.*
collusive tendering also **dummy tendering, level tendering** when companies making tenders secretly share information or make arrangements among themselves in order to control the result: *banned practices such as price fixing and collusive tendering*

tender issue —see under ISSUE²

tender offer —see under OFFER²

ten•e•ment /ˈtenəmənt/ *n* **1** [U] LAW REAL PROPERTY (=land and buildings) belonging to one owner
2 [C] LAW a house
3 [C] a large building divided into apartments, especially in a poor area of a city: *He was owner and manager of a tenement in the Bronx.*

ten•ner /ˈtenə‖-ər/ *n* [C] *BrE informal* ten pounds, especially in the form of a ten pound note: *Can you lend me a tenner?*

ten•or /ˈtenə‖-ər/ *n* [C] the period of time before a BILL OF EXCHANGE or PROMISSORY NOTE has to be paid, which is stated on the bill or note: *Local Government Promissory Notes normally have a tenor of 91 days or less.*

ten•ure /ˈtenjə, -jʊə‖-jər/ *n* [U] **1** the period of time when someone has an important job or position: *During Mr Tilly's four-year tenure as president, the firm's annual revenue rose dramatically.*
2 the right to stay permanently in a job, for example a teaching job in a university: *Mr. Armstrong is not worried about the effect of the study on his job, as he has tenure.*
3 LAW the legal right to live in a house or use a piece of land: *inequalities in land tenure* —see also SECURITY OF TENURE

term¹ /tɜːm‖tɜːrm/ *n* **1** [C] a word or expression that has a particular meaning, especially in a technical or scientific subject: *a glossary of **business terms*** + **for**:

'Multimedia' is the industry term for any technique that uses computers to combine sound and images.

2 in real terms a change of a price or cost in real terms has been calculated to include the effects of other changes such as INFLATION (=price rises over time): *Cocoa prices fell to their lowest in real terms for over 50 years.*

3 [C] one of the conditions of an agreement, contract, or other legal document: ***Under the terms of** the contract, Hydro-Quebec was to deliver 1,000 megawatts of electricity to New York.*

delivery terms [plural] an agreement in a contract between a buyer and seller about when goods will be delivered, how they will be paid for etc: *Customs require information comprising such details as the delivery terms, weight, method of transport and country of origin.*

draft terms [plural] the conditions of an agreement before they become final: *draft terms of the credit agreement currently being negotiated*

express term [C] LAW a term in a contract which is stated clearly and openly: *Helix Electronics was permitted to transfer the software because there were no express terms in the licence agreement prohibiting this.*

fleet terms [plural] reduced prices which a car dealer offers to a company with a FLEET (=group) of cars if the company agrees to buy all its vehicles from that dealer

implied term [C] LAW a condition in a contract that is not written, but is understood to exist because of the general purpose of the contract: *There is also an implied term that the supplier of a service will supply the service with reasonable care and skill.*

price terms [plural] ◆ in a sales agreement or contract, the price that the buyer must pay, and often showing how it is calculated: *The agency is prohibited from using price terms which are not industry standard.*

◆ if a price is given in relation to particular price terms, it is calculated using those prices as a guide: *Wool prices are projected to average around 743 cents a kilo by 2002, in 1996 price terms.*

settlement terms [plural] the conditions under which two sides involved in a legal or industrial disagreement agree to end a law case, STRIKE etc, for example by an amount of money that one side will pay to the other: *Under the settlement terms, both companies agreed not to run the ads any more.*

4 terms [plural] the conditions under which you agree to buy or sell something: *You may be able to find another policy offering the same cover **on more favourable terms*** (=more cheaply, with easier ways to pay etc).

account terms [plural] the arrangement that a seller makes with a buyer for goods or services to be paid for using an account, including the amount of time a buyer can wait before payment must be made, the method of payment etc: *The goods were sold **on monthly account terms**. | Many exporters are reluctant to sell **on open account terms*** (=where no particular date or method of payment has been agreed).

credit terms [plural] the conditions under which someone agrees to give a customer credit: *They offer overseas buyers credit terms of as long as 360 days.*

payment terms [plural] the conditions of a sales agreement that concern how the customer will pay, and especially how much time is allowed for payment: *We might consider extending the normal payment terms from 30 days to 40 days or more.*

preferential terms [plural] conditions that make it easier for a particular person or group to buy something, for example because they are allowed to pay a lower price or pay over a longer period of time: *Employees will be allowed to purchase their company's shares on preferential terms.*

settlement terms [plural] conditions under which customers receive price reductions for paying within certain periods of time, for example a 5% reduction for paying within 30 days and a 2% reduction for paying within 60 days

trade terms [plural] ◆ the conditions under which countries or companies agree to buy from and sell to each other: *These are the most favorable trade terms generally available to our country's trading partners.*

◆ also **terms to the trade** price reductions given to customers that are businesses rather than members of the public

5 on equal terms/on the same terms having the same advantages, rights etc as anyone else: *US companies want to be able to compete on equal terms with their overseas rivals.*

6 terms of reference [plural] the agreed limits of what an official committee or report has been asked to study: *The matter of compensation is not within the committee's terms of reference.*

7 in the long/short/medium term over a period of time from now until a long, short etc time into the future: *The company's prospects look good in the long term.* —see also LONG-TERM, MEDIUM-TERM, SHORT-TERM

8 [C] a period of time for which someone has an important job or position, or that a government has power: *The chairman's term is six years. | The President hopes to be elected to a second **term of office**.*

9 [singular] the period of time that a legal right or agreement continues for + **of**: *New legislation would lengthen the term of patent protection to 20 years. | Expenses are refundable **over the term of the contract** during the time that it continues.*

10 [singular] the period of time before something has to be paid or repaid: *We're trying to extend the term on our mortgage.* + **of**: *a promissory note with a term of 6 months*

11 [singular] the end of the period of a business agreement: *The policy reaches its term next year.*

12 [singular] INSURANCE the period of time that an insurance contract lasts for, especially when this is less than one year

13 [C] STATISTICS one of the numbers or signs used in a mathematical calculation

term² *v* [T] to use a particular word or expression to name or describe something **be termed sth**: *He discussed the formation of what he termed strategic alliances'.*

term³ *adj* [only before a noun] **term deposit/loan etc** money that is put in a bank or a loan that is given for a particular length of time: *Pension-GICs are term deposits held for corporate employee pension and savings funds. | Its credit line was converted to a term loan that matures Oct. 31.*

term assurance —see under ASSURANCE

term bill —see under BILL¹

term deposit —see under DEPOSIT¹

ter·mi·nal /ˈtɜːmɨnəl‖ˈtɜːr-/ *n* [C] **1** a large building that is part of an airport, bus station, or port, where people wait to get onto planes, buses, or ships: *Your plane leaves from Terminal 4.*

2 COMPUTING a piece of computer equipment that consists of a keyboard and a screen, used as part of a network of computers that are all connected to each other or to one large computer: *A PC can work as a terminal on a network.*

dumb terminal a terminal that cannot be used by itself as a computer, but can be used to look at or work on information that is on a network or larger computer

intelligent terminal a terminal that can also be used by itself as a computer

terminal bonus —see under BONUS

terminal market —see under MARKET¹

ter·mi·nate /ˈtɜːmɨneɪt‖ˈtɜːr-/ *v* **1** [I,T] if something terminates, or if you terminate it, it ends: *Their three-*

year partnership was terminated. | *The contract terminated in April.*

2 [T] to remove someone from their job: *The company has terminated several managers.*

ter•mi•na•tion /ˌtɜːmə̇ˈneɪʃən‖ˌtɜːr-/ *n* [C,U] **1** the act of ending something, or the end of something: *No reason was given for the termination of the discussions.* | *Some investors will continue with payments until the plan's termination in 15 years' time.*

2 when someone is removed from their job by their employer: *Some partners were selected for termination.* | *The planned job terminations will affect various locations.*

wrongful termination LAW when someone is removed from their job in a way that is unfair and illegal, for example because the proper processes are not followed: *The employees sued, claiming wrongful termination.*

term insurance —see under INSURANCE

term loan —see under LOAN[1]

terms of employment *n* [U] another name for CONTRACT OF EMPLOYMENT

terms of engagment —see under ENGAGEMENT

territorial waters *n* [plural] the sea near a country's coast, which that country has legal control over: *Tankers in Spain's territorial waters are affected by strict new safety regulations.*

ter•ri•to•ry /ˈterə̇təri‖-tɔːri/ *n* plural **territories**
1 [C,U] an area which is the responsibility of a particular salesperson: *His sales force's territory comprises Minnesota, the Dakotas, Iowa and Wisconsin.*

2 [C,U] land that is owned or controlled by a particular government, ruler, or military force: *The parliament has jurisdiction over minerals mined on its territory.* | *Until 1997 Hong Kong was a British territory.*

3 [U] an area of experience or knowledge: *Statistical analysis is not the exclusive territory of a handful of specialists.* | *The very competitive market is pushing firms into unfamiliar territory.*

4 FINANCE **in negative/positive/record etc territory** falling or rising in value, higher than ever before in value etc: *On the world's major exchanges, stocks ended in negative territory.* | *A late spurt of buying pulled the Dow Jones into positive territory.*

ter•tia•ry /ˈtɜːʃəri‖ˈtɜːrʃieri, -ʃəri/ *adj* [only before a noun] tertiary industries or companies are involved in providing services, rather than the production of RAW MATERIALS (=materials used in manufacturing) or manufacturing: *The government plans to transform the current farm-based rural economy into a mixture of primary, secondary and* ***tertiary industries***. | *The city's economy has moved away from heavy industries towards an expanded* ***tertiary sector***.

tertiary education —see under EDUCATION

tertiary industry —see under INDUSTRY

TESSA /ˈtesə/ *n* [C] Tax Exempt Special Savings Account; a type of savings account introduced by the British Government in 1991 to encourage people to save money, replaced in 1999 by ISAs

test[1] /test/ *n* [C] **1** a set of questions, exercises, or practical activities to measure someone's skill, ability, or knowledge

aptitude test a test to find out if you have the necessary skills to do a particular job or activity: *After the interview you will be asked to take an aptitude test.*

EQ test emotional quotient test; a test that employers give to possible future EMPLOYEES to find out if they have the character, CREATIVITY (=ability to produce new ideas), and social skills necessary to be good at their jobs

IQ test intelligence quotient test; a test to measure a person's level of intelligence, with 100 being the average result. The test consists of problems related to letters, numbers, and shapes

2 a process used to find out whether something is of the right quality or works correctly, or to find out whether it contains a particular substance: *nuclear weapons tests* + **for**: *a test for chemicals in the water*

blind test [C] MARKETING ◆ a way of testing a product in which people are asked to try the product and give their opinion about it without telling them the product's name: *In a blind test, 58% of those tested preferred Coors Extra Gold.*

◆ a test carried out on a new medicine to see whether it works or not. Some people are given the real medicine and others are given something that looks like it but contains none of the new medicine. The results are checked to prove whether the medicine had an effect; BLIND TRIAL

field test a test on a new piece of equipment done in the place where it is to be used rather than in a LABORATORY, factory etc; FIELD TRIAL

hall test MARKETING a type of market research in which a group of consumers are asked what they think of specific products, advertisements etc: *We got paid $35 an hour to participate in a hall test this weekend.*

liquid ratio test FINANCE another name for ACID RATIO —see also ***acid test ratio*** under RATIO, MEANS-TEST

test[2] *v* **1** [T] to ask someone spoken or written questions, or make them do a practical activity, to find out how much they know about something or how well they can do something: *We will be testing your knowledge of computers.* **test sb on sth**: *Candidates were tested on their typing skills.*

2 [T] to use something for a short time to see if it works properly: *The software has not been fully tested.* **test sth on sb**: *The new drug has not been tested on humans.*

3 [I,T] to examine a substance in order to find out something about it, for example whether it contains something **test sth for sth**: *We test the ore samples for quality.* **test for sth**: *They are currently testing for oil at the site.* **test sb for sth**: *Employees can be randomly tested for drugs.*

tes•ta•ment /ˈtestəmənt/ *n* [C] a WILL

tes•tate /ˈtesteɪt/ *adj* LAW **die testate** to die after having made a WILL (=official document stating who will have your money, property etc after you die) —compare INTESTATE

tes•ta•tor /teˈsteɪtə‖ˈtesteɪtər/ *n* [C] LAW a person who makes a WILL (=official document stating who will have their money, property etc after they die): *The witnesses must sign the will in the testator's presence.*

test case —see under CASE

test•deck /ˈtestdek/ *n* [C] ACCOUNTING, COMPUTING a computer program which is used to check a small amount of DATA (=information held by a computer). The results of the calculations are then compared with the results of calculations done by a person to make sure the computer is operating correctly. Testdecks are often used as part of an AUDIT: *The testdeck will reveal errors in the income and expenditure account operation.*

test-drive *n* [C] an occasion when someone, especially a customer, drives a car to find out whether they want to buy it: *More auto shoppers are taking extended test drives by renting, perhaps for a weekend, the models they are considering buying.* —**test-drive** *v* [T] *Consumers who test-drive any Cadillac next week get a free weekend rental of a Cadillac through Avis.*

tes•ti•mo•ni•al /ˌtestə̇ˈməʊniəl‖-ˈmoʊ-/ *n* [C] **1** a statement about the quality or value of a product, especially one made by a respected or famous person as part of an advertisement: *The ads feature testimonials from*

T

car owners who credit the air bag with saving their lives.
2 a formal written statement describing someone's character and abilities that they can use when looking for work: *You may need a testimonial from a senior manager or employer.* —compare REFERENCE

tes·ti·mo·ny /'testəməni‖-mouni/ *n* plural **testimonies** [C,U] a formal statement that something is true, such as the one a WITNESS makes in a court of law: *In her testimony, Ms. Jones denied that she knew about the transactions.* | *A federal grand jury has called a number of witnesses to* ***give testimony*** *in the pension-fund case.*

test market —see under MARKET[1]

test-market *v* [T] MARKETING to introduce a new product or service in a small area of a country to find out whether people are likely to buy it when it becomes more widely available: *Anheuser-Busch Cos. will test-market a new light beer in six states beginning next week.* | *The low-fat eggs, which were testmarketed in Cincinnati probably won't be back on the shelves for some time.*

test-run *n* [C] an occasion when a new machine, piece of equipment, or procedure is tested to find out whether it works correctly: *Fire during a test-run seriously damaged an experimental Japanese supertrain.*

text file —see under FILE[1]

tex·tile /'tekstaɪl/ *n* **1** [C] cloth made in large quantities: *Their main exports are textiles, especially silk and cotton.* | *the British* ***textile company*** *Coats Viyella PLC* | *the US* ***textile market***
2 textiles [plural] the industry involved in making cloth: *Half a million jobs were lost in steel and textiles.*

theft /θeft/ *n* [C,U] the crime of stealing or an act of stealing something: *An employee was fired for theft.* | *Your property should be insured against theft.* + **of**: *Thefts of property from cars rose 24%.*

theo·ry /'θɪəri‖'θi:əri/ *n* plural **theories** **1** [C] an idea or set of ideas that is intended to explain why something happens or how it works + **of**: *Schumpeter's Theory of Economic Development* | *The theory is that a healthy employee is cheaper and more productive.*
2 [U] the general principles or ideas of a subject, especially a scientific subject: *They found that* ***theory and practice*** *are two different things* (=things do not always happen according to the theory).

economic theory ♦ [U] all the different ways of explaining and understanding economics: *One lesson from economic theory is that high-saving economies grow quickly.*
♦ [C] a particular way of explaining economics or an economic activity: *Shatalin worked on an economic theory known as 'optimal planning'.*

Elliot wave theory [singular] ECONOMICS the idea that prices on the stockmarkets go up and down over time in a regular way, like a series of waves. People who believe in this theory think it can be used to see how stockmarket prices will change in the future and to say when particular shares will reach their highest and lowest price

employment theory [U] ECONOMICS the part of economics concerned with the level and type of employment in an economy, what causes it to change etc

game theory [U] STATISTICS a method of guessing how the activities of competing organizations could affect your own company. It involves imagining what other companies will do and calculating the economic results of these actions: *Game theory is different from other forms of theorizing because it recognizes that the outcome of a transaction often depends on what other people are doing.*

monetary theory [U] ideas about how monetary systems operate, what effect monetary policies have etc: *In simple monetary theory, the growth in the money supply equals the growth in the economy plus the rate of inflation.*

price theory [U] ECONOMICS the study of how prices are set and how they go up and down in relation to changing supply, demand etc

queuing theory also **queueing theory** STATISTICS ideas to do with the way in which people wait in line for goods and services, used for example by service organizations to make the best use of employees so that customers do not wait for longer than necessary —see also COST OF PRODUCTION THEORY OF VALUE

Theory X *n* [singular] HUMAN RESOURCES the theory that employees will not work well unless managers pay close attention to their work and control them by encouraging or threatening them

Theory Y *n* [singular] HUMAN RESOURCES the theory that employees will generally work well and take responsibility for their own work, if they have the right conditions and rewards

Theory Z *n* [singular] HUMAN RESOURCES the theory that when employees are very involved in their organization and in making decisions, as in the Japanese style of management, they work better and produce more

therm /θɜ:m‖θɜ:rm/ *n* [C] a measurement of heat equal to 100,000 British Thermal Units, used in Britain for measuring how much gas someone has used

thin /θɪn/ *adj* if trading on a financial market is thin, there is not much activity: *Trade was thin in the currency markets yesterday, heading into a Japanese long weekend.*

think-tank also **think tank** *n* [C] a committee of people with special experience or knowledge in a particular area which is established by a government to produce ideas and advice on something: *a government-sponsored think-tank*

third /θɜ:d‖θɜ:rd/ *adj* **third half/quarter/period** the third half, quarter etc of the financial year

third market —see under MARKET[1]

third party *n* plural **third parties** [C] **1** LAW someone who is not one of the two main people or organizations involved in an agreement or legal case: *The preference tests were conducted by an independent third party.*
2 INSURANCE in an insurance contract, someone who is not the insurer or the insured person, but who will get money if the insured person causes them loss or injury: *The insurance only covers loss or injury to a third party.*

third party, fire and theft insurance —see under INSURANCE

Third World *n* **the Third World** the poorer countries of the world, that are not industrially developed: *The bank had stakes in several operations in the Third World.* —**Third World** *adj*: *Third World debt*

Third World debt —see under DEBT

Thirty-Share index —see ***FTSE 30 Index*** under INDEX[1]

thresh·old /'θreʃhəuld, -ʃəuld‖-ould/ *n* [C] the level at which something belongs in a particular class or is affected by a particular rule: *Cash transactions over a $10,000 threshold must be reported to the IRS.* + **for**: *The vehicles will have 70% U.S. content, which is the legal threshold for being an American car.*

thrift /θrɪft/ *n* **1** [C] also **thrift institution** in the US, a SAVINGS AND LOAN ASSOCIATION or SAVINGS BANK: *Before it collapsed, Lamar Savings was the 12th largest thrift in Texas.*
2 [U] wise and careful use of money, especially when this involves saving money for the future: *Savings banks spread new ideas about independence and thrift.*

thrive /θraɪv/ *v* past tense **thrived** or **throve** [I] if a company, market, or place is thriving, it is very successful

T

and making a lot of money: *Our natural food supermarkets are thriving.* —**thriving** *adj*: *He has a thriving computer-consultancy business.*

through•put /'θruːpʊt/ *n* [U] the amount of work, materials etc that can be dealt with in a particular period of time: *an airport with a weekly throughput of 100,000 passengers* | *The ATF has the* ***throughput capacity*** *of seven of our old computers* (=can deal with seven times as much information in the same period of time).

throw /θrəʊ‖θroʊ/ *v* past tense **threw** past participle **thrown** [T] **1 throw money at** to try to solve a problem by spending a lot of money, without really thinking about the problem: *There is no point throwing money at the pollution problem.*

2 throw money away also **throw good money after bad** *BrE*, **throw money down the drain** *BrE*, **throw money down a rat hole** *AmE* to waste money by spending it on something that has already failed: *As the project devoured more than £4 million, we began to wonder if we were throwing money down the drain.*

throw sth ↔ **out** *phr v* [T] **1** to get rid of something that you do not want or need: *They are throwing out their old mainframe computers.*

2 to decide not to accept a plan, suggestion, or legal decision: *The appeals court threw out the verdict.* | *The bill was thrown out by the Senate.*

throw•a•way /'θrəʊəweɪ‖'θroʊ-/ *adj* **1 throwaway cup/plate/razor etc** a cup, plate etc that has been produced cheaply so that it can be thrown away after it has been used; DISPOSABLE

2 the throwaway society used to show disapproval when talking about modern societies in which products are not made to last a long time and people do not care about things because they can buy new ones whenever they want

tick[1] /tɪk/ *n* [C] **1** a mark that you put next to an answer to show that it is correct or against an item on a list to show that you have dealt with it; CHECK *AmE*: *Put a tick in the column that applies to you.*

2 on tick *BrE informal* if you get something on tick, you arrange to take it now and pay for it later

3 FINANCE an occasion when the price of a share, bond etc moves up or down: *He had the trades done near the close of the trading day on either a* ***plus tick*** (=a price higher than the previous trade) *or a* ***zero-plus tick*** (=an unchanged price following upward price movement).

4 FINANCE in interest rates, bond prices etc one hundredth of one per cent: *The price of the December Eurodollar future quickly rose four ticks, from 94.15 to 94.19.*

tick[2] *v* [T] to make a mark next to an answer or something on a list to show that it is correct or has been dealt with; CHECK *AmE*: *Which of the following features do you feel are important when choosing a bed? (Please tick all that apply).*

tick over *phr v* [I] *BrE* if a system, business etc ticks over, it goes on working but without producing much or without much happening: *The market did little more than tick over.*

ticker tape *n* **1** [U] long narrow paper on which information or news is printed by a special machine as soon as events have happened

2 [singular] FINANCE a computer screen that shows information about the buying and selling of shares: *Several large trades showed on the ticker tape.*

tick•et /'tɪkɨt/ *n* [C] a printed piece of paper which shows that you have paid to travel on a bus or plane, enter a cinema, go to a sports game etc: *The price includes* ***theatre tickets*** *and taxis.* + **to**: *The airline is offering frequent fliers a free ticket to Europe.* + **for**: *He bought an Underground ticket for Piccadilly.* | *United Airlines has nearly 14,000* ***ticket agents***.

one-way ticket a ticket for travelling from one place to another but not back again: *A first-class one-way ticket between New York and Boston cost $89.*

return ticket also **round-trip ticket** *AmE* a ticket for a trip from one place to another and back again: *The airline's New York-London round-trip ticket will be $428 on weekdays.*

season ticket a ticket for several journeys, performances, games etc that costs less than paying separately each time: *a* ***season ticket holder*** (=someone who has one)

single ticket *BrE* another name for a ONE-WAY TICKET

tie /taɪ/ *v* past tense and past participle **tied** present participle **tying**

tie sth **up** *phr v* [T] **1** to use money for something so that it is not easily available to be used for anything else: *These securities could be a good choice for investors who can afford to tie up their money for two to seven years.* + **in:** *Her cash is all tied up in real estate.* | *The bank had too high a percentage of its assets, about 20%, tied up in one borrower.*

2 to use a telephone line so that it cannot be used for anything else or by anyone else: *computerized dialing machines that tie up phone lines*

3 be tied up to be very busy so that you do not have time to see someone or to do something: *I can't see you tomorrow – I'm going to be tied up all day.*

4 to finish arranging all the details of a contract, deal, or plan: *Our sales team were able to tie up a new contract.*

5 *AmE* to block the movement of vehicles or people so that they cannot move freely: *a free roadside service for stranded vehicles that tie up traffic*

tie up with sb/sth *phr v* [T] if one organization ties up with another, they decide to work together as partners on a particular activity: *Neither airline has announced plans to tie up with a foreign carrier.*

tie-in *n* [C] **1** a product such as a record, book, or toy that is connected with a new film, TV show etc: *Many of the books in the bestseller lists are TV tie-ins.*

2 a way of PROMOTING (=attracting people's attention to) a new film, TV show etc by connecting it with something such as a free gift or well-known product: *Walt Disney is working with Burger King on a tie-in with the release of Disney's 'Beauty & the Beast' movie.*

tier /tɪə‖tɪr/ *n* [C] one of several levels of quality, usually three: *Investors are going for the better value represented by* ***middle-tier*** *and* ***lower-tier*** *junk bonds* (=bonds that have a high risk of not being repaid). | *Iberia will build its Viva subsidiary into a* ***second-tier*** *airline offering discounted flights.* | *three* ***top-tier*** *accounting firms*

Tier 1 capital —see under CAPITAL

Tier 2 capital —see under CAPITAL

tier 1 equity —see under EQUITY

tie-up *n* [C] an agreement to become business partners + **with**: *Asahi Breweries Ltd. will market beer in Britain in a tie-up with Courage Breweries.*

Ti•gers /'taɪgəz‖-ərz/ also **Asian Tigers** *n* [plural] *journalism* the successful economies of South East Asia including South Korea, Taiwan, Singapore, Malaysia, and Hong Kong: *Japan and the Asian tigers have managed perfectly well without domestic sources of oil.*

till /tɪl, tl/ *n* [C] a machine used in shops, restaurants etc for calculating the amount you have to pay, and for storing the money; CASH REGISTER: *Two armed men ordered the assistant to open the till.* | *There were queues* ***at the till***.

tim•ber /'tɪmbə‖-ər/ *n* [U] *especially BrE* wood used for building or making things, or the trees that produce this wood; LUMBER *AmE*: *The region has huge exports of timber.*

time /taɪm/ *n* **1** [U] the quantity that is measured in minutes, hours, years etc using clocks: *The company needs more time to restructure its finances.* | *The Channel Tunnel has cut the* ***journey time*** *from London to Paris.*

air time ◆ [U] MARKETING the amount of time that a particular advertisement is seen on television, heard on radio etc: *Banks are now allowed only 375 seconds of air time monthly on each television station.*
◆ [U] the amount of time that a MOBILE PHONE user talks on his or her phone in a particular period of time: *Cellular customers will pay normal air time charges for the service.*
dead time [U] time that is not being used: *A business person spends 60 hours a year on hold on the phone, but until now little imagination has been applied to using this dead time.*
delivery time [C] the amount of time that a company takes to get goods ready for delivery, for example the time it takes to obtain them or make them: *They reported increases in delivery times and unfilled orders.*
down time ◆ [U] time that a machine is not being used, usually because it is broken: *To reduce down time, the designers made all parts modular. Parts needing service can be popped out and quickly replaced.*
◆ [U] time that a factory is not working, usually because there is not enough demand for its products: *GM is idling seven assembly plants next week, which includes the extension of down time at its factory in Bowling Green, Ohio.*
dwell time [U] MARKETING a calculation of the amount of time people spend waiting for something, such as a train, airline etc, and therefore the length of time they are likely to spend doing things while they wait, such as reading advertisements, buying food etc: *With airline delays increasing passenger dwell time in terminals, it is in the financial self-interest of airports to serve up appealing distractions.*
lead time [C] the time it takes to prepare, make, or deliver something: *It takes **long lead times** to propose and build new nuclear power plants.*
lost time [U] the time when a piece of machinery cannot be used or a worker is unable to work, for example because of injury: *The number of **lost time accidents** occurring on site was 14.*
new time [U] FINANCE the beginning of a new period of time for trading on a financial market: *new time buying on the futures market*
play time [U] the length of time that a particular record is heard on radio, used to calculate ROYALTIES (=payments to those that made it): *Each record is cataloged according to its play time and schedule for airing.*
prime time [U] the time when most people are watching the television or listening to the radio, and therefore the most expensive time for advertising: *Mr Clinton used **prime time television** for a brief, personalised appeal to voters.* | *NPR's prime time is just before the 8 o'clock news.*
quality time [U] time that is set aside for a particular activity, especially something that is usually forgotten because you are very busy: *Nicola Horlick's high-powered career didn't prevent her from spending quality time with her five children.*
2 time and a half/time and a quarter one and a half times or one and a quarter times the normal rate of pay: *You get time and a half if you come into the office on Saturday.*
3 double/triple time twice or three times the normal rate of pay: *We worked Sundays and holidays at double time.*
4 [singular] a particular point in time: ***What time is** the meeting?*
5 [U] the time in one particular part of the world, or the time used in one particular area: *We will be arriving in New York at 3 a.m. **local time**.*
6 on time arriving or happening at the correct time or the time that was arranged: *86% of our flights were on time last year.* | *The card rewards customers for paying bills on time.*
7 [C] an occasion when something happens or someone does something: *The committee meets six times a year.* | *Customers resented being charged $100 every time they brought a vehicle in for repairs.*
8 five/ten/many etc times used to say how much bigger, better etc one thing is than another: *The stock was recently selling for more than 200 times the past four quarters' earnings.* —see also FULL-TIME, LAPSE OF TIME, PART-TIME, RIGHT FIRST TIME

time and motion study —see under STUDY[1]

time charter —see under CHARTER[2]

time clock *n* [C] a clock, often connected to a computer, that records the exact time that someone arrives at and leaves work

time-frame *n* [C] the period of time during which you expect or agree that something will happen or be done + **for**: *The 60-day time-frame for completion of the report seems reasonable.* + **on**: *Santa Cruz Operation Inc. declined to **put a time-frame** on delivery of its products.*

time lag —see under LAG[2]

time management —see under MANAGEMENT

time-sharing *n* [U] **1** COMPUTING a way for a computer to deal with more than one program at the same time, or for a telephone line to deal with more than one set of signals at the same time: *Connections are rapidly switched on a time-sharing basis.*
2 when people buy a holiday home with other people so that they can each spend a period of time there every year: *the sale of time-sharing real estate units* —**time-share** *adj* [only before a noun] *golf courses, marinas, hotels and **time-share developments***

time sheet *n* [C] a record of the hours you have worked and what work you have been doing in that time, written on a piece of paper or put onto a computer: *He ordered his staff to fill in time sheets, accounting for every hour.*

time·ta·ble /ˈtaɪmˌteɪbəl/ *n* [C] **1** a plan giving dates and times when events will take place or things must be done; SCHEDULE: *It is your responsibility to produce the report according to the timetable agreed with us.* + **for**: *They drew up a timetable for the development of a prototype.*
2 a list of the times at which buses, trains, planes etc arrive and leave; SCHEDULE *AmE*: *A full railway timetable is available on the Internet.* —**timetabled** *adj*: *penalties paid by operating companies for failing to run timetabled trains*

time to market *n* [U] the time it takes to design and make a new product and make it available to buy: *The electronics industry is looking for ways to accelerate time to market.*

time value also **time value of money** *n* [C] the fact that an amount of money to be received or paid in the future is worth less than the same amount today, and the further it is in the future, the less it is worth: *We recognise that money has a time value by discounting future cash flows at an appropriate discount rate.*

time zone —see under ZONE[1]

tip[1] /tɪp/ *n* [C] **1** a piece of advice about what is likely to happen, for example about which shares are likely to go up or down in value: *to receive a stock market tip* | *Many dealers' clients boast to friends of their broker or their man in the City, who gives them tips.*
2 a small amount of additional money that you give to someone such as a waiter in order to thank them for their services: *She gave the taxi driver a £5 tip.*

tip[2] *v* past tense and past participle **tipped** present participle **tipping** **1** [T] to say who you think is most likely to do something or be successful **be tipped to do sth**: *Cadbury has been tipped to buy Perrier's soft drinks business.* | *Mr Zhu is tipped to replace the cautious Mr Li eventually.* **tip sb for sth**: *Journalists are tipping her for rapid promotion.*

T

2 [I,T] a give advice about something, for example about which shares are likely to go up or down in value: *These shares were tipped in the Investor's Chronicle.*
3 [I,T] to give a small amount of additional money to someone such as a waiter in order to thank them for their services: *He tipped the taxi driver £2.* | *According to the waiters, she always tips generously.*

tip•pee /tɪˈpiː/ *n* [C] FINANCE someone who receives information about financial deals, especially those involving buying or selling shares: *Under the regulations, a tippee may not deal in the securities of a company if he holds unpublished price-sensitive information about them.* —compare TIPPER

tippee trading —see under TRADING

tip•per /ˈtɪpə‖-ər/ *n* [C] FINANCE someone who supplies information about financial deals, especially those involving buying or selling shares: *The ruling of the Supreme Court has reduced the liability of both tippers and tippees considerably.* —compare TIPPEE

tip sheets *n* [plural] FINANCE *informal* newspapers which give information and advice about which shares should be bought or sold: *Licensed dealers still deal in certain shares the punter reads about in the tip sheets.*

TIR *n* Transports Internationaux Routiers; the French name for international road TRANSPORT. Vehicles in some countries that are taking goods abroad carry a sign with the letters TIR

ti•ta•ni•um /taɪˈteɪniəm/ *n* [U] a strong, light, and very expensive metal used in manufacturing and traded on COMMODITIES MARKETS: *The company plans to mine titanium deposits in South Africa.*

ti•tle /ˈtaɪtl/ *n* **1** [C] a name that describes a person's job or position: *What is your **job title**?* | *Her official title is Human Resources Manager.*
2 [C] a particular book, magazine, piece of software etc sold by a company: *We publish 200 new titles a year.*
3 [singular, U] LAW the legal right to own property: *You must demonstrate that you have **proof of title**.* + **to**: *Who holds the title to the land?*
absolute title [singular, U] a right of ownership of land that cannot be doubted and where there is no risk of anyone else claiming to be the owner
abstract of title plural **abstracts of title** [C,U] a legal document that proves someone's right to own a particular property, listing all the documents relating to the ownership of the property: *Examine your abstract of title against the deeds to check for inconsistencies.* —compare CERTIFICATE OF SEARCH
bad title [singular, U] a title that is not clear about who is the owner of a property, especially property that is for sale
deducing title [singular, U] proving who is the legal owner of a property: *As a seller, deducing title will consist in almost all cases merely of supplying the buyer's conveyancer with office copy entries on the Register.*
defective title [singular, U] in Britain, a right of ownership of land which is not recorded with the LAND REGISTRY and so there is a risk that someone else can claim to be the owner
document of title plural **documents of title** [C] a document that shows the ownership of property or that gives the person possessing it the right to deal with the property as if they owned it
marketable title [singular, U] a title to land which shows that the person selling the land is the only legal owner and so has the right to sell it: *Solicitors should be able to say whether there is **good and marketable title** to the relevant property.*
paper title [singular, U] ownership of something and the legal document that shows this: *a person who can **establish paper title*** (=prove that they own something)
proof of title [U] a legal document that proves that someone owns a particular property: *There was a difficulty getting proof of title from the Land Registry.*
registered title [singular, U] in Britain, a right of ownership of land which has been recorded with the LAND REGISTRY
root of title [singular, U] documents showing ownership of property, even if the property is not REGISTERED: *The Law of Property Act 1969 provides that a good root of title is a conveyance on sale or legal mortgage which is at least 15 years old* —see also CHAIN OF TITLE, CLOUD ON TITLE, EVIDENCE OF TITLE, EXAMINATION OF TITLE

title deed —see under DEED

TM written abbreviation for TRADEMARK

toe•hold /ˈtəʊhəʊld‖ˈtoʊhoʊld/ *n* [singular] someone's first involvement in a particular business activity from which they can develop and become stronger: *The company has struggled for a toehold in the fiercely competitive workstation market.*

to•ken[1] /ˈtəʊkən‖ˈtoʊ-/ *n* [C] a piece of paper, card, plastic etc that can be exchanged for goods: *Collect eight of these tokens and send off for a free recipe book.*
book token *BrE* a piece of paper worth a particular amount of money which can be exchanged for a book in a shop: *a £10 book token*
gift token also **gift voucher** *BrE* a piece of paper worth a particular amount of money which can be exchanged for goods in a shop; GIFT CERTIFICATE *AmE*

token[2] *adj* [only before a noun] done or given only as a small sign of something larger or more important: *a token cut in interest rates* | *There is a **token charge*** (=a small charge that does not cover the actual cost of something) *for the use of the database.* | *The players were amateurs and received only a token payment plus expenses*

token coinage —see under COINAGE

to•ken•ism /ˈtəʊkənɪzəm‖ˈtoʊ-/ *n* [U] when an organization includes a representative of a particular group such as women, black people etc in an activity or position only in order to give an appearance of fairness: *Appointing her to the committee strikes me as little more than tokenism.*

token strike —see under STRIKE[1]

toll[1] /təʊl‖toʊl/ *n* **1** [C] the money you have to pay to use a particular road, bridge etc: *In France and in parts of the USA tolls are charged for motorways.* | *to raise revenue through customs duties and road tolls*
2 take a/its toll on sth/sb to have a very bad effect on something or someone over a long period of time: *Mounting debts were taking a toll on its finances.* | *Rising unemployment has taken its toll on the consumer lending market.*

toll[2] *adj* **toll bridge/road/tunnel etc** *BrE* a bridge etc where you have to pay to drive

toll-free *adv AmE* if you telephone a number toll-free, you do not have to pay for the call —**toll-free** *adj*: *Call this toll-free number for details.*

tomb•stone /ˈtuːmstəʊn‖-stoʊn/ *n* [C] *informal* FINANCE an advertisement in a newspaper that lists the banks that are taking part in a share or bond ISSUE: *KPMG reserve the right to publish at its own expense and subject to your prior approval a tombstone recording the completed transaction.*

ton /tʌn/ *n* plural **tons** or **ton** [C] **1** a unit for measuring weight, equal to 2240 pounds or 1016 kilograms in Britain, and 2000 pounds or 907.2 kilograms in the US: *The quarry produces about 6000 tons per annum.* | *a price of $150 a ton* —compare TONNE
American ton another name for SHORT TON
British ton another name for LONG TON
long ton a unit for measuring weight, equal to 2240 pounds or 1016 kilograms; BRITISH TON
metric ton a unit for measuring weight, equal to 1000 kilograms; TONNE

T

net ton *AmE* another name for SHORT TON: *Steel exports in July were 303,000 net tons.*

short ton a unit for measuring weight, equal to 2000 pounds or 907.2 kilograms; AMERICAN TON

2 *informal* used when talking about money to mean a hundred', for example £100 or $100 million

ton•nage /ˈtʌnɪdʒ/ *n* [C,U] **1** the total number of tons that something weighs: *The aim is to obtain the maximum saleable tonnage at reasonable cost.*

2 the size of a ship or the amount of goods it can carry, measured in tons

gross registered tonnage abbreviation **GRT** ♦ a measurement of the space for carrying goods in a ship. Gross measurement tonnage is obtained by dividing the number of CUBIC FEET of space by 100

♦ the total gross registered tonnage of all the ships belonging to a particular shipping company, country etc: *Liberia held the third largest gross registered tonnage on the Lloyds Register of Shipping in that year.*

net registered tonnage abbreviation **NRT** gross registered tonnage less the space taken by stores, fuel, machinery etc

tonne /tʌn/ *n* plural **tonnes** or **tonne** [C] a metric unit for measuring weight, equal to 1000 kilograms; METRIC TON: *Brazil produced more than 50,000 tonnes of tin in 1989.* | *Cash LME copper jumped by £54.50 a tonne.*

tool¹ /tuːl/ *n* [C] **1** an object, piece of equipment, or device used for making things: *Something like sixty tools may be used to machine a workpiece.* | *Black and Decker, the tool manufacturer*

machine tool MANUFACTURING a powerful tool used for cutting and shaping metal, for example for making parts for cars, engines, machinery etc: *a slump in demand for machine tools and other capital goods*

2 a skill or method of doing a particular task: *Praise is a hugely powerful* ***management tool.*** | *Using a preferred currency can be a strong* ***marketing tool*** *when negotiating a contract.* | *Reports and accounts are a useful publicity tool.*

3 COMPUTING a piece of software designed to do a particular task: *an editing tool allowing colour to be added* | *The files are textual, to allow the use of most UNIX tools.*

tool² *v*

tool up *phr v* [I,T] to prepare a factory for production by providing the necessary tools and machinery: *Nimslo received £3 million in government grants to tool up for production at the Timex factory.* | *Ford was tooled up to produce their new car, the Mondeo, in large numbers.*

top¹ /tɒp‖tɑːp/ *adj* [only before a noun] **1** at the highest level: *The top rate of income tax has been cut sharply.* | *the pay of top executives* | *She spent five years in the* ***top job.*** | *He is among the top 5% of earners in this country.*

2 biggest or most successful: *the top 100 companies in the UK*

3 best: *We sell only top-quality goods.*

top² *v* past tense and past participle **topped** present participle **topping** [T] **1** to be higher than a particular amount: *Profits this year should top £1.2 billion.* | *Last year bilateral trade topped $1 billion.*

2 top an offer/bid etc to offer more money than someone else: *A rival company has topped our offer by $5 million.*

top out *phr v* [I] if something such as a price that is increasing tops out, it reaches its highest point and stops rising: *Do you think interest rates have topped out now?*

top sth ↔ **up** *phr v* [T] *BrE* to add to something in order to bring it up to the level you want: *to top up your pension contributions* —see also TOP-UP

top³ *n* **the top** the most important or most successful position in an organization, company, group etc: *He started life at the bottom and worked his way up to the top.* | *This decision has come* ***from the top*** (=was made by the most important managers).

top brass *n* [singular, U] *informal* the top managers in an organization; BRASS: *Unix System Labs' top brass has been meeting with the Russian Minister of Higher Education.*

top copy —see under COPY¹

top-down *adj* [only before a noun] a top-down plan etc is one in which you start with a general idea of what you want and then add the details later: *a top-down or bottom-up approach to management*

top-end *adj* [only before a noun] used to describe the most expensive products in a range of products or a market: *a top-end retailer*

top grosser *n* [C] *journalism* a product, especially a film, play etc that makes more money than any other film etc in a particular period of time: *By the end of this week, 'Star Wars: The Phantom Menace' could surpass the original movie as the studio's top grosser.*

top-hat pension —see under PENSION¹

top-heavy *adj* an organization that is top-heavy has too many managers compared to the number of ordinary workers: *The company was burdened with a top-heavy bureaucracy.*

TOPIC /ˈtɒpɪk‖ˈtɑː-/ *n* FINANCE Teletext Output of Price Information on Computer; a computer system used on the London Stock Exchange which gives information on share prices, currency exchange rates etc: *When a bargain has been struck the TOPIC price displays are altered to show the last trades made.*

top line *n* [singular] the amount of money received before costs have been taken away; REVENUE: *Last year we focused on cost-cutting rather than revenue, but this year we need to focus on the top line.* **—top-line** *adj* [only before a noun] *top-line revenue growth*

top-line *adj* also **top-of-the-line** top-line goods are expensive and thought to be of high quality: *makers of top-line cars such as Mercedes, BMW and Porsche*

top management —see under MANAGEMENT

top-of-the-range *adj* used to describe the most expensive products in a range of products or a market: *top-of-the-range PCs* | *This is our* ***top-of-the-range model.***

top-up *n* [C] *BrE* an amount added to something in order to bring it up to the level you want: *Factoring finance sometimes provides the top-up needed to make a buyout possible.* **—top-up** *adj* [only before a noun] ***a top-up loan*** | *top-up fees*

top-up pension —see under PENSION¹

tort /tɔːt‖tɔːrt/ *n* [C,U] LAW an action that is wrong but not criminal and can be dealt with in a CIVIL court of law: *the tort of negligence* | *claiming damages* ***in tort*** | *a reform of the US tort system*

to•tal¹ /ˈtəʊtl‖ˈtoʊ-/ *adj* [only before a noun] with everything added together: *The* ***total cost*** *of the project is put at £450 million.* | *a company with total sales of £12 billion last year* | *His total income is around £40,000.*

total² *n* [C] the final number or amount of things when everything has been counted or added together: *What does the total come to?* | *We expect to raise a total of £3.6 million.* | *The jobless total is steadily increasing.*

total³ *v* **totalled totalling** *BrE* **totaled totaling** *AmE* [T] to add up to a particular total: *Last year their sales totalled £364 million.* | *The company has debts totalling $7.9 million.* | *In order to receive benefits your savings must total less than £6,000.*

total quality management —see under MANAGEMENT

touch /tʌtʃ/ *v* [T] **touch base (with sb)** to telephone someone you work with, or visit them for a short time,

T

while you are spending time somewhere else: *I need to touch base with the office back in Boston.*

touch screen —see under SCREEN[1]

touch-type *v* [I] to be able to use a TYPEWRITER or computer KEYBOARD without needing to look at the KEYS (=letters) while you are using it: *I wish I'd learnt to touch-type.*

tour•is•m /ˈtʊərɪzəm‖ˈtʊr-/ *n* [U] the business of providing hotels, entertainment, meals etc for people while they are on holiday: *Most of the country's income derives from tourism.*

tour operator —see under OPERATOR

tout[1] /taʊt/ *v* **1 tout for business/custom/trade** *especially BrE* to try to persuade people to buy goods or services you are offering: *I've been on the phone all morning touting for business.*
2 [T] to praise something or someone in order to persuade people that they are worth accepting, using etc **be touted as sth**: *She is being touted as the best candidate for the job.*

tout[2] *n* [C] also **ticket tout** *BrE* someone who buys tickets for a concert, sports match etc and sells them for more than the official price; SCALPER *AmE*

TQM abbreviation for TOTAL QUALITY MANAGEMENT

tracker fund —see under FUND[1]

track record *n* [C usually singular] all the things that a person or organization has done in the past, which shows how good they are at doing their job, dealing with problems etc: *This is a company with a* ***proven track record*** (=they have shown in the past how good they are). | *a track record of success* + **in**: *He has a* ***good track record*** *in improving efficiency.*

trad•a•ble also **tradeable** /ˈtreɪdəbəl/ *adj* if something is tradable, you can buy and sell it: *The potential pool of tradable bank loans is huge.* | *big,* ***easily tradable*** *stocks such as Johnson & Johnson, Merck and Coca-Cola*

trade[1] /treɪd/ *n* **1** [U] the activity of buying, selling, or exchanging goods within a country or between countries: *Trade between Hong Kong and eastern European countries has been very limited.* | *Restrictive practices in their home market have given Japanese industries an unfair advantage in* ***international trade***. | *The list will provide a basis for a* ***trade agreement between*** *Canada and Mexico.* + **in**: *The Reptile Protection Trust wants to ban the trade in pet turtles.*
2 [U] ECONOMICS the value of a country's imports and exports, especially when these are compared: *The statistics on UK trade provided some basis for optimism.* | *Hungary's total net trade fell between the last two quarters of the year.* | *The new* ***trade figures*** *were released today.*
external trade [U] buying and selling goods and services abroad: *Luxembourg's external trade increased considerably, reflecting a boost in exports.*
fair trade ♦ [U] a system in which two countries which are TRADING PARTNERS agree not to charge import taxes on particular goods they buy from each other: *The EU has fixed a date by which members should comply with its fair trade rules.*
♦ [U] trading practices that do not restrict the rights of consumers: *Japan's Fair Trade Commission issued new anti-monopoly guidelines.* | *America's fair trade laws*
foreign trade [U] trade with other countries: *China's expanding foreign trade.*
free trade [U] a system in which goods can be bought and sold between countries without any restrictions such as TARIFFS (=taxes) or QUOTAS (=limits on imports) + **with**: *Quebec Liberals strongly support free trade with the US.* | *an agreement on bilateral free trade* (=free trade between two countries) *between Brazil and Venezuela.* | *We aim at bringing the Pacific region rapidly into a US-sponsored Free Trade Area, en route to* ***multilateral free trade*** (=free trade between many countries) *with all of the WTO.* | *the creation of a* ***free trade area*** *that would give South African exporters and South Africa's neighbours improved access to EU markets*
international trade [U] trade in goods and services between different countries: *the GATT international trade talks* + **in**: *efforts to end the international trade in toxic wastes*
invisible trade [U] trade in services such as tourism and banking: *Transport represents 12.6% of the world's total invisible trade.*
overseas trade [U] trade with countries abroad: *a new exporters' organization, intended to help companies get round obstacles to overseas trade*
3 the hotel/banking/motor etc trade(s) the business done by hotels, banks etc: *The figures suggest an improvement in the* ***retail trade*** (=business done by shops). | *The building trades are riddled with bad business practices.*
4 the rag trade *informal* the business of making and selling clothes
5 [singular, U] the level of activity in a company, industry etc: *Trade is very slow at the moment.* | *Garden centres do most of their trade at weekends.* | *They were* ***doing a brisk trade*** (=doing a lot of business) *in Christmas trees right up to the 24th.* | *The restaurants on Boat Quay were* ***doing a roaring trade*** (=doing a lot of business) *despite the fall in tourist arrivals.*
passing trade [U] *BrE* people who go into a shop, restaurant etc because they happen to see it, rather than being regular customers: *businesses which rely on passing trade*
6 [C] a particular job, especially one needing special skills with your hands: *Similar rates of pay apply in other trades, including carpentry, plumbing and joinery.*
7 [C usually plural] FINANCE an occasion when an investment is bought and sold on a financial market: *For trades of 2,000 or more shares, the charge will be $60 plus five cents a share.* | *NASDAQ is the computerized market that handles OTC trades.*
insider trade [C usually plural] when someone working at a high level in a company buys or sells shares in the company: *The executive vice president who heads the bank's equity markets division sold 40,000 shares in November, says Invest/Net, an organization that tracks insider trades.*
wash trade [C] an occasion when the buyer and seller of shares is the same person or organization. Wash trades are illegal —see also BALANCE OF TRADE, BARRIER TO TRADE, CHAMBER OF TRADE

trade[2] *v* **1** [I,T] to buy and sell goods, services etc as part of your business: *The agreement allows metals and plastics to be traded among 24 countries.* + **in**: *They intended to start up a business trading in electronics equipment.* + **with**: *These countries can trade with Britain without having to pay import duties.*
2 [I] to exist and operate as a business: *The joint venture will* ***trade under the name*** *of Do It All chain.* | *The company currently trades on the American Stock Exchange.*
3 [T] FINANCE to buy or sell shares, bonds, currencies, COMMODITIES (=oil, metal, farm products) etc: *115 million shares were traded, more than 15% of the company's stock.*

trade at sth *phr v* [T] if shares etc trade at a particular price, that is how much they cost to buy: *US currency was trading at 1.7407 marks, down from Tuesday's close.*

trade down *phr v* [I] to buy cheaper goods that are of poorer quality: *Consumers aren't trading down in quality, but they are cutting costs in other ways.* + **to**: *Winston loyalists have increasingly traded down to cheaper cigarettes.*

trade sth ↔ **in** *phr v* [T] to give something, such as a car, as part of the payment for something you are buying: *The Toyota dealer only offered him $4,000 to trade it in.* —see also TRADE-IN

T

trade sth ↔ **off** to balance two situations against each other in order to get an acceptable result: *Companies are under pressure to trade off price stability for short-term gains* —see also TRADE-OFF

trade up *phr v* [I] to buy more expensive goods that are of better quality: *Thousands of small-apartment owners are trading up for more luxurious accommodation.* + to: *Home-computer buyers are trading up to machines with more power and speed.*

tradeable *adj* another spelling of TRADABLE

trade association —see under ASSOCIATION

trade balance —see under BALANCE OF TRADE

trade barrier another name for BARRIER TO TRADE

trade bill —see under BILL OF EXCHANGE

trade credit —see under CREDIT[1]

trade creditor —see under CREDITOR

trade cycle —see under CYCLE

trade debt —see under DEBT

trade deficit —see under DEFICIT

trade description *n* [C] *BrE* a description of goods or services by the person or company selling them, for example in an advertisement or a price list: *Even a spoken statement about a product is a trade description.*

Trade Descriptions Act *n* [singular] in Britain, a law which controls how companies can describe their products and services so that customers are not deceived about what they are buying: *The purpose of the Trade Descriptions Act is to promote good business practice.*

trade discount —see under DISCOUNT[1]

traded option —see under OPTION

trade exhibition —see under EXHIBITION

trade gap another name for TRADE DEFICIT —see under DEFICIT

trade-in *n* [C,U] *AmE* a way of buying a new car, television etc in which you give the seller your old car as part of the payment, or a car etc as part of the payment for something new; PART-EXCHANGE *BrE*: *AT&T offer customers a trade-in on their telephone systems for an AT&T product.* | *They can't afford a new car because the* ***trade-in value*** *of the old one has dropped so much.*

T

trade magazine —see under MAGAZINE

trade•mark /ˈtreɪdmɑːk‖-mɑːrk/ *n* [C] a name, sign, or design used on a product to show it is made by a particular company. Trademarks are protected by law: *The company used names similar to well-known trademarks to sell cheap imitations.*

trade mission —see under MISSION

trade•name /ˈtreɪdneɪm/ *n* [C] **1** a name used for a particular product, especially to help customers recognize it: *The new drug will be marketed under the tradename Ciproxin.* —compare BRAND NAME
2 another name for TRADEMARK

trade-off *n* [C] a balance between two situations in order to get an acceptable result: *The legal restrictions will remain as a trade-off for allowing interstate investment.*

trade price —see under PRICE[1]

trad•er /ˈtreɪdə‖-ər/ *n* [C] **1** FINANCE someone who deals in shares, bonds, currencies, COMMODITIES (=oil, metal, farm products) etc on a market either for themselves or for a financial institution: *To the surprise of many traders, the dollar rose in European markets.*
2 someone who buys and sells goods

sole trader a legal form of company in some countries for someone who has their own business, with no other shareholders: *The bank has over one million business accounts, from sole traders to the largest corporations.*

trade sales —see under SALE

Trades Union Congress —see TUC

trade surplus —see under SURPLUS[1]

trade terms —see under TERM[1]

trade union —see under UNION

trade war —see under WAR

trade-weighted exchange rate —see under EXCHANGE RATE

trade-weighted index —see under INDEX[1]

trad•ing /ˈtreɪdɪŋ/ *n* [U] **1** the activity of operating as a business, or the level of this activity: *Unlike other recruitment companies, Burns has not found trading becoming more difficult.*

fair trading when companies do business and compete in a legal and moral way: *We will look closely at mergers in the brewing industry under the fair trading legislation* —see also HORSE-TRADING

2 FINANCE buying and selling activity on a financial market or COMMODITIES MARKET (=one for oil, metals, farm products etc); DEALING *BrE*: *Shares were weak from the outset of London trading.* | *British government bond prices surged in brisk trading.* —see also CROSS-TRADING

active trading ◆ when many shares, COMMODITIES (=oil, metals, farm products etc) are being bought and sold: *Stock prices rose in active trading of 170.3 million shares on the New York Stock Exchange.*
◆ when a company's shares are being bought and sold on a stockmarket, and have not been SUSPENDED (=prevented from being traded by the authorities): *Ferranti's shares return to active trading today after a three-week suspension.*

after-hours trading also **off-hours trading** *AmE* buying and selling shares, bonds etc after a financial market has officially closed for the day: *The NYSE approved a limited form of off-hours trading for large investors, in a move that marks a step toward 24-hour stock trading.*

heavy trading when there is a lot of buying and selling on a stockmarket: *In Hong Kong, shares staged a powerful surge in extremely heavy trading.*

insider trading when someone uses knowledge of a particular company, situation etc that is not available to other people in order to buy or sell shares. Insider trading is illegal: *Shares in both banks jumped 20% two weeks before confirmation of their merger, which led to an insider trading inquiry being opened.*

mixed trading when prices on a financial market go up and down, without a clear movement in either direction: *In mixed trading the Dow Jones average struggled to hold recently won high ground.*

moderate trading when the amount of buying and selling on the stockmarket is neither very large nor very small: *Stock prices closed higher in moderate trading on London's Stock Exchange.*

off-board trading the buying and selling of shares in large US companies without using the NEW YORK STOCK EXCHANGE: *It wasn't clear why Salomon didn't execute the trade on the Big Board. It could have been because off-board trading rules are less strict in some circumstances.*

over-the-counter trading the buying and selling of shares etc when dealers buy and sell shares etc directly between themselves using telephones and computers; OVER-THE-COUNTER DEALING

principal trading also **proprietary trading** when a financial institution buys and sells investments for its own profit, rather than for its clients: *Some 41% of program trading reflected firms' trading for their own accounts, or principal trading, while 44.7% involved trading for customers.*

programme trading *BrE*, **program trading** *AmE* ◆ trading that is done by computers automatically when prices reach particular levels. Some people think that programme trading is responsible for big price changes and may cause markets to CRASH (=an occasion when prices fall very quickly by a very large amount): *Heavy computer-driven programme trading pushed prices down.*

◆ when there is a large order to buy or sell a number of different shares etc in large quantities: *By market close, program trading activity amounted to 14 buys and 7 sells, with a net effect of adding 538.73 points to the Dow.*

tippee trading a type of INSIDER DEALING in which someone who receives secret information from another person passes it to a third person, who then uses it to gain a financial advantage

trading company —see under COMPANY

trading desk *n* [C] FINANCE the area of a financial market where a particular company does business: *The market was quiet and most dealers closed their trading desks at 3 pm.*

trading estate —see under ESTATE

trading loss —see under LOSS

trading manager —see under MANAGER

trading partner —see under PARTNER

trading post *n* [C] *AmE informal* an area in the stockmarket where a particular company does business; TRADING DESK: *A crowd swarmed around the Lasker, Stone & Stern trading post.*

trading profit —see under PROFIT[1]

trading stamp —see under STAMP[1]

traf•fic[1] /ˈtræfɪk/ *n* [U] **1** the movement of planes, ships, trains etc from one place to another: *a telecommunications network for controlling* ***air traffic****.*

2 the movement of people or goods by air, ship, train etc: *The airline said* ***passenger traffic*** *dropped 29% in February.* + **of**: *the extensive traffic of Chinese goods to Canada*

container traffic the movement of goods using containers: *By some estimates, US container traffic will rise by 4% next year.*

3 the movement of computer DATA or other electronic information from one place to another: *American Telephone uses the satellite to carry* ***phone traffic*** *between the US and Russia.* | *a digital service used for* ***data traffic***

4 the number of people buying a particular product or using a particular service: *If consumer spending picks up, there will be keen competition for* ***consumer traffic****.* —see also PAGE TRAFFIC

traffic[2] *v* past tense and past participle **trafficked** present participle **trafficking**

traffic in sth *phr v* [T] to buy and sell illegal goods: *They were accused of trafficking in arms and drugs.*

traf•fick•er /ˈtræfɪkə‖-ər/ *n* [C] someone who buys and sells illegal goods: *international traffickers in stolen art*

trail•blaz•er /ˈtreɪlˌbleɪzə‖-ər/ *n* [C] someone who is the first to do something new, such as develop a new method or product: *His radical management methods gave him the reputation of a trailblazer among American executives.*

trail•er /ˈtreɪlə‖-ər/ *n* [C] an advertisement for a new film, television show etc showing small scenes from it: *The trailer was put through rigorous consumer testing.*

train[1] /treɪn/ *n* [C] a number of connected carriages pulled by an engine on a railway line

goods train *BrE*, **freight train** *AmE* a train for carrying goods, rather than passengers: *The fuel arrives inside special containers on goods trains from nuclear reactors all over the country.* —see also GRAVY TRAIN

train[2] *v* [I,T] to teach someone or to be taught the skills and knowledge needed for a particular job: *Both my sons want to train as chartered accountants.* **train sb in sth**: *One of the major costs of implementing the technology was the need to train workers in new skills.* **train sb to do sth**: *He trains his people to identify customer needs clearly.* —**trained** *adj*: *The recession makes it even more essential to have properly* ***trained staff****.*

train•ee /ˌtreɪˈniː◂/ *n* [C] someone who is being taught the skills and knowledge to do a particular job: *He joined the company as a* ***management trainee****.* | *The company will shed some 300 jobs among trainees and junior management.*

train•ing /ˈtreɪnɪŋ/ *n* [singular, U] the process of training someone or of being trained: *Seiko is sending 30 workers to Japan for training.* | *90% of the graduates were offered* ***on-the-job training*** (=training while working for an employer).

assertiveness training [U] HUMAN RESOURCES training which helps people deal confidently with difficult situations, especially when these involve opposing other people: *Assertiveness training is aimed at improving the effectiveness of our communication style.*

computer-based training [U] when you learn how to use a computer or particular software by doing the special exercises displayed on screen and typing your answers to the questions etc directly into the computer. This training method allows people with different levels of ability to work at different speeds: *Computer-based training is expected to be the biggest professional market for multimedia products in the future.*

management training [U] actions, courses etc to improve the skills of managers in a company: *British companies have doubled their level of management training and development in the last 10 years.*

sensitivity training [U] HUMAN RESOURCES special training to help employees to be aware of the different types of people they deal with in their job: *Sensitivity training alerts employees to customer needs.* | *The study recommends cross-cultural sensitivity training for court personnel.*

tranche /trɑːnʃ/ *n* [C] FINANCE part of a larger sum of money or collection of shares: *The government has traded 200 million Eurobonds in two tranches.* | *The second tranche of the loan would be repaid over three years.*

tranch•ette /trɑːnˈʃet/ *n* [C] a small number of GILTS (=British government bonds) sold in addition to bonds already sold in a particular ISSUE (=amount made available): *The auction was successful and the following day the Bank announced the issue of three new tranchettes of tap stock.*

trans•act /trænˈzækt/ *v* [I,T] *formal* to do business, such as buying or selling, with another company: *The new networks offer the opportunity to* ***transact business*** *electronically with other companies.* | *The good negotiator knows the price at which he is prepared to transact.*

trans•ac•tion /trænˈzækʃən/ *n* [C] **1** a payment, or the process of making one: *The auditors will conduct regular checks on all* ***financial transactions****.* | *HSBC offers a current account aimed at businesses with regular* ***international transactions****.*

2 a business deal: *Corning and Vitro S.A. of Mexico completed a $300 million transaction to combine their consumer businesses.*

3 FINANCE an occasion when a company sells shares, bonds etc or exchanges them for other shares etc: *Amstar Corp. and Essex Industries Inc. carried out a swap of junk bonds in a complicated debt-reduction transaction.*

transaction cost —see under COST[1]

transaction tax —see under TAX[1]

trans•ceiv•er /trænˈsiːvə‖-ər/ *n* [C] a piece of equipment that can receive and send electronic signals: *The new network will use transceivers placed around the city to transmit and relay calls.*

trans•con•tain•er /ˈtrænskənˈteɪnə‖-ər/ *n* [C] a container designed for carrying a particular type of goods, for example soft fruit

trans•fer[1] /træns'fɜː‖-'fɜːr/ *v* past tense and past participle **transferred** present participle **transferring** **1** [T] to move money or investments from one account or institution to another: *Customers can **transfer money** instantly, using the bank's automated machines.* | *One reason investors **transfer annuities** is to get a higher level of benefit.*

2 [T] to move something from one place or position to another: ***Production** from both units **will be transferred** to other centres.* | *Brazil is in the process of transferring its state-owned mills to private ownership.*

3 [I,T] to move from one place or job to another, or to arrange for someone to do this: *The company transferred hundreds of jobs to Mexico.* | *Ms. Martin transferred from Houston to her current job in Los Angeles after being promised promotion.*

4 [T] to pass a telephone call from one telephone to another, or computer files from one computer to another: *Hold on, let me transfer you.* | *The technology will be very useful to companies that routinely **transfer documents electronically**.*

trans•fer[2] /'trænsfɜː‖-fɜːr/ *n* [C,U] **1** the process by which someone or something is moved from one place or position to another: *The cuts will be achieved through a combination of layoffs, retirements and **job transfers**.*

file transfer COMPUTING the process of moving computer FILES from one computer to another: *IBM Workstation One enables file transfers and use of local area networks.* | *the UK's JANET system, which allows **file transfer between** computers nationally and internationally.*

2 a change in the ownership of money, property etc from one person or organization to another, or the arrangements for doing this: *The legal environment for **share transfers** in Russia is still unclear.* | *The Land Registry records every **property transfer**.*

bank transfer when money is sent, usually electronically, from an account in one bank to an account in another: *Payment can be made either by credit card or bank transfer.*

blank transfer FINANCE a document given to someone lending money when shares are being offered as SECURITY in case the loan is not repaid. The lender's name can be written onto the blank transfer if the loan is not repaid, and the shares will then belong to them

capital transfer FINANCE when money for investment goes from one country to another; CAPITAL FLOWS: *Capital transfers from rich to developing countries have grown sharply.*

credit transfer a way of sending money directly from one bank account to another without using a cheque etc: *Electronic credit transfer is an increasingly popular method of sending money abroad.*

telegraphic transfer a quick method of sending money abroad, by moving money from one account to another using TELEX: *Charges will be made for any extra services such as telegraphic transfers.* | *We will send the money by telegraphic transfer.* —see also DEED OF TRANSFER

trans•fer•a•ble /træns'fɜːrəbəl/ *adj* able to be moved from one place or position to another: *Preferred stock is generally **freely transferable*** (=easily sold). | *easily transferable pensions*

transferable skill —see under SKILL

transfer agent —see under AGENT

trans•fe•ree /ˌtrænsfɜː'riː/ *n* [C] *formal* a person or company to whom money, shares, property etc is transferred: *The case is disputed because it is not clear what rights were accepted by the transferee.*

transfer fee —see under FEE

trans•fer•or /træns'fɜːrə‖ˌtrænsfə'rɔːr/ *n* [C] *formal* a person or company who transfers money, shares, property etc to another person

transfer payment —see under PAYMENT

transfer price —see under PRICE[1]

transfer register —see under REGISTER[1]

tran•ship also **transship** /ˌtræns'ʃɪp/ *v* past tense and past participle **transhipped** present participle **transhipping** [T] to move goods from one ship to another, or from a ship to a different form of transport: *Customs and Excise authorities uncovered illegal traffic in cargo transhipped from larger vessels into small local boats.* —**transhipment** *n* [U] *a pipeline that would carry natural gas to port for transhipment*

tran•si•ent /'trænziənt‖'trænʃənt/ *adj formal* only lasting for a short period of time: *Customer loyalty in the health drinks market appears transient at the best of times.*

transient worker —see under WORKER

tran•sit /'trænsɨt, -zɨt/ *n* [U] **1** the process of moving people or goods from one place to another: *Smaller cities are finding that attractive **public transit services*** (=buses, trains etc used by the general public) *are essential to their survival.*

2 **in transit** if goods are in transit, they are being taken by train, plane etc from one place to another: *An insurance policy will cover the risk of damage to goods in transit.* —see also STOPPAGE IN TRANSIT

tran•si•tion /træn'zɪʃən, -'sɪ-/ *n* [C,U] *formal* the act or process of changing from one state or form to another: *Compaq is going through a difficult **transition period**.* | *Three directors are expected to retire after the **management transitions** are completed.* | *Hungary, **in transition** to a free-market economy, has 3% unemployment.*

tran•si•to•ry /'trænzɨtəri‖-tɔːri/ *adj formal* continuing or existing for only a short period of time: *The current weakness in gold is transitory and will eventually produce greater profits.* | *The last decade saw powerful but **transitory** economic **changes**.*

trans•late /træns'leɪt, trænz-/ *v* **1** [T] FINANCE to change one currency into another **translate sth into sth**: *A strong dollar reduces the value of overseas profits when they are translated back into dollars.* | *The company sustained losses as revenue was translated from weak dollars to strong marks.*

2 [I,T] to change something from one form to another, especially to produce a final result: *This task previously required an extra machine to translate computer files.* **+ into**: *£100m of private investment should translate into 5,000 new inner-city jobs.* | *The production team translates the architect's specifications into high-quality systems.*

trans•la•tion /træns'leɪʃən, trænz-/ *n* **1** [C,U] FINANCE the process of changing one currency into another: *Favorable **foreign currency translations** boosted profits.* **+ into**: *After translation into Swiss francs, the only division showing a decline in sales was agriculture.*

2 [U] *formal* the process of changing something into a different form, usually to produce a final result: *The rapid translation from prototype to new product gives companies little time to rest between projects.*

trans•mis•sion /trænz'mɪʃən‖træns-/ *n* [C,U] the process of sending out electrical signals by radio, telephone, or similar equipment: *This feature enables the machine to recognize whether an incoming call is a voice or **fax transmission**.* **+ of**: *The system is intended to speed the **transmission of data**.*

trans•na•tion•al /ˌtrænz'næʃənəl/ *adj* [only before a noun] a transnational company, organization etc does business in many countries: *GM and Ford are **transnational corporations** with huge investments outside the US.*

trans•par•ent /træn'spærənt, -'speər-‖-'spær-, -'sper-/ *adj* if rules, methods, or business dealings are transparent, they are clear and people can see that they are fair

T

and honest: *The trade agreement between Japan and the US is more transparent, and there are no secret documents.* | *The regulations will force large corporations to conduct their contract awards **in a transparent manner**.* —**transparency** *n* [U] *EU laws on transparency and competition*

trans•port[1] /ˈtrænspɔːt‖-ɔːrt/ *n* [U] **1** the process or business of moving goods from one place to another by rail, air, ship etc: *the development of swifter modes of communication and transport*

surface transport the transport of goods by road or rail

2 *BrE* a system for carrying passengers or goods from one place to another; TRANSPORTATION *AmE*: *Critics have pointed to the lack of **transport links** to the Millennium Dome.*

trans•port[2] /trænˈspɔːt‖-ɔːrt/ *v* [T] to take goods from one place to another by rail, air, ship etc: *The Midwest's crops are transported down the Mississippi River for export.*

trans•por•ta•tion /ˌtrænspɔːˈteɪʃən‖-spər-/ *n* [U] **1** the process or business of moving goods from one place to another by rail, air, ship etc: *Prices include transportation from London.*

2 *AmE* a system for carrying passengers or goods from one place to another; TRANSPORT *BrE*: *Dial will manufacture motor coaches for Taiwan's **public transportation system**.*

trans•port•er /trænˈspɔːtə‖-ˈspɔːrtər/ *n* [C] **1** a long heavy vehicle used for moving other vehicles from one place to another: *a car transporter*

2 a company that moves goods from one place to another: *a five-day strike by private transporters*

Transports Internationaux Routiers —see TIR

trans•put•er /trænzˈpjuːtə‖trænsˈpjuːtər/ *n* [C] COMPUTING a very powerful computer MICROCHIP that can deal with large amounts of information very quickly

transship another spelling of TRANSHIP

trav•el[1] /ˈtrævəl/ *n* [U] the activity of going from one place to another, or to several different places, by air, road, rail etc: *The drop in revenue reflected lower levels of **domestic travel*** (=within your own country). | *American Express has strengthened its lead in the **corporate travel business**.* | ***Air travel** continued its recovery from a year earlier.*

travel[2] *v* **travelled travelling** *BrE* **traveled traveling** *AmE* [I,T] to go from one place to another, or to several different places, by air, road, rail etc: *the increasing trend among Japanese to **travel abroad*** | *Channel Tunnel trains travel between London and Paris in 3 hours.*

travel expense —see under EXPENSE

travel insurance —see under INSURANCE

trav•el•ler *BrE*, **traveler** *AmE* /ˈtrævələ‖-ər/ *n* [C] someone who travels from one place to another, or to several different places by air, road, rail etc: *The most important thing for a **business traveller** is to get there on time.*

commercial traveller *BrE* another name for TRAVELLING SALESMAN: *hotels catering for commercial travellers*

traveller's cheque —see under CHEQUE

travelling salesman —see under SALESMAN

Treasure Island *n informal* Britain, where prices of many goods are higher than elsewhere, meaning that companies can make higher profits

treas•ur•er /ˈtreʒərə‖-ər/ *n* [C] someone who is in charge of the money for an organization, company etc: *general manager and deputy treasurer of the Bank of Scotland* | *Money managers and **corporate treasurers** readily switch funds on the market.*

Treas•ur•ies /ˈtreʒəriz/ *n* [plural] —see ***Treasury bonds*** under BOND

Treas•ur•y /ˈtreʒəri/ *n* **the Treasury** the government department in charge of the money that a country collects in taxes and from borrowing, and the money that it spends

Treasury bill —see under BILL[1]

Treasury bond —see under BOND

treasury management —see under MANAGEMENT

Treasury notes —see under NOTE[1]

Treasury stock —see under STOCK[1]

treat /triːt/ *v* [T] **1** to deal with someone or something in a particular way: *We treat all complaints very seriously.* **treat sb/sth as**: *Proceeds from the asset transfers won't be treated as income.* | *Some information ought to be **treated as confidential**.*

2 to put a special substance on something to clean or protect it, or to make it safe: *The convention insists that countries should treat their own hazardous wastes.*

treat•ment /ˈtriːtmənt/ *n* **1** [C,U] a particular way of dealing with someone or something: *The range of permissible **accounting treatments** is amazingly broad.* | *The investigation found that some contractors received **preferential treatment*** (=were given an unfair advantage).

2 [U] a process by which something is protected, cleaned, or made safe: *an organic waste treatment plant*

treat•y /ˈtriːti/ *n* plural **treaties** [C] **1** a formal agreement between two countries or governments: *The US-Taiwan **trade treaty** is still valid, despite the ending of diplomatic ties.*

commercial treaty an agreement on trade between two countries: *When Cobden negotiated a commercial treaty with France, it seemed that an era of universal free trade was beginning.* —see also MAASTRICHT TREATY

2 LAW a formal agreement between two people or companies; CONTRACT

private treaty a private agreement for the sale of property or a work of art: *Redrow sourced 95% of its development land through private treaty.*

treb•le /ˈtrebəl/ *v* [I,T] to become three times as big in amount; TRIPLE: *Net income more than trebled, to £5.7 million.* | *A federal jury awarded $2 million in damages, to be trebled under antitrust law.*

treble damages —see under DAMAGE[1]

trend /trend/ *n* [C] **1** the general way in which a particular situation is changing or developing: *a New Jersey firm that tracks financial **market trends*** | *The **price trend** in food grains continued upwards.* + **toward**: *Credit card issuers are fighting a trend among consumers toward more conservative spending habits.*

2 buck the trend if something bucks the trend, it does not develop in the same way as most other similar things: *Two of the country's airlines have bucked the **industry trend** by cutting fares during the winter season.*

3 reverse the trend if something reverses a trend, it changes the way things were developing before: *To try to reverse the downward trend in its profits, Tandy will focus on its retail business.*

4 set the trend to start doing something in a way that other people begin to copy: *The public sector pay awards have **set an inflationary trend** for wage settlements this year.*

tres•pass /ˈtrespəs‖-pəs, -pæs/ *v* [I] to go onto someone's land or into their property without their permission + **on**: *Union organizers had trespassed on company premises to try and recruit new members.* —**trespass** *n* [U] *state laws against trespass* —**trespasser** *n* [C] *a sign to deter trespassers*

tri•al /ˈtraɪəl/ *n* [C] **1** a legal process in which a court of law examines a case to decide whether someone is guilty

T

of a crime: *Three former brokers were ordered to* ***stand trial*** *for securities fraud.*

2 a process of testing a product to see whether it is safe, effective etc: *The company expects* ***clinical trials*** (=scientific tests on a drug to see if it is safe before it is sold) *to continue for two years.* —**trial** *v* [T] *The language awareness course has been trialled with encouraging results.* —**trialling** *n* [U] *the development, trialling and pre-testing of materials*

acceptance trial MANUFACTURING testing by a customer of newly delivered equipment to check that it works correctly: *He required some modifications to be carried out, after which final acceptance trials took place.*

blind trial MARKETING a test carried out on a new medicine to see whether it works or not. Some people are given the real medicine and others are given something that looks like it but contains none of the new medicine. The results are checked to prove whether the medicine had an effect; BLIND TEST: *In the double-blind test, neither the patients nor the researchers know which samples contain the active drug.*

field trial a test on a new piece of equipment done in the place where it is to be used rather than in a LABORATORY, factory etc; FIELD TEST: *The system is designed to be carried on emergency vehicles and has undergone successful field trials with the Seattle Fire Department.* —compare PILOT

3 by/through trial and error if you do something by or through trial and error, you try several different ways of doing it to get the result you want: *I got these machine settings right purely by trial and error.*

trial balance —see under BALANCE[1]

trial offer —see under OFFER[2]

tri·bu·nal /traɪˈbjuːnl/ *n* [C] a court that is given official authority to deal with a particular situation or problem: *The case of your redundancy* (=loss of your job) *will be heard by an* ***independent tribunal.*** | *an Australian Broadcasting Tribunal report on television violence* | *a brief to be read out at a* ***tribunal hearing***

administrative tribunal in Britain, a tribunal that deals with special government problems: *administrative tribunals operating in the areas of National Insurance and rent assessment*

industrial tribunal in Britain, a tribunal where employees can bring complaints about their employers: *An industrial tribunal dismissed Mr Gilbert's claim of unfair dismissal.*

trick·le /ˈtrɪkəl/ *v* [I] to move somewhere slowly and in very small numbers or amounts: *Only four or five customers had trickled in by 11:30.* | *Details of the programs have trickled out over the past weeks, but haven't been widely publicized.* —**trickle** *n* [singular] *Trading activity* ***slowed to a trickle*** *as traders waited for a sign that war could be avoided.*

trickle down *phr v* [I] if something trickles down from one group to another, the people in the lower group start to feel the effects of something that has been done to the higher one: *As Mexico made the painful conversion to a market economy, less wealth trickled down from the bosses to the masses.*

trickle-down *adj* [only before a noun] the trickle-down effect is the belief that additional wealth gained by the richest people in society will have a good economic effect on the lives of everyone: *Bush was criticized for his trickle-down economic policies.*

trig·ger[1] /ˈtrɪgə‖-ər/ also **trigger off** *v* [T] to make something start happening, especially a series of events: *The move could trigger a rush by investors to buy annuities.* | *a sales rush triggered by cuts in interest rates*

trigger[2] *n* **be the trigger (for)** to be the thing that quickly causes something to happen, especially a problem: *A quick-fix solution could be a trigger for higher inflation.*

trigger point —see under POINT[1]

tril·lion /ˈtrɪljən/ *number* plural **trillion** or **trillions** one million million; 1,000,000,000,000: *The bank has assets of about eight trillion pesetas.*

trim[1] /trɪm/ *v* past tense and past participle **trimmed** present participle **trimming** [T] to remove parts of a plan, set of activities, company etc in order to reduce its costs: *We need to trim the Defence budget by another £500m.* | *The company is to trim its workforce* (=reduce the number of people it employs) *by 10%.* | *Itel is working on ways to* ***trim*** *its* ***debt load*** (=reduce the amount of debt it has).

trim[2] *n* [U] MANUFACTURING an additional part on a car etc to make it look more attractive: *Voplex, a supplier of automotive plastic interior trim*

trip·le[1] /ˈtrɪpəl/ *adj* [only before a noun] having three parts or members: *Blockbusters' triple-digit earnings gains* | *a triple alliance of the government, state industries and foreign firms*

triple[2] *v* [I,T] to become three times as much or as many, or to make something do this; TREBLE: *Fourth quarter profits have tripled.* | *The newspaper tripled its circulation in less than a year.*

triple-A *adj* FINANCE a triple-A RATING for a company shows that it is one of the safest to lend money to: *the only major bank based in New York that still has a triple-A credit rating*

triple-witching also **triple-witching hour** *n* [singular] *informal* FINANCE a time on a financial market when FUTURES, STOCK INDEX FUTURES, and STOCK OPTIONS all EXPIRE (=reach the end of their life) at the same time: *Volume was low ahead of Friday's "triple witching hour," when three sets of options and futures contracts expire on the German Futures and Options Exchange, and stock investors fear volatility and uncertainty.* —compare DOUBLE-WITCHING

trip·li·cate /ˈtrɪplɨkɨt/ *n* **in triplicate** if you copy something in triplicate, you make three copies of it

Tro·jan horse /ˌtrəʊdʒən ˈhɔːs‖ˌtroʊdʒən ˈhɔːrs/ *n* [C usually singular] something that looks attractive but that is intended to deceive: *The bank's CEO described Japanese investments in the UK as a Trojan horse, destroying Europe's defences against unfair competition.*

troub·led /ˈtrʌbəld/ *adj* having many problems: *These are troubled times for the coal industry.* | ***financially troubled*** *companies*

troub·le·shoot·er /ˈtrʌbəlˌʃuːtə‖-ər/ *n* [C] someone who is employed by a company to deal with serious problems it is having: *He was hired as a troubleshooter, and began by slashing costs.*

trough /trɒf‖trɒːf/ *n* [C] the lowest point in a series of prices, values etc: *the* ***peaks and troughs*** *of investing in stocks and shares* | *When would the nation come out of its* ***economic trough?*** —**trough** *v* [I] *This is the biggest fall in economic activity since the recession troughed five years ago.*

truck[1] /trʌk/ *n* [C] **1** a large road vehicle used to carry goods; LORRY *BrE*

2 *BrE* a railway vehicle that is part of a train and carries goods; CAR *AmE*: *coal trucks*

truck[2] *v* [T] *AmE* to take something somewhere by truck: *Crude oil would be imported on tankers and trucked to the pipeline.* —**trucking** *n* [U] *The company has operations in trucking and air freight.*

truck farm —see under FARM[1]

true /truː/ *adj* used to describe the actual amount of something, when extra hidden amounts are added to or taken from it: *The APR is the annual percentage rate of the total charge for credit or the **true cost** of borrowing.*

true and fair view *n* [singular] ACCOUNTING words used in a company's accounts by AUDITORS to show that they think the accounts give correct and complete information about a company's financial situation: *Price Waterhouse's said the accounts gave a true and fair view of the company's business.*

true interest —see under INTEREST

true yield —see under YIELD[1]

trust /trʌst/ *n* **1** [U] a belief in the honesty or goodness of someone or something: *The measures are necessary to restore public trust in the futures markets.* | *He abused his **position of trust*** (=a job with responsibility for making important decisions) *and defrauded the institution.*
2 take sth on trust to believe that something is true without having any proof: *I just had to take it on trust that he would deliver the money.*
3 [U] an arrangement by which someone has legal control over your money or property until you are old enough to use it: *The money your father left you will be **held in trust** until you are 21.*
4 [C] LAW an arrangement by which someone has legal control over your money and usually invests it for you, or an organization that does this: *He put his assets in a variety of trusts.* | *a bank trust department*
blind trust [C] a trust that belongs to someone who does not know what investments have been made with the money in the trust. Blind trusts are used by politicians and others so that they can show that their decisions are not being influenced by their personal investments
business trust [C] in the US, an association of investors who give cash and other property to others to manage: *Jones is seeking approval to structure its next offering as a Delaware business trust.*
charitable trust [C] a TRUST formed with the purpose of giving money to a charity; PUBLIC TRUST: *Local people raised £600,000 and set up a charitable trust to run the hospital.*
constructive trust [C] a trust that is created by the law of EQUITY rather than by the people who will gain from it; IMPLIED TRUST —opposite ***express trust***
debenture trust [C] a trust made by a company, that holds the company's assets that are security for DEBENTURE STOCK (=borrowed capital)
discretionary trust ◆ [C] a trust whose managers are allowed to decide the best way of managing the trust and the best way of sharing its income and capital: *a discretionary trust fund which was set up to help disabled people living at home*
◆ [C] an arrangement for leaving money to someone in a TRUST after you die, where the person managing the trust decides when to make payments, how much to pay etc: *If you are worried about your relative not being able to manage money, you could leave a sum of money on discretionary trust.*
executed trust [C] a trust that has clear instructions about how it is to be used, usually one formed by a person in their WILL (=a document saying how someone's property is to be shared out when they die)
executory trust [C] a trust that does not give full details about how it is to be used, usually one formed by a person in their WILL (=a document saying how someone's property is to be shared out when they die). A further document is needed before the person's intentions can be carried out
express trust [C] a trust that has been formed by clearly stated words, rather than by the law of EQUITY —opposite ***constructive trust, implied trust***
fixed trust [C] a trust whose funds can only be invested in a particular range of bonds, shares etc —opposite ***flexible trust***
flexible trust *BrE*, **general management trust** *AmE* [C] a trust whose funds can be invested in any type of shares etc, within agreed limits —opposite ***fixed trust***
implied trust [C] another name for a CONSTRUCTIVE TRUST
living trust [C] a trust in which someone's assets are passed to another person before they die, done to avoid the trust having to go through PROBATE (=the sometimes long legal process of dealing with a dead person's will): *She has transferred her properties to a living trust.*
private trust [C] a trust set up for a named person or group of people: *The publicly quoted company never seemed to do as well as the family's own private trusts.*
public trust [C] a trust formed to provide financial support for groups that are poor or in urgent need of help. Public trusts do not have to pay tax in most countries; CHARITABLE TRUST —compare ***private trust***
unit trust [C] *BrE* a company that invests money in stocks and shares of many different businesses for small investors; MUTUAL FUND *AmE*: *The best way to invest in a portfolio of international bonds is through a managed fund, such as a unit trust.*
5 [C] *especially AmE* a group of companies that illegally work together to reduce competition and control prices: *anti-trust laws* —see also BREACH OF TRUST, DECLARATION OF TRUST, DEED OF TRUST, INVESTMENT TRUST, REAL ESTATE INVESTMENT TRUST

trust-busting *n* [U] *AmE informal* when officials bring to a court of law cases where they believe companies have been illegally working together to reduce competition and control prices —**trust-buster** *n* [C] *Trust-busters appear most concerned with airports dominated by only one or two airlines.*

trust company —see under COMPANY

trust deed —see under DEED

trust•ee /ˌtrʌˈstiː◂/ *n* [C] LAW **1** someone who controls money or property that is in a trust for someone else: *the trustees of the pension fund*
active trustee a trustee who invests the money they have control over, rather than simply passing it on to someone at the particular time they are allowed to have it
bare trustee a trustee who holds property and passes it on to someone at the particular time they are allowed to have it
constructive trustee someone who is in charge of a CONSTRUCTIVE TRUST
2 a member of a group that controls the money of a company, college, or other organization: *It is being operated by a trustee appointed by the federal Bankruptcy Court.*

trustee for sale *n* plural **trustees for sale** [C] *BrE* LAW someone who controls a TRUST FOR SALE: *land held by trustees for sale*

trustee in bankruptcy —see under BANKRUPTCY

trust•ee•ship /trʌˈstiːʃɪp/ *n* [C,U] LAW the job of controlling a trust or when property is controlled by a trustee: *The company was placed **into trusteeship** in April 1999 through a bankruptcy court.* | *pension fund trusteeships*

trust for sale *n* plural **trusts for sale** [C] *BrE* LAW trust that contains instructions to sell land or other property immediately and to give the money made from the sale to a named person or named people

trust fund —see under FUND[1]

trust receipt —see under RECEIPT[1]

trust•wor•thy /ˈtrʌstˌwɜːði‖-ɜːr-/ *adj* a person or organization that is trustworthy can be trusted and depended upon: *The staff are honest, trustworthy, intensely loyal and hard-working.* —**trustworthiness** *n* [U] *The brand conveyed quality, modernity and trustworthiness.*

T

Truth in Lending Act *n* [singular] in the US, a law under which money lenders such as banks must tell borrowers the real cost of credit, including all charges, so they can decide which lender offers the best deal. It also gives borrowers who decide to use their property as SECURITY a three-day period in which to change their minds

try /traɪ/ *v* past tense and past participle **tried** [T usually passive] to examine and judge a legal case, or someone who is thought to be guilty of a crime in a court: *Savings-and-loan directors are being tried for fraud.*

TUC *n* Trades Union Congress; the association of British trade unions

tu·i·tion /tjuˈɪʃən‖tu-/ *n* [U] **1** teaching, especially in small groups: *Trainees have a week of intensive tuition at the management training centre.*
2 *AmE* the money you pay for being taught: *Big tuition increases are due at public colleges and universities.* | *funding that comes from students' **tuition fees***

tuition fees —see under FEE

tum·ble /ˈtʌmbəl/ *v* [I] *journalism* if prices, figures etc tumble, they go down suddenly and by a large amount: *Stock market prices have tumbled over the past week.* —**tumble** *n* [C usually singular] *The announcement sparked a 10% tumble in the company's stock price.*

tune /tjuːn‖tuːn/ *n* **to the tune of $1000/£100 etc** *informal* used to emphasize how large an amount or number is: *The company is in debt to the tune of £1.2 billion.*

turn¹ /tɜːn‖tɜːrn/ *n* **1** [C] FINANCE the difference between the price at which a MARKETMAKER will buy and sell a particular share; SPREAD
2 [singular] if something takes a particular turn, it starts developing in a completely different way: *Things may **take a** bad **turn** and the economic situation may deteriorate.* | *The economy seems to be **taking a turn for the worse*** (=suddenly become worse).

turn² *v* **turn a profit** to make a profit: *The China operation has just started turning a profit.*

turn sth ↔ **around** also **turn round** *BrE phr v* [T]
1 to make a business that is having difficulties successful again: *New models and new ideas have turned the company around and saved the factory from closure.*
2 to complete the process of making a product or providing a service: *Federal reduced the average time it takes to turn around a new product to 20 days.* —see also TURNAROUND

turn down *phr v* **1** [T] **turn** sth ↔ **down** to refuse an offer or request: *He turned down a job at Georgia-Pacific.*
2 [I] if an economy etc turns down, the level of activity etc falls, companies become less profitable etc: *When the economy turns down, the aerospace industry suffers too, however exciting the projects.* —see also DOWNTURN

turn sth ↔ **out** *phr v* [T] to produce or make a lot of a particular product: *The factory turns out 300 units a day.*

turn over sth *phr v* [T] if a business turns over a particular amount of money, it makes that amount in a particular period of time: *We were turning over $2000 a week when business was good.* —see also TURNOVER

turn sth **over to** sb *phr v* [T] to give someone ownership of property, a business etc, or responsibility for doing something, so that you no longer have it: *I'm turning the shop over to my son when I retire.* | *Half of BCCI's assets were turned over to government agencies.*

turn·a·round /ˈtɜːnəraʊnd‖ˈtɜːrn-/ also **turnround** *BrE* — *n* [C usually singular] **1** the time between receiving an order for goods, dealing with it, and sending the goods to the customer: *Some drivers are on a bonus for **fast turnaround** and deliveries.*
2 a complete change from a bad situation to a good one: *The large increase in sales indicates a turnaround for the company, which ran into tough times during the early 1990s.* + **in**: *Managers don't expect a turnaround in profits yet.* —see also ***turn around*** under TURN¹
3 a complete change in someone's opinion or ideas + **in**: *a turnaround in government policy*

turn·key /ˈtɜːnkiː‖ˈtɜːrn-/ *adj* [only before a noun] turnkey PROJECTS or systems are ones that have been produced in such a way that they are ready to be used immediately by a customer: *The unit provides turnkey software systems to credit unions.* | *a $115 million **turnkey contract** to build a wastewater treatment plant in Egypt*

turnkey contract —see under CONTRACT¹

turn·out /ˈtɜːnaʊt‖ˈtɜːrn-/ *n* [singular] the number of people who vote in an election or go to a meeting or other organized event: *Voting drew a record turnout of 85%.* —see also ***turn out*** under TURN¹

turn·o·ver /ˈtɜːnˌəʊvə‖ˈtɜːrnˌoʊvər/ *n* **1** *BrE* the amount of business done in a particular period of time, measured by the amount of money obtained from customers for goods or services that have been sold; SALES —see also ***turn over*** under TURN¹ + **of**: *The commercial services business unit had an **annual turnover** of 3.9 billion kronor.*

asset turnover ACCOUNTING, FINANCE a company's sales in relation to its assets, calculated to see how efficiently a business uses its assets

capital turnover also **investment turnover** FINANCE the relationship between the total sales of a business and its share capital. For example, if a business has total sales of £10 million and the share capital was £2 million, the capital turnover is 5:1: *Inferior quality, enormous waste in construction, and **slow capital turnover** are to be found throughout the industry.*

stock turnover also **stock turn** *BrE* the average value of stock held by a business in relation to the total value of its sales during a year, showing how quickly a business sells its stock: *New book purchases must be based on a stock turn of one year – in other words, the whole print run has to sell out within one year.*

2 the rate at which workers leave an organization and are replaced by others: *Morale among child-care workers is low, and turnover is more than 40% a year.* | *the problem of **high** employee **turnover** at the IRS* | *Contract workers have a **high turnover rate**.*
3 the rate at which goods are sold + **of**: *Tri-Star's **fast turnover** of stock*
4 FINANCE the number of shares traded on a stockmarket during a particular period of time, usually a day, or the number of shares traded in a particular company: *Paris stocks' rise occurred on extremely light turnover.* | *Wellcome shares gained 20p to 463p on turnover of 1.1 million shares.*

turnover tax —see under TAX¹

turn·round /ˈtɜːnraʊnd‖ˈtɜːrn-/ *n* [C usually singular] another name for TURNAROUND

twist·ing /ˈtwɪstɪŋ/ *n* [U] *disapproving* when a salesperson persuades a customer to trade when they do not need to, so that the salesperson earns COMMISSION (=an amount of money they get every time they make a sale); CHURNING

ty·coon /taɪˈkuːn/ *n* [C] someone who is successful in business and industry and has a lot of money and power: *Australian-born business tycoon Rupert Murdoch*

type /taɪp/ *v* [I,T] to write something using a typewriter or WORD PROCESSOR: *Does the report need to be typed?* | *How fast can you type?*

type·face /ˈtaɪpfeɪs/ *n* [C] a group of letters, numbers etc of the same style and size, used in printing: *a sans serif typeface* | *The headings are set in bold typeface.*

type·set·ter /ˈtaɪpˌsetə‖-ər/ *n* [C] a person, company, or machine that arranges the letters, words etc on a page for printing

type•set•ting /ˈtaɪpˌsetɪŋ/ *n* [U] the job or activity of arranging the letters, words etc on a page for printing: *Publishers have now switched over to computerized typesetting.* —**typeset** *v* [I,T] *The article is typeset in two columns.*

type•writ•er /ˈtaɪpˌraɪtə‖-ər/ *n* [C] a machine that prints letters of the alphabet onto paper

type•writ•ten /ˈtaɪpˌrɪtn/ *adj* written using a typewriter or WORD PROCESSOR: *a typewritten letter*

typ•ist /ˈtaɪpəst/ *n* [C] a secretary whose main job is to write letters and other documents using a WORD PROCESSOR

ty•po /ˈtaɪpəʊ‖-poʊ/ *n* [C] *informal* a small mistake in the way something has been TYPED or printed

T

U

UBR abbreviation for UNIFORM BUSINESS RATE

ultimate consumer —see under CONSUMER

ultimate customer —see under CUSTOMER

ul·tra vi·res /ˌʌltrə ˈvaɪriːz/ *adj* LAW beyond legal or official powers: *All these transactions could be declared ultra vires.* | *an ultra vires demand by the revenue*

u/m written abbreviation for UNDERMENTIONED

um·brel·la /ʌmˈbrelə/ *n* [C] something which covers or includes a wide range of different parts: *C&W World has to pull together a huge number of companies* ***under the umbrella of*** *the parent group.* | *an EU* ***umbrella organization***

umbrella fund —see under FUND[1]

u·nan·i·mous /juːˈnænəməs/ *adj* a unanimous decision, statement etc is one that everyone agrees with: *If the value of the shares is not to be determined by the auditors, there has to be* ***unanimous agreement*** *of the shareholders.* | *The vote in favour of the merger was unanimous.*

un·au·dit·ed /ʌnˈɔːdətəd‖-ˈɒː-/ *adj* unaudited accounts etc have not been checked by an AUDITOR: *unaudited management accounts* | *Unaudited financial data must be clearly marked as such.*

unbalanced budget —see under BUDGET[1]

un·bun·dle /ʌnˈbʌndl/ *v* [T] **1** to provide products or services separately that were previously sold together: *Sky TV's refusal to unbundle its programme package to allow the cable companies to offer customers channels of their choice*

2 to separate activities that were previously managed together, usually in order to sell them: *Lonrho is expected to unbundle some of its Zimbabwe goldmining interests to local investors.* —**unbundling** *n* [C,U] *a complex unbundling that divides the group into 13 different companies* | *corporate unbundlings*

uncalled capital —see under CAPITAL

un·cer·tain·ty /ʌnˈsɜːtnti‖-ɜːr-/ *n* [U] a situation when what will happen in the future is likely to change, often in a way that is bad: *Exchange rate uncertainty is bound to reduce investment.* + **over/about**: *The announcement ends months of uncertainty over the contract's future.*

unclean bill of lading —see under BILL OF LADING

uncleared effects —see under EFFECT

un·col·lect·ed /ˌʌnkəˈlektəd◂/ *adj* debts, payments etc that are uncollected have not yet been paid: *Newco will be required to buy the uncollected trade debts for the amount of the interest-free loan which remains outstanding.* | *uncollected taxes*

un·con·di·tion·al /ˌʌnkənˈdɪʃənəl◂/ *adj* **1 unconditional offer/bid** a takeover offer which does not depend on any conditions: *The Hong Kong and Shanghai Bank declared that its £3.7 billion bid for Midland Bank was unconditional.*

2 go/become unconditional if a takeover offer goes or becomes unconditional, it is accepted by more than half the existing shareholders: *Mr Franklin would not say when the bid would go unconditional.* | *Once the offer document is posted, a takeover offer can become unconditional within four weeks.*

UNCTAD /ˈʌŋktæd/ *n* abbreviation for UNITED NATIONS CONFERENCE ON TRADE AND DEVELOPMENT

un·dat·ed /ʌnˈdeɪtəd/ *adj* **1 undated bond/security etc** a bond etc that has no MATURITY (=date at which it will be repaid). A few British government bonds are undated

2 undated cheque/document an undated cheque etc has no date written on it —compare POST-DATED

undated gilts —see under GILTS

undated security —see under SECURITY

un·der·bid /ˌʌndəˈbɪd‖-ər-/ *v* past tense and past participle **underbid** present participle **underbidding** [T] to offer a lower price for something than someone else, for example in an AUCTION (=when the buyer offering the highest price obtains the thing being sold): *We applied for the tender but were underbid by another company.*

un·der·cap·i·tal·ized /ˌʌndəˈkæpətl-aɪzd‖-ər-/ also **undercapitalised** *BrE adj* FINANCE if a company is undercapitalized, it has less capital than it needs in order to operate effectively and grow: *If you set up a store and you're undercapitalized, you're going to go bust* (=bankrupt). —**undercapitalization** also **undercapitalisation** *BrE n* [U] *The business is suffering from undercapitalization.*

und·er·charge /ˌʌndəˈtʃɑːdʒ‖ˌʌndərˈtʃɑːrdʒ/ *v* [I,T] to charge too little or less than the correct amount of money for something: *The city was grossly undercharging the tannery for the use of the sewage treatment plant.* **undercharge sb by £10/$20 etc**: *They undercharged me by about two dollars.* —opposite OVERCHARGE —**undercharge** /ˈʌndətʃɑːdʒ‖-dərtʃɑːrdʒ/ *n* [C] *an undercharge of £15*

un·der·cut /ˌʌndəˈkʌt‖-ər-/ *v* past tense and past participle **undercut** present participle **undercutting** [T] to sell goods or services more cheaply than another company: *Our competitors have been undercutting our prices.* | *The firm that expands output will always be able to reduce costs and undercut its rivals.*

underdeveloped country *n* plural **underdeveloped countries** [C] a country that is poor and where there is not much modern industry —compare DEVELOPING COUNTRY, LDC

un·der·em·ployed /ˌʌndərɪmˈplɔɪd◂/ *adj* not having enough work to do: *A large proportion of our staff is underemployed.*

un·der·es·ti·mate /ˌʌndərˈestəmeɪt/ *v* [T] to think that something is smaller than it really is: *We underestimated our operating costs.* | *The official statistics seriously underestimate actual unemployment.* —**underestimate** /ˈʌndəˈestəmət‖-dər-/ *n* [C] *These unemployment figures should be regarded as underestimates.*

un·der·fund·ed /ˌʌndəˈfʌndəd‖-ər-/ *adj* if an organization is underfunded, it receives too little money in relation to its needs: *Many charities are badly underfunded.*

un·der·fund·ing /ˈʌndəˈfʌndɪŋ‖-ər-/ *n* [U] when an organization receives too little money in relation to its needs: *Some departments may, through overfunding, be absorbing resources unfairly.*

un·der·hand /ˌʌndəˈhænd◂‖ˈʌndərhænd/ *adj* dishonest and done secretly: *He has a reputation for underhand dealings.*

under-insurance —see under INSURANCE

un·der·in·sured /ˌʌndərɪnˈʃʊəd◂‖-ʃʊrd◂/ also **under-insured** *adj* INSURANCE **1** if a person care, the value of the health care for which they are insured is less than what they really need: *tax vouchers and deductions to help millions of uninsured or underinsured Americans buy private medical coverage*

2 if property or its owners are underinsured and the property is stolen, damaged etc, and the owners make a claim, they will receive less from the insurance company than the property is really worth: *With our revaluation scheme, providing you were not underinsured to start with, you need no longer worry about becoming underinsured as a result of inflation.* —**underinsurance** *n* [U] *In the event of a serious loss considerable hardship can be caused by underinsurance.*

un·der·lease /ˈʌndəliːs‖-ər-/ *n* [C] another name for SUBLEASE

un·der·let /ˈʌndəˈlet‖-ər-/ *v* past tense and past participle **underlet** present participle **underletting** [T] another name for SUBLET

un·der·ly·ing /ˌʌndəˈlaɪ-ɪŋ◂‖-ər-/ *adj* **1 underlying figure/rate** a rate or figure that shows the real level of inflation, EARNINGS etc although it is not immediately obvious: *The underlying rate of interest went up last month.* —compare HEADLINE

2 underlying security/share etc FINANCE the investment to which a DERIVATIVE such as an OPTION (=the right to buy or sell particular shares etc during a particular period of time) relates: *If the warrant is held for its full 18-month life, the value of the underlying shares would have to rise at least 18.6% to make it profitable for holders.*

underlying assets —see under ASSET

underlying inflation —see under INFLATION

underlying loan —see under LOAN[1]

underlying share —see under SHARE

underlying stock —see under STOCK[1]

un·der·manned /ˌʌndəˈmænd◂‖-ər-/ *adj* an office, department, organization etc that is undermanned has fewer people working in it than it really needs: *The department is poorly funded and hopelessly undermanned.* —**undermanning** *n* [U] *an undermanning problem*

un·der·men·tioned /ˌʌndəˈmenʃənd◂‖-ər-/ written abbreviation **u/m** *adj formal* mentioned later in the same piece of writing: *Please supply me with the undermentioned goods.*

un·der·paid /ˌʌndəˈpeɪd◂‖-ər-/ *adj* paid less money than you deserve for your work: *Most of the staff feel they are overworked and underpaid.*

un·der·pay /ˌʌndəˈpeɪ‖-ər-/ *v* past tense and past participle **underpaid** [I,T] **1** to pay less money to people than they deserve for their work: *In an interview, the star said that the studio underpays and misuses him.*

2 to pay less money to a person or organization than is owed to them: *The IRS claimed that the construction company underpaid its income, employment and excise taxes by $3.2 billion over an eleven-year period.*

un·der·per·form /ˌʌndəpəˈfɔːm‖-dərpərˈfɔːrm/ *v* [I,T] if a company, investment etc underperforms, it is not as profitable as it should be, or as profitable as similar companies investments etc: *One reason Champion has underperformed is too much capital spending.* | *In Canada, stocks underperformed their U.S. counterparts.* —**underperformance** *n* [U] *the group's underperformance in the market* —**underperformer** *n* [C] *operations that were considered underperformers*

un·der·re·port /ˌʌndərɪˈpɔːt‖-ˈpɔːrt/ *v* [T] **1** to calculate a figure wrongly, and so produce a figure that is less than the real one: *The study estimated that the U.S. underreports its exports of goods by $10 billion to $20 billion annually.*

2 *AmE* TAX to say that your income is less than it really is on your TAX RETURN —**underreported** *adj*: *The IRS estimates about $100 billion in taxes weren't paid because of underreported income.*

un·der·sell /ˌʌndəˈsel‖-ər-/ *v* past tense and past participle **undersold** [T] **1** to sell goods etc at a lower price than someone else: *We undersell all our rivals.* | *They claim never to be undersold* (=that nobody sells goods as cheaply as they do).

2 to sell something for less than its real value: *When it was privatized, the water industry was massively undersold.*

3 to make people think that someone or something is less good, effective, skilful etc than they really are: *Don't undersell yourself at the interview*

un·der·shoot /ˌʌndəˈʃuːt‖-ər-/ *v* past tense and past participle **undershot** [T] to not reach a figure or level that was set as a limit or target: *IRC said results for its fiscal first quarter will undershoot analysts' expectations.* —opposite OVERSHOOT —**undershooting** *n* [U] *There would be a continuing problem of overshooting or undershooting.*

un·der·spend /ˌʌndəˈspend‖-ər-/ *v* past tense and past participle **underspent** [I,T] to spend less than you intended or than you are allowed to: *If the budget is underspent, then the amount will be lost or next year's budget will be reduced to the lower amount.* + **by**: *We underspent last year by about 30%.* —**underspend** *n* [C] *Departments are not allowed to carry forward underspends into the next financial year.*

un·der·staffed /ˌʌndəˈstɑːft◂‖ˌʌndərˈstæft◂/ *adj* a company, organization etc that is understaffed has fewer people working for it than it really needs: *The factory inspectorate is seriously understaffed at the moment.* —opposite OVERSTAFFED

un·der·sub·scribed /ˌʌndəsəbˈskraɪbd◂‖-dər-/ *adj* FINANCE a share or bond ISSUE (=when they are made available for sale) is undersubscribed if people ask for fewer shares etc than are available: *Tender issues that are undersubscribed are taken up by the Bank.*

un·der·take /ˌʌndəˈteɪk‖-ər-/ *v* past tense **undertook** past participle **undertaken** [T] **1** to accept that you are responsible for a piece of work and start to do it: *His first task was to undertake a major reorganization of production methods.* | *LCH has just undertaken a major review of its clearing system.*

2 undertake to do sth to promise or agree to do something: *The ferry operators undertook not to reduce services or increase fares.*

un·der·tak·ing /ˌʌndəˈteɪkɪŋ‖ˈʌndərteɪ-/ *n* **1** [C usually singular] an important job, piece of work, or activity that you are responsible for: *Starting a new business can be a risky undertaking.*

2 [C] a business: *The railway's **commercial undertaking** was divided into its separate elements.* | *the parent company and its **subsidiary undertakings***

3 [C] a promise to do something, especially one that has legal force: *He **gave an undertaking** that he would repay the money in full.*

un·der·val·ued /ˌʌndəˈvæljuːd‖-ər-/ *v* [T] FINANCE if someone describes a currency, shares etc as undervalued, they think that its value is lower than it should be: *Share prices remain relatively undervalued.* + **against**: *The dollar is significantly undervalued against European currencies.*

un·der·weight /ˌʌndəˈweɪt◂‖-ər-/ *adj* FINANCE used to show that an investor has less of a particular investment than usual, or less of it than they should have: *Investors would be wise to be underweight in the German banking and retailing sectors at the moment.* —**underweight** *v* [T] *You should underweight the Deutsche mark-bloc markets of Germany, the Netherlands and Switzerland.*

un·der·write /ˌʌndəˈraɪt/ *v* past tense **underwrote** past participle **underwritten** [T] **1** FINANCE if a financial institution underwrites a SHARE ISSUE, it arranges to sell shares to investors and agrees to buy any shares that are not bought by them: *An underwritten offer may be the only way a company can raise money.*

2 INSURANCE if an insurance company underwrites an insurance contract, it agrees to pay for any loss covered by the contract

U

3 to agree to pay the cost of something and to take financial responsibility for it if it fails: *A local company has underwritten some of the development costs.* | *The government has agreed to underwrite the project with a grant of £5 million.*

un•der•writ•er /ˈʌndəˌraɪtə‖-dərˌraɪtər/ *n* [C] **1** FINANCE a financial institution that underwrites a SHARE ISSUE, that arranges to sell shares to investors and agrees to buy any shares that are not bought by them
2 INSURANCE a person, usually someone who works for an insurance company, who calculates the risk involved in an activity and decides how much insurance will cost to cover it
3 INSURANCE a person who agrees to accept the risk of any loss under an insurance contract: *a Lloyd's **insurance underwriter***
marine underwriter a person or company that makes marine insurance contracts

underwriting loss —see under LOSS

underwriting power —see under POWER[1]

underwriting risk —see under RISK[1]

underwriting syndicate —see under SYNDICATE[1]

undeveloped land —see under LAND[1]

undischarged bankrupt —see under BANKRUPT[2]

undistributed earnings —see under EARNINGS

undistributed profit —see under PROFIT[1]

undue influence *n* [U] LAW when unfair pressure is put on someone to enter into an agreement: *He was found guilty of misrepresentation and undue influence.*

unearned income —see under INCOME

un•e•co•nom•ic /ˌʌniːkəˈnɒmɪk◂, ˌʌnekə-‖-ˈnɑː-/ *adj* **1** not making enough money or profit: *Uneconomic coal mines will have to be closed.* | *Vast subsidies were going to uneconomic nationalized industries.*
2 using too much effort, money, or materials: *Firms find it uneconomic to keep opening up and shutting down.*

un•e•co•nom•ic•al /ˌʌniːkəˈnɒmɪkəl, ˌʌnekə-‖-ˈnɑː-/ *adj* using too much effort, money, or materials: *Stockbrokers' minimum commission charges can make small deals uneconomical for shareholders.* | *Some train routes became uneconomical to run.* —**uneconomically** *adv*: *Only a handful of goods traffic was being conveyed on these branch lines – uneconomically.*

un•em•ploy•able /ˌʌnɪmˈplɔɪəbəl◂/ *adj* not having the skills or qualities needed to get a job: *People over 40 can suddenly find themselves unemployable.* —opposite EMPLOYABLE

U

un•em•ployed[1] /ˌʌnɪmˈplɔɪd◂/ *adj* without a job: *I have been unemployed for two years.* | *an unemployed accountant*

unemployed[2] *n* [plural] **the unemployed** people without jobs: *She may soon **be joining the ranks of the unemployed*** (=lose her job). | *a £230 million jobs package aimed at helping **the long-term unemployed*** (=people who have not had a job for a long time)

un•em•ploy•ment /ˌʌnɪmˈplɔɪmənt/ *n* [U] **1** when you do not have a job: *Closure of the plant will mean unemployment for 500 workers.* | *Most of our staff now **face unemployment**.*
2 the number of people in a country who do not have a job: ***Unemployment rose** by 32,000 in May.* | *The region suffers from **high unemployment*** (=many people do not have a job). | *the unemployment figures*
disguised unemployment another name for HIDDEN UNEMPLOYMENT
frictional unemployment when people are unemployed because they are in the process of changing jobs and are taking time to look for the most suitable job; SEARCH UNEMPLOYMENT
hard-core unemployment unemployment among people who have been without work for a long time and who are the least likely to want or find jobs
hidden unemployment unemployment which is known to exist but is not included in the official government figures
involuntary unemployment when people are unemployed but do not want to be, and are looking for a job
long-term unemployment when people have been unemployed for a long time, for example more than a year
search unemployment another name for FRICTIONAL UNEMPLOYMENT
seasonal unemployment when people are unemployed at certain times of the year, because they work in industries where they are not needed all year round
structural unemployment when people are unemployed because the industry they work in is getting smaller or disappearing
voluntary unemployment when people are unemployed and do not want to work and are not looking for a job, especially because they are satisfied with the money they are getting from the government in the form of UNEMPLOYMENT BENEFIT
3 *AmE informal* money paid regularly by the government to people who have no job: *I've never **claimed unemployment**.* —see also NAIRU

unemployment benefit —see under BENEFIT[1]

unemployment insurance —see under INSURANCE

unenforceable contract —see under CONTRACT[1]

un•fair /ˌʌnˈfeə◂‖-ˈfer◂/ *adj* **1** not right or fair: *Warner-Lambert criticized the FDA advisory panel's ruling against its drug as unfair.* | *poverty wages and unfair working conditions*
2 not giving a fair opportunity to everyone: *The current law is not equitable, since it gives an **unfair advantage** to those pilots who belong to a union.* | *American workers feel threatened by **unfair competition** from abroad.*

unfair dismissal —see under DISMISSAL

un•fa•vou•ra•ble *BrE*, **unfavorable** *AmE* *adj* /ʌnˈfeɪvərəbəl/ opposite to what is needed or wanted: *Market conditions had become unfavourable.* | *an unfavourable balance of payments* (=when a country imports more than it exports)

unfriendly takeover —see under TAKEOVER

uniform business rate —see under RATE[1]

u•ni•lat•e•ral /ˌjuːnɪˈlætərəl◂/ *adj* a unilateral action or decision is done or made by only one of the groups involved in a situation: *In the 19th-century, Britain announced and largely followed a policy of unilateral free trade.* —**unilateralism** *n* [U] —**unilaterally** *adv*: *The Russian central bank president suggested that interest payments on commercial debt would be unilaterally suspended* (=stopped for a period of time without the agreement of lenders).

unilateral contract —see under CONTRACT[1]

uninsurable risk —see under RISK[1]

un•in•sured /ˌʌnɪnˈʃʊəd‖-ˈʃʊrd/ *adj* having no insurance: *It was revealed that they were uninsured.*

u•nion /ˈjuːnjən/ *n* **1** [C] an organization representing people working in a particular industry or profession that protects their rights; TRADE UNION *BrE*; LABOR UNION *AmE*: *TGWU, the transport union* | ***Union membership** has increased steadily over the past 5 years.* | *a union agreement* (=an agreement between a trade union and management about wages, conditions etc) | *the factory's official **trade union representative***
company union [C] HUMAN RESOURCES a TRADE UNION established by a company for its workers, perhaps not

part of the official trade union system: *Under pressure from the company union, Toyota has promised to reduce work schedules.*

craft union [C] a trade union whose members all work in skilled jobs that involve making or doing things with their hands

2 [C] a group of countries with the same central government: *the former Soviet Union*

3 [U] the act of joining two or more things together or the state of being joined together: *The countries of the EU are in a process of ever closer economic and political union.* —see also CREDIT UNION, CUSTOMS UNION

u·nion·ize also **unionise** *BrE* /ˈjuːnjənaɪz/ *v* [I,T] if workers unionize or are unionized, they become members of a TRADE UNION: *More than 50% of the labour force is unionized.* | *unionized workers*

unique selling point —see under POINT[1]

unique selling proposition *n* [C] another name for UNIQUE SELLING POINT

unissued capital —see under CAPITAL

u·nit /ˈjuːnət/ *n* [C] **1** a single complete product made by a company: *Output is now up to 150,000 units each month.* | *The* ***unit cost*** (=cost to make one unit) *of the computer system comprised about 80% materials, 15% overheads and 5% labour.* | ***Unit sales*** (=number of units sold) *of watches climbed about 35% last year.*

2 a company, organization, or group that is part of a larger company, organization, or group: *The computer maker Wang agreed to sell its Network Services unit.* + **of**: *Coors Brewing Co. is a unit of Adolph Coors Co.* | *She works in* ***the production unit.***

bargaining unit in the US, a group of employees officially appointed to take part in discussions between employers and unions about levels of pay, working conditions etc

decision-making unit abbreviation **DMU** a group of people in a company or other organization involved in making an important decision, especially a decision about buying something: *It is useful for a seller to know the degree of pressure on key members of the decision-making unit.*

strategic business unit abbreviation **SBU** a part of a business that can be thought of as separate from the rest of the business because it has its own market and needs to make a profit in its own right: *One vice-president is accountable for several strategic business units.*

3 an amount or quantity of something used as a standard of measurement + **of**: *The dollar is the basic unit of currency in the US.*

accumulation unit FINANCE an amount of money held in a particular type of INVESTMENT TRUST, in which profit is invested back into the trust rather than paid as a regular DIVIDEND

4 FINANCE a single share in a UNIT TRUST: *The company is splitting its 5p nominal shares into units of 2.5p to increase their marketability*

5 a single building on an INDUSTRIAL ESTATE: *He is renting a* ***factory unit*** *as a workshop.*

6 a piece of machinery which is part of a larger machine: *This is the* ***control unit*** *for the central heating.*

central processing unit abbreviation **CPU** COMPUTING the part of a computer that controls and organizes all its activities: *systems that need a big expensive central processing unit to work*

storage unit COMPUTING the part of a computer in which information is stored; MEMORY

unitary tax —see under TAX[1]

unit cost —see under COST[1]

United Nations Conference on Trade and Development abbreviation **UNCTAD** *n* an organization set up by the United Nations in 1964 to encourage international trade, especially by helping DEVELOPING COUNTRIES to increase their exports

United Nations Industrial Development Organization abbreviation **UNIDO** *n* an organization that became part of the United Nations in 1986, which helps the development of industry, especially manufacturing, in DEVELOPING COUNTRIES

u·nit·ize also **unitise** *BrE* /ˈjuːnətaɪz/ *v* [T] FINANCE to change an INVESTMENT TRUST into a UNIT TRUST —**unitization** also **unitisation** *BrE n* [U] *the unitization of an investment trust*

unit-linked *adj BrE* **unit-linked policy/plan/insurance** a life insurance policy, PENSION PLAN etc in which all or part of the PREMIUMS (=regular payments) are invested in an INVESTMENT FUND: *Midland Pensions are unit-linked plans, and since the value of units can go down as well as up it is possible that the value may fall below that of the original investment.*

unit of account *n* plural **units of account** [C] **1** the unit of money used in accounts: *Although the ECU was used as the unit of account for most official EU business, it was not used much privately.*

2 the unit of currency of a country

unit share —see under SHARE

unit trust —see under TRUST

unit trust company —see under COMPANY

universal banking —see under BANKING

Universal Product Code —see under CODE

Unix also **UNIX** /ˈjuːnɪks/ *n* [U] COMPUTING an OPERATING SYSTEM (=a computer's most basic program) for computers that is often used by universities, and was important in the development of the INTERNET: *engineers experienced in working with Unix* | *a fast* ***Unix computer*** *that can serve a network of 500 users*

un·la·den /ʌnˈleɪdn/ *adj* not carrying a load: *goods vehicles of an* ***unladen weight*** *exceeding 1525 kg*

un·li·censed /ʌnˈlaɪsənst/ *adj* without a LICENCE (=official document that allows you to do or have something): *He was accused of trading as an unlicensed dealer.* | *an unlicensed insurance agent*

unlimited company —see under COMPANY

unlimited liability —see under LIABILITY

un·list·ed /ʌnˈlɪstəd/ *adj* **1** FINANCE unlisted shares are in smaller companies that are not traded on the main stockmarket of a country, such as OVER-THE-COUNTER SHARES in the US: *Unlisted stocks were unable to match the gains posted by New York Stock Exchange issues yesterday.*

2 *AmE* not in the list of numbers in the telephone directory; EX-DIRECTORY *BrE*

unlisted company —see under COMPANY

unlisted security —see under SECURITY

unlisted share —see under SHARE

unlisted stock —see under STOCK[1]

un·load /ʌnˈləʊd‖-ˈloʊd/ *v* **1** [I,T] to remove a load from a vehicle, ship etc: *Delivery people were unloading fax machines.* | *This is where the ships load and unload.*

2 [T] to get rid of something quickly, especially by selling large quantities, for example because its price is falling: *The poor economy prompted investors to unload shares.* | *Their U.S. government bond desk unloaded $20 billion in government securities.* —**unloading** *n* [U] *the unloading of more than 2,000 tons of bananas* | *The company has been hurt by recent unloading of its stock.*

un·of·fi·cial /ˌʌnəˈfɪʃəl◂/ *adj* **1** without formal approval and permission from the organization or person in authority: *He made his complaint through unofficial channels.*

2 not made publicly known as part of an official plan:

Our unofficial policy is to grant two days' paternity leave. —**unofficially** *adv*: *countries that link their currencies, officially or unofficially, to the U.S. dollar*

unofficial exchange rate —see under EXCHANGE RATE

unofficial strike —see under STRIKE[1]

unpaid dividend —see under DIVIDEND

un•prof•it•a•ble /ʌn'prɒfɪtəbəl‖-'prɑː-/ *adj* an unprofitable business or activity does not make a profit: *The factory was unprofitable and was closed down.* —**unprofitably** *adv*: *Ferro's plastics business continued to operate unprofitably in the first quarter of this year.*

un•re•cov•er•a•ble /ˌʌnri'kʌvərəbəl◂/ *adj* if a loss, debt etc is unrecoverable, it is impossible to get back what is lost or owed: *Roughly 80% of the £15 million losses is unrecoverable.* | *He used the blank checks to make* ***unrecoverable loans.***

unrecoverable error —see under ERROR

unreported income —see under INCOME

un•scru•pu•lous /ʌn'skruːpjʊləs/ *adj* behaving in an unfair or dishonest way: *a campaign to protect consumers and make unscrupulous insurers obey the law* —**unscrupulously** *adv*

un•se•cured /ˌʌnsɪ'kjʊəd◂‖-'kjʊrd◂/ *adj* FINANCE **1** an unsecured loan, debt etc is not protected by an agreement that if it is not paid the company borrowing the money has to give the lender certain assets, such as property or shares: *Lenders typically collect less than 10 cents on the dollar on unsecured loans in personal bankruptcy proceedings.*
2 unsecured lender/creditor someone who lends money, without an agreement that if the debt is not paid, the company borrowing or owing the money has to give the lender certain assets, such as property or shares: *Under the terms of the reorganization, unsecured creditors will also receive newly issued common stock in the company.*

unsecured credit —see under CREDIT[1]

unsecured creditor —see under CREDITOR

unsecured debt —see under DEBT

unsecured loan —see under LOAN[1]

unsecured notes —see under NOTE[1]

un•skilled /ˌʌn'skɪld◂/ *adj* **1** an unskilled worker has not been trained for any job that needs special skills: *Half the plant's* ***unskilled workers*** *risk losing their jobs.* | ***Unskilled labour*** *costs four times as much in Britain as in Malaysia.*
2 unskilled work does not need people with special skills: *Unskilled industrial jobs are declining.* —compare SEMI-SKILLED, SKILLED

U

unskilled worker —see under WORKER

un•so•cial /ˌʌn'səʊʃəl◂‖-'soʊ-/ *adj BrE* **unsocial hours** [plural] if someone works unsocial hours, they work at times when most people do not work, such as early in the morning or during the night

un•sold /ˌʌnsəʊld◂‖-'soʊld◂/ *adj* unsold goods, shares etc have not yet been bought by a customer: *Stocks of unsold cars are lower this year.* | *£4.3 million shares remain unsold.*

unsold balance —see under BALANCE[1]

un•sol•i•cit•ed /ˌʌnsə'lɪsɪtɪd◂/ *adj* an unsolicited offer, request etc is made without being asked for by anyone: *PacifiCorp made an unsolicited $1.82 billion takeover offer for Pinnacle West.* | *Philadelphia Electric Co. said it will no longer accept unsolicited job applications.*

unsolicited offer —see under OFFER[2]

unspecified damages —see under DAMAGE[1]

un•su•stain•a•ble /ˌʌnsə'steɪnəbəl◂/ *adj* **1** impossible to continue doing for any length of time: *The company's growth strategy proved unsustainable in a slow sales environment.* | *The banks claim that the cost of running the system has become unsustainable.*
2 involving the use of materials that cannot be grown or produced again: *unsustainable products such as hardwoods* —compare SUSTAINABLE

unsustainable growth —see under GROWTH

unsystematic risk —see under RISK[1]

un•veil /ʌn'veɪl/ *v* [T] *journalism* to inform people about something, especially financial results or a new product: *Moulinex yesterday unveiled improved first-half results, marking a new step in its recovery.* | *They have unveiled a new series of multimedia products, including a double CD-Rom with an interactive game.*

un•wind /ʌn'waɪnd/ *v* past tense and past participle **unwound** FINANCE **1 unwind a long position** to sell bonds, shares etc because you think their price will fall: *Investors decided to unwind their money-losing long-term bond positions, using proceeds to buy short-term securities.*
2 unwind a short position to obtain the bonds, shares etc that you borrowed to sell, and deliver them: *When the market rose instead of falling, these speculators rushed to unwind their short positions.* —**unwinding** *n* [U] *the unwinding of some long, or overbought, dollar positions*

up /ʌp/ *adj* [not before a noun] if a computer, machine etc is up, it is working normally and not broken: *Is the network up now?* —opposite DOWN[2]

up and running *adj* [not before a noun] if a system is up and running, it has just started to work: *The longer it takes Kuwait to get its industry up and running, the more markets it loses to other producers.*

up•date[1] /ʌp'deɪt/ *v* [T] **1** to change something such as a report or computer file so that it includes new information: *These staff have responsibility for updating the database.* | *The July savings figures have been updated to include projections from managers.*
2 to give someone the most recent information about something **update sb on sth**: *The company has agreed to meet creditors to update them on its financial status.*
3 to change something to make it more modern: *We are updating our telephone system.*

up•date[2] /'ʌpdeɪt/ *n* [C] **1** the most recent news or information about something + **of**: *The GAO report is an update of a 1995 survey.* + **on**: *Let me* ***give you an update*** *on how the project is going.*
2 a new copy of something such a piece of software, that has been changed to make it better and able to do more things + **of**: *Release 3.0 is an update of the company's popular 1-2-3 spreadsheet software.*

up•front /ˌʌp'frʌnt◂/ *adj* **upfront payment/cost/fee etc** money that is paid as soon as a deal has been agreed, before any work has been done or any goods have been supplied: *The company offered an upfront payment of 25% of his first year's salary.* | *The fund charges a 3.75% upfront sales commission.* —**up front** *adv*: *Investors will need to pay about $9.25 per share up front, with $7.50 payable a year later.*

upfront fee —see under FEE

up•grade[1] /ˌʌp'greɪd/ *v* **1** [I,T] to make a computer, machine etc better and able to do more things: *AT&T is upgrading its office systems to include desktop videophones.* + **to**: *The way the computer is designed means you can easily upgrade to 128 megabytes of RAM.*
2 [I,T] to buy a new computer, machine etc that is better and able to do more things than your old one: *The money will be used to upgrade machinery and trucks.* + **to**: *word processor users who want to upgrade to a computer*
3 [I,T] to get a better seat on a plane, a better rented car

etc than the one you paid for + **to**: *You can use your frequent flier mileage to upgrade to business class.*

4 [T] to put something in a better class or at a higher level on a scale than before: *Moody's Investors Service Inc. said it upgraded $1.3 billion of United Airlines long-term debt* (=gave it a higher rating according to the borrower's ability to repay the debt).

up·grade² /ˈʌpgreɪd/ *n* [C] **1** the act of improving a product or service, or one that has been improved: *a £220 million upgrade on the freight route linking Glasgow with the Channel tunnel*

2 also **upgrade program** COMPUTING new computer software that replaces previous software of the same type + **to**: *The next version of Windows will cost less when it is bought as an upgrade to the existing version.*

3 an occasion when someone is given a better seat on a plane, or a better rented car, than the one they paid for: *If you're lucky you might* ***get an upgrade****.*

up·keep /ˈʌpkiːp/ *n* [U] the care and money needed to keep something in good condition: *We are introducing a user fee to finance the building and upkeep of state roads.*

up·load /ˌʌpˈləʊd‖-ˈloʊd/ *v* [T] COMPUTING to move information or programs from your computer onto another computer, especially onto a larger central computer: *If you are uploading and downloading big files you need a quicker modem.*

up·mar·ket¹ /ˌʌpˈmɑːkɨt◂‖-ɑːr-/ also **up·scale** /ˌʌpˈskeɪl◂/ *AmE* — *adj* involving goods and services that are expensive and perhaps of good quality compared to other goods etc of the same type, or the people that buy them: *an upmarket ski resort* | *an upscale family car*

upmarket² also **up·scale** /ˌʌpˈskeɪl◂/ *AmE* — *adv* **1** **go/move upmarket/upscale** to start buying or selling more expensive goods or services: *The travel operator is trying to lose its cheap image and move upmarket with more exotic destinations.*

2 **take sth upmarket/upscale** to change a product or a service, or people's ideas about it, so that it is or seems to be more expensive and of better quality: *He took the retailer upmarket, adding European designer clothing to its range.*

up·side /ˈʌpsaɪd/ *n* [singular] FINANCE the amount that the price of a share, bond etc is expected to rise: *The bonds' upside is limited – they are unlikely to rise above 100% of their face value.* | *The stock is at a low and could have* ***upside potential*** (=could rise).

up·stream /ˌʌpˈstriːm◂/ *adj* relating to an activity, product etc on which other activities etc depend or that happen before other activities: *Upstream technologies such as electronics and optics improve the performance of manufacturing machinery* —**upstream** *adv* —compare DOWNSTREAM

up·swing /ˈʌpˌswɪŋ/ *n* [C] an improvement or increase in the number or level of something + **in**: *The airline has noticed an upswing in bookings recently.* | *an upswing in business confidence*

up·tick /ˈʌptɪk/ *n* **1** [C usually singular] FINANCE a trade of shares at a higher price than that of its previous trade: *290 of the stocks in the S&P 500 were* ***trading on an uptick****.* —compare DOWNTICK

2 [C] an increase or improvement in the level of something + **in**: *There may be an uptick in housing construction.*

up·time /ˈʌptaɪm/ *n* [U] COMPUTING the period of time when a computer is working normally and able to be used: *customers that need 99% or better uptime from their mainframe computers*

up-to-date also **up to date** *adj* **1** modern or fashionable: *the most up-to-date equipment* | *a $400 million investment program to* ***bring*** *the company's plants* ***up-to-date***

2 including all the newest information: *The database includes up-to-date information on 50 key industries.* | *Our clients are always* ***kept up to date on*** (=told the latest information about) *costs.*

up-to-the-min·ute *adj* including all the newest information: *The American Stock Exchange began providing up-to-the-minute information on six overseas stock indexes.*

up·trend /ˈʌptrend/ *n* [C] a period of time when business or economic activity increases or improves: *Reflecting a steady uptrend, orders for machinery climbed 13.4%.*

up·turn /ˈʌptɜːn‖-ɜːrn/ *n* [C] an increase or improvement in the level of something + **in**: *There seems to be no sign of an upturn in business.* | *The prospects are good for an* ***economic upturn****.*

upwardly mobile *adj* moving up through the social classes and becoming richer: *young, upwardly mobile professionals*

ur·ban /ˈɜːbən‖ˈɜːr-/ *adj* [only before a noun] connected with towns or cities: ***urban areas*** *that have pollution problems* | *money to help finance* ***urban development*** *projects*

ur·ban·ize also **urbanise** *BrE* /ˈɜːbənaɪz‖ˈɜːr-/ *v* [I,T] to build houses, towns etc in the countryside: *a semi-urbanized town outside Mexico city* —**urbanization** *n* [U] *Taiwan's small size and heavy urbanization causes problems.*

urban renewal —see ***inner city renewal*** under RENEWAL

used /juːzd/ *adj* **used car/clothes etc** cars, clothes etc that have had one or more previous owners; PRE-OWNED *AmE*; SECOND HAND

useful life —see under LIFE

us·er /ˈjuːzə‖-ər/ *n* [C] someone or something that uses a product or service: ***Computer users*** *can send messages electronically.*

end user also **end-user** the person who actually uses a particular product, rather than someone involved in its production or sale: *End users used to get very little say in what software they got.* | *The company is examining the feasibility of retail outlets or catalogues, instead of selling direct to the end-user as in the past.*

user-friendly *adj* easy to use or operate: *a user-friendly computer manual* | *If gas isn't perceived as user-friendly, a lot of customers will find alternatives.* —**user-friendliness** *n* [U] *research into the factors which affect the user-friendliness of man-machine systems*

USP MARKETING abbreviation for UNIQUE SELLING POINT or UNIQUE SELLING PROPOSITION: *how to become the unique brand with the USP you need to succeed*

u·su·fruct /ˈjuːzjuːfrʌkt/ *n* [U] LAW the legal right to use a person's property in whatever way you like during your life, on condition that you return it to its owner in a reasonable condition: *usufruct rights over agricultural land*

u·su·ry /ˈjuːʒəri/ *n* [U] when someone lends people money and makes them pay an unfairly high rate of interest —**usurer** *n* [C]

u·til·i·ty /juːˈtɪlɨti/ *n* plural **utilities** [C usually plural] **1** a large company that provides services such as gas or electricity: *PacifiCorp is an* ***electric utility*** *whose service territories cover seven states.* | *the* ***public utilities***

2 *AmE* a service such as gas or electricity, provided for people to use: *Does your rent include utilities?*

u·til·ize also **utilise** *BrE* /ˈjuːtɨlaɪz/ *v* [T] to use something effectively: *a heating system that utilizes solar energy* —**utilization** *n* [U] *the full utilization of the oil pipeline* —see also PLANT UTILIZATION

V

v. —see VS.

va•can•cy /'veɪkənsi/ *n* plural **vacancies** [C] **1** a job that is available for someone to start doing: *We have **job vacancies** for graduates in engineering and information technology.* | *A **vacancy has arisen*** (=become available) *in the department for a senior accountant.* | *We haven't been able to find anyone to **fill** this **vacancy**.*
2 a hotel room, flat, or office which has not been taken and which is therefore available for rent: ***Apartment vacancies** are still high in several markets.*

va•cant /'veɪkənt/ *adj* **1** property that is vacant is not being used and may be available to rent or buy: *GM is adapting the vacant factory to build Opel cars.* | *Richcraft Homes has acquired a block of **vacant land** for development.*
2 vacant jobs or positions in a company are available for someone to start doing: *She turned down two job offers before accepting the **vacant post** of deputy administrator.* | *nine seats **left vacant** by recent board resignations.*
3 situations vacant the part of a newspaper in which jobs are advertised

vacant land —see under LAND[1]

vacant lot —see under LOT

vacant possession —see under POSSESSION

va•cate /və'keɪt, veɪ-‖'veɪkeɪt/ *v* [T] *formal* **1** to leave a job, position etc: *Mr Jones was elected to fill the board seat vacated by Mr. Carlisle*
2 *AmE* LAW to officially cancel a decision made by a court of law: *The court vacated the compensation award and sent it for new hearings.*

va•ca•tion /və'keɪʃən‖veɪ-/ *n* [C] **1** *AmE* a period of time when people are on holiday or not working: *Most factories close for a few weeks in the summer for vacations and plant maintenance.* | *Mr Williams was **on vacation** and couldn't be reached.*
2 a period of time when universities and certain law courts or other organizations are closed: *The process may take longer if the timetable is interrupted by a **court vacation**.*

vacation pay —see under PAY[1]

vac•il•late /'væsəleɪt/ *v* [I] if prices or rates vacillate, they continually change by small amounts: *Prices will vacillate near or slightly below current levels.* | *The rate of inflation has been vacillating between 4% and 5%.*

V

val•id /'væləd/ *adj* a valid document or agreement is legally acceptable, often for a fixed period of time: *The court ruled that P&G's patent is valid and enforceable.* | *Investors with valid claims against the company could receive payments within a few months.* | *The voucher is valid for 12 months.*

val•i•date /'vælədeɪt/ *v* [T] *formal* to prove that something is true, correct, or acceptable: *The federal court overturned court rulings validating the company's patent.* | *Our **data is validated** to ensure reliability.* —**validation** *n* [U] *A sample **validation check** showed there were two suspect areas of information.*

va•lid•i•ty /və'lɪdəti/ *n* [U] when a document is legally acceptable: *The shareholder group may question the **legal validity** of the merger in court.*
face validity STATISTICS figures, results, or DATA with face validity appear to be correct, but they may not be completely correct or may hide important facts: *A feeling of unease persists about the face validity of these accounts.*

val•u•a•ble /'væljuəbəl, -jəbəl‖'væljəbəl/ *adj* worth a lot of money: *The falling dollar makes US company profits less valuable.* | *The fuel oil will be converted into more valuable products, such as gasoline.*

val•u•a•bles /'væljuəbəlz, -jəbəlz‖-jəbəlz/ *n* [plural] things someone owns that are worth a lot of money, such as jewellery and electronic equipment: *The insurance policy covers valuables up to £3,000.*

val•u•a•tion /ˌvælju'eɪʃən/ *n* [C,U] a judgement about how much money something is worth: *There have been some rather unrealistic valuations put on businesses recently.* | *disagreements over the valuation of the bank's shares* | *property valuation*
inventory valuation the amount of stock that a company has compared with the amount of goods that they have sold in a particular period of time: *In September, U.S. retailers' inventory-to-sales ratio was 1.57.*
stock valuation FINANCE a judgement about the total value of a company's shares at a particular time: *conservative forms of stock valuation based on earnings*

val•ue[1] /'vælju:/ *n* **1** [C,U] the amount of money something is worth: *The dangers associated with hazardous waste clearly outweigh its **commercial value**.* | *The company's **current value** is estimated at £300 million.* | *A price rise would **increase** the **dollar value** of US oil production by $31 billion a year.*
2 good/excellent etc value (for money) if something is good, excellent etc value, it is of good quality, considering its price or you get a large amount for the price: *Local firms seem to offer **the best value for money**.*
3 values [plural] the principles and practices that a business or organization thinks are important and which it tries to follow: *Our vision for the new century calls for less consumerism and more attention to human values.*
added value [U] an increase in the value of something that has been worked on, combined with other things etc so that it can be sold in a new form: *In the past, producers ignored the potential 25% added value that could be gained from selling gold as jewellery.* | *The emphasis will be on putting new refining joint ventures in Venezuela to provide added value there for its oil industry.* | *Clients will look to computer systems for the answers to all legal questions, and will be willing to pay for personal service only when the added value justifies the expense.*
annual value *BrE* [C,U] PROPERTY the value of a property, used to calculate the amount of local tax that must be paid on it; ASSURED VALUE *AmE*: *In 1445, his English estates had an annual value of over £1,061.* | *The tax base, or rateable value, is the net annual value of the property occupied.*
asset value [C,U] FINANCE the total NET BOOK VALUE of a company's assets: *"Selling something like this for below its asset value indicates either that it's a very bad deal or a very bad business," he said.*
asset value per share [U] FINANCE the total value of the assets that a company has, divided by the number of shares that the company has issued; ASSET BACKING: *The share price remains below the bank's net asset value per share.*
assured value *AmE* [C,U] FINANCE the value of a property, used to calculate the amount of local tax that must be paid on it; ANNUAL VALUE *BrE*
book value ◆ [C,U] ACCOUNTING the value of an asset or group of assets in a company's accounts, not necessarily the amount they could be sold for: *The company owns a ski resort on Lake Tahoe that could be worth double its $19 million book value.* —compare ***market value***
◆ [C,U] FINANCE the value of a company measured as its total assets minus total liabilities except liabilities to

shareholders: *Value investors buy a stock when it seems cheap compared with a company's earnings, dividends, or book value.*

break-up value [C,U] FINANCE the total value of a company if each part of the company is sold separately, rather than if it is sold as a working company: *The mining company has a break-up value put at £2.6 billion more than its current £5.8 billion capitalisation.*

capital value [U] FINANCE the total worth of one or more investments: *London & Associated Properties said that 50% of the capital value of its portfolio was now invested in town centre retail malls.*

declared value [U] the value of goods on which DUTY must be paid when passing through CUSTOMS

deprival value [C] ACCOUNTING the amount a business would lose if an asset was lost or damaged etc. This amount represents what it would cost to replace the asset or the amount a business would have received from the asset's sale: *Assets under deprival value accounting could be significantly higher than the book values of assets with related outstanding debt.*

economic value [U] a calculation of the profits produced by an asset, or the amount of profit it might produce in the future: *The economic value of the oil and gas field could become uncertain if electricity generating companies are forced to use more British coal.*

expected value [C] STATISTICS an average figure that would appear if a set of figures was studied many times

extrinsic value [U] *formal* the amount of money something is worth, based on its outer appearance or price: *Your personal belongings may have little extrinsic value, but when they are lost or stolen, the cost of replacement can be surprisingly high.*

face value ◆ [C,U] the amount that appears on a coin, cheque etc which shows how much money it is worth: *A voucher issued to passengers whose flights have been cancelled is redeemable by KLF Airlines for its face value.* + **of**: *A bank manager had issued false deposit certificates with a face value of 342,000 yen.*

◆ [C,U] FINANCE the stated value of a share, bond etc when it is ISSUED (=sold for the first time). This is not necessarily the price that is really paid for it. Bonds, for example, may be sold slightly above or below their face amount. This value is used to calculate YIELD (=how much profit bonds make for the investor); FACE AMOUNT; NOMINAL VALUE; PAR VALUE + **of**: *30-year bonds with a discounted face value of 35%* —compare ***market value***

fair value also **fair market value** [C usually singular] FINANCE the value of a business's assets based on the amount of money that could probably be obtained if they were sold: *The price of the shares was to be the fair value, as determined by the company's auditors.* | *a proposal to sell the company's headquarters at its current fair market value*

future value written abbreviation **fv** [C,U] FINANCE the value of an investment on a future date, used for example in calculating the value of an asset after it has been rented out for a period of time, or in calculating how much profit a particular activity will make: *With Rover Select, you have the peace of mind of a guaranteed future value at the end of the agreement.*

imputed value [U] TAX, STATISTICS a value given to something because the actual value is not known, for example because exact figures are not available

intrinsic value [U] the amount of money something is worth, based on its personal value to someone

market value ◆ [C,U] how much people would be willing to pay for something, rather than a value calculated in another way: *Continental officials said they estimate the market value of Pirelli's world-wide tire assets at roughly DM800 million.*

◆ [C,U] FINANCE the total value of all the shares on a stockmarket, or the value of the shares of a particular company: *UnionFed shares lost almost half their market value yesterday, losing $2.25.*

net annual value [C,U] PROPERTY the amount of rent that could be charged for a house, land etc, used in Britain as a basis for calculating local taxes: *The tax base, or rateable value, is the net annual value of the property occupied.*

net asset value written abbreviation **NAV** [U] ◆ FINANCE the value of a company's assets, less its liabilities except to shareholders at a particular time. Net asset value is used as an indicator of how much a company is worth to a buyer; NET WORTH: *ICI has estimated the net asset value of the subsidiary at £700 million, but analysts have forecast a selling price of £500 million.*

◆ [C,U] FINANCE the value of the investments of a MUTUAL FUND (=a financial institution that invests its shareholders' money in other companies) at a particular time: *If the net asset value of the trust were £50 million and there were 5 million units in existence, then the net asset value of one unit would be £10.*

net book value abbreviation **NBV** [C,U] FINANCE the value of an asset or group of assets in a company's financial records after DEPRECIATION (=amounts to allow for their estimated loss of value as they get older, less productive etc) or REVALUATIONS (=amounts to show estimated increases in the value of property, buildings etc). This may be more or less than what they could actually be sold for: *The net book value of Hondo's domestic oil and gas properties was $112.3 million as of last Sept. 30.* | *Is property and plant at net book value or are they included at current valuation or depreciated replacement cost?*

net present value written abbreviation **NPV** [C,U] FINANCE the value of the income from a business investment using a particular percentage to calculate its DISCOUNTED CASH FLOW (=the money it will bring in the future, reduced at a particular rate to take account of the delay in receiving it). The rate is based on present interest rates increased by an amount to take account of risk. If, using this rate, the NPV is positive in relation to the cost of the investment, the investment will be profitable: *By investing in projects that have positive net present value, finance managers will create value.*

net realizable value also **net realisable value** *BrE* [C,U] FINANCE the realistic value of an asset if it were sold, after taking off any costs relating to selling it: *Turner will take a $21 million reserve against future declines in the net realizable value of its real estate properties.*

nominal value ◆ [C,U] in shares and bonds, another name for PAR VALUE: *Under a new law, Swiss companies will be able to lower the nominal value of their shares to 10 Swiss francs from 100.*

◆ [C,U] the nominal value of a BANKNOTE is the amount printed on it: *A system of banknotes is economical when the nominal value of each note is about double that of the lesser note.*

par value [C,U] FINANCE the stated value of a bond, share etc when it is ISSUED (=sold for the first time). This is not necessarily the actual price paid for it. Bonds, for example, may be sold slightly above or below this value. The par value of bonds is used to calculate YIELD (=their profitability to the investor); FACE AMOUNT; FACE VALUE; NOMINAL VALUE: *The bonds were trading at about 97% of their par value.* | *Currently denominated at 500 yen par value, the shares will be changed to 50 yen.* —see also PAR

rateable value [C,U] PROPERTY a value given to buildings in Britain before 1990 in order to calculate how much local tax the owner had to pay

replacement value [C,U] INSURANCE the amount of money something would cost to replace: *Airlines insured their aircraft for replacement value because the industry was booming.*

residual value [C,U] ACCOUNTING the amount of

money something is worth after a particular length of time: *The machinery has a useful life of 10 years, and the residual value is likely to be very small.*

surplus value [U] ECONOMICS the difference between what it costs to make a product and the amount of money it can be sold for; PROFIT: *The main purpose of Marx's theory is to explain the phenomenon of surplus value in the capitalist system.*

surrender value [C,U] FINANCE the value of an insurance policy when it MATURES (=becomes due for payment), or when you stop it before it matures: *If the holder drops the policy before death, the person gets to walk away with some of the accumulated savings, the policy's surrender value.*

written-down value [C,U] ACCOUNTING the value of an asset or group of assets in a company's financial records after DEPRECIATION (=amounts to allow for their estimated loss of value as they get older, less productive etc): *The written-down value has no relation to the market value of an asset.* —see also TIME VALUE

value[2] *v* [T] to decide how much something is worth, especially by comparing it with other, similar things: *It's almost impossible to value a media property fairly in the current economic climate.* **value sth at**: *Legal & General plc agreed to sell its insurance unit in a* ***deal valued at*** *£140 million.*

value-added *adj* [only before a noun] value-added products or services have an increased value because work has been done on them, they have been combined with other products etc. This increase in value to the buyer is what the buyer pays for: *ConAgra Inc. is the top supplier of value-added foods for the catering industry.* | *The new Russian economy could increase the supply of* ***low-value-added*** *manufactured* ***goods***.

value-added product —see under PRODUCT

value-added reseller —see under RESELLER

value-added tax —see under TAX[1]

value chain —see under CHAIN

val•ued /ˈvæljuːd/ *adj* [only before a noun] a valued customer, worker etc is important and useful to you: *Harvard is a* ***valued client*** *and we're delighted to resume business relations.*

valued insurance —see under INSURANCE

value fund —see under FUND[1]

value investor —see under INVESTOR

value judgment —see under JUDGMENT

val•u•er /ˈvæljuə‖-ər/ *n* [C] someone whose job is to calculate how much something is worth: *The property is inspected by a valuer who tells the bank whether the house you want to buy is worth the price.*

value share —see under SHARE

value stock —see under STOCK[1]

V

van•guard /ˈvængɑːd‖-gɑːrd/ *n* **be in/at the vanguard (of sth)** to be the most advanced or developed business, person etc in a particular area of work: *IBM considers itself in the vanguard of employee benefits.*

va•pour•ware *BrE*, **vaporware** *AmE* /ˈveɪpəweə‖-pərwer/ *n* [U] *informal* COMPUTING software that computer companies say will soon be available, but that may never appear: *major embarrassments brought by "vaporware," products that end up existing for years only on press releases*

VAR written abbreviation for VALUE-ADDED RESELLER —see under RESELLER

var•i•a•ble[1] /ˈveəriəbəl‖ˈver-/ *n* [C] something that affects a situation in a way that means you cannot be sure what will happen: *Interest rates and earnings are the two most important variables in forecasting stock prices.* | *The Japanese are subject to the same* ***economic variables*** *as everybody else.*

variable[2] *adj* variable costs, prices, interest rates etc change or can change and are not fixed: *The value of both fixed- and* ***variable-rate loans*** *fell nearly half a per cent.* | *The new management will offer more attractive* ***variable annuities***.

variable cost —see under COST[1]

variable-rate gilts —see under GILTS

variable-rate mortgage —see under MORTGAGE[1]

var•i•ance /ˈveəriəns‖ˈver-/ *n* **1** [U] the amount by which two or more things are different: *the wide variance in the language used in contracts*

2 [C,U] ACCOUNTING the difference between what something actually costs and its usual or standard cost, or its cost when calculated earlier: *A significant variance is one amounting to more than 10% of the allocated budget.*

3 [C] *AmE* an arrangement in which a court of law allows a company to do something that would not normally be allowed; EXEMPTION *BrE*: *The authority* ***granted a variance*** *so the company could install the satellite dish.*

4 [C] *AmE* an arrangement in which a local government authority allows someone to do something to their property that would not normally be allowed

var•i•a•tion /ˌveəriˈeɪʃən‖ˌver-/ *n* [C,U] a difference or change in the normal amount or appearance of something: *Labor figures in both reports are adjusted for* ***seasonal variation*** (=variation that depends on the time of year). + **on**: *Miller Lite has been using the same campaign with variations on its slogan, for well over ten years.*

va•ri•e•ty /vəˈraɪəti/ *n* plural **varieties** [C] a particular type of a product: *Intel expects to be selling 30 new varieties of its latest microprocessors.* | *We sell over 50 different varieties of beer.*

var•y /ˈveəri‖ˈveri/ *v* past tense and past participle **varied**

1 [I,T] if rates, costs, prices etc vary, or something varies them, they change when economic conditions change: *Many professional investors vary the proportions of their portfolios invested in stocks.* | *The returns on bonds for the first five months vary considerably.* + **with**: *Premiums vary with the age of the person insured and length of cover.*

2 [I] if several things of the same type vary, they are all different from each other: *Though estimates vary widely, analysts generally expect investors to earn between £1 to £2 a share.* | *The offices* ***varied in size*** *from three to 14 rooms.* —**varied** *adj*: *Motorola increased revenue 16%, reflecting gains in* ***varied product lines***. | *Katmandu wants investors in varied industrial ventures.*

VAT /ˌviː eɪ ˈtiː, væt/ *n* [U] Value-Added Tax; a tax on some goods and services. Businesses pay VAT on most goods and services they buy and if they are over a certain size, charge VAT on the goods and services they sell. At regular periods of time, the total amount of tax paid is taken away from the total amount charged to arrive at an amount that is owed to or by the business. Final customers pay VAT on these goods in shops and on services. VAT is a way of charging tax on the increase in value of goods and services at each stage as they are produced, rather than just on their final selling price to customers: *Our quotes exclude VAT, currently 17.5%.* | *Some goods and services are zero-rated, which means that no VAT is charged on them.* —see also EX VAT

VAT man *n* **the VAT man** *informal BrE* the British government department that collects VAT: *The VAT rules have previously been so complex that they have confused even the VAT man.*

vault[1] /vɔːlt‖vɒːlt/ *n* [C] also **vaults** [plural] part of a bank or other organization where money is kept safely: *More than $425 million currently sit in vaults in the Treasury Department.*

bonded vault a special building for storing wines and spirits that have been brought into a country until import tax has been paid on them

vault² *v* [I,T] to move into a higher or more successful position: *When rates vaulted, selling accelerated.* + **to/into/above etc**: *The Hang Seng Index vaulted 2.6% to 3722.39.* | *The acquisition vaulted the company to the top of the workstation market.*

vault cash —see under CASH¹

VDT *n* [C] visual display terminal; another name for VDU

VDU *n* [C] visual display unit; a computer screen; MONITOR: *VDU operators find their work unpleasant because they look at the screen for long, uninterrupted periods.*

ve·hi·cle /ˈviːɪkəl/ *n* **1** *formal* **a vehicle for (doing) sth** something used as a way of achieving a particular result: *Hechinger Co. expects its subsidiary to become the primary* ***growth vehicle*** *for the company.* | *Corporations are more efficient vehicles for reinvestment than partnerships.*

2 a particular type of investment: *Mutual funds are an appropriate vehicle for investors who don't want to lock their money up.* | *Analysts see the stock market as the* ***investment vehicle*** *of choice this year.*

3 a car, bus etc

commercial vehicle a vehicle such as a TRUCK or VAN, used for transporting goods: *Daewoo produces a wide range of passenger and commercial vehicles.*

goods vehicle *BrE* a road vehicle used for carrying goods: *In Britain in 1918 there were 78,000 cars, and nearly as many buses and goods vehicles.*

heavy goods vehicle abbreviation **HGV** *BrE* a very large road vehicle for carrying goods: *The volume of movement of heavy goods vehicles along the approach roads seriously affected the residents' enjoyment of their properties.*

public service vehicle abbreviation **PSV** *BrE* LAW a bus used by the public

ve·lo·ci·ty /vəˈlɒsəti‖vəˈlɑː-/ *n* [U] ECONOMICS the number of times a particular unit of money is spent over a period of time. A country's GDP is the total amount of money available and its velocity: *Unless there is a sharp* ***rise in velocity****, a more inflationary monetary policy would be appropriate.*

vend /vend/ *v* [T] *formal* to sell something: *This was the first move by Adobe into vending hardware.* —**vending** *n* [U] *Los Angeles has finally legalized* ***sidewalk vending*** (=selling things on the street)

ven·dee /ˌvenˈdiː/ *n* [C] LAW someone who is buying something; BUYER, PURCHASER

ven·der /ˌvendə‖-ər/ *n* [C] another spelling of VENDOR

vending machine —see under MACHINE¹

vend·or /ˈvendə‖-ər/ *n* [C] *formal* someone who is selling something, especially a house or a piece of land; SELLER: *House sales could dry up as vendors refuse to accept drastic price cuts.* | *leading software vendors*

vendor placing —see under PLACING

ven·ture¹ /ˈventʃə‖-ər/ *n* [C] a new business activity or project that involves taking risks: *She identified potential customers for a new* ***business venture*** *she was evaluating.* | *American Aviation* ENTERED INTO A ***joint venture*** *with GE to rebuild the Lockheed plant.*

joint venture a business activity in which two or more companies have invested together: *Saudi Arabian and Japanese officials agreed on a joint venture to build oil refineries in both countries.*

venture² *v*

venture into sth *phr v* [T] if a company or investor ventures into an area of business or investment, they become involved in it for the first time: *The entertainment concern is venturing into a different field of computer animation.* | *Some investors ventured into blue chips to put idle cash back to work.*

venture capital —see under CAPITAL

venture capitalist —see under CAPITALIST¹

ven·ue /ˈvenjuː/ *n* [C] a place where a large event is arranged to take place: *All parts of the* ***conference venue*** *have access for people with disabilities.*

VER —see ***voluntary export restraint*** under RESTRAINT

verb·al /ˈvɜːbəl‖ˈvɜːr-/ *adj* a verbal contract, agreement etc is one that is spoken rather than written: *The bank manager gave* ***verbal assurances*** *of the security of the investments.*

ver·dict /ˈvɜːdɪkt‖ˈvɜːr-/ *n* [C] an official decision made in a court of law or other organization that has authority: *It took 16 hours for the* ***jury to reach a verdict****.* | *Debt-rating agencies had a split* (=divided) *verdict on Coca-Cola Enterprises Inc.'s reorganization plan announced this week.*

ver·sion /ˈvɜːʃən‖ˈvɜːrʒən/ *n* [C] a particular product that is slightly different from other products of the same type, in the same range etc: *A new version of the computer spreadsheet will be launched this year.* | *Honda's version of the S200 will be built in Birmingham.*

beta version COMPUTING a VERSION of software that has been tested by the people who developed it and then given to a specially chosen group of users to find out if there are any more small problems with it, before it is made available to the public: *Even with this beta version, no major problems have surfaced, so we expect the release version to be very solid.*

ver·sion·ing /ˈvɜːʃənɪŋ‖ˈvɜːrʒ-/ *n* [U] when a company makes particular versions of products for different markets, customers etc: *versioning of computer software for individual clients* | *Any* ***electronic versioning*** *of the book shall be the subject of a separate agreement between the author and the publisher.*

ver·so /ˈvɜːsəʊ‖ˈvɜːrsoʊ/ *n* [C] the page on the left-hand side of a book: *The verso always carries the even page number and the recto the odd number.* —opposite RECTO

ver·sus /ˈvɜːsəs‖ˈvɜːr-/ abbreviation **v.** or **vs.** *AmE prep* used to show that two people or companies are against each other in a legal case: *The judge agreed with the decision in White versus Illinois.*

ver·ti·cal /ˈvɜːtɪkəl‖ˈvɜːr-/ *adj* **1** HUMAN RESOURCES a vertical organization, system etc is one in which decisions and rules are passed on to employees through several different levels of management: *Our team has abandoned the* ***vertical structure*** *because it didn't let people interact.* | *Our goal is to improve vertical communications.*

2 vertical restraint/price-fixing FINANCE methods used by manufacturers to control the price at which their products are sold by other companies: *Retail price maintenance is a simple example of a vertical restraint.* | *a crackdown on vertical price-fixing affecting distributors* —compare FLAT¹

vertical amalgamation —see under AMALGAMATION

vertical combination —see under COMBINATION

vertical equity —see under EQUITY

vertical expansion —see under EXPANSION

vertical integration —see under INTEGRATION

vertical merger —see under MERGER

vest /vest/ *v* [T] FINANCE if shares, stocks etc are vested, they are owned by someone: *About one-third of these options are vested and can be exercised by shareholders at any time.*

vest sth **in** sb *phr v* [T] LAW to give someone the legal right to own something, such as property or investments: *The plan gives employees the right to become fully vested in stock and other incentive options.*

vest sb **with** sth *phr v* [T] LAW to give someone the legal right to use their authority, property etc: *Voting responsibility is vested with fund officials.*

vested interest —see under INTEREST

vest•ing /ˈvestɪŋ/ *n* [U] *AmE* the right of a worker to receive a PENSION (=money you receive after you stop working) from the company they work for: *Pension plans are moving toward quicker vesting for employees of five years' service or more.*

vet /vet/ *v* past tense and past participle **vetted** present participle **vetting** [T] *BrE* to examine someone's previous jobs and activities to find out whether they are suitable to do a job, especially one that involves dealing with secret information: *The key requirement is to vet people for the most senior posts.* | *After passing the selection board, candidates are vetted by one of the organization's professionals.* —**vetting** *n* [U] *The company said standard* ***vetting procedures*** *were carried out.*

ve•to /ˈviːtəʊ‖-toʊ/ *v* [T] to officially refuse to allow something to happen, especially something other people have agreed: *An attempt to use £35 million to strengthen the bank's capital was vetoed by bank regulators.* —**veto** *n* [C] *Senior advisers have recommended a veto to the President.*

vex•a•tious /vekˈseɪʃəs/ *adj* LAW vexatious legal actions are not serious or based on the truth, but are done only to annoy someone: *We may have found a way to get around* ***vexatious*** *shareholder* ***litigation****.*

vi•a•ble /ˈvaɪəbəl/ *adj* **1** a viable plan, system, suggestion etc is realistic and therefore may succeed: *We had two months to come up with a* ***viable proposal*** *for saving the factory.* | *If investors find that approach viable, there are no rules to stop them doing that.*

2 a viable company or organization is making a profit and can continue to do business: *We had to reduce staff to survive as a viable firm.* | *The auditors will decide whether or not the bank is* ***economically viable****.*

vicarious liability —see under LIABILITY

vice chairman —see under CHAIRMAN

vice president —see under PRESIDENT

vid•e•o /ˈvɪdiəʊ‖-dioʊ/ *n* **1** [C] a copy of a film or television programme recorded on videotape: *a video shop*

2 [C,U] a videotape: *a blank video* | *'Titanic' is now available* ***on video****.*

3 [C] *BrE* a video cassette recorder; VCR

4 [U] the process of recording and showing television programmes, films, real events etc using video equipment: *Interactive learning has been greatly advanced by the introduction of video.* | *video games*

video-conferencing *n* [U] a system that allows a lot of people in different places to communicate with each other, using special equipment that can send sound and pictures: *Corporations use video-conferencing as a low-cost alternative to travelling for meetings.* —**video-conference** *n* [C] *The device made video-conferences practical though expensive at $1,000 an hour for the lines and $250,000 for a fully equipped room.*

video display terminal —see VDT

vid•e•o•tape /ˈvɪdiəʊteɪp‖-dioʊ-/ *n* [C,U] a long thin band of MAGNETIC material used to record pictures and sound —**videotape** *v* [T] *AmE FBI agents videotaped lawmakers taking cash from lobbyists.* | *The President can give a* ***videotaped desposition*** *or a written reply to the court's questions.*

vi•o•late /ˈvaɪəleɪt/ *v* [T] **1** to disobey a law or do something that is against an official agreement, rule etc: *The contractors* ***violated the law*** *by laying off workers without notice.* | *The proposed legislation would violate existing trade agreements.*

2 violate the rights/privacy of to do something that does not respect someone's rights, such as their right to be private: *There was concern that the company was violating customers' privacy.*

vi•o•la•tion /ˌvaɪəˈleɪʃən/ *n* **1** [C,U] an action that breaks a law, agreement, principle etc: *Employers who fail to comply can be fined £5,000 per violation.* | *their blatant violation of the law*

2 in violation of if something is in violation of a law, agreement, principle etc, it breaks it: *She was accused of starting a competing business in violation of her contract.*

vir•tu•al /ˈvɜːtʃuəl‖ˈvɜːr-/ *adj* **1** [only before a noun] a virtual monopoly, ban, takeover etc is so nearly a complete monopoly, ban etc that any difference is unimportant: *They enjoy a virtual monopoly in sales of pickup trucks.* | *Trading activity reached a virtual standstill.*

2 virtual office/library/classroom etc COMPUTING computer software that gives you the experience of being in a place, or allows you to do the things that you would do in a real office, library etc: *the virtual library, where people can explore information resources from their desks*

3 virtual document/companion etc COMPUTING a document etc that exists on a computer rather than in physical form: *Buying an air ticket involves the creation of several virtual documents.*

virtual memory —see under MEMORY

virtual reality abbreviation **VR** *n* [U] images produced by a computer that give you the experience of seeing or being inside a real place or physical object. It can be used, for example, to make models of new products or to train people to use new machines: *Video game makers were the first mainstream users of virtual reality.*

vi•rus /ˈvaɪərəs‖ˈvaɪrəs/ *n* [C] a set of instructions secretly put onto a computer, that can destroy or change information on the computer: *The virus had already destroyed data at several US companies.* —compare BUG

vi•sa /ˈviːzə/ *n* [C] an official mark put on your PASSPORT by the representative of a foreign country, that allows you to enter, pass through, or leave that country: *In Saudi Arabia foreigners need both an* ***entry visa*** *and an* ***exit visa****.*

visible exports —see under EXPORT[1]

vis•i•bles /ˈvɪzəbəlz/ *n* [plural] imports and exports of goods rather than services —compare INVISIBLES

visual display terminal —see VDT

visual display unit —see VDU

vivos —see INTER VIVOS

vo•ca•tion /vəʊˈkeɪʃən‖voʊ-/ *n* [C] a job, especially one that involves helping people, that you do because you enjoy it or because you have a strong feeling that it is the purpose of your life to do it: *As a nurse, she felt she had* ***found her vocation****.* | *He was happy in his new vocation, but sad about the money he wasn't making.*

vo•ca•tion•al /vəʊˈkeɪʃənəl‖voʊ-/ *adj* **vocational training/guidance/course etc** training etc that teaches you the skills you need to do a particular job: *He argued for better vocational education, saying many students were not interested in academic courses.*

voice mail —see under MAIL[1]

voice recognition —see under RECOGNITION

void /vɔɪd/ *adj* LAW a contract or agreement that is void has no legal effect because it is against the law: *Under state law, a contract to pay money knowingly lent for gambling is void.* —**void** *v* [T] *Mr. Mullen's termination agreement was voided and he had to return more than $5 million.*

void•a•ble /ˈvɔɪdəbəl/ *adj* LAW a voidable contract, agreement etc can be declared void: *The contract was voidable on the grounds of fraud, but not void.*

voidable contract —see under CONTRACT[1]

void contract —see under CONTRACT[1]

vol. written abbreviation for VOLUME

vol•a•tile /ˈvɒlətaɪl‖ˈvɑːlətl/ *adj* a volatile market, situation etc is changing quickly and suddenly, for example rising and falling without much warning: *Bonds started the year in a highly volatile trading environment.* —**volatility** *n* [U] *The report questioned whether **market volatility** should be blamed on foreign investors.*

volatile stock —see under STOCK[1]

vol•ume /ˈvɒljuːm‖ˈvɑːljəm/ *n* [C,U] **1** the amount of space that a substance or object contains or fills: *The US gallon is about five-sixths the volume of the UK gallon.*
2 the total amount of something + **of**: *The volume of exports was up 4% on the previous 4 months.* | *the **high volume** of traffic at O'Hare airport* | *59% of companies reported that **sales volume** was lower than a year ago.* | *The telephone company AT&T began offering a new **volume discount** price reduction for using a large amount of goods or services for business customers.*
3 FINANCE the total amount of activity on a stockmarket, usually measured by the number of shares that have been traded in a particular period of time: *Volume dropped sharply to 113.5 million shares.*

volume discount —see under DISCOUNT[1]

vol•un•ta•ry /ˈvɒləntəri‖ˈvɑːlənteri/ *adj* **1** done or agreed to willingly and without being forced: *He suggested that workers take voluntary pay cuts to help the economy.* | *Cigar advertising on television is banned under a **voluntary agreement**.* | *The company was wound up **on a voluntary basis**.*
2 voluntary work/service etc work etc that is done by people who do it because they want to and are not paid, or are paid very little: *In her spare time, Elaine does voluntary work for a mental health charity.*

voluntary bankruptcy —see under BANKRUPTCY

voluntary liquidation —see under LIQUIDATION

voluntary restraint agreement —see under AGREEMENT

voluntary unemployment —see under UNEMPLOYMENT

voluntary winding up —see under WINDING UP

vostro account —see under ACCOUNT[1]

vote[1] /vəʊt‖voʊt/ *v* [I,T] to show by marking a paper, raising your hand etc which person you want to elect or whether you support a particular plan + **for/against**: *23% of shareholders voted for him as a new director.* | *The board voted against filing a suit to recover the money.* **vote to do sth**: *Committee members voted 9–2 to raise interest rates.* **vote sth down** (=reject it in a vote): *The settlement offer collapsed after the House of Representatives voted it down.* **vote sb in** (=elect them): *The chairman was voted in by a 12–1 majority.* —**voter** *n* [C] *Voters did not like their anti-European stance.*

vote[2] *n* **1** [C] when a group of people vote in order to decide or choose something: *The results of the vote were surprising – 80% of workers favoured strike action.* | *Creditors will **take a vote on** the reorganization plan later this year.*
2 [C] a choice or decision that someone makes by voting in an election or meeting: *The union was only 23 votes short of the majority it needed.*
block vote [C] in Britain, the system of voting used at a meeting of the TRADES UNION CONGRESS. When heads of trades unions vote, each head does not have just one vote, but has as many votes as he or she has members: *The outcome turned on the block votes of union delegations at opposite ends of the conflict.*
casting vote [C] an extra vote that someone in charge of a meeting can have, which is only used if there are exactly the same number of votes for and against something: *He missed being sacked only by the Chairman's casting vote.*
3 [C] the right to vote: *Each share carries a vote.*
4 [singular] the total number of votes made in an election or the total number of people who vote: *AT&T's proposal to oust the board got 78% of the vote.*

voting rights —see under RIGHT

voting share —see under SHARE

voting stock —see under STOCK[1]

vouch•er /ˈvaʊtʃə‖-ər/ *n* [C] **1** a ticket that can be used instead of money for a particular purpose + **for**: *The tour price includes a voucher for a meal in a pub of your choice.* | *She was given a **travel voucher** from Belfast to London.*
2 money that a government gives people to use for a particular purpose such as health or education: *The White House is proposing tax credits or vouchers, worth perhaps as much as $5,000 a family, to help low-income people buy health insurance.* | *The nursery voucher scheme gave parents vouchers worth £1000 to buy the nursery provision of their choice in state or private schools.*
3 ACCOUNTING an official RECEIPT given for money that has been paid: *On receiving payment the subcontractor should give the builder a completed voucher.*
4 ACCOUNTING any document that proves that someone's accounts are correct

vouch•ing /ˈvaʊtʃɪŋ/ *n* [U] ACCOUNTING the act of checking all the vouchers and other documents, such as INVOICES, that prove that a company's accounts are correct

voyage charter —see under CHARTER[2]

VP abbreviation for VICE PRESIDENT: *I sat outside the VP's office waiting for him to arrive.*

vs. also **v.** *BrE* written abbreviation for VERSUS

vulture fund —see under FUND[1]

vulture investor —see under INVESTOR

W

wage /weɪdʒ/ *n* [C] also **wages** money that someone earns according to the number of hours, days, or weeks that they work, especially money that is paid each week: *The average **hourly wage** in the industry is $6.* | *Workers were demanding a 10% **wage increase**.* | *The new law would mean a 5% pay cut for most **wage earners**.* | *For the average worker, wages rose 4.6%.* | *She worked long hours for **low wages**.*

basic wage also **base wage** *AmE* [singular] the amount of money that workers are paid for each normal hour, week etc that they work, not including any extra payments + **of**: *a base wage of $11 an hour* | *The company proposed a 2% basic wage increase.*

living wage [singular] a wage high enough to allow someone to live a fairly comfortable life: *Trade Unions are still fighting for a living wage in many industries.*

minimum wage [singular] the lowest amount of money that can legally be paid per hour to a worker: *He claimed that Labour's plans to introduce a **national minimum wage** would lead to job losses.* | *a **statutory minimum wage***

money wages [plural] the amount of money that someone receives as their wages, rather than payments in the form of goods, a place to live etc: *Both money wages and prices are rising, leaving real wages unchanged.*

real wages [plural] the amount of goods and services that can be bought with someone's wages, after taking into account INFLATION (=rising prices): *Since 1975, real wages for US manual workers have fallen.*

wage assignment —see under ASSIGNMENT

wage bargaining —see under BARGAINING

wage inflation —see under INFLATION

wage packet *n* [C] *BrE* another name for PAY PACKET

wage payment —see under PAYMENT

wage-price spiral —see under SPIRAL[1]

wage-push inflation —see under INFLATION

wage restraint —see under RESTRAINT

waive /weɪv/ *v* [T] to state officially that a right, rule etc can be ignored in a particular case: *The government has **waived restrictions** on dealing in foreign currencies.* | *American Express offered to **waive fees** for additional cards held by family members.* | *The defendant **waived his right to** an attorney.*

waiv•er /ˈweɪvə‖-ər/ *n* [C] an official statement that a right, rule etc can be waived + **of**: *Creditors agreed to a 30-day waiver of interest payments.*

collision damage waiver abbreviation **CDW** a payment that you make when renting a car so that you do not have to pay the cost of any damage to the car. If you do not pay the CDW, you have to pay a part of the cost of repair if the car is damaged

walk•out /ˈwɔːk-aʊt‖ˈwɒːk-/ also **walk-out** *n* [C usually singular] an occasion when workers stop working and leave their office or factory as a protest: *The talks broke off on Tuesday, prompting a **nationwide walkout** of about 200,000 rail workers.* | *Workers **staged a walkout** at the company's engine factory as the union continued its strike action.*

wall /wɔːl‖wɒːl/ *n* **1 go to the wall** if a business goes to the wall, it fails, especially because of financial difficulties: *One of highest-flyers in the computer industry went to the wall a year ago because of trouble handling a large acquisition.*

2 hit a wall if sales, profits etc hit a wall, they reach their highest point before beginning to fall: *Booming car sales in Germany hit a wall in August, plummeting 40%.* —see also CHINESE WALL, GLASS WALL, PARTY WALL

wall•flow•er /ˈwɔːlˌflaʊə‖ˈwɒːlˌflaʊər/ *n* [C] FINANCE *journalism* an investment that is not popular with investors because it is not profitable enough: *Investors started buying the new issue in large numbers, turning a Wall Street wallflower into one of the hottest financial products.*

wall•pa•per /ˈwɔːlˌpeɪpə‖ˈwɒːlˌpeɪpər/ *n* [U] *disapproving* FINANCE when a company sells a lot of new shares to finance a series of takeovers; PAPERCHASE

Wall Street *n* **1** the NEW YORK STOCK EXCHANGE, situated in Wall Street in Manhattan

2 American financial institutions and investors in general: *Wall Street analysts projected that the issue would sell at 94 cents a share.* —compare CITY

Wall Street Crash *n* **1** FINANCE the period in October 1929 when shares and other investments in the US fell in value by very large amounts, and that was followed by the DEPRESSION

2 October 19, 1987, when shares in the US fell in value by very large amounts, with similar declines in stockmarkets elsewhere

WAN /wæn/ *n* [C] COMPUTING wide area network; an arrangement in which computers in different areas or buildings are connected to each other and users in different places can look at and work on the same information: *Sumitomi uses a WAN to link all three of its global sites.* —compare LAN

wane[1] /weɪn/ *v* [I] if something such as influence, interest, or power wanes, it gradually becomes less strong: *Trading activity quickly waned after the initial flurry, leaving prices stuck at the lower levels.* | *evidence that inflation is waning*

wane[2] *n* **on the wane** becoming smaller, weaker, or less important: *The positive signs are that economic growth is steady and unemployment is on the wane.*

want-ad —see under AD

war /wɔː‖wɔːr/ *n* [C] **price/trade/sales war** a situation in which countries or companies compete against each other very strongly: *Manufacturers of basic commodity products are vulnerable to price wars when demand is slow.* | *Progress in talks with Japan have averted the risk of a protectionist trade war.* | *A price war may break out as tire makers try to grab market share and put spare capacity to work.* | *Gasoline retailers have been **waging price wars*** (=taking part in them).

war chest *n* [C usually singular] *journalism* FINANCE a large amount of money that a company has in its RESERVES (=profits from earlier periods of time not paid out to shareholders, or cash from the sale of assets) that it can use to buy other companies: *Roche seems to be building up a war chest for a big merger or acquisition.*

ware•house /ˈweəhaʊs‖ˈwer-/ *n* [C] a large building used for storing goods in large quantities: *The unit will add 14 warehouses to its current distribution centers.*

bonded warehouse also **Customs warehouse** a warehouse in which imported goods are stored until taxes on them have been paid: *The measures include creating a bonded warehouse to make the port a point of entry for imported goods.*

data warehouse COMPUTING a place where business information is stored electronically: *the mainframe's role as a data warehouse for core business applications such as billing, distribution, and accounting*

distribution warehouse a warehouse in which goods that are ready to be sent to shops or direct to customers are stored: *An Idaho supermarket chain is considering buying Super Food's wholesale food distribution warehouse and delivery equipment.* —**warehouse** *v* [T] *AT&T is studying the systems it uses to warehouse and deliver its products.* —**warehousing** *n* [U] *They take on such tasks as warehousing, inventory management, labeling, and packaging.*

warehouse club *n* [C] *AmE* a group of very large shops selling many different kinds of goods cheaply: *The aggressive warehouse clubs could take as much as 10% of the auto spares market.* | *Consumers continue to favor discount stores and warehouse clubs over pricey department stores.*

warehouse receipt —see under RECEIPT[1]

wares /weəz‖werz/ *n* [plural] things that are for sale: *Shoppers are willing to spend extra money for environmentally conscious wares.* | *The companies will develop products together, and may even sell some of each others' wares.*

war•rant[1] /ˈwɒrənt‖ˈwɔː-, ˈwɑː-/ *n* [C] **1** FINANCE also **share warrant**, **stock warrant** an official document giving someone, usually an existing shareholder, the right to buy shares in a company. Warrants are similar to RIGHTS ISSUES, except that holders usually have longer to use them: *LDCA has a warrant entitling it to buy 300,000 Carolco common shares for $18.50 each.* | *Each £5,000 bond carries one stock warrant exercisable five years from now.*

bond warrant the right to buy particular bonds in the future at a particular price: *DM1 million of bond warrants at DM2.85 per warrant; each warrant entitles the holder to buy DM5,000 bonds by Kaufhof Finance*

covered warrant a warrant that is owned by a person selling the related shares and who is able to sell them without having to first buy the shares elsewhere

dividend warrant *BrE* a cheque sent by a company to a shareholder in payment of dividends; DIVIDEND CHECK *AmE*

2 an official document giving someone the legal authority to do something: *The attorney's office* ***filed a warrant*** *seeking the forfeiture of the illegal assets.* | *According to the* ***arrest warrant****, one of his victims was a widow with nine children.*

warrant[2] *v* [T] to promise that something is true or to guarantee that something will happen: *Investors expect the auditors to warrant information contained in the accountants' report.* | *If the purchaser wishes specific matters to be warranted, these should be set out in detail in the contract.*

war•ran•tee /ˌwɒrənˈtiː‖ˌwɔː-, ˌwɑː-/ *n* [C] a person who is given a warranty

war•ran•tor /ˈwɒrəntɔː‖ˈwɔːrəntər, ˈwɑː-/ *n* [C] a person who gives someone else a warranty

war•ran•ty /ˈwɒrənti‖ˈwɔː-, ˈwɑː-/ *n* plural **warranties** [C,U] a written promise that a company gives to a customer, stating that it will repair or replace a product they have bought if it breaks during a certain period of time; GUARANTEE: *Ford offers a 12-month basic warranty on all car parts.* | *If the set isn't* ***under warranty****, repairs by a registered dealer could cost up to 25% more.*

express warranty [C] a warranty that is actually stated in writing rather than an implied warranty: *The buyer is advised to demand an express warranty as to the suitability of the goods for their intended purpose.*

implied warranty [C] a warranty that is not actually stated in writing, but that is understood to exist: *an implied warranty that the goods are of merchantable quality* —see also BREACH OF WARRANTY

wash sale —see under SALE

wash trade —see under TRADE[1]

wast•age /ˈweɪstɪdʒ/ *n* [U] **1** an amount of something that is lost or destroyed: *Penalties should be introduced for excessive wastage of materials.* | *Our courses are designed to maximise the learning process and minimise time and money wastage.*

2 natural wastage HUMAN RESOURCES a reduction in the number of people working for a company, organization etc because workers decide to leave or stop working, not because they have lost their jobs: *We achieved a 40% reduction in staff through natural wastage and redeployment to other offices.*

waste[1] /weɪst/ *n* **1** [U] unwanted materials or substances that are left after a particular process: *The factory's byproduct waste is used to feed pigs.* | *illegal disposal of* ***hazardous waste***

2 [singular, U] things such as money or skills that should be used effectively, but are not: *Try as he might, the new manager couldn't overcome the waste and inefficiency that had plagued the plant for years.* | *Sales of natural gas at present prices would be a* ***waste of*** *company* ***assets***. —**waste** *adj*: *Chambers is a waste collection, hauling, and disposal concern.* | *government guidelines for* ***toxic waste disposal***

waste[2] *v* [T] to use more of something, especially time or money, than you need to, or use it in a way that is not sensible: *A prominent economist has suggested that the government wasted $200 billion during the oil-price boom.* | *We waste a lot of time and legal fees on defending our trademarks rather than tending to business.*

waste•ful /ˈweɪstfəl/ *adj* using things such as money, materials or energy in a way that is not sensible or effective: *Local government is seen as slow, wasteful, and incompetent.*

wasting asset —see under ASSET

watch•dog /ˈwɒtʃdɒg‖ˈwɑːtʃdɒːg, ˈwɒːtʃ-/ *n* [C] an independent organization responsible for making sure that companies in a particular industry or business do not do anything illegal: *France's stock market watchdog is conducting a routine investigation of trading.* | *This week, the* ***consumer watchdog*** *updated its guidelines on selling white goods.*

watching brief —see under BRIEF[1]

watch list —see under LIST[1]

wa•ter /ˈwɔːtə‖ˈwɒːtər, ˈwɑː-/ *v*

water sth ↔ **down** *phr v* [T] to make a suggestion, rule, or proposal less forceful by removing some parts of it: *A late amendment watered down the insider-trading penalties to a £100,000 maximum fine instead of the earlier £500,000.* —**watered-down** *adj* [only before a noun] *Legislators want to offer a* ***watered-down version*** *in hopes that it will satisfy voters.*

watered stock —see under STOCK[1]

wa•ter•mark /ˈwɔːtəmɑːk‖ˈwɒːtərmɑːrk, ˈwɑː-/ *n* [C] **1** a design that is put into paper that you can see when you hold it up to the light: *Banknotes have a watermark to prevent forgery.*

2 COMPUTING an electronic device in text, pictures, music etc in DIGITAL form, showing where they came from. Watermarks can be used to fight against illegal copying: *A* ***digital watermark*** *through music bought over the Internet will show the original purchaser.*

WATS /wɒts‖wɑːts/ *n* [singular] *AmE* wide area telephone service; a system which allows companies to use long distance telephone lines at reduced rates. Calls made by a customer to a WATS number are free, and the company pays for these calls at the lower rate: *Users of overseas WATS can get monthly discounts of 2%.* —compare FREEFONE

way•bill /ˈweɪbɪl/ *n* [C] a document stating the number of goods being carried on a ship, train, plane etc and the place they are going to: *This* ***air waybill*** *can be issued only by the airline whose name appears on it.*

Ways and Means Committee *n* a group of people in the US government whose job is to find methods of raising money for the work that the government wants to do: *The Ways and Means committee will vote on the proposals this afternoon.*

weak /wiːk/ *adj* **1** FINANCE if markets, investments, currencies etc are weak, their prices are falling: *The company reported a loss of C$16 million, mostly because of **weak** metals **prices**. | The **weak dollar** has made many US products cheaper than those from Japan. | Revenue continued to decline in the **weak economy**.*
2 if a company is weak, it is not strong or successful financially: *our **weak financial position** will force us to merge with our rivals. | The Trump Taj Mahal is considered the weakest of the three casinos because it has the heaviest debt load.*

weak·en /ˈwiːkən/ *v* **1** [I,T] if investments, prices, currencies etc weaken, or something weakens them, they begin to fall in value: *A combination of low US interest rates and a rising Euro will weaken the dollar. | Work stoppages will cause an already **weakening economy** to slow further. | London shares weakened, while Frankfurt stocks finished strong.*
2 [T] to make something less powerful, successful, or profitable: *Further weakened by the recession, the airline filed for bankruptcy. | Many agencies fear that revealing the use of subcontractors may weaken their reputations as full-service shops.*

weak·ness /ˈwiːknəs/ *n* **1** [U] a lack of power, success, or influence: *The stock market doesn't fully reflect the weakness in the economy. | Citing continued weakness in computer sales, analyst William Milton lowered his profit forecast.*
2 [C] part of something that can be criticized easily: *A major weakness of the firm has been its reliance on its headquarters in Atlanta for making decisions. | a serious weakness in the system*

wealth /welθ/ *n* [U] a large amount of money or valuable possessions: *Colombia's economy needn't rely solely on its mineral wealth. | The legislation is designed to give American firms the ability to **generate wealth** from overseas operations.* —**wealthy** *adj*: *a maker of high-priced electronic goods for wealthy consumers*
national wealth ECONOMICS the total value of goods and services produced in a country in a particular period of time: *The key task for industrial policy is to create the right climate for the creation of national wealth.*

wealth effect —see under EFFECT

wealth tax —see under TAX[1]

wear /weə‖wer/ *n* **(fair) wear and tear** INSURANCE the amount of damage that can be expected to affect a product or property in normal use. Wear and tear is often taken into consideration by an insurance company when paying an insurance claim: *The sum insured should be based on current replacement costs, less an allowance for wear and tear.*

wear·out /ˈweəraʊt‖ˈwer-/ *n* [U] MARKETING used to describe a situation in which customers are no longer interested in a product or an advertising campaign: *With market saturation* (=too many products available) ***consumer wearout** is a very likely outcome. | Some advertisers get around the **wearout factor** by repackaging an old idea.*

weath·er /ˈweðə‖-ər/ *v* [T] if a company, business etc weathers a difficult situation, it manages to come through it safely: *Courtaulds Textiles is continuing to **weather the recession** well. | The company has **weathered the slump** better than its competitors.*

web /web/ *n* **the (Worldwide) Web** abbreviation **WWW** a system of millions of computers all over the world connected to the INTERNET, which allows people to create and look at websites

web·page /ˈwebpeɪdʒ/ *n* [C] one of the areas you can go to on a website —compare HOMEPAGE

web·site /ˈwebsaɪt/ *n* [C] a programme on a computer that is connected to the INTERNET, showing information about a particular company, organization, subject etc. All websites have an address which is used to find them and which begins with 'http://www': *our website, at http://www.awl.-elt.com/dictionaries*

weigh·bridge /ˈweɪˌbrɪdʒ/ *n* [C] *BrE* a machine for weighing vehicles and their loads, with a flat area that you drive the vehicle onto; SCALE; SCALES

weight[1] /weɪt/ *n* [C,U] how heavy something is, measured using a particular system: *The weight of the new noise reduction kits may limit the aircraft's capacity by up to 10%.*
gross weight [U] the weight of goods, including any packaging or the vehicle in which they are being carried: *goods vehicles with a maximum gross weight not exceeding 3,500 kg*
net weight [U] the weight of a product, after the weight of packaging has been taken away

weight[2] *v* [T] STATISTICS to allow for the differences between sets of figures that are being compared by increasing or lowering the value of some of them, and so creating a balance between them: *The mid-cap index is weighted according to the market values of the stocks. | The results of the survey were weighted by age to make sure the poll accurately reflects voters nationwide. | In its tender exercise, Pearl weighted certain questions* (=gave more marks for them) *to provide an insight into the strengths and weaknesses of all four suppliers.*

weighted average —see under AVERAGE[2]

weighted index —see under INDEX[1]

weight·ing /ˈweɪtɪŋ/ *n* [singular, U] **1** *BrE* additional money paid to someone because of the higher costs of living in a particular area; COST OF LIVING ALLOWANCE: *The salary is £35,000 a year, including a **London weighting allowance**.*
2 STATISTICS an additional value given to certain figures in a calculation, in order to allow for their importance: *Chrysler's bonus formula assigns a 20% weighting to profits and another 20% weighting to market share.*

weighting factor —see under FACTOR[1]

welch also **welsh** /welʃ‖welʃ, weltʃ/ *v* [I] *informal* if someone welches on a deal, they fail to do what they promised to: *If they welch on this agreement, who will want to deal with them in future?*

wel·fare /ˈwelfeə‖-fer/ *n* [U] **1** help that is given by government to people with social or financial problems: *a drastic reform of the welfare system*
2 *AmE* money paid by the government to people who are poor, unemployed etc: *Non-profit companies are providing job placement for welfare recipients. | large families **on welfare***

welfare benefit —see under BENEFIT[1]

welfare economics —see under ECONOMICS

welfare payment —see under PAYMENT

welfare state —see under STATE

welfare-to-work *n* [U] in Britain, a government policy of encouraging people who are unemployed to stop receiving BENEFIT (=money from the government) and to get jobs instead: *Welfare-to-work has become a central plank of government policy.*

well /wel/ *n* [C] another name for an OIL WELL

wellness program —see under PROGRAM[1]

well off *adj* having more money than other people, or enough money to live comfortably: *There should be some safeguards to protect **less well-off people** who live on fixed, low incomes.* —opposite BADLY OFF

wet goods —see under GOODS

wet lease —see under LEASE[2]

wharf /wɔːf‖wɔːrf/ *n* plural **wharves** [C] the place where a ship can stop and unload goods; DOCK: *an application for a wharf expansion at Long Beach*

what-if *adj* **what-if? question/analysis etc** a way of examining a situation by deciding what you would do if something happened to change it: *A risk management consultant can kick-start the process by providing a few, objective what-if? questions.*

what you see is what you get —see WYSIWYG

wheeling and dealing —see under DEALING

when-issued abbreviation **WI** *adj* [only before a noun] FINANCE when-issued shares and bonds have been planned and agreed but not yet made available officially, and unofficial trading in them has begun: *The company rolled out two new when-issued stocks, providing shareholders with a choice of investing in either the company's steel or oil operations*

when-issued share —see under SHARE

when-issued stock —see under STOCK[1]

whip•saw /ˈwɪpsɔː‖-sɒː/ *v* [T] FINANCE **be whipsawed** if investments or investors are whipsawed, they are trapped in a market where prices are falling and rising very quickly, and it is difficult to say what might happen: *The bond market was whipsawed in extremely volatile trading yesterday.* | *Currency traders have been whipsawed by a combination of political crises and changing sentiments about the economic recovery.*

whis•tle•blow•er /ˈwɪsəlˌbləʊə‖-ˌbloʊər/ *n* [C] someone working for an organization who tells the authorities that people in the organization are doing something illegal, dishonest, or wrong: *The company had paid out substantial sums to silence would-be whistleblowers.*

white•board /ˈwaɪtbɔːd‖-bɔːrd/ *n* [C] a large white board on which you write information that you are presenting to a group of people —compare FLIPCHART

white-coat *adj* **white-coat ban/rule** in the US, a law which makes it illegal to use a real doctor to help sell or advertise health products: *Even some drug company executives are nervous about lifting the white-coat ban.*

white-collar *adj* [only before a noun] white-collar workers work in offices, banks etc, rather than in factories, mines etc: *The redundancies have devastated **white-collar workers**.* | *The car maker will cut 9,000 **white-collar jobs**.* —compare BLUE-COLLAR

white-collar crime —see under CRIME

white-collar worker —see under WORKER

white elephant *n* [C] something that is completely useless, even though it cost a lot of money: *The hotel is unfinished and structurally unsound – a white elephant of epic proportions.*

white goods —see under GOODS

White•hall /ˈwaɪthɔːl, ˌwaɪtˈhɔːl‖-hɒːl/ *n* the British government administration, especially government departments rather than Parliament

White House *n* **the White House** the US President and the people who advise him or her

white knight *n* [C] FINANCE someone who buys shares in a company to prevent another company taking it over completely: *Morgan has been looking for a white knight since insurance broker Willis Faber announced it was selling its 20% stake in the company.* —compare BLACK KNIGHT

White Pages *n* [plural] *AmE* in the US, the part of the telephone book containing the names, addresses, and phone numbers of people with phones in a particular area: *Southwestern Bell is considering putting a special mark on its White Pages that will prevent them from being photocopied.* —compare YELLOW PAGES

white sale —see under SALE

whizz also **whiz** *AmE* /wɪz/ *n* [C] *informal* **financial/computer/technology etc whizz** someone who is very skilled in a particular activity or is successful in a particular area of work: *He dismissed rumours that Wall Street whizz Asher Edelman is the gallery's money source.* | *Top managers may be **financial whizzes**, but they aren't marketing geniuses.*

whizz-kid *n* [C] a young person who is very skilled in a particular activity or is very successful in a particular area of work

whole-life *adj* [only before a noun] INSURANCE whole-life insurance contracts, arrangements etc are ones in which the person whose life is insured pays a fixed sum each year, and the insurance company pays out a sum when that person dies: *A whole-life policy could provide protection if a parent dies.*

whole-life insurance —see under INSURANCE

whole•sale[1] /ˈhəʊlseɪl‖ˈhoʊl-/ *n* [U] the business of selling large quantities of goods at low prices to other businesses, rather than to the general public

wholesale[2] *adj* **1** involving the business of selling goods in large quantities to businesses, rather than to the general public: *The **wholesale trade sector** lost 14,000 jobs.* | *Japan's overall **wholesale prices** in December were unchanged.*

2 involving the business of providing services to other businesses, rather than to the general public: *Japan's long-term credit banks are primarily **wholesale lenders*** (=banks that lend to other financial institutions and to companies). —**wholesale** *adv*: *Dealing wholesale requires certification by a local authority.* —compare RETAIL[1]

wholesale co-operative —see under CO-OPERATIVE

wholesale price —see under PRICE[1]

whole•sal•er /ˈhəʊlˌseɪlə‖ˈhoʊlˌseɪlər/ *n* [C] a person or company that sells goods in large quantities to businesses, rather than to the general public: *Carrollton makes and distributes own-label products for supermarket retailers and wholesalers.* —compare RETAILER

wholly-owned subsidiary —see under SUBSIDIARY[1]

WI written abbreviation for WHEN-ISSUED

wide area network —see under NETWORK[1]

wide area telephone service —see WATS

wide price —see under PRICE[1]

wid•get /ˈwɪdʒɪt/ *n* [C] *informal* **1** any small piece of equipment, used especially to talk about something that you do not know the name of: *Rear-view mirrors are just the kind of widget that car makers could easily buy from cheap-labor plants in Asia.*

2 an imaginary product that a company might produce: *Company A produces 6000 widgets a month at a price of $0.33.*

widow-and-orphan stock —see under STOCK[1]

wild card *n* [C] **1** something that has an unexpected effect on a situation + **in**: *A wild card in the company's prospects is the disagreement that has broken out between the company and some of its 16,000 workers.*

2 COMPUTING a sign that can represent any letter in some computer commands

wild•cat[1] /ˈwaɪldkæt/ *adj* [only before a noun] *AmE* a wildcat oil well or discovery of oil is one that is in a place where no one has found oil before

wildcat[2] *v* [I] *AmE* to look for oil in a place where no one has found it yet —**wildcatter** *n* [C] *Oklahoma wildcatters struck oil in the late 1920s.*

wildcat strike —see under STRIKE[1]

wilderness area —see under AREA

will[1] /wɪl/ *n* [C] a legal document that says who you want your money and property to be given to when you die: *They found a lawyer to **draft their wills**. | This is the **last will and testament** of John Smith.*

living will a document explaining what medical or legal decisions should be made if you become too ill to make those decisions yourself —see also TENANT AT WILL

will[2] *v* [T] to leave something to someone in your will: *Taylor willed £604,521 to his family.*

Wil·shire 5000 /ˌwɪlʃə faɪv ˈhʌndrɪ̈d‖-ʃər-/ *n* in the US, a stock INDEX of shares in 5000 companies that gives a general picture of the way US stocks are performing

wind /waɪnd/ *v* past tense and past participle **wound**

wind sth ↔ **down** *phr v* [T] to gradually reduce the work of a business or organization so that it can be closed down completely: *The company has been winding down its business for 10 months because it was operating unprofitably.*

wind sth ↔ **up** *phr v* [T] **1** *BrE* to close down a company, especially because it cannot pay its debts: *The Bank of England presented a petition to the court for an order that the firm be wound up.*
2 to bring something, especially a discussion or meeting, to an end: *Mr Reid wound up the debate.*

wind·fall /ˈwɪndfɔːl‖-fɒːl/ *n* [C] an amount of money that a person or business gets unexpectedly: *Falling interest rates **are a windfall for** homeowners refinancing their mortgages. | The group earned a **windfall profit** on the sale of part of an office building in Paris.*

windfall profit —see under PROFIT[1]

windfall tax —see under TAX[1]

winding up *n* [singular, U] when a business or organization is closed down, especially because it cannot pay its debts: *the way a company's assets are distributed **on a winding up** | the presentation of a **winding up petition***

compulsory winding up a winding up that is controlled by a court of law, with an officer of the court in charge

voluntary winding up a winding up that is not controlled by a court of law but happens because the owners of the company decide it should happen

win·dow /ˈwɪndəʊ‖-doʊ/ *n* [C] **1** one of the separate areas on a computer screen where different processes or programs are operating: *You can make a window larger or smaller by dragging its corner with the mouse.*
2 a short period of time that is available for a particular activity: *There is a 12- to 24-month buying window in the domestic real estate markets before prices start going up again.*
3 in the window if a product is in the window, it is on display at the front of a shop to encourage customers to come in: *Showcased in the window is a Murphy bed set inside a large cabinet.* —see also DISCOUNT WINDOW, DRIVE-UP WINDOW

window dressing *n* [U] **1** when people try to give the public a favourable idea about something, sometimes hiding the true situation: *Stock prices benefited from window dressing by some money managers anxious to present good reports to clients.*
2 the art of arranging goods in a shop window so that they look attractive to customers —**window dresser** *n* [C] *Window dressers have created strong demand for the stock.*

Win·dows /ˈwɪndəʊz‖-doʊz/ *n* [U] *trademark* a system produced by the Microsoft Corporation for organizing information on a personal computer, which can run several programs in separate areas of the computer screen: *Most of today's software is designed for Windows. | the latest version of Windows*

window shopping —see under SHOPPING

win-win *adj* [only before a noun] used to describe a situation in which both sides involved gain something or are successful: *The extra earnings available to lenders and the facility provided for borrowers make it a **win-win situation**. | A spokesman said the company was "pleased" and called the contract a 'win-win' settlement.*

WIP abbreviation for WORK IN PROGRESS; WORK IN PROCESS

Wipo /ˈwaɪpəʊ‖-poʊ/ *n* World Intellectual Property Organization; an organization that protects the rights of the owners of INTELLECTUAL PROPERTY (=something on which someone owns the legal rights to be the only producer or seller)

Wi·pon·et /ˈwaɪpəʊˌnet‖-poʊ-/ *n* a computer NETWORK that connects Wipo and the offices of its members across the world

wire /waɪə‖waɪr/ *v* [T] *AmE* to send money electronically from one bank to another: *Each institution wired $99,000 to Settlers, which in turn deposited the money in another bank.*

wire·less /ˈwaɪələs‖ˈwaɪr-/ *adj* [only before a noun] wireless communications, systems etc use signals that pass through the air rather than using wires and CABLES: *The Federal Communications Commission is encouraging phone companies to offer **wireless telephony*** (=telephone services).

wireless communications —see under COMMUNICATION

with·draw /wɪðˈdrɔː, wɪθ-‖-ˈdrɒː/ *v* past tense **withdrew** past participle **withdrawn** **1** [T] to take money out of a bank account: *You can withdraw cash from ATMs in any town or city.*
2 [T] to remove something or take it back, often because of an official decision: *a government decision to withdraw funding | They offered her the job but then withdrew the offer after checking her references.*
3 [T] MARKETING if a company withdraws a product or service, it stops making it available, either for a period of time or permanently: *Previous testing showed no safety problems, but the company decided to withdraw the product so the incidents could be investigated. | The drug has been withdrawn from the market for further testing.*
4 withdraw a remark/claim/accusation etc to say that something you said earlier was completely untrue: *The newspaper has agreed to withdraw its allegations.*
5 [I] to no longer take part in something or to no longer belong to a particular organization + **as**: *The Bank of New York withdrew as a primary dealer of U.S. government securities.* + **from**: *His decision to withdraw from active management was a blow to the company.*

with·draw·al /wɪðˈdrɔːəl, wɪθ-‖-ˈdrɒːəl-/ *n* **1** [C,U] the act of taking money from a bank account, or the amount you take out + **of**: *There are penalties for the early withdrawal of savings. | **cash withdrawals** from ATMs*
2 [U] the removal or stopping of something such as support, an offer, or a service + **of**: *the withdrawal of government aid*
3 [C,U] also **product withdrawal** when a product is made no longer available, either for a period of time or permanently: *It stopped producing the drug after the death of a patient and took a $100 million pretax charge for the product withdrawal.*
4 [U] when someone no longer takes part in an activity or is no longer a member of an organization + **from**: *the company's withdrawal from its unprofitable games and entertainment computer business*
5 [U] when you say that something you previously said was in fact untrue + **of**: *the withdrawal of all allegations*

with·hold /wɪðˈhəʊld, wɪθ-‖-ˈhoʊld/ past tense and past participle **withheld** *v* [T] **1** to refuse to let someone have something: *I **withheld payment** until they had* *completed the work.* | *the part of your salary withheld for income tax*

2 withhold facts/evidence/information to refuse to give information: *Apple has hinted that it has some big plans, but has withheld details.*

withholding tax —see under TAX[1]

without-profits policy —see under INSURANCE POLICY

with profits *adj* [only before a noun] INSURANCE a with profits insurance policy pays a guaranteed amount in BONUSES (=profits from the insurer's fund)

with-profits policy —see under INSURANCE POLICY

wit•ness[1] /ˈwɪtnəs/ *n* [C] **1** someone in a court of law who tells the court what they saw or what they know about a crime: *The government's case rested on one* ***key*** (=important) ***witness.*** | *I was asked to testify as a* ***defense witness*** (=acting to defend the person accused of committing a crime). | *the main* ***prosecution witness*** (=acting to show that the accused person is guilty)

expert witness someone who has expert knowledge in a particular area and comes to a court of law to give their opinion about it: *Professor Wheeler has served as an expert witness for the IRS in transfer-pricing cases.*

2 someone who is present when an official paper is signed and who also signs it to prove this + **to**: *a witness to a will*

witness[2] *v* [T] to be present when someone signs an official document, and to sign it yourself to show this: *Will you witness my signature?*

witness summons —see under SUMMONS[1]

wiz•ard /ˈwɪzəd‖-ərd/ *n* [C] COMPUTING a piece of software that allows you to INSTALL (=put) a program on your computer

wk. written abbreviation for week

wonk /wɒŋk‖wɑːŋk/ *n* [C] *informal AmE* someone who works very hard, is very serious, and knows a lot about a particular subject: *policy wonks surrounding the President*

word-of-mouth *n* [U] MARKETING when people hear about something from their friends, people they work with etc: *College students rated the film as either 'excellent' or 'very good', a favourable indicator for films that rely on word-of-mouth.*

word-processing software —see under SOFTWARE

word processor *n* [C] **1** a small computer, used especially for writing documents

2 software for writing documents on a PERSONAL COMPUTER —**word processing** *n* [U] *software for word processing and database storage*

words per minute —see WPM

work[1] /wɜːk‖wɜːrk/ *v* **1** [I] to do a job that you are paid for: *Harry is 78 and still working.* | *Most of the people I went to school with work in factories.* + **for**: *David works for the BBC.* + **as**: *She works as a consultant for a design company.*

2 [I,T] to do the activities or duties that are part of your job: *Sally isn't working tomorrow.* | *I'm tired of working ten-hour days.*

3 [T] to travel around a particular area as part of your job, especially in order to sell something: *Markovitz works the Tri-State area.*

4 [I] to do an activity which needs time and effort: *We had to work non-stop to get the book finished on time.*

5 work sb hard to make someone use a lot of time and effort in a job or activity: *The company is famous for working its employees hard.*

6 [T] if you work a particular material such as metal, leather etc, you cut or shape it in order to make something

7 work the land/soil to do all the work necessary to grow crops on a piece of land: *Our family has worked this land for generations.*

8 work a mine to remove a substance such as coal, gold, or oil from a mine

9 [I] if a machine or piece of equipment works, it does what it is supposed to do: *Is the photocopier working now?*

10 [T] to operate a machine or piece of equipment: *The check-out is slow, because only two clerks work the cash registers.*

11 [I] if a method, plan, or system works, it produces the results you want: *The article gives a good understanding of how the pharmaceutical research process works.*

12 [I] if something such as a fact, situation, or system works in a particular way, it has a particular effect on somebody or something: *The tax laws tend to work against small companies.*

13 work an organization/system etc to know how to influence an organization etc in order to achieve something: *He knows how to work the Moscow government for all the necessary approvals.*

14 work your way up if you work your way up, or work your way up in an organization, your jobs in it become more and more important: *They have spent their entire careers at the firm and worked their way up the ranks.*

15 work to rule *BrE* **work to contract** *AmE* to protest about a situation at work by doing your job less quickly or effectively than usual, but without breaking your employer's rules or the terms of your contract: *The staff are not on strike but are working to rule.* —see also WORK-TO-RULE

work out *phr v* **1** [T] **work** sth ↔ **out** to calculate an amount, price, or value: *We need to work out how much they owe us.* | *Can anyone work this bill out?*

2 [I] if something works out at a particular amount, you calculate that it costs that amount + **at**: *The bill works out at £15 each.* | *If we employ contract workers, its going to work out very expensive.*

3 work sth ↔ **out** [T] to think carefully about how you are going to do something and plan a good way of doing it: *The Group of Seven leading industrial nations agreed to work out some arrangements for debt rescheduling.*

4 be worked out if a mine is worked out, all the coal, gold etc has been removed from it

work[2] *n* [U] **1** the job you are paid to do or an activity that you do regularly to earn money: *My father started work when he was 14.* | *The work was interesting and well paid.* | *He eventually* ***found work*** *on a construction site.* | *She's been* ***out of work*** (=not had a job) *for almost a year now.* | *He has been* ***off work*** (=not working because of illness) *for four weeks because of his wrist condition.* | *women who have been laid off, taken* ***part-time work*** *or dropped out to raise children* | *6.3 million people are working part time but would prefer* ***full-time work.***

casual work work that uses workers employed for a short period of time

piece work also **piecework** work that is paid according to the number of things you produce rather than the number of hours you work: *Much demolition work is done on a piece work basis.*

2 a place where you do your job, which is not your home: *He* ***left work*** *at the usual time.* | *Jo's still* ***at work.***

3 the duties and activities that are part of your job: *What kind of work are you looking for?* | *A large part of the work we do involves using computers.* | *I wouldn't be very good at* ***manual work*** (=hard physical work).

4 work in progress abbreviation **WIP** *BrE* work or products that are in the process of being done or made, but are not yet finished: *Some journals expect editors to retain responsibility for work in progress when they leave.*

5 work in process abbreviation **WIP** *AmE* work or products that are in the process of being done or made, but are not yet finished —see also WORKS

work·a·hol·ic /ˌwɜːkəˈhɒlɪk‖ˌwɜːrkəˈhɒː-/ *n* [C] *informal* someone who cannot seem to stop working, and does not have time for anything else

work day also **workday** *n* [C] the amount of time that you spend working in a day: *The company has shortened the work day at some of its plants.*

work·er /ˈwɜːkə‖ˈwɜːrkər/ *n* [C] one of the people who work for an organization or business, and are below the level of manager: *new health and safety regulations for factory workers* | *Many* ***office workers*** *suffer from eye-strain.* —see also TELEWORKER

blue-collar worker [C] a worker who does physical work, rather than work in management or administration: *The company hopes to reduce back injuries amongst its blue-collar workers.*

contract worker [C] a worker who has a temporary contract to do a particular piece of work, but is not an employee of the company who they are working for: *A report that said contract workers receive less safety training than permanent workers.*

core workers [plural] the most necessary or important workers in an organization: *A strike by even a small number of core workers such as train drivers or signalmen can paralyse the network*

factory worker [C] someone who works in a factory; BLUE-COLLAR WORKER: *women factory workers fighting for equal pay*

farm worker [C] a person who works for a farmer: *30,000 EU farm workers demonstrated in Brussels about low pay and bad conditions.*

guest worker [C] someone who comes to another country to work in a low paid job, usually for a limited period of time: *Vu had to go back to Vietnam when he completed his education, but came back three years later as a guest worker in a factory.*

home worker [C] someone who does their job from home rather than an office

manual worker [C] a worker who does physical work: *a dispute among manual workers at the Ford Motor Company*

mobile worker [C] someone whose job involves working in different places: *mobile workers such as field service engineers*

nomadic worker [C] someone who works while they are away from the office, travelling on business etc, using modern means of communication: *nomadic workers who are no longer tied to a desk but can review or change their documents and data on the move*

pink-collar worker [C] *AmE* a worker, usually a female one, who does a low-paid job, for example in an office or restaurant

portfolio worker [C] a professional person who works for many different companies or individuals; FREELANCER

skilled worker [C] a worker who does work that involves special skills that they have gained through training: *skilled workers such as pipefitters and electricians*

transient worker [C] someone who passes quickly through a place, doing a series of usually badly paid jobs that do not need special skills

unskilled worker [C] a worker who does work that does not involve any special skill or training: *unskilled workers such as those who work in the clothing industry*

white-collar worker [C] a worker who works in management or administration, rather than one who does physical work: *The overall cost-cutting effort will largely affect white-collar workers.*

work experience —see under EXPERIENCE

work·fare /ˈwɜːkfeə‖ˈwɜːrkfer/ *n* [U] *especially AmE* a principle, policy, or system of requiring people who are unemployed to work or train before they are allowed to receive WELFARE (=money from the government): *The trend toward workfare is well-established in Europe. Sweden ties unemployment benefits to training programs, and France introduced measures in which the long-term unemployed must attend jobcentres to qualify for state welfare.* —compare WELFARE-TO-WORK

work·force /ˈwɜːkfɔːs‖ˈwɜːrkfɔːrs/ *n* [C] all the people who work in a particular country, industry, or factory: *State industry employs almost one-third of China's urban workforce of 150 million.* | *Ames closed 311 stores and* ***cut its workforce*** *to 29,500.*

work·horse /ˈwɜːkhɔːs‖ˈwɜːrkhɔːrs/ *n* [C] a machine or vehicle that can be used to do a lot of work: *a graphics software program that is rapidly becoming the architect's workhorse*

work·ing /ˈwɜːkɪŋ‖ˈwɜːr-/ *adj* [only before a noun]
1 working people have jobs that they are paid for: *the effect of the tax changes on* ***working couples*** | *the growth rate of the* ***working population*** (=all the people in a country who have a job) —see also REMOTE WORKING, SHORT-TIME WORKING
2 a working man or woman does physical work, rather than work in management or administration: *an ordinary working man*
3 working conditions or practices are ones that you have in your job: *Workers want better pay and* ***working conditions.*** | *Productivity is up 18% since a new labor pact last year swept away decades-old* ***working practices.***
4 your working hours, day etc are the period of time during the day when you are doing your job: ***Working hours*** *are flexible here and the dress is casual.* | *We want a shorter* ***working day.***
5 working breakfast/lunch/dinner a breakfast, lunch etc that is also a business meeting
6 be in (good) working order to be working properly and not broken: *He agreed to buy back the $130,000 machine, which he says is in good working order.*

working capital —see under CAPITAL

working class —see under CLASS

working group *n* [C] a committee that is formed to examine a particular situation or problem and suggest ways of dealing with it; WORKING PARTY *BrE*: *A working group will evaluate costs and set deadlines.*

working interest —see under INTEREST

working life *n* plural **working lives** [C] the part of your adult life when you work: *Geoff spent all his working life with the same company.*

working papers —see under PAPER

working partner —see under PARTNER

working party *n* plural **working parties** [C] *BrE* a group of people with specialist knowledge, brought together by an official organization to give advice on a particular issue; WORKING GROUP: *Coopers & Lybrand* ***formed a working party*** *to survey and examine interim reporting.* | *He was a member of the the working party which submitted evidence to the Select Committee on BSE.*

working stiff *n* [C] *AmE informal* an ordinary person who works to earn enough money to live: *a working stiff with money problems*

work load also **workload** —see under LOAD[1]

work·man /ˈwɜːkmən‖ˈwɜːrk-/ *n* plural **workmen** [C] someone who does physical work such as building, repairing things etc

work·man·like /ˈwɜːkmənlaɪk‖ˈwɜːrk-/ *adj* a workmanlike piece of work has been done in a careful, skilful way: *Ted Bates had a reputation for extraordinarily workmanlike advertisements.*

work·man·ship /ˈwɜːkmənʃɪp‖ˈwɜːrk-/ *n* [U] the ability to make things in a careful, skilful way so that what is

W

produced is of a high standard: *complaints about **shoddy*** (=bad and careless) ***workmanship***

work measurement *n* [U] the process of measuring and calculating the time taken by a worker to do a particular job to a fixed standard or quality: *Surveyors fees are dependent on work measurement.*

work•out /ˈwɜːkaʊt‖ˈwɜːrk-/ *n* [C] FINANCE a way for a borrower in financial difficulty to repay loans, debts etc: *The bank's lending services department develops workouts for business customers when they get into trouble or go bankrupt.* | *a **workout specialist***

work permit —see under PERMIT

work•place /ˈwɜːkpleɪs‖ˈwɜːrk-/ *n* [C usually singular] the room or building where you work: *Good design involves adapting the workplace environment to the needs of workers, rather than trying to make workers adjust to the workplace.*

workplace democracy —see under DEMOCRACY

work-related injury —see under INJURY

works /wɜːks‖wɜːrks/ *n* [plural] **1** *old-fashioned* a building or group of buildings in which goods are produced in large quantities or an industrial process happens: *The brick works closed last year.*
2 the activity involved in doing something on a large scale: *the official in charge of the **engineering works***
public works the building of something on a large scale, paid for by a government: *He called for spending on highways and public works to revive the economy.* —see also SKUNK WORKS

works council —see under COUNCIL

work•shop /ˈwɜːkʃɒp‖ˈwɜːrkʃɑːp/ *n* [C] **1** a fairly small room or building in which tools and machines are used for making or repairing things: *a small engineering workshop*
2 a meeting at which people discuss their experiences and do practical exercises, especially in order to find solutions to problems + **on**: *a small-business workshop on combating drug use in the workplace*

work-shy *adj BrE disapproving* lazy and not wanting to work: *The minister was criticized for branding the young unemployed as work-shy.*

work•sta•tion /ˈwɜːkˌsteɪʃən‖ˈwɜːrk-/ *n* [C] **1** the part of an office where you work, where your desk, computer etc are
2 a computer and all the equipment that goes with it

work-to-rule *BrE*, **work-to-contract** *AmE* — *n* [singular] an occasion when people protest about a situation at work by doing their job less quickly or effectively, but without breaking their employer's rules or the terms of their contract: *The work-to-rule exposed the chronic staffing problems in the London Ambulance Service.* —see also ***work to rule*** under WORK[1]

work•week /ˈwɜːkwiːk‖ˈwɜːrk-/ also **working week** *BrE* — *n* [singular] the number of hours or days people in a particular industry or job work in a week: *The plant will resume its normal five-day workweek on March 16 to catch up on orders.*

World Bank *n* **the World Bank** a bank based in Washington, D.C. that gives financial help to countries that need money for development. Its capital is provided by the countries of the INTERNATIONAL MONETARY FUND. The World Bank is also known as the INTERNATIONAL BANK FOR RECONSTRUCTION AND DEVELOPMENT: *The dams, funded by the World Bank, were among many ambitious projects to open up the Amazon.*

World Economic Forum abbreviation **WEF** *n* an organization that arranges meetings and makes information available on economic problems, the performance of different countries etc: *the World Economic Forum's latest report on international competitiveness*

World Intellectual Property Organization also **World Intellectual Property Organisation** *BrE* —see WIPO

world language —see under LANGUAGE

World Trade Organization abbreviation **WTO** *n* an organization that was formed in 1995 to control trade agreements between countries and to set rules on international trade. It replaced GATT (=the General Agreement on Tariffs and Trade)

World Wide Web written abbreviation **WWW** *n* **the World Wide Web** a system that connects documents stored in computers in many different parts of the world, and that people all over the world can use with a single program on their computer

worth[1] /wɜːθ‖wɜːrθ/ *n* [U] **1** the value of something in money: *The balance sheet will not show the current worth of the company.* | *I am willing to buy £100,000 worth of bonds.*
2 ten hours' worth/a week's etc worth of sth something that takes ten hours, a week etc to happen or to do: *You may be faced with two days worth of maintenance.* | *Investors risk losing a few months' worth of interest.* —see also COMPARABLE WORTH, NET WORTH

worth[2] *prep* [U] **1 be worth** to have a particular value in money: *What is Pearson Education worth?* | *The company's assets are worth $70 a share.* | *defense contracts worth $10 billion*
2 be worth millions/a fortune *informal* to be extremely rich: *The man who founded CNN must be worth a fortune.*
3 if it is worth doing something, or if something is worth doing, an advantage will be gained by doing it: *If commission fees are cut any further, it simply won't be worth doing business anymore.*

worth•less /ˈwɜːθləs‖ˈwɜːrθ-/ *adj* having no value or importance: *Inflation made the old Argentinian currency virtually worthless.* | *a completely worthless exercise*

wpm words per minute; used to show how fast someone can type or do SHORTHAND: *My typing speed is 60 wpm.*

wreck•age /ˈrekɪdʒ/ *n* [U] *journalism* a business activity, company, system etc that has failed, is in extremely bad financial condition etc: *Communism's economic wreckage was visible even in this small place.* | *the wreckage caused by overbuilding* (=building too much) *in the Southwest*

writ /rɪt/ *n* [C,U] LAW a document from a court that orders someone to do or not to do something: *A number of BCCI depositors **issued a writ** against the central bank, alleging that it had failed to exercise proper supervision.* | *an action begun **by writ***

write /raɪt/ *v* past tense **wrote** past participle **written**
1 [I,T] to form letters or numbers with a pen or pencil: *The price is written on the label.*
2 also **write out** [T] to write information on a cheque or document: *He wrote out a cheque for £4000.*
3 [T] INSURANCE to sell a particular amount of insurance: *We have written £5 million of insurance this month.*
write sth ↔ **back** *phr v* [T] ACCOUNTING to increase the value of an asset that had been written off or written down. This happens, for example, when a debt that you thought would not be paid is unexpectedly paid —see also WRITE-BACK
write sth ↔ **down** *phr v* [T] ACCOUNTING to reduce the value of an asset as shown in a company's accounts: *The giant hospital chain said it will write down about $100 million in assets and reserves.* —see also WRITE-DOWN
write sth **into** sth *phr v* [T] to include something such as a rule or condition in a document, agreement etc: *I have to attend regular training sessions – it's written into my contract.*

write off *phr v* [T] **1 write** sb/sth ↔ **off** to decide that someone or something is useless, unimportant, or a failure + **as**: *We've written the project off as a non-starter.*
2 write sth ↔ **off** to officially say that someone does not have to pay a debt: *As part of the deal, all their debts were written off.*
3 ACCOUNTING **write** sth ↔**off** to reduce the value of an asset to nothing, for example in the case of a bad debt (=money you have lent but that will never be repaid): *Businesses write off capital assets over a period of years.*
4 write sth ↔ **off** *BrE* INSURANCE if an insurance company writes off a vehicle, it decides that it has been damaged so badly that it is not worth repairing: *The car has been written off, so they have to pay out for a new one.* —see also WRITE-OFF

write sth ↔ **up** *phr v* [T] ACCOUNTING to increase the value of an asset, usually land or a building, as shown in a company's accounts: *The company can periodically write up the value of certain assets if its directors think the assets are worth more than the purchase price.*

write-back *n* [C,U] ACCOUNTING when the value of an asset that had been written off or written down increases, for example when a debt that you thought would not be paid is unexpectedly paid

write-down also **writedown** *n* [C,U] ACCOUNTING when the value of an asset as shown in a company's accounts is reduced: *The charge includes $2.7 million from the write-down of assets.*

write-off also **writeoff** *n* **1** [C,U] an official agreement stating that someone does not have to pay a debt: *The 20% write-off of Argentinian debt had been expected.*
2 [C,U] ACCOUNTING when all or part of the value of an asset as shown in a company's accounts is reduced: *a one-year depreciation write-off of 15% of the cost of new equipment*
3 [C] *BrE* INSURANCE a vehicle that an insurance company decides has been so badly damaged that it is not worth repairing

write-protect *v* [T] COMPUTING to make it impossible for a computer user to write information onto a computer disk, or change the details of an existing file, so that information is not changed or destroyed: *Once write-protected, a disk can't be infected by a virus.*

writ·er /ˈraɪtə‖-ər/ *n* [C] **1** FINANCE someone who sells PUT OPTION and CALL OPTION contracts
naked writer someone who sells OPTIONS (=the right to buy shares etc at a particular price at a later date) for shares etc that they do not own
2 INSURANCE a person or company that provides insurance contracts; UNDERWRITER: *Universal Security Insurance Co., a writer of property and casualty policies*

write-up *n* **1** [C,U] ACCOUNTING when the value of an asset is increased: *Shvets had expected a total asset write-up of about A$1 billion.*
2 [C] a written opinion about a new product, book etc: *Their PC had a good write-up but the purchase price had increased by £50.*

writing-down allowance —see under ALLOWANCE

writ of execution *n* plural **writs of execution** [C] LAW a writ to put into effect a court's judgement by forcing someone to pay an amount of money or do something. It is usually addressed to a court officer, ordering him or her to do something such as take property from the person

writ of fie·ri fa·ci·as /ˌrɪt əv ˌfaɪəraɪ ˈfeɪʃiəs‖-ˌfaɪri-/ abbreviation **fi fa** *n* plural **writs of fieri facias** [C] LAW a writ ordering an officer to take and sell property belonging to someone who owes money, until the value of the property taken is equal to the amount of their debt

writ of summons —see under SUMMONS[1]

written-down value —see under VALUE[1]

wrong·ful /ˈrɒŋfəl‖ˈrɒːŋ-/ *adj* [only before a noun] wrongful actions or activities are unfair or illegal: *Mr. Campeau has filed a lawsuit alleging **wrongful dismissal*** (=being dismissed unfairly from his job). —**wrongfully** *adv*: *The company had wrongfully fired him after he refused to violate environmental policies.*

wt. written abbreviation for weight

WTO abbreviation for WORLD TRADE ORGANIZATION

WWW abbreviation for WORLD WIDE WEB, used in the addresses of some web pages

WYSIWYG /ˈwɪziwɪg/ *n* [U] COMPUTING What You See Is What You Get; a word meaning what you see on the computer screen is exactly what will be printed on paper: *text and graphics with full **WYSIWYG display***

x also **xd** FINANCE ex dividend; used after a share price to show that a DIVIDEND (=payment of part of a company's profits to shareholders) has been announced but that the seller of the share will receive it, not the buyer: *a closing fall of 7p to 731p xd*

xa FINANCE ex all; used after a share price to show that it is sold without any of the advantages that have been or will soon be available, for example DIVIDENDs or RIGHTS ISSUEs (=rights for existing shareholders to buy new shares)

xc FINANCE ex capitalization; used after a share price to show that the buyer does not have the right to a BONUS ISSUE that has been or will soon be made, where existing shareholders are paid part of a company's profits in the form of new shares

Xe•rox[1] /ˈzɪərɒks‖ˈziːrɑːks/ *n* [C] *trademark especially AmE* **1** also **Xerox machine** a machine that makes photographic copies of documents; PHOTOCOPIER
2 also **Xerox copy**, or **Xerox sheet** a photographic copy of a document, made on a Xerox machine; PHOTOCOPY

Xerox[2] *v* [T] *trademark especially AmE* to make a photographic copy of a document; PHOTOCOPY: *xeroxed pages*

x-inefficient *adj* an x-inefficient business produces a particular level of goods or services at a higher cost than could be possible: *A public sector monopoly can be as x-inefficient as a private sector one.* —**x-inefficiency** *n* [U] *Reductions in x- inefficiency do not necessarily lead to net welfare improvements for consumers.*

xr FINANCE ex-rights; used after a share price to show that the buyer does not have the right to new shares in a particular RIGHTS ISSUE (=rights for existing shareholders to buy new shares) that has been or will soon be made

X

Y2K *n* [U] the year 2000, used especially when people are talking about the MILLENNIUM BUG (=the problem that some computers had when the date changed in the year 2000): *the effect of the* ***Y2K problem*** *on earnings in the computer industry*

Yankee bond —see under BOND

yankee dollar certificate of deposit —see under CERTIFICATE OF DEPOSIT

YAP /jæp/ *n* [C] *AmE* Young Aspiring Professional; another name for YUPPIE

yard /jɑːd‖jɑːrd/ *n* [C] **1** written abbreviation **yd.** a unit for measuring length, equal to 3 feet or 0.9144 metres
2 an enclosed area next to a building or group of buildings, used for a special purpose, activity, or business: *Their house is next to a builder's yard.* | *a* ***timber yard*** —see also STOCKYARD

yard·stick /ˈjɑːdˌstɪk‖ˈjɑːrd-/ *n* [C] something that you use to compare another thing with, in order to judge how good or successful it is + **of**: *Is profit the only yardstick of success?* | *The annual percentage rate is the best yardstick to use when comparing the costs of the different forms of credit.*

year /jɪə, jɜː‖jɪr/ written abbreviation **yr** *n* [C] **1** also **calendar year** the period of time beginning on January 1 and ending on December 31: *The Small Business Administration arranged 55,000 small business loans* ***last year***.
2 any period of time equal to about 12 months: *My passport expires* ***in a year***.
financial year *especially BrE* the 12-month period over which a company's accounts are calculated. In Britain, many companies have the end of March or the end of December as the end of their financial year: *Beazer said pretax earnings for its latest financial year fell to £160.6 million.*
fiscal year ◆ *especially AmE* a company's financial year: *For the first nine months of its fiscal year, the company's after-tax profit rose 21% to $364 million.*
◆ the 12-month period used by government departments for calculating BUDGETs etc, in Britain ending on April 5: *the cabinet's approval for an austere budget for the next fiscal year* | *Emergency medical care cost the city $66.5 million in fiscal year 1998.*
tax year a 12-month period at the end of which your taxable income is calculated. In Britain the tax year ends on April 5: *By the end of the tax year, the company had invested £39.7 billion.*

year·book /ˈjɪəbʊk, ˈjɜː-‖ˈjɪr-/ *n* [C] a book that is produced once a year, and to which the most recent information is added each year: *the British Yearbook of International Law*

year end *n* [singular, U] the end of a company's financial year: *Shareholders' funds were almost £50 million at the year end.* | *The world's biggest household appliance maker has seen its* ***year-end profits*** *fall.* | *individuals who get* ***year-end bonuses*** *from their employers*

year·ling /ˈjɪəlɪŋ, ˈjɜː-‖ˈjɪr-/ also **yearling bond** *n* [C] FINANCE money borrowed by a LOCAL AUTHORITY in the form of a bond that must be paid back within a year: *The duration of local authority bonds is typically between one and five years, although most are for one year and are known as yearling bonds.*

year·ly /ˈjɪəli, ˈjɜː-‖ˈjɪrli/ *adj* happening or appearing every year or once a year: *a* ***yearly pay award*** | *the* ***yearly advertising budget*** | *Tenneco Corp. reported its best* ***yearly earnings*** *since 1998.* —**yearly** *adv*: *We pay the fee yearly.*

year planner *n* [C] a large CHART showing the days, weeks, and months of a particular year, which you use to write your planned activities on

year to date written abbreviation **YTD** *n* [singular] ACCOUNTING the period from the beginning of a CALENDAR YEAR or FINANCIAL YEAR until the present time, used especially to talk about the amount of sales or profit in a particular period: *For the year to date, sales of domestically made cars and trucks were down 17%.* —**year-to-date** *adj*: *GM's* ***year-to-date*** *car* ***sales*** *were down 5.7%.*

Yellow Book *n* **the Yellow Book** FINANCE *informal* Admission of Securities to Listing, a book produced by the LONDON STOCK EXCHANGE containing the rules that companies must follow if they want their shares to be traded there: *The Stock Exchange is considering a change to its Yellow Book rules to enable young biotechnology companies to be floated* (=have their shares sold) *in London even if they are years away from making profits.*

Yellow Pages *n trademark* a book that contains the telephone numbers of businesses and organizations in an area, arranged according to the type of business they do —compare WHITE PAGES

Yellow Sheets also **yellow sheets** *n* [plural] information published daily by the NATIONAL QUOTATION BUREAU in the US, about bonds traded in the OVER-THE-COUNTER market for bonds in smaller companies —see also PINK SHEETS

yen /jen/ *n* plural **yen** [C] the standard unit of money in Japan: *The company already has debts of 127 billion Yen.* | *The dollar closed at 125.75 yen on the Tokyo foreign exchange market.*

yield[1] /jiːld/ *n* **1** FINANCE the amount of money that you get from an investment, especially bonds: *investments with* ***high yields*** | *Many investors are buying stocks because of* ***low yields*** *in other securities.*
bond yield [C] the interest paid on a bond: *Government bond yields of nearly 8% look highly attractive when inflation is running at only 3%.*
current yield [C] the income received from a bond, calculated as a percentage of its present market price: *The current yield on the bond is 11.76%.*
dividend yield [C] the GROSS DIVIDEND (=part of profit divided among shareholders, before tax) calculated as a percentage of the price of a share, or of a group of shares: *The dividend yield on FT-SE 100 Index companies is 3.88%.*
earnings yield [C usually singular] the amount that a particular type of investment earns, expressed as a percentage of its value: *The 8.6% interest that investors can collect on 10-year government bonds is almost 2.5 percentage points higher than the earnings yield on stocks.*
effective yield also **flat yield**, **running yield** the income received from a FIXED-INTEREST BOND etc, calculated as a percentage of the price paid for it: *Bond prices fell Friday, raising the effective yield on bonds to 8.06 %.*
equity yield [C,U] the percentage rate of money earned on shares in general: *In the UK, dividend payouts have been rising sharply; in the US, the situation is the other way, with the equity yield at an all-time low.* —compare RETURN ON EQUITY
gilt yields [plural] income from British government bonds: *UK gilt yields remain the second highest within the EU.*
gross yield [C] the income received from a bond etc before tax: *Estimated gross yield at 100p is 4.5% a year.*

initial yield [C] the income received from a bond etc when it is first bought: *Total return for fixed-income investments comprises not just the initial yield, but also interest on reinvested interest, and price change.* | *notes due June 1, 2010, priced at 99.866 for an initial yield of 8.60%*

maturity yield [C] another name for REDEMPTION YIELD

net yield [C] the profit from an investment to an investor after taking off dealing costs, taxes etc, usually given as a percentage of its value: *The average net yield on assets was down to 4.45% from 5% a year earlier, a result of declining interest rates.*

nominal yield [C] the interest received from a FIXED-INTEREST INVESTMENT, calculated as a percentage of its price when it was first bought

prospective yield [C] the income that you expect to get from an investment

redemption yield also **yield to redemption** [C] other phrases for YIELD TO MATURITY: *In general, low-coupon bonds will have a lower* ***gross redemption yield*** *before tax because they will be attractive to tax-paying investors concerned to maximize their* ***net redemption yield*** *after payment of taxes.*

running yield [C] the income that an investor receives from an investment such as GOVERNMENT STOCK. It is calculated by multiplying the COUPON (=the investment's interest rate) by 100, and dividing the result by the price paid for the investment

true yield [C] the yearly income that an investor receives from a SECURITY, calculated by dividing its NOMINAL VALUE by its market price and then multiplying by the DIVIDEND per cent

2 the amount of something that is produced, such as crops: *Farmers who practise intensive farming are aiming for maximum yields for minimum cost.*

3 the average amount of money that an AIRLINE gets from each of its passengers for each mile that they fly or by a hotel from each of its guests for each night they stay: *BA's passenger revenue yield rose from 12.8 cents to 12.95 cents.* | *Airlines have sophisticated* ***yield management*** *systems for maximizing passenger revenue.* —see also LOAD FACTOR

yield² *v* **1** [T] to produce income or profits: *Mining shares often yield a high level of return.*

2 [T] to produce a product, crop etc: *These rice fields now yield 145,000 tons a year.*

3 [T] to produce a result, answer, or a piece of information: *The discussions failed to* ***yield*** *any useful* ***results.*** | *Writing to the agents yielded no reply.*

yield curve —see under CURVE

yield equivalence *n* [U] when a TAX-EXEMPT investment (=one that is not taxed) and a taxable investment of a similar quality provide the same after-tax RETURN, at a particular INTEREST RATE

yield gap *n* [C] FINANCE the difference between the amounts of interest on two types of bonds: *The yield gap between the three-month bill and the 30-year bond widened to 213 basis points from 212.*

yield spread —see under SPREAD²

yield to call *n* plural **yields to call** [C] FINANCE the yield that an investor will get from a bond if they REDEEM it (=change it into cash) at the first CALL DATE (=when they can be redeemed before MATURITY): *Many junk bonds currently are trading at their 'yield-to-call' price, which assumes that the bonds will be redeemed by the issuer at the first call date.*

yield to maturity also **maturity yield** *n* plural **yields to maturity** [C] FINANCE the yield of a bond calculated from the time when it was bought, taking into account the price paid for it, interest payments on it, and its value at MATURITY (=when it becomes ready to be paid); REDEMPTION YIELD; YIELD TO REDEMPTION: *A disadvantage of yield to maturity is that investors do not typically hold bonds to maturity.*

yield to redemption *n* plural **yields to redemption** [C] another name for YIELD TO MATURITY

Yours /jɔːz‖jɔːrz/ *pron* **1 Yours faithfully** used to end a formal letter that begins 'Dear Sir' or 'Dear Madam'

2 Yours sincerely/Yours used to end a less formal letter that begins with the name of the person you are writing to, for example 'Dear Mr Graves' or 'Dear Miss Hope'

yr. written abbreviation for YEAR

Yrs written abbreviation for YOURS

YTD written abbreviation for YEAR-TO-DATE

YTM written abbreviation for YIELD TO MATURITY

yup·pie also **yuppy** /ˈjʌpi/ *n* plural **yuppies** [C] *informal* a young person in a professional job with a high income, especially one who enjoys spending money and having a fashionable way of life; YAP: *The area has been converted into smart flats for yuppies.*

Z

zai•bat•su /zaɪˈbætsuː/ *n* plural **zaibatsu** or **zaibatsus** [C] in Japan in former times, a group of related companies often owned by members of the same family, with a bank at its centre in which the companies owned shares: *The group comprised one of the three most powerful zaibatsu before and during the war.* —compare KEIRETSU

zai•tech /ˈzaɪtek/ *n* [U] FINANCE in Japan, when a company buys valuable paintings, objects etc in order to hide the profits it has made: *Many Japanese corporate collectors appear to have used high-priced art for tax purposes, a practice known here as 'zaitech'.*

ZBB abbreviation for ZERO-BASED BUDGETING

ze•ro[1] /ˈzɪərəʊ‖ˈziːroʊ/ *n* plural **zeros** or **zeroes** [C]
1 the number 0
2 zero growth/inflation etc no growth, inflation etc at all: *Government officials are predicting zero inflation for April.* | *The figures show zero growth in industrial output value.*
3 zero [C usually plural] *informal* another name for ZERO COUPON BONDS —see under BOND

zero[2] *v*
zero in on sb/sth *phr v* [T] to direct all your attention towards a particular person or thing: *Companies are looking to zero in on specific markets.*

zero-based budgeting —see under BUDGETING

zero-coupon bond —see under BOND

zero defects —see under DEFECT[1]

zero inflation —see under INFLATION

zero-rated *adj* TAX zero-rated goods and services are those on which you do not have to pay VAT (=a type of sales tax). In Britain, most food and books are zero-rated —**zero-rating** *n* [U] *the decision to abolish the zero rating of VAT on gas and electricity bills for individual homes*

zero-sum game *n* [C] *AmE* a situation in which a balance is achieved between something such as money received and something given away: *a zero-sum game in which every dollar of tax relief for one group means a dollar lost by another*

zinc /zɪŋk/ *n* [U] a white metal used in manufacturing and traded on COMMODITIES MARKETS: *On the London Metal Exchange, zinc fell in afternoon trading to a fresh 10-month low.*

zip code *n* [C] *AmE* a number that you put below the address on an envelope to help the postal service deliver the mail more quickly; POSTCODE *BrE*

zip file —see under FILE[1]

zone[1] /zəʊn‖zoʊn/ *n* [C] **1** a large area that is different from others around it in some way: *This is a no-parking zone.* | *Buckinghamshire County Council's headquarters is now a* ***smoke free zone*** (=where smoking is not allowed).
2 licence-free/passport-free etc zone a group of countries where you do not need a licence to import goods, you do not need special documents to travel etc
3 residential/industrial/commercial etc zone an area of a city that is used for a particular purpose or activity, such as houses or shops: *The trucks are limited by federal law to the commercial zone.* | *The company's five factories are situated in Tai Po, a new industrial zone in the New Territories.*
development zone another name for ENTERPRISE ZONE
duty-free zone an area where goods can be imported and exported without paying CUSTOMS DUTIES: *The Malaysian government has declared Langkawi a duty-free zone.*
economic zone also **exclusive economic zone** an area of sea around a country, where that country alone is allowed to fish, mine etc
enterprise zone an area which the government is helping by supporting new businesses and encouraging companies to move there by offering money or by allowing them not to pay certain taxes for a period of time; DEVELOPMENT ZONE: *One of Asia's most ambitious projects is the Multimedia Super Corridor, a 30-mile-long high-technology enterprise zone in Malaysia.*
euro-zone the euro-zone the part of Europe where the euro is used as currency: *The new currency is due to be physically introduced across the euro zone between January and July 2002.*
foreign trade zone an area, often a port, where goods can be re-exported free of DUTY, or with low taxes etc: *The Baltic port cities are thinking about creating foreign trade zones.* —see also ***free port*** under PORT[1]
free zone also **free trade zone** another name for DUTY-FREE ZONE or TAX-FREE ZONE: *Ilo will be developed jointly as a free zone with full industrial and commercial facilities, with Peru allowing free access to Bolivian goods.*
special economic zone an area where economic development is encouraged by the government. Materials can be exported into special economic zones, used to manufacture goods, and then re-exported tax-free: *The special economic zone of Xiamen in southeast China approved 128 Taiwan investment projects worth $275 million.*
tax free zone another name for DUTY FREE ZONE
time zone one of the 24 areas that the world is divided into, each of which has its own time: *Investors want to trade in Europe's stocks in a single market within the European time zone.*

zone[2] *v* [T] *AmE* to divide a town or city into different areas for different purposes: *The privately owned land is currently zoned for residential use* (=for houses). —see also DOWNZONING —**zoning** *adj*: ***zoning laws*** *to allow used-car lots in commercial service areas*

Z-score *n* [C] FINANCE, STATISTICS a figure that shows how likely it is that a business will fail. The Z-score is calculated using information about the relative levels of a business's assets, sales, profits etc and is correct about 90% of the time in calculating if a business will go bankrupt within one year: *Auditors at one point gave McDonnell Douglas a Z-score of 2.27.*

Parts of Speech

adj	adjective
adv	adverb
n	noun
number	number
phr v	phrasal verb
prefix	prefix
prep	preposition
suffix	suffix
v	verb

Grammar Codes

[C]	COUNTABLE: countable nouns can be made plural
[U]	UNCOUNTABLE: uncountable nouns have no plural form
[plural]	shows that a noun is always plural and must be followed by a plural form of a verb
[singular]	shows that a noun is always singular and must be followed by a singular form of a verb
[T]	TRANSITIVE: transitive verbs must have an object
[I]	INTRANSITIVE: intransitive verbs do not have an object
[not before a noun]	shows that an adjective is never used before a noun
[only before a noun]	shows that an adjective is only used before a noun
[only after a noun]	shows that an adjective is only used after a noun

Labels

AmE	American English
BrE	British English
formal	used in formal or official situations, but not usually in ordinary conversation
informal	used in letters and conversations with friends or people at work who you know well, but not in official letters or formal situations
spoken	used in spoken English, but not usually in written English
written	used in written English, but not usually in spoken English
old-fashioned	not used in normal English anymore
trademark	used as the official name of a product or service by the company that made it, developed it, etc
approving	used when a word praises people or things, although this may not be clear from its meaning
disapproving	used when a word shows that you disapprove of someone or something, although this may not be clear from the meaning
journalism	used in newspapers or news reports, but not in normal English

Subject Area Labels

The following labels are used when the meaning of a word is related to a particular subject or profession:

- ACCOUNTING
- BANKING
- COMPUTING
- ECONOMICS
- FINANCE
- HUMAN RESOURCES
- INSURANCE
- LAW
- MANUFACTURING
- MARKETING
- PROPERTY
- TAX
- STATISTICS